Auditing Practices

Standards and Guidance
2007

January 2007

PREFACE

This is the third edition of 'APB Standards and Guidance'. It contains a summary of The Auditing Practices Board (APB)'s activities during 2006 and an overview of its plans for 2007. A full list of extant APB standards and guidance at 1 January 2007 is provided in the appendix on page 1207.

The APB is one of the operating bodies of the Financial Reporting Council (FRC). The FRC is a unified, independent regulator with a mission of promoting confidence in corporate reporting and governance. In addition to the APB, the FRC incorporates five other operating bodies: the Accounting Standards Board, the Financial Reporting Review Panel, the Accountancy Discipline and Investigation Board, the Board for Actuarial Standards and the Professional Oversight Board.

The APB is committed to leading the development of auditing practice in the United Kingdom and the Republic of Ireland so as to:

- Establish high standards of auditing;

- Meet the developing needs of users of financial information; and

- Ensure public confidence in the auditing process.

Further information regarding the APB's remit and processes is provided in the statement of its scope and authority of pronouncements on page 5 and on its website www.frc.org.uk/apb.

Neither the Auditing Practices Board Limited nor the APB accepts any liability to any party for any loss, damage or costs howsoever arising, whether directly or indirectly, whether in contract, tort or otherwise from any action or decision taken (or not taken) as a result of any person relying on or otherwise using this document or arising from any omission from it.

References to legislation and regulations

Some APB pronouncements include cross references to legislation and regulations that apply at the time of issuance of those pronouncements. Such references may have become out of date due to changes in the relevant legislation or regulations and users are advised to check the continuing relevance of them as necessary when applying the APB's pronouncements.

CONTENTS

Section 1: THE AUDITING PRACTICES BOARD
SUMMARY OF 2006 AND FUTURE APB ACTIVITIES

The APB's activities during 2006 and its planned work for 2007 are summarised below, organised under each of the APB's strategic objectives.

Objective: Establishing Auditing Standards which set out the basic principles and essential procedures with which external auditors in the United Kingdom and the Republic of Ireland are required to comply.

2006 ACTIVITIES

New auditing standards were implemented in 2005; these were the ISAs as issued by the International Auditing and Assurance Standards Board (IAASB), supplemented, where necessary, by standards and guidance from the UK auditing standards previously in issue.

In 2006 the APB has not made changes to these ISAs (UK and Ireland) other than to revise ISA (UK and Ireland) 720 to reflect a change in UK company law relating to auditors reporting on directors' reports. This does not mean, however, that the APB has been inactive. Rather the APB has concentrated its efforts on contributing to IAASB's work to revise a number of the ISAs and to reformat all of them as part of its 'Clarity Project'. The Clarity Project, which is expected to be completed in late 2008, has major significance to auditors in the UK and Ireland as the ISAs are likely to be adopted within the European Union under the provisions of the Statutory Audit Directive.

As well as contributing directly to a number of IAASB projects and commenting on all exposure drafts the APB, through its press releases and other material published on its website (www.frc.org.uk/apb) is seeking to raise the awareness of auditors, investors and preparers of financial statements to the important changes that are being made to the ISAs and to facilitate their input to the process.

PLANNED FUTURE ACTIVITIES

During 2007 the APB will continue its contribution to the IAASB's Clarity Project and the revision of 'older' ISAs including:

- ISA 200 on the objective and general principles of audits;

- ISA 540 on auditing accounting estimates (including fair values);

- ISA 550 on auditing related parties; and

- ISA 600 on group audits.

Objective: Issuing guidance on the application of Auditing Standards in particular circumstances and industries and timely guidance on new and emerging issues.

2006 ACTIVITIES

As more fully described in Section 6, in 2006 the APB issued 16 documents, these being:

- three revised Practice Notes;

- two updated Practice Notes containing interim guidance;

- five consultation drafts of revised Practice Notes; and

- six Bulletins.

PLANNED FUTURE ACTIVITIES

The main areas of activity in 2007 are likely to be:

- Continuing to update industry specific Practice Notes to reflect the adoption of ISAs (UK and Ireland) and changes in regulatory requirements including those relating to charities, pension schemes and investment businesses;

- Updating Practice Note 8 *'Reports by auditors under company legislation'* and Bulletins (including Bulletin 2006/6 which sets out illustrative audit reports) in the light of the Companies Act 2006.

Objective: Establishing Standards and related guidance for accountants providing assurance services.

2006 ACTIVITIES

During 2005 the Standards for Investment Reporting (SIRs) were updated to reflect the requirements of the EC Prospectus Directive and new standards were issued on public reporting engagements on profit forecasts and pro forma financial information. During 2006 the APB finalised Ethical Standards for Reporting Accountants (ESRA) (see page 109).

PLANNED FUTURE ACTIVITIES

In 2007, the focus will be on:

- Finalisation of a new standard on the review of interim financial information performed by the independent auditor of the entity based on International Standard on Review Engagements (ISRE) 2410; and

- Work on a new SIR addressing the work of the reporting accountant on GAAP reconciliations.

Objective: Establishing Ethical Standards in relation to the independence, objectivity and integrity of external auditors and those providing assurance services.

2006 ACTIVITIES

New ethical standards for auditors (ESs) were implemented in 2005. During 2006 the APB focused on developing ethical standards for reporting accountants; the ESRA is applicable for investment circular reporting engagements commencing on or after 1 April 2007.

PLANNED FUTURE ACTIVITIES

IFAC are in the process of making significant revisions to its Code of Ethics with respect to auditor independence. In 2007 the APB will comment on IFAC's exposure draft and commence a review of the ESs.

Objective: Taking an appropriate role in the development of statutes, regulations and accounting standards which affect the conduct of auditing and assurance services, both domestically and internationally.

2006 ACTIVITIES

In 2006 the APB contributed views on proposed company law reforms affecting auditors that culminated in the Companies Act 2006. In 2007, in conjunction with the FRC and the POB, the APB will continue to contribute to the maintenance of a robust audit regulatory environment in the UK, Republic of Ireland, Europe and internationally.

Objective: Contributing to efforts to advance public understanding of the roles and responsibilities of external auditors and the providers of assurance services including the sponsorship of research.

2006 ACTIVITIES

During 2006 the APB made a significant contribution to the FRC's Discussion Paper 'Promoting Audit Quality' which was published in November 2006. This Discussion Paper addresses the FRC's objective of promoting and maintaining confidence in the audit process and the resulting audit report. The Discussion Paper:

- Identifies those drivers that the FRC believes are central to achieving a high quality audit of listed companies;

- Considers whether there are 'threats' which weaken the effective operation of those drivers; and

- Seeks opinions as to whether, within the existing legal and regulatory framework, all appropriate steps are being taken to maintain and enhance the quality of audits and, if not, seeks views as to what more could or should be done.

The Discussion Paper has been prepared in the context of the financial reporting framework in the UK and the Republic of Ireland. However, because of the increasingly international context in which standard setting takes place, the FRC is keen to receive the views of all those interested in promoting high quality audits wherever they may be located.

PLANNED FUTURE ACTIVITIES

Future activities will include:

- Considering comments received on 'Promoting Audit Quality' (due date: 31 March 2007); and

- Considering the actions taken in response to the POB's research into the accounting and auditing needs of smaller entities in the context of standards for SME audits.

**THE AUDITING
PRACTICES BOARD**

Section 2: THE AUDITING PRACTICES BOARD – SCOPE AND AUTHORITY OF PRONOUNCEMENTS (REVISED)

CONTENTS

> This statement, which describes the scope and authority of the Auditing Practices Board's (APB's) pronouncements, replaces a previous document of the same title which was issued in April 2003. The revised statement reflects the position of the APB (and of the Auditing Practices Board Limited) at the date of issue.

Introduction

1. The objectives of the Auditing Practices Board Limited, which is a constituent body of the Financial Reporting Council[1], are to:

    *   Establish Auditing Standards which set out the basic principles and essential procedures with which external auditors in the United Kingdom and the Republic of Ireland are required to comply;

    *   Issue guidance on the application of Auditing Standards in particular circumstances and industries and timely guidance on new and emerging issues;

    *   Establish Standards and related guidance for accountants providing assurance services where they relate to activities that are reported in the public domain, and are therefore within the "public interest";

    *   Establish Ethical Standards in relation to the independence, objectivity and integrity of external auditors and those providing assurance services;

    *   Participate in the development of statutes, regulations and standards which affect the conduct of auditing and assurance services, both domestically and internationally; and

    *   Contribute to efforts to advance public understanding of the roles and responsibilities of external auditors and the providers of assurance services including the sponsorship of research.

2. The Auditing Practices Board Limited discharges its responsibilities through a Board ('the APB'), comprising individuals who are eligible for appointment as company auditors and those who are not so eligible. Those who are eligible for appointment as company auditors may not exceed 40% of the APB by number.

3. The Nomination Committee of the Financial Reporting Council appoints members of the Board.

Nature and Scope of APB Pronouncements

4. APB pronouncements include:

    *   'Quality control standards' for firms that perform audits of financial statements, reports in connection with investment circulars and other assurance engagements;

---

[1] Information about the Financial Reporting Council (FRC) and its structure, including its subsidiary bodies, can be found on the FRC's website (www.frc.org.uk).

- A framework of fundamental principles which the APB expects to guide the conduct of auditors (see Appendix 2);

- 'Engagement standards' for audits of financial statements, reports in connection with investment circulars and other assurance engagements; and

- Guidance for auditors of financial statements, reporting accountants acting in connection with an investment circular and auditors involved in other assurance engagements.

The structure of APB pronouncements is shown in Appendix 1.

5. Auditors and reporting accountants should not claim compliance with APB standards unless they have complied fully with all of those standards relevant to an engagement.

6. APB quality control and engagement standards contain basic principles and essential procedures (identified in bold type lettering[2]) together with related guidance in the form of explanatory and other material, including appendices. The basic principles and essential procedures are to be understood and applied in the context of the explanatory and other material that provide guidance for their application. It is therefore necessary to consider the whole text of a Standard to understand and apply the basic principles and essential procedures.

7. In order to support the international harmonisation of auditing standards APB has decided to adopt the International Standard on Quality Control 1 (ISQC 1) and International Standards on Auditing (ISAs) issued by the International Auditing and Assurance Standards Board[3] (IAASB). Where necessary APB has augmented such international standards by additional standards and guidance to maintain the requirements and clarity of previous UK and Irish auditing standards. This additional material is clearly differentiated from the original text of the international standards by the use of grey shading.

8. The APB has not at this time adopted ISA 700 (Revised) "The independent auditor's report on a complete set of general purpose financial statements" and the related conforming amendments made to ISA 200 "Objective and general principles governing an audit of financial statements" and ISA 560 "Subsequent events". The main effect of this is that the form of UK and Ireland auditor's reports dated on or after 31 December 2006 may not be exactly aligned with that required by ISA 700 (Revised). However, the APB believes that there are no significant differences of substance that would affect the actual performance of audits in the UK and Ireland, and accordingly

---

[2] In addition to the use of bold type lettering, the level of authority of the text in these paragraphs is identified by use of the expression "the auditor should ...". In some of the explanatory and other material the expression the "the auditor would ..." is used; the use of the word "would" in these paragraphs does not give them the same level of authority as the use of the word "should" in bold text.

[3] IAASB is a committee of the International Federation of Accountants (IFAC). The IAASB's constitution and due process is described in its 'Preface to the international standards on Quality Control, Auditing, Assurance and Related Services'.

that the differences do not cause audits performed in accordance with ISAs (UK and Ireland) to not comply with ISAs as issued by the IAASB.[4]

9. The ISAs (UK and Ireland) and ISQC 1 (UK and Ireland) require compliance with the APB's Ethical Standards and relevant ethical pronouncements relating to the work of auditors issued by the auditor's relevant professional body. This contrasts with the ISAs and ISQC 1 as issued by the IAASB, which refer to compliance ordinarily with Parts A and B of the IFAC Code of Ethics for Professional Accountants (the IFAC Code[5]) together with national requirements that are more restrictive.

10. When preparing them, the APB sought to ensure that the Ethical Standards adhered to the principles of the IFAC Code[6]. The APB is not aware of any significant instances where the relevant parts of the IFAC Code are more restrictive than the Ethical Standards[7].

Standards and Guidance for Audits of Financial Statements

11. The Auditors' Code, which is set out as Appendix 2, provides a framework of fundamental principles which encapsulate the concepts that govern the conduct of audits and underlie the APB's ethical and auditing standards.

12. APB engagement standards, which comprise APB Ethical Standards and International Standards on Auditing (UK and Ireland), apply to auditors carrying out:

- Statutory audits of companies in accordance with the Companies Acts[8];

- Audits of financial statements of entities in accordance with other UK or Irish legislation e.g. building societies, credit unions, friendly societies, pension funds, charities and registered social landlords;

- Public sector audits in the UK, including those carried out either on behalf of the national audit agencies or under contract to those agencies. (The standards

---

[4] The APB notes that ISA 700 (Revised) specifically recognises that national auditing standards may require using a different layout or wording for the auditor's report. In such circumstances, ISA 700 (Revised) provides that audits can still be referred to as being conducted in accordance with ISAs if the auditor's report includes all specified elements (and the audit complies with all the other relevant requirements of ISAs). Those elements are included in auditor's reports prepared in compliance with ISA (UK and Ireland) 700.

[5] The IFAC Code is included in the IFAC "Handbook of International Auditing, Assurance, and Ethics Pronouncements" and can be downloaded free of charge from the publications section of the IAASB website (www.ifac.org/IAASB).

[6] The Ethical Standards have also been designed to implement the requirements of the EC Recommendation on "Statutory auditors' independence in the EU: a set of fundamental principles" in the UK and Ireland.

[7] Should auditors wish to state that an audit has been conducted in compliance with ISAs as issued by IAASB they will need to ensure that they have complied with the relevant parts of the IFAC Code.

[8] Companies Act 1985 in the UK and the Companies Acts 1963 - 2003 in the Republic of Ireland.

**THE AUDITING
PRACTICES BOARD**

governing the conduct and reporting of the audit of financial statements are a matter for the national audit agencies to determine. However, the heads of the national audit agencies[9] in the UK have chosen to adopt the APB's engagement standards and quality control standards for audits as the basis of their approach to the audit of financial statements);

- Other audits performed by audit firms registered with the members of the Consultative Committee of Accountancy Bodies (CCAB)[10] unless the nature of the engagement requires the use of other recognised auditing standards; and

- Other audits where audit firms not registered with members of the CCAB elect, or are required by contract, to perform the work in accordance with UK or Irish auditing standards.

13. The APB also issues guidance to auditors of financial statements in the form of Practice Notes and Bulletins. Practice Notes and Bulletins are persuasive rather than prescriptive and are indicative of good practice. Practice Notes assist auditors in applying APB engagement standards to particular circumstances and industries and Bulletins provide timely guidance on new or emerging issues. Auditors should be aware of and consider Practice Notes applicable to the engagement. Auditors who do not consider and apply the guidance included in a relevant Practice Note should be prepared to explain how the basic principles and essential procedures in APB standards have been complied with.

14. The APB also issues consultative documents, briefing papers and research studies to stimulate public debate and comment.

Standards and Guidance for Reporting Accountants Acting in Connection With an Investment Circular

15. APB engagement standards apply to reporting accountants when carrying out engagements involving investment circulars intended to be issued in connection with a securities transaction governed wholly or in part by the laws and regulations of the United Kingdom or the Republic of Ireland. They comprise APB Ethical Standards for Reporting Accountants (ESRA) and Standards for Investment Reporting (SIRs).

16. SIRs and Bulletins adopt the same style and format and have the same status as equivalent APB pronouncements applying to auditors of financial statements.

---

[9] National audit agencies in the UK are the National Audit Office (for the Comptroller and Auditor General), the Welsh Audit Office (for the Auditor General for Wales), the Audit Commission, Audit Scotland (for the Auditor General for Scotland and the Accounts Commission) and the Northern Ireland Audit Office (for the Comptroller and Auditor General (Northern Ireland)).

[10] Members of CCAB are The Institute of Chartered Accountants in England & Wales, The Institute of Chartered Accountants of Scotland, The Institute of Chartered Accountants in Ireland, The Association of Chartered Certified Accountants, The Chartered Institute of Management Accountants and The Chartered Institute of Public Finance and Accountancy.

Guidance for Auditors Involved in Other Assurance Engagements.

17. The APB also issues standards and guidance for accountants on assurance engagements closely related to an audit of the financial statements. To date most of its pronouncements have taken the form of Bulletins (e.g. the auditors' statement on summary financial statements). However, the APB intends to issue standards for other assurance engagements as practice evolves and when APB believes that this is in the public interest.

Authority of APB Pronouncements

18. In order to be eligible for appointment in Great Britain as auditors of companies, or of any of the other entities which require their auditors to be eligible for appointment as auditors under section 25 of the Companies Act 1989, persons must be registered with a Recognised Supervisory Body (RSB)[11] recognised under that Act and must be eligible for appointment under the rules of that RSB. The Companies Act 1989 requires RSBs to have rules and practices as to the technical standards to be applied in company audit work and as to the manner in which these standards are to be applied in practice[12]. Each RSB is also required to have arrangements in place for the effective monitoring and enforcement of compliance with these standards.

19. In the Republic of Ireland legislative requirements concerning qualifications for appointment as auditor and recognition of bodies[13] of accountants are contained in the Companies Act 1990. This Act requires bodies of accountants to have satisfactory rules and practices as to technical and other standards. The Act also empowers the Minister for Enterprise, Trade and Employment to revoke or suspend recognition or authorisation of a body of accountants or individual auditor[14].

20. The members of the CCAB have undertaken to adopt APB standards and guidance developed by the APB within three months of promulgation by the APB of such Standards and guidance. In the Republic of Ireland, accountancy bodies which are not members of the CCAB but which are also recognised bodies for the supervision of auditors may choose to require their members to comply with APB standards.

---

[11] The Institute of Chartered Accountants in England & Wales, The Institute of Chartered Accountants of Scotland, The Institute of Chartered Accountants in Ireland, the Association of Authorised Public Accountants and The Association of Chartered Certified Accountants are Recognised Supervisory Bodies for the purpose of regulating auditors in the UK.

[12] In Northern Ireland, equivalent requirements are contained in Part III of the Companies (Northern Ireland) Order 1990.

[13] The Institute of Chartered Accountants in Ireland, the Institute of Certified Public Accountants in Ireland, the Institute of Incorporated Public Accountants, The Association of Chartered Certified Accountants, The Institute of Chartered Accountants in England and Wales and The Institute of Chartered Accountants in Scotland are "Recognised Bodies" in the Republic of Ireland.

[14] In the Republic of Ireland, the Companies (Auditing and Accounting) Act 2003, has made provision for the establishment of The Irish Auditing and Accounting Supervisory Authority (IAASA), a new statutory supervisory body. The functions of IAASA will include a role in cooperating and working in partnership with the auditing profession and other interested parties in developing standards in relation to the independence of auditors and in developing auditing standards and practice notes.

21. Apparent failures by auditors to comply with APB standards are liable to be investigated by the relevant accountancy body. Auditors who do not comply with auditing standards when performing company or other audits make themselves liable to regulatory action which may include the withdrawal of registration and hence of eligibility to perform company audits.

22. All relevant APB pronouncements and in particular auditing standards are likely to be taken into account when the adequacy of the work of auditors is being considered in a court of law or in other contested situations.

23. The nature of APB standards and associated guidance requires professional accountants to exercise professional judgment in applying them. In exceptional circumstances, auditors and reporting accountants may judge it necessary to depart from a basic principle or essential procedure of a standard to achieve more effectively the objective of the engagement. When such a situation arises, the auditor or reporting accountant documents the reasons for the departure.

Development of APB Pronouncements

24. Before publishing or amending its standards or Practice Notes the APB publishes an exposure draft on its website and sends a copy of the exposure draft to the members of the CCAB and to other parties.

25. The APB's aim is to allow three months for representations to be made on draft standards and Practice Notes. Where the draft standards are based on international standards the APB intends to co-ordinate its exposure process with that of IAASB.

26. Where exposure drafts would cause changes to be made to other previously issued publications, any such consequential changes will also be exposed for comment and published simultaneously. Representations received on exposure drafts will be given full and proper consideration by the APB, and will be available for public inspection.

27. Bulletins and other publications may be developed without the full process of consultation and exposure used for APB standards and Practice Notes. However, in the development of such documents, and before publication, the APB will decide the means by which it will obtain external views on them.

28. Each year the APB considers its priorities and consults on its proposed work programme with interested parties.

Appendix 1

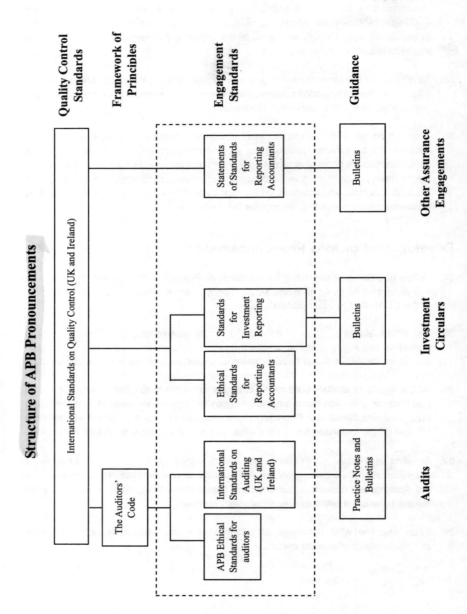

Structure of APB Pronouncements

Quality Control Standards

International Standards on Quality Control (UK and Ireland)

Framework of Principles

The Auditors' Code

Engagement Standards

Statements of Standards for Reporting Accountants

Standards for Investment Reporting

Ethical Standards for Reporting Accountants

International Standards on Auditing (UK and Ireland)

APB Ethical Standards for auditors

Guidance

Bulletins

Bulletins

Practice Notes and Bulletins

Other Assurance Engagements

Investment Circulars

Audits

Appendix 2

The Auditors' Code

Accountability	Auditors act in the interests of primary stakeholders, whilst having regard to the wider public interest. The identity of primary stakeholders is determined by reference to the statute or agreement requiring an audit: in the case of companies, the primary stakeholder is the general body of shareholders
Integrity	Auditors act with integrity, fulfilling their responsibilities with honesty, fairness, candour, courage and confidentiality. Confidential information obtained in the course of the audit is disclosed only when required in the public interest, or by operation of law.
Objectivity and independence	Auditors are objective and provide impartial opinions unaffected by bias, prejudice, compromise and conflicts of interest. Auditors are also independent, this requires them to be free from situations and relationships which would make it probable that a reasonable and informed third party would conclude that the auditors' objectivity either is impaired or could be impaired.
Competence	Auditors act with professional skill, derived from their qualification, training and practical experience. This demands an understanding of financial reporting and business issues, together with expertise in accumulating and assessing the evidence necessary to form an opinion.
Rigour	Auditors approach their work with thoroughness and with an attitude of professional scepticism. They assess critically the information and explanations obtained in the course of their work and such additional evidence as they consider necessary for the purposes of their audit.
Judgment	Auditors apply professional judgment taking account of materiality in the context of the matter on which they are reporting.
Clear, complete and effective communication	Auditors' reports contain clear expressions of opinion and set out information necessary for a proper understanding of the opinion. Auditors communicate audit matters of governance interest arising from the audit of financial statements with those charged with governance of an entity.
Association	Auditors allow their reports to be included in documents containing other information only if they consider that the additional information is not in conflict with the matters covered by their report and they have no cause to believe it to be misleading.
Providing value	Auditors add to the reliability and quality of financial reporting; they provide to directors and officers constructive observations arising from the audit process; and thereby contribute to the effective operation of business capital markets and the public sector.

Appendix 3

Conforming Amendment to This Statement on Scope and Authority of Pronouncements as a Result of ISA (UK and Ireland) 230 (Revised) – Effective for Engagements Performed by Auditors and Reporting Accountants for Periods Beginning on or After June 15, 2006

The revision of ISA (UK and Ireland) 230 *"Audit Documentation"* gave rise to conforming amendments to the APB's Statement on the Scope and Authority of Pronouncements.

The following paragraph in the APB Statement is amended as marked:

23. The nature of APB standards and associated guidance requires professional accountants to exercise professional judgment in applying them. Where, in exceptional circumstances, auditors and reporting accountants may judge it necessary to depart from a basic principle or essential procedure that is relevant in the circumstances of a standard to achieve more effectively the objective of the engagement. When such a situation arises, the auditor or reporting accountant documents how the alternative procedures performed achieve the objective of the engagement and, unless otherwise clear, the reasons for the departure.

This amendment is effective for engagements performed by auditors and reporting accountants for periods beginning on or after June 15, 2006.

Section 3: ETHICAL STANDARDS

2006 ACTIVITIES

APB Ethical Standards for Auditors (ESs) were issued in December 2004 and are effective for audits of financial statements for periods commencing on or after 15 December 2004. As stated in the APB work programme for 2006/07, the APB believes that use of the standards for at least two audit cycles (i.e. completion of December 2005 and December 2006 audits) will be needed before any systematic review of them should be undertaken. Such a review is currently planned for 2007/08.

In January 2006 the APB issued a consultation paper and exposure draft of the *Ethical Standard for Reporting Accountants* (ESRA) which proposed how the principles and independence requirements of ES 1 to 5 would apply to investment circular reporting engagements. The APB's goal in the development of the ESRA has been to keep independence standards for audit and investment circular reporting engagements as closely aligned as possible.

The main issues raised by commentators on the exposure draft of the ESRA related to the practical implications that result from the complexity of relationships with the engagement client and other parties who are connected with the investment circular and the level of confidentiality required where price sensitive transactions are involved. The APB gave careful consideration to these comments in order to provide a practical approach in the final standard.

In October 2006 the APB finalised the ESRA, which is effective for investment circular reporting engagements commencing on or after 1 April 2007. A feedback paper explaining the comments received on the consultation and the actions taken by the APB is available on the APB website at: www.frc.org.uk/apb/publications/exposure.cfm.

APB ETHICAL STANDARD 1

INTEGRITY, OBJECTIVITY AND INDEPENDENCE

(Re-issued December 2004)

CONTENTS

PREFACE

APB Ethical Standards apply in the audit of financial statements. They should be read in the context of the Auditing Practices Board's Statement "The Auditing Practices Board – Scope and Authority of Pronouncements (Revised)" which sets out the application and authority of APB Ethical Standards.

The terms used in APB Ethical Standards for Auditors are explained in the Glossary.

APB Ethical Standards apply to audits of financial statements in both the private and the public sectors. However, auditors in the public sector are subject to more complex ethical requirements than their private sector counterparts. This includes, for example, compliance with legislation such as the Prevention of Corruption Act 1916, concerning gifts and hospitality, and with Cabinet Office guidance.

INTRODUCTION

1   The financial statements of an entity may have a number of different users. For example, they may be used by suppliers and customers, joint venture partners, bankers and other suppliers of finance, taxation and regulatory authorities, employees, trades unions and environmental groups. In the case of a listed company, the financial statements are an important source of information to the capital markets. But the primary purpose of the financial statements of an entity is to provide its owners – the shareholders (or those in an equivalent position) – with information on the state of affairs of the entity and its performance and to assist them in assessing the stewardship exercised by the directors (or those in an equivalent position) over the business that has been entrusted to them.

2   The financial statements of an entity are the responsibility of its board of directors and are prepared by them, or by others on their behalf, for the shareholders or, in some circumstances, for other third parties.

3   The primary objective of an audit of the financial statements is for the auditors to provide independent assurance to the shareholders that the directors have prepared the financial statements properly. The auditors issue a report that includes their opinion as to whether or not the financial statements give a true and fair view in accordance with the relevant financial reporting framework.[1] Thus the auditors assist the shareholders to exercise their proprietary powers as shareholders in the Annual General Meeting.

4   Public confidence in the operation of the capital markets and in the conduct of public interest entities depends, in part, upon the credibility of the opinions and reports issued by the auditors in connection with the audit of the financial statements. Such credibility depends on beliefs concerning the integrity, objectivity and independence of the auditors and the quality of audit work they perform. APB establishes quality control, auditing and ethical standards to provide a framework for audit practice. The Auditors' Code underlies APB's standards and sets out the fundamental principles, which APB expects should guide the conduct of auditors.

5   APB Ethical Standards are concerned with the integrity, objectivity and independence of auditors. Ethical guidance on other matters, together with statements of fundamental ethical principles governing the work of all professional accountants, are issued by professional accountancy bodies.

6   **Auditors should conduct the audit of the financial statements of an entity with integrity, objectivity and independence.**

---

[1]   In the case of certain bodies in the public sector, the auditors express an opinion as to whether the financial statements 'present fairly' the financial position.

Integrity

7   Integrity is a prerequisite for all those who act in the public interest. It is essential that auditors act, and are seen to act, with integrity, which requires not only honesty but a broad range of related qualities such as fairness, candour, courage, intellectual honesty and confidentiality.

8   It is important that the directors and management of an audit client can rely on the auditors to treat the information obtained during an audit as confidential, unless they have authorised its disclosure, unless it is already known to third parties or unless the auditors have a legal right or duty to disclose it. Without this, there is a danger that the directors and management will fail to disclose such information to the auditors and that the effectiveness of the audit will thereby be impaired.

Objectivity

9   Objectivity is a state of mind that excludes bias, prejudice and compromise and that gives fair and impartial consideration to all matters that are relevant to the task in hand, disregarding those that are not. Objectivity requires that the auditors' judgment is not affected by conflicts of interests. Like integrity, objectivity is a fundamental ethical principle.

10   The need for auditors to be objective arises from the fact that many of the important issues involved in the preparation of financial statements do not relate to questions of fact but rather to questions of judgment. For example, there are choices to be made by the board of directors in deciding on the accounting policies to be adopted by the entity: the directors have to select the ones that they consider most appropriate and this decision can have a material impact on the financial statements. Furthermore, many items included in the financial statements cannot be measured with absolute precision and certainty. In many cases, estimates have to be made and the directors may have to choose one value from a range of possible outcomes. When exercising discretion in these areas, the directors have regard to the applicable financial reporting framework. If the directors, whether deliberately or inadvertently, make a biased judgment or an otherwise inappropriate decision, the financial statements may be misstated or misleading.

11   It is against this background that the auditors are required to express an opinion on the financial statements. Their audit involves considering the process followed and the choices made by the directors in preparing the financial statements and concluding whether the result gives a true and fair view in accordance with the relevant financial reporting framework. The auditors' objectivity requires that they express an impartial opinion in the light of all the available audit evidence and their professional judgment. Objectivity also requires that the auditors adopt a rigorous and robust approach and that they are prepared to disagree, where necessary, with the directors' judgments.

Independence

12   Independence is freedom from situations and relationships which make it probable that a reasonable and informed third party would conclude that objectivity either is impaired or could be impaired. Independence is related to and underpins objectivity. However, whereas objectivity is a personal behavioural characteristic concerning the auditors' state of mind, independence relates to the circumstances surrounding the audit, including the financial, employment, business and personal relationships between the auditors and their client.

13   The need for independence arises because, in most cases, users of the financial statements and other third parties do not have all the information necessary for judging whether the auditors are, in fact, objective. Although the auditors themselves may be satisfied that their objectivity is not impaired by a particular situation, a third party may reach a different conclusion. For example, if a third party were aware that the auditors had certain financial, employment, business or personal relationships with the audit client, that individual might reasonably conclude that the auditors could be subject to undue influence from the directors or would not be impartial or unbiased. Public confidence in the auditors' objectivity could therefore suffer as a result of this perception, irrespective of whether there is any actual impairment.

14   Accordingly, in evaluating the likely consequences of such situations and relationships, the test to be applied is not whether the auditors consider that their objectivity is impaired but whether it is probable that a reasonable and informed third party would conclude that the auditors' objectivity either is impaired or is likely to be impaired. There are inherent threats to the level of independence (both actual and perceived) that auditors can achieve as a result of the influence that the board of directors and management have over the appointment and remuneration of the auditors. The auditors consider the application of safeguards where there are threats to their independence (both actual and perceived).

COMPLIANCE WITH ETHICAL STANDARDS

15   **The audit firm should establish policies and procedures, appropriately documented and communicated, designed to ensure that, in relation to each audit engagement, the audit firm, and all those who are in a position to influence the conduct and outcome of the audit, act with integrity, objectivity and independence.**

16   For the purposes of APB Ethical Standards, a person in a position to influence the conduct and outcome of the audit is:

    (a)   any person who is directly involved in the audit ('the engagement team'), including:

        (i)   the audit partners, audit managers and audit staff ('the audit team');

(ii) professional personnel from other disciplines involved in the audit (for example, lawyers, actuaries, taxation specialists, IT specialists, treasury management specialists);[2]

(iii) those who provide quality control or direct oversight of the audit;

(b) any person, who forms part of the chain of command for the audit within the audit firm;

(c) any person within the audit firm who, due to any other circumstances, may be in a position to exert such influence.

17 Compliance with the requirements regarding the auditors' integrity, objectivity and independence is a responsibility of both the audit firm and of individual partners and professional staff. The audit firm establishes policies and procedures, appropriate to the size and nature of the audit firm, to promote and monitor compliance with those requirements by any person who is in a position to influence the conduct and outcome of the audit.[3]

18 The leadership of the audit firm should take responsibility for establishing a control environment within the firm that places adherence to ethical principles and compliance with APB Ethical Standards above commercial considerations.

19 The leadership of the audit firm influences the internal culture of the firm by its actions and by its example ('the tone at the top'). Achieving a robust control environment requires that the leadership gives clear, consistent and frequent messages, backed up by appropriate actions, which emphasise the importance of compliance with APB Ethical Standards.

20 In order to promote a strong control environment, the audit firm establishes policies and procedures that include:

(a) requirements for partners and staff to report where applicable:

- family and other personal relationships involving an audit client of the firm;

- financial interests in an audit client of the firm;

- decisions to join an audit client.

---

[2] Where external consultants are involved in the audit, ISA (UK and Ireland) 620 *'Using the work of an Expert'* states that the auditor should evaluate the objectivity of the expert.

[3] Monitoring of compliance with ethical requirements will often be performed as part of a broader quality control process. ISQC (UK & Ireland) 1 *'Quality Control for firms that perform audits and reviews of historical financial information and other assurance and related services engagements'* establishes the basic principles and essential procedures in relation to a firm's responsibilities for its system of quality control for audits.

(b) monitoring of compliance with the firm's policies and procedures relating to integrity, objectivity and independence. Such monitoring procedures include, on a test basis, periodic review of the audit engagement partners' documentation of their consideration of the auditors' objectivity and independence, addressing, for example:

- financial interests in audit clients;

- economic dependence on audit clients;

- the performance of non-audit services;

- audit partner rotation;

(c) prompt communication of possible or actual breaches of the firm's policies and procedures to the relevant audit engagement partners;

(d) evaluation by audit engagement partners of the implications of any identified possible or actual breaches of the firm's policies and procedures that are reported to them;

(e) reporting by audit engagement partners of particular circumstances or relationships as required by APB Ethical Standards;

(f) prohibiting members of the audit team from making, or assuming responsibility for, management decisions for the audit client;

(g) operation of an enforcement mechanism to promote compliance with policies and procedures;

(h) empowerment of staff to communicate to senior levels within the firm any issue of objectivity or independence that concerns them; this includes establishing clear communication channels open to staff, encouraging staff to use these channels and ensuring that staff who use these channels are not subject to disciplinary proceedings as a result.

21 **Save where the circumstances contemplated in paragraph 23 apply, the audit firm should designate a partner in the firm ('the ethics partner') as having responsibility for:**

(a) **the adequacy of the firm's policies and procedures relating to integrity, objectivity and independence, their compliance with APB Ethical Standards, and the effectiveness of their communication to partners and staff within the firm; and**

(b) **providing related guidance to individual partners.** *see D02/08/02 slide 6*

22 In assessing the effectiveness of the firm's communication of its policies and procedures relating to integrity, objectivity and independence, ethics partners

consider whether they are properly covered in induction programmes, professional training and continuing professional development for all partners and staff. Ethics partners also provide guidance on matters referred to them and on matters which they otherwise become aware of, where a difficult and objective judgment needs to be made or a consistent position reached.

23 In audit firms with three or less partners who are 'responsible individuals'[4], it may not be practicable for an ethics partner to be designated. In these circumstances all partners will regularly discuss ethical issues amongst themselves, so ensuring that they act in a consistent manner and observe the principles set out in APB Ethical Standards. In the case of a sole practitioner, advice on matters where a difficult and objective judgment needs to be made is obtained through the ethics helpline of their professional body, or through discussion with a practitioner from another firm. In all cases, it is important that such discussions are documented.

24 To be able to discharge his or her responsibilities, the ethics partner is an individual possessing seniority, relevant experience and authority within the firm and is provided with sufficient staff support and other resources, commensurate with the size of the firm. Alternative arrangements are established to allow for:

- the provision of guidance on those audits where the ethics partner is the audit engagement partner; and

- situations where the ethics partner is unavailable, for example due to illness or holidays.

25 Whenever a possible or actual breach of an APB Ethical Standard, or of policies and procedures established pursuant to the requirements of an APB Ethical Standard, is identified, the audit engagement partner, in the first instance, and the ethics partner, where appropriate, assesses the implications of the breach, determines whether there are safeguards that can be put in place or other actions that can be taken to address any potential adverse consequences and considers whether there is a need to resign from the audit engagement.

26 An inadvertent violation of this Standard does not necessarily call into question the audit firm's ability to give an audit opinion, provided that:

(a) the audit firm has established policies and procedures that require all partners and staff to report any breach promptly to the audit engagement partner or to the ethics partner, as appropriate;

(b) the audit engagement partner or ethics partner promptly notifies the relevant partner or member of staff that any matter which has given rise to a breach is to be addressed as soon as possible and ensures that such action is taken;

---

[4] A 'responsible individual' is a partner or employee of the audit firm who is responsible for audit work and designated as such under the audit regulations of a Recognised Supervisory Body.

(c)   safeguards, where appropriate, are applied, (for example, having another partner review the work done by the relevant partner or member of staff or removing him or her from the engagement team); and

(d)   the actions taken and the rationale for them are documented.

IDENTIFICATION AND ASSESSMENT OF THREATS

27   Auditors identify and assess the circumstances, which could adversely affect the auditors' objectivity ('threats'), including any perceived loss of independence, and apply procedures ('safeguards'), which will either:

(a)   eliminate the threat (for example, by eliminating the circumstances, such as removing an individual from the engagement team or disposing of a financial interest in the audit client); or

(b)   reduce the threat to an acceptable level, that is a level at which it is not probable that a reasonable and informed third party would conclude that the auditors' objectivity is impaired or is likely to be impaired (for example, by having the audit work reviewed by another partner or by another audit firm).

When considering safeguards, where the audit engagement partner chooses to reduce rather than to eliminate a threat to objectivity and independence, he or she recognises that this judgment may not be shared by users of the financial statements and that he or she may be required to justify the decision.

Threats to objectivity and independence

28   The principal types of threats to the auditors' objectivity and independence are:

most important focus on nature see relation to non-audit ES5

*   **self-interest threat**
    A self-interest threat arises when auditors have financial or other interests which might cause them to be reluctant to take actions that would be adverse to the interests of the audit firm or any individual in a position to influence the conduct or outcome of the audit (for example, where they have an investment in the client, are seeking to provide additional services to the client or need to recover long-outstanding fees from the client).

*   **self-review threat**
    A self-review threat arises when the results of a non-audit service performed by the auditors or by others within the audit firm are reflected in the amounts included or disclosed in the financial statements (for example, where the audit firm has been involved in maintaining the accounting records, or undertaking valuations that are incorporated in the financial statements). In the course of the audit, the auditors may need to re-evaluate the work performed in the non-audit service. As, by virtue of providing the non-audit service, the audit firm is associated with aspects of the

preparation of the financial statements, it may be (or may be perceived to be) unable to take an impartial view of relevant aspects of those financial statements.

- **management threat**
  A management threat arises when the audit firm undertakes work that involves making judgments and taking decisions, which are the responsibility of management (for example, where it has been involved in the design, selection and implementation of financial information technology systems). In such work, the audit firm may become closely aligned with the views and interests of management and the auditors' objectivity and independence may be impaired, or may be perceived to be, impaired.

- **advocacy threat**
  An advocacy threat arises when the audit firm undertakes work that involves acting as an advocate for an audit client and supporting a position taken by management in an adversarial context (for example, by acting as a legal advocate for the client in litigation). In order to act in an advocacy role, the audit firm has to adopt a position closely aligned to that of management. This creates both actual and perceived threats to the auditors' objectivity and independence.

- **familiarity (or trust) threat**
  A familiarity (or trust) threat arises when the auditors are predisposed to accept or are insufficiently questioning of the client's point of view (for example, where they develop close personal relationships with client personnel through long association with the client).

- **intimidation threat**
  An intimidation threat arises when the auditors' conduct is influenced by fear or threats (for example, where they encounter an aggressive and dominating individual).

These categories may not be entirely distinct: certain circumstances may give rise to more than one type of threat. For example, where an audit firm wishes to retain the fee income from a large audit client, but encounters an aggressive and dominating individual, there may be a self-interest threat as well as an intimidation threat.

29   Threats to the auditors' objectivity, including a perceived loss of independence, may arise where the audit firm is appointed to a non-audit service engagement for a non-audit client, but where an audit client makes this decision. In such cases, even if the non-audit client pays the fee for the non-audit service engagement, the auditors consider the implication of the threats (especially the self-interest threat) that arise from the appointment.

30   **The audit firm should establish policies and procedures to require persons in a position to influence the conduct and outcome of the audit to be constantly alert to circumstances that might reasonably be considered threats to their objectivity or the perceived loss of independence and, where such circumstances are identified, to report them to the audit engagement partner or to the ethics partner, as appropriate.**

31 Such policies and procedures require that threats to the auditors' objectivity and independence are communicated to the appropriate person, having regard to the nature of the threats and to the part of the firm and the identity of any person involved. The consideration of all threats and the action taken is documented. If the audit engagement partner is personally involved, or if he or she is unsure about the action to be taken, the matter is resolved through consultation with the ethics partner.

32 **The audit firm should establish policies and procedures to require the audit engagement partner to identify and assess the significance of threats to the auditors' objectivity, including any perceived loss of independence:**

(a) **when considering whether to accept or retain an audit engagement;[5]**

(b) **when planning the audit;**

(c) **when forming an opinion on the financial statements;[6]**

(d) **when considering whether to accept or retain an engagement to provide non-audit services to an audit client; and**

(e) **when potential threats are reported to him or her.**

33 An initial assessment of the threats to objectivity and independence is required when the audit engagement partner is considering whether to accept or retain an audit engagement. That assessment is reviewed and updated at the planning stage of each audit. At the end of the audit process, when forming an opinion on the financial statements but before issuing the report, the audit engagement partner draws an overall conclusion as to whether any threats to objectivity and independence have been properly addressed in accordance with APB Ethical Standards. If, at any time, the auditors are invited to accept an engagement to provide non-audit services to an audit client, the audit engagement partner considers the impact this may have on the auditors' objectivity and independence.

34 When identifying and assessing threats to their objectivity and independence, auditors take into account their current relationships with the audit client (including non-audit service engagements), those that existed prior to the current audit engagement and any known to be in prospect following the current audit engagement. This is because those prior and subsequent relationships may be perceived as likely to influence the auditors in the performance of the audit or as otherwise impairing the auditors' objectivity and independence.

---

[5] Consideration of whether to accept or retain an audit engagement does not arise with those bodies in the public sector where responsibility for the audit is assigned by legislation.

[6] In the case of listed companies, the auditors also assess whether there is any threat to their objectivity and independence when discharging their responsibilities in relation to preliminary announcements and when reporting on interim results.

35 Where the audit client or a third party calls into question the objectivity and independence of the audit firm in relation to a particular client, the ethics partner carries out such investigations as may be appropriate.

IDENTIFICATION AND ASSESSMENT OF SAFEGUARDS

36 **If the audit engagement partner identifies threats to the auditors' objectivity, including any perceived loss of independence, he or she should identify and assess the effectiveness of the available safeguards and apply such safeguards as are sufficient to eliminate the threats or reduce them to an acceptable level.**

37 The nature and extent of safeguards to be applied depend on the significance of the threats. Where a threat is clearly insignificant, no safeguards are needed.

38 Other APB Ethical Standards address specific circumstances which can create threats to the auditors' objectivity or loss of independence. They give examples of safeguards that can, in some circumstances, eliminate the threat or reduce it to an acceptable level. In circumstances where this is not possible, either the auditors do not accept or withdraw from the audit engagement.

39 **The audit engagement partner should not accept or should not continue an audit engagement if he or she concludes that any threats to the auditors' objectivity and independence cannot be reduced to an acceptable level.**

40 Where a reasonable and informed third party would regard ceasing to act as the auditor as detrimental to the shareholders (or equivalent) of the audit client, then resignation may not be immediate. However, the audit firm discloses full details of the position to those charged with governance of the audit client, and establishes appropriate safeguards.

REVIEW BY AN INDEPENDENT PARTNER

See pg 114 glossary

41 **In the case of listed companies the independent partner[7] should:**

(a) **consider the audit firm's compliance with APB Ethical Standards in relation to the audit engagement;**

(b) **form an independent opinion as to the appropriateness and adequacy of the safeguards applied; and**

(c) **consider the adequacy of the documentation of the audit engagement partner's consideration of the auditors' objectivity and independence.**

---

[7] ISA (UK and Ireland) 220 'Quality control for audits of historical financial information', requires the audit engagement partner to appoint an engagement quality control reviewer for all audits of listed entities...The engagement quality control review involves consideration of...the engagement team's evaluation of the independence of the firm...'

42 The audit firm's policies and procedures will also set out the circumstances in which an independent review is performed for other audit engagements. These policies will take into consideration the nature of the entity's business, its size, the number of its employees and the range of its stakeholders.

OVERALL CONCLUSION

43 **At the end of the audit process, when forming an opinion but before issuing the report on the financial statements, the audit engagement partner should reach an overall conclusion that any threats to objectivity and independence have been properly addressed in accordance with APB Ethical Standards. If the audit engagement partner cannot make such a conclusion, he or she should not report and the audit firm should resign as auditors.**

44 If the audit engagement partner remains unable to conclude that any threat to objectivity and independence has been properly addressed in accordance with APB Ethical Standards, or if there is a disagreement between the audit engagement partner and the independent partner, he or she consults the ethics partner.

45 In concluding on compliance with the requirements for objectivity and independence, the audit engagement partner is entitled to rely on the completeness and accuracy of the data developed by the audit firm's systems relating to independence (for example, in relation to the reporting of financial interests by staff), unless informed otherwise by the firm.

OTHER AUDITORS INVOLVED IN THE AUDIT OF GROUP FINANCIAL STATEMENTS

46 **The group audit engagement partner should be satisfied that other auditors (whether a network firm or another audit firm) involved in the audit of the group financial statements, who are not subject to APB Ethical Standards, are objective and document the rationale for that conclusion.**

47 The group audit engagement partner obtains written confirmation from the other auditors that they have a sufficient understanding of and have complied with the IFAC Code of Ethics for Professional Accountants, including the independence requirements[8].

48 In the case of a listed company, the group audit engagement partner establishes that the company has communicated its policy on the engagement of external auditors to

---

[8] Section 8 of the International Federation of Accountants (IFAC) Code of Ethics for Professional Accountants (the IFAC Code) establishes a conceptual framework for independence requirements for assurance engagements that is the international standard on which national standards should be based. No Member Body of IFAC is allowed to apply less stringent standards than those stated in that section. In addition, members of the IFAC Forum of Firms have agreed to apply ethical standards, which are at least as rigorous as those of the IFAC Code.

supply non-audit services to its affiliates and obtains confirmation that the other auditors will comply with this policy.

COMMUNICATION WITH THOSE CHARGED WITH GOVERNANCE

49 **The audit engagement partner should ensure that those charged with governance of the audit client are appropriately informed on a timely basis of all significant facts and matters that bear upon the auditors' objectivity and independence.**

nonlisted

50 The audit committee, where one exists, is usually responsible for oversight of the relationship between the auditors and the entity and of the conduct of the audit process. It therefore has a particular interest in being informed about the auditors' ability to express an objective opinion on the financial statements. Where there is no audit committee, this role is undertaken by the board of directors.[9, 10]

listed

51 The aim of these communications is to ensure full and fair disclosure by the auditors to those charged with governance of the audit client on matters in which they have an interest. These will generally include the key elements of the audit engagement partner's consideration of objectivity and independence, such as:

nonlisted

- the principal threats, if any, to objectivity and independence identified by the auditors, including consideration of all relationships between the audit client, its affiliates and directors and the audit firm;

- any safeguards adopted and the reasons why they are considered to be effective;

- any independent partner review;

- the overall assessment of threats and safeguards;

- information about the general policies and processes within the audit firm for maintaining objectivity and independence.

52 In the case of listed companies, the auditors, as a minimum:

listed

(a) disclose in writing:

    (i) details of all relationships between the auditors and the client, its directors and senior management and its affiliates, including all services provided by the audit firm and its network to the client, its directors and senior management and its affiliates, that the auditors consider may reasonably be thought to bear on their objectivity and independence;

---

[9] Where there is no audit committee, references to communication with the audit committee are to be construed as including communication with the board of directors.

[10] Some bodies in the public sector have audit committees but others have different governance models.

(ii)   the related safeguards that are in place; and

(iii) the total amount of fees that the auditors and their network firms have charged to the client and its affiliates for the provision of services during the reporting period, analysed into appropriate categories, for example, statutory audit services, further audit services, tax advisory services and other non-audit services.[11] For each category, the amounts of any future services which have been contracted or where a written proposal has been submitted, are separately disclosed;

(b)   confirm in writing that they comply with APB Ethical Standards and that, in their professional judgment, they are independent and their objectivity is not compromised, or otherwise declare that they have concerns that their objectivity and independence may be compromised (including instances where the group audit engagement partner does not consider the other auditors to be objective); and explaining the actions which necessarily follow from this; and

(c)   seek to discuss these matters with the audit committee.

53   The most appropriate time for final confirmation of such matters is usually at the conclusion of the audit. However, communications between the auditors and those charged with the governance of the audit client will also be needed at the planning stage and whenever significant judgments are made about threats to objectivity and independence and the appropriateness of safeguards put in place, for example, when accepting an engagement to provide non-audit services.

DOCUMENTATION

54   **The audit engagement partner should ensure that his or her consideration of the auditors' objectivity and independence is appropriately documented on a timely basis.**

55   The requirement to document these issues contributes to the clarity and rigour of the audit engagement partner's thinking and the quality of his or her judgments. In addition, such documentation provides evidence that the audit engagement partner's consideration of the auditors' objectivity and independence was properly performed and, for listed companies, provides the basis for review by the independent partner.

56   Matters to be documented[12] include all key elements of the process and any significant judgments concerning:

---

[11] When considering how to present this analysis of fees, the auditors take account of any applicable legislation and whether the types of non-audit services provided differ substantially.

[12] The necessary working papers can be combined with those prepared pursuant to paragraph 12 of ISA (UK and Ireland) 220 'Quality control for audits of historical financial information', which states that: 'The engagement partner should ... document conclusions on independence and any relevant discussions with the firm that support these conclusions.'

- threats identified and the process used in identifying them;

- safeguards adopted and the reasons why they are considered to be effective;

- review by an independent partner;

- overall assessment of threats and safeguards; and

- communication with those charged with governance.

EFFECTIVE DATE

57   Effective for audits of financial statements for periods commencing on or after 15 December 2004.

58   Firms may complete audit engagements relating to periods commencing prior to 15 December 2004 in accordance with existing ethical guidance from the relevant professional body, putting in place any necessary changes in the subsequent engagement period.

59   Firms may implement revisions to their policies and procedures as required under paragraphs 15 and 21 during the year commencing 15 December 2004.

APB ETHICAL STANDARD 2

FINANCIAL, BUSINESS, EMPLOYMENT AND PERSONAL RELATIONSHIPS

(Re-issued December 2004)

CONTENTS

PREFACE

APB Ethical Standards apply in the audit of financial statements. They should be read in the context of the Auditing Practices Board's Statement "The Auditing Practices Board – Scope and Authority of Pronouncements (Revised)" which sets out the application and authority of APB Ethical Standards.

The terms used in APB Ethical Standards for Auditors are explained in the Glossary.

APB Ethical Standards apply to audits of financial statements in both the private and the public sectors. However, auditors in the public sector are subject to more complex ethical requirements than their private sector counterparts. This includes, for example, compliance with legislation such as the Prevention of Corruption Act 1916, concerning gifts and hospitality, and with Cabinet Office guidance.

INTRODUCTION

1   APB Ethical Standard 1 requires the audit engagement partner to identify and assess the circumstances which could adversely affect the auditors' objectivity ('threats'), including any perceived loss of independence, and to apply procedures ('safeguards') which will either:

(a)   eliminate the threat; or

(b)   reduce the threat to an acceptable level (that is, a level at which it is not probable that a reasonable and informed third party would conclude that the auditors' objectivity and independence is impaired or is likely to be impaired).

When considering safeguards, where the audit engagement partner chooses to reduce rather than to eliminate a threat to objectivity and independence, he or she recognises that this judgment may not be shared by users of the financial statements and that he or she may be required to justify the decision.

2   This Standard provides requirements and guidance on specific circumstances arising out of financial, business, employment and personal relationships with the audit client, which may create threats to the auditors' objectivity or perceived loss of independence. It gives examples of safeguards that can, in some circumstances, eliminate the threat or reduce it to an acceptable level. In circumstances where this is not possible, either the relationship in question is not entered into or the auditors either do not accept or withdraw from the audit engagement, as appropriate.

3   Whenever a possible or actual breach of an APB Ethical Standard is identified, the audit engagement partner, in the first instance, and the ethics partner, where appropriate, assesses the implications of the breach, determines whether there are safeguards that can be put in place or other actions that can be taken to address any potential adverse consequences and considers whether there is a need to resign from the audit engagement.

4   An inadvertent violation of this Standard does not necessarily call into question the audit firm's ability to give an audit opinion provided that:

(a)   the audit firm has established policies and procedures that require all partners and staff to report any breach promptly to the audit engagement partner or to the ethics partner as appropriate;

(b)   the audit engagement partner or ethics partner promptly notifies the partner or member of staff that any matter which has given rise to a breach is to be addressed as soon as possible and ensures that such action is taken;

(c)   safeguards, if appropriate, are applied (for example, having another partner review the work done by the relevant partner or member of staff or by removing him or her from the engagement team); and

(d)   the actions taken and the rationale for them are documented.

FINANCIAL RELATIONSHIPS

General considerations

5   A financial interest is an equity or other security, debenture, loan or other debt instrument of an entity, including rights and obligations to acquire such an interest and derivatives directly related to such an interest.

6   Financial interests may be:

(a)   owned directly, rather than through intermediaries (a 'direct financial interest'); or

(b)   owned through intermediaries, for example, an open ended investment company or a pension scheme (an 'indirect financial interest').

7   **The audit firm, any partner in the audit firm, a person in a position to influence the conduct and outcome of the audit or an immediate family member of such a person should not hold:**

(a)   **any direct financial interest in an audit client or an affiliate of an audit client; or**

(b)   **any indirect financial interest in an audit client or an affiliate of an audit client, where the investment is material to the audit firm or the individual and to the intermediary; or**

(c)   **any indirect financial interest in an audit client or an affiliate of an audit client, where the person holding it has both:**

(i)   **the ability to influence the investment decisions of the intermediary; and**

(ii)   **actual knowledge of the existence of the underlying investment in the audit client.**

8   The threats to the auditors' objectivity and independence, where a direct financial interest or a material indirect financial interest in the audit client is held by the audit firm or by one of the individuals specified in paragraph 7 are such that no safeguards can eliminate them or reduce them to an acceptable level.

9   For the purposes of paragraph 7, where holdings in an authorised unit or investment trust, an open ended investment company or an equivalent investment vehicle which is audited by the audit firm, are held by a partner in the audit firm, who is not in a position to influence the conduct and outcome of the audit, or an immediate family member of such a partner, these are to be treated as indirect financial interests. Such interests can therefore be held as long as:

(a)   they are not material to the individual; and

(b)   the individual has no influence over the investment decisions of the audit client.

10   Where a person in a position to influence the conduct and outcome of the audit, or a partner in the audit firm, or any of their immediate family members, are members or shareholders of an audit client, as a result of membership requirements, or equivalent, the audit firm ensures that no more than the minimum number of shares necessary to comply with the requirement are held and that this shareholding is not material to either the audit client or the individual. Disclosure of such shareholdings will be made to those charged with governance of the audit client, in accordance with APB Ethical Standard 1, paragraph 49.

11   Where one of the financial interests specified in paragraph 7 is held by:

(a)   *the audit firm, a partner in the audit firm or an immediate family member of such a partner:* the entire financial interest is disposed of, a sufficient amount of an indirect financial interest is disposed of so that the remaining interest is no longer material, or the firm does not accept (or withdraws from) the audit engagement;

(b)   *a person in a position to influence the conduct and outcome of the audit:* the entire financial interest is disposed of, a sufficient amount of an indirect financial interest is disposed of so that the remaining interest is no longer material, or that person does not retain a position in which they exert such influence on the audit engagement;

(c)   *an immediate family member of a person in a position to influence the conduct and outcome of the audit:* the entire financial interest is disposed of, a sufficient amount of an indirect financial interest is disposed of so that the remaining interest is no longer material, or the person in a position to influence the conduct and outcome of the audit does not retain a position in which they exert such influence on the audit engagement.

12   Where one of the financial interests specified in paragraph 7 is acquired unintentionally, as a result of an external event (for example, inheritance, gift, or merger of firms or companies), the disposal of the financial interest is required immediately, or as soon as possible after the relevant person has actual knowledge of and the right to dispose of the interest.

13   Where the disposal of a financial interest does not take place immediately, the audit firm adopts safeguards to preserve its objectivity until the financial interest is disposed. These may include the temporary exclusion of the person in a position to influence the conduct and outcome of the audit from such influence on the audit or a review of the relevant person's audit work by an audit partner having sufficient experience and authority to fulfill the role, who is not involved in the audit engagement.

14   Where the audit firm or one of the individuals specified in paragraph 7 holds an indirect financial interest but does not have both:

(a)   the ability to influence the investment decisions of the intermediary; and

(b)   actual knowledge of the existence of the underlying investment in the audit client, there may not be a threat to the auditors' objectivity and independence. For example, where the indirect financial interest takes the form of an investment in a pension fund, the composition of the funds and the size and nature of any underlying investment in the audit client may be known but there is unlikely to be any influence on investment decisions, as the fund will generally be managed independently on a discretionary basis. In the case of an 'index tracker' fund, the investment in the audit client is determined by the composition of the relevant index and there may be no threat to objectivity. As long as the person holding the indirect interest is not directly involved in the audit of the intermediary, nor able to influence the individual investment decisions of the intermediary, any threat to the auditors' objectivity and independence may be regarded as insignificant.

15   Where the audit firm or one of the individuals specified in paragraph 7 holds a beneficial interest in a properly operated 'blind' trust, they are (by definition) completely unaware of the identity of the underlying investments. If these include an investment in the audit client, this means that they are unaware of the existence of an indirect financial interest. In these circumstances, there is no threat to the auditors' objectivity and independence.

16   **Where a person in a position to influence the conduct and outcome of the audit or a partner in the audit firm becomes aware that a close family member holds one of the financial interests specified in paragraph 7, that individual should report the matter to the audit engagement partner to take appropriate action. If it is a close family member of the audit engagement partner, or if the audit engagement partner is in doubt as to the action to be taken, the audit engagement partner should resolve the matter through consultation with the ethics partner.**

Financial interests held as trustee

17   Where a direct or an indirect financial interest in the audit client or its affiliates is held in a trustee capacity by a person in a position to influence the conduct and outcome of the audit, or an immediate family member of such a person, a self-interest threat may be created because either the existence of the trustee interest may influence the conduct of the audit or the trust may influence the actions of the audit client. Accordingly, such a trustee interest is only held when:

- the relevant person is not an identified potential beneficiary of the trust; and

- the financial interest held by the trust in the audit client is not material to the trust; and

- the trust is not able to exercise significant influence over the audit client or an affiliate of the audit client; and

- the relevant person does not have significant influence over the investment decisions made by the trust, in so far as they relate to the financial interest in the audit client.

18   Where it is not clear whether the financial interest held by the trust in the audit client is material to the trust or whether the trust is able to exercise significant influence over the audit client, the financial interest is reported to the ethics partner, so that a decision can be made as to the steps that need to be taken.

Financial interests held by audit firm pension schemes

19   Where the pension scheme of an audit firm has a financial interest in an audit client or its affiliates and the firm has any influence over the trustees' investment decisions (other than indirect strategic and policy decisions), the self-interest threat created is such that no safeguards can eliminate it or reduce it to an acceptable level. In other cases (for example, where the pension scheme invests through a collective investment scheme and the firm's influence is limited to investment policy decisions, such as the allocation between different categories of investment), the ethics partner considers the acceptability of the position, having regard to the materiality of the financial interest to the pension scheme.

Loans and guarantees

20   Where audit firms, persons in a position to influence the conduct and outcome of the audit or immediate family members of such persons:

(a)   accept a loan[1] or a guarantee of their borrowings from an audit client; or

(b)   make a loan to or guarantee the borrowings of an audit client,

a self-interest threat and an intimidation threat to the auditors' objectivity can be created or there may be a perceived loss of independence. In a number of situations, no safeguards can eliminate this threat or reduce it to an acceptable level.

21   **Audit firms, persons in a position to influence the conduct and outcome of the audit and immediate family members of such persons should not make a loan to, or guarantee the borrowings of, an audit client or its affiliates unless this represents a deposit made with a bank or similar deposit taking institution in the ordinary course of business and on normal business terms.**

22   **Audit firms should not accept a loan from, or have their borrowings guaranteed by, the audit client or its affiliates unless:**

(a)   **the audit client is a bank or similar deposit taking institution; and**

(b)   **the loan or guarantee is made in the ordinary course of business on normal business terms; and**

---

[1]   For the purpose of this standard, the term 'loan' does not include ordinary trade credit arrangements or deposits placed for goods or services, unless they are material to either party (see paragraph 26).

(c) the loan or guarantee is not material to both the audit firm and the audit client.

23 Persons in a position to influence the conduct and outcome of the audit and immediate family members of such persons should not accept a loan from, or have their borrowings guaranteed by, the audit client or its affiliates unless:

(a) the audit client is a bank or similar deposit taking institution; and

(b) the loan or guarantee is made in the ordinary course of business on normal business terms; and

(c) the loan or guarantee is not material to the audit client.

24 Loans by an audit client that is a bank or similar institution to a person in a position to influence the conduct and outcome of the audit, or an immediate family member of such a person (for example, home mortgages, bank overdrafts or car loans), do not create an unacceptable threat to objectivity and independence, provided that normal business terms apply. However, where such loans are in arrears by a significant amount, this creates an intimidation threat that is unacceptable. Where such a situation arises, the person in a position to influence the conduct and outcome of the audit reports the matter to the audit engagement partner, or to the ethics partner, as appropriate and ceases to have any involvement with the audit. The audit engagement partner or, where appropriate, the ethics partner considers whether any audit work is to be reperformed.

BUSINESS RELATIONSHIPS

25 A business relationship between:

(a) the audit firm or a person who is in a position to influence the conduct and outcome of the audit, or an immediate family member of such a person, and

(b) the audit client or its affiliates, or its management

involves the two parties having a common commercial interest. Business relationships may create self-interest, advocacy or intimidation threats to the auditors' objectivity and perceived loss of independence. Examples include:

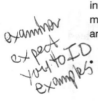
examiner expect you to ID examples

- joint ventures with the audit client or with a director, officer or other individual who performs senior managerial functions for the client;

- arrangements to combine one or more services or products of the audit firm with one or more services or products of the audit client and to market the package with reference to both parties;

- distribution or marketing arrangements under which the audit firm acts as a distributor or marketer of any of the audit client's products or services, or the audit client acts as the distributor or marketer of any of the products or services of the audit firm;

- other commercial transactions, such as the audit firm leasing its office space from the audit client.

26 **Audit firms, persons in a position to influence the conduct and outcome of the audit and immediate family members of such persons should not enter into business relationships with an audit client or its affiliates except where they involve the purchase of goods and services from the audit firm or the audit client in the ordinary course of business and on an arm's length basis and the value involved is not material to either party.**

27 Where a business relationship is not in the ordinary course of business, or where it is not on an arm's length basis, or where the value involved is material, and has been entered into by:

(a) *the audit firm:* either the relationship is terminated or the firm does not accept (or withdraws from) the audit engagement;

(b) *a person in a position to influence the conduct and outcome of the audit:* either the relationship is terminated or that person does not retain a position in which they exert such influence on the audit engagement;

(c) *an immediate family member of a person in a position to influence the conduct and outcome of the audit:* either the relationship is terminated or that person does not retain a position in which they exert such influence on the audit engagement.

Where there is an unavoidable delay in the termination of a business relationship, the audit firm adopts safeguards to preserve its objectivity until the relationship is terminated. These may include a review of the relevant person's audit work or a temporary exclusion of the relevant person from influence on conduct and outcome of the audit.

28 **Where a person in a position to influence the conduct and outcome of the audit becomes aware that a close family member has entered into one of the business relationships specified in paragraph 25, that individual should report the matter to the audit engagement partner to take appropriate action. If it is a close family member of the audit engagement partner or if the audit engagement partner is in doubt as to the action to be taken, the audit engagement partner should resolve the matter through consultation with the ethics partner.**

29 Where there are doubts as to whether a transaction or series of transactions are either in the ordinary course of business and on an arm's length basis or of such materiality that they constitute a threat to the audit firm's objectivity and independence, the audit engagement partner reports the issue:

- to the ethics partner, so that a decision can be made as to the appropriate action that needs to be taken to ensure that the matter is resolved; and

- to those charged with governance of the audit client, together with other significant facts and matters that bear upon the auditors' objectivity and independence, to obtain their views on the matter.

30 **An audit firm should not provide audit services to any entity or person able to influence the affairs of the audit firm or the performance of any audit engagement undertaken by the audit firm.**

31 This prohibition applies to:

(a) any entity that owns any significant part of an audit firm, or is an affiliate of such an entity; or

(b) any shareholder, director or other person in a position to direct the affairs of such an entity or its affiliate.

A significant ownership is one that carries the ability materially to influence the policy of an entity.[2]

EMPLOYMENT RELATIONSHIPS

MANAGEMENT ROLE WITH AUDIT CLIENT

32 **An audit firm should not admit to the partnership or employ a person to undertake audit work if that person is also employed by the audit client or its affiliates ('dual employment').**

Loan staff assignments

33 **An audit firm should not enter into an agreement with an audit client to provide a partner or employee to work for a temporary period as if that individual were an employee of the audit client or its affiliates (a 'loan staff assignment') unless the audit client:**

(a) **agrees that the individual concerned will not hold a management position; and**

(b) **acknowledges its responsibility for directing and supervising the work to be performed, which will not include such matters as:**

- **making management decisions; or**

---

[2] For companies, competition authorities have generally treated a 15% shareholding as sufficient to provide a material ability to influence policy.

- **exercising discretionary authority to commit the audit client to a particular position or accounting treatment.**

34   Where an audit firm agrees to assist an audit client by providing loan staff, threats to objectivity and independence may be created. A management threat may arise if the employee undertakes work that involves making judgments and taking decisions that are properly the responsibility of management. Thus, for example, interim management arrangements involving participation in the financial reporting function are not acceptable.

35   A self-review threat may also arise if the individual, during the loan staff assignment, is in a position to influence the preparation of the client's financial statements and then, on completion of that assignment, is assigned to the engagement team for that client, with responsibility to report on matters for which he or she was responsible whilst on that loan staff assignment.

36   **Where a partner or employee returns to the firm on completion of a loan staff assignment, that individual should not be given any role on the audit involving any function or activity that he or she performed or supervised during that assignment.**

37   In considering for how long this restriction is to be observed, the need to realise the potential value to the effectiveness of the audit of the increased knowledge of the client's business gained through the assignment has to be weighed against the potential threats to objectivity and independence. Those threats increase with the length of the assignment and with the intended level of responsibility of the individual within the engagement team. As a minimum, this restriction will apply to at least the first audit of the financial statements following the completion of the loan staff assignment.

Partners and engagement team members joining an audit client

38   **Where a former partner in the audit firm joins the audit client, the audit firm should take action as quickly as possible - and, in any event, before any further work is done by the audit firm in connection with the audit - to ensure that no significant connections remain between the firm and the individual.**

39   Ensuring that no significant connections remain between the firm and the individual requires that:

- all capital balances and similar financial interests be fully settled (including retirement benefits) unless these are made in accordance with pre-determined arrangements that cannot be influenced by any remaining connections between the individual and the firm; and

- the individual does not participate or appear to participate in the audit firm's business or professional activities.

From should do

40   Audit firms should establish policies and procedures that require:

   (a)   all partners in the audit firm to notify the firm of any situation involving their potential employment with any audit client of the firm; and

   (b)   senior members of any engagement team to notify the audit firm of any situation involving their potential employment with the relevant audit client; and

   (c)   other members of any engagement team to notify the audit firm of any situation involving their probable employment with the relevant audit client; and

   (d)   anyone who has given such notice to be removed from the engagement team; and

   (e)   a review of the audit work performed by the resigning or former engagement team member in the current and, where appropriate, the most recent audit.

41   Objectivity and independence may be threatened where a director, an officer or an employee of the audit client who is in a position to exert direct and significant influence over the preparation of the financial statements has recently been a partner in the audit firm or a member of the engagement team. Such circumstances may create self-interest, familiarity and intimidation threats, particularly when significant connections remain between the individual and the audit firm. Similarly, objectivity and independence may be threatened when an individual knows, or has reason to believe that he or she will or may be joining the audit client at some time in the future.

42   Where a partner in the audit firm or a member of the engagement team for a particular audit client has left the audit firm and taken up employment with that audit client, the significance of the self-interest, familiarity and intimidation threats is assessed and normally depends on such factors as:

   •   the position that individual had in the engagement team or firm;

   •   the position that individual has taken at the audit client;

   •   the amount of involvement that individual will have with the engagement team (especially where it includes former colleagues with whom he or she worked);

   •   the length of time since that individual was a member of the engagement team or employed by the audit firm.

   Following the assessment of any such threats, appropriate safeguards are applied where necessary.

43   Any review of audit work is performed by a more senior audit professional. If the individual joining the client is an audit partner, the review is performed by an audit partner who is not involved in the audit engagement. Where, due to its size, the audit

firm does not have a partner who was not involved in the audit engagement, it seeks either a review by another audit firm or advice from its professional body.

44   **Where a partner leaves the firm and is appointed as a director (including as a non-executive director) or to a key management position with an audit client, having acted as audit engagement partner (or as an independent partner, key audit partner or a partner in the chain of command) at any time in the two years prior to this appointment, the firm should resign as auditors.[3] The firm should not accept re-appointment as auditors until a two-year period, commencing when the former partner ceased to act for the client, has elapsed or the former partner ceases employment with the former client, whichever is the sooner.**

45   **Where a former member of the engagement team (other than an audit engagement partner, a key audit partner or a partner in the chain of command) leaves the audit firm and, within two years of ceasing to hold that position, joins the audit client as a director (including as a non-executive director) or in a key management position, the audit firm should consider whether the composition of the audit team is appropriate.**

46   In such circumstances, the audit firm evaluates the appropriateness of the composition of the audit team by reference to the factors listed in paragraph 42 and alters or strengthens the audit team to address any threat to the auditors' objectivity and independence that may be identified.

Family members employed by an audit client

47   **Where a person in a position to influence the conduct and outcome of the audit, or a partner in the audit firm, becomes aware that an immediate or close family member is employed by an audit client in a position to exercise influence on the accounting records or financial statements, that individual should either:**

  (a) **in the case of an immediate family member of a person in a position to influence the conduct and outcome of the audit, cease to hold a position in which they exert such influence on the audit; or**

  (b) **in the case of a close family member of a person in a position to influence the conduct and outcome of the audit, or any family member of a partner in the audit firm, report the matter to the audit engagement partner to take appropriate action. If it is a close family member of the audit engagement partner or if the audit engagement partner is in doubt as to the action to be taken, the audit engagement partner should resolve the matter in consultation with the ethics partner.**

---

[3]   The timing of the audit firm's resignation as auditors is determined in accordance with paragraph 40 of APB Ethical Standard 1. In the case of those public sector bodies where the responsibility for the audit is assigned by legislation, the auditors cannot resign from the audit engagement and they consider alternative safeguards that they can put in place.

GOVERNANCE ROLE WITH AUDIT CLIENT

48   Paragraphs 49 to 51 are supplementary to certain statutory or regulatory provisions that prohibit directors of entities from being appointed as their auditors.[4]

49   **A partner or employee of the audit firm who undertakes audit work should not accept appointment:**

    (a)   to the board of directors of the audit client;

    (b)   to any subcommittee of that board; or

    (c)   to such a position in an entity which holds directly or indirectly more than 20% of the voting rights in the audit client, or in which the audit client holds directly or indirectly more than 20% of the voting rights.

50   **Where a person in a position to influence the conduct and outcome of the audit has an immediate or close family member who holds a position described in paragraph 49, the audit firm should take appropriate steps to ensure that the relevant person does not retain a position in which they exert influence on the conduct and outcome of the audit engagement.**

51   **Where a partner or employee of the audit firm, not being a member of the engagement team, has an immediate or close family member who holds a position described in paragraph 49, that individual should report that fact to the audit engagement partner, who should consider whether the relationship might be regarded by a reasonable and informed third party as impairing, or being thought to impair, the auditors' objectivity. If the audit engagement partner concludes that the auditors' objectivity may be impaired, that individual should consult with the ethics partner to determine whether appropriate safeguards exist. If no such safeguards exist, the audit firm withdraws from the audit engagement.**

EMPLOYMENT WITH AUDIT FIRM

52   Objectivity and independence may be threatened where a former director or employee of the audit client becomes a member of the engagement team. Self-interest, self-review and familiarity threats may be created where a member of the engagement team has to report on, for example, financial statements which he or she prepared, or elements of the financial statements for which he or she had responsibility, while with the audit client.

---

[4]   In the case of limited companies, for example, section 27 of the Companies Act 1989 contains detailed provisions. Amongst other things, these state that:
'...A person is ineligible for appointment as company auditor of a company if he is (a) an officer or employee of the company, or (b) a partner or employee of such a person, or a partnership of which such a person is a partner, or if he is ineligible by virtue of paragraph (a) or (b) for appointment as company auditor of any associated undertaking of the company.'

53 **Where a former director or a former employee of an audit client, who was in a position to exert significant influence over the preparation of the financial statements, joins the audit firm, that individual should not be assigned to a position in which he or she is able to influence the conduct and outcome of the audit for that client or its affiliates for a period of two years following the date of leaving the audit client.**

54 In certain circumstances, a longer period of exclusion from the engagement team may be appropriate. For example, threats to objectivity and independence may exist in relation to the audit of the financial statements of any period which are materially affected by the work of that person whilst occupying his or her former position of influence with the audit client. The significance of these threats depends on factors such as:

- the position the individual held with the audit client;

- the length of time since the individual left the audit client;

- the position the individual holds in the engagement team.

FAMILY AND OTHER PERSONAL RELATIONSHIPS

55 A relationship between a person who is in a position to influence the conduct and outcome of the audit and another party does not generally affect the consideration of the auditors' objectivity and independence. However, if it is a family relationship, and if the family member also has a financial, business or employment relationship with the audit client, then self-interest, familiarity or intimidation threats to the auditors' objectivity and independence may be created. The significance of any such threats depends on such factors as:

- the relevant person's involvement in the audit;

- the nature of the relationship between the relevant person and his or her family member;

- the family member's relationship with the audit client.

56 A distinction is made between immediate family relationships and close family relationships. Immediate family members comprise an individual's spouse (or equivalent) and dependents, whereas close family members comprise parents, non-dependent children and siblings. While an individual can usually be presumed to be aware of matters concerning his or her immediate family members and to be able to influence their behaviour, it is generally recognised that the same levels of knowledge and influence do not exist in the case of close family members.

57 When considering family relationships, it needs to be acknowledged that, in an increasingly secular, open and inclusive society, the concept of what constitutes a family is evolving and relationships between individuals which have no status formally

recognised by law may nevertheless be considered as significant as those which do. It may therefore be appropriate to regard certain other personal relationships, particularly those that would be considered close personal relationships, as if they are family relationships.

58   **The audit firm should establish policies and procedures that require:**

   (a)   partners and professional staff to report to the audit firm any immediate family, close family and other personal relationships involving an audit client of the firm, to which they are a party and which they consider might create a threat to the auditors' objectivity or a perceived loss of independence;

   (b)   the relevant audit engagement partners to be notified promptly of any immediate family, close family and other personal relationships reported by partners and other professional staff.

59   **The audit engagement partner should:**

   (a)   assess the threats to the auditors' objectivity and independence arising from immediate family, close family and other personal relationships on the basis of the information reported to the firm by persons in a position to influence the conduct and outcome of the audit;

   (b)   apply appropriate safeguards to eliminate the threat or reduce it to an acceptable level; and

   (c)   where there are unresolved matters or the need for clarification, consult with the ethics partner.

60   Where such matters are identified or reported, the audit engagement partner or the ethics partner assesses the information available and the potential for there to be a threat to the auditors' objectivity and independence, treating any personal relationship as if it were a family relationship.

EXTERNAL CONSULTANTS INVOLVED IN THE AUDIT

61   Audit firms may employ external consultants as experts in order to obtain sufficient appropriate audit evidence regarding certain financial statement assertions.[5] There is a risk that an expert's objectivity and independence will be impaired if the expert is related to the entity, for example by being financially dependent upon or having an investment in, the entity.

---

[5]   ISA (UK and Ireland) 620 *'Using the work of an Expert'* states that the auditor should evaluate the objectivity of the expert.

62 **The audit engagement partner should be satisfied that any external consultant involved in the audit will be objective and document the rationale for that conclusion.**

63 The audit engagement partner obtains information from the external consultant as to the existence of any connections that they have with the audit client including:

* financial interests;

* business relationships;

* employment (past, present and future);

* family and other personal relationships.

EFFECTIVE DATE

64 Effective for audits of financial statements for periods commencing on or after 15 December 2004.

65 Firms may complete audit engagements relating to periods commencing prior to 15 December 2004 in accordance with existing ethical guidance from the relevant professional body, putting in place any necessary changes in the subsequent engagement period.

66 Financial interests held at 15 December 2004 that were permissible in accordance with existing ethical guidance (including transitional arrangements) from the relevant professional body, but are prohibited by the requirements of paragraphs 5 to 24, may continue to be held for up to twelve months after that date provided that:

* no new interest is acquired; and

* the audit firm satisfies itself that there are adequate safeguards in place to reduce the threat to acceptable levels.

67 Business relationships existing at 15 December 2004 that were permissible in accordance with existing ethical guidance (including transitional arrangements) from the relevant professional body, but are prohibited by the requirements of paragraphs 25 to 31, may continue to exist for up to twelve months after that date provided that:

* no new contracts under the business relationship are entered into; and

* the audit firm satisfies itself that there are adequate safeguards in place to reduce the threat to acceptable levels.

68 The requirements of paragraph 44 in respect of employment with the audit client do not apply if:

- the relevant person has notified an intention to join the client prior to 5 October 2004 or has entered into contractual arrangements prior to that date; and

- the continuation of the audit relationship was permitted by existing ethical guidance (including transitional arrangements) from the relevant professional body.

APB ETHICAL STANDARD 3

LONG ASSOCIATION WITH THE AUDIT ENGAGEMENT

(Re-issued December 2004)

CONTENTS

PREFACE

APB Ethical Standards apply in the audit of financial statements. They should be read in the context of the Auditing Practices Board's Statement "The Auditing Practices Board – Scope and Authority of Pronouncements (Revised)" which sets out the application and authority of APB Ethical Standards.

The terms used in APB Ethical Standards for Auditors are explained in the Glossary.

APB Ethical Standards apply to audits of financial statements in both the private and the public sectors. However, auditors in the public sector are subject to more complex ethical requirements than their private sector counterparts. This includes, for example, compliance with legislation such as the Prevention of Corruption Act 1916, concerning gifts and hospitality, and with Cabinet Office guidance.

INTRODUCTION

1   APB Ethical Standard 1 requires the audit engagement partner to identify and assess the circumstances which could adversely affect the auditors' objectivity ('threats'), including any perceived loss of independence, and to apply procedures ('safeguards') which will either:

(a)   eliminate the threat; or

(b)   reduce the threat to an acceptable level (that is, a level at which it is not probable that a reasonable and informed third party would conclude that the auditors' objectivity and independence either is impaired or is likely to be impaired).

When considering safeguards, where the audit engagement partner chooses to reduce rather than to eliminate a threat to objectivity and independence, he or she recognises that this judgment may not be shared by users of the financial statements and that he or she may be required to justify the decision.

2   This Standard provides requirements and guidance on specific circumstances arising out of long association with the audit engagement, which may create threats to the auditors' objectivity or perceived loss of independence. It gives examples of safeguards that can, in some circumstances, eliminate the threat or reduce it to an acceptable level. In circumstances where this is not possible, the auditors either do not accept or withdraw from the audit engagement, as appropriate.

3   Whenever a possible or actual breach of an APB Ethical Standard is identified, the audit engagement partner, in the first instance, and the ethics partner, where appropriate, assesses the implications of the breach, determines whether there are safeguards that can be put in place or other actions that can be taken to address any potential adverse consequences and considers whether there is a need to resign from the audit engagement.

4   An inadvertent violation of this Standard does not necessarily call into question the audit firm's ability to give an audit opinion provided that:

(a)   the audit firm has established policies and procedures that require all partners and staff to report any breach promptly to the audit engagement partner or to the ethics partner, as appropriate;

(b)   the audit engagement partner or ethics partner ensures that any matter which has given rise to a breach is addressed as soon as possible;

(c)   safeguards, if appropriate, are applied (for example, by having another partner review the work done by the relevant partner or member of staff or by removing him or her from the engagement team): and

(d)   the actions taken and the rationale for them are documented.

GENERAL PROVISIONS

5   The audit firm should establish policies and procedures to monitor the length of time that audit engagement partners, key audit partners and staff in senior positions serve as members of the engagement team for each audit.

6   Where audit engagement partners, key audit partners and staff in senior positions have a long association with the audit, the audit firm should assess the threats to the auditors' objectivity and independence and, where the threats are other than clearly insignificant, should apply safeguards to reduce the threats to an acceptable level. Where appropriate safeguards cannot be applied, the audit firm should either resign as auditors or not stand for reappointment, as appropriate.[1]

7   Where audit engagement partners, key audit partners and staff in senior positions have a long association with the audit client, self-interest, self-review and familiarity threats to the auditors' objectivity may arise. Similarly, such circumstances may result in an actual or perceived loss of independence. The significance of such threats depends upon factors such as:

*   the role of the individual in the engagement team;

*   the proportion of time that the audit client contributes to the individual's annual billable hours;

*   the length of time that the individual has been associated with that audit engagement.

8   In order to address such threats, audit firms apply safeguards. Appropriate safeguards may include:

*   removing ('rotating') the audit partners and the other senior members of the engagement team after a pre-determined number of years;

*   involving an additional partner, who is not and has not recently been a member of the engagement team, to review the work done by the audit partners and the other senior members of the engagement team and to advise as necessary;

*   applying independent internal quality reviews to the engagement in question.

9   Once an audit engagement partner has held this role for a continuous period of ten years, careful consideration is given as to whether a reasonable and informed third party would consider the audit firm's objectivity and independence to be impaired. Where the individual concerned is not rotated after ten years, it is important that:

---

[1]   In the case of those public sector bodies where the responsibility for the audit is assigned by legislation, the auditors cannot resign from the audit engagement.

(a)   alternative safeguards such as those noted in paragraph 8 are applied; or

(b)   (i)   the reasoning as to why the individual continues to participate in the audit engagement is documented; and

(ii)   the facts are communicated to those charged with governance of the audit client in accordance with paragraphs 49-53 of APB Ethical Standard 1.

10   The audit firm's policies and procedures set out the circumstances in which the audit engagement partners responsible for the audits of non-listed clients are subject to accelerated rotation requirements, such as those set out in paragraph 12. These policies take into consideration the nature of the entity's business, its size, the number of its employees and the range of its stakeholders in addition to the factors set out in paragraph 7.

11   Any scheme of rotation of audit partners and other senior members of the engagement team needs to take into account the factors which affect the quality of the audit work, including the experience and continuity of members of the engagement team and the need to ensure appropriate succession planning.

ADDITIONAL PROVISIONS RELATED TO AUDITS OF LISTED COMPANIES

The audit engagement partner and the independent partner

12   In the case of listed companies, save where the circumstances contemplated in paragraph 13 and 14 apply, the audit firm should establish policies and procedures to ensure that:

(a)   no one should act as audit engagement partner or as independent partner for a continuous period longer than five years;

(b)   where an independent partner becomes the audit engagement partner, the combined period of service in these positions should not exceed five years; and

(c)   anyone who has acted as the audit engagement partner or the independent partner, or held a combination of such positions, for a particular audit client for a period of five years, whether continuously or in aggregate, should not hold any position of responsibility in relation to the audit engagement, until a further period of five years has elapsed.

13   When an audit client becomes a listed company, the length of time the audit engagement partner has served the audit client in that capacity is taken into account in calculating the period before the audit engagement partner is rotated off the engagement team. However, where the audit engagement partner has already served for four or more years, that individual may continue to serve as the audit

engagement partner for not more than two years after the audit client becomes a listed company.

14   Some degree of flexibility over the timing of rotation may be necessary in circumstances where a reasonable and informed third party would regard the audit engagement partner's continuity as being especially important to the shareholders of the audit client. For example, where major changes to the audit client's structure or its senior management are expected that would otherwise coincide with the rotation of the audit engagement partner. In these circumstances alternative safeguards are applied to reduce any threats to an acceptable level. Such safeguards may include ensuring that an expanded review of the audit work is undertaken by an audit partner, who is not involved in the audit engagement.

15   In the case of joint audit arrangements for listed companies, audit firms will make arrangements for changes of audit engagement partners and independent partners over a five-year period so that the familiarity threat is avoided, whilst also taking into consideration factors that affect the quality of the audit work.

Key audit partners

16   **In the case of listed companies, the audit firm should establish policies and procedures to ensure that:**

   (a)   **no one should act as a key audit partner for a continuous period longer than seven years;**   see glossary ¶ 1195

   (b)   **where a key audit partner becomes the audit engagement partner, the combined period of service in these positions should not exceed seven years; and**

   (c)   **anyone who has acted as a key audit partner for a particular audit client for a period of seven years, whether continuously or in aggregate, should not hold any position of responsibility in relation to the audit engagement until a further period of two years has elapsed.**

Other partners and staff in senior positions

17   **In the case of listed companies, the audit engagement partner should review the safeguards put in place to address the threats to the auditors' objectivity and independence arising where:**

   (a)   **partners have been responsible for significant affiliates (but not as key audit partners); or**

   (b)   **staff have been involved in the audit in senior positions;**

for a continuous period longer than seven years and should discuss those situations with the independent partner. Any unresolved problems or issues should be referred to the ethics partner.

18 Such safeguards might include the removal of the member of staff from, or the rotation of roles within, the engagement team.

EFFECTIVE DATE

19 Effective for audits of financial statements for periods commencing on or after 15 December 2004.

20 Firms may complete audit engagements relating to periods commencing prior to 15 December 2004 in accordance with existing ethical guidance from the relevant professional body, putting in place any necessary changes in the subsequent engagement period.

21 Firms may implement revisions to their policies and procedures as required under paragraph 5 during the year commencing 15 December 2004.

22 Where the provisions of paragraphs 12 and 16 require audit partners to rotate off the audit engagement prior to the period allowed by existing ethical guidance (including transitional arrangements) from the relevant professional body, they may continue where a change would impair audit quality. However, this extension beyond the period permitted by paragraphs 12 and 16 can be applied only for audits of financial statements for periods commencing on or prior to 15 December 2006.

APB ETHICAL STANDARD 4

FEES, REMUNERATION AND EVALUATION POLICIES, LITIGATION, GIFTS AND HOSPITALITY

(Re-issued December 2004)

CONTENTS

PREFACE

APB Ethical Standards apply in the audit of financial statements. They should be read in the context of the Auditing Practices Board's Statement "The Auditing Practices Board – Scope and Authority of Pronouncements (Revised)" which sets out the application and authority of APB Ethical Standards.

The terms used in APB Ethical Standards for Auditors are explained in the Glossary.

APB Ethical Standards apply to audits of financial statements in both the private and the public sectors. However, auditors in the public sector are subject to more complex ethical requirements than their private sector counterparts. This includes, for example, compliance with legislation such as the Prevention of Corruption Act 1916, concerning gifts and hospitality, and with Cabinet Office guidance.

INTRODUCTION

1   APB Ethical Standard 1 requires the audit engagement partner to identify and assess the circumstances which could adversely affect the auditors' objectivity ('threats'), including any perceived loss of independence, and to apply procedures ('safeguards') which will either:

(a)   eliminate the threat; or

(b)   reduce the threat to an acceptable level (that is, a level at which it is not probable that a reasonable and informed third party would conclude that the auditors' objectivity and independence either is impaired or is likely to be impaired).

When considering safeguards, where the audit engagement partner chooses to reduce rather than to eliminate a threat to objectivity and independence, he or she recognises that this judgment may not be shared by users of the financial statements and that he or she may be required to justify the decision.

2   This Standard provides requirements and guidance on specific circumstances arising out of fees, economic dependence, litigation, remuneration and evaluation of partners and staff, and gifts and hospitality, which may create threats to the auditors' objectivity or perceived loss of independence. It gives examples of safeguards that can, in some situations, eliminate the threat or reduce it to an acceptable level. In circumstances where this is not possible, either the situation is avoided or the auditors either do not accept or withdraw from the audit engagement, as appropriate.

3   Whenever a possible or actual breach of an APB Ethical Standard is identified, the audit engagement partner, in the first instance, and the ethics partner, where appropriate, assesses the implications of the breach, determines whether there are safeguards that can be put in place or other actions that can be taken to address any potential adverse consequences and considers whether there is a need to resign from the audit engagement.

4   An inadvertent violation of this Standard does not necessarily call into question the audit firm's ability to give an audit opinion provided that:

(a)   the audit firm has established policies and procedures that require all partners and staff to report any breach promptly to the audit engagement partner or to the ethics partner, as appropriate;

(b)   the audit engagement partner or ethics partner ensures that any matter which has given rise to a breach is addressed as soon as possible;

(c)   safeguards, if appropriate, are applied (for example, having another partner review the work done by the relevant partner or member of staff or by removing him or her from the engagement team); and

(d)   the actions taken and the rationale for them are documented.

FEES

5   **The audit engagement partner should be satisfied and able to demonstrate that the audit engagement has assigned to it sufficient partners and staff with appropriate time and skill to perform the audit in accordance with all applicable Auditing and Ethical Standards, irrespective of the audit fee to be charged.**

6   Paragraph 5 is not intended to prescribe the approach to be taken by audit firms to the setting of audit fees, but rather to emphasise that there are no circumstances where the amount of the audit fee can justify any lack of appropriate resource or time taken to perform a proper audit in accordance with applicable Auditing and Ethical Standards.

7   **An audit should not be undertaken on a contingent fee basis.**

8   A contingent fee basis is any arrangement made at the outset of an engagement under which a pre-determined amount or a specified commission on or percentage of any consideration or saving is payable to the audit firm upon the happening of a specified event or the achievement of an outcome (or alternative outcomes). Differential hourly fee rates, or arrangements under which the fee payable will be negotiated after the completion of the engagement, do not constitute contingent fee arrangements.

9   Contingent fee arrangements in respect of audit engagements create self-interest threats to the auditors' objectivity and independence that are so significant that they cannot be eliminated or reduced to an acceptable level by the application of any safeguards.

10   The audit fee ordinarily reflects the time spent and the skills and experience of the personnel performing the audit in accordance with all the relevant requirements. It does not depend on whether the auditors' report on the financial statements is qualified or unqualified.

11   The basis for the calculation of the audit fee is agreed with the audit client each year before significant audit work is undertaken. The audit engagement partner explains to the audit client that the estimated audit fee is based on the expected level of audit work required and that, if unforeseen problems are encountered, the cost of any additional audit work found to be necessary will be reflected in the audit fee actually charged. This is not a contingent fee arrangement.

12   **The audit firm should establish policies and procedures to ensure that the audit engagement partner and the ethics partner are notified where others within the audit firm propose to adopt contingent fee arrangements in relation to the provision of non-audit services to the audit client or its affiliates.**

13   Contingent fee arrangements in respect of non-audit services provided by the auditors to an audit client may create a threat to the auditors' objectivity and independence. The circumstances in which such fee arrangements are not permitted for such non-audit services are dealt with in APB Ethical Standard 5.

THE AUDITING PRACTICES BOARD

14 **In the case of listed companies the audit engagement partner should disclose to the audit committee, in writing, any contingent fee arrangements for non-audit services provided by the auditors or their network firms.**

15 In the case of a group audit of a listed company, which involves other auditors, the letter of instruction sent by the group audit engagement partner to the other auditors requests disclosure of any contingent fees for non-audit services charged or proposed to be charged by the other auditors.

16 **The actual amount of the audit fee for the previous audit and the arrangements for its payment should be agreed with the audit client before the audit firm formally accepts appointment as auditors in respect of the following period.**

17 Ordinarily, any outstanding fees for the previous audit period are paid before the audit firm commences any new audit work. Where they are not, it is important for the audit engagement partner to understand the nature of any disagreement or other issue.

18 **Where fees for professional services from the audit client are overdue and the amount cannot be regarded as trivial, the audit engagement partner, in consultation with the ethics partner, should consider whether the audit firm can continue as auditors or whether it is necessary to resign.**

19 Where fees due from an audit client, whether for audit or for non-audit services, remain unpaid for a long time - and, in particular, where a significant part is not paid before the auditors' report on the financial statements for the following year is due to be issued - a self-interest threat to the auditors' objectivity and independence is created because the issue of an unqualified audit report may enhance the audit firm's prospects of securing payment of such overdue fees.

20 Where the outstanding fees are in dispute and the amount involved is significant, the threats to the auditors' objectivity and independence may be such that no safeguards can eliminate them or reduce them to an acceptable level. The audit engagement partner therefore considers whether the audit firm can continue with the audit engagement.

21 Where the outstanding fees are unpaid because of exceptional circumstances (including financial distress), the audit engagement partner considers whether the audit client will be able to resolve its difficulties. In deciding what action to take, the audit engagement partner weighs the threats to the auditors' objectivity and independence, if the audit firm were to remain in office, against the difficulties the audit client would be likely to face in finding a successor, and therefore the public interest considerations, if the audit firm were to resign.

22 In any case where the audit firm does not resign from the audit engagement, the audit engagement partner applies appropriate safeguards (such as a review by an audit partner who is not involved in the audit engagement) and notifies the ethics partner of the facts concerning the overdue fees.

Listed

23 **Where it is expected that the total fees for both audit and non-audit services receivable from a listed audit client and its subsidiaries audited by the audit firm[1] will regularly exceed 10% of the annual fee income of the audit firm or, where profits are not shared on a firm-wide basis, of the part of the firm by reference to which the audit engagement partner's profit share is calculated, the firm should not act as the auditors of that entity and should either resign as auditors or not stand for reappointment, as appropriate.[2]**

Non-Listed

24 **Where it is expected that the total fees for both audit and non-audit services receivable from a non-listed audit client and its subsidiaries audited by the audit firm will regularly exceed 15% of the annual fee income of the audit firm or, where profits are not shared on a firm-wide basis, of the part of the firm by reference to which the audit engagement partner's profit share is calculated, the firm should not act as the auditors of that entity and should either resign as auditors or not stand for reappointment, as appropriate.**

25 Where it is expected that the total fees for both audit and non-audit services receivable from an audit client and its subsidiaries that are audited by the audit firm will regularly exceed 10% in the case of listed companies and 15% in the case of non-listed entities of the annual fee income of the part of the firm by reference to which the audit engagement partner's profit share is calculated, it may be possible to assign the audit client to another part of the firm.

26 Paragraphs 23 and 24 are not intended to require the audit firm to resign as auditors or not stand for reappointment as a result of an individual event or engagement, the nature or size of which was unpredictable and where a reasonable and informed third party would regard ceasing to act as detrimental to the shareholders (or equivalent) of the audit client. However, in such circumstances, the audit firm discloses full details of the position to the ethics partner and to those charged with governance of the audit client and discusses with both what, if any, safeguards may be appropriate.

Listed

27 **Where it is expected that the total fees for both audit and non-audit services receivable from a listed audit client and its subsidiaries audited by the audit firm will regularly exceed 5% of the annual fee income of the audit firm or the part of the firm by reference to which the audit engagement partner's profit share is calculated, but will not regularly exceed 10%, the audit engagement partner should disclose that expectation to the ethics partner and to those charged with governance of the audit client and consider whether appropriate safeguards should be applied to eliminate or reduce to an acceptable level the threat to the auditors' objectivity and independence.**

28 It is fundamental to the auditors' objectivity that they be willing and able, if necessary, to disagree with the directors and management, regardless of the consequences to

---

[1] Total fees will include those billed by others where the audit firm is entitled to the fees, but will not include fees billed by the audit firm where it is acting as agent for another party.

[2] Paragraphs 23 to 32 do not apply to the audits of those public sector bodies where the responsibility for the audit is assigned by legislation. In such cases, the auditors cannot resign from the audit engagement, irrespective of considerations of economic dependence.

their own position. Where the auditors are, to any significant extent, economically dependent on the audit client, this may inhibit their willingness or constrain their ability to express a qualified opinion on the financial statements, since this could be viewed as likely to lead to them losing the audit client.

29   An audit firm is deemed to be economically dependent on a listed audit client if the total fees for audit and all other services from that client and its subsidiaries which are audited by the audit firm represent 10% of the total fees of the audit firm or the part of the firm by reference to which the audit engagement partner's profit share is calculated. Where such fees are between 5% and 10%, the audit engagement partner and the ethics partner consider the significance of the threat and the need for appropriate safeguards.

30   Such safeguards might include:

a   taking steps to reduce the non-audit work to be undertaken and therefore the fees earned from the audit client;

b   applying independent internal quality control reviews.

31   **Where it is expected that the total fees for both audit and non-audit services receivable from a non-listed audit client and its subsidiaries audited by the audit firm will regularly exceed 10% of the annual fee income of the audit firm or the part of the firm by reference to which the audit engagement partner's profit share is calculated, but will not regularly exceed 15%, the audit engagement partner should disclose that expectation to the ethics partner and to those charged with governance of the audit client and the firm should arrange an external independent quality control review of the audit engagement to be undertaken before the auditors' report is finalised[3].**

32   A quality control review involves discussion with the audit engagement partner, a review of the financial statements and the auditors' report, and consideration of whether the report is appropriate. It also involves a review of selected working papers relating to the significant judgments the engagement team has made and the conclusions they have reached. The extent of the review depends on the complexity of the engagement and the risk that the report might not be appropriate in the circumstances. The review includes considering the following:

a   Significant risks identified during the audit and the responses to those risks.

b   Judgments made, particularly with respect to materiality and significant risks.

c   Whether appropriate consultation has taken place on matters involving differences of opinion or other difficult or contentious matters, and the conclusions arising from those consultations.

---

[3]   As provided in APB Ethical Standard – Provisions Available for Small Entities, auditors of Small Entities are not required to comply with this paragraph.

- The significance and disposition of corrected and uncorrected misstatements identified during the audit.

- The appropriateness of the report to be issued.

Where the quality control reviewer makes recommendations that the audit engagement partner does not accept and the matter is not resolved to the reviewer's satisfaction, the report is not issued until the matter is resolved by following the audit firm's procedures for dealing with differences of opinion.

33 A new audit firm seeking to establish itself may find the requirements relating to economic dependence difficult to comply with in the short term. In these circumstances, such firms would:

(a) not undertake any audits of listed companies, where fees from such a client would represent 10% or more of the annual fee income of the firm; and

(b) for a period not exceeding two years, require external independent quality control reviews of those audits of unlisted entities that represent more than 15% of the annual fee income before the audit opinion is issued.

The firm might also develop its practice by accepting work from non-audit clients so as to bring the fees payable by each audit client below 15%.

34 A self-interest threat may also be created where an audit partner in the engagement team:

- is employed exclusively or principally on that audit engagement;

- is remunerated on the basis of the performance of part of the firm which is substantially dependent on fees from that audit client.

35 Where the circumstances described in paragraph 34 arise, the audit firm assesses the significance of the threat and, if it is other than clearly insignificant, applies safeguards to reduce the threat to an acceptable level. Such safeguards might include:

- reducing the dependence of the office, partner or person in a position to influence the conduct and outcome of the audit by reallocating the work within the practice;

- a review by an audit partner who is not involved with the audit engagement to ensure that the auditors' objectivity and independence is not affected by the self-interest threat.

REMUNERATION AND EVALUATION POLICIES

36 **The audit firm should establish policies and procedures to ensure that, in relation to each audit client:**

(a) the objectives of the members of the audit team do not include selling non-audit services to the audit client;

(b) the criteria for evaluating the performance of members of the audit team do not include success in selling non-audit services to the audit client; and

(c) no specific element of the remuneration of a member of the audit team and no decision concerning promotion within the audit firm is based on his or her success in selling non-audit services to the audit client.

37 Where auditors identify areas for possible improvement in a client they may provide general business advice, which might include suggested solutions to problems. Before discussing any non-audit service that might be provided by the audit firm or effecting any introductions to colleagues from outside the audit team, the audit engagement partner considers the threats that such a service would have on the audit engagement, in line with the requirements of APB Ethical Standard 5.

38 The policies and procedures required for compliance with paragraph 36 are not intended to inhibit normal profit-sharing arrangements. However, such policies and procedures are central to an audit firm's ability to demonstrate its objectivity and independence and to rebut any suggestion that an audit that it has undertaken and the opinion that it has given are influenced by the nature and extent of any non-audit services that it has provided to that audit client. Because it is possible that, despite such policies and procedures, such factors may be taken into account in the evaluation and remuneration of members of an audit team, the ethics partner pays particular attention to the actual implementation of those policies and procedures and makes himself or herself available for consultation when needed.

THREATENED AND ACTUAL LITIGATION

39 Where litigation in relation to audit or non-audit services between the audit client or its affiliates and the audit firm, which is other than insignificant, is already in progress, or where the audit engagement partner considers such litigation to be probable, the audit firm should either not continue with or not accept the audit engagement.[4]

40 Where litigation (in relation to audit or non-audit services) actually takes place between the audit firm (or any person in a position to influence the conduct and outcome of the audit) and the audit client, or where litigation is threatened and there is a realistic prospect of such litigation being commenced, self-interest, advocacy and intimidation threats to the auditors' objectivity and independence are created because the audit firm's interest will be the achievement of an outcome to the dispute or litigation that is favourable to itself. In addition, an effective audit process requires complete candour and full disclosure between the audit client management and the engagement team:

---

[4] Paragraphs 39 to 41 do not apply to the audits of those public sector bodies where the responsibility for the audit is assigned by legislation. In such cases, the auditors cannot resign from the audit engagement: the auditors report significant litigation to the relevant legislative authority.

such disputes or litigation may place the two parties in opposing adversarial positions and may affect management's willingness to make complete disclosure of relevant information. Where the auditors can foresee that such a threat may arise, they inform the audit committee of their intention to resign or, where there is no audit committee, the board of directors.

41 The auditors are not required to resign immediately in circumstances where a reasonable and informed third party would not regard it as being in the interests of the shareholders for them to do so. Such circumstances might arise, for example, where:

- the litigation was commenced as the audit was about to be completed and shareholder interests would be adversely affected by a delay in the audit of the financial statements;

- on appropriate legal advice, the audit firm deems that the threatened or actual litigation is vexatious or designed solely to bring pressure to bear on the opinion to be expressed by the auditors.

GIFTS AND HOSPITALITY

42 **The audit firm, those in a position to influence the conduct and outcome of the audit and immediate family members of such persons should not accept gifts from the audit client, unless the value is clearly insignificant.**

43 **Those in a position to influence the conduct and outcome of the audit and immediate family members of such persons should not accept hospitality from the audit client, unless it is reasonable in terms of its frequency, nature and cost.**

44 Where gifts or hospitality are accepted from an audit client, self-interest and familiarity threats to the auditors' objectivity and independence are created. Familiarity threats also arise where gifts or hospitality are offered to an audit client.

45 Gifts from the audit client, unless their value is clearly insignificant, create threats to objectivity and independence which no safeguards can eliminate or reduce.

46 Hospitality is a component of many business relationships and can provide valuable opportunities for developing an understanding of the client's business and for gaining the insight on which an effective and successful working relationship depends. Therefore, the auditors' objectivity and independence is not necessarily impaired as a result of accepting hospitality from the audit client, provided it is reasonable in terms of its frequency, its nature and its cost.

47 **The audit firm should establish policies on the nature and value of gifts and hospitality that may be accepted from and offered to audit clients, their directors, officers and employees, and should issue guidance to assist partners and staff to comply with such policies.**

48 In assessing the acceptability of gifts and hospitality, the test to be applied is not whether the auditors consider that their objectivity is impaired but whether it is probable that a reasonable and informed third party would conclude that it is or is likely to be impaired. *3rd party viewpoint*

49 Where there is any doubt as to the acceptability of gifts or hospitality offered by the audit client, members of the engagement team discuss the position with the audit engagement partner. If there is any doubt as to the acceptability of gifts or hospitality offered to the audit engagement partner, or if the audit engagement partner has any residual doubt about the acceptability of gifts or hospitality to other individuals, the audit engagement partner reports the facts to the ethics partner, for further consideration regarding any action to be taken.

50 Where the cumulative amount of gifts or hospitality accepted from the audit client appears abnormally high, the audit engagement partner reports the facts to both:

- the ethics partner; and

- the audit committee (or, where there is no audit committee, the board of directors),

together with other significant facts and matters that bear upon the auditors' objectivity and independence.

EFFECTIVE DATE

51 Effective for audits of financial statements for periods commencing on or after 15 December 2004.

52 Firms may complete audit engagements relating to periods commencing prior to 15 December 2004 in accordance with existing ethical guidance from the relevant professional body, putting in place any necessary changes in the subsequent engagement period.

53 Firms may implement revisions to their policies and procedures as required under paragraphs 12, 36 and 47 during the year commencing 15 December 2004.

54 Where the requirements of paragraph 23 or 24 would result in an audit firm being required to resign from providing one or more services to an entity, the firm may continue to provide services under existing arrangements, until the appointment as auditors for the first period commencing on or after 15 December 2005 is considered, provided that:

- the engagements held at 15 December 2004 were permitted by existing ethical guidance from the relevant professional body;

- the level of dependence on the audit client is not increased from that in existence at 15 December 2004;

- any safeguards required by existing ethical guidance continue to be applied; and

- the need for additional safeguards is assessed and, if considered necessary, those additional safeguards are applied.

APB ETHICAL STANDARD 5

NON-AUDIT SERVICES PROVIDED TO AUDIT CLIENTS

(Re-issued December 2004)

CONTENTS

PREFACE

APB Ethical Standards apply in the audit of financial statements. They should be read in the context of the Auditing Practices Board's Statement "The Auditing Practices Board – Scope and Authority of Pronouncements (Revised)" which sets out the application and authority of APB Ethical Standards.

The terms used in APB Ethical Standards for Auditors are explained in the Glossary.

APB Ethical Standards apply to audits of financial statements in both the private and the public sectors. However, auditors in the public sector are subject to more complex ethical requirements than their private sector counterparts. This includes, for example, compliance with legislation such as the Prevention of Corruption Act 1916, concerning gifts and hospitality, and with Cabinet Office guidance.

INTRODUCTION

1   APB Ethical Standard 1 requires the audit engagement partner to identify and assess the circumstances which could adversely affect the auditors' objectivity ('threats'), including any perceived loss of independence, and to apply procedures ('safeguards') which will either:

(a)   eliminate the threat; or

(b)   reduce the threat to an acceptable level (that is, a level at which it is not probable that a reasonable and informed third party would conclude that the auditors' objectivity and independence either is impaired or is likely to be impaired).

When considering safeguards, where the audit engagement partner chooses to reduce rather than to eliminate a threat to objectivity and independence, he or she recognises that this judgment may not be shared by users of the financial statements and that he or she may be required to justify the decision.

2   This Standard provides requirements and guidance on specific circumstances arising from the provision of non-audit services by audit firms to their audit clients, which may create threats to the auditors' objectivity or perceived loss of independence. It gives examples of safeguards that can, in some circumstances, eliminate the threat or reduce it to an acceptable level. In circumstances where this is not possible, either the non-audit service engagement in question is not undertaken or the auditors either do not accept or withdraw from the audit engagement, as appropriate.

3   Whenever a possible or actual breach of an APB Ethical Standard is identified, the audit engagement partner, in the first instance, and the ethics partner, where appropriate, assess the implications of the breach, determine whether there are safeguards that can be put in place or other actions that can be taken to address any potential adverse consequences and consider whether there is a need to resign from the audit engagement.

4   An inadvertent violation of this Standard does not necessarily call into question the audit firm's ability to give an audit opinion provided that:

(a)   the audit firm has established policies and procedures that require all partners and staff to report any breach promptly to the audit engagement partner or to the ethics partner, as appropriate;

(b)   the audit engagement partner promptly notifies the partner or member of staff that any matter which has given rise to a breach is to be addressed as soon as possible and ensures that such action is taken;

(c)   safeguards, if appropriate, are applied (for example, by having another partner review the work done by the relevant partner or member of staff or by removing him or her from the engagement team); and

(d)   the actions taken and the rationale for them are documented.

GENERAL APPROACH TO NON-AUDIT SERVICES

5   Paragraphs 6 to 38 of this Standard set out the general approach to be adopted by audit firms and auditors in relation to the provision of non-audit services to their audit clients. This approach is applicable irrespective of the nature of the non-audit services, which may be in question in a given case. (Paragraphs 39 to 125 of this Standard illustrate the application of the general approach to a number of common non-audit services.)

6   In this Standard, 'non-audit services' comprise any engagement in which an audit firm provides professional services to an audit client other than pursuant to:

   (a)   the audit of financial statements; and

   (b)   those other roles which legislation or regulation specify can be performed by the auditors of the entity (for example, considering the preliminary announcements of listed companies, complying with the procedural and reporting requirements of regulators, such as requirements relating to the audit of the client's internal controls and reports in accordance with Section 151 or 173 of the Companies Act 1985).

7   There may be circumstances where the audit firm is engaged to provide a non-audit service and where that engagement and its scope are determined by a client which is not an audit client. However, it might be contemplated that an audit client may gain some benefit from that engagement[1]. In these circumstances, whilst there may be no threat to the audit firm's objectivity and independence at the time of appointment, the audit firm considers how the engagement may be expected to develop, whether there are any threats that the audit firm may be subject to if additional relevant parties which are audit clients are identified and whether any safeguards should be put in place.

8   In the case of a group, non-audit services, for the purposes of this Standard, include:

   •   services provided by the audit firm, to the parent company or to any affiliate;

   •   services provided by a network firm to the audit client or any of its significant affiliates; and

   •   services provided by the audit firm of a significant affiliate to the parent company.

9   **The audit firm should establish policies and procedures that require others within the firm, and its network, when considering whether to accept a proposed engagement to provide a non-audit service to an audit client or any of its affiliates, to communicate details of the proposed engagement to the audit engagement partner.**

---

[1]   For example, in a vendor due diligence engagement, the engagement is initiated and scoped by the vendor before the purchaser is identified. If an audit client of the firm undertaking the due diligence engagement is the purchaser, that audit client may gain the benefit of the report issued by its auditor, it may be a party to the engagement letter and it may pay an element of the fee.

10   The audit firm establishes appropriate channels of internal communication to ensure that, in relation to an existing audit client, the audit engagement partner (or their delegate) is informed about any proposed engagement to provide a non-audit service to the audit client or any of its affiliates and that he or she considers the implications for the auditors' objectivity and independence before the engagement is accepted.

11   In the case of a listed company, the group audit engagement partner establishes that the company has communicated its policy on the engagement of external auditors to supply non-audit services to its affiliates and obtains confirmation that the auditors of the affiliates will comply with this policy.[2]

IDENTIFICATION AND ASSESSMENT OF THREATS AND SAFEGUARDS

12   Before the audit firm accepts a proposed engagement to provide a non-audit service to an audit client, the audit engagement partner should:

(a)   consider whether it is probable that a reasonable and informed third party would regard the objectives of the proposed engagement as being inconsistent with the objectives of the audit of the financial statements; and   *Test*

(b)   identify and assess the significance of any related threats to the auditors' objectivity, including any perceived loss of independence; and   *Threat*

(c)   identify and assess the effectiveness of the available safeguards to eliminate the threats or reduce them to an acceptable level.   *Safeguard*

13   The objective of the audit of financial statements is to express an opinion on the preparation and presentation of those financial statements. For example, in the case of a limited company, legislation requires the auditors to make a report to the members on all annual accounts laid before the company in general meeting during their tenure of office. The report must state whether, in the auditors' opinion, the accounts have been properly prepared in accordance with the requirements of the legislation, and, in particular, whether they give a true and fair view in accordance with the relevant financial reporting framework.

14   Where the audit engagement partner considers that it is probable that a reasonable and informed third party would regard the objectives of the proposed non-audit service engagement as being inconsistent with the objectives of the audit of the financial statements, the audit firm should either:

(a)   not undertake the non-audit service engagement; or

(b)   not accept or withdraw from the audit engagement.

---

[2]   The Combined Code on Corporate Governance requires audit committees to develop the company's policy on the engagement of the external auditors to supply non-audit services.

15   The objectives of engagements to provide non-audit services vary and depend on the specific terms of the engagement. In some cases these objectives may be inconsistent with those of the audit, and, in such cases, this may give rise to a threat to the auditors' objectivity and to the appearance of their independence. Audit firms do not undertake non-audit service engagements where the objectives of such engagements are inconsistent with the objectives of the audit, or do not accept or withdraw from the audit engagement.

16   Similarly, in relation to a possible new audit client, consideration needs to be given to recent, current and potential engagements to provide non-audit services by the audit firm for the prospective audit client and whether the scope and objectives of those engagements are consistent with the proposed audit engagement. In the case of listed companies, when tendering for a new audit engagement, the audit firm ensures that relevant information on recent non-audit services is drawn to the attention of the audit committee, including:

•   when recent non-audit services were provided to the potential client;

•   the materiality of those non-audit services to the proposed audit engagement;

•   whether those non-audit services would have been prohibited if the client had been an audit client at the time when they were undertaken; and

•   the extent to which the outcomes of non-audit services have been audited or reviewed by another audit firm.

Threats to objectivity and independence

17   The principal types of threats to the auditors' objectivity and independence are:

a   self-interest threat;

b   self-review threat;

c   management threat;

d   advocacy threat;

e   familiarity (or trust) threat; and

f   intimidation threat.

The auditors remain alert to the possibility that any of these threats may occur in connection with non-audit services. However, the threats most commonly associated with non-audit services are self-interest threat, self-review threat, management threat and advocacy threat.

18   A **self-interest threat** exists when auditors have financial or other interests which might cause them to be reluctant to take actions that would be adverse to the interests

of the audit firm or any individual in a position to influence the conduct or outcome of the audit. In relation to non-audit services, the main self-interest threat concerns fees and economic dependence and these are addressed in APB Ethical Standard 4.

19 Where substantial fees are regularly generated from the provision of non-audit services, and the fees for non-audit services are significantly greater than the annual audit and audit-related fees, the audit firm has regard to the possibility that there may be perceived to be a loss of independence. The audit firm addresses such perceived loss of independence by determining whether there is any risk that there will be an actual loss of independence and objectivity by the audit engagement team. The audit firm ensures that those charged with governance are informed of the position on a timely basis.

20 Where fees for non-audit services are calculated on a contingent fee basis, the perception may be that the audit firm's interests are so closely aligned with the audit client that it threatens the auditor's objectivity and independence. Any contingent fee that is material to the audit firm, or that part of the firm by reference to which the audit engagement partner's profit share is calculated, will create an unacceptable self-interest threat and the audit firm does not undertake such an engagement.

21 A **self-review threat** exists when the results of a non-audit service performed by the engagement team or by others within the audit firm are reflected in the amounts included or disclosed in the financial statements.

22 A threat to objectivity and independence arises because, in the course of the audit, the auditors may need to re-evaluate the work performed in the non-audit service. As, by virtue of providing the non-audit service, the audit firm is associated with aspects of the preparation of the financial statements, it may be (or may appear to be) unable to take an impartial view of relevant aspects of those financial statements.

23 In assessing the significance of the self-review threat, the auditors consider the extent to which the non-audit service will:

* involve a significant degree of subjective judgment; and

* have a material effect on the preparation and presentation of the financial statements.

24 Where a significant degree of judgment relating to the financial statements is involved in a non-audit service engagement, the auditors may be inhibited from questioning that judgment in the course of the audit. Whether a significant degree of subjective judgment is involved will depend upon whether the non-audit service involves the application of well-established principles and procedures, and whether reliable information is available. If such circumstances do not exist because the non-audit service is based on concepts, methodologies or assumptions that require judgment and are not established by the client or by authoritative guidance, the auditors' objectivity and the appearance of their independence may be adversely affected. Where the provision of a proposed non-audit service would also have a material effect

on the financial statements, it is unlikely that any safeguard can eliminate or reduce to an acceptable level the self-review threat.

25 A **management threat** exists when the audit firm undertakes work that involves making judgments and taking decisions that are properly the responsibility of management.

26 A threat to objectivity and independence arises because, by making judgments and taking decisions that are properly the responsibility of management, the audit firm erodes the distinction between the audit client and the audit firm. The auditors may become closely aligned with the views and interests of management and this may, in turn, impair or call into question the auditors' ability to apply a proper degree of professional scepticism in auditing the financial statements. The auditors' objectivity and the appearance of their independence therefore may be, or may be perceived to be, impaired.

27 Factors to be considered in determining whether a non-audit service does or does not give rise to a management threat include whether:

- the non-audit service results in recommendations by the audit firm justified by objective and transparent analyses or the client being given the opportunity to decide between reasonable alternatives;

- the auditors are satisfied that a member of management (or senior employee of the audit client) has been designated by the audit client to receive the results of the non-audit service and make any judgments and decisions that are needed; and

- that member of management has the capability to make independent management judgments and decisions on the basis of the information provided ('informed management').

28 Where there is 'informed management', the auditors assess whether there are safeguards that can be introduced that would be effective to avoid a management threat or to reduce it to a level at which it can be disregarded. In the absence of such circumstances, it is unlikely that any safeguards can eliminate the management threat or reduce it to an acceptable level.

29 An **advocacy threat** exists when the audit firm undertakes work that involves acting as an advocate for an audit client and supporting a position taken by management in an adversarial context.

30 A threat to objectivity and independence arises because, in order to act in an advocacy role, the audit firm has to adopt a position closely aligned to that of management. This creates both actual and perceived threats to the auditors' objectivity and independence. For example, where the audit firm, acting as advocate, has supported a particular contention of management, it may be difficult for the auditors to take an impartial view of this in the context of the audit of the financial statements.

31 Where the provision of a non-audit service would require the auditors to act as advocates for the audit client in relation to matters that are material to the financial statements, it is unlikely that any safeguards can eliminate or reduce to an acceptable level the advocacy threat that would exist.

Safeguards

32 Where any threat to the auditors' objectivity and the appearance of their independence is identified, the audit engagement partner assesses the significance of that threat and considers whether there are safeguards that could be applied and which would be effective to eliminate the threat or reduce it to an acceptable level. If such safeguards can be identified and are applied, the non-audit service may be provided. However, where no such safeguards are applied, the only course is for the audit firm either not to undertake the engagement to provide the non-audit service in question or not to accept (or to withdraw from) the audit engagement.

33 **Where the audit engagement partner concludes that no appropriate safeguards are available to eliminate or reduce to an acceptable level the threats to the auditors' objectivity, including any perceived loss of independence, related to a proposed engagement to provide a non-audit service to an audit client, he or she should inform the others concerned within the audit firm of that conclusion and the firm should either:**

   (a) not undertake the non-audit service engagement; or

   (b) not accept or withdraw from the audit engagement.

   If the audit engagement partner is in doubt as to the appropriate action to be taken, he or she should resolve the matter through consultation with the ethics partner.

34 An initial assessment of the threats to objectivity and independence and the safeguards to be applied is required when the audit engagement partner is considering the acceptance of an engagement to provide a non-audit service. That assessment is reviewed whenever the scope and objectives of the non-audit service change significantly. If such a review suggests that safeguards cannot reduce the threat to an acceptable level, the audit firm withdraws from the non-audit service engagement, or does not accept re-appointment or withdraws from the audit engagement.

COMMUNICATION WITH THOSE CHARGED WITH GOVERNANCE

35 **The audit engagement partner should ensure that those charged with governance of the audit client are appropriately informed on a timely basis of:**

(a) **all significant facts and matters that bear upon the auditors' objectivity and independence, related to the provision of non-audit services, including the safeguards put in place; and**

(b) **for listed companies, any inconsistencies between APB Ethical Standards and the company's policy for the supply of non-audit services by the audit firm and any apparent breach of that policy.[2]**

36 Transparency is a key element in addressing the issues raised by the provision of non-audit services by audit firms to their audit clients. This can be facilitated by timely communication with those charged with governance of the audit client (see APB Ethical Standard 1, paragraphs 49 to 53). Such communications are addressed to the audit committee, where there is one; in other circumstances, they are addressed to the board of directors (or those in an equivalent position). In the case of listed companies, ensuring that the audit committee is properly informed about the issues associated with the provision of non-audit services will assist them to comply with the provisions of the Combined Code on Corporate Governance relating to reviewing and monitoring the external auditors' independence and objectivity and to developing a policy on the engagement of external auditors to supply non-audit services. This will include discussion of any inconsistencies between the company's policy and APB Ethical Standards and ensuring that the policy is communicated to affiliates.

DOCUMENTATION

37 **The audit engagement partner should ensure that the reasoning for a decision to undertake an engagement to provide non-audit services to an audit client, and any safeguards adopted, is appropriately documented.**

38 Matters to be documented include any significant judgments concerning:

- threats identified;

- safeguards adopted and the reasons why they are considered to be effective; and

- communication with those charged with governance.

APPLICATION OF GENERAL PRINCIPLES TO SPECIFIC NON-AUDIT SERVICES

INTERNAL AUDIT SERVICES

39 The range of 'internal audit services' is wide and they may not be termed as such by the audit client. For example, the audit firm may be engaged:

- to outsource the audit client's entire internal audit function; or

- to supplement the audit client's internal audit function in specific areas (for example, by providing specialised technical services or resources in particular locations); or

- to provide occasional internal audit services to the audit client on an *ad hoc* basis.

All such engagements would fall within the term 'internal audit services'.

40   The main threats to the auditors' objectivity and independence arising from the provision of internal audit services are the self-review threat and the management threat.

41   Engagements to provide internal audit services - other than those prohibited in paragraph 43 - may be undertaken, provided that the auditors are satisfied that 'informed management'[3] has been designated by the audit client and provided that appropriate safeguards are applied.

42   Examples of safeguards that may be appropriate when internal audit services are provided to an audit client include ensuring that:

- internal audit projects undertaken by the audit firm are performed by partners and staff who have no involvement in the external audit of the financial statements;

- the audit of the financial statements is reviewed by an audit partner who is not involved in the audit engagement, to ensure that the internal audit work performed by the audit firm has been properly and effectively assessed in the context of the audit of the financial statements.

43   **The audit firm should not undertake an engagement to provide internal audit services to an audit client where it is reasonably foreseeable that:**

   (a)   for the purposes of the audit of the financial statements, the auditors would place significant reliance on the internal audit work performed by the audit firm; or

   (b)   for the purposes of the internal audit services, the audit firm would undertake part of the role of management.

44   The self-review threat is unacceptably high where the auditors cannot perform the audit of the financial statements without placing significant reliance on the work performed for the purposes of the internal audit services engagement. For example, the provision of internal audit services on the internal financial controls for an audit client which is a large bank, is likely to be unacceptable as the external audit team is likely to place significant reliance on the work performed by the internal audit team in relation to the bank's internal financial controls.

---

[3]   The nature of 'informed management' is discussed in paragraph 27.

45   The management threat is unacceptably high where the audit firm provides internal audit services that involve audit firm personnel taking decisions or making judgments, which are properly the responsibility of management. For example, such situations can arise where the nature of the internal audit work involves the audit firm in taking decisions as to:

- the scope and nature of the internal audit services to be provided to the audit client, or

- the design of internal controls or implementing changes thereto.

46   During the course of the audit the auditors generally evaluate the design and test the operating effectiveness of some of the entity's internal financial controls, including the operation of any internal audit function and provide management with observations on matters that have come to their attention, including comments on weaknesses in the internal control systems (including the internal audit function) and suggestions for addressing them. This work is a by-product of the audit service rather than the result of a specific engagement to provide non-audit services and therefore does not constitute internal audit services for the purposes of this Standard.

[handwritten margin note: Control assessment by-product not a problem]

47   In some circumstances, additional internal financial controls work is performed during the course of the audit in response to a specific request for an extended scope to the external audit. Whether it is appropriate for this work to be undertaken by the audit firm will depend on the extent to which it gives rise to a management threat to the auditor's objectivity and independence. The audit engagement partner reviews the scope and objectives of the proposed work and assesses the threats to which it gives rise and the safeguards available.

INFORMATION TECHNOLOGY SERVICES

48   Design, provision and implementation of information technology (including financial information technology) systems by audit firms for their audit clients creates threats to the auditors' objectivity and independence. The principal threats are the self-review threat and the management threat.

49   Engagements to design, provide or implement information technology systems that are not important to any significant part of the accounting system or to the production of the financial statements and do not have significant reliance placed on them by the auditors, may be undertaken, provided that 'informed management'[3] has been designated by the audit client and provided that appropriate safeguards are applied.

50   Examples of safeguards that may be appropriate when information technology services are provided to an audit client include ensuring that:

- information technology projects undertaken by the audit firm are performed by partners and staff who have no involvement in the external audit of the financial statements;

- the audit of the financial statements is reviewed by an audit partner who is not involved in the audit engagement to ensure that the information technology work performed has been properly and effectively assessed in the context of the audit of the financial statements.

51 **The audit firm should not undertake an engagement to design, provide or implement information technology systems for an audit client where:**

(a) **the systems concerned would be important to any significant part of the accounting system or to the production of the financial statements and the auditors would place significant reliance upon them as part of the audit of the financial statements; or**

(b) **for the purposes of the information technology services, the audit firm would undertake part of the role of management.**

52 Where it is reasonably apparent that, having regard to the activities and size of the audit client and the range and complexity of the proposed system, the management lacks the expertise required to take responsibility for the systems concerned, it is unlikely that any safeguards would be sufficient to eliminate these threats or to reduce them to an acceptable level. In particular, formal acceptance by management of the systems designed and installed by the audit firm is unlikely to be an effective safeguard when, in substance, the audit firm have been retained by management as experts and they make important decisions in relation to the design or implementation of systems of internal control and financial reporting.

53 The provision and installation of information technology services associated with a standard 'off the shelf accounting package' (including basic set-up procedures to make the package operate on the client's existing platform and peripherals, setting up the chart of accounts and the entry of standard data such as the client's product names and prices) is unlikely to create a level of threat to the auditor's objectivity and independence that cannot be addressed through applying appropriate safeguards.

VALUATION SERVICES

54 **The audit firm should not undertake an engagement to provide a valuation to an audit client where the valuation would both:**

Both

(a) **involve a significant degree of subjective judgment; and**

(b) **have a material effect on the financial statements.**

55 The main threats to the auditors' objectivity and independence arising from the provision of valuation services are the self-review threat and the management threat. The self-review threat is considered too high to allow the provision of valuation services which involve the valuation of amounts with a significant degree of subjectivity that may have a material effect on the financial statements.

56 This restriction does not apply in circumstances where the auditors are designated by legislation or regulation as being eligible to carry out a valuation.[4] In such circumstances, the audit engagement partner applies relevant safeguards.

57 It is usual for the auditors to provide the management with accounting advice in relation to valuation matters that have come to their attention during the course of the audit. Such matters might typically include:

- comments on valuation assumptions and their appropriateness;

- errors identified in a valuation calculation and suggestions for correcting them;

- advice on accounting policies and any valuation methodologies used in their application.

Advice on such matters does not constitute valuation services for the purpose of this Standard.

58 Where auditors are engaged to collect and verify the accuracy of data to be used in a valuation to be performed by others, such engagements do not constitute valuation services under this Standard.

ACTUARIAL VALUATION SERVICES

59 **The audit firm should not undertake an engagement to provide actuarial valuation services to an audit client, unless the firm is satisfied that either:**

(a) **all significant judgments, including the assumptions, are made by 'informed management'; or**

(b) **the valuation has no material effect on the financial statements.**

60 Actuarial valuation services are subject to the same general principles as other valuation services. Where they involve the audit firm in making a subjective judgment and have a material effect on the financial statements, actuarial valuations give rise to an unacceptable level of self-review threat and so may not be performed by audit firms for their audit clients.

61 However, in cases where all significant judgments concerning the assumptions, methodology and data for the actuarial valuation are made by 'informed management' and the audit firm's role is limited to applying proven methodologies using the given data, for which the management takes responsibility, it may be possible to establish effective safeguards to protect the auditors' objectivity and the appearance of their independence.

---

[4] For example, Section 103 of the Companies Act 1985 requires a public company to obtain a report on the value of assets to be received in payment for shares to be allotted from independent accountants who either are the auditors or are qualified to act as auditors, of the allotting company.

Section 30/32 Companies Amendment Act 1983

TAX SERVICES

62 The range of activities encompassed by the term 'tax services' is wide. Three broad categories of tax service can be distinguished. They are where the audit firm:

(a) provides advice to the audit client on one or more specific matters at the request of the audit client; or

(b) undertakes a substantial proportion of the tax planning or compliance work for the audit client; or

(c) promotes tax structures or products to the audit client, the effectiveness of which is likely to be influenced by the manner in which they are accounted for in the financial statements.

Whilst it is possible to consider tax services under broad headings, such as tax planning or compliance, in practice these services are often interrelated and it is impracticable to analyse services in this way for the purposes of attempting to identify generically the threats to which specific engagements give rise. As a result, audit firms need to identify and assess, on a case-by-case basis, the potential threats to the auditors' objectivity and independence before deciding whether to undertake a proposed engagement to provide tax services to an audit client.

63 The provision of tax services by audit firms to their audit clients may give rise to a number of threats to the auditors' objectivity and independence, including the self-interest threat, the management threat, the advocacy threat and, where the work involves a significant degree of subjective judgment and has a material effect on the financial statements, the self-review threat.

64 Where the audit firm provides advice to the audit client on one or more specific matters at the request of the audit client, a self-review threat may be created. This self-review threat is more significant where the audit firm undertakes a substantial proportion of the tax planning and compliance work for the audit client. However, the auditors may be able to adopt appropriate safeguards.

65 Examples of such safeguards that may be appropriate when tax services are provided to an audit client include ensuring that:

• the tax services are provided by partners and staff who have no involvement in the audit of the financial statements;

• the tax services are reviewed by an independent tax partner, or other senior tax employee;

• external independent advice is obtained on the tax work;

• tax computations prepared by the audit team are reviewed by a partner or senior staff member with appropriate expertise who is not a member of the audit team; or

- an audit partner not involved in the audit engagement reviews whether the tax work has been properly and effectively addressed in the context of the audit of the financial statements.

66 **The audit firm should not promote tax structures or products or undertake an engagement to provide tax advice to an audit client where the audit engagement partner has, or ought to have, reasonable doubt as to the appropriateness of the related accounting treatment involved, having regard to the requirement for the financial statements to give a true and fair view in accordance with the relevant financial reporting framework.**

67 Where the audit firm promotes tax structures or products or undertakes an engagement to provide tax advice to the audit client, it may be necessary to adopt an accounting treatment about which there is reasonable doubt as to its appropriateness, in order to achieve the desired result. A self-review threat arises in the course of an audit because the auditors may be unable to form an impartial view of the accounting treatment to be adopted for the purposes of the proposed arrangements. Accordingly, this Standard does not permit the promotion of tax structures or products by audit firms to their audit clients where, in the view of the audit engagement partner, after such consultation as is appropriate, the effectiveness of the tax structure or product depends on an accounting treatment about which there is reasonable doubt as to its appropriateness.

68 **The audit firm should not undertake an engagement to provide tax services to an audit client wholly or partly on a contingent fee basis where:**

(a) **the engagement fees are material to the audit firm or the part of the firm by reference to which the audit engagement partner's profit share is calculated; or**

(b) **the outcome of those tax services (and, therefore, the entitlement to the fee) is dependent on:**

(i) **the application of tax law which is uncertain or has not been established; and**

(ii) **a future or contemporary audit judgment relating to a material balance in the financial statements of the audit client.**

69 Where tax services, such as advising on corporate structures and structuring transactions to achieve a particular effect, are undertaken on a contingent fee basis, self-interest threats to the auditors' objectivity and independence may arise. The auditors may have, or may appear to have, an interest in the success of the tax services, causing them to make an audit judgment about which there is reasonable doubt as to its appropriateness. Where the contingent fee is determined by the outcome of the application of tax law, which is uncertain or has not been established, and where the tax implications are material to the financial statements, the self-interest threat cannot be eliminated or reduced to an acceptable level by the application of any safeguards.

70   **The audit firm should not undertake an engagement to provide tax services to an audit client where the engagement would involve the audit firm undertaking a management role.**

71   When providing tax services to an audit client, there is a risk that the audit firm undertakes a management role, unless the firm is working with 'informed management'[3] and appropriate safeguards are applied.

72   For entities other than listed companies or significant affiliates of listed companies, auditors may undertake an engagement to prepare accounting entries relating to tax and deferred tax calculations, provided that:

(a)   such services:

(i)   do not involve initiating transactions or taking management decisions; and

(ii)   are of a technical, mechanical or an informative nature; and

(b)   appropriate safeguards are applied.

73   **The audit firm should not undertake an engagement to provide tax services to an audit client where this would involve acting as an advocate for the audit client, before an appeals tribunal or court[5] in the resolution of an issue:**

(a)   **that is material to the financial statements; or**

(b)   **where the outcome of the tax issue is dependent on a future or contemporary audit judgment.**

74   Where the tax services to be provided by the audit firm include representing the client in any negotiations or proceedings involving the tax authorities, advocacy threats to the auditors' objectivity and independence may arise.

75   The audit firm is not acting as an advocate where the tax services involve the provision of information to the tax authorities (including an explanation of the approach being taken and the arguments being advanced by the audit client). In such circumstances effective safeguards may exist and the tax authorities will undertake their own review of the issues.

76   Where the tax authorities indicate that they are minded to reject the audit client's arguments on a particular issue and the matter is likely to be determined by an appeals tribunal or court, the audit firm may become so closely identified with management's arguments that the auditors are inhibited from forming an impartial view of the treatment of the issue in the financial statements. In such circumstances, if the issue is material to the financial statements or is dependent on a future or contemporary audit

---

[5]   The restriction applies to the first level of Tax Court that is independent of the tax authorities and to more authoritative bodies. In the UK this would be the General or Special Commissioners of the Inland Revenue or the VAT and Duties Tribunal.

judgment, the audit firm discusses the matter with the audit client and makes it clear to the client that it will have to withdraw from that element of the engagement to provide tax services that requires it to act as advocate for the audit client, or resign from the audit engagement from the time when the matter is formally listed for hearing before the appeals tribunal.

77 The audit firm is not, however, precluded from having a continuing role (for example, responding to specific requests for information) for the audit client in relation to the appeal. The audit firm assesses the threat associated with any continuing role in accordance with the provisions of paragraphs 78 to 80 of this Standard.

LITIGATION SUPPORT SERVICES

Self review
Threat

78 **The audit firm should not undertake an engagement to provide litigation support services to an audit client where this would involve the estimation by the audit firm of the likely outcome of a pending legal matter that could be material to the amounts to be included or the disclosures to be made in the financial statements and there is a significant degree of subjectivity involved.**

79 Although management and advocacy threats may arise in litigation support services, such as acting as an expert witness, the primary issue is that a self-review threat will arise where such services involve a subjective estimation of the likely outcome of a matter that is material to the amounts to be included or the disclosures to be made in the financial statements.

80 Litigation support services that do not involve such subjective estimations are not prohibited, provided that the audit firm has carefully considered the implications of any threats and established appropriate safeguards.

LEGAL SERVICES

81 **The audit firm should not undertake an engagement to provide legal services to an audit client where this would involve acting as the solicitor formally nominated to represent the client in the resolution of a dispute or litigation which is material to the amounts to be included or the disclosures to be made in the financial statements.**

82 Although the provision by auditors of certain types of legal services to their audit clients may create advocacy, self-review and management threats, this Standard does not impose a general prohibition on the provision of legal services. However, in view of the degree of advocacy involved in litigation or other types of dispute resolution procedures and the potential importance of any assessment by the auditors of the merits of the audit client's position when auditing its financial statements, this Standard prohibits an audit firm from acting as the formally nominated representative for an audit client in the resolution of a dispute or litigation which is material to the financial statements (either in terms of the amounts recognised or disclosed in the financial statements).

RECRUITMENT AND REMUNERATION SERVICES

83 **The audit firm should not undertake an engagement to provide recruitment services to an audit client that would involve the firm taking responsibility for the appointment of any director or employee of the audit client.**

all companies

84 A management threat arises where audit firm personnel take responsibility for any decision as to who should be appointed by the audit client.

management threat

85 **For an audit client that is a listed company, the audit firm should not undertake an engagement to provide recruitment services in relation to a key management position of the audit client, or a significant affiliate of such an entity.**

listed companies

86 A familiarity threat arises if the audit firm plays a significant role in relation to the identification and recruitment of senior members of management within the company, as the audit engagement team may be less likely to be critical of the information or explanations provided by such individuals than might otherwise be the case. Accordingly, for listed companies, and for significant affiliates of such entities, the audit firm does not undertake engagements that involve the recruitment of individuals for key management positions.

87 The audit firm's policies and procedures will set out circumstances in which recruitment services are not undertaken for non-listed audit clients. These policies will take into consideration the nature of the entity's business, its size, the number of its employees and the range of its stakeholders.

88 Recruitment services involve a specifically identifiable, and separately remunerated, engagement. Audit firms and engagement teams may contribute to an entity's recruitment process in less formal ways. The prohibition set out in paragraph 85 does not extend to senior members of an audit team interviewing prospective employees of the audit client or to the audit entity using information gathered by the audit firm, including that relating to salary surveys.

familiarity threat

89 **The audit firm should not undertake an engagement to provide advice on the quantum of the remuneration package or the measurement criteria on which the quantum is calculated, for a director or key management position of an audit client.**

90 The provision of advice on remuneration packages (including bonus arrangements, incentive plans and other benefits) to existing or prospective employees of the audit client gives rise to familiarity threats. The significance of the familiarity threat is considered too high to allow advice on the overall amounts to be paid or on the quantitative measurement criteria included in remuneration packages for directors and key management positions.

91 For other employees, these threats can be adequately addressed by the application of safeguards, such as the advice being provided by partners and staff who have no involvement in the audit of the financial statements.

92 In cases where all significant judgments concerning the assumptions, methodology and data for the calculation of remuneration packages for directors and key management are made by 'informed management' or a third party and the audit firm's role is limited to applying proven methodologies using the given data, for which the management takes responsibility, it may be possible to establish effective safeguards to protect the auditors' objectivity and independence.

93 Advice on tax, pensions and interpretation of accounting standards relating to remuneration packages for directors and key management can be provided by the audit firm, provided they are not prohibited by the requirements of this Standard relating to tax, actuarial valuations and accounting services. Disclosure of the provision of any such advice would be made to those charged with governance of the audit client (see APB Ethical Standard 1, paragraphs 49 to 53).

CORPORATE FINANCE SERVICES

94 The range of services encompassed by the term 'corporate finance services' is wide. For example, the audit firm may be engaged:

- to identify possible purchasers for parts of the audit client's business and provide advisory services in the course of such sales; or

- to identify possible 'targets' for the audit client to acquire; or

- to advise the audit client on how to fund its financing requirements, including advising on debt restructuring and securitisation programmes; or

- to act as sponsor on admission to listing on the London Stock Exchange, or as Nominated Advisor on the admission of the audit client on the Alternative Investments Market (AIM); or

- to act as financial adviser to audit client offerors or offerees in connection with public takeovers.

95 The potential for the auditors' objectivity and independence to be impaired through the provision of corporate finance services varies considerably depending on the precise nature of the service provided. The main threats to auditors' objectivity and independence arising from the provision of corporate finance services are the self-review, management and advocacy threats. Self-interest threats may also arise, especially in situations where the audit firm is paid on a contingent fee basis.

96 When providing corporate finance services to an audit client, there is a risk that the audit firm undertakes a management role, unless the firm is working with 'informed management'[3] and appropriate safeguards are applied.

97 Examples of safeguards that may be appropriate when corporate finance services are provided to an audit client include ensuring that:

- the corporate finance advice is provided by partners and staff who have no involvement in the audit of the financial statements;

- any advice provided is reviewed by an independent corporate finance partner within the audit firm;

- external independent advice on the corporate finance work is obtained;

- an audit partner who is not involved in the audit engagement reviews the audit work performed in relation to the subject matter of the corporate finance services provided to ensure that such audit work has been properly and effectively reviewed and assessed in the context of the audit of the financial statements.

98   Where the audit firm undertakes an engagement to provide corporate finance services to an audit client in connection with conducting the sale or purchase of a material part of the audit client's business, the audit engagement partner should inform the audit committee (or equivalent) about the engagement, as set out in paragraphs 49 to 53 of APB Ethical Standard 1.

99   **The audit firm should not undertake an engagement to provide corporate finance services to an audit client where:**

   (a) **the engagement would involve the audit firm taking responsibility for dealing in, underwriting or promoting shares; or**

   (b) **the audit engagement partner has, or ought to have, reasonable doubt as to the appropriateness of an accounting treatment that is related to the advice provided, having regard to the requirement for the financial statements to give a true and fair view in accordance with the relevant financial reporting framework; or**

   (c) **such corporate finance services are to be provided on a contingent fee basis and:**

   (i) **the engagement fees are material to the audit firm or the part of the firm by reference to which the audit engagement partner's profit share is calculated; or**

   (ii) **the outcome of those corporate finance services (and, therefore, the entitlement to the fee) is dependent on a future or contemporary audit judgment relating to a material balance in the financial statements of the audit client; or**

   (d) **the engagement would involve the audit firm undertaking a management role.**

100 An unacceptable advocacy threat arises where, in the course of providing a corporate finance service, the audit firm promotes the interests of the audit client by taking responsibility for dealing in, underwriting, or promoting shares.

101 Where the audit firm acts as a sponsor under the Listing Rules[6], or as Nominated Adviser on the admission of the audit client to the AIM, the audit firm is required to confirm that the audit client has satisfied all applicable conditions for listing and other relevant requirements of the listing (or AIM) rules. Where there is, or there ought to be, reasonable doubt that the audit firm will be able to give that confirmation, it does not enter into such an engagement.

102 A self-review threat arises where the outcome or consequences of the corporate finance service provided by the audit firm may be material to the financial statements of the audit client, which are, or will be, subject to audit by the same firm. Where the audit firm provides corporate finance services, for example advice to the audit client on financing arrangements, it may be necessary to adopt an accounting treatment about which there is reasonable doubt as to its appropriateness in order to achieve the desired result. A self-review threat is created because the auditors may be unable to form an impartial view of the accounting treatment to be adopted for the purposes of the proposed arrangements. Accordingly, this Standard does not permit the provision of advice by audit firms to their audit clients where there is reasonable doubt about the appropriateness of the related accounting treatments.

103 Advice to audit clients on funding issues and banking arrangements, where there is no reasonable doubt as to the appropriateness of the accounting treatment, is not prohibited provided this does not involve the audit firm in taking decisions or making judgments which are properly the responsibility of management.

104 Where a corporate finance engagement is undertaken on a contingent fee basis, self-interest threats to the auditors' objectivity and independence also arise as the auditors may have, or may appear to have, an interest in the success of the corporate finance services. The significance of the self-interest threat is primarily determined by the materiality of the contingent fee to the audit firm, or to the part of the firm by reference to which the audit engagement partner's profit share is calculated. Where the contingent fee and the outcome of the corporate finance services is dependent on a future or contemporary audit judgment relating to a material balance included in the financial statements of the audit client, the self-interest threat cannot be eliminated or reduced to an acceptable level by the application of any safeguards.

105 These restrictions do not apply in circumstances where the auditors are designated by legislation or regulation as being eligible to carry out a particular service. In such circumstances, the audit engagement partner establishes appropriate safeguards.

TRANSACTION RELATED SERVICES

106 In addition to corporate finance services, there are other non-audit services associated with transactions that an audit firm may undertake for an audit client. For example:

---

[6] In the United Kingdom, the UK Listing Authority's publication the 'Listing Rules'. In the Republic of Ireland, the United Kingdom 'Listing Rules' as modified by the 'Notes on the Listing Rules' published by the Irish Stock Exchange.

- investigations into possible acquisitions or disposals ('due diligence' investigations); or

- investigations into the tax affairs of possible acquisitions or disposals; or

- the provision of information to sponsors in relation to prospectuses and other investment circulars (for example, long form reports, comfort letters on the adequacy of working capital).

107 When providing transaction related services to an audit client, unless the firm is working with 'informed management'[3] and appropriate safeguards are applied, there is a risk that the audit firm undertakes a management role.

108 Examples of safeguards that may be appropriate when transaction related services are provided to an audit client include ensuring that:

- the transaction related advice is provided by partners and staff who have no involvement in the audit of the financial statements;

- any advice provided is reviewed by an independent transactions partner within the audit firm;

- external independent advice on the transaction related work is obtained;

- an audit partner who is not involved in the audit engagement reviews the audit work performed in relation to the subject matter of the transaction related service provided to ensure that such audit work has been properly and effectively reviewed and assessed in the context of the audit of the financial statements.

109 **The audit firm should not undertake an engagement to provide transaction related services to an audit client where:**

(a) **the audit engagement partner has, or ought to have, reasonable doubt as to the appropriateness of an accounting treatment that is related to the advice provided, having regard to the requirement for the financial statements to give a true and fair view in accordance with the relevant financial reporting framework; or**   *(110)*

(b) **such transaction related services are to be provided on a contingent fee basis and:**   *(111)*

(i) **the engagement fees are material to the audit firm or the part of the firm by reference to which the audit engagement partner's profit share is calculated; or**

(ii) **the outcome of those transaction related services (and, therefore, the entitlement to the fee) is dependent on a future or contemporary audit judgment relating to a material balance in the financial statements of the audit client; or**

(c) **the engagement would involve the audit firm undertaking a management role.**

110 A self-review threat arises where the outcome of the transaction related service undertaken by the audit firm may be material to the financial statements of the audit client which are, or will be, subject to audit by the same firm. Where the audit client proposes to undertake a transaction, it may be necessary to adopt an inappropriate accounting treatment in order to achieve the desired result. A self-review threat is created if the auditors undertake transaction related services in connection with such a transaction. Accordingly, this Standard does not permit the provision of advice by audit firms to their audit clients where there is reasonable doubt about the appropriateness of the accounting treatments related to the transaction advice given.

111 Where a transaction related services engagement is undertaken on a contingent fee basis, self-interest threats to the auditors' objectivity and independence also arise as the auditors may have, or may appear to have, an interest in the success of the transaction. The significance of the self-interest threat is primarily determined by the materiality of the contingent fee to the audit firm, or to the part of the firm by reference to which the audit engagement partner's profit share is calculated. Where the contingent fee and the outcome of the transaction related services is dependent on a future or contemporary audit judgment on a material balance included in the financial statements of the audit client, the self-interest threat cannot be eliminated or reduced to an acceptable level by the application of any safeguards, other than where the transaction is subject to a pre-established dispute resolution procedure.

112 These restrictions do not apply in circumstances where the auditors are designated by legislation or regulation as being eligible to carry out a particular service. In such circumstances, the audit engagement partner establishes appropriate safeguards.

ACCOUNTING SERVICES

113 In this Standard, the term 'accounting services' is defined as the provision of services that involve the maintenance of accounting records or the preparation of financial statements that are then subject to audit. Advice on the implementation of current and proposed accounting standards is not included in the term 'accounting services'.

114 The range of activities encompassed by the term 'accounting services' is wide. In some cases, the audit client may ask the audit firm to provide a complete service including maintaining all of the accounting records and the preparation of the financial statements. Other common situations are:

- the audit firm may take over the provision of a specific accounting function on an outsourced basis (for example, payroll);

- the audit client maintains the accounting records, undertakes basic bookkeeping and prepares a year-end trial balance and asks the audit firm to assist with the preparation of the necessary adjustments and the financial statements.

115 The provision of accounting services by the audit firm to the audit client creates threats to the auditors' objectivity and independence, principally self-review and management threats, the significance of which depends on the nature and extent of the accounting services in question and upon the level of public interest in the audit client.

116 When providing accounting services to an audit client, unless the firm is working with 'informed management'[3], there is a risk that the audit firm undertakes a management role.

117 **The audit firm should not undertake an engagement to provide accounting services to:**

(a) an audit client that is a listed company or a significant affiliate of such an entity, save where the circumstances contemplated in paragraph 121 apply; or

(b) any other audit client, where those accounting services would involve the audit firm undertaking part of the role of management.

118 Even where there is no engagement to provide any accounting services, it is usual for the auditors to provide the management with accounting advice on matters that have come to their attention during the course of the audit. Such matters might typically include:

- comments on weaknesses in the accounting records and suggestions for addressing them;

- errors identified in the accounting records and in the financial statements and suggestions for correcting them;

- advice on the accounting policies in use and on the application of current and proposed accounting standards.

This advice is a by-product of the audit service rather than the result of any engagement to provide non-audit services. Consequently, as it is part of the audit service, such advice cannot be regarded as giving rise to any threat to the auditors' objectivity and independence.

119 For listed companies or significant affiliates of such entities, the threats to the auditors' objectivity and independence that would be created are too high to allow the audit firm to undertake an engagement to provide any accounting services, save where the circumstances contemplated in paragraph 121 apply.

120 The audit firm's policies and procedures will set out circumstances in which accounting services are not undertaken for non-listed audit clients. These policies will take into consideration the nature of the entity's business, its size, the number of its employees and the range of its stakeholders.

listed companies exception

121 In emergency situations, the audit firm may provide a listed audit client, or a significant affiliate of such a company, with accounting services to assist the company in the timely preparation of its financial statements. This might arise when, due to external and unforeseeable events, the audit firm personnel are the only people with the necessary knowledge of the audit client's systems and procedures. A situation could be considered an emergency where the audit firm's refusal to provide these services would result in a severe burden for the audit client (for example, withdrawal of credit lines), or would even threaten its going concern status. In such circumstances, the audit firm ensures that:

(a) any staff involved in the accounting services have no involvement in the audit of the financial statements; and

(b) the engagement would not lead to any audit firm staff or partners taking decisions or making judgments which are properly the responsibility of management.

non listed

122 For entities other than listed companies or significant affiliates of listed companies, auditors may undertake an engagement to provide accounting services, provided that:

(a) such services:

123 (i) do not involve initiating transactions or taking management decisions; and

124 (ii) are of a technical, mechanical or an informative nature; and

125 (b) appropriate safeguards are applied.

123 The maintenance of the accounting records and the preparation of the financial statements are the responsibility of the management of the audit client. Accordingly, in any engagement to provide the audit client with accounting services, the audit firm does not initiate any transactions or take any decisions or make any judgments, which are properly the responsibility of the management. These include:

• authorising or approving transactions;

• preparing originating data (including valuation assumptions);

• determining or changing journal entries, or the classifications for accounts or transactions, or other accounting records without management approval.

124 Examples of accounting services of a technical or mechanical nature or of an informative nature include:

• recording transactions for which management has determined the appropriate account classification, posting coded transactions to the general ledger, posting entries approved by management to the trial balance or providing certain data-processing services (for example, payroll);

- assistance with the preparation of the financial statements where management takes all decisions on issues requiring the exercise of judgment and has prepared the underlying accounting records.

125 Examples of safeguards that may be appropriate when accounting services are provided to an audit client include:

- accounting services provided by the audit firm are performed by partners and staff who have no involvement in the external audit of the financial statements;

- the accounting services are reviewed by a partner or other senior staff member with appropriate expertise who is not a member of the audit team;

- the audit of the financial statements is reviewed by an audit partner who is not involved in the audit engagement to ensure that the accounting services performed have been properly and effectively assessed in the context of the audit of the financial statements.

EFFECTIVE DATE

126 Effective for audits of financial statements for periods commencing on or after 15 December 2004.

127 Firms may complete audit engagements relating to periods commencing prior to 15 December 2004 in accordance with existing ethical guidance from the relevant professional body, putting in place any necessary changes in the subsequent engagement period.

128 Where compliance with the requirements of ES 5 would result in a service not being supplied, services contracted before 5 October 2004 may continue to be provided until either:

(a) the completion of the specific task or the end of the contract term, where this is set out in the contract; or

(b) 15 December 2005, where a task or term is not defined,

as long as the following apply:

- the engagement was permitted by existing ethical guidance (including transitional provisions) from the relevant professional body;

- any safeguards required by existing ethical guidance continue to be applied; and

- the need for additional safeguards is assessed, including where possible any additional safeguards specified by ES5, and if considered necessary, those additional safeguards are applied.

129 In the first year of appointment as auditors to an audit client, an audit firm may continue to provide non-audit services which are already contracted at the date of appointment, until either:

(i)   the completion of the specific task or the end of the contract term, where this is set out in the contract; or

(ii)   one year after the date of appointment, where a task or term is not defined,

provided that the need for additional safeguards is assessed and if considered necessary, those additional safeguards are applied.

APB ETHICAL STANDARD

PROVISIONS AVAILABLE FOR SMALL ENTITIES

(Re-issued April 2005)

CONTENTS

PREFACE

APB Ethical Standards apply in the audit of financial statements. They should be read in the context of the Auditing Practices Board's Statement "The Auditing Practices Board – Scope and Authority of Pronouncements (Revised)" which sets out the application and authority of APB Ethical Standards.

The terms used in APB Ethical Standards for Auditors are explained in the Glossary.

INTRODUCTION

1   The APB issues Ethical Standards which set out the standards that auditors are required to comply with in order to discharge their responsibilities in respect of their integrity, objectivity and independence. The Ethical Standards issued in October 2004 address such matters as:

- How audit firms set policies and procedures to ensure that, in relation to each audit, the audit firm and all those who are in a position to influence the conduct and outcome of an audit act with integrity, objectivity and independence;

- Financial, business, employment and personal relationships;

- Long association with the audit engagement;

- Fees, remuneration and evaluation policies, litigation, gifts and hospitality;

- Non-audit services provided to audit clients.

Such Ethical Standards apply to all audit firms and to all audits and must be read in order to understand the alternative provisions and exemptions contained in this Standard.

2   The APB is aware that a limited number of the requirements in Ethical Standards 1 to 5 are difficult for certain audit firms to comply with, particularly when auditing a small entity. Whilst the APB is clear that those standards are appropriate in the interests of establishing the integrity, objectivity and independence of auditors, it accepts that certain dispensations, as set out in this Standard, are appropriate to facilitate the cost effective audit of the financial statements of Small Entities (as defined below).

3   This Standard provides alternative provisions for auditors of Small Entities to apply in respect of the threats arising from economic dependence and where tax or accounting services are provided and allows the option of taking advantage of exemptions from certain of the requirements in APB Ethical Standards 1 to 5 for a Small Entity audit engagement. Where an audit firm takes advantage of the exemptions within this Standard, it is required to:

(a)   take the steps described in this Standard; and

(b)   disclose in the audit report the fact that the firm has applied APB Ethical Standard – Provisions Available for Small Entities.

4   (i)   In this Standard, for the UK a 'Small Entity' is:

        (a)   any company, which is not a UK listed company or an affiliate thereof, that meets two or more of the following requirements in both the current financial year and the preceding financial year:

           • not more than £5.6 million turnover;

           • not more than £2.8 million balance sheet total;

           • not more than 50 employees.

        (b)   any charity with an income of less than £5.6 million;

        (c)   any pension fund with less than 1,000 members (including active, deferred and pensioner members)[1];

        (d)   any firm regulated by the FSA, which is not required to appoint an auditor in accordance with chapter 3 of the FSA Supervision Manual which forms a part of the FSA Handbook[2];

        (e)   any credit union which is a mutually owned financial co-operative established under the Credit Unions Act 1979 and the Industrial and Provident Societies Act 1965 (or equivalent legislation), which meets the criteria set out in (a) above;

        (f)   any entity registered under the Industrial and Provident Societies Act 1965, incorporated under the Friendly Societies Act 1992 or registered under the Friendly Societies Act 1974 (or equivalent legislation), which meets the criteria set out in (a) above;

        (g)   any registered social landlord with less than 250 units; and

        (h)   any other entity, such as a club, which would be a Small Entity if it were a company.

    (ii)   In this Standard, for the Republic of Ireland a 'Small Entity' is:

        (a)   any company, which is not an Irish listed company or an affiliate thereof, that meets two or more of the following requirements in both the current financial year and the preceding financial year:

           • not more than €7.3 million turnover;

---

[1] In cases where a scheme with more than 1,000 members has been in wind-up over a number of years, such a scheme does not qualify as a Small Entity, even where the remaining number of members falls below 1,000.

[2] This relates to those firms that are not required to appoint an auditor under rule 3.3.2 of the FSA Supervision Manual.

- not more than €3.65 million balance sheet total;

- not more than 50 employees.

(b) any charity with an income of less than €7.3 million;

(c) any pension fund with less than 1,000 members (including active, deferred and pensioner members)[1]; and

(d) any other entity, such as a club or credit union, which would be a Small Entity if it were a company.

Where an entity falls into more than one of the above categories, it is only regarded as a 'Small Entity' if it meets the criteria of all relevant categories.

ALTERNATIVE PROVISIONS
ECONOMIC DEPENDENCE

5 **When auditing the financial statements of a Small Entity an audit firm is not required to comply with the requirement in APB Ethical Standard 4, paragraph 31 that an external independent quality control review is performed.**

6 APB Ethical Standard 4, paragraph 31 provides that, where it is expected that the total fees for both audit and non-audit services receivable from a non-listed audit client and its subsidiaries audited by the audit firm will regularly exceed 10% of the annual fee income of the audit firm or the part of the firm by reference to which the audit engagement partner's profit share is calculated, but will not regularly exceed 15% the firm should arrange an external independent quality control review of the audit engagement to be undertaken before the auditors' report is finalised. Although an external independent quality control review is not required, nevertheless the audit engagement partner discloses the expectation that fees will amount to between 10% and 15% of the firm's annual fee income to the ethics partner and to those charged with governance of the audit client.

SELF-REVIEW THREAT – NON-AUDIT SERVICES

7 **When undertaking non-audit services for a Small Entity audit client, the audit firm is not required to apply safeguards to address a self-review threat provided:**

(a) **the audit client has 'informed management'; and**

(b) **the audit firm extends the cyclical inspection of completed engagements that is performed for quality control purposes.**

8 APB Ethical Standard 5 requires that, when an audit firm provides non-audit services to an audit client, appropriate safeguards are applied in order to reduce any self-review

threat to an acceptable level. APB Ethical Standard 5 provides examples of safeguards that may be appropriate when non-audit services are provided to an audit client (for example in paragraphs 65 for tax services and 125 for accounting services). In the case of an audit of a Small Entity, alternative procedures involve discussions with 'informed management', supplemented by an extension of the firm's cyclical inspection of completed engagements that is performed for quality control purposes.

9   The audit firm extends the number of engagements inspected under the requirements of ISQC (UK and Ireland) 1 *'Quality control for firms that perform audits and reviews of historical financial information, and other assurance and related services engagements'*[3] to include a random selection of audit engagements where non-audit services have been provided. Particular attention is given to ensuring that there is documentary evidence that 'informed management' has made such judgments and decisions that are needed in relation to the presentation and disclosure of information in the financial statements.

10   Those inspecting the engagements are not involved in performing the engagement. Small audit firms may wish to use a suitably qualified external person or another firm to carry out engagement inspections.

11   In addition to the documentation requirements of ISQC (UK and Ireland) 1, those inspecting the engagements document their evaluation of whether the documentary evidence that 'informed management' made such judgments and decisions that were needed in relation to the presentation and disclosure of information in the financial statements.

EXEMPTIONS

MANAGEMENT THREAT – NON-AUDIT SERVICES

12   **When undertaking non-audit services for Small Entity audit clients, the audit firm is not required to adhere to the prohibitions in APB Ethical Standard 5, relating to providing non-audit services that involve the audit firm undertaking part of the role of management, provided that:**

   (a)   **it discusses objectivity and independence issues related to the provision of non-audit services with those charged with governance; and**

   (b)   **it discloses the fact that it has applied this Standard in accordance with paragraph 22.**

13   APB Ethical Standard 5, paragraph 28 provides that where an audit firm provides non-audit services to an audit client that does not have 'informed management', it is

---

[3]   ISQC (UK and Ireland) 1 requires audit firms to establish policies and procedures which include a periodic inspection of a selection of completed engagements. Engagements selected for inspection include at least one engagement for each engagement partner over the inspection cycle, which ordinarily spans no more than three years.

unlikely that any safeguards can eliminate the management threat or reduce it to an acceptable level with the consequence that such non-audit services may not be provided to that audit client. This is because the absence of a capable member of management, who has been designated by the audit client to:

- receive the results of the non-audit services provided by the audit firm; and

- make any judgments and decisions that are needed, on the basis of the information provided,

means that there is an increased threat that the audit firm takes certain decisions and makes certain judgments, which are properly the responsibility of management.

14 An audit firm auditing a Small Entity is exempted from the requirements of APB Ethical Standard 5, paragraphs 43(b) (internal audit services), 51(b) (information technology services), 70 (tax services), 99(d) (corporate finance services) 109(c) (transaction related services) and 117(b) (accounting services) in circumstances when there is no 'informed management' as envisioned by APB Ethical Standard 5, provided it discusses objectivity and independence issues related to the provision of non-audit services with those charged with governance and discloses the fact that it has applied this Standard in accordance with paragraph 22.

ADVOCACY THREAT – TAX SERVICES

15 **The audit firm of a Small Entity is not required to comply with APB Ethical Standard 5, paragraph 73 provided that it discloses the fact that it has applied this Standard in accordance with paragraph 22.**

16 APB Ethical Standard 5, paragraph 73 provides that 'the audit firm should not undertake an engagement to provide tax services to an audit client where this would involve acting as an advocate for the audit client, before an appeals tribunal or court in the resolution of an issue:

(a) that is material to the financial statements; or

(b) where the outcome of the tax issue is dependent on a future or contemporary audit judgment'.

Such circumstances may create an advocacy threat which it is unlikely any safeguards can eliminate or reduce to an acceptable level.

17 Where an audit firm auditing a Small Entity takes advantage of the dispensation in paragraph 15, it discloses the fact that it has applied this Standard in accordance with paragraph 22.

PARTNERS JOINING AN AUDIT CLIENT

18   **The audit firm of a Small Entity is not required to comply with APB Ethical Standard 2, paragraph 44 provided that:**

(a) **it takes appropriate steps to determine that there has been no significant threat to the audit team's integrity, objectivity and independence; and**

(b) **it discloses the fact that it has applied this Standard in accordance with paragraph 22.**

19   APB Ethical Standard 2, paragraph 44 provides that 'where a former partner is appointed as a director or to a key management position with an audit client, having acted as audit engagement partner (or as an independent partner, key audit partner or a partner in the chain of command) at any time in the two years prior to this appointment, the firm should resign as auditors and should not accept re-appointment until a two-year period, commencing when the former partner ceased to act for the client, has elapsed or the former partner ceases employment with the former client, whichever is the sooner'. Such circumstances may create self-interest, familiarity and intimidation threats.

20   An audit firm takes appropriate steps to determine that there has been no significant threat to the audit team's integrity, objectivity and independence as a result of the former partner's employment by an audit client that is a Small Entity by:

(a) assessing the significance of the self-interest, familiarity or intimidation threats, having regard to the following factors:

  •   the position the individual has taken at the audit client;

  •   the nature and amount of any involvement the individual will have with the audit team or the audit process;

  •   the length of time that has passed since the individual was a member of the audit team or firm; and

  •   the former position of the individual within the audit team or firm, and

(b) if the threat is other than clearly insignificant, applying alternative procedures such as:

  •   considering the appropriateness or necessity of modifying the audit plan for the audit engagement;

  •   assigning an audit team to the subsequent audit engagement that is of sufficient experience in relation to the individual who has joined the audit client;

- involving an audit partner or senior staff member with appropriate expertise, who was not a member of the audit team, to review the work done or otherwise advise as necessary; or

- undertaking an engagement quality control review of the audit engagement.

21 When an audit firm auditing a Small Entity takes advantage of paragraph 18 it discloses the fact that it has applied this Standard in accordance with paragraph 22 and documents the steps that it has taken to comply with this Standard.

DISCLOSURE REQUIREMENTS

22 Where the audit firm has taken advantage of an exemption provided in paragraphs 12, 15 or 18 of this Standard, the audit engagement partner should ensure that:

(a) the auditors' report discloses this fact, and

(b) either the financial statements, or the auditors' report, discloses the type of non-audit services provided to the audit client or the fact that a former audit engagement partner has joined the client.

23 The fact that an audit firm has taken advantage of an exemption from APB Ethical Standard – Provisions Available for Small Entities is set out in a separate paragraph of the audit report as part of the Basis of audit opinion. It does not affect the Opinion paragraph. An illustrative example of such disclosure is set out in the Appendix.

24 The audit engagement partner ensures that within the financial statements reference is made to the type of non-audit services provided to the audit client or the fact that a former partner has joined the client. An illustration of possible disclosures is set out in the Appendix. Where such a disclosure is not made within the financial statements it is included in the auditors' report.

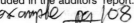

EFFECTIVE DATE

25 Effective for audits of financial statements for periods commencing on or after 15 December 2004.

APPENDIX: Illustrative disclosures

(a) Illustrative disclosure of the fact that the audit firm has taken advantage of an exemption within the auditors' report

Basis of audit opinion

We conducted our audit in accordance with United Kingdom Auditing Standards issued by the Auditing Practices Board. An audit includes examination, on a test basis, of evidence relevant to the amounts and disclosures in the financial statements. It also includes an assessment of the significant estimates and judgments made by [the directors] in the preparation of the financial statements, and of whether the accounting policies are appropriate to the [company's] circumstances, consistently applied and adequately disclosed.

We planned and performed our audit so as to obtain all the information and explanations which we considered necessary in order to provide us with sufficient evidence to give reasonable assurance that the financial statements are free from material misstatement, whether caused by fraud or other irregularity or error. In forming our opinion we also evaluated the overall adequacy of the presentation of information in the financial statements.

We have undertaken the audit in accordance with the requirements of APB Ethical Standards including APB Ethical Standard – Provisions Available for Small Entities, in the circumstances set out in note [x] to the financial statements.

Opinion

In our opinion the financial statements give a true and fair view of the state of the [company's] affairs as at .... .

[Date of the auditors' report, *auditors' signature and* address]

(b) Illustrative disclosure of relevant circumstances within the financial statements

Note [x] In common with many other businesses of our size and nature we use our auditors to prepare and submit returns to the tax authorities and assist with the preparation of the financial statements[4].

Note [x] In common with many other businesses of our size and nature we use our auditors to provide tax advice and to represent us, as necessary, at tax tribunals[5].

Note [x] XYZ, a former partner of [audit firm] joined [audit client] as [a director] on [date][6].

---

[4] Where exemption in paragraph 12 (Management threat in relation non-audit services) is applied.
[5] Where exemption in paragraph 15 (Advocacy threat – tax services) is applied.
[6] Where exemption in paragraph 18 (Partners joining an audit client) is applied.

THE AUDITING
PRACTICES BOARD

ETHICAL STANDARD FOR REPORTING ACCOUNTANTS

(Issued October 2006)

CONTENTS

PREFACE

The APB Ethical Standard for Reporting Accountants applies to all engagements:

- that are subject to the requirements of the Standards for Investment Reporting (SIRs), and

- which are in connection with an investment circular in which a report from the reporting accountant is to be published.

It should be read in the context of the Auditing Practices Board's Statement "The Auditing Practices Board – Scope and Authority of Pronouncements (Revised)" which sets out the application and authority of APB Ethical Standards.

The terms used in the APB Ethical Standard for Reporting Accountants are explained in the Glossary of terms at Appendix 1.

SECTION 1

INTRODUCTION

1.1 APB Ethical Standards for Auditors require an auditor to be independent from the entity that it is appointed to audit. There is a substantial degree of similarity between an audit opinion and the nature of assurance provided by accountants reporting for the purposes of an investment circular prepared in accordance with the statutory or regulatory requirements of a recognised stock exchange. Accordingly, the Auditing Practices Board (APB) believes that users of investment circulars will expect an equivalent standard of independence of reporting accountants to that required of auditors.

1.2 This standard is based on the APB Ethical Standards for Auditors and applies to all engagements:

- that are subject to the requirements of the Standards for Investment Reporting (SIRs) issued by the APB, and

- which are in connection with an investment circular in which a report from the reporting accountant is to be published.

This standard applies to all public reporting engagements undertaken in accordance with the SIRs. It also applies to all private reporting engagements that are directly linked to such public reporting engagements.

1.3 Where a private reporting engagement is undertaken, but it is not intended that the reporting accountant will issue a public report, the reporting accountant follows the ethical guidance issued by the professional accountancy body of which the reporting accountant is a member. The APB is not aware of any significant instances where the relevant parts of the ethical guidance issued by professional accountancy bodies in the UK and Ireland are more restrictive than this standard.

1.4 An investment circular is a document issued by an entity pursuant to statutory or regulatory requirements relating to securities on which it is intended that a third party should make an investment decision, including a prospectus, listing particulars, a circular to shareholders or similar document.

1.5 Public confidence in the operation of the capital markets and in the conduct of public interest entities depends, in part, upon the credibility of the opinions and reports issued by reporting accountants in connection with investment circulars. Such credibility depends on beliefs concerning the integrity, objectivity and independence of reporting accountants and the quality of work they perform. The APB establishes quality control, investment reporting[1] and ethical standards to provide a framework for the practice of reporting accountants.

---

[1] SIR 1000 paragraph 18 states *'In the conduct of an engagement involving an investment circular, the reporting accountant should comply with the applicable ethical standards issued by the Auditing Practices Board'*.

1.6 **Reporting Accountants should conduct an investment circular reporting engagement with integrity, objectivity and independence.**

Integrity

1.7 Integrity is a prerequisite for all those who act in the public interest. It is essential that reporting accountants act, and are seen to act, with integrity, which requires not only honesty but a broad range of related qualities such as fairness, candour, courage, intellectual honesty and confidentiality.

1.8 It is important that the directors and management of an engagement client can rely on the reporting accountant to treat the information obtained during an engagement as confidential, unless they have authorised its disclosure, it is already known to third parties or the reporting accountant has a legal right or duty to disclose it. Without this, there is a danger that the directors and management will fail to disclose such information to the reporting accountant and that the outcome of the engagement will thereby be impaired.

Objectivity

1.9 Objectivity is a state of mind that excludes bias, prejudice and compromise and that gives fair and impartial consideration to all matters that are relevant to the task in hand, disregarding those that are not. Objectivity requires that the reporting accountant's judgment is not affected by conflicts of interests. Like integrity, objectivity is a fundamental ethical principle.

1.10 The need for reporting accountants to be objective arises from the fact that the important issues involved in an engagement are likely to relate to questions of judgment rather than to questions of fact. For example, in relation to historical financial information included in an investment circular directors have to form a view as to whether it is necessary to make adjustments to previously published financial statements. If the directors, whether deliberately or inadvertently, make a biased judgment or an otherwise inappropriate decision, the financial information may be misstated or misleading.

1.11 It is against this background that reporting accountants are engaged to undertake an investment circular reporting engagement. The reporting accountant's objectivity requires that it expresses an impartial opinion in the light of all the available information and its professional judgment. Objectivity also requires that the reporting accountant adopts a rigorous and robust approach and is prepared to disagree, where necessary, with the directors' judgments.

Independence

1.12 Independence is freedom from situations and relationships which make it probable that a reasonable and informed third party would conclude that objectivity either is impaired or could be impaired. Independence is related to and underpins objectivity. However, whereas objectivity is a personal behavioural characteristic concerning the reporting accountant's state of mind, independence relates to the circumstances surrounding the engagement, including the financial, employment, business and personal relationships between the reporting accountant and its engagement client and other parties who are connected with the investment circular.

1.13 The need for independence arises because, in most cases, users of the financial information and other third parties do not have all the information necessary to assess whether reporting accountants are, in fact, objective. Although reporting accountants themselves may be satisfied that their objectivity is not impaired by a particular situation, a third party may reach a different conclusion. For example, if a third party were aware that the reporting accountant had certain financial, employment, business or personal relationships with the engagement client, that individual might reasonably conclude that the reporting accountant could be subject to undue influence from the engagement client or would not be impartial or unbiased. Public confidence in the reporting accountant's objectivity could therefore suffer as a result of this perception, irrespective of whether there is any actual impairment.

1.14 Accordingly, in evaluating the likely consequences of such situations and relationships, the test to be applied is not whether the reporting accountant considers that its objectivity is impaired but whether it is probable that a reasonable and informed third party would conclude that the reporting accountant's objectivity either is impaired or is likely to be impaired. There are inherent threats to the level of independence (both actual and perceived) that the reporting accountant can achieve as a result of the influence that the board of directors and management have over its appointment and remuneration. The reporting accountant considers the application of safeguards where there are threats to their independence (both actual and perceived).

COMPLIANCE WITH ETHICAL STANDARDS

1.15 **The reporting accountant should establish policies and procedures, appropriately documented and communicated, designed to ensure that, in relation to each investment circular reporting engagement, the firm, and all those who are in a position directly to influence the conduct and outcome of the investment circular reporting engagement, act with integrity, objectivity and independence.**

1.16 For the purposes of the APB Ethical Standard for Reporting Accountants, a person in a position directly to influence the conduct and outcome of the investment circular reporting engagement is:

(a) any person within the firm who is directly involved in the investment circular reporting engagement ('the engagement team'), including:

(i) the partners, managers and staff from assurance and other disciplines involved in the engagement (for example, taxation specialists, IT specialists, treasury management specialists, lawyers, actuaries);[2]

(ii) those who provide quality control or direct oversight of the engagement;

(b) any person within the firm who can directly influence the conduct and outcome of the investment circular reporting engagement through the provision of direct supervisory, management or other oversight of the engagement team in the context of the investment circular reporting engagement.

1.17 Because investment circulars may relate to transactions that are price sensitive and therefore confidential, the fact that a firm has been engaged to undertake an investment circular reporting engagement is likely to be known by only a limited number of individuals within the firm. For this reason, the requirements of this standard apply only to:

(a) individuals within the engagement team and those with a direct supervisory, management or other oversight responsibility for the engagement team who have actual knowledge of the investment circular reporting engagement; and

(b) where required by this Standard, the firm.

1.18 Compliance with the requirements regarding the reporting accountant's integrity, objectivity and independence is a responsibility of both the firm and of individual partners and professional staff. The firm establishes policies and procedures, appropriate to the size and nature of the firm, to promote and monitor compliance with those requirements by any person who is in a position directly to influence the conduct and outcome of the investment circular reporting engagement.[3]

1.19 **The leadership of the firm should take responsibility for establishing a control environment within the firm that places adherence to ethical principles and compliance with the APB Ethical Standard for Reporting Accountants above commercial considerations.**

1.20 The leadership of the firm influences the internal culture of the organisation by its actions and by its example ('the tone at the top'). Achieving a robust control environment requires that the leadership gives clear, consistent and frequent messages, backed up by appropriate actions, which emphasise the importance of compliance with the APB Ethical Standard for Reporting Accountants.

---

[2] Where external consultants are engaged by the reporting accountant and involved in the engagement, the reporting accountant should evaluate the objectivity of the expert in accordance with paragraphs 2.53 to 2.55 of this Standard.

[3] Monitoring of compliance with ethical requirements will often be performed as part of a broader quality control process. ISQC (UK & Ireland) 1 'Quality Control for firms that perform audits and reviews of historical financial information and other assurance and related services engagements' establishes the basic principles and essential procedures in relation to a firm's responsibilities for its system of quality control for engagements in connection with an investment circular.

1.21 In order to promote a strong control environment, the firm establishes policies and procedures (including the maintenance of appropriate records) that include:

(a) reporting by partners and staff as required by the APB Ethical Standard for Reporting Accountants of particular circumstances including:

- family and other personal relationships involving an engagement client of the firm;

- financial interests in an engagement client of the firm; and

- decisions to join an engagement client;

(b) monitoring of compliance with the firm's policies and procedures relating to integrity, objectivity and independence. Such monitoring procedures include, on a test basis, periodic review of the engagement partners' documentation of their consideration of the reporting accountant's objectivity and independence, addressing, for example:

- financial interests in engagement clients;

- contingent fee arrangements;

- economic dependence on clients;

- the performance of other service engagements for the engagement client;

(c) a mechanism for prompt communication of possible or actual breaches of the firm's policies and procedures to the relevant engagement partners;

(d) evaluation by engagement partners of the implications of any identified possible or actual breaches of the firm's policies and procedures that are reported to them;

(e) prohibiting members of the engagement team from making, or assuming responsibility for, management decisions for the engagement client;

(f) operation of an enforcement mechanism to promote compliance with policies and procedures; and

(g) empowerment of staff to communicate to senior levels within the firm any issue of objectivity or independence that concerns them; this includes establishing clear communication channels open to staff, encouraging staff to use these channels and ensuring that staff who use these channels are not subject to disciplinary proceedings as a result.

1.22 **Save where the circumstances contemplated in paragraph 1.24 apply, the firm should designate a partner in the firm ('the ethics partner'[4]) as having responsibility for:**

(a) **the adequacy of the firm's policies and procedures relating to integrity, objectivity and independence, their compliance with the APB Ethical Standard for Reporting Accountants, and the effectiveness of their communication to partners and staff within the firm; and**

(b) **providing related guidance to individual partners.**

1.23 In assessing the effectiveness of the firm's communication of its policies and procedures relating to integrity, objectivity and independence, ethics partners consider whether these matters are properly covered in induction programmes, professional training and continuing professional development for all partners and staff with direct involvement in investment circular reporting engagements. Ethics partners also provide guidance on matters referred to them and on matters which they otherwise become aware of, where a difficult and objective judgment needs to be made or a consistent position reached.

1.24 In firms with three or less partners, it may not be practicable for an ethics partner to be designated. In these circumstances all partners will regularly discuss ethical issues amongst themselves, so ensuring that they act in a consistent manner and observe the principles set out in the APB Ethical Standard for Reporting Accountants. In the case of a sole practitioner, advice on matters where a difficult and objective judgment needs to be made is obtained through the ethics helpline of their professional body, or through discussion with a practitioner from another firm. In all cases, it is important that such discussions are documented.

1.25 To be able to discharge his or her responsibilities, the ethics partner is an individual possessing seniority, relevant experience and authority within the firm and is provided with sufficient staff support and other resources, commensurate with the size of the firm. Alternative arrangements are established to allow for:

• the provision of guidance on those engagements where the ethics partner is the engagement partner; and

• situations where the ethics partner is unavailable, for example due to illness or holidays.

1.26 Whenever a possible or actual breach of the APB Ethical Standard for Reporting Accountants, or of policies and procedures established pursuant to the requirements of the APB Ethical Standard for Reporting Accountants, is identified, the engagement partner, in the first instance, and the ethics partner, where appropriate, assesses the implications of the breach, determines whether there are safeguards that can be put

---

[4]   This individual may be the same person who is designated as the ethics partner for the purposes of the APB Ethical Standards for Auditors.

in place or other actions that can be taken to address any potential adverse consequences and considers whether there is a need to withdraw from the investment circular reporting engagement.

1.27 An inadvertent violation of this Standard does not necessarily call into question the firm's ability to undertake an investment circular reporting engagement, provided that:

(a) the firm has established policies and procedures that require all partners and staff to report any breach promptly to the engagement partner or to the ethics partner, as appropriate;

(b) the engagement partner or ethics partner promptly notifies the relevant partner or member of staff that any matter which has given rise to a breach is to be addressed as soon as possible and ensures that such action is taken;

(c) safeguards, where appropriate, are applied, (for example, having another partner review the work done by the relevant partner or member of staff or removing him or her from the engagement team); and

(d) the actions taken and the rationale for them are documented.

IDENTIFICATION AND ASSESSMENT OF THREATS

1.28 Reporting accountants identify and assess the circumstances, which could adversely affect their objectivity ('threats'), including any perceived loss of independence, and apply procedures ('safeguards'), which will either:

(a) eliminate the threat (for example, by eliminating the circumstances, such as removing an individual from the engagement team or disposing of a financial interest in the engagement client); or

(b) reduce the threat to an acceptable level; that is a level at which it is not probable that a reasonable and informed third party would conclude that the reporting accountant's objectivity is impaired or is likely to be impaired (for example, by having the work reviewed by another partner or by another firm).

When considering safeguards, where the engagement partner chooses to reduce rather than to eliminate a threat to objectivity and independence, he or she recognises that this judgment may not be shared by third parties and that he or she may be required to justify the decision.

Threats to objectivity and independence

1.29 The principal types of threats to the reporting accountant's objectivity and independence are:

- self-interest threat;

- self-review threat;

- management threat;

- advocacy threat;

- familiarity (or trust) threat; and

- intimidation threat.

1.30 A **self-interest threat** arises when reporting accountants have financial or other interests which might cause them to be reluctant to take actions that would be adverse to the interests of the firm or any individual in a position directly to influence the conduct or outcome of the engagement (for example, when the engagement partner has a financial interest in the company issuing the investment circular).

1.31 A **self-review threat** arises when the results of a service performed by the engagement team or others within the firm are reflected in the amounts included or disclosed in the financial information that is the subject of the investment circular reporting engagement (for example, when reporting in relation to an initial public offering for a company where the firm has been involved in maintaining the accounting records of that company). A threat to objectivity arises because, in the course of the investment circular reporting engagement, the reporting accountant may need to re-evaluate the work performed in the course of the other service previously provided by the firm. As, by virtue of providing the other service, the firm is associated with aspects of the financial information being reported upon, the reporting accountant may be (or may be perceived to be) unable to take an impartial view of relevant aspects of that financial information.

1.32 There is a self-review threat where a firm prepares an accountant's report on historical financial information which has been included in, or formed part of, financial statements which have already been subject to audit by the same firm. In such situations, where the two engagement teams are not completely independent of each other, the engagement partner evaluates the significance of the self-review threat created. If this is other than clearly insignificant, safeguards are applied, such as the appointment of an engagement quality control reviewer who has not been involved in the audit.

1.33 In assessing the significance of the self-review threat in relation to an investment circular reporting engagement, the reporting accountant considers the extent to which the other service will:

- involve a significant degree of subjective judgment; and

- have a material effect on the preparation and presentation of the financial information that is the subject of the investment circular reporting engagement.

1.34 Where a significant degree of subjective judgment relating to the financial information is involved in an other service engagement, the reporting accountant may be inhibited from questioning that judgment in the course of the investment circular reporting engagement. Whether a significant degree of subjective judgment is involved will depend upon whether the other service involves the application of well-established principles and procedures, and whether reliable information is available. If such circumstances do not exist because the other service is based on concepts, methodologies or assumptions that require judgment and are not established by the engagement client or by authoritative guidance, the reporting accountant's objectivity and the appearance of its independence may be adversely affected. Where the provision of the other service during the relevant period also has a material effect on the financial information that is the subject of the investment circular reporting engagement, it is unlikely that any safeguard can eliminate or reduce to an acceptable level the self-review threat.

1.35   A **management threat** arises when the firm undertakes work that involves making judgments and taking decisions, which are the responsibility of the management of the party responsible for issuing the investment circular containing the financial information or the party on whose financial information the firm is reporting (the engagement client) in relation to:

- the transaction (for example, where it has been working closely with a company in developing a divestment strategy); or

- the financial information that is the subject of the investment circular reporting engagement (for example, deciding on the assumptions to be used in a profit forecast).

A threat to objectivity and independence arises because, by making judgments and taking decisions that are properly the responsibility of management, the firm erodes the distinction between the engagement client and the reporting accountant. The firm may become closely aligned with the views and interests of management and this may, in turn, impair or call into question the reporting accountant's ability to apply a proper degree of professional scepticism in performing the investment circular reporting engagement. The reporting accountant's objectivity and independence therefore may be impaired, or may be perceived to be, impaired.

1.36   Factors to be considered in determining whether an other service does or does not give rise to a management threat include whether:

- the other service results in recommendations by the firm justified by objective and transparent analyses or the engagement client being given the opportunity to decide between reasonable alternatives;

- the reporting accountant is satisfied that a member of management (or senior employee) has been designated by the engagement client to receive the results of the other service and make any judgments and decisions that are needed; and

- that member of management has the capability to make independent management judgments and decisions on the basis of the information provided ('informed management').

1.37   Where there is 'informed management', the reporting accountant assesses whether there are safeguards that can be introduced that would be effective to avoid a management threat or to reduce it to a level at which it can be disregarded. Such safeguards would include the investment circular reporting engagement being provided by partners and staff who have no involvement in those other services. In the absence of 'informed management', it is unlikely that any safeguards can eliminate the management threat or reduce it to an acceptable level.

1.38   An **advocacy threat** arises when the firm undertakes work that involves acting as an advocate for an engagement client and supporting a position taken by management in an adversarial context (for example, by undertaking an active responsibility for the marketing of an entity's shares). In order to act in an advocacy role, the firm has to adopt a position closely aligned to that of management. This creates both actual and perceived threats to the reporting accountant's objectivity and independence. For example, where the firm, acting as advocate, has supported a particular contention of management, it may be difficult for the reporting accountant to take an impartial view of this in the context of its review of the financial information.

1.39   Where the provision of an other service would require the reporting accountant to act as an advocate for the engagement client in relation to matters that are material to the financial information that is the subject of the investment circular reporting engagement, it is unlikely that any safeguards can eliminate or reduce to an acceptable level the advocacy threat that would exist.

1.40   A **familiarity threat** arises when reporting accountants are predisposed to accept or are insufficiently questioning of the engagement client's point of view (for example, where they develop close personal relationships with client personnel through long association with the engagement client).

1.41   An **intimidation threat** arises when the conduct of reporting accountants is influenced by fear or threats (for example, where they encounter an aggressive and dominating party).

1.42   These categories may not be entirely distinct: certain circumstances may give rise to more than one type of threat. For example, where a firm wishes to retain the fee income from a large client, but encounters an aggressive and dominating individual, there may be a self-interest threat as well as an intimidation threat.

1.43   When identifying threats to objectivity and independence, reporting accountants consider circumstances and relationships with a number of different parties. The engagement client may constitute one or more parties, dependent on the circumstances of the transaction which is the subject of the investment circular[5]. Where the party responsible for issuing the investment circular is different from the party whose financial information is included in the investment circular, the reporting

---

[5]   For example, where a report on a target company's financial statements is included in the acquiring company's investment circular.

accountant makes an assessment of independence with respect to both these parties, applying the alternative procedures set out in paragraph 1.44 as necessary.

1.44 Where either:

- an investment circular reporting engagement is undertaken to provide a report on the financial information relating to an audit client but the reporting accountant's report is to be published in an investment circular issued by another entity that is not an audit client; or

- the reporting accountant's report is to be published in an investment circular issued by an audit client but the reporting accountant's report is on financial information relating to another entity that is not an audit client,

it may not be practicable in the time available to identify all relationships and other service engagements recently undertaken by the firm for the non-audit client and its significant affiliates. In such instances the reporting accountant undertakes those enquiries[6] that are practical in the time available into the relationships and other service engagements that the firm has with the non-audit client and, having regard to its obligations to maintain confidentiality, addresses any identified threats. Having done so, the reporting accountant discloses to those charged with governance of the issuing engagement client that a consideration of all known threats has been undertaken and, where appropriate, safeguards applied, but this does not constitute a full evaluation of all relationships and other services provided to the non-audit client.

1.45 **The firm should establish policies and procedures to require persons in a position directly to influence the conduct and outcome of the investment circular reporting engagement to be constantly alert to circumstances and relationships with:**

(a) **the engagement client, and**

(b) **other parties who are connected with the investment circular,**

that might reasonably be considered threats to their objectivity or the perceived loss of their independence, and, where such circumstances or relationships are identified, to report them to the engagement partner or to the ethics partner, as appropriate.

1.46 Such policies and procedures require that threats to the reporting accountant's objectivity and independence are communicated to the appropriate person, having regard to the nature of the threats and the part of the firm and the identity of any person involved. The consideration of all threats and the action taken is documented.

---

[6] For example, these enquiries are likely to include reviewing the list of engagements recorded in the firm's accounting systems and an enquiry of individuals within the firm who are responsible for maintaining such systems as to whether any confidentially coded engagements could be relevant.

If the engagement partner is personally involved, or if he or she is unsure about the action to be taken, the matter is resolved through consultation with the ethics partner.

1.47 In addition to considering independence in the context of the engagement client, the reporting accountant also considers relationships with other parties who are connected with the investment circular. These parties will include the sponsor or nominated advisor, other parties from whom, in accordance with the engagement letter, the reporting accountant takes instructions and other entities directly involved in the transaction which is the subject of the investment circular.[7] The reporting accountant considers the circumstances involved and uses judgment to assess whether it is probable that a reasonable and informed third party would conclude that the reporting accountant's objectivity either is impaired or is likely to be impaired as a result of relationships held with any of these parties.

1.48 In the case of established financial institutions or advisers, the reporting accountant may have extensive relationships with these parties, including for the provision of other services or the purchase of goods and services in the ordinary course of business. These relationships will not generally give rise to a significant threat to the reporting accountant's objectivity.

1.49 Relationships with other parties who are connected with the investment circular which are outside the ordinary course of business or which are material to any party are more likely to give rise to a significant threat to the reporting accountant's objectivity. Consideration of the threats to the reporting accountant's objectivity in relation to other entities will primarily be concerned with matters that could give rise to self-interest and intimidation threats, for example:

- where there is financial dependence on the relationship with the other party arising from fees (including any contingent element) for investment circular reporting engagements undertaken by the firm as a result of connections with the other parties;

- joint ventures or similar relationships with the other party or with a senior member of their management;

- significant purchases of goods or services which are not in the ordinary course of business or are not on an arm's length basis;

- personal relationships between engagement team members and individuals in senior positions within the other party; or

- large direct financial interests in, or loans made by, the other party.

---

[7] Where such entities are part of a complex group or corporate structure, the reporting accountant considers issues relating to the wider group and not just the entity directly involved in the transaction.

1.50 **The firm should establish policies and procedures to require the engagement partner to identify and assess the significance of threats to the reporting accountant's objectivity, including any perceived loss of independence:**

    (a) **when considering whether to accept an investment circular reporting engagement and planning the work to be undertaken;**

    (b) **when signing the report;**

    (c) **when considering whether the firm can accept or retain an engagement to provide other services to an engagement client during the relevant period; and**

    (d) **when potential threats are reported to him or her.**

1.51 An initial assessment of the threats to objectivity and independence is required when the engagement partner is considering whether to accept an investment circular reporting engagement and planning the engagement. At the end of the engagement, when reporting on the work undertaken but before issuing the report, the engagement partner draws an overall conclusion as to whether any threats to objectivity and independence have been properly addressed in accordance with the APB Ethical Standard for Reporting Accountants. If, at any time, the reporting accountant is invited to accept an engagement to provide other services to an engagement client for which the firm is undertaking an investment circular reporting engagement, the engagement partner considers the impact this new engagement may have on the reporting accountant's objectivity and independence.

1.52 When identifying and assessing threats to their objectivity and independence, reporting accountants take into account their current relationships with the engagement client (including other service engagements) and those that existed prior to the current engagement in the relevant period. The relevant period covers the period during which the engagement is undertaken and any additional period before the engagement period but subsequent to the balance sheet date of the most recent audited financial statements[8]. This is because those prior relationships may be perceived as likely to influence the reporting accountant in the performance of the investment circular reporting engagement or as otherwise impairing the reporting accountant's objectivity and independence.

1.53 A firm's procedures will include reference to records of past and current engagements whenever a new investment circular reporting engagement is proposed.

1.54 Where the engagement client or a third party calls into question the objectivity and independence of the firm in relation to a particular client, the ethics partner carries out such investigations as may be appropriate.

---

[8] In the case of newly incorporated clients (not part of an established group of companies), where there has been no financial statement audit, this period is from the date of incorporation.

IDENTIFICATION AND ASSESSMENT OF SAFEGUARDS

1.55 **If the engagement partner identifies threats to the reporting accountant's objectivity, including any perceived loss of independence, he or she should identify and assess the effectiveness of the available safeguards and apply such safeguards as are sufficient to eliminate the threats or reduce them to an acceptable level.**

1.56 The nature and extent of safeguards to be applied depend on the significance of the threats. Where a threat is clearly insignificant, no safeguards are needed.

1.57 Sections 2 and 3 of this Standard address specific circumstances which can create threats to the reporting accountant's objectivity or loss of independence. They give examples of safeguards that can, in some circumstances, eliminate the threat or reduce it to an acceptable level. In circumstances where this is not possible, either the reporting accountant does not accept (or withdraws from) the investment circular reporting engagement or, in the case of threats arising from the current provision of other services, does not undertake the engagement to provide the other service.

1.58 **The engagement partner should not accept or should not continue an investment circular reporting engagement if he or she concludes that any threats to the reporting accountant's objectivity and independence cannot be reduced to an acceptable level.**

1.59 If during the conduct of the investment circular reporting engagement the engagement partner becomes aware of a threat and concludes that it cannot be reduced to an acceptable level, the firm withdraws immediately from the engagement, save in circumstances where a reasonable and informed third party would regard ceasing to act as the reporting accountant would be contrary to the public interest. In such cases withdrawal from the investment circular reporting engagement may not be appropriate. The firm discloses on a timely basis full details of the position to those charged with governance of the issuing engagement client and those the reporting accountant is instructed to advise, as set out in paragraphs 1.68 to 1.76, and establishes appropriate safeguards.

ENGAGEMENT QUALITY CONTROL REVIEW

1.60 Paragraph 22 of SIR 1000 requires the reporting accountant to comply with applicable standards and guidance set out in ISQC (UK and Ireland) 1 *'Quality control for firms that perform audits and reviews of historical financial information and other assurance and related services engagements'* and ISA (UK and Ireland) 220 *'Quality control for audits of historical financial information'*. This includes the appointment of an engagement quality control reviewer for all public reporting engagements.

1.61 **The engagement quality control reviewer should:**

   (a) **consider the firm's compliance with the APB Ethical Standard for Reporting Accountants in relation to the investment circular reporting engagement;**

(b) **form an independent opinion as to the appropriateness and adequacy of the safeguards applied; and**

(c) **consider the adequacy of the documentation of the engagement partner's consideration of the reporting accountant's objectivity and independence.**

1.62 The requirements of paragraph 1.61 supplement the requirements relating to the engagement quality control review established by ISA (UK and Ireland) 220. The engagement quality control reviewer will be a partner or other person performing the function of a partner who is not otherwise involved in the engagement. The experience required of the engagement quality control reviewer is determined by the nature of the engagement and the seniority and experience of the engagement partner.

OVERALL CONCLUSION

1.63 **At the end of the investment circular reporting engagement, when reporting on the work undertaken but before issuing the report, the engagement partner should reach an overall conclusion that any threats to objectivity and independence have been properly addressed in accordance with the APB Ethical Standard for Reporting Accountants. If the engagement partner cannot make such a conclusion, he or she should not report and the firm should withdraw from the investment circular reporting engagement.**

1.64 If the engagement partner remains unable to conclude that any threat to objectivity and independence has been properly addressed in accordance with the APB Ethical Standard for Reporting Accountants, or if there is a disagreement between the engagement partner and the engagement quality control reviewer, he or she consults the ethics partner.

1.65 In concluding on compliance with the requirements for objectivity and independence, the engagement partner is entitled to rely on the completeness and accuracy of the data developed by the firm's systems relating to independence (for example, in relation to the reporting of financial interests by staff), unless informed otherwise by the firm.

OTHER ACCOUNTANTS INVOLVED IN AN INVESTMENT CIRCULAR REPORTING ENGAGEMENT

1.66 **The engagement partner should be satisfied that other accountants (whether a network firm or another firm) involved in the investment circular reporting engagement, who are not subject to the APB Ethical Standard for Reporting Accountants, are objective and document the rationale for that conclusion.**

1.67 The engagement partner obtains written confirmation from the other accountants that they have a sufficient understanding of and have complied with the applicable provisions of the IFAC Code of Ethics for Professional Accountants, including the independence requirements.[9]

COMMUNICATION WITH THOSE CHARGED WITH GOVERNANCE

1.68 **The engagement partner should ensure that those charged with governance of the issuing engagement client, and any other persons or entities the reporting accountant is instructed to advise, are appropriately informed on a timely basis of all significant facts and matters that bear upon the reporting accountant's objectivity and independence.**

1.69 Those charged with governance of the issuing engagement client are responsible for oversight of the relationship between the reporting accountant and the entity and of the conduct of the investment circular reporting engagement. This group therefore has a particular interest in being informed about the reporting accountant's ability to report objectively on the engagement.

1.70 The aim of these communications by the reporting accountant is to ensure full and fair disclosure to those charged with governance of the issuing engagement client and to those from whom, in accordance with the engagement letter, the reporting accountant takes instructions of matters in which they have an interest.

1.71 It may be that all of the parties to the engagement letter wish to be informed about all significant facts and matters that bear upon the reporting accountant's objectivity and independence. In other cases, however, the parties to the engagement letter (other than the engagement client) may not wish to be directly involved and may appoint one or more of their number to review these matters on their behalf. At the time of appointment, the reporting accountant ensures that it is clear in the engagement letter to whom these communications are provided. If no such provision is included in the engagement letter, the reporting accountant will make disclosures to all those from whom, in accordance with the engagement letter, the reporting accountant takes instructions.

1.72 Matters communicated will generally include the key elements of the engagement partner's consideration of objectivity and independence, such as:

- the principal threats, if any, to objectivity and independence identified by the reporting accountant, including consideration of relationships between the firm and:

---

[9] The International Federation of Accountants Code of Ethics for Professional Accountants (the IFAC Code) establishes a conceptual framework for ethical requirements for professional accountants and includes independence requirements for assurance engagements. No Member Body of IFAC is allowed to apply less stringent standards than those stated in the IFAC Code. In addition, members of the IFAC Forum of Firms have agreed to apply ethical standards, which are at least as rigorous as those of the IFAC Code.

- the engagement client, its affiliates and directors, and

- the sponsor and such other parties from whom the reporting accountant takes instructions, and

- other entities directly involved in the transaction which is the subject of the investment circular;

- any safeguards adopted and the reasons why they are considered to be effective;

- the considerations of the engagement quality control review;

- the overall assessment of threats and safeguards;

- information about the general policies and processes within the firm for maintaining objectivity and independence.

1.73 The reporting accountant, as a minimum:

(a) discloses in writing to those charged with governance of the issuing engagement client, and any other persons or entities the reporting accountant is instructed to advise:

(i) details of all relationships that the reporting accountant considers may reasonably be thought to bear on the objectivity and independence of the reporting accountant,[10] having regard to its relationships with the engagement client, its directors and senior management and its affiliates;

(ii) details of all relationships that the reporting accountant considers give rise to a threat to its objectivity between the reporting accountant and:

- the sponsor and such other parties from whom the reporting accountant takes instructions[11];

- other entities directly involved in the transaction which is the subject of the investment circular;

(iii) whether the total amount of fees that the reporting accountant is likely to charge to the engagement client and its significant affiliates for the provision of services relating to the transaction which is the subject of the

---

[10] Relationships include significant services previously provided by the firm and network firms involved in the investment circular reporting engagement to the engagement client and its significant affiliates. In considering the significance of such services the reporting accountant takes into account whether those services have been the subject of independent review after they were provided.

[11] Where a party to the engagement letter is an established financial institution or adviser, a generic disclosure that the firm has extensive relationships entered into in the ordinary course of business with these parties is sufficient with specific disclosure only being made in the case of relationships which are outside the ordinary course of business or which are material to any party.

investment circular during the relevant period is greater than 5% of the fee income of the firm in the relevant period or the part of the firm by reference to which the engagement partner's profit share is calculated during the relevant period; and

(iv) the related safeguards that are in place;

(b) confirms in writing that:

(i) it complies with the APB Ethical Standard for Reporting Accountants and that it is independent and its objectivity is not compromised, and

(ii) where relevant, the circumstances contemplated in paragraph 1.44 exist and a consideration of all known threats and safeguards has been undertaken, but this does not constitute a full evaluation of all business relationships and other services provided to the entity.

1.74 The reporting accountant seeks to discuss these matters with those charged with governance of the issuing engagement client and those others the reporting accountant is instructed to advise.

1.75 The most appropriate time for final confirmation of such matters is usually at the conclusion of the investment circular reporting engagement. However, communications between the reporting accountant and those charged with governance of the issuing engagement client and those others the reporting accountant is instructed to advise will also be needed at the planning stage and whenever significant judgments are made about threats to objectivity and independence and the appropriateness of safeguards put in place, for example, when accepting an engagement to provide other services.

1.76 Transparency is a key element in addressing the issues raised by the provision of other services by reporting accountants to their clients. This can be facilitated by timely communication with those charged with governance of the issuing engagement client. In the case of companies that are seeking a listing, ensuring that the audit committee is properly informed about the issues associated with the provision of other services will assist the audit committee to comply on an ongoing basis with the provisions of the Combined Code on Corporate Governance[12] relating to reviewing and monitoring the external auditors' independence and objectivity.

DOCUMENTATION

1.77 **The engagement partner should ensure that his or her consideration of the reporting accountant's objectivity and independence is appropriately documented on a timely basis.**

---

[12] Provision C.3.2 provides that 'the main role and responsibilities of the audit committee should be set out in written terms of reference and should include ... to develop and implement a policy on the engagement of the external auditor to supply non-audit services ...'

1.78 The requirement to document these issues contributes to the clarity and rigour of the engagement partner's thinking and the quality of his or her judgments. In addition, such documentation provides evidence that the engagement partner's consideration of the reporting accountant's objectivity and independence was properly performed and provides the basis for the engagement quality control review.

1.79 Matters to be documented include all key elements of the process and any significant judgments concerning:

- threats identified (in relation to the engagement client, those from whom, in accordance with the engagement letter, the reporting accountant takes instructions and other entities directly involved in the transaction which is the subject of the investment circular) and the process used in identifying them;

- safeguards adopted and the reasons why they are considered to be effective;

- the engagement quality control review;

- overall assessment of threats and safeguards; and

- communication with those charged with governance of the issuing engagement client and those others the reporting accountant is instructed to advise.

SECTION 2 - SPECIFIC CIRCUMSTANCES CREATING THREATS TO A REPORTING ACCOUNTANT'S OBJECTIVITY AND INDEPENDENCE

INTRODUCTION

2.1 Paragraphs 1.50 and 1.55 require the engagement partner to identify and assess the circumstances which could adversely affect the reporting accountant's objectivity ('threats'), including any perceived loss of independence, and to apply procedures ('safeguards') which will either:

(a) eliminate the threat; or

(b) reduce the threat to an acceptable level (that is, a level at which it is not probable that a reasonable and informed third party would conclude that the reporting accountant's objectivity and independence is impaired or is likely to be impaired).

When considering safeguards, where the engagement partner chooses to reduce rather than to eliminate a threat to objectivity and independence, he or she recognises that this judgment may not be shared by third parties and that he or she may be required to justify the decision.

2.2 This section of the APB Ethical Standard for Reporting Accountants provides requirements and guidance on specific circumstances arising out of relationships with the engagement client, which may create threats to the reporting accountant's objectivity or a perceived loss of independence. It gives examples of safeguards that can, in some circumstances, eliminate the threat or reduce it to an acceptable level. In circumstances where this is not possible, either the relationship in question is not entered into or the reporting accountant either does not accept or withdraws from the investment circular reporting engagement, as appropriate.

FINANCIAL RELATIONSHIPS

General considerations

2.3 A financial interest is an interest in an equity or other security, debenture, loan or other debt instrument of an entity, including rights and obligations to acquire such an interest and derivatives directly related to such an interest.

2.4 Financial interests may be:

- owned directly, rather than through intermediaries (a 'direct financial interest'); or

- owned through intermediaries, for example, an open ended investment company or a pension scheme (an 'indirect financial interest').

2.5 **Where a firm is engaged to undertake an investment circular reporting engagement for a client, the firm, a person in a position directly to influence the conduct and outcome of the investment circular reporting engagement or an immediate family member of such a person should not hold during the engagement period:**

(a) **any direct financial interest in the engagement client or an affiliate of the engagement client; or**

(b) **any indirect financial interest in the engagement client or an affiliate of the engagement client, where the investment is material to the firm or the individual and to the intermediary; or**

(c) **any indirect financial interest in the engagement client or an affiliate of the engagement client, where the person holding it has both:**

(i) **the ability to influence the investment decisions of the intermediary; and**

(ii) **actual knowledge of the existence of the underlying investment in the engagement client.**

2.6 The threats to the reporting accountant's objectivity and independence, where a direct financial interest or a material indirect financial interest in the engagement client is held by the firm or by one of the individuals specified in paragraph 2.5 are such that no safeguards can eliminate them or reduce them to an acceptable level. If the existence of the transaction which is connected with the investment circular is price sensitive information then disposal of the financial interest may not be possible and the firm either does not accept the engagement or the relevant individuals are not included in the engagement team. Where a partner with one of the financial interests specified normally has direct supervisory or management responsibility over the engagement team, he or she is excluded from this responsibility for the purposes of the particular investment circular reporting engagement.

2.7 Where one of the financial interests specified in paragraph 2.5 is held by:

(a) *the firm:* the entire financial interest is disposed of, a sufficient amount of an indirect financial interest is disposed of so that the remaining interest is no longer material, or the firm does not accept (or withdraws from) the investment circular reporting engagement;

(b) *a person in a position directly to influence the conduct and outcome of the investment circular reporting engagement:* the entire financial interest is disposed of, a sufficient amount of an indirect financial interest is disposed of so that the remaining interest is no longer material, or that person does not retain a position in which they exert such direct influence on the investment circular reporting engagement;

**THE AUDITING
PRACTICES BOARD**

(c) *an immediate family member of a person in a position directly to influence the conduct and outcome of the investment circular reporting engagement:* the entire financial interest is disposed of, a sufficient amount of an indirect financial interest is disposed of so that the remaining interest is no longer material, or the person in a position directly to influence the conduct and outcome of the investment circular reporting engagement does not retain a position in which they exert such direct influence on the investment circular reporting engagement.

2.8 Where the firm or one of the individuals specified in paragraph 2.5 holds an indirect financial interest but does not have both:

(a) the ability to influence the investment decisions of the intermediary; and

(b) actual knowledge of the existence of the underlying investment in the engagement client,

there may not be a threat to the reporting accountant's objectivity and independence. For example, where the indirect financial interest takes the form of an investment in a pension fund, the composition of the funds and the size and nature of any underlying investment in the engagement client may be known but there is unlikely to be any influence on investment decisions, as the fund will generally be managed independently on a discretionary basis. In the case of an 'index tracker' fund, the investment in the engagement client is determined by the composition of the relevant index and there may be no threat to objectivity. As long as the person holding the indirect interest is not directly involved in an investment circular reporting engagement involving the intermediary, nor able to influence the individual investment decisions of the intermediary, any threat to the reporting accountant's objectivity and independence may be regarded as insignificant.

2.9 Where the firm or one of the individuals specified in paragraph 2.5 holds a beneficial interest in a properly operated 'blind' trust, they are (by definition) completely unaware of the identity of the underlying investments. If these include an investment in the engagement client, this means that they are unaware of the existence of an indirect financial interest. In these circumstances, there is no threat to the reporting accountant's objectivity and independence.

2.10 **Where a person in a position directly to influence the conduct and outcome of the investment circular reporting engagement becomes aware that a close family member holds one of the financial interests specified in paragraph 2.5, that individual should report the matter to the engagement partner to take appropriate action. If it is a close family member of the engagement partner, or if the engagement partner is in doubt as to the action to be taken, the engagement partner should resolve the matter through consultation with the ethics partner.**

Financial interests held as trustee

2.11 Where a direct or an indirect financial interest in the engagement client or its affiliates is held in a trustee capacity by a person in a position directly to influence the conduct and outcome of the investment circular reporting engagement, or an immediate family member of such a person, a self-interest threat may be created because either the existence of the trustee interest may influence the conduct of the investment circular reporting engagement or the trust may influence the actions of the engagement client. Accordingly, such a trustee interest is only held when:

- the relevant person is not an identified potential beneficiary of the trust; and

- the financial interest held by the trust in the engagement client is not material to the trust; and

- the trust is not able to exercise significant influence over the engagement client or an affiliate of the engagement client; and

- the relevant person does not have significant influence over the investment decisions made by the trust, in so far as they relate to the financial interest in the engagement client.

2.12 Where it is not clear whether the financial interest held by the trust in the engagement client is material to the trust or whether the trust is able to exercise significant influence over the engagement client, the financial interest is reported to the ethics partner, so that a decision can be made as to the steps that need to be taken.

Financial interests held by firm pension schemes

2.13 Where the pension scheme of a firm has a financial interest in an engagement client or its affiliates and the firm has any influence over the trustees' investment decisions (other than indirect strategic and policy decisions), the self-interest threat created is such that no safeguards can eliminate it or reduce it to an acceptable level. In other cases (for example, where the pension scheme invests through a collective investment scheme and the firm's influence is limited to investment policy decisions, such as the allocation between different categories of investment), the ethics partner considers the acceptability of the position, having regard to the materiality of the financial interest to the pension scheme.

Loans and guarantees

2.14 Where reporting accountants, persons in a position directly to influence the conduct and outcome of the investment circular reporting engagement or immediate family members of such persons:

(a) accept a loan[13] or a guarantee of their borrowings from an engagement client; or

(b) make a loan to or guarantee the borrowings of an engagement client,

---

[13] For the purpose of this standard, the term 'loan' does not include ordinary trade credit arrangements or deposits placed for goods or services (see paragraph 2.20).

a self-interest threat and an intimidation threat to the reporting accountant's objectivity can be created or there may be a perceived loss of independence. No safeguards can eliminate this threat or reduce it to an acceptable level.

2.15 **The firm, persons in a position directly to influence the conduct and outcome of the investment circular reporting engagement and immediate family members of such persons should not during the engagement period have a loan outstanding to, or guarantee the borrowings of, an engagement client or its affiliates unless this represents a deposit made with a bank or similar deposit taking institution in the ordinary course of business and on normal business terms.**

2.16 **The firm should not during the engagement period have a loan from, or have its borrowings guaranteed by, the engagement client or its affiliates unless:**

 (a) **the engagement client is a bank or similar deposit taking institution; and**

 (b) **the loan or guarantee is made in the ordinary course of business on normal business terms; and**

 (c) **the loan or guarantee is not material to both the firm and the engagement client.**

2.17 **Persons in a position directly to influence the conduct and outcome of the investment circular reporting engagement and immediate family members of such persons should not during the engagement period have a loan from, or have their borrowings guaranteed by, the engagement client or its affiliates unless:**

 (a) **the engagement client is a bank or similar deposit taking institution; and**

 (b) **the loan or guarantee is made in the ordinary course of business on normal business terms; and**

 (c) **the loan or guarantee is not material to the engagement client.**

2.18 Loans by an engagement client that is a bank or similar institution to a person in a position directly to influence the conduct and outcome of the investment circular reporting engagement, or an immediate family member of such a person (for example, home mortgages, bank overdrafts or car loans), do not create an unacceptable threat to objectivity and independence, provided that normal business terms apply. However, where such loans are in arrears by a significant amount, this creates an intimidation threat that is unacceptable. Where such a situation arises, the person in a position directly to influence the conduct and outcome of the investment circular reporting engagement reports the matter to the engagement partner, or to the ethics partner, as appropriate and ceases to have any involvement with the investment circular reporting engagement. The engagement partner or, where appropriate, the ethics partner considers whether any work is to be reperformed.

BUSINESS RELATIONSHIPS

2.19   A business relationship between:

(a)   the firm or a person who is in a position directly to influence the conduct and outcome of the investment circular reporting engagement, or an immediate family member of such a person, and

(b)   the engagement client or its affiliates, or its management

involves the two parties having a common commercial interest. Business relationships may create self-interest, advocacy or intimidation threats to the reporting accountant's objectivity and perceived loss of independence. Examples include:

- joint ventures with the engagement client or with a director, officer or other individual who performs senior managerial functions for the client;

- arrangements to combine one or more services or products of the firm with one or more services or products of the engagement client and to market the package with reference to both parties;

- distribution or marketing arrangements under which the firm acts as a distributor or marketer of any of the engagement client's products or services, or the engagement client acts as the distributor or marketer of any of the products or services of the firm;

- other commercial transactions, such as the firm leasing its office space from the engagement client.

Subject to the alternative procedures outlined in paragraphs 1.44, a firm will identify all business relationships entered into by the firm, persons in a position directly to influence the conduct and outcome of the investment circular reporting engagement, or an immediate family member of such a person.

2.20   **Where a firm is engaged to undertake an investment circular reporting engagement for a client, the firm, persons in a position directly to influence the conduct and outcome of the investment circular reporting engagement and immediate family members of such persons should not have business relationships with the engagement client, its management or its affiliates during the relevant period except where they:**

- **are entered into in the ordinary course of business and are clearly trivial; or**

- **involve the purchase of goods and services from the firm or the engagement client in the ordinary course of business and on an arm's length basis.**

2.21   Where a business relationship exists, that is not permitted under paragraph 2.20, and has been entered into by:

(a) *the firm:* either the relationship is terminated before the start of the relevant period or the firm does not accept (or withdraws from) the investment circular reporting engagement;

(b) *a person in a position directly to influence the conduct and outcome of the investment circular reporting engagement:* either the relationship is terminated before the start of the relevant period or that person does not retain a position in which they exert such direct influence on the investment circular reporting engagement[14];

(c) *an immediate family member of a person in a position directly to influence the conduct and outcome of the investment circular reporting engagement:* either the relationship is terminated before the start of the relevant period or that person does not retain a position in which they exert such direct influence on the investment circular reporting engagement[14].

2.22 **Where a person in a position directly to influence the conduct and outcome of the investment circular reporting engagement becomes aware that a close family member has one of the business relationships specified in paragraph 2.20, that individual should report the matter to the engagement partner to take appropriate action. If it is a close family member of the engagement partner or if the engagement partner is in doubt as to the action to be taken, the engagement partner should resolve the matter through consultation with the ethics partner.**

2.23 Where there are doubts as to whether a transaction or series of transactions are either in the ordinary course of business or on an arm's length basis, the engagement partner reports the issue to the ethics partner, so that a decision can be made as to the appropriate action that needs to be taken to ensure that the matter is resolved.

2.24 **A firm should not act as reporting accountant to any entity or person able to influence the affairs of the firm or the performance of any investment circular reporting engagement undertaken by the firm.**

2.25 This prohibition applies to:

(a) any entity that owns any significant part of a firm, or is an affiliate of such an entity; or

(b) any shareholder, director or other person in a position to direct the affairs of such an entity or its affiliate.

---

[14] If the existence of the transaction which is connected with the investment circular is price sensitive information then termination of the business relationship may not be possible and the firm either does not accept the engagement or the relevant individuals are not included in the engagement team. Where a partner with one of the business relationships specified normally has direct supervisory or management responsibility over the engagement team, he or she is excluded from this responsibility for the purposes of the particular investment circular reporting engagement.

A significant ownership is one that carries the ability materially to influence the policy of an entity.[15]

EMPLOYMENT RELATIONSHIPS

MANAGEMENT ROLE WITH ENGAGEMENT CLIENT

2.26 **A firm undertaking an investment circular reporting engagement should not have as a partner or employ a person in a position directly to influence the conduct and outcome of the investment circular reporting engagement any person who is also employed by the engagement client or its affiliates ('dual employment').**

Loan staff assignments

2.27 **A reporting accountant should not enter into an agreement with an engagement client to provide a partner or employee to work for a temporary period as if that individual were an employee of the engagement client or its affiliates (a 'loan staff assignment') during the relevant period or for a period of one year before it, unless the client:**

(a) **agrees that the individual concerned will not hold a management position in relation to the transaction or the financial information that is the subject of the investment circular reporting engagement, and**

(b) **acknowledges its responsibility for directing and supervising the work to be performed, which will not include such matters as:**

- **making management decisions; or**

- **exercising discretionary authority to commit the engagement client to a particular position or accounting treatment.**

2.28 Where a firm agrees to assist an engagement client by providing loan staff, threats to objectivity and independence may be created. A management threat may arise if the employee undertakes work that involves making judgments and taking decisions that are properly the responsibility of management of the engagement client in relation to the transaction or the financial information that is the subject of the investment circular reporting engagement. Thus, for example, interim management arrangements involving participation in the financial reporting function involved in producing the financial information that is the subject of the investment circular reporting engagement are not acceptable.

---

[15] For companies, competition authorities have generally treated a 15% shareholding as sufficient to provide a material ability to influence policy.

2.29   A self-review threat may also arise if the individual, during the loan staff assignment, is in a position directly to influence the preparation of the engagement client's financial information and then, on completion of that assignment, is assigned to the engagement team for that client.

2.30   **Where a partner or employee returns to the firm on completion of a loan staff assignment, that individual should not be given any role on an investment circular reporting engagement for the engagement client which involves a review of, or any work in relation to, any function or activity that he or she performed or supervised during that assignment.**

2.31   In considering for how long this restriction is to be observed, the need to realise the potential value to the effectiveness of the investment circular reporting engagement of the increased knowledge of the client's business gained through the assignment has to be weighed against the potential threats to objectivity and independence. Those threats increase with the length of the assignment and with the intended level of responsibility of the individual within the engagement team. As a minimum, this restriction will apply to at least the period until an audit has been undertaken of the financial statements following the completion of the loan staff assignment.

Partners and engagement team members joining an engagement client

2.32   **Where a former partner in the firm joins the engagement client, the firm should take action before any further work is done by the firm in connection with the investment circular reporting engagement to ensure that no significant connections remain between the firm and the individual.**

2.33   Ensuring that no significant connections remain between the firm and the individual requires that:

   • all capital balances and similar financial interests be fully settled (including retirement benefits) unless these are made in accordance with pre-determined arrangements that cannot be influenced by any remaining connections between the individual and the firm; and

   • the individual does not participate or appear to participate in the firm's business or professional activities.

2.34   **Reporting accountants should establish policies and procedures that require:**

   (a)   senior members of the engagement team to notify the firm of any situation involving their potential employment with the engagement client; and

   (b)   other members of the engagement team to notify the firm of any situation involving their probable employment with the engagement client; and

   (c)   anyone who has given such notice to be removed from the engagement team; and

(d)   a review of the work performed by the resigning or former engagement team member in relation to the investment circular reporting engagement.

2.35   Objectivity and independence may be threatened where a director, an officer or an employee of the engagement client who is in a position to exert direct and significant influence over the preparation of the financial information has recently been a partner in the firm or a member of an engagement team. Such circumstances may create self-interest, familiarity and intimidation threats, particularly when significant connections remain between the individual and the firm. Similarly, objectivity and independence may be threatened when an individual knows, or has reason to believe that he or she will or may be joining the engagement client at some time in the future.

2.36   Where a partner in the firm or a member of the engagement team for a particular client has left the firm and taken up employment with that client, the significance of the self-interest, familiarity and intimidation threats is assessed and normally depends on such factors as:

•   the position that individual had in an engagement team or the firm;

•   the position that individual has taken at the engagement client;

•   the amount of involvement that individual will have with the engagement team (especially where it includes former colleagues with whom he or she worked);

•   the length of time since that individual was a member of an engagement team or employed by the firm.

Following the assessment of any such threats, appropriate safeguards are applied where necessary.

2.37   Any review of work is performed by a more senior professional. If the individual joining the engagement client is a partner, the review is performed by a partner who is not involved in the engagement. Where, due to its size, the firm does not have a partner who was not involved in the engagement, it seeks either a review by another firm or advice from its professional body.

2.38   **Where a partner leaves the firm and is appointed as a director (including as a non-executive director) or to a key management position with an engagement client, having acted as an audit engagement partner, engagement quality control reviewer, key audit partner, reporting accountant or a partner in the chain of command at any time in the two years prior to such appointment, the firm should not accept an appointment as reporting accountant for a period of two years commencing when the former partner ceased to act for the engagement client or the former partner ceases employment with the engagement client, whichever is the sooner.**

2.39   **Where a partner (other than as specified in paragraph 2.38) or an employee joins the engagement client as a director (including as a non-executive director)** or in a key management position, the firm should consider whether the composition of the engagement team is appropriate.

2.40 In such circumstances, the firm evaluates the appropriateness of the composition of the engagement team by reference to the factors listed in paragraph 2.36 and alters or strengthens the team to address any threat to the reporting accountant's objectivity and independence that may be identified.

Family members employed by an engagement client

2.41 Where a person in a position directly to influence the conduct and outcome of the investment circular reporting engagement becomes aware that an immediate or close family member is employed by the engagement client in a position to exercise influence on the accounting records or financial information, that individual should either:

(a) in the case of an immediate family member, cease to hold a position in which they exert such direct influence on the investment circular reporting engagement; or

(b) in the case of a close family member, report the matter to the engagement partner to take appropriate action. If it is a close family member of the engagement partner or if the engagement partner is in doubt as to the action to be taken, the engagement partner should resolve the matter in consultation with the ethics partner.

GOVERNANCE ROLE WITH ENGAGEMENT CLIENT

2.42 A firm that undertakes an investment circular reporting engagement should not have as a partner or employ a person who during the engagement period is:

(a) on the board of directors of the engagement client;

(b) on any subcommittee of that board; or

(c) in such a position in an entity which holds directly or indirectly more than 20% of the voting rights in the engagement client, or in which the engagement client holds directly or indirectly more than 20% of the voting rights.

2.43 Where a person in a position directly to influence the conduct and outcome of the investment circular reporting engagement has an immediate or close family member who holds a position described in paragraph 2.42, the firm should take appropriate steps to ensure that the relevant person does not retain a position in which they exert direct influence on the conduct and outcome of the investment circular reporting engagement.

EMPLOYMENT WITH FIRM

2.44 Objectivity and independence may be threatened where a former director or employee of the engagement client becomes a member of the engagement team. Self-interest, self-review and familiarity threats may be created where a member of the engagement team has to report on, for example, financial information which he or she prepared, or elements of the financial information for which he or she had responsibility, while with the client.

2.45 **Where a former director or a former employee of an engagement client, who was in a position to exert significant influence over the preparation of the financial information, joins the firm, that individual should not be assigned to a position in which he or she is able directly to influence the conduct and outcome of an investment circular reporting engagement for that client or its affiliates for a period of two years following the date of leaving the client.**

2.46 In certain circumstances, a longer period of exclusion from the engagement team may be appropriate. For example, threats to objectivity and independence may exist in relation to an investment circular reporting engagement relating to the financial information of any period which was materially affected by the work of that person whilst occupying his or her former position of influence with the engagement client. The significance of these threats depends on factors such as:

- the position the individual held with the engagement client;

- the length of time since the individual left the engagement client;

- the position the individual holds in the engagement team.

FAMILY AND OTHER PERSONAL RELATIONSHIPS

2.47 A relationship between a person who is in a position directly to influence the conduct and outcome of the investment circular reporting engagement and another party does not generally affect the consideration of the reporting accountant's objectivity and independence. However, if it is a family relationship, and if the family member also has a financial, business or employment relationship with the engagement client, then self-interest, familiarity or intimidation threats to the reporting accountant's objectivity and independence may be created. The significance of any such threats depends on such factors as:

- the relevant person's involvement in the investment circular reporting engagement;

- the nature of the relationship between the relevant person and his or her family member;

- the family member's relationship with the engagement client.

2.48 A distinction is made between immediate family relationships and close family relationships. Immediate family members comprise an individual's spouse (or equivalent) and dependents, whereas close family members comprise parents, non-dependent children and siblings. While an individual can usually be presumed to be aware of matters concerning his or her immediate family members and to be able to influence their behaviour, it is generally recognised that the same levels of knowledge and influence do not exist in the case of close family members.

2.49 When considering family relationships, it needs to be acknowledged that, in an increasingly secular, open and inclusive society, the concept of what constitutes a family is evolving and relationships between individuals which have no status formally recognised by law may nevertheless be considered as significant as those which do. It may therefore be appropriate to regard certain other personal relationships, particularly those that would be considered close personal relationships, as if they are family relationships.

2.50 **The reporting accountant should establish policies and procedures that require:**

(a) **partners and professional staff to report to the firm where they become aware of any immediate family, close family and other relationships involving an engagement client of the firm and which they consider might create a threat to the reporting accountant's objectivity or a perceived loss of independence;**

(b) **the relevant engagement partners to be notified promptly of any immediate family, close family and other personal relationships reported by partners and other professional staff.**

2.51 **The engagement partner should:**

(a) **assess the threats to the reporting accountant's objectivity and independence arising from immediate family, close family and other personal relationships on the basis of the information reported to the firm;**

(b) **apply appropriate safeguards to eliminate the threat or reduce it to an acceptable level; and**

(c) **where there are unresolved matters or the need for clarification, consult with the ethics partner.**

2.52 Where such matters are identified or reported, the engagement partner or the ethics partner assesses the information available and the potential for there to be a threat to the reporting accountant's objectivity and independence, treating any personal relationship as if it were a family relationship.

EXTERNAL CONSULTANTS INVOLVED IN AN INVESTMENT CIRCULAR REPORTING ENGAGEMENT

2.53 Reporting accountants may employ external consultants as part of their investment circular reporting engagement. There is a risk that an expert's objectivity and independence will be impaired if the expert is related to the entity, for example by being financially dependent upon or having an investment in, the entity.

2.54 **The engagement partner should be satisfied that any external consultant engaged by the reporting accountant in the investment circular reporting engagement will be objective and document the rationale for that conclusion.**

2.55 The engagement partner obtains information from the external consultant as to the existence of any connections that they have with the engagement client including:

- financial interests;

- business relationships;

- employment (past, present and future);

- family and other personal relationships.

ASSOCIATION WITH AN ENGAGEMENT CLIENT

2.56 Where partners and staff in senior positions have been part of engagement teams acting for a client on a number of audit, corporate finance or other transaction related engagements they gain a deep knowledge of the client and its operations. This association may also create close personal relationships with client personnel, which may create threats to the reporting accountant's objectivity or perceived loss of independence.

2.57 **The firm should establish policies and procedures to monitor the extent of involvement of partners and staff in senior positions where the firm acts in connection with investment circulars on a regular basis for an engagement client.**

2.58 **Where partners and staff in senior positions in the engagement team have had extensive involvement with the engagement client, the firm should assess the threats to the reporting accountant's objectivity and independence and, where the threats are other than clearly insignificant, should:**

- **disclose the engagements previously undertaken by the reporting accountant for the engagement client to those charged with governance of the issuing engagement client and any other persons or entities the reporting accountant is instructed to advise, and**

- **apply safeguards to reduce the threats to an acceptable level.**

Where appropriate safeguards cannot be applied, the firm should either not accept or withdraw from the investment circular reporting engagement as appropriate.

2.59   Where partners and staff in senior positions in the engagement team have had extensive involvement with a particular engagement client, self-interest, self-review and familiarity threats to the reporting accountant's objectivity may arise. Similarly, such circumstances may result in an actual or perceived loss of independence.

2.60   To evaluate such threats, the reporting accountant gives careful consideration to which individual is appointed as the engagement partner on an investment circular reporting engagement. This consideration will reflect the need for relevant expertise[16] as well as factors such as:

- the nature of the investment circular reporting engagement and whether it will involve the reappraisal of previously audited financial information,

- the length of time that the audit engagement partner has been associated with the audit engagement,

- the length of time that other partners have acted for the client on corporate finance and other transaction related engagements,

- whether the objectivity of the engagement partner on a subsequent audit could be adversely affected by an opinion on a profit forecast included in the investment circular, and

- the scope of the engagement quality control review.

2.61   A self-interest threat may be created where a partner in the engagement team:

- is employed exclusively or principally on an investment circular reporting engagement that extends for a significant period of time; or

- is remunerated on the basis of the performance of a part of the firm which is substantially dependent on fees from that engagement client.

2.62   In order to address those threats that are identified, firms apply safeguards to reduce the threat to an acceptable level. Appropriate safeguards may include:

- appointing a partner who has no previous involvement with the engagement client as the engagement partner;

- arranging an engagement quality control review of the investment circular reporting engagement by a partner who is not involved with the client and, if

---

[16] Paragraph 25 of SIR 1000 requires that a partner with appropriate experience should be involved in the conduct of the work.

relevant, is not remunerated on the basis of the performance of part of the firm which is substantially dependent on fees from that client;

- arranging an external engagement quality control review of the investment circular reporting engagement.

FEES

2.63　**The engagement partner should be satisfied and able to demonstrate that the investment circular reporting engagement has assigned to it sufficient partners and staff with appropriate time and skill to perform the investment circular reporting engagement in accordance with all applicable Investment Reporting and Ethical Standards, irrespective of the fee to be charged.**

2.64　Paragraph 2.63 is not intended to prescribe the approach to be taken by reporting accountants to the setting of fees, but rather to emphasise that there are no circumstances where the amount of the fee can justify any lack of appropriate resource or time taken to perform an investment circular reporting engagement in accordance with applicable Investment Reporting and Ethical Standards.

2.65　**An investment circular reporting engagement should not be undertaken on a contingent fee basis.**

2.66　A contingent fee basis is any arrangement made at the outset of an engagement under which a pre-determined amount or a specified commission on or percentage of any consideration or saving is payable to the firm upon the happening of a specified event or the achievement of an outcome (or alternative outcomes). Differential hourly fee rates, or arrangements under which the fee payable will be negotiated after the completion of the engagement, do not constitute contingent fee arrangements.

2.67　Contingent fee arrangements in respect of investment circular reporting engagements create self-interest threats to the reporting accountant's objectivity and independence that are so significant that they cannot be eliminated or reduced to an acceptable level by the application of any safeguards.

2.68　The fee ordinarily reflects the time spent and the skills and experience of the personnel performing the engagement in accordance with all the relevant requirements.

2.69　The basis for the calculation of the fee is agreed with the engagement client prior to the commencement of the engagement. The engagement partner explains to the engagement client that the estimated fee is based on the expected level of work required and that, if unforeseen problems are encountered, the cost of any additional work found to be necessary will be reflected in the fee actually charged. This is not a contingent fee arrangement.

2.70   Investigations into possible acquisitions or disposals ('due diligence engagements'), particularly those performed in relation to a prospective transaction, typically involve a high level of risk and responsibility. A firm carrying out a due diligence engagement may charge a higher fee for work relating to a completed transaction than for the same transaction if it is not completed, for whatever reason, provided that the difference is related to such additional risk and responsibility and not the outcome of the due diligence engagement.

2.71   Where the reporting accountant is aware that the engagement client has a record of seeking substantial discounts to the fee payable where a transaction is unsuccessful or abortive, the engagement partner discusses the position with the ethics partner. An appropriate safeguard may involve arranging an engagement quality control review of the investment circular reporting engagement.

2.72   **The firm should establish policies and procedures to ensure that the engagement partner and the ethics partner are notified where others within the firm have agreed contingent fee arrangements in relation to the provision of other services to the engagement client or its affiliates.**

2.73   Contingent fee arrangements in respect of other services provided by the firm to an engagement client may create a threat to the reporting accountant's objectivity and independence. Where fees for other services are calculated on a contingent fee basis, the perception may be that the firm's interests are so closely aligned with the engagement client that it threatens the reporting accountant's objectivity and independence. Any contingent fee that is material to the firm, or that part of the firm by reference to which the engagement partner's profit share is calculated, will create an unacceptable self-interest threat and the firm does not undertake such an engagement at the same time as an investment circular reporting engagement.

2.74   **Where fees for professional services from the engagement client are overdue and the amount cannot be regarded as trivial, the engagement partner, in consultation with the ethics partner, should consider whether the firm should not accept or should withdraw from the investment circular reporting engagement.**

2.75   Where fees due from an engagement client, whether for audit, investment circular reporting engagements or for other professional services, remain unpaid for a long time a self-interest threat to the reporting accountant's objectivity and independence is created because the signing of a report may enhance the firm's prospects of securing payment of such overdue fees.

2.76   Where the outstanding fees are in dispute and the amount involved is significant, the threats to the reporting accountant's objectivity and independence may be such that no safeguards can eliminate them or reduce them to an acceptable level. The engagement partner therefore considers whether the firm can continue with the investment circular reporting engagement.

2.77   Where the outstanding fees are unpaid because of exceptional circumstances (including financial distress), the engagement partner considers whether the engagement client will be able to resolve its difficulties. In deciding what action to take, the engagement partner weighs the threats to the reporting accountant's objectivity and independence if the firm were to continue with the investment circular reporting engagement, against the difficulties the engagement client would be likely to face in finding a successor, and therefore the public interest considerations, if the firm were to withdraw from the investment circular reporting engagement.

2.78   In any case where the firm does not withdraw from the investment circular reporting engagement, the engagement partner applies appropriate safeguards (such as a review by a partner who is not involved in the engagement) and notifies the ethics partner of the facts concerning the overdue fees.

THREATENED AND ACTUAL LITIGATION

2.79   **Where litigation in relation to professional services between the engagement client or its affiliates and the firm, which is other than insignificant, is already in progress, or where the engagement partner considers such litigation to be probable, the reporting accountant should either not continue with or not accept the investment circular reporting engagement.**

2.80   Where litigation actually takes place between the firm (or any person in a position directly to influence the conduct and outcome of the investment circular reporting engagement) and the engagement client, or where litigation is threatened and there is a realistic prospect of such litigation being commenced, self-interest, advocacy and intimidation threats to the reporting accountant's objectivity and independence are created because the firm's interest will be the achievement of an outcome to the dispute or litigation that is favourable to itself. In addition, an effective investment circular reporting engagement requires complete candour and full disclosure between the engagement client management and the engagement team: such disputes or litigation may place the two parties in opposing adversarial positions and may affect management's willingness to make complete disclosure of relevant information. Where the reporting accountant can foresee that such a threat may arise, it informs those charged with governance of the issuing engagement client and any other persons or entities the reporting accountant is instructed to advise of its intention to withdraw from the investment circular reporting engagement.

2.81   The reporting accountant is not required to withdraw from the investment circular reporting engagement in circumstances where a reasonable and informed third party would not regard it as being in the public interest for it to do so. Such circumstances might arise, for example, where:

• the litigation was commenced as the investment circular reporting engagement was about to be completed and stakeholder interests would be adversely affected by a delay in the completion of the work (for example where the engagement relates to the restructuring of a company to avoid its imminent collapse);

- on appropriate legal advice, the firm deems that the threatened or actual litigation is vexatious or designed solely to bring pressure to bear on the opinion to be expressed by the reporting accountant.

GIFTS AND HOSPITALITY

2.82 **The reporting accountant, those in a position directly to influence the conduct and outcome of the investment circular reporting engagement and immediate family members of such persons should not accept gifts from the engagement client, unless the value is clearly insignificant.**

2.83 **Those in a position directly to influence the conduct and outcome of the investment circular reporting engagement and immediate family members of such persons should not accept hospitality from the engagement client, unless it is reasonable in terms of its frequency, nature and cost.**

2.84 Where gifts or hospitality are accepted from an engagement client, self-interest and familiarity threats to the reporting accountant's objectivity and independence are created. Familiarity threats also arise where gifts or hospitality are offered to an engagement client.

2.85 Gifts from the engagement client, unless their value is clearly insignificant, create threats to objectivity and independence which no safeguards can eliminate or reduce.

2.86 Hospitality is a component of many business relationships and can provide valuable opportunities for developing an understanding of the client's business and for gaining the insight on which an effective and successful working relationship depends. Therefore, the reporting accountant's objectivity and independence is not necessarily impaired as a result of accepting hospitality from the engagement client, provided it is reasonable in terms of its frequency, its nature and its cost.

2.87 **The firm should establish policies on the nature and value of gifts and hospitality that may be accepted from and offered to clients, their directors, officers and employees, and should issue guidance to assist partners and staff to comply with such policies.**

2.88 In assessing the acceptability of gifts and hospitality, the test to be applied is not whether the reporting accountant considers that its objectivity is impaired but whether it is probable that a reasonable and informed third party would conclude that it is or is likely to be impaired.

2.89 Where there is any doubt as to the acceptability of gifts or hospitality offered by the engagement client, members of the engagement team discuss the position with the engagement partner. If the cumulative amount of gifts or hospitality accepted from the engagement client appears abnormally high or there is any doubt as to the acceptability of gifts or hospitality offered to the engagement partner, or if the engagement partner has any residual doubt about the acceptability of gifts or hospitality to other individuals, the engagement partner reports the facts to the ethics partner, for further consideration regarding any action to be taken.

SECTION 3 - THE PROVISION OF OTHER SERVICES

INTRODUCTION

3.1 The provision of other services by reporting accountants to the engagement client may create threats to their objectivity or perceived loss of independence. The threats and safeguards approach set out in Section 1 sets out the general approach to be adopted by reporting accountants in relation to the provision of other services to their clients. This approach is applicable irrespective of the nature of the services, which may be in question in a given case. This Section illustrates the application of the general approach to a number of commonly provided services.

3.2 In this Standard, 'other services' comprise any engagement in which a reporting accountant provides professional services to an engagement client other than pursuant to:

(a) any investment circular reporting engagement;

(b) the audit of financial statements; and

(c) those other roles which legislation or regulation specify can be performed by the auditors of the entity (for example, considering the preliminary announcements of listed companies, complying with the procedural and reporting requirements of regulators, such as requirements relating to the audit of the client's internal controls and reports in accordance with Section 151 or 173 of the Companies Act 1985).

3.3 Where the engagement client is a member of a group, other services, for the purposes of this Standard, include:

• services provided by the firm, to the parent company or to any of its significant affiliates; and

• services provided by a network firm which is involved in the investment circular reporting engagement to the engagement client or any of its significant affiliates.

3.4 The provisions of this section apply only to those other services provided by the reporting accountant to the engagement client during the relevant period. The relevant period covers the period during which the engagement is undertaken and any additional period subsequent to the date of the most recent audited financial statements. Other services provided prior to that date are unlikely to create threats to the reporting accountant's objectivity because:

• where the reporting accountant undertook the last audit of the engagement client's financial statements and complied with the APB Ethical Standards for Auditors, the requirements applicable to the provision of other services will have been observed; or

- where the last audit of the engagement client's financial statements was undertaken by a different firm, the work done by the reporting accountant in providing other services will have been the subject of independent review in the course of the audit.

3.5 **The firm should establish policies and procedures, including the alternative procedures outlined in paragraphs 1.44, that enable it to identify circumstances where others within the firm and network firms involved in the investment circular reporting engagement have accepted an engagement to provide during the relevant period, an other service to an engagement client or any of that client's significant affiliates.**

3.6 The firm establishes appropriate policies and procedures to ensure that, in relation to an engagement client, any engagement to provide an other service to the client or any of its significant affiliates during the relevant period is identified so that the engagement partner can consider the implications for the reporting accountant's objectivity and independence before the investment circular reporting engagement is accepted. Such policies and procedures are likely to involve:

i) enquiries of the engagement client;

ii) reference to records of past and current other service engagements provided by the firm;

iii) enquiries of network firms involved in the investment circular reporting engagement as to whether they have provided any other service engagement to the client or any of its significant affiliates during the relevant period.

Such enquiries are undertaken in a manner which seeks to protect confidentiality.

3.7 **Where the engagement partner considers that it is probable that a reasonable and informed third party would regard the objectives of an other service engagement[17] undertaken during the relevant period as being inconsistent with the objectives of the investment circular reporting engagement, the firm should not accept or withdraw from the investment circular reporting engagement.**

3.8 The objectives of engagements to provide other services vary and depend on the specific terms of the engagement. In some cases these objectives may be inconsistent with those of the investment circular reporting engagement, and, in such cases, this may give rise to a threat to the reporting accountant's objectivity and to the appearance of its independence. Firms do not undertake other service engagements during the relevant period, where the objectives of such engagements are inconsistent with the objectives of the investment circular reporting engagement, or do not accept or withdraw from the investment circular reporting engagement.

---

[17] This includes consideration of any private reporting engagements associated with the transaction which is the subject of the investment circular that were undertaken before the investment circular was contemplated.

3.9   Similarly, in relation to a possible new investment circular reporting engagement, consideration needs to be given to recent and current engagements to provide other services by the firm to the client and whether the scope and objectives of those engagements are consistent with the proposed investment circular reporting engagement. In making this assessment, the engagement partner gives consideration to the provisions and guidance given on specific other services in paragraphs 3.13 to 3.89.

3.10   When tendering for a new investment circular reporting engagement, the firm ensures that relevant information on recent other services is drawn to the attention of those charged with governance of the issuing engagement client and any other persons or entities the reporting accountant is instructed to advise, including:

- when recent services were provided to the client;

- the materiality of those services to the proposed investment circular reporting engagement;

- whether those services would have been prohibited if the firm had been undertaking an investment circular reporting engagement at the time when they were undertaken; and

- the extent to which the outcomes of other services have been reviewed by another firm.

3.11   Where both an investment circular reporting engagement and an engagement to undertake other services are provided concurrently the initial assessment of the threats to objectivity and independence and the safeguards to be applied are reviewed whenever the scope and objectives of the other service or the investment circular reporting engagement change significantly. If such a review suggests that safeguards cannot reduce the threat to an acceptable level, the firm withdraws from the other service engagement, or withdraws from the investment circular reporting engagement.

3.12   The following paragraphs provide requirements and guidance on the provision of specific other services by the reporting accountant during the relevant period to the engagement client once the assessment of threats to independence and objectivity at the time of appointment has been made.

INTERNAL AUDIT SERVICES

3.13   The range of 'internal audit services' is wide and they may not be termed as such by the engagement client. For example, the firm may be engaged:

- to outsource the engagement client's entire internal audit function; or

- to supplement the engagement client's internal audit function in specific areas (for example, by providing specialised technical services or resources in particular locations); or

- to provide occasional internal audit services to the engagement client on an *ad hoc* basis.

All such engagements would fall within the term 'internal audit services'.

3.14 The main threats to the reporting accountant's objectivity and independence arising from the provision of internal audit services are the self-review threat and the management threat.

3.15 Engagements to provide internal audit services - other than those prohibited in paragraph 3.17 - may be undertaken, provided that the reporting accountant is satisfied that 'informed management'[18] has been designated by the client and provided that appropriate safeguards are applied.

3.16 Examples of safeguards that may be appropriate when internal audit services are provided to an engagement client include ensuring that:

- internal audit projects undertaken by the firm are performed by partners and staff who have no involvement in the investment circular reporting engagement;

- the work of the reporting accountant is reviewed by a partner who is not involved in the engagement, to ensure that the internal audit work performed by the firm has been properly and effectively assessed in the context of the investment circular reporting engagement.

3.17 **The firm should not undertake an engagement to provide internal audit services to an engagement client where it is reasonably foreseeable that:**

(a) **for the purposes of the investment circular reporting engagement, the reporting accountant would place significant reliance on the internal audit work performed by the firm; or**

(b) **for the purposes of the internal audit services, the firm would undertake part of the role of management of the engagement client in relation to the transaction or the financial information that is the subject of the investment circular reporting engagement.**

3.18 The self-review threat is unacceptably high where the reporting accountant cannot perform the investment circular reporting engagement without placing significant reliance on the work performed for the purposes of the internal audit services engagement. For example, the provision of internal audit services on the internal financial controls for an engagement client which is a large bank, is likely to be

---

[18] See paragraph 1.36.

unacceptable as the reporting accountant is likely to place significant reliance on the work performed by the internal audit team in relation to the bank's internal financial controls.

3.19 The management threat is unacceptably high where the firm provides internal audit services that involve firm personnel taking decisions or making judgments which are properly the responsibility of management. For example, such situations can arise where the nature of the internal audit work involves the firm in taking decisions in relation to the transaction or the financial information that is the subject of the investment circular reporting engagement, as to:

- the scope and nature of the internal audit services to be provided to the engagement client, or

- the design of internal controls or implementing changes thereto.

3.20 During the course of an investment circular reporting engagement the reporting accountant may evaluate the design and test the operating effectiveness of some of the entity's internal financial controls, including the operation of any internal audit function and provide management with observations on matters that have come to their attention, including comments on weaknesses in the internal control systems (including the internal audit function) and suggestions for addressing them. This work is a by-product of the investment circular reporting engagement rather than the result of a specific engagement to provide other services and therefore does not constitute internal audit services for the purposes of this Standard.

3.21 In some circumstances, additional internal financial controls work is performed during the course of the investment circular reporting engagement in response to a specific request. Whether it is appropriate for this work to be undertaken by the firm will depend on the extent to which it gives rise to a management threat to the reporting accountant's objectivity and independence. The engagement partner reviews the scope and objectives of the proposed work and assesses the threats to which it gives rise and the safeguards available.

INFORMATION TECHNOLOGY SERVICES

3.22 Design, provision and implementation of information technology (including financial information technology) systems by firms for their clients creates threats to the reporting accountant's objectivity and independence. The principal threats are the self-review threat and the management threat.

3.23 Engagements to design, provide or implement information technology systems that are not important to any significant part of the accounting system or to the production of the financial information that is the subject of the investment circular reporting engagement and do not have significant reliance placed on them by the reporting accountant, may be undertaken, provided that 'informed management'[18] has been designated by the engagement client and provided that appropriate safeguards are applied.

3.24 Examples of safeguards that may be appropriate when information technology services are provided to an engagement client include ensuring that:

- information technology projects undertaken by the firm are performed by partners and staff who have no involvement in the investment circular reporting engagement;

- the work undertaken in the course of the investment circular reporting engagement is reviewed by a partner who is not involved in the engagement to ensure that the information technology work performed has been properly and effectively assessed.

3.25 **The firm should not undertake an engagement to design, provide or implement information technology systems for an engagement client where:**

   (a) **the systems concerned would be important to any significant part of the accounting system or to the production of the financial information that is the subject of an investment circular reporting engagement and the reporting accountant would place significant reliance upon them as part of the investment circular reporting engagement; or**

   (b) **for the purposes of the information technology services, the firm would undertake part of the role of management of the engagement client in relation to the transaction or the financial information that is the subject of the investment circular reporting engagement.**

3.26 Where it is reasonably apparent that, having regard to the activities and size of the engagement client and the range and complexity of the system, the management lacks the expertise required to take responsibility for the systems concerned, it is unlikely that any safeguards would be sufficient to eliminate these threats or to reduce them to an acceptable level. In particular, formal acceptance by management of the systems designed and installed by the firm is unlikely to be an effective safeguard when, in substance, the firm has been retained by management for its expertise and has made important decisions in relation to the design or implementation of systems of internal control and financial reporting in relation to the transaction or the financial information that is the subject of the investment circular reporting engagement.

3.27 The provision and installation of information technology services associated with a standard 'off the shelf accounting package' (including basic set-up procedures to make the package operate on the client's existing platform and peripherals, setting up the chart of accounts and the entry of standard data such as the client's product names and prices) is unlikely to create a level of threat to the reporting accountant's objectivity and independence that cannot be addressed through applying appropriate safeguards.

VALUATION SERVICES

3.28 **The firm should not undertake an engagement to provide a valuation to an engagement client where the valuation would both:**

   (a) **involve a significant degree of subjective judgment; and**

   (b) **have a material effect on the financial information that is the subject of the investment circular reporting engagement.**

3.29 The main threats to the reporting accountant's objectivity and independence arising from the provision of valuation services are the self-review threat and the management threat. The self-review threat is considered too high to allow the provision of valuation services which involve the valuation of amounts with a significant degree of subjectivity that may have a material effect on the financial information that is the subject of the investment circular reporting engagement.

3.30 It is usual for the reporting accountant to provide the management with accounting advice in relation to valuation matters that have come to its attention during the course of the investment circular reporting engagement. Such matters might typically include:

   • comments on valuation assumptions and their appropriateness;

   • errors identified in a valuation calculation and suggestions for correcting them;

   • advice on accounting policies and any valuation methodologies used in their application.

   Advice on such matters does not constitute valuation services for the purpose of this Standard.

3.31 Where reporting accountants are engaged to collect and verify the accuracy of data to be used in a valuation to be performed by others, such engagements do not constitute valuation services under this Standard.

ACTUARIAL VALUATION SERVICES

3.32 **The firm should not undertake an engagement to provide actuarial valuation services to an engagement client, unless the firm is satisfied that either:**

   (a) **all significant judgments, including the assumptions, are made by 'informed management'[18]; or**

   (b) **the valuation has no material effect on the financial information that is the subject of the investment circular reporting engagement.**

3.33 Actuarial valuation services are subject to the same general principles as other valuation services. Where they involve the firm in making a subjective judgment and have a material effect on the financial information that is the subject of the investment circular reporting engagement, actuarial valuations give rise to an unacceptable level of self-review threat and so may not be performed by reporting accountants for their clients.

3.34 However, in cases where all significant judgments concerning the assumptions, methodology and data for the actuarial valuation are made by 'informed management' and the firm's role is limited to applying proven methodologies using the given data, for which the management takes responsibility, it may be possible to establish effective safeguards to protect the reporting accountant's objectivity and the appearance of its independence.

TAX SERVICES

3.35 The range of activities encompassed by the term 'tax services' is wide. Three broad categories of tax service can be distinguished. They are where the firm:

(a) provides advice to the engagement client on one or more specific matters at the request of the client; or

(b) undertakes a substantial proportion of the tax planning or compliance work for the engagement client; or

(c) promotes tax structures or products to the engagement client, the effectiveness of which is likely to be influenced by the manner in which they are accounted for in the financial information that is the subject of the investment circular reporting engagement.

Whilst it is possible to consider tax services under broad headings, such as tax planning or compliance, in practice these services are often interrelated and it is impracticable to analyse services in this way for the purposes of attempting to identify generically the threats to which specific engagements give rise. As a result, firms need to identify and assess, on a case-by-case basis, the potential threats to the reporting accountant's objectivity and independence before deciding whether to undertake an engagement to provide tax services to an engagement client.

3.36 The provision of tax services by firms to their engagement clients may give rise to a number of threats to the reporting accountant's objectivity and independence, including the self-interest threat, the management threat, the advocacy threat and, where the work involves a significant degree of subjective judgment and has a material effect on the financial information that is the subject of the investment circular reporting engagement, the self-review threat.

3.37 Where the firm provides advice to the engagement client on one or more specific matters at the request of the client, a self-review threat may be created. This self-review threat is more significant where the firm undertakes a substantial proportion of the tax planning and compliance work for the engagement client. However, the reporting accountant may be able to adopt appropriate safeguards.

3.38 Examples of such safeguards that may be appropriate when tax services are provided to an engagement client include ensuring that:

- the tax services are provided by partners and staff who have no involvement in the investment circular reporting engagement;

- the tax services are reviewed by an independent tax partner, or other senior tax employee;

- external independent advice is obtained on the tax work;

- tax computations prepared by the firm are reviewed by a partner or senior staff member with appropriate expertise who is not a member of the investment circular reporting engagement team; or

- a partner not involved in the engagement reviews whether the tax work has been properly and effectively addressed in the context of the investment circular reporting engagement.

3.39 **The firm should not promote tax structures or products or undertake an engagement to provide tax advice to an engagement client where the engagement partner has, or ought to have, reasonable doubt as to the appropriateness of the related accounting treatment involved, having regard to the requirement for the financial information to give a true and fair view, in the context of the relevant financial reporting framework.**

3.40 Where the firm promotes tax structures or products or undertakes an engagement to provide tax advice to the engagement client, it may be necessary to adopt an accounting treatment about which there is reasonable doubt as to its appropriateness, in order to achieve the desired result. A self-review threat arises in the course of an investment circular reporting engagement because the reporting accountant may be unable to form an impartial view of the accounting treatment to be adopted for the purposes of the proposed arrangements. Accordingly, this Standard does not permit the promotion of tax structures or products by firms to their engagement clients where, in the view of the engagement partner, after such consultation as is appropriate, the effectiveness of the tax structure or product depends on an accounting treatment about which there is reasonable doubt as to its appropriateness.

3.41 **The firm should not undertake an engagement to provide tax services to an engagement client wholly or partly on a contingent fee basis where:**

(a) **the engagement fees are material to the firm or the part of the firm by reference to which the engagement partner's profit share is calculated; or**

(b) **the outcome of those tax services (and, therefore, the entitlement to the fee) is dependent on:**

(i) **the application of tax law which is uncertain or has not been established; and**

(ii) **a judgment made by the reporting accountant in relation to a material aspect of the investment circular reporting engagement.**

3.42 Where tax services, such as advising on corporate structures and structuring transactions to achieve a particular effect, are undertaken on a contingent fee basis, self-interest threats to the reporting accountant's objectivity and independence may arise. The reporting accountant may have, or may appear to have, an interest in the success of the tax services, causing it to make a judgment about which there is reasonable doubt as to its appropriateness. Where the contingent fee is determined by the outcome of the application of tax law, which is uncertain or has not been established, and a judgment made by the reporting accountant in relation to a material aspect of the investment circular reporting engagement, the self-interest threat cannot be eliminated or reduced to an acceptable level by the application of any safeguards.

3.43 **The firm should not undertake an engagement to provide tax services to an engagement client where the engagement would involve the firm undertaking a management role for the engagement client in relation to the transaction or the financial information that is the subject of the investment circular reporting engagement.**

3.44 When providing tax services to an engagement client, there is a risk that the reporting accountant undertakes a management role, unless the firm is working with 'informed management'[18] and appropriate safeguards are applied, such as the tax services being provided by partners and staff who have no involvement in the investment circular reporting engagement.

3.45 **The firm should not undertake an engagement to provide tax services to an engagement client where this would involve acting as an advocate for the client, before an appeals tribunal or court[19] in the resolution of an issue:**

(a) **that is material to the financial information that is the subject of the investment circular reporting engagement; or**

(b) **where the outcome of the tax issue is dependent on a judgment made by the reporting accountant in relation to a material aspect of the investment circular reporting engagement.**

---

[19] The restriction applies to the first level of Tax Court that is independent of the tax authorities and to more authoritative bodies. In the UK this would be the General or Special Commissioners of the Inland Revenue or the VAT and Duties Tribunal.

3.46 Where the tax services to be provided by the firm include representing the client in any negotiations or proceedings involving the tax authorities, advocacy threats to the reporting accountant's objectivity and independence may arise.

3.47 The firm is not acting as an advocate where the tax services involve the provision of information to the tax authorities (including an explanation of the approach being taken and the arguments being advanced by the client). In such circumstances effective safeguards may exist and the tax authorities will undertake their own review of the issues.

3.48 Where the tax authorities indicate that they are minded to reject the client's arguments on a particular issue and the matter is likely to be determined by an appeals tribunal or court, the firm may become so closely identified with management's arguments that the reporting accountant is inhibited from forming an impartial view of the treatment of the issue in the financial information that is the subject of the investment circular reporting engagement. In such circumstances, if the issue is material to the financial information or is dependent on a judgment made by the reporting accountant in relation to a material aspect of the investment circular reporting engagement, the firm discusses the matter with the engagement client and makes it clear to the engagement client that it will have to withdraw from that element of the engagement to provide tax services that requires it to act as advocate for the engagement client, or withdraw from the investment circular reporting engagement from the time when the matter is formally listed for hearing before the appeals tribunal.

3.49 The firm is not, however, precluded from having a continuing role (for example, responding to specific requests for information) for the engagement client in relation to the appeal. The firm assesses the threat associated with any continuing role in accordance with the provisions of paragraphs 3.50 to 3.52 of this Standard.

LITIGATION SUPPORT SERVICES

3.50 **The firm should not undertake an engagement to provide litigation support services to an engagement client where this would involve the estimation by the firm of the likely outcome of a pending legal matter that could be material to the amounts to be included or the disclosures to be made in the financial information that is the subject of the investment circular reporting engagement and there is a significant degree of subjectivity involved.**

3.51 Although management and advocacy threats may arise in litigation support services, such as acting as an expert witness, the primary issue is that a self-review threat will arise where such services involve a subjective estimation of the likely outcome of a matter that is material to the amounts to be included or the disclosures to be made in the financial information that is the subject of the investment circular reporting engagement.

3.52 Litigation support services that do not involve such subjective estimations are not prohibited, provided that the firm has carefully considered the implications of any threats and established appropriate safeguards.

LEGAL SERVICES

3.53 **The firm should not undertake an engagement to provide legal services to an engagement client where this would involve acting as the solicitor formally nominated to represent the client in the resolution of a dispute or litigation which is material to the amounts to be included or the disclosures to be made in the financial information that is the subject of the investment circular reporting engagement.**

3.54 Although the provision by reporting accountants of certain types of legal services to their clients may create advocacy, self-review and management threats, this Standard does not impose a general prohibition on the provision of legal services. However, in view of the degree of advocacy involved in litigation or other types of dispute resolution procedures and the potential importance of any assessment by the reporting accountant of the merits of the client's position when reviewing the financial information, this Standard prohibits a reporting accountant from acting as the formally nominated representative for an engagement client in the resolution of a dispute or litigation which is material to the financial information that is the subject of the investment circular reporting engagement (either in terms of the amounts recognised or disclosed in the financial information).

RECRUITMENT AND REMUNERATION SERVICES

3.55 **The firm should not undertake an engagement to provide recruitment services to an engagement client in relation to the appointment of:**

* **any director or**

* **any employee of the engagement client who will be involved in an area that is directly concerned with the transaction which is the subject of the investment circular.**

3.56 A management threat arises where firm personnel take responsibility for any decision as to who should be appointed by the engagement client. Furthermore, a familiarity threat arises if the firm plays a significant role in relation to the identification and recruitment of senior members of management within the company, as the engagement team may be less likely to be critical of the information or explanations provided by such individuals than might otherwise be the case. Accordingly, the firm does not undertake engagements that involve the recruitment of individuals for key management positions during the relevant period.

3.57 Where the firm has played a significant role in relation to the identification and recruitment of a senior member of management within the company, including all directors, prior to the relevant period, the engagement partner considers whether a familiarity threat exists, taking account of factors such as:

- the closeness of personal relationships between the firm's partners and staff and client personnel;

- the length of time since the recruitment of the individual in question;

- the position held by the individual at the engagement client;

- the extent of involvement that the individual will have with the transaction which is the subject of the investment circular;

- whether the individual is in a position to exercise influence on the accounting records or financial information.

Following the assessment of any such threats, appropriate safeguards are applied where necessary, such as ensuring that the engagement team does not include individuals with a close relationship to the senior member of management or who were involved in the recruitment exercise.

3.58 Recruitment services involve a specifically identifiable, and separately remunerated, engagement. Reporting accountants may contribute to an entity's recruitment process in less formal ways. The prohibition set out in paragraph 3.55 does not extend to senior members of an engagement team interviewing prospective employees of the engagement client or to the entity using information gathered by the firm, including that relating to salary surveys.

3.59 **The firm should not undertake an engagement to provide advice on the quantum of the remuneration package or the measurement criteria on which the quantum is calculated, for a director or key management position of an engagement client.**

3.60 The provision of advice on remuneration packages (including bonus arrangements, incentive plans and other benefits) to existing or prospective employees of the engagement client gives rise to familiarity threats. The significance of the familiarity threat is considered too high to allow advice on the overall amounts to be paid or on the quantitative measurement criteria included in remuneration packages for directors and key management positions.

3.61 For other employees, these threats can be adequately addressed by the application of safeguards, such as the advice being provided by partners and staff who have no involvement in the investment circular reporting engagement.

3.62 In cases where all significant judgments concerning the assumptions, methodology and data for the calculation of remuneration packages for directors and key management are made by 'informed management'[18] or a third party and the firm's role is limited to applying proven methodologies using the given data, for which the management takes responsibility, it may be possible to establish effective safeguards to protect the reporting accountant's objectivity and independence.

3.63 Advice on tax, pensions and interpretation of accounting standards relating to remuneration packages for directors and key management can be provided by the firm, provided they are not prohibited by the requirements of this Standard relating to tax, actuarial valuations and accounting services.

CORPORATE FINANCE SERVICES

3.64 The range of services encompassed by the term 'corporate finance services' is wide. For example, the firm may be engaged:

- to identify possible purchasers for parts of the client's business and provide advisory services in the course of such sales; or

- to identify possible 'targets' for the client to acquire; or

- to advise the client on how to fund its financing requirements, including advising on debt restructuring and securitisation programmes; or

- to act as sponsor on admission to listing on the London Stock Exchange or the Irish Stock Exchange, as Nominated Advisor on the admission of the client on the Alternative Investments Market (AIM); or as an IEX Adviser on the admission of the client to the Irish Enterprise Exchange (IEX) of the Irish Stock Exchange; or

- to act as financial adviser to client offerors or offerees in connection with public takeovers.

3.65 The potential for the reporting accountant's objectivity and independence to be impaired through the provision of corporate finance services varies considerably depending on the precise nature of the service provided. The main threats to reporting accountant's objectivity and independence arising from the provision of corporate finance services are the self-review, management and advocacy threats. Self-interest threats may also arise, especially in situations where the firm is paid on a contingent fee basis.

3.66 When providing corporate finance services to an engagement client, there is a risk that the firm undertakes a management role, unless the firm is working with 'informed management'[18] and appropriate safeguards are applied.

3.67 Examples of safeguards that may be appropriate when corporate finance services are provided to an engagement client include ensuring that:

- the corporate finance advice is provided by partners and staff who have no involvement in the investment circular reporting engagement,

- any advice provided is reviewed by an independent corporate finance partner within the firm,

- external independent advice on the corporate finance work is obtained,

- a partner who is not involved in the investment circular reporting engagement or the corporate finance services reviews the work performed in the investment circular reporting engagement.

3.68 Where the firm undertakes an engagement to provide corporate finance services to an engagement client in connection with conducting the sale or purchase of a material part of the client's business, the engagement partner should inform those charged with governance of the issuing engagement client and any other person or entity the reporting accountant is instructed to advise about the engagement, as set out in paragraphs 1.68 to 1.76.

3.69 **The firm should not undertake an engagement to provide corporate finance services to an engagement client where:**

(a) **the engagement would involve the firm taking responsibility for dealing in, underwriting or promoting shares; or**

(b) **the engagement partner has, or ought to have, reasonable doubt as to the appropriateness of an accounting treatment that is related to the advice provided, having regard to the requirement for the financial information to give a true and fair view in accordance with the relevant financial reporting framework; or**

(c) **such corporate finance services are to be provided on a contingent fee basis and:**

(i) **the engagement fees are material to the firm or the part of the firm by reference to which the engagement partner's profit share is calculated; or**

(ii) **the outcome of those corporate finance services (and, therefore, the entitlement to the fee) is dependent on a judgment made by the reporting accountant in relation to a material aspect of the investment circular reporting engagement[20]; or**

(d) **the engagement would involve the firm undertaking a management role for the engagement client in relation to the transaction or the financial**

---

[20] A reporting accountant judgment made in relation to a material aspect of the investment circular reporting engagement would be one which could adversely affect the successful completion of the transaction to which the investment circular relates, for example, where a reporting accountant is considering a qualification to an accountant's report as a result of a disagreement in relation to an accounting treatment which would affect revenue recognition and where a qualified opinion would be likely to render the company unsuitable for listing.

information that is the subject of the investment circular reporting engagement.

3.70 An unacceptable advocacy threat arises where, in the course of providing a corporate finance service, the firm promotes the interests of the engagement client by taking responsibility for dealing in, underwriting, or promoting shares.

3.71 Where the firm acts as a Sponsor under the Listing Rules[21], as Nominated Adviser on the admission of the engagement client to the AIM or as IEX Adviser on the admission of the engagement client to IEX, the firm is required to confirm that the client has satisfied all applicable conditions for listing and other relevant requirements of the Listing Rules, AIM Rules or IEX Rules, respectively. Where there is, or there ought to be, reasonable doubt that the firm will be able to give that confirmation, it does not enter into such an engagement.

3.72 A self-review threat arises where the outcome or consequences of the corporate finance service provided by the firm may be material to the financial information that is the subject of the investment circular reporting engagement. Where the firm provides corporate finance services, for example advice to the engagement client on financing arrangements, it may be necessary to adopt an accounting treatment about which there is reasonable doubt as to its appropriateness in order to achieve the desired result. A self-review threat is created because the reporting accountant may be unable to form an impartial view of the accounting treatment to be adopted for the purposes of the proposed arrangements. Accordingly, this Standard does not permit the provision of advice by firms to their engagement clients where there is reasonable doubt about the appropriateness of the related accounting treatments.

3.73 Advice to engagement clients on issues such as funding and banking arrangements, where there is no reasonable doubt as to the appropriateness of the accounting treatment, is not prohibited provided this does not involve the firm in taking decisions or making judgments which are properly the responsibility of management.

3.74 Where a corporate finance engagement is undertaken on a contingent fee basis, self-interest threats to the reporting accountant's objectivity and independence also arise as the reporting accountant may have, or may appear to have, an interest in the success of the corporate finance services. The significance of the self-interest threat is primarily determined by the materiality of the contingent fee to the firm, or to the part of the firm by reference to which the engagement partner's profit share is calculated. Where the contingent fee and the outcome of the corporate finance services is dependent on a judgment made by the reporting accountant in relation to a material aspect of the investment circular reporting engagement, the self-interest threat cannot be eliminated or reduced to an acceptable level by the application of any safeguards.

---

[21] In the United Kingdom, the UK Listing Authority's publication the 'Listing Rules'. In the Republic of Ireland, the Irish Stock Exchange's publication the 'Listing Rules'.

3.75 In situations where a reporting accountant can see at the outset of the investment circular reporting engagement that there is likely to be a judgment that will be made in relation to a material aspect of the investment circular reporting engagement which could adversely affect the successful completion of the transaction to which the investment circular relates, the firm will not agree to undertake any corporate finance engagements in relation to the transaction on a contingent fee basis, or will not accept the investment circular reporting engagement. Where corporate finance engagements are entered into on a contingent fee basis and a judgment needs to be made in relation to a material aspect of the investment circular reporting engagement during the course of an investment circular reporting engagement, then the firm changes the terms of the corporate finance engagement so that it no longer involves a contingent fee or withdraws from either the relevant corporate finance engagement or the investment circular reporting engagement.

3.76 Where the firm provides a range of corporate finance services to the engagement client, including acting as a Sponsor, Nominated Advisor or IEX Adviser on terms that involve a contingent fee, and that firm also undertakes a public reporting engagement for the engagement client, the self-interest threat caused by contingent fee arrangements may be reduced to an acceptable level by the application of safeguards, such as the corporate finance services being provided by partners and staff who have no involvement in the investment circular reporting engagement. In such circumstances the reporting accountant ensures that the situation is fully disclosed to the Financial Services Authority, the Irish Stock Exchange or the London Stock Exchange and any related regulatory requirements have been complied with.[22]

TRANSACTION RELATED SERVICES

3.77 In addition to corporate finance services, there are other services associated with transactions that a firm may undertake for an engagement client. For example:

- investigations into possible acquisitions or disposals ('due diligence' engagements); or

- investigations into the tax implications of possible acquisitions or disposals.

---

[22] At the date of issue:
- FSA Listing Rule 8.7.12 states that a sponsor must provide written confirmation to the UKLA that it is independent of the issuer or new applicant by way of a 'Sponsor's Confirmation of Independence' form.
- Irish Stock Exchange Listing Rule 2.2.1(2) requires that for each transaction in respect of which a firm acts as sponsor in accordance with the listing rules, the sponsor must submit to the Exchange at an early stage a confirmation of independence in the form set out in 'Schedule 1'.
- Part Two of the *AIM Nominated Adviser eligibility criteria* states that a nominated adviser may not act as both reporting accountant and nominated adviser to an AIM company unless it has satisfied the London Stock Exchange that appropriate safeguards are in place.
- Part Two of the *IEX Adviser Eligibility Criteria* states that an IEX adviser may not act as both reporting accountant and IEX adviser to an IEX company unless it has satisfied the Irish Stock Exchange that appropriate safeguards are in place.

3.78   When providing transaction related services to an engagement client, unless the firm is working with 'informed management'[18] and appropriate safeguards are applied, there is a risk that the firm undertakes a management role.

3.79   Examples of safeguards that may be appropriate when transaction related services are provided to an engagement client include ensuring that:

- the transaction related advice is provided by partners and staff who have no involvement in the investment circular reporting engagement,

- any advice provided is reviewed by an independent transactions partner within the firm,

- external independent advice on the transaction related work is obtained,

- a partner who is not involved in the investment circular reporting engagement reviews the work performed in relation to the subject matter of the transaction related service provided to ensure that such work has been properly and effectively reviewed and assessed in the context of the investment circular reporting engagement.

3.80   **The reporting accountant should not undertake an engagement to provide transaction related services to an engagement client where:**

(a)   **the engagement partner has, or ought to have, reasonable doubt as to the appropriateness of an accounting treatment that is related to the advice provided, having regard to the requirement for the financial information to give a true and fair view in accordance with the relevant financial reporting framework; or**

(b)   **such transaction related services are to be provided on a contingent fee basis and:**

    (i)   **the engagement fees are material to the firm or the part of the firm by reference to which the engagement partner's profit share is calculated; or**

    (ii)   **the outcome of those transaction related services (and, therefore, the entitlement to the fee) is dependent on a judgment made by the reporting accountant in relation to a material aspect of the investment circular reporting engagement; or**

(c)   **the engagement would involve the firm undertaking a management role for the engagement client in relation to the transaction or the financial information that is the subject of the investment circular reporting engagement.**

3.81   A self-review threat arises where the outcome of the transaction related service undertaken by the firm may be material to the financial information that is the subject of the investment circular reporting engagement. Where the engagement client proposes to undertake a transaction, it may be necessary to adopt an inappropriate accounting treatment in order to achieve the desired result. A self-review threat is created if the reporting accountant undertakes transaction related services in connection with such a transaction. Accordingly, this Standard does not permit the provision of advice by firms to their engagement clients where there is reasonable doubt about the appropriateness of the accounting treatments related to the transaction advice given.

3.82   Where a transaction related services engagement is undertaken on a contingent fee basis, self-interest threats to the reporting accountant's objectivity and independence also arise as the reporting accountant may have, or may appear to have, an interest in the success of the transaction. The significance of the self-interest threat is primarily determined by the materiality of the contingent fee to the firm, or to the part of the firm by reference to which the engagement partner's profit share is calculated. Where the contingent fee and the outcome of the transaction related services is dependent on a judgment made by the reporting accountant in relation to a material aspect of the investment circular reporting engagement, the self-interest threat cannot be eliminated or reduced to an acceptable level by the application of any safeguards, other than where the transaction is subject to a pre-established dispute resolution procedure.

ACCOUNTING SERVICES

3.83   In this Standard, the term 'accounting services' is defined as the provision of services that involve the maintenance of accounting records or the preparation of financial statements or information that is then subject to review in an investment circular reporting engagement. Advice on the implementation of current and proposed accounting standards is not included in the term 'accounting services'.

3.84   The range of activities encompassed by the term 'accounting services' is wide. In some cases, the client may ask the firm to provide a complete service including maintaining all of the accounting records and the preparation of the financial information. Other common situations are:

• the firm may take over the provision of a specific accounting function on an outsourced basis (for example, payroll);

• the client maintains the accounting records, undertakes basic bookkeeping and prepares trial balance information and asks the firm to assist with the preparation of the necessary adjustments and financial information.

3.85   The provision of accounting services by the firm to the engagement client creates threats to the reporting accountant's objectivity and independence, principally self-review and management threats, the significance of which depends on the nature and extent of the accounting services in question and upon the level of public interest in the client.

3.86 **The firm should not undertake an engagement to provide accounting services in relation to the financial information that is the subject of the investment circular reporting engagement save where the circumstances contemplated in paragraph 3.89 apply.**

3.87 Even where there is no engagement to provide any accounting services, it is usual for the reporting accountant to provide the management with accounting advice on matters that have come to its attention during the course of an engagement. Such matters might typically include:

- comments on weaknesses in the accounting records and suggestions for addressing them;

- errors identified in the accounting records and in the financial information and suggestions for correcting them;

- advice on the accounting policies in use and on the application of current and proposed accounting standards.

This advice is a by-product of the investment circular reporting engagement rather than the result of any engagement to provide other services. Consequently, as it is part of the reporting accountant's engagement, such advice cannot be regarded as giving rise to any threat to the reporting accountant's objectivity and independence.

3.88 The threats to the reporting accountant's objectivity and independence that would be created are too high to allow the firm to undertake an engagement to provide any accounting services in relation to the financial information that is the subject of the investment circular reporting engagement, save where the circumstances contemplated in paragraph 3.89 apply.

3.89 In emergency situations, the firm may provide an engagement client, or a significant affiliate of such a company, with accounting services to assist the company in the timely preparation of its financial statements or information. This might arise when, due to external and unforeseeable events, the firm personnel are the only people with the necessary knowledge of the client's systems and procedures. A situation could be considered an emergency where the firm's refusal to provide these services would result in a severe burden for the client (for example, withdrawal of credit lines), or would even threaten its going concern status. In such circumstances, the firm ensures that:

(a) any staff involved in the accounting services have no involvement in the investment circular reporting engagement; and

(b) the engagement would not lead to any firm staff or partners taking decisions or making judgments which are properly the responsibility of management.

SECTION 4 - EFFECTIVE DATE

4.1 Effective for investment circular reporting engagements commencing on or after 1 April 2007.

4.2 Firms may complete investment circular reporting engagements commenced prior to 1 April 2007 in accordance with existing ethical guidance applicable to them at the time of their engagement from the relevant professional body.

4.3 Business relationships existing at 31 October 2006 that were permissible in accordance with existing ethical guidance from the relevant professional body, but are prohibited by the requirements of paragraph 2.20, may continue until 31 December 2007 provided that:

- no new contracts (or extensions of contracts) under the business relationship are entered into;

- the reporting accountant satisfies itself that there are adequate safeguards in place to reduce the threat to acceptable levels; and

- disclosure is made to those charged with governance of the issuing engagement client and those the reporting accountant is instructed to advise.

4.4 Loan staff assignments existing at 31 October 2006 that are prohibited by the requirements of paragraph 2.27, may continue until the earlier of:

(a) the completion of the specific task or the end of the contract term, where this is set out in the contract; or

(b) 31 December 2007, where a task or term is not defined,

as long as the following apply:

- the investment circular reporting engagement was permitted by existing ethical guidance from the relevant professional body;

- any safeguards required by existing ethical guidance continue to be applied;

- the need for additional safeguards is assessed, including where possible safeguards specified in section 3, and if considered necessary, those additional safeguards are applied; and

- disclosure is made to those charged with governance of the issuing engagement client and those the reporting accountant is instructed to advise.

4.5 The requirements of paragraph 2.38 in respect of employment with the engagement client do not apply if:

- the relevant person has notified an intention to join the client, or has entered into contractual arrangements, prior to 31 October 2006;

- undertaking the investment circular reporting engagement was permitted by existing ethical guidance from the relevant professional body; and

- disclosure is made to those charged with governance of the issuing engagement client and those the reporting accountant is instructed to advise.

4.6 Where compliance with the requirements of section 3 would result in an investment circular reporting engagement or other service not being supplied, other services contracted before 31 October 2006 may continue to be provided until the earlier of:

(a) the completion of the specific task or the end of the contract term, where this is set out in the contract; or

(b) 31 December 2007, where a task or term is not defined,

as long as the following apply:

- the investment circular reporting engagement was permitted by existing ethical guidance from the relevant professional body;

- any safeguards required by existing ethical guidance continue to be applied;

- the need for additional safeguards is assessed, including where possible safeguards specified in section 3, and if considered necessary, those additional safeguards are applied; and

- disclosure is made to those charged with governance of the issuing engagement client and those the reporting accountant is instructed to advise.

APPENDIX 1 – GLOSSARY OF TERMS

accounting services The provision of services that involve the maintenance of accounting records or the preparation of financial statements or information that is then subject to review in an investment circular reporting engagement

affiliate Any undertaking which is connected to another by means of common ownership, control or management.

audit engagement partner The partner or other person in the firm who is responsible for the audit engagement and its performance and for the report that is issued on behalf of the firm, and who, where required, has the appropriate authority from a professional, legal or regulatory body.

chain of command All persons who have a direct supervisory, management or other oversight responsibility for the engagement team who have actual knowledge of the investment circular reporting engagement. This includes all partners, principals and shareholders who prepare, review or directly influence the performance appraisal of any partner of the engagement team as a result of their involvement with the investment circular reporting engagement.

close family A non-dependent parent, child or sibling.

contingent fee basis Any arrangement made at the outset of an engagement under which a pre-determined amount or a specified commission on or percentage of any consideration or saving is payable to the firm upon the happening of a specified event or the achievement of an outcome (or alternative outcomes).
Differential hourly fee rates, or arrangements under which the fee payable will be negotiated after the completion of the engagement, do not constitute contingent fee arrangements.

engagement client The party responsible for issuing the investment circular containing the financial information[23] (the issuing engagement client) and, if different the party on whose financial information the firm is reporting.

engagement partner The partner or other person in the firm who is responsible for the investment circular reporting engagement and its performance and for the report that is issued on behalf of the firm, and who, where required, has the appropriate authority from a professional, legal or regulatory body.

engagement period The engagement period starts when the firm accepts the investment circular reporting engagement and ends on the date of the report.

---

[23] The financial information is described in SIR 1000 as being the 'outcome' of a reporting engagement.

engagement team	All professional personnel who are directly involved in the acceptance and performance of a particular investment circular reporting engagement. This includes those who provide quality control or direct oversight of the engagement.
ethics partner	The partner or other person in the firm having responsibility for the adequacy of the firm's policies and procedures relating to integrity, objectivity and independence, their compliance with APB Ethical Standards and the effectiveness of their communication to partners and staff within the firm and providing related guidance to individual partners.
financial interest	An interest in an equity or other security, debenture, loan or other debt instrument of an entity, including rights and obligations to acquire such an interest and derivatives directly related to such an interest.
firm	The sole practitioner, partnership, limited liability partnership or other corporate entity engaged as a reporting accountant. For the purpose of APB Ethical Standards, the firm includes network firms in the UK and Ireland, which are controlled by the firm or its partners.
immediate family	A spouse (or equivalent) or dependent.
issuing engagement client	The party responsible for issuing the investment circular containing the financial information being reported on.
investment circular	An investment circular is a document issued by an entity pursuant to statutory or regulatory requirements relating to securities on which it is intended that a third party should make an investment decision, including a prospectus, listing particulars, a circular to shareholders or similar document.
investment circular reporting engagement	Any public or private reporting engagement in connection with an investment circular where the engagement is undertaken in accordance with Standards for Investment Reporting (SIRs).
key audit partner	An audit partner, or other person performing the function of an audit partner, of the engagement team (other than the audit engagement partner) who is involved at the group level and is responsible for key decisions or judgments on significant matters, such as on significant subsidiaries or divisions of the audit client, or on significant risk factors that relate to the audit of that client.

key management position	Any position at the engagement client which involves the responsibility for fundamental management decisions at the client (e.g. as a CEO or CFO), including an ability to influence the accounting policies and the preparation of the financial statements of the client. A key management position also arises where there are contractual and factual arrangements which in substance allow an individual to participate in exercising such a management function in a different way (e.g. via a consulting contract).

network firm	Any entity:
	(i) controlled by the firm or
	(ii) under common control, ownership or management or
	(iii) otherwise affiliated or associated with the firm through the use of a common name or through the sharing of significant common professional resources.

person in a position directly to influence the conduct and outcome of the investment circular reporting engagement	(a) Any person who is directly involved in the investment circular reporting engagement (the engagement team), including:
	(i) professional personnel from all disciplines involved in the engagement, for example, lawyers, actuaries, taxation specialists, IT specialists, treasury management specialists;
	(ii) those who provide quality control or direct oversight of the engagement;
	(b) Any person within the firm who can directly influence the conduct and outcome of the investment circular reporting engagement through the provision of direct supervisory, management or other oversight of the engagement team in the context of the investment circular reporting engagement.

private reporting engagement	An engagement, in connection with an investment circular, in which a reporting accountant does not express a conclusion that is published in an investment circular

public reporting engagement	An engagement in which a reporting accountant expresses a conclusion that is published in an investment circular and which is designed to enhance the degree of confidence of the intended users of the report about the 'outcome' of the directors' evaluation or measurement of 'subject matter' (usually financial information) against 'suitable criteria'.

relevant period	The engagement period and any additional period before the engagement period but subsequent to the balance sheet date of the most recent audited financial statements of the engagement client.

reporting accountant An accountant engaged to prepare a report for inclusion in, or in connection with, an investment circular. The reporting accountant may or may not be the auditor of the entity issuing the investment circular. The term "reporting accountant" is used to describe either the engagement partner or the engagement partner's firm[24]. The reporting accountant could be a limited company or a principal employed by the company.

---

[24] Where the term applies to the engagement partner, it describes the responsibilities or obligations of the engagement partner. Such obligations or responsibilities may be fulfilled by either the engagement partner or another member of the engagement team.

Section 4: AUDITING STANDARDS

2006 ACTIVITIES

During the year the APB has:

(a) Issued a revised International Standard on Auditing (UK and Ireland) (ISA (UK and Ireland) 720 which addresses the auditor's consideration of other information in documents containing audited financial statements;

(b) Invited comments on two exposure drafts issued by the International Auditing and Assurance Standards Board (IAASB) containing substantive revisions to existing ISAs; and

(c) Invited comments on three exposure drafts issued by the IAASB of revised ISAs that have been redrafted in the 'Clarity Project' format.

ISA (UK and Ireland) 720 (Revised)

In April 2006, the APB issued ISA (UK and Ireland) 720 (Revised) which addresses the auditor's consideration of other information in documents containing audited financial statements, including the auditor's new statutory reporting responsibilities in relation to directors' reports. The revised standard has two sections:

Section A – 'Other Information in Documents Containing Audited Financial Statements'. The standards and guidance in this section apply to all 'other information', including the directors' report. This section is largely unchanged from the previous standard.

Section B – 'The Auditor's Statutory Reporting Responsibility in relation to Directors' Reports'. This section introduces further standards and guidance specifically in respect of the auditor's new statutory responsibility to report whether, in the auditor's opinion, the information given in the directors' report is consistent with the financial statements. This takes account of changes to the UK Companies Act applicable to financial years which begin on or after 1 April 2005.

The exposure draft of this revised standard, issued in October 2005, also included a section with proposed standards and guidance in respect of the then statutory requirement for auditors to report on statutory Operating and Financial Reviews. That section is not included in the final revised standard as the related legislation was repealed by the Government (SI 2005/3442 – Companies Act 1985 (Operating and Financial Review) (Repeal) Regulations 2005 – which came into effect on 12 January 2006).

Exposure Drafts Issued by the IAASB of Proposed Revised ISAs

ISA 550 (Revised) 'Related Parties'

The IAASB had been encouraged to review its current auditing standard on related parties because of the involvement of related parties in many high profile corporate scandals of the last decade. In January 2006, the IAASB issued an exposure draft of revisions to ISA 550, 'Related Parties', with a comment period that ended on 30 April 2006.

The proposed revision of ISA 550 places greater emphasis on a risk-based approach to the consideration of related parties. The auditor is required to obtain an understanding of the nature and business rationale of an entity's related party relationships and transactions sufficient to identify, assess and respond to the risks of material misstatement resulting from them. It also seeks to improve auditor performance with the difficult task of identifying related party relationships and transactions not disclosed to them by management.

The APB's letter of comment on the exposure draft, and an analysis by the APB staff of the main changes from the requirements of the current ISA (UK and Ireland) 550, can be found in the Publications (IAASB Clarity Documentation) section of the APB's website[1].

ISA 600 (Revised) 'The Audit of Group Financial Statements'

In March 2006, the IAASB issued an exposure draft of ISA 600 (Revised), 'The Audit of Group Financial Statements', with a comment period that ended on 31 July 2006.

The revision of ISA 600, currently titled 'Using the Work of Another Auditor', commenced in 2003 with the objective of dealing in more detail with the special considerations in group audits. There have been two previous exposure drafts (December 2003 and March 2005). The 2006 exposure draft reflected the changes the IAASB proposed to make in response to the previous comments received and was also presented in the 'Clarity Project' format (see below). The primary issues highlighted by the IAASB for commentators to consider related to the extent to which the group auditor needs to be involved in the audits of components that are audited by other auditors.

The APB's letter of comment on the exposure draft, and the highlighted version of the exposure draft prepared by the APB staff to distinguish the sources of the 'shall' requirements, can be found in the Publications (IAASB Clarity Documentation) section of the APB's website.

Exposure Drafts Issued by the IAASB of Revised ISAs Redrafted in the Clarity Project Format

In November 2006, the IAASB issued exposure drafts of:

- ISA 260 (Revised and Redrafted), 'Communication With Those Charged With Governance';

- ISA 320 (Revised and Redrafted), 'Materiality in Planning and Performing an Audit';

- ISA 450 (Redrafted), 'Evaluation of Misstatements Identified During the Audit'.

The comment period ends on 15 February 2007.

---

[1] www.frc.org.uk/apb/publications/iaasb.cfm

The IAASB has approved 'close off' documents of revisions to these ISAs after taking into consideration responses to previous exposure drafts issued in December 2004 (for ISA 320) and March 2005 (for ISA 260). The current exposure drafts are based on those close off documents and redrafted using the IAASB's Clarity Project drafting conventions.

The IAASB is seeking comments only on changes resulting from applying the Clarity Project drafting conventions and their effect on the content of the ISAs. The IAASB is not seeking repetition of comments made on the previous exposure drafts.

The IAASB has also issued explanatory memoranda prepared by the IAASB staff that summarise the significant responses received to the December 2004 and March 2005 exposure drafts and how they have been addressed by the IAASB. It has also issued detailed mapping documents that demonstrate how the material in the close off documents has been reflected in the proposed redrafted ISAs (including sections that identify present tense sentences in the close off documents and indicate whether they have been treated as requirements or application material in accordance with the Clarity Project drafting conventions).

To further help interested parties in the UK and Ireland understand the source of the 'shall' requirements in the current exposure drafts, the staff of the APB have prepared versions with colour highlighting applied to identify the requirements that derive from those in the original exposure drafts of these ISAs and those that have been elevated from guidance under the Clarity Project or introduced in response to comments received by the IAASB. These can be found in the Publications (IAASB Clarity Documentation) section of the APB's website.

ISA 260 (Revised and Redrafted), 'Communication With Those Charged With Governance'

The revisions incorporated in the close off document bring the ISA much closer in substance to ISA (UK and Ireland) 260 which includes a number of supplementary requirements carried forward from the APB's pre-existing SAS 610.

Requirements relating to the communication of misstatements are addressed in the proposed new ISA 450 'Evaluation of Misstatements Identified During the Audit'.

ISA 320 (Revised and Redrafted), 'Materiality in Planning and Performing an Audit' and ISA 450 (Redrafted), 'Evaluation of Misstatements Identified During the Audit'

The proposed ISAs 320 (Revised and Redrafted) and 450 (Redrafted) taken together represent a revision of the current ISA 320, 'Audit Materiality'. Following consideration of the responses to the December 2004 exposure draft, the IAASB concluded that the clarity and flow of the requirements and guidance would be enhanced by addressing materiality and misstatements in separate ISAs.

The revision exercise undertaken by the IAASB has resulted in a significant number of new requirements and guidance.

The IAASB Clarity Project

On 31 October 2005 the IAASB announced that it intends to improve the clarity of its ISAs. The Clarity Project drafting conventions aim to improve the overall readability and understandability of ISAs through structural and drafting improvements, including:

- Setting an overall objective for each ISA;

- Presenting the requirements and application guidance in separate sections;

- Clarifying the obligations imposed on the auditor by the requirements of the ISA, and by using the word 'shall' instead of the current 'should' to emphasise the expectation that these requirements are applicable in virtually all engagements to which the ISA is relevant; and

- Eliminating any ambiguity about the status of the non-bold text in the ISA by modifying the language of current present tense statements, either by elevating them to 'shall' statements or by eliminating the present tense to make it clear that there is no intention to create a requirement.

The IAASB's current criteria for determining the requirements of a Standard are:

- The requirement is necessary to achieve the objective stated in the Standard;

- The requirement is expected to be applicable in virtually all engagements to which the Standard is relevant; and

- The objective stated in the Standard is unlikely to have been met by the requirements of other Standards.

In determining the requirements of a Standard, the IAASB will consider whether the requirements are proportionate to the importance of the subject matter of the Standard in relation to the overall objective of the engagement.

The target completion date for the IAASB completing the Clarity Project is autumn 2008. A brief status report prepared by the APB staff, updated on a regular basis, can be found in the Publications (IAASB Clarity Documentation) section of the APB's website.

In November 2005, the APB issued a Consultation Paper setting out its proposed approach to the exposure drafts issued by IAASB in connection with the Clarity Project. In the Consultation Paper the APB proposed that it should not issue exposure drafts of corresponding 'clarified' ISAs (UK and Ireland) at this stage; rather the APB believes that the timing of formal exposure of such standards should take place after the ISAs have been finalised by the IAASB and also take account of the European Commission's forthcoming process for the adoption of ISAs in the European Union. Responses to the Consultation Paper generally supported the proposed approach.

INTERNATIONAL STANDARD ON QUALITY CONTROL (UK AND IRELAND) 1

QUALITY CONTROL FOR FIRMS THAT PERFORM AUDITS AND REVIEWS OF HISTORICAL FINANCIAL INFORMATION, AND OTHER ASSURANCE AND RELATED SERVICES ENGAGEMENTS*

CONTENTS

International Standard on Quality Control (UK and Ireland) (ISQC (UK and Ireland)) 1 "Quality Control for Firms that Perform Audits and Reviews of Historical Financial Information, and Other Assurance and Related Services Engagements" should be read in the context of the Auditing Practices Board's Statement "The Auditing Practices Board - Scope and Authority of Pronouncements (Revised)" which sets out the application and authority of ISQCs (UK and Ireland).

---

* Paragraphs 6(a) and 73a – 73l are conforming amendments introduced by ISA (UK and Ireland) 230 (Revised); associated changes to systems to be established by June 15, 2006

Introduction

1. The purpose of this International Standard on Quality Control (UK and Ireland) (ISQC (UK and Ireland)) is to establish standards and provide guidance regarding a firm's responsibilities for its system of quality control for audits and reviews of historical financial information, and for other assurance and related services engagements. This ISQC (UK and Ireland) is to be read in conjunction with Parts A and B of the IFAC *Code of Ethics for Professional Accountants* (the IFAC Code).

1-1. In the UK and Ireland the relevant ethical pronouncements with which the auditor complies are the APB's Ethical Standards and the ethical pronouncements relating to the work of auditors issued by the auditor's relevant professional body – see the Statement "The Auditing practices Board – Scope and Authority of Pronouncements".

2. Additional standards and guidance on the responsibilities of firm personnel regarding quality control procedures for specific types of engagements are set out in other pronouncements of the International Auditing and Assurance Standards Board (IAASB). ISA (UK and Ireland) 220, "Quality Control for Audits of Historical Financial Information," for example, establishes standards and provides guidance on quality control procedures for audits of historical financial information.

3. **The firm should establish a system of quality control designed to provide it with reasonable assurance that the firm and its personnel comply with professional standards and regulatory and legal requirements, and that reports issued by the firm or engagement partners are appropriate in the circumstances.**

4. A system of quality control consists of policies designed to achieve the objectives set out in paragraph 3 and the procedures necessary to implement and monitor compliance with those policies.

5. This ISQC (UK and Ireland) applies to all firms. The nature of the policies and procedures developed by individual firms to comply with this ISQC (UK and Ireland) will depend on various factors such as the size and operating characteristics of the firm, and whether it is part of a network.

Definitions

6. In this ISQC (UK and Ireland), the following terms have the meanings attributed below:

   (a) "Engagement documentation" – the record of work performed, results obtained, and conclusions the practitioner reached (terms such as "working papers" or "workpapers" are sometimes used). The documentation for a specific engagement is assembled in an engagement file;

   (b) "Engagement partner" – the partner or other person in the firm who is responsible for the engagement and its performance, and for the report that is issued on behalf of the firm, and who, where required, has the appropriate authority from a professional, legal or regulatory body;

(c) "Engagement quality control review" – a process designed to provide an objective evaluation, before the report is issued, of the significant judgments the engagement team made and the conclusions they reached in formulating the report;

(d) "Engagement quality control reviewer" – a partner, other person in the firm, suitably qualified external person, or a team made up of such individuals, with sufficient and appropriate experience and authority to objectively evaluate, before the report is issued, the significant judgments the engagement team made and the conclusions they reached in formulating the report;

(e) "Engagement team" – all personnel performing an engagement, including any experts contracted by the firm in connection with that engagement;

(f) "Firm"* – a sole practitioner, partnership, corporation or other entity of professional accountants;

(g) "Inspection" – in relation to completed engagements, procedures designed to provide evidence of compliance by engagement teams with the firm's quality control policies and procedures;

(h) "Listed entity"* – an entity whose shares, stock or debt are quoted or listed on a recognized stock exchange, or are marketed under the regulations of a recognized stock exchange or other equivalent body;

(i) "Monitoring" – a process comprising an ongoing consideration and evaluation of the firm's system of quality control, including a periodic inspection of a selection of completed engagements, designed to enable the firm to obtain reasonable assurance that its system of quality control is operating effectively;

(j) "Network firm"* – an entity under common control, ownership or management with the firm or any entity that a reasonable and informed third party having knowledge of all relevant information would reasonably conclude as being part of the firm nationally or internationally;

(k) "Partner" – any individual with authority to bind the firm with respect to the performance of a professional services engagement;

(l) "Personnel" – partners and staff;

(m) "Professional standards" – IAASB Engagement Standards, as defined in the IAASB's "Preface to the International Standards on Quality Control, Auditing, Assurance and Related Services," and relevant ethical requirements, which

---

* As defined in the IFAC Code published in November 2001.

ordinarily comprise Parts A and B of the IFAC Code and relevant national ethical requirements[1];

(n) "Reasonable assurance" – in the context of this ISQC (UK and Ireland), a high, but not absolute, level of assurance;

(o) "Staff" – professionals, other than partners, including any experts the firm employs; and

(p) "Suitably qualified external person" – an individual outside the firm with the capabilities and competence to act as an engagement partner, for example a partner of another firm, or an employee (with appropriate experience) of either a professional accountancy body whose members may perform audits and reviews of historical financial information, or other assurance or related services engagements, or of an organization that provides relevant quality control services.

Elements of a System of Quality Control

7. **The firm's system of quality control should include policies and procedures addressing each of the following elements:**

   (a) **Leadership responsibilities for quality within the firm.**

   (b) **Ethical requirements.**

   (c) **Acceptance and continuance of client relationships and specific engagements.**

   (d) **Human resources.**

   (e) **Engagement performance.**

   (f) **Monitoring.**

8. **The quality control policies and procedures should be documented and communicated to the firm's personnel.** Such communication describes the quality control policies and procedures and the objectives they are designed to achieve, and includes the message that each individual has a personal responsibility for quality and is expected to comply with these policies and procedures. In addition, the firm recognizes the importance of obtaining feedback on its quality control system from its personnel. Therefore, the firm encourages its personnel to communicate their views or concerns on quality control matters.

---

[1] In the UK and Ireland the relevant ethical pronouncements with which the auditor complies are the APB's Ethical Standards and the ethical pronouncements relating to the work of auditors issued by the auditor's relevant professional body – see the Statement "The Auditing Practices Board – Scope and Authority of Pronouncements".

Leadership Responsibilities for Quality Within the Firm

9. **The firm should establish policies and procedures designed to promote an internal culture based on the recognition that quality is essential in performing engagements. Such policies and procedures should require the firm's chief executive officer (or equivalent) or, if appropriate, the firm's managing board of partners (or equivalent), to assume ultimate responsibility for the firm's system of quality control.**

10. The firm's leadership and the examples it sets significantly influence the internal culture of the firm. The promotion of a quality-oriented internal culture depends on clear, consistent and frequent actions and messages from all levels of the firm's management emphasizing the firm's quality control policies and procedures, and the requirement to:

    (a) Perform work that complies with professional standards and regulatory and legal requirements; and

    (b) Issue reports that are appropriate in the circumstances.

    Such actions and messages encourage a culture that recognizes and rewards high quality work. They may be communicated by training seminars, meetings, formal or informal dialogue, mission statements, newsletters, or briefing memoranda. They are incorporated in the firm's internal documentation and training materials, and in partner and staff appraisal procedures such that they will support and reinforce the firm's view on the importance of quality and how, practically, it is to be achieved.

11. Of particular importance is the need for the firm's leadership to recognize that the firm's business strategy is subject to the overriding requirement for the firm to achieve quality in all the engagements that the firm performs. Accordingly:

    (a) The firm assigns its management responsibilities so that commercial considerations do not override the quality of work performed;

    (b) The firm's policies and procedures addressing performance evaluation, compensation, and promotion (including incentive systems) with regard to its personnel, are designed to demonstrate the firm's overriding commitment to quality; and

    (c) The firm devotes sufficient resources for the development, documentation and support of its quality control policies and procedures.

12. **Any person or persons assigned operational responsibility for the firm's quality control system by the firm's chief executive officer or managing board of partners should have sufficient and appropriate experience and ability, and the necessary authority, to assume that responsibility.**

13. Sufficient and appropriate experience and ability enables the responsible person or persons to identify and understand quality control issues and to develop appropriate

policies and procedures. Necessary authority enables the person or persons to implement those policies and procedures.

Ethical Requirements

14. **The firm should establish policies and procedures designed to provide it with reasonable assurance that the firm and its personnel comply with relevant ethical requirements.**

15. Ethical requirements relating to audits and reviews of historical financial information, and other assurance and related services engagements ordinarily comprise Parts A and B of the IFAC Code together with national requirements that are more restrictive[1]. The IFAC Code establishes the fundamental principles of professional ethics, which include:

    (a) Integrity;

    (b) Objectivity;

    (c) Professional competence and due care;

    (d) Confidentiality; and

    (e) Professional behavior.

16. Part B of the IFAC Code includes a conceptual approach to independence for assurance engagements that takes into account threats to independence, accepted safeguards and the public interest[1].

17. The firm's policies and procedures emphasize the fundamental principles, which are reinforced in particular by (a) the leadership of the firm, (b) education and training, (c) monitoring and (d) a process for dealing with non-compliance. Independence for assurance engagements is so significant that it is addressed separately in paragraphs 18-27 below. These paragraphs need to be read in conjunction with the IFAC Code[1].

Independence

18. **The firm should establish policies and procedures designed to provide it with reasonable assurance that the firm, its personnel and, where applicable, others subject to independence requirements (including experts contracted by the firm and network firm personnel), maintain independence where required by the IFAC Code and national ethical requirements[1]. Such policies and procedures should enable the firm to:**

    (a) **Communicate its independence requirements to its personnel and, where applicable, others subject to them; and**

(b) Identify and evaluate circumstances and relationships that create threats to independence, and to take appropriate action to eliminate those threats or reduce them to an acceptable level by applying safeguards, or, if considered appropriate, to withdraw from the engagement.

19. Such policies and procedures should require:

(a) Engagement partners to provide the firm with relevant information about client engagements, including the scope of services, to enable the firm to evaluate the overall impact, if any, on independence requirements;

(b) Personnel to promptly notify the firm of circumstances and relationships that create a threat to independence so that appropriate action can be taken; and

(c) The accumulation and communication of relevant information to appropriate personnel so that:

(i) The firm and its personnel can readily determine whether they satisfy independence requirements;

(ii) The firm can maintain and update its records relating to independence; and

(iii) The firm can take appropriate action regarding identified threats to independence.

20. The firm should establish policies and procedures designed to provide it with reasonable assurance that it is notified of breaches of independence requirements, and to enable it to take appropriate actions to resolve such situations. The policies and procedures should include requirements for:

(a) All who are subject to independence requirements to promptly notify the firm of independence breaches of which they become aware;

(b) The firm to promptly communicate identified breaches of these policies and procedures to:

(i) The engagement partner who, with the firm, needs to address the breach; and

(ii) Other relevant personnel in the firm and those subject to the independence requirements who need to take appropriate action; and

(c) Prompt communication to the firm, if necessary, by the engagement partner and the other individuals referred to in subparagraph (b)(ii) of the actions taken to resolve the matter, so that the firm can determine whether it should take further action.

21. Comprehensive guidance on threats to independence and safeguards, including application to specific situations, is set out in Section 8 of the IFAC Code[1].

22. A firm receiving notice of a breach of independence policies and procedures promptly communicates relevant information to engagement partners, others in the firm as appropriate and, where applicable, experts contracted by the firm and network firm personnel, for appropriate action. Appropriate action by the firm and the relevant engagement partner includes applying appropriate safeguards to eliminate the threats to independence or to reduce them to an acceptable level, or withdrawing from the engagement. In addition, the firm provides independence education to personnel who are required to be independent.

23. **At least annually, the firm should obtain written confirmation of compliance with its policies and procedures on independence from all firm personnel required to be independent by the IFAC Code and national ethical requirements[1].**

24. Written confirmation may be in paper or electronic form. By obtaining confirmation and taking appropriate action on information indicating non-compliance, the firm demonstrates the importance that it attaches to independence and makes the issue current for, and visible to, its personnel.

25. The IFAC Code[1] discusses the familiarity threat that may be created by using the same senior personnel on an assurance engagement over a long period of time and the safeguards that might be appropriate to address such a threat. **Accordingly, the firm should establish policies and procedures:**

    (a) **Setting out criteria for determining the need for safeguards to reduce the familiarity threat to an acceptable level when using the same senior personnel on an assurance engagement over a long period of time; and**

    (b) **For all audits of financial statements of listed entities, requiring the rotation of the engagement partner after a specified period in compliance with the IFAC Code and national ethical requirements that are more restrictive[1].**

26. Using the same senior personnel on assurance engagements over a prolonged period may create a familiarity threat or otherwise impair the quality of performance of the engagement. Therefore, the firm establishes criteria for determining the need for safeguards to address this threat. In determining appropriate criteria, the firm considers such matters as (a) the nature of the engagement, including the extent to which it involves a matter of public interest, and (b) the length of service of the senior personnel on the engagement. Examples of safeguards include rotating the senior personnel or requiring an engagement quality control review.

27. The IFAC Code[1] recognizes that the familiarity threat is particularly relevant in the context of financial statement audits of listed entities. For these audits, the IFAC Code[1] requires the rotation of the engagement partner after a pre-defined period, normally no

more than seven years[2], and provides related standards and guidance. National requirements may establish shorter rotation periods.

Acceptance and Continuance of Client Relationships and Specific Engagements

28. **The firm should establish policies and procedures for the acceptance and continuance of client relationships and specific engagements, designed to provide it with reasonable assurance that it will only undertake or continue relationships and engagements where it:**

    (a) **Has considered the integrity of the client and does not have information that would lead it to conclude that the client lacks integrity;**

    (b) **Is competent to perform the engagement and has the capabilities, time and resources to do so; and**

    (c) **Can comply with ethical requirements.**

    The firm should obtain such information as it considers necessary in the circumstances before accepting an engagement with a new client, when deciding whether to continue an existing engagement, and when considering acceptance of a new engagement with an existing client. Where issues have been identified, and the firm decides to accept or continue the client relationship or a specific engagement, it should document how the issues were resolved.

29. With regard to the integrity of a client, matters that the firm considers include, for example:

    • The identity and business reputation of the client's principal owners, key management, related parties and those charged with its governance.

    • The nature of the client's operations, including its business practices.

    • Information concerning the attitude of the client's principal owners, key management and those charged with its governance towards such matters as aggressive interpretation of accounting standards and the internal control environment.

    • Whether the client is aggressively concerned with maintaining the firm's fees as low as possible.

    • Indications of an inappropriate limitation in the scope of work.

---

[2] APB Ethical Standard 3, "Long Association With The Audit Engagement," requires that, save for particular circumstances described therein, no one should act as audit engagement partner or as independent partner for a listed company for a continuous period longer than 5 years.

- Indications that the client might be involved in money laundering or other criminal activities.

- The reasons for the proposed appointment of the firm and non-reappointment of the previous firm.

The extent of knowledge a firm will have regarding the integrity of a client will generally grow within the context of an ongoing relationship with that client.

30. Information on such matters that the firm obtains may come from, for example:

- Communications with existing or previous providers of professional accountancy services to the client in accordance with the IFAC Code[1], and discussions with other third parties.

- Inquiry of other firm personnel or third parties such as bankers, legal counsel and industry peers.

- Background searches of relevant databases.

31. In considering whether the firm has the capabilities, competence, time and resources to undertake a new engagement from a new or an existing client, the firm reviews the specific requirements of the engagement and existing partner and staff profiles at all relevant levels. Matters the firm considers include whether:

- Firm personnel have knowledge of relevant industries or subject matters;

- Firm personnel have experience with relevant regulatory or reporting requirements, or the ability to gain the necessary skills and knowledge effectively;

- The firm has sufficient personnel with the necessary capabilities and competence;

- Experts are available, if needed;

- Individuals meeting the criteria and eligibility requirements to perform engagement quality control review are available, where applicable; and

- The firm is able to complete the engagement within the reporting deadline.

32. The firm also considers whether accepting an engagement from a new or an existing client may give rise to an actual or perceived conflict of interest. Where a potential conflict is identified, the firm considers whether it is appropriate to accept the engagement.

33. Deciding whether to continue a client relationship includes consideration of significant matters that have arisen during the current or previous engagements, and their implications for continuing the relationship. For example, a client may have started to expand its business operations into an area where the firm does not possess the necessary knowledge or expertise.

34. Where the firm obtains information that would have caused it to decline an engagement if that information had been available earlier, policies and procedures on the continuance of the engagement and the client relationship should include consideration of:

    (a) The professional and legal responsibilities that apply to the circumstances, including whether there is a requirement for the firm to report to the person or persons who made the appointment or, in some cases, to regulatory authorities; and

    (b) The possibility of withdrawing from the engagement or from both the engagement and the client relationship.

35. Policies and procedures on withdrawal from an engagement or from both the engagement and the client relationship address issues that include the following:

    • Discussing with the appropriate level of the client's management and those charged with its governance regarding the appropriate action that the firm might take based on the relevant facts and circumstances.

    • If the firm determines that it is appropriate to withdraw, discussing with the appropriate level of the client's management and those charged with its governance withdrawal from the engagement or from both the engagement and the client relationship, and the reasons for the withdrawal.

    • Considering whether there is a professional, regulatory or legal requirement for the firm to remain in place, or for the firm to report the withdrawal from the engagement, or from both the engagement and the client relationship, together with the reasons for the withdrawal, to regulatory authorities.

    • Documenting significant issues, consultations, conclusions and the basis for the conclusions.

Human Resources

36. The firm should establish policies and procedures designed to provide it with reasonable assurance that it has sufficient personnel with the capabilities, competence, and commitment to ethical principles necessary to perform its engagements in accordance with professional standards and regulatory and legal requirements, and to enable the firm or engagement partners to issue reports that are appropriate in the circumstances.

37. Such policies and procedures address the following personnel issues:

    • Recruitment;

    • Performance evaluation;

- Capabilities;

- Competence;

- Career development;

- Promotion;

- Compensation; and

- The estimation of personnel needs.

Addressing these issues enables the firm to ascertain the number and characteristics of the individuals required for the firm's engagements. The firm's recruitment processes include procedures that help the firm select individuals of integrity with the capacity to develop the capabilities and competence necessary to perform the firm's work.

38. Capabilities and competence are developed through a variety of methods, including the following:

- Professional education.

- Continuing professional development, including training.

- Work experience.

- Coaching by more experienced staff, for example, other members of the engagement team.

39. The continuing competence of the firm's personnel depends to a significant extent on an appropriate level of continuing professional development so that personnel maintain their knowledge and capabilities. The firm therefore emphasizes in its policies and procedures the need for continuing training for all levels of firm personnel, and provides the necessary training resources and assistance to enable personnel to develop and maintain the required capabilities and competence. Where internal technical and training resources are unavailable, or for any other reason, the firm may use a suitably qualified external person for that purpose.

40. The firm's performance evaluation, compensation and promotion procedures give due recognition and reward to the development and maintenance of competence and commitment to ethical principles. In particular, the firm:

(a) Makes personnel aware of the firm's expectations regarding performance and ethical principles;

(b) Provides personnel with evaluation of, and counseling on, performance, progress and career development; and

(c) Helps personnel understand that advancement to positions of greater responsibility depends, among other things, upon performance quality and adherence to ethical principles, and that failure to comply with the firm's policies and procedures may result in disciplinary action.

41. The size and circumstances of the firm will influence the structure of the firm's performance evaluation process. Smaller firms, in particular, may employ less formal methods of evaluating the performance of their personnel.

Assignment of Engagement Teams

42. **The firm should assign responsibility for each engagement to an engagement partner. The firm should establish policies and procedures requiring that:**

    (a) **The identity and role of the engagement partner are communicated to key members of client management and those charged with governance;**

    (b) **The engagement partner has the appropriate capabilities, competence, authority and time to perform the role; and**

    (c) **The responsibilities of the engagement partner are clearly defined and communicated to that partner.**

43. Policies and procedures include systems to monitor the workload and availability of engagement partners so as to enable these individuals to have sufficient time to adequately discharge their responsibilities.

44. **The firm should also assign appropriate staff with the necessary capabilities, competence and time to perform engagements in accordance with professional standards and regulatory and legal requirements, and to enable the firm or engagement partners to issue reports that are appropriate in the circumstances.**

45. The firm establishes procedures to assess its staff's capabilities and competence. The capabilities and competence considered when assigning engagement teams, and in determining the level of supervision required, include the following:

    - An understanding of, and practical experience with, engagements of a similar nature and complexity through appropriate training and participation.

    - An understanding of professional standards and regulatory and legal requirements.

    - Appropriate technical knowledge, including knowledge of relevant information technology.

    - Knowledge of relevant industries in which the clients operate.

    - Ability to apply professional judgment.

    - An understanding of the firm's quality control policies and procedures.

Engagement Performance

46. **The firm should establish policies and procedures designed to provide it with reasonable assurance that engagements are performed in accordance with professional standards and regulatory and legal requirements, and that the firm or the engagement partner issue reports that are appropriate in the circumstances.**

47. Through its policies and procedures, the firm seeks to establish consistency in the quality of engagement performance. This is often accomplished through written or electronic manuals, software tools or other forms of standardized documentation, and industry or subject matter-specific guidance materials. Matters addressed include the following:

    • How engagement teams are briefed on the engagement to obtain an understanding of the objectives of their work.

    • Processes for complying with applicable engagement standards.

    • Processes of engagement supervision, staff training and coaching.

    • Methods of reviewing the work performed, the significant judgments made and the form of report being issued.

    • Appropriate documentation of the work performed and of the timing and extent of the review.

    • Processes to keep all policies and procedures current.

48. It is important that all members of the engagement team understand the objectives of the work they are to perform. Appropriate team-working and training are necessary to assist less experienced members of the engagement team to clearly understand the objectives of the assigned work.

49. Supervision includes the following:

    • Tracking the progress of the engagement.

    • Considering the capabilities and competence of individual members of the engagement team, whether they have sufficient time to carry out their work, whether they understand their instructions and whether the work is being carried out in accordance with the planned approach to the engagement.

    • Addressing significant issues arising during the engagement, considering their significance and modifying the planned approach appropriately.

    • Identifying matters for consultation or consideration by more experienced engagement team members during the engagement.

50. Review responsibilities are determined on the basis that more experienced engagement team members, including the engagement partner, review work performed by less experienced team members. Reviewers consider whether:

   (a) The work has been performed in accordance with professional standards and regulatory and legal requirements;

   (b) Significant matters have been raised for further consideration;

   (c) Appropriate consultations have taken place and the resulting conclusions have been documented and implemented;

   (d) There is a need to revise the nature, timing and extent of work performed;

   (e) The work performed supports the conclusions reached and is appropriately documented;

   (f) The evidence obtained is sufficient and appropriate to support the report; and

   (g) The objectives of the engagement procedures have been achieved.

Consultation

51. **The firm should establish policies and procedures designed to provide it with reasonable assurance that:**

   (a) **Appropriate consultation takes place on difficult or contentious matters;**

   (b) **Sufficient resources are available to enable appropriate consultation to take place;**

   (c) **The nature and scope of such consultations are documented; and**

   (d) **Conclusions resulting from consultations are documented and implemented.**

52. Consultation includes discussion, at the appropriate professional level, with individuals within or outside the firm who have specialized expertise, to resolve a difficult or contentious matter.

53. Consultation uses appropriate research resources as well as the collective experience and technical expertise of the firm. Consultation helps to promote quality and improves the application of professional judgment. The firm seeks to establish a culture in which consultation is recognized as a strength and encourages personnel to consult on difficult or contentious matters.

54. Effective consultation with other professionals requires that those consulted be given all the relevant facts that will enable them to provide informed advice on technical, ethical or other matters. Consultation procedures require consultation with those having appropriate knowledge, seniority and experience within the firm (or, where

applicable, outside the firm) on significant technical, ethical and other matters, and appropriate documentation and implementation of conclusions resulting from consultations.

55. A firm needing to consult externally, for example, a firm without appropriate internal resources, may take advantage of advisory services provided by (a) other firms, (b) professional and regulatory bodies, or (c) commercial organizations that provide relevant quality control services. Before contracting for such services, the firm considers whether the external provider is suitably qualified for that purpose.

56. The documentation of consultations with other professionals that involve difficult or contentious matters is agreed by both the individual seeking consultation and the individual consulted. The documentation is sufficiently complete and detailed to enable an understanding of:

   (a) The issue on which consultation was sought; and

   (b) The results of the consultation, including any decisions taken, the basis for those decisions and how they were implemented.

Differences of Opinion

57. **The firm should establish policies and procedures for dealing with and resolving differences of opinion within the engagement team, with those consulted and, where applicable, between the engagement partner and the engagement quality control reviewer. Conclusions reached should be documented and implemented.**

58. Such procedures encourage identification of differences of opinion at an early stage, provide clear guidelines as to the successive steps to be taken thereafter, and require documentation regarding the resolution of the differences and the implementation of the conclusions reached. **The report should not be issued until the matter is resolved**.

59. A firm using a suitably qualified external person to conduct an engagement quality control review recognizes that differences of opinion can occur and establishes procedures to resolve such differences, for example, by consulting with another practitioner or firm, or a professional or regulatory body.

Engagement Quality Control Review

60. **The firm should establish policies and procedures requiring, for appropriate engagements, an engagement quality control review that provides an objective evaluation of the significant judgments made by the engagement team and the conclusions reached in formulating the report. Such policies and procedures should:**

   (a) **Require an engagement quality control review for all audits of financial statements of listed entities;**

(b) **Set out criteria against which all other audits and reviews of historical financial information, and other assurance and related services engagements should be evaluated to determine whether an engagement quality control review should be performed; and**

(c) **Require an engagement quality control review for all engagements meeting the criteria established in compliance with subparagraph (b).**

61. **The firm's policies and procedures should require the completion of the engagement quality control review before the report is issued.**

62. Criteria that a firm considers when determining which engagements other than audits of financial statements of listed entities are to be subject to an engagement quality control review include the following:

- The nature of the engagement, including the extent to which it involves a matter of public interest.

- The identification of unusual circumstances or risks in an engagement or class of engagements.

- Whether laws or regulations require an engagement quality control review.

63. **The firm should establish policies and procedures setting out:**

(a) **The nature, timing and extent of an engagement quality control review;**

(b) **Criteria for the eligibility of engagement quality control reviewers; and**

(c) **Documentation requirements for an engagement quality control review.**

Nature, Timing and Extent of the Engagement Quality Control Review

64. An engagement quality control review ordinarily involves discussion with the engagement partner, a review of the financial statements or other subject matter information and the report, and, in particular, consideration of whether the report is appropriate. It also involves a review of selected working papers relating to the significant judgments the engagement team made and the conclusions they reached. The extent of the review depends on the complexity of the engagement and the risk that the report might not be appropriate in the circumstances. The review does not reduce the responsibilities of the engagement partner.

65. An engagement quality control review for audits of financial statements of listed entities includes considering the following:

- The engagement team's evaluation of the firm's independence in relation to the specific engagement.

- Significant risks identified during the engagement and the responses to those risks.

- Judgments made, particularly with respect to materiality and significant risks.

- Whether appropriate consultation has taken place on matters involving differences of opinion or other difficult or contentious matters, and the conclusions arising from those consultations.

- The significance and disposition of corrected and uncorrected misstatements identified during the engagement.

- The matters to be communicated to management and those charged with governance and, where applicable, other parties such as regulatory bodies.

- Whether working papers selected for review reflect the work performed in relation to the significant judgments and support the conclusions reached.

- The appropriateness of the report to be issued.

Engagement quality control reviews for engagements other than audits of financial statements of listed entities may, depending on the circumstances, include some or all of these considerations.

66. The engagement quality control reviewer conducts the review in a timely manner at appropriate stages during the engagement so that significant matters may be promptly resolved to the reviewer's satisfaction before the report is issued.

67. Where the engagement quality control reviewer makes recommendations that the engagement partner does not accept and the matter is not resolved to the reviewer's satisfaction, the report is not issued until the matter is resolved by following the firm's procedures for dealing with differences of opinion.

Criteria for the Eligibility of Engagement Quality Control Reviewers

68. **The firm's policies and procedures should address the appointment of engagement quality control reviewers and establish their eligibility through:**

    (a) **The technical qualifications required to perform the role, including the necessary experience and authority; and**

    (b) **The degree to which an engagement quality control reviewer can be consulted on the engagement without compromising the reviewer's objectivity.**

69. The firm's policies and procedures on the technical qualifications of engagement quality control reviewers address the technical expertise, experience and authority necessary to perform the role. What constitutes sufficient and appropriate technical expertise, experience and authority depends on the circumstances of the

engagement. In addition, the engagement quality control reviewer for an audit of the financial statements of a listed entity is an individual with sufficient and appropriate experience and authority to act as an audit engagement partner on audits of financial statements of listed entities.

70. The firm's policies and procedures are designed to maintain the objectivity of the engagement quality control reviewer. For example, the engagement quality control reviewer:

    (a) Is not selected by the engagement partner;

    (b) Does not otherwise participate in the engagement during the period of review;

    (c) Does not make decisions for the engagement team; and

    (d) Is not subject to other considerations that would threaten the reviewer's objectivity.

71. The engagement partner may consult the engagement quality control reviewer during the engagement. Such consultation need not compromise the engagement quality control reviewer's eligibility to perform the role. Where the nature and extent of the consultations become significant, however, care is taken by both the engagement team and the reviewer to maintain the reviewer's objectivity. Where this is not possible, another individual within the firm or a suitably qualified external person is appointed to take on the role of either the engagement quality control reviewer or the person to be consulted on the engagement. The firm's policies provide for the replacement of the engagement quality control reviewer where the ability to perform an objective review may be impaired.

72. Suitably qualified external persons may be contracted where sole practitioners or small firms identify engagements requiring engagement quality control reviews. Alternatively, some sole practitioners or small firms may wish to use other firms to facilitate engagement quality control reviews. Where the firm contracts suitably qualified external persons, the firm follows the requirements and guidance in paragraphs 68-71.

Documentation of the Engagement Quality Control Review

73. **Policies and procedures on documentation of the engagement quality control review should require documentation that:**

    (a) **The procedures required by the firm's policies on engagement quality control review have been performed;**

    (b) **The engagement quality control review has been completed before the report is issued; and**

(c) **The reviewer is not aware of any unresolved matters that would cause the reviewer to believe that the significant judgments the engagement team made and the conclusions they reached were not appropriate.**

Engagement Documentation

Completion of the Assembly of Final Engagement Files

73a. **The firm should establish policies and procedures for engagement teams to complete the assembly of final engagement files on a timely basis after the engagement reports have been finalized.**

73b. Law or regulation may prescribe the time limits by which the assembly of final engagement files for specific types of engagement should be completed. Where no such time limits are prescribed in law or regulation, the firm establishes time limits appropriate to the nature of the engagements that reflect the need to complete the assembly of final engagement files on a timely basis. In the case of an audit, for example, such a time limit is ordinarily not more than 60 days after the date of the auditor's report.

73c. Where two or more different reports are issued in respect of the same subject matter information of an entity, the firm's policies and procedures relating to time limits for the assembly of final engagement files address each report as if it were for a separate engagement. This may, for example, be the case when the firm issues an auditor's report on a component's financial information for group consolidation purposes and, at a subsequent date, an auditor's report on the same financial information for statutory purposes.

Confidentiality, Safe Custody, Integrity, Accessibility and Retrievability of Engagement Documentation

73d. **The firm should establish policies and procedures designed to maintain the confidentiality, safe custody, integrity, accessibility and retrievability of engagement documentation.**

73e. Relevant ethical requirements establish an obligation for the firm's personnel to observe at all times the confidentiality of information contained in engagement documentation, unless specific client authority has been given to disclose information, or there is a legal or professional duty to do so. Specific laws or regulations may impose additional obligations on the firm's personnel to maintain client confidentiality, particularly where data of a personal nature are concerned.

73f. Whether engagement documentation is in paper, electronic or other media, the integrity, accessibility or retrievability of the underlying data may be compromised if the documentation could be altered, added to or deleted without the firm's knowledge, or if it could be permanently lost or damaged. Accordingly, the firm designs and implements appropriate controls for engagement documentation to:

(a) Enable the determinination of when and by whom engagement documentation was created, changed or reviewed;

(b) Protect the integrity of the information at all stages of the engagement, especially when the information is shared within the engagement team or transmitted to other parties via the Internet;

(c) Prevent unauthorized changes to the engagement documentation; and

(d) Allow access to the engagement documentation by the engagement team and other authorized parties as necessary to properly discharge their responsibilities.

73g. Controls that the firm may design and implement to maintain the confidentiality, safe custody, integrity, accessibility and retrievability of engagement documentation include, for example:

- The use of a password among engagement team members to restrict access to electronic engagement documentation to authorized users.

- Appropriate back-up routines for electronic engagement documentation at appropriate stages during the engagement.

- Procedures for properly distributing engagement documentation to the team members at the start of engagement, processing it during engagement, and collating it at the end of engagement.

- Procedures for restricting access to, and enabling proper distribution and confidential storage of, hardcopy engagement documentation.

73h. For practical reasons, original paper documentation may be electronically scanned for inclusion in engagement files. In that case, the firm implements appropriate procedures requiring engagement teams to:

(a) Generate scanned copies that reflect the entire content of the original paper documentation, including manual signatures, cross-references and annotations;

(b) Integrate the scanned copies into the engagement files, including indexing and signing off on the scanned copies as necessary; and

(c) Enable the scanned copies to be retrieved and printed as necessary.

The firm considers whether to retain original paper documentation that has been scanned for legal, regulatory or other reasons.

Retention of Engagement Documentation

73i. **The firm should establish policies and procedures for the retention of engagement documentation for a period sufficient to meet the needs of the firm or as required by law or regulation.**

73j. The needs of the firm for retention of engagement documentation, and the period of such retention, will vary with the nature of the engagement and the firm's circumstances, for example, whether the engagement documentation is needed to provide a record of matters of continuing significance to future engagements. The retention period may also depend on other factors, such as whether local law or regulation prescribes specific retention periods for certain types of engagements, or whether there are generally accepted retention periods in the jurisdiction in the absence of specific legal or regulatory requirements. In the specific case of audit engagements, the retention period ordinarily is no shorter than five years from the date of the auditor's report, or, if later, the date of the group auditor's report.

73k. Procedures that the firm adopts for retention of engagement documentation include those that:

- Enable the retrieval of, and access to, the engagement documentation during the retention period, particularly in the case of electronic documentation since the underlying technology may be upgraded or changed over time.

- Provide, where necessary, a record of changes made to engagement documentation after the engagement files have been completed.

- Enable authorized external parties to access and review specific engagement documentation for quality control or other purposes.

Ownership of Engagement Documentation

73l. Unless otherwise specified by law or regulation, engagement documentation is the property of the firm. The firm may, at its discretion, make portions of, or extracts from, engagement documentation available to clients, provided such disclosure does not undermine the validity of the work performed, or, in the case of assurance engagements, the independence of the firm or its personnel.

Monitoring

74. **The firm should establish policies and procedures designed to provide it with reasonable assurance that the policies and procedures relating to the system of quality control are relevant, adequate, operating effectively and complied with in practice. Such policies and procedures should include an ongoing consideration and evaluation of the firm's system of quality control, including a periodic inspection of a selection of completed engagements.**

75. The purpose of monitoring compliance with quality control policies and procedures is to provide an evaluation of:

    (a) Adherence to professional standards and regulatory and legal requirements;

    (b) Whether the quality control system has been appropriately designed and effectively implemented; and

    (c) Whether the firm's quality control policies and procedures have been appropriately applied, so that reports that are issued by the firm or engagement partners are appropriate in the circumstances.

76. The firm entrusts responsibility for the monitoring process to a partner or partners or other persons with sufficient and appropriate experience and authority in the firm to assume that responsibility. Monitoring of the firm's system of quality control is performed by competent individuals and covers both the appropriateness of the design and the effectiveness of the operation of the system of quality control.

77. Ongoing consideration and evaluation of the system of quality control includes matters such as the following:

    • Analysis of:

        ○ New developments in professional standards and regulatory and legal requirements, and how they are reflected in the firm's policies and procedures where appropriate;

        ○ Written confirmation of compliance with policies and procedures on independence;

        ○ Continuing professional development, including training; and

        ○ Decisions related to acceptance and continuance of client relationships and specific engagements.

    • Determination of corrective actions to be taken and improvements to be made in the system, including the provision of feedback into the firm's policies and procedures relating to education and training.

    • Communication to appropriate firm personnel of weaknesses identified in the system, in the level of understanding of the system, or compliance with it.

    • Follow-up by appropriate firm personnel so that necessary modifications are promptly made to the quality control policies and procedures.

78. The inspection of a selection of completed engagements is ordinarily performed on a cyclical basis. Engagements selected for inspection include at least one engagement for each engagement partner over an inspection cycle, which ordinarily spans no more than three years. The manner in which the inspection cycle is organized, including the

timing of selection of individual engagements, depends on many factors, including the following:

- The size of the firm.

- The number and geographical location of offices.

- The results of previous monitoring procedures.

- The degree of authority both personnel and offices have (for example, whether individual offices are authorized to conduct their own inspections or whether only the head office may conduct them).

- The nature and complexity of the firm's practice and organization.

- The risks associated with the firm's clients and specific engagements.

79. The inspection process includes the selection of individual engagements, some of which may be selected without prior notification to the engagement team. Those inspecting the engagements are not involved in performing the engagement or the engagement quality control review. In determining the scope of the inspections, the firm may take into account the scope or conclusions of an independent external inspection program. However, an independent external inspection program does not act as a substitute for the firm's own internal monitoring program.

80. Small firms and sole practitioners may wish to use a suitably qualified external person or another firm to carry out engagement inspections and other monitoring procedures. Alternatively, they may wish to establish arrangements to share resources with other appropriate organizations to facilitate monitoring activities.

81. **The firm should evaluate the effect of deficiencies noted as a result of the monitoring process and should determine whether they are either:**

    (a) **Instances that do not necessarily indicate that the firm's system of quality control is insufficient to provide it with reasonable assurance that it complies with professional standards and regulatory and legal requirements, and that the reports issued by the firm or engagement partners are appropriate in the circumstances; or**

    (b) **Systemic, repetitive or other significant deficiencies that require prompt corrective action.**

82. **The firm should communicate to relevant engagement partners and other appropriate personnel deficiencies noted as a result of the monitoring process and recommendations for appropriate remedial action.**

83. **The firm's evaluation of each type of deficiency should result in recommendations for one or more of the following:**

(a) Taking appropriate remedial action in relation to an individual engagement or member of personnel;

(b) The communication of the findings to those responsible for training and professional development;

(c) Changes to the quality control policies and procedures; and

(d) Disciplinary action against those who fail to comply with the policies and procedures of the firm, especially those who do so repeatedly.

84. Where the results of the monitoring procedures indicate that a report may be inappropriate or that procedures were omitted during the performance of the engagement, the firm should determine what further action is appropriate to comply with relevant professional standards and regulatory and legal requirements. It should also consider obtaining legal advice.

85. At least annually, the firm should communicate the results of the monitoring of its quality control system to engagement partners and other appropriate individuals within the firm, including the firm's chief executive officer or, if appropriate, its managing board of partners. Such communication should enable the firm and these individuals to take prompt and appropriate action where necessary in accordance with their defined roles and responsibilities. Information communicated should include the following:

(a) A description of the monitoring procedures performed.

(b) The conclusions drawn from the monitoring procedures.

(c) Where relevant, a description of systemic, repetitive or other significant deficiencies and of the actions taken to resolve or amend those deficiencies.

86. The reporting of identified deficiencies to individuals other than the relevant engagement partners ordinarily does not include an identification of the specific engagements concerned, unless such identification is necessary for the proper discharge of the responsibilities of the individuals other than the engagement partners.

87. Some firms operate as part of a network and, for consistency, may implement some or all of their monitoring procedures on a network basis. Where firms within a network operate under common monitoring policies and procedures designed to comply with this ISQC (UK and Ireland), and these firms place reliance on such a monitoring system:

(a) At least annually, the network communicates the overall scope, extent and results of the monitoring process to appropriate individuals within the network firms;

(b) The network communicates promptly any identified deficiencies in the quality control system to appropriate individuals within the relevant network firm or firms so that the necessary action can be taken; and

(c) Engagement partners in the network firms are entitled to rely on the results of the monitoring process implemented within the network, unless the firms or the network advises otherwise.

88. Appropriate documentation relating to monitoring:

(a) Sets out monitoring procedures, including the procedure for selecting completed engagements to be inspected;

(b) Records the evaluation of:

(i) Adherence to professional standards and regulatory and legal requirements;

(ii) Whether the quality control system has been appropriately designed and effectively implemented; and

(iii) Whether the firm's quality control policies and procedures have been appropriately applied, so that reports that are issued by the firm or engagement partners are appropriate in the circumstances; and

(c) Identifies the deficiencies noted, evaluates their effect, and sets out the basis for determining whether and what further action is necessary.

Complaints and Allegations

89. **The firm should establish policies and procedures designed to provide it with reasonable assurance that it deals appropriately with:**

(a) **Complaints and allegations that the work performed by the firm fails to comply with professional standards and regulatory and legal requirements; and**

(b) **Allegations of non-compliance with the firm's system of quality control.**

90. Complaints and allegations (which do not include those that are clearly frivolous) may originate from within or outside the firm. They may be made by firm personnel, clients or other third parties. They may be received by engagement team members or other firm personnel.

91. As part of this process, the firm establishes clearly defined channels for firm personnel to raise any concerns in a manner that enables them to come forward without fear of reprisals.

92. The firm investigates such complaints and allegations in accordance with established policies and procedures. The investigation is supervised by a partner with sufficient and appropriate experience and authority within the firm but who is not otherwise involved in the engagement, and includes involving legal counsel as necessary. Small firms and sole practitioners may use the services of a suitably qualified external person

or another firm to carry out the investigation. Complaints, allegations and the responses to them are documented.

93. Where the results of the investigations indicate deficiencies in the design or operation of the firm's quality control policies and procedures, or non-compliance with the firm's system of quality control by an individual or individuals, the firm takes appropriate action as discussed in paragraph 83.

Documentation

94. **The firm should establish policies and procedures requiring appropriate documentation to provide evidence of the operation of each element of its system of quality control.**

95. How such matters are documented is the firm's decision. For example, large firms may use electronic databases to document matters such as independence confirmations, performance evaluations and the results of monitoring inspections. Smaller firms may use more informal methods such as manual notes, checklists and forms.

96. Factors to consider when determining the form and content of documentation evidencing the operation of each of the elements of the system of quality control include the following:

- The size of the firm and the number of offices.

- The degree of authority both personnel and offices have.

- The nature and complexity of the firm's practice and organization.

97. The firm retains this documentation for a period of time sufficient to permit those performing monitoring procedures to evaluate the firm's compliance with its system of quality control, or for a longer period if required by law or regulation.

Effective Date

98. Systems of quality control in compliance with this ISQC (UK and Ireland) are required to be established by firms in the UK and Ireland by 15 June 2005 (15 June 2006 for paragraphs 6(a) and 73a – 73l). Firms consider the appropriate transitional arrangements for engagements in process at these dates.

Public Sector Perspective

1. *This ISQC (UK and Ireland) is applicable in all material respects to the public sector.*

2. *Some of the terms in the ISQC (UK and Ireland), such as "engagement partner" and "firm," should be read as referring to their public sector equivalents. However, with limited exceptions, there is no public sector equivalent of "listed entities," although there may be audits of particularly significant public sector entities which should be*

subject to the listed entity requirements of mandatory rotation of the engagement partner (or equivalent) and engagement quality control review. There are no fixed objective criteria on which this determination of significance should be based. However, such an assessment should encompass an evaluation of all factors relevant to the audited entity. Such factors include size, complexity, commercial risk, parliamentary or media interest and the number and range of stakeholders affected.

3. ISQC (UK and Ireland) 1, paragraph 70, states that "The firm's policies and procedures are designed to maintain the objectivity of the engagement quality control reviewer." Subparagraph (a) notes as an example that the engagement quality control reviewer is not selected by the engagement partner. In many jurisdictions there is a single statutorily appointed auditor-general. In such circumstances, where applicable, the engagement reviewer should be selected having regard to the need for independence and objectivity.

4. In the public sector, auditors may be appointed in accordance with statutory procedures. Accordingly, considerations regarding the acceptance and continuance of client relationships and specific engagements, as set out in paragraphs 28-35 of ISQC (UK and Ireland) 1, may not apply.

5. Similarly, the independence of public sector auditors may be protected by statutory measures, with the consequence that certain of the threats to independence of the nature envisaged by paragraphs 18-27 of ISQC (UK and Ireland) 1 are unlikely to occur.

INTERNATIONAL STANDARD ON AUDITING
(UK AND IRELAND) 200*

OBJECTIVE AND GENERAL PRINCIPLES GOVERNING AN AUDIT OF FINANCIAL STATEMENTS

CONTENTS

International Standard on Auditing (UK and Ireland) (ISA (UK and Ireland)) 200 "Objective and General Principles Governing an Audit of Financial Statements" should be read in the context of the Auditing Practices Board's Statement "The Auditing Practices Board - Scope and Authority of Pronouncements (Revised)" which sets out the application and authority of ISAs (UK and Ireland).

---

* This ISA (UK and Ireland) does not include the conforming amendments that were promulgated with ISA 700 (Revised) by the IAASB in December 2004. This is because the APB has decided to defer revising the current ISA (UK and Ireland) 700 until progress has been made in resolving a number of issues, including whether ISA 700 (Revised) will be adopted for use in Europe.

Introduction

1. The purpose of this International Standard on Auditing (UK and Ireland) (ISA (UK and Ireland)) is to establish standards and provide guidance on the objective and general principles governing an audit of financial statements.

1-1. This ISA (UK and Ireland) uses the terms 'those charged with governance' and 'management'. The term 'governance' describes the role of persons entrusted with the supervision, control and direction of an entity. Ordinarily, those charged with governance are accountable for ensuring that the entity achieves its objectives, and for the quality of its financial reporting and reporting to interested parties. Those charged with governance include management only when they perform such functions.

1-2. In the UK and Ireland, those charged with governance include the directors (executive and non-executive) of a company or other body, the members of an audit committee where one exists, the partners, proprietors, committee of management or trustees of other forms of entity, or equivalent persons responsible for directing the entity's affairs and preparing its financial statements.

1-3. 'Management' comprises those persons who perform senior managerial functions.

1-4. In the UK and Ireland, depending on the nature and circumstances of the entity, management may include some or all of those charged with governance (e.g. executive directors). Management will not normally include non-executive directors.

Objective of an Audit

2. The objective of an audit of financial statements is to enable the auditor to express an opinion whether the financial statements are prepared, in all material respects, in accordance with an applicable financial reporting framework. The phrases used to express the auditor's opinion are "give a true and fair view" or "present fairly, in all material respects," which are equivalent terms.

2-1. The "applicable financial reporting framework" comprises those requirements of accounting standards, law and regulations applicable to the entity that determine the form and content of its financial statements.

3. Although the auditor's opinion enhances the credibility of the financial statements, the user cannot assume that the audit opinion is an assurance as to the future viability of the entity nor the efficiency or effectiveness with which management has conducted the affairs of the entity.

General Principles of an Audit

4. **The auditor should comply with the *Code of Ethics for Professional Accountants* issued by the International Federation of Accountants.** Ethical principles governing the auditor's professional responsibilities are:

    (a) Independence;

    (b) Integrity;

    (c) Objectivity;

    (d) Professional competence and due care;

    (e) Confidentiality;

    (f) Professional behavior; and

    (g) Technical standards.

4-1. **In the UK and Ireland the relevant ethical pronouncements with which the auditor should comply are the APB's Ethical Standards and the ethical pronouncements relating to the work of auditors issued by the auditor's relevant professional body.**

4-2. Auditors in the UK and Ireland are subject to ethical requirements from two sources: the Ethical Standards established by APB concerning the integrity, objectivity and independence of the auditor, and the ethical pronouncements established by the auditor's relevant professional body. The APB is not aware of any significant instances where the relevant parts of the IFAC Code of Ethics are more restrictive than the Ethical Standards.

5. **The auditor should conduct an audit in accordance with ISAs (UK and Ireland).** These contain basic principles and essential procedures together with related guidance in the form of explanatory and other material.

6. **The auditor should plan and perform an audit with an attitude of professional skepticism recognizing that circumstances may exist that cause the financial statements to be materially misstated.** An attitude of professional skepticism means the auditor makes a critical assessment, with a questioning mind, of the validity of audit evidence obtained and is alert to audit evidence that contradicts or brings into question the reliability of documents or management representations. For example, an attitude of professional skepticism is necessary throughout the audit process for the auditor to reduce the risk of overlooking suspicious circumstances, of over generalizing when drawing conclusions from audit observations, and of using faulty assumptions in determining the nature, timing, and extent of the audit procedures and evaluating the results thereof. In planning and performing an audit, the auditor neither assumes that management is dishonest nor assumes unquestioned honesty. Accordingly, representations from management are not a substitute for obtaining

sufficient appropriate audit evidence to be able to draw reasonable conclusions on which to base the audit opinion.

Scope of an Audit

7.   The term "scope of an audit" refers to the audit procedures deemed necessary in the circumstances to achieve the objective of the audit. **The audit procedures required to conduct an audit in accordance with ISAs (UK and Ireland) should be determined by the auditor having regard to the requirements of ISAs (UK and Ireland), relevant professional bodies, legislation, regulations and, where appropriate, the terms of the audit engagement and reporting requirements.**

7-1. Although the basic principles of auditing are the same in the public and the private sectors, the auditor of a public service body often has wider objectives and additional duties and statutory responsibilities, laid down in legislation, directives or codes of practice.

Reasonable Assurance

8.   An audit in accordance with ISAs (UK and Ireland) is designed to provide reasonable assurance that the financial statements taken as a whole are free from material misstatement. Reasonable assurance is a concept relating to the accumulation of the audit evidence necessary for the auditor to conclude that there are no material misstatements in the financial statements taken as a whole. Reasonable assurance relates to the whole audit process.

9.   An auditor cannot obtain absolute assurance because there are inherent limitations in an audit that affect the auditor's ability to detect material misstatements. These limitations result from factors such as:

   *   The use of testing.

   *   The inherent limitations of internal control (for example, the possibility of management override or collusion).

   *   The fact that most audit evidence is persuasive rather than conclusive.

   *   The impracticality of examining all items within a class of transactions or account balance.

   *   The possibility of collusion or misrepresentation for fraudulent purposes.

9-1. The view given in financial statements is itself based on a combination of fact and judgment and, consequently, cannot be characterized as either 'absolute' or 'correct'. A degree of imprecision is inevitable in the preparation of all but the simplest of financial statements because of inherent uncertainties and the need to use judgment in making accounting estimates and selecting appropriate accounting policies.

10. Also, the work undertaken by the auditor to form an audit opinion is permeated by judgment, in particular regarding:

    (a) The gathering of audit evidence, for example, in deciding the nature, timing, and extent of audit procedures; and

    (b) The drawing of conclusions based on the audit evidence gathered, for example, assessing the reasonableness of the estimates made by management[1a] in preparing the financial statements.

11. Further, other limitations may affect the persuasiveness of audit evidence available to draw conclusions on particular assertions[1] (for example, transactions between related parties). In these cases certain ISAs (UK and Ireland) identify specified audit procedures which will, because of the nature of the particular assertions, provide sufficient appropriate audit evidence in the absence of:

    (a) Unusual circumstances which increase the risk of material misstatement beyond that which would ordinarily be expected; or

    (b) Any indication that a material misstatement has occurred.

12. Accordingly, because of the factors described above, an audit is not a guarantee that the financial statements are free of material misstatement.

Audit Risk and Materiality

13. Entities pursue strategies to achieve their objectives, and depending on the nature of their operations and industry, the regulatory environment in which they operate, and their size and complexity, they face a variety of business risks.[2] Management[1a] is responsible for identifying such risks and responding to them. However, not all risks relate to the preparation of the financial statements. The auditor is ultimately concerned only with risks that may affect the financial statements.

14. The auditor obtains and evaluates audit evidence to obtain reasonable assurance about whether the financial statements give a true and fair view (or are presented fairly, in all material respects) in accordance with the applicable financial reporting framework. The concept of reasonable assurance acknowledges that there is a risk the audit opinion is inappropriate. The risk that the auditor expresses an inappropriate

---

[1a] In the UK and Ireland, those charged with governance are responsible for the preparation of the financial statements.

[1] Paragraphs 15–18 of ISA (UK and Ireland) 500, "Audit Evidence" discuss the use of assertions in obtaining audit evidence.

[2] Paragraphs 30 – 34 of ISA (UK and Ireland) 315, "Understanding the Entity and Its Environment and Assessing the Risks of Material Misstatement," discuss the concept of business risks and how they relate to risks of material misstatement.

audit opinion when the financial statements are materially misstated is known as "audit risk".[3]

15. **The auditor should plan and perform the audit to reduce audit risk to an acceptably low level that is consistent with the objective of an audit.** The auditor reduces audit risk by designing and performing audit procedures to obtain sufficient appropriate audit evidence to be able to draw reasonable conclusions on which to base an audit opinion. Reasonable assurance is obtained when the auditor has reduced audit risk to an acceptably low level.

16. Audit risk is a function of the risk of material misstatement of the financial statements (or simply, the "risk of material misstatement") (*i.e.*, the risk that the financial statements are materially misstated prior to audit) and the risk that the auditor will not detect such misstatement ("detection risk"). The auditor performs audit procedures to assess the risk of material misstatement and seeks to limit detection risk by performing further audit procedures based on that assessment (see ISA (UK and Ireland) 315, "Understanding the Entity and Its Environment and Assessing the Risks of Material Misstatement" and ISA (UK and Ireland) 330, "The Auditor's Procedures in Response to Assessed Risks"). The audit process involves the exercise of professional judgment in designing the audit approach, through focusing on what can go wrong (*i.e.*, what are the potential misstatements that may arise) at the assertion level (see ISA (UK and Ireland) 500, "Audit Evidence") and performing audit procedures in response to the assessed risks in order to obtain sufficient appropriate audit evidence.

17. The auditor is concerned with material misstatements, and is not responsible for the detection of misstatements that are not material to the financial statements taken as a whole. The auditor considers whether the effect of identified uncorrected misstatements, both individually and in the aggregate, is material to the financial statements taken as a whole. Materiality and audit risk are related (see ISA (UK and Ireland) 320, "Audit Materiality"). In order to design audit procedures to determine whether there are misstatements that are material to the financial statements taken as a whole, the auditor considers the risk of material misstatement at two levels: the overall financial statement level and in relation to classes of transactions, account balances, and disclosures and the related assertions.[4]

18. The auditor considers the risk of material misstatement at the overall financial statement level, which refers to risks of material misstatement that relate pervasively to the financial statements as a whole and potentially affect many assertions. Risks of this nature often relate to the entity's control environment (although these risks may also relate to other factors, such as declining economic conditions), and are not necessarily risks identifiable with specific assertions at the class of transactions, account balance, or disclosure level. Rather, this overall risk represents circumstances that increase the risk that there could be material misstatements in any number of different assertions,

---

[3] This definition of audit risk does not include the risk that the auditor might erroneously express an opinion that the financial statements are materially misstated.

[4] ISA (UK and Ireland) 315, "Understanding the Entity and Its Environment and Assessing the Risks of Material Misstatement" provides additional guidance on the auditor's requirement to assess risks of material misstatement at the financial statement level and at the assertion level.

for example, through management override of internal control. Such risks may be especially relevant to the auditor's consideration of the risk of material misstatement arising from fraud. The auditor's response to the assessed risk of material misstatement at the overall financial statement level includes consideration of the knowledge, skill, and ability of personnel assigned significant engagement responsibilities, including whether to involve experts; the appropriate levels of supervision; and whether there are events or conditions that may cast significant doubt on the entity's ability to continue as a going concern.

19. The auditor also considers the risk of material misstatement at the class of transactions, account balance, and disclosure level because such consideration directly assists in determining the nature, timing, and extent of further audit procedures at the assertion level.[5] The auditor seeks to obtain sufficient appropriate audit evidence at the class of transactions, account balance, and disclosure level in such a way that enables the auditor, at the completion of the audit, to express an opinion on the financial statements taken as a whole at an acceptably low level of audit risk. Auditors use various approaches to accomplish that objective.[6]

20. The discussion in the following paragraphs provides an explanation of the components of audit risk. The risk of material misstatement at the assertion level consists of two components as follows:

- "Inherent risk" is the susceptibility of an assertion to a misstatement that could be material, either individually or when aggregated with other misstatements, assuming that there are no related controls. The risk of such misstatement is greater for some assertions and related classes of transactions, account balances, and disclosures than for others. For example, complex calculations are more likely to be misstated than simple calculations. Accounts consisting of amounts derived from accounting estimates that are subject to significant measurement uncertainty pose greater risks than do accounts consisting of relatively routine, factual data. External circumstances giving rise to business risks may also influence inherent risk. For example, technological developments might make a particular product obsolete, thereby causing inventory to be more susceptible to overstatement. In addition to those circumstances that are peculiar to a specific assertion, factors in the entity and its environment that relate to several or all of the classes of transactions, account balances, or disclosures may influence the inherent risk related to a specific assertion. These latter factors include, for example, a lack of sufficient working capital to continue operations or a declining industry characterized by a large number of business failures.

---

[5] ISA (UK and Ireland) 330, "The Auditor's Procedures in Response to Assessed Risks" provides additional guidance on the requirement for the auditor to design and perform further audit procedures in response to the assessed risks at the assertion level.

[6] The auditor may make use of a model that expresses the general relationship of the components of audit risk in mathematical terms to arrive at an appropriate level of detection risk. Some auditors find such a model to be useful when planning audit procedures to achieve a desired audit risk though the use of such a model does not eliminate the judgment inherent in the audit process.

- "Control risk" is the risk that a misstatement that could occur in an assertion and that could be material, either individually or when aggregated with other misstatements, will not be prevented, or detected and corrected, on a timely basis by the entity's internal control. That risk is a function of the effectiveness of the design and operation of internal control in achieving the entity's objectives relevant to preparation of the entity's financial statements. Some control risk will always exist because of the inherent limitations of internal control.

21. Inherent risk and control risk are the entity's risks; they exist independently of the audit of the financial statements. The auditor is required to assess the risk of material misstatement at the assertion level as a basis for further audit procedures, though that assessment is a judgment, rather than a precise measurement of risk. When the auditor's assessment of the risk of material misstatement includes an expectation of the operating effectiveness of controls, the auditor performs tests of controls to support the risk assessment. The ISAs (UK and Ireland) do not ordinarily refer to inherent risk and control risk separately, but rather to a combined assessment of the "risk of material misstatement." Although the ISAs (UK and Ireland) ordinarily describe a combined assessment of the risk of material misstatement, the auditor may make separate or combined assessments of inherent and control risk depending on preferred audit techniques or methodologies and practical considerations. The assessment of the risk of material misstatement may be expressed in quantitative terms, such as in percentages, or in non-quantitative terms. In any case, the need for the auditor to make appropriate risk assessments is more important than the different approaches by which they may be made.

22. "Detection risk" is the risk that the auditor will not detect a misstatement that exists in an assertion that could be material, either individually or when aggregated with other misstatements. Detection risk is a function of the effectiveness of an audit procedure and of its application by the auditor. Detection risk cannot be reduced to zero because the auditor usually does not examine all of a class of transactions, account balance, or disclosure and because of other factors. Such other factors include the possibility that an auditor might select an inappropriate audit procedure, misapply an appropriate audit procedure, or misinterpret the audit results. These other factors ordinarily can be addressed through adequate planning, proper assignment of personnel to the engagement team, the application of professional skepticism, and supervision and review of the audit work performed.

23. Detection risk relates to the nature, timing, and extent of the auditor's procedures that are determined by the auditor to reduce audit risk to an acceptably low level. For a given level of audit risk, the acceptable level of detection risk bears an inverse relationship to the assessment of the risk of material misstatement at the assertion level. The greater the risk of material misstatement the auditor believes exists, the less the detection risk that can be accepted. Conversely, the less risk of material misstatement the auditor believes exist, the greater the detection risk that can be accepted.

Responsibility for the Financial Statements

24. While the auditor is responsible for forming and expressing an opinion on the financial statements, the responsibility for preparing and presenting the financial statements in accordance with the applicable financial reporting framework is that of the management of the entity, with oversight from those charged with governance.[71a] The audit of the financial statements does not relieve management or those charged with governance of their responsibilities.

Effective Date

25. This ISA (UK and Ireland) is effective for audits of financial statements for periods commencing on or after 15 December 2004.

---

[7] The structures of governance vary from country to country reflecting cultural and legal backgrounds. Therefore, the respective responsibilities of management and those charged with governance vary depending on the legal responsibilities in the particular jurisdiction.

Appendix

Conforming Amendments to ISA (UK and Ireland) 200 as a Result of ISA (UK and Ireland) 230 (Revised) – Effective for Audits of Financial Statements for Periods Beginning on or After June, 15 2006

The revision of ISA (UK and Ireland) 230 "Audit Documentation" gave rise to conforming amendments to ISA (UK and Ireland) 200. Once effective the conforming amendments set out below will be incorporated in the body of ISA (UK and Ireland) 200 and this appendix will be deleted.

The following paragraph is added as 7a.*

The auditor may, in exceptional circumstances, judge it necessary to depart from a basic principle or an essential procedure that is relevant in the circumstances of the audit, in order to achieve the objective of the audit. In such a case, the auditor is not precluded from representing compliance with ISAs (UK and Ireland), provided the departure is appropriately documented as required by ISA (UK and Ireland) 230 (Revised), "Audit Documentation."

This amendment is effective for audits of financial statements for periods beginning on or after June 15, 2006.

---

* This conforming amendment is inserted in a different location to that indicated by the IAASB to take account of the fact that the APB has not promulgated ISA 700 (Revised), relating to auditor's reports, and the conforming changes related to that standard.

THE AUDITING PRACTICES BOARD

INTERNATIONAL STANDARD ON AUDITING
(UK AND IRELAND) 210

TERMS OF AUDIT ENGAGEMENTS

CONTENTS

International Standard on Auditing (UK and Ireland) (ISA (UK and Ireland)) 210 "Terms of Audit Engagements" should be read in the context of the Auditing Practices Board's Statement "The Auditing Practices Board - Scope and Authority of Pronouncements (Revised)" which sets out the application and authority of ISAs (UK and Ireland).

Introduction

1. The purpose of this International Standard on Auditing (UK and Ireland) (ISA (UK and Ireland)) is to establish standards and provide guidance on:

    (a) agreeing the terms of the engagement with the client; and

    (b) the auditor's response to a request by a client to change the terms of an engagement to one that provides a lower level of assurance.

1-1. This ISA (UK and Ireland) uses the terms 'those charged with governance' and 'management'. The term 'governance' describes the role of persons entrusted with the supervision, control and direction of an entity. Ordinarily, those charged with governance are accountable for ensuring that the entity achieves its objectives, and for the quality of its financial reporting and reporting to interested parties. Those charged with governance include management only when they perform such functions.

1-2. In the UK and Ireland, those charged with governance include the directors (executive and non-executive) of a company or other body, the members of an audit committee where one exists, the partners, proprietors, committee of management or trustees of other forms of entity, or equivalent persons responsible for directing the entity's affairs and preparing its financial statements.

1-3. 'Management' comprises those persons who perform senior managerial functions.

1-4. In the UK and Ireland, depending on the nature and circumstances of the entity, management may include some or all of those charged with governance (e.g. executive directors). Management will not normally include non-executive directors.

1-5. For the purpose of this ISA (UK and Ireland) 'client' means the addressees of the auditor's report or, when as often will be the case it is not practical to agree such terms with the addressees, the entity itself through those charged with governance.

2. **The auditor and the client should agree on the terms of the engagement.** The agreed terms would need to be recorded in an audit engagement letter or other suitable form of contract.

2-1. **The terms of the engagement should be recorded in writing.**

3. This ISA is intended to assist the auditor in the preparation of engagement letters relating to audits of financial statements. The guidance is also applicable to related services. When other services such as tax, accounting, or management advisory services are to be provided, separate letters may be appropriate.

4. In some countries, the objective and scope of an audit and the auditor's obligations are established by law. Even in those situations the auditor may still find audit engagement letters informative for their clients.

Audit Engagement Letters

5.   It is in the interest of both client and auditor that the auditor sends an engagement letter, preferably before the commencement of the engagement, to help in avoiding misunderstandings with respect to the engagement. The engagement letter documents and confirms the auditor's acceptance of the appointment, the objective and scope of the audit, the extent of the auditor's responsibilities to the client and the form of any reports.

5-1. **In the UK and Ireland, the auditor should ensure that the engagement letter documents and confirms the auditor's acceptance of the appointment, and includes a summary of the responsibilities of those charged with governance and of the auditor, the scope of the engagement and the form of any reports.**

5-2. Appendix 2 sets out illustrative wording to describe the responsibilities of the directors and the auditor and the scope of the audit, for a limited (non-listed) company client for an audit conducted in accordance with ISAs (UK and Ireland).

Principal Contents

6.   The form and content of audit engagement letters may vary for each client, but they would generally include reference to:

- The objective of the audit of financial statements.

- Management's responsibility for the financial statements[1].

- The scope of the audit, including reference to applicable legislation, regulations, or pronouncements of professional bodies to which the auditor adheres.

- The form of any reports or other communication of results of the engagement.

- The fact that because of the test nature and other inherent limitations of an audit, together with the inherent limitations of internal control, there is an unavoidable risk that even some material misstatement may remain undiscovered.

- Unrestricted access to whatever records, documentation and other information requested in connection with the audit.

7.   The auditor may also wish to include in the letter:

- Arrangements regarding the planning and performance of the audit.

- Expectation of receiving from management written confirmation concerning representations made in connection with the audit.

---

[1]   In the UK and Ireland, those charged with governance are responsible for the preparation of the financial statements.

- Request for the client to confirm the terms of the engagement by acknowledging receipt of the engagement letter.[2]

- Description of any other letters or reports the auditor expects to issue to the client.

- Any confidentiality of other letters or reports to be issued and, where appropriate, the conditions, if any, on which permission might be given to those charged with governance to make those reports available to others.

- Basis on which fees are computed and any billing arrangements.

8. When relevant, the following points could also be made:

- Arrangements concerning the involvement of other auditors and experts in some aspects of the audit.

- Arrangements concerning the involvement of internal auditors and other client staff.

- Arrangements to be made with the predecessor auditor, if any, in the case of an initial audit.

- Any restriction of the auditor's liability when such possibility exists.

- A reference to any further agreements between the auditor and the client.

An example of an audit engagement letter is set out in the Appendix.[3]

Audits of Components

9. When the auditor of a parent entity is also the auditor of its subsidiary, branch or division (component), the factors that influence the decision whether to send a separate engagement letter to the component include:

- Who appoints the auditor of the component.

- Whether the terms for each component are the same.

- Whether a separate audit report is to be issued on the component.

- Legal requirements.

- Regulatory requirements.

---

[2] Acceptance by the client of the terms of the engagement is normally evidenced by signature by a person at an appropriate level within the entity, for example the finance director or equivalent.
[3] The example letter in the Appendix is not tailored for the United Kingdom and Ireland.

- The extent of any work performed by other auditors.

- Degree of ownership by parent.

- Degree of independence of the component's management.

9-1. If the auditor sends one letter relating to the group as a whole, it identifies the components for which the auditor is appointed as auditor. Those charged with governance of the parent entity are requested to forward the letter to those charged with governance of the components concerned. Each board is requested to confirm that the terms of the engagement letter are accepted.

Recurring Audits

10. **On recurring audits, the auditor should consider whether circumstances require the terms of the engagement to be revised and whether there is a need to remind the client of the existing terms of the engagement.**

11. The auditor may decide not to send a new engagement letter each period. However, the following factors may make it appropriate to send a new letter:

- Any indication that the client misunderstands the objective and scope of the audit.

- Any revised or special terms of the engagement.

- A recent change of senior management or those charged with governance.

- A significant change in ownership.

- A significant change in nature or size of the client's business.

- Legal or regulatory requirements.

Acceptance of a Change in Engagement

12. **An auditor who, before the completion of the engagement, is requested to change the engagement to one which provides a lower level of assurance, should consider the appropriateness of doing so.**

13. A request from the client for the auditor to change the engagement may result from a change in circumstances affecting the need for the service, a misunderstanding as to the nature of an audit or related service originally requested or a restriction on the scope of the engagement, whether imposed by management or caused by circumstances. The auditor would consider carefully the reason given for the request, particularly the implications of a restriction on the scope of the engagement.

14. A change in circumstances that affects the entity's requirements or a misunderstanding concerning the nature of service originally requested would ordinarily be considered a reasonable basis for requesting a change in the engagement. In contrast a change would not be considered reasonable if it appeared that the change relates to information that is incorrect, incomplete or otherwise unsatisfactory.

15. Before agreeing to change an audit engagement to a related service, an auditor who was engaged to perform an audit in accordance with ISAs (UK and Ireland) would consider, in addition to the above matters, any legal or contractual implications of the change.

16. If the auditor concludes, that there is reasonable justification to change the engagement and if the audit work performed complies with the ISAs (UK and Ireland) applicable to the changed engagement, the report issued would be that appropriate for the revised terms of engagement. In order to avoid confusing the reader, the report would not include reference to:

    (a) The original engagement; or

    (b) Any procedures that may have been performed in the original engagement, except where the engagement is changed to an engagement to undertake agreed-upon procedures and thus reference to the procedures performed is a normal part of the report.

17. **Where the terms of the engagement are changed, the auditor and the client should agree on the new terms.**

18. **The auditor should not agree to a change of engagement where there is no reasonable justification for doing so.** An example might be an audit engagement where the auditor is unable to obtain sufficient appropriate audit evidence regarding receivables and the client asks for the engagement to be changed to a review engagement to avoid a qualified audit opinion or a disclaimer of opinion.

19. **If the auditor is unable to agree to a change of the engagement and is not permitted to continue the original engagement, the auditor should withdraw and consider whether there is any obligation, either contractual or otherwise, to report to other parties, such as those charged with governance or shareholders, the circumstances necessitating the withdrawal.**

19-1. The auditor of a limited company in Great Britain who ceases to hold office as auditor is required to comply with the requirements of section 394 of the Companies Act 1985 regarding the statement to be made by the auditor in relation to ceasing to hold office. Equivalent requirements for Northern Ireland are contained in Article 401A of the Companies (Northern Ireland) Order 1986 and, for the Republic of Ireland, are contained in section 185 of the Companies Act 1990.

Effective Date

19-2. This ISA (UK and Ireland) is effective for audits of financial statements for periods commencing on or after 15 December 2004.

Public Sector Perspective

Additional guidance for auditors of public sector bodies in the UK and Ireland is given in:

- Practice Note 10 "Audit of Financial Statements of Public Sector Bodies in the United Kingdom (Revised)"

- Practice Note 10(I) "Audit of Central Government Financial Statements in the Republic of Ireland (Revised)"

1. The purpose of the engagement letter is to inform the auditee of the nature of the engagement and to clarify the responsibilities of the parties involved. The legislation and regulations governing the operations of public sector audits generally mandate the appointment of a public sector auditor and the use of audit engagement letters may not be a widespread practice. Nevertheless, a letter setting out the nature of the engagement or recognizing an engagement not indicated in the legislative mandate may be useful to both parties. Public sector auditors have to give serious consideration to issuing audit engagements letters when undertaking an audit.

2. Paragraphs 12-19 of this ISA (UK and Ireland)deal with the action a private sector auditor may take when there are attempts to change an audit engagement to one which provides a lower level of assurance. In the public sector specific requirements may exist within the legislation governing the audit mandate; for example, the auditor may be required to report directly to a minister, the legislature or the public if management (including the department head) attempts to limit the scope of the audit.

Appendix

Example of an Audit Engagement Letter

The following letter is for use as a guide in conjunction with the considerations outlined in this ISA and will need to be varied according to individual requirements and circumstances.

To the Board of Directors or the appropriate representative of senior management:

You have requested that we audit the balance sheet of .... as of ...., and the related statements of income and cash flows for the year then ending. We are pleased to confirm our acceptance and our understanding of this engagement by means of this letter. Our audit will be made with the objective of our expressing an opinion on the financial statements.

We will conduct our audit in accordance with International Standards on Auditing (or refer to relevant national standards or practices). Those Standards require that we plan and perform the audit to obtain reasonable assurance about whether the financial statements are free of material misstatements. An audit includes examining, on a test basis, evidence supporting the amounts and disclosures in the financial statements. An audit also includes assessing the accounting principles used and significant estimates made by management, as well as evaluating the overall financial statement presentation.

Because of the test nature and other inherent limitations of an audit, together with the inherent limitations of any accounting and internal control system, there is an unavoidable risk that even some material misstatements may remain undiscovered.

In addition to our report on the financial statements, we expect to provide you with a separate letter concerning any material weaknesses in accounting and internal control systems which come to our notice.

We remind you that the responsibility for the preparation of financial statements including adequate disclosure is that of the management of the company. This includes the maintenance of adequate accounting records and internal controls, the selection and application of accounting policies, and the safeguarding of the assets of the company. As part of our audit process, we will request from management written confirmation concerning representations made to us in connection with the audit.

We look forward to full cooperation with your staff and we trust that they will make available to us whatever records, documentation and other information are requested in connection with our audit. Our fees, which will be billed as work progresses, are based on the time required by the individuals assigned to the engagement plus out-of-pocket expenses. Individual hourly rates vary according to the degree of responsibility involved and the experience and skill required.

This letter will be effective for future years unless it is terminated, amended or superseded.

Please sign and return the attached copy of this letter to indicate that it is in accordance with your understanding of the arrangements for our audit of the financial statements.

XYZ & Co.
Acknowledged on behalf of
ABC Company by

(signed)
....
Name and Title
Date

Appendix 2

Illustrative wording to describe the responsibilities of the directors and the auditor and the scope of the audit, for a limited (non-listed) company client for an audit conducted in accordance with ISAs (UK and Ireland)

The illustrative wording set out below is not necessarily comprehensive or appropriate to be used in relation to every non-listed company, and it must be tailored to specific circumstances - for example, to the special reporting requirements of regulated entities *(note 1)*, or of small companies to which certain exemptions are given.

The wording reflects legal and professional responsibilities as at 15 December 2004. The wording should be amended as necessary to take account of changes in the responsibilities of the directors and the auditor after that date, for example as a result of changes in company legislation.

The auditor includes other wording as appropriate to address the matters set out in paragraphs 6 to 9-1 of this ISA (UK and Ireland).

Responsibilities of directors and auditors

As directors of xxxxxx, you are responsible for ensuring that the company maintains proper accounting records and for preparing financial statements which give a true and fair view and have been prepared in accordance with the Companies Act 1985 *(or other relevant legislation - note 2)*. You are also responsible for making available to us, as and when required, all the company's accounting records and all other relevant records and related information, including minutes of all management and shareholders' meetings. We are entitled to require from the company's officers such other information and explanations as we think necessary for the performance of our duties as auditors.

We have a statutory responsibility to report to the members whether in our opinion the financial statements give a true and fair view and whether they have been properly prepared in accordance with the Companies Act 1985 *(or other relevant legislation)*. In arriving at our opinion, we are required to consider the following matters, and to report on any in respect of which we are not satisfied *(note 3)*:

(a) Whether proper accounting records have been kept by the company *(note 4)* and proper returns adequate for our audit have been received from branches not visited by us;

(b) Whether the company's *(note 4)* balance sheet and profit and loss account are in agreement with the accounting records and returns;

(c) Whether we have obtained all the information and explanations which we consider necessary for the purposes of our audit; and

(d) Whether the information given in the directors' report is consistent with the financial statements.

In addition, there are certain other matters which, according to the circumstances, may need to be dealt with in our report. For example, where the financial statements do not give details of directors' remuneration or of their transactions with the company, the Companies Act 1985 requires us to disclose such matters in our report.

We have a professional responsibility to report if the financial statements do not comply in any material respect with applicable accounting standards, unless in our opinion the non-compliance is justified in the circumstances. In determining whether or not the departure is justified we consider:

(a) Whether the departure is required in order for the financial statements to give a true and fair view; and

(b) Whether adequate disclosure has been made concerning the departure.

Our professional responsibilities also include:

• Including in our report a description of the directors' responsibilities for the financial statements where the financial statements or accompanying information do not include such a description; and

• Considering whether other information in documents containing audited financial statements is consistent with those financial statements.

(note 5)

Scope of audit

Our audit will be conducted in accordance with the International Standards on Auditing (UK and Ireland) issued by the Auditing Practices Board, and will include such tests of transactions and of the existence, ownership and valuation of assets and liabilities as we consider necessary. We shall obtain an understanding of the accounting and internal control systems in order to assess their adequacy as a basis for the preparation of the financial statements and to establish whether proper accounting records have been maintained by the company. We shall expect to obtain such appropriate evidence as we consider sufficient to enable us to draw reasonable conclusions therefrom.

The nature and extent of our procedures will vary according to our assessment of the company's accounting system and, where we wish to place reliance on it, the internal control system, and may cover any aspect of the business's operations that we consider appropriate. Our audit is not designed to identify all significant weaknesses in the company's systems but, if such weaknesses come to our notice during the course of our audit which we think should be brought to your attention, we shall report them to you. Any such report may not be provided to third parties without our prior written consent. Such consent will be granted only on the basis that such reports are not prepared with the interests of anyone other than the company in mind and that we accept no duty or responsibility to any other party as concerns the reports.

As part of our normal audit procedures, we may request you to provide written confirmation of certain oral representations which we have received from you during the course of the audit on matters having a material effect on the financial statements. In connection with representations and the supply of information to us generally, we draw your attention to section 389A of the Companies Act 1985 (*note 6*) under which it is an offence for an officer of the company to mislead the auditors.

In order to assist us with the examination of your financial statements, we shall request sight of all documents or statements, including the chairman's statement, operating and financial review and the directors' report, which are due to be issued with the financial statements. We are also entitled to attend all general meetings of the company and to receive notice of all such meetings.

The responsibility for safeguarding the assets of the company and for the prevention and detection of fraud, error and non-compliance with law or regulations rests with yourselves. However, we shall endeavour to plan our audit so that we have a reasonable expectation of detecting material misstatements in the financial statements or accounting records (including those resulting from fraud, error or non-compliance with law or regulations), but our examination should not be relied upon to disclose all such material misstatements or frauds, errors or instances of non-compliance as may exist.

(*Where appropriate - note 7*) We shall not be treated as having notice, for the purposes of our audit responsibilities, of information provided to members of our firm other than those engaged on the audit (for example information provided in connection with accounting, taxation and other services).

Once we have issued our report we have no further direct responsibility in relation to the financial statements for that financial year. However, we expect that you will inform us of any material event occurring between the date of our report and that of the Annual General Meeting which may affect the financial statements.

Notes

1   *Additional guidance is provided in APB Practice Notes.*

2   *Relevant legislation for the Republic of Ireland is the Companies Acts 1963 to 2003 and for Northern Ireland is the Companies (Northern Ireland) Order 1986.*

3   *In the Republic of Ireland, auditors are required to report additionally on matters (a) to (d) as identified in the section 'Responsibilities of directors and auditors' of the example engagement letter, and on whether there existed at the balance sheet date a financial situation which, under section 40(1) of the Companies (Amendment) Act 1983, would require the convening of an extraordinary general meeting of the company. Hence this sentence would read:*

'... we are required to consider the following matters and to report on:'

4   *The reference to 'company' does not need to be altered in the case of groups as section 237 of the Companies Act 1985 refers only to the company being audited and not to any parent company or subsidiary or associated undertaking.*

5   *In the Republic of Ireland, auditors have the following additional legal responsibilities which are set out in the engagement letter:*

Company law

To report whether, in their opinion, proper books of account have been kept by the entity.

Where suspected indictable offences under the Companies Acts come to the attention of auditors, while carrying out their audit examination, they are obliged to report these to the Director of Corporate Enforcement. This reporting obligation imposed by Section 194, Companies Act, 1990, as amended by Section 74, Company Law Enforcement Act, 2001, applies regardless of the apparent materiality of the suspected offence, or whether the suspected offence has already been reported to the relevant authorities.

Criminal law

Where, in the course of conducting professional work, it comes to the attention of certain "relevant persons" (as defined), that information or documents indicate that an offence may have been committed under Section 59 Criminal Justice (Theft and Fraud Offences) Act 2001, auditors have a reporting obligation to the Garda Siochana. This applies regardless of the apparent materiality of the suspected offence, or whether the suspected offence has already been reported to the relevant authorities.

Taxation

Auditors must report material relevant offences, as defined in Section 1079 of the Taxes Consolidation Act 1997, to the directors of the company in writing, requesting them to rectify the matter or notify an appropriate officer of the Revenue Commissioners of the offence within 6 months. In the event that the auditors request is not complied with, the auditor must cease to act as auditor to the company or to assist the company in any taxation matter. The auditor must also send a copy of the auditor's notice of resignation to an appropriate officer of the Revenue Commissioners within 14 days

6   *Relevant references for the Republic of Ireland are sections 193(3), 196 and 197 of the Companies Act 1990. The relevant reference for Northern Ireland is Article 397A of the Companies (Northern Ireland) Order 1986.*

7   *When accounting, taxation or other services are undertaken on behalf of an audit client, information may be provided to members of the audit firm other than those engaged on the audit. In such cases, it may be appropriate for the audit engagement letter to include this or a similar paragraph to indicate that the auditors are not to be treated as having notice, for the purposes of their audit responsibilities, of such information, to make it clear that a company would not be absolved from informing the auditors directly of a material matter.*

INTERNATIONAL STANDARD ON AUDITING
(UK AND IRELAND) 220

QUALITY CONTROL FOR AUDITS OF HISTORICAL
FINANCIAL INFORMATION

CONTENTS

International Standard on Auditing (UK and Ireland) (ISA (UK and Ireland)) 220 "Quality Control for Audits of Historical Financial Information" should be read in the context of the Auditing Practices Board's Statement "The Auditing Practices Board - Scope and Authority of Pronouncements (Revised)" which sets out the application and authority of ISAs (UK and Ireland).

Introduction

1. The purpose of this International Standard on Auditing (UK and Ireland) (ISA(UK and Ireland)) is to establish standards and provide guidance on specific responsibilities of firm personnel regarding quality control procedures for audits of historical financial information, including audits of financial statements. This ISA (UK and Ireland) is to be read in conjunction with Parts A and B of the IFAC *Code of Ethics for Professional Accountants* (the IFAC Code).

1-1. In the UK and Ireland the relevant ethical pronouncements with which the auditor complies are the APB's Ethical Standards and the ethical pronouncements relating to the work of auditors issued by the auditor's relevant professional body - see the Statement "The Auditing practices Board – Scope and Authority of Pronouncements."

2. **The engagement team should implement quality control procedures that are applicable to the individual audit engagement.**

3. Under International Standard on Quality Control (UK and Ireland) (ISQC (UK and Ireland)) 1, "Quality Control for Firms that Perform Audits and Reviews of Historical Financial Information, and Other Assurance and Related Services Engagements," a firm has an obligation to establish a system of quality control designed to provide it with reasonable assurance that the firm and its personnel comply with professional standards and regulatory and legal requirements, and that the auditors' reports issued by the firm or engagement partners are appropriate in the circumstances.

4. Engagement teams:

    (a) Implement quality control procedures that are applicable to the audit engagement;

    (b) Provide the firm with relevant information to enable the functioning of that part of the firm's system of quality control relating to independence; and

    (c) Are entitled to rely on the firm's systems (for example in relation to capabilities and competence of personnel through their recruitment and formal training; independence through the accumulation and communication of relevant independence information; maintenance of client relationships through acceptance and continuance systems; and adherence to regulatory and legal requirements through the monitoring process), unless information provided by the firm or other parties suggests otherwise.

Definitions

5. In this ISA (UK and Ireland), the following terms have the meanings attributed below:

    (a) "Engagement partner" – the partner or other person in the firm who is responsible for the audit engagement and its performance, and for the auditor's report that is issued on behalf of the firm, and who, where required, has the appropriate authority from a professional, legal or regulatory body;

(b) "Engagement quality control review" – a process designed to provide an objective evaluation, before the auditor's report is issued, of the significant judgments the engagement team made and the conclusions they reached in formulating the auditor's report;

(c) "Engagement quality control reviewer" – a partner, other person in the firm, suitably qualified external person, or a team made up of such individuals, with sufficient and appropriate experience and authority to objectively evaluate, before the auditor's report is issued, the significant judgments the engagement team made and the conclusions they reached in formulating the auditor's report;

(d) "Engagement team" – all personnel performing an audit engagement, including any experts contracted by the firm in connection with that audit engagement;

(e) "Firm"* – a sole practitioner, partnership, corporation or other entity of professional accountants;

(f) "Inspection" – in relation to completed audit engagements, procedures designed to provide evidence of compliance by engagement teams with the firm's quality control policies and procedures;

(g) "Listed entity"* – an entity whose shares, stock or debt are quoted or listed on a recognized stock exchange, or are marketed under the regulations of a recognized stock exchange or other equivalent body;

(h) "Monitoring" – a process comprising an ongoing consideration and evaluation of the firm's system of quality control, including a periodic inspection of a selection of completed engagements, designed to enable the firm to obtain reasonable assurance that its system of quality control is operating effectively;

(i) "Network firm"* – an entity under common control, ownership or management with the firm or any entity that a reasonable and informed third party having knowledge of all relevant information would reasonably conclude as being part of the firm nationally or internationally;

(j) "Partner" – any individual with authority to bind the firm with respect to the performance of a professional services engagement;

(k) "Personnel" – partners and staff;

(l) "Professional standards" – IAASB Engagement Standards, as defined in the IAASB's "Preface to the International Standards on Quality Control, Auditing, Assurance and Related Services," and relevant ethical requirements, which

---

* As defined in the IFAC Code published in November 2001.

ordinarily comprise Parts A and B of the IFAC Code and relevant national ethical requirements[1];

(m) "Reasonable assurance" – in the context of this ISA (UK and Ireland), a high, but not absolute, level of assurance;

(n) "Staff" – professionals, other than partners, including any experts the firm employs; and

(o) "Suitably qualified external person" – an individual outside the firm with the capabilities and competence to act as an engagement partner, for example a partner of another firm, or an employee (with appropriate experience) of either a professional accountancy body whose members may perform audits of historical financial information or of an organization that provides relevant quality control services.

5-1. This ISA (UK and Ireland) uses the terms 'those charged with governance' and 'management'. The term 'governance' describes the role of persons entrusted with the supervision, control and direction of an entity. Ordinarily, those charged with governance are accountable for ensuring that the entity achieves its objectives, and for the quality of its financial reporting and reporting to interested parties. Those charged with governance include management only when they perform such functions.

5-2. In the UK and Ireland, those charged with governance include the directors (executive and non-executive) of a company or other body, the members of an audit committee where one exists, the partners, proprietors, committee of management or trustees of other forms of entity, or equivalent persons responsible for directing the entity's affairs and preparing its financial statements.

5-3. 'Management' comprises those persons who perform senior managerial functions.

5-4. In the UK and Ireland, depending on the nature and circumstances of the entity, management may include some or all of those charged with governance (e.g. executive directors). Management will not normally include non-executive directors.

Leadership Responsibilities for Quality on Audits

6. **The engagement partner should take responsibility for the overall quality on each audit engagement to which that partner is assigned.**

7. The engagement partner sets an example regarding audit quality to the other members of the engagement team through all stages of the audit engagement.

---

[1] In the UK and Ireland the relevant ethical pronouncements with which the auditor complies are the APB's Ethical Standards and the ethical pronouncements relating to the work of auditors issued by the auditor's relevant professional body - see the Statement "The Auditing practices Board – Scope and Authority of Pronouncements."

Ordinarily, this example is provided through the actions of the engagement partner and through appropriate messages to the engagement team. Such actions and messages emphasize:

(a) The importance of:

    (i) Performing work that complies with professional standards and regulatory and legal requirements;

    (ii) Complying with the firm's quality control policies and procedures as applicable; and

    (iii) Issuing auditor's reports that are appropriate in the circumstances; and

(b) The fact that quality is essential in performing audit engagements.

Ethical Requirements

8. **The engagement partner should consider whether members of the engagement team have complied with ethical requirements.**

9. Ethical requirements relating to audit engagements ordinarily comprise Parts A and B of the IFAC Code together with national requirements that are more restrictive[1]. The IFAC Code establishes the fundamental principles of professional ethics, which include:

(a) Integrity;

(b) Objectivity;

(c) Professional competence and due care;

(d) Confidentiality; and

(e) Professional behavior.

10. The engagement partner remains alert for evidence of non-compliance with ethical requirements. Inquiry and observation regarding ethical matters amongst the engagement partner and other members of the engagement team occur as necessary throughout the audit engagement. If matters come to the engagement partner's attention through the firm's systems or otherwise that indicate that members of the engagement team have not complied with ethical requirements, the partner, in consultation with others in the firm, determines the appropriate action.

11. The engagement partner and, where appropriate, other members of the engagement team, document issues identified and how they were resolved.

Independence

12. The engagement partner should form a conclusion on compliance with independence requirements that apply to the audit engagement. In doing so, the engagement partner should:

    (a) Obtain relevant information from the firm and, where applicable, network firms, to identify and evaluate circumstances and relationships that create threats to independence;

    (b) Evaluate information on identified breaches, if any, of the firm's independence policies and procedures to determine whether they create a threat to independence for the audit engagement;

    (c) Take appropriate action to eliminate such threats or reduce them to an acceptable level by applying safeguards. The engagement partner should promptly report to the firm any failure to resolve the matter for appropriate action; and

    (d) Document conclusions on independence and any relevant discussions with the firm that support these conclusions.

13. The engagement partner may identify a threat to independence regarding the audit engagement that safeguards may not be able to eliminate or reduce to an acceptable level. In that case, the engagement partner consults within the firm to determine appropriate action, which may include eliminating the activity or interest that creates the threat, or withdrawing from the audit engagement. Such discussion and conclusions are documented.

Acceptance and Continuance of Client Relationships and Specific Audit Engagements

14. The engagement partner should be satisfied that appropriate procedures regarding the acceptance and continuance of client relationships and specific audit engagements have been followed, and that conclusions reached in this regard are appropriate and have been documented.

15. The engagement partner may or may not initiate the decision-making process for acceptance or continuance regarding the audit engagement. Regardless of whether the engagement partner initiated that process, the partner determines whether the most recent decision remains appropriate.

16. Acceptance and continuance of client relationships and specific audit engagements include considering:

    • The integrity of the principal owners, key management and those charged with governance of the entity;

- Whether the engagement team is competent to perform the audit engagement and has the necessary time and resources; and

- Whether the firm and the engagement team can comply with ethical requirements.

Where issues arise out of any of these considerations, the engagement team conducts the appropriate consultations set out in paragraphs 30-33, and documents how issues were resolved.

17. Deciding whether to continue a client relationship includes consideration of significant matters that have arisen during the current or previous audit engagement, and their implications for continuing the relationship. For example, a client may have started to expand its business operations into an area where the firm does not possess the necessary knowledge or expertise.

18. **Where the engagement partner obtains information that would have caused the firm to decline the audit engagement if that information had been available earlier, the engagement partner should communicate that information promptly to the firm, so that the firm and the engagement partner can take the necessary action.**

Assignment of Engagement Teams

19. **The engagement partner should be satisfied that the engagement team collectively has the appropriate capabilities, competence and time to perform the audit engagement in accordance with professional standards and regulatory and legal requirements, and to enable an auditor's report that is appropriate in the circumstances to be issued.**

20. The appropriate capabilities and competence expected of the engagement team as a whole include the following:

- An understanding of, and practical experience with, audit engagements of a similar nature and complexity through appropriate training and participation.

- An understanding of professional standards and regulatory and legal requirements.

- Appropriate technical knowledge, including knowledge of relevant information technology.

- Knowledge of relevant industries in which the client operates.

- Ability to apply professional judgment.

- An understanding of the firm's quality control policies and procedures.

Engagement Performance

21. **The engagement partner should take responsibility for the direction, supervision and performance of the audit engagement in compliance with professional standards and regulatory and legal requirements, and for the auditor's report that is issued to be appropriate in the circumstances.**

22. The engagement partner directs the audit engagement by informing the members of the engagement team of:

    (a) Their responsibilities;

    (b) The nature of the entity's business;

    (c) Risk-related issues;

    (d) Problems that may arise; and

    (e) The detailed approach to the performance of the engagement.

    The engagement team's responsibilities include maintaining an objective state of mind and an appropriate level of professional skepticism, and performing the work delegated to them in accordance with the ethical principle of due care. Members of the engagement team are encouraged to raise questions with more experienced team members. Appropriate communication occurs within the engagement team.

23. It is important that all members of the engagement team understand the objectives of the work they are to perform. Appropriate team-working and training are necessary to assist less experienced members of the engagement team to clearly understand the objectives of the assigned work.

24. Supervision includes the following:

    • Tracking the progress of the audit engagement.

    • Considering the capabilities and competence of individual members of the engagement team, whether they have sufficient time to carry out their work, whether they understand their instructions, and whether the work is being carried out in accordance with the planned approach to the audit engagement.

    • Addressing significant issues arising during the audit engagement, considering their significance and modifying the planned approach appropriately.

    • Identifying matters for consultation or consideration by more experienced engagement team members during the audit engagement.

25. Review responsibilities are determined on the basis that more experienced team members, including the engagement partner, review work performed by less experienced team members. Reviewers consider whether:

(a) The work has been performed in accordance with professional standards and regulatory and legal requirements;

(b) Significant matters have been raised for further consideration;

(c) Appropriate consultations have taken place and the resulting conclusions have been documented and implemented;

(d) There is a need to revise the nature, timing and extent of work performed;

(e) The work performed supports the conclusions reached and is appropriately documented;

(f) The evidence obtained is sufficient and appropriate to support the auditor's report; and

(g) The objectives of the engagement procedures have been achieved.

26. **Before the auditor's report is issued, the engagement partner, through review of the audit documentation and discussion with the engagement team, should be satisfied that sufficient appropriate audit evidence has been obtained to support the conclusions reached and for the auditor's report to be issued.**

27. The engagement partner conducts timely reviews at appropriate stages during the engagement. This allows significant matters to be resolved on a timely basis to the engagement partner's satisfaction before the auditor's report is issued. The reviews cover critical areas of judgment, especially those relating to difficult or contentious matters identified during the course of the engagement, significant risks, and other areas the engagement partner considers important. The engagement partner need not review all audit documentation. However, the partner documents the extent and timing of the reviews. Issues arising from the reviews are resolved to the satisfaction of the engagement partner.

28. A new engagement partner taking over an audit during the engagement reviews the work performed to the date of the change. The review procedures are sufficient to satisfy the new engagement partner that the work performed to the date of the review has been planned and performed in accordance with professional standards and regulatory and legal requirements.

29. Where more than one partner is involved in the conduct of an audit engagement, it is important that the responsibilities of the respective partners are clearly defined and understood by the engagement team.

Consultation

30. **The engagement partner should:**

(a) **Be responsible for the engagement team undertaking appropriate consultation on difficult or contentious matters;**

(b) **Be satisfied that members of the engagement team have undertaken appropriate consultation during the course of the engagement, both within the engagement team and between the engagement team and others at the appropriate level within or outside the firm;**

(c) **Be satisfied that the nature and scope of, and conclusions resulting from, such consultations are documented and agreed with the party consulted; and**

(d) **Determine that conclusions resulting from consultations have been implemented.**

31. Effective consultation with other professionals requires that those consulted be given all the relevant facts that will enable them to provide informed advice on technical, ethical or other matters. Where appropriate, the engagement team consults individuals with appropriate knowledge, seniority and experience within the firm or, where applicable, outside the firm. Conclusions resulting from consultations are appropriately documented and implemented.

32. It may be appropriate for the engagement team to consult outside the firm, for example, where the firm lacks appropriate internal resources. They may take advantage of advisory services provided by other firms, professional and regulatory bodies, or commercial organizations that provide relevant quality control services.

33. The documentation of consultations with other professionals that involve difficult or contentious matters is agreed by both the individual seeking consultation and the individual consulted. The documentation is sufficiently complete and detailed to enable an understanding of:

(a) The issue on which consultation was sought; and

(b) The results of the consultation, including any decisions taken, the basis for those decisions and how they were implemented.

Differences of Opinion

34. **Where differences of opinion arise within the engagement team, with those consulted and, where applicable, between the engagement partner and the engagement quality control reviewer, the engagement team should follow the firm's policies and procedures for dealing with and resolving differences of opinion.**

35. As necessary, the engagement partner informs members of the engagement team that they may bring matters involving differences of opinion to the attention of the engagement partner or others within the firm as appropriate without fear of reprisals.

Engagement Quality Control Review

36. **For audits of financial statements of listed entities, the engagement partner should:**

    (a) **Determine that an engagement quality control reviewer has been appointed;**

    (b) **Discuss significant matters arising during the audit engagement, including those identified during the engagement quality control review, with the engagement quality control reviewer; and**

    (c) **Not issue the auditor's report until the completion of the engagement quality control review.**

    For other audit engagements where an engagement quality control review is performed, the engagement partner follows the requirements set out in subparagraphs (a) to (c).

37. Where, at the start of the engagement, an engagement quality control review is not considered necessary, the engagement partner is alert for changes in circumstances that would require such a review.

38. **An engagement quality control review should include an objective evaluation of:**

    (a) **The significant judgments made by the engagement team; and**

    (b) **The conclusions reached in formulating the auditor's report.**

39. An engagement quality control review ordinarily involves discussion with the engagement partner, a review of the financial information and the auditor's report, and, in particular, consideration of whether the auditor's report is appropriate. It also involves a review of selected audit documentation relating to the significant judgments the engagement team made and the conclusions they reached. The extent of the review depends on the complexity of the audit engagement and the risk that the auditor's report might not be appropriate in the circumstances. The review does not reduce the responsibilities of the engagement partner.

40. An engagement quality control review for audits of financial statements of listed entities includes considering the following:

    • The engagement team's evaluation of the firm's independence in relation to the specific audit engagement.

    • Significant risks identified during the engagement (in accordance with ISA (UK and Ireland) 315, "Understanding the Entity and its Environment and Assessing the Risks of Material Misstatement"), and the responses to those risks (in accordance with ISA (UK and Ireland) 320, "Auditor's Procedures in Response to Assessed Risks"), including the engagement team's assessment of, and response to, the risk of fraud.

- Judgments made, particularly with respect to materiality and significant risks.

- Whether appropriate consultation has taken place on matters involving differences of opinion or other difficult or contentious matters, and the conclusions arising from those consultations.

- The significance and disposition of corrected and uncorrected misstatements identified during the audit.

- The matters to be communicated to management and those charged with governance and, where applicable, other parties such as regulatory bodies.

- Whether audit documentation selected for review reflects the work performed in relation to the significant judgments and supports the conclusions reached.

- The appropriateness of the auditor's report to be issued.

Engagement quality control reviews for audits of historical financial information other than audits of financial statements of listed entities may, depending on the circumstances, include some or all of these considerations.

Monitoring

41. ISQC 1 requires the firm to establish policies and procedures designed to provide it with reasonable assurance that the policies and procedures relating to the system of quality control are relevant, adequate, operating effectively and complied with in practice. The engagement partner considers the results of the monitoring process as evidenced in the latest information circulated by the firm and, if applicable, other network firms. The engagement partner considers:

    (a) Whether deficiencies noted in that information may affect the audit engagement; and

    (b) Whether the measures the firm took to rectify the situation are sufficient in the context of that audit.

42. A deficiency in the firm's system of quality control does not indicate that a particular audit engagement was not performed in accordance with professional standards and regulatory and legal requirements, or that the auditor's report was not appropriate.

Effective Date

43. For firms in the UK and Ireland, this ISA (UK and Ireland) is effective for audits of financial statements for periods commencing on or after 15 December 2004. For network firms outside the UK and Ireland, this ISA (UK and Ireland) is effective for audits of financial statements for periods commencing on or after 15 June 2005.

Public Sector Perspective

Additional guidance for auditors of public sector bodies in the UK and Ireland is given in:

- Practice Note 10 "Audit of Financial Statements of Public Sector Bodies in the United Kingdom (Revised)"

- Practice Note 10(I) "Audit of Central Government Financial Statements in the Republic of Ireland (Revised)"

1. *Some of the terms in the ISA (UK and Ireland), such as "engagement partner" and "firm," should be read as referring to their public sector equivalents. However, with limited exceptions, there is no public sector equivalent of "listed entities," although there may be audits of particularly significant public sector entities which should be subject to the listed entity requirements of mandatory rotation of the engagement partner (or equivalent) and engagement quality control review. There are no fixed objective criteria on which this determination of significance should be based. However, such an assessment should encompass an evaluation of all factors relevant to the audited entity. Such factors include size, complexity, commercial risk, parliamentary or media interest and the number and range of stakeholders affected.*

2. *In many jurisdictions there is a single statutorily appointed auditor-general. In such circumstances, where applicable, the engagement reviewer should be selected having regard to the need for independence and objectivity.*

3. *In the public sector, auditors may be appointed in accordance with statutory procedures. Accordingly, certain of the considerations regarding the acceptance and continuance of client relationships and specific engagements, as set out in paragraphs 16-17 of this ISA (UK and Ireland), may not be relevant.*

4. *Similarly, the independence of public sector auditors may be protected by statutory measures. However, public sector auditors or audit firms carrying out public sector audits on behalf of the statutory auditor may, depending on the terms of the mandate in a particular jurisdiction, need to adapt their approach in order to ensure compliance with the spirit of paragraphs 12 and 13. This may include, where the public sector auditor's mandate does not permit withdrawal from the engagement, disclosure through a public report, of circumstances that have arisen that would, if they were in the private sector, lead the auditor to withdraw.*

5. *Paragraph 20 sets out capabilities and competence expected of the engagement team. Additional capabilities may be required in public sector audits, dependent upon the terms of the mandate in a particular jurisdiction. Such additional capabilities may include an understanding of the applicable reporting arrangements, including reporting to parliament or in the public interest. The wider scope of a public sector audit may include, for example, some aspects of performance auditing or a comprehensive assessment of the arrangements for ensuring legality and preventing and detecting fraud and corruption.*

INTERNATIONAL STANDARD ON AUDITING
(UK AND IRELAND) 230*

DOCUMENTATION

CONTENTS

International Standard on Auditing (UK and Ireland) (ISA (UK and Ireland)) 230 "Documentation" should be read in the context of the Auditing Practices Board's Statement "The Auditing Practices Board - Scope and Authority of Pronouncements (Revised)" which sets out the application and authority of ISAs (UK and Ireland).

---

* This ISA (UK and Ireland) is superseded by ISA (UK and Ireland) 230 (Revised) for audits of financial information beginning on or after 15 June 2006.

Introduction

1. The purpose of this International Standard on Auditing (UK and Ireland) (ISA (UK and Ireland)) is to establish standards and provide guidance regarding documentation in the context of the audit of financial statements.

1-1. This ISA (UK and Ireland) uses the terms 'those charged with governance' and 'management'. The term 'governance' describes the role of persons entrusted with the supervision, control and direction of an entity. Ordinarily, those charged with governance are accountable for ensuring that the entity achieves its objectives, and for the quality of its financial reporting and reporting to interested parties. Those charged with governance include management only when they perform such functions.

1-2. In the UK and Ireland, those charged with governance include the directors (executive and non-executive) of a company or other body, the members of an audit committee where one exists, the partners, proprietors, committee of management or trustees of other forms of entity, or equivalent persons responsible for directing the entity's affairs and preparing its financial statements.

1-3. 'Management' comprises those persons who perform senior managerial functions.

1-4. In the UK and Ireland, depending on the nature and circumstances of the entity, management may include some or all of those charged with governance (e.g. executive directors). Management will not normally include non-executive directors.

2. **The auditor should document matters which are important in providing audit evidence to support the auditor's opinion and evidence that the audit was carried out in accordance with ISAs (UK and Ireland).**

3. "Documentation" means the material (working papers) prepared by and for, or obtained and retained by the auditor in connection with the performance of the audit. Working papers may be in the form of data stored on paper, film, electronic media or other media.

4. Working papers:

    (a) Assist in the planning and performance of the audit;

    (b) Assist in the supervision and review of the audit work; and

    (c) Record the audit evidence resulting from the audit work performed to support the auditor's opinion.

Form and Content of Working Papers

5. **The auditor should prepare working papers which are sufficiently complete and detailed to provide an overall understanding of the audit.**

6. **The auditor should record in the working papers information on planning the audit, the nature, timing and extent of the audit procedures performed and the results thereof, and the conclusions drawn from the audit evidence obtained.** Working papers include the auditor's reasoning on all significant matters which require the exercise of judgment, together with the auditor's conclusion thereon. In areas involving difficult questions of principle or judgment, working papers record the relevant facts that were known by the auditor at the time the conclusions were reached.

6-1. **In the UK and Ireland, the auditor should record in the working papers the auditor's reasoning on all significant matters which require the exercise of judgment, and the auditor's conclusions thereon.**

7. The extent of working papers is a matter of professional judgment since it is neither necessary nor practical to document every matter the auditor considers. In assessing the extent of working papers to be prepared and retained, it may be useful for the auditor to consider what would be necessary to provide another auditor who has no previous experience with the audit with an understanding of the work performed and the basis of the principle decisions taken but not the detailed aspects of the audit. That other auditor may only be able to obtain an understanding of detailed aspects of the audit by discussing them with the auditors who prepared the working papers.

8. The form and content of working papers are affected by matters such as the following:

    - Nature of the engagement.

    - Form of the auditor's report.

    - Nature, size and complexity of the business.

    - Nature and complexity of the entity's internal control.

    - Needs in the particular circumstances for direction, supervision and review of work performed by assistants.

    - Specific audit methodology and technology used in the course of the audit.

9. Working papers are designed and organized to meet the circumstances and the auditor's needs for each individual audit. The use of standardized working papers (for example, checklists, specimen letters, standard organization of working papers) may improve the efficiency with which such working papers are prepared and reviewed. They facilitate the delegation of work while providing a means to control its quality.

10. To improve audit efficiency, the auditor may utilize schedules, analyses and other documentation prepared by the entity. In such circumstances, the auditor would need to be satisfied that those materials have been properly prepared.

11. Working papers ordinarily include the following:

- Information obtained in understanding the entity and its environment, including its internal control, such as the following:

  ○ Information concerning the legal and organizational structure of the entity.

  ○ Extracts or copies of important legal documents, agreements and minutes.

  ○ Information concerning the industry, economic environment and legislative environment within which the entity operates.

  ○ Extracts from the entity's internal control manual.

- Evidence of the planning process including audit programs and any changes thereto.

- Evidence of the auditor's consideration of the work of internal auditing and conclusions reached.

- Analyses of transactions and balances.

- Analyses of significant ratios and trends.

- The identified and assessed risks of material misstatements at the financial statement and the assertion level.

- A record of the nature, timing and extent of audit procedures performed in response to risks at the assertion level and the results of such procedures.

- Evidence that the work performed by assistants was supervised and reviewed.

- An indication as to who performed the audit procedures and when they were performed.

- Details of audit procedures applied regarding components whose financial statements are audited by another auditor.

- Copies of communications with other auditors, experts and other third parties.

- Copies of letters or notes concerning audit matters communicated to or discussed with management or those charged with governance, including the terms of the engagement and material weaknesses in internal control.

- Letters of representation received from the entity.

- Conclusions reached by the auditor concerning significant aspects of the audit, including how exceptions and unusual matters, if any, disclosed by the auditor's procedures were resolved or treated.

- Copies of the financial statements and auditor's report.

12. In the case of recurring audits, some working paper files may be classified as "permanent" audit files which are updated with new information of continuing importance, as distinct from current audit files which contain information relating primarily to the audit of a single period.

Confidentiality, Safe Custody, Retention and Ownership of Working Papers

13. **The auditor should adopt appropriate procedures for maintaining the confidentiality and safe custody of the working papers and for retaining them for a period sufficient to meet the needs of the practice and in accordance with legal and professional requirements of record retention.[1]**

14. Working papers are the property of the auditor. Although portions of or extracts from the working papers may be made available to the entity at the discretion of the auditor, they are not a substitute for the entity's accounting records.

Effective Date

14-1. This ISA (UK and Ireland) is effective for audits of financial statements for periods commencing on or after 15 December 2004.

---

[1] In the UK and Republic of Ireland this requirement must be applied having regard to specific requirements of the Audit Regulations.
Audit Regulation 3.08b states that "A Registered Auditor must keep all audit working papers which auditing standards require for a period of at least six years. The period starts with the end of the accounting period to which the papers relate."

INTERNATIONAL STANDARD ON AUDITING (UK AND IRELAND) 230 (REVISED)

AUDIT DOCUMENTATION

(Effective for audits of financial information for periods beginning on or after June 15, 2006)*

CONTENTS

---

* This revised ISA (UK and Ireland) gave rise to amendments to ISA (UK and Ireland) 200, "Objective and General Principles Governing and Audit of Financial Statements," ISA (UK and Ireland) 330, "The Auditor's Procedures in Response to Assessed Risks," and the APB Statement, "The Auditing Practices Board – Scope and Authority of Pronouncements (Revised)." Those amendments are reflected in appendices to those pronouncments and are effective for audits of fiancial statements beginning on or after June 15, 2006. Conforming amendments have also been made to ISQC (UK and Ireland) 1, "Quality Control for Firms that Perform Audits and Reviews of Historical Financial Information and Other Assurance and Related Services Engagements", which required associated changes to systems to be established by June 15, 2006.

International Standard on Auditing (UK and Ireland) (ISA (UK and Ireland)) 230 (Revised), "Audit Documentation," should be read in the context of the Auditing Practices Board's Statement "The Auditing Practices Board - Scope and Authority of Pronouncements (Revised)" which sets out the application and authority of ISAs (UK and Ireland).

Introduction

1. The purpose of this International Standard on Auditing (UK and Ireland) (ISA (UK and Ireland)) is to establish standards and provide guidance on audit documentation. The Appendix lists other ISAs (UK and Ireland) containing subject matter-specific documentation requirements and guidance. Laws or regulations may establish additional documentation requirements.

2. **The auditor should prepare, on a timely basis, audit documentation that provides:**

    (a) **A sufficient and appropriate record of the basis for the auditor's report; and**

    (b) **Evidence that the audit was performed in accordance with ISAs (UK and Ireland) and applicable legal and regulatory requirements.**

3. Preparing sufficient and appropriate audit documentation on a timely basis helps to enhance the quality of the audit and facilitates the effective review and evaluation of the audit evidence obtained and conclusions reached before the auditor's report is finalized. Documentation prepared at the time the work is performed is likely to be more accurate than documentation prepared subsequently.

4. Compliance with the requirements of this ISA (UK and Ireland) together with the specific documentation requirements of other relevant ISAs (UK and Ireland) is ordinarily sufficient to achieve the objectives in paragraph 2.

5. In addition to these objectives, audit documentation serves a number of purposes, including:

    (a) Assisting the audit team to plan and perform the audit;

    (b) Assisting members of the audit team responsible for supervision to direct and supervise the audit work, and to discharge their review responsibilities in accordance with ISA (UK and Ireland) 220, "Quality Control for Audits of Historical Financial Information;"

    (c) Enabling the audit team to be accountable for its work;

    (d) Retaining a record of matters of continuing significance to future audits;

    (e) Enabling an experienced auditor to conduct quality control reviews and inspections[1] in accordance with ISQC (UK and Ireland) 1, "Quality Control for Firms that Perform Audits and Reviews of Historical Financial Information, and Other Assurance and Related Services Engagements;" and

    (f) Enabling an experienced auditor to conduct external inspections in accordance with applicable legal, regulatory or other requirements.

---

[1] As defined in ISA (UK and Ireland) 220.

Definitions

6.   In this ISA (UK and Ireland):

(a)   "Audit documentation" means the record of audit procedures performed,[2] relevant audit evidence obtained, and conclusions the auditor reached (terms such as "working papers" or "workpapers" are also sometimes used); and

(b)   "Experienced auditor" means an individual (whether internal or external to the firm) who has a reasonable understanding of (i) audit processes, (ii) ISAs (UK and Ireland) and applicable legal and regulatory requirements, (iii) the business environment in which the entity operates, and (iv) auditing and financial reporting issues relevant to the entity's industry.

Nature of Audit Documentation

7.   Audit documentation may be recorded on paper or on electronic or other media. It includes, for example, audit programs, analyses, issues memoranda, summaries of significant matters, letters of confirmation and representation, checklists, and correspondence (including e-mail) concerning significant matters. Abstracts or copies of the entity's records, for example, significant and specific contracts and agreements, may be included as part of audit documentation if considered appropriate. Audit documentation, however, is not a substitute for the entity's accounting records. The audit documentation for a specific audit engagement is assembled in an audit file.

8.   The auditor ordinarily excludes from audit documentation superseded drafts of working papers and financial statements, notes that reflect incomplete or preliminary thinking, previous copies of documents corrected for typographical or other errors, and duplicates of documents.

Form, Content and Extent of Audit Documentation

9.   **The auditor should prepare the audit documentation so as to enable an experienced auditor, having no previous connection with the audit, to understand:**

(a)   **The nature, timing, and extent of the audit procedures performed to comply with ISAs (UK and Ireland) and applicable legal and regulatory requirements;**

(b)   **The results of the audit procedures and the audit evidence obtained; and**

(c)   **Significant matters arising during the audit and the conclusions reached thereon.**

---

[2]   Audit procedures performed include audit planning, as addressed in ISA (UK and Ireland) 300, "Planning an Audit of Financial Statements."

10. The form, content and extent of audit documentation depend on factors such as:

   • The nature of the audit procedures to be performed;

   • The identified risks of material misstatement;

   • The extent of judgment required in performing the work and evaluating the results;

   • The significance of the audit evidence obtained;

   • The nature and extent of exceptions identified;

   • The need to document a conclusion or the basis for a conclusion not readily determinable from the documentation of the work performed or audit evidence obtained; and

   • The audit methodology and tools used.

   It is, however, neither necessary nor practicable to document every matter the auditor considers during the audit.

11. Oral explanations by the auditor, on their own, do not represent adequate support for the work the auditor performed or conclusions the auditor reached, but may be used to explain or clarify information contained in the audit documentation.

Documentation of the Identifying Characteristics of Specific Items or Matters Being Tested

12. **In documenting the nature, timing and extent of audit procedures performed, the auditor should record the identifying characteristics of the specific items or matters being tested.**

13. Recording the identifying characteristics serves a number of purposes. For example, it enables the audit team to be accountable for its work and facilitates the investigation of exceptions or inconsistencies. Identifying characteristics will vary with the nature of the audit procedure and the item or matter being tested. For example:

   • For a detailed test of entity-generated purchase orders, the auditor may identify the documents selected for testing by their dates and unique purchase order numbers.

   • For a procedure requiring selection or review of all items over a specific amount from a given population, the auditor may record the scope of the procedure and identify the population (for example, all journal entries over a specified amount from the journal register).

   • For a procedure requiring systematic sampling from a population of documents, the auditor may identify the documents selected by recording their source, the starting point and the sampling interval (for example, a systematic sample of shipping reports selected from the shipping log for the period from April 1 to September 30, starting with report number 12345 and selecting every 125th report).

- For a procedure requiring inquiries of specific entity personnel, the auditor may record the dates of the inquiries and the names and job designations of the entity personnel.

- For an observation procedure, the auditor may record the process or subject matter being observed, the relevant individuals, their respective responsibilities, and where and when the observation was carried out.

Significant Matters

14. Judging the significance of a matter requires an objective analysis of the facts and circumstances. Significant matters include, amongst others:

- Matters that give rise to significant risks (as defined in ISA (UK and Ireland) 315, "Understanding the Entity and its Environment and Assessing the Risks of Material Misstatement").

- Results of audit procedures indicating (a) that the financial information could be materially misstated, or (b) a need to revise the auditor's previous assessment of the risks of material misstatement and the auditor's responses to those risks.

- Circumstances that cause the auditor significant difficulty in applying necessary audit procedures.

- Findings that could result in a modification to the auditor's report.

15. The auditor may consider it helpful to prepare and retain as part of the audit documentation a summary (sometimes known as a completion memorandum) that describes the significant matters identified during the audit and how they were addressed, or that includes cross-references to other relevant supporting audit documentation that provides such information. Such a summary may facilitate effective and efficient reviews and inspections of the audit documentation, particularly for large and complex audits. Further, the preparation of such a summary may assist the auditor's consideration of the significant matters.

16. **The auditor should document discussions of significant matters with management and others on a timely basis.**

17. The audit documentation includes records of the significant matters discussed, and when and with whom the discussions took place. It is not limited to records prepared by the auditor but may include other appropriate records such as agreed minutes of meetings prepared by the entity's personnel. Others with whom the auditor may discuss significant matters include those charged with governance, other personnel within the entity, and external parties, such as persons providing professional advice to the entity.

18. **If the auditor has identified information that contradicts or is inconsistent with the auditor's final conclusion regarding a significant matter, the auditor should document how the auditor addressed the contradiction or inconsistency in forming the final conclusion.**

19. The documentation of how the auditor addressed the contradiction or inconsistency, however, does not imply that the auditor needs to retain documentation that is incorrect or superseded.

Documentation of Departures from Basic Principles or Essential Procedures

20. The basic principles and essential procedures in ISAs (UK and Ireland) are designed to assist the auditor in meeting the overall objective of the audit. Accordingly, other than in exceptional circumstances, the auditor complies with each basic principle and essential procedure that is relevant in the circumstances of the audit.

21. **Where, in exceptional circumstances, the auditor judges it necessary to depart from a basic principle or an essential procedure that is relevant in the circumstances of the audit, the auditor should document how the alternative audit procedures performed achieve the objective of the audit, and, unless otherwise clear, the reasons for the departure.** This involves the auditor documenting how the alternative audit procedures performed were sufficient and appropriate to replace that basic principle or essential procedure.

22. The documentation requirement does not apply to basic principles and essential procedures that are not relevant in the circumstances, i.e., where the circumstances envisaged in the specified basic principle or essential procedure do not apply. For example, in a continuing engagement, nothing in ISA (UK and Ireland) 510, "Initial Engagements—Opening Balances and Continuing Engagements–Opening Balances," related to intial engagements is relevant. Similarly, if an ISA (UK and Ireland) includes conditional requirements, they are not relevant if the specified conditions do not exist (for example, the requirement to modify the auditor's report where there is a limitation of scope).

Identification of Preparer and Reviewer

23. **In documenting the nature, timing and extent of audit procedures performed, the auditor should record:**

    (a) **Who performed the audit work and the date such work was completed; and**

    (b) **Who reviewed the audit work performed and the date and extent of such review.[3]**

24. The requirement to document who reviewed the audit work performed does not imply a need for each specific working paper to include evidence of review. The audit

---

[3] Paragraph 26 of ISA (UK and Ireland) 220 establishes the requirement for the auditor to review the audit work performed through review of the audit documentation, which involves the auditor documenting the extent and timing of the reviews. Paragraph 25 of ISA (UK and Ireland) 220 describes the nature of a review of work performed.

documentation, however, evidences who reviewed specified elements of the audit work performed and when.

Assembly of the Final Audit File

25. **The auditor should complete the assembly of the final audit file on a timely basis after the date of the auditor's report.**

26. ISQC (UK and Ireland) 1 requires firms to establish policies and procedures for the timely completion of the assembly of audit files. As ISQC (UK and Ireland) 1 indicates, 60 days after the date of the auditor's report is ordinarily an appropriate time limit within which to complete the assembly of the final audit file.

27. The completion of the assembly of the final audit file after the date of the auditor's report is an administrative process that does not involve the performance of new audit procedures or the drawing of new conclusions. Changes may, however, be made to the audit documentation during the final assembly process if they are administrative in nature. Examples of such changes include:

    - Deleting or discarding superseded documentation.

    - Sorting, collating and cross-referencing working papers.

    - Signing off on completion checklists relating to the file assembly process.

    - Documenting audit evidence that the auditor has obtained, discussed and agreed with the relevant members of the audit team before the date of the auditor's report.

28. **After the assembly of the final audit file has been completed, the auditor should not delete or discard audit documentation before the end of its retention period.**

29. ISQC (UK and Ireland) 1 requires firms to establish policies and procedures for the retention of engagement documentation. As ISQC (UK and Ireland) 1 indicates, the retention period for audit engagements ordinarily is no shorter than five years from the date of the auditor's report, or, if later, the date of the group auditor's report[3a].

3a In the UK and Republic of Ireland this requirement is applied having regard to specific requirements of the Audit Regulations.
Audit Regulation 3.08b states that "A Registered Auditor must keep all audit working papers which auditing standards require for a period of at least six years. The period starts with the end of the accounting period to which the papers relate."
Audit Regulation 7.06 states that "In carrying out its responsibilities under regulation 7.03, the Registration Committee, any sub-committee, the secretariat, or a monitoring unit may, to the extent necessary for the review of a firm's audit work or how it is complying or intends to comply with these regulations, require a Registered Auditor or an applicant for registration to provide any information, held in whatsoever form (including electronic), about the firm or its clients and to allow access to the firm's systems and personnel."
The Audit Regulations referred to above were originally published in December 1995 and updated in June 2005 (Audit News 40).

30. When the auditor finds it necessary to modify existing audit documentation or add new audit documentation after the assembly of the final audit file has been completed, the auditor should, regardless of the nature of the modifications or additions, document:

   (a)   When and by whom they were made, and (where applicable) reviewed;

   (b)   The specific reasons for making them; and

   (c)   Their effect, if any, on the auditor's conclusions.

Changes to Audit Documentation in Exceptional Circumstances after the Date of the Auditor's Report

31. When exceptional circumstances arise after the date of the auditor's report that require the auditor to perform new or additional audit procedures or that lead the auditor to reach new conclusions, the auditor should document:

   (a)   The circumstances encountered;

   (b)   The new or additional audit procedures performed, audit evidence obtained, and conclusions reached; and

   (c)   When and by whom the resulting changes to audit documentation were made, and (where applicable) reviewed.

32. Such exceptional circumstances include the discovery of facts regarding the audited financial information that existed at the date of the auditor's report that might have affected the auditor's report had the auditor then been aware of them.

Effective Date

33. This ISA (UK and Ireland) is effective for audits of financial information for periods beginning on or after June 15, 2006.

Appendix

Specific Audit Documentation Requirements and Guidance in Other ISAs (UK and Ireland)

The following lists the main paragraphs that contain specific documentation requirements and guidance in other ISAs (UK and Ireland):

- ISA (UK and Ireland) 210, "Terms of Audit Engagements"–Paragraph 5 –5-2;

- ISA (UK and Ireland) 220, "Quality Control for Audits of Historical Financial Information"–Paragraphs 11–14, 16, 25, 27, 30, 31 and 33;

- ISA (UK and Ireland) 240, "The Auditor's Responsibility to Consider Fraud in an Audit of Financial Statements"–Paragraphs 60 and 107–111;

- ISA (UK and Ireland) 250, Section A "Consideration of Laws and Regulations"– Paragraph 28; Section B "The Auditor's Right and Duty to Report to Regulators in the Financial Sector"-Paragraph 46;

- ISA (UK and Ireland) 260, "Communication of Audit Matters with Those Charged with Governance"–Paragraph 16;

- ISA (UK and Ireland) 300, "Planning an Audit of Financial Statements"–Paragraphs 22-26;

- ISA (Ireland) 315, "Understanding the Entity and its Environment and Assessing the Risks of Material Misstatement"–Paragraphs 122 and 123;

- ISA (UK and Ireland) 330, "The Auditor's Procedures in Response to Assessed Risks"–Paragraphs 73 and 74;

- ISA (UK and Ireland) 402, "Audit Considerations in Relation to Entities using Service Organizations" – Paragraphs 5-3 and 9-13;

- ISA (UK and Ireland) 505, "External Confirmations"–Paragraph 33;

- ISA (UK and Ireland) 570, "Going Concern" – Paragraph 30-1;

- ISA (UK and Ireland) 580, "Management Representations"–Paragraph 10; and

- ISA (UK and Ireland) 600, "Using the Work of Another Auditor"–Paragraph 14.

INTERNATIONAL STANDARD ON AUDITING
(UK AND IRELAND) 240

THE AUDITOR'S RESPONSIBILITY TO CONSIDER FRAUD IN AN AUDIT OF FINANCIAL STATEMENTS

CONTENTS

International Standard on Auditing (UK and Ireland) (ISA (UK and Ireland)) 240 "The Auditor's Responsibility to Consider Fraud in an Audit of Financial Statements" should be read in the context of the Auditing Practices Board's Statement "The Auditing Practices Board - Scope and Authority of Pronouncements (Revised)" which sets out the application and authority of ISAs (UK and Ireland).

Introduction

1. The purpose of this International Standard on Auditing (UK and Ireland) (ISA (UK and Ireland)) is to establish standards and provide guidance on the auditor's responsibility to consider fraud in an audit of financial statements[1] and expand on how the standards and guidance in ISA (UK and Ireland) 315, "Understanding the Entity and its Environment and Assessing the Risks of Material Misstatement" and ISA (UK and Ireland) 330, "The Auditor's Procedures in Response to Assessed Risks" are to be applied in relation to the risks of material misstatement due to fraud. The standards and guidance in this ISA (UK and Ireland) are intended to be integrated into the overall audit process.

1-1. This ISA (UK and Ireland) uses the terms 'those charged with governance' and 'management'. The term 'governance' describes the role of persons entrusted with the supervision, control and direction of an entity. Ordinarily, those charged with governance are accountable for ensuring that the entity achieves its objectives, and for the quality of its financial reporting and reporting to interested parties. Those charged with governance include management only when they perform such functions.

1-2. In the UK and Ireland, those charged with governance include the directors (executive and non-executive) of a company or other body, the members of an audit committee where one exists, the partners, proprietors, committee of management or trustees of other forms of entity, or equivalent persons responsible for directing the entity's affairs and preparing its financial statements.

1-3. 'Management' comprises those persons who perform senior managerial functions.

1-4. In the UK and Ireland, depending on the nature and circumstances of the entity, management may include some or all of those charged with governance (e.g. executive directors). Management will not normally include non-executive directors.

2. This standard:

    *   Distinguishes fraud from error and describes the two types of fraud that are relevant to the auditor, that is, misstatements resulting from misappropriation of assets and misstatements resulting from fraudulent financial reporting; describes the respective responsibilities of those charged with governance and the management of the entity for the prevention and detection of fraud, describes the inherent limitations of an audit in the context of fraud, and sets out the responsibilities of the auditor for detecting material misstatements due to fraud;

    *   Requires the auditor to maintain an attitude of professional skepticism recognizing the possibility that a material misstatement due to fraud could exist,

---

[1] The auditor's responsibility to consider laws and regulations in an audit of financial statements is established in ISA (UK and Ireland) 250, "Consideration of Laws and Regulations."

notwithstanding the auditor's past experience with the entity about the honesty and integrity of management and those charged with governance;

- Requires members of the engagement team to discuss the susceptibility of the entity's financial statements to material misstatement due to fraud and requires the engagement partner to consider which matters are to be communicated to members of the engagement team not involved in the discussion;

- Requires the auditor to:

  o Perform procedures to obtain information that is used to identify the risks of material misstatement due to fraud;

  o Identify and assess the risks of material misstatement due to fraud at the financial statement level and the assertion level; and for those assessed risks that could result in a material misstatement due to fraud, evaluate the design of the entity's related controls, including relevant control activities, and to determine whether they have been implemented;

  o Determine overall responses to address the risks of material misstatement due to fraud at the financial statement level and consider the assignment and supervision of personnel; consider the accounting policies used by the entity and incorporate an element of unpredictability in the selection of the nature, timing and extent of the audit procedures to be performed;

  o Design and perform audit procedures to respond to the risk of management override of controls;

  o Determine responses to address the assessed risks of material misstatement due to fraud;

  o Consider whether an identified misstatement may be indicative of fraud;

  o Obtain written representations from management[1a] relating to fraud; and

  o Communicate with management and those charged with governance;

- Provides guidance on communications with regulatory and enforcement authorities;

- Provides guidance if, as a result of a misstatement resulting from fraud or suspected fraud, the auditor encounters exceptional circumstances that bring into question the auditor's ability to continue performing the audit; and

- Establishes documentation requirements.

[1a] In the UK and Ireland, the auditor obtains written representations from those charged with governance.

3.   **In planning and performing the audit to reduce audit risk to an acceptably low level, the auditor should consider the risks of material misstatements in the financial statements due to fraud.**

Characteristics of Fraud

4.   Misstatements in the financial statements can arise from fraud or error. The distinguishing factor between fraud and error is whether the underlying action that results in the misstatement of the financial statements is intentional or unintentional.

5.   The term "error" refers to an unintentional misstatement in financial statements, including the omission of an amount or a disclosure, such as the following:

   •   A mistake in gathering or processing data from which financial statements are prepared.

   •   An incorrect accounting estimate arising from oversight or misinterpretation of facts.

   •   A mistake in the application of accounting principles relating to measurement, recognition, classification, presentation or disclosure.

6.   The term "fraud" refers to an intentional act by one or more individuals among management, those charged with governance, employees, or third parties, involving the use of deception to obtain an unjust or illegal advantage. Although fraud is a broad legal concept, for the purposes of this ISA (UK and Ireland), the auditor is concerned with fraud that causes a material misstatement in the financial statements. Auditors do not make legal determinations of whether fraud has actually occurred. Fraud involving one or more members of management or those charged with governance is referred to as "management fraud;" fraud involving only employees of the entity is referred to as "employee fraud." In either case, there may be collusion within the entity or with third parties outside of the entity.

7.   Two types of intentional misstatements are relevant to the auditor, that is, misstatements resulting from fraudulent financial reporting and misstatements resulting from misappropriation of assets.

8.   Fraudulent financial reporting involves intentional misstatements including omissions of amounts or disclosures in financial statements to deceive financial statement users. Fraudulent financial reporting may be accomplished by the following:

   •   Manipulation, falsification (including forgery), or alteration of accounting records or supporting documentation from which the financial statements are prepared.

   •   Misrepresentation in, or intentional omission from, the financial statements of events, transactions or other significant information.

- Intentional misapplication of accounting principles relating to amounts, classification, manner of presentation, or disclosure.

9. Fraudulent financial reporting often involves management override of controls that otherwise may appear to be operating effectively. Fraud can be committed by management overriding controls using such techniques as:

- Recording fictitious journal entries, particularly close to the end of an accounting period, to manipulate operating results or achieve other objectives;

- Inappropriately adjusting assumptions and changing judgments used to estimate account balances;

- Omitting, advancing or delaying recognition in the financial statements of events and transactions that have occurred during the reporting period;

- Concealing, or not disclosing, facts that could affect the amounts recorded in the financial statements;

- Engaging in complex transactions that are structured to misrepresent the financial position or financial performance of the entity; and

- Altering records and terms related to significant and unusual transactions.

10. Fraudulent financial reporting can be caused by the efforts of management to manage earnings in order to deceive financial statement users by influencing their perceptions as to the entity's performance and profitability. Such earnings management may start out with small actions or inappropriate adjustment of assumptions and changes in judgments by management. Pressures and incentives may lead these actions to increase to the extent that they result in fraudulent financial reporting. Such a situation could occur when, due to pressures to meet market expectations or a desire to maximize compensation based on performance, management intentionally takes positions that lead to fraudulent financial reporting by materially misstating the financial statements. In some other entities, management may be motivated to reduce earnings by a material amount to minimize tax or to inflate earnings to secure bank financing.

11. Misappropriation of assets involves the theft of an entity's assets and is often perpetrated by employees in relatively small and immaterial amounts. However, it can also involve management who are usually more able to disguise or conceal misappropriations in ways that are difficult to detect. Misappropriation of assets can be accomplished in a variety of ways including:

- Embezzling receipts (for example, misappropriating collections on accounts receivable or diverting receipts in respect of written-off accounts to personal bank accounts);

- Stealing physical assets or intellectual property (for example, stealing inventory for personal use or for sale, stealing scrap for resale, colluding with a competitor by disclosing technological data in return for payment);

- Causing an entity to pay for goods and services not received (for example, payments to fictitious vendors, kickbacks paid by vendors to the entity's purchasing agents in return for inflating prices, payments to fictitious employees); and

- Using an entity's assets for personal use (for example, using the entity's assets as collateral for a personal loan or a loan to a related party).

Misappropriation of assets is often accompanied by false or misleading records or documents in order to conceal the fact that the assets are missing or have been pledged without proper authorization.

12. Fraud involves incentive or pressure to commit fraud, a perceived opportunity to do so and some rationalization of the act. Individuals may have an incentive to misappropriate assets for example, because the individuals are living beyond their means. Fraudulent financial reporting may be committed because management is under pressure, from sources outside or inside the entity, to achieve an expected (and perhaps unrealistic) earnings target – particularly since the consequences to management for failing to meet financial goals can be significant. A perceived opportunity for fraudulent financial reporting or misappropriation of assets may exist when an individual believes internal control can be overridden, for example, because the individual is in a position of trust or has knowledge of specific weaknesses in internal control. Individuals may be able to rationalize committing a fraudulent act. Some individuals possess an attitude, character or set of ethical values that allow them knowingly and intentionally to commit a dishonest act. However, even otherwise honest individuals can commit fraud in an environment that imposes sufficient pressure on them.

Responsibilities of Those Charged With Governance and of Management

13. The primary responsibility for the prevention and detection of fraud rests with both those charged with governance of the entity and with management. The respective responsibilities of those charged with governance and of management may vary by entity and from country to country. In some entities, the governance structure may be more informal as those charged with governance may be the same individuals as management of the entity.

14. It is important that management, with the oversight of those charged with governance, place a strong emphasis on fraud prevention, which may reduce opportunities for fraud to take place, and fraud deterrence, which could persuade individuals not to commit fraud because of the likelihood of detection and punishment. This involves a culture of honesty and ethical behavior. Such a culture, based on a strong set of core values, is communicated and demonstrated by management and by those charged

with governance and provides the foundation for employees as to how the entity conducts its business. Creating a culture of honesty and ethical behavior includes setting the proper tone; creating a positive workplace environment; hiring, training and promoting appropriate employees; requiring periodic confirmation by employees of their responsibilities and taking appropriate action in response to actual, suspected or alleged fraud.

15. It is the responsibility of those charged with governance of the entity to ensure, through oversight of management, that the entity establishes and maintains internal control to provide reasonable assurance with regard to reliability of financial reporting, effectiveness and efficiency of operations and compliance with applicable laws and regulations. Active oversight by those charged with governance can help reinforce management's commitment to create a culture of honesty and ethical behavior. In exercising oversight responsibility, those charged with governance consider the potential for management override of controls or other inappropriate influence over the financial reporting process, such as efforts by management to manage earnings in order to influence the perceptions of analysts as to the entity's performance and profitability.

16. It is the responsibility of management, with oversight from those charged with governance, to establish a control environment and maintain policies and procedures to assist in achieving the objective of ensuring, as far as possible, the orderly and efficient conduct of the entity's business. This responsibility includes establishing and maintaining controls pertaining to the entity's objective of preparing financial statements that give a true and fair view (or are presented fairly in all material respects) in accordance with the applicable financial reporting framework and managing risks that may give rise to material misstatements in those financial statements. Such controls reduce but do not eliminate the risks of misstatement. In determining which controls to implement to prevent and detect fraud, management considers the risks that the financial statements may be materially misstated as a result of fraud. As part of this consideration, management may conclude that it is not cost effective to implement and maintain a particular control in relation to the reduction in the risks of material misstatement due to fraud to be achieved.

Inherent Limitations of an Audit in the Context of Fraud

17. As described in ISA (UK and Ireland) 200, "Objective and General Principles Governing an Audit of Financial Statements," the objective of an audit of financial statements is to enable the auditor to express an opinion whether the financial statements are prepared, in all material respects, in accordance with an applicable financial reporting framework. Owing to the inherent limitations of an audit, there is an unavoidable risk that some material misstatements of the financial statements will not be detected, even though the audit is properly planned and performed in accordance with ISAs (UK and Ireland).

18. The risk of not detecting a material misstatement resulting from fraud is higher than the risk of not detecting a material misstatement resulting from error because fraud may involve sophisticated and carefully organized schemes designed to conceal it, such as

forgery, deliberate failure to record transactions, or intentional misrepresentations being made to the auditor. Such attempts at concealment may be even more difficult to detect when accompanied by collusion. Collusion may cause the auditor to believe that audit evidence is persuasive when it is, in fact, false. The auditor's ability to detect a fraud depends on factors such as the skillfulness of the perpetrator, the frequency and extent of manipulation, the degree of collusion involved, the relative size of individual amounts manipulated, and the seniority of those individuals involved. While the auditor may be able to identify potential opportunities for fraud to be perpetrated, it is difficult for the auditor to determine whether misstatements in judgment areas such as accounting estimates are caused by fraud or error.

19. Furthermore, the risk of the auditor not detecting a material misstatement resulting from management fraud is greater than for employee fraud, because management is frequently in a position to directly or indirectly manipulate accounting records and present fraudulent financial information. Certain levels of management may be in a position to override control procedures designed to prevent similar frauds by other employees, for example, by directing subordinates to record transactions incorrectly or to conceal them. Given its position of authority within an entity, management has the ability to either direct employees to do something or solicit their help to assist in carrying out a fraud, with or without the employees' knowledge.

20. The subsequent discovery of a material misstatement of the financial statements resulting from fraud does not, in and of itself, indicate a failure to comply with ISAs (UK and Ireland). This is particularly the case for certain kinds of intentional misstatements, since audit procedures may be ineffective for detecting an intentional misstatement that is concealed through collusion between or among one or more individuals among management, those charged with governance, employees, or third parties, or that involves falsified documentation. Whether the auditor has performed an audit in accordance with ISAs (UK and Ireland) is determined by the audit procedures performed in the circumstances, the sufficiency and appropriateness of the audit evidence obtained as a result thereof and the suitability of the auditor's report based on an evaluation of that evidence.

Responsibilities of the Auditor for Detecting Material Misstatement Due to Fraud

21. An auditor conducting an audit in accordance with ISAs (UK and Ireland) obtains reasonable assurance that the financial statements taken as a whole are free from material misstatement, whether caused by fraud or error. An auditor cannot obtain absolute assurance that material misstatements in the financial statements will be detected because of such factors as the use of judgment, the use of testing, the inherent limitations of internal control and the fact that much of the audit evidence available to the auditor is persuasive rather than conclusive in nature.

22. When obtaining reasonable assurance, an auditor maintains an attitude of professional skepticism throughout the audit, considers the potential for management override of controls and recognizes the fact that audit procedures that are effective for detecting error may not be appropriate in the context of an identified risk of material

misstatement due to fraud. The remainder of this ISA (UK and Ireland) provides additional guidance on considering the risks of fraud in an audit and designing procedures to detect material misstatements due to fraud.

Professional Skepticism

23. As required by ISA (UK and Ireland) 200, the auditor plans and performs an audit with an attitude of professional skepticism recognizing that circumstances may exist that cause the financial statements to be materially misstated. Due to the characteristics of fraud, the auditor's attitude of professional skepticism is particularly important when considering the risks of material misstatement due to fraud. Professional skepticism is an attitude that includes a questioning mind and a critical assessment of audit evidence. Professional skepticism requires an ongoing questioning of whether the information and audit evidence obtained suggests that a material misstatement due to fraud may exist.

24. **The auditor should maintain an attitude of professional skepticism throughout the audit, recognizing the possibility that a material misstatement due to fraud could exist, notwithstanding the auditor's past experience with the entity about the honesty and integrity of management and those charged with governance.**

25. As discussed in ISA (UK and Ireland) 315, the auditor's previous experience with the entity contributes to an understanding of the entity. However, although the auditor cannot be expected to fully disregard past experience with the entity about the honesty and integrity of management and those charged with governance, the maintenance of an attitude of professional skepticism is important because there may have been changes in circumstances. When making inquiries and performing other audit procedures, the auditor exercises professional skepticism and is not satisfied with less-than-persuasive audit evidence based on a belief that management and those charged with governance are honest and have integrity. With respect to those charged with governance, maintaining an attitude of professional skepticism means that the auditor carefully considers the reasonableness of responses to inquiries of those charged with governance, and other information obtained from them, in light of all other evidence obtained during the audit.

26. An audit performed in accordance with ISAs (UK and Ireland) rarely involves the authentication of documents, nor is the auditor trained as or expected to be an expert in such authentication. Furthermore, an auditor may not discover the existence of a modification to the terms contained in a document, for example through a side agreement that management or a third party has not disclosed to the auditor. During the audit, the auditor considers the reliability of the information to be used as audit evidence including consideration of controls over its preparation and maintenance where relevant. Unless the auditor has reason to believe the contrary, the auditor ordinarily accepts records and documents as genuine. However, if conditions identified during the audit cause the auditor to believe that a document may not be authentic or that terms in a document have been modified, the auditor investigates further, for example confirming directly with the third party or considering using the work of an expert to assess the document's authenticity.

Discussion Among the Engagement Team

27. **Members of the engagement team should discuss the susceptibility of the entity's financial statements to material misstatement due to fraud.**

28. ISA (UK and Ireland) 315 requires members of the engagement team to discuss the susceptibility of the entity to material misstatement of the financial statements. This discussion places particular emphasis on the susceptibility of the entity's financial statements to material misstatement due to fraud. The discussion includes the engagement partner who uses professional judgment, prior experience with the entity and knowledge of current developments to determine which other members of the engagement team are included in the discussion. Ordinarily, the discussion involves the key members of the engagement team. The discussion provides an opportunity for more experienced engagement team members to share their insights about how and where the financial statements may be susceptible to material misstatement due to fraud.

29. **The engagement partner should consider which matters are to be communicated to members of the engagement team not involved in the discussion.** All of the members of the engagement team do not necessarily need to be informed of all of the decisions reached in the discussion. For example, a member of the engagement team involved in audit of a component of the entity may not need to know the decisions reached regarding another component of the entity.

30. The discussion occurs with a questioning mind setting aside any beliefs that the engagement team members may have that management and those charged with governance are honest and have integrity. The discussion ordinarily includes:

    • An exchange of ideas among engagement team members about how and where they believe the entity's financial statements may be susceptible to material misstatement due to fraud, how management could perpetrate and conceal fraudulent financial reporting, and how assets of the entity could be misappropriated;

    • A consideration of circumstances that might be indicative of earnings management and the practices that might be followed by management to manage earnings that could lead to fraudulent financial reporting;

    • A consideration of the known external and internal factors affecting the entity that may create an incentive or pressure for management or others to commit fraud, provide the opportunity for fraud to be perpetrated, and indicate a culture or environment that enables management or others to rationalize committing fraud;

    • A consideration of management's involvement in overseeing employees with access to cash or other assets susceptible to misappropriation;

    • A consideration of any unusual or unexplained changes in behavior or lifestyle of management or employees which have come to the attention of the engagement team;

- An emphasis on the importance of maintaining a proper state of mind throughout the audit regarding the potential for material misstatement due to fraud;

- A consideration of the types of circumstances that, if encountered, might indicate the possibility of fraud;

- A consideration of how an element of unpredictability will be incorporated into the nature, timing and extent of the audit procedures to be performed;

- A consideration of the audit procedures that might be selected to respond to the susceptibility of the entity's financial statement to material misstatements due to fraud and whether certain types of audit procedures are more effective than others;

- A consideration of any allegations of fraud that have come to the auditor's attention; and

- A consideration of the risk of management override of controls.

31. Discussing the susceptibility of the entity's financial statements to material misstatement due to fraud is an important part of the audit. It enables the auditor to consider an appropriate response to the susceptibility of the entity's financial statements to material misstatement due to fraud and to determine which members of the engagement team will conduct certain audit procedures. It also permits the auditor to determine how the results of audit procedures will be shared among the engagement team and how to deal with any allegations of fraud that may come to the auditor's attention. Many small audits are carried out entirely by the engagement partner (who may be a sole practitioner). In such situations, the engagement partner, having personally conducted the planning of the audit, considers the susceptibility of the entity's financial statements to material misstatement due to fraud.

32. It is important that after the initial discussion while planning the audit, and also at intervals throughout the audit, engagement team members continue to communicate and share information obtained that may affect the assessment of risks of material misstatement due to fraud or the audit procedures performed to address these risks. For example, for some entities it may be appropriate to update the discussion when reviewing the entity's interim financial information.

Risk Assessment Procedures

33. As required by ISA (UK and Ireland) 315, to obtain an understanding of the entity and its environment, including its internal control, the auditor performs risk assessment procedures. As part of this work the auditor performs the following procedures to obtain information that is used to identify the risks of material misstatement due to fraud:

    (a) Makes inquiries of management, of those charged with governance, and of others within the entity as appropriate and obtains an understanding of how those charged with governance exercise oversight of management's processes for identifying and responding to the risks of fraud and the internal control that management has established to mitigate these risks.

(b) Considers whether one or more fraud risk factors are present.

(c) Considers any unusual or unexpected relationships that have been identified in performing analytical procedures.

(d) Considers other information that may be helpful in identifying the risks of material misstatement due to fraud.

Inquiries and Obtaining an Understanding of Oversight Exercised by Those Charged With Governance

34. **When obtaining an understanding of the entity and its environment, including its internal control, the auditor should make inquiries of management regarding:**

    (a) **Management's assessment of the risk that the financial statements may be materially misstated due to fraud;**

    (b) **Management's process for identifying and responding to the risks of fraud in the entity, including any specific risks of fraud that management has identified or account balances, classes of transactions or disclosures for which a risk of fraud is likely to exist;**

    (c) **Management's communication, if any, to those charged with governance regarding its processes for identifying and responding to the risks of fraud in the entity; and**

    (d) **Management's communication, if any, to employees regarding its views on business practices and ethical behavior.**

35. As management[1b] is responsible for the entity's internal control and for the preparation of the financial statements, it is appropriate for the auditor to make inquiries of management regarding management's own assessment of the risk of fraud and the controls in place to prevent and detect it. The nature, extent and frequency of management's assessment of such risk and controls vary from entity to entity. In some entities, management may make detailed assessments on an annual basis or as part of continuous monitoring. In other entities, management's assessment may be less formal and less frequent. In some entities, particularly smaller entities, the focus of the assessment may be on the risks of employee fraud or misappropriation of assets. The nature, extent and frequency of management's assessment are relevant to the auditor's understanding of the entity's control environment. For example, the fact that management has not made an assessment of the risk of fraud may in some

---

[1b] In the UK and Ireland, those charged with governance are responsible for the preparation of the financial statements.

circumstances be indicative of the lack of importance that management places on internal control.

36. In a small owner managed entity, the owner-manager may be able to exercise more effective oversight than in a larger entity, thereby compensating for the generally more limited opportunities for segregation of duties. On the other hand, the owner-manager may be more able to override controls because of the informal system of internal control. This is taken into account by the auditor when identifying the risks of material misstatement due to fraud.

37. When making inquiries as part of obtaining an understanding of management's process for identifying and responding to the risks of fraud in the entity, the auditor inquires about the process to respond to internal or external allegations of fraud affecting the entity. For entities with multiple locations, the auditor inquires about the nature and extent of monitoring of operating locations or business segments and whether there are particular operating locations or business segments for which a risk of fraud may be more likely to exist.

38. **The auditor should make inquiries of management, internal audit, and others within the entity as appropriate, to determine whether they have knowledge of any actual, suspected or alleged fraud affecting the entity.**

39. Although the auditor's inquiries of management may provide useful information concerning the risks of material misstatements in the financial statements resulting from employee fraud, such inquiries are unlikely to provide useful information regarding the risks of material misstatement in the financial statements resulting from management fraud. Making inquiries of others within the entity, in addition to management, may be useful in providing the auditor with a perspective that is different from management and those responsible for the financial reporting process. Such inquiries may provide individuals with an opportunity to convey information to the auditor that may not otherwise be communicated. The auditor uses professional judgment in determining those others within the entity to whom inquiries are directed and the extent of such inquiries. In making this determination the auditor considers whether others within the entity may be able to provide information that will be helpful to the auditor in identifying the risks of material misstatement due to fraud.

40. The auditor makes inquiries of internal audit personnel, for those entities that have an internal audit function. The inquiries address the views of the internal auditors regarding the risks of fraud, whether during the year the internal auditors have performed any procedures to detect fraud, whether management has satisfactorily responded to any findings resulting from these procedures, and whether the internal auditors have knowledge of any actual, suspected or alleged fraud.

41. Examples of others within the entity to whom the auditor may direct inquiries about the existence or suspicion of fraud include:

- Operating personnel not directly involved in the financial reporting process;

- Employees with different levels of authority;

**THE AUDITING
PRACTICES BOARD**

- Employees involved in initiating, processing or recording complex or unusual transactions and those who supervise or monitor such employees;

- In-house legal counsel;

- Chief ethics officer or equivalent person; and

- The person or persons charged with dealing with allegations of fraud.

42. When evaluating management's responses to inquiries, the auditor maintains an attitude of professional skepticism recognizing that management is often in the best position to perpetrate fraud. Therefore, the auditor uses professional judgment in deciding when it is necessary to corroborate responses to inquiries with other information. When responses to inquiries are inconsistent, the auditor seeks to resolve the inconsistencies.

43. **The auditor should obtain an understanding of how those charged with governance exercise oversight of management's processes for identifying and responding to the risks of fraud in the entity and the internal control that management has established to mitigate these risks.**

44. Those charged with governance of an entity have oversight responsibility for systems for monitoring risk, financial control and compliance with the law. In many countries, corporate governance practices are well developed and those charged with governance play an active role in oversight of the entity's assessment of the risks of fraud and of the internal control the entity has established to mitigate specific risks of fraud that the entity has identified. Since the responsibilities of those charged with governance and management may vary by entity and by country, it is important that the auditor understands their respective responsibilities to enable the auditor to obtain an understanding of the oversight exercised by the appropriate individuals.[2] Those charged with governance include management when management performs such functions, such as may be the case in smaller entities.

45. Obtaining an understanding of how those charged with governance exercise oversight of management's processes for identifying and responding to the risks of fraud in the entity, and the internal control that management has established to mitigate these risks, may provide insights regarding the susceptibility of the entity to management fraud, the adequacy of such internal control and the competence and integrity of management. The auditor may obtain this understanding by performing procedures such as attending meetings where such discussions take place, reading the minutes from such meetings or by making inquiries of those charged with governance.

46. **The auditor should make inquiries of those charged with governance to determine whether they have knowledge of any actual, suspected or alleged fraud affecting the entity.**

---

[2] ISA (UK and Ireland) 260, "Communication of Audit Matters With Those Charged With Governance," paragraph 8, discusses with whom the auditor communicates when the entity's governance structure is not well defined.

47. The auditor makes inquiries of those charged with governance in part to corroborate the responses to the inquiries from management. When responses to these inquiries are inconsistent, the auditor obtains additional audit evidence to resolve the inconsistencies. Inquiries of those charged with governance may also assist the auditor in identifying risks of material misstatement due to fraud.

Consideration of Fraud Risk Factors

48. **When obtaining an understanding of the entity and its environment, including its internal control, the auditor should consider whether the information obtained indicates that one or more fraud risk factors are present.**

49. The fact that fraud is usually concealed can make it very difficult to detect. Nevertheless, when obtaining an understanding of the entity and its environment, including its internal control, the auditor may identify events or conditions that indicate an incentive or pressure to commit fraud or provide an opportunity to commit fraud. Such events or conditions are referred to as "fraud risk factors." For example:

- The need to meet expectations of third parties to obtain additional equity financing may create pressure to commit fraud;

- The granting of significant bonuses if unrealistic profit targets are met may create an incentive to commit fraud; and

An ineffective control environment may create an opportunity to commit fraud. While fraud risk factors may not necessarily indicate the existence of fraud, they have often been present in circumstances where frauds have occurred. The presence of fraud risk factors may affect the auditor's assessment of the risks of material misstatement.

50. Fraud risk factors cannot easily be ranked in order of importance. The significance of fraud risk factors varies widely. Some of these factors will be present in entities where the specific conditions do not present risks of material misstatement. Accordingly, the auditor exercises professional judgment in determining whether a fraud risk factor is present and whether it is to be considered in assessing the risks of material misstatement of the financial statements due to fraud.

51. Examples of fraud risk factors related to fraudulent financial reporting and misappropriation of assets are presented in Appendix 1 to this ISA (UK and Ireland). These illustrative risk factors are classified based on the three conditions that are generally present when fraud exists: an incentive or pressure to commit fraud; a perceived opportunity to commit fraud; and an ability to rationalize the fraudulent action. Risk factors reflective of an attitude that permits rationalization of the fraudulent action may not be susceptible to observation by the auditor. Nevertheless, the auditor may become aware of the existence of such information. Although the fraud risk factors described in Appendix 1 cover a broad range of situations that may be faced by auditors, they are only examples and other risk factors may exist. The auditor also has to be alert for risk factors specific to the entity that are not included in Appendix 1. Not all of the examples in Appendix 1 are relevant in all circumstances, and some may be of greater or lesser significance in entities of different size, with different ownership

characteristics, in different industries, or because of other differing characteristics or circumstances.

52. The size, complexity, and ownership characteristics of the entity have a significant influence on the consideration of relevant fraud risk factors. For example, in the case of a large entity, the auditor ordinarily considers factors that generally constrain improper conduct by management, such as the effectiveness of those charged with governance and of the internal audit function and the existence and enforcement of a formal code of conduct. Furthermore, fraud risk factors considered at a business segment operating level may provide different insights than the consideration thereof at an entity-wide level. In the case of a small entity, some or all of these considerations may be inapplicable or less important. For example, a smaller entity may not have a written code of conduct but, instead, may have developed a culture that emphasizes the importance of integrity and ethical behavior through oral communication and by management example. Domination of management by a single individual in a small entity does not generally, in and of itself, indicate a failure by management to display and communicate an appropriate attitude regarding internal control and the financial reporting process. In some entities, the need for management authorization can compensate for otherwise weak controls and reduce the risk of employee fraud. However, domination of management by a single individual can be a potential weakness since there is an opportunity for management override of controls.

Consideration of Unusual or Unexpected Relationships

53. **When performing analytical procedures to obtain an understanding of the entity and its environment, including its internal control, the auditor should consider unusual or unexpected relationships that may indicate risks of material misstatement due to fraud.**

54. Analytical procedures may be helpful in identifying the existence of unusual transactions or events, and amounts, ratios, and trends that might indicate matters that have financial statement and audit implications. In performing analytical procedures the auditor develops expectations about plausible relationships that are reasonably expected to exist based on the auditor's understanding of the entity and its environment, including its internal control. When a comparison of those expectations with recorded amounts, or with ratios developed from recorded amounts, yields unusual or unexpected relationships, the auditor considers those results in identifying risks of material misstatement due to fraud. Analytical procedures include procedures related to revenue accounts with the objective of identifying unusual or unexpected relationships that may indicate risks of material misstatement due to fraudulent financial reporting, such as, for example, fictitious sales or significant returns from customers that might indicate undisclosed side agreements.

Consideration of Other Information

55. **When obtaining an understanding of the entity and its environment, including its internal control, the auditor should consider whether other information obtained indicates risks of material misstatement due to fraud.**

56. In addition to information obtained from applying analytical procedures, the auditor considers other information obtained about the entity and its environment that may be helpful in identifying the risks of material misstatement due to fraud. The discussion among team members described in paragraphs 27-32 may provide information that is helpful in identifying such risks. In addition, information obtained from the auditor's client acceptance and retention processes, and experience gained on other engagements performed for the entity, for example engagements to review interim financial information, may be relevant in the identification of the risks of material misstatement due to fraud.

Identification and Assessment of the Risks of Material Misstatement Due to Fraud

57. **When identifying and assessing the risks of material misstatement at the financial statement level, and at the assertion level for classes of transactions, account balances and disclosures, the auditor should identify and assess the risks of material misstatement due to fraud. Those assessed risks that could result in a material misstatement due to fraud are significant risks and accordingly, to the extent not already done so, the auditor should evaluate the design of the entity's related controls, including relevant control activities, and determine whether they have been implemented.**

58. To assess the risks of material misstatement due to fraud the auditor uses professional judgment and:

    (a) Identifies risks of fraud by considering the information obtained through performing risk assessment procedures and by considering the classes of transactions, account balances and disclosures in the financial statements;

    (b) Relates the identified risks of fraud to what can go wrong at the assertion level; and

    (c) Considers the likely magnitude of the potential misstatement including the possibility that the risk might give rise to multiple misstatements and the likelihood of the risk occurring.

59. It is important for the auditor to obtain an understanding of the controls that management has designed and implemented to prevent and detect fraud because in designing and implementing such controls, management may make informed judgments on the nature and extent of the controls it chooses to implement, and the nature and extent of the risks it chooses to assume. The auditor may learn, for example, that management has consciously chosen to accept the risks associated with a lack of segregation of duties. This may often be the case in small entities where the owner provides day-to-day supervision of operations. Information from obtaining this understanding may also be useful in identifying fraud risk factors that may affect the auditor's assessment of the risks that the financial statements may contain material misstatement due to fraud.

Risks of Fraud in Revenue Recognition

60. Material misstatements due to fraudulent financial reporting often result from an overstatement of revenues (for example, through premature revenue recognition or recording fictitious revenues) or an understatement of revenues (for example, through improperly shifting revenues to a later period). Therefore, the auditor ordinarily presumes that there are risks of fraud in revenue recognition and considers which types of revenue, revenue transactions or assertions may give rise to such risks. Those assessed risks of material misstatement due to fraud related to revenue recognition are significant risks to be addressed in accordance with paragraphs 57 and 61. Appendix 3 includes examples of responses to the auditor's assessment of the risk of material misstatement due to fraudulent financial reporting resulting from revenue recognition. If the auditor has not identified, in a particular circumstance, revenue recognition as a risk of material misstatement due to fraud, the auditor documents the reasons supporting the auditor's conclusion as required by paragraph 110.

Responses to the Risks of Material Misstatement Due to Fraud

61. **The auditor should determine overall responses to address the assessed risks of material misstatement due to fraud at the financial statement level and should design and perform further audit procedures whose nature, timing and extent are responsive to the assessed risks at the assertion level.**

62. ISA (UK and Ireland) 330 requires the auditor to perform substantive procedures that are specifically responsive to risks that are assessed as significant risks.

63. The auditor responds to the risks of material misstatement due to fraud in the following ways:

    (a) A response that has an overall effect on how the audit is conducted, that is, increased professional skepticism and a response involving more general considerations apart from the specific procedures otherwise planned.

    (b) A response to identified risks at the assertion level involving the nature, timing and extent of audit procedures to be performed.

    (c) A response to identified risks involving the performance of certain audit procedures to address the risks of material misstatement due to fraud involving management override of controls, given the unpredictable ways in which such override could occur.

64. The response to address the assessed risks of material misstatement due to fraud may affect the auditor's professional skepticism in the following ways:

    (a) Increased sensitivity in the selection of the nature and extent of documentation to be examined in support of material transactions.

(b) Increased recognition of the need to corroborate management explanations or representations concerning material matters.

65. The auditor may conclude that it would not be practicable to design audit procedures that sufficiently address the risks of material misstatement due to fraud. In such circumstances the auditor considers the implications for the audit (see paragraphs 89 and 103).

Overall Responses

66. **In determining overall responses to address the risks of material misstatement due to fraud at the financial statement level the auditor should:**

    (a) **Consider the assignment and supervision of personnel;**

    (b) **Consider the accounting policies used by the entity; and**

    (c) **Incorporate an element of unpredictability in the selection of the nature, timing and extent of audit procedures.**

67. The knowledge, skill and ability of the individuals assigned significant engagement responsibilities are commensurate with the auditor's assessment of the risks of material misstatement due to fraud for the engagement. For example, the auditor may respond to identified risks of material misstatement due to fraud by assigning additional individuals with specialized skill and knowledge, such as forensic and IT experts, or by assigning more experienced individuals to the engagement. In addition, the extent of supervision reflects the auditor's assessment of risks of material misstatement due to fraud and the competencies of the engagement team members performing the work.

68. The auditor considers management's selection and application of significant accounting policies, particularly those related to subjective measurements and complex transactions. The auditor considers whether the selection and application of accounting policies may be indicative of fraudulent financial reporting resulting from management's effort to manage earnings in order to deceive financial statement users by influencing their perceptions as to the entity's performance and profitability.

69. Individuals within the entity who are familiar with the audit procedures normally performed on engagements may be more able to conceal fraudulent financial reporting. Therefore, the auditor incorporates an element of unpredictability in the selection of the nature, extent and timing of audit procedures to be performed. This can be achieved by, for example, performing substantive procedures on selected account balances and assertions not otherwise tested due to their materiality or risk, adjusting the timing of audit procedures from that otherwise expected, using different sampling methods, and performing audit procedures at different locations or at locations on an unannounced basis.

Audit Procedures Responsive to Risks of Material Misstatement Due to Fraud at the Assertion Level

70. The auditor's responses to address the assessed risks of material misstatement due to fraud at the assertion level may include changing the nature, timing, and extent of audit procedures in the following ways:

- The nature of audit procedures to be performed may need to be changed to obtain audit evidence that is more reliable and relevant or to obtain additional corroborative information. This may affect both the type of audit procedures to be performed and their combination. Physical observation or inspection of certain assets may become more important or the auditor may choose to use computer-assisted audit techniques to gather more evidence about data contained in significant accounts or electronic transaction files. In addition, the auditor may design procedures to obtain additional corroborative information. For example, if the auditor identifies that management is under pressure to meet earnings expectations, there may be a related risk that management is inflating sales by entering into sales agreements that include terms that preclude revenue recognition or by invoicing sales before delivery. In these circumstances, the auditor may, for example, design external confirmations not only to confirm outstanding amounts, but also to confirm the details of the sales agreements, including date, any rights of return and delivery terms. In addition, the auditor might find it effective to supplement such external confirmations with inquiries of non-financial personnel in the entity regarding any changes in sales agreements and delivery terms.

- The timing of substantive procedures may need to be modified. The auditor may conclude that performing substantive testing at or near the period end better addresses an assessed risk of material misstatement due to fraud. The auditor may conclude that, given the risks of intentional misstatement or manipulation, audit procedures to extend audit conclusions from an interim date to the period end would not be effective. In contrast, because an intentional misstatement, for example a misstatement involving improper revenue recognition, may have been initiated in an interim period, the auditor may elect to apply substantive procedures to transactions occurring earlier in or throughout the reporting period.

- The extent of the procedures applied reflects the assessment of the risks of material misstatement due to fraud. For example, increasing sample sizes or performing analytical procedures at a more detailed level may be appropriate. Also, computer-assisted audit techniques may enable more extensive testing of electronic transactions and account files. Such techniques can be used to select sample transactions from key electronic files, to sort transactions with specific characteristics, or to test an entire population instead of a sample.

71. If the auditor identifies a risk of material misstatement due to fraud that affects inventory quantities, examining the entity's inventory records may help to identify locations or items that require specific attention during or after the physical inventory count. Such a review may lead to a decision to observe inventory counts at certain

locations on an unannounced basis or to conduct inventory counts at all locations on the same date.

72. The auditor may identify a risk of material misstatement due to fraud affecting a number of accounts and assertions, including asset valuation, estimates relating to specific transactions (such as acquisitions, restructurings, or disposals of a segment of the business), and other significant accrued liabilities (such as pension and other post-employment benefit obligations, or environmental remediation liabilities). The risk may also relate to significant changes in assumptions relating to recurring estimates. Information gathered through obtaining an understanding of the entity and its environment may assist the auditor in evaluating the reasonableness of such management estimates and underlying judgments and assumptions. A retrospective review of similar management judgments and assumptions applied in prior periods may also provide insight about the reasonableness of judgments and assumptions supporting management estimates.

73. Examples of possible audit procedures to address the assessed risks of material misstatement due to fraud are presented in Appendix 2 to this ISA (UK and Ireland). The appendix includes examples of responses to the auditor's assessment of the risks of material misstatement resulting from both fraudulent financial reporting and misappropriation of assets.

Audit Procedures Responsive to Management Override of Controls

74. As noted in paragraph 19, management is in a unique position to perpetrate fraud because of management's ability to directly or indirectly manipulate accounting records and prepare fraudulent financial statements by overriding controls that otherwise appear to be operating effectively. While the level of risk of management override of controls will vary from entity to entity, the risk is nevertheless present in all entities and is a significant risk of material misstatement due to fraud. Accordingly, in addition to overall responses to address the risks of material misstatement due to fraud and responses to address the assessed risks of material misstatement due to fraud at the assertion level, the auditor performs audit procedures to respond to the risk of management override of controls.

75. Paragraphs 76-82 set out the audit procedures required to respond to risk of management override of controls. However, the auditor also considers whether there are risks of management override of controls for which the auditor needs to perform procedures other than those specifically referred to in these paragraphs.

76. **To respond to the risk of management override of controls, the auditor should design and perform audit procedures to:**

   (a) **Test the appropriateness of journal entries recorded in the general ledger and other adjustments made in the preparation of financial statements;**

   (b) **Review accounting estimates for biases that could result in material misstatement due to fraud; and**

(c) **Obtain an understanding of the business rationale of significant transactions that the auditor becomes aware of that are outside of the normal course of business for the entity, or that otherwise appear to be unusual given the auditor's understanding of the entity and its environment.**

Journal Entries and Other Adjustments

77. Material misstatements of financial statements due to fraud often involve the manipulation of the financial reporting process by recording inappropriate or unauthorized journal entries throughout the year or at period end, or making adjustments to amounts reported in the financial statements that are not reflected in formal journal entries, such as through consolidating adjustments and reclassifications. In designing and performing audit procedures to test the appropriateness of journal entries recorded in the general ledger and other adjustments made in the preparation of the financial statements the auditor:

(a) Obtains an understanding of the entity's financial reporting process and the controls over journal entries and other adjustments;

(b) Evaluates the design of the controls over journal entries and other adjustments and determines whether they have been implemented;

(c) Makes inquiries of individuals involved in the financial reporting process about inappropriate or unusual activity relating to the processing of journal entries and other adjustments;

(d) Determines the timing of the testing; and

(e) Identifies and selects journal entries and other adjustments for testing.

78. For the purposes of identifying and selecting journal entries and other adjustments for testing, and determining the appropriate method of examining the underlying support for the items selected, the auditor considers the following:

- *The assessment of the risks of material misstatement due to fraud* – the presence of fraud risk factors and other information obtained during the auditor's assessment of the risks of material misstatement due to fraud may assist the auditor to identify specific classes of journal entries and other adjustments for testing.

- *Controls that have been implemented over journal entries and other adjustments* – effective controls over the preparation and posting of journal entries and other adjustments may reduce the extent of substantive testing necessary, provided that the auditor has tested the operating effectiveness of the controls.

- *The entity's financial reporting process and the nature of evidence that can be obtained* – for many entities routine processing of transactions involves a combination of manual and automated steps and procedures. Similarly, the processing of journal entries and other adjustments may involve both manual and automated procedures and controls. When information technology is used in the financial reporting process, journal entries and other adjustments may exist only in electronic form.

- *The characteristics of fraudulent journal entries or other adjustments* – inappropriate journal entries or other adjustments often have unique identifying characteristics. Such characteristics may include entries (a) made to unrelated, unusual, or seldom-used accounts, (b) made by individuals who typically do not make journal entries, (c) recorded at the end of the period or as post-closing entries that have little or no explanation or description, (d) made either before or during the preparation of the financial statements that do not have account numbers, or (e) containing round numbers or consistent ending numbers.

- *The nature and complexity of the accounts* – inappropriate journal entries or adjustments may be applied to accounts that (a) contain transactions that are complex or unusual in nature, (b) contain significant estimates and period-end adjustments, (c) have been prone to misstatements in the past, (d) have not been reconciled on a timely basis or contain unreconciled differences, (e) contain inter-company transactions, or (f) are otherwise associated with an identified risk of material misstatement due to fraud. In audits of entities that have several locations or components, consideration is given to the need to select journal entries from multiple locations.

- *Journal entries or other adjustments processed outside the normal course of business* – non standard journal entries may not be subject to the same level of internal control as those journal entries used on a recurring basis to record transactions such as monthly sales, purchases and cash disbursements.

79. The auditor uses professional judgment in determining the nature, timing and extent of testing of journal entries and other adjustments. Because fraudulent journal entries and other adjustments are often made at the end of a reporting period, the auditor ordinarily selects the journal entries and other adjustments made at that time. However, because material misstatements in financial statements due to fraud can occur throughout the period and may involve extensive efforts to conceal how the fraud is accomplished, the auditor considers whether there is also a need to test journal entries and other adjustments throughout the period.

Accounting Estimates

80. In preparing financial statements, management is responsible for making a number of judgments or assumptions that affect significant accounting estimates and for monitoring the reasonableness of such estimates on an ongoing basis. Fraudulent financial reporting is often accomplished through intentional misstatement of accounting estimates. In reviewing accounting estimates for biases that could result in material misstatement due to fraud the auditor:

(a) Considers whether differences between estimates best supported by audit evidence and the estimates included in the financial statements, even if they are individually reasonable, indicate a possible bias on the part of the entity's management, in which case the auditor reconsiders the estimates taken as a whole; and

(b) Performs a retrospective review of management judgments and assumptions related to significant accounting estimates reflected in the financial statements of the prior year. The objective of this review is to determine whether there is an indication of a possible bias on the part of management, and it is not intended to call into question the auditor's professional judgments made in the prior year that were based on information available at the time.

81. If the auditor identifies a possible bias on the part of management in making accounting estimates, the auditor evaluates whether the circumstances producing such a bias represent a risk of material misstatement due to fraud. The auditor considers whether, in making accounting estimates, management's actions appear to understate or overstate all provisions or reserves in the same fashion so as to be designed either to smooth earnings over two or more accounting periods, or to achieve a designated earnings level in order to deceive financial statement users by influencing their perceptions as to the entity's performance and profitability.

Business Rationale for Significant Transactions

82. The auditor obtains an understanding of the business rationale for significant transactions that are outside the normal course of business for the entity, or that otherwise appear to be unusual given the auditor's understanding of the entity and its environment and other information obtained during the audit. The purpose of obtaining this understanding is to consider whether the rationale (or the lack thereof) suggests that the transactions may have been entered into to engage in fraudulent financial reporting or to conceal misappropriation of assets. In gaining such an understanding the auditor considers the following:

- Whether the form of such transactions appears overly complex (for example, the transaction involves multiple entities within a consolidated group or multiple unrelated third parties).

- Whether management has discussed the nature of and accounting for such transactions with those charged with governance of the entity, and whether there is adequate documentation.

- Whether management is placing more emphasis on the need for a particular accounting treatment than on the underlying economics of the transaction.

- Whether transactions that involve non-consolidated related parties, including special purpose entities, have been properly reviewed and approved by those charged with governance of the entity.

- Whether the transactions involve previously unidentified related parties or parties that do not have the substance or the financial strength to support the transaction without assistance from the entity under audit.

Evaluation of Audit Evidence

83. As required by ISA (UK and Ireland) 330, the auditor, based on the audit procedures performed and the audit evidence obtained, evaluates whether the assessments of the risks of material misstatement at the assertion level remain appropriate. This evaluation is primarily a qualitative matter based on the auditor's judgment. Such an evaluation may provide further insight about the risks of material misstatement due to fraud and whether there is a need to perform additional or different audit procedures. As part of this evaluation, the auditor considers whether there has been appropriate communication with other engagement team members throughout the audit regarding information or conditions indicative of risks of material misstatement due to fraud.

84. An audit of financial statements is a cumulative and iterative process. As the auditor performs planned audit procedures information may come to the auditor's attention that differs significantly from the information on which the assessment of the risks of material misstatement due to fraud was based. For example, the auditor may become aware of discrepancies in accounting records or conflicting or missing evidence. Also, relationships between the auditor and management may become problematic or unusual. Appendix 3 to this ISA (UK and Ireland) contains examples of circumstances that may indicate the possibility of fraud.

85. **The auditor should consider whether analytical procedures that are performed at or near the end of the audit when forming an overall conclusion as to whether the financial statement as a whole are consistent with the auditor's knowledge of the business indicate a previously unrecognized risk of material misstatement due to fraud.** Determining which particular trends and relationships may indicate a risk of material misstatement due to fraud requires professional judgment. Unusual relationships involving year-end revenue and income are particularly relevant. These might include, for example, uncharacteristically large amounts of income being reported in the last few weeks of the reporting period or unusual transactions; or income that is inconsistent with trends in cash flow from operations.

86. **When the auditor identifies a misstatement, the auditor should consider whether such a misstatement may be indicative of fraud and if there is such an indication, the auditor should consider the implications of the misstatement in relation to other aspects of the audit, particularly the reliability of management[1a] representations.**

87. The auditor cannot assume that an instance of fraud is an isolated occurrence. The auditor also considers whether misstatements identified may be indicative of a higher risk of material misstatement due to fraud at a specific location. For example, numerous misstatements at a specific location, even though the cumulative effect is not material, may be indicative of a risk of material misstatement due to fraud.

88. If the auditor believes that a misstatement is or may be the result of fraud, but the effect of the misstatement is not material to the financial statements, the auditor evaluates the implications, especially those dealing with the organizational position of the individual(s) involved. For example, fraud involving a misappropriation of cash from

a small petty cash fund normally would be of little significance to the auditor in assessing the risks of material misstatement due to fraud because both the manner of operating the fund and its size would tend to establish a limit on the amount of potential loss, and the custodianship of such funds normally is entrusted to a non-management employee. Conversely, if the matter involves higher-level management, even though the amount itself is not material to the financial statements, it may be indicative of a more pervasive problem, for example, implications about the integrity of management. In such circumstances, the auditor re-evaluates the assessment of the risks of material misstatement due to fraud and its resulting impact on the nature, timing, and extent of audit procedures to respond to the assessed risks. The auditor also reconsiders the reliability of evidence previously obtained since there may be doubts about the completeness and truthfulness of representations made and about the genuineness of accounting records and documentation. The auditor also considers the possibility of collusion involving employees, management or third parties when reconsidering the reliability of evidence.

89. **When the auditor confirms that, or is unable to conclude whether, the financial statements are materially misstated as a result of fraud, the auditor should consider the implications for the audit.** ISA (UK and Ireland) 320, "Audit Materiality" and ISA (UK and Ireland) 700, "The Auditor's Report on Financial Statements" provide guidance on the evaluation and disposition of misstatements and the effect on the auditor's report.

Management Representations

90. **The auditor should obtain written representations from management[1a] that:**

   (a) **It acknowledges its responsibility for the design and implementation of internal control to prevent and detect fraud;**

   (b) **It has disclosed to the auditor the results of its assessment of the risk that the financial statements may be materially misstated as a result of fraud;**

   (c) **It has disclosed to the auditor its knowledge of fraud or suspected fraud affecting the entity involving:**

   (i) **Management[2a]**

   (ii) **Employees who have significant roles in internal control; or**

   (iii) **Others where the fraud could have a material effect on the financial statements; and**

[2a] In the UK and Ireland, and those charged with governance.

(d) **It has disclosed to the auditor its knowledge of any allegations of fraud, or suspected fraud, affecting the entity's financial statements communicated by employees, former employees, analysts, regulators or others.**

91. ISA (UK and Ireland) 580, "Management Representations" provides guidance on obtaining appropriate representations from management[1a] in the audit. In addition to acknowledging its responsibility for the financial statements, it is important that, irrespective of the size of the entity, management acknowledges its responsibility for internal control designed and implemented to prevent and detect fraud.

92. Because of the nature of fraud and the difficulties encountered by auditors in detecting material misstatements in the financial statements resulting from fraud, it is important that the auditor obtains a written representation from management[1a] confirming that it has disclosed to the auditor the results of management's assessment of the risk that the financial statements may be materially misstated as a result of fraud and its knowledge of actual, suspected or alleged fraud affecting the entity.

Communications With Management and Those Charged With Governance

93. **If the auditor has identified a fraud or has obtained information that indicates that a fraud may exist, the auditor should communicate these matters as soon as practicable to the appropriate level of management.**

94. When the auditor has obtained evidence that fraud exists or may exist, it is important that the matter be brought to the attention of the appropriate level of management as soon as practicable. This is so even if the matter might be considered inconsequential (for example, a minor defalcation by an employee at a low level in the entity's organization). The determination of which level of management is the appropriate one is a matter of professional judgment and is affected by such factors as the likelihood of collusion and the nature and magnitude of the suspected fraud. Ordinarily, the appropriate level of management is at least one level above the persons who appear to be involved with the suspected fraud.

95. **If the auditor has identified fraud involving:**

    (a) **Management;**

    (b) **Employees who have significant roles in internal control; or**

    (c) **Others where the fraud results in a material misstatement in the financial statements,**

    the auditor should communicate these matters to those charged with governance as soon as practicable.

96. The auditor's communication with those charged with governance may be made orally or in writing. ISA (UK and Ireland) 260, "Communication of Audit Matters With Those

Charged With Governance" identifies factors the auditor considers in determining whether to communicate orally or in writing. Due to the nature and sensitivity of fraud involving senior management, or fraud that results in a material misstatement in the financial statements, the auditor reports such matters as soon as practicable and considers whether it is necessary to also report such matters in writing. If the auditor suspects fraud involving management, the auditor communicates these suspicions to those charged with governance and also discusses with them the nature, timing and extent of audit procedures necessary to complete the audit.

97. If the integrity or honesty of management or those charged with governance is doubted, the auditor considers seeking legal advice to assist in the determination of the appropriate course of action.

98. At an early stage in the audit, the auditor reaches an understanding with those charged with governance about the nature and extent of the auditor's communications regarding fraud that the auditor becomes aware of involving employees other than management that does not result in a material misstatement.

99. **The auditor should make those charged with governance and management aware, as soon as practicable, and at the appropriate level of responsibility, of material weaknesses in the design or implementation of internal control to prevent and detect fraud which may have come to the auditor's attention.**

100. If the auditor identifies a risk of material misstatement of the financial statements due to fraud, which management has either not controlled, or for which the relevant control is inadequate, or if in the auditor's judgment there is a material weakness in management's risk assessment process, the auditor includes such internal control deficiencies in the communication of audit matters of governance interest (see ISA (UK and Ireland) 260).

101. **The auditor should consider whether there are any other matters related to fraud to be discussed with those charged with governance of the entity.**[3] Such matters may include for example:

- Concerns about the nature, extent and frequency of management's assessments of the controls in place to prevent and detect fraud and of the risk that the financial statements may be misstated.

- A failure by management to appropriately address identified material weaknesses in internal control.

- A failure by management to appropriately respond to an identified fraud.

- The auditor's evaluation of the entity's control environment, including questions regarding the competence and integrity of management.

---

[3] For a discussion of these matters, see ISA (UK and Ireland) 260, "Communication of Audit Matters With Those Charged With Governance," paragraphs 11-12.

- Actions by management that may be indicative of fraudulent financial reporting, such as management's selection and application of accounting policies that may be indicative of management's effort to manage earnings in order to deceive financial statement users by influencing their perceptions as to the entity's performance and profitability.

- Concerns about the adequacy and completeness of the authorization of transactions that appear to be outside the normal course of business.

Communications to Regulatory and Enforcement Authorities

102. The auditor's professional duty to maintain the confidentiality of client information may preclude reporting fraud to a party outside the client entity. The auditor considers obtaining legal advice to determine the appropriate course of action in such circumstances. The auditor's legal responsibilities vary by country[3a] and in certain circumstances, the duty of confidentiality may be overridden by statute, the law or courts of law. For example, in some countries, the auditor of a financial institution has a statutory duty to report the occurrence of fraud to supervisory authorities. Also, in some countries the auditor has a duty to report misstatements to authorities in those cases where management and those charged with governance fail to take corrective action.

Auditor Unable to Continue the Engagement

103. **If, as a result of a misstatement resulting from fraud or suspected fraud, the auditor encounters exceptional circumstances that bring into question the auditor's ability to continue performing the audit the auditor should:**

  (a) **Consider the professional and legal responsibilities applicable in the circumstances, including whether there is a requirement for the auditor to report to the person or persons who made the audit appointment or, in some cases, to regulatory authorities;**

  (b) **Consider the possibility of withdrawing from the engagement; and**

  (c) **If the auditor withdraws:**

  (i) **Discuss with the appropriate level of management and those charged with governance the auditor's withdrawal from the engagement and the reasons for the withdrawal; and**

[3a] In the UK and Ireland, anti-money laundering legislation (see footnote 15 to ISA (UK and Ireland) 250, "Consideration of laws and regulations") imposes a duty on auditors to report all suspicions that a criminal offence giving rise to any direct or indirect benefit from criminal conduct has been committed regardless of whether that offence has been committed by a client or a third party. Suspicions relating to fraud are likely to be required to be reported under this legislation.

(ii) **Consider whether there is a professional or legal requirement to report to the person or persons who made the audit appointment or, in some cases, to regulatory authorities, the auditor's withdrawal from the engagement and the reasons for the withdrawal.**

104. Such exceptional circumstances can arise, for example, when:

(a) The entity does not take the appropriate action regarding fraud that the auditor considers necessary in the circumstances, even when the fraud is not material to the financial statements;

(b) The auditor's consideration of the risks of material misstatement due to fraud and the results of audit tests indicate a significant risk of material and pervasive fraud; or

(c) The auditor has significant concern about the competence or integrity of management or those charged with governance.

105. Because of the variety of the circumstances that may arise, it is not possible to describe definitively when withdrawal from an engagement is appropriate. Factors that affect the auditor's conclusion include the implications of the involvement of a member of management or of those charged with governance (which may affect the reliability of management[1a] representations) and the effects on the auditor of a continuing association with the entity.

106. The auditor has professional and legal responsibilities in such circumstances and these responsibilities may vary by country. In some countries, for example, the auditor may be entitled to, or required to, make a statement or report to the person or persons who made the audit appointment or, in some cases, to regulatory authorities. Given the exceptional nature of the circumstances and the need to consider the legal requirements, the auditor considers seeking legal advice when deciding whether to withdraw from an engagement and in determining an appropriate course of action, including the possibility of reporting to shareholders, regulators or others.[4]

Documentation

107. **The documentation of the auditor's understanding of the entity and its environment and the auditor's assessment of the risks of material misstatement required by paragraph 122 of ISA (UK and Ireland) 315 should include:**

---

[4] The IFAC *Code of Ethics for Professional Accountants* provides guidance on communications with a proposed successor auditor.
In the UK and Ireland the relevant ethical guidance on proposed communications with a successor auditor is provided by the ethical pronouncements relating to the work of auditors issued by the auditor's relevant professional body.

(a) **The significant decisions reached during the discussion among the engagement team regarding the susceptibility of the entity's financial statements to material misstatement due to fraud; and**

(b) **The identified and assessed risks of material misstatement due to fraud at the financial statement level and at the assertion level.**

108. **The documentation of the auditor's responses to the assessed risks of material misstatement required by paragraph 73 of ISA (UK and Ireland) 330 should include:**

(a) **The overall responses to the assessed risks of material misstatements due to fraud at the financial statement level and the nature, timing and extent of audit procedures, and the linkage of those procedures with the assessed risks of material misstatement due to fraud at the assertion level; and**

(b) **The results of the audit procedures, including those designed to address the risk of management override of controls.**

109. **The auditor should document communications about fraud made to management, those charged with governance, regulators and others.**

110. **When the auditor has concluded that the presumption that there is a risk of material misstatement due to fraud related to revenue recognition is not applicable in the circumstances of the engagement, the auditor should document the reasons for that conclusion.**

111. The extent to which these matters are documented is for the auditor to determine using professional judgment.

Effective Date

112. This ISA (UK and Ireland) is effective for audits of financial statements for periods commencing on or after 15 December 2004.

Public Sector Perspective

Additional guidance for auditors of public sector bodies in the UK and Ireland is given in:

- Practice Note 10 "Audit of Financial Statements of Public Sector Bodies in the United Kingdom (Revised)"

- Practice Note 10(I) "Audit of Central Government Financial Statements in the Republic of Ireland (Revised)"

1. ISA (UK and Ireland) 240 is applicable in all material respects to audits of public sector entities.

2. In the public sector the scope and nature of the audit relating to the prevention and detection of fraud may be affected by legislation, regulation, ordinances or ministerial directives. The terms of the mandate may be a factor that the auditor needs to take into account when exercising judgment.

3. Requirements for reporting fraud, whether or not discovered through the audit process often may be subject to specific provisions of the audit mandate or related legislation or regulation in line with paragraph 102 of the ISA (UK and Ireland).

4. In many cases in the public sector the option of withdrawing from the engagement as suggested in paragraph 103 of the ISA (UK and Ireland) may not be available to the auditor due to the nature of the mandate or public interest considerations.

Appendix 1

Examples of Fraud Risk Factors

The fraud risk factors identified in this Appendix are examples of such factors that may be faced by auditors in a broad range of situations. Separately presented are examples relating to the two types of fraud relevant to the auditor's consideration, that is, fraudulent financial reporting and misappropriation of assets. For each of these types of fraud, the risk factors are further classified based on the three conditions generally present when material misstatements due to fraud occur: (a) incentives/pressures, (b) opportunities, and (c) attitudes/rationalizations. Although the risk factors cover a broad range of situations, they are only examples and, accordingly, the auditor may identify additional or different risk factors. Not all of these examples are relevant in all circumstances, and some may be of greater or lesser significance in entities of different size or with different ownership characteristics or circumstances. Also, the order of the examples of risk factors provided is not intended to reflect their relative importance or frequency of occurrence.

Risk Factors Relating to Misstatements Arising from Fraudulent Financial Reporting

The following are examples of risk factors relating to misstatements arising from fraudulent financial reporting.

Incentives/Pressures

1.   Financial stability or profitability is threatened by economic, industry, or entity operating conditions, such as (or as indicated by) the following:

     •   High degree of competition or market saturation, accompanied by declining margins.

     •   High vulnerability to rapid changes, such as changes in technology, product obsolescence, or interest rates.

     •   Significant declines in customer demand and increasing business failures in either the industry or overall economy.

     •   Operating losses making the threat of bankruptcy, foreclosure, or hostile takeover imminent.

     •   Recurring negative cash flows from operations or an inability to generate cash flows from operations while reporting earnings and earnings growth.

     •   Rapid growth or unusual profitability especially compared to that of other companies in the same industry.

     •   New accounting, statutory, or regulatory requirements.

THE AUDITING PRACTICES BOARD

2. Excessive pressure exists for management to meet the requirements or expectations of third parties due to the following:

    *   Profitability or trend level expectations of investment analysts, institutional investors, significant creditors, or other external parties (particularly expectations that are unduly aggressive or unrealistic), including expectations created by management in, for example, overly optimistic press releases or annual report messages.

    *   Need to obtain additional debt or equity financing to stay competitive, including financing of major research and development or capital expenditures.

    *   Marginal ability to meet exchange listing requirements or debt repayment or other debt covenant requirements.

    *   Perceived or real adverse effects of reporting poor financial results on significant pending transactions, such as business combinations or contract awards.

3. Information available indicates that the personal financial situation of management or those charged with governance is threatened by the entity's financial performance arising from the following:

    *   Significant financial interests in the entity.

    *   Significant portions of their compensation (for example, bonuses, stock options, and earn-out arrangements) being contingent upon achieving aggressive targets for stock price, operating results, financial position, or cash flow.[5]

    *   Personal guarantees of debts of the entity.

4. There is excessive pressure on management or operating personnel to meet financial targets established by those charged with governance, including sales or profitability incentive goals.

Opportunities

1. The nature of the industry or the entity's operations provides opportunities to engage in fraudulent financial reporting that can arise from the following:

    *   Significant related-party transactions not in the ordinary course of business or with related entities not audited or audited by another firm.

    *   A strong financial presence or ability to dominate a certain industry sector that allows the entity to dictate terms or conditions to suppliers or customers that may result in inappropriate or non-arm's length transactions.

---

[5] Management incentive plans may be contingent upon achieving targets relating only to certain accounts or selected activities of the entity, even though the related accounts or activities may not be material to the entity as a whole.

- Assets, liabilities, revenues, or expenses based on significant estimates that involve subjective judgments or uncertainties that are difficult to corroborate.

- Significant, unusual, or highly complex transactions, especially those close to period end that pose difficult "substance over form" questions.

- Significant operations located or conducted across international borders in jurisdictions where differing business environments and cultures exist.

- Use of business intermediaries for which there appears to be no clear business justification.

- Significant bank accounts or subsidiary or branch operations in tax-haven jurisdictions for which there appears to be no clear business justification.

2. There is ineffective monitoring of management as a result of the following:

- Domination of management by a single person or small group (in a non owner-managed business) without compensating controls.

- Ineffective oversight by those charged with governance over the financial reporting process and internal control.

3. There is a complex or unstable organizational structure, as evidenced by the following:

- Difficulty in determining the organization or individuals that have controlling interest in the entity.

- Overly complex organizational structure involving unusual legal entities or managerial lines of authority.

- High turnover of senior management, legal counsel, or those charged with governance.

4. Internal control components are deficient as a result of the following:

- Inadequate monitoring of controls, including automated controls and controls over interim financial reporting (where external reporting is required).

- High turnover rates or employment of ineffective accounting, internal audit, or information technology staff.

- Ineffective accounting and information systems, including situations involving material weaknesses in internal control.

Attitudes/Rationalizations

- Ineffective communication, implementation, support, or enforcement of the entity's values or ethical standards by management or the communication of inappropriate values or ethical standards.

- Nonfinancial management's excessive participation in or preoccupation with the selection of accounting policies or the determination of significant estimates.

- Known history of violations of securities laws or other laws and regulations, or claims against the entity, its senior management, or those charged with governance alleging fraud or violations of laws and regulations.

- Excessive interest by management in maintaining or increasing the entity's stock price or earnings trend.

- A practice by management of committing to analysts, creditors, and other third parties to achieve aggressive or unrealistic forecasts.

- Management failing to correct known material weaknesses in internal control on a timely basis.

- An interest by management in employing inappropriate means to minimize reported earnings for tax-motivated reasons.

- Low morale among senior management.

- The owner-manager makes no distinction between personal and business transactions.

- Dispute between shareholders in a closely held entity.

- Recurring attempts by management to justify marginal or inappropriate accounting on the basis of materiality.

- The relationship between management and the current or predecessor auditor is strained, as exhibited by the following:

  ○ Frequent disputes with the current or predecessor auditor on accounting, auditing, or reporting matters.

  ○ Unreasonable demands on the auditor, such as unreasonable time constraints regarding the completion of the audit or the issuance of the auditor's report.

  ○ Formal or informal restrictions on the auditor that inappropriately limit access to people or information or the ability to communicate effectively with those charged with governance.

      ○ Domineering management behavior in dealing with the auditor, especially involving attempts to influence the scope of the auditor's work or the selection or continuance of personnel assigned to or consulted on the audit engagement.

Risk Factors Arising from Misstatements Arising from Misappropriation of Assets

Risk factors that relate to misstatements arising from misappropriation of assets are also classified according to the three conditions generally present when fraud exists: (a) incentives/pressures, (b) opportunities, and (c) attitudes/rationalizations. Some of the risk factors related to misstatements arising from fraudulent financial reporting also may be present when misstatements arising from misappropriation of assets occur. For example, ineffective monitoring of management and weaknesses in internal control may be present when misstatements due to either fraudulent financial reporting or misappropriation of assets exist. The following are examples of risk factors related to misstatements arising from misappropriation of assets.

Incentives/Pressures

1. Personal financial obligations may create pressure on management or employees with access to cash or other assets susceptible to theft to misappropriate those assets.

2. Adverse relationships between the entity and employees with access to cash or other assets susceptible to theft may motivate those employees to misappropriate those assets. For example, adverse relationships may be created by the following:

    *   Known or anticipated future employee layoffs.

    *   Recent or anticipated changes to employee compensation or benefit plans.

    *   Promotions, compensation, or other rewards inconsistent with expectations.

Opportunities

1. Certain characteristics or circumstances may increase the susceptibility of assets to misappropriation. For example, opportunities to misappropriate assets increase when there are the following:

    *   Large amounts of cash on hand or processed.

    *   Inventory items that are small in size, of high value, or in high demand.

    *   Easily convertible assets, such as bearer bonds, diamonds, or computer chips.

    *   Fixed assets which are small in size, marketable, or lacking observable identification of ownership.

2. Inadequate internal control over assets may increase the susceptibility of misappropriation of those assets. For example, misappropriation of assets may occur because there is the following:

    *   Inadequate segregation of duties or independent checks.

    *   Inadequate oversight of senior management expenditures, such as travel and other re-imbursements.

    *   Inadequate management oversight of employees responsible for assets, for example, inadequate supervision or monitoring of remote locations.

    *   Inadequate job applicant screening of employees with access to assets.

    *   Inadequate record keeping with respect to assets.

    *   Inadequate system of authorization and approval of transactions (for example, in purchasing).

    *   Inadequate physical safeguards over cash, investments, inventory, or fixed assets.

    *   Lack of complete and timely reconciliations of assets.

    *   Lack of timely and appropriate documentation of transactions, for example, credits for merchandise returns.

    *   Lack of mandatory vacations for employees performing key control functions.

    *   Inadequate management understanding of information technology, which enables information technology employees to perpetrate a misappropriation.

    *   Inadequate access controls over automated records, including controls over and review of computer systems event logs.

Attitudes/Rationalizations

*   Disregard for the need for monitoring or reducing risks related to misappropriations of assets.

*   Disregard for internal control over misappropriation of assets by overriding existing controls or by failing to correct known internal control deficiencies.

*   Behavior indicating displeasure or dissatisfaction with the entity or its treatment of the employee.

*   Changes in behavior or lifestyle that may indicate assets have been misappropriated.

*   Tolerance of petty theft.

Appendix 2

Examples of Possible Audit Procedures to Address the Assessed Risks of Material Misstatement Due to Fraud

The following are examples of possible audit procedures to address the assessed risks of material misstatement due to fraud resulting from both fraudulent financial reporting and misappropriation of assets. Although these procedures cover a broad range of situations, they are only examples and, accordingly they may not be the most appropriate nor necessary in each circumstance. Also the order of the procedures provided is not intended to reflect their relative importance.

Consideration at the Assertion Level

Specific responses to the auditor's assessment of the risks of material misstatement due to fraud will vary depending upon the types or combinations of fraud risk factors or conditions identified, and the account balances, classes of transactions and assertions they may affect.

The following are specific examples of responses:

- Visiting locations or performing certain tests on a surprise or unannounced basis. For example, observing inventory at locations where auditor attendance has not been previously announced or counting cash at a particular date on a surprise basis.

- Requesting that inventories be counted at the end of the reporting period or on a date closer to period end to minimize the risk of manipulation of balances in the period between the date of completion of the count and the end of the reporting period.

- Altering the audit approach in the current year. For example, contacting major customers and suppliers orally in addition to sending written confirmation, sending confirmation requests to a specific party within an organization, or seeking more or different information.

- Performing a detailed review of the entity's quarter-end or year-end adjusting entries and investigating any that appear unusual as to nature or amount.

- For significant and unusual transactions, particularly those occurring at or near year-end, investigating the possibility of related parties and the sources of financial resources supporting the transactions.

- Performing substantive analytical procedures using disaggregated data. For example, comparing sales and cost of sales by location, line of business or month to expectations developed by the auditor.

- Conducting interviews of personnel involved in areas where a risk of material misstatement due to fraud has been identified, to obtain their insights about the risk and whether, or how, controls address the risk.

- When other independent auditors are auditing the financial statements of one or more subsidiaries, divisions or branches, discussing with them the extent of work necessary to be performed to address the risk of material misstatement due to fraud resulting from transactions and activities among these components.

- If the work of an expert becomes particularly significant with respect to a financial statement item for which the risk of misstatement due to fraud is high, performing additional procedures relating to some or all of the expert's assumptions, methods or findings to determine that the findings are not unreasonable, or engaging another expert for that purpose.

- Performing audit procedures to analyze selected opening balance sheet accounts of previously audited financial statements to assess how certain issues involving accounting estimates and judgments, for example an allowance for sales returns, were resolved with the benefit of hindsight.

- Performing procedures on account or other reconciliations prepared by the entity, including considering reconciliations performed at interim periods.

- Performing computer-assisted techniques, such as data mining to test for anomalies in a population.

- Testing the integrity of computer-produced records and transactions.

- Seeking additional audit evidence from sources outside of the entity being audited.

Specific Responses—Misstatement Resulting from Fraudulent Financial Reporting

Examples of responses to the auditor's assessment of the risk of material misstatements due to fraudulent financial reporting are as follows:

Revenue recognition

- Performing substantive analytical procedures relating to revenue using disaggregated data, for example, comparing revenue reported by month and by product line or business segment during the current reporting period with comparable prior periods. Computer-assisted audit techniques may be useful in identifying unusual or unexpected revenue relationships or transactions.

- Confirming with customers certain relevant contract terms and the absence of side agreements, because the appropriate accounting often is influenced by such terms or agreements and basis for rebates or the period to which they relate are often poorly documented. For example, acceptance criteria, delivery and payment terms, the absence of future or continuing vendor obligations, the right to return the product, guaranteed resale amounts, and cancellation or refund provisions often are relevant in such circumstances.

- Inquiring of the entity's sales and marketing personnel or in-house legal counsel regarding sales or shipments near the end of the period and their knowledge of any unusual terms or conditions associated with these transactions.

- Being physically present at one or more locations at period end to observe goods being shipped or being readied for shipment (or returns awaiting processing) and performing other appropriate sales and inventory cutoff procedures.

- For those situations for which revenue transactions are electronically initiated, processed, and recorded, testing controls to determine whether they provide assurance that recorded revenue transactions occurred and are properly recorded.

Inventory Quantities

- Examining the entity's inventory records to identify locations or items that require specific attention during or after the physical inventory count.

- Observing inventory counts at certain locations on an unannounced basis or conducting inventory counts at all locations on the same date.

- Conducting inventory counts at or near the end of the reporting period to minimize the risk of inappropriate manipulation during the period between the count and the end of the reporting period.

- Performing additional procedures during the observation of the count, for example, more rigorously examining the contents of boxed items, the manner in which the goods are stacked (for example, hollow squares) or labeled, and the quality (that is, purity, grade, or concentration) of liquid substances such as perfumes or specialty chemicals. Using the work of an expert may be helpful in this regard.

- Comparing the quantities for the current period with prior periods by class or category of inventory, location or other criteria, or comparison of quantities counted with perpetual records.

- Using computer-assisted audit techniques to further test the compilation of the physical inventory counts—for example, sorting by tag number to test tag controls or by item serial number to test the possibility of item omission or duplication.

Management estimates

- Using an expert to develop an independent estimate for comparison to management's estimate.

- Extending inquiries to individuals outside of management and the accounting department to corroborate management's ability and intent to carry out plans that are relevant to developing the estimate.

Specific Responses—Misstatements Due to Misappropriation of Assets

Differing circumstances would necessarily dictate different responses. Ordinarily, the audit response to a risk of material misstatement due to fraud relating to misappropriation of assets will be directed toward certain account balances and classes of transactions. Although some of the audit responses noted in the two categories above may apply in such circumstances, the scope of the work is to be linked to the specific information about the misappropriation risk that has been identified.

Examples of responses to the auditor's assessment of the risk of material misstatements due to misappropriation of assets are as follows:

- Counting cash or securities at or near year-end.

- Confirming directly with customers the account activity (including credit memo and sales return activity as well as dates payments were made) for the period under audit.

- Analyzing recoveries of written-off accounts.

- Analyzing inventory shortages by location or product type.

- Comparing key inventory ratios to industry norm.

- Reviewing supporting documentation for reductions to the perpetual inventory records.

- Performing a computerized match of the vendor list with a list of employees to identify matches of addresses or phone numbers.

- Performing a computerized search of payroll records to identify duplicate addresses, employee identification or taxing authority numbers or bank accounts

- Reviewing personnel files for those that contain little or no evidence of activity, for example, lack of performance evaluations.

- Analyzing sales discounts and returns for unusual patterns or trends.

- Confirming specific terms of contracts with third parties.

- Obtaining evidence that contracts are being carried out in accordance with their terms.

- Reviewing the propriety of large and unusual expenses.

- Reviewing the authorization and carrying value of senior management and related party loans.

- Reviewing the level and propriety of expense reports submitted by senior management.

Appendix 3

Examples of Circumstances that Indicate the Possibility of Fraud

The following are examples of circumstances that may indicate the possibility that the financial statements may contain a material misstatement resulting from fraud.

Discrepancies in the accounting records, including the following:

- Transactions that are not recorded in a complete or timely manner or are improperly recorded as to amount, accounting period, classification, or entity policy.

- Unsupported or unauthorized balances or transactions.

- Last-minute adjustments that significantly affect financial results.

- Evidence of employees' access to systems and records inconsistent with that necessary to perform their authorized duties.

- Tips or complaints to the auditor about alleged fraud.

Conflicting or missing evidence, including the following:

- Missing documents.

- Documents that appear to have been altered.

- Unavailability of other than photocopied or electronically transmitted documents when documents in original form are expected to exist.

- Significant unexplained items on reconciliations.

- Unusual balance sheet changes, or changes in trends or important financial statement ratios or relationships, for example receivables growing faster than revenues.

- Inconsistent, vague, or implausible responses from management or employees arising from inquiries or analytical procedures.

- Unusual discrepancies between the entity's records and confirmation replies.

- Large numbers of credit entries and other adjustments made to accounts receivable records.

- Unexplained or inadequately explained differences between the accounts receivable sub-ledger and the control account, or between the customer statements and the accounts receivable sub-ledger.

- Missing or non-existent cancelled checks in circumstances where cancelled checks are ordinarily returned to the entity with the bank statement.

- Missing inventory or physical assets of significant magnitude.

- Unavailable or missing electronic evidence, inconsistent with the entity's record retention practices or policies.

- Fewer responses to confirmations than anticipated or a greater number of responses than anticipated.

- Inability to produce evidence of key systems development and program change testing and implementation activities for current-year system changes and deployments.

Problematic or unusual relationships between the auditor and management, including the following:

- Denial of access to records, facilities, certain employees, customers, vendors, or others from whom audit evidence might be sought.

- Undue time pressures imposed by management to resolve complex or contentious issues.

- Complaints by management about the conduct of the audit or management intimidation of engagement team members, particularly in connection with the auditor's critical assessment of audit evidence or in the resolution of potential disagreements with management.

- Unusual delays by the entity in providing requested information.

- Unwillingness to facilitate auditor access to key electronic files for testing through the use of computer-assisted audit techniques.

- Denial of access to key IT operations staff and facilities, including security, operations, and systems development personnel.

- An unwillingness to add or revise disclosures in the financial statements to make them more complete and understandable.

- An unwillingness to address identified weaknesses in internal control on a timely basis.

Other includes the following:

- Unwillingness by management to permit the auditor to meet privately with those charged with governance.

- Accounting policies that appear to be at variance with industry norms.

- Frequent changes in accounting estimates that do not appear to result from changes circumstances.

- Tolerance of violations of the entity's code of conduct.

THE AUDITING
PRACTICES BOARD

INTERNATIONAL STANDARD ON AUDITING (UK AND IRELAND) 250

SECTION A – CONSIDERATION OF LAWS AND REGULATIONS IN AN AUDIT OF FINANCIAL STATEMENTS

SECTION B – THE AUDITOR'S RIGHT AND DUTY TO REPORT TO REGULATORS IN THE FINANCIAL SECTOR

CONTENTS

International Standard on Auditing (UK and Ireland) (ISA (UK and Ireland)) 250 "Consideration of Laws and Regulations in an Audit of Financial Statements" should be read in the context of the Auditing Practices Board's Statement "The Auditing Practices Board - Scope and Authority of Pronouncements" which sets out the application and authority of ISAs (UK and Ireland).

Section A

Introduction

1. The purpose of this International Standard on Auditing (UK and Ireland) (ISA (UK and Ireland)) is to establish standards and provide guidance on the auditor's responsibility to consider laws and regulations in an audit of financial statements.

1-1. This ISA (UK and Ireland) uses the terms 'those charged with governance' and 'management'. The term 'governance' describes the role of persons entrusted with the supervision, control and direction of an entity. Ordinarily, those charged with governance are accountable for ensuring that the entity achieves its objectives, and for the quality of its financial reporting and reporting to interested parties. Those charged with governance include management only when they perform such functions.

1-2. In the UK and Ireland, those charged with governance include the directors (executive and non-executive) of a company or other body, the members of an audit committee where one exists, the partners, proprietors, committee of management or trustees of other forms of entity, or equivalent persons responsible for directing the entity's affairs and preparing its financial statements.

1-3. 'Management' comprises those persons who perform senior managerial functions.

1-4. In the UK and Ireland, depending on the nature and circumstances of the entity, management may include some or all of those charged with governance (e.g. executive directors). Management will not normally include non-executive directors.

2. **When designing and performing audit procedures and in evaluating and reporting the results thereof, the auditor should recognize that noncompliance by the entity with laws and regulations may materially affect the financial statements.** However, an audit cannot be expected to detect noncompliance with all laws and regulations. Detection of noncompliance, regardless of materiality, requires consideration of the implications for the integrity of management[1] or employees and the possible effect on other aspects of the audit.

3. The term "noncompliance" as used in this ISA (UK and Ireland) refers to acts of omission or commission by the entity being audited, either intentional or unintentional, which are contrary to the prevailing laws or regulations. Such acts, include transactions entered into by, or in the name of, the entity or on its behalf by its management[2] or employees. For the purpose of this ISA (UK and Ireland), noncompliance does not include personal misconduct (unrelated to the business activities of the entity) by the entity's management or employees.

---

[1] In the UK and Ireland, the auditor also considers the implications for the integrity of those charged with governance.

[2] In the UK and Ireland, such acts include transactions entered into by, or in the name of, the entity or on its behalf by those charged with governance.

4. Whether an act constitutes noncompliance is a legal determination that is ordinarily beyond the auditor's professional competence. The auditor's training, experience and understanding of the entity and its industry may provide a basis for recognition that some acts coming to the auditor's attention may constitute noncompliance with laws and regulations. The determination as to whether a particular act constitutes or is likely to constitute noncompliance is generally based on the advice of an informed expert qualified to practice law but ultimately can only be determined by a court of law.

5. Laws and regulations vary considerably in their relation to the financial statements. Some laws or regulations determine the form or content of an entity's financial statements or the amounts to be recorded or disclosures to be made in financial statements. Other laws or regulations are to be complied with by management[3] or set the provisions under which the entity is allowed to conduct its business. Some entities operate in heavily regulated industries (such as banks and chemical companies). Others are only subject to the many laws and regulations that generally relate to the operating aspects of the business (such as those related to occupational safety and health and equal employment). Noncompliance with laws and regulations could result in financial consequences for the entity such as fines, litigation, etc. Generally, the further removed noncompliance is from the events and transactions ordinarily reflected in financial statements, the less likely the auditor is to become aware of it or to recognize its possible noncompliance.

5-1. When determining the type of procedures necessary in a particular instance the auditor takes account of the particular entity concerned and the complexity of the regulations with which it is required to comply. In general, a small company which does not operate in a regulated area will require few specific procedures compared with a large multinational corporation carrying on complex, regulated business.

6. Laws and regulations vary from country to country. National accounting and auditing standards are therefore likely to be more specific as to the relevance of laws and regulations to an audit.

7. This ISA (UK and Ireland) applies to audits of financial statements and does not apply to other engagements in which the auditor is specifically engaged to test and report separately on compliance with specific laws or regulations.

8. Guidance on the auditor's responsibility to consider fraud and error in an audit of financial statements is provided in ISA (UK and Ireland) 240, "The Auditor's Responsibility to Consider Fraud in an Audit of Financial Statements."

8-1. Guidance on the auditor's responsibility to report direct to regulators in the financial sector is provided in Section B of this ISA (UK and Ireland).

---

[3] In the UK and Ireland, there are also laws or regulations that are to be complied with by those charged with governance.

Responsibility of Management[4] for the Compliance With Laws and Regulations

9. It is management's responsibility to ensure that the entity's operations are conducted in accordance with laws and regulations[4]. The responsibility for the prevention and detection of noncompliance rests with management[4].

10. The following policies and procedures, among others, may assist management[5] in discharging its responsibilities for the prevention and detection of noncompliance:

    •   Monitoring legal requirements and ensuring that operating procedures are designed to meet these requirements.

    •   Instituting and operating appropriate internal control.

    •   Developing, publicizing and following a code of conduct.

    •   Ensuring employees are properly trained and understand the code of conduct.

    •   Monitoring compliance with the code of conduct and acting appropriately to discipline employees who fail to comply with it.

    •   Engaging legal advisors to assist in monitoring legal requirements.

    •   Maintaining a register of significant laws with which the entity has to comply within its particular industry and a record of complaints.

    In larger entities, these policies and procedures may be supplemented by assigning appropriate responsibilities to the following:

    •   An internal audit function.

    •   An audit committee.

    •   A legal department.

    •   A compliance function.

10-1.   In the UK and Ireland, in certain sectors or activities (for example financial services), there are detailed laws and regulations that specifically require directors to have systems to ensure compliance. These laws and regulations could, if breached, have a material effect on the financial statements. In addition, the directors are required to

---

[4]   In the UK and Ireland, this responsibility rests with those charged with governance.
[5]   In the UK and Ireland, the policies and procedures may also assist those charged with governance in discharging their responsibilities for the prevention and detection of noncompliance.

report certain instances of non-compliance to the proper authorities on a timely basis.

10-2. In the UK and Ireland, it is the directors' responsibility to prepare financial statements that give a true and fair view of the state of affairs of a company or group and of its profit or loss for the financial year. Accordingly it is necessary, where possible non-compliance with law or regulations has occurred which may result in a material misstatement in the financial statements, for them to ensure that the matter is appropriately reflected and/or disclosed in the financial statements.

10-3. In the UK and Ireland, in addition, directors and officers of companies have responsibility to provide information required by the auditor, to which they have a legal right of access[6]. Such legislation also provides that it is a criminal offence to give to the auditor information or explanations which are misleading, false or deceptive.

The Auditor's Consideration of Compliance With Laws and Regulations

11. The auditor is not, and cannot be held responsible for preventing noncompliance. The fact that an annual audit is carried out may, however, act as a deterrent.

12. An audit is subject to the unavoidable risk that some material misstatements of the financial statements will not be detected, even though the audit is properly planned and performed in accordance with ISAs (UK and Ireland). This risk is higher with regard to material misstatements resulting from noncompliance with laws and regulations due to factors such as the following:

- There are many laws and regulations, relating principally to the operating aspects of the entity, that typically do not have a material effect on the financial statements and are not captured by the entity's information systems relevant to financial reporting.

- The effectiveness of audit procedures is affected by the inherent limitations of internal control and by the use of testing.

- Much of the audit evidence obtained by the auditor is persuasive rather than conclusive in nature.

- Noncompliance may involve conduct designed to conceal it, such as collusion, forgery, deliberate failure to record transactions, senior management[7] override of controls or intentional misrepresentations being made to the auditor.

---

[6] In the UK under Section 389A of the Companies Act 1985 or Sections 193(3) and 197 of the Companies Act, 1990 in Ireland.

[7] In the UK and Ireland, an additional factor is override of controls by those charged with governance.

13. **In accordance with ISA (UK and Ireland) 200, "Objective and General Principles Governing an Audit of Financial Statements" the auditor should plan and perform the audit with an attitude of professional skepticism recognizing that the audit may reveal conditions or events that would lead to questioning whether an entity is complying with laws and regulations.**

14. In accordance with specific statutory requirements, the auditor may be specifically required to report as part of the audit of the financial statements whether the entity complies with certain provisions of laws or regulations[8]. In these circumstances, the auditor would plan to test for compliance with these provisions of the laws and regulations.

15. **In order to plan the audit, the auditor should obtain a general understanding of the legal and regulatory framework applicable to the entity and the industry and how the entity is complying with that framework.**

15-1. **In the UK and Ireland, the auditor should obtain a general understanding of the procedures followed by the entity to ensure compliance with that framework.**

16. In obtaining this general understanding, the auditor would particularly recognize that some laws and regulations may give rise to business risks that have a fundamental effect on the operations of the entity. That is, noncompliance with certain laws and regulations may cause the entity to cease operations, or call into question the entity's continuance as a going concern. For example, noncompliance with the requirements of the entity's license or other title to perform its operations could have such an impact (for example, for a bank, noncompliance with capital or investment requirements)[9].

17. To obtain the general understanding of laws and regulations, the auditor would ordinarily:

     •   Use the existing understanding of the entity's industry, regulatory and other external factors;

     •   Inquire of management[10] concerning the entity's policies and procedures regarding compliance with laws and regulations;

---

[8] In Ireland, the Companies (Auditing and Accounting) Act 2003 contains provisions that will require, when commenced, directors of "large" companies to make statements regarding compliance with the Companies Acts, tax laws and any other elements that provide a legal framework within which the company operates and that may materially affect the company's financial statements. Auditors of such companies will be required to review the statements to determine whether they are fair and reasonable having regard to information obtained by the auditor in the course of the audit or other work undertaken for the company. The auditors' review requirements are not addressed in this ISA (UK and Ireland)).

[9] Such requirements exist in the UK under the Financial Services and Markets Act 2000 and in Ireland under the Investment Intermediaries Act 1995, the Central Bank Acts 1942 to 1989 and the Credit Union Act , 1997.

[10] In the UK and Ireland, the auditor makes inquiries of such matters with those charged with governance.

- Inquire of management[10] as to the laws or regulations that may be expected to have a fundamental effect on the operations of the entity;

- Discuss with management[11] the policies or procedures adopted for identifying, evaluating and accounting for litigation claims and assessments; and

- Discuss the legal and regulatory framework with auditors of subsidiaries in other countries (for example, if the subsidiary is required to adhere to the securities regulations of the parent company).

18.   **After obtaining the general understanding, the auditor should perform further audit procedures to help identify instances of noncompliance with those laws and regulations where noncompliance should be considered when preparing financial statements, specifically:**

   (a)   **Inquiring of management as to whether the entity is in compliance with such laws and regulations; and**

   (b)   **Inspecting correspondence with the relevant licensing or regulatory authorities.**

   (c)   **Enquiring of those charged with governance as to whether they are on notice of any such possible instances of non-compliance with law or regulations.**

18-1. **In the UK and Ireland, the auditor's procedures should be designed to help identify possible or actual instances of non-compliance with those laws and regulations which provide a legal framework within which the entity conducts its business and which are central to the entity's ability to conduct its business and hence to its financial statements.**

19.   **Further, the auditor should obtain sufficient appropriate audit evidence about compliance with those laws and regulations generally recognized by the auditor to have an effect on the determination of material amounts and disclosures in financial statements. The auditor should have a sufficient understanding of these laws and regulations in order to consider them when auditing the assertions related to the determination of the amounts to be recorded and the disclosures to be made.**

20.   Such laws and regulations would be well established and known to the entity and within the industry; they would be considered on a recurring basis each time financial statements are issued. These laws and regulations, may relate, for example, to the form and content of financial statements[12], including industry specific requirements;

---

[11]   In the UK and Ireland, the auditor discusses such matters with those charged with governance.
[12]   In the UK under Schedule 4 to the Companies Act 1985 or The Companies (Amendment) Act, 1986 in Ireland.

accounting for transactions under government contracts; or the accrual or recognition of expenses for income taxes or pension costs.

20-1. In the UK and Ireland, these laws and regulations include:

- Those which determine the circumstances under which a company is prohibited from making a distribution except out of profits available for the purpose[13].

- Those laws which require auditors expressly to report non-compliance, such as the requirements relating to the maintenance of proper accounting records or the disclosure of particulars of directors' remuneration in a company's financial statements[14].

21. Other than as described in paragraphs 18-20, the auditor does not perform other audit procedures on the entity's compliance with laws and regulations since this would be outside the scope of an audit of financial statements.

22. **The auditor should be alert to the fact that audit procedures applied for the purpose of forming an opinion on the financial statements may bring instances of possible noncompliance with laws and regulations to the auditor's attention.** For example, such audit procedures include reading minutes; inquiring of the entity's management[10] and legal counsel concerning litigation, claims and assessments; and performing substantive tests of details of classes of transactions, account balances, or disclosures.

22-1. **In the UK and Ireland, when carrying out procedures for the purpose of forming an opinion on the financial statements, the auditor should be alert for those instances of possible or actual noncompliance with laws and regulations that might incur obligations for partners and staff in audit firms to report money laundering offences.**

22-2. There may be a wide range of laws and regulations falling into this category, many of which fall outside the expertise of individuals trained in financial auditing. There can therefore be no assurance that the auditor appointed to report on an entity's statements will detect all material breaches of such laws and regulations. However, when the auditor suspects the existence of breaches which could be material, the auditor needs to consider whether and how the matter ought to be reported, as set out later in this ISA (UK and Ireland).

---

[13] In the UK under Section 263 of the Companies Act 1985 or Section 45 of the Companies (Amendment) Act, 1983 in Ireland.
[14] In the UK under Sections 237(2) and 237(4)(a) of the Companies Act 1985 or Section 193 and 194 of the Companies Act, 1990 in Ireland.

22-3. Anti-money laundering legislation[15] in the UK and Ireland extends further than the laundering of money that is derived from drug trafficking or is related to terrorist[16] offences and has specific auditor reporting responsibilities[17]. The new anti-money laundering legislation imposes a duty to report money laundering in respect of the proceeds of all crime. The detailed legislation in both countries differs but the impact on the auditor can broadly be summarised as follows:

- Money laundering includes concealing, disguising, converting, transferring, removing, using, acquiring or possessing property[18] which constitutes or represents a benefit from criminal conduct[19]. Although the anti-money laundering legislation does not contain de minimis concessions in the UK the National Criminal Intelligence Service ("NCIS") has introduced guidance on reports of limited intelligence value.

- Partners and staff in audit firms are required to report suspicions[20] that a criminal

---

[15] In the UK, with effect from 1 March 2004 The Money Laundering Regulations 2003 replaced the 1993 and 2001 regulations and the requirements of the Proceeds of Crime Act 2002 were extended to the provision by way of business of audit services by a person who is eligible for appointment as a company auditor under section 25 of the Companies Act 1989.
In Ireland, with effect from 15 September 2003 the Criminal Justice Act 1994 (Section 32) Regulations 2003 designate accountants, auditors, and tax advisors and others for the purposes of the anti-money laundering provisions of the Criminal Justice Act, 1994, as amended.

[16] In the UK, the Terrorism Act 2000 (as amended by the Anti-terrorism, Crime and Security Act 2001) and associated regulations. The duty to report drug trafficking related money laundering has been subsumed into the general requirement to report the proceeds of crime.
In Ireland, there is similar proposed legislation that the auditor will need to consider in due course.

[17] Anti-money laundering legislation differs in the UK and Ireland, references to such legislation in the main body of the SAS uses generalised wording with the specific requirements of the UK and Irish legislation described in footnotes.

[18] In the UK, "property" is criminal property if it constitutes a person's benefit from criminal conduct or it represents such a benefit (in whole or part and whether directly or indirectly), and the alleged offender knows or suspects that it constitutes or represents such a benefit.
In Ireland, "property" is defined as including money and all other property, real or personal, heritable or moveable, including choses in action and other intangible or incorporeal property.

[19] In the UK, "criminal conduct" is defined as conduct which constitutes an offence in any part of the UK or would constitute such an offence if it occurred in any part of the UK.
In Ireland, "criminal conduct" means conduct which constitutes an 'indictable offence', or where the conduct occurs outside the State, would constitute such an offence if it occurred within the State and also constitutes an offence under the law of the country or territorial unit in which it occurs, and includes participation in such conduct.

[20] In the UK, as a result of the Proceeds of Crime Act 2002 and the 2003 Money Laundering Regulations auditors are required to report where they know or suspect, or have reasonable grounds to know or suspect, that another person is engaged in money laundering. Partners and staff in audit firms discharge their responsibilities by reporting to their Money Laundering Reporting Officer ("MLRO") or, in the case of sole practitioners, to NCIS.
In Ireland, the Criminal Justice Act, 1994, as amended, and the Criminal Justice Act, 1994 (Section 32) Regulations, 2003 require auditors and other defined persons to report to the Garda Síochána and the Revenue Commissioners where they suspect that an offence, as defined in the legislation, in relation to the business of that person has been or is being committed. Two further reporting duties exist in Irish law, Section 74 of the Company Law Enforcement Act 2001 requires auditors to report to the Director of Corporate Enforcement instances of the suspected commission of indictable offences under the Companies Acts and Section 59 of the Criminal Justice (Theft and Fraud Offences) Act, 2001 requires 'relevant persons', as defined in the section and which includes auditors of companies, to report 'indications' that specified offences under the Act have been committed to the Garda Síochána. Additionally, auditors may report direct to the Revenue Commissioners certain offences under Section 1079 of the Taxes Consolidation Act, 1997.

offence, giving rise to direct or indirect benefit has been committed, regardless of whether that offence has been committed by a client or by a third party.

- Partners and staff in audit firms need to be alert to the dangers of making disclosures that are likely to tip off a money launderer or prejudice an investigation ('tipping-off[21]'), as this will constitute a criminal offence under the anti-money laundering legislation.

23. **The auditor should obtain written representations that management[22] has disclosed to the auditor all known actual or possible noncompliance with laws and regulations whose effects should be considered when preparing financial statements.**

23-1. **Where applicable, the written representations should include the actual or contingent consequences which may arise from the non-compliance.**

24. In the absence of audit evidence to the contrary, the auditor is entitled to assume the entity is in compliance with these laws and regulations.

Compliance with Tax Legislation

24-1. In the UK and Ireland, the auditor's responsibility to express an opinion on an entity's financial statements does not extend to determining whether the entity has complied in every respect with applicable tax legislation. The auditor needs to obtain sufficient appropriate evidence to give reasonable assurance that the amounts included in the financial statements in respect of taxation are not materially misstated. This will usually include making appropriate enquiries of those advising the entity on taxation matters (whether within the audit firm or elsewhere).

24-2. In the UK and Ireland, if the auditor becomes aware that the entity has failed to comply with the requirements of tax legislation, the auditor follows the procedures for reporting set out in paragraphs 38 to 38-1 of this ISA (UK and Ireland).

---

[21] In the UK, 'tipping off' is an offence under section 333 of the Proceeds of Crime Act 2002. It arises when an individual discloses matters where:
(a) There is knowledge or suspicion that a report has already been made, and
(b) That disclosure is likely to prejudice any investigation which might be conducted following the report.
Whilst "tipping off" requires a person to have knowledge or suspicion that a report has been or will be made, a further offence of prejudicing an investigation is included in section 342 of POCA. Under this provision, it is an offence to make any disclosure which may prejudice an investigation of which a person has knowledge or suspicion, or to falsify, conceal, destroy or otherwise dispose of, or cause or permit the falsification, concealment, destruction or disposal of, documents relevant to such an investigation.
In Ireland Section 58 of the Criminal Justice Act, 1994, as amended, establishes the offence of "prejudicing an investigation". This relates both to when a person, knowing or suspecting that an investigation is taking place, makes any disclosure likely to prejudice the investigation or when a person, knowing that a report has been made, makes any disclosure likely to prejudice any investigation arising from the report.
[22] In the UK and Ireland the auditor obtains this written representation from those charged with governance.

Audit Procedures When Noncompliance is Discovered

25. The Appendix to this ISA (UK and Ireland) sets out examples of the type of information that might come to the auditor's attention that may indicate noncompliance.

26. **When the auditor becomes aware of information concerning a possible instance of noncompliance, the auditor should[23] obtain an understanding of the nature of the act and the circumstances in which it has occurred, and sufficient other information to evaluate the possible effect on the financial statements.**

27. When evaluating the possible effect on the financial statements, the auditor considers:

   • The potential financial consequences, such as fines, penalties, damages, threat of expropriation of assets[24], enforced discontinuation of operations and litigation.

   • Whether the potential financial consequences require disclosure.

   • Whether the potential financial consequences are so serious as to call into question the true and fair view (fair presentation) given by the financial statements.

27-1. As the consideration of compliance with laws and regulations may involve consideration of matters which do not lie within the competence and experience of individuals trained in the audit of financial information, it may be necessary for the auditor to obtain appropriate expert advice (whether through the entity or independently) in order to evaluate the possible effect on the entity's financial statements. Where this is the case, the auditor is required to meet the Standards set out in ISA (UK and Ireland) 620 "Using the work of an expert".

28. **When the auditor believes there may be noncompliance, the auditor should document the findings and discuss them with management[11].** Documentation of findings would include copies of records and documents and making minutes of conversations, if appropriate.

28-1. **Any discussion of findings with those charged with governance and with management should be subject to compliance with legislation relating to 'tipping off' and any requirement to report the findings direct to a third party.**

---

[23] Subject to compliance with legislation relating to 'tipping off'. See footnote 21.

[24] The Proceeds of Crime Act 2002 ("POCA") establishes an independent Government Department, the Assets Recovery Agency.
In Ireland, the Criminal Assets Bureau, a similar agency responsible for the confiscation of assets was established by the Criminal Assets Bureau Act, 1996.

29.   If management[25] does not provide satisfactory information that it is in fact in compliance, the auditor would consult with the entity's lawyer about the application of the laws and regulations to the circumstances and the possible effects on the financial statements. When it is not considered appropriate to consult with the entity's lawyer or when the auditor is not satisfied with the opinion, the auditor would consider consulting the auditor's own lawyer as to whether a violation of a law or regulation is involved, the possible legal consequences and what further action, if any, the auditor would take.

30.   **When adequate information about the suspected noncompliance cannot be obtained, the auditor should consider the effect of the lack of sufficient appropriate audit evidence on the auditor's report.**

31.   **The auditor should consider the implications of noncompliance in relation to other aspects of the audit, particularly the reliability of management[26] representations.** In this regard, the auditor reconsiders the risk assessment and the validity of management representations, in case of noncompliance not detected by the entity's internal controls or not included in management representations. The implications of particular instances of noncompliance discovered by the auditor will depend on the relationship of the perpetration and concealment, if any, of the act to specific control activities and the level of management or employees involved.

Reporting of Noncompliance

To Management

32.   **The auditor should, as soon as practicable, either communicate with those charged with governance, or obtain audit evidence that they are appropriately informed, regarding noncompliance that comes to the auditor's attention.** However, the auditor need not do so for matters that are clearly inconsequential or trivial and may reach agreement in advance on the nature of such matters to be communicated.

33.   **If in the auditor's judgment the noncompliance is believed to be intentional and material, the auditor should communicate the finding without delay.**

33-1. **In the UK and Ireland the auditor should communicate the finding where the non-compliance is material or is believed to be intentional. The non-compliance does not have to be both material and intentional.**

33-2. Any communication with those charged with governance, or action by the auditor to obtain evidence that they are appropriately informed is subject to compliance with legislation relating to 'tipping off'.

---

[25] In the UK and Ireland, the auditor obtains such information from those charged with governance.
[26] In the UK and Ireland, the auditor also considers the reliability of representations from those charged with governance.

34. **If the auditor suspects that members of senior management, including members of the board of directors[27], are involved in noncompliance, the auditor should report the matter to the next higher level of authority at the entity, if it exists, such as an audit committee or a supervisory board.** Where no higher authority exists, or if the auditor believes that the report may not be acted upon or is unsure as to the person to whom to report, the auditor would consider seeking legal advice.

34-1. In the case of suspected Money Laundering it may be appropriate to report the matter direct to the appropriate authority.

To the Users of the Auditor's Report on the Financial Statements

35. **If the auditor concludes that the noncompliance has a material effect on the financial statements, and has not been properly reflected in the financial statements, the auditor should[23] express a qualified or an adverse opinion.**

36. **If the auditor is precluded by the entity from obtaining sufficient appropriate audit evidence to evaluate whether noncompliance that may be material to the financial statements, has, or is likely to have, occurred, the auditor should[23] express a qualified opinion or a disclaimer of opinion on the financial statements on the basis of a limitation on the scope of the audit.**

37. **If the auditor is unable to determine whether noncompliance has occurred because of limitations imposed by the circumstances rather than by the entity, the auditor should[23] consider the effect on the auditor's report.**

37-1. In the UK and Ireland, if the auditor concludes that the view given by the financial statements could be affected by a level of uncertainty concerning the consequences of a suspected or actual noncompliance which, in the auditor's opinion, is significant, the auditor, subject to compliance with legislation relating to 'tipping off', includes an explanatory paragraph referring to the matter in the auditor's report.

37-2. In the UK and Ireland, in determining whether disclosures concerning the matter are adequate, or whether an explanatory paragraph needs to be included in the auditor's report, the auditor bases the decision primarily on the adequacy of the overall view given by the financial statements. Steps taken to regularize the position (for example, where there has been an unauthorized material transaction for which authority has subsequently been obtained), or the possible consequences of qualification, are not, on their own, grounds on which the auditor may refrain from expressing a qualified opinion or from including an explanatory paragraph reflecting a significant uncertainty.

37-3. In the UK and Ireland, when determining whether a suspected or actual instance of non-compliance with laws or regulations requires disclosure in the financial statements, the auditor has regard to whether shareholders require the information

---

[27] In the UK and Ireland, the auditor also reports such matters if those charged with governance are suspected of being involved in non compliance.

to enable them to assess the performance of the company and any potential implications for its future operations or standing. Where a suspected or actual instance of non-compliance needs to be reflected in the financial statements, a true and fair view will require that sufficient particulars are provided to enable users of the financial statements to appreciate the significance of the information disclosed. This would usually require the full potential consequences to be disclosed and, in some cases, it may be necessary for this purpose that the financial statements indicate that non-compliance with laws or regulations is or may be involved.

37-4. In the UK and Ireland, when considering whether the financial statements reflect the possible consequences of any suspected or actual non-compliance, the auditor has regard to the requirements of FRS 12 "Provisions, contingent liabilities and contingent assets"/IAS 37, "Provisions, contingent liabilities and contingent assets". Suspected or actual non-compliance with laws or regulations may require disclosure in the financial statements because, although the immediate financial effect on the entity may not be material, there could be future material consequences such as fines or litigation. For example, an illegal payment may not itself be material but may result in criminal proceedings against the entity or loss of business which could have a material effect on the true and fair view given by the financial statements.

To Regulatory and Enforcement Authorities

38. The auditor's duty of confidentiality would ordinarily preclude reporting noncompliance to a third party. However, in certain circumstances, that duty of confidentiality is overridden by statute, law or by courts of law (for example, in some countries the auditor is required to report noncompliance by financial institutions to the supervisory authorities). The auditor may need to seek legal advice in such circumstances, giving due consideration to the auditor's responsibility to the public interest.

38-1. **If the auditor becomes aware of a suspected or actual non-compliance with law and regulations which gives rise to a statutory duty to report, the auditor should, subject to compliance with legislation relating to "tipping off", make a report to the appropriate authority without undue delay.**

38-2. Legislation in the UK and Ireland establishes specific responsibilities for the auditor to report suspicions regarding certain criminal offences. In addition, the auditor of entities subject to statutory regulation[28], has separate responsibilities to report certain information direct to the relevant regulator. Standards and guidance on these responsibilities is given in Section B of this ISA (UK and Ireland) and relevant APB Practice Notes.

---

[28] Auditors of financial service entities, pension schemes and, in the UK, charities have a statutory responsibility, subject to compliance with legislation relating to "tipping off", to report matters that are likely to be of material significance to the regulator.

38-3. The procedures and guidance in Section B of this ISA (UK and Ireland) can be adapted to circumstances in which the auditor of other types of entity becomes aware of a suspected instance of non-compliance with laws or regulations which the auditor is under a statutory duty to report.

38-4. Where the auditor becomes aware of a suspected or actual instance of non-compliance with law or regulations which does not give rise to a statutory duty to report to an appropriate authority the auditor considers whether the matter may be one that ought to be reported to a proper authority in the public interest and, where this is the case, except in the circumstances covered in paragraph 38-6 below, discusses the matter with those charged with governance, including any audit committee.

38-5. If, having considered any views expressed on behalf of the entity and in the light of any legal advice obtained, the auditor concludes that the matter ought to be reported to an appropriate authority in the public interest, the auditor notifies those charged with governance in writing of the view and, if the entity does not voluntarily do so itself or is unable to provide evidence that the matter has been reported, the auditor reports it.

38-6. The auditor reports a matter direct to a proper authority in the public interest and without discussing the matter with the entity if the auditor concludes that the suspected or actual instance of non-compliance has caused the auditor no longer to have confidence in the integrity of the those charged with governance.

38-7. Examples of circumstances which may cause the auditor no longer to have confidence in the integrity of those charged with governance include situations:

- Where the auditor suspects or has evidence of the involvement or intended involvement of those charged with governance in possible non-compliance with law or regulations which could have a material effect on the financial statements; or

- Where the auditor is aware that those charged with governance are aware of such non-compliance and, contrary to regulatory requirements or the public interest, have not reported it to a proper authority within a reasonable period.

38-8. Determination of where the balance of public interest lies requires careful consideration. An auditor whose suspicions have been aroused uses professional judgment to determine whether the auditor's misgivings justify the auditor in carrying the matter further or are too insubstantial to deserve reporting. The auditor is protected from the risk of liability for breach of confidence or defamation provided that:

- In the case of breach of confidence, disclosure is made in the public interest, and such disclosure is made to an appropriate body or person[29], and there is no malice motivating the disclosure; and

- In the case of defamation disclosure is made in the auditor's capacity as auditor of the entity concerned, and there is no malice motivating the disclosure.

In addition, the auditor is protected from such risks where the auditor is expressly permitted or required by legislation to disclose information.

38-9. 'Public interest' is a concept that is not capable of general definition. Each situation must be considered individually. Matters to be taken into account when considering whether disclosure is justified in the public interest may include:

- The extent to which the suspected or actual non-compliance with law or regulations is likely to affect members of the public;

- Whether those charged with governance have rectified the matter or are taking, or are likely to take, effective corrective action;

- The extent to which non-disclosure is likely to enable the suspected or actual non-compliance with law or regulations to recur with impunity;

- The gravity of the matter;

- Whether there is a general ethos within the entity of disregarding law or regulations; and

- The weight of evidence and the degree of the auditor's suspicion that there has been an instance of non-compliance with law or regulations.

38-10. An auditor who can demonstrate having acted reasonably and in good faith in informing an authority of a breach of law or regulations which the auditor thinks has been committed would not be held by the court to be in breach of duty to the client even if, an investigation or prosecution having occurred, it were found that there had been no offence.

38-11. The auditor needs to remember that the auditor's decision as to whether to report, and if so to whom, may be called into question at a future date, for example on the basis of:

---

[29] In the UK, proper authorities could include the Serious Fraud Office, the Crown Prosecution Service, police forces, the Financial Services Authority the Panel on Takeovers and Mergers, the Society of Lloyd's, local authorities, the Charity Commissioners for England and Wales, the Scottish Office For Scottish Charities, the Inland Revenue, HM Customs and Excise, the Department of Trade and Industry and the Health and Safety Executive.
In Ireland, comparable bodies could include the Garda Bureau of Fraud Investigation, the Revenue Commissioners, the Irish Stock Exchange, the Irish Financial Services Regulatory Authority, the Pensions Board, the Director of Corporate Enforcement and the Department of Enterprise Trade and Employment.

- What the auditor knew at the time;

- What the auditor to have known in the course of the audit;

- What the auditor ought to have concluded; and

- What the auditor ought to have done.

  The auditor may also wish to consider the possible consequences if financial loss is occasioned by non-compliance with law or regulations which the auditor suspects (or ought to suspect) has occurred but decided not to report.

38-12. The auditor may need to take legal advice before making a decision on whether the matter needs to be reported to a proper authority in the public interest.

Withdrawal From the Engagement

39.   The auditor may conclude that withdrawal from the engagement is necessary when the entity does not take the remedial action that the auditor considers necessary in the circumstances, even when the noncompliance is not material to the financial statements. Factors that would affect the auditor's conclusion include the implications of the involvement of the highest authority within the entity which may affect the reliability of management[26] representations, and the effects on the auditor of continuing association with the entity. In reaching such a conclusion, the auditor would ordinarily seek legal advice.

39-1.   Resignation by the auditor is a step of last resort. It is normally preferable for the auditor to remain in office to fulfil the auditor's statutory duties, particularly where minority interests are involved. However, there are circumstances where there may be no alternative to resignation, for example where the directors of a company refuse to issue its financial statements or the auditor wishes to inform the shareholders or creditors of the company of the auditor's concerns and there is no immediate occasion to do so.

40.   **As stated in the *Code of Ethics for Professional Accountants*[30] issued by the International Federation of Accountants, on receipt of an inquiry from the proposed auditor, the existing auditor should advise whether there are any professional reasons why the proposed auditor should not accept the appointment.** The extent to which an existing auditor can discuss the affairs of a client with a proposed auditor will depend on whether the client's permission to do so has been obtained and/or the legal or ethical requirements that apply in each country relating to such disclosure. If there are any such reasons or other matters which need to be disclosed, the existing auditor would, taking account of the legal

---

[30] In the UK and Ireland the relevant ethical pronouncements with which the auditor complies are the APB's Ethical Standards and the ethical pronouncements relating to the work of auditors issued by the auditor's relevant professional body - see the Statement "The Auditing practices Board – Scope and Authority of Pronouncements.

and ethical constraints, including where appropriate permission of the client, give details of the information and discuss freely with the proposed auditor all matters relevant to the appointment. **If permission from the client to discuss its affairs with the proposed auditor is denied by the client, that fact should be disclosed to the proposed auditor.**

Effective Date

40-1. This ISA (UK and Ireland) is effective for audits of financial statements for periods commencing on or after 15 December 2004.

40-2. In the UK, the Money Laundering Regulations 2003 came into force on 1 March 2004. In Ireland, the Criminal Justice Act 1994 (Section 32) Regulations 2003 are effective from 15 September 2003.

Public Sector Perspective

Additional guidance for auditors of public sector bodies in the UK and Ireland is given in:

- Practice Note 10 "Audit of Financial Statements of Public Sector Bodies in the United Kingdom (Revised)"

- Practice Note 10(I) "Audit of Central Government Financial Statements in the Republic of Ireland (Revised)"

1. *Many public sector engagements include additional audit responsibilities with respect to consideration of laws and regulations. Even if the auditor's responsibilities do not extend beyond those of the private sector auditor, reporting responsibilities may be different as the public sector auditor may be obliged to report on instances of noncompliance to governing authorities or to report them in the audit report. In respect to public sector entities, the Public Sector Committee (PSC) has supplemented the guidance included in this ISA (UK and Ireland) in its Study 3, "Auditing for Compliance with Authorities—A Public Sector Perspective."*

Appendix

Indications That Noncompliance May Have Occurred

Examples of the type of information that may come to the auditor's attention that may indicate that noncompliance with laws or regulations has occurred are listed below:

- Investigation by government departments.

- Payment of fines or penalties.

- Payments for unspecified services or loans to consultants, related parties, employees or government employees.

- Sales commissions or agent's fees that appear excessive in relation to those ordinarily paid by the entity or in its industry or to the services actually received.

- Purchasing at prices significantly above or below market price.

- Unusual payments in cash, purchases in the form of cashiers' checks payable to bearer or transfers to numbered bank accounts.

- Complex corporate structures including offshore companies where ownership cannot be identified.

- Unusual transactions with companies registered in tax havens.

- Tax evasion such as the under declaring of income and over claiming of expenses.

- Payments for goods or services made other than to the country from which the goods or services originated.

- Payments without proper exchange control documentation.

- Existence of an information system which fails, whether by design or by accident, to provide an adequate audit trail or sufficient evidence.

- Unauthorized transactions or improperly recorded transactions.

- Media comment.

- Transactions undertaken by the entity that have no apparent purpose or that make no obvious economic sense.

- Where those charged with governance of the entity refuse to provide necessary information and explanations to support transactions and other dealings of the company.

Section B

The Auditor's Right and Duty to Report to Regulators in the Financial Sector

Introduction

1. The purpose of this Section of this ISA (UK and Ireland) is to establish standards and provide guidance on the circumstances in which the auditor of a financial institution subject to statutory regulation (a 'regulated entity') is required to report direct to a regulator information which comes to the auditor's attention in the course of the work undertaken in the auditor's capacity as auditor of the regulated entity. This may include work undertaken to express an opinion on the entity's financial statements, other financial information or on other matters specified by legislation or by a regulator.

2. **The auditor of a regulated entity should bring information of which the auditor has become aware in the ordinary course of performing work undertaken to fulfil the auditor's audit responsibilities to the attention of the appropriate regulator without delay when:**

    (a) **The auditor concludes that it is relevant to the regulator's functions having regard to such matters as may be specified in statute or any related regulations; and**

    (b) **In the auditor's opinion there is reasonable cause to believe it is or may be of material significance to the regulator.**

3. The auditor of a regulated entity generally has special reporting responsibilities in addition to the responsibility to report on financial statements. These special reporting responsibilities take two forms:

    (a) *A responsibility to provide a report on matters specified in legislation or by a regulator.* This form of report is often made on an annual or other routine basis and does not derive from another set of reporting responsibilities. The auditor is required to carry out appropriate procedures sufficient to form an opinion on the matters concerned. These procedures may be in addition to those carried out to form an opinion on the financial statements; and

    (b) *A statutory duty to report certain information, relevant to the regulators' functions, that come to the auditor's attention in the course of the audit work.* The auditor has no responsibility to carry out procedures to search out the information relevant to the regulator. This form of report is derivative in nature, arising only in the context of another set of reporting responsibilities, and is initiated by the auditor on discovery of a reportable matter.

4.   The statutory duty to report to a regulator applies to information which comes to the attention of the auditor in the auditor's capacity as auditor. In determining whether information is obtained in that capacity, two criteria in particular need to be considered: first, whether the person who obtained the information also undertook the audit work; and if so, whether it was obtained in the course of or as a result of undertaking the audit work. Appendix 2 to this section of this ISA (UK and Ireland) sets out guidance on the application of these criteria.

5.   The auditor may have a statutory right to bring information to the attention of the regulator in particular circumstances which lie outside those giving rise to a statutory duty to initiate a direct report. Where this is so, the auditor may use that right to make a direct report relevant to the regulator on a specific matter which comes to the auditor's attention when the auditor concludes that doing so is necessary to protect the interests of those for whose benefit the regulator is required to act.

6.   This section of this ISA (UK and Ireland) deals with both forms of direct reports. Guidance on the auditor's responsibility to provide special reports on a routine basis on other matters specified in legislation or by a regulator is given in the Practice Notes dealing with regulated business, for example banks, building societies, investment businesses and insurers.

7.   The standards and explanatory material in this section of this ISA (UK and Ireland) complement but do not replace the legal and regulatory requirements applicable to each regulated entity. Where the application of those requirements, taking into account any published interpretations, is insufficiently clear for the auditor to determine whether a particular circumstance results in a legal duty to make a report to a regulator, or a right to make such a report, it may be appropriate to take legal advice.

Definitions

8.   **The Act**: In the United Kingdom, this comprises the Financial Services and Markets Act 2000 and regulations made under that Act, and any future legislation including provisions relating to the duties of auditors similar to those contained in that statute.

9.   In the Republic of Ireland, *the Acts* comprise the Central Bank Acts 1942 to 1989, the Building Societies Act 1989, The Central Bank and Financial Services Authority of Ireland Act, 2003, the Trustees Savings Bank Act 1989, the Insurance Act 1989, the European Communities (Undertakings for Collective Investment in Transferable Securities) Regulations 1989, the Unit Trusts Act 1990, the ICC Bank Act (section 3) Regulations 1993 and, in the case of investment companies, the Companies Act 1990 and any future legislation[1] including provisions relating to the duties of auditors similar to those contained in those Acts, together with other regulations made under them.

---

[1]   Specifically, the Central Bank and Financial Services Authority of Ireland (no. 2) Bill published in December 2003 is also likely to introduce changes to the duties of auditors.

10. **Audit**: for the purpose of this Section of this ISA (UK and Ireland), the term *audit* refers both to an engagement to report on the financial statements of a regulated entity and to an engagement to provide a report on other matters specified by statute or by a regulator undertaken in the capacity of auditor.

11. **Auditor**: the term 'auditor' should be interpreted in accordance with the requirements of the Acts. Guidance on its interpretation is contained in Practice Notes relating to each area of the financial sector to which the duty applies.

12. **Control environment**: the overall attitude, awareness and actions of those charged with governance and management regarding internal controls and their importance in the entity. Factors reflected in the control environment include:

    • Management's philosophy and operating style;

    • The entity's organisational structure and methods of assigning authority and responsibility (including segregation of duties and management supervisory controls); and

    • Management's methods of imposing control including the internal audit function, the functions of those charged with governance and personnel policies and procedures.

13. **Those charged with governance**: In the UK and Ireland, those charged with governance include the directors (executive and non-executive) of a company or other body, the members of an audit committee where one exists, the partners, proprietors, committee of management or trustees of other forms of entity, or equivalent persons responsible for directing the entity's affairs and preparing its financial statements.

14. **Material significance**: the term 'material significance' requires interpretation in the context of the specific legislation applicable to the regulated entity. A matter or group of matters is normally of material significance to a regulator's functions when, due either to its nature or its potential financial impact, it is likely of itself to require investigation by the regulator. Further guidance on the interpretation of the term in the context of specific legislation is contained in Practice Notes dealing with the rights and duties of auditors of regulated entities to report direct to regulators.

15. **Regulated entity**: an individual, company or other type of entity authorised to carry on business in the financial sector which is subject to statutory regulation.

16. **Regulator**: such persons as are empowered by the Act to regulate business in the financial sector. The term includes the Financial Services Authority (FSA), Irish Financial Services Regulatory Authority (IFSRA) and such other bodies as may be so empowered in future legislation.

Appointment as Auditor and Ceasing to Hold Office

17. Before accepting appointment, the auditor follows the procedures identified in the APB's Ethical Standards and the ethical pronouncements and Audit Regulations issued by the auditor's relevant professional body.

18. In the case of regulated entities, the auditor would in particular obtain an understanding of the appropriate statutory and regulatory requirements and a preliminary knowledge of the management and operations of the entity, so as to enable the auditor to determine whether a level of knowledge of the business adequate to perform the audit can be obtained. The procedures carried out by the auditor in seeking to obtain this preliminary understanding may include discussion with the previous auditor and, in some circumstances, with the regulator.

19. On ceasing to hold office, the auditor may be required by statute or by regulation to make specific reports concerning the circumstances relating to that event, and would also follow the procedures identified in the ethical guidance issued by the relevant professional body.

20. In addition, the auditor of a regulated entity would assess whether it is appropriate to bring any matters of which the auditor is then aware to the notice of the regulator. Under legislation in the UK, this may be done either before or after ceasing to hold office, as the auditor's statutory right to disclose to a regulator information obtained in the course of the auditor's appointment is not affected by the auditor's removal, resignation or otherwise ceasing to hold office.

Conduct of the Audit

21. The duty to make a report direct to a regulator does not impose upon the auditor a duty to carry out specific work: it arises solely in the context of work carried out to fulfil other reporting responsibilities. Accordingly, no auditing procedures in addition to those carried out in the normal course of auditing the financial statements, or for the purpose of making any other specified report, are necessary for the fulfilment of the auditor's responsibilities.

22. It will, however, be necessary for the auditor to take additional time in carrying out a financial statement audit or other engagement to assess whether matters which come to the auditor's attention should be included in a direct report and, where appropriate, to prepare and submit the report. These additional planning and follow-up procedures do not constitute an extension of the scope of the financial statement audit or of other work undertaken to provide a specified report relating to a regulated entity. They are necessary solely in order to understand and clarify the reporting responsibility and, where appropriate, to make a report.

23. The circumstances in which the auditor is required by statute to make a report direct to a regulator include matters which are not considered as part of the audit of financial statements or of work undertaken to discharge other routine responsibilities. For example, the duty to report would apply to information of which the auditor became aware in the course of the auditor's work which is relevant to the FSA's criteria for approved persons, although the auditor is not otherwise required to express an opinion on such matters. However, the legislation imposing a duty to make reports direct to regulators does not require the auditor to change the scope of the audit work, nor does it place on the auditor an obligation to conduct the audit work in such a way that there is reasonable certainty that the auditor will discover all matters which regulators might consider as being of material significance. Therefore, whilst the auditor of a regulated entity is required to be alert to matters which may require a report, the auditor is not expected to be aware of all circumstances which, had the auditor known of them, would have led the auditor to make such a report. It is only when the auditor becomes aware of such a matter during the conduct of the normal audit work that the auditor has an obligation to determine whether a report to the regulator is required by statute or appropriate for other reasons.

24. Similarly, the auditor is not responsible for reporting on a regulated entity's overall compliance with rules with which it is required to comply nor is the auditor required to conduct the audit work in such a way that there is reasonable certainty that the auditor will discover breaches. Nevertheless, breaches of rules with which a regulated entity is required to comply may have implications for the financial statements and, accordingly, the auditor of a regulated entity needs to consider whether any actual or contingent liabilities may have arisen from breaches of regulatory requirements. Breaches of a regulator's requirements may also have consequences for other matters on which the auditor of a regulated entity is required to express an opinion and, if such breaches represent criminal conduct, could give rise to the need to report to specified authorities.

Planning

25. **When gaining a knowledge of the business for the purpose of the audit, the auditor of a regulated entity should obtain an understanding of its current activities, the scope of its authorisation and the effectiveness of its control environment.**

26. ISAs (UK and Ireland) require the auditor to gain a sufficient understanding of the reporting entity's business to plan and perform the audit effectively and to assess the risk of material misstatements in the financial statements.

27. In the context of a regulated entity, the auditor's understanding of its business needs to extend to the applicable statutory provisions, the rules of the regulator concerned and any guidance issued by the regulator on the interpretation of those rules, together with other guidance issued by the APB.

28. The auditor is also required to assess the risk of misstatements in the financial statements, or of other errors in relation to other matters on which the auditor is required to report. In making such an assessment the auditor takes into account the control environment, including the entity's higher level procedures for complying with the requirements of its regulator. Such a review gives an indication of the extent to which the general atmosphere and controls in the regulated entity are conducive to compliance, for example through consideration of *inter alia:*

- The adequacy of procedures and training to inform staff of the requirements of relevant legislation and the rules or other regulations of the regulator;

- The adequacy of procedures for authorisation of transactions;

- Procedures for internal review of the entity's compliance with regulatory or other requirements;

- The authority of, and any resources available to, the compliance officer/Money Laundering Reporting Officer ('MLRO'); and

- Procedures to ensure that possible breaches of requirements are investigated by an appropriate person and are brought to the attention of senior management.

29. In some areas of the financial sector, conducting business outside the scope of the entity's authorisation is a serious regulatory breach, and therefore of material significance to the regulator. In addition, it may result in fines, suspension or loss of authorisation.

30. Where the auditor's review of the reporting entity's activities indicates that published guidance by the regulator may not be sufficiently precise to enable the auditor to identify circumstances in which it is necessary to initiate a report, the auditor would consider whether it is necessary to discuss the matters specified in legislation with the appropriate regulator with a view to reaching agreement on its interpretation.

31. Similarly, where a group includes two or more companies separately regulated by different regulators, there may be a need to clarify the regulators' requirements in any overlapping areas of activity. However, the statutory duty to make a report as presently defined arises only in respect of the legal entity subject to regulation. Therefore the auditor of an unregulated company in a group that includes one or more other companies which are authorised by regulators would not have a duty to report matters to the regulators of those companies.

32. When a regulated entity is subject to provisions of two or more regulators, the auditor needs to take account of the separate reporting requirements in planning and conducting the audit work. Arrangements may exist for one regulatory body to rely on financial monitoring being carried out by another body (the 'lead regulator') and where this is the case, routine reports by the regulated entity's auditor may be made to the lead regulator alone.

33. However, the auditor's statutory duty to report cannot be discharged by reliance on the lead regulator informing others. Therefore, where the auditor concludes that a matter is of material significance to one regulator, the auditor needs to assess the need for separate reports informing each regulator of matters which the auditor concludes are or may be of material significance to it.

Supervision and Control

34. **The auditor should ensure that all staff involved in the audit of a regulated entity have an understanding of:**

    (a) **The provisions of applicable legislation;**

    (b) **The regulator's rules and any guidance issued by the regulator; and**

    (c) **Any specific requirements which apply to the particular regulated entity,**

    appropriate to their role in the audit and sufficient (in the context of that role) to enable them to identify situations which may give reasonable cause to believe that a matter should be reported to the regulator.

35. ISAs (UK and Ireland) require the auditor to exercise adequate control and supervision over staff conducting work on an audit. Consequently, in planning and conducting the audit of a regulated entity the auditor needs to ensure that staff are alert to the possibility that a report to its regulator may be required.

36. Auditing firms also need to establish adequate procedures to ensure that any matters which are discovered in the course of or as a result of audit work and may give rise to a duty to report are brought to the attention of the partner responsible for the audit on a timely basis.

37. The right and duty to report to a regulator applies to information of which the auditor becomes aware in the auditor's capacity as such. They do not extend automatically to any information obtained by an accounting firm regardless of its source. Consequently partners and staff undertaking work in another capacity are not required to have detailed knowledge of the regulator's requirements (unless necessary for that other work) nor to bring information to the attention of the partner responsible for the audit on a routine basis.

38. However, as discussed further in Appendix 2, firms need to establish lines of communications, commensurate with their size and complexity, sufficient to ensure that non-audit work undertaken for a regulated entity which is likely to have an effect on the audit is brought to the attention of the partner responsible for the audit, who will need to determine whether the results of non-audit work undertaken for a regulated entity ought to be assessed as part of the audit process.

Identifying Matters Requiring a Report Direct to Regulators

39. **Where an apparent breach of statutory or regulatory requirements comes to the auditor's attention, the auditor should:**

    (a) **Obtain such evidence as is available to assess its implications for the auditor's reporting responsibilities;**

    (b) **Determine whether, in the auditor's opinion, there is reasonable cause to believe that the breach is of material significance to the regulator; and**

    (c) **Consider whether the apparent breach is criminal conduct that gives rise to criminal property and, as such, should be reported to the specified authorities.**

40. The precise matters which give rise to a statutory duty on auditors to make a report to a regulator derive from the relevant Acts. Broadly, such matters fall into three general categories:

    (a) The financial position of the regulated entity;

    (b) Its compliance with requirements for the management of its business; and

    (c) The status of those charged with governance as fit and proper persons.

    Further detailed guidance on the interpretation of these matters in the context of specific legislation applicable to each type of regulated entity is contained in Practice Notes dealing with the rights and duties of auditors of regulated entities to report direct to regulators.

41. In assessing the effect of an apparent breach, the auditor takes into account the quantity and type of evidence concerning such a matter which may reasonably be expected to be available. If the auditor concludes that the auditor has been prevented from obtaining all such evidence concerning a matter which may give rise to a duty to report, the auditor would normally make a report direct to the regulator without delay.

42. An apparent breach of statutory or regulatory requirements may not of itself give rise to a statutory duty to make a report to a regulator. There will normally be a need for some further investigation and discussion of the circumstances surrounding the apparent breach with the directors in order to obtain sufficient information to determine whether it points to a matter which is or may be of material significance to the regulator. For example, a minor breach which has been corrected by the regulated entity and reported (if appropriate) to the regulator, and which from the evidence available to the auditor appears to be an isolated occurrence, would not normally give the auditor reasonable cause to believe that it is or may be of material significance to the regulator. However a minor breach that results in a criminal offence that gave rise to the criminal property would be reportable to the specified authorities under the anti-money laundering legislation.

43. When determining whether a breach of statutory or regulatory requirements gives rise to a statutory duty to make a report direct to a regulator, the auditor considers factors such as:

- Whether the breach, though minor, is indicative of a general lack of compliance with the regulator's requirements or otherwise casts doubt on the status of those charged with governance as fit and proper persons;

- Whether a breach which occurred before the auditor's visit to the regulated entity was reported by the entity itself and has since been corrected, such that, at the date of the auditor's discovery, no breach exists;

- Whether the circumstances giving rise to a breach which occurred before the auditors visit to the regulated entity continue to exist, or those charged with governance have not taken corrective action, or the breach has re-occurred; and

- Whether the circumstances suggest that an immediate report to the regulator is necessary in order to protect the interests of depositors, investors, policyholders, clients of the entity or others in whose interests the regulator is required to act.

44. The auditor would normally seek evidence to assess the implications of a suspected breach before reporting a matter to the regulator. However, the auditor's responsibility to make a report does not require the auditor to determine the full implications of a matter before reporting: the auditor is required to exercise professional judgment as to whether or not there is reasonable cause to believe that a matter is or may be of material significance to the regulator. In forming that judgment, the auditor undertakes appropriate investigations to determine the circumstances but does not require the degree of evidence which would be a normal part of forming an opinion on financial statements. Such investigations, subject to compliance with legislation relating to 'tipping off'[2], would normally include:

---

[2] In the UK, 'tipping off' is an offence under section 333 of the Proceeds of Crime Act 2002 (POCA). It arises when an individual discloses matters where:
  (a) There is knowledge or suspicion that a report has already been made; and
  (b) That disclosure is likely to prejudice any investigation which might be conducted following the report.
Whilst 'tipping off' requires a person to have knowledge or suspicion that a report has been or will be made, a further offence of prejudicing an investigation is included in section 342 of POCA. Under this provision, it is an offence to make any disclosure which may prejudice an investigation of which a person has knowledge or suspicion, or to falsify, conceal, destroy or otherwise dispose of, or cause or permit the falsification, concealment, destruction or disposal of, documents relevant to such an investigation.
In Ireland, Section 58 of the Criminal Justice Act, 1994, as amended, establishes the offence of 'prejudicing an investigation'. This relates both to when a person, knowing or suspecting that an investigation is taking place, makes any disclosure likely to prejudice the investigation or when a person, knowing that a report has been made, makes any disclosure likely to prejudice any investigation arising from the report.

- Enquiry of appropriate level of staff;

- Review of correspondence and documents relating to the transaction or event concerned; and

- Discussion with those charged with governance, or other senior management where appropriate.

In the case of a life company, it would also be appropriate to consult with the appointed actuary, who also has various statutory duties under insurance companies legislation.

45. The potential gravity of some apparent breaches may be such that an immediate report to the regulator is essential in order to enable the regulator to take appropriate action: in particular, prompt reporting of a loss of client assets may be necessary to avoid further loss to investors or others in whose interests the regulator is required to act. The auditor is therefore required to balance the need for further investigation of the matter with the need, subject to compliance with legislation relating to 'tipping off', for prompt reporting.

46. On completion of the auditor's investigations, the auditor needs to ensure that the facts and the basis for the auditor's decision (whether to report or not) is adequately documented such that the reasons for that decision may be clearly demonstrated should the need to do so arise in future.

Reliance on Other Auditors

47. An auditor with responsibilities for reporting on financial statements including financial information of one or more components audited by other auditors is required to obtain sufficient appropriate audit evidence that the work of the other auditors is adequate for the purposes of the audit. The same principle applies to reliance on another auditor in a different type of engagement. The auditor of a regulated entity who relies on work undertaken by other auditors needs to establish reporting arrangements such that the other auditors bring to the attention of the auditor of the regulated entity matters arising from their work which may give rise to a duty to report to a regulator.

48. The nature of the reporting arrangements will depend on the nature of the work undertaken by the other auditors. For example, the statutory duty to make a report relates to the legal entity subject to regulation rather than to the entire group to which that entity may belong. Consequently, the auditor of a holding company authorised by one regulator would not be expected to have knowledge of all matters which come to the attention of a subsidiary's auditor. The auditor of the regulated entity would, however, have a duty to report, where appropriate, matters which arise from the audit of the regulated entity's own financial statements and of the consolidated group figures.

49. Where the audit of a regulated entity is undertaken by joint auditors, knowledge obtained by one auditing firm is likely to be deemed to be known by the other. Care will therefore be needed in agreeing and implementing arrangements to exchange information relating to matters which may give rise to a duty to report to a regulator including compliance with legislation relating to tipping off.

Reporting

The Auditor's Statutory Duty to Report Direct to Regulators

50. **When the auditor concludes, after appropriate discussion and investigations, that a matter which has come to the auditor's attention gives rise to a statutory duty to make a report, subject to compliance with legislation relating to 'tipping off', the auditor should bring the matter to the attention of the regulator without undue delay in a form and manner which will facilitate appropriate action by the regulator. When the initial report is made orally, the auditor should make a contemporaneous written record of the oral report and should confirm the matter in writing to the regulator.**

51. Except in the circumstances referred to in paragraph 54 the auditor seeks to reach agreement with those charged with governance on the circumstances giving rise to a report direct to the regulator. However, where a statutory duty to report arises, the auditor is required to make such a report regardless of:

    (a) Whether the matter has been referred to the regulator by other parties (including the company, whether by those charged with governance or otherwise); and

    (b) Any duty owed to other parties, including the those charged with governance of the regulated entity and its shareholders (or equivalent persons).

52. Except in the circumstances set out in paragraph 54, the auditor sends a copy of the auditor's written report to those charged with governance and (where appropriate) audit committee of the regulated entity.

53. In normal circumstances, the auditor would wish to communicate with the regulator with the knowledge and agreement of those charged with governance of the regulated entity. However, in some circumstances immediate notification of the discovery of a matter giving reasonable grounds to believe that a reportable matter exists will be necessary - for example, a phone call to alert the regulator followed by a meeting to discuss the circumstances.

54. **When the matter giving rise to a statutory duty to make a report direct to a regulator casts doubt on the integrity of those charged with governance or their competence to conduct the business of the regulated entity, the auditor should, subject to compliance with legislation relating to 'tipping off', make the report to the regulator without delay and without informing those charged with governance in advance.**

55. Speed of reporting is essential where the circumstances cause the auditor no longer to have confidence in the integrity of those charged with governance. In such circumstances, there may be a serious and immediate threat to the interests of depositors or other persons for whose protection the regulator is required to act; for example where the auditor believes that a fraud or other irregularity may have been committed by, or with the knowledge of, those charged with governance, or have evidence of the intention of those charged with governance to commit or condone a suspected fraud or other irregularity.

56. In circumstances where the auditor no longer has confidence in the integrity of those charged with governance, it is not appropriate to provide those charged with governance with copies of the auditor's report. Since such circumstances will be exceptional and extreme, the auditor may wish to seek legal advice as to the auditor's responsibilities and the appropriate course of action.

Money Laundering

57. For a number of years auditors in the UK have been required to report to an appropriate authority where they suspect the laundering of money which either derived from drug trafficking or was related to terrorist offences. In the UK, partners and staff in audit firms must continue to report non-compliance with certain laws related to terrorism[3] but new anti-money laundering legislation[4] in the UK and Ireland has extended both the definition of what money laundering comprises and the auditor's reporting responsibilities[5]. The anti-money laundering legislation now imposes a duty to report money laundering in respect of the proceeds of all crime. The detailed legislation in both countries differs but common features include:

  - Money laundering includes concealing, disguising, converting, transferring, removing, using, acquiring or possessing property[6] which constitutes or

---

[3] In the UK, the Terrorism Act 2000 (as amended by the Anti-terrorism, Crime and Security Act 2001) and associated regulations. The duty to report drug trafficking related money laundering has been subsumed into the general requirement to report the proceeds of crime.

In Ireland, there is similar proposed legislation that auditors will need to consider in due course.

[4] In the UK, with effect from 1 March 2004 The Money Laundering Regulations 2003 replaced the 1993 and 2001 regulations and the requirements of the Proceeds of Crime Act 2002 were extended to the provision by way of business of audit services by a person who is eligible for appointment as a company auditor under section 25 of the Companies Act 1989 or Article 28 of the Companies (Northern Ireland) Order 1990.

In Ireland, with effect from 15 September 2003 the Criminal Justice Act 1994 (Section 32) Regulations 2003 designate accountants, auditors, and tax advisors and others for the purposes of the anti-money laundering provisions of the Criminal Justice Act, 1994, as amended.

[5] Anti-money laundering legislation differs in the UK and Ireland, references to such legislation in the main body of this ISA (UK and Ireland) use generalised wording with the specific requirements of the UK and Irish legislation described in footnotes.

[6] In the UK, 'property' is criminal property if it constitutes a person's benefit from criminal conduct or it represents such a benefit (in whole or part and whether directly or indirectly), and the alleged offender knows or suspects that it constitutes or represents such a benefit.

In Ireland, 'property' is defined as including money and all other property, real or personal, heritable or moveable, including choses in action and other intangible or incorporeal property.

represents a benefit from criminal conduct[7]. Although the anti-money laundering legislation does not contain de minimis concessions in the UK the National Criminal Intelligence Service (NCIS) has introduced guidance on reports of limited intelligence value;

- Partners and staff in audit firms are required to report all suspicions[8] that a criminal offence, giving rise to any direct or indirect benefit has been committed, regardless of whether that offence has been committed by a client or by a third party;

- Partners and staff in audit firms need to be alert to the dangers of making disclosures that are likely to tip off a money launderer or prejudice an investigation ('tipping off'), as this will constitute a criminal offence under the anti-money laundering legislation.

This ISA (UK and Ireland) does not address these responsibilities although, when reporting to a regulator (whether under a statutory duty or right) the auditor has regard to the offence of 'tipping off'.

The Auditor's Right to Report Direct to Regulators

58. **When a matter comes to the auditor's attention which the auditor concludes does not give rise to a statutory duty to report but nevertheless may be relevant to the regulator's exercise of its functions, the auditor should, subject to compliance with legislation relating to 'tipping off':**

    (a) **Consider whether the matter should be brought to the attention of the regulator under the terms of the appropriate legal provisions enabling the auditor to report direct to the regulator; and, if so**

---

[7] In the UK, 'criminal conduct' is defined as conduct which constitutes an offence in any part of the United Kingdom or would constitute such an offence if it occurred in any part of the UK.
In Ireland, 'criminal conduct' means conduct which constitutes an 'indictable offence', or where the conduct occurs outside the State, would constitute such an offence if it occurred within the State and also constitutes an offence under the law of the country or territorial unit in which it occurs, and includes participation in such conduct.

[8] In the UK, as a result of the Proceeds of Crime Act 2002 and the 2003 Money Laundering Regulations auditors are required to report where they know or suspect or have reasonable grounds to know or suspect that another person is engaged in money laundering. Partners and staff in audit firms discharge their responsibilities by reporting to their Money Laundering Reporting Officer ('MLRO') or, in the case of sole practitioners, to the National Criminal Intelligence Service.
In Ireland, the Criminal Justice Act, 1994, as amended, and the Criminal Justice Act, 1994 (Section 32) Regulations, 2003 require auditors and other defined persons to report to the Garda Síochána and the Revenue Commissioners where they suspect that an offence as defined in the legislation in relation to the business of that person has been or is being committed. Two further reporting duties exist in Irish law, Section 74 of the Company Law Enforcement Act 2001 requires auditors to report to the Director of Corporate Enforcement instances of the suspected commission of indictable offences under the Companies Acts and Section 59 of the Criminal Justice (Theft and Fraud Offences) Act, 2001 requires 'relevant persons', as defined in the section and which includes auditors of companies, to report 'indications' that specified offences under the Act have been committed to the Garda Síochána. Additionally, auditors may report direct to the Revenue Commissioners certain offences under Section 1079 of the Taxes Consolidation Act, 1997.

(b) **Advise those charged with governance that in the auditor's opinion the matter should be drawn to the regulators' attention.**

Where the auditor is unable to obtain, within a reasonable period, adequate evidence that those charged with governance have properly informed the regulator of the matter, the auditor should, subject to compliance with legislation relating to 'tipping off', make a report direct to the regulator without undue delay.

59. The auditor may become aware of matters which the auditor concludes are relevant to the exercise of the regulator's functions even though they fall outside the statutory definition of matters which must be reported to a regulator. In such circumstances, the Acts provide the auditor with protection for making disclosure of the matter to the appropriate regulator.

60. Where the auditor considers that a matter which does not give rise to a statutory duty to report is nevertheless, in the auditor's professional judgment, such that it should be brought to the attention of the regulator, it is normally appropriate for the auditor to request those charged with governance of the regulated entity in writing to draw it to the attention of the regulator.

Contents of a Report Initiated by the Auditor

61. **When making or confirming in writing a report direct to a regulator, the auditor should:**

    (a) **State the name of the regulated entity concerned;**

    (b) **State the statutory power under which the report is made;**

    (c) **State that the report has been prepared in accordance with ISA (UK and Ireland) 250, Section B 'The auditor's Right and Duty to Report to Regulators in the Financial Sector';**

    (d) **Describe the context in which the report is given;**

    (e) **Describe the matter giving rise to the report;**

    (f) **Request the regulator to confirm that the report has been received; and**

    (g) **State the name of the auditor, the date of the written report and, where appropriate, the date on which an oral report was made to the regulator and the name and title of the individual to whom the oral report was made.**

62. Such a report is a by-product of other work undertaken by the auditor. As a result it is not possible for the auditor or the regulator to conclude that all matters relevant to the regulator were encountered in the course of the auditor's work. The auditor's report therefore sets out the context in which the information reported was identified and

indicates the extent to which the matter has been investigated and discussed with those charged with governance.

Context of a Report

63. Matters to which the auditor may wish to refer when describing the context in which a report is made direct to a regulator include:

   - The nature of the appointment from which the report derives. For example, it may be appropriate to distinguish between a report made in the course of an audit of financial statements and one which arises in the course of a more limited engagement, such as an appointment to report on specified matters by the FSA or IFSRA;

   - The applicable legislative requirements and interpretations of those requirements which have informed the auditor's judgment;

   - The extent to which the auditor has investigated the circumstances giving rise to the matter reported;

   - Whether the matter reported has been discussed with those charged with governance;

   - Whether steps to rectify the matter have been taken.

Communication of Information by the Regulator

64. The Acts provide that, in certain exceptional circumstances, regulators may pass confidential information to another party. The precise circumstances in which regulators may disclose information varies, but in general they may do so if considered necessary to fulfil their own obligations under the appropriate Act, or, in some cases, to enable the auditor to fulfil the auditor's duties either to the regulated entity or, in other cases, to the regulator. Confidential information remains confidential in the hands of the recipient.

65. In so far as the law permits, regulators have confirmed that they will consider taking the initiative in bringing a matter to the attention of the auditor of a regulated entity in circumstances where:

   (a) They believe the matter is of such importance that the auditor's knowledge of it could significantly affect the form of the auditor's report on the entity's financial statements or other matters on which the auditor is required to report, or the way in which the auditor discharges the auditor's reporting responsibilities; and

   (b) The disclosure is for the purpose of enabling or assisting the regulator to discharge its functions under the Acts.

66. The auditor needs to be aware that there may be circumstances in which the regulators are unable to disclose such information. Where the auditor of a regulated entity is not informed by the regulator of any matter, therefore, the auditor cannot assume that there are no matters known to the regulator which could affect the auditor's judgment as to whether information is of material significance. However, in the absence of disclosure by the regulator, the auditor can only form a judgment in the light of evidence to which the auditor has access.

Relationship With Other Reporting Responsibilities

67. **When issuing a report expressing an opinion on a regulated entity's financial statements or on other matters specified by legislation or a regulator, the auditor:**

    (a) **Should consider whether there are consequential reporting issues affecting the auditor's opinion which arise from any report previously made direct to the regulator in the course of the auditor's appointment; and**

    (b) **Should assess whether any matters encountered in the course of the audit indicate a need for a further direct report.**

68. The circumstances which give rise to a report direct to a regulator may involve an uncertainty or other matter which requires disclosure in the financial statements. The auditor will therefore need to consider whether the disclosures made in the financial statements are adequate for the purposes of giving a true and fair view of the regulated entity's state of affairs and profit or loss. Where the auditor concludes that an uncertainty which has resulted in such a report is significant, the auditor is required by ISA (UK and Ireland) 700 "The Auditor's Report on Financial Statements" to consider whether to add an explanatory paragraph drawing attention to the matter in the auditor's report.

69. Similarly, circumstances giving rise to a report direct to a regulator may also require reflection in the auditor's reports on other matters required by legislation or another regulator.

70. In fulfilling the responsibility to report direct to a regulator, it is important that the auditor not only assess the significance of individual transactions or events but also consider whether a combination of such items over the course of the work undertaken for the auditor's primary reporting responsibilities may give the auditor reasonable grounds to believe that they constitute a matter of material significance to the regulator, and so give rise to a statutory duty to make a report.

71. As there is no requirement for the auditor to extend the scope of the audit work to search for matters which may give rise to a statutory duty to report, such an assessment of the cumulative effect of evidence obtained in the course of an audit would be made when reviewing the evidence in support of the opinions to be expressed in the reports the auditor has been appointed to make. Where such a review leads to the conclusion that the cumulative effect of matters noted in the course of the audit is of material significance to the regulator, it will be appropriate for a report to be made as set out in paragraph 61 above. However, reports indicating a 'nil return' are not appropriate.

THE AUDITING PRACTICES BOARD

Effective Date

72. In the United Kingdom, the Money Laundering Regulations 2003 came into force on 1 March 2004. In Ireland, the Criminal Justice Act 1994 (Section 32) Regulations 2003 are effective from 15 September 2003. This Section of this ISA (UK and Ireland) is effective for audits of financial statements for periods commencing on or after 15 December 2004.

Note on Legal Requirements

i   Reference should be made to the legislation itself for an understanding of the relevant points of law. In interpreting the legal requirements it is also appropriate to refer to guidance published by the regulators and that contained in Practice Notes issued by the Auditing Practices Board.

Legal Requirements in the United Kingdom

ii   The auditor's right to report to a regulator is contained in The Financial Services and Markets Act 2000, sections 342 and 343.

iii   The auditor's duty to report to a regulator is set out in the Statutory Instrument The Financial Services and Markets Act 2000 (Communication by Auditors) Regulations 2001.

Legal Requirements in the Republic of Ireland

iv   The auditor's duty to report to a regulator is set out in:

    (a)   The Building Societies Act 1989, section 89(i);

    (b)   The Central Bank Act 1989, section 47;

    (c)   The Trustee Savings Bank Act 1989, section 38(i);

    (d)   The Insurance Act 1989, section 35(i);

    (e)   The European Communities (Undertakings for Collective Investment in Transferable Securities) Regulations 1989, sections 83(2) to (7);

    (f)   The Unit Trusts Act 1990, section 15;

    (g)   The Stock Exchange Act 1995, section 34;

    (h)   The Investment Intermediaries Act 1995, section 33 (applicable to investment and insurance intermediaries;

    (i)   The Pensions (Amendment) Act 1996, section 83;

    (j)   The Credit Unions Act 1997, section 122; and

    (k)   The Companies Act 1990, section 258.

Further reporting duties are included in the Central Bank and Financial Services Authority of Ireland (no. 2) Bill published in December 2003.

Appendix 1

The Regulatory Framework

1. In both the UK and Ireland, legislation exists in the principal areas of financial services to protect the interests of investors, depositors in banks and other users of financial services. Regulated entities operating in the financial sector are required to comply with legal and regulatory requirements concerning the way their business is conducted. Compliance with those rules is monitored in four principal ways:

    *   Internal monitoring by those charged with governance of the regulated entity;

    *   Submission of regular returns by the regulated entity to the regulator;

    *   Monitoring and, in some cases, inspection of the entity by the regulator;

    *   Subject to compliance with legislation relating to 'tipping off', reports by the reporting entity's auditor on its financial statements and other specified matters required by legislation or by the regulator.

Responsibility for Ensuring Compliance

2. Ensuring compliance with the requirements with which a regulated entity is required to comply in carrying out its business is the responsibility of those charged with governance of a regulated entity. It requires adequate organisation and systems of controls. The regulatory framework provides that adequate procedures for compliance must be established and maintained. Those charged with governance of a regulated entity are also normally required to undertake regular reviews of compliance and to inform the regulator of any breach of the rules and regulations applicable to its regulated business. In addition, regulators may undertake compliance visits.

3. The auditor of regulated entity normally has responsibilities for reporting, subject to compliance with legislation relating to 'tipping off', on particular aspects of its compliance with the regulator's requirements. However, the auditor has no direct responsibility for expressing an opinion on an entity's overall compliance with the requirements for the conduct of its business, nor does an audit provide any assurance that breaches of requirements which are not the subject of regular auditors' reports will be detected.

The Role of Auditors

4. Those charged with governance of regulated entities have primary responsibility for ensuring that all appropriate information is made available to regulators. Normal reporting procedures (including auditor's reports on records, systems and returns, and regular meetings with those charged with governance and/or management and auditors) supplemented by any inspection visits considered necessary by the regulators should provide the regulators with all the information they need to carry out their responsibilities under the relevant Act.

Routine Reporting by Auditors

5.   Regulators' requirements for reports by auditors vary. In general terms, however, such reports may include opinions on:

   • The regulated entity's annual financial statements;

   • The regulated entity's compliance with requirements for financial resources; and

   • The adequacy of the regulated entity's system of controls over its transactions and in particular over its clients' money and other property.

6.   As a result of performing the work necessary to discharge their routine reporting responsibilities, or those arising from an appointment to provide a special report required by the regulator, the auditor of a regulated entity may become aware of matters which the auditor considers need to be brought to the regulator's attention sooner than would be achieved by routine reports by the entity or its auditor.

7.   The auditor of a regulated entity normally has a right to communicate in good faith, subject to compliance with legislation relating to 'tipping off', information the auditor considers is relevant to the regulators' functions.

The Auditor's Statutory Duty to Report to the Regulator

8.   In addition, the auditor is required by law to report, subject to compliance with legislation relating to 'tipping off', direct to a regulator when the auditor concludes that there is reasonable cause to believe that a matter is or may be of material significance to the regulator. The precise matters which result in a statutory duty to make such a report vary, depending upon the specific requirements of relevant legislation and the regulator's rules. In general, however, a duty to report to a regulator arises when the auditor becomes aware that:

   • The regulated entity is in serious breach of:

      ○ Requirements to maintain adequate financial resources; or

      ○ Of requirements for those charged with governance to conduct its business in a sound and prudent manner (including the maintenance of systems of control over transactions and over any clients' assets held by the business); or

   • There are circumstances which give reason to doubt the status of those charged with governance or senior management as fit and proper persons.

Confidentiality

9.   Confidentiality is an implied term of the auditor's contracts with client entities. However, subject to compliance with legislation relating to 'tipping off', in the circumstances leading to a right or duty to report, the auditor is entitled to

communicate to regulators in good faith information or opinions relating to the business or affairs of the entity or any associated body without contravening the duty of confidence owed to the entity and, in the case of a bank, building society and friendly society, its associated bodies.

10. The statutory provisions permitting the auditor to communicate information to regulators relate to information obtained in the auditor's capacity as auditor of the regulated entity concerned. Auditors and regulators therefore should be aware that confidential information obtained in other capacities may not normally be disclosed to another party.

Appendix 2

The Application of the Statutory Duty to Report to Regulators

Introduction

1. The statutory duty to report to a regulator, subject to compliance with legislation relating to 'tipping off', applies to information which comes to the attention of the auditor in the auditor's capacity as auditor. However, neither the term 'auditor' nor the phrase "in the capacity of auditor" are defined in the legislation, nor has the court determined how these expressions should be construed.

2. As a result, it is not always clearly apparent when an accounting firm should regard itself as having a duty to report to a regulator. For example, information about a regulated entity may be obtained when partners or staff of the firm which is appointed as its auditor carry out work for another client entity; or when the firm undertakes other work for the regulated entity. Auditors, regulated entities and regulators need to be clear as to when the normal duty of confidentiality will be overridden by the auditor's statutory duty to report to the regulator.

3. In order to clarify whether or not an accounting firm should regard itself as bound by the duty, the APB has developed, in conjunction with HM Treasury, the IFSRA and the regulators, guidance on the interpretation of the key conditions for the existence of that duty, namely that the firm is to be regarded as auditor of a regulated entity and that information is obtained in the capacity of auditor.

4. Guidance on the interpretation of the term 'auditor' in the context of each Act is contained in the separate Practice Notes dealing with each area affected by the legislation.

5. This appendix sets out guidance on the interpretation of the phrase "in the capacity of auditor". The Board nevertheless continues to hold the view that the meaning of the phrase should be clarified in legislation in the longer term.

In the Capacity of Auditor

6. In determining whether information is obtained in the capacity of auditor, two criteria in particular should be considered:

   (a) Whether the person who obtained the information also undertook the audit work; and if so

   (b) Whether it was obtained in the course of or as a result of undertaking the audit work.

7. It is then necessary to apply these criteria to information about a regulated entity which may become known from a number of sources, and by a number of different individuals within an accounting firm. Within a large firm, for example, information may come to the attention of the partner responsible for the audit of a regulated entity, a

partner in another office who undertakes a different type of work, or members of the firm's staff at any level. In the case of a sole practitioner who is the auditor of a regulated entity, information about a regulated entity may also be obtained by the practitioner in the course of work other than its audit.

Non-Audit Work Carried out in Relation to a Regulated Entity

8. Where partners or staff involved in the audit of a regulated entity carry out work other than its audit (non-audit work) information about the regulated entity will be known to them as individuals. In circumstances which suggest that a matter would otherwise give rise to a statutory duty to report, subject to compliance with legislation relating to 'tipping off', if obtained in the capacity of auditor, it will be prudent for them to make enquiries in the course of their audit work in order to establish whether this is the case from information obtained in that capacity.

9. However where non-audit work is carried out by other partners or staff, neither of the criteria set out in paragraph 6 is met in respect of information which becomes known to them. Nevertheless the firm should take proper account of such information when it could affect the audit so that it is treated in a responsible manner, particularly since in partnership law the knowledge obtained by one partner in the course of the partnership business may be imputed to the entire partnership. In doing so, two types of work may be distinguished: first, work which could affect the firm's work as auditor and, secondly, work which is undertaken purely in an advisory capacity.

10. A firm appointed as auditor of a regulated entity needs to have in place appropriate procedures to ensure that the partner responsible for the audit function is made aware of any other relationship which exists between any department of the firm and the regulated entity when that relationship could affect the firm's work as auditor. Common examples of such work include accounting work, particularly for smaller entities, and provision of tax services to the regulated entity.

11. *Prima facie*, information obtained in the course of non-audit work is not covered by either the right or the duty to report to a regulator. However, the firm appointed as auditor needs to consider whether the results of other work undertaken for a regulated entity need to be assessed as part of the audit process. In principle, this is no different to seeking to review a report prepared by outside consultants on, say, the entity's accounting systems so as to ensure that the auditor makes a proper assessment of the risks of misstatement in the financial statements and of the work needed to form an opinion. Consequently, the partner responsible for the audit needs to make appropriate enquiries in the process of planning and completing the audit (see paragraph 67 above). Such enquiries would be directed to those aspects of the non-audit work which might reasonably be expected to be relevant to the audit. When, as a result of such enquiries, those involved in the audit become aware of issues which may be of material significance to a regulator such issues should be considered, and if appropriate reported, subject to compliance with legislation relating to 'tipping off, following the requirements set out in this Section of this ISA (UK and Ireland).

12. Work which is undertaken in an advisory capacity, for example to assist the directors of a regulated entity to determine effective and efficient methods of discharging their duties, would not normally affect the work undertaken for the audit. Nevertheless, in rare instances, the partner responsible for such advisory work may conclude that steps considered necessary in order to comply with the regulator's requirements have not been taken by the directors or that the directors intend in some respect not to comply with the regulator's requirements. Such circumstances would require consideration in the course of work undertaken for the audit, both to consider the effect on the auditor's routine reports and to determine whether the possible non-compliance is or is likely to be of material significance to the regulator.

Work Relating to a Separate Entity

13. Information obtained in the course of work relating to another entity audited by the same firm (or the same practitioner) is confidential to that other entity. The auditor is not required, and has no right, to report to a regulator confidential information which arises from work undertaken by the same auditing firm for another client. However, as a matter of sound practice, individuals involved in the audit of a regulated entity who become aware (in a capacity other than that of auditor of a regulated entity) of a matter which could otherwise give rise to a statutory duty to report would normally make enquiries in the course of their audit of the regulated entity to establish whether the information concerned is substantiated.

14. In carrying out the audit work, the auditor is required to have due regard to whether disclosure of non-compliance with laws and regulations to a proper authority is appropriate in the public interest. standards and guidance on this general professional obligation is set out in Section A of this ISA (UK and Ireland).

Conclusion

15. The phrase "in his capacity as auditor" limits information subject to the duty to report to matters of which the auditor becomes aware in the auditor's capacity as such. Consequently, it is unlikely that a partnership can be said to be acting in its capacity as auditor of a particular regulated entity whenever any apparently unrelated material comes to the attention of a partner or member of staff not engaged in that audit, particularly if that material is confidential to another client.

16. The statutory duty to report to a regulator, subject to compliance with legislation relating to 'tipping off', therefore does not extend automatically to any information obtained by an accounting firm regardless of its source. Accounting firms undertaking audits of regulated entities need, however, to establish lines of communication, commensurate with their size and organisational structure, sufficient to ensure that non-audit work undertaken for a regulated entity which is likely to have an effect on the audit is brought to the attention of the partner responsible for the audit and to establish procedures for the partner responsible for the audit to make appropriate enquiries of those conducting such other work as part of the process of planning and completing the audit.

Appendix 3

Action by the Auditor on Discovery of a Breach of a Regulator's Requirements

1. This appendix sets out in the form of a flowchart the steps involved in assessing whether a report to a regulator is required when a breach of the regulator's requirements comes to the attention of the auditor.

2. The flowchart is intended to provide guidance to readers in understanding this Section of this ISA (UK and Ireland). It does not form part of the auditing standards contained in the ISA (UK and Ireland).

Action by the Auditor on Discovery of a Breach of a Regulator's Requirements

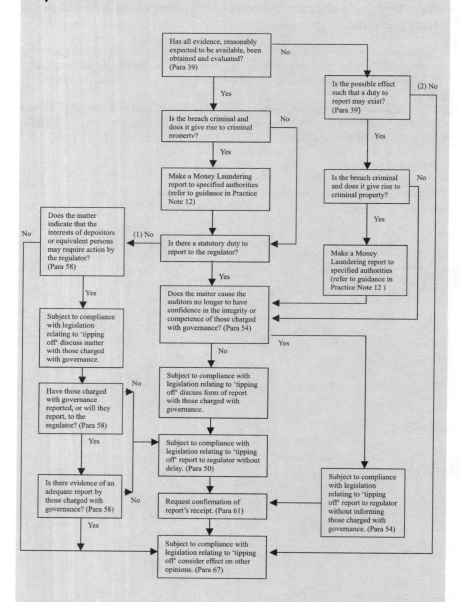

(1) This note would only be followed when a distinct right to report to the regulator exists. Otherwise, where no duty to report exists, the auditor would next consider the effect on other opinions.

(2) Where the auditor considers that a distinct right to report to the regulator exists, the auditor would next consider the question marked (1).

INTERNATIONAL STANDARD ON AUDITING (UK AND IRELAND) 260

COMMUNICATION OF AUDIT MATTERS WITH THOSE CHARGED WITH GOVERNANCE

CONTENTS

International Standard on Auditing (UK and Ireland) (ISA (UK and Ireland)) 260 "Communication of Audit Matters With Those Charged With Governance" should be read in the context of the Auditing Practices Board's Statement "The Auditing Practices Board - Scope and Authority of Pronouncements (Revised)" which sets out the application and authority of ISAs (UK and Ireland).

Introduction

1.   The purpose of this International Standard on Auditing (UK and Ireland) (ISA (UK and Ireland)) is to establish standards and provide guidance on communication of audit matters arising from the audit of financial statements between the auditor and those charged with governance of an entity. These communications relate to audit matters of governance interest as defined in this ISA (UK and Ireland). This ISA (UK and Ireland) does not provide guidance on communications by the auditor to parties outside the entity, for example, external regulatory or supervisory agencies.

2.   **The auditor should communicate audit matters of governance interest arising from the audit of financial statements with those charged with governance of an entity.**

2-1. For the purposes of this ISA (UK and Ireland) the term "communicate" is used in the sense of an active two-way communication (dialogue) between the auditor and those charged with governance. Effective communication is unlikely to be achieved when the auditor communicates with those charged with governance solely by means of formal written reports.

2-2. The auditor discusses issues clearly and unequivocally with those charged with governance so that the implications of those issues are likely to be fully comprehended by them.

3.   For the purposes of this ISA (UK and Ireland), "governance" is the term used to describe the role of persons entrusted with the supervision, control and direction of an entity.[1] Those charged with governance ordinarily are accountable for ensuring that the entity achieves its objectives, with regard to reliability of financial reporting, effectiveness and efficiency of operations, compliance with applicable laws, and reporting to interested parties. Those charged with governance include management only when it performs such functions.

3-1. In the UK and Ireland, those charged with governance include the directors (executive and non-executive) of a company or other body, the members of an audit committee where one exists, the partners, proprietors, committee of management or trustees of other forms of entity, or equivalent persons responsible for directing the entity's affairs and preparing its financial statements.

3-2. 'Management' comprises those persons who perform senior managerial functions.

---

[1] Principles of corporate governance have been developed by many countries as a point of reference for the establishment of good corporate behavior. Such principles generally focus on publicly traded companies; however, they may also serve to improve governance in other forms of entities. There is no single model of good corporate governance. Board structures and practices vary from country to country. A common principle is that the entity should have in place a governance structure which enables the board to exercise objective judgment on corporate affairs, including financial reporting, independent in particular from management.

THE AUDITING PRACTICES BOARD

3-3. In the UK and Ireland, depending on the nature and circumstances of the entity, management may include some or all of those charged with governance (e.g. executive directors). Management will not normally include non-executive directors.

4. For the purpose of this ISA (UK and Ireland), "audit matters of governance interest" are those that arise from the audit of financial statements and, in the opinion of the auditor, are both important and relevant to those charged with governance in overseeing the financial reporting and disclosure process. Audit matters of governance interest include only those matters that have come to the attention of the auditor as a result of the performance of the audit. The auditor is not required, in an audit in accordance with ISAs (UK and Ireland), to design audit procedures for the specific purpose of identifying matters of governance interest.

4-1. The principal purposes of communications with those charged with governance are to:

(a) Reach a mutual understanding of the scope of the audit and the respective responsibilities of the auditor and those charged with governance;

(b) Share information to assist both the auditor and those charged with governance fulfill their respective responsibilities; and

(c) Provide to those charged with governance constructive observations arising from the audit process.

4-2. Although the requirements of this ISA (UK and Ireland) focus on the auditor's communications to those charged with governance, it is important that there is effective two-way communication (see paragraphs 2-1 and 2-2). The auditor reasonably expects those charged with governance to give the auditor such information and explanations as the auditor requires for the purposes of the audit[1a].

4-3. The extent, form and frequency of communications with those charged with governance will vary, reflecting the size and nature of the entity and the manner in which those charged with governance operate, as well as the auditor's views as to the importance of the audit matters of governance interest relating to the audit. In particular, communications with those charged with governance of listed companies might be more formal than communications with those charged with governance of smaller entities, or of subsidiary undertakings.

Relevant Persons

5. **The auditor should determine the relevant persons who are charged with governance and with whom audit matters of governance interest are communicated.**

[1a] Section 389A of the Companies Act 1985 sets legal requirements in relation to the communication of information to the auditor. (For Northern Ireland and the Republic of Ireland, relevant requirements are set out in Article 245(3) of the Companies (Northern Ireland) Order 1986 and Section 193(3), Companies Act 1990, respectively.)

6. The structures of governance vary from country to country reflecting cultural and legal backgrounds. For example, in some countries, the supervision function, and the management function are legally separated into different bodies, such as a supervisory (wholly or mainly non-executive) board and a management (executive) board. In other countries, both functions are the legal responsibility of a single, unitary board, although there may be an audit committee that assists that board in its governance responsibilities with respect to financial reporting.

7. This diversity makes it difficult to establish a universal identification of the persons who are charged with governance and with whom the auditor communicates audit matters of governance interest. The auditor uses judgment to determine those persons with whom audit matters of governance interest are communicated, taking into account the governance structure of the entity, the circumstances of the engagement and any relevant legislation. The auditor also considers the legal responsibilities of those persons. For example, in entities with supervisory boards or with audit committees, the relevant persons may be those bodies. However, in entities where a unitary board has established an audit committee, the auditor may decide to communicate with the audit committee, or with the whole board, depending on the importance of the audit matters of governance interest.

7-1. In most UK and Irish entities a board or equivalent governing body comprises individuals who are collectively charged with governance, including financial reporting. In some smaller entities a single individual may be charged with governance. In other cases, committees of a board or individual members of it may be charged with specific tasks in order to assist a board to meet its governance responsibilities (e.g. there may be an audit committee, a remuneration committee or a nomination committee).

7-2. When considering communicating with a committee the auditor considers whether the committee is in a position to provide the information and explanations the auditor needs for the purpose of the audit, whether the committee has the authority to act on the auditor's findings and whether there may be a need to repeat the communication to the board or governing body. Irrespective of what may be agreed, the auditor may judge it necessary to communicate directly with the board or governing body when a matter is sufficiently important.

7-3. The establishment of audit committees by the boards of listed companies, many public sector bodies and some other organizations has meant that communication with the audit committee[2], where one exists, has become a key element in the auditor's communication with those charged with governance. It is to be expected that the engagement partner will be invited regularly to attend meetings of the audit committee and that the audit committee chairman, and to a lesser extent the other members of the audit committee, will wish to liaise on a continuing basis with the engagement partner.

---

[2] The Combined Code on Corporate Governance, and the Guidance on Audit Committees (The Smith Guidance) appended to it, contain, inter alia, recommendations about the conduct of the audit committee's relationship with the auditor.

7-4 The audit committee ordinarily will, at least annually, meet the auditor, without management, to discuss matters relating to the audit committee's remit and issues arising from the audit.

7-5. As part of obtaining an understanding of the control environment, the auditor obtains an understanding of how the audit committee operates, including the particular remit given to the committee by the entity's board and its role in relation to governance matters such as reviewing the identification, evaluation and management of business risks. An entity's board and its auditor bear in mind that communication to audit committees forms only part of the auditor's overall obligation to communicate effectively with those charged with governance.

8. When the entity's governance structure is not well defined, or those charged with governance are not clearly identified by the circumstances of the engagement, or by legislation, the auditor comes to an agreement with the entity about with whom audit matters of governance interest are to be communicated. Examples include some owner-managed entities, some not for profit organizations, and some government agencies.

8-1. In order to ensure that effective two-way communication is established, the expectations both of the auditor and those charged with governance regarding the form, level of detail and timing of communications are established at an early stage in the audit process. The manner in which these expectations are established will vary, reflecting the size and nature of the entity and the manner in which those charged with governance operate.

8-2. **The auditor should ensure that those charged with governance are provided with a copy of the audit engagement letter on a timely basis.**

9. To avoid misunderstandings, an audit engagement letter may explain that the auditor will communicate only those matters of governance interest that come to attention as a result of the performance of an audit and that the auditor is not required to design audit procedures for the specific purpose of identifying matters of governance interest. The engagement letter may also:

- Describe the form in which any communications on audit matters of governance interest will be made.

- Identify the relevant persons with whom such communications will be made.

- Identify any specific audit matters of governance interest that it has been agreed are to be communicated.

9-1. ISA (UK and Ireland) 210, "Terms of Audit Engagements," requires that the auditor and the client should agree on the terms of the engagement. "Client" means the addressees of the of the auditor's report or, when as often will be the case it is not practical to agree such terms with the addressees, the entity itself through those charged with governance.

9-2. The provision of copies of the audit engagement letter to those charged with governance facilitates the review and agreement of the audit engagement letter by the Audit Committee, as recommended by the Combined Code Guidance on Audit Committees. As part of their review, the guidance further recommends the audit committee to consider whether the audit engagement letter has been updated to reflect changes in circumstances since the previous year.

10. The effectiveness of communications is enhanced by developing a constructive working relationship between the auditor and those charged with governance. This relationship is developed while maintaining an attitude of professional independence and objectivity.

Groups

10-1. Where a parent undertaking is preparing group financial statements, the auditor of the parent undertaking communicates to those charged with governance of the parent undertaking such matters brought to the attention of those charged with governance of its subsidiary undertakings, by the auditors of the subsidiary undertakings, as they judge to be of significance in the context of the group (e.g. weaknesses in systems of internal control that have resulted, or could result, in material errors in the group financial statements).

10-2. There are statutory obligations on corporate subsidiary undertakings, and their auditors, in the UK and Ireland to provide the auditor of a corporate parent undertaking with such information and explanations as that auditor may reasonably require for the purposes of the audit[3]. Where there is no such statutory obligation (e.g. for non corporate entities and overseas subsidiary undertakings), permission may be needed by the auditors of the subsidiary undertakings, from those charged with governance of the subsidiary undertakings, to disclose the contents of any communication to them to the auditor of the parent undertaking and also for the auditor of the parent undertaking to pass those disclosures onto those charged with governance of the parent undertaking. The auditor of the parent undertaking seeks to ensure that appropriate arrangements are made at the planning stage for these disclosures. Normally, such arrangements for groups are recorded in the instructions to the auditors of subsidiary undertakings and relevant engagement letters.

---

[3] As at 15 December 2004, section 389A of the Companies Act 1985 requires a subsidiary undertaking which is a body corporate incorporated in Great Britain, and its auditors, to give to the auditors of any parent company of the undertaking such information and explanations as they may reasonably require for the purposes of their duties as auditors of that company. If a parent company has a subsidiary undertaking which is not a body corporate incorporated in Great Britain, section 389A requires that it shall, if required by its auditors to do so, take all such steps as are reasonably open to it to obtain from the subsidiary undertaking such information and explanations as the parent company auditors may reasonably require for the purposes of their duties as auditors of that company. (Similar obligations regarding companies incorporated in Northern Ireland and the Republic of Ireland are set out in Article 397A of the Companies (Northern Ireland) Order 1986 and Section 196, Companies Act 1990, respectively.)

10-3. The auditor of the parent undertaking considers the manner in which the group is managed and the wishes of those charged with governance of the parent undertaking when deciding with whom the auditor should communicate in the group about particular matters. In recognition of the responsibilities of those charged with governance of subsidiary undertakings, the auditors of those subsidiary undertakings communicate audit matters of governance interest to those charged with governance of the subsidiary undertakings.

Audit Matters of Governance Interest to be Communicated

11. **The auditor should consider audit matters of governance interest that arise from the audit of the financial statements and communicate them with those charged with governance.** Ordinarily such matters include the following:

- Relationships that may bear on the firm's independence and the integrity and objectivity of the audit engagement partner and audit staff.

    See paragraphs 11-2 - 11-6 below.

- The general approach and overall scope of the audit, including any expected limitations thereon, or any additional requirements.

    See paragraphs 11-7 - 11-11 below.

- The selection of, or changes in, significant accounting policies and practices that have, or could have, a material effect on the entity's financial statements.

    See paragraph 11-13 - 11-14 below.

- The potential effect on the financial statements of any material risks and exposures, such as pending litigation, that are required to be disclosed in the financial statements.

- Audit adjustments, whether or not recorded by the entity that have, or could have, a material effect on the entity's financial statements.

    See paragraphs 11-16 - 11-20 below.

- Material uncertainties related to events and conditions that may cast significant doubt on the entity's ability to continue as a going concern.

- Disagreements with management about matters that, individually or in aggregate, could be significant to the entity's financial statements or the auditor's report. These communications include consideration of whether the matter has, or has not, been resolved and the significance of the matter.

- Expected modifications to the auditor's report.

See paragraph 11-21 below.

- Other matters warranting attention by those charged with governance, such as material weaknesses in internal control, questions regarding management integrity, and fraud involving management.

See paragraph 11-22 - 11-23 below.

- Any other matters agreed upon in the terms of the audit engagement.

11.a. **The auditor should inform those charged with governance of those uncorrected misstatements aggregated[4] by the auditor during the audit that were determined by management to be immaterial, both individually and in the aggregate, to the financial statements taken as a whole.**

11.b. The uncorrected misstatements communicated to those charged with governance need not include the misstatements below a designated amount[5].

11-1. Additional standards and guidance, for auditors in the UK and Ireland, relating to the communication of uncorrected misstatements are set out in paragraphs 11-16 to 11-20 below.

Integrity, Objectivity and Independence

11-2. APB Ethical Standard 1, "Integrity, objectivity and independence" requires the audit engagement partner to ensure that those charged with the governance of the audit client are appropriately informed on a timely basis of all significant facts and matters that bear upon the auditor's objectivity and independence.

11-3. The audit committee where one exists, is usually responsible for oversight of the relationship between the auditor and the entity and of the conduct of the audit process. It therefore has a particular interest in being informed about the auditor's ability to express an objective opinion on the financial statements. Where there is no audit committee, this role is taken by the board of directors.

11-4. The aim of these communications is to ensure full and fair disclosure by the auditor to those charged with governance of the audit client on matters in which they have an interest. These will generally include the key elements of the audit engagement partner's consideration of objectivity and independence such as:

- The principal threats, if any to objectivity and independence identified by the auditor, including consideration of all relationships between the audit client, its affiliates and directors and the audit firm.

---

[4] In the UK and Ireland, the term "aggregated" used in this particular context is taken to mean "identified".

[5] In the UK and Ireland, the auditor communicates all uncorrected misstatements other than those that the auditor believes are clearly trivial (see paragraph 11-16).

- Any safeguards adopted and the reasons why they are considered to be effective.

- Any independent partner review.

- The overall assessment of threats and safeguards.

- Information about the general policies and processes within the audit firm for maintaining objectivity and independence.

11-5. In the case of listed companies, the auditor, as a minimum:

(a) Discloses in writing:

  (i) Details of all relationships between the auditor and the client, its directors and senior management and its affiliates, including all services provided by the audit firm and its network to the client, its directors and senior management and its affiliates, that the auditor considers may reasonably be thought to bear on the auditor's objectivity and independence;

  (ii) The related safeguards that are in place; and

  (iii) The total amount of fees that the auditor and the auditor's network firms have charged to the client and its affiliates for the provision of services during the reporting period, analyzed into appropriate categories, for example, statutory audit services, further audit services, tax advisory services and other non-audit services. For each category, the amounts of any future services which have been contracted or where a written proposal has been submitted, are separately disclosed;

(b) Confirms in writing that the auditor complies with APB Ethical Standards and that, in the auditor's professional judgment, the auditor is independent and the auditor's objectivity is not compromised, or otherwise declare that the auditor has concerns that the auditor's objectivity and independence may be compromised (including instances where the group audit engagement partner does not consider the other auditors to be objective); and explaining the actions which necessarily follow from this; and

(c) Seeks to discuss these matters with the audit committee.

11-6. The most appropriate time for such communications is usually at the conclusion of the audit. However, communications between the auditor and those charged with governance of the audit client will also be needed at the planning stage and whenever significant judgments are made about threats to objectivity and the appropriateness of safeguards put in place, for example, when accepting an engagement to provide non audit services.

Planning Information

11-7. **The auditor should communicate to those charged with governance an outline of the nature and scope, including, where relevant, any limitations thereon, of the work the auditor proposes to undertake and the form of the reports the auditor expects to make.**

11-8. The nature and detail of the planning information communicated will reflect the size and nature of the entity and the manner in which those charged with governance operate.

11-9. The auditor communicates in outline the principal ways in which the auditor proposes to address the risks of material misstatement, with particular reference to areas of higher risk. As part of the two-way communication process the auditor seeks to gain an understanding of the attitude of those charged with governance to the business risks of the entity. When describing the planned approach to addressing the risk of material misstatement, the auditor does not describe the plan in such detail that the "surprise" element of the audit is lost. Other matters that might be communicated in outline include:

- The concept of materiality and its application to the audit approach.

- The auditor's approach to the assessment of, and reliance on, internal controls.

- The extent, if any, to which reliance will be placed on the work of internal audit and on the way in which the external and internal auditors can best work together on a constructive and complementary basis.

- Where relevant, the work to be undertaken by any other firms of auditors (including related firms) and how the principal auditor intends to obtain assurance as to the adequacy of the other auditors' procedures in so far as it relates to the principal auditor's role.

11-10. In any particular year, the auditor may decide that there are no significant changes from audit matters of governance interest that have been communicated previously and judge that it is unnecessary to remind those charged with governance of all or part of that information. In these circumstances, the auditor need only make those charged with governance aware that the auditor has no new audit matters of governance interest to communicate. Matters that are included in the audit engagement letter need not be repeated.

11-11. Other matters that the auditor may, for the purpose of the audit, find beneficial to discuss with those charged with governance include:

- The views of those charged with governance of the nature and extent of significant internal and external operational, financial, compliance and other risks facing the entity which might affect the financial statements, including the likelihood of those risks materializing and how they are managed.

- The control environment within the entity, including the attitude of management to controls, and whether those charged with governance have a process for keeping under review the effectiveness of the system of internal control and, where a review of the effectiveness of internal control has been carried out, the results of that review.

- Actions those charged with governance plan to take in response to matters such as developments in law, accounting standards, corporate governance reporting, Listing Rules, and other developments relevant to the entity's financial statements and annual report.

Findings From the Audit

11-12. **The auditor should communicate the following findings from the audit to those charged with governance:**

    (a) **The auditor's views about the qualitative aspects of the entity's accounting practices and financial reporting;**

    (b) **The final draft of the representation letter, that the auditor is requesting management and those charged with governance to sign. The communication should specifically refer to any matters where management is reluctant to make the representations requested by the auditor;**

    (c) **Uncorrected misstatements;**

    (d) **Expected modifications to the auditor's report;**

    (e) **Material weaknesses in internal control identified during the audit;**

    (f) **Matters specifically required by other ISAs (UK and Ireland) to be communicated to those charged with governance; and**

    (g) **Any other audit matters of governance interest.**

Qualitative Aspects of Accounting Practices and Financial Reporting

11-13. The accounting requirements of company law, accounting standards and interpretations issued by the relevant accounting standard setters, permit a degree of choice in some areas as to the specific accounting policies and practices that may be adopted by an entity. Additionally, there are matters for which those charged with governance have to make accounting estimates and judgments.

11-14. In the course of the audit of the financial statements, the auditor considers the qualitative aspects of the financial reporting process, including items that have a significant impact on the relevance, reliability, comparability, understandability and materiality of the information provided by the financial statements. The auditor discusses in an open and frank manner with those charged with governance the auditor's views on the quality and acceptability of the entity's accounting practices and financial reporting. Such discussions may include:

- The appropriateness of the accounting policies to the particular circumstances of the entity, judged against the objectives of relevance, reliability, comparability and understandability but having regard also to the need to balance the different objectives and the need to balance the cost of providing information with the likely benefit to users of the entity's financial statements.

  The auditor explains to those charged with governance why the auditor considers any accounting policy not to be appropriate, and requests those charged with governance to make appropriate changes. If those charged with governance decline to make the changes on the grounds that the effect is not material, the auditor informs them that the auditor will consider qualifying the auditor's report when the effect of not using an appropriate policy can reasonably be expected to influence the economic decisions of users of the financial statements.

- The timing of transactions and the period in which they are recorded.

- The appropriateness of accounting estimates and judgments, for example in relation to provisions, including the consistency of assumptions and degree of prudence reflected in the recorded amounts.

- The potential effect on the financial statements of any material risks and exposures, such as pending litigation, that are required to be disclosed in the financial statements.

- Material uncertainties related to events and conditions that may cast significant doubt on the entity's ability to continue as a going concern.

- The extent to which the financial statements are affected by any unusual transactions including non-recurring profits and losses recognized during the period and the extent to which such transactions are separately disclosed in the financial statements.

- Apparent misstatements in the other information in the document containing the audited financial statements or material inconsistencies between it and the audited financial statements.

- The overall balance and clarity of the information contained in the annual report.

- Disagreements about matters that, individually or in aggregate, could be significant to the entity's financial statements or the auditor's report. These communications include consideration of whether the matters have, or have not, been resolved and the significance of the matters.

Management Representation Letter

11-15. The auditor reviews the content of management's representation letter with those charged with governance. The auditor explains the significance of representations that have been requested relating to non-standard issues.

Uncorrected Misstatements

11-16. The auditor communicates all uncorrected misstatements, other than those that the auditor believes are clearly trivial[6], to the entity's management and requests that management correct them. When communicating misstatements, the auditor distinguishes between misstatements that are errors of fact and misstatements that arise from differences in judgment and explain why the latter are considered misstatements. When such misstatements identified by the auditor are not corrected by management the auditor communicates the misstatements to those charged with governance, in accordance with the requirement set out in paragraph 11a, and requests them to make the corrections. Where those charged with governance refuse to make some or all of the corrections, the auditor discusses with them the reasons for, and appropriateness of, not making those corrections, having regard to qualitative as well as quantitative considerations, and considers the implications for their audit report of the effect of misstatements that remain uncorrected.

11-17. If management have corrected material misstatements, the auditor considers whether those corrections of which the auditor is aware should be communicated to those charged with governance so as to assist them to fulfill their governance responsibilities, including reviewing the effectiveness of the system of internal control.

11-18. Paragraph 5a.(b) of ISA (UK and Ireland) 580, "Management Representations," requires the auditor to obtain written representations from management that it believes the effects of those uncorrected misstatements identified by the auditor during the audit are immaterial, both individually and in the aggregate, to the financial statements taken as a whole. A summary of such misstatements is required to be included in or attached to the written representations.

11-19. **The auditor should seek to obtain a written representation from those charged with governance that explains their reasons for not correcting misstatements brought to their attention by the auditor.**

11-20. If those charged with governance refuse to make some or all of the corrections the auditor has requested, a representation is obtained to reduce the possibility of

---

[6] This is not another expression for 'immaterial'. Matters which are 'clearly trivial' will be of an wholly different (smaller) order of magnitude than the materiality thresholds used in the audit, and will be matters that are clearly inconsequential, whether taken individually or in aggregate and whether judged by any quantitative and/or qualitative criteria. Further, whenever there is any uncertainty about whether one or more items are 'clearly trivial' (in accordance with this definition), the presumption should be that the matter is not 'clearly trivial'.

misunderstandings concerning their reasons for not making the corrections. A summary of the uncorrected misstatements[7] is included in, or attached to, the representation letter. Obtaining the representation does not relieve the auditor of the need to form an independent opinion as to the materiality of uncorrected misstatements.

Expected Modifications to the Auditor's Report

11-21. The auditor discusses expected modifications to the auditor's report on the financial statements with those charged with governance to ensure that:

(a) Those charged with governance are aware of the proposed modification and the reasons for it before the report is finalized;

(b) There are no disputed facts in respect of the matter(s) giving rise to the proposed modification (or that matters of disagreement are confirmed as such); and

(c) Those charged with governance have an opportunity, where appropriate, to provide the auditor with further information and explanations in respect of the matter(s) giving rise to the proposed modification.

Material Weaknesses in Internal Control

11-22. A material weakness in internal control is a deficiency in design or operation which could adversely affect the entity's ability to record, process, summarize and report financial and other relevant data so as to result in a material misstatement in the financial statements. The auditor normally does not need to communicate information concerning a material weakness of which those charged with governance are aware and in respect of which, in the view of the auditor, appropriate corrective action has been taken, unless the weakness is symptomatic of broader weaknesses in the overall control environment and there is a risk that other material weaknesses may occur. Material weaknesses of which the auditor is aware are communicated where they have been corrected by management without the knowledge of those charged with governance.

11-23. The auditor explains to those charged with governance that the auditor has not provided a comprehensive statement of all weaknesses which may exist in internal control or of all improvements which may be made, but has addressed only those matters which have come to the auditor's attention as a result of the audit procedures performed.

12. As part of the auditor's communications, those charged with governance are informed that:

---

[7] The summary need not include any misstatements that the auditors believe are 'clearly trivial' (see footnote 6).

- The auditor's communications of matters include only those audit matters of governance interest that have come to the attention of the auditor as a result of the performance of the audit.

- An audit of financial statements is not designed to identify all matters that may be relevant to those charged with governance. Accordingly, the audit does not ordinarily identify all such matters.

Timing of Communications

13. **The auditor should communicate audit matters of governance interest on a timely basis.** This enables those charged with governance to take appropriate action.

13-1. **The auditor should plan with those charged with governance the form and timing of communications to them.**

14. In order to achieve timely communications, the auditor discusses with those charged with governance the basis and timing of such communications. In certain cases, because of the nature of the matter, the auditor may communicate that matter sooner than previously agreed.

14-1. In certain circumstances the auditor may identify matters that need to be communicated to those charged with governance without delay (e.g. the existence of a material weakness in internal control). Findings from the audit that are relevant to the financial statements, including the auditor's views about the qualitative aspects of the entity's accounting and financial reporting, are communicated to those charged with governance before they approve the financial statements.

Forms of Communications

15. The auditor's communications with those charged with governance may be made orally or in writing. The auditor's decision whether to communicate orally or in writing is affected by factors such as:

- The size, operating structure, legal structure, and communications processes of the entity being audited;

- The nature, sensitivity and significance of the audit matters of governance interest to be communicated;

- The arrangements made with respect to periodic meetings or reporting of audit matters of governance interest;

- The amount of on-going contact and dialogue the auditor has with those charged with governance.

- Statutory and regulatory requirements.

15-1. As stated in paragraph 10-3, in relation to the audit of groups, the auditor of the parent undertaking considers the manner in which the group is managed and the wishes of those charged with governance of the parent undertaking when deciding with whom the auditor should communicate in the group about particular matters. These considerations include whether it is necessary and appropriate to communicate in writing with those charged with governance of subsidiary undertakings.

16. When audit matters of governance interest are communicated orally, the auditor documents in the working papers the matters communicated and any responses to those matters. This documentation may take the form of a copy of the minutes of the auditor's discussion with those charged with governance. In certain circumstances, depending on the nature, sensitivity, and significance of the matter, it may be advisable for the auditor to confirm in writing with those charged with governance any oral communications on audit matters of governance interest.

16-1. **In the UK and Ireland, the auditor should communicate in writing with those charged with governance regarding the significant findings from the audit.**

16-2. This written communication is issued even if its content is limited to explaining that there is nothing the auditor wishes to draw to the attention of those charged with governance. To avoid doubt where there are no matters the auditor wishes to communicate in writing, the auditor communicates that fact in writing to those charged with governance.

17. Ordinarily, the auditor initially discusses audit matters of governance interest with management, except where those matters relate to questions of management competence or integrity. These initial discussions with management are important in order to clarify facts and issues, and to give management an opportunity to provide further information. If management agrees to communicate a matter of governance interest with those charged with governance, the auditor may not need to repeat the communications, provided that the auditor is satisfied that such communications have effectively and appropriately been made.

17-1. The auditor incorporates in the communication of audit matters of governance interest to those charged with governance comments made by management, where those comments will aid the understanding of those charged with governance, and any actions management have indicated that they will take.

Effectiveness of Communications

17-2. **The auditor should consider whether the two-way communication between the auditor and those charged with governance has been adequate for an effective audit and, if it has not, should take appropriate action.**

17-3. Paragraph 69 of ISA 315 "Understanding the Entity and Its Environment and Assessing the Risks of Material Misstatement", identifies participation by those charged with governance, including their interaction with internal and external auditors, as an element the auditor considers when evaluating the design of the entity's control environment. Inadequate two-way communication may indicate an unsatisfactory control environment, which will influence the auditor's assessment of the risks of material misstatements. Examples of evidence about the adequacy of the two-way communication process may include:

- The appropriateness and timeliness of actions taken by those charged with governance in response to the recommendations made by the auditor. (See also paragraph 19-1 regarding significant matters raised in previous communications.)

- The apparent openness of those charged with governance in their communications with the auditor.

- The willingness and capacity of those charged with governance to meet with the auditor without management present.

- The apparent ability of those charged with governance to fully comprehend the recommendations made by the auditor. For example, the extent to which those charged with governance probe issues and question recommendations made to them.

17-4. If the two-way communication between the auditor and those charged with governance is inadequate, there is a risk that the auditor may not obtain all the audit evidence required to form an opinion on the financial statements. In such a situation, the auditor considers taking actions such as:

- Obtaining legal advice about the consequences of different courses of action.

- Communicating with third parties (e.g. an appropriate regulator), or higher authority in the governance structure that is outside the entity (such as the owners of a small business).

If the auditor concludes that the two way communication is unlikely to become adequate for the purposes of the audit, the auditor considers withdrawing from the engagement.

Other Matters

18. If the auditor considers that a modification of the auditor's report on the financial statements is required, as described in ISA (UK and Ireland) 700, "The Auditor's Report on Financial Statements," communications between the auditor and those charged with governance cannot be regarded as a substitute.

19. The auditor considers whether audit matters of governance interest previously communicated may have an effect on the current year's financial statements. The

auditor considers whether the point continues to be a matter of governance interest and whether to communicate the matter again with those charged with governance.

19-1. The auditor considers the actions taken by those charged with governance in response to previous communications. Where significant matters raised in previous communications to those charged with governance have not been dealt with effectively, the auditor enquires as to why appropriate action has not been taken. If the auditor considers that a matter raised previously has not been adequately addressed, consideration is given to repeating the point in a current communication; otherwise there is a risk that the auditor may give an impression that the auditor is satisfied that the matter has been adequately addressed or is no longer significant.

Confidentiality

20. The requirements of national professional accountancy bodies, legislation or regulation may impose obligations of confidentiality that restrict the auditor's communications of audit matters of governance interest. The auditor refers to such requirements, laws and regulations before communicating with those charged with governance. In some circumstances, the potential conflicts with the auditor's ethical and legal obligations of confidentiality and reporting may be complex. In these cases, the auditor may wish to consult with legal counsel.

20-1. Occasionally those charged with governance may wish to provide third parties, for example bankers or certain regulatory authorities, with copies of a written communication from the auditor. It is appropriate to ensure that third parties who see the communication understand that it was not prepared with third parties in mind. Furthermore, where the written communications contain open and frank discussion of aspects of the entity's accounting and financial reporting practices, it may not be appropriate for such communications to be disclosed to third parties. Thus the auditor normally states in the communication to those charged with governance that:

   (a) The report has been prepared for the sole use of the entity and, where appropriate, any parent undertaking and its auditor;

   (b) It must not be disclosed to a third party, or quoted or referred to, without the written consent of the auditor; and

   (c) No responsibility is assumed by the auditor to any other person.

20-2. In the public or regulated sectors, the auditor may have a duty to submit a report to those charged with governance annually, and also to submit copies of the report to relevant regulatory or funding bodies. In the public sector, there may also be a requirement or expectation that reports will be made public and in such circumstances some or all of the restrictions set out in the preceding paragraph may not be appropriate.

20-3. Any communication with those charged with governance is confidential information. Thus, when the auditor communicates in writing with those charged with governance, the auditor requires the prior consent of those charged with governance if the auditor is to provide a copy of the communication to a third party.

Laws and Regulations

21. The requirements of national professional accountancy bodies, legislation or regulation may impose obligations on the auditor to make communications on governance related matters. These additional communications requirements are not covered by this ISA (UK and Ireland); however, they may affect the content, form and timing of communications with those charged with governance.

Effective Date

22. This ISA (UK and Ireland) is effective for audits of financial statements for periods commencing on or after 15 December 2004.

Public Sector Perspective

Additional guidance for auditors of public sector bodies in the UK and Ireland is given in:

- Practice Note 10 "Audit of Financial Statements of Public Sector Bodies in the United Kingdom (Revised)"

- Practice Note 10(I) "Audit of Central Government Financial Statements in the Republic of Ireland (Revised)"

1. While the basic principles contained in this ISA (UK and Ireland) apply to the audit of financial statements in the public sector, the legislation giving rise to the audit mandate may specify the nature, content and form of the communications with those charged with governance of the entity.

2. For public sector audits, the types of matters that may be of interest to the governing body may be broader than the types of matters discussed in the ISA (UK and Ireland), which are directly related to the audit of financial statements. Public sector auditors' mandates may require them to report matters that come to their attention that relate to:

- Compliance with legislative or regulatory requirements and related authorities;

- Adequacy of internal control;

- Economy, efficiency and effectiveness of programs, projects and activities.

3. For public sector auditors, the auditors' written communications may be placed on the public record. For that reason, the public sector auditor needs to be aware that their

written communications may be distributed to a wider audience than solely those persons charged with governance of the entity.

Appendix

Other ISAs (UK and Ireland) Referring to Communication With Those Charged With Governance and With Management

210 - Terms of Audit Engagements

2. The auditor and the client should agree on the terms of the engagement.

2-1. The terms of the engagement should be recorded in writing.

5-1. In the UK and Ireland, the auditor should ensure that the engagement letter documents and confirms the auditor's acceptance of the appointment, and includes a summary of the responsibilities of those charged with governance and of the auditor, the scope of the engagement and the form of any reports.

10. On recurring audits, the auditor should consider whether circumstances require the terms of the engagement to be revised and whether there is a need to remind the client of the existing terms of the engagement.

17. Where the terms of the engagement are changed, the auditor and the client should agree on the new terms.

19. If the auditor is unable to agree to a change of the engagement and is not permitted to continue the original engagement, the auditor should withdraw and consider whether there is any obligation, either contractual or otherwise, to report to other parties, such as those charged with governance or shareholders, the circumstances necessitating the withdrawal.

240 - Fraud

90. The auditor should obtain written representations from management[8] that:

   (a) It acknowledges its responsibility for the design and implementation of internal control to prevent and detect fraud;

   (b) It has disclosed to the auditor the results of its assessment of the risk that the financial statements may be materially misstated as a result of fraud;

   (c) It has disclosed to the auditor its knowledge of fraud or suspected fraud affecting the entity involving:

   (i) Management[9];

---

[8] In the UK and Ireland, the auditor obtains written representations from those charged with governance.

[9] In the UK and Ireland, and those charged with governance.

(ii) Employees who have significant roles in internal control; or

(iii) Others where the fraud could have a material effect on the financial statements; and

(d) It has disclosed to the auditor its knowledge of any allegations of fraud, or suspected fraud, affecting the entity's financial statements communicated by employees, former employees, analysts, regulators or others.

93. If the auditor has identified a fraud or has obtained information that indicates that a fraud may exist, the auditor should communicate these matters as soon as practicable to the appropriate level of management.

95. If the auditor has identified fraud involving:

(a) Management;

(b) Employees who have significant roles in internal control; or

(c) Others where the fraud results in a material misstatement in the financial statements,

the auditor should communicate these matters to those charged with governance as soon as practicable.

99. The auditor should make those charged with governance and management aware, as soon as practicable, and at the appropriate level of responsibility, of material weaknesses in the design or implementation of internal control to prevent and detect fraud which may have come to the auditor's attention.

101. The auditor should consider whether there are any other matters related to fraud to be discussed with those charged with governance of the entity.

103. If, as a result of a misstatement resulting from fraud or suspected fraud, the auditor encounters exceptional circumstances that bring into question the auditor's ability to continue performing the audit the auditor should:

(a) Consider the professional and legal responsibilities applicable in the circumstances, including whether there is a requirement for the auditor to report to the person or persons who made the audit appointment or, in some cases, to regulatory authorities;

(b) Consider the possibility of withdrawing from the engagement; and

(c) If the auditor withdraws:

(i) Discuss with the appropriate level of management and those charged with governance the auditor's withdrawal from the engagement and the reasons for the withdrawal; and

(ii) Consider whether there is a professional or legal requirement to report to the person or persons who made the audit appointment or, in some cases, to regulatory authorities, the auditor's withdrawal from the engagement and the reasons for the withdrawal.

250 Section A - Consideration of Laws and Regulations

23. The auditor should obtain written representations that management[10] has disclosed to the auditor all known actual or possible noncompliance with laws and regulations whose effects should be considered when preparing financial statements.

23-1. Where applicable, the written representations should include the actual or contingent consequences which may arise from the non-compliance.

28. When the auditor believes there may be noncompliance, the auditor should document the findings and discuss them with management[11].

28-1. Any discussion of findings with those charged with governance and with management should be subject to compliance with legislation relating to 'tipping off' and any requirement to report the findings direct to a third party.

32. The auditor should, as soon as practicable, either communicate with those charged with governance, or obtain evidence that they are appropriately informed, regarding noncompliance that comes to the auditor's attention.

33. If in the auditor's judgment the noncompliance is believed to be intentional and material, the auditor should communicate the finding without delay.

33-1. In the UK and Ireland the auditor should communicate the finding where the non-compliance is material or is believed to be intentional. The non-compliance does not have to be both material and intentional.

34. If the auditor suspects that members of senior management, including members of the board of directors[12], are involved in noncompliance, the auditor should report the matter to the next higher level of authority at the entity, if it exists, such as an audit committee or a supervisory board.

---

[10] In the UK and Ireland the auditor obtains this written representations from those charged with governance.

[11] In the UK and Ireland, the auditor discusses such matters with those charged with governance.

[12] In the UK and Ireland, the auditor also reports such matters if those charged with governance are suspected of being involved in non compliance.

315 - Understanding the Entity and Its Environment and Assessing the Risks of Material Misstatement

120. The auditor should make those charged with governance or management aware, as soon as practicable, and at an appropriate level of responsibility, of material weaknesses in the design or implementation of internal control which have come to the auditor's attention.

320 – Audit Materiality

17. If the auditor has identified a material misstatement resulting from error, the auditor should communicate the misstatement to the appropriate level of management on a timely basis, and consider the need to report it to those charged with governance in accordance with ISA (UK and Ireland) 260, "Communication of Audit Matters to Those Charged with Governance."

545 - Fair Value Measurements and Disclosures

63. The auditor should obtain written representations from management regarding the reasonableness of significant assumptions, including whether they appropriately reflect management's intent and ability to carry out specific courses of action on behalf of the entity where relevant to the fair value measurements or disclosures.

550 - Related Parties

15. The auditor should obtain a written representation from management[13] concerning:

    (a) The completeness of information provided regarding the identification of related parties; and

    (b) The adequacy of related party disclosures in the financial statements.

115. The auditor should obtain a written representation from management[14] concerning:

    (a) The completeness of information provided regarding the identification of related parties; and

    (b) The adequacy of related party disclosures in the financial statements.

---

[13] In the UK and Ireland the auditor obtains written representations from those charged with governance.

[14] In the UK and Ireland the auditor obtains written representations from those charged with governance.

560 - Subsequent Events

9.   When, after the date of the auditor's report but before the financial statements are issued, the auditor becomes aware of a fact which may materially affect the financial statements, the auditor should consider whether the financial statements need amendment, should discuss the matter with management[15], and should take the action appropriate in the circumstances.

14.   When, after the financial statements have been issued, the auditor becomes aware of a fact which existed at the date of the auditor's report and which, if known at that date, may have caused the auditor to modify the auditor's report, the auditor should consider whether the financial statements need revision[16], should discuss the matter with management[15], and should take the action appropriate in the circumstances.

570 - Going Concern

26.   When events or conditions have been identified which may cast significant doubt on the entity's ability to continue as a going concern, the auditor should:

      (a) Review management's[17] plans for future actions based on its going concern assessment;

      (b) Gather sufficient appropriate audit evidence to confirm or dispel whether or not a material uncertainty exists through carrying out procedures considered necessary, including considering the effect of any plans of management and other mitigating factors; and

      (c) Seek written representations from management[18] regarding its plans for future action.

26-1. The auditor should consider the need to obtain written confirmations of representations from those charged with governance regarding:

      (a) The assessment of those charged with governance that the company is a going concern;

---

[15] In the UK and Ireland the auditor discusses these matters with those charged with governance. Those charged with governance are responsible for the preparation of the financial statements.

[16] In the UK the detailed regulations governing revised financial statements and directors' reports, where the revision is voluntary, are set out in sections 245 to 245C of the Companies Act 1985 and in the Articles 253 to 253C of the Companies (Northern Ireland) Order 1986. There are no provisions in the Companies Acts of the Republic of Ireland for revising financial statements

[17] In the UK and Ireland, those charged with governance are responsible for the preparation of the entity's financial statements and the assessment of the entity's ability to continue as a going concern.

[18] In the UK and Ireland the auditor obtains written representations from those charged with governance.

(b) Any relevant disclosures in the financial statements.

580 - Management Representations

2.   The auditor should obtain appropriate representations from management.

2-1. Written confirmation of appropriate representations from management, as required by paragraph 4 below, should be obtained before the audit report is issued.

3-1. In the UK and Ireland, the auditor should obtain evidence that those charged with governance acknowledge their collective responsibility for the preparation of the financial statements and have approved the financial statements.

4.   The auditor should obtain written representations from management on matters material to the financial statements when other sufficient appropriate audit evidence cannot reasonably be expected to exist.

5.a. The auditor should obtain written representations from management that:

(a) It acknowledges its responsibility for the design and implementation of internal control to prevent and detect error; and

(b) It believes the effects of those uncorrected financial statements misstatements aggregated by the auditor during the audit are immaterial, both individually and in the aggregate, to the financial statements taken as a whole. A summary of such items should be included in or attached to the written representations.

15.   If management refuses to provide a representation that the auditor considers necessary, this constitutes a scope limitation and the auditor should express a qualified opinion or a disclaimer of opinion.

720 - Other Information (Section A)

11-1. If the auditor identifies a material inconsistency the auditor should seek to resolve the matter through discussion with those charged with governance.

16.   If the auditor becomes aware that the other information appears to include a material misstatement of fact, the auditor should discuss the matter with the entity's management[19].

---

[19] In the UK and Ireland the auditor discusses such matters with, and obtains responses from, those charged with governance.

INTERNATIONAL STANDARD ON AUDITING (UK AND IRELAND) 300

PLANNING AN AUDIT OF FINANCIAL STATEMENTS

CONTENTS

International Standard on Auditing (UK and Ireland) (ISA (UK and Ireland)) 300 "Planning an Audit of Financial Statements" should be read in the context of the Auditing Practices Board's Statement "The Auditing Practices Board - Scope and Authority of Pronouncements" which sets out the application and authority of ISAs (UK and Ireland).

Introduction

1. The purpose of this International Standard on Auditing (UK and Ireland) (ISA (UK and Ireland)) is to establish standards and provide guidance on the considerations and activities applicable to planning an audit of financial statements. This ISA (UK and Ireland) is framed in the context of recurring audits. In addition, matters the auditor considers in initial audit engagements are included in paragraphs 28 and 29.

1-1. This ISA (UK and Ireland) uses the terms 'those charged with governance' and 'management'. The term 'governance' describes the role of persons entrusted with the supervision, control and direction of an entity. Ordinarily, those charged with governance are accountable for ensuring that the entity achieves its objectives, and for the quality of its financial reporting and reporting to interested parties. Those charged with governance include management only when they perform such functions.

1-2. In the UK and Ireland, those charged with governance include the directors (executive and non-executive) of a company or other body, the members of an audit committee where one exists, the partners, proprietors, committee of management or trustees of other forms of entity, or equivalent persons responsible for directing the entity's affairs and preparing its financial statements.

1-3. 'Management' comprises those persons who perform senior managerial functions.

1-4. In the UK and Ireland, depending on the nature and circumstances of the entity, management may include some or all of those charged with governance (e.g. executive directors). Management will not normally include non-executive directors.

2. **The auditor should plan the audit so that the engagement will be performed in an effective manner.**

3. Planning an audit involves establishing the overall audit strategy for the engagement and developing an audit plan, in order to reduce audit risk to an acceptably low level. Planning involves the engagement partner and other key members of the engagement team to benefit from their experience and insight and to enhance the effectiveness and efficiency of the planning process.

4. Adequate planning helps to ensure that appropriate attention is devoted to important areas of the audit, that potential problems are identified and resolved on a timely basis and that the audit engagement is properly organized and managed in order to be performed in an effective and efficient manner. Adequate planning also assists in the proper assignment of work to engagement team members, facilitates the direction and supervision of engagement team members and the review of their work, and assists, where applicable, in coordination of work done by auditors of components and experts. The nature and extent of planning activities will vary according to the size and complexity of the entity, the auditor's previous experience with the entity, and changes in circumstances that occur during the audit engagement.

5.   Planning is not a discrete phase of an audit, but rather a continual and iterative process that often begins shortly after (or in connection with) the completion of the previous audit and continues until the completion of the current audit engagement. However, in planning an audit, the auditor considers the timing of certain planning activities and audit procedures that need to be completed prior to the performance of further audit procedures. For example, the auditor plans the discussion among engagement team members,[1] the analytical procedures to be applied as risk assessment procedures, the obtaining of a general understanding of the legal and regulatory framework applicable to the entity and how the entity is complying with that framework, the determination of materiality, the involvement of experts and the performance of other risk assessment procedures prior to identifying and assessing the risks of material misstatement and performing further audit procedures at the assertion level for classes of transactions, account balances, and disclosures that are responsive to those risks.

Preliminary Engagement Activities

6.   **The auditor should perform the following activities at the beginning of the current audit engagement:**

- **Perform procedures regarding the continuance of the client relationship and the specific audit engagement** (see ISA (UK and Ireland) 220, "Quality Control for Audits of Historical Financial Information" for additional guidance).

- **Evaluate compliance with ethical requirements, including independence** (see ISA (UK and Ireland) 220 for additional guidance).

- **Establish an understanding of the terms of the engagement** (see ISA (UK and Ireland) 210, "Terms of Audit Engagements" for additional guidance).

The auditor's consideration of client continuance and ethical requirements, including independence, occurs throughout the performance of the audit engagement as conditions and changes in circumstances occur. However, the auditor's initial procedures on both client continuance and evaluation of ethical requirements (including independence) are performed prior to performing other significant activities for the current audit engagement. For continuing audit engagements, such initial procedures often occur shortly after (or in connection with) the completion of the previous audit.

7.   The purpose of performing these preliminary engagement activities is to help ensure that the auditor has considered any events or circumstances that may adversely affect the auditor's ability to plan and perform the audit engagement to reduce audit risk to

---

[1]   ISA (UK and Ireland) 315, "Understanding the Entity and Its Environment and Assessing the Risks of Material Misstatement" paragraphs 14-19 provide guidance on the engagement team's discussion of the susceptibility of the entity to material misstatements of the financial statements. ISA (UK and Ireland) 240, "The Auditor's Responsibility to Consider Fraud in an Audit of Financial Statements" paragraphs 27-32 provide guidance on the emphasis given during this discussion to the susceptibility of the entity's financial statements to material misstatement due to fraud.

an acceptably low level. Performing these preliminary engagement activities helps to ensure that the auditor plans an audit engagement for which:

- The auditor maintains the necessary independence and ability to perform the engagement.

- There are no issues with management integrity[2] that may affect the auditor's willingness to continue the engagement.

- There is no misunderstanding with the client as to the terms of the engagement.

Planning Activities

The Overall Audit Strategy

8. **The auditor should establish the overall audit strategy for the audit.**

9. The overall audit strategy sets the scope, timing and direction of the audit, and guides the development of the more detailed audit plan. The establishment of the overall audit strategy involves:

(a) Determining the characteristics of the engagement that define its scope, such as the financial reporting framework used, industry-specific reporting requirements and the locations of the components of the entity;

(b) Ascertaining the reporting objectives of the engagement to plan the timing of the audit and the nature of the communications required, such as deadlines for interim and final reporting, and key dates for expected communications with management and those charged with governance; and

(c) Considering the important factors that will determine the focus of the engagement team's efforts, such as determination of appropriate materiality levels, preliminary identification of areas where there may be higher risks of material misstatement, preliminary identification of material components and account balances, evaluation of whether the auditor may plan to obtain evidence regarding the effectiveness of internal control, and identification of recent significant entity-specific, industry, financial reporting or other relevant developments.

In developing the overall audit strategy, the auditor also considers the results of preliminary engagement activities (see paragraphs 6 and 7) and, where practicable, experience gained on other engagements performed for the entity. The Appendix to this ISA (UK and Ireland) lists examples of matters the auditor may consider in establishing the overall audit strategy for an engagement.

---

[2] In the UK and Ireland, the auditor is also concerned to establish that there are no issues with the integrity of those charged with governance that may affect the auditor's willingness to continue the engagement.

10. The process of developing the audit strategy helps the auditor to ascertain the nature, timing and extent of resources necessary to perform the engagement. The overall audit strategy sets out clearly, in response to the matters identified in paragraph 9, and subject to the completion of the auditor's risk assessment procedures:

   (a) The resources to deploy for specific audit areas, such as the use of appropriately experienced team members for high risk areas or the involvement of experts on complex matters;

   (b) The amount of resources to allocate to specific audit areas, such as the number of team members assigned to observe the inventory count at material locations, the extent of review of other auditors' work in the case of group audits, or the audit budget in hours to allocate to high risk areas;

   (c) When these resources are deployed, such as whether at an interim audit stage or at key cut-off dates; and

   (d) How such resources are managed, directed and supervised, such as when team briefing and debriefing meetings are expected to be held, how engagement partner and manager reviews are expected to take place (for example, on-site or off-site), and whether to complete engagement quality control reviews.

11. Once the audit strategy has been established, the auditor is able to start the development of a more detailed audit plan to address the various matters identified in the overall audit strategy, taking into account the need to achieve the audit objectives through the efficient use of the auditor's resources. Although the auditor ordinarily establishes the overall audit strategy before developing the detailed audit plan, the two planning activities are not necessarily discrete or sequential processes but are closely inter-related since changes in one may result in consequential changes to the other. Paragraphs 14 and 15 provide further guidance on developing the audit plan.

12. In audits of small entities, the entire audit may be conducted by a very small audit team. Many audits of small entities involve the audit engagement partner (who may be a sole practitioner) working with one engagement team member (or without any engagement team members). With a smaller team, co-ordination and communication between team members are easier. Establishing the overall audit strategy for the audit of a small entity need not be a complex or time-consuming exercise; it varies according to the size of the entity and the complexity of the audit. For example, a brief memorandum prepared at the completion of the previous audit, based on a review of the working papers and highlighting issues identified in the audit just completed, updated and changed in the current period based on discussions with the owner-manager, can serve as the basis for planning the current audit engagement.

The Audit Plan

13. **The auditor should develop an audit plan for the audit in order to reduce audit risk to an acceptably low level.**

14. The audit plan is more detailed than the audit strategy and includes the nature, timing and extent of audit procedures to be performed by engagement team members in order to obtain sufficient appropriate audit evidence to reduce audit risk to an acceptably low level. Documentation of the audit plan also serves as a record of the proper planning and performance of the audit procedures that can be reviewed and approved prior to the performance of further audit procedures.

15. The audit plan includes:

- A description of the nature, timing and extent of planned risk assessment procedures sufficient to assess the risks of material misstatement, as determined under ISA (UK and Ireland) 315, "Understanding the Entity and Its Environment and Assessing the Risks of Material Misstatement;"

- A description of the nature, timing and extent of planned further audit procedures at the assertion level for each material class of transactions, account balance, and disclosure, as determined under ISA (UK and Ireland) 330, "The Auditor's Procedures in Response to Assessed Risks." The plan for further audit procedures reflects the auditor's decision whether to test the operating effectiveness of controls, and the nature, timing and extent of planned substantive procedures; and

- Such other audit procedures required to be carried out for the engagement in order to comply with ISAs (UK and Ireland) (for example, seeking direct communication with the entity's lawyers).

Planning for these audit procedures takes place over the course of the audit as the audit plan for the engagement develops. For example, planning of the auditor's risk assessment procedures ordinarily occurs early in the audit process. However, planning of the nature, timing and extent of specific further audit procedures depends on the outcome of those risk assessment procedures. In addition, the auditor may begin the execution of further audit procedures for some classes of transactions, account balances and disclosures before completing the more detailed audit plan of all remaining further audit procedures.

Changes to Planning Decisions During the Course of the Audit

16. **The overall audit strategy and the audit plan should be updated and changed as necessary during the course of the audit.**

17. Planning an audit is a continual and iterative process throughout the audit engagement. As a result of unexpected events, changes in conditions, or the audit evidence obtained from the results of audit procedures, the auditor may need to modify the overall audit strategy and audit plan, and thereby the resulting planned nature, timing and extent of further audit procedures. Information may come to the auditor's attention that differs significantly from the information available when the auditor planned the audit procedures. For example, the auditor may obtain audit evidence through the performance of substantive procedures that contradicts the audit evidence obtained with respect to the testing of the operating effectiveness of controls. In such circumstances, the auditor re-evaluates the planned audit procedures, based

on the revised consideration of assessed risks at the assertion level for all or some of the classes of transactions, account balances or disclosures.

Direction, Supervision and Review

18. **The auditor should plan the nature, timing and extent of direction and supervision of engagement team members and review of their work.**

19. The nature, timing and extent of the direction and supervision of engagement team members and review of their work vary depending on many factors, including the size and complexity of the entity, the area of audit, the risks of material misstatement, and the capabilities and competence of personnel performing the audit work. ISA (UK and Ireland) 220 contains detailed guidance on the direction, supervision and review of audit work.

20. The auditor plans the nature, timing and extent of direction and supervision of engagement team members based on the assessed risk of material misstatement. As the assessed risk of material misstatement increases, for the area of audit risk, the auditor ordinarily increases the extent and timeliness of direction and supervision of engagement team members and performs a more detailed review of their work. Similarly, the auditor plans the nature, timing and extent of review of the engagement team's work based on the capabilities and competence of the individual team members performing the audit work.

21. In audits of small entities, an audit may be carried out entirely by the audit engagement partner (who may be a sole practitioner). In such situations, questions of direction and supervision of engagement team members and review of their work do not arise as the audit engagement partner, having personally conducted all aspects of the work, is aware of all material issues. The audit engagement partner (or sole practitioner) nevertheless needs to be satisfied that the audit has been conducted in accordance with ISAs (UK and Ireland). Forming an objective view on the appropriateness of the judgments made in the course of the audit can present practical problems when the same individual also performed the entire audit. When particularly complex or unusual issues are involved, and the audit is performed by a sole practitioner, it may be desirable to plan to consult with other suitably-experienced auditors or the auditor's professional body.

Documentation

22. **The auditor should document the overall audit strategy and the audit plan, including any significant changes made during the audit engagement.**

23. The auditor's documentation of the overall audit strategy records the key decisions considered necessary to properly plan the audit and to communicate significant matters to the engagement team. For example, the auditor may summarize the overall audit strategy in the form of a memorandum that contains key decisions regarding the overall scope, timing and conduct of the audit.

24. The auditor's documentation of the audit plan is sufficient to demonstrate the planned nature, timing and extent of risk assessment procedures, and further audit procedures at the assertion level for each material class of transaction, account balance, and disclosure in response to the assessed risks. The auditor may use standard audit programs or audit completion checklists. However, when such standard programs or checklists are used, the auditor appropriately tailors them to reflect the particular engagement circumstances.

25. The auditor's documentation of any significant changes to the originally planned overall audit strategy and to the detailed audit plan includes the reasons for the significant changes and the auditor's response to the events, conditions, or results of audit procedures that resulted in such changes. For example, the auditor may significantly change the planned overall audit strategy and the audit plan as a result of a material business combination or the identification of a material misstatement of the financial statements. A record of the significant changes to the overall audit strategy and the audit plan, and resulting changes to the planned nature, timing and extent of audit procedures, explains the overall strategy and audit plan finally adopted for the audit and demonstrates the appropriate response to significant changes occurring during the audit.

26. The form and extent of documentation depend on such matters as the size and complexity of the entity, materiality, the extent of other documentation, and the circumstances of the specific audit engagement.

Communications With Those Charged With Governance and Management

27. The auditor may discuss elements of planning with those charged with governance and the entity's management. These discussions may be a part of overall communications required to be made to those charged with governance of the entity or may be made to improve the effectiveness and efficiency of the audit. Discussions with those charged with governance ordinarily include the overall audit strategy and timing of the audit, including any limitations thereon, or any additional requirements[3]. Discussions with management often occur to facilitate the conduct and management of the audit engagement (for example, to coordinate some of the planned audit procedures with the work of the entity's personnel). Although these discussions often occur, the overall audit strategy and the audit plan remain the auditor's responsibility. When discussions of matters included in the overall audit strategy or audit plan occur, care is required in order to not compromise the effectiveness of the audit. For example, the auditor considers whether discussing the nature and timing of detailed audit procedures with management compromises the effectiveness of the audit by making the audit procedures too predictable.

---

[3] ISA (UK and Ireland) 260, "Communication of Audit Matters With Those Charged With Governance," requires the auditor to communicate to those charged with governance an outline of the nature and scope, including, where relevant, any limitations thereon, of the work the auditor proposes to undertake. Examples are given of planning information that might be communicated.

Additional Considerations in Initial Audit Engagements

28. **The auditor should perform the following activities prior to starting an initial audit:**

    (a) **Perform procedures regarding the acceptance of the client relationship and the specific audit engagement (see ISA (UK and Ireland) 220 for additional guidance).**

    (b) **Communicate with the previous auditor, where there has been a change of auditors, in compliance with relevant ethical requirements.**

29. The purpose and objective of planning the audit are the same whether the audit is an initial or recurring engagement. However, for an initial audit, the auditor may need to expand the planning activities because the auditor does not ordinarily have the previous experience with the entity that is considered when planning recurring engagements. For initial audits, additional matters the auditor may consider in developing the overall audit strategy and audit plan include the following:

    • Unless prohibited by law or regulation, arrangements to be made with the previous auditor, for example, to review the previous auditor's working papers.

    • Any major issues (including the application of accounting principles or of auditing and reporting standards) discussed with management in connection with the initial selection as auditors, the communication of these matters to those charged with governance and how these matters affect the overall audit strategy and audit plan.

    • The planned audit procedures to obtain sufficient appropriate audit evidence regarding opening balances (see paragraph 2 of ISA (UK and Ireland) 510, "Initial Engagements - Opening Balances").

    • The assignment of firm personnel with appropriate levels of capabilities and competence to respond to anticipated significant risks.

    • Other procedures required by the firm's system of quality control for initial audit engagements (for example, the firm's system of quality control may require the involvement of another partner or senior individual to review the overall audit strategy prior to commencing significant audit procedures or to review reports prior to their issuance).

Effective Date

30. This ISA (UK and Ireland) is effective for audits of financial statements for periods commencing on or after 15 December 2004.

Public Sector Perspective

Additional guidance for auditors of public sector bodies in the UK and Ireland is given in:

- Practice Note 10 "Audit of Financial Statements of Public Sector Bodies in the United Kingdom (Revised)"

- Practice Note 10(I) "Audit of Central Government Financial Statements in the Republic of Ireland (Revised)"

1. *This ISA (UK and Ireland) is applicable in all material respects to audits of public sector entities.*

2. *Some of the terms used in this ISA (UK and Ireland) such as "engagement partner" and "firm" should be read as referring to their public sector equivalents.*

3. *Paragraph 6 of this ISA (UK and Ireland) refers to ISA (UK and Ireland) 210, "Terms of Audit Engagements," and ISA (UK and Ireland) 220, "Quality Control for Audits of Historical Financial Information." The Public Sector Perspectives to those ISAs (UK and Ireland) contain a discussion of their applicability to audits of public sector entities, and are therefore relevant to the application of this ISA (UK and Ireland) in the public sector.*

Appendix

Examples of Matters the Auditor May Consider in Establishing the Overall Audit Strategy

This appendix provides examples of matters the auditor may consider in establishing the overall audit strategy. Many of these matters will also influence the auditor's detailed audit plan. The examples provided cover a broad range of matters applicable to many engagements. While some of the matters referred to below may be required to be performed by other ISAs (UK and Ireland), not all matters are relevant to every audit engagement and the list is not necessarily complete. In addition, the auditor may consider these matters in an order different from that shown below.

Scope of the Audit Engagement

The auditor may consider the following matters when establishing the scope of the audit engagement:

- The financial reporting framework on which the financial information to be audited has been prepared, including any need for reconciliations to another financial reporting framework.

- Industry-specific reporting requirements such as reports mandated by industry regulators.

- The expected audit coverage, including the number and locations of components to be included.

- The nature of the control relationships between a parent and its components that determine how the group is to be consolidated.

- The extent to which components are audited by other auditors.

- The nature of the business segments to be audited, including the need for specialized knowledge.

- The reporting currency to be used, including any need for currency translation for the financial information audited.

- The need for a statutory audit of standalone financial statements in addition to an audit for consolidation purposes.

- The availability of the work of internal auditors and the extent of the auditor's potential reliance on such work.

- The entity's use of service organizations and how the auditor may obtain evidence concerning the design or operation of controls performed by them.

- The expected use of audit evidence obtained in prior audits, for example, audit evidence related to risk assessment procedures and tests of controls.

- The effect of information technology on the audit procedures, including the availability of data and the expected use of computer-assisted audit techniques.

- The coordination of the expected coverage and timing of the audit work with any reviews of interim financial information and the effect on the audit of the information obtained during such reviews.

- The discussion of matters that may affect the audit with firm personnel responsible for performing other services to the entity.

- The availability of client personnel and data.

Reporting Objectives, Timing of the Audit and Communications Required

The auditor may consider the following matters when ascertaining the reporting objectives of the engagement, the timing of the audit and the nature of communications required:

- The entity's timetable for reporting, such as at interim and final stages.

- The organization of meetings with management and those charged with governance to discuss the nature, extent and timing of the audit work.

- The discussion with management and those charged with governance regarding the expected type and timing of reports to be issued and other communications, both written and oral, including the auditor's report, management letters and communications to those charged with governance.

- The discussion with management regarding the expected communications on the status of audit work throughout the engagement and the expected deliverables resulting from the audit procedures.

- Communication with auditors of components regarding the expected types and timing of reports to be issued and other communications in connection with the audit of components.

- The expected nature and timing of communications among engagement team members, including the nature and timing of team meetings and timing of the review of work performed.

- Whether there are any other expected communications with third parties, including any statutory or contractual reporting responsibilities arising from the audit.

Direction of the Audit

The auditor may consider the following matters when setting the direction of the audit:

- With respect to materiality:

    - Setting materiality for planning purposes.

    - Setting and communicating materiality for auditors of components.

    - Reconsidering materiality as audit procedures are performed during the course of the audit.

    - Identifying the material components and account balances.

- Audit areas where there is a higher risk of material misstatement.

- The impact of the assessed risk of material misstatement at the overall financial statement level on direction, supervision and review.

- The selection of the engagement team (including, where necessary, the engagement quality control reviewer) and the assignment of audit work to the team members, including the assignment of appropriately experienced team members to areas where there may be higher risks of material misstatement.

- Engagement budgeting, including considering the appropriate amount of time to set aside for areas where there may be higher risks of material misstatement.

- The manner in which the auditor emphasizes to engagement team members the need to maintain a questioning mind and to exercise professional skepticism in gathering and evaluating audit evidence.

- Results of previous audits that involved evaluating the operating effectiveness of internal control, including the nature of identified weaknesses and action taken to address them.

- Evidence of management's[4] commitment to the design and operation of sound internal control, including evidence of appropriate documentation of such internal control.

- Volume of transactions, which may determine whether it is more efficient for the auditor to rely on internal control.

- Importance attached to internal control throughout the entity to the successful operation of the business.

- Significant business developments affecting the entity, including changes in information technology and business processes, changes in key management, and acquisitions, mergers and divestments.

---

[4] In the UK and Ireland, the auditor also considers evidence of the commitment of those charged with governance to the design and operation of sound internal control.

- Significant industry developments such as changes in industry regulations and new reporting requirements.

- Significant changes in the financial reporting framework, such as changes in accounting standards.

- Other significant relevant developments, such as changes in the legal environment affecting the entity.

INTERNATIONAL STANDARD ON AUDITING
(UK AND IRELAND) 315

UNDERSTANDING THE ENTITY AND ITS ENVIRONMENT AND ASSESSING THE RISKS OF MATERIAL MISSTATEMENT

CONTENTS

Appendix 3: Conditions and Events That May Indicate Risks of Material
Misstatement

International Standard on Auditing (UK and Ireland) (ISA (UK and Ireland)) 315 "Understanding the Entity and its Environment and Assessing the Risks of Material Misstatement" should be read in the context of the Auditing Practices Board's Statement "The Auditing Practices Board - Scope and Authority of Pronouncements (Revised)" which sets out the application and authority of ISAs (UK and Ireland).

Introduction

1. The purpose of this International Standard on Auditing (UK and Ireland) (ISA (UK and Ireland)) is to establish standards and provide guidance on obtaining an understanding of the entity and its environment, including its internal control, and on assessing the risks of material misstatement in a financial statement audit. The importance of the auditor's risk assessment as a basis for further audit procedures is discussed in the explanation of audit risk in ISA (UK and Ireland) 200, "Objective and General Principles Governing an Audit of Financial Statements."

1-1. This ISA (UK and Ireland) uses the terms 'those charged with governance' and 'management'. The term 'governance' describes the role of persons entrusted with the supervision, control and direction of an entity. Ordinarily, those charged with governance are accountable for ensuring that the entity achieves its objectives, and for the quality of its financial reporting and reporting to interested parties. Those charged with governance include management only when they perform such functions.

1-2. In the UK and Ireland, those charged with governance include the directors (executive and non-executive) of a company or other body, the members of an audit committee where one exists, the partners, proprietors, committee of management or trustees of other forms of entity, or equivalent persons responsible for directing the entity's affairs and preparing its financial statements.

1-3. 'Management' comprises those persons who perform senior managerial functions.

1-4. In the UK and Ireland, depending on the nature and circumstances of the entity, management may include some or all of those charged with governance (e.g. executive directors). Management will not normally include non-executive directors.

2. **The auditor should obtain an understanding of the entity and its environment, including its internal control, sufficient to identify and assess the risks of material misstatement of the financial statements whether due to fraud or error, and sufficient to design and perform further audit procedures.** ISA (UK and Ireland) 500, "Audit Evidence," requires the auditor to use assertions in sufficient detail to form a basis for the assessment of risks of material misstatement and the design and performance of further audit procedures. This ISA (UK and Ireland) requires the auditor to make risk assessments at the financial statement and assertion levels based on an appropriate understanding of the entity and its environment, including its internal control. ISA (UK and Ireland) 330, "The Auditor's Procedures in Response to Assessed Risks" discusses the auditor's responsibility to determine overall responses and to design and perform further audit procedures whose nature, timing, and extent are responsive to the risk assessments. The requirements and guidance of this ISA (UK and Ireland) are to be applied in conjunction with the requirements and guidance provided in other ISAs (UK and Ireland). In particular, further guidance in relation to the auditor's responsibility to assess the risks of material misstatement due to fraud is discussed in ISA (UK and Ireland) 240, "The Auditor's Responsibility to Consider Fraud in an Audit of Financial Statements."

3.   The following is an overview of the requirements of this standard:

*   *Risk assessment procedures and sources of information about the entity and its environment, including its internal control.* This section explains the audit procedures that the auditor is required to perform to obtain the understanding of the entity and its environment, including its internal control (risk assessment procedures). It also requires discussion among the engagement team about the susceptibility of the entity's financial statements to material misstatement.

*   *Understanding the entity and its environment, including its internal control.* This section requires the auditor to understand specified aspects of the entity and its environment, and components of its internal control, in order to identify and assess the risks of material misstatement.

*   *Assessing the risks of material misstatement.* This section requires the auditor to identify and assess the risks of material misstatement at the financial statement and assertion levels. The auditor:

    –   Identifies risks by considering the entity and its environment, including relevant controls, and by considering the classes of transactions, account balances, and disclosures in the financial statements;

    –   Relates the identified risks to what can go wrong at the assertion level; and

    –   Considers the significance and likelihood of the risks.

This section also requires the auditor to determine whether any of the assessed risks are significant risks that require special audit consideration or risks for which substantive procedures alone do not provide sufficient appropriate audit evidence. The auditor is required to evaluate the design of the entity's controls, including relevant control activities, over such risks and determine whether they have been implemented.

*   *Communicating with those charged with governance and management.* This section deals with matters relating to internal control that the auditor communicates to those charged with governance and management.

*   *Documentation.* This section establishes related documentation requirements.

4.   Obtaining an understanding of the entity and its environment is an essential aspect of performing an audit in accordance with ISAs (UK and Ireland). In particular, that understanding establishes a frame of reference within which the auditor plans the audit and exercises professional judgment about assessing risks of material misstatement of the financial statements and responding to those risks throughout the audit, for example when:

*   Establishing materiality and evaluating whether the judgment about materiality remains appropriate as the audit progresses;

THE AUDITING PRACTICES BOARD

- Considering the appropriateness of the selection and application of accounting policies, and the adequacy of financial statement disclosures;

- Identifying areas where special audit consideration may be necessary, for example, related party transactions, the appropriateness of management's use of the going concern assumption, or considering the business purpose of transactions;

- Developing expectations for use when performing analytical procedures;

- Designing and performing further audit procedures to reduce audit risk to an acceptably low level; and

- Evaluating the sufficiency and appropriateness of audit evidence obtained, such as the appropriateness of assumptions and of management's oral and written representations[1a].

5.   The auditor uses professional judgment to determine the extent of the understanding required of the entity and its environment, including its internal control. The auditor's primary consideration is whether the understanding that has been obtained is sufficient to assess the risks of material misstatement of the financial statements and to design and perform further audit procedures. The depth of the overall understanding that is required by the auditor in performing the audit is less than that possessed by management in managing the entity.

Risk Assessment Procedures and Sources of Information About the Entity and Its Environment, Including Its Internal Control

6.   Obtaining an understanding of the entity and its environment, including its internal control, is a continuous, dynamic process of gathering, updating and analyzing information throughout the audit. As described in ISA (UK and Ireland) 500, audit procedures to obtain an understanding are referred to as "risk assessment procedures" because some of the information obtained by performing such procedures may be used by the auditor as audit evidence to support assessments of the risks of material misstatement. In addition, in performing risk assessment procedures, the auditor may obtain audit evidence about classes of transactions, account balances, or disclosures and related assertions and about the operating effectiveness of controls, even though such audit procedures were not specifically planned as substantive procedures or as tests of controls. The auditor also may choose to perform substantive procedures or tests of controls concurrently with risk assessment procedures because it is efficient to do so.

[1a] In the UK and Ireland, the auditor obtains written representations from those charged with governance.

Risk Assessment Procedures

7. **The auditor should perform the following risk assessment procedures to obtain an understanding of the entity and its environment, including its internal control:**

    (a) **Inquiries of management and others within the entity;**

    (b) **Analytical procedures; and**

    (c) **Observation and inspection.**

    The auditor is not required to perform all the risk assessment procedures described above for each aspect of the understanding described in paragraph 20. However, all the risk assessment procedures are performed by the auditor in the course of obtaining the required understanding.

8. In addition, the auditor performs other audit procedures where the information obtained may be helpful in identifying risks of material misstatement. For example, the auditor may consider making inquiries of the entity's external legal counsel or of valuation experts that the entity has used. Reviewing information obtained from external sources such as reports by analysts, banks, or rating agencies; trade and economic journals; or regulatory or financial publications may also be useful in obtaining information about the entity.

9. Although much of the information the auditor obtains by inquiries can be obtained from management and those responsible for financial reporting, inquiries of others within the entity, such as production and internal audit personnel, and other employees with different levels of authority, may be useful in providing the auditor with a different perspective in identifying risks of material misstatement. In determining others within the entity to whom inquiries may be directed, and the extent of those inquiries, the auditor considers what information may be obtained that helps the auditor in identifying risks of material misstatement. For example:

    *   Inquiries directed towards those charged with governance may help the auditor understand the environment in which the financial statements are prepared.

    *   Inquiries directed toward internal audit personnel may relate to their activities concerning the design and effectiveness of the entity's internal control and whether management has satisfactorily responded to any findings from these activities.

    *   Inquiries of employees involved in initiating, processing or recording complex or unusual transactions may help the auditor in evaluating the appropriateness of the selection and application of certain accounting policies.

    *   Inquiries directed toward in-house legal counsel may relate to such matters as litigation, compliance with laws and regulations, knowledge of fraud or suspected fraud affecting the entity, warranties, post-sales obligations, arrangements (such as joint ventures) with business partners and the meaning of contract terms.

- Inquiries directed towards marketing or sales personnel may relate to changes in the entity's marketing strategies, sales trends, or contractual arrangements with its customers.

10. Analytical procedures may be helpful in identifying the existence of unusual transactions or events, and amounts, ratios, and trends that might indicate matters that have financial statement and audit implications. In performing analytical procedures as risk assessment procedures, the auditor develops expectations about plausible relationships that are reasonably expected to exist. When comparison of those expectations with recorded amounts or ratios developed from recorded amounts yields unusual or unexpected relationships, the auditor considers those results in identifying risks of material misstatement. However, when such analytical procedures use data aggregated at a high level (which is often the situation), the results of those analytical procedures only provide a broad initial indication about whether a material misstatement may exist. Accordingly, the auditor considers the results of such analytical procedures along with other information gathered in identifying the risks of material misstatement. See ISA (UK and Ireland) 520, "Analytical Procedures" for additional guidance on the use of analytical procedures.

11. Observation and inspection may support inquiries of management and others, and also provide information about the entity and its environment. Such audit procedures ordinarily include the following:

- Observation of entity activities and operations.

- Inspection of documents (such as business plans and strategies), records, and internal control manuals.

- Reading reports prepared by management (such as quarterly management reports and interim financial statements) and those charged with governance (such as minutes of board of directors' meetings).

- Visits to the entity's premises and plant facilities.

- Tracing transactions through the information system relevant to financial reporting (walk-throughs).

12. **When the auditor intends to use information about the entity and its environment obtained in prior periods, the auditor should determine whether changes have occurred that may affect the relevance of such information in the current audit.** For continuing engagements, the auditor's previous experience with the entity contributes to the understanding of the entity. For example, audit procedures performed in previous audits ordinarily provide audit evidence about the entity's organizational structure, business and controls, as well as information about past misstatements and whether or not they were corrected on a timely basis, which assists the auditor in assessing risks of material misstatement in the current audit. However, such information may have been rendered irrelevant by changes in the entity or its environment. The auditor makes inquiries and performs other appropriate audit

procedures, such as walk-throughs of systems, to determine whether changes have occurred that may affect the relevance of such information.

13. When relevant to the audit, the auditor also considers other information such as that obtained from the auditor's client acceptance or continuance process or, where practicable, experience gained on other engagements performed for the entity, for example, engagements to review interim financial information.

Discussion Among the Engagement Team

14. **The members of the engagement team should discuss the susceptibility of the entity's financial statements to material misstatements.**

15. The objective of this discussion is for members of the engagement team to gain a better understanding of the potential for material misstatements of the financial statements resulting from fraud or error in the specific areas assigned to them, and to understand how the results of the audit procedures that they perform may affect other aspects of the audit including the decisions about the nature, timing, and extent of further audit procedures.

16. The discussion provides an opportunity for more experienced engagement team members, including the engagement partner, to share their insights based on their knowledge of the entity, and for the team members to exchange information about the business risks[1] to which the entity is subject and about how and where the financial statements might be susceptible to material misstatement. As required by ISA (UK and Ireland) 240, particular emphasis is given to the susceptibility of the entity's financial statements to material misstatement due to fraud. The discussion also addresses application of the applicable financial reporting framework to the entity's facts and circumstances.

17. Professional judgment is used to determine which members of the engagement team are included in the discussion, how and when it occurs, and the extent of the discussion. The key members of the engagement team are ordinarily involved in the discussion; however, it is not necessary for all team members to have a comprehensive knowledge of all aspects of the audit. The extent of the discussion is influenced by the roles, experience, and information needs of the engagement team members. In a multi-location audit, for example, there may be multiple discussions that involve the key members of the engagement team in each significant location. Another factor to consider in planning the discussions is whether to include experts assigned to the engagement team. For example, the auditor may determine that including a professional possessing specialist information technology (IT)[2] or other skills is needed on the engagement team and therefore includes that individual in the discussion.

---

[1] See paragraph 30.

[2] Information technology (IT) encompasses automated means of originating, processing, storing and communicating information, and includes recording devices, communication systems, computer systems (including hardware and software components and data), and other electronic devices.

18. As required by ISA (UK and Ireland) 200, the auditor plans and performs the audit with an attitude of professional skepticism. The discussion among the engagement team members emphasizes the need to maintain professional skepticism throughout the engagement, to be alert for information or other conditions that indicate that a material misstatement due to fraud or error may have occurred, and to be rigorous in following up on such indications.

19. Depending on the circumstances of the audit, there may be further discussions in order to facilitate the ongoing exchange of information between engagement team members regarding the susceptibility of the entity's financial statements to material misstatements. The purpose is for engagement team members to communicate and share information obtained throughout the audit that may affect the assessment of the risks of material misstatement due to fraud or error or the audit procedures performed to address the risks.

Understanding the Entity and Its Environment, Including Its Internal Control

20. The auditor's understanding of the entity and its environment consists of an understanding of the following aspects:

    (a) Industry, regulatory, and other external factors, including the applicable financial reporting framework.

    (b) Nature of the entity, including the entity's selection and application of accounting policies.

    (c) Objectives and strategies and the related business risks that may result in a material misstatement of the financial statements.

    (d) Measurement and review of the entity's financial performance.

    (e) Internal control.

    Appendix 1 contains examples of matters that the auditor may consider in obtaining an understanding of the entity and its environment relating to categories (a) through (d) above. Appendix 2 contains a detailed explanation of the internal control components.

21. The nature, timing, and extent of the risk assessment procedures performed depend on the circumstances of the engagement such as the size and complexity of the entity and the auditor's experience with it. In addition, identifying significant changes in any of the above aspects of the entity from prior periods is particularly important in gaining a sufficient understanding of the entity to identify and assess risks of material misstatement.

Industry, Regulatory and Other External Factors, Including the Applicable Financial Reporting Framework

22. **The auditor should obtain an understanding of relevant industry, regulatory, and other external factors including the applicable financial reporting framework.** These factors include industry conditions such as the competitive environment, supplier and customer relationships, and technological developments; the regulatory environment encompassing, among other matters, the applicable financial reporting framework, the legal and political environment, and environmental requirements affecting the industry and the entity; and other external factors such as general economic conditions. See ISA (UK and Ireland) 250, "Consideration of Laws and Regulations in an Audit of Financial Statements" for additional requirements related to the legal and regulatory framework applicable to the entity and the industry.

23. The industry in which the entity operates may give rise to specific risks of material misstatement arising from the nature of the business or the degree of regulation. For example, long-term contracts may involve significant estimates of revenues and costs that give rise to risks of material misstatement. In such cases, the auditor considers whether the engagement team includes members with sufficient relevant knowledge and experience.

24. Legislative and regulatory requirements often determine the applicable financial reporting framework to be used by management[2a] in preparing the entity's financial statements. In most cases, the applicable financial reporting framework will be that of the jurisdiction in which the entity is registered or operates and the auditor is based, and the auditor and the entity will have a common understanding of that framework. In some cases there may be no local financial reporting framework, in which case the entity's choice will be governed by local practice, industry practice, user needs, or other factors. For example, the entity's competitors may apply International Financial Reporting Standards (IFRS) and the entity may determine that IFRS are also appropriate for its financial reporting requirements. The auditor considers whether local regulations specify certain financial reporting requirements for the industry in which the entity operates, since the financial statements may be materially misstated in the context of the applicable financial reporting framework if management[2a] fails to prepare the financial statements in accordance with such regulations.

Nature of the Entity

25. **The auditor should obtain an understanding of the nature of the entity.** The nature of an entity refers to the entity's operations, its ownership and governance, the types of investments that it is making and plans to make, the way that the entity is structured and how it is financed. An understanding of the nature of an entity enables the auditor to understand the classes of transactions, account balances, and disclosures to be expected in the financial statements.

[2a] In the UK and Ireland, those charged with governance are responsible for preparing the financial statements.

26. The entity may have a complex structure with subsidiaries or other components in multiple locations. In addition to the difficulties of consolidation in such cases, other issues with complex structures that may give rise to risks of material misstatement include: the allocation of goodwill to business segments, and its impairment; whether investments are joint ventures, subsidiaries, or investments accounted for using the equity method; and whether special-purpose entities are accounted for appropriately.

27. An understanding of the ownership and relations between owners and other people or entities is also important in determining whether related party transactions have been identified and accounted for appropriately. ISA (UK and Ireland) 550, "Related Parties" provides additional guidance on the auditor's considerations relevant to related parties.

28. **The auditor should obtain an understanding of the entity's selection and application of accounting policies and consider whether they are appropriate for its business and consistent with the applicable financial reporting framework and accounting polices used in the relevant industry.** The understanding encompasses the methods the entity uses to account for significant and unusual transactions; the effect of significant accounting policies in controversial or emerging areas for which there is a lack of authoritative guidance or consensus; and changes in the entity's accounting policies. The auditor also identifies financial reporting standards and regulations that are new to the entity and considers when and how the entity will adopt such requirements. Where the entity has changed its selection of or method of applying a significant accounting policy, the auditor considers the reasons for the change and whether it is appropriate and consistent with the requirements of the applicable financial reporting framework.

29. The presentation of financial statements in conformity with the applicable financial reporting framework includes adequate disclosure of material matters. These matters relate to the form, arrangement, and content of the financial statements and their appended notes, including, for example, the terminology used, the amount of detail given, the classification of items in the statements, and the basis of amounts set forth. The auditor considers whether the entity has disclosed a particular matter appropriately in light of the circumstances and facts of which the auditor is aware at the time.

Objectives and Strategies and Related Business Risks

30. **The auditor should obtain an understanding of the entity's objectives and strategies, and the related business risks that may result in material misstatement of the financial statements.** The entity conducts its business in the context of industry, regulatory and other internal and external factors. To respond to these factors, the entity's management or those charged with governance define objectives, which are the overall plans for the entity. Strategies are the operational approaches by which management intends to achieve its objectives. Business risks result from significant conditions, events, circumstances, actions or inactions that could adversely affect the entity's ability to achieve its objectives and execute its strategies, or through the setting of inappropriate objectives and strategies. Just as the external environment

changes, the conduct of the entity's business is also dynamic and the entity's strategies and objectives change over time.

31. Business risk is broader than the risk of material misstatement of the financial statements, though it includes the latter. Business risk particularly may arise from change or complexity, though a failure to recognize the need for change may also give rise to risk. Change may arise, for example, from the development of new products that may fail; from an inadequate market, even if successfully developed; or from flaws that may result in liabilities and reputational risk. An understanding of business risks increases the likelihood of identifying risks of material misstatement. However, the auditor does not have a responsibility to identify or assess all business risks.

32. Most business risks will eventually have financial consequences and, therefore, an effect on the financial statements. However, not all business risks give rise to risks of material misstatement. A business risk may have an immediate consequence for the risk of misstatement for classes of transactions, account balances, and disclosures at the assertion level or the financial statements as a whole. For example, the business risk arising from a contracting customer base due to industry consolidation may increase the risk of misstatement associated with the valuation of receivables. However, the same risk, particularly in combination with a contracting economy, may also have a longer-term consequence, which the auditor considers when assessing the appropriateness of the going concern assumption. The auditor's consideration of whether a business risk may result in material misstatement is, therefore, made in light of the entity's circumstances. Examples of conditions and events that may indicate risks of material misstatement are given in Appendix 3.

33. Usually management identifies business risks and develops approaches to address them. Such a risk assessment process is part of internal control and is discussed in paragraphs 76-79.

34. Smaller entities often do not set their objectives and strategies, or manage the related business risks, through formal plans or processes. In many cases there may be no documentation of such matters. In such entities, the auditor's understanding is ordinarily obtained through inquiries of management and observation of how the entity responds to such matters.

Measurement and Review of the Entity's Financial Performance

35. **The auditor should obtain an understanding of the measurement and review of the entity's financial performance.** Performance measures and their review indicate to the auditor aspects of the entity's performance that management and others consider to be of importance. Performance measures, whether external or internal, create pressures on the entity that, in turn, may motivate management to take action to improve the business performance or to misstate the financial statements. Obtaining an understanding of the entity's performance measures assists the auditor in considering whether such pressures result in management actions that may have increased the risks of material misstatement.

36. Management's measurement and review of the entity's financial performance is to be distinguished from the monitoring of controls (discussed as a component of internal control in paragraphs 96-99), though their purposes may overlap. Monitoring of controls, however, is specifically concerned with the effective operation of internal control through consideration of information about the control. The measurement and review of performance is directed at whether business performance is meeting the objectives set by management (or third parties), but in some cases performance indicators also provide information that enables management to identify deficiencies in internal control.

37. Internally-generated information used by management for this purpose may include key performance indicators (financial and non-financial), budgets, variance analysis, segment information and divisional, departmental or other level performance reports, and comparisons of an entity's performance with that of competitors. External parties may also measure and review the entity's financial performance. For example, external information such as analysts' reports and credit rating agency reports may provide information useful to the auditor's understanding of the entity and its environment. Such reports often are obtained from the entity being audited.

38. Internal measures may highlight unexpected results or trends requiring management's inquiry of others in order to determine their cause and take corrective action (including, in some cases, the detection and correction of misstatements on a timely basis). Performance measures may also indicate to the auditor a risk of misstatement of related financial statement information. For example, performance measures may indicate that the entity has unusually rapid growth or profitability when compared to that of other entities in the same industry. Such information, particularly if combined with other factors such as performance-based bonus or incentive remuneration, may indicate the potential risk of management[2a] bias in the preparation of the financial statements.

39. Much of the information used in performance measurement may be produced by the entity's information system. If management assumes that data used for reviewing the entity's performance are accurate without having a basis for that assumption, errors may exist in the information, potentially leading management to incorrect conclusions about performance. When the auditor intends to make use of the performance measures for the purpose of the audit (for example, for analytical procedures), the auditor considers whether the information related to management's review of the entity's performance provides a reliable basis and is sufficiently precise for such a purpose. If making use of performance measures, the auditor considers whether they are precise enough to detect material misstatements.

40. Smaller entities ordinarily do not have formal processes to measure and review the entity's financial performance. Management nevertheless often relies on certain key indicators which knowledge and experience of the business suggest are reliable bases for evaluating financial performance and taking appropriate action.

Internal Control

41. **The auditor should obtain an understanding of internal control relevant to the audit.** The auditor uses the understanding of internal control to identify types of potential misstatements, consider factors that affect the risks of material misstatement, and design the nature, timing, and extent of further audit procedures. Internal control relevant to the audit is discussed in paragraphs 47-53 below. In addition, the depth of the understanding is discussed in paragraphs 54-56 below.

42. Internal control is the process designed and effected by those charged with governance, management, and other personnel to provide reasonable assurance about the achievement of the entity's objectives with regard to reliability of financial reporting, effectiveness and efficiency of operations and compliance with applicable laws and regulations. It follows that internal control is designed and implemented to address identified business risks that threaten the achievement of any of these objectives.

43. Internal control, as discussed in this ISA (UK and Ireland), consists of the following components:

    (a) The control environment.

    (b) The entity's risk assessment process.

    (c) The information system, including the related business processes, relevant to financial reporting, and communication.

    (d) Control activities.

    (e) Monitoring of controls.

    Appendix 2 contains a detailed discussion of the internal control components.

44. The division of internal control into the five components provides a useful framework for auditors to consider how different aspects of an entity's internal control may affect the audit. The division does not necessarily reflect how an entity considers and implements internal control. Also, the auditor's primary consideration is whether, and how, a specific control prevents, or detects and corrects, material misstatements in classes of transactions, account balances, or disclosures, and their related assertions, rather than its classification into any particular component. Accordingly, auditors may use different terminology or frameworks to describe the various aspects of internal control, and their effect on the audit than those used in this ISA (UK and Ireland), provided all the components described in this ISA (UK and Ireland) are addressed.

45. The way in which internal control is designed and implemented varies with an entity's size and complexity. Specifically, smaller entities may use less formal means and simpler processes and procedures to achieve their objectives. For example, smaller entities with active management involvement in the financial reporting process may not have extensive descriptions of accounting procedures or detailed written policies. For

some entities, in particular very small entities, the owner-manager[3] may perform functions which in a larger entity would be regarded as belonging to several of the components of internal control. Therefore, the components of internal control may not be clearly distinguished within smaller entities, but their underlying purposes are equally valid.

46. For the purposes of this ISA (UK and Ireland), the term "internal control" encompasses all five components of internal control stated above. In addition, the term "controls" refers to one or more of the components, or any aspect thereof.

Controls Relevant to the Audit

47. There is a direct relationship between an entity's objectives and the controls it implements to provide reasonable assurance about their achievement. The entity's objectives, and therefore controls, relate to financial reporting, operations and compliance; however, not all of these objectives and controls are relevant to the auditor's risk assessment.

48. Ordinarily, controls that are relevant to an audit pertain to the entity's objective of preparing financial statements for external purposes that give a true and fair view (or are presented fairly, in all material respects) in accordance with the applicable financial reporting framework and the management of risk that may give rise to a material misstatement in those financial statements. It is a matter of the auditor's professional judgment, subject to the requirements of this ISA (UK and Ireland), whether a control, individually or in combination with others, is relevant to the auditor's considerations in assessing the risks of material misstatement and designing and performing further procedures in response to assessed risks. In exercising that judgment, the auditor considers the circumstances, the applicable component and factors such as the following:

- The auditor's judgment about materiality.

- The size of the entity.

- The nature of the entity's business, including its organization and ownership characteristics.

- The diversity and complexity of the entity's operations.

- Applicable legal and regulatory requirements.

- The nature and complexity of the systems that are part of the entity's internal control, including the use of service organizations.

---

[3] This ISA (UK and Ireland) uses the term "owner-manager" to indicate the proprietors of entities who are involved in the running of the entity on a day-to-day basis.

49. Controls over the completeness and accuracy of information produced by the entity may also be relevant to the audit if the auditor intends to make use of the information in designing and performing further procedures. The auditor's previous experience with the entity and information obtained in understanding the entity and its environment and throughout the audit assists the auditor in identifying controls relevant to the audit. Further, although internal control applies to the entire entity or to any of its operating units or business processes, an understanding of internal control relating to each of the entity's operating units and business processes may not be relevant to the audit.

50. Controls relating to operations and compliance objectives may, however, be relevant to an audit if they pertain to data the auditor evaluates or uses in applying audit procedures. For example, controls pertaining to non-financial data that the auditor uses in analytical procedures, such as production statistics, or controls pertaining to detecting non-compliance with laws and regulations that may have a direct and material effect on the financial statements, such as controls over compliance with income tax laws and regulations used to determine the income tax provision, may be relevant to an audit.

51. An entity generally has controls relating to objectives that are not relevant to an audit and therefore need not be considered. For example, an entity may rely on a sophisticated system of automated controls to provide efficient and effective operations (such as a commercial airline's system of automated controls to maintain flight schedules), but these controls ordinarily would not be relevant to the audit.

52. Internal control over safeguarding of assets against unauthorized acquisition, use, or disposition may include controls relating to financial reporting and operations objectives. In obtaining an understanding of each of the components of internal control, the auditor's consideration of safeguarding controls is generally limited to those relevant to the reliability of financial reporting. For example, use of access controls, such as passwords, that limit access to the data and programs that process cash disbursements may be relevant to a financial statement audit. Conversely, controls to prevent the excessive use of materials in production generally are not relevant to a financial statement audit.

53. Controls relevant to the audit may exist in any of the components of internal control and a further discussion of controls relevant to the audit is included under the heading of each internal control component below. In addition, paragraphs 113 and 115 discuss certain risks for which the auditor is required to evaluate the design of the entity's controls over such risks and determine whether they have been implemented.

Depth of Understanding of Internal Control

54. Obtaining an understanding of internal control involves evaluating the design of a control and determining whether it has been implemented. Evaluating the design of a control involves considering whether the control, individually or in combination with other controls, is capable of effectively preventing, or detecting and correcting, material misstatements. Further explanation is contained in the discussion of each internal control component below. Implementation of a control means that the control exists and that the entity is using it. The auditor considers the design of a control in

determining whether to consider its implementation. An improperly designed control may represent a material weakness[4] in the entity's internal control and the auditor considers whether to communicate this to those charged with governance and management as required by paragraph 120.

55. Risk assessment procedures to obtain audit evidence about the design and implementation of relevant controls may include inquiring of entity personnel, observing the application of specific controls, inspecting documents and reports, and tracing transactions through the information system relevant to financial reporting. Inquiry alone is not sufficient to evaluate the design of a control relevant to an audit and to determine whether it has been implemented.

56. Obtaining an understanding of an entity's controls is not sufficient to serve as testing the operating effectiveness of controls, unless there is some automation that provides for the consistent application of the operation of the control (manual and automated elements of internal control relevant to the audit are further described below). For example, obtaining audit evidence about the implementation of a manually operated control at a point in time does not provide audit evidence about the operating effectiveness of the control at other times during the period under audit. However, IT enables an entity to process large volumes of data consistently and enhances the entity's ability to monitor the performance of control activities and to achieve effective segregation of duties by implementing security controls in applications, databases, and operating systems. Therefore, because of the inherent consistency of IT processing, performing audit procedures to determine whether an automated control has been implemented may serve as a test of that control's operating effectiveness, depending on the auditor's assessment and testing of controls such as those over program changes. Tests of the operating effectiveness of controls are further described in ISA (UK and Ireland) 330.

Characteristics of Manual and Automated Elements of Internal Control Relevant to the Auditor's Risk Assessment

57. Most entities make use of IT systems for financial reporting and operational purposes. However, even when IT is extensively used, there will be manual elements to the systems. The balance between manual and automated elements varies. In certain cases, particularly smaller, less complex entities, the systems may be primarily manual. In other cases, the extent of automation may vary with some systems substantially automated with few related manual elements and others, even within the same entity, predominantly manual. As a result, an entity's system of internal control is likely to contain manual and automated elements, the characteristics of which are relevant to the auditor's risk assessment and further audit procedures based thereon.

58. The use of manual or automated elements in internal control also affects the manner in which transactions are initiated, recorded, processed, and reported.[5] Controls in a

---

[4] A material weakness in internal control is one that could have a material effect on the financial statements.

[5] Paragraph 9 of Appendix 2 defines initiation, recording, processing, and reporting as used throughout this ISA (UK and Ireland).

manual system may include such procedures as approvals and reviews of activities, and reconciliations and follow-up of reconciling items. Alternatively, an entity may use automated procedures to initiate, record, process, and report transactions, in which case records in electronic format replace such paper documents as purchase orders, invoices, shipping documents, and related accounting records. Controls in IT systems consist of a combination of automated controls (for example, controls embedded in computer programs) and manual controls. Further, manual controls may be independent of IT, may use information produced by IT, or may be limited to monitoring the effective functioning of IT and of automated controls, and to handling exceptions. When IT is used to initiate, record, process or report transactions, or other financial data for inclusion in financial statements, the systems and programs may include controls related to the corresponding assertions for material accounts or may be critical to the effective functioning of manual controls that depend on IT. An entity's mix of manual and automated controls varies with the nature and complexity of the entity's use of IT.

59. Generally, IT provides potential benefits of effectiveness and efficiency for an entity's internal control because it enables an entity to:

- Consistently apply predefined business rules and perform complex calculations in processing large volumes of transactions or data;

- Enhance the timeliness, availability, and accuracy of information;

- Facilitate the additional analysis of information;

- Enhance the ability to monitor the performance of the entity's activities and its policies and procedures;

- Reduce the risk that controls will be circumvented; and

- Enhance the ability to achieve effective segregation of duties by implementing security controls in applications, databases, and operating systems.

60. IT also poses specific risks to an entity's internal control, including the following:

- Reliance on systems or programs that are inaccurately processing data, processing inaccurate data, or both.

- Unauthorized access to data that may result in destruction of data or improper changes to data, including the recording of unauthorized or non-existent transactions, or inaccurate recording of transactions. Particular risks may arise where multiple users access a common database.

- The possibility of IT personnel gaining access privileges beyond those necessary to perform their assigned duties thereby breaking down segregation of duties.

- Unauthorized changes to data in master files.

- Unauthorized changes to systems or programs.

- Failure to make necessary changes to systems or programs.

- Inappropriate manual intervention.

- Potential loss of data or inability to access data as required.

61. Manual aspects of systems may be more suitable where judgment and discretion are required such as for the following circumstances:

- Large, unusual or non-recurring transactions.

- Circumstances where errors are difficult to define, anticipate or predict.

- In changing circumstances that require a control response outside the scope of an existing automated control.

- In monitoring the effectiveness of automated controls.

62. Manual controls are performed by people, and therefore pose specific risks to the entity's internal control. Manual controls may be less reliable than automated controls because they can be more easily bypassed, ignored, or overridden and they are also more prone to simple errors and mistakes. Consistency of application of a manual control element cannot therefore be assumed. Manual systems may be less suitable for the following:

- High volume or recurring transactions, or in situations where errors that can be anticipated or predicted can be prevented or detected by control parameters that are automated.

- Control activities where the specific ways to perform the control can be adequately designed and automated.

63. The extent and nature of the risks to internal control vary depending on the nature and characteristics of the entity's information system. Therefore in understanding internal control, the auditor considers whether the entity has responded adequately to the risks arising from the use of IT or manual systems by establishing effective controls.

Limitations of Internal Control

64. Internal control, no matter how well designed and operated, can provide an entity with only reasonable assurance about achieving the entity's financial reporting objectives. The likelihood of achievement is affected by limitations inherent to internal control. These include the realities that human judgment in decision-making can be faulty and that breakdowns in internal control can occur because of human failures, such as simple errors or mistakes. For example, if an entity's information system personnel do not completely understand how an order entry system processes sales transactions, they may erroneously design changes to the system to process sales for a new line of

products. On the other hand, such changes may be correctly designed but misunderstood by individuals who translate the design into program code. Errors also may occur in the use of information produced by IT. For example, automated controls may be designed to report transactions over a specified amount for management review, but individuals responsible for conducting the review may not understand the purpose of such reports and, accordingly, may fail to review them or investigate unusual items.

65. Additionally, controls can be circumvented by the collusion of two or more people or inappropriate management override of internal control. For example, management may enter into side agreements with customers that alter the terms and conditions of the entity's standard sales contracts, which may result in improper revenue recognition. Also, edit checks in a software program that are designed to identify and report transactions that exceed specified credit limits may be overridden or disabled.

66. Smaller entities often have fewer employees which may limit the extent to which segregation of duties is practicable. However, for key areas, even in a very small entity, it can be practicable to implement some degree of segregation of duties or other form of unsophisticated but effective controls. The potential for override of controls by the owner-manager depends to a great extent on the control environment and in particular, the owner-manager's attitudes about the importance of internal control.

Control Environment

67. **The auditor should obtain an understanding of the control environment.** The control environment includes the governance and management functions and the attitudes, awareness, and actions of those charged with governance and management concerning the entity's internal control and its importance in the entity. The control environment sets the tone of an organization, influencing the control consciousness of its people. It is the foundation for effective internal control, providing discipline and structure.

68. The primary responsibility for the prevention and detection of fraud and error rests with both those charged with governance and the management of an entity. In evaluating the design of the control environment and determining whether it has been implemented, the auditor understands how management, with the oversight of those charged with governance, has created and maintained a culture of honesty and ethical behavior, and established appropriate controls to prevent and detect fraud and error within the entity.

69. In evaluating the design of the entity's control environment, the auditor considers the following elements and how they have been incorporated into the entity's processes:

(a) Communication and enforcement of integrity and ethical values—essential elements which influence the effectiveness of the design, administration and monitoring of controls.

(b) Commitment to competence—management's consideration of the competence levels for particular jobs and how those levels translate into requisite skills and knowledge.

(c) Participation by those charged with governance—independence from management, their experience and stature, the extent of their involvement and scrutiny of activities, the information they receive, the degree to which difficult questions are raised and pursued with management and their interaction with internal and external auditors.

(d) Management's philosophy and operating style—management's approach to taking and managing business risks, and management's attitudes and actions toward financial reporting, information processing and accounting functions and personnel.

(e) Organizational structure—the framework within which an entity's activities for achieving its objectives are planned, executed, controlled and reviewed.

(f) Assignment of authority and responsibility—how authority and responsibility for operating activities are assigned and how reporting relationships and authorization hierarchies are established.

(g) Human resource policies and practices—recruitment, orientation, training, evaluating, counseling, promoting, compensating and remedial actions.

70. In understanding the control environment elements, the auditor also considers whether they have been implemented. Ordinarily, the auditor obtains relevant audit evidence through a combination of inquiries and other risk assessment procedures, for example, corroborating inquiries through observation or inspection of documents. For example, through inquiries of management and employees, the auditor may obtain an understanding of how management communicates to employees its views on business practices and ethical behavior. The auditor determines whether controls have been implemented by considering, for example, whether management has established a formal code of conduct and whether it acts in a manner that supports the code or condones violations of, or authorizes exceptions to the code.

71. Audit evidence for elements of the control environment may not be available in documentary form, in particular for smaller entities where communication between management and other personnel may be informal, yet effective. For example, management's commitment to ethical values and competence are often implemented through the behavior and attitude they demonstrate in managing the entity's business instead of in a written code of conduct. Consequently, management's attitudes, awareness and actions are of particular importance in the design of a smaller entity's control environment. In addition, the role of those charged with governance is often undertaken by the owner-manager where there are no other owners.

72. The overall responsibilities of those charged with governance are recognized in codes of practice and other regulations or guidance produced for the benefit of those charged with governance. It is one, but not the only, role of those charged with

governance to counterbalance pressures on management in relation to financial reporting. For example, the basis for management remuneration may place stress on management arising from the conflicting demands of fair reporting and the perceived benefits of improved results. In understanding the design of the control environment, the auditor considers such matters as the independence of the directors and their ability to evaluate the actions of management. The auditor also considers whether there is an audit committee that understands the entity's business transactions and evaluates whether the financial statements give a true and fair view (or are presented fairly, in all material respects) in accordance with the applicable financial reporting framework.

73. The nature of an entity's control environment is such that it has a pervasive effect on assessing the risks of material misstatement. For example, owner-manager controls may mitigate a lack of segregation of duties in a small business, or an active and independent board of directors may influence the philosophy and operating style of senior management in larger entities. The auditor's evaluation of the design of the entity's control environment includes considering whether the strengths in the control environment elements collectively provide an appropriate foundation for the other components of internal control, and are not undermined by control environment weaknesses. For example, human resource policies and practices directed toward hiring competent financial, accounting, and IT personnel may not mitigate a strong bias by top management to overstate earnings. Changes in the control environment may affect the relevance of information obtained in prior audits. For example, management's decision to commit additional resources for training and awareness of financial reporting activities may reduce the risk of errors in processing financial information. Alternatively, management's failure to commit sufficient resources to address security risks presented by IT may adversely affect internal control by allowing improper changes to be made to computer programs or to data, or by allowing unauthorized transactions to be processed.

74. The existence of a satisfactory control environment can be a positive factor when the auditor assesses the risks of material misstatement and as explained in paragraph 5 of ISA (UK and Ireland) 330, influences the nature, timing, and extent of the auditor's further procedures. In particular, it may help reduce the risk of fraud, although a satisfactory control environment is not an absolute deterrent to fraud. Conversely, weaknesses in the control environment may undermine the effectiveness of controls and therefore be negative factors in the auditor's assessment of the risks of material misstatement, in particular in relation to fraud.

75. The control environment in itself does not prevent, or detect and correct, a material misstatement in classes of transactions, account balances, and disclosures and related assertions. The auditor, therefore, ordinarily considers the effect of other components along with the control environment when assessing the risks of material misstatement; for example, the monitoring of controls and the operation of specific control activities.

The Entity's Risk Assessment Process

76. **The auditor should obtain an understanding of the entity's process for identifying business risks relevant to financial reporting objectives and deciding about actions to address those risks, and the results thereof.** The process is described as the "entity's risk assessment process" and forms the basis for how management determines the risks to be managed.

77. In evaluating the design and implementation of the entity's risk assessment process, the auditor determines how management identifies business risks relevant to financial reporting, estimates the significance of the risks, assesses the likelihood of their occurrence, and decides upon actions to manage them. If the entity's risk assessment process is appropriate to the circumstances, it assists the auditor in identifying risks of material misstatement.

78. The auditor inquires about business risks that management has identified and considers whether they may result in material misstatement. During the audit, the auditor may identify risks of material misstatement that management failed to identify. In such cases, the auditor considers whether there was an underlying risk of a kind that should have been identified by the entity's risk assessment process, and if so, why that process failed to do so and whether the process is appropriate to its circumstances. If, as a result, the auditor judges that there is a material weakness in the entity's risk assessment process, the auditor communicates to those charged with governance as required by paragraph 120.

79. In a smaller entity, management may not have a formal risk assessment process as described in paragraph 76. For such entities, the auditor discusses with management how risks to the business are identified by management and how they are addressed.

Information System, Including the Related Business Processes, Relevant to Financial Reporting, and Communication

80. The information system relevant to financial reporting objectives, which includes the accounting system, consists of the procedures and records established to initiate, record, process, and report entity transactions (as well as events and conditions) and to maintain accountability for the related assets, liabilities, and equity.

81. **The auditor should obtain an understanding of the information system, including the related business processes, relevant to financial reporting, including the following areas:**

   • **The classes of transactions in the entity's operations that are significant to the financial statements.**

   • **The procedures, within both IT and manual systems, by which those transactions are initiated, recorded, processed and reported in the financial statements.**

- **The related accounting records, whether electronic or manual, supporting information, and specific accounts in the financial statements, in respect of initiating, recording, processing and reporting transactions.**

- **How the information system captures events and conditions, other than classes of transactions, that are significant to the financial statements.**

- **The financial reporting process used to prepare the entity's financial statements, including significant accounting estimates and disclosures.**

82. In obtaining this understanding, the auditor considers the procedures used to transfer information from transaction processing systems to general ledger or financial reporting systems. The auditor also understands the entity's procedures to capture information relevant to financial reporting for events and conditions other than transactions, such as the depreciation and amortization of assets and changes in the recoverability of accounts receivables.

83. An entity's information system typically includes the use of standard journal entries that are required on a recurring basis to record transactions such as sales, purchases, and cash disbursements in the general ledger, or to record accounting estimates that are periodically made by management, such as changes in the estimate of uncollectible accounts receivable.

84. An entity's financial reporting process also includes the use of non-standard journal entries to record non-recurring, unusual transactions or adjustments. Examples of such entries include consolidating adjustments and entries for a business combination or disposal or non-recurring estimates such as an asset impairment. In manual, paper-based general ledger systems, non-standard journal entries may be identified through inspection of ledgers, journals, and supporting documentation. However, when automated procedures are used to maintain the general ledger and prepare financial statements, such entries may exist only in electronic form and may be more easily identified through the use of computer-assisted audit techniques.

85. Preparation of the entity's financial statements include procedures that are designed to ensure information required to be disclosed by the applicable financial reporting framework is accumulated, recorded, processed, summarized and appropriately reported in the financial statements.

86. In obtaining an understanding, the auditor considers risks of material misstatement associated with inappropriate override of controls over journal entries and the controls surrounding non-standard journal entries. For example, automated processes and controls may reduce the risk of inadvertent error but do not overcome the risk that individuals may inappropriately override such automated processes, for example, by changing the amounts being automatically passed to the general ledger or financial reporting system. Furthermore, the auditor maintains an awareness that when IT is used to transfer information automatically, there may be little or no visible evidence of such intervention in the information systems.

87. The auditor also understands how the incorrect processing of transactions is resolved, for example, whether there is an automated suspense file and how it is used by the entity to ensure that suspense items are cleared out on a timely basis, and how system overrides or bypasses to controls are processed and accounted for.

88. The auditor obtains an understanding of the entity's information system relevant to financial reporting in a manner that is appropriate to the entity's circumstances. This includes obtaining an understanding of how transactions originate within the entity's business processes. An entity's business processes are the activities designed to develop, purchase, produce, sell and distribute an entity's products and services; ensure compliance with laws and regulations; and record information, including accounting and financial reporting information.

89. **The auditor should understand how the entity communicates financial reporting roles and responsibilities and significant matters relating to financial reporting.** Communication involves providing an understanding of individual roles and responsibilities pertaining to internal control over financial reporting and may take such forms as policy manuals and financial reporting manuals. It includes the extent to which personnel understand how their activities in the financial reporting information system relate to the work of others and the means of reporting exceptions to an appropriate higher level within the entity. Open communication channels help ensure that exceptions are reported and acted on. The auditor's understanding of communication pertaining to financial reporting matters also includes communications between management and those charged with governance, particularly the audit committee, as well as external communications such as those with regulatory authorities.

Control Activities

90. **The auditor should obtain a sufficient understanding of control activities to assess the risks of material misstatement at the assertion level and to design further audit procedures responsive to assessed risks.** Control activities are the policies and procedures that help ensure that management directives are carried out; for example, that necessary actions are taken to address risks that threaten the achievement of the entity's objectives. Control activities, whether within IT or manual systems, have various objectives and are applied at various organizational and functional levels. Examples of specific control activities include those relating to the following:

- Authorization.

- Performance reviews.

- Information processing.

- Physical controls.

- Segregation of duties.

91. In obtaining an understanding of control activities, the auditor's primary consideration is whether, and how, a specific control activity, individually or in combination with others, prevents, or detects and corrects, material misstatements in classes of transactions, account balances, or disclosures. Control activities relevant to the audit are those for which the auditor considers it necessary to obtain an understanding in order to assess risks of material misstatement at the assertion level and to design and perform further audit procedures responsive to the assessed risks. An audit does not require an understanding of all the control activities related to each significant class of transactions, account balance, and disclosure in the financial statements or to every assertion relevant to them. The auditor's emphasis is on identifying and obtaining an understanding of control activities that address the areas where the auditor considers that material misstatements are more likely to occur. When multiple control activities achieve the same objective, it is unnecessary to obtain an understanding of each of the control activities related to such objective.

92. The auditor considers the knowledge about the presence or absence of control activities obtained from the understanding of the other components of internal control in determining whether it is necessary to devote additional attention to obtaining an understanding of control activities. In considering whether control activities are relevant to the audit, the auditor considers the risks the auditor has identified that may give rise to material misstatement. Also, control activities are relevant to the audit if the auditor is required to evaluate them as discussed in paragraphs 113 and 115.

93. **The auditor should obtain an understanding of how the entity has responded to risks arising from IT.** The use of IT affects the way that control activities are implemented. The auditor considers whether the entity has responded adequately to the risks arising from IT by establishing effective general IT-controls and application controls. From the auditor's perspective, controls over IT systems are effective when they maintain the integrity of information and the security of the data such systems process.

94. General IT-controls are policies and procedures that relate to many applications and support the effective functioning of application controls by helping to ensure the continued proper operation of information systems. General IT-controls that maintain the integrity of information and security of data commonly include controls over the following:

- Data center and network operations.

- System software acquisition, change and maintenance.

- Access security.

- Application system acquisition, development, and maintenance.

They are generally implemented to deal with the risks referred to in paragraph 60 above.

95. Application controls are manual or automated procedures that typically operate at a business process level. Application controls can be preventative or detective in nature and are designed to ensure the integrity of the accounting records. Accordingly, application controls relate to procedures used to initiate, record, process and report transactions or other financial data. These controls help ensure that transactions occurred, are authorized, and are completely and accurately recorded and processed. Examples include edit checks of input data, and numerical sequence checks with manual follow-up of exception reports or correction at the point of data entry.

Monitoring of Controls

96. **The auditor should obtain an understanding of the major types of activities that the entity uses to monitor internal control over financial reporting, including those related to those control activities relevant to the audit, and how the entity initiates corrective actions to its controls.**

97. Monitoring of controls is a process to assess the effectiveness of internal control performance over time. It involves assessing the design and operation of controls on a timely basis and taking necessary corrective actions modified for changes in conditions. Management accomplishes monitoring of controls through ongoing activities, separate evaluations, or a combination of the two. Ongoing monitoring activities are often built into the normal recurring activities of an entity and include regular management and supervisory activities.

98. In many entities, internal auditors or personnel performing similar functions contribute to the monitoring of an entity's activities. See ISA (UK and Ireland) 610, "Considering the Work of Internal Auditing" for additional guidance. Management's monitoring activities may also include using information from communications from external parties such as customer complaints and regulator comments that may indicate problems or highlight areas in need of improvement.

99. Much of the information used in monitoring may be produced by the entity's information system. If management assumes that data used for monitoring are accurate without having a basis for that assumption, errors may exist in the information, potentially leading management to incorrect conclusions from its monitoring activities. The auditor obtains an understanding of the sources of the information related to the entity's monitoring activities, and the basis upon which management considers the information to be sufficiently reliable for the purpose. When the auditor intends to make use of the entity's information produced for monitoring activities, such as internal auditor's reports, the auditor considers whether the information provides a reliable basis and is sufficiently detailed for the auditor's purpose.

Assessing the Risks of Material Misstatement

100. **The auditor should identify and assess the risks of material misstatement at the financial statement level, and at the assertion level for classes of transactions, account balances, and disclosures.** For this purpose, the auditor:

- Identifies risks throughout the process of obtaining an understanding of the entity and its environment, including relevant controls that relate to the risks, and by considering the classes of transactions, account balances, and disclosures in the financial statements;

- Relates the identified risks to what can go wrong at the assertion level;

- Considers whether the risks are of a magnitude that could result in a material misstatement of the financial statements; and

- Considers the likelihood that the risks could result in a material misstatement of the financial statements.

101. The auditor uses information gathered by performing risk assessment procedures, including the audit evidence obtained in evaluating the design of controls and determining whether they have been implemented, as audit evidence to support the risk assessment. The auditor uses the risk assessment to determine the nature, timing, and extent of further audit procedures to be performed.

102. The auditor determines whether the identified risks of material misstatement relate to specific classes of transactions, account balances, and disclosures and related assertions, or whether they relate more pervasively to the financial statements as a whole and potentially affect many assertions. The latter risks (risks at the financial statement level) may derive in particular from a weak control environment.

103. The nature of the risks arising from a weak control environment is such that they are not likely to be confined to specific individual risks of material misstatement in particular classes of transactions, account balances, and disclosures. Rather, weaknesses such as management's lack of competence may have a more pervasive effect on the financial statements and may require an overall response by the auditor.

104. In making risk assessments, the auditor may identify the controls that are likely to prevent, or detect and correct, material misstatement in specific assertions. Generally, the auditor gains an understanding of controls and relates them to assertions in the context of processes and systems in which they exist. Doing so is useful because individual control activities often do not in themselves address a risk. Often only multiple control activities, together with other elements of internal control, will be sufficient to address a risk.

105. Conversely, some control activities may have a specific effect on an individual assertion embodied in a particular class of transactions or account balance. For example, the control activities that an entity established to ensure that its personnel are properly counting and recording the annual physical inventory relate directly to the existence and completeness assertions for the inventory account balance.

106. Controls can be either directly or indirectly related to an assertion. The more indirect the relationship, the less effective that control may be in preventing, or detecting and correcting, misstatements in that assertion. For example, a sales manager's review of a

summary of sales activity for specific stores by region ordinarily is only indirectly related to the completeness assertion for sales revenue. Accordingly, it may be less effective in reducing risk for that assertion than controls more directly related to that assertion, such as matching shipping documents with billing documents.

107. The auditor's understanding of internal control may raise doubts about the auditability of an entity's financial statements. Concerns about the integrity of the entity's management may be so serious as to cause the auditor to conclude that the risk of management misrepresentation in the financial statements is such that an audit cannot be conducted. Also, concerns about the condition and reliability of an entity's records may cause the auditor to conclude that it is unlikely that sufficient appropriate audit evidence will be available to support an unqualified opinion on the financial statements. In such circumstances, the auditor considers a qualification or disclaimer of opinion, but in some cases the auditor's only recourse may be to withdraw from the engagement.

Significant Risks That Require Special Audit Consideration

108. **As part of the risk assessment as described in paragraph 100, the auditor should determine which of the risks identified are, in the auditor's judgment, risks that require special audit consideration (such risks are defined as "significant risks").** In addition, ISA (UK and Ireland) 330, paragraphs 44 and 51 describe the consequences for further audit procedures of identifying a risk as significant.

109. The determination of significant risks, which arise on most audits, is a matter for the auditor's professional judgment. In exercising this judgment, the auditor excludes the effect of identified controls related to the risk to determine whether the nature of the risk, the likely magnitude of the potential misstatement including the possibility that the risk may give rise to multiple misstatements, and the likelihood of the risk occurring are such that they require special audit consideration. Routine, non-complex transactions that are subject to systematic processing are less likely to give rise to significant risks because they have lower inherent risks. On the other hand, significant risks are often derived from business risks that may result in a material misstatement. In considering the nature of the risks, the auditor considers a number of matters, including the following:

- Whether the risk is a risk of fraud.

- Whether the risk is related to recent significant economic, accounting or other developments and, therefore, requires specific attention.

- The complexity of transactions.

- Whether the risk involves significant transactions with related parties.

- The degree of subjectivity in the measurement of financial information related to the risk especially those involving a wide range of measurement uncertainty.

- Whether the risk involves significant transactions that are outside the normal course of business for the entity, or that otherwise appear to be unusual.

110. Significant risks often relate to significant non-routine transactions and judgmental matters. Non-routine transactions are transactions that are unusual, either due to size or nature, and that therefore occur infrequently. Judgmental matters may include the development of accounting estimates for which there is significant measurement uncertainty.

111. Risks of material misstatement may be greater for risks relating to significant non-routine transactions arising from matters such as the following:

- Greater management intervention to specify the accounting treatment.

- Greater manual intervention for data collection and processing.

- Complex calculations or accounting principles.

- The nature of non-routine transactions, which may make it difficult for the entity to implement effective controls over the risks.

112. Risks of material misstatement may be greater for risks relating to significant judgmental matters that require the development of accounting estimates, arising from matters such as the following:

- Accounting principles for accounting estimates or revenue recognition may be subject to differing interpretation.

- Required judgment may be subjective, complex or require assumptions about the effects of future events, for example, judgment about fair value.

113. **For significant risks, to the extent the auditor has not already done so, the auditor should evaluate the design of the entity's related controls, including relevant control activities, and determine whether they have been implemented.** An understanding of the entity's controls related to significant risks is required to provide the auditor with adequate information to develop an effective audit approach. Management ought to be aware of significant risks; however, risks relating to significant non-routine or judgmental matters are often less likely to be subject to routine controls. Therefore, the auditor's understanding of whether the entity has designed and implemented controls for such significant risks includes whether and how management responds to the risks and whether control activities such as a review of assumptions by senior management or experts, formal processes for estimations or approval by those charged with governance have been implemented to address the risks. For example, where there are one-off events such as the receipt of notice of a significant lawsuit, consideration of the entity's response will include such matters as whether it has been referred to appropriate experts (such as internal or external legal counsel), whether an assessment has been made of the potential effect, and how it is proposed that the circumstances are to be disclosed in the financial statements.

114. If management has not appropriately responded by implementing controls over significant risks and if, as a result, the auditor judges that there is a material weakness in the entity's internal control, the auditor communicates this matter to those charged with governance as required by paragraph 120. In these circumstances, the auditor also considers the implications for the auditor's risk assessment.

Risks for Which Substantive Procedures Alone Do Not Provide Sufficient Appropriate Audit Evidence

115. **As part of the risk assessment as described in paragraph 100, the auditor should evaluate the design and determine the implementation of the entity's controls, including relevant control activities, over those risks for which, in the auditor's judgment, it is not possible or practicable to reduce the risks of material misstatement at the assertion level to an acceptably low level with audit evidence obtained only from substantive procedures.** The consequences for further audit procedures of identifying such risks are described in paragraph 25 of ISA (UK and Ireland) 330.

116. The understanding of the entity's information system relevant to financial reporting enables the auditor to identify risks of material misstatement that relate directly to the recording of routine classes of transactions or account balances, and the preparation of reliable financial statements; these include risks of inaccurate or incomplete processing. Ordinarily, such risks relate to significant classes of transactions such as an entity's revenue, purchases, and cash receipts or cash payments.

117. The characteristics of routine day-to-day business transactions often permit highly automated processing with little or no manual intervention. In such circumstances, it may not be possible to perform only substantive procedures in relation to the risk. For example, in circumstances where a significant amount of an entity's information is initiated, recorded, processed, or reported electronically such as in an integrated system, the auditor may determine that it is not possible to design effective substantive procedures that by themselves would provide sufficient appropriate audit evidence that relevant classes of transactions or account balances, are not materially misstated. In such cases, audit evidence may be available only in electronic form, and its sufficiency and appropriateness usually depend on the effectiveness of controls over its accuracy and completeness. Furthermore, the potential for improper initiation or alteration of information to occur and not be detected may be greater if information is initiated, recorded, processed or reported only in electronic form and appropriate controls are not operating effectively.

118. Examples of situations where the auditor may find it impossible to design effective substantive procedures that by themselves provide sufficient appropriate audit evidence that certain assertions are not materially misstated include the following:

- An entity that conducts its business using IT to initiate orders for the purchase and delivery of goods based on predetermined rules of what to order and in what quantities and to pay the related accounts payable based on system-generated decisions initiated upon the confirmed receipt of goods and terms of payment. No other documentation of orders placed or goods received is produced or maintained, other than through the IT system.

- An entity that provides services to customers via electronic media (for example, an Internet service provider or a telecommunications company) and uses IT to create a log of the services provided to its customers, initiate and process its billings for the services and automatically record such amounts in electronic accounting records that are part of the system used to produce the entity's financial statements.

Revision of Risk Assessment

119. The auditor's assessment of the risks of material misstatement at the assertion level is based on available audit evidence and may change during the course of the audit as additional audit evidence is obtained. In particular, the risk assessment may be based on an expectation that controls are operating effectively to prevent, or detect and correct, a material misstatement at the assertion level. In performing tests of controls to obtain audit evidence about their operating effectiveness, the auditor may obtain audit evidence that controls are not operating effectively at relevant times during the audit. Similarly, in performing substantive procedures the auditor may detect misstatements in amounts or frequency greater than is consistent with the auditor's risk assessments. In circumstances where the auditor obtains audit evidence from performing further audit procedures that tends to contradict the audit evidence on which the auditor originally based the assessment, the auditor revises the assessment and modifies the further planned audit procedures accordingly. See paragraphs 66 and 70 of ISA (UK and Ireland) 330 for further guidance.

Communicating With Those Charged With Governance and Management

120. **The auditor should make those charged with governance or management aware, as soon as practicable, and at an appropriate level of responsibility, of material weaknesses in the design or implementation of internal control which have come to the auditor's attention.**

121. If the auditor identifies risks of material misstatement which the entity has either not controlled, or for which the relevant control is inadequate, or if in the auditor's judgment there is a material weakness in the entity's risk assessment process, then the auditor includes such internal control weaknesses in the communication of audit matters of governance interest. See ISA (UK and Ireland) 260, "Communications of Audit Matters with Those Charged with Governance."

Documentation

122. **The auditor should document:**

(a)   The discussion among the engagement team regarding the susceptibility of the entity's financial statements to material misstatement due to error or fraud, and the significant decisions reached;

(b)   Key elements of the understanding obtained regarding each of the aspects of the entity and its environment identified in paragraph 20, including each of the internal control components identified in paragraph 43, to assess the risks of material misstatement of the financial statements; the sources of information from which the understanding was obtained; and the risk assessment procedures;

(c)   The identified and assessed risks of material misstatement at the financial statement level and at the assertion level as required by paragraph 100; and

(d)   The risks identified and related controls evaluated as a result of the requirements in paragraphs 113 and 115.

123. The manner in which these matters are documented is for the auditor to determine using professional judgment. In particular, the results of the risk assessment may be documented separately, or may be documented as part of the auditor's documentation of further procedures (see paragraph 73 of ISA (UK and Ireland) 330 for additional guidance). Examples of common techniques, used alone or in combination include narrative descriptions, questionnaires, check lists and flow charts. Such techniques may also be useful in documenting the auditor's assessment of the risks of material misstatement at the overall financial statement and assertions level. The form and extent of this documentation is influenced by the nature, size and complexity of the entity and its internal control, availability of information from the entity and the specific audit methodology and technology used in the course of the audit. For example, documentation of the understanding of a complex information system in which a large volume of transactions are electronically initiated, recorded, processed, or reported may include flowcharts, questionnaires, or decision tables. For an information system making limited or no use of IT or for which few transactions are processed (for example, long-term debt), documentation in the form of a memorandum may be sufficient. Ordinarily, the more complex the entity and the more extensive the audit procedures performed by the auditor, the more extensive the auditor's documentation will be. ISA (UK and Ireland) 230, "Documentation" provides guidance regarding documentation in the context of the audit of financial statements.

Effective Date

124. This ISA (UK and Ireland) is effective for audits of financial statements for periods commencing on or after 15 December 2004.

Public Sector Perspective

Additional guidance for auditors of public sector bodies in the UK and Ireland is given in:

- Practice Note 10 "Audit of Financial Statements of Public Sector Bodies in the United Kingdom (Revised)"

- Practice Note 10(I) "Audit of Central Government Financial Statements in the Republic of Ireland (Revised)"

1. When carrying out audits of public sector entities, the auditor takes into account the legislative framework and any other relevant regulations, ordinances or ministerial directives that affect the audit mandate and any other special auditing requirements. Therefore in obtaining an understanding of the regulatory framework as required in paragraph 22 of this ISA (UK and Ireland), auditors will have regard to the legislation and proper authority governing the operation of an entity. Similarly in respect of paragraph 30 of this ISA (UK and Ireland) the auditor should be aware that the "management objectives" of public sector entities may be influenced by concerns regarding public accountability and may include objectives which have their source in legislation, regulations, government ordinances, and ministerial directives.

2. Paragraphs 47-53 of this ISA UK and Ireland) explain the controls relevant to the audit. Public sector auditors often have additional responsibilities with respect to internal controls, for example to report on compliance with an established Code of Practice. Public sector auditors can also have responsibilities to report on the compliance with legislative authorities. Their review of internal controls may be broader and more detailed.

3. Paragraphs 120 and 121 of this ISA (UK and Ireland) deals with communication of weaknesses. There may be additional communication or reporting requirements for public sector auditors. For example, internal control weaknesses may have to be reported to the legislature or other governing body.

Appendix 1

Understanding the Entity and Its Environment

This appendix provides additional guidance on matters the auditor may consider when obtaining an understanding of the industry, regulatory, and other external factors that affect the entity, including the applicable financial reporting framework; the nature of the entity; objectives and strategies and related business risks; and measurement and review of the entity's financial performance. The examples provided cover a broad range of matters applicable to many engagements; however, not all matters are relevant to every engagement and the list of examples is not necessarily complete. Additional guidance on internal control is contained in Appendix 2.

Industry, Regulatory and Other External Factors, Including The Applicable Financial Reporting Framework

Examples of matters an auditor may consider include the following:

- Industry conditions

    - The market and competition, including demand, capacity, and price competition

    - Cyclical or seasonal activity

    - Product technology relating to the entity's products

    - Energy supply and cost

- Regulatory environment

    - Accounting principles and industry specific practices

    - Regulatory framework for a regulated industry

    - Legislation and regulation that significantly affect the entity's operations

        ○ Regulatory requirements

        ○ Direct supervisory activities

    - Taxation (corporate and other)

    - Government policies currently affecting the conduct of the entity's business

        ○ Monetary, including foreign exchange controls

        ○ Fiscal

  - ○ Financial incentives (for example, government aid programs)

  - ○ Tariffs, trade restrictions

 - Environmental requirements affecting the industry and the entity's business

- Other external factors currently affecting the entity's business

 - General level of economic activity (for example, recession, growth)

 - Interest rates and availability of financing

 - Inflation, currency revaluation

Nature of the Entity

Examples of matters an auditor may consider include the following:

Business Operations

- Nature of revenue sources (for example, manufacturer, wholesaler, banking, insurance or other financial services, import/export trading, utility, transportation, and technology products and services)

- Products or services and markets (for example, major customers and contracts, terms of payment, profit margins, market share, competitors, exports, pricing policies, reputation of products, warranties, order book, trends, marketing strategy and objectives, manufacturing processes)

- Conduct of operations (for example, stages and methods of production, business segments, delivery or products and services, details of declining or expanding operations)

- Alliances, joint ventures, and outsourcing activities

Involvement in electronic commerce, including Internet sales and marketing activities

- Geographic dispersion and industry segmentation

- Location of production facilities, warehouses, and offices

- Key customers

- Important suppliers of goods and services (for example, long-term contracts, stability of supply, terms of payment, imports, methods of delivery such as "just-in-time")

- Employment (for example, by location, supply, wage levels, union contracts, pension and other post employment benefits, stock option or incentive bonus arrangements, and government regulation related to employment matters)

- Research and development activities and expenditures

- Transactions with related parties

Investments

- Acquisitions, mergers or disposals of business activities (planned or recently executed)

- Investments and dispositions of securities and loans

- Capital investment activities, including investments in plant and equipment and technology, and any recent or planned changes

- Investments in non-consolidated entities, including partnerships, joint ventures and special-purpose entities

Financing

- Group structure – major subsidiaries and associated entities, including consolidated and non-consolidated structures

- Debt structure, including covenants, restrictions, guarantees, and off-balance-sheet financing arrangements

- Leasing of property, plant or equipment for use in the business

- Beneficial owners (local, foreign, business reputation and experience)

- Related parties

- Use of derivative financial instruments

Financial Reporting

- Accounting principles and industry specific practices

- Revenue recognition practices

- Accounting for fair values

- Inventories (for example, locations, quantities)

- Foreign currency assets, liabilities and transactions

- Industry-specific significant categories (for example, loans and investments for banks, accounts receivable and inventory for manufacturers, research and development for pharmaceuticals)

- Accounting for unusual or complex transactions including those in controversial or emerging areas (for example, accounting for stock-based compensation)

- Financial statement presentation and disclosure

Objectives and Strategies and Related Business Risks

Examples of matters an auditor may consider include the following:

- Existence of objectives (*i.e.*, how the entity addresses industry, regulatory and other external factors) relating to, for example, the following:

    - Industry developments (a potential related business risk might be, for example, that the entity does not have the personnel or expertise to deal with the changes in the industry)

    - New products and services (a potential related business risk might be, for example, that there is increased product liability)

    - Expansion of the business (a potential related business risk might be, for example, that the demand has not been accurately estimated)

    - New accounting requirements (a potential related business risk might be, for example, incomplete or improper implementation, or increased costs)

    - Regulatory requirements (a potential related business risk might be, for example, that there is increased legal exposure)

    - Current and prospective financing requirements (a potential related business risk might be, for example, the loss of financing due to the entity's inability to meet requirements)

    - Use of IT (a potential related business risk might be, for example, that systems and processes are incompatible)

- Effects of implementing a strategy, particularly any effects that will lead to new accounting requirements (a potential related business risk might be, for example, incomplete or improper implementation)

Measurement and review of the Entity's Financial Performance

Examples of matters an auditor may consider include the following:

- Key ratios and operating statistics

- Key performance indicators

- Employee performance measures and incentive compensation policies

- Trends

- Use of forecasts, budgets and variance analysis

- Analyst reports and credit rating reports

- Competitor analysis

- Period-on-period financial performance (revenue growth, profitability, leverage)

Appendix 2

Internal Control Components

1. As set out in paragraph 43 and described in paragraphs 67-99, internal control consists of the following components:

    (a) The control environment;

    (b) The entity's risk assessment process;

    (c) The information system, including the related business processes, relevant to financial reporting, and communication;

    (d) Control activities; and

    (e) Monitoring of controls.

    This appendix further explains the above components as they relate to a financial statement audit.

Control Environment

2. The control environment includes the attitudes, awareness, and actions of management and those charged with governance concerning the entity's internal control and its importance in the entity. The control environment also includes the governance and management functions and sets the tone of an organization, influencing the control consciousness of its people. It is the foundation for effective internal control, providing discipline and structure.

3. The control environment encompasses the following elements:

    (a) *Communication and enforcement of integrity and ethical values*. The effectiveness of controls cannot rise above the integrity and ethical values of the people who create, administer, and monitor them. Integrity and ethical values are essential elements of the control environment which influence the effectiveness of the design, administration, and monitoring of other components of internal control. Integrity and ethical behavior are the product of the entity's ethical and behavioral standards, how they are communicated, and how they are reinforced in practice. They include management's actions to remove or reduce incentives and temptations that might prompt personnel to engage in dishonest, illegal, or unethical acts. They also include the communication of entity values and behavioral standards to personnel through policy statements and codes of conduct and by example.

    (b) *Commitment to competence*. Competence is the knowledge and skills necessary to accomplish tasks that define the individual's job. Commitment to competence includes management's consideration of the competence levels for particular jobs and how those levels translate into requisite skills and knowledge.

(c) *Participation by those charged with governance.* An entity's control consciousness is influenced significantly by those charged with governance. Attributes of those charged with governance include independence from management, their experience and stature, the extent of their involvement and scrutiny of activities, the appropriateness of their actions, the information they receive, the degree to which difficult questions are raised and pursued with management, and their interaction with internal and external auditors. The importance of responsibilities of those charged with governance is recognized in codes of practice and other regulations or guidance produced for the benefit of those charged with governance. Other responsibilities of those charged with governance include oversight of the design and effective operation of whistle blower procedures and the process for reviewing the effectiveness of the entity's internal control.

(d) *Management's philosophy and operating style.* Management's philosophy and operating style encompass a broad range of characteristics. Such characteristics may include the following: management's approach to taking and monitoring business risks; management's attitudes and actions toward financial reporting (conservative or aggressive selection from available alternative accounting principles, and conscientiousness and conservatism with which accounting estimates are developed); and management's attitudes toward information processing and accounting functions and personnel.

(e) *Organizational structure.* An entity's organizational structure provides the framework within which its activities for achieving entity-wide objectives are planned, executed, controlled, and reviewed. Establishing a relevant organizational structure includes considering key areas of authority and responsibility and appropriate lines of reporting. An entity develops an organizational structure suited to its needs. The appropriateness of an entity's organizational structure depends, in part, on its size and the nature of its activities.

(f) *Assignment of authority and responsibility.* This factor includes how authority and responsibility for operating activities are assigned and how reporting relationships and authorization hierarchies are established. It also includes policies relating to appropriate business practices, knowledge and experience of key personnel, and resources provided for carrying out duties. In addition, it includes policies and communications directed at ensuring that all personnel understand the entity's objectives, know how their individual actions interrelate and contribute to those objectives, and recognize how and for what they will be held accountable.

(g) *Human resource policies and practices.* Human resource policies and practices relate to recruitment, orientation, training, evaluating, counseling, promoting, compensating, and remedial actions. For example, standards for recruiting the most qualified individuals – with emphasis on educational background, prior work experience, past accomplishments, and evidence of integrity and ethical behavior – demonstrate an entity's commitment to competent and trustworthy people. Training policies that communicate prospective roles and responsibilities and include practices such as training schools and seminars illustrate expected levels of performance and behavior. Promotions driven by periodic performance appraisals demonstrate the entity's commitment to the advancement of qualified personnel to higher levels of responsibility.

Application to Small Entities

4. Small entities may implement the control environment elements differently than larger entities. For example, small entities might not have a written code of conduct but, instead, develop a culture that emphasizes the importance of integrity and ethical behavior through oral communication and by management example. Similarly, those charged with governance in small entities may not include an independent or outside member.

Entity's Risk Assessment Process

5. An entity's risk assessment process is its process for identifying and responding to business risks and the results thereof. For financial reporting purposes, the entity's risk assessment process includes how management identifies risks relevant to the preparation of financial statements that give a true and fair view (or are presented fairly, in all material respects) in accordance with the entity's applicable financial reporting framework, estimates their significance, assesses the likelihood of their occurrence, and decides upon actions to manage them. For example, the entity's risk assessment process may address how the entity considers the possibility of unrecorded transactions or identifies and analyzes significant estimates recorded in the financial statements. Risks relevant to reliable financial reporting also relate to specific events or transactions.

6. Risks relevant to financial reporting include external and internal events and circumstances that may occur and adversely affect an entity's ability to initiate, record, process, and report financial data consistent with the assertions of management in the financial statements. Once risks are identified, management considers their significance, the likelihood of their occurrence, and how they should be managed. Management may initiate plans, programs, or actions to address specific risks or it may decide to accept a risk because of cost or other considerations. Risks can arise or change due to circumstances such as the following:

- *Changes in operating environment.* Changes in the regulatory or operating environment can result in changes in competitive pressures and significantly different risks.

- *New personnel.* New personnel may have a different focus on or understanding of internal control.

- *New or revamped information systems.* Significant and rapid changes in information systems can change the risk relating to internal control.

- *Rapid growth.* Significant and rapid expansion of operations can strain controls and increase the risk of a breakdown in controls.

- *New technology*. Incorporating new technologies into production processes or information systems may change the risk associated with internal control.

- *New business models, products, or activities*. Entering into business areas or transactions with which an entity has little experience may introduce new risks associated with internal control.

- *Corporate restructurings*. Restructurings may be accompanied by staff reductions and changes in supervision and segregation of duties that may change the risk associated with internal control.

- *Expanded foreign operations*. The expansion or acquisition of foreign operations carries new and often unique risks that may affect internal control, for example, additional or changed risks from foreign currency transactions.

- *New accounting pronouncements*. Adoption of new accounting principles or changing accounting principles may affect risks in preparing financial statements.

Application to Small Entities

7.   The basic concepts of the entity's risk assessment process are relevant to every entity, regardless of size, but the risk assessment process is likely to be less formal and less structured in small entities than in larger ones. All entities should have established financial reporting objectives, but they may be recognized implicitly rather than explicitly in small entities. Management may be aware of risks related to these objectives without the use of a formal process but through direct personal involvement with employees and outside parties.

Information System, Including the Related Business Processes, Relevant To Financial Reporting, And Communication

8.   An information system consists of infrastructure (physical and hardware components), software, people, procedures, and data. Infrastructure and software will be absent, or have less significance, in systems that are exclusively or primarily manual. Many information systems make extensive use of information technology (IT).

9.   The information system relevant to financial reporting objectives, which includes the financial reporting system, consists of the procedures and records established to initiate, record, process, and report entity transactions (as well as events and conditions) and to maintain accountability for the related assets, liabilities, and equity. Transactions may be initiated manually or automatically by programmed procedures. Recording includes identifying and capturing the relevant information for transactions or events. Processing includes functions such as edit and validation, calculation, measurement, valuation, summarization, and reconciliation, whether performed by automated or manual procedures. Reporting relates to the preparation of financial reports as well as other information, in electronic or printed format, that the entity uses in measuring and reviewing the entity's financial performance and in other functions. The quality of system-generated information affects management's ability to make

appropriate decisions in managing and controlling the entity's activities and to prepare reliable financial reports.

10. Accordingly, an information system encompasses methods and records that:

- Identify and record all valid transactions.

- Describe on a timely basis the transactions in sufficient detail to permit proper classification of transactions for financial reporting.

- Measure the value of transactions in a manner that permits recording their proper monetary value in the financial statements.

- Determine the time period in which transactions occurred to permit recording of transactions in the proper accounting period.

- Present properly the transactions and related disclosures in the financial statements.

11. Communication involves providing an understanding of individual roles and responsibilities pertaining to internal control over financial reporting. It includes the extent to which personnel understand how their activities in the financial reporting information system relate to the work of others and the means of reporting exceptions to an appropriate higher level within the entity. Open communication channels help ensure that exceptions are reported and acted on.

12. Communication takes such forms as policy manuals, accounting and financial reporting manuals, and memoranda. Communication also can be made electronically, orally, and through the actions of management.

Application to Small Entities

13. Information systems and related business processes relevant to financial reporting in small entities are likely to be less formal than in larger entities, but their role is just as significant. Small entities with active management involvement may not need extensive descriptions of accounting procedures, sophisticated accounting records, or written policies. Communication may be less formal and easier to achieve in a small entity than in a larger entity due to the small entity's size and fewer levels as well as management's greater visibility and availability.

Control Activities

14. Control activities are the policies and procedures that help ensure that management directives are carried out, for example, that necessary actions are taken to address risks that threaten the achievement of the entity's objectives. Control activities, whether within IT or manual systems, have various objectives and are applied at various organizational and functional levels.

15. Generally, control activities that may be relevant to an audit may be categorized as policies and procedures that pertain to the following:

- *Performance reviews*. These control activities include reviews and analyses of actual performance versus budgets, forecasts, and prior period performance; relating different sets of data – operating or financial – to one another, together with analyses of the relationships and investigative and corrective actions; comparing internal data with external sources of information; and review of functional or activity performance, such as a bank's consumer loan manager's review of reports by branch, region, and loan type for loan approvals and collections.

- *Information processing*. A variety of controls are performed to check accuracy, completeness, and authorization of transactions. The two broad groupings of information systems control activities are application controls and general IT-controls. Application controls apply to the processing of individual applications. These controls help ensure that transactions occurred, are authorized, and are completely and accurately recorded and processed. Examples of application controls include checking the arithmetical accuracy of records, maintaining and reviewing accounts and trial balances, automated controls such as edit checks of input data and numerical sequence checks, and manual follow-up of exception reports. General IT-controls are polices and procedures that relate to many applications and support the effective functioning of application controls by helping to ensure the continued proper operation of information systems. General IT-controls commonly include controls over data center and network operations; system software acquisition, change and maintenance; access security; and application system acquisition, development, and maintenance. These controls apply to mainframe, miniframe, and end-user environments. Examples of such general IT-controls are program change controls, controls that restrict access to programs or data, controls over the implementation of new releases of packaged software applications, and controls over system software that restrict access to or monitor the use of system utilities that could change financial data or records without leaving an audit trail.

- *Physical controls*. These activities encompass the physical security of assets, including adequate safeguards such as secured facilities over access to assets and records; authorization for access to computer programs and data files; and periodic counting and comparison with amounts shown on control records (for example comparing the results of cash, security and inventory counts with accounting records). The extent to which physical controls intended to prevent theft of assets are relevant to the reliability of financial statement preparation, and therefore the audit, depends on circumstances such as when assets are highly susceptible to misappropriation. For example, these controls would ordinarily not be relevant when any inventory losses would be detected pursuant to periodic physical inspection and recorded in the financial statements. However, if for financial reporting purposes management relies solely on perpetual inventory records, the physical security controls would be relevant to the audit.

- *Segregation of duties*. Assigning different people the responsibilities of authorizing transactions, recording transactions, and maintaining custody of assets is intended to reduce the opportunities to allow any person to be in a position to both perpetrate and conceal errors or fraud in the normal course of the person's duties. Examples of segregation of duties include reporting, reviewing and approving reconciliations, and approval and control of documents.

16. Certain control activities may depend on the existence of appropriate higher level policies established by management or those charged with governance. For example, authorization controls may be delegated under established guidelines, such as investment criteria set by those charged with governance; alternatively, non-routine transactions such as major acquisitions or divestments may require specific high level approval, including in some cases that of shareholders.

Application to Small Entities

17. The concepts underlying control activities in small entities are likely to be similar to those in larger entities, but the formality with which they operate varies. Further, small entities may find that certain types of control activities are not relevant because of controls applied by management. For example, management's retention of authority for approving credit sales, significant purchases, and draw-downs on lines of credit can provide strong control over those activities, lessening or removing the need for more detailed control activities. An appropriate segregation of duties often appears to present difficulties in small entities. Even companies that have only a few employees, however, may be able to assign their responsibilities to achieve appropriate segregation or, if that is not possible, to use management oversight of the incompatible activities to achieve control objectives.

Monitoring of Controls

18. An important management responsibility is to establish and maintain internal control on an ongoing basis. Management's monitoring of controls includes considering whether they are operating as intended and that they are modified as appropriate for changes in conditions. Monitoring of controls may include activities such as management's review of whether bank reconciliations are being prepared on a timely basis, internal auditors' evaluation of sales personnel's compliance with the entity's policies on terms of sales contracts, and a legal department's oversight of compliance with the entity's ethical or business practice policies.

19. Monitoring of controls is a process to assess the quality of internal control performance over time. It involves assessing the design and operation of controls on a timely basis and taking necessary corrective actions. Monitoring is done to ensure that controls continue to operate effectively. For example, if the timeliness and accuracy of bank reconciliations are not monitored, personnel are likely to stop preparing them. Monitoring of controls is accomplished through ongoing monitoring activities, separate evaluations, or a combination of the two.

20. Ongoing monitoring activities are built into the normal recurring activities of an entity and include regular management and supervisory activities. Managers of sales, purchasing, and production at divisional and corporate levels are in touch with

operations and may question reports that differ significantly from their knowledge of operations.

21. In many entities, internal auditors or personnel performing similar functions contribute to the monitoring of an entity's controls through separate evaluations. They regularly provide information about the functioning of internal control, focusing considerable attention on evaluating the design and operation of internal control. They communicate information about strengths and weaknesses and recommendations for improving internal control.

22. Monitoring activities may include using information from communications from external parties that may indicate problems or highlight areas in need of improvement. Customers implicitly corroborate billing data by paying their invoices or complaining about their charges. In addition, regulators may communicate with the entity concerning matters that affect the functioning of internal control, for example, communications concerning examinations by bank regulatory agencies. Also, management may consider communications relating to internal control from external auditors in performing monitoring activities.

Application to Small Entities

23. Ongoing monitoring activities of small entities are more likely to be informal and are typically performed as a part of the overall management of the entity's operations. Management's close involvement in operations often will identify significant variances from expectations and inaccuracies in financial data leading to corrective action to the control.

Appendix 3

Conditions and Events That May Indicate Risks of Material Misstatement

The following are examples of conditions and events that may indicate the existence of risks of material misstatement. The examples provided cover a broad range of conditions and events; however, not all conditions and events are relevant to every audit engagement and the list of examples is not necessarily complete.

- Operations in regions that are economically unstable, for example, countries with significant currency devaluation or highly inflationary economies.

- Operations exposed to volatile markets, for example, futures trading.

- High degree of complex regulation.

- Going concern and liquidity issues including loss of significant customers.

- Constraints on the availability of capital and credit.

- Changes in the industry in which the entity operates.

- Changes in the supply chain.

- Developing or offering new products or services, or moving into new lines of business.

- Expanding into new locations.

- Changes in the entity such as large acquisitions or reorganizations or other unusual events.

- Entities or business segments likely to be sold.

- Complex alliances and joint ventures.

- Use of off-balance-sheet finance, special-purpose entities, and other complex financing arrangements.

- Significant transactions with related parties.

- Lack of personnel with appropriate accounting and financial reporting skills.

- Changes in key personnel including departure of key executives.

- Weaknesses in internal control, especially those not addressed by management.

- Inconsistencies between the entity's IT strategy and its business strategies.

- Changes in the IT environment.

- Installation of significant new IT systems related to financial reporting.

- Inquiries into the entity's operations or financial results by regulatory or government bodies.

- Past misstatements, history of errors or a significant amount of adjustments at period end.

- Significant amount of non-routine or non-systematic transactions including intercompany transactions and large revenue transactions at period end.

- Transactions that are recorded based on management's intent, for example, debt refinancing, assets to be sold and classification of marketable securities.

- Application of new accounting pronouncements.

- Accounting measurements that involve complex processes.

- Events or transactions that involve significant measurement uncertainty, including accounting estimates.

- Pending litigation and contingent liabilities, for example, sales warranties, financial guarantees and environmental remediation.

INTERNATIONAL STANDARD ON AUDITING (UK AND IRELAND) 320

AUDIT MATERIALITY

CONTENTS

International Standard on Auditing (UK and Ireland) (ISA (UK and Ireland)) 320 "Audit Materiality" should be read in the context of the Auditing Practices Board's Statement "The Auditing Practices Board - Scope and Authority of Pronouncements (Revised)" which sets out the application and authority of ISAs (UK and Ireland).

Introduction

1. The purpose of this International Standard on Auditing (UK and Ireland) (ISA (UK and Ireland)) is to establish standards and provide guidance on the concept of materiality and its relationship with audit risk.

1-1. This ISA (UK and Ireland) uses the terms 'those charged with governance' and 'management'. The term 'governance' describes the role of persons entrusted with the supervision, control and direction of an entity. Ordinarily, those charged with governance are accountable for ensuring that the entity achieves its objectives, and for the quality of its financial reporting and reporting to interested parties. Those charged with governance include management only when they perform such functions.

1-2. In the UK and Ireland, those charged with governance include the directors (executive and non-executive) of a company or other body, the members of an audit committee where one exists, the partners, proprietors, committee of management or trustees of other forms of entity, or equivalent persons responsible for directing the entity's affairs and preparing its financial statements.

1-3. 'Management' comprises those persons who perform senior managerial functions.

1-4. In the UK and Ireland, depending on the nature and circumstances of the entity, management may include some or all of those charged with governance. (e.g. executive directors). Management will not normally include non-executive directors.

2. **The auditor should consider materiality and its relationship with audit risk when conducting an audit.**

3. "Materiality" is defined in the International Accounting Standards Board's "Framework for the Preparation and Presentation of Financial Statements" in the following terms:

    "Information is material if its omission or misstatement could influence the economic decisions of users taken on the basis of the financial statements. Materiality depends on the size of the item or error judged in the particular circumstances of its omission or misstatement. Thus, materiality provides a threshold or cut-off point rather than being a primary qualitative characteristic which information must have if it is to be useful."

Materiality

4. **The objective of an audit of financial statements is to enable the auditor to express an opinion whether the financial statements are prepared, in all material respects, in accordance with an applicable financial reporting framework.** The assessment of what is material is a matter of professional judgment.

5. In designing the audit plan, the auditor establishes an acceptable materiality level so as to detect quantitatively material misstatements. However, both the amount

(quantity) and nature (quality) of misstatements need to be considered. Examples of qualitative misstatements would be the inadequate or improper description of an accounting policy when it is likely that a user of the financial statements would be misled by the description, and failure to disclose the breach of regulatory requirements when it is likely that the consequent imposition of regulatory restrictions will significantly impair operating capability.

6.   The auditor needs to consider the possibility of misstatements of relatively small amounts that, cumulatively, could have a material effect on the financial statements. For example, an error in a month end procedure could be an indication of a potential material misstatement if that error is repeated each month.

7.   The auditor considers materiality at both the overall financial statement level and in relation to classes of transactions, account balances, and disclosures. Materiality may be influenced by considerations such as legal and regulatory requirements and considerations relating to classes of transactions, account balances, and disclosures and their relationships. This process may result in different materiality levels depending on the aspect of the financial statements being considered.

7-1. For example, in the UK and Ireland, the expected degree of accuracy of certain statutory disclosures, such as directors' emoluments, may make normal materiality considerations irrelevant.

8.   **Materiality should be considered by the auditor when:**

   (a) **Determining the nature, timing and extent of audit procedures; and**

   (b) **Evaluating the effect of misstatements.**

The Relationship between Materiality and Audit Risk

9.   When planning the audit, the auditor considers what would make the financial statements materially misstated. The auditor's understanding of the entity and its environment establishes a frame of reference within which the auditor plans the audit and exercises professional judgment about assessing the risks of material misstatement of the financial statements and responding to those risks throughout the audit. It also assists the auditor to establish materiality and in evaluating whether the judgment about materiality remains appropriate as the audit progresses. The auditor's assessment of materiality, related to classes of transactions, account balances, and disclosures helps the auditor decide such questions as what items to examine and whether to use sampling and substantive analytical procedures. This enables the auditor to select audit procedures that, in combination, can be expected to reduce audit risk to an acceptably low level.

9-1. If the auditor identifies factors which result in the revision of the preliminary materiality assessment, the auditor considers the implications for the audit approach and may modify the nature, timing and extent of planned audit procedures.

10. There is an inverse relationship between materiality and the level of audit risk, that is, the higher the materiality level, the lower the audit risk and vice versa. The auditor takes the inverse relationship between materiality and audit risk into account when determining the nature, timing and extent of audit procedures. For example, if, after planning for specific audit procedures, the auditor determines that the acceptable materiality level is lower, audit risk is increased. The auditor would compensate for this by either:

(a) Reducing the assessed risk of material misstatement, where this is possible, and supporting the reduced level by carrying out extended or additional tests of control; or

(b) Reducing detection risk by modifying the nature, timing and extent of planned substantive procedures.

Materiality and Audit Risk in Evaluating Audit Evidence

11. The auditor's assessment of materiality and audit risk may be different at the time of initially planning the engagement from at the time of evaluating the results of audit procedures. This could be because of a change in circumstances or because of a change in the auditor's knowledge as a result of performing audit procedures. For example, if audit procedures are performed prior to period end, the auditor will anticipate the results of operations and the financial position. If actual results of operations and financial position are substantially different, the assessment of materiality and audit risk may also change. Additionally, the auditor may, in planning the audit work, intentionally set the acceptable materiality level at a lower level than is intended to be used to evaluate the results of the audit. This may be done to reduce the likelihood of undiscovered misstatements and to provide the auditor with a margin of safety when evaluating the effect of misstatements discovered during the audit.

Evaluating the Effect of Misstatements

12. **In evaluating whether the financial statements are prepared, in all material respects, in accordance with an applicable financial reporting framework, the auditor should assess whether the aggregate of uncorrected misstatements that have been identified during the audit is material.**

12-1. In the UK and Ireland the auditor ordinarily evaluates whether the financial statements give a true and fair view.

13. The aggregate of uncorrected misstatements comprises:

(a) Specific misstatements identified by the auditor including the net effect of uncorrected misstatements identified during the audit of previous periods; and

(b) The auditor's best estimate of other misstatements which cannot be specifically identified (*i.e.*, projected errors).

14. The auditor needs to consider whether the aggregate of uncorrected misstatements is material. If the auditor concludes that the misstatements may be material, the auditor needs to consider reducing audit risk by extending audit procedures or requesting management to adjust the financial statements. In any event, management may want to adjust the financial statements for the misstatements identified.

15. **If management refuses to adjust the financial statements and the results of extended audit procedures do not enable the auditor to conclude that the aggregate of uncorrected misstatements is not material, the auditor should consider the appropriate modification to the auditor's report in accordance with ISA (UK and Ireland) 700 "The Auditor's Report on Financial Statements."**

16. If the aggregate of the uncorrected misstatements that the auditor has identified approaches the materiality level, the auditor would consider whether it is likely that undetected misstatements, when taken with aggregate uncorrected misstatements could exceed materiality level. Thus, as aggregate uncorrected misstatements approach the materiality level the auditor would consider reducing audit risk by performing additional audit procedures or by requesting management to adjust the financial statements for identified misstatements.

Communication of Errors

17. **If the auditor has identified a material misstatement resulting from error, the auditor should communicate the misstatement to the appropriate level of management on a timely basis, and consider the need to report it to those charged with governance in accordance with ISA (UK and Ireland) 260, "Communication of Audit Matters to Those Charged with Governance."**

Effective Date

17-1. This ISA (UK and Ireland) is effective for audits of financial statements for periods commencing on or after 15 December 2004.

Public Sector Perspective

Additional guidance for auditors of public sector bodies in the UK and Ireland is given in:

- Practice Note 10 "Audit of Financial Statements of Public Sector Bodies in the United Kingdom (Revised)"

- Practice Note 10(I) "Audit of Central Government Financial Statements in the Republic of Ireland (Revised)"

1. *In assessing materiality, the public sector auditor must, in addition to exercising professional judgment, consider any legislation or regulation which may impact that assessment. In the public sector, materiality is also based on the "context and nature" of*

an item and includes, for example, sensitivity as well as value. Sensitivity covers a variety of matters such as compliance with authorities, legislative concern or public interest.

INTERNATIONAL STANDARD ON AUDITING (UK AND IRELAND) 330

THE AUDITOR'S PROCEDURES IN RESPONSE TO ASSESSED RISKS

CONTENTS

International Standard on Auditing (UK and Ireland) (ISA (UK and Ireland)) 330 "The Auditor's Procedures in Response to Assessed Risks" should be read in the context of the Auditing Practices Board's Statement "The Auditing Practices Board - Scope and Authority of Pronouncements (Revised)" which sets out the application and authority of ISAs (UK and Ireland).

Introduction

1. The purpose of this International Standard on Auditing (UK and Ireland) (ISA (UK and Ireland)) is to establish standards and provide guidance on determining overall responses and designing and performing further audit procedures to respond to the assessed risks of material misstatement at the financial statement and assertion levels in a financial statement audit. The auditor's understanding of the entity and its environment, including its internal control, and assessment of the risks of material misstatement are described in ISA (UK and Ireland) 315, "Understanding the Entity and Its Environment and Assessing the Risks of Material Misstatement."

1-1. This ISA (UK and Ireland) uses the terms 'those charged with governance' and 'management'. The term 'governance' describes the role of persons entrusted with the supervision, control and direction of an entity. Ordinarily, those charged with governance are accountable for ensuring that the entity achieves its objectives, and for the quality of its financial reporting and reporting to interested parties. Those charged with governance include management only when they perform such functions.

1-2. In the UK and Ireland, those charged with governance include the directors (executive and non-executive) of a company or other body, the members of an audit committee where one exists, the partners, proprietors, committee of management or trustees of other forms of entity, or equivalent persons responsible for directing the entity's affairs and preparing its financial statements.

1-3. 'Management' comprises those persons who perform senior managerial functions.

1-4. In the UK and Ireland, depending on the nature and circumstances of the entity, management may include some or all of those charged with governance (e.g. executive directors). Management will not normally include non-executive directors.

2. The following is an overview of the requirements of this standard:

   - *Overall responses.* This section requires the auditor to determine overall responses to address risks of material misstatement at the financial statement level and provides guidance on the nature of those responses.

   - *Audit procedures responsive to risks of material misstatement at the assertion level.* This section requires the auditor to design and perform further audit procedures, including tests of the operating effectiveness of controls, when relevant or required, and substantive procedures, whose nature, timing, and extent are responsive to the assessed risks of material misstatement at the assertion level. In addition, this section includes matters the auditor considers in determining the nature, timing, and extent of such audit procedures.

   - *Evaluating the sufficiency and appropriateness of audit evidence obtained.* This section requires the auditor to evaluate whether the risk assessment remains appropriate and to conclude whether sufficient appropriate audit evidence has been obtained.

THE AUDITING PRACTICES BOARD

- *Documentation*. This section establishes related documentation requirements.

3. **In order to reduce audit risk to an acceptably low level, the auditor should determine overall responses to assessed risks at the financial statement level, and should design and perform further audit procedures to respond to assessed risks at the assertion level.** The overall responses and the nature, timing, and extent of the further audit procedures are matters for the professional judgment of the auditor. In addition to the requirements of this ISA (UK and Ireland), the auditor also complies with the requirements and guidance in ISA (UK and Ireland) 240, "The Auditor's Responsibility to Consider Fraud in an Audit of Financial Statements" in responding to assessed risks of material misstatement due to fraud.

Overall Responses

4. **The auditor should determine overall responses to address the risks of material misstatement at the financial statement level.** Such responses may include emphasizing to the audit team the need to maintain professional skepticism in gathering and evaluating audit evidence, assigning more experienced staff or those with special skills or using experts,[1] providing more supervision, or incorporating additional elements of unpredictability in the selection of further audit procedures to be performed. Additionally, the auditor may make general changes to the nature, timing, or extent of audit procedures as an overall response, for example, performing substantive procedures at period end instead of at an interim date.

5. The assessment of the risks of material misstatement at the financial statement level is affected by the auditor's understanding of the control environment. An effective control environment may allow the auditor to have more confidence in internal control and the reliability of audit evidence generated internally within the entity and thus, for example, allow the auditor to conduct some audit procedures at an interim date rather than at period end. If there are weaknesses in the control environment, the auditor ordinarily conducts more audit procedures as of the period end rather than at an interim date, seeks more extensive audit evidence from substantive procedures, modifies the nature of audit procedures to obtain more persuasive audit evidence, or increases the number of locations to be included in the audit scope.

6. Such considerations, therefore, have a significant bearing on the auditor's general approach, for example, an emphasis on substantive procedures (substantive approach), or an approach that uses tests of controls as well as substantive procedures (combined approach).

---

[1] The assignment of engagement personnel to the particular engagement reflects the auditor's risk assessment, which is based on the auditor's understanding of the entity.

Audit Procedures Responsive to Risks of Material Misstatement at the Assertion Level

7. **The auditor should design and perform further audit procedures whose nature, timing, and extent are responsive to the assessed risks of material misstatement at the assertion level.** The purpose is to provide a clear linkage between the nature, timing, and extent of the auditor's further audit procedures and the risk assessment. In designing further audit procedures, the auditor considers such matters as the following:

- The significance of the risk.

- The likelihood that a material misstatement will occur.

- The characteristics of the class of transactions, account balance, or disclosure involved.

- The nature of the specific controls used by the entity and in particular whether they are manual or automated.

- Whether the auditor expects to obtain audit evidence to determine if the entity's controls are effective in preventing, or detecting and correcting, material misstatements.

The nature of the audit procedures is of most importance in responding to the assessed risks.

8. The auditor's assessment of the identified risks at the assertion level provides a basis for considering the appropriate audit approach for designing and performing further audit procedures. In some cases, the auditor may determine that only by performing tests of controls may the auditor achieve an effective response to the assessed risk of material misstatement for a particular assertion. In other cases, the auditor may determine that performing only substantive procedures is appropriate for specific assertions and, therefore, the auditor excludes the effect of controls from the relevant risk assessment. This may be because the auditor's risk assessment procedures have not identified any effective controls relevant to the assertion, or because testing the operating effectiveness of controls would be inefficient. However, the auditor needs to be satisfied that performing only substantive procedures for the relevant assertion would be effective in reducing the risk of material misstatement to an acceptably low level. Often the auditor may determine that a combined approach using both tests of the operating effectiveness of controls and substantive procedures is an effective approach. Irrespective of the approach selected, the auditor designs and performs substantive procedures for each material class of transactions, account balance, and disclosure as required by paragraph 49.

9. In the case of very small entities, there may not be many control activities that could be identified by the auditor. For this reason, the auditor's further audit procedures are likely to be primarily substantive procedures. In such cases, in addition to the matters

referred to in paragraph 8 above, the auditor considers whether in the absence of controls it is possible to obtain sufficient appropriate audit evidence.

Considering the Nature, Timing, and Extent of Further Audit Procedures

Nature

10. The nature of further audit procedures refers to their purpose (tests of controls or substantive procedures) and their type, that is, inspection, observation, inquiry, confirmation, recalculation, reperformance, or analytical procedures. Certain audit procedures may be more appropriate for some assertions than others. For example, in relation to revenue, tests of controls may be most responsive to the assessed risk of misstatement of the completeness assertion, whereas substantive procedures may be most responsive to the assessed risk of misstatement of the occurrence assertion.

11. The auditor's selection of audit procedures is based on the assessment of risk. The higher the auditor's assessment of risk, the more reliable and relevant is the audit evidence sought by the auditor from substantive procedures. This may affect both the types of audit procedures to be performed and their combination. For example, the auditor may confirm the completeness of the terms of a contract with a third party, in addition to inspecting the document.

12. In determining the audit procedures to be performed, the auditor considers the reasons for the assessment of the risk of material misstatement at the assertion level for each class of transactions, account balance, and disclosure. This includes considering both the particular characteristics of each class of transactions, account balance, or disclosure (*i.e.*, the inherent risks) and whether the auditor's risk assessment takes account of the entity's controls (*i.e.*, the control risk). For example, if the auditor considers that there is a lower risk that a material misstatement may occur because of the particular characteristics of a class of transactions without consideration of the related controls, the auditor may determine that substantive analytical procedures alone may provide sufficient appropriate audit evidence. On the other hand, if the auditor expects that there is a lower risk that a material misstatement may arise because an entity has effective controls and the auditor intends to design substantive procedures based on the effective operation of those controls, then the auditor performs tests of controls to obtain audit evidence about their operating effectiveness. This may be the case, for example, for a class of transactions of reasonably uniform, non-complex characteristics that are routinely processed and controlled by the entity's information system.

13. The auditor is required to obtain audit evidence about the accuracy and completeness of information produced by the entity's information system when that information is used in performing audit procedures. For example, if the auditor uses non-financial information or budget data produced by the entity's information system in performing audit procedures, such as substantive analytical procedures or tests of controls, the auditor obtains audit evidence about the accuracy and completeness of such information. See ISA (UK and Ireland) 500, "Audit Evidence" paragraph 11 for further guidance.

Timing

14. Timing refers to when audit procedures are performed or the period or date to which the audit evidence applies.

15. The auditor may perform tests of controls or substantive procedures at an interim date or at period end. The higher the risk of material misstatement, the more likely it is that the auditor may decide it is more effective to perform substantive procedures nearer to, or at, the period end rather than at an earlier date, or to perform audit procedures unannounced or at unpredictable times (for example, performing audit procedures at selected locations on an unannounced basis). On the other hand, performing audit procedures before the period end may assist the auditor in identifying significant matters at an early stage of the audit, and consequently resolving them with the assistance of management or developing an effective audit approach to address such matters. If the auditor performs tests of controls or substantive procedures prior to period end, the auditor considers the additional evidence required for the remaining period (see paragraphs 37-38 and 56-61).

16. In considering when to perform audit procedures, the auditor also considers such matters as the following:

    • The control environment.

    • When relevant information is available (for example, electronic files may subsequently be overwritten, or procedures to be observed may occur only at certain times).

    • The nature of the risk (for example, if there is a risk of inflated revenues to meet earnings expectations by subsequent creation of false sales agreements, the auditor may wish to examine contracts available on the date of the period end).

    • The period or date to which the audit evidence relates.

17. Certain audit procedures can be performed only at or after period end, for example, agreeing the financial statements to the accounting records and examining adjustments made during the course of preparing the financial statements. If there is a risk that the entity may have entered into improper sales contracts or transactions may not have been finalized at period end, the auditor performs procedures to respond to that specific risk. For example, when transactions are individually material or an error in cutoff may lead to a material misstatement, the auditor ordinarily inspects transactions near the period end.

Extent

18. Extent includes the quantity of a specific audit procedure to be performed, for example, a sample size or the number of observations of a control activity. The extent of an audit procedure is determined by the judgment of the auditor after considering the materiality, the assessed risk, and the degree of assurance the auditor plans to obtain. In particular, the auditor ordinarily increases the extent of audit procedures as

the risk of material misstatement increases. However, increasing the extent of an audit procedure is effective only if the audit procedure itself is relevant to the specific risk; therefore, the nature of the audit procedure is the most important consideration.

19. The use of computer-assisted audit techniques (CAATs) may enable more extensive testing of electronic transactions and account files. Such techniques can be used to select sample transactions from key electronic files, to sort transactions with specific characteristics, or to test an entire population instead of a sample.

20. Valid conclusions may ordinarily be drawn using sampling approaches. However, if the quantity of selections made from a population is too small, the sampling approach selected is not appropriate to achieve the specific audit objective, or if exceptions are not appropriately followed up, there will be an unacceptable risk that the auditor's conclusion based on a sample may be different from the conclusion reached if the entire population was subjected to the same audit procedure. ISA (UK and Ireland) 530, "Audit Sampling and Other Means of Testing" contains guidance on the use of sampling.

21. This standard regards the use of different audit procedures in combination as an aspect of the nature of testing as discussed above. However, the auditor considers whether the extent of testing is appropriate when performing different audit procedures in combination.

Tests of Controls

22. The auditor is required to perform tests of controls when the auditor's risk assessment includes an expectation of the operating effectiveness of controls or when substantive procedures alone do not provide sufficient appropriate audit evidence at the assertion level.

23. **When the auditor's assessment of risks of material misstatement at the assertion level includes an expectation that controls are operating effectively, the auditor should perform tests of controls to obtain sufficient appropriate audit evidence that the controls were operating effectively at relevant times during the period under audit.** See paragraphs 39-44 below for discussion of using audit evidence about the operating effectiveness of controls obtained in prior audits.

24. The auditor's assessment of risk of material misstatement at the assertion level may include an expectation of the operating effectiveness of controls, in which case the auditor performs tests of controls to obtain audit evidence as to their operating effectiveness. Tests of the operating effectiveness of controls are performed only on those controls that the auditor has determined are suitably designed to prevent, or detect and correct, a material misstatement in an assertion. Paragraphs 104-106 of ISA (UK and Ireland) 315 discuss the identification of controls at the assertion level likely to prevent, or detect and correct, a material misstatement in a class of transactions, account balance or disclosure.

25. **When, in accordance with paragraph 115 of ISA (UK and Ireland) 315, the auditor has determined that it is not possible or practicable to reduce the risks of material**

misstatement at the assertion level to an acceptably low level with audit evidence obtained only from substantive procedures, the auditor should perform tests of relevant controls to obtain audit evidence about their operating effectiveness. For example, as discussed in paragraph 115 of ISA (UK and Ireland) 315, the auditor may find it impossible to design effective substantive procedures that by themselves provide sufficient appropriate audit evidence at the assertion level when an entity conducts its business using IT and no documentation of transactions is produced or maintained, other than through the IT system.

26. Testing the operating effectiveness of controls is different from obtaining audit evidence that controls have been implemented. When obtaining audit evidence of implementation by performing risk assessment procedures, the auditor determines that the relevant controls exist and that the entity is using them. When performing tests of the operating effectiveness of controls, the auditor obtains audit evidence that controls operate effectively. This includes obtaining audit evidence about how controls were applied at relevant times during the period under audit, the consistency with which they were applied, and by whom or by what means they were applied. If substantially different controls were used at different times during the period under audit, the auditor considers each separately. The auditor may determine that testing the operating effectiveness of controls at the same time as evaluating their design and obtaining audit evidence of their implementation is efficient.

27. Although some risk assessment procedures that the auditor performs to evaluate the design of controls and to determine that they have been implemented may not have been specifically designed as tests of controls, they may nevertheless provide audit evidence about the operating effectiveness of the controls and, consequently, serve as tests of controls. For example, the auditor may have made inquiries about management's use of budgets, observed management's comparison of monthly budgeted and actual expenses, and inspected reports pertaining to the investigation of variances between budgeted and actual amounts. These audit procedures provide knowledge about the design of the entity's budgeting policies and whether they have been implemented, and may also provide audit evidence about the effectiveness of the operation of budgeting policies in preventing or detecting material misstatements in the classification of expenses. In such circumstances, the auditor considers whether the audit evidence provided by those audit procedures is sufficient.

Nature of Tests of Controls

28. The auditor selects audit procedures to obtain assurance about the operating effectiveness of controls. As the planned level of assurance increases, the auditor seeks more reliable audit evidence. In circumstances when the auditor adopts an approach consisting primarily of tests of controls, in particular related to those risks where it is not possible or practicable to obtain sufficient appropriate audit evidence only from substantive procedures, the auditor ordinarily performs tests of controls to obtain a higher level of assurance about their operating effectiveness.

29. The auditor should perform other audit procedures in combination with inquiry to test the operating effectiveness of controls. Although different from obtaining an understanding of the design and implementation of controls, tests of the operating

effectiveness of controls ordinarily include the same types of audit procedures used to evaluate the design and implementation of controls, and may also include reperformance of the application of the control by the auditor. Since inquiry alone is not sufficient, the auditor uses a combination of audit procedures to obtain sufficient appropriate audit evidence regarding the operating effectiveness of controls. Those controls subject to testing by performing inquiry combined with inspection or reperformance ordinarily provide more assurance than those controls for which the audit evidence consists solely of inquiry and observation. For example, an auditor may inquire about and observe the entity's procedures for opening the mail and processing cash receipts to test the operating effectiveness of controls over cash receipts. Because an observation is pertinent only at the point in time at which it is made, the auditor ordinarily supplements the observation with inquiries of entity personnel, and may also inspect documentation about the operation of such controls at other times during the audit period in order to obtain sufficient appropriate audit evidence.

30. The nature of the particular control influences the type of audit procedure required to obtain audit evidence about whether the control was operating effectively at relevant times during the period under audit. For some controls, operating effectiveness is evidenced by documentation. In such circumstances, the auditor may decide to inspect the documentation to obtain audit evidence about operating effectiveness. For other controls, however, such documentation may not be available or relevant. For example, documentation of operation may not exist for some factors in the control environment, such as assignment of authority and responsibility, or for some types of control activities, such as control activities performed by a computer. In such circumstances, audit evidence about operating effectiveness may be obtained through inquiry in combination with other audit procedures such as observation or the use of CAATs.

31. In designing tests of controls, the auditor considers the need to obtain audit evidence supporting the effective operation of controls directly related to the assertions as well as other indirect controls on which these controls depend. For example, the auditor may identify a user review of an exception report of credit sales over a customer's authorized credit limit as a direct control related to an assertion. In such cases, the auditor considers the effectiveness of the user review of the report and also the controls related to the accuracy of the information in the report (for example, the general IT-controls).

32. In the case of an automated application control, because of the inherent consistency of IT processing, audit evidence about the implementation of the control, when considered in combination with audit evidence obtained regarding the operating effectiveness of the entity's general controls (and in particular, change controls) may provide substantial audit evidence about its operating effectiveness during the relevant period.

33. When responding to the risk assessment, the auditor may design a test of controls to be performed concurrently with a test of details on the same transaction. The objective of tests of controls is to evaluate whether a control operated effectively. The objective of tests of details is to detect material misstatements at the assertion level. Although these objectives are different, both may be accomplished concurrently through

performance of a test of controls and a test of details on the same transaction, also known as a dual-purpose test. For example, the auditor may examine an invoice to determine whether it has been approved and to provide substantive audit evidence of a transaction. The auditor carefully considers the design and evaluation of such tests to accomplish both objectives.

34. The absence of misstatements detected by a substantive procedure does not provide audit evidence that controls related to the assertion being tested are effective. However, misstatements that the auditor detects by performing substantive procedures are considered by the auditor when assessing the operating effectiveness of related controls. A material misstatement detected by the auditor's procedures that was not identified by the entity ordinarily is indicative of the existence of a material weakness in internal control, which is communicated to management and those charged with governance.

Timing of Tests of Controls

35. The timing of tests of controls depends on the auditor's objective and determines the period of reliance on those controls. If the auditor tests controls at a particular time, the auditor only obtains audit evidence that the controls operated effectively at that time However, if the auditor tests controls throughout a period, the auditor obtains audit evidence of the effectiveness of the operation of the controls during that period.

36. Audit evidence pertaining only to a point in time may be sufficient for the auditor's purpose, for example, when testing controls over the entity's physical inventory counting at the period end. If, on the other hand, the auditor requires audit evidence of the effectiveness of a control over a period, audit evidence pertaining only to a point in time may be insufficient and the auditor supplements those tests with other tests of controls that are capable of providing audit evidence that the control operated effectively at relevant times during the period under audit. Such other tests may consist of tests of the entity's monitoring of controls.

37. **When the auditor obtains audit evidence about the operating effectiveness of controls during an interim period, the auditor should determine what additional audit evidence should be obtained for the remaining period.** In making that determination, the auditor considers the significance of the assessed risks of material misstatement at the assertion level, the specific controls that were tested during the interim period, the degree to which audit evidence about the operating effectiveness of those controls was obtained, the length of the remaining period, the extent to which the auditor intends to reduce further substantive procedures based on the reliance of controls, and the control environment. The auditor obtains audit evidence about the nature and extent of any significant changes in internal control, including changes in the information system, processes, and personnel that occur subsequent to the interim period.

38. Additional audit evidence may be obtained, for example, by extending the testing of the operating effectiveness of controls over the remaining period or testing the entity's monitoring of controls.

39. **If the auditor plans to use audit evidence about the operating effectiveness of controls obtained in prior audits, the auditor should obtain audit evidence about whether changes in those specific controls have occurred subsequent to the prior audit. The auditor should obtain audit evidence about whether such changes have occurred by performing inquiry in combination with observation or inspection to confirm the understanding of those specific controls.** Paragraph 23 of ISA (UK and Ireland) 500 states that the auditor performs audit procedures to establish the continuing relevance of audit evidence obtained in prior periods when the auditor plans to use the audit evidence in the current period. For example, in performing the prior audit, the auditor may have determined that an automated control was functioning as intended. The auditor obtains audit evidence to determine whether changes to the automated control have been made that affect its continued effective functioning, for example, through inquiries of management and the inspection of logs to indicate what controls have been changed. Consideration of audit evidence about these changes may support either increasing or decreasing the expected audit evidence to be obtained in the current period about the operating effectiveness of the controls.

40. **If the auditor plans to rely on controls that have changed since they were last tested, the auditor should test the operating effectiveness of such controls in the current audit.** Changes may affect the relevance of the audit evidence obtained in prior periods such that there may no longer be a basis for continued reliance. For example, changes in a system that enable an entity to receive a new report from the system probably do not affect the relevance of prior period audit evidence; however, a change that causes data to be accumulated or calculated differently does affect it.

41. **If the auditor plans to rely on controls that have not changed since they were last tested, the auditor should test the operating effectiveness of such controls at least once in every third audit.** As indicated in paragraphs 40 and 44, the auditor may not rely on audit evidence about the operating effectiveness of controls obtained in prior audits for controls that have changed since they were last tested or controls that mitigate a significant risk. The auditor's decision on whether to rely on audit evidence obtained in prior audits for other controls is a matter of professional judgment. In addition, the length of time period between retesting such controls is also a matter of professional judgment, but cannot exceed two years.

42. In considering whether it is appropriate to use audit evidence about the operating effectiveness of controls obtained in prior audits, and, if so, the length of the time period that may elapse before retesting a control, the auditor considers the following:

   • The effectiveness of other elements of internal control, including the control environment, the entity's monitoring of controls, and the entity's risk assessment process.

   • The risks arising from the characteristics of the control, including whether controls are manual or automated (see ISA (UK and Ireland) 315, paragraphs 57-63 for a discussion of specific risks arising from manual and automated elements of a control).

- The effectiveness of general IT-controls.

- The effectiveness of the control and its application by the entity, including the nature and extent of deviations in the application of the control from tests of operating effectiveness in prior audits.

- Whether the lack of a change in a particular control poses a risk due to changing circumstances.

- The risk of material misstatement and the extent of reliance on the control.

In general, the higher the risk of material misstatement, or the greater the reliance on controls, the shorter the time period elapsed, if any, is likely to be. Factors that ordinarily decrease the period for retesting a control, or result in not relying on audit evidence obtained in prior audits at all, include the following:

- A weak control environment.

- Weak monitoring of controls.

- A significant manual element to the relevant controls.

- Personnel changes that significantly affect the application of the control.

- Changing circumstances that indicate the need for changes in the control.

- Weak general IT-controls.

43. **When there are a number of controls for which the auditor determines that it is appropriate to use audit evidence obtained in prior audits, the auditor should test the operating effectiveness of some controls each audit.** The purpose of this requirement is to avoid the possibility that the auditor might apply the approach of paragraph 41 to all controls on which the auditor proposes to rely, but test all those controls in a single audit period with no testing of controls in the subsequent two audit periods. In addition to providing audit evidence about the operating effectiveness of the controls being tested in the current audit, performing such tests provides collateral evidence about the continuing effectiveness of the control environment and therefore contributes to the decision about whether it is appropriate to rely on audit evidence obtained in prior audits. Therefore, when the auditor determines in accordance with paragraphs 39-42 that it is appropriate to use audit evidence obtained in prior audits for a number of controls, the auditor plans to test a sufficient portion of the controls in that population in each audit period, and at a minimum, each control is tested at least every third audit.

44. **When, in accordance with paragraph 108 of ISA (UK and Ireland) 315, the auditor has determined that an assessed risk of material misstatement at the assertion level is a significant risk and the auditor plans to rely on the operating effectiveness of controls intended to mitigate that significant risk, the auditor should obtain the audit evidence about the operating effectiveness of those**

controls from tests of controls performed in the current period. The greater the risk of material misstatement, the more audit evidence the auditor obtains that relevant controls are operating effectively. Accordingly, although the auditor often considers information obtained in prior audits in designing tests of controls to mitigate a significant risk, the auditor does not rely on audit evidence obtained in a prior audit about the operating effectiveness of controls over such risks, but instead obtains the audit evidence about the operating effectiveness of controls over such risks in the current period.

Extent of Tests of Controls

45. The auditor designs tests of controls to obtain sufficient appropriate audit evidence that the controls operated effectively throughout the period of reliance. Matters the auditor may consider in determining the extent of the auditor's tests of controls include the following:

    • The frequency of the performance of the control by the entity during the period.

    • The length of time during the audit period that the auditor is relying on the operating effectiveness of the control.

    • The relevance and reliability of the audit evidence to be obtained in supporting that the control prevents, or detects and corrects, material misstatements at the assertion level.

    • The extent to which audit evidence is obtained from tests of other controls related to the assertion.

    • The extent to which the auditor plans to rely on the operating effectiveness of the control in the assessment of risk (and thereby reduce substantive procedures based on the reliance of such control).

    • The expected deviation from the control.

46. The more the auditor relies on the operating effectiveness of controls in the assessment of risk, the greater is the extent of the auditor's tests of controls. In addition, as the rate of expected deviation from a control increases, the auditor increases the extent of testing of the control. However, the auditor considers whether the rate of expected deviation indicates that the control will not be sufficient to reduce the risk of material misstatement at the assertion level to that assessed by the auditor. If the rate of expected deviation is expected to be too high, the auditor may determine that tests of controls for a particular assertion may not be effective.

47. Because of the inherent consistency of IT processing, the auditor may not need to increase the extent of testing of an automated control. An automated control should function consistently unless the program (including the tables, files, or other permanent data used by the program) is changed. Once the auditor determines that an automated control is functioning as intended (which could be done at the time the control is initially implemented or at some other date), the auditor considers

performing tests to determine that the control continues to function effectively. Such tests might include determining that changes to the program are not made without being subject to the appropriate program change controls, that the authorized version of the program is used for processing transactions, and that other relevant general controls are effective. Such tests also might include determining that changes to the programs have not been made, as may be the case when the entity uses packaged software applications without modifying or maintaining them. For example, the auditor may inspect the record of the administration of IT security to obtain audit evidence that unauthorized access has not occurred during the period.

Substantive Procedures

48. Substantive procedures are performed in order to detect material misstatements at the assertion level, and include tests of details of classes of transactions, account balances, and disclosures and substantive analytical procedures. The auditor plans and performs substantive procedures to be responsive to the related assessment of the risk of material misstatement.

49. **Irrespective of the assessed risk of material misstatement, the auditor should design and perform substantive procedures for each material class of transactions, account balance, and disclosure.** This requirement reflects the fact that the auditor's assessment of risk is judgmental and may not be sufficiently precise to identify all risks of material misstatement. Further, there are inherent limitations to internal control including management override. Accordingly, while the auditor may determine that the risk of material misstatement may be reduced to an acceptably low level by performing only tests of controls for a particular assertion related to a class of transactions, account balance or disclosure (see paragraph 8), the auditor always performs substantive procedures for each material class of transactions, account balance, and disclosure.

50. **The auditor's substantive procedures should include the following audit procedures related to the financial statement closing process:**

    • **Agreeing the financial statements to the underlying accounting records; and**

    • **Examining material journal entries and other adjustments made during the course of preparing the financial statements.**

    The nature and extent of the auditor's examination of journal entries and other adjustments depends on the nature and complexity of the entity's financial reporting process and the associated risks of material misstatement.

51. **When, in accordance with paragraph 108 of ISA (UK and Ireland) 315, the auditor has determined that an assessed risk of material misstatement at the assertion level is a significant risk, the auditor should perform substantive procedures that are specifically responsive to that risk.** For example, if the auditor identifies that management is under pressure to meet earnings expectations, there may be a risk that management is inflating sales by improperly recognizing revenue related to sales agreements with terms that preclude revenue recognition or by invoicing sales before

shipment. In these circumstances, the auditor may, for example, design external confirmations not only to confirm outstanding amounts, but also to confirm the details of the sales agreements, including date, any rights of return and delivery terms. In addition, the auditor may find it effective to supplement such external confirmations with inquiries of non-financial personnel in the entity regarding any changes in sales agreements and delivery terms.

52. When the approach to significant risks consists only of substantive procedures, the audit procedures appropriate to address such significant risks consist of tests of details only, or a combination of tests of details and substantive analytical procedures The auditor considers the guidance in paragraphs 53-64 in designing the nature, timing, and extent of substantive procedures for significant risks. In order to obtain sufficient appropriate audit evidence, the substantive procedures related to significant risks are most often designed to obtain audit evidence with high reliability.

Nature of Substantive Procedures

53. Substantive analytical procedures are generally more applicable to large volumes of transactions that tend to be predictable over time. Tests of details are ordinarily more appropriate to obtain audit evidence regarding certain assertions about account balances, including existence and valuation. In some situations, the auditor may determine that performing only substantive analytical procedures may be sufficient to reduce the risk of material misstatement to an acceptably low level. For example, the auditor may determine that performing only substantive analytical procedures is responsive to the assessed risk of material misstatement for a class of transactions where the auditor's assessment of risk is supported by obtaining audit evidence from performance of tests of the operating effectiveness of controls. In other situations, the auditor may determine that only tests of details are appropriate, or that a combination of substantive analytical procedures and tests of details are most responsive to the assessed risks.

54. The auditor designs tests of details responsive to the assessed risk with the objective of obtaining sufficient appropriate audit evidence to achieve the planned level of assurance at the assertion level. In designing substantive procedures related to the existence or occurrence assertion, the auditor selects from items contained in a financial statement amount and obtains the relevant audit evidence. On the other hand, in designing audit procedures related to the completeness assertion, the auditor selects from audit evidence indicating that an item should be included in the relevant financial statement amount and investigates whether that item is so included. For example, the auditor might inspect subsequent cash disbursements to determine whether any purchases had been omitted from accounts payable.

55. In designing substantive analytical procedures, the auditor considers such matters as the following:

- The suitability of using substantive analytical procedures given the assertions.

- The reliability of the data, whether internal or external, from which the expectation of recorded amounts or ratios is developed.

- Whether the expectation is sufficiently precise to identify a material misstatement at the desired level of assurance.

- The amount of any difference in recorded amounts from expected values that is acceptable.

The auditor considers testing the controls, if any, over the entity's preparation of information used by the auditor in applying analytical procedures. When such controls are effective, the auditor has greater confidence in the reliability of the information and, therefore, in the results of analytical procedures. Alternatively, the auditor may consider whether the information was subjected to audit testing in the current or prior period. In determining the audit procedures to apply to the information upon which the expectation for substantive analytical procedures is based, the auditor considers the guidance in paragraph 11 of ISA (UK and Ireland) 500.

Timing of Substantive Procedures

56. **When substantive procedures are performed at an interim date, the auditor should perform further substantive procedures or substantive procedures combined with tests of controls to cover the remaining period that provide a reasonable basis for extending the audit conclusions from the interim date to the period end.**

57. In some circumstances, substantive procedures may be performed at an interim date. This increases the risk that misstatements that may exist at the period end are not detected by the auditor. This risk increases as the remaining period is lengthened. In considering whether to perform substantive procedures at an interim date, the auditor considers such factors as the following:

- The control environment and other relevant controls.

- The availability of information at a later date that is necessary for the auditor's procedures.

- The objective of the substantive procedure.

- The assessed risk of material misstatement.

- The nature of the class of transactions or account balance and related assertions.

- The ability of the auditor to perform appropriate substantive procedures or substantive procedures combined with tests of controls to cover the remaining period in order to reduce the risk that misstatements that exist at period end are not detected.

58. Although the auditor is not required to obtain audit evidence about the operating effectiveness of controls in order to have a reasonable basis for extending audit conclusions from an interim date to the period end, the auditor considers whether

performing only substantive procedures to cover the remaining period is sufficient. If the auditor concludes that substantive procedures alone would not be sufficient, tests of the operating effectiveness of relevant controls are performed or the substantive procedures are performed as of the period end.

59. In circumstances where the auditor has identified risks of material misstatement due to fraud, the auditor's response to address those risks may include changing the timing of audit procedures. For example, the auditor might conclude that, given the risks of intentional misstatement or manipulation, audit procedures to extend audit conclusions from an interim date to the period end would not be effective. In such circumstances, the auditor might conclude that substantive procedures need to be performed at or near the end of the reporting period to address an identified risk of material misstatement due to fraud (see ISA (UK and Ireland) 240).

60. Ordinarily, the auditor compares and reconciles information concerning the balance at the period end with the comparable information at the interim date to identify amounts that appear unusual, investigates any such amounts, and performs substantive analytical procedures or tests of details to test the intervening period. When the auditor plans to perform substantive analytical procedures with respect to the intervening period, the auditor considers whether the period end balances of the particular classes of transactions or account balances are reasonably predictable with respect to amount, relative significance, and composition. The auditor considers whether the entity's procedures for analyzing and adjusting such classes of transactions or account balances at interim dates and for establishing proper accounting cutoffs are appropriate. In addition, the auditor considers whether the information system relevant to financial reporting will provide information concerning the balances at the period end and the transactions in the remaining period that is sufficient to permit investigation of: significant unusual transactions or entries (including those at or near period end); other causes of significant fluctuations, or expected fluctuations that did not occur; and changes in the composition of the classes of transactions or account balances. The substantive procedures related to the remaining period depend on whether the auditor has performed tests of controls.

61. If misstatements are detected in classes of transactions or account balances at an interim date, the auditor ordinarily modifies the related assessment of risk and the planned nature, timing, or extent of the substantive procedures covering the remaining period that relate to such classes of transactions or account balances, or extends or repeats such audit procedures at the period end.

62. The use of audit evidence from the performance of substantive procedures in a prior audit is not sufficient to address a risk of material misstatement in the current period. In most cases, audit evidence from the performance of substantive procedures in a prior audit provides little or no audit evidence for the current period. In order for audit evidence obtained in a prior audit to be used in the current period as substantive audit evidence, the audit evidence and the related subject matter must not fundamentally change. An example of audit evidence obtained from the performance of substantive procedures in a prior period that may be relevant in the current year is a legal opinion related to the structure of a securitization to which no changes have occurred during the current period. As required by paragraph 23 of ISA (UK and Ireland) 500, if the

auditor plans to use audit evidence obtained from the performance of substantive procedures in a prior audit, the auditor performs audit procedures during the current period to establish the continuing relevance of the audit evidence.

Extent of the Performance of Substantive Procedures

63. The greater the risk of material misstatement, the greater the extent of substantive procedures. Because the risk of material misstatement takes account of internal control, the extent of substantive procedures may be increased as a result of unsatisfactory results from tests of the operating effectiveness of controls. However, increasing the extent of an audit procedure is appropriate only if the audit procedure itself is relevant to the specific risk.

64. In designing tests of details, the extent of testing is ordinarily thought of in terms of the sample size, which is affected by the risk of material misstatement. However, the auditor also considers other matters, including whether it is more effective to use other selective means of testing, such as selecting large or unusual items from a population as opposed to performing representative sampling or stratifying the population into homogeneous subpopulations for sampling. ISA (UK and Ireland) 530 contains guidance on the use of sampling and other means of selecting items for testing. In designing substantive analytical procedures, the auditor considers the amount of difference from the expectation that can be accepted without further investigation. This consideration is influenced primarily by materiality and the consistency with the desired level of assurance. Determination of this amount involves considering the possibility that a combination of misstatements in the specific account balance, class of transactions, or disclosure could aggregate to an unacceptable amount. In designing substantive analytical procedures, the auditor increases the desired level of assurance as the risk of material misstatement increases. ISA (UK and Ireland) 520, "Analytical Procedures" contains guidance on the application of analytical procedures during an audit.

Adequacy of Presentation and Disclosure

65. **The auditor should perform audit procedures to evaluate whether the overall presentation of the financial statements, including the related disclosures, are in accordance with the applicable financial reporting framework.** The auditor considers whether the individual financial statements are presented in a manner that reflects the appropriate classification and description of financial information. The presentation of financial statements in conformity with the applicable financial reporting framework also includes adequate disclosure of material matters. These matters relate to the form, arrangement, and content of the financial statements and their appended notes, including, for example, the terminology used, the amount of detail given, the classification of items in the statements, and the bases of amounts set forth. The auditor considers whether management should have disclosed a particular matter in light of the circumstances and facts of which the auditor is aware at the time. In performing the evaluation of the overall presentation of the financial statements, including the related disclosures, the auditor considers the assessed risk of material misstatement at the assertion level. See paragraph 17 of ISA (UK and Ireland) 500 for a description of the assertions related to presentation and disclosure.

Evaluating the Sufficiency and Appropriateness of Audit Evidence Obtained

66. **Based on the audit procedures performed and the audit evidence obtained, the auditor should evaluate whether the assessments of the risks of material misstatement at the assertion level remain appropriate.**

67. An audit of financial statements is a cumulative and iterative process. As the auditor performs planned audit procedures, the audit evidence obtained may cause the auditor to modify the nature, timing, or extent of other planned audit procedures. Information may come to the auditor's attention that differs significantly from the information on which the risk assessment was based. For example, the extent of misstatements that the auditor detects by performing substantive procedures may alter the auditor's judgment about the risk assessments and may indicate a material weakness in internal control. In addition, analytical procedures performed at the overall review stage of the audit may indicate a previously unrecognized risk of material misstatement. In such circumstances, the auditor may need to reevaluate the planned audit procedures, based on the revised consideration of assessed risks for all or some of the classes of transactions, account balances, or disclosures and related assertions. Paragraph 119 of ISA (UK and Ireland) 315 contains further guidance on revising the auditor's risk assessment.

68. The concept of effectiveness of the operation of controls recognizes that some deviations in the way controls are applied by the entity may occur. Deviations from prescribed controls may be caused by such factors as changes in key personnel, significant seasonal fluctuations in volume of transactions and human error. When such deviations are detected during the performance of tests of controls, the auditor makes specific inquiries to understand these matters and their potential consequences, for example, by inquiring about the timing of personnel changes in key internal control functions. The auditor determines whether the tests of controls performed provide an appropriate basis for reliance on the controls, whether additional tests of controls are necessary, or whether the potential risks of misstatement need to be addressed using substantive procedures.

69. The auditor cannot assume that an instance of fraud or error is an isolated occurrence, and therefore considers how the detection of a misstatement affects the assessed risks of material misstatement. Before the conclusion of the audit, the auditor evaluates whether audit risk has been reduced to an acceptably low level and whether the nature, timing, and extent of the audit procedures may need to be reconsidered. For example, the auditor reconsiders the following:

• The nature, timing, and extent of substantive procedures.

• The audit evidence of the operating effectiveness of relevant controls, including the entity's risk assessment process.

70. **The auditor should conclude whether sufficient appropriate audit evidence has been obtained to reduce to an acceptably low level the risk of material misstatement in the financial statements.** In developing an opinion, the auditor

considers all relevant audit evidence, regardless of whether it appears to corroborate or to contradict the assertions in the financial statements.

71. The sufficiency and appropriateness of audit evidence to support the auditor's conclusions throughout the audit are a matter of professional judgment. The auditor's judgment as to what constitutes sufficient appropriate audit evidence is influenced by such factors as the following:

- Significance of the potential misstatement in the assertion and the likelihood of its having a material effect, individually or aggregated with other potential misstatements, on the financial statements.

- Effectiveness of management's responses and controls to address the risks.

- Experience gained during previous audits with respect to similar potential misstatements.

- Results of audit procedures performed, including whether such audit procedures identified specific instances of fraud or error.

- Source and reliability of the available information.

- Persuasiveness of the audit evidence.

- Understanding of the entity and its environment, including its internal control.

72. **If the auditor has not obtained sufficient appropriate audit evidence as to a material financial statement assertion, the auditor should attempt to obtain further audit evidence. If the auditor is unable to obtain sufficient appropriate audit evidence, the auditor should express a qualified opinion or a disclaimer of opinion.** See ISA (UK and Ireland) 700, "The Auditor's Report on Financial Statements" for further guidance.

Documentation

73. **The auditor should document the overall responses to address the assessed risks of material misstatement at the financial statement level and the nature, timing, and extent of the further audit procedures, the linkage of those procedures with the assessed risks at the assertion level, and the results of the audit procedures. In addition, if the auditor plans to use audit evidence about the operating effectiveness of controls obtained in prior audits, the auditor should document the conclusions reached with regard to relying on such controls that were tested in a prior audit.** The manner in which these matters are documented is based on the auditor's professional judgment. ISA (UK and Ireland) 230, "Documentation" establishes standards and provides guidance regarding documentation in the context of the audit of financial statements.

Effective Date

74. This ISA (UK and Ireland) is effective for audits of financial statements for periods commencing on or after 15 December 2004.

Public Sector Perspective

Additional guidance for auditors of public sector bodies in the UK and Ireland is given in:

- Practice Note 10 "Audit of Financial Statements of Public Sector Bodies in the United Kingdom (Revised)"

- Practice Note 10(I) "Audit of Central Government Financial Statements in the Republic of Ireland (Revised)"

1. *When carrying out audits of public sector entities, the auditor takes into account the legislative framework and any other relevant regulations, ordinances or ministerial directives that affect the audit mandate and any other special auditing requirements. Such factors might affect, for example, the extent of the auditor's discretion in establishing materiality and judgments on the nature and scope of audit procedures to be applied. Paragraph 3 of this ISA (UK and Ireland) may have to be applied only after giving consideration to such restrictions.*

Appendix

Conforming Amendments to ISA (UK and Ireland) 330 as a Result of ISA (UK and Ireland) 230 (Revised) – Effective for Audits of Financial Statements for Periods Beginning on or After June 15, 2006

The revision of ISA (UK and Ireland) 230 "Audit Documentation" gave rise to conforming amendments to ISA (UK and Ireland) 330. Once effective the conforming amendments set out below will be incorporated in the body of ISA (UK and Ireland) 330 and this appendix will be deleted.

The following paragraphs in ISA (UK and Ireland) 330 are amended as marked:

50. **The auditor's substantive procedures should include the following audit procedures related to the financial statement closing process:**

    • **Agreeing or reconciling the financial statements with to the underlying accounting records; and**

    • **Examining material journal entries and other adjustments made during the course of preparing the financial statements.**

    The nature and extent of the auditor's examination of journal entries and other adjustments depends on the nature and complexity of the entity's financial reporting process and the associated risks of material misstatement.

73. **The auditor should document the overall responses to address the assessed risks of material misstatement at the financial statement level and the nature, timing, and extent of the further audit procedures, the linkage of those procedures with the assessed risks at the assertion level, and the results of those audit procedures, including the conclusions where these are not otherwise clear. In addition, if the auditor plans to use audit evidence about the operating effectiveness of controls obtained in prior audits, the auditor should document the conclusions reached with regard to relying on such controls that were tested in a prior audit.** The manner in which these matters are documented is based on the auditor's professional judgment. ISA (UK and Ireland) 230, "Documentation" establishes standards and provides guidance regarding documentation in the context of the audit of financial statements.

The following paragraphs are added to ISA (UK and Ireland) 330:

73a. **The auditor's documentation should demonstrate that the financial statements agree or reconcile with the underlying accounting records.**

73b. The manner in which the matters referred to in paragraphs 73 and 73a are documented is based on the auditor's professional judgment. ISA (UK and Ireland) 230 (Revised), "Audit Documentation" establishes standards and provides guidance regarding documentation in the context of the audit of financial statements.

These amendments to ISA (UK and Ireland) 330 are effective for audits of financial statements for periods beginning on or after June 15, 2006.

INTERNATIONAL STANDARD ON AUDITING
(UK AND IRELAND) 402

AUDIT CONSIDERTIONS RELATING TO ENTITIES USING SERVICE ORGANIZATIONS

CONTENTS

International Standard on Auditing (UK and Ireland) (ISA (UK and Ireland)) 402, "Audit Considerations Relating to Entities Using Service Organizations" should be read in the context of the Auditing Practices Board's Statement "The Auditing Practices Board - Scope and Authority of Pronouncements (Revised)" which sets out the application and authority of ISAs (UK and Ireland).

Introduction

1. The purpose of this International Standard on Auditing (UK and Ireland) (ISA (UK and Ireland)) is to establish standards and provide guidance to an auditor where the entity uses a service organization. This ISA (UK and Ireland) also describes the service organization auditor's reports which may be obtained by the entity's auditors.

1-1. This ISA (UK and Ireland) uses the terms 'those charged with governance' and 'management'. The term 'governance' describes the role of persons entrusted with the supervision, control and direction of an entity. Ordinarily, those charged with governance are accountable for ensuring that the entity achieves its objectives, and for the quality of its financial reporting and reporting to interested parties. Those charged with governance include management only when they performs such functions.

1-2. In the UK and Ireland, those charged with governance include the directors (executive and non-executive) of a company or other body, the members of an audit committee where one exists, the partners, proprietors, committee of management or trustees of other forms of entity, or equivalent persons responsible for directing the entity's affairs and preparing its financial statements.

1-3. 'Management' comprises those persons who perform senior managerial functions.

1-4. In the UK and Ireland, depending on the nature and circumstances of the entity, management may include some or all of those charged with governance (e.g. executive directors). Management will not normally include non-executive directors.

2. **The auditor should consider how an entity's use of a service organization affects the entity's internal control so as to identify and assess the risk of material misstatement and to design and perform further audit procedures.**

3. A client may use a service organization such as one that executes transactions and maintains related accountability or records transactions and processes related data (for example, a computer systems service organization). If the entity uses a service organization, certain policies, procedures and records maintained by the service organization may be relevant to the audit of the financial statements of the client.

3-1. Use of a service organisation does not diminish the ultimate responsibility of those charged with governance for conducting its business in a manner which meets their legal responsibilities, including those of safeguarding the entity's assets, maintaining proper accounting records and preparing financial statements which provide information about its economic activities and financial position. Practical issues, including the way in which accounting records will be kept and the manner in which those charged with governance assess the quality of the service, need to be addressed.

Additional Statutory or Regulatory Responsibilities

3-2. An auditor appointed to report on a client's financial statements may have additional reporting responsibilities, which could be affected by the client's use of a service organisation (for example, reporting on compliance with the requirement of company law concerning maintenance of adequate accounting records; or the expression of an opinion on reports by the entity to its regulator).

Definitions

3-3. *Service organisation*: the term 'service organisation' is used in this ISA (UK and Ireland) to refer to any entity that provides services to another. Service organisations undertake a wide variety of activities, including:

- Information processing.

- Maintenance of accounting records.

- Facilities management.

- Maintenance of safe custody of assets, such as investments.

- Initiation or execution of transactions on behalf of the other entity.

Service organisations may undertake activities on a dedicated basis for one entity, or on a shared basis, either for members of a single group of entities or for unrelated customers.

3-4. *Relevant activities*: this term is used to refer to activities undertaken by a service organisation that are relevant to the audit. Relevant activities are those that:

(a) Relate directly to:

    (i) The preparation of the entity's financial statements, including the maintenance of material elements of its accounting records which form the basis for those financial statements; and

    (ii) The reporting of material assets, liabilities and transactions which are required to be included or disclosed in the financial statements (excluding the charge for provision of the service concerned); or

(b) Are subject to law and regulations that are central to the entity's ability to conduct its business.[1]

---

[1] ISA (UK and Ireland) 250, paragraph 18-1.

Understanding the entity and its environment

Service Organization Activities Relevant to the Audit

4. A service organization may establish and execute policies and procedures that affect the entity's internal control. These policies and procedures are physically and operationally separate from the entity. When the services provided by the service organization are limited to recording and processing the entity's transactions and the entity retains authorization and maintenance of accountability, the entity may be able to implement effective policies and procedures within its organization. When the service organization executes the entity's transactions and maintains accountability, the entity may deem it necessary to rely on policies and procedures at the service organization.

5. **In obtaining an understanding of the entity and its environment, the auditor should determine the significance of service organization activities to the entity and the relevance to the audit.** In doing so, the auditor obtains an understanding of the following, as appropriate:

    *   Nature of the services provided by the service organization.

    *   Terms of contract and relationship between the entity and the service organization.

    *   Extent to which the entity's internal control interact with the systems at the service organization.

    *   The entity's internal control relevant to the service organization activities such as:

        o   Those that are applied to the transactions processed by the service organization.

        o   How the entity identifies and manages risks related to use of the service organization.

    *   Service organization's capability and financial strength, including the possible effect of the failure of the service organization on the entity.

    *   Information about the service organization such as that reflected in user and technical manuals.

    *   Information available on controls relevant to the service organization's information systems such as general IT controls and application controls.

5-1. Examples of service organisation activities that are relevant to the audit include:

    *   Maintenance of the entity's accounting records.

- Other finance functions (such as the computation of tax liabilities, or debtor management and credit risk analysis) which involve establishing the carrying value of items in the financial statements.

- Management of assets.

- Undertaking or making arrangements for transactions as agent of the entity.

5-2. Other types of services, for example facilities management, may involve activities which do not fall within the definition of relevant activities.

Understanding the Contractual Terms and Monitoring Arrangements

5-3. **The auditor should obtain and document an understanding of the contractual terms which apply to relevant activities undertaken by the service organization and the way that the entity monitors those activities so as to ensure that it meets its fiduciary and other legal responsibilities.**

5-4. Matters which the auditor may consider include:

- Whether the terms contain an adequate specification of the information to be provided to the entity and responsibilities for initiating transactions relating to the activity undertaken by the service organization.

- The way that accounting records relating to relevant activities are maintained.

- Whether the entity has rights of access to accounting records prepared by the service organisation concerning the activities undertaken, and relevant underlying information held by it, and the conditions in which such access may be sought.

- Whether the terms take proper account of any applicable requirements of regulatory bodies concerning the form of records to be maintained, or access to them.

- The nature of relevant performance standards.

- The way in which the entity monitors performance of relevant activities and the extent to which its monitoring process relies on controls operated by the service organization.

- Whether the service organisation has agreed to indemnify the entity in the event of a performance failure.

- Whether the contractual terms permit the auditor access to sources of audit evidence, including accounting records of the entity and other information necessary for the conduct of the audit.

Considering Access to Sources of Evidence

6. The auditor would also consider the existence of third-party reports from service organization auditors, internal auditors, or regulatory agencies as a means of obtaining information about the internal control of the service organization and about its operation and effectiveness. When the auditor intends to use work of the internal auditor, ISA (UK and Ireland) 610, "Considering the Work of Internal Auditing" provides guidance on evaluating the adequacy of the internal auditor's work for the auditor's purposes.

6a. The understanding obtained may lead the auditor to decide that the control risk assessment of the risk of material misstatement will not be affected by controls at the service organization; if so, further consideration of this ISA (UK and Ireland) is unnecessary.

6-1. Access to information held by the service organisation is not always necessary in order to obtain sufficient appropriate audit evidence: sufficient evidence may, depending on the nature of activities undertaken by the service organisation, be available at the client itself. If the auditor concludes that access to information or records held by the service organisation is necessary for the purposes of the audit, and the contract terms do not provide for such access, the auditor requests those charged with governance to make appropriate arrangements to obtain it.

6-2 The auditor evaluates the efficiency and effectiveness of visiting the service organisation or using evidence provided by the service organisation's auditor, by;

(a) Requesting the service organisation auditor or the entity's internal audit function to perform specified procedures: where information necessary to form an opinion on the entity's financial statements is not available without access to the service organisation's underlying records, its auditor may conclude that the most effective manner to obtain that information is to request the service organisation's auditor or the entity's internal audit function (where the function is established on a suitable basis[2]) to do so. The feasibility of this approach will depend on whether the contractual arrangements with the service organisation entitle the entity to obtain supplementary information when considered necessary;

(b) Reviewing information from the service organisation and its auditor concerning the design and operation of its controls systems: those charged with governance may use such information as part of their arrangements for monitoring the activities undertaken by a service organisation. Where this is the case, those charged with governance of the entity periodically obtain reports from the service organisation, its auditor, or both, confirming that controls have operated as agreed. Such reports may provide information on the operation of controls at the service organisation relevant to the auditor's judgment as to the extent to which controls reduce the necessity to obtain evidence from substantive procedures.

---

[2] The auditor determines whether this is the case by applying the criteria set out in ISA (UK and Ireland) 610 'Considering the work of internal auditing'.

6-3. Where the contractual terms do not provide for access to information held by the service organisation which the auditor considers necessary in order to report on the entity's financial statements, the auditor discusses with the those charged with governance at the entity the way in which such information may be obtained and, unless it is made available, qualify the auditor's opinion on the entity's financial statements. If, following discussions with those charged with governance, the auditor concludes that necessary changes in arrangements agreed between the entity and service organisation will not be made in the future, the auditor considers withdrawing from the engagement.

Indemnities

6-4. Agreement by a service organisation to provide an indemnity does not provide information directly relevant to the auditor's assessment of the risk of material misstatements relating to financial statement assertions. However, such agreements may help to inform the auditor's judgment concerning the effect of performance failure on the entity's financial statements: this may be relevant in instances of performance failure, when the existence of an indemnity may help to ensure that the entity's status as a going concern is not threatened. Where the auditor wishes to rely on the operation of the indemnity for this purpose, the resources available to the service organisation also need to be considered.

Compliance with Law and Regulations

6-5. Additionally, the auditor considers whether the activities undertaken by the service organisation are in an area in which the entity is required to comply with requirements of law and regulations. In such circumstances, non-compliance may have a significant effect on the financial statements. The auditor therefore determines whether the law and regulations concerned are to be regarded as relevant to the audit[3] in order to meet the requirements of ISA (UK and Ireland) 250 "Consideration of laws and regulations in an audit of financial statements" and undertake procedures to assess the risk of a misstatement arising from non-compliance as set out in that ISA (UK and Ireland).

Assessing Risks

7. **If the auditor concludes that the activities of the service organization are significant to the entity and relevant to the audit, the auditor should obtain a sufficient understanding of the entity and its environment, including its internal control, to identify and assess the risks of material misstatement and design further audit procedures in response to the assessed risk.** The auditor assesses the risk of material misstatement at the financial statement level and at the assertion level for classes of transactions, account balances and disclosures.

---

[3] Laws and regulations are relevant to the audit when they either relate directly to the preparation of the financial statements of the entity, or are central to its ability to conduct its business - [ISA (UK and Ireland) 250 – Section A, paragraphs 18-1 and 19]

8. If the understanding obtained is insufficient, the auditor would consider the need to request the service organization to have its auditor perform such risk assessment procedures to supply the necessary information, or the need to visit the service organization to obtain the information. An auditor wishing to visit a service organization may advise the entity to request the service organization to give the auditor access to the necessary information.

9. The auditor may be able to obtain a sufficient understanding of internal control affected by the service organization by reading the third-party report of the service organization auditor. In addition, when assessing the risks of material misstatement, for assertions affected by the service organization's internal controls, the auditor may also use the service organization auditor's report. **If the auditor uses the report of a service organization auditor, the auditor should consider making inquiries concerning that auditor's professional competence in the context of the specific assignment undertaken by the service organization auditor.**

9-1. **The auditor should determine the effect of relevant activities on their assessment of risk and the client's control environment.**

9-2. The auditor assesses risk in relation to financial statement assertions. An entity's decision to commission a service organisation to undertake activities which are relevant to the audit (as defined in paragraph 3-4) affects risk in relation to financial statement assertions about material account balances and classes of transactions arising from those activities. The auditor's assessment of risk will be affected inter alia by:

- *The nature of the services provided*: the complexity of activities undertaken by the service organisation may affect the auditor's assessment of risk. For example, outsourcing the treasury function involves a considerably greater degree of risk than straightforward custody of investments.

- *The degree to which authority is delegated to the service organisations*: the provision of accounting services consisting of maintenance of accounting records limited to recording completed transactions carries a relatively low risk of error compared with accounting services which involve initiating transactions (for example, VAT payments). In some cases, the entity may delegate wide powers of decision-making to the service provider, as is the case where an investment manager is given discretionary powers in relation to an entity's investment portfolio.

- *The arrangements for ensuring quality of the service provided*: such arrangements may vary considerably, depending upon the nature of the service and the degree of delegation involved. In general, the greater degree of delegation, the more likely it is that the entity's management will rely on controls operated by the service organisation over the completeness and integrity of information and records of the entity.

- *Whether the activities involve assets which are susceptible to loss or misappropriation.*

- *The reputation for integrity of those responsible for direction and management of the service organisation*: the extent to which a service organisation has a proven record for ensuring quality both of service and of information may provide indicative factors relating to the likely reliability of information it provides to the entity. The auditor therefore considers the extent and frequency of errors in and adjustments to information provided by the service organisation.

9-3. Some outsourced activities are the subject of regulation, notably investment management. However, the existence of regulation does not eliminate the need for the auditor to obtain independent evidence because controls required by regulators, and inspection work undertaken by them in service organisations, may not be relevant to or sufficiently focussed on aspects of importance to the entity. Furthermore, reports from the service organisation's auditor required by its regulator are not ordinarily available to an entity or its auditor.

9-4. The financial standing of a service organisation is relevant to the audit insofar as the auditor considers it necessary to rely on the operation of an indemnity from the service organisation in assessing the entity's status as a going concern (see paragraph 6-4). However, a service organisation whose cash and/or capital resources are low in relation to the nature of services provided or the volume of its customers may be susceptible to pressures resulting in errors or deliberate misstatements in reporting to the entity, or fraud. If the auditor considers that this factor may be relevant to the assessment of risk, the auditor also takes into account the existence of binding arrangements to provide resources to the service organisations from a holding company or other group company, and the financial strength of the group as a whole.

9-5. The arrangements made by those charged with governance to monitor the way in which activities are undertaken by a service organisation may include a number of factors relevant to the auditor's assessment of risk. These include:

- The extent and nature of controls operated by the entity's personnel.

- Undertakings by the service organisation for the operation of internal controls, and whether such controls are adequately specified, having regard to the size and complexity of the activities undertaken by the service organization.

- Actual experience of adjustments to, or errors and omissions in, reports received from the service organization.

- The way in which the entity determines whether the service organisation complies with its contractual undertakings, in particular the way in which it monitors compliance with applicable law and regulations.

- Whether the service organisation provides information on the design and operation of systems of controls, possibly accompanied by reports from its external auditor.

9-6.　When a service organisation undertakes maintenance of accounting records, factors of particular importance to the auditor's assessment of risk include the following:

- The knowledge and expertise of service organisation staff in matters relevant to the entity's business.

- The practicability of control by the entity's management, and the nature of controls actually implemented. Some types of business facilitate the use of analytical control techniques subsequent to completion of transactions (for example payroll processing); others need detailed processing controls operated on a concurrent basis (for example, distribution centres which hold stock belonging to the entity and arrange deliveries for the entity).

- The use of quality assurance processes by the service organisation (e.g. its internal audit function).

9-7.　Examples of ways in which different activities undertaken by service organisations can affect the risk of misstatement are given in the Appendix to this ISA (UK and Ireland).

Designing Audit Procedures

9-8.　Following the assessment of risk, the auditor determines the nature, timing and extent of tests of control and substantive procedures required to provide sufficient appropriate audit evidence as to whether the financial statements are free of material misstatement.

9-9.　Assessing the sufficiency and appropriateness of audit evidence as a basis for reporting on financial statements requires the auditor to exercise judgment concerning both the quantity of evidence required and its quality. This judgment is affected by the degree of risk of material misstatements in the financial statements, the quality of the entity's accounting and internal control systems and the reliability of information available.

9-10.　The reliability of information for use as audit evidence is determined by a number of factors, including its source. In general terms, evidence supporting an item in an entity's financial statements is more reliable when it is obtained from an independent source; similarly, documentary evidence is normally regarded as more reliable than oral representations.

9-11.　The use of service organisations to undertake particular activities introduces an additional element in the auditor's judgment as to whether evidence can be regarded as coming from an independent source. Whilst the service organisation is a third party, the nature of the activities undertaken or the arrangements for their management may mean that information it provides concerning transactions initiated, processed or recorded on behalf of the entity cannot be regarded as independent for audit purposes. Hence the auditor needs to assess carefully the nature and source of information available in order to establish the most effective way to obtain evidence competent to support an independent opinion on its financial statements.

Accounting Records

9-12. **If a service organisation maintains all or part of an entity's accounting records, the auditor should assess whether the arrangements affect the auditor's reporting responsibilities in relation to accounting records arising from law or regulation.**

9-13. For each relevant activity involving maintenance of material elements of the entity's accounting records by a service organisation, the auditor obtains and documents an understanding as to the way that the accounting records are maintained, including the way in which those charged with governance ensure that its accounting records meet any relevant legal obligations. Such obligations may arise under statute, regulation (for example, specific requirements apply to authorised investment businesses) or under the terms of the entity's governing document (for example, the trust deed establishing a charity may require it to maintain particular records).

9-14. Key obligations of entities incorporated under company law are:

    (a) To maintain accounting records which are sufficient to:

        (i) Disclose with reasonable accuracy, at any time, the financial position of the company at that time, and

        (ii) Enable the directors to ensure that the company's financial statements meet statutory requirements;

    (b) To guard against falsification; and

    (c) To provide its directors, officers and auditor with access to its accounting records at any time[4].

9.15. When an entity incorporated under company law arranges for a service organisation to maintain its accounting records, the contractual arrangements can only be regarded as appropriate if they establish the company's legal ownership of the records and provide for access to them at any time by those charged with governance of the company and by its auditor.

9-16. An auditor of entities incorporated under company law has statutory reporting obligations relating to compliance with requirements for companies to maintain proper accounting records. Where such an entity outsources the preparation of its

---

[4] In the UK, Companies Act 1985, sections 221, 222, 389A and 722 and in Ireland, Companies Act 1963, section 378 and Companies Act 1990, sections 193 and 202.

accounting records to a service organisation, issues relating to whether the arrangements with the service organisation are such as to permit the entity to meet its statutory obligations may require careful consideration, by both those charged with governance and the auditor. Where there is doubt, the auditor may wish to encourage the those charged with governance to take legal advice before issuing their report on its financial statements.

9-17. A particular issue arises in relation to companies incorporated in the United Kingdom. The wording of UK company law appears to be prescriptive and to require the company itself to keep accounting records. Consequently, whether a company 'keeps' records (as opposed to 'causes records to be kept') will depend upon the particular terms of the outsourcing arrangements and, in particular, the extent to which the company retains ownership of, has access to, or holds copies of, those records[5].

Obtaining Audit Evidence.

9-18. **Based on the auditor's understanding of the aspects of the entity's accounting system and control environment relating to relevant activities, the auditor should:**

    (a) **Assess whether sufficient appropriate audit evidence concerning the relevant financial statement assertions is available from records held at the entity; and if not,**

    (b) **Determine effective procedures to obtain evidence necessary for the audit, either by direct access to records kept by service organisations or through information obtained from the service organisations or their auditor.**

9-19. In general, the most cost effective audit approach is likely to be based on information obtained from the entity, together with confirmations from the service organisation, where these provide independent evidence. However, such an approach may not always be feasible, particularly in instances where the service organisation can initiate transactions or payments on the entity's behalf without prior agreement or approval.

9-20. When the service organisation maintains material elements of the accounting records of the entity, the auditor may require direct access to those records in order to obtain sufficient appropriate audit evidence relating to the operation of controls over those records or to substantiate transactions and balances recorded in them, or both. Such access may involve either physical inspection of records at the service organisation's premises or interrogation of records maintained electronically from the entity or another location, or both. Where direct access is achieved electronically, the auditor may also need to consider obtaining evidence as to the adequacy of controls

---

[5] In Ireland, company law requires that companies shall cause records to be kept in accordance with its requirements.

operated by the service organisation over the completeness and integrity of the entity's data for which it is responsible.

9-21. In determining the extent and nature of audit evidence to be obtained in relation to balances representing assets held or transactions undertaken by service organisations undertaking relevant activities, the auditor evaluates the efficiency and effectiveness of the following procedures:

(a) Inspecting records and documents held by the entity: the effectiveness of this source of evidence is determined by the nature and extent of the accounting records and supporting documentation retained by the entity. In some cases the entity may not maintain detailed records or documentation initiating transactions, nor will it receive documentation confirming specific transactions undertaken on its behalf;

(b) Establishing the effectiveness of controls: entities may monitor performance of activities undertaken by a service organisation in a variety of ways. Where a entity has established direct controls over such activities, its auditor may, if the auditor proposes to place reliance on their operation, undertake tests of those controls. Alternatively, the arrangements for monitoring the activity concerned may include obtaining an undertaking from the service organisation that its control systems will provide assurance as to the reliability of financial information;

(c) Obtaining representations to confirm balances and transactions from the service organisation: where the entity maintains independent records of balances and transactions and a service organisation executes transactions only at the specific authorisation of the entity or acts as a simple custodian of assets, confirmation from the service provider corroborating those records usually constitutes reliable audit evidence concerning the existence of the transactions and assets concerned.

If the entity does not maintain independent records, information obtained in representations from the service provider is merely a statement of what is reflected in the records maintained by the service organisation. Hence such representations do not, taken alone, constitute reliable audit evidence. In these circumstances, the auditor considers whether there is a separation of functions for the services provided such that an alternative source of independent evidence can be identified. For example:

• When one service organisation initiates transactions and another independent organisation holds related documents of title or other records (for example an investment manager initiates trades and another entity acts as custodian), the auditor may confirm year end balances with the latter, apply other substantive procedures to transactions reported by the first service organisation and review the reconciliation of differences between the records of the two organizations.

- If one organisation both initiates transactions on behalf of the entity and also holds related documents of title, all the information available to the auditor is based on that organisation's information. In such circumstances, the auditor is unable to obtain reliable audit evidence to corroborate representations from the service organisation unless effective separation of functions exists, for example where there are separate departments to provide the investment management and custodian services, which operate independently and whose records are independently generated and maintained.

(d) Performing analytical review procedures on the records maintained by the entity or on the returns received from the service organisation: the effectiveness of analytical procedures is likely to vary by assertion and will be affected by the extent and detail of information available;

(e) Inspecting records and documents held by the service organisation: the auditor's access to the records of the service organisation is likely to be established as part of the contractual arrangements between the entity and the service organisation.

10. The auditor obtains audit evidence about the operating effectiveness of controls when the auditor's risk assessment includes an expectation of the operating effectiveness of the service organization's controls or when substantive procedures alone do not provide sufficient appropriate audit evidence at the assertion level. The auditor may also conclude that it would be efficient to obtain audit evidence from tests of controls. Audit evidence about the operating effectiveness of controls may be obtained by the following:

- Performing tests of the entity's controls over activities of the service organization.

- Obtaining a service organization auditor's report that expresses an opinion as to the operating effectiveness of the service organization's internal control for the service organization activities relevant to the audit.

- Visiting the service organization and performing tests of controls.

Service Organization Auditor's Reports

11. **When using a service organization auditor's report, the auditor should consider the nature of and content of that report.**

12. The report of the service organization auditor will ordinarily be one of two types as follows:

Type A—Report on the Design and Implementation of Internal Control

(a) A description of the service organization's internal control, ordinarily prepared by the management of the service organization; and

(b) An opinion by the service organization auditor that:

  (i) The above description is accurate;

  (ii) The internal control is suitably designed to achieve their stated objectives; and

  (iii) The internal controls have been implemented.

Type B—Report on the Design, Implementation and Operating Effectiveness of Internal Control

(a) A description of the service organization's internal control, ordinarily prepared by the management of the service organization; and

(b) An opinion by the service organization auditor that:

  (i) The above description is accurate;

  (ii) The internal controls is suitably designed to achieve their stated objectives;

  (iii) The internal controls have been implemented; and

  (iv) The internal controls are operating effectively based on the results from the tests of controls. In addition to the opinion on operating effectiveness, the service organization auditor would identify the tests of controls performed and related results.

The report of the service organization auditor will ordinarily contain restrictions as to use (generally to management, the service organization and its customers, and the entity's auditors).

13. **The auditor should consider the scope of work performed by the service organization auditor and should evaluate the usefulness and appropriateness of reports issued by the service organization auditor.**

13-1. **The auditor should consider whether the report issued by the service organization auditor is sufficient for its intended use.**

13-2. In assessing the relevance of reports from the auditor of the service organisation or from the client's internal audit function regarding the operation of its accounting and internal control systems, the auditor considers whether the report:

(a) Addresses controls and procedures concerning financial statement assertions that are relevant to the auditor's examination;

(b) Provides an adequate level of information concerning relevant aspects of the systems' design, implementation and operation over a specified period, including:

    (i) The way in which the service organization monitors the completeness and integrity of data relating to reports to its customers; and

    (ii) Whether the service organization auditor's testing of operational effectiveness of controls was undertaken in relation to all customers (or all customers of a specified type, that includes the entity) and addressed transactions and balances that could be expected to be representative of the population as a whole; and

(c) Covers the period during which the entity auditor intends to rely on an assessment of control risk at the service organization.

14. While Type A reports may be useful to the auditor in obtaining an understanding of the internal control, an auditor would not use such reports as audit evidence about the operating effectiveness of controls.

15. In contrast, Type B reports may provide such audit evidence since tests of control have been performed. When a Type B report is to be used as audit evidence about operating effectiveness of controls, the auditor would consider whether the controls tested by the service organization auditor are relevant to the entity's transactions, account balances, and disclosures, and related assertions, and whether the service organization auditor's tests of control and the results are adequate. With respect to the latter, two key considerations are the length of the period covered by the service organization auditor's tests and the time since the performance of those tests.

15-1. If the service organization auditor's Type B reports do not fully cover the period during which the auditor intends to rely on internal control at the service organization, the auditor determines whether additional auditing procedures or a change in audit strategy are necessary. In making this determination, the length of the period not covered by the report is considered.

15-2. Additional auditing procedures which may be carried out with respect to a period not covered by such test include:

• Review of stewardship reports or any other correspondence from the service organization to the client relating to the intervening period.

• Consideration of any previous or subsequent reports issued by the service organization's auditor.

• Consideration of the reputation of the service organization as a provider of reliable information (in order to form a judgment about the risk of error in the 'stub period').

- A request for assurance from the service organization, or possibly its auditor, that there were no significant changes in the intervening period to the stated control objectives or control procedures designed to achieve those objectives that are relevant to the auditor.

16. **For those specific tests of control and results that are relevant, the auditor should consider whether the nature, timing and extent of such tests provide sufficient appropriate audit evidence about the operating effectiveness of the internal control to support the auditor's assessed risks of material misstatement.**

17. The auditor of a service organization may be engaged to perform substantive procedures that are of use to the entity's auditor. Such engagements may involve the performance of procedures agreed upon by the entity and its auditor and by the service organization and its auditor.

18. **When the auditor uses a report from the auditor of a service organization, no reference should be made in the entity's auditor's report to the auditor's report on the service organization.**

Reporting

18-1. **If an auditor concludes that evidence from records held by a service organization is necessary in order to form an opinion on the client's financial statements and the auditor is unable to obtain such evidence, the auditor should include a description of the factors leading to the lack of evidence in the basis of opinion section of their report and qualify their opinion or issue a disclaimer of opinion on the financial statements.**

18-2. The auditor is unlikely to be able to obtain sufficient appropriate evidence to express an unqualified opinion if all of the following three conditions exist:

(a) The client does not maintain adequate records of, or controls over, the activities undertaken by the service organisation or cause such records to be maintained independently of the service organisation;

(b) The service organization has not made available a report from its auditor concerning the operation of aspects of its systems of controls which the auditor considers sufficient for the purposes of their audit; and

(c) The auditor is unable to carry out such tests as the auditor considers appropriate at the service organization itself, nor has it been possible for those tests to be undertaken by the service organization's auditor.

In such circumstances, the auditor issues a disclaimer of opinion when the possible effect of the resulting limitation on the scope of their work is so material or pervasive that the auditor is unable to express an opinion. When the effect of the limitation is not so material or pervasive, the auditor indicates that the auditor's opinion is qualified as to the possible adjustments to the financial statements that might have been determined to be necessary had the limitation not existed.

Effective Date

18-3. This ISA (UK and Ireland) is effective for audits of financial statements for periods commencing on or after 15 December 2004.

Appendix

Examples of Factors Relating to Activities Undertaken by Service Organizations Which May Increase the Risk of Material Misstatements

1 Outsourced Accounting Functions

Degree of risk	Characteristics	Examples
High	• Complex transactions • Those undertaking accounting work need extensive business or specialist knowledge • Delegated authority to initiate and execute transactions • Effective controls only possible on 'real time' basis • Reversal of outsourcing costly/ difficult • High cost of performance failure (e.g. misleading management reports leading to poor decision making) • High proportion of finance functions outsourced	• Maintenance of both accounting records and preparation of budgets and control reports • Accounting records of retail business
Medium	• Some business knowledge needed but parameters for necessary judgements can be identified and agreed in advance • Transactions can be initiated but execution requires approval from entity	• Outsourcing of accounting records by a supplier of raw materials • Credit control • Leasing arrangements

Degree of risk	Characteristics	Examples
	• Execution of transactions on instruction from entity • Analytical techniques insufficient for adequate degree of control • Discrete functions outsourced.	
Low	• Little requirement for judgment in processing transactions • Non-complex transactions • Little business knowledge required • Analytical control techniques effective • Effects of failure can be contained. • Easy to rearrange/ find alternate service organisations • Low proportion of discrete functions outsourced	• Processing salary payments • Preparation of invoices • Data entry

2 Outsourced Investment Custody and Management

Degree of risk	Characteristics	Examples
High	• Transactions can be initiated on a discretionary basis • Entity does not maintain and cannot generate independent records of assets and interest, dividends or other income • Complex financial instruments • Custody and investment management undertaken by two separate entities but records are not independently generated, or one combined report is provided to the entity	• Discretionary trading, same custodian
Medium	• Combination of custody and execution of transactions/ collection of income but entity maintains or can generate (for example by reference to Extel) independent records of income • Custody and investment management undertaken by two unrelated entities which maintain independently generated records (i.e. derived from different source data) and report separately direct to the entity	• Custodian responsible for collection of dividends and reporting of income: entity reviews information • Independent custodian and investment manager

Degree of risk	Characteristics	Examples
Low	• Entity initiates and maintains records of transactions • Separation of execution and custody functions • Low frequency of transactions and/or counterparties • Non-complex financial instruments • Analytical control techniques effective	• Custody of assets only • Execution of investment transactions pursuant to entity's instructions

INTERNATIONAL STANDARD ON AUDITING (UK AND IRELAND) 500

AUDIT EVIDENCE

CONTENTS

International Standard on Auditing (UK and Ireland) (ISA (UK and Ireland)) 500 "Audit Evidence" should be read in the context of the Auditing Practices Board's Statement "The Auditing Practices Board - Scope and Authority of Pronouncements (Revised)" which sets out the application and authority of ISAs (UK and Ireland).

Introduction

1.   The purpose of this International Standard on Auditing (UK and Ireland) (ISA (UK and Ireland)) is to establish standards and provide guidance on what constitutes audit evidence in an audit of financial statements, the quantity and quality of audit evidence to be obtained, and the audit procedures that auditors use for obtaining that audit evidence.

1-1. This ISA (UK and Ireland) uses the terms 'those charged with governance' and 'management'. The term 'governance' describes the role of persons entrusted with the supervision, control and direction of an entity. Ordinarily, those charged with governance are accountable for ensuring that the entity achieves its objectives, and for the quality of its financial reporting and reporting to interested parties. Those charged with governance include management only when they perform such functions.

1-2. In the UK and Ireland, those charged with governance include the directors (executive and non-executive) of a company or other body, the members of an audit committee where one exists, the partners, proprietors, committee of management or trustees of other forms of entity, or equivalent persons responsible for directing the entity's affairs and preparing its financial statements.

1-3. 'Management' comprises those persons who perform senior managerial functions.

1-4. In the UK and Ireland, depending on the nature and circumstances of the entity, management may include some or all of those charged with governance (e.g. executive directors). Management will not normally include non-executive directors.

2.   **The auditor should obtain sufficient appropriate audit evidence to be able to draw reasonable conclusions on which to base the audit opinion.**

Concept of Audit Evidence

3.   "Audit evidence" is all the information used by the auditor in arriving at the conclusions on which the audit opinion is based, and includes the information contained in the accounting records underlying the financial statements and other information. Auditors are not expected to address all information that may exist.[1] Audit evidence, which is cumulative in nature, includes audit evidence obtained from audit procedures performed during the course of the audit and may include audit evidence obtained from other sources such as previous audits and a firm's quality control procedures for client acceptance and continuance.

4.   Accounting records generally include the records of initial entries and supporting records, such as checks and records of electronic fund transfers; invoices; contracts; the general and subsidiary ledgers, journal entries and other adjustments to the

---

[1]   See paragraph 14.

financial statements that are not reflected in formal journal entries; and records such as work sheets and spreadsheets supporting cost allocations, computations, reconciliations and disclosures. The entries in the accounting records are often initiated, recorded, processed and reported in electronic form. In addition, the accounting records may be part of integrated systems that share data and support all aspects of the entity's financial reporting, operations and compliance objectives.

5. Management[1a] is responsible for the preparation of the financial statements based upon the accounting records of the entity. The auditor obtains some audit evidence by testing the accounting records, for example, through analysis and review, reperforming procedures followed in the financial reporting process, and reconciling related types and applications of the same information. Through the performance of such audit procedures, the auditor may determine that the accounting records are internally consistent and agree to the financial statements. However, because accounting records alone do not provide sufficient audit evidence on which to base an audit opinion on the financial statements, the auditor obtains other audit evidence.

6. Other information that the auditor may use as audit evidence includes minutes of meetings; confirmations from third parties; analysts' reports; comparable data about competitors (benchmarking); controls manuals; information obtained by the auditor from such audit procedures as inquiry, observation, and inspection; and other information developed by, or available to, the auditor that permits the auditor to reach conclusions through valid reasoning.

Sufficient Appropriate Audit Evidence

7. Sufficiency is the measure of the quantity of audit evidence. Appropriateness is the measure of the quality of audit evidence; that is, its relevance and its reliability in providing support for, or detecting misstatements in, the classes of transactions, account balances, and disclosures and related assertions. The quantity of audit evidence needed is affected by the risk of misstatement (the greater the risk, the more audit evidence is likely to be required) and also by the quality of such audit evidence (the higher the quality, the less may be required). Accordingly, the sufficiency and appropriateness of audit evidence are interrelated. However, merely obtaining more audit evidence may not compensate for its poor quality.

8. A given set of audit procedures may provide audit evidence that is relevant to certain assertions, but not others. For example, inspection of records and documents related to the collection of receivables after the period end may provide audit evidence regarding both existence and valuation, although not necessarily the appropriateness of period-end cutoffs. On the other hand, the auditor often obtains audit evidence from different sources or of a different nature that is relevant to the same assertion. For example, the auditor may analyze the aging of accounts receivable and the subsequent collection of receivables to obtain audit evidence relating to the

---

[1a] In the UK and Ireland, the auditor obtains written representations from those charged with governance.

valuation of the allowance for doubtful accounts. Furthermore, obtaining audit evidence relating to a particular assertion, for example, the physical existence of inventory, is not a substitute for obtaining audit evidence regarding another assertion, for example, the valuation of inventory.

9. The reliability of audit evidence is influenced by its source and by its nature and is dependent on the individual circumstances under which it is obtained. Generalizations about the reliability of various kinds of audit evidence can be made; however, such generalizations are subject to important exceptions. Even when audit evidence is obtained from sources external to the entity, circumstances may exist that could affect the reliability of the information obtained. For example, audit evidence obtained from an independent external source may not be reliable if the source is not knowledgeable. While recognizing that exceptions may exist, the following generalizations about the reliability of audit evidence may be useful:

- Audit evidence is more reliable when it is obtained from independent sources outside the entity.

- Audit evidence that is generated internally is more reliable when the related controls imposed by the entity are effective.

- Audit evidence obtained directly by the auditor (for example, observation of the application of a control) is more reliable than audit evidence obtained indirectly or by inference (for example, inquiry about the application of a control).

- Audit evidence is more reliable when it exists in documentary form, whether paper, electronic, or other medium (for example, a contemporaneously written record of a meeting is more reliable than a subsequent oral representation of the matters discussed).

- Audit evidence provided by original documents is more reliable than audit evidence provided by photocopies or facsimiles.

10. An audit rarely involves the authentication of documentation, nor is the auditor trained as or expected to be an expert in such authentication. However, the auditor considers the reliability of the information to be used as audit evidence, for example, photocopies, facsimiles, filmed, digitized or other electronic documents, including consideration of controls over their preparation and maintenance where relevant.

11. **When information produced by the entity is used by the auditor to perform audit procedures, the auditor should obtain audit evidence about the accuracy and completeness of the information.** In order for the auditor to obtain reliable audit evidence, the information upon which the audit procedures are based needs to be sufficiently complete and accurate. For example, in auditing revenue by applying standard prices to records of sales volume, the auditor considers the accuracy of the price information and the completeness and accuracy of the sales volume data. Obtaining audit evidence about the completeness and accuracy of the information produced by the entity's information system may be performed concurrently with the actual audit procedure applied to the information when obtaining such audit evidence

is an integral part of the audit procedure itself. In other situations, the auditor may have obtained audit evidence of the accuracy and completeness of such information by testing controls over the production and maintenance of the information. However, in some situations the auditor may determine that additional audit procedures are needed. For example, these additional procedures may include using computer-assisted audit techniques (CAATs) to recalculate the information.

12. The auditor ordinarily obtains more assurance from consistent audit evidence obtained from different sources or of a different nature than from items of audit evidence considered individually. In addition, obtaining audit evidence from different sources or of a different nature may indicate that an individual item of audit evidence is not reliable. For example, corroborating information obtained from a source independent of the entity may increase the assurance the auditor obtains from a management[1a] representation. Conversely, when audit evidence obtained from one source is inconsistent with that obtained from another, the auditor determines what additional audit procedures are necessary to resolve the inconsistency.

13. The auditor considers the relationship between the cost of obtaining audit evidence and the usefulness of the information obtained. However, the matter of difficulty or expense involved is not in itself a valid basis for omitting an audit procedure for which there is no alternative.

14. In forming the audit opinion the auditor does not examine all the information available because conclusions ordinarily can be reached by using sampling approaches and other means of selecting items for testing. Also, the auditor ordinarily finds it necessary to rely on audit evidence that is persuasive rather than conclusive; however, to obtain reasonable assurance,[2] the auditor is not satisfied with audit evidence that is less than persuasive. The auditor uses professional judgment and exercises professional skepticism in evaluating the quantity and quality of audit evidence, and thus its sufficiency and appropriateness, to support the audit opinion.

The Use of Assertions in Obtaining Audit Evidence

ISA 315
pwa 19
pg 424

15. Management[3] is responsible for the fair presentation of financial statements that reflect the nature and operations of the entity. In representing that the financial statements give a true and fair view (or are presented fairly, in all material respects) in accordance with the applicable financial reporting framework, management implicitly or explicitly makes assertions regarding the recognition, measurement, presentation and disclosure of the various elements of financial statements and related disclosures.

16. **The auditor should use assertions for classes of transactions, account balances, and presentation and disclosures in sufficient detail to form a basis for the**

---

[2] Paragraphs 8-12 of ISA (UK and Ireland) 200, "Objective and General Principles Governing an Audit of Financial Statements," provide discussion of reasonable assurance as it relates to an audit of financial statements.

[3] In the UK and Ireland, those charged with governance are responsible for the preparation of the financial statements.

assessment of risks of material misstatement and the design and performance of further audit procedures. The auditor uses assertions in assessing risks by considering the different types of potential misstatements that may occur, and thereby designing audit procedures that are responsive to the assessed risks. Other ISAs (UK and Ireland) discuss specific situations where the auditor is required to obtain audit evidence at the assertion level.

17. Assertions used by the auditor fall into the following categories:

(a) Assertions about classes of transactions and events for the period under audit:

(i) Occurrence—transactions and events that have been recorded have occurred and pertain to the entity.

(ii) Completeness—all transactions and events that should have been recorded have been recorded.

(iii) Accuracy—amounts and other data relating to recorded transactions and events have been recorded appropriately.

(iv) Cutoff—transactions and events have been recorded in the correct accounting period.

(v) Classification—transactions and events have been recorded in the proper accounts.

(b) Assertions about account balances at the period end:

(i) Existence—assets, liabilities, and equity interests exist.

(ii) Rights and obligations—the entity holds or controls the rights to assets, and liabilities are the obligations of the entity.

(iii) Completeness—all assets, liabilities and equity interests that should have been recorded have been recorded.

(iv) Valuation and allocation —assets, liabilities, and equity interests are included in the financial statements at appropriate amounts and any resulting valuation or allocation adjustments are appropriately recorded.

(c) Assertions about presentation and disclosure:

(i) Occurrence and rights and obligations—disclosed events, transactions, and other matters have occurred and pertain to the entity.

(ii) Completeness—all disclosures that should have been included in the financial statements have been included.

THE AUDITING PRACTICES BOARD

(iii) Classification and understandability.—financial information is appropriately presented and described, and disclosures are clearly expressed.

(iv) Accuracy and valuation—financial and other information are disclosed fairly and at appropriate amounts.

18. The auditor may use the assertions as described above or may express them differently provided all aspects described above have been covered. For example, the auditor may choose to combine the assertions about transactions and events with the assertions about account balances. As another example, there may not be a separate assertion related to cutoff of transactions and events when the occurrence and completeness assertions include appropriate consideration of recording transactions in the correct accounting period.

Audit Procedures for Obtaining Audit Evidence

19. The auditor obtains audit evidence to draw reasonable conclusions on which to base the audit opinion by performing audit procedures to:

(a) Obtain an understanding of the entity and its environment, including its internal control, to assess the risks of material misstatement at the financial statement and assertion levels (audit procedures performed for this purpose are referred to in the ISAs (UK and Ireland) as "risk assessment procedures");

(b) When necessary or when the auditor has determined to do so, test the operating effectiveness of controls in preventing, or detecting and correcting, material misstatements at the assertion level (audit procedures performed for this purpose are referred to in the ISAs (UK and Ireland) as "tests of controls"); and

(c) Detect material misstatements at the assertion level (audit procedures performed for this purpose are referred to in the ISAs (UK and Ireland) as "substantive procedures" and include tests of details of classes of transactions, account balances, and disclosures and substantive analytical procedures).

20. The auditor always performs risk assessment procedures to provide a satisfactory basis for the assessment of risks at the financial statement and assertion levels. Risk assessment procedures by themselves do not provide sufficient appropriate audit evidence on which to base the audit opinion, however, and are supplemented by further audit procedures in the form of tests of controls, when necessary, and substantive procedures.

21. Tests of controls are necessary in two circumstances. When the auditor's risk assessment includes an expectation of the operating effectiveness of controls, the auditor is required to test those controls to support the risk assessment. In addition, when substantive procedures alone do not provide sufficient appropriate audit evidence, the auditor is required to perform tests of controls to obtain audit evidence about their operating effectiveness.

22. The auditor plans and performs substantive procedures to be responsive to the related assessment of the risks of material misstatement, which includes the results of tests of controls, if any. The auditor's risk assessment is judgmental, however, and may not be sufficiently precise to identify all risks of material misstatement. Further, there are inherent limitations to internal control, including the risk of management override, the possibility of human error and the effect of systems changes. Therefore, substantive procedures for material classes of transactions, account balances, and disclosures are always required to obtain sufficient appropriate audit evidence.

23. The auditor uses one or more types of audit procedures described in paragraphs 26-38 below. These audit procedures, or combinations thereof, may be used as risk assessment procedures, tests of controls or substantive procedures, depending on the context in which they are applied by the auditor. In certain circumstances, audit evidence obtained from previous audits may provide audit evidence where the auditor performs audit procedures to establish its continuing relevance.

24. The nature and timing of the audit procedures to be used may be affected by the fact that some of the accounting data and other information may be available only in electronic form or only at certain points or periods in time. Source documents, such as purchase orders, bills of lading, invoices, and checks, may be replaced with electronic messages. For example, entities may use electronic commerce or image processing systems. In electronic commerce, the entity and its customers or suppliers use connected computers over a public network, such as the Internet, to transact business electronically. Purchase, shipping, billing, cash receipt, and cash disbursement transactions are often consummated entirely by the exchange of electronic messages between the parties. In image processing systems, documents are scanned and converted into electronic images to facilitate storage and reference, and the source documents may not be retained after conversion. Certain electronic information may exist at a certain point in time. However, such information may not be retrievable after a specified period of time if files are changed and if backup files do not exist. An entity's data retention policies may require the auditor to request retention of some information for the auditor's review or to perform audit procedures at a time when the information is available.

25. When the information is in electronic form, the auditor may carry out certain of the audit procedures described below through CAATs.

Inspection of Records or Documents

26. Inspection consists of examining records or documents, whether internal or external, in paper form, electronic form, or other media. Inspection of records and documents provides audit evidence of varying degrees of reliability, depending on their nature and source and, in the case of internal records and documents, on the effectiveness of the controls over their production. An example of inspection used as a test of controls is inspection of records or documents for evidence of authorization.

27. Some documents represent direct audit evidence of the existence of an asset, for example, a document constituting a financial instrument such as a stock or bond. Inspection of such documents may not necessarily provide audit evidence about

ownership or value. In addition, inspecting an executed contract may provide audit evidence relevant to the entity's application of accounting policies, such as revenue recognition.

Inspection of Tangible Assets

28. Inspection of tangible assets consists of physical examination of the assets. Inspection of tangible assets may provide reliable audit evidence with respect to their existence, but not necessarily about the entity's rights and obligations or the valuation of the assets. Inspection of individual inventory items ordinarily accompanies the observation of inventory counting.

Observation

29. Observation consists of looking at a process or procedure being performed by others. Examples include observation of the counting of inventories by the entity's personnel and observation of the performance of control activities. Observation provides audit evidence about the performance of a process or procedure, but is limited to the point in time at which the observation takes place and by the fact that the act of being observed may affect how the process or procedure is performed. See ISA (UK and Ireland) 501, "Audit Evidence—Additional Considerations for Specific Items" for further guidance on observation of the counting of inventory.

Inquiry

30. Inquiry consists of seeking information of knowledgeable persons, both financial and non-financial, throughout the entity or outside the entity. Inquiry is an audit procedure that is used extensively throughout the audit and often is complementary to performing other audit procedures. Inquiries may range from formal written inquiries to informal oral inquiries. Evaluating responses to inquiries is an integral part of the inquiry process.

31. Responses to inquiries may provide the auditor with information not previously possessed or with corroborative audit evidence. Alternatively, responses might provide information that differs significantly from other information that the auditor has obtained, for example, information regarding the possibility of management override of controls. In some cases, responses to inquiries provide a basis for the auditor to modify or perform additional audit procedures.

32. The auditor performs audit procedures in addition to the use of inquiry to obtain sufficient appropriate audit evidence. Inquiry alone ordinarily does not provide sufficient audit evidence to detect a material misstatement at the assertion level. Moreover, inquiry alone is not sufficient to test the operating effectiveness of controls.

33. Although corroboration of evidence obtained through inquiry is often of particular importance, in the case of inquiries about management intent, the information available to support management's intent may be limited. In these cases, understanding management's past history of carrying out its stated intentions with respect to assets or liabilities, management's stated reasons for choosing a particular

course of action, and management's ability to pursue a specific course of action may provide relevant information about management's intent.

34. In respect of some matters, the auditor obtains written representations from management[1a] to confirm responses to oral inquiries. For example, the auditor ordinarily obtains written representations from management[1a] on material matters when other sufficient appropriate audit evidence cannot reasonably be expected to exist or when the other audit evidence obtained is of a lower quality. See ISA (UK and Ireland) 580, "Management Representations" for further guidance on written representations.

Confirmation

35. Confirmation, which is a specific type of inquiry, is the process of obtaining a representation of information or of an existing condition directly from a third party. For example, the auditor may seek direct confirmation of receivables by communication with debtors. Confirmations are frequently used in relation to account balances and their components, but need not be restricted to these items. For example, the auditor may request confirmation of the terms of agreements or transactions an entity has with third parties; the confirmation request is designed to ask if any modifications have been made to the agreement and, if so, what the relevant details are. Confirmations also are used to obtain audit evidence about the absence of certain conditions, for example, the absence of a "side agreement" that may influence revenue recognition. See ISA (UK and Ireland) 505, "External Confirmations" for further guidance on confirmations.

Recalculation

36. Recalculation consists of checking the mathematical accuracy of documents or records. Recalculation can be performed through the use of information technology, for example, by obtaining an electronic file from the entity and using CAATs to check the accuracy of the summarization of the file.

Reperformance

37. Reperformance is the auditor's independent execution of procedures or controls that were originally performed as part of the entity's internal control, either manually or through the use of CAATs, for example, reperforming the aging of accounts receivable.

Analytical Procedures

38. Analytical procedures consist of evaluations of financial information made by a study of plausible relationships among both financial and non-financial data. Analytical procedures also encompass the investigation of identified fluctuations and relationships that are inconsistent with other relevant information or deviate significantly from predicted amounts. See ISA (UK and Ireland) 520, "Analytical Procedures," for further guidance on analytical procedures.

Effective Date

39. This ISA (UK and Ireland) is effective for audits of financial statements for periods commencing on or after 15 December 2004.

Public Sector Perspective

Additional guidance for auditors of public sector bodies in the UK and Ireland is given in:

- Practice Note 10 "Audit of Financial Statements of Public Sector Bodies in the United Kingdom (Revised)"

- Practice Note 10(I) "Audit of Central Government Financial Statements in the Republic of Ireland (Revised)"

1. *When carrying out audits of public sector entities, the auditor takes into account the legislative framework and any other relevant regulations, ordinances or ministerial directives that affect the audit mandate and any other special auditing requirements. In making assertions about the financial statements, management asserts that transactions and events have been in accordance with legislation or proper authority in addition to the assertions in paragraph 15 of this ISA (UK and Ireland).*

**THE AUDITING
PRACTICES BOARD**

INTERNATIONAL STANDARD ON AUDITING
(UK AND IRELAND) 501

AUDIT EVIDENCE – ADDITIONAL CONSIDERATIONS
FOR SPECIFIC ITEMS

CONTENTS

International Standard on Auditing (UK and Ireland) (ISA (UK and Ireland)) 501, "Audit Evidence—Additional Considerations for Specific Items" should be read in the context of the Auditing Practices Board's Statement "The Auditing Practices Board – Scope and Authority of Pronouncements (Revised)" which sets out the application and authority of ISAs (UK and Ireland).

Introduction

1. The purpose of this International Standard on Auditing (UK and Ireland) (ISA (UK and Ireland)) is to establish standards and provide guidance additional to that contained in ISA (UK and Ireland) 500, "Audit Evidence" with respect to certain specific financial statement account balances and other disclosures.

1-1. This ISA (UK and Ireland) uses the terms 'those charged with governance' and 'management'. The term 'governance' describes the role of persons entrusted with the supervision, control and direction of an entity. Ordinarily, those charged with governance are accountable for ensuring that the entity achieves its objectives, and for the quality of its financial reporting and reporting to interested parties. Those charged with governance include management only when they perform such functions.

1-2. In the UK and Ireland, those charged with governance include the directors (executive and non-executive) of a company or other body, the members of an audit committee where one exists, the partners, proprietors, committee of management or trustees of other forms of entity, or equivalent persons responsible for directing the entity's affairs and preparing its financial statements.

1-3. 'Management' comprises those persons who perform senior managerial functions.

1-4. In the UK and Ireland, depending on the nature and circumstances of the entity, management may include some or all of those charged with governance (e.g. executive directors). Management will not normally include non-executive directors.

2. Application of the standards and guidance provided in this ISA (UK and Ireland) will assist the auditor in obtaining audit evidence with respect to the specific financial statement account balances and other disclosures addressed.

3. This ISA (UK and Ireland) comprises the following parts:

   (a) Attendance at Physical Inventory Counting

   (b) Superceded by ISA (UK and Ireland) 505—Part B has been deleted.

   (c) Inquiry Regarding Litigation and Claims

   (d) Valuation and Disclosure of Long-term Investments

   (e) Segment Information

Part A: Attendance at Physical Inventory Counting

4.   Management[1] ordinarily establishes procedures under which inventory is physically counted at least once a year to serve as a basis for the preparation of the financial statements or to ascertain the reliability of the perpetual inventory system.

4-1. In accordance with ISA (UK and Ireland) 315, "Understanding the Entity and its Environment and Assessing the Risks of Material misstatement" the auditor uses professional judgment to assess the risks of material misstatement. Risk factors relating to the existence assertion in the context of the audit of inventory include the:

- Reliability of accounting and inventory recording systems including, in relation to work in progress, the systems that track location, quantities and stages of completion.

- Timing of physical inventory counts relative to the year-end date, and the reliability of records used in any 'roll-forward' of balances.

- Location of inventory, including inventory on 'consignment' and inventory held at third-party warehouses.

- Physical controls over the inventory, and its susceptibility to theft or deterioration.

- Objectivity, experience and reliability of the inventory counters and of those monitoring their work.

- The degree of fluctuation in inventory levels.

- Nature of the inventory, for example whether specialist knowledge is needed to identify the quantity, quality and/or identity of inventory items.

- Difficulty in carrying out the assessment of quantity, for example whether a significant degree of estimation is involved.

4-2. When planning the audit, the auditor also assesses the risk of material misstatements due to fraud. Based on this risk assessment, the auditor designs audit procedures so as to have a reasonable expectation of detecting material misstatements arising from fraud. Fraudulent activities which can occur in relation to inventory include:

- 'False sales' involving the movement of inventory still owned by the entity to a location not normally used for storing inventory.

- Movement of inventory between entity sites with physical inventory counts at different dates.

---

[1] In the UK and Ireland, those charged with governance are responsible for the preparation and presentation of the financial statements.

- The appearance of inventory and work in progress being misrepresented so that they seem to be of a higher value/greater quantity.

- The application of inappropriate estimating techniques.

- Inventory count records prepared during physical inventory counts deliberately being incorrectly completed or altered after the event.

- Additional (false) inventory count records being added to those prepared during the count.

5. **When inventory is material to the financial statements, the auditor should obtain sufficient appropriate audit evidence regarding its existence and condition by attendance at physical inventory counting unless impracticable.** The auditor's attendance serves as a test of controls or substantive procedure over inventory depending on the auditor's risk assessment and planned approach. Such attendance enables the auditor to inspect the inventory, to observe compliance with the operation of management's procedures for recording and controlling the results of the count and to provide audit evidence as to the reliability of management's procedures.

5-1. The principal sources of evidence relating to the existence of inventory are:

(a) Evidence from audit procedures which confirm the reliability of the accounting records upon which the amount in the financial statements is based;

(b) Evidence from tests of the operation of internal controls over inventory, including the reliability of inventory counting procedures applied by the entity; and

(c) Substantive evidence from the physical inspection tests undertaken by the auditor.

6. **If unable to attend the physical inventory count on the date planned due to unforeseen circumstances, the auditor should take or observe some physical counts on an alternative date and, when necessary, perform audit procedures on intervening transactions.**

7. **Where attendance is impracticable, due to factors such as the nature and location of the inventory, the auditor should consider whether alternative procedures provide sufficient appropriate audit evidence of existence and condition to conclude that the auditor need not make reference to a scope limitation.** For example, documentation of the subsequent sale of specific inventory items acquired or purchased prior to the physical inventory count may provide sufficient appropriate audit evidence.

8. In planning attendance at the physical inventory count or the alternative procedures, the auditor considers the following:

- The risks of material misstatement related to inventory.

- The nature of the internal control related to inventory.

- Whether adequate procedures are expected to be established and proper instructions issued for physical inventory counting.

- The timing of the count.

- The locations at which inventory is held.

- Whether an expert's assistance is needed.

8-1. The effectiveness of the auditor's attendance at a physical inventory count is increased by the use of audit staff who are familiar with the entity's business and where advance planning has been undertaken. Planning procedures include:

- Performing analytical procedures, and discussing with management any significant changes in inventory over the year and any problems with inventory that have recently occurred, for example unexpected 'stock-out' reports and negative inventory balances.

- Discussing inventory counting arrangements and instructions with management.

- Familiarisation with the nature and volume of the inventory, the identification of high value items, the method of accounting for inventory and the conditions giving rise to obsolescence.

- Assessing the implications of the locations at which inventory is held for inventory control and recording.

- Considering the quantity and nature of work in progress, the quantity of inventory held by third parties, and whether expert valuers or inventory counters will be engaged (further guidance on these issues is set out in paragraphs 8-2 and 8-3 below).

- Reviewing internal control relating to inventory, so as to identify potential areas of difficulty (for example cut-off).

- Considering any internal audit involvement, with a view to deciding the reliance which can be placed on it.

- Considering the results of previous physical inventory counts made by the entity.

- Reviewing the auditor's working papers for the previous year.

8-2. Prior to attending a physical inventory count, the auditor establishes whether expert help, such as that provided by a quantity surveyor, needs to be obtained by management to substantiate quantities, or to identify the nature and condition of the inventories, where they are very specialised. In cases where the entity engages a third party expert the auditor assesses, in accordance with ISA (UK and Ireland) 620 "Using the Work of an Expert", the objectivity and professional qualifications, experience and resources of the expert engaged to carry out this work, and also the instructions given to the expert.

8-3. Management may from time to time appoint inventory counters from outside the entity, a practice common for inventory at, for example, farms, petrol stations and public houses. The use of independent inventory counters does not eliminate the need for the auditor to obtain audit evidence as to the existence of inventory. In addition, as well as obtaining satisfaction as to the competence and objectivity of the independent inventory counters, the auditor considers how to obtain evidence as to the procedures followed by them to ensure that the inventory count records have been properly prepared. In this connection, the auditor has regard to the relevant guidance set out in ISA (UK and Ireland) 402, "Auditor's Considerations Relating to Entities Using Service Organizations".

9.   When the quantities are to be determined by a physical inventory count and the auditor attends such a count, or when the entity operates a perpetual system and the auditor attends a count one or more times during the year, the auditor would ordinarily observe count procedures and perform test counts.

9-1. The nature of the auditor's procedures during their attendance at a physical inventory count will depend upon the results of the assessment of risks of material misstatements carried out in accordance with ISA (UK and Ireland) 315. In cases where the auditor decides to place reliance on accounting systems and internal controls, the auditor attends a physical inventory count primarily to obtain evidence regarding the design and operating effectiveness of management procedures for confirming inventory quantities.

9-2. Where entities maintain detailed inventory records and check these by regular test counts the auditor performs audit procedures designed to confirm whether management:

(a)   Maintains adequate inventory records that are kept up-to-date;

(b)   Has satisfactory procedures for inventory counting and test-counting; and

(c)   Investigates and corrects all material differences between the book inventory records and the physical counts.

The auditor attends a physical inventory count to gain assurance that the inventory checking as a whole is effective in confirming that accurate inventory records are maintained. If the entity's inventory records are not reliable the auditor may need to request management to perform alternative procedures which may include a full count at the year end.

9-3. In entities that do not maintain detailed inventory records the quantification of inventory for financial statement purposes is likely to be based on a full physical count of all inventory held at a date close to the company's year end. In such circumstances the auditor will consider the date of the physical inventory count recognising that the evidence of the existence of inventory provided by the inventory count is greater when the inventory count is carried out at the end of the financial year. Physical inventory counts carried out before or after the year end may also be acceptable for audit purposes provided the auditor is satisfied that the records of inventory movements in the intervening period are reliable.

10. If the entity uses procedures to estimate the physical quantity, such as estimating a coal pile, the auditor would need to be satisfied regarding the reasonableness of those procedures.

11. When inventory is situated in several locations, the auditor would consider at which locations attendance is appropriate, taking into account the materiality of the inventory and the risk of material misstatement at different locations.

12. The auditor would review management's instructions regarding:

   (a) The application of control activities, for example, collection of used stocksheets, accounting for unused stocksheets and count and re-count procedures;

   (b) Accurate identification of the stage of completion of work in progress, of slow moving, obsolete or damaged items and of inventory owned by a third party, for example, on consignment; and

   (c) Whether appropriate arrangements are made regarding the movement of inventory between areas and the shipping and receipt of inventory before and after the cutoff date.

12-1. The auditor examines the way the physical inventory count is organised and evaluates the adequacy of the client's instructions for the physical inventory count. Such instructions, preferably in writing, should cover all phases of the inventory counting procedures, be issued in good time and be discussed with the person responsible for the physical inventory count to check that the procedures are understood and that potential difficulties are anticipated. If the instructions are found to be inadequate, the auditor seeks improvements to them.

13. To obtain audit evidence that management's control activities are adequately implemented, the auditor would observe employees' procedures and perform test counts. When performing test counts, the auditor performs procedures over both the completeness and the accuracy of the count records by tracing items selected from those records to the physical inventory and items selected from the physical inventory to the count records. The auditor considers the extent to which copies of such count records need to be retained for subsequent audit procedures and comparison.

13-1. If the manner of carrying out the inventory count or the results of the test-counts are not satisfactory, the auditor immediately draws the matter to the attention of the management supervising the inventory count and may have to request a recount of part, or all of the inventory.

13-2. When carrying out test counts, the auditor gives particular consideration to those inventory items which the auditor believes to have a high value either individually or as a category of inventory. The auditor includes in the audit working papers items for any subsequent testing considered necessary, such as copies of (or extracts from) inventory count records and details of the sequence of those records, and any differences noted between the records and the physical inventory counted.

13-3 The auditor determines whether the procedures for identifying damaged, obsolete and slow moving stock operate properly. The auditor obtains (from observation and by discussion e.g. with storekeepers and inventory counters) information about the inventory condition, age, usage and, in the case of work in progress, its stage of completion. Further, the auditor ascertains that stock held on behalf of third parties is separately identified and accounted for.

14. The auditor also considers cutoff procedures including details of the movement of inventory just prior to, during and after the count so that the accounting for such movements can be checked at a later date.

14-1. The auditor considers whether management has instituted adequate cut-off procedures, i.e. procedures intended to ensure that movements into, within and out of inventory are properly identified and reflected in the accounting records in the correct period. The auditor's procedures during the inventory count will depend on the manner in which the year end inventory value is to be determined. For example, where inventory is determined by a full count and evaluation at the year end, the auditor tests the arrangements made to identify inventory that corresponds to sales made before the cut-off point and the auditor identifies goods movement documents for reconciliation with financial records of purchases and sales. Alternatively, where the full count and evaluation is at an interim date and year end inventory is determined by updating such valuation by the cost of purchases and sales, the auditor performs appropriate procedures during attendance at the physical inventory count and in addition tests the financial cut-off (involving the matching of costs with revenues) at the year end.

15. For practical reasons, the physical inventory count may be conducted at a date other than period end. This will ordinarily be adequate for audit purposes only when the entity has designed and implemented controls over changes in inventory. The auditor would determine whether, through the performance of appropriate audit procedures, changes in inventory between the count date and period end are correctly recorded.

16. When the entity operates a perpetual inventory system which is used to determine the period end balance, the auditor would evaluate whether, through the performance of additional procedures, the reasons for any significant differences

between the physical count and the perpetual inventory records are understood and the records are properly adjusted.

17. The auditor performs audit procedures over the final inventory listing to determine whether it accurately reflects actual inventory counts.

18. When inventory is under the custody and control of a third party, the auditor would ordinarily obtain direct confirmation from the third party as to the quantities and condition of inventory held on behalf of the entity. Depending on materiality of this inventory the auditor would also consider the following:

- The integrity and independence of the third party.

- Observing, or arranging for another auditor to observe, the physical inventory count.

- Obtaining another auditor's report on the adequacy of the third party's internal control for ensuring that inventory is correctly counted and adequately safeguarded.

- Inspecting documentation regarding inventory held by third parties, for example, warehouse receipts, or obtaining confirmation from other parties when such inventory has been pledged as collateral.

- Testing the owner's procedures for investigating the custodian and evaluating the custodian's performance.

- The guidance set out in ISA (UK and Ireland) 402.

18-1. The auditor's working papers include details of the auditor's observations and tests (for example, of physical quantity, cut-off date and controls over inventory count records), the manner in which points that are relevant and material to the inventory being counted or measured have been dealt with by the entity, instances where the entity's procedures have not been satisfactorily carried out and the auditor's conclusions.

18-2. Although the principal reason for attendance at a physical inventory count is usually to obtain evidence to substantiate the existence of the inventory, attendance can also enhance the auditor's understanding of the business by providing an opportunity to observe the production process and/or business locations at first hand and providing evidence regarding the completeness and valuation of inventory and the entity's internal control. Matters that the auditor may wish to observe whilst attending a physical inventory count include:

Understanding the business

- The production process.

- Evidence of significant pollution and environmental damage.

- Unused buildings and machinery.

Completeness and valuation of inventory

- Physical controls.

- Obsolete inventory (for example goods beyond their sale date).

- Scrap, and goods marked for re-awork.

- Returned goods.

Internal control

- Exceptions identified by the production process (for example missing work tickets).

- The operation of 'shop-floor' disciplines regarding the inputting of data such as inventory movements into the computer systems.

18-3. Some entities use computer-assisted techniques to perform inventory counts; for example hand held scanners can be used to record inventory items which update computerised records. In some situations there are no stock-sheets, no physical count records, and no paper records available at the time of the count. In these circumstances the auditor considers the IT environment surrounding the inventory count and considers the need for specialist assistance when evaluating the techniques used and the controls surrounding them. Relevant issues involve systems interfaces, and the controls over ensuring that the computerised inventory records are properly updated for the inventory count information.

The auditor considers the following aspects of the physical inventory count:

(a) How the test counts (and double counts where two people are checking) are recorded;

(b) How differences are investigated before the computerised inventory records are updated for the counts; and

(c) How the computerised inventory records are updated, and how inventory differences are recorded.

After the Physical Inventory Count

18-4. After the physical inventory count, the matters recorded in the auditor's working papers at the time of the count or measurement, including apparent instances of obsolete or deteriorating inventory, are followed up. For example, details of the last serial numbers of goods inwards and outwards records and of movements during the inventory count may be used in order to check cut-off. Further, copies of (or extracts from) the inventory count records and details of test counts, and of the sequence of inventory count records may be used to check that the results of the count have been properly reflected in the accounting records of the entity.

18-5. Where appropriate, the auditor considers whether management has instituted procedures to ensure that all inventory movements between the observed inventory count and the period end have been adjusted in the accounting records, and the auditor tests these procedures to the extent considered necessary to address the assessed risk of material misstatement. In addition, the auditor follows up all queries and notifies senior management of serious problems encountered during the physical inventory count.

18-6. In conclusion, the auditor considers whether attendance at the physical inventory count has provided sufficient reliable audit evidence in relation to relevant assertions (principally existence) and, if not, the other procedures that should be performed.

Work in Progress

18-7. Management may place substantial reliance on internal controls designed to ensure the completeness and accuracy of records of work in progress. In such circumstances there may not be a physical inventory count which can be attended by the auditor. Nevertheless, inspection of the work in progress may assist the auditor in understanding the entity's control systems and processes. It will also assist the auditor in planning further audit procedures, and it may also help on such matters as the determination of the stage of completion of construction or engineering work in progress. For this purpose, the auditor identifies the accounting records that will be used by management to produce the work in progress figure in the year-end accounts and, where unfinished items are uniquely identifiable (for example by reference to work tickets or labels), the auditor physically examine items to obtain evidence that supports the recorded stage of completion. In some cases, for example in connection with building projects, photographic evidence can also be useful evidence as to the state of work in progress at the date of the physical inventory count, particularly if provided by independent third parties or the auditor.

Part B: Superceded by ISA (UK and Ireland) 505 (paragraphs 19-30 have been deleted.)

Part C: Procedures Regarding Litigation and Claims

31. Litigation and claims involving an entity may have a material effect on the financial statements and thus may be required to be disclosed and/or provided for in the financial statements.

32. **The auditor should carry out audit procedures in order to become aware of any litigation and claims involving the entity which may result in a material misstatement of the financial statements.** Such procedures would include the following:

- Make appropriate inquiries of management[2] including obtaining representations.

- Review minutes of those charged with governance and correspondence with the entity's legal counsel.

- Examine legal expense accounts.

- Use any information obtained regarding the entity's business including information obtained from discussions with any in-house legal department.

33. **When the auditor assesses a risk of material misstatement regarding litigation or claims that have been identified or when the auditor believes they may exist, the auditor should seek direct communication with the entity's legal counsel.** Such communication will assist in obtaining sufficient appropriate audit evidence as to whether potentially material litigation and claims are known and management's[1] estimates of the financial implications, including costs, are reliable. When the auditor determines that the risk of material misstatement is a significant risk, the auditor evaluates the design of the entity's related controls and determines whether they have been implemented. Paragraphs 108-114 of ISA (UK and Ireland) 315, "Understanding the Entity and Assessing the Risks of Material Misstatement" provides further guidance on the determination of significant risks.

34. **The letter, which should be prepared by management[3] and sent by the auditor, should request the entity's legal counsel to communicate directly with the auditor.** When it is considered unlikely that the entity's legal counsel will respond to a general inquiry[4], the letter would ordinarily specify the following:

- A list of litigation and claims.

- Management's[1] assessment of the outcome of the litigation or claim and its estimate of the financial implications, including costs involved.

- A request that the entity's legal counsel confirm the reasonableness of management's assessments and provide the auditor with further information if the list is considered by the entity's legal counsel to be incomplete or incorrect.

35. The auditor considers the status of legal matters up to the date of the audit report. In some instances, the auditor may need to obtain updated information from entity's legal counsel.

36. In certain circumstances, for example, where the auditor determines that the matter is a significant risk, the matter is complex or there is disagreement between management and the entity's legal counsel, it may be necessary for the auditor to meet with the entity's legal counsel to discuss the likely outcome of litigation and

---

[2] In the UK and Ireland the auditor makes appropriate enquiries of those charged with governance.
[3] In the UK and Ireland the letter should be prepared by those charged with governance.
[4] In the UK, the Council of the Law Society has advised solicitors that it is unable to recommend them to comply with non-specific requests for information.

claims. Such meetings would take place with management's[5] permission and, preferably, with a representative of management in attendance.

37. **If management[4] refuses to give the auditor permission to communicate with the entity's legal counsel, this would be a scope limitation and should ordinarily lead to a qualified opinion or a disclaimer of opinion.** Where the entity's legal counsel refuses to respond in an appropriate manner and the auditor is unable to obtain sufficient appropriate audit evidence by applying alternative audit procedures, the auditor would consider whether there is a scope limitation which may lead to a qualified opinion or a disclaimer of opinion.

Part D: Valuation and Disclosure of Long-term Investments

38. **When long-term investments are material to the financial statements, the auditor should obtain sufficient appropriate audit evidence regarding their valuation and disclosure.**

39. Audit procedures regarding long-term investments ordinarily include obtaining audit evidence as to whether the entity has the ability to continue to hold the investments on a long term basis and discussing with management whether the entity will continue to hold the investments as long-term investments and obtaining written representations to that effect.

40. Other audit procedures would ordinarily include considering related financial statements and other information, such as market quotations, which provide an indication of value and comparing such values to the carrying amount of the investments up to the date of the auditor's report.

41. If such values do not exceed the carrying amounts, the auditor would consider whether a write-down is required. If there is an uncertainty as to whether the carrying amount will be recovered, the auditor would consider whether appropriate adjustments and/or disclosures have been made.

Part E: Segment Information

42. **When segment information is material to the financial statements, the auditor should obtain sufficient appropriate audit evidence regarding its presentation and disclosure in accordance with the applicable financial reporting framework.**

43. The auditor considers segment information in relation to the financial statements taken as a whole, and is not ordinarily required to apply audit procedures that would be necessary to express an opinion on the segment information standing alone. However, the concept of materiality encompasses both quantitative and qualitative factors and the auditor's procedures recognize this.

---

[5] In the UK and Ireland the auditor seeks the permission of those charged with governance.

44. Audit procedures regarding segment information ordinarily consist of analytical procedures and other audit procedures as appropriate in the circumstances.

45. The auditor would discuss with management[1] the methods used in determining segment information, and consider whether such methods are likely to result in disclosure in accordance with the applicable financial reporting framework and perform audit procedures over the application of such methods. The auditor would consider sales, transfers and charges between segments, elimination of inter-segment amounts, comparisons with budgets and other expected results, for example, operating profits as a percentage of sales, and the allocation of assets and costs among segments including consistency with prior periods and the adequacy of the disclosures with respect to inconsistencies.

Effective Date

45-1. This ISA (UK and Ireland) is effective for audits of financial statements for periods commencing on or after 15 December 2004.

INTERNATIONAL STANDARD ON AUDITING (UK AND IRELAND) 505

EXTERNAL CONFIRMATIONS

CONTENTS

International Standard on Auditing (UK and Ireland) (ISA (UK and Ireland)) 505 "External Confirmations" should be read in the context of the Auditing Practices Board's Statement "The Auditing Practices Board - Scope and Authority of Pronouncements (Revised)" which sets out the application and authority of ISAs (UK and Ireland).

Introduction

1. The purpose of this International Standard on Auditing (UK and Ireland) (ISA (UK and Ireland)) is to establish standards and provide guidance on the auditor's use of external confirmations as a means of obtaining audit evidence.

1-1. This ISA (UK and Ireland) uses the terms 'those charged with governance' and 'management'. The term 'governance' describes the role of persons entrusted with the supervision, control and direction of an entity. Ordinarily, those charged with governance are accountable for ensuring that the entity achieves its objectives, and for the quality of its financial reporting and reporting to interested parties. Those charged with governance include management only when they perform such functions.

1-2. In the UK and Ireland, those charged with governance include the directors (executive and non-executive) of a company or other body, the members of an audit committee where one exists, the partners, proprietors, committee of management or trustees of other forms of entity, or equivalent persons responsible for directing the entity's affairs and preparing its financial statements.

1-3. 'Management' comprises those persons who perform senior managerial functions.

1-4. In the UK and Ireland, depending on the nature and circumstances of the entity, management may include some or all of those charged with governance (e.g. executive directors). Management will not normally include non-executive directors.

2. **The auditor should determine whether the use of external confirmations is necessary to obtain sufficient appropriate audit evidence at the assertion level. In making this determination, the auditor should consider the assessed risk of material misstatement at the assertion level and how the audit evidence from other planned audit procedures will reduce the risk of material misstatement at the assertion level to an acceptably low level.**

3. ISA (UK and Ireland) 500, "Audit Evidence" states that the reliability of audit evidence is influenced by its source and by its nature, and is dependent on the individual circumstances under which it is obtained. It indicates that, while recognizing exceptions may exist, the following generalization about the reliability of audit evidence may be useful:

    *   Audit evidence is more reliable when it is obtained from independent sources outside the entity.

    *   Audit evidence obtained directly by the auditor is more reliable than audit evidence obtained indirectly or by inference.

    *   Audit evidence is more reliable when it exists in documentary form.

    *   Audit evidence provided by original documents is more reliable than audit evidence provided by photocopies or facsimiles.

Accordingly, audit evidence in the form of original written responses to confirmation requests received directly by the auditor from third parties who are not related to the entity being audited, when considered individually or cumulatively with audit evidence from other audit procedures, may assist in reducing the risk of material misstatement for the related assertions to an acceptably low level.

4. External confirmation is the process of obtaining and evaluating audit evidence through a representation of information or an existing condition directly from a third party in response to a request for information about a particular item affecting assertions in the financial statements or related disclosures. In deciding to what extent to use external confirmations the auditor considers the characteristics of the environment in which the entity being audited operates and the practice of potential respondents in dealing with requests for direct confirmation.

5. External confirmations are frequently used in relation to account balances and their components, but need not be restricted to these items. For example, the auditor may request external confirmation of the terms of agreements or transactions an entity has with third parties. The confirmation request is designed to ask if any modifications have been made to the agreement, and if so what the relevant details are. External confirmations may also be used to obtain audit evidence about the absence of certain conditions, for example, the absence of a "side agreement" that may influence revenue recognition. Other examples of situations where external confirmations may be used include the following:

    • Bank balances and other information from bankers.

    • Accounts receivable balances.

    • Stocks held by third parties at bonded warehouses for processing or on consignment.

    • Property title deeds held by lawyers or financiers for safe custody or as security.

    • Investments purchased from stockbrokers but not delivered at the balance sheet date.

    • Loans from lenders.

    • Accounts payable balances.

6. The reliability of the audit evidence obtained by external confirmations depends, among other factors, upon the auditor applying appropriate audit procedures in designing the external confirmation request, performing the external confirmation procedures, and evaluating the results of the external confirmation procedures. Factors affecting the reliability of confirmations include the control the auditor exercises over confirmation requests and responses, the characteristics of the

respondents, and any restrictions included in the response or imposed by management[1].

Relationship of External Confirmation Procedures to the Auditor's Assessments of the Risk of Material Misstatement

7. ISA (UK and Ireland) 315, "Understanding the Entity and Its Environment and Assessing the Risks of Material Misstatement" discusses the auditor's responsibility to obtain an understanding of the entity and its environment including its internal control; and to assess the risks of material misstatement. It outlines the audit procedures performed to assess the risks of material misstatements of the financial statements sufficient to design and perform further audit procedures.

8. ISA (UK and Ireland) 330, "The Auditor's Procedures in Response to Assessed Risks" discusses the auditor's responsibility to determine overall responses and to design and perform further audit procedures whose nature, timing and extent are responsive to the assessed risks of material misstatement at the financial statement and assertion levels. In particular, ISA (UK and Ireland) 330 indicates that the auditor determines the nature and extent of audit evidence to be obtained from the performance of substantive procedures in response to the related assessment of the risk of material misstatement, and that, irrespective of the assessed risk of material misstatement, the auditor designs and performs substantive procedures for each material class of transactions, account balance, and disclosure. These substantive procedures may include the use of external confirmations for certain assertions.

9. Paragraph 11 of ISA (UK and Ireland) 330 indicates that the higher the auditor's assessment of risk, the more reliable and relevant is the audit evidence sought by the auditor from substantive procedures. Consequently as the assessed risk of material misstatement increases, the auditor designs substantive procedures to obtain more reliable and relevant audit evidence, or more persuasive audit evidence, at the assertion level. In these situations, the use of confirmation procedures may be effective in providing sufficient appropriate audit evidence.

10. The lower the assessed risk of material misstatement, the less assurance the auditor needs from substantive procedures to form a conclusion about an assertion. For example, an entity may have a loan that it is repaying according to an agreed schedule, the terms of which the auditor has confirmed in previous years. If the other work carried out by the auditor (including such tests of controls as are necessary) indicates that the terms of the loan have not changed and has lead to the risk of material misstatement over the balance of the loan outstanding being assessed as lower, the auditor might limit substantive procedures to testing details of the payments made, rather than again confirming the balance directly with the lender.

11. When the auditor has identified a risk as being significant (see paragraph 108 of ISA (UK and Ireland) 315), the auditor may give particular consideration to whether

---

[1] In the UK and Ireland such restrictions might be imposed by those charged with governance.

confirmations of certain matters may be an appropriate way of reducing the risk of misstatement. For example, unusual or complex transactions may be associated with higher assessed risk than simple transactions. If the entity has entered into an unusual or complex transaction that results in a higher assessed risk of material misstatement, the auditor considers confirming the terms of the transaction with the other parties in addition to examining documentation held by the entity.

Assertions Addressed by External Confirmations

12. ISA (UK and Ireland) 500 requires the use of assertions in assessing risks and designing and performing audit procedures in response to the assessed risks. ISA (UK and Ireland) 500 categorizes the assertions into those relating to classes of transactions, account balances, and disclosures. While external confirmations may provide audit evidence regarding these assertions, the ability of an external confirmation to provide audit evidence relevant to a particular assertion varies.

13. External confirmation of an account receivable provides reliable and relevant audit evidence regarding the existence of the account as at a certain date. Confirmation also provides audit evidence regarding the operation of cutoff procedures. However, such confirmation does not ordinarily provide all the necessary audit evidence relating to the valuation assertion, since it is not practicable to ask the debtor to confirm detailed information relating to its ability to pay the account.

14. Similarly, in the case of goods held on consignment, external confirmation is likely to provide reliable and relevant audit evidence to support the existence and the rights and obligations assertions, but might not provide audit evidence that supports the valuation assertion.

15. The relevance of external confirmations to auditing a particular assertion is also affected by the objective of the auditor in selecting information for confirmation. For example, when auditing the completeness assertion for accounts payable, the auditor needs to obtain audit evidence that there is no material unrecorded liability. Accordingly, sending confirmation requests to an entity's principal suppliers asking them to provide copies of their statements of account directly to the auditor, even if the records show no amount currently owing to them, will usually be more effective in detecting unrecorded liabilities than selecting accounts for confirmation based on the larger amounts recorded in the accounts payable subsidiary ledger.

16. When obtaining audit evidence for assertions not adequately addressed by confirmations, the auditor considers other audit procedures to complement confirmation procedures or to be used instead of confirmation procedures.

Design of the External Confirmation Request

17. **The auditor should tailor external confirmation requests to the specific audit objective.** When designing the request, the auditor considers the assertions being addressed and the factors that are likely to affect the reliability of the confirmations.

Factors such as the form of the external confirmation request, prior experience on the audit or similar engagements, the nature of the information being confirmed, and the intended respondent, affect the design of the requests because these factors have a direct effect on the reliability of the audit evidence obtained through external confirmation procedures.

18. Also, in designing the request, the auditor considers the type of information respondents will be able to confirm readily since this may affect the response rate and the nature of the audit evidence obtained. For example, certain respondents' information systems may facilitate the external confirmation of single transactions rather than of entire account balances. In addition, respondents may not always be able to confirm certain types of information, such as the overall accounts receivable balance, but may be able to confirm individual invoice amounts within the total balance.

19. Confirmation requests ordinarily include management's authorization to the respondent to disclose the information to the auditor. Respondents may be more willing to respond to a confirmation request containing management's authorization, and in some cases may be unable to respond unless the request contains management's authorization.

Use of Positive and Negative Confirmations

20. The auditor may use positive or negative external confirmation requests or a combination of both.

21. A positive external confirmation request asks the respondent to reply to the auditor in all cases either by indicating the respondent's agreement with the given information, or by asking the respondent to fill in information. A response to a positive confirmation request is ordinarily expected to provide reliable audit evidence. There is a risk, however, that a respondent may reply to the confirmation request without verifying that the information is correct. The auditor is not ordinarily able to detect whether this has occurred. The auditor may reduce this risk, however, by using positive confirmation requests that do not state the amount (or other information) on the confirmation request, but ask the respondent to fill in the amount or furnish other information. On the other hand, use of this type of "blank" confirmation request may result in lower response rates because additional effort is required of the respondents.

22. A negative external confirmation request asks the respondent to reply only in the event of disagreement with the information provided in the request. However, when no response has been received to a negative confirmation request, the auditor remains aware that there will be no explicit audit evidence that intended third parties have received the confirmation requests and verified that the information contained therein is correct. Accordingly, the use of negative confirmation requests ordinarily provides less reliable audit evidence than the use of positive confirmation requests, and the auditor considers performing other substantive procedures to supplement the use of negative confirmations.

23. Negative confirmation requests may be used to reduce the risk of material misstatement to an acceptable level when:

    (a) The assessed risk of material misstatement is lower;

    (b) A large number of small balances is involved;

    (c) A substantial number of errors is not expected; and

    (d) The auditor has no reason to believe that respondents will disregard these requests.

24. A combination of positive and negative external confirmations may be used. For example, where the total accounts receivable balance comprises a small number of large balances and a large number of small balances, the auditor may decide that it is appropriate to confirm all or a sample of the large balances with positive confirmation requests and a sample of the small balances using negative confirmation requests.

Management Requests

25. **When the auditor seeks to confirm certain balances or other information, and management requests the auditor not to do so, the auditor should consider whether there are valid grounds for such a request and obtain audit evidence to support the validity of management's requests. If the auditor agrees to management's request not to seek external confirmation regarding a particular matter, the auditor should apply alternative audit procedures to obtain sufficient appropriate audit evidence regarding that matter.**

26. **If the auditor does not accept the validity of management's request and is prevented from carrying out the confirmations, there has been a limitation on the scope of the auditor's work and the auditor should consider the possible impact on the auditor's report.**

27. When considering the reasons provided by management, the auditor applies an attitude of professional skepticism and considers whether the request has any implications regarding management's integrity. The auditor considers whether management's request may indicate the possible existence of fraud or error. If the auditor believes that fraud or error exists, the auditor applies the guidance in ISA (UK and Ireland) 240, "The Auditor's Responsibility to Consider Fraud in an Audit of Financial Statements." The auditor also considers whether the alternative audit procedures will provide sufficient appropriate audit evidence regarding that matter.

Characteristics of Respondents

28. The reliability of audit evidence provided by a confirmation is affected by the respondent's competence, independence, authority to respond, knowledge of the matter being confirmed, and objectivity. For this reason, the auditor attempts to

ensure, where practicable, that the confirmation request is directed to an appropriate individual. For example, when confirming that a covenant related to an entity's long-term debt has been waived, the auditor directs the request to an official of the creditor who has knowledge about the waiver and has the authority to provide the information.

29. The auditor also assesses whether certain parties may not provide an objective or unbiased response to a confirmation request. Information about the respondent's competence, knowledge, motivation, ability or willingness to respond may come to the auditor's attention. The auditor considers the effect of such information on designing the confirmation request and evaluating the results, including determining whether additional audit procedures are necessary. The auditor also considers whether there is sufficient basis for concluding that the confirmation request is being sent to a respondent from whom the auditor can expect a response that will provide sufficient appropriate audit evidence. For example, the auditor may encounter significant unusual year-end transactions that have a material effect on the financial statements, the transactions being with a third party that is economically dependent upon the entity. In such circumstances, the auditor considers whether the third party may be motivated to provide an inaccurate response.

The External Confirmation Process

30. **When performing confirmation procedures, the auditor should maintain control over the process of selecting those to whom a request will be sent, the preparation and sending of confirmation requests, and the responses to those requests.** Control is maintained over communications between the intended recipients and the auditor to minimize the possibility that the results of the confirmation process will be biased because of the interception and alteration of confirmation requests or responses. The auditor ensures that it is the auditor who sends out the confirmation requests, that the requests are properly addressed, and that it is requested that all replies are sent directly to the auditor. The auditor considers whether replies have come from the purported senders.

No Response to a Positive Confirmation Request

31. **The auditor should perform alternative audit procedures where no response is received to a positive external confirmation request. The alternative audit procedures should be such as to provide audit evidence about the assertions that the confirmation request was intended to provide.**

32. Where no response is received, the auditor ordinarily contacts the recipient of the request to elicit a response. Where the auditor is unable to obtain a response, the auditor uses alternative audit procedures. The nature of alternative audit procedures varies according to the account and assertion in question. In the examination of accounts receivable, alternative audit procedures may include examination of subsequent cash receipts, examination of shipping documentation or other client documentation to provide audit evidence for the existence assertion, and examination of sales near the period-end to provide audit evidence for the cutoff assertion. In the examination of accounts payable, alternative audit procedures may include

examination of subsequent cash disbursements or correspondence from third parties to provide audit evidence of the existence assertion, and examination of other records, such as goods received notes, to provide audit evidence of the completeness assertion.

Reliability of Responses Received

33. The auditor considers whether there is any indication that external confirmations received may not be reliable. The auditor considers the response's authenticity and performs audit procedures to dispel any concern. The auditor may choose to verify the source and contents of a response in a telephone call to the purported sender. In addition, the auditor requests the purported sender to mail the original confirmation directly to the auditor. With ever-increasing use of technology, the auditor considers validating the source of replies received in electronic format (for example, fax or electronic mail). Oral confirmations are documented in the work papers. If the information in the oral confirmations is significant, the auditor requests the parties involved to submit written confirmation of the specific information directly to the auditor.

Causes and Frequency of Exceptions

34. **When the auditor forms a conclusion that the confirmation process and alternative audit procedures have not provided sufficient appropriate audit evidence regarding an assertion, the auditor should perform additional audit procedures to obtain sufficient appropriate audit evidence.**

   In forming the conclusion, the auditor considers the:

   (a)   Reliability of the confirmations and alternative audit procedures;

   (b)   Nature of any exceptions, including the implications, both quantitative and qualitative of those exceptions; and

   (c)   Audit evidence provided by other audit procedures.

   Based on this evaluation, the auditor determines whether additional audit procedures are needed to obtain sufficient appropriate audit evidence.

35. The auditor also considers the causes and frequency of exceptions reported by respondents. An exception may indicate a misstatement in the entity's records, in which case, the auditor determines the reasons for the misstatement and assesses whether it has a material effect on the financial statements. If an exception indicates a misstatement, the auditor reconsiders the nature, timing and extent of audit procedures necessary to provide the audit evidence required.

Evaluating the Results of the Confirmation Process

36. **The auditor should evaluate whether the results of the external confirmation process together with the results from any other audit procedures performed, provide sufficient appropriate audit evidence regarding the assertion being audited.** In conducting this evaluation the auditor considers the guidance provided by ISA (UK and Ireland) 330 and ISA (UK and Ireland) 530, "Audit Sampling and Other Means of Testing."

External Confirmations Prior to the Year-end

37. When the auditor uses confirmation as at a date prior to the balance sheet to obtain audit evidence to support an assertion, the auditor obtains sufficient appropriate audit evidence that transactions relevant to the assertion in the intervening period have not been materially misstated. Depending on the assessed risk of material misstatement, the auditor may decide to confirm balances at a date other than the period end, for example, when the audit is to be completed within a short time after the balance sheet date. As with all types of pre-year-end work, the auditor considers the need to obtain further audit evidence relating to the remainder of the period. ISA (UK and Ireland) 330 provides additional guidance when audit procedures are performed at an interim date.

Effective Date

38. This ISA (UK and Ireland) is effective for audits of financial statements for periods commencing on or after 15 December 2004.

INTERNATIONAL STANDARD ON AUDITING (UK AND IRELAND) 510

INITIAL ENGAGEMENTS – OPENING BALANCES AND CONTINUING ENGAGEMENTS – OPENING BALANCES

CONTENTS

International Standard on Auditing (UK and Ireland) (ISA (UK and Ireland)) 510 "Initial Engagements - Opening Balances and Continuing Engagements - Opening Balances" should be read in the context of the Auditing Practices Board's Statement "The Auditing Practices Board - Scope and Authority of Pronouncements (Revised)" which sets out the application and authority of ISAs (UK and Ireland).

Introduction

1. The purpose of this International Standard on Auditing (UK and Ireland) (ISA (UK and Ireland)) is to establish standards and provide guidance regarding opening balances when the financial statements are audited for the first time or when the financial statements for the prior period were audited by another auditor. This ISA (UK and Ireland) would also be considered when the auditor becomes aware of contingencies and commitments existing at the beginning of the period. Guidance on the audit and reporting requirements regarding comparatives is provided in ISA (UK and Ireland) 710 "Comparatives."

1-1. This ISA (UK and Ireland) also provides guidance regarding opening balances for a continuing auditor (an auditor who audited and reported on the preceding periods financial statements and continues as auditor for the current period).

1-2. This ISA (UK and Ireland) uses the terms 'those charged with governance' and 'management'. The term 'governance' describes the role of persons entrusted with the supervision, control and direction of an entity. Ordinarily, those charged with governance are accountable for ensuring that the entity achieves its objectives, and for the quality of its financial reporting and reporting to interested parties. Those charged with governance include management only when they perform such functions.

1-3. In the UK and Ireland, those charged with governance include the directors (executive and non-executive) of a company or other body, the members of an audit committee where one exists, the partners, proprietors, committee of management or trustees of other forms of entity, or equivalent persons responsible for directing the entity's affairs and preparing its financial statements.

1-4. 'Management' comprises those persons who perform senior managerial functions.

1-5. In the UK and Ireland, depending on the nature and circumstances of the entity, management may include some or all of those persons charged with governance (e.g. executive directors). Management will not normally include non-executive directors.

2. **For initial audit engagements, the auditor should obtain sufficient appropriate audit evidence that:**

    (a) **The opening balances do not contain misstatements that materially affect the current period's financial statements;**

    (b) **The prior period's closing balances have been correctly brought forward to the current period or, when appropriate, have been restated; and**

    (c) **Appropriate accounting policies are consistently applied or changes in accounting policies have been properly accounted for and adequately presented and disclosed.**

2-1. **The auditor should also obtain sufficient appropriate audit evidence for the matters set out in paragraph 2 for continuing audit engagements (see paragraphs 10-1 and 10-2).**

3. "Opening balances" means those account balances which exist at the beginning of the period. Opening balances are based upon the closing balances of the prior period and reflect the effects of:

   (a) Transactions of prior periods; and

   (b) Accounting policies applied in the prior period.

   In an initial audit engagement, the auditor will not have previously obtained audit evidence supporting such opening balances.

Audit Procedures

4. The sufficiency and appropriateness of the audit evidence the auditor will need to obtain regarding opening balances depends on such matters as:

   - The accounting policies followed by the entity.

   - Whether the prior period's financial statements were audited, and if so whether the auditor's report was modified.

   - The nature of the accounts and the risk of material misstatement in the current period's financial statements.

   - The materiality of the opening balances relative to the current period's financial statements.

5. The auditor will need to consider whether opening balances reflect the application of appropriate accounting policies and that those policies are consistently applied in the current period's financial statements. When there are any changes in the accounting policies or application thereof, the auditor would consider whether they are appropriate and properly accounted for and adequately presented and disclosed.

6. When the prior period's financial statements were audited by another auditor, the current auditor may be able to obtain sufficient appropriate audit evidence regarding opening balances by reviewing the predecessor auditor's working papers. In these circumstances, the current auditor would also consider the professional competence and independence of the predecessor auditor. If the prior period's auditor's report was modified, the auditor would pay particular attention in the current period to the matter which resulted in the modification.

7. Prior to communicating with the predecessor auditor, the current auditor will need to consider the *Code of Ethics for Professional Accountants* issued by the International Federation of Accountants.

7-1. In the UK and Ireland the relevant ethical guidance on proposed communications with a predecessor auditor is provided by the ethical pronouncements relating to the work of auditors issued by the auditor's relevant professional body.

8. When the prior period's financial statements were not audited or when the auditor is not able to be satisfied by using the audit procedures described in paragraph 6, the auditor will need to perform other audit procedures such as those discussed in paragraphs 9 and 10.

9. For current assets and liabilities some audit evidence can ordinarily be obtained as part of the current period's audit procedures. For example, the collection (payment) of opening accounts receivable (accounts payable) during the current period will provide some audit evidence of their existence, rights and obligations, completeness and valuation at the beginning of the period. In the case of inventories, however, it is more difficult for the auditor to be satisfied as to inventory on hand at the beginning of the period. Therefore, additional audit procedures are ordinarily necessary such as observing a current physical inventory taking and reconciling it back to the opening inventory quantities, performing audit procedures on the valuation of the opening inventory items, and performing audit procedures on gross profit and cutoff. A combination of these procedures may provide sufficient appropriate audit evidence.

10. For noncurrent assets and liabilities, such as fixed assets, investments and long-term debt, the auditor will ordinarily examine the accounting records and other information underlying the opening balances. In certain cases, the auditor may be able to obtain confirmation of opening balances with third parties, for example, for long-term debt and investments. In other cases, the auditor may need to carry out additional audit procedures.

Continuing Auditor

10-1. If a continuing auditor issued an unqualified report on the preceding period's financial statements and the audit of the current period has not revealed any matters which cast doubt on those financial statements, the procedures regarding opening balances need not extend beyond ensuring that opening balances have been appropriately brought forward and that current accounting policies have been consistently applied.

10-2. If a qualified report was issued on the preceding period's financial statements the auditor, in addition to carrying out the procedures in paragraph 10-1, considers whether the matter which gave rise to the qualification has been resolved and properly dealt with in the current period's financial statements.

Audit Conclusions and Reporting

11. **If, after performing audit procedures including those set out above, the auditor is unable to obtain sufficient appropriate audit evidence concerning opening balances, the auditor's report should include:**

(a) **A qualified opinion,** for example:

"We did not observe the counting of the physical inventory stated at XXX as at December 31, 19X1, since that date was prior to our appointment as auditors. We were unable to satisfy ourselves as to the inventory quantities at that date by other audit procedures.

In our opinion, except for the effects of such adjustments, if any, as might have been determined to be necessary had we been able to observe the counting of physical inventory and satisfy ourselves as to the opening balance of inventory, the financial statements give a true and fair view of (present fairly, in all material respects,) the financial position of ... as at December 31, 19X2 and the results of its operations and its cash flows for the year then ended in accordance with ...;"

Illustrative examples of auditor's reports tailored for use with audits conducted in accordance with ISAs (UK and Ireland) are given in the most recent version of the APB Bulletin, "Auditor's Reports on Financial Statements".

(b) **A disclaimer of opinion; or**

(c) **In those jurisdictions where it is permitted[1], an opinion which is qualified or disclaimed regarding the results of operations and unqualified regarding financial position,** for example:

"We did not observe the counting of the physical inventory stated at XXX as at December 31, 19X1, since that date was prior to our appointment as auditors. We were unable to satisfy ourselves as to the inventory quantities at that date by other audit procedures.

Because of the significance of the above matter in relation to the results of the Company's operations for the year to December 31, 19X2, we are not in a position to, and do not, express an opinion on the results of its operations and its cash flows for the year then ended.

In our opinion, the balance sheet gives a true and fair view of (or 'presents fairly in all material respects,') the financial position of the Company as at December 31, 19X2, in accordance with ....."

Illustrative examples of auditor's reports tailored for use with audits conducted in accordance with ISAs (UK and Ireland) are given in the most recent version of the APB Bulletin, "Auditor's Reports on Financial Statements".

12. If the opening balances contain misstatements which could materially affect the current period's financial statements, the auditor would inform management[2] and, after

---

[1] This form of opinion is permitted in the UK and Ireland.
[2] In the UK and Ireland the auditor would inform those charged with governance and seek their authorization to inform the predecessor auditor, if any.

having obtained management's authorization, the predecessor auditor, if any. **If the effect of the misstatement is not properly accounted for and adequately presented and disclosed, the auditor should express a qualified opinion or an adverse opinion, as appropriate.**

13. **If the current period's accounting policies have not been consistently applied in relation to opening balances and if the change has not been properly accounted for and adequately presented and disclosed, the auditor should express a qualified opinion or an adverse opinion as appropriate.**

14. If the entity's prior period auditor's report was modified, the auditor would consider the effect thereof on the current period's financial statements. For example, if there was a scope limitation, such as one due to the inability to determine opening inventory in the prior period, the auditor may not need to qualify or disclaim the current period's audit opinion. **However, if a modification regarding the prior period's financial statements remains relevant and material to the current period's financial statements, the auditor should modify the current auditor's report accordingly.**

Effective Date

14-1. This ISA (UK and Ireland) is effective for audits of financial statements for periods commencing on or after 15 December 2004.

INTERNATIONAL STANDARD ON AUDITING (UK AND IRELAND) 520

ANALYTICAL PROCEDURES

CONTENTS

International Standard on Auditing (UK and Ireland) (ISA (UK and Ireland)) 520 "Analytical Procedures" should be read in the context of the Auditing Practices Board's Statement "The Auditing Practices Board - Scope and Authority of Pronouncements (Revised)" which sets out the application and authority of ISAs (UK and Ireland).

Introduction

1. The purpose of this International Standard on Auditing (UK and Ireland) (ISA (UK and Ireland)) is to establish standards and provide guidance on the application of analytical procedures during an audit.

2. **The auditor should apply analytical procedures as risk assessment procedures to obtain an understanding of the entity and its environment and in the overall review at the end of the audit.** Analytical procedures may also be applied as substantive procedures.

3. "Analytical procedures" means evaluations of financial information made by a study of plausible relationships among both financial and non-financial data. Analytical procedures also encompass the investigation of identified fluctuations and relationships that are inconsistent with other relevant information or deviate significantly from predicted amounts.

3-1. This ISA (UK and Ireland) uses the terms 'those charged with governance' and 'management'. The term 'governance' describes the role of persons entrusted with the supervision, control and direction of an entity. Ordinarily, those charged with governance are accountable for ensuring that the entity achieves its objectives, and for the quality of its financial reporting and reporting to interested parties. Those charged with governance include management only when they perform such functions.

3-2. In the UK and Ireland, those charged with governance include the directors (executive and non-executive) of a company or other body, the members of an audit committee where one exists, the partners, proprietors, committee of management or trustees of other forms of entity, or equivalent persons responsible for directing the entity's affairs and preparing its financial statements.

3-3. 'Management' comprises those persons who perform senior managerial functions.

3-4. In the UK and Ireland, depending on the nature and circumstances of the entity, management may include some or all of those charged with governance (e.g. executive directors). Management will not normally include non-executive directors.

Nature and Purpose of Analytical Procedures

4. Analytical procedures include the consideration of comparisons of the entity's financial information with, for example:

    *   Comparable information for prior periods.

    *   Anticipated results of the entity, such as budgets or forecasts, or expectations of the auditor, such as an estimation of depreciation.

- Similar industry information, such as a comparison of the entity's ratio of sales to accounts receivable with industry averages or with other entities of comparable size in the same industry.

5. Analytical procedures also include consideration of relationships:

- Among elements of financial information that would be expected to conform to a predictable pattern based on the entity's experience, such as gross margin percentages.

- Between financial information and relevant non-financial information, such as payroll costs to number of employees.

6. Various methods may be used in performing the above audit procedures. These range from simple comparisons to complex analyses using advanced statistical techniques. Analytical procedures may be applied to consolidated financial statements, financial statements of components (such as subsidiaries, divisions or segments) and individual elements of financial information. The auditor's choice of audit procedures, methods and level of application is a matter of professional judgment.

7. Analytical procedures are used for the following purposes:

(a) As risk assessment procedures to obtain an understanding of the entity and its environment (paragraphs 8-9).

(b) As substantive procedures when their use can be more effective or efficient than tests of details in reducing the risk of material misstatement at the assertion level to an acceptably low level (paragraphs 10-19).

(c) As an overall review of the financial statements at the end of the audit (paragraph 13).

Analytical Procedures as Risk Assessment Procedures

8. **The auditor should apply analytical procedures as risk assessment procedures to obtain an understanding of the entity and its environment.** Application of analytical procedures may indicate aspects of the entity of which the auditor was unaware and will assist in assessing the risks of material misstatement in order to determine the nature, timing and extent of further audit procedures.

9. Analytical procedures applied as risk assessment procedures use both financial and non-financial information, for example, the relationship between sales and square footage of selling space or volume of goods sold. Paragraph 10 of ISA (UK and Ireland) 315, "Understanding the Entity and Its Environment and Assessing the Risks of Material Misstatement" contains additional guidance on applying analytical procedures as risk assessment procedures.

9-1 Analytical procedures at this stage are usually based on interim financial information, budgets and management accounts. However, for those entities with less formal means of controlling and monitoring performance, it may be possible to extract relevant financial information from the accounting system, VAT returns and bank statements. Discussions with management, focused on identifying significant changes in the business since the prior financial period, may also be useful.

Analytical Procedures as Substantive Procedures

10. The auditor designs and performs substantive procedures to be responsive to the related assessment of the risk of material misstatement at the assertion level. The auditor's substantive procedures at the assertion level may be derived from tests of details, from substantive analytical procedures, or from a combination of both. The decision about which audit procedures to use to achieve a particular audit objective is based on the auditor's judgment about the expected effectiveness and efficiency of the available audit procedures in reducing the assessed risk of material misstatement at the assertion level to an acceptably low level.

11. The auditor will ordinarily inquire of management as to the availability and reliability of information needed to apply substantive analytical procedures and the results of any such procedures performed by the entity. It may be efficient to use analytical data prepared by the entity, provided the auditor is satisfied that such data is properly prepared.

12. When designing and performing analytical procedures as substantive procedures, the auditor will need to consider a number of factors such as the following:

- The suitability of using substantive analytical procedures given the assertions (paragraphs 12a and 12b).

- The reliability of the data, whether internal or external, from which the expectation of recorded amounts or ratios is developed (paragraphs 12c and 12d).

- Whether the expectation is sufficiently precise to identify a material misstatement at the desired level of assurance (paragraph 112e).

- The amount of any difference of recorded amounts from expected values that is acceptable (paragraph 12f).

Suitability of Using Substantive Analytical Procedures Given the Assertions

12a. Substantive analytical procedures are generally more applicable to large volumes of transactions that tend to be predictable over time. The application of substantive analytical procedures is based on the expectation that relationships among data exist and continue in the absence of known conditions to the contrary. The presence of these relationships provides audit evidence as to the completeness, accuracy and occurrence of transactions captured in the information produced by the entity's information system. However, reliance on the results of substantive analytical procedures will depend on the auditor's assessment of the risk that the analytical procedures may identify relationships as expected when, in fact, a material misstatement exists.

12b. In determining the suitability of substantive analytical procedures given the assertions, the auditor considers:

(a) *The assessment of the risk of material misstatement.* The auditor considers the understanding of the entity and its internal control, the materiality and likelihood of misstatement of the items involved, and the nature of the assertion in determining whether substantive analytical procedures are suitable. For example, if controls over sales order processing are weak, the auditor may place more reliance on tests of details rather than substantive analytical procedures for assertions related to receivables. As another example, when inventory balances are material, the auditor ordinarily does not rely only on substantive analytical procedures when performing audit procedures on the existence assertion. ISA (UK and Ireland) 330, "The Auditor's Procedures in Response to Assessed Risks" indicates that when the approach to significant risks consists only of substantive procedures, the audit procedures appropriate to address such significant risks consist of tests of details only, or a combination of tests of details and substantive analytical procedures.

(b) *Any tests of details directed toward the same assertion.* Substantive analytical procedures may also be considered appropriate when tests of details are performed on the same assertion. For example, when auditing the collectibility of accounts receivable, the auditor may apply substantive analytical procedures to an aging of customers' accounts in addition to tests of details on subsequent cash receipts.

The Reliability of the Data

12c. The reliability of data is influenced by its source and by its nature and is dependent on the circumstances under which it is obtained. In determining whether data is reliable for purposes of designing substantive analytical procedures, the auditor considers:

(a) *Source of the information available.* For example, information is ordinarily more reliable when it is obtained from independent sources outside the entity.

(b) *Comparability of the information available.* For example, broad industry data may need to be supplemented to be comparable to that of an entity that produces and sells specialized products.

(c) *Nature and relevance of the information available.* For example, whether budgets have been established as results to be expected rather than as goals to be achieved.

(d) *Controls over the preparation of the information.* For example, controls over the preparation, review and maintenance of budgets.

(e) *Prior year knowledge and understanding.* For example, the knowledge gained during previous audits, together with the auditor's understanding of the effectiveness of the accounting and internal control systems and the types of problems that in prior periods have given rise to accounting adjustments.

(f) *Whether the information is produced internally.* For example, if the information is produced internally, its reliability is enhanced if it is produced independently of the accounting system or there are adequate controls over its preparation. The necessity for evidence on the reliability of such information depends on the results of the other audit procedures and on the importance of the results of analytical procedures as a basis for the auditor's opinion.

12d. The auditor considers testing the controls, if any, over the entity's preparation of information used by the auditor in applying substantive analytical procedures. When such controls are effective, the auditor has greater confidence in the reliability of the information and, therefore, in the results of substantive analytical procedures. The controls over non-financial information can often be tested in conjunction with other tests of controls. For example, an entity in establishing controls over the processing of sales invoices may include controls over the recording of unit sales. In these circumstances, the auditor could test the operating effectiveness of controls over the recording of unit sales in conjunction with tests of the operating effectiveness of controls over the processing of sales invoices. Alternatively, the auditor may consider whether the information was subjected to audit testing in the current or prior period. In determining the audit procedures to apply to the information upon which the expectation for substantive analytical procedures is based, the auditor considers the guidance in paragraph 11 of ISA (UK and Ireland) 500, "Audit Evidence."

Whether the Expectation is Sufficiently Precise

12e. In assessing whether the expectation can be developed sufficiently precise to identify a material misstatement at the desired level of assurance, the auditor considers factors such as:

- *The accuracy with which the expected results of substantive analytical procedures can be predicted.* For example, the auditor will ordinarily expect greater consistency in comparing gross profit margins from one period to another than in comparing discretionary expenses, such as research or advertising.

- *The degree to which information can be disaggregated.* For example, substantive analytical procedures may be more effective when applied to financial information on individual sections of an operation or to financial statements of components of a diversified entity, than when applied to the financial statements of the entity as a whole.

- *The availability of the information, both financial and nonfinancial.* For example, the auditor considers whether financial information, such as budgets or forecasts, and non-financial information, such as the number of units produced or sold, is available to design substantive analytical procedures. If the information is available, the auditor also considers the reliability of the information as discussed in paragraphs 12c and 12d above.

> • *The frequency with which a relationship is observed.* For example, a pattern repeated monthly as opposed to annually.

Amount of Difference of Recorded Amounts from Expected Values that is Acceptable

12f. In designing and performing substantive analytical procedures, the auditor considers the amount of difference from expectation that can be accepted without further investigation. This consideration is influenced primarily by materiality and the consistency with the desired level of assurance. Determination of this amount involves considering the possibility that a combination of misstatements in the specific account balance, class of transactions, or disclosure could aggregate to an unacceptable amount. The auditor increases the desired level of assurance as the risk of material misstatement increases by reducing the amount of difference from the expectation that can be accepted without further investigation. Paragraphs 17 and 18 below discuss the auditor's response when the amount of difference between the expected value and the reported value exceeds the amount that can be accepted without further investigation.

12g. When the auditor performs substantive procedures at an interim date and plans to perform substantive analytical procedures with respect to the intervening period, the auditor considers how the matters discussed in paragraphs 12a-12f affect the ability to obtain sufficient appropriate audit evidence for the remaining period. This includes considering whether the period end balances of the particular classes of transactions or account balances are reasonably predictable with respect to amount, relative significance, and composition. See ISA (UK and Ireland) 330 paragraphs 56-61 for additional guidance.

Analytical Procedures in the Overall Review at the End of the Audit

13. **The auditor should apply analytical procedures at or near the end of the audit when forming an overall conclusion as to whether the financial statements as a whole are consistent with the auditor's understanding of the entity.** The conclusions drawn from the results of such audit procedures are intended to corroborate conclusions formed during the audit of individual components or elements of the financial statements and assist in arriving at the overall conclusion as to the reasonableness of the financial statements. However, they may also identify a previously unrecognized risk of material misstatement. In such circumstances, the auditor may need to re-evaluate the planned audit procedures, based on the revised consideration of assessed risks for all or some of the classes of transactions, account balances, or disclosures and related assertions.

13-1. These procedures will also involve consideration of whether the assertions contained in the financial statements are consistent with the auditor's understanding of the entity.

13-2. The principal considerations when carrying out such procedures are:

(a) Whether the financial statements adequately reflect the information and explanations previously obtained and conclusions previously reached during the course of the audit;

(b) Whether the procedures reveal any new factors which may affect the presentation of, or disclosures in, the financial statements;

(c) Whether analytical procedures applied when completing the audit, such as comparing the information in the financial statements with other pertinent data, produce results which assist in arriving at the overall conclusion as to whether the financial statements as a whole are consistent with the auditor's knowledge of the entity's business;

(d) Whether the presentation adopted in the financial statements may have been unduly influenced by the desire of those charged with governance to present matters in a favourable or unfavourable light; and

(e) The potential impact on the financial statements of the aggregate of uncorrected misstatements (including those arising from bias in making accounting estimates) identified during the course of the audit and the preceding period's audit, if any.

[Paragraphs 14-16 were deleted when the audit risk standards[1] became effective.]

Investigating Unusual Items

17. When analytical procedures identify significant fluctuations or relationships that are inconsistent with other relevant information or that deviate from predicted amounts, the auditor should investigate and obtain adequate explanations and appropriate corroborative audit evidence.

18. The investigation of unusual fluctuations and relationships ordinarily begins with inquiries of management, followed by:

---

[1] The audit risk standards comprise ISA (UK and Ireland) 315, "Understanding the Entity and its Environment and Assessing the Risks of Material Misstatement," ISA (UK and Ireland) 330, "The Auditor's Procedures in Response to Assessed Risks," and ISA (UK and Ireland) 500 (Revised), "Audit Evidence." The audit risk standards gave rise to amendments to this and other ISAs (UK and Ireland).

(a) Corroboration of management's responses, for example, by comparing them with the auditor's understanding of the entity and other audit evidence obtained during the course of the audit; and

(b) Consideration of the need to apply other audit procedures based on the results of such inquiries, if management is unable to provide an explanation or if the explanation is not considered adequate.

Effective Date

18-1. This ISA (UK and Ireland) is effective for audits of financial statements for periods commencing on or after 15 December 2004.

Public Sector Perspective

Additional guidance for auditors of public sector bodies in the UK and Ireland is given in:

- Practice Note 10 "Audit of Financial Statements of Public Sector Bodies in the United Kingdom (Revised)"

- Practice Note 10(I) "Audit of Central Government Financial Statements in the Republic of Ireland (Revised)"

1. *The relationships between individual financial statement items traditionally considered in the audit of business entities may not always be appropriate in the audit of governments or other non-business public sector entities; for example, in many such public sector entities there is often little direct relationship between revenues and expenditures. In addition, because expenditure on the acquisition of assets is frequently noncapitalized, there may be no relationship between expenditures on, for example, inventories and fixed assets and the amount of those assets reported in the financial statements. In addition, in the public sector, industry data or statistics for comparative purposes may not be available. However, other relationships may be relevant, for example, variations in the cost per kilometer of road construction or the number of vehicles acquired compared with vehicles retired. Where appropriate, reference has to be made to available private sector industry data and statistics. In certain instances, it may also be appropriate for the auditor to generate an in-house database of reference information.*

THE AUDITING PRACTICES BOARD

INTERNATIONAL STANDARD ON AUDITING (UK AND IRELAND) 530

AUDIT SAMPLING AND OTHER MEANS OF TESTING

CONTENTS

International Standard on Auditing (UK and Ireland) (ISA (UK and Ireland)) 530 "Audit Sampling and Other Means of Testing" should be read in the context of the Auditing Practices Board's Statement "The Auditing Practices Board - Scope and Authority of Pronouncements (Revised)" which sets out the application and authority of ISAs (UK and Ireland).

Introduction

1. The purpose of this International Standard on Auditing (UK and Ireland) (ISA (UK and Ireland)) is to establish standards and provide guidance on the use of audit sampling and other means of selecting items for testing when designing audit procedures to gather audit evidence.

1-1. This ISA (UK and Ireland) applies to any audit using sampling whether related to financial statements or not. Nothing contained in this statement is intended to preclude non-statistically based samples where there are reasonable grounds for believing that the results may be relied on for the purpose of the test. Statistically based sampling involves the use of techniques from which mathematically constructed conclusions about the population can be drawn. An auditor draws a judgmental opinion about the population from non-statistical methods.

1-2. This ISA (UK and Ireland) uses the terms 'those charged with governance' and 'management'. The term 'governance' describes the role of persons entrusted with the supervision, control and direction of an entity. Ordinarily, those charged with governance are accountable for ensuring that the entity achieves its objectives, and for the quality of its financial reporting and reporting to interested parties. Those charged with governance include management only when they perform such functions.

1-3. In the UK and Ireland, those charged with governance include the directors (executive and non-executive) of a company or other body, the members of an audit committee where one exists, the partners, proprietors, committee of management or trustees of other forms of entity, or equivalent persons responsible for directing the entity's affairs and preparing its financial statements.

1-4. 'Management' comprises those persons who perform senior managerial functions.

1-5. In the UK and Ireland, depending on the nature and circumstances of the entity, management may include some or all of those charged with governance (e.g. executive directors). Management will not normally include non-executive directors.

2. **When designing audit procedures, the auditor should determine appropriate means for selecting items for testing so as to gather sufficient appropriate audit evidence to meet the objectives of the audit procedures.**

Definitions

3. "Audit sampling" (sampling) involves the application of audit procedures to less than 100% of items within a class of transactions or account balance such that all sampling units have a chance of selection. This will enable the auditor to obtain and evaluate audit evidence about some characteristic of the items selected in order to form or assist in forming a conclusion concerning the population from which the sample is drawn. Audit sampling can use either a statistical or a non-statistical approach.

4. For purposes of this ISA (UK and Ireland), "error" means either control deviations, when performing tests of controls, or misstatements, when performing tests of details. Similarly, total error is used to mean either the rate of deviation or total misstatement.

5. "Anomalous error" means an error that arises from an isolated event that has not recurred other than on specifically identifiable occasions and is therefore not representative of errors in the population.

6. "Population" means the entire set of data from which a sample is selected and about which the auditor wishes to draw conclusions. For example, all of the items in a class of transactions or account balance constitute a population. A population may be divided into strata, or sub-populations, with each stratum being examined separately. The term population is used to include the term stratum.

7. "Sampling risk" arises from the possibility that the auditor's conclusion, based on a sample may be different from the conclusion reached if the entire population were subjected to the same audit procedure. There are two types of sampling risk:

    (a) The risk the auditor will conclude, in the case of a test of controls, that controls are more effective than they actually are, or in the case of a test of details, that a material error does not exist when in fact it does. This type of risk affects audit effectiveness and is more likely to lead to an inappropriate audit opinion; and

    (b) The risk the auditor will conclude, in the case of a test of controls, that controls are less effective than they actually are, or in the case of a test of details, that a material error exists when in fact it does not. This type of risk affects audit efficiency as it would usually lead to additional work to establish that initial conclusions were incorrect.

    The mathematical complements of these risks are termed confidence levels.

8. "Non-sampling risk" arises from factors that cause the auditor to reach an erroneous conclusion for any reason not related to the size of the sample. For example, ordinarily the auditor finds it necessary to rely on audit evidence that is persuasive rather than conclusive, the auditor might use inappropriate audit procedures, or the auditor might misinterpret audit evidence and fail to recognize an error.

9. "Sampling unit" means the individual items constituting a population, for example checks listed on deposit slips, credit entries on bank statements, sales invoices or debtors' balances, or a monetary unit.

10. "Statistical sampling" means any approach to sampling that has the following characteristics:

    (a) Random selection of a sample; and

    (b) Use of probability theory to evaluate sample results, including measurement of sampling risk.

A sampling approach that does not have characteristics (a) and (b) is considered non-statistical sampling.

11. "Stratification" is the process of dividing a population into subpopulations, each of which is a group of sampling units which have similar characteristics (often monetary value).

12. "Tolerable error" means the maximum error in a population that the auditor is willing to accept.

Audit Evidence

13. In accordance with ISA (UK and Ireland) 500, "Audit Evidence" audit evidence is obtained by performing risk assessment procedures, tests of controls and substantive procedures. The type of audit procedure to be performed is important to an understanding of the application of audit sampling in gathering audit evidence.

Risk Assessment Procedures

13a. In accordance with ISA (UK and Ireland) 315, "Understanding the Entity and Its Environment and Assessing the Risks of Material Misstatement," the auditor performs risk assessment procedures to obtain an understanding of the entity and its environment, including its internal control. Ordinarily, risk assessment procedures do not involve the use of audit sampling. However, the auditor often plans and performs tests of controls concurrently with obtaining an understanding of the design of controls and determining whether they have been implemented. In such cases, the following discussion of tests of controls is relevant.

Tests of Control

14. In accordance with ISA (UK and Ireland) 330, "The Auditor's Procedures in Response to Assessed Risks" tests of controls are performed when the auditor's risk assessment includes an expectation of the operating effectiveness of controls.

15. Based on the auditor's understanding of internal control, the auditor identifies the characteristics or attributes that indicate performance of a control, as well as possible deviation conditions which indicate departures from adequate performance. The presence or absence of attributes can then be tested by the auditor.

16. Audit sampling for tests of controls is generally appropriate when application of the control leaves audit evidence of performance (for example, initials of the credit manager on a sales invoice indicating credit approval, or evidence of authorization of data input to a microcomputer based data processing system).

Substantive Procedures

17. Substantive procedures are concerned with amounts and are of two types: tests of details of classes of transactions, account balances, and disclosures and substantive

analytical procedures. The purpose of substantive procedures is to obtain audit evidence to detect material misstatements at the assertion level. In the context of substantive procedures, audit sampling and other means of selecting items for testing, as discussed in this ISA (UK and Ireland), relate only to tests of details. When performing tests of details, audit sampling and other means of selecting items for testing and gathering audit evidence may be used to verify one or more assertions about a financial statement amount (for example, the existence of accounts receivable), or to make an independent estimate of some amount (for example, the value of obsolete inventories).

Risk Considerations in Obtaining Audit Evidence

18. **In obtaining audit evidence, the auditor should use professional judgment to assess the risk of material misstatement (which includes inherent and control risk) and design further audit procedures to ensure this risk is reduced to an acceptably low level.**

19. [Paragraph 19 was deleted when the audit risk standards[1] became effective.]

20. Sampling risk and non-sampling risk can affect the components of the risk of material misstatement. For example, when performing tests of controls, the auditor may find no errors in a sample and conclude that controls are operating effectively, when the rate of error in the population is, in fact, unacceptably high (sampling risk). Or there may be errors in the sample which the auditor fails to recognize (non-sampling risk). With respect to substantive procedures, the auditor may use a variety of methods to reduce detection risk to an acceptable level. Depending on their nature, these methods will be subject to sampling and/or non-sampling risks. For example, the auditor may choose an inappropriate substantive analytical procedure (non-sampling risk) or may find only minor misstatements in a test of details when, in fact, the population misstatement is greater than the tolerable amount (sampling risk). For both tests of controls and substantive tests of details, sampling risk can be reduced by increasing sample size, while non-sampling risk can be reduced by proper engagement planning supervision and review.

Audit Procedures for Obtaining Audit Evidence

21. Audit procedures for obtaining audit evidence include inspection, observation, inquiry and confirmation, recalculation, reperformance and analytical procedures. The choice of appropriate audit procedures is a matter of professional judgment in the circumstances. Application of these audit procedures will often involve the selection

---

[1] The audit risk standards comprise ISA (UK and Ireland) 315, "Understanding the Entity and its Environment and Assessing the Risks of Material Misstatement," ISA (UK and Ireland) 330, "The Auditor's Procedures in Response to Assessed Risks," and ISA (UK and Ireland) 500 (Revised), "Audit Evidence." The audit risk standards gave rise to amendments to this and other ISAs (UK and Ireland).

of items for testing from a population. Paragraphs 19-38 of ISA (UK and Ireland) 500 contain additional discussion on audit procedures for obtaining audit evidence.

Selecting Items for Testing to Gather Audit Evidence

22. **When designing audit procedures, the auditor should determine appropriate means of selecting items for testing.** The means available to the auditor are:

    (a) Selecting all items (100% examination);

    (b) Selecting specific items, and

    (c) Audit sampling.

23. The decision as to which approach to use will depend on the circumstances, and the application of any one or combination of the above means may be appropriate in particular circumstances. While the decision as to which means, or combination of means, to use is made on the basis of the risk of material misstatement related to the assertion being tested and audit efficiency, the auditor needs to be satisfied that methods used are effective in providing sufficient appropriate audit evidence to meet the objectives of the audit procedure.

Selecting All Items

24. The auditor may decide that it will be most appropriate to examine the entire population of items that make up a class of transactions or account balance (or a stratum within that population). 100% examination is unlikely in the case of tests of controls; however, it is more common for tests of details. For example, 100% examination may be appropriate when the population constitutes a small number of large value items, when there is a significant risk and other means do not provide sufficient appropriate audit evidence, or when the repetitive nature of a calculation or other process performed automatically by an information system makes a 100% examination cost effective, for example, through the use of computer-assisted audit techniques (CAATs).

Selecting Specific Items

25. The auditor may decide to select specific items from a population based on such factors as the auditor's understanding of the entity, the assessed risk of material misstatement, and the characteristics of the population being tested. The judgmental selection of specific items is subject to non-sampling risk. Specific items selected may include:

    • *High value or key items*. The auditor may decide to select specific items within a population because they are of high value, or exhibit some other characteristic, for example items that are suspicious, unusual, particularly risk-prone or that have a history of error.

- *All items over a certain amount*. The auditor may decide to examine items whose values exceed a certain amount so as to verify a large proportion of the total amount of class of transactions or account balance.

- *Items to obtain information*. The auditor may examine items to obtain information about matters such as the nature of the entity, the nature of transactions, and internal control.

- *Items to test control activities*. The auditor may use judgment to select and examine specific items to determine whether or not a particular control activity is being performed.

26. While selective examination of specific items from a class of transactions or account balance will often be an efficient means of gathering audit evidence, it does not constitute audit sampling. The results of audit procedures applied to items selected in this way cannot be projected to the entire population. The auditor considers the need to obtain sufficient appropriate audit evidence regarding the remainder of the population when that remainder is material.

Audit Sampling

27. The auditor may decide to apply audit sampling to a class of transactions or account balance. Audit sampling can be applied using either non-statistical or statistical sampling methods. Audit sampling is discussed in detail in paragraphs 30-55.

Statistical Versus Non-statistical Sampling Approaches

28. The decision whether to use a statistical or non-statistical sampling approach is a matter for the auditor's judgment regarding the most efficient manner to obtain sufficient appropriate audit evidence in the particular circumstances. For example, in the case of tests of controls the auditor's analysis of the nature and cause of errors will often be more important than the statistical analysis of the mere presence or absence (that is, the count) of errors. In such a situation, non-statistical sampling may be most appropriate.

29. When applying statistical sampling, the sample size can be determined using either probability theory or professional judgment. Moreover, sample size is not a valid criterion to distinguish between statistical and non-statistical approaches. Sample size is a function of factors such as those identified in Appendices 1 and 2. When circumstances are similar, the effect on sample size of factors such as those identified in Appendices 1 and 2 will be similar regardless of whether a statistical or non-statistical approach is chosen.

30. Often, while the approach adopted does not meet the definition of statistical sampling, elements of a statistical approach are used, for example the use of random selection using computer generated random numbers. However, only when the approach adopted has the characteristics of statistical sampling are statistical measurements of sampling risk valid.

Design of the Sample

31. **When designing an audit sample, the auditor should consider the objectives of the audit procedure and the attributes of the population from which the sample will be drawn.**

31-1. **When designing an audit sample the auditor should also consider the sampling and selection methods.**

32. The auditor first considers the specific objectives to be achieved and the combination of audit procedures which is likely to best achieve those objectives. Consideration of the nature of the audit evidence sought and possible error conditions or other characteristics relating to that audit evidence will assist the auditor in defining what constitutes an error and what population to use for sampling.

33. The auditor considers what conditions constitute an error by reference to the objectives of the audit procedure. A clear understanding of what constitutes an error is important to ensure that all, and only, those conditions that are relevant to the objectives of the audit procedure are included in the projection of errors. For example, in a test of details relating to the existence of accounts receivable, such as confirmation, payments made by the customer before the confirmation date but received shortly after that date by the client are not considered an error. Also, a misposting between customer accounts does not affect the total accounts receivable balance. Therefore, it is not appropriate to consider this an error in evaluating the sample results of this particular audit procedure, even though it may have an important effect on other areas of the audit, such as the assessment of the likelihood of fraud or the adequacy of the allowance for doubtful accounts.

34. When performing tests of controls, the auditor generally makes an assessment of the rate of error the auditor expects to find in the population to be tested. This assessment is based on the auditor's understanding of the design of the relevant controls and whether they have been implemented or the examination of a small number of items from the population. Similarly, for tests of details, the auditor generally makes an assessment of the expected amount of error in the population. These assessments are useful for designing an audit sample and in determining sample size. For example, if the expected rate of error is unacceptably high, tests of controls will normally not be performed. However, when performing tests of details, if the expected amount of error is high, 100% examination or the use of a large sample size may be appropriate.

Population

35. It is important for the auditor to ensure that the population is:

    (a) *Appropriate* to the objective of the audit procedure, which will include consideration of the direction of testing. For example, if the auditor's objective is to test for overstatement of accounts payable, the population could be defined as the accounts payable listing. On the other hand, when testing for understatement of accounts payable, the population is not the accounts payable listing but rather subsequent disbursements, unpaid invoices, suppliers' statements, unmatched receiving reports or other populations that provide audit evidence of understatement of accounts payable; and

(b) *Complete*. For example, if the auditor intends to select payment vouchers from a file, conclusions cannot be drawn about all vouchers for the period unless the auditor is satisfied that all vouchers have in fact been filed. Similarly, if the auditor intends to use the sample to draw conclusions about whether a control activity operated effectively during the financial reporting period, the population needs to include all relevant items from throughout the entire period. A different approach may be to stratify the population and use sampling only to draw conclusions about the control activity during, say, the first 10 months of a year, and to use alternative audit procedures or a separate sample regarding the remaining two months. ISA (UK and Ireland) 330 contains additional guidance on performing audit procedures at an interim period.

35a. The auditor is required to obtain audit evidence about the accuracy and completeness of information produced by the entity's information system when that information is used in performing audit procedures. When performing audit sampling, the auditor performs audit procedures to ensure that the information upon which the audit sampling is performed is sufficiently complete and accurate. ISA (UK and Ireland) 500 paragraph 11 contains additional guidance on the audit procedures to perform regarding the accuracy and completeness of such information.

Stratification

36. Audit efficiency may be improved if the auditor stratifies a population by dividing it into discrete sub-populations which have an identifying characteristic. The objective of stratification is to reduce the variability of items within each stratum and therefore allow sample size to be reduced without a proportional increase in sampling risk. Sub-populations need to be carefully defined such that any sampling unit can only belong to one stratum.

37. When performing tests of details, a class of transaction or account balance or is often stratified by monetary value. This allows greater audit effort to be directed to the larger value items which may contain the greatest potential monetary error in terms of overstatement. Similarly, a population may be stratified according to a particular characteristic that indicates a higher risk of error, for example, when testing the valuation of accounts receivable, balances may be stratified by age.

38. The results of audit procedures applied to a sample of items within a stratum can only be projected to the items that make up that stratum. To draw a conclusion on the entire population, the auditor will need to consider the risk of material misstatement in relation to whatever other strata make up the entire population. For example, 20% of the items in a population may make up 90% of the value of an account balance. The auditor may decide to examine a sample of these items. The auditor evaluates the results of this sample and reaches a conclusion on the 90% of value separately from the remaining 10% (on which a further sample or other means of gathering audit evidence will be used, or which may be considered immaterial).

Value Weighted Selection

39. It will often be efficient in performing tests of details, particularly when testing for overstatements, to identify the sampling unit as the individual monetary units (for example, dollars) that make up a class of transactions or account balance. Having selected specific monetary units from within the population, for example, the accounts receivable balance, the auditor then examines the particular items, for example, individual balances, that contain those monetary units. This approach to defining the sampling unit ensures that audit effort is directed to the larger value items because they have a greater chance of selection, and can result in smaller sample sizes. This approach is ordinarily used in conjunction with the systematic method of sample selection (described in Appendix 3) and is most efficient when selecting items using CAATs.

Sample Size

40. **In determining the sample size, the auditor should consider whether sampling risk is reduced to an acceptably low level.** Sample size is affected by the level of sampling risk that the auditor is willing to accept. The lower the risk the auditor is willing to accept, the greater the sample size will need to be.

41. The sample size can be determined by the application of a statistically-based formula or through the exercise of professional judgment objectively applied to the circumstances. Appendices 1 and 2 indicate the influences that various factors typically have on the determination of sample size, and hence the level of sampling risk.

Selecting the Sample

42. **The auditor should select items for the sample with the expectation that all sampling units in the population have a chance of selection.** Statistical sampling requires that sample items are selected at random so that each sampling unit has a known chance of being selected. The sampling units might be physical items (such as invoices) or monetary units. With non-statistical sampling, an auditor uses professional judgment to select the items for a sample. Because the purpose of sampling is to draw conclusions about the entire population, the auditor endeavors to select a representative sample by choosing sample items which have characteristics typical of the population, and the sample needs to be selected so that bias is avoided.

43. The principal methods of selecting samples are the use of random number tables or CAATs, systematic selection and haphazard selection. Each of these methods is discussed in Appendix 3.

Performing the Audit Procedure

44. **The auditor should perform audit procedures appropriate to the particular audit objective on each item selected.**

45. If a selected item is not appropriate for the application of the audit procedure, the audit procedure is ordinarily performed on a replacement item. For example, a voided check may be selected when testing for evidence of payment authorization. If the auditor is satisfied that the check had been properly voided such that it does not constitute an error, an appropriately chosen replacement is examined.

46. Sometimes however, the auditor is unable to apply the designed audit procedures to a selected item because, for instance, documentation relating to that item has been lost. If suitable alternative audit procedures cannot be performed on that item, the auditor ordinarily considers that item to be in error. An example of a suitable alternative audit procedure might be the examination of subsequent receipts when no reply has been received in response to a positive confirmation request.

Nature and Cause of Errors

47. **The auditor should consider the sample results, the nature and cause of any errors identified, and their possible effect on the particular audit objective and on other areas of the audit.**

48. When performing tests of controls, the auditor is primarily concerned with obtaining audit evidence that controls operated effectively throughout the period of reliance. This includes obtaining audit evidence about how controls were applied at relevant times during the period under audit, the consistency with which they were applied, and by whom or by what means they were applied. The concept of effectiveness of the operation of controls recognizes that some errors in the way controls are applied by the entity may occur. However, when such errors are identified, the auditor makes specific inquiries to understand these matters and also needs to consider matters such as:

    (a) The direct effect of identified errors on the financial statements; and

    (b) The effectiveness of internal control and their effect on the audit approach when, for example, the errors result from management override of a control.

    In these cases, the auditor determines whether the tests of controls performed provide an appropriate basis for use as audit evidence, whether additional tests of controls are necessary, or whether the potential risks of misstatement need to be addressed using substantive procedures.

49. In analyzing the errors discovered, the auditor may observe that many have a common feature, for example, type of transaction, location, product line or period of time. In such circumstances, the auditor may decide to identify all items in the population that

possess the common feature, and extend audit procedures in that stratum. In addition, such errors may be intentional, and may indicate the possibility of fraud.

50. Sometimes, the auditor may be able to establish that an error arises from an isolated event that has not recurred other than on specifically identifiable occasions and is therefore not representative of similar errors in the population (an anomalous error). To be considered an anomalous error, the auditor has to have a high degree of certainty that such error is not representative of the population. The auditor obtains this certainty by performing additional audit procedures. The additional audit procedures depend on the situation, but are adequate to provide the auditor with sufficient appropriate audit evidence that the error does not affect the remaining part of the population. One example is an error caused by a computer breakdown that is known to have occurred on only one day during the period. In that case, the auditor assesses the effect of the breakdown, for example by examining specific transactions processed on that day, and considers the effect of the cause of the breakdown on audit procedures and conclusions. Another example is an error that is found to be caused by use of an incorrect formula in calculating all inventory values at one particular branch. To establish that this is an anomalous error, the auditor needs to ensure the correct formula has been used at other branches.

Projecting Errors

51. **For tests of details, the auditor should project monetary errors found in the sample to the population, and should consider the effect of the projected error on the particular audit objective and on other areas of the audit.** The auditor projects the total error for the population to obtain a broad view of the scale of errors, and to compare this to the tolerable error. For tests of details, tolerable error is the tolerable misstatement, and will be an amount less than or equal to the auditor's materiality used for the individual class of transactions or account balances being audited.

52. When an error has been established as an anomalous error, it may be excluded when projecting sample errors to the population. The effect of any such error, if uncorrected, still needs to be considered in addition to the projection of the non-anomalous errors. If a class of transactions or account balance has been divided into strata, the error is projected for each stratum separately. Projected errors plus anomalous errors for each stratum are then combined when considering the possible effect of errors on the total class of transactions or account balance.

53. For tests of controls, no explicit projection of errors is necessary since the sample error rate is also the projected rate of error for the population as a whole.

Evaluating the Sample Results

54. **The auditor should evaluate the sample results to determine whether the assessment of the relevant characteristic of the population is confirmed or needs to be revised.** In the case of tests of controls, an unexpectedly high sample error rate may lead to an increase in the assessed risk of material misstatement, unless

further audit evidence substantiating the initial assessment is obtained. In the case of tests of details, an unexpectedly high error amount in a sample may cause the auditor to believe that a class of transactions or account balance is materially misstated, in the absence of further audit evidence that no material misstatement exists.

55. If the total amount of projected error plus anomalous error is less than but close to that which the auditor deems tolerable, the auditor considers the persuasiveness of the sample results in the light of other audit procedures, and may consider it appropriate to obtain additional audit evidence. The total of projected error plus anomalous error is the auditor's best estimate of error in the population. However, sampling results are affected by sampling risk. Thus when the best estimate of error is close to the tolerable error, the auditor recognizes the risk that a different sample would result in a different best estimate that could exceed the tolerable error. Considering the results of other audit procedures helps the auditor to assess this risk, while the risk is reduced if additional audit evidence is obtained.

56. If the evaluation of sample results indicates that the assessment of the relevant characteristic of the population needs to be revised, the auditor may:

   (a) Request management to investigate identified errors and the potential for further errors, and to make any necessary adjustments; and/or

   (b) Modify the nature, timing and extent of further audit procedures. For example, in the case of tests of controls, the auditor might extend the sample size, test an alternative control or modify related substantive procedures; and/or

   (c) Consider the effect on the audit report.

Effective Date

57. This ISA (UK and Ireland) is effective for audits of financial statements for periods commencing on or after 15 December 2004.

Appendix 1

Examples of Factors Influencing Sample Size for Tests of Controls

The following are factors that the auditor considers when determining the sample size for tests of controls. These factors, which need to be considered together, assume the auditor does not modify the nature or timing of tests of controls or otherwise modify the approach to substantive procedures in response to assessed risks.

FACTOR	EFFECT ON SAMPLE SIZE
An increase in the extent to which the risk of material misstatement is reduced by the operating effectiveness of controls	Increase
An increase in the rate of deviation from the prescribed control activity that the auditor is willing to accept	Decrease
An increase in the rate of deviation from the prescribed control activity that the auditor expects to find in the population	Increase
An increase in the auditor's required confidence level (or conversely, a decrease in the risk that the auditor will conclude that the risk of material misstatement is lower than the actual risk of material misstatement in the population)	Increase
An increase in the number of sampling units in the population	Negligible effect

1. *The extent to which the risk of material misstatement is reduced by the operating effectiveness of controls.* The more assurance the auditor intends to obtain from the operating effectiveness of controls, the lower the auditor's assessment of the risk of material misstatement will be, and the larger the sample size will need to be. When the auditor's assessment of the risk of material misstatement at the assertion level includes an expectation of the operating effectiveness of controls, the auditor is required to perform tests of controls. Other things being equal, the more the auditor relies on the operating effectiveness of controls in the risk assessment, the greater is the extent of the auditor's tests of controls (and therefore, the sample size is increased).

2. *The rate of deviation from the prescribed control activity the auditor is willing to accept (tolerable error).* The lower the rate of deviation that the auditor is willing to accept, the larger the sample size needs to be.

3. *The rate of deviation from the prescribed control activity the auditor expects to find in the population (expected error).* The higher the rate of deviation that the auditor expects, the larger the sample size needs to be so as to be in a position to make a reasonable estimate of the actual rate of deviation. Factors relevant to the auditor's consideration of the expected error rate include the auditor's understanding of the business (in particular, risk assessment procedures undertaken to obtain an understanding of internal control), changes in personnel or in internal control, the results of audit procedures applied in prior periods and the results of other audit procedures. High

expected error rates ordinarily warrant little, if any, reduction of the assessed risk of material misstatement, and therefore in such circumstances tests of controls would ordinarily be omitted.

4. *The auditor's required confidence level.* The greater the degree of confidence that the auditor requires that the results of the sample are in fact indicative of the actual incidence of error in the population, the larger the sample size needs to be.

5. *The number of sampling units in the population.* For large populations, the actual size of the population has little, if any, effect on sample size. For small populations however, audit sampling is often not as efficient as alternative means of obtaining sufficient appropriate audit evidence.

Appendix 2

Examples of Factors Influencing Sample Size for Tests of Details

The following are factors that the auditor considers when determining the sample size for tests of details. These factors, which need to be considered together, assume the auditor does not modify the approach to tests of controls or otherwise modify the nature or timing of substantive procedures in response to the assessed risks.

FACTOR	EFFECT ON SAMPLE SIZE
An increase in the auditor's assessment of the risk of material misstatement	Increase
An increase in the use of other substantive procedures directed at the same assertion	Decrease
An increase in the auditor's required confidence level (or conversely, a decrease in the risk that the auditor will conclude that a material error does not exist, when in fact it does exist)	Increase
An increase in the total error that the auditor is willing to accept (tolerable error)	Decrease
An increase in the amount of error the auditor expects to find in the population	Increase
Stratification of the population when appropriate	Decrease
The number of sampling units in the population	Negligible Effect

1.   [Deleted by IAASB]

2.   *The auditor's assessment of the risk of material misstatement.* The higher the auditor's assessment of the risk of material misstatement, the larger the sample size needs to be. The auditor's assessment of the risk of material misstatement is affected by inherent risk and control risk. For example, if the auditor does not perform tests of controls, the auditor's risk assessment cannot be reduced for the effective operation of internal controls with respect to the particular assertion. Therefore, in order to reduce audit risk to an acceptably low level, the auditor needs a low detection risk and will rely more on substantive procedures. The more audit evidence that is obtained from tests of details (that is, the lower the detection risk), the larger the sample size will need to be.

3.   *The use of other substantive procedures directed at the same assertion.* The more the auditor is relying on other substantive procedures (tests of details or substantive analytical procedures) to reduce to an acceptable level the detection risk regarding a particular class of transactions or account balance, the less assurance the auditor will require from sampling and, therefore, the smaller the sample size can be.

4. *The auditor's required confidence level.* The greater the degree of confidence that the auditor requires that the results of the sample are in fact indicative of the actual amount of error in the population, the larger the sample size needs to be.

5. *The total error the auditor is willing to accept (tolerable error).* The lower the total error that the auditor is willing to accept, the larger the sample size needs to be.

6. *The amount of error the auditor expects to find in the population (expected error).* The greater the amount of error the auditor expects to find in the population, the larger the sample size needs to be in order to make a reasonable estimate of the actual amount of error in the population. Factors relevant to the auditor's consideration of the expected error amount include the extent to which item values are determined subjectively, the results of risk assessment procedures, the results of tests of control, the results of audit procedures applied in prior periods, and the results of other substantive procedures.

7. *Stratification.* When there is a wide range (variability) in the monetary size of items in the population. It may be useful to group items of similar size into separate sub-populations or strata. This is referred to as stratification. When a population can be appropriately stratified, the aggregate of the sample sizes from the strata generally will be less than the sample size that would have been required to attain a given level of sampling risk, had one sample been drawn from the whole population.

8. *The number of sampling units in the population.* For large populations, the actual size of the population has little, if any, effect on sample size. Thus, for small populations, audit sampling is often not as efficient as alternative means of obtaining sufficient appropriate audit evidence. (However, when using monetary unit sampling, an increase in the monetary value of the population increases sample size, unless this is offset by a proportional increase in materiality.)

Appendix 3

Sample Selection Methods

The principal methods of selecting samples are as follows:

(a) Use of a computerized random number generator (through CAATs) or random number tables.

(b) Systematic selection, in which the number of sampling units in the population is divided by the sample size to give a sampling interval, for example 50, and having determined a starting point within the first 50, each 50th sampling unit thereafter is selected. Although the starting point may be determined haphazardly, the sample is more likely to be truly random if it is determined by use of a computerized random number generator or random number tables. When using systematic selection, the auditor would need to determine that sampling units within the population are not structured in such a way that the sampling interval corresponds with a particular pattern in the population.

(c) Haphazard selection, in which the auditor selects the sample without following a structured technique. Although no structured technique is used, the auditor would nonetheless avoid any conscious bias or predictability (for example, avoiding difficult to locate items, or always choosing or avoiding the first or last entries on a page) and thus attempt to ensure that all items in the population have a chance of selection. Haphazard selection is not appropriate when using statistical sampling.

(d) Block selection involves selecting a block(s) of contiguous items from within the population. Block selection cannot ordinarily be used in audit sampling because most populations are structured such that items in a sequence can be expected to have similar characteristics to each other, but different characteristics from items elsewhere in the population. Although in some circumstances it may be an appropriate audit procedure to examine a block of items, it would rarely be an appropriate sample selection technique when the auditor intends to draw valid inferences about the entire population based on the sample.

INTERNATIONAL STANDARD ON AUDITING (UK AND IRELAND) 540

AUDIT OF ACCOUNTING ESTIMATES

CONTENTS

International Standard on Auditing (UK and Ireland) (ISA (UK and Ireland)) 540 "Audit of Accounting Estimates" should be read in the context of the Auditing Practices Board's Statement "The Auditing Practices Board - Scope and Authority of Pronouncements (Revised)" which sets out the application and authority of ISAs (UK and Ireland).

Introduction

1. The purpose of this International Standard on Auditing (UK and Ireland) (ISA (UK and Ireland)) is to establish standards and provide guidance on the audit of accounting estimates contained in financial statements. This ISA (UK and Ireland) is not intended to be applicable to the examination of prospective financial information, though many of the audit procedures outlined herein may be suitable for that purpose.

1-1. This ISA (UK and Ireland) uses the terms 'those charged with governance' and 'management'. The term 'governance' describes the role of persons entrusted with the supervision, control and direction of an entity. Ordinarily, those charged with governance are accountable for ensuring that the entity achieves its objectives, and for the quality of its financial reporting and reporting to interested parties. Those charged with governance include management only when they perform such functions.

1-2. In the UK and Ireland, those charged with governance include the directors (executive and non-executive) of a company or other body, the members of an audit committee where one exists, the partners, proprietors, committee of management or trustees of other forms of entity, or equivalent persons responsible for directing the entity's affairs and preparing its financial statements.

1-3. 'Management' comprises those persons who perform senior managerial functions.

1-4. In the UK and Ireland, depending on the nature and circumstances of the entity, management may include some or all of those charged with governance (e.g. executive directors). Management will not normally include non-executive directors.

2. **The auditor should obtain sufficient appropriate audit evidence regarding accounting estimates.**

3. "Accounting estimate" means an approximation of the amount of an item in the absence of a precise means of measurement. Examples are:

    *   Allowances to reduce inventory and accounts receivable to their estimated realizable value.

    *   Provisions to allocate the cost of fixed assets over their estimated useful lives.

    *   Accrued revenue.

    *   Deferred tax.

    *   Provision for a loss from a lawsuit.

    *   Losses on construction contracts in progress.

    *   Provision to meet warranty claims.

4.   Management[1] is responsible for making accounting estimates included in financial statements. These estimates are often made in conditions of uncertainty regarding the outcome of events that have occurred or are likely to occur and involve the use of judgment. As a result, the risk of material misstatement is greater when accounting estimates are involved and in some cases the auditor may determine that the risk of material misstatement related to an accounting estimate is a significant risk that requires special audit consideration. See paragraphs 108-114 of ISA (UK and Ireland) 315, "Understanding the Entity and Its Environment and Assessing the Risks of Material Misstatement."

4-1. In addition, audit evidence obtained is generally less conclusive when accounting estimates are involved. Consequently, in assessing the sufficiency and appropriateness of audit evidence on which to base the audit opinion, the auditor is more likely to need to exercise judgment when considering accounting estimates than in other areas of the audit.

The Nature of Accounting Estimates

5.   The determination of an accounting estimate may be simple or complex depending upon the nature of the item. For example, accruing a charge for rent may be a simple calculation, whereas estimating a provision for slow-moving or surplus inventory may involve considerable analyses of current data and a forecast of future sales. In complex estimates, there may be a high degree of special knowledge and judgment required.

6.   Accounting estimates may be determined as part of the routine information system relevant to financial reporting operating on a continuing basis, or may be nonroutine, operating only at period end. In many cases, accounting estimates are made by using a formula based on experience, such as the use of standard rates for depreciating each category of fixed assets or a standard percentage of sales revenue for computing a warranty provision. In such cases, the formula needs to be reviewed regularly by management, for example, by reassessing the remaining useful lives of assets or by comparing actual results with the estimate and adjusting the formula when necessary.

7.   The uncertainty associated with an item, or the lack of objective data may make it incapable of reasonable estimation, in which case, the auditor needs to consider whether the auditor's report needs modification to comply with ISA (UK and Ireland) 700 "The Auditor's Report on Financial Statements."

Audit Procedures Responsive to the Risk of Material Misstatement of the Entity's Accounting Estimates

8.   **The auditor should design and perform further audit procedures to obtain sufficient appropriate audit evidence as to whether the entity's accounting**

---

[1]   In the UK and Ireland those charged with governance are responsible for the preparation of the financial statements.

estimates are reasonable in the circumstances and, when required, appropriately disclosed. The audit evidence available to detect a material misstatement in an accounting estimate will often be more difficult to obtain and less persuasive than audit evidence available to detect a material misstatement in other items in the financial statements. The auditor's understanding of the entity and its environment, including its internal control, assists the auditor in identifying and assessing the risks of material misstatement of the entity's accounting estimates.

9. An understanding of the procedures and methods, including relevant control activities, used by management in making the accounting estimates is important for the auditor to identify and assess risks of material misstatement in order to design the nature, timing and extent of the further audit procedures.

10. **The auditor should adopt one or a combination of the following approaches in the audit of an accounting estimate:**

   (a) **Review and test the process used by management to develop the estimate;**

   (b) **Use an independent estimate for comparison with that prepared by management; or**

   (c) **Review of subsequent events which provide audit evidence of the reasonableness of the estimate made.**

Reviewing and Testing the Process Used by Management

11. The steps ordinarily involved in reviewing and testing of the process used by management are:

   (a) Evaluation of the data and consideration of assumptions on which the estimate is based;

   (b) Testing of the calculations involved in the estimate;

   (c) Comparison, when possible, of estimates made for prior periods with actual results of those periods; and

   (d) Consideration of management's approval procedures.

Evaluation of Data and Consideration of Assumptions

12. The auditor would evaluate whether the data on which the estimate is based is accurate, complete and relevant. When information produced by the entity is used, it will need to be consistent with the data processed through the information system relevant to financial reporting. For example, in substantiating a warranty provision, the auditor would obtain audit evidence that the data relating to products still within the warranty period at period end agree with the sales information within the information system relevant to financial reporting. ISA (UK and Ireland) 500, "Audit Evidence"

paragraph 11 provides additional guidance on the requirement to obtain audit evidence about the accuracy and completeness of information produced by the entity when it is used in performing audit procedures.

13. The auditor may also seek audit evidence from sources outside the entity. For example, when examining a provision for inventory obsolescence calculated by reference to anticipated future sales, the auditor may, in addition to examining internal data such as past levels of sales, orders on hand and marketing trends, seek audit evidence from industry-produced sales projections and market analyses. Similarly, when examining management's estimates of the financial implications of litigation and claims, the auditor would seek direct communication with the entity's lawyers.

14. The auditor would evaluate whether the data collected is appropriately analyzed and projected to form a reasonable basis for determining the accounting estimate. Examples are the analysis of the age of accounts receivable and the projection of the number of months of supply on hand of an item of inventory based on past and forecast usage.

15. The auditor would evaluate whether the entity has an appropriate base for the principal assumptions used in the accounting estimate. In some cases, the assumptions will be based on industry or government statistics, such as future inflation rates, interest rates, employment rates and anticipated market growth. In other cases, the assumptions will be specific to the entity and will be based on internally generated data.

16. In evaluating the assumptions on which the estimate is based, the auditor would consider, among other things, whether they are:

- Reasonable in light of actual results in prior periods.

- Consistent with those used for other accounting estimates.

- Consistent with management's plans which appear appropriate.

The auditor would need to pay particular attention to assumptions which are sensitive to variation, subjective or susceptible to material misstatement.

17. In the case of complex estimating processes involving specialized techniques, it may be necessary for the auditor to use the work of an expert, for example, engineers for estimating quantities in stock piles of mineral ores. Guidance on how to use the work of an expert is provided in ISA (UK and Ireland) 620 "Using the Work of an Expert."

18. The auditor would review the continuing appropriateness of formulae used by management in the preparation of accounting estimates. Such a review would reflect the auditor's knowledge of the financial results of the entity in prior periods, practices used by other entities in the industry and the future plans of management as disclosed to the auditor.

Testing of Calculations

19. The auditor would perform audit procedures on the calculation procedures used by management. The nature, timing and extent of the auditor's procedures will depend on the assessed risk of material misstatement, which is impacted by such factors as the complexity involved in calculating the accounting estimate, the auditor's understanding and evaluation of the procedures and methods, including relevant control activities used by the entity in producing the estimate and the materiality of the estimate in the context of the financial statements.

Comparison of Previous Estimates with Actual Results

20. When possible, the auditor would compare accounting estimates made for prior periods with actual results of those periods to assist in:

    (a) Obtaining audit evidence about the general reliability of the entity's estimating procedures and methods, including relevant control activities;

    (b) Considering whether adjustments to estimating formulae may be required; and

    (c) Evaluating whether differences between actual results and previous estimates have been quantified and that, where necessary, appropriate adjustments or disclosures have been made.

Consideration of Management's Approval Procedures

21. Material accounting estimates are ordinarily reviewed and approved by management. The auditor would consider whether such review and approval is performed by the appropriate level of management and that it is evidenced in the documentation supporting the determination of the accounting estimate.

Use of an Independent Estimate

22. The auditor may make or obtain an independent estimate and compare it with the accounting estimate prepared by management. When using an independent estimate the auditor would ordinarily evaluate the data, consider the assumptions and perform audit procedures on the calculation procedures used in its development. It may also be appropriate to compare accounting estimates made for prior periods with actual results of those periods.

Review of Subsequent Events

23. Transactions and events which occur after period end, but prior to completion of the audit, may provide audit evidence regarding an accounting estimate made by management. The auditor's review of such transactions and events may reduce, or even remove, the need for the auditor to review and perform audit procedures on the

process used by management to develop the accounting estimate or to use an independent estimate in assessing the reasonableness of the accounting estimate.

Evaluation of Results of Audit Procedures

24. **The auditor should make a final assessment of the reasonableness of the entity's accounting estimates based on the auditor's understanding of the entity and its environment and whether the estimates are consistent with other audit evidence obtained during the audit.**

25. The auditor would consider whether there are any significant subsequent transactions or events which affect the data and the assumptions used in determining the accounting estimates.

26. Because of the uncertainties inherent in accounting estimates, evaluating differences can be more difficult than in other areas of the audit. When there is a difference between the auditor's estimate of the amount best supported by the available audit evidence and the estimated amount included in the financial statements, the auditor would determine whether such a difference requires adjustment. If the difference is reasonable, for example, because the amount in the financial statements falls within a range of acceptable results, it may not require adjustment. However, if the auditor believes the difference is unreasonable, management would be requested to revise the estimate. If management refuses to revise the estimate, the difference would be considered a misstatement and would be considered with all other misstatements in assessing whether the effect on the financial statements is material.

27. The auditor would also consider whether individual differences which have been accepted as reasonable are biased in one direction, so that, on a cumulative basis, they may have a material effect on the financial statements. In such circumstances, the auditor would evaluate the accounting estimates taken as a whole.

Effective Date

27-1. This ISA (UK and Ireland) is effective for audits of financial statements for periods commencing on or after 15 December 2004.

See 2006 paper

INTERNATIONAL STANDARD ON AUDITING
(UK AND IRELAND) 545

AUDITING FAIR VALUE MEASUREMENTS AND DISCLOSURES

CONTENTS

International Standard on Auditing (UK and Ireland) (ISA (UK and Ireland)) 545 "Auditing Fair Value Measurements and Disclosures" should be read in the context of the Auditing Practices Board's Statement "The Auditing Practices Board - Scope and Authority of Pronouncements (Revised)" which sets out the application and authority of ISAs (UK and Ireland).

Introduction

1. The purpose of this International Standard on Auditing (UK and Ireland) (ISA (UK and Ireland)) is to establish standards and provide guidance on auditing fair value measurements and disclosures contained in financial statements. In particular, this ISA (UK and Ireland) addresses audit considerations relating to the measurement, presentation and disclosure of material assets, liabilities and specific components of equity presented or disclosed at fair value in financial statements. Fair value measurements of assets, liabilities and components of equity may arise from both the initial recording of transactions and later changes in value. Changes in fair value measurements that occur over time may be treated in different ways under different financial reporting frameworks. For example, some financial reporting frameworks may require that such changes be reflected directly in equity, while others may require them to be reflected in income.

1-1. Many of the examples of accounting principles given in this ISA (UK and Ireland) are based on International Accounting Standards. If other accounting standards are used (e.g. Financial Reporting Standards issued by the UK Accounting Standards Board) the auditor recognizes that, whilst the accounting principles may differ, the audit principles remain the same.

1-2. Paragraph 22 of ISA (UK and Ireland) 315 "Understanding the Entity and its Environment and Assessing the Risks of Material Misstatement" requires that "the auditor should obtain an understanding of ... the applicable financial reporting framework." That understanding includes the requirements of the particular accounting standards that the entity is required or chooses, where a choice is possible, to comply with. The auditor takes that understanding into account when complying with the requirements of this ISA (UK and Ireland). The auditor also takes into account requirements of legislation pertaining to fair value accounting (e.g. Schedule 4 of the UK Companies Act 1985 as amended by "The Companies Act 1985 (International Accounting Standards and Other Accounting Amendments) Regulations 2004").

1-3. This ISA (UK and Ireland) uses the terms 'those charged with governance' and 'management'. The term 'governance' describes the role of persons entrusted with the supervision, control and direction of an entity. Ordinarily, those charged with governance are accountable for ensuring that the entity achieves its objectives, and for the quality of its financial reporting and reporting to interested parties. Those charged with governance include management only when they perform such functions.

1-4. In the UK and Ireland, those charged with governance include the directors (executive and non-executive) of a company or other body, the members of an audit committee where one exists, the partners, proprietors, committee of management or trustees of other forms of entity, or equivalent persons responsible for directing the entity's affairs and preparing its financial statements.

1-5. 'Management' comprises those persons who perform senior managerial functions.

1-6.   In the UK and Ireland, depending on the nature and circumstances of the entity, management may include some or all of those charged with governance (e.g. executive directors). Management will not normally include non-executive directors.

2.   While this ISA (UK and Ireland) provides guidance on auditing fair value measurements and disclosures, audit evidence obtained from other audit procedures also may provide audit evidence relevant to the measurement and disclosure of fair values. For example, inspection procedures to verify existence of an asset measured at fair value also may provide relevant audit evidence about its valuation (such as the physical condition of an investment property).

2a.   ISA (UK and Ireland) 500, "Audit Evidence" paragraph 16 requires the auditor to use assertions in sufficient detail to form a basis for the assessment of risks of material misstatements and the design and performance of further audit procedures in response to the assessed risks. Fair value measurements and disclosures are not in themselves assertions, but may be relevant to specific assertions, depending on the applicable financial reporting framework.

3.   **The auditor should obtain sufficient appropriate audit evidence that fair value measurements and disclosures are in accordance with the entity's applicable financial reporting framework.** Paragraph 22 of ISA (UK and Ireland) 315, "Understanding the Entity and Its Environment and Assessing the Risks of Material Misstatement" requires the auditor to obtain an understanding of the entity's applicable financial reporting framework.

4.   Management[1] is responsible for making the fair value measurements and disclosures included in the financial statements. As part of fulfilling its responsibility, management needs to establish an accounting and financial reporting process for determining the fair value measurements and disclosures, select appropriate valuation methods, identify and adequately support any significant assumptions used, prepare the valuation and ensure that the presentation and disclosure of the fair value measurements are in accordance with the entity's applicable financial reporting framework.

5.   Many measurements based on estimates, including fair value measurements, are inherently imprecise. In the case of fair value measurements, particularly those that do not involve contractual cash flows or for which market information is not available when making the estimate, fair value estimates often involve uncertainty in both the amount and timing of future cash flows. Fair value measurements also may be based on assumptions about future conditions, transactions or events whose outcome is uncertain and will therefore be subject to change over time. The auditor's consideration of such assumptions is based on information available to the auditor at the time of the audit and the auditor is not responsible for predicting future conditions, transactions or events which, had they been known at the time of the audit, may have had a significant effect on management's actions or management's

---

[1]   In the UK and Ireland, those charged with governance are responsible for the preparation of the financial statements.

assumptions underlying the fair value measurements and disclosures. Assumptions used in fair value measurements are similar in nature to those required when developing other accounting estimates. ISA (UK and Ireland) 540, "Audit of Accounting Estimates" provides guidance on auditing accounting estimates. This ISA (UK and Ireland), however, addresses considerations similar to those in ISA (UK and Ireland) 540 as well as others in the specific context of fair value measurements and disclosures in accordance with an applicable financial reporting framework.

6.   Different financial reporting frameworks require or permit a variety of fair value measurements and disclosures in financial statements. They also vary in the level of guidance that they provide on the basis for measuring assets and liabilities or the related disclosures. Some financial reporting frameworks give prescriptive guidance, others give general guidance, and some give no guidance at all. In addition, certain industry-specific measurement and disclosure practices for fair values also exist. While this ISA (UK and Ireland) provides guidance on auditing fair value measurements and disclosures, it does not address specific types of assets or liabilities, transactions, or industry-specific practices. The Appendix to this ISA (UK and Ireland) discusses fair value measurements and disclosures under different financial reporting frameworks and the prevalence of fair value measurements, including the fact that different definitions of "fair value" may exist under such frameworks. For example, International Accounting Standard (IAS) 39, "Financial Instruments: Recognition and Measurement" defines fair value as "the amount for which an asset could be exchanged, or a liability settled, between knowledgeable, willing parties in an arm's length transaction."

7.   In most financial reporting frameworks, underlying the concept of fair value measurements is a presumption that the entity is a going concern without any intention or need to liquidate, curtail materially the scale of its operations, or undertake a transaction on adverse terms. Therefore, in this case, fair value would not be the amount that an entity would receive or pay in a forced transaction, involuntary liquidation, or distress sale. An entity, however, may need to take its current economic or operating situation into account in determining the fair values of its assets and liabilities if prescribed or permitted to do so by its financial reporting framework and such framework may or may not specify how that is done. For example, management's plan to dispose of an asset on an accelerated basis to meet specific business objectives may be relevant to the determination of the fair value of that asset.

8.   The measurement of fair value may be relatively simple for certain assets or liabilities, for example, assets that are bought and sold in active and open markets that provide readily available and reliable information on the prices at which actual exchanges occur. The measurement of fair value for other assets or liabilities may be more complex. A specific asset may not have an active market or may possess characteristics that make it necessary for management to estimate its fair value (for example, an investment property or a complex derivative financial instrument). The estimation of fair value may be achieved through the use of a valuation model (for example, a model premised on projections and discounting of future cash flows) or through the assistance of an expert, such as an independent valuer.

9.   The uncertainty associated with an item, or the lack of objective data may make it incapable of reasonable estimation, in which case, the auditor considers whether the auditor's report needs modification to comply with ISA (UK and Ireland) 700, "The Auditor's Report on Financial Statements."

Understanding the Entity's Process for Determining Fair Value Measurements and Disclosures and Relevant Control Activities, and Assessing Risk

10.   **As part of the understanding of the entity and its environment, including its internal control, the auditor should obtain an understanding of the entity's process for determining fair value measurements and disclosures and of the relevant control activities sufficient to identify and assess the risks of material misstatement at the assertion level and to design and perform further audit procedures.**

11.   Management[1] is responsible for establishing an accounting and financial reporting process for determining fair value measurements. In some cases, the measurement of fair value and therefore the process set up by management to determine fair value may be simple and reliable. For example, management may be able to refer to published price quotations to determine fair value for marketable securities held by the entity. Some fair value measurements, however, are inherently more complex than others and involve uncertainty about the occurrence of future events or their outcome, and therefore assumptions that may involve the use of judgment need to be made as part of the measurement process. The auditor's understanding of the measurement process, including its complexity, helps identify and assess the risks of material misstatement in order to determine the nature, timing and extent of the further audit procedures.

12.   When obtaining an understanding of the entity's process for determining fair value measurements and disclosures, the auditor considers, for example:

*   The relevant control activities over the process used to determine fair value measurements, including, for example, controls over data and the segregation of duties between those committing the entity to the underlying transactions and those responsible for undertaking the valuations.

*   The expertise and experience of those persons determining the fair value measurements.

*   The role that information technology has in the process.

*   The types of accounts or transactions requiring fair value measurements or disclosures (for example, whether the accounts arise from the recording of routine and recurring transactions or whether they arise from non-routine or unusual transactions).

- The extent to which the entity's process relies on a service organization to provide fair value measurements or the data that supports the measurement. When an entity uses a service organization, the auditor complies with the requirements of ISA (UK and Ireland) 402, "Audit Considerations Relating to Entities Using Service Organizations."

- The extent to which the entity uses the work of experts in determining fair value measurements and disclosures (see paragraphs 29–32 of this Standard).

- The significant management assumptions used in determining fair value.

- The documentation supporting management's assumptions.

- The methods used to develop and apply management assumptions and to monitor changes in those assumptions.

- The integrity of change controls and security procedures for valuation models and relevant information systems, including approval processes.

- The controls over the consistency, timeliness and reliability of the data used in valuation models.

13. ISA (UK and Ireland) 315, "Understanding the Entity and its Environment and Assessing the Risks of Material Misstatement," requires the auditor to obtain an understanding of the components of internal control. In particular, the auditor obtains a sufficient understanding of control activities related to the determination of the entity's fair value measurements and disclosures in order to identify and assess the risks of material misstatement and to design the nature, timing and extent of the further audit procedures.

14. **After obtaining an understanding of the entity's process for determining fair value measurements and disclosures, the auditor should identify and assess the risks of material misstatement at the assertion level related to the fair value measurements and disclosures in the financial statements to determine the nature, timing and extent of the further audit procedures.**

15. The degree to which a fair value measurement is susceptible to misstatement is an inherent risk. Consequently, the nature, timing and extent of the further audit procedures will depend upon the susceptibility to misstatement of a fair value measurement and whether the process for determining fair value measurements is relatively simple or complex.

15a Where the auditor has determined that the risk of material misstatement related to a fair value measurement or disclosure is a significant risk that requires special audit considerations, the auditor follows the requirements of ISA (UK and Ireland) 315.

16. ISA (UK and Ireland) 315 discusses the inherent limitations of internal controls. As fair value determinations often involve subjective judgments by management, this may affect the nature of control activities that are capable of being implemented. The

susceptibility to misstatement of fair value measurements also may increase as the accounting and financial reporting requirements for fair value measurements become more complex. The auditor considers the inherent limitations of controls in such circumstances in assessing the risk of material misstatement.

Evaluating the Appropriateness of Fair Value Measurements and Disclosures

17. **The auditor should evaluate whether the fair value measurements and disclosures in the financial statements are in accordance with the entity's applicable financial reporting framework.**

18. The auditor's understanding of the requirements of the applicable financial reporting framework and knowledge of the business and industry, together with the results of other audit procedures, are used to assess whether the accounting for assets or liabilities requiring fair value measurements is appropriate, and whether the disclosures about the fair value measurements and significant uncertainties related thereto are appropriate under the entity's applicable financial reporting framework.

19. The evaluation of the appropriateness of the entity's fair value measurements under its applicable financial reporting framework and the evaluation of audit evidence depends, in part, on the auditor's knowledge of the nature of the business. This is particularly true where the asset or liability or the valuation method is highly complex. For example, derivative financial instruments may be highly complex, with a risk that differing interpretations of how to determine fair values will result in different conclusions. The measurement of the fair value of some items, for example "in-process research and development" or intangible assets acquired in a business combination, may involve special considerations that are affected by the nature of the entity and its operations if such considerations are appropriate under the entity's applicable financial reporting framework. Also, the auditor's knowledge of the business, together with the results of other audit procedures, may help identify assets for which management[1] needs to recognize an impairment by using a fair value measurement pursuant to the entity's applicable financial reporting framework.

20. Where the method for measuring fair value is specified by the applicable financial reporting framework, for example, the requirement that the fair value of a marketable security be measured using quoted market prices as opposed to using a valuation model, the auditor considers whether the measurement of fair value is consistent with that method.

21. Some financial reporting frameworks presume that fair value can be measured reliably for assets or liabilities as a prerequisite to either requiring or permitting fair value measurements or disclosures. In some cases, this presumption may be overcome when an asset or liability does not have a quoted market price in an active market and for which other methods of reasonably estimating fair value are clearly inappropriate or unworkable. When management[1] has determined that it has overcome the presumption that fair value can be reliably determined, the auditor obtains sufficient

appropriate audit evidence to support such determination, and whether the item is properly accounted for under the applicable financial reporting framework.

22. **The auditor should obtain audit evidence about management's intent to carry out specific courses of action, and consider its ability to do so, where relevant to the fair value measurements and disclosures under the entity's applicable financial reporting framework.**

23. In some financial reporting frameworks, management's[1] intentions with respect to an asset or liability are criteria for determining measurement, presentation, and disclosure requirements, and how changes in fair values are reported within financial statements. In such financial reporting frameworks, management's intent is important in determining the appropriateness of the entity's use of fair value. Management often documents plans and intentions relevant to specific assets or liabilities and the applicable financial reporting framework may require it to do so. While the extent of audit evidence to be obtained about management's intent is a matter of professional judgment, the auditor's procedures ordinarily include inquiries of management, with appropriate corroboration of responses, for example, by:

- Considering management's past history of carrying out its stated intentions with respect to assets or liabilities.

- Reviewing written plans and other documentation, including, where applicable, budgets, minutes, *etc.*

- Considering management's stated reasons for choosing a particular course of action.

- Considering management's ability to carry out a particular course of action given the entity's economic circumstances, including the implications of its contractual commitments.

The auditor also considers management's ability to pursue a specific course of action if ability is relevant to the use, or exemption from the use, of fair value measurement under the entity's applicable financial reporting framework.

24. **Where alternative methods for measuring fair value are available under the entity's applicable financial reporting framework, or where the method of measurement is not prescribed, the auditor should evaluate whether the method of measurement is appropriate in the circumstances under the entity's applicable financial reporting framework.**

25. Evaluating whether the method of measurement of fair value is appropriate in the circumstances requires the use of professional judgment. When management selects one particular valuation method from alternative methods available under the entity's applicable financial reporting framework, the auditor obtains an understanding of management's rationale for its selection by discussing with management its reasons for selecting the valuation method. The auditor considers whether:

(a) Management has sufficiently evaluated and appropriately applied the criteria, if any, provided in the applicable financial reporting framework to support the selected method;

(b) The valuation method is appropriate in the circumstances given the nature of the asset or liability being valued and the entity's applicable financial reporting framework; and

(c) The valuation method is appropriate in relation to the business, industry and environment in which the entity operates.

26. Management may have determined that different valuation methods result in a range of significantly different fair value measurements. In such cases, the auditor evaluates how the entity has investigated the reasons for these differences in establishing its fair value measurements.

27. **The auditor should evaluate whether the entity's method for its fair value measurements is applied consistently.**

28. Once management has selected a specific valuation method, the auditor evaluates whether the entity has consistently applied that basis in its fair value measurement, and if so, whether the consistency is appropriate considering possible changes in the environment or circumstances affecting the entity, or changes in the requirements of the entity's applicable financial reporting framework. If management has changed the valuation method, the auditor considers whether management can adequately demonstrate that the valuation method to which it has changed provides a more appropriate basis of measurement, or whether the change is supported by a change in the requirements of the entity's applicable financial reporting framework or a change in circumstances. For example, the introduction of an active market for a particular class of asset or liability may indicate that the use of discounted cash flows to estimate the fair value of such asset or liability is no longer appropriate.

Using the Work of an Expert

29. **The auditor should determine the need to use the work of an expert.** The auditor may have the necessary skill and knowledge to plan and perform audit procedures related to fair values or may decide to use the work of an expert. In making such a determination, the auditor considers the matters discussed in paragraph 7 of ISA (UK and Ireland) 620.

30. If the use of such an expert is planned, the auditor obtains sufficient appropriate audit evidence that such work is adequate for the purposes of the audit, and complies with the requirements of ISA (UK and Ireland) 620.

31. When planning to use the work of an expert, the auditor considers whether the expert's understanding of the definition of fair value and the method that the expert will use to determine fair value are consistent with that of management and the requirements of the applicable financial reporting framework. For example, the method used by an

expert for estimating the fair value of real estate or a complex derivative, or the actuarial methodologies developed for making fair value estimates of insurance obligations, reinsurance receivables and similar items, may not be consistent with the measurement principles of the applicable financial reporting framework. Accordingly, the auditor considers such matters, often by discussing, providing or reviewing instructions given to the expert or when reading the report of the expert.

32. In accordance with ISA (UK and Ireland) 620, the auditor assesses the appropriateness of the expert's work as audit evidence. While the reasonableness of assumptions and the appropriateness of the methods used and their application are the responsibility of the expert, the auditor obtains an understanding of the significant assumptions and methods used, and considers whether they are appropriate, complete and reasonable, based on the auditor's knowledge of the business and the results of other audit procedures. The auditor often considers these matters by discussing them with the expert. Paragraphs 39-49 discuss the auditor's evaluation of significant assumptions used by management, including assumptions relied upon by management based on the work of an expert.

Audit Procedures Responsive to the Risk of Material Misstatement of the Entity's Fair Value Measurements and Disclosures

33. **The auditor should design and perform further audit procedures in response to assessed risks of material misstatement of assertions relating to the entity's fair value measurements and disclosures.** ISA (UK and Ireland) 330, "The Auditor's Procedures in Response to Assessed Risks" discusses the auditor's responsibility to design and perform further audit procedures whose nature, timing and extent are responsive to the assessed risk of material misstatement at the assertion level. Such further audit procedures include tests of control and substantive procedures, as appropriate. Paragraphs 34-55 below provide additional specific guidance on substantive procedures that may be relevant in the context of the entity's fair value measurements and disclosures.

34. Because of the wide range of possible fair value measurements, from relatively simple to complex, the auditor's procedures can vary significantly in nature, timing and extent. For example, substantive procedures relating to the fair value measurements may involve (a) testing management's significant assumptions, the valuation model, and the underlying data (see paragraphs 39–49), (b) developing independent fair value estimates to corroborate the appropriateness of the fair value measurement (see paragraph 52), or (c) considering the effect of subsequent events on the fair value measurement and disclosures (see paragraphs 53–55).

35. The existence of published price quotations in an active market ordinarily is the best audit evidence of fair value. Some fair value measurements, however, are inherently more complex than others. This complexity arises either because of the nature of the item being measured at fair value or because of the valuation method required by the applicable financial reporting framework or selected by management. For example, in the absence of quoted prices in an active market, some financial reporting frameworks

permit an estimate of fair value based on an alternative basis such as a discounted cash flow analysis or a comparative transaction model. Complex fair value measurements normally are characterized by greater uncertainty regarding the reliability of the measurement process. This greater uncertainty may be a result of:

• Length of the forecast period.

• The number of significant and complex assumptions associated with the process.

• A higher degree of subjectivity associated with the assumptions and factors used in the process.

• A higher degree of uncertainty associated with the future occurrence or outcome of events underlying the assumptions used.

• Lack of objective data when highly subjective factors are used.

36. The auditor's understanding of the measurement process, including its complexity, helps guide the auditor's determination of the nature, timing and extent of audit procedures to be performed. The following are examples of considerations in the development of audit procedures:

• Using a price quotation to obtain audit evidence about valuation may require an understanding of the circumstances in which the quotation was developed. For example, where quoted securities are held for investment purposes, valuation at the listed market price may require adjustment under the entity's applicable financial reporting framework if the holding is significantly large in size or is subject to restrictions in marketability.

• When using audit evidence provided by a third party, the auditor considers its reliability. For example, when information is obtained through the use of external confirmations, the auditor considers the respondent's competence, independence, authority to respond, knowledge of the matter being confirmed, and objectivity in order to be satisfied with the reliability of the evidence. The extent of such audit procedures will vary according to the assessed risk of material misstatement associated with the fair value measurements. The auditor complies with ISA (UK and Ireland) 505, "External Confirmations" in this regard.

• Audit evidence supporting fair value measurements, for example, a valuation by an independent valuer, may be obtained at a date that does not coincide with the date at which the entity is required to measure and report that information in its financial statements. In such cases, the auditor obtains audit evidence that management has taken into account the effect of events, transactions and changes in circumstances occurring between the date of fair value measurement and the reporting date.

• Collateral often is assigned for certain types of investments in debt instruments that either are required to be measured at fair value or are evaluated for possible impairment. If the collateral is an important factor in measuring the fair value of the investment or evaluating its carrying amount, the auditor obtains sufficient appropriate audit evidence regarding the existence, value, rights and access to or transferability of such collateral, including consideration whether all appropriate liens have been filed, and considers whether appropriate disclosures about the collateral have been made under the entity's applicable financial reporting framework.

- In some situations, additional audit procedures, such as the inspection of an asset by the auditor, may be necessary to obtain sufficient appropriate audit evidence about the appropriateness of a fair value measurement. For example, inspection of an investment property may be necessary to obtain information about the current physical condition of the asset relevant to its fair value, or inspection of a security may reveal a restriction on its marketability that may affect its value.

Testing Management's Significant Assumptions, the Valuation Model, and the Underlying Data

37. The auditor's understanding of the reliability of the process used by management to determine fair value is an important element in support of the resulting amounts and therefore affects the nature, timing, and extent of further audit procedures. A reliable process for determining fair value is one that results in reasonably consistent measurement and, where relevant, presentation and disclosure of fair value when used in similar circumstances. When obtaining audit evidence about the entity's fair value measurements and disclosures, the auditor evaluates whether:

    (a)   The assumptions used by management are reasonable;

    (b)   The fair value measurement was determined using an appropriate model, if applicable;

    (c)   Management used relevant information that was reasonably available at the time.

38. Estimation techniques and assumptions and the auditor's consideration and comparison of fair value measurements determined in prior periods, if any, to results obtained in the current period may provide audit evidence of the reliability of management's processes. However, the auditor also considers whether such variances result from changes in economic circumstances.

39. **Where the auditor determines there is a significant risk related to fair value, or where otherwise applicable, the auditor should evaluate whether the significant assumptions used by management[1] in measuring fair values, taken individually and as a whole, provide a reasonable basis for the fair value measurements and disclosures in the entity's financial statements.**

40. It is necessary for management to make assumptions, including assumptions relied upon by management based upon the work of an expert, to develop fair value measurements. For these purposes, management's assumptions also include those assumptions developed under the guidance of those charged with governance. Assumptions are integral components of more complex valuation methods, for

example valuation methods that employ a combination of estimates of expected future cash flows together with estimates of the values of assets or liabilities in the future, discounted to the present. Auditors pay particular attention to the significant assumptions underlying a valuation method and evaluate whether such assumptions are reasonable. To provide a reasonable basis for the fair value measurements and disclosures, assumptions need to be relevant, reliable, neutral, understandable and complete. Paragraph 36 of the "International Framework for Assurance Engagements" describes these characteristics in more detail.

41. Specific assumptions will vary with the characteristics of the asset or liability being valued and the valuation method used (e.g., replacement cost, market or an income-based approach). For example, where discounted cash flows (an income-based approach) are used as the valuation method, there will be assumptions about the level of cash flows, the period of time used in the analysis, and the discount rate.

42. Assumptions ordinarily are supported by differing types of audit evidence from internal and external sources that provide objective support for the assumptions used. The auditor assesses the source and reliability of audit evidence supporting management's assumptions, including consideration of the assumptions in light of historical information and an evaluation of whether they are based on plans that are within the entity's capacity.

43. Audit procedures dealing with management's assumptions are performed in the context of the audit of the entity's financial statements. The objective of the audit procedures is therefore not intended to obtain sufficient appropriate audit evidence to provide an opinion on the assumptions themselves. Rather, the auditor performs audit procedures to consider whether the assumptions provide a reasonable basis in measuring fair values in the context of an audit of the financial statements taken as a whole.

44. Identifying those assumptions that appear to be significant to the fair value measurement requires the exercise of judgment by management. The auditor focuses attention on significant assumptions. Generally, significant assumptions cover matters that materially affect the fair value measurement and may include those that are:

(a) Sensitive to variation or uncertainty in amount or nature. For example, assumptions about short-term interest rates may be less susceptible to significant variation compared to assumptions about long-term interest rates;

(b) Susceptible to misapplication or bias.

45. The auditor considers the sensitivity of the valuation to changes in significant assumptions, including market conditions that may affect the value. Where applicable, the auditor encourages management to use such techniques as sensitivity analysis to help identify particularly sensitive assumptions. In the absence of such management analysis, the auditor considers whether to employ such techniques. The auditor also considers whether the uncertainty associated with a fair value measurement, or the

lack of objective data may make it incapable of reasonable estimation under the entity's applicable financial reporting framework (see paragraph 9).

46. The consideration of whether the assumptions provide a reasonable basis for the fair value measurements relates to the whole set of assumptions as well as to each assumption individually. Assumptions are frequently interdependent, and therefore, need to be internally consistent. A particular assumption that may appear reasonable when taken in isolation may not be reasonable when used in conjunction with other assumptions. The auditor considers whether management has identified the significant assumptions and factors influencing the measurement of fair value.

47. The assumptions on which the fair value measurements are based (for example, the discount rate used in calculating the present value of future cash flows) ordinarily will reflect what management expects will be the outcome of specific objectives and strategies. To be reasonable, such assumptions, individually and taken as a whole, also need to be realistic and consistent with:

   (a)   The general economic environment and the entity's economic circumstances;

   (b)   The plans of the entity;

   (c)   Assumptions made in prior periods, if appropriate

   (d)   Past experience of, or previous conditions experienced by, the entity to the extent currently applicable;

   (e)   Other matters relating to the financial statements, for example, assumptions used by management in accounting estimates for financial statement accounts other than those relating to fair value measurements and disclosures; and

   (f)   If applicable, the risk associated with cash flows, including the potential variability of the cash flows and the related effect on the discounted rate.

   Where assumptions are reflective of management's intent and ability to carry out specific courses of action, the auditor considers whether they are consistent with the entity's plans and past experience (see paragraphs 22 and 23).

48. If management relies on historical financial information in the development of assumptions, the auditor considers the extent to which such reliance is justified. However, historical information might not be representative of future conditions or events, for example, if management intends to engage in new activities or circumstances change.

49. For items valued by the entity using a valuation model, the auditor is not expected to substitute his or her judgment for that of the entity's management. Rather, the auditor reviews the model, and evaluates whether the model is appropriate and the assumptions used are reasonable. For example, it may be inappropriate to use a discounted cash flow method in valuing an equity investment in a start-up enterprise if

there are no current revenues on which to base the forecast of future earnings or cash flows.

50. **The auditor should perform audit procedures on the data used to develop the fair value measurements and disclosures and evaluate whether the fair value measurements have been properly determined from such data and management's assumptions.**

51. The auditor evaluates whether the data on which the fair value measurements are based, including the data used in the work of an expert, are accurate, complete and relevant; and whether the fair value measurements have been properly determined using such data and management's assumptions. The auditor's procedures also may include, for example, audit procedures such as verifying the source of the data, mathematical recalculation and reviewing of information for internal consistency, including whether such information is consistent with management's intent to carry out specific courses of action discussed in paragraphs 22 and 23.

Developing Independent Fair Value Estimates for Corroborative Purposes

52. The auditor may make an independent estimate of fair value (for example, by using an auditor-developed model) to corroborate the entity's fair value measurement. When developing an independent estimate using management's assumptions, the auditor evaluates those assumptions as discussed in paragraphs 39-49. Instead of using management's assumptions the auditor may develop separate assumptions to make a comparison with management's fair value measurements. In that situation, the auditor nevertheless understands management's assumptions. The auditor uses that understanding to determine that the auditor's model considers the significant variables and to evaluate any significant difference from management's estimate. The auditor also performs audit procedures on the data used to develop the fair value measurements and disclosures as discussed in paragraphs 50 and 51. The auditor considers the guidance contained in ISA (UK and Ireland) 520, "Analytical Procedures" when performing these procedures during an audit.

Subsequent Events

53. **The auditor should consider the effect of subsequent events on the fair value measurements and disclosures in the financial statements.**

54. Transactions and events that occur after period-end but prior to completion of the audit, may provide appropriate audit evidence regarding the fair value measurements made by management. For example, a sale of investment property shortly after the period-end may provide audit evidence relating to the fair value measurement.

55. In the period after a financial statement period-end, however, circumstances may change from those existing at the period-end. Fair value information after the period-end may reflect events occurring after the period-end and not the circumstances existing at the balance sheet date. For example, the prices of actively traded marketable securities that change after the period-end ordinarily do not constitute appropriate audit evidence of the values of the securities that existed at the period-end.

The auditor complies with ISA (UK and Ireland) 560, "Subsequent Events" when evaluating audit evidence relating to such events.

Disclosures About Fair Values

56. **The auditor should evaluate whether the disclosures about fair values made by the entity are in accordance with its financial reporting framework.**

57. Disclosure of fair value information is an important aspect of financial statements in many financial reporting frameworks. Often, fair value disclosure is required because of the relevance to users in the evaluation of an entity's performance and financial position. In addition to the fair value information required by the applicable financial reporting framework, some entities disclose voluntary additional fair value information in the notes to the financial statements.

58. When auditing fair value measurements and related disclosures included in the notes to the financial statements, whether required by the applicable financial reporting framework or disclosed voluntarily, the auditor ordinarily performs essentially the same types of audit procedures as those employed in auditing a fair value measurement recognized in the financial statements. The auditor obtains sufficient appropriate audit evidence that the valuation principles are appropriate under the entity's applicable financial reporting framework, are being consistently applied, and the method of estimation and significant assumptions used are properly disclosed in accordance with the entity's applicable financial reporting framework. The auditor also considers whether voluntary information may be inappropriate in the context of the financial statements. For example, management[1] may disclose a current sales value for an asset without mentioning that significant restrictions under contractual arrangements preclude the sale in the immediate future.

59. The auditor evaluates whether the entity has made appropriate disclosures about fair value information as called for by its financial reporting framework. If an item contains a high degree of measurement uncertainty, the auditor assesses whether the disclosures are sufficient to inform users of such uncertainty. For example, the auditor might evaluate whether disclosures about a range of amounts, and the assumptions used in determining the range, within which the fair value is reasonably believed to lie is appropriate under the entity's applicable financial reporting framework, when management[1] considers a single amount presentation not appropriate. Where applicable, the auditor also considers whether the entity has complied with the accounting and disclosure requirements relating to changes in the valuation method used to determine fair value measurements.

60. When disclosure of fair value information under the applicable financial reporting framework is omitted because it is not practicable to determine fair value with sufficient reliability, the auditor evaluates the adequacy of disclosures required in these circumstances. If the entity has not appropriately disclosed fair value information required by the applicable financial reporting framework, the auditor evaluates whether the financial statements are materially misstated by the departure from the applicable financial reporting framework.

Evaluating the Results of Audit Procedures

61. **In making a final assessment of whether the fair value measurements and disclosures in the financial statements are in accordance with the entity's applicable financial reporting framework, the auditor should evaluate the sufficiency and appropriateness of the audit evidence obtained as well as the consistency of that evidence with other audit evidence obtained and evaluated during the audit.**

62. When assessing whether the fair value measurements and disclosures in the financial statements are in accordance with the entity's applicable financial reporting framework, the auditor evaluates the consistency of the information and audit evidence obtained during the audit of fair value measurements with other audit evidence obtained during the audit, in the context of the financial statements taken as a whole. For example, the auditor considers whether there is or should be a relationship or correlation between the interest rates used to discount estimated future cash flows in determining the fair value of an investment property and interest rates on borrowings currently being incurred by the entity to acquire investment property.

Management Representations

63. **The auditor should obtain written representations from management regarding the reasonableness of significant assumptions, including whether they appropriately reflect management's intent and ability to carry out specific courses of action on behalf of the entity where relevant to the fair value measurements or disclosures.**

64. ISA (UK and Ireland) 580, "Management Representations" discusses the use of management representations as audit evidence. Depending on the nature, materiality and complexity of fair values, management[3] representations about fair value measurements and disclosures contained in the financial statements also may include representations about:

- The appropriateness of the measurement methods, including related assumptions, used by management in determining fair values within the applicable financial reporting framework, and the consistency in application of the methods.

- The basis used by management to overcome the presumption relating to the use of fair value set forth under the entity's applicable financial reporting framework.

- The completeness and appropriateness of disclosures related to fair values under the entity's applicable financial reporting framework.

- Whether subsequent events require adjustment to the fair value measurements and disclosures included in the financial statements.

Communication with Those Charged with Governance

65. ISA (UK and Ireland) 260, "Communication of Audit Matters with Those Charged with Governance" requires auditors to communicate audit matters of governance interest with those charged with governance. Because of the uncertainties often involved with some fair value measurements, the potential effect on the financial statements of any significant risks may be of governance interest. For example, the auditor considers communicating the nature of significant assumptions used in fair value measurements, the degree of subjectivity involved in the development of the assumptions, and the relative materiality of the items being measured at fair value to the financial statements as a whole. The auditor considers the guidance contained in ISA (UK and Ireland) 260 when determining the nature and form of communication.

Effective Date

66. This ISA (UK and Ireland) is effective for audits of financial statements for periods commencing on or after 15 December 2004.

Public Sector Perspective

Additional guidance for auditors of public sector bodies in the UK and Ireland is given in:

* Practice Note 10 "Audit of Financial Statements of Public Sector Bodies in the United Kingdom (Revised)"

* Practice Note 10(I) "Audit of Central Government Financial Statements in the Republic of Ireland (Revised)"

1. *Many governments are moving to accrual accounting and are adopting fair value as the basis of valuation for many classes of the assets and liabilities that they hold, or for disclosures of items in the financial statements. The broad principles of this ISA (UK and Ireland) are therefore applicable to the consideration of the audit of fair value measurements and disclosures included in the financial statements of public sector entities.*

2. *Paragraph 3 of the ISA (UK and Ireland) states that when fair value measurements and disclosures are material to the financial statements, the auditor should obtain sufficient appropriate audit evidence that such measurements and disclosures are in accordance with the entity's applicable financial reporting framework. The International Public Sector Accounting Standards accounting framework include a number of standards that require or allow the recognition or disclosure of fair values.*

3. *As noted in paragraph 8 of the ISA (UK and Ireland), determining the fair value of certain assets or liabilities may be complex where there is no active market. This can be a particular issue in the Public Sector, where entities have significant holdings of specialized assets. Furthermore many assets held by public sector entities do not generate cash flows. In these circumstances a fair value or similar current value may be*

estimated by reference to other valuation methods including, but not limited to, depreciated replacement cost and indexed price method.

Appendix

Fair Value Measurements and Disclosures under Different Financial Reporting Frameworks

1. Different financial reporting frameworks require or permit a variety of fair value measurements and disclosures in financial statements. They also vary in the level of guidance that they provide on the basis for measuring assets and liabilities or the related disclosures. Some financial reporting frameworks give prescriptive guidance, others give general guidance, and some give no guidance at all. In addition, certain industry-specific measurement and disclosure practices for fair values also exist.

2. Different definitions of fair value may exist among financial reporting frameworks, or for different assets, liabilities or disclosures within a particular framework. For example, International Accounting Standard (IAS) 39, "Financial Instruments: Recognition and Measurement" defines fair value as "the amount for which an asset could be exchanged, or a liability settled, between knowledgeable, willing parties in an arm's length transaction". The concept of fair value ordinarily assumes a current transaction, rather than settlement at some past or future date. Accordingly, the process of measuring fair value would be a search for the estimated price at which that transaction would occur. Additionally, different financial reporting frameworks may use such terms as "entity-specific value", "value in use", or similar terms, but may still fall within the concept of fair value in this ISA (UK and Ireland).

3. Different financial reporting frameworks may treat changes in fair value measurements that occur over time in different ways. For example, a particular financial reporting framework may require that changes in fair value measurements of certain assets or liabilities be reflected directly in equity, while such changes might be reflected in income under another framework. In some frameworks, the determination of whether to use fair value accounting or how it is applied is influenced by management's intent to carry out certain courses of action with respect to the specific asset or liability.

4. Different financial reporting frameworks may require certain specific fair value measurements and disclosures in financial statements and prescribe or permit them in varying degrees. The financial reporting frameworks may:

    *   Prescribe measurement, presentation and disclosure requirements for certain information included in the financial statements or for information disclosed in notes to financial statements or presented as supplementary information.

    *   Permit certain measurements using fair values at the option of an entity or only when certain criteria have been met.

    *   Prescribe a specific method for determining fair value, for example, through the use of an independent appraisal or specified ways of using discounted cash flows.

    *   Permit a choice of method for determining fair value from among several alternative methods (the criteria for selection may or may not be provided by the financial reporting framework).

- Provide no guidance on the fair value measurements or disclosures of fair value other than their use being evident through custom or practice, for example, an industry practice.

5. Some financial reporting frameworks presume that fair value can be measured reliably for assets or liabilities as a prerequisite to either requiring or permitting fair value measurements or disclosures. In some cases, this presumption may be overcome when an asset or liability does not have a quoted market price in an active market and for which other methods of reasonably estimating fair value are clearly inappropriate or unworkable.

6. Some financial reporting frameworks require certain specified adjustments or modifications to valuation information, or other considerations unique to a particular asset or liability. For example, accounting for investment properties may require adjustments to be made to an appraised market value, such as adjustments for estimated closing costs on sale, adjustments related to the property's condition and location, and other matters. Similarly, if the market for a particular asset is not an active market, published price quotations may have to be adjusted or modified to arrive at a more suitable measure of fair value. For example, quoted market prices may not be indicative of fair value if there is infrequent activity in the market, the market is not well established, or small volumes of units are traded relative to the aggregate number of trading units in existence. Accordingly, such market prices may have to be adjusted or modified. Alternative sources of market information may be needed to make such adjustments or modifications.

Prevalence of Fair Value Measurements

7. Measurements and disclosures based on fair value are becoming increasingly prevalent in financial reporting frameworks. Fair values may occur in, and affect the determination of, financial statements in a number of ways, including the measurement at fair value of:

- Specific assets or liabilities, such as marketable securities or liabilities to settle an obligation under a financial instrument, routinely or periodically "marked-to-market".

- Specific components of equity, for example when accounting for the recognition, measurement and presentation of certain financial instruments with equity features, such as a bond convertible by the holder into common shares of the issuer.

- Specific assets or liabilities acquired in a business combination. For example, the initial determination of goodwill arising on the purchase of an entity in a business combination usually is based on the fair value measurement of the identifiable assets and liabilities acquired and the fair value of the consideration given.

- Specific assets or liabilities adjusted to fair value on a one-time basis. Some financial reporting frameworks may require the use of a fair value measurement to quantify an adjustment to an asset or a group of assets as part of an asset impairment determination, for example, a test of impairment of goodwill acquired in a business combination based on the fair value of a defined operating entity or reporting unit, the value of which is then allocated among the entity's or unit's group of assets and liabilities in order to derive an implied goodwill for comparison to the recorded goodwill.

- Aggregations of assets and liabilities. In some circumstances, the measurement of a class or group of assets or liabilities calls for an aggregation of fair values of some of the individual assets or liabilities in such class or group. For example, under an entity's applicable financial reporting framework, the measurement of a diversified loan portfolio might be determined based on the fair value of some categories of loans comprising the portfolio.

- Transactions involving the exchange of assets between independent parties without monetary consideration. For example, a non-monetary exchange of plant facilities in different lines of business.

- Information disclosed in notes to financial statements or presented as supplementary information, but not recognized in the financial statements.

INTERNATIONAL STANDARD ON AUDITING (UK AND IRELAND) 550

RELATED PARTIES

CONTENTS

For accounting periods commencing on or after 1 January 2005, the consolidated financial statements of listed companies must be prepared under EU adopted IFRS. Other companies will be able to continue to prepare their financial statements in accordance with UK and Irish accounting standards. Paragraphs 1 to 17 of this ISA (UK and Ireland) apply to the audit of financial statements prepared under IAS 24 and paragraphs 101 to 117 of this ISA (UK and Ireland) apply to the audit of financial statements prepared under FRS 8.

International Standard on Auditing (UK and Ireland) (ISA (UK and Ireland)) 550 "Related Parties" should be read in the context of the Auditing Practices Board's Statement "The Auditing Practices Board - Scope and Authority of Pronouncements (Revised)" which sets out the application and authority of ISAs (UK and Ireland).

ISA (UK and Ireland) 550 to be used where IAS 24, "Related Party Disclosures" applies

Introduction

1. The purpose of this International Standard on Auditing (UK and Ireland) (ISA (UK and Ireland)) is to establish standards and provide guidance on the auditor's responsibilities and audit procedures regarding related parties and transactions with such parties regardless of whether International Accounting Standard (IAS) 24, "Related Party Disclosures," or similar requirement, is part of the applicable financial reporting framework.

1-1. In the UK and Ireland, for accounting periods commencing on or after 1 January 2005, the consolidated financial statements of listed companies must be prepared under EU adopted IFRS. From the same date other companies will be able, either to make an irrevocable election to prepare their financial statements under EU adopted IFRS, or to prepare their financial statements in accordance with UK and Irish accounting standards. Paragraphs 1 to 16-2 of this ISA (UK and Ireland) apply to financial statements prepared under EU adopted IFRS, including IAS 24. Paragraphs 101 to 116-2 of this ISA (UK and Ireland) apply to financial statements prepared under UK and Irish accounting standards, including FRS 8, "Related Party Disclosures".

1-2. This ISA (UK and Ireland) uses the terms 'those charged with governance' and 'management'. The term 'governance' describes the role of persons entrusted with the supervision, control and direction of an entity. Ordinarily, those charged with governance are accountable for ensuring that the entity achieves its objectives, and for the quality of its financial reporting and reporting to interested parties. Those charged with governance include management only when they perform such functions.

1-3. In the UK and Ireland, those charged with governance include the directors (executive and non-executive) of a company or other body, the members of an audit committee where one exists, the partners, proprietors, committee of management or trustees of other forms of entity, or equivalent persons responsible for directing the entity's affairs and preparing its financial statements.

1-4. 'Management' comprises those persons who perform senior managerial functions.

1-5. In the UK and Ireland, depending on the nature and circumstances of the entity, management may include some or all of those charged with governance (e.g. executive directors). Management will not normally include non-executive directors.

2. **The auditor should perform audit procedures designed to obtain sufficient appropriate audit evidence regarding the identification and disclosure by management[1] of related parties and the effect of related party transactions that**

---

[1] In the UK and Ireland those charged with governance are responsible for the preparation of the financial statements

are material to the financial statements. However, an audit cannot be expected to detect all related party transactions.

3. As indicated in ISA (UK and Ireland) 200 "Objective and General Principles Governing an Audit of Financial Statements," in certain circumstances there are limitations that may affect the persuasiveness of audit evidence available to draw conclusions on particular assertions. Because of the degree of uncertainty associated with the assertions regarding the completeness of related parties, the audit procedures identified in this ISA (UK and Ireland) will provide sufficient appropriate audit evidence regarding those assertions in the absence of any circumstance identified by the auditor that:

    (a) Increases the risk of material misstatement beyond that which would ordinarily be expected; or

    (b) Indicates that a material misstatement regarding related parties has occurred.

    Where there is any indication that such circumstances exist, the auditor should perform modified, extended or additional audit procedures as are appropriate in the circumstances.

4. Definitions regarding related parties are given in IAS 24 and are adopted for the purposes of this ISA (UK and Ireland)[2]

4-1. IAS 24 does not override the disclosure requirements of either companies legislation or listing rules. Similarly, the requirements of IAS 24 do not override exemptions from disclosures given by law to, and utilized by, certain types of entity. For the purposes of this ISA (UK and Ireland) companies legislation is defined as:

    (a) In Great Britain, the Companies Act 1985;

    (b) In Northern Ireland, The Companies (Northern Ireland) Order 1986; and

    (c) In the Republic of Ireland, the Companies Acts 1963 to 2003 and the European Communities (Companies: Group Accounts) Regulations 1992.

5. Management[1] is responsible for the identification and disclosure of related parties and transactions with such parties. This responsibility requires management to implement adequate internal control to ensure that transactions with related parties are appropriately identified in the information system and disclosed in the financial statements.

5-1. As transactions between related parties may not be on an arm's length basis and there may be an actual, or perceived, conflict of interest those charged with governance

[2] Definitions from IAS 24, "Related Party Disclosures," are set out in the Appendix.

usually ensure that such transactions are subject to appropriate approval procedures. The approval of material related party transactions is often recorded in the minutes of meetings of those charged with governance.

5-2. In owner managed entities, as the risks associated with such transactions are the same, similar approval procedures would ideally apply. Often, however, procedures are less formalized because the owner manager is often personally aware of, and implicitly or explicitly approves, all such transactions.

5-3. The definition of a related party is complex and in part subjective and it may not always be self-evident to management whether a party is related. Furthermore, many information systems are not designed to either distinguish or summarize related party transactions and outstanding balances between an entity and its related parties. Management may, therefore, have to carry out additional analysis of the accounting records to identify related party transactions. Accordingly related party transactions are often inherently difficult for the auditor to detect.

high risk area

6. The auditor needs to have a sufficient understanding of the entity and its environment to enable identification of the events, transactions and practices that may result in a risk of material misstatement regarding related parties and transactions with such parties. While the existence of related parties and transactions between such parties are considered ordinary features of business, the auditor needs to be aware of them because:

(a) The applicable financial reporting framework may require disclosure in the financial statements of certain related party relationships and transactions, such as those required by IAS 24;

(b) The existence of related parties or related party transactions may affect the financial statements. For example, the entity's tax liability and expense may be affected by the tax laws in various jurisdictions which require special consideration when related parties exist;

(c) The source of audit evidence affects the auditor's assessment of its reliability. Generally a greater degree of reliance may be placed on audit evidence that is obtained from or created by unrelated third parties;

(d) A related party transaction may be motivated by other than ordinary business considerations, for example, profit sharing or even fraud; and

(e) The entity may be engaged in transfers of goods and services with related parties in accordance with specified transfer pricing policies or under reciprocal trading arrangements, such as barter transactions, which may give rise to accounting recognition and measurement issues. In particular an entity may have received or provided management services at no charge.

6-1. The risk that undisclosed related party transactions, or outstanding balances between an entity and its related parties, will not be detected by the auditor is especially high when:

(a) Related party transactions have taken place without charge;

(b) Related party transactions are not self-evident to the auditor;

(c) Transactions are with a party that the auditor could not reasonably be expected to know is a related party;

(d) Transactions undertaken with a related party in an earlier period have remained unsettled for a considerable period of time; or

(e) Active steps have been taken by those charged with governance or management to conceal either the full terms of a transaction or that a transaction is, in substance, with a related party.

6-2. Those charged with governance or management may wish to conceal the fact that a transaction, or an outstanding balance is with a related party because:

(a) Its disclosure may be sensitive to the parties involved and they may be reticent about disclosing it; and

(b) The transaction may be motivated by other than ordinary business considerations, for example to enhance the presentation of the financial statements (for example fraud or window dressing).

Related party transactions may be concealed in whole or in part from the auditor for fraudulent or other purposes. The likelihood of detecting fraudulent related party transactions depends upon the nature of the fraud and, in particular, the degree of collusion, the seniority of those involved and the level of deception concerned. ISA (UK and Ireland) 240 "The Auditor's responsibility to Consider Fraud in an Audit of Financial Statements" establishes the standards and provides the guidance on the auditor's responsibility to consider fraud in an audit of financial statements, including related party transactions.

Existence and Disclosure of Related Parties

6-3. **When planning the audit the auditor should assess the risk that material undisclosed related party transactions, or undisclosed outstanding balances between an entity and its related parties may exist.**

6-4 The responsibility of those charged with governance to identify, approve and disclose related party transactions requires them to implement adequate information systems to identify related parties and internal control to ensure that related party transactions are appropriately identified in the accounting records and disclosed in the financial statements. As part of the risk assessment the auditor obtains an understanding of such information systems and internal control.

6-5 The extent to which formal policies and codes of conduct dealing with relationships with related parties are maintained normally depends on the significance of related parties and on the philosophy and operating style of the management of the entity and of those charged with governance. Such policies often cover the approval, recording and reporting of related party transactions entered into, on behalf of the entity, by employees and those charged with governance.

6-6 In respect of entities that do not have formal policies and codes of conduct concerning related party transactions, for example owner managed entities, the auditor may only be able to perform substantive procedures. If the auditor assesses the risk of undisclosed related party transactions as low such planned substantive procedures may not need to be extensive.

7. **The auditor should review information provided by those charged with governance and management identifying the names of all known related parties and should perform the following audit procedures in respect of the completeness of this information:**

    (a) **Review prior year working papers for names of known related parties;**

    (b) **Review the entity's procedures for identification of related parties;**

    (c) **Inquire as to the affiliation of those charged with governance and officers with other entities;**

    (d) **Review shareholder records to determine the names of principal shareholders or, if appropriate, obtain a listing of principal shareholders from the share register;**

    (e) **Review minutes of the meetings of shareholders and those charged with governance and other relevant statutory records such as the register of directors' interests;**

    (f) **Inquire of other auditors currently involved in the audit, or predecessor auditors, as to their knowledge of additional related parties;**

    (g) **Review the entity's income tax returns and other information supplied to regulatory agencies;**

    (h) **Review invoices and correspondence from lawyers for indications of the existence of related parties or related party transactions; and**

    (i) **Inquire of the names of all pension and other trusts established for the benefit of employees and the names of their management.**

If, in the auditor's judgment, there is a lower risk of significant related parties remaining undetected, these procedures may be modified as appropriate.

7-1. After evaluating the results of:

(a) Determining the implementation of the entity's internal control with respect to related party transactions; and

(b) The audit procedures described in the preceding paragraph

The auditor may determine that few additional substantive procedures are required to obtain sufficient appropriate audit evidence that no other material related party transactions have occurred. However, if the auditor assesses the controls with respect to related party transactions as weak, it may be necessary to perform additional substantive procedures to obtain reasonable assurance that no material undisclosed related party transactions have occurred.

8. **Where the applicable financial reporting framework requires disclosure of related party relationships, the auditor should be satisfied that the disclosure is adequate.**

Transactions with Related Parties

9. **The auditor should review information provided by those charged with governance and management identifying related party transactions and should be alert for other material related party transactions.**

10. **When obtaining an understanding of the entity's internal control, the auditor should consider the adequacy of control activities over the authorization and recording of related party transactions.**

11. During the course of the audit, the auditor needs to be alert for transactions which appear unusual in the circumstances and may indicate the existence of previously unidentified related parties. Examples include:

- Transactions which have abnormal terms of trade, such as unusual prices, interest rates, guarantees, and repayment terms.

- Transactions which lack an apparent logical business reason for their occurrence.

- Transactions in which substance differs from form.

- Transactions processed in an unusual manner.

- High volume or significant transactions with certain customers or suppliers as compared with others.

- Unrecorded transactions such as the receipt or provision of management services at no charge.

12. During the course of the audit, the auditor carries out audit procedures which may identify the existence of transactions with related parties. Examples include:

pro cedures

- Performing detailed tests of transactions and balances.

- Reviewing minutes of meetings of shareholders and those charged with governance.

- Reviewing accounting records for large or unusual transactions or balances, paying particular attention to transactions recognized at or near the end of the reporting period.

- Reviewing confirmations of loans receivable and payable and confirmations from banks. Such a review may indicate guarantor relationship and other related party transactions.

- Reviewing investment transactions, for example, purchase or sale of an equity interest in a joint venture or other entity.

Examining Identified Related Party Transactions

13. **In examining the identified related party transactions, the auditor should obtain sufficient appropriate audit evidence as to whether these transactions have been properly recorded and disclosed.**

14. Given the nature of related party relationships, audit evidence of a related party transaction may be limited, for example, regarding the existence of inventory held by a related party on consignment or an instruction from a parent company to a subsidiary to record a royalty expense. Because of the limited availability of appropriate audit evidence about such transactions, the auditor considers performing audit procedures such as:

- Discussing the purpose of the transaction with management or those charged with governance.

- Confirming the terms and amount of the transaction with the related party.

- Inspecting information in possession of the related party.

- Corroborating with the related party the explanation of the purpose of the transaction and, if necessary, confirming that the transaction is bona fide.

- Obtaining information from an unrelated third party.

- Confirming or discussing information with persons associated with the transaction, such as banks, lawyers, guarantors and agents.

14-1. IAS 24 requires that "an entity shall disclose the nature of the related party relationship as well as information about the transactions and outstanding balances necessary for an understanding of the potential effect of the relationship on the financial statements". An example of a disclosure falling within this requirement would be noting that the transfer of a major asset had taken place at an amount materially different from that obtainable on normal commercial terms. The auditor, therefore, is alert for related party transactions that have occurred on other than normal commercial terms. In particular, the auditor is alert for unrecorded transactions such as the receipt or provision of management services at no charge.

14-2. The auditor considers the implications for other aspects of the audit if they identify material related party transactions not included in the information provided by management or those charged with governance. In particular, the auditor considers the impact on their assessment of audit risk and the reliance placed on other representations made by those charged with governance during the audit.

Disclosures Relating to Control of the Entity

14-3. **The auditor should obtain sufficient appropriate audit evidence that disclosures in the financial statements relating to control of the entity are properly stated.**

14-4. IAS 24 requires "Relationships between parents and subsidiaries shall be disclosed irrespective of whether there have been transactions between those related parties. An entity shall disclose the name of the entity's parent and, if different, the ultimate controlling party. If neither the entity's parent nor the ultimate controlling party produces financial statements available for public use, the name of the next most senior parent that does so shall also be disclosed." Companies legislation contains additional detailed disclosures requirements relating to control of a company[3].

14-5. The next most senior parent is the first parent in the group above the immediate parent that produces consolidated financial statements available for public use.

14-6. The auditor may only be able to determine the name of the entity's ultimate controlling party through specific inquiry of management or those charged with governance. When the auditor considers it necessary, the auditor obtains corroboration from the ultimate controlling party confirming representations received in this regard.

---

[3] In Great Britain these requirements are set out in S. 231 and Schedule 5 Parts I and II of the Companies Act 1985. In Northern Ireland these requirements are set out in Article 239 and Schedule 5 Parts I and II of the Companies (Northern Ireland) Order 1986. In the Republic of Ireland these requirements are set out in S 16 of the Companies (Amendment) Act 1986 and Regulations 36 and 44 of the European Communities (Companies: Group Accounts) Regulations 1992.

Management Representations

15.   The auditor should obtain a written representation from management[4] concerning:

(a)   **The completeness of information provided regarding the identification of related parties; and**

(b)   **The adequacy of related party disclosures in the financial statements.**

15-1. The written representations obtained by the auditor include confirmation from those charged with governance that they (and any key managers or other individuals who are in a position to influence, or who are accountable for the stewardship of the reporting entity) have disclosed all transactions relevant to the entity and that they are not aware of any other such matters required to be disclosed in the financial statements, whether under IAS 24 or other requirements.

15-2. An entity may require its management and those charged with governance to sign individual declarations on these disclosure matters. In view of the inherent difficulties of detecting undisclosed related party transactions, and having regard to the conclusions drawn from other audit evidence, the auditor may wish to inspect the individual declarations. For this purpose, it may be helpful if they are addressed jointly to a designated official of the entity and also to the auditor. In other cases, the auditor may wish to obtain representations directly from each of those charged with governance and from members of management.

Audit Conclusions and Reporting

16.   **If the auditor is unable to obtain sufficient appropriate audit evidence concerning related parties and transactions with such parties or concludes that their disclosure in the financial statements is not adequate, the auditor should modify the audit report appropriately.**

16-1. If the auditor is unable to obtain sufficient appropriate audit evidence concerning related party transactions and transactions with such parties, this is a limitation on the scope of the audit. Accordingly the auditor considers the need to issue either a qualified opinion or disclaimer of opinion in accordance with eh requirements of ISA (UK and Ireland) 700, "The Auditor's Report on Financial Statements."

16-2. If the auditor concludes that the disclosure of related party transactions is not adequate the auditor considers the need to issue either a qualified or adverse opinion depending on the particular circumstances. Where the auditor is aware of material undisclosed related party transactions or an undisclosed control relationship, that in the auditor's opinion is required to be disclosed, the opinion

---

[4]   In the UK and Ireland the auditor obtains written representations from those charged with governance.

section of the auditor's report, whenever practicable, includes the information that would have been included in the financial statements had the relevant requirements been followed.

Effective Date

16-3. This ISA (UK and Ireland) is effective for audits of financial statements for, periods commencing on or after 15 December 2004.

Public Sector Perspective

Additional guidance for auditors of public sector bodies in the UK and Ireland is given in:

* Practice Note 10 "Audit of Financial Statements of Public Sector Bodies in the United Kingdom (Revised)"

* Practice Note 10(I) "Audit of Central Government Financial Statements in the Republic of Ireland (Revised)"

1. *In applying the audit principles in this ISA (UK and Ireland), auditors have to make reference to legislative requirements which are applicable to public sector entities and employees in respect of related party transactions. Such legislation may prohibit entities and employees from entering into transactions with related parties. There may also be a requirement for public sector employees to declare their interests in entities with which they transact on a professional and/or commercial basis. Where such legislative requirements exist, the audit procedures would need to be expanded to detect instances of noncompliance with these requirements.*

2. *While International Public Sector Guideline 1, "Financial Reporting by Government Business Enterprises," indicates that all International Accounting Standards (IASs) apply to business enterprises in the public sector, IAS 24, Related Party Disclosures does not require that transactions between state controlled enterprises be disclosed. Definitions of related parties included in IAS 24 and this ISA (UK and Ireland) do not address all circumstances relevant to public sector entities. For example, the status, for purposes of application of this ISA (UK and Ireland), of the relationship between ministers and departments of state, and departments of state and statutory authorities or government agencies is not discussed.*

Appendix

Definitions adopted from IAS 24

<u>Related party</u>. A party is related to an entity if:

(a) directly, or indirectly through one or more intermediaries, the party:

    (i) Controls, is controlled by, or is under common control with, the entity (this includes parents, subsidiaries and fellow subsidiaries);

    (ii) Has an interest in the entity that gives it significant influence over the entity; or

    (iii) Has joint control over the entity;

(b) The party is an associate (as defined in IAS 28 Investments in Associates) of the entity;

(c) The party is a joint venture in which the entity is a venturer (see IAS 31 Interests in Joint Ventures);

(d) The party is a member of the key management personnel of the entity or its parent;

(e) The party is a close member of the family of any individual referred to in (a) or (d);

(f) The party is an entity that is controlled, jointly controlled or significantly influenced by or for which significant voting power in such entity resides with, directly or indirectly, any individual referred to in (d) or (e); or

(g) The party is a post-employment benefit plan for the benefit of employees of the entity, or of any entity that is a related party of the entity.

A <u>related party transaction</u> is a transfer of resources, services or obligations between related parties, regardless of whether a price is charged.

<u>Close members of the family of an individual</u> are those family members who may be expected to influence, or be influenced by, that individual in their dealings with the entity. They may include:

(a) The individual's domestic partner and children;

(b) Children of the individual's domestic partner; and

(c) Dependents of the individual or the individual's domestic partner.

<u>Control</u> is the power to govern the financial and operating policies of an entity so as to obtain benefits from its activities.

Joint control is the contractually agreed sharing of control over an economic activity.

Key management personnel are those persons having authority and responsibility for planning, directing and controlling the activities of the entity, directly or indirectly, including any director (whether executive or otherwise) of that entity.

Significant influence is the power to participate in the financial and operating policy decisions of an entity, but is not control over those policies. Significant influence may be gained by share ownership, statute or agreement.

ISA (UK and Ireland) 550 to be used where FRS 8, "Related Party Disclosures" applies

Introduction

101. The purpose of this International Standard on Auditing (UK and Ireland) (ISA (UK and Ireland)) is to establish standards and provide guidance on the auditor's responsibilities and audit procedures regarding related parties and transactions with such parties regardless of whether International Accounting Standard (IAS) 24, "Related Party Disclosures," or similar requirement, is part of the applicable financial reporting framework.

101-1. In the UK and Ireland for accounting periods commencing on or after 1 January 2005, the following companies will continue to be able, if they wish, to prepare their financial statements in accordance with UK and Irish accounting standards;

(a) All companies within a listed group for their individual financial statements (and, where a consolidation is prepared by an unlisted subsidiary, for those consolidated financial statements);

(b) Unlisted companies; and

(c) Other entities, including many public benefit entities.

Paragraphs 101 to 116-2 apply to financial statements prepared under UK and Irish accounting standards, including FRS 8, "Related Party Disclosures". Paragraphs 1 to 16-2 of this ISA (UK and Ireland) apply to financial statements prepared under EU adopted IFRS, including IAS 24.

101-2. This ISA (UK and Ireland) uses the terms 'those charged with governance' and 'management'. The term 'governance' describes the role of persons entrusted with the supervision, control and direction of an entity. Ordinarily, those charged with governance are accountable for ensuring that the entity achieves its objectives, and for the quality of its financial reporting and reporting to interested parties. Those charged with governance include management only when they perform such functions.

101-3. In the UK and Ireland, those charged with governance include the directors (executive and non-executive) of a company or other body, the members of an audit committee where one exists, the partners, proprietors, committee of management or trustees of other forms of entity, or equivalent persons responsible for directing the entity's affairs and preparing its financial statements.

101-4. 'Management' comprises those persons who perform senior managerial functions.

101-5. In the UK and Ireland, depending on the nature and circumstances of the entity, management may include some or all of those charged with governance (e.g. executive directors). Management will not normally include non-executive directors.

102. **The auditor should perform audit procedures designed to obtain sufficient appropriate audit evidence regarding the identification and disclosure by management[1] of related parties and the effect of related party transactions that are material to the financial statements.** However, an audit cannot be expected to detect all related party transactions.

103. As indicated in ISA (UK and Ireland) 200 "Objective and General Principles Governing an Audit of Financial Statements," in certain circumstances there are limitations that may affect the persuasiveness of audit evidence available to draw conclusions on particular assertions. Because of the degree of uncertainty associated with the assertions regarding the completeness of related parties, the audit procedures identified in this ISA (UK and Ireland) will provide sufficient appropriate audit evidence regarding those assertions in the absence of any circumstance identified by the auditor that:

(a) Increases the risk of material misstatement beyond that which would ordinarily be expected; or

(b) Indicates that a material misstatement regarding related parties has occurred.

Where there is any indication that such circumstances exist, the auditor should perform modified, extended or additional audit procedures as are appropriate in the circumstances.

104. Definitions regarding related parties are given in FRS 8 and are adopted for the purposes of this ISA (UK and Ireland)[2]

104-1. FRS 8 does not override the disclosure requirements of either companies legislation or listing rules. Similarly, the requirements of FRS 8 do not override exemptions from disclosures given by law to, and utilized by, certain types of entity. For the purposes of this ISA (UK and Ireland) companies legislation is defined as:

(a) In Great Britain, the Companies Act 1985;

(b) In Northern Ireland, The Companies (Northern Ireland) Order 1986; and

(c) In the Republic of Ireland, the Companies Acts 1963 to 2003 and the European Communities (Companies: Group Accounts) Regulations 1992.

104-2. FRS 8 exempts the disclosure of certain related party transactions undertaken by an entity. In exceptional circumstances if an entity avails itself of an exemption contained in an accounting standard this may be inconsistent with the overriding requirement for the financial statements to give a true and fair view of the state of the entity's affairs. In the course of an audit the auditor may become aware of transactions that

---

[1] In the UK and Ireland those charged with governance are responsible for the preparation of the financial statements.
[2] Definitions from FRS 8, "Related Party Disclosures," are set out in the Appendix.

are exempt from disclosure under FRS 8. The auditor assesses whether such related party transactions need to be disclosed in order for the financial statements to give a true and fair view.

105. Management[1] is responsible for the identification and disclosure of related parties and transactions with such parties. This responsibility requires management to implement adequate internal control to ensure that transactions with related parties are appropriately identified in the information system and disclosed in the financial statements.

105-1. As transactions between related parties may not be on an arm's length basis and there may be an actual, or perceived, conflict of interest those charged with governance usually ensure that such transactions are subject to appropriate approval procedures. The approval of material related party transactions is often recorded in the minutes of meetings of those charged with governance.

105-2. In owner managed entities, as the risks associated with such transactions are the same, similar approval procedures would ideally apply. Often, however, procedures are less formalized because the owner manager is often personally aware of, and implicitly or explicitly approves, all such transactions.

105-3. The definition of a related party is complex and in part subjective and it may not always be self-evident to management whether a party is related. Furthermore, many information systems are not designed to either distinguish or summarize related party transactions and outstanding balances between an entity and its related parties. Management may, therefore, have to carry out additional analysis of the accounting records to identify related party transactions. Accordingly related party transactions are often inherently difficult for the auditor to detect.

105-4. These difficulties are heightened by the particular perspective to the concept of materiality introduced by FRS 8 which states: "The materiality of related party transactions is to be judged, not only in terms of their significance to the reporting entity, but also in relation to the other related party when that party is:

(a) A director, key manager or other individual in a position to influence, or accountable for stewardship of, the reporting entity; or

(b) A member of the close family of any individual mentioned in (a) above; or

(c) An entity controlled by any individual mentioned in (a) or (b) above".

Although the auditor designs audit procedures so as to have a reasonable expectation of detecting undisclosed related party transactions that are material to the reporting entity, an audit cannot necessarily be expected to detect all such transactions; nor can it be expected to detect transactions that are not material to the entity, even though they may be material to the other related party.

106. The auditor needs to have a sufficient understanding of the entity and its environment to enable identification of the events, transactions and practices that may result in a risk of material misstatement regarding related parties and transactions with such parties. While the existence of related parties and transactions between such parties are considered ordinary features of business, the auditor needs to be aware of them because:

(a) The applicable financial reporting framework may require disclosure in the financial statements of certain related party relationships and transactions, such as those required by FRS 8;

(b) The existence of related parties or related party transactions may affect the financial statements. For example, the entity's tax liability and expense may be affected by the tax laws in various jurisdictions which require special consideration when related parties exist;

(c) The source of audit evidence affects the auditor's assessment of its reliability. Generally a greater degree of reliance may be placed on audit evidence that is obtained from or created by unrelated third parties;

(d) A related party transaction may be motivated by other than ordinary business considerations, for example, profit sharing or even fraud; and

(e) The entity may be engaged in transfers of goods and services with related parties in accordance with specified transfer pricing policies or under reciprocal trading arrangements, such as barter transactions, which may give rise to accounting recognition and measurement issues. In particular an entity may have received or provided management services at no charge.

106-1. The risk that undisclosed related party transactions, or outstanding balances between an entity and its related parties, will not be detected by the auditor is especially high when:

(a) Related party transactions have taken place without charge;

(b) Related party transactions are not self-evident to the auditor;

(c) Transactions are with a party that the auditor could not reasonably be expected to know is a related party;

(d) Transactions undertaken with a related party in an earlier period have remained unsettled for a considerable period of time; or

(e) Active steps have been taken by those charged with governance or management to conceal either the full terms of a transaction or that a transaction is, in substance, with a related party.

106-2. Those charged with governance or management may wish to conceal the fact that a transaction, or an outstanding balance is with a related party because:

(a) Its disclosure may be sensitive to the parties involved and they may be reticent about disclosing it; and

(b) The transaction may be motivated by other than ordinary business considerations, for example to enhance the presentation of the financial statements (for example fraud or window dressing).

Related party transactions may be concealed in whole or in part from the auditor for fraudulent or other purposes. The likelihood of detecting fraudulent related party transactions depends upon the nature of the fraud and, in particular, the degree of collusion, the seniority of those involved and the level of deception concerned. ISA (UK and Ireland) 240 "The Auditor's responsibility to Consider Fraud in an Audit of Financial Statements" establishes the standards and provides the guidance on the auditor's responsibility to consider fraud in an audit of financial statements, including related party transactions.

Existence and Disclosure of Related Parties

106-3. **When planning the audit the auditor should assess the risk that material undisclosed related party transactions, or undisclosed outstanding balances between an entity and its related parties may exist.**

106-4. The responsibility of those charged with governance to identify, approve and disclose related party transactions requires them to implement adequate information systems to identify related parties and internal control to ensure that related party transactions are appropriately identified in the accounting records and disclosed in the financial statements. As part of the risk assessment the auditor obtains an understanding of such information systems and internal control.

106-5. The extent to which formal policies and codes of conduct dealing with relationships with related parties are maintained normally depends on the significance of related parties and on the philosophy and operating style of the management of the entity and of those charged with governance. Such policies often cover the approval, recording and reporting of related party transactions entered into, on behalf of the entity, by employees and those charged with governance.

106-6. In respect of entities that do not have formal policies and codes of conduct concerning related party transactions, for example owner managed entities, the auditor may only be able to perform substantive procedures. If the auditor assesses the risk of undisclosed related party transactions as low such planned substantive procedures may not need to be extensive.

107. **The auditor should review information provided by those charged with governance and management identifying the names of all known related parties and should perform the following audit procedures in respect of the completeness of this information:**

(a) **Review prior year working papers for names of known related parties;**

(b)   Review the entity's procedures for identification of related parties;

(c)   Inquire as to the affiliation of those charged with governance and officers with other entities;

(d)   Review shareholder records to determine the names of principal shareholders or, if appropriate, obtain a listing of principal shareholders from the share register;

(e)   Review minutes of the meetings of shareholders and those charged with governance and other relevant statutory records such as the register of directors' interests;

(f)   Inquire of other auditors currently involved in the audit, or predecessor auditors, as to their knowledge of additional related parties;

(g)   Review the entity's income tax returns and other information supplied to regulatory agencies;

(h)   Review invoices and correspondence from lawyers for indications of the existence of related parties or related party transactions; and

(i)   Inquire of the names of all pension and other trusts established for the benefit of employees and the names of their management.

If, in the auditor's judgment, there is a lower risk of significant related parties remaining undetected, these procedures may be modified as appropriate.

107-1. After evaluating the results of:

(a)   Determining the implementation of the entity's internal control with respect to related party transactions; and

(b)   The audit procedures described in the preceding paragraph

the auditor may determine that few additional substantive procedures are required to obtain sufficient appropriate audit evidence that no other material related party transactions have occurred. However, if the auditor assesses the controls with respect to related party transactions as weak, it may be necessary to perform additional substantive procedures to obtain reasonable assurance that no material undisclosed related party transactions have occurred.

108.   Where the applicable financial reporting framework requires disclosure of related party relationships, the auditor should be satisfied that the disclosure is adequate.

Transactions with Related Parties

109. **The auditor should review information provided by those charged with governance and management identifying related party transactions and should be alert for other material related party transactions.**

110. **When obtaining an understanding of the entity's internal control, the auditor should consider the adequacy of control activities over the authorization and recording of related party transactions.**

111. During the course of the audit, the auditor needs to be alert for transactions which appear unusual in the circumstances and may indicate the existence of previously unidentified related parties. Examples include:

   • Transactions which have abnormal terms of trade, such as unusual prices, interest rates, guarantees, and repayment terms.

   • Transactions which lack an apparent logical business reason for their occurrence.

   • Transactions in which substance differs from form.

   • Transactions processed in an unusual manner.

   • High volume or significant transactions with certain customers or suppliers as compared with others.

   • Unrecorded transactions such as the receipt or provision of management services at no charge.

112. During the course of the audit, the auditor carries out audit procedures which may identify the existence of transactions with related parties. Examples include:

   • Performing detailed tests of transactions and balances.

   • Reviewing minutes of meetings of shareholders and those charged with governance.

   • Reviewing accounting records for large or unusual transactions or balances, paying particular attention to transactions recognized at or near the end of the reporting period.

   • Reviewing confirmations of loans receivable and payable and confirmations from banks. Such a review may indicate guarantor relationship and other related party transactions.

   • Reviewing investment transactions, for example, purchase or sale of an equity interest in a joint venture or other entity.

Examining Identified Related Party Transactions

113. **In examining the identified related party transactions, the auditor should obtain sufficient appropriate audit evidence as to whether these transactions have been properly recorded and disclosed.**

114. Given the nature of related party relationships, audit evidence of a related party transaction may be limited, for example, regarding the existence of inventory held by a related party on consignment or an instruction from a parent company to a subsidiary to record a royalty expense. Because of the limited availability of appropriate audit evidence about such transactions, the auditor considers performing audit procedures such as:

   • Discussing the purpose of the transaction with management or those charged with governance.

   • Confirming the terms and amount of the transaction with the related party.

   • Inspecting information in possession of the related party.

   • Corroborating with the related party the explanation of the purpose of the transaction and, if necessary, confirming that the transaction is bona fide.

   • Obtaining information from an unrelated third party.

   • Confirming or discussing information with persons associated with the transaction, such as banks, lawyers, guarantors and agents.

114-1. FRS 8 requires "disclosure of any other elements of the [related party] transactions necessary for an understanding of the financial statements. An example falling within this requirement would be the need to give an indication that the transfer of a major asset had taken place at an amount materially different from that obtainable on normal commercial terms". The auditor, therefore, is alert for related party transactions that have occurred on other than normal commercial terms. In particular, the auditor is alert for unrecorded transactions such as the receipt or provision of management services at no charge.

114-2. The auditor considers the implications for other aspects of the audit if they identify material related party transactions not included in the information provided by management or those charged with governance. In particular, the auditor considers the impact on their assessment of audit risk and the reliance placed on other representations made by those charged with governance during the audit.

Disclosures Relating to Control of the Entity

114-3. **The auditor should obtain sufficient appropriate audit evidence that disclosures in the financial statements relating to control of the entity are properly stated.**

114-4. FRS 8 requires, "when the reporting entity is controlled by another party, there should be disclosure of the related party relationship and the name of that party and, if different, that of the ultimate controlling party. If the controlling party or ultimate controlling party of the entity is not known, that fact should be disclosed". Companies legislation contains additional detailed disclosures requirements relating to control of a company[3].

114-5. The auditor may only be able to determine the name of the entity's ultimate controlling party through specific inquiry of management or those charged with governance. When the auditor considers it necessary, the auditor obtains corroboration from the ultimate controlling party confirming representations received in this regard.

Management Representations

115. **The auditor should obtain a written representation from management[4] concerning:**

    (a) **The completeness of information provided regarding the identification of related parties; and**

    (b) **The adequacy of related party disclosures in the financial statements.**

115-1. The written representations obtained by the auditor include confirmation from those charged with governance that they (and any key managers or other individuals who are in a position to influence, or who are accountable for the stewardship of the reporting entity) have disclosed all transactions relevant to the entity and that they are not aware of any other such matters required to be disclosed in the financial statements, whether under FRS 8 or other requirements.

115-2. An entity may require its management and those charged with governance to sign individual declarations on these disclosure matters. In view of the inherent difficulties of detecting undisclosed related party transactions (in particular transactions that are not material to the entity), and having regard to the conclusions drawn from other audit evidence, the auditor may wish to inspect the individual declarations. For this purpose, it may be helpful if they are addressed jointly to a designated official of the entity and also to the auditor. In other cases, the auditor may wish to obtain representations directly from each of those charged with governance and from members of management.

---

[3] In Great Britain these requirements are set out in S. 231 and Schedule 5 Parts I and II of the Companies Act 1985. In Northern Ireland these requirements are set out in Article 239 and Schedule 5 Parts I and II of the Companies (Northern Ireland) Order 1986. In the Republic of Ireland these requirements are set out in S 16 of the Companies (Amendment) Act 1986 and Regulations 36 and 44 of the European Communities (Companies: Group Accounts) Regulations 1992.

[4] In the UK and Ireland the auditor obtains written representations from those charged with governance.

Audit Conclusions and Reporting

116. **If the auditor is unable to obtain sufficient appropriate audit evidence concerning related parties and transactions with such parties or concludes that their disclosure in the financial statements is not adequate, the auditor should modify the audit report appropriately.**

116-1. If the auditor is unable to obtain sufficient appropriate audit evidence concerning related party transactions and transactions with such parties, this is a limitation on the scope of the audit. Accordingly the auditor considers the need to issue either a qualified opinion or disclaimer of opinion in accordance with eh requirements of ISA (UK and Ireland) 700, "The Auditor's Report on Financial Statements."

116-2. If the auditor concludes that the disclosure of related party transactions is not adequate the auditor considers the need to issue either a qualified or adverse opinion depending on the particular circumstances. Where the auditor is aware of material undisclosed related party transactions or an undisclosed control relationship, that in the auditor's opinion is required to be disclosed, the opinion section of the auditor's report, whenever practicable, includes the information that would have been included in the financial statements had the relevant requirements been followed.

Effective Date

116-3. This ISA (UK and Ireland) is effective for audits of financial statements for, periods commencing on or after 15 December 2004.

Public Sector Perspective

Additional guidance for auditors of public sector bodies in the UK and Ireland is given in:

- Practice Note 10 "Audit of Financial Statements of Public Sector Bodies in the United Kingdom (Revised)"

- Practice Note 10(I) "Audit of Central Government Financial Statements in the Republic of Ireland (Revised)"

1. *In applying the audit principles in this ISA (UK and Ireland), auditors have to make reference to legislative requirements which are applicable to public sector entities and employees in respect of related party transactions. Such legislation may prohibit entities and employees from entering into transactions with related parties. There may also be a requirement for public sector employees to declare their interests in entities with which they transact on a professional and/or commercial basis. Where such legislative requirements exist, the audit procedures would need to be expanded to detect instances of noncompliance with these requirements.*

2.   *While International Public Sector Guideline 1, "Financial Reporting by Government Business Enterprises," indicates that all International Accounting Standards (IASs) apply to business enterprises in the public sector, IAS 24, Related Party Disclosures does not require that transactions between state controlled enterprises be disclosed. Definitions of related parties included in IAS 24 and this ISA (UK and Ireland) do not address all circumstances relevant to public sector entities. For example, the status, for purposes of application of this ISA (UK and Ireland), of the relationship between ministers and departments of state, and departments of state and statutory authorities or government agencies is not discussed.*

Appendix

Definitions Adopted From FRS 8

Related parties

(a) Two or more parties are related parties when at any time during the financial period:

   (i) One party has direct or indirect control of the other party; or;

   (ii) The parties are subject to common control from the same source; or

   (iii) One party has influence over the financial and operating policies of the other party to an extent that that other party might be inhibited from pursuing at all times its own separate interests; or

   (iv) The parties, in entering a transaction, are subject to influence from the same source to such an extent that one of the parties to the transaction has subordinated its own separate interests.

(b) For the avoidance of doubt, the following are related parties of the reporting entity;

   (i) Its ultimate and intermediate parent undertakings, subsidiary undertakings and fellow subsidiary undertakings;

   (ii) Its associates and joint ventures;

   (iii) The investor or venturer in respect of which the reporting entity is an associate or a joint venture;

   (iv) Directors[5] of the reporting entity and the directors of its ultimate and intermediate parent undertakings; and

   (v) Pension funds for the benefit of employees of the reporting entity or of any entity that is a related party of the reporting entity;

(c) And the following are presumed to be related parties of the reporting entity unless it can be demonstrated that neither party has influenced the financial and operating policies of the other in such a way as to inhibit the pursuit of separate interests:

---

[5] Directors include shadow directors, which are defined in companies legislation as persons in accordance with whose directions or instructions the directors of the company are accustomed to act.

(i)　The key management of the reporting entity and the key management of its parent undertaking or undertakings;

(ii)　A person owning or able to exercise control over 20 per cent or more of the voting rights of the reporting entity, whether directly or through nominees;

(iii)　Each person acting in concert in such a way as to be able to exercise control or influence (in terms of (a) (iii) above) over the reporting entity; and

(iv)　An entity managing or managed by the reporting entity under a management contract.

(d)　Additionally, because of their relationship with certain parties that are, or are presumed to be, related parties of the reporting entity, the following are also presumed to be related parties of the reporting entity:

(i)　Members of the close family of any individual falling under parties mentioned in (a) – (c) above; and

(ii)　Partnerships, companies, trusts or other entities in which any individual or member of the close family in (a) – (c) above has a controlling interest.

Sub-paragraphs (b), (c) and (d) are not intended to be an exhaustive list of related parties.

Related party transaction: The transfer of assets or liabilities or the performance of services by, to or for a related party irrespective of whether a price is charged.

Close family: Close members of the family of an individual are those family members, or members of the same household, who may be expected to influence, or be influenced by, that person in their dealings with the reporting entity.

Control: The ability to direct the financial and operating policies of an entity with a view to gaining economic benefits from its activities.

Key management: Those persons in senior positions having authority or responsibility for directing or controlling the major activities and resources of the reporting entity.

Persons acting in concert: Persons who, pursuant to an agreement or understanding (whether formal or informal), actively co-operate, whether by the ownership by any of them of shares in an undertaking or otherwise, to exercise control or influence (in terms of (a) (iii) above in the definition of related parties) over that undertaking.

INTERNATIONAL STANDARD ON AUDITING
(UK AND IRELAND) 560*

SUBSEQUENT EVENTS

CONTENTS

International Standard on Auditing (UK and Ireland) (ISA (UK and Ireland)) 560 "Subsequent Events" should be read in the context of the Auditing Practices Board's Statement "The Auditing Practices Board - Scope and Authority of Pronouncements (Revised)" which sets out the application and authority of ISAs (UK and Ireland).

---

* This ISA (UK and Ireland) does not include the conforming amendments that were promulgated with ISA 700 (Revised) by the IAASB in December 2004. This is because the APB has decided to defer revising the current ISA (UK and Ireland) 700 until progress has been made in resolving a number of issues, including whether ISA 700 (Revised) will be adopted for use in Europe.

Introduction

1. The purpose of this International Standard on Auditing (UK and Ireland) (ISA (UK and Ireland)) is to establish standards and provide guidance on the auditor's responsibility regarding subsequent events. In this ISA (UK and Ireland), the term "subsequent events" is used to refer to both events occurring between period end and the date of the auditor's report, and facts discovered after the date of the auditor's report.

1-1. This ISA (UK and Ireland) uses the terms 'those charged with governance' and 'management'. The term 'governance' describes the role of persons entrusted with the supervision, control and direction of an entity. Ordinarily, those charged with governance are accountable for ensuring that the entity achieves its objectives, and for the quality of its financial reporting and reporting to interested parties. Those charged with governance include management only when they perform such functions.

1-2. In the UK and Ireland, those charged with governance include the directors (executive and non-executive) of a company or other body, the members of an audit committee where one exists, the partners, proprietors, committee of management or trustees of other forms of entity, or equivalent persons responsible for directing the entity's affairs and preparing its financial statements.

1.3. 'Management' comprises those persons who perform senior managerial functions.

1-4. In the UK and Ireland, depending on the nature and circumstances of the entity, management may include some or all of those charged with governance (e.g. executive directors). Management will not normally include non-executive directors.

1-5. In the UK and Ireland the auditor has responsibility for three phases when considering subsequent events. The ISA (UK and Ireland) provides guidance on the auditor's responsibilities in relation to:

   (a) Events occurring between period end and the date of the auditor's report;

   (b) Facts discovered after the date of the auditor's report but before the financial statements are issued; and

   (c) Facts discovered after financial statements have been issued but before the laying of the financial statements before the members, or equivalent.

1-6. These three phases - and auditor's responsibilities in relation to them - leading to the laying of financial statements before members apply to all entities. However, in practice one or more of the phases may be so short as not to require separate consideration by the auditor, for example where the meeting at which those charged with governance of a small owner-managed entity approve the financial statements, and the auditor's report is signed, is immediately followed by the entity's annual general meeting.

Facts discovered after the laying of the financial statements before the members may result in those charged with governance issuing revised accounts as defined by relevant legislation. The auditor's considerations in relation to revised financial statements are covered in paragraphs 14 to 18 below.

2. **The auditor should consider the effect of subsequent events on the financial statements and on the auditor's report.**

3. International Accounting Standard 10, "Events After the Balance Sheet Date" deals with the treatment in financial statements of events, both favorable and unfavorable, that occur between the balance sheet date and the date when the financial statements are authorised for issue and identifies two types of events:

    (a) Those that provide evidence of conditions that existed at the balance sheet date (adjusting events after the balance sheet date); and

    (b) Those that are indicative of conditions that arose after the balance sheet date (non-adjusting events after the balance sheet date).

Events Occurring Up to the Date of the Auditor's Report

4. **The auditor should perform audit procedures designed to obtain sufficient appropriate audit evidence that all events up to the date of the auditor's report that may require adjustment of, or disclosure in, the financial statements have been identified.** These procedures are in addition to procedures which may be applied to specific transactions occurring after period end to obtain audit evidence as to account balances as at period end, for example, the testing of inventory cutoff and payments to creditors. The auditor is not, however, expected to conduct a continuing review of all matters to which previously applied audit procedures have provided satisfactory conclusions.

5. The audit procedures to identify events that may require adjustment of, or disclosure in, the financial statements would be performed as near as practicable to the date of the auditor's report. Such audit procedures take into account the auditor's risk assessment and ordinarily include the following:

    •   Reviewing procedures management has established to ensure that subsequent events are identified.

    •   Reading minutes of the meetings of shareholders, those charged with governance, including established committees such as relevant executive committees and the audit committee, held after period end and inquiring about matters discussed at meetings for which minutes are not yet available.

    •   Reading the entity's latest available interim financial statements and, as considered necessary and appropriate, budgets, cash flow forecasts and other related management reports.

- Inquiring, or extending previous oral or written inquiries, of the entity's legal counsel concerning litigation and claims.

- Inquiring of management as to whether any subsequent events have occurred which might affect the financial statements. Examples of inquiries of management on specific matters are:

  o The current status of items that were accounted for on the basis of preliminary or inconclusive data.

  o Whether new commitments, borrowings or guarantees have been entered into.

  o Whether sales or acquisition of assets have occurred or are planned.

  o Whether the issue of new shares or debentures or an agreement to merge or liquidate has been made or is planned.

  o Whether any assets have been appropriated by government or destroyed, for example, by fire or flood.

  o Whether there have been any developments regarding risk areas and contingencies.

  o Whether any unusual accounting adjustments have been made or are contemplated.

  o Whether any events have occurred or are likely to occur which will bring into question the appropriateness of accounting policies used in the financial statements as would be the case, for example, if such events call into question the validity of the going concern assumption.

5-1. In the UK and Ireland the auditor reviews procedures established by those charged with governance and inquires of those charged with governance as to whether any subsequent events have occurred which might affect the financial statements.

6. When a component, such as a division, branch or subsidiary, is audited by another auditor, the auditor would consider the other auditor's procedures regarding events after period end and the need to inform the other auditor of the planned date of the auditor's report.

7. **When the auditor becomes aware of events which materially affect the financial statements, the auditor should consider whether such events are properly accounted for and adequately disclosed in the financial statements.**

Facts Discovered After the Date of the Auditor's Report But Before the Financial Statements are Issued

8. The auditor does not have any responsibility to perform audit procedures or make any inquiry regarding the financial statements after the date of the auditor's report. During the period from the date of the auditor's report to the date the financial statements are issued, the responsibility to inform the auditor of facts which may affect the financial statements rests with management[1].

9. **When, after the date of the auditor's report but before the financial statements are issued, the auditor becomes aware of a fact which may materially affect the financial statements, the auditor should consider whether the financial statements need amendment, should discuss the matter with management[2], and should take the action appropriate in the circumstances.**

10. When management[3] amends the financial statements, the auditor would carry out the audit procedures necessary in the circumstances and would provide management with a new report on the amended financial statements. The new auditor's report would be dated not earlier than the date the amended financial statements are signed or approved and, accordingly, the audit procedures referred to in paragraphs 4 and 5 would be extended to the date of the new auditor's report.

11. **When management[3] does not amend the financial statements in circumstances where the auditor believes they need to be amended and the auditor's report has not been released to the entity, the auditor should express a qualified opinion or an adverse opinion.**

12. When the auditor's report has been released to the entity, the auditor would notify those charged with governance not to issue the financial statements and the auditor's report thereon to third parties. If the financial statements are subsequently released, the auditor needs to take action to prevent reliance on the auditor's report. The action taken will depend on the auditor's legal rights and obligations and the recommendations of the auditor's lawyer.

Facts Discovered After the Financial Statements Have Been Issued

13. After the financial statements have been issued, the auditor has no obligation to make any inquiry regarding such financial statements.

---

[1] In the UK and Ireland the responsibility to inform the auditor of facts which may affect the financial statements rests with those charged with governance.
[2] In the UK and Ireland the auditor discusses these matters with those charged with governance. Those charged with governance are responsible for the preparation of the financial statements.
[3] In the UK and Ireland the responsibility for amending the financial statements rests with those charged with governance.

13-1. For the purposes of this ISA (UK and Ireland), in the UK and the Republic of Ireland the term "after the financial statements have been issued" includes the period after the financial statements have been issued but before they have been laid before members, or equivalent. In the UK or the Republic of Ireland the auditor has a statutory right to attend the AGM and be heard on any part of the business of the meeting which concerns them as auditor, including making a statement about facts discovered after the date of the auditor's report and this implies that where subsequent events come to the attention of the auditor, the auditor needs to consider what to do in relation to them.

14. **When, after the financial statements have been issued, the auditor becomes aware of a fact which existed at the date of the auditor's report and which, if known at that date, may have caused the auditor to modify the auditor's report, the auditor should consider whether the financial statements need revision[4], should discuss the matter with management[2], and should take the action appropriate in the circumstances.**

14-1. Where the auditor becomes aware of a fact relevant to the audited financial statements which did not exist at the date of the auditor's report there are no statutory provisions for revising financial statements. The auditor discusses with those charged with governance whether they should withdraw the financial statements and where those charged with governance decide not to do so the auditor may wish to take advice on whether it might be possible to withdraw their report. In both cases, other possible courses of action include the making of a statement by those charged with governance or the auditor at the annual general meeting. In any event legal advice may be helpful.

15. When management[3] revises the financial statements, the auditor would carry out the audit procedures necessary in the circumstances, would review the steps taken by management to ensure that anyone in receipt of the previously issued financial statements together with the auditor's report thereon is informed of the situation, and would issue a new report on the revised financial statements.

16. **The new auditor's report should include an emphasis of a matter paragraph referring to a note to the financial statements that more extensively discusses the reason for the revision of the previously issued financial statements and to the earlier report issued by the auditor.** The new auditor's report would be dated not earlier than the date the revised financial statements are approved and, accordingly, the audit procedures referred to in paragraphs 4 and 5 would ordinarily be extended to the date of the new auditor's report. Local regulations of some countries permit the auditor to restrict the audit procedures regarding the revised financial statements to the effects of the subsequent event that necessitated the

---

[4] In the UK the detailed regulations governing revised financial statements and directors' reports, where the revision is voluntary, are set out in sections 245 to 245C of the Companies Act 1985 and in the Articles 253 to 253C of the Companies (Northern Ireland) Order 1986. There are no provisions in the Companies Acts of the Republic of Ireland for revising financial statements.

revision. In such cases, the new auditor's report would contain a statement to that effect.

16-1. When issuing a new report the auditor has regard to the regulations relating to reports on revised annual financial statements and directors' reports[5].

17. When management[5] does not take the necessary steps to ensure that anyone in receipt of the previously issued financial statements together with the auditor's report thereon is informed of the situation and does not revise the financial statements in circumstances where the auditor believes they need to be revised, the auditor would notify those charged with governance of the entity that action will be taken by the auditor to prevent future reliance on the auditor's report. The action taken will depend on the auditor's legal rights and obligations and the recommendations of the auditor's lawyers.

17-1. For example, where the financial statements are issued but have not yet been laid before the members or equivalent, or if those charged with governance do not intend to make an appropriate statement at the annual general meeting, then the auditor may consider making an appropriate statement at the annual general meeting. The auditor does not have a statutory right to communicate directly in writing with the members although, if the auditor resigns or is removed or is not reappointed, the auditor has, for example, various duties under company law[6].

18. It may not be necessary to revise the financial statements and issue a new auditor's report when issue of the financial statements for the following period is imminent, provided appropriate disclosures are to be made in such statements.

Offering of Securities to the Public

In the UK and Ireland, standards and guidance for accountants engaged to prepare a report and/or letter for inclusion in, or in connection with, an investment circular are set out in APB's Statements of Investment Circular Reporting Standards (SIRS).

19. **In cases involving the offering of securities to the public, the auditor should consider any legal and related requirements applicable to the auditor in all jurisdictions in which the securities are being offered.** For example, the auditor may be required to carry out additional audit procedures to the date of the final offering document. These procedures would ordinarily include carrying out the audit procedures referred to in paragraphs 4 and 5 up to a date at or near the effective date

---

[5] In the UK and Ireland, those charged with governance have responsibility for taking the steps referred to in paragraph 17.

[6] The auditor of a limited company in Great Britain who ceases to hold office as auditor is required to comply with the requirements of section 394 of the Companies Act 1985 regarding the statement to be made by the auditor in relation to ceasing to hold office. Equivalent requirements for Northern Ireland are contained in Article 401A of the Companies (Northern Ireland) Order 1986 and, for the Republic of Ireland, are contained in section 185 of the Companies Act 1990.

of the final offering document and reading the offering document to assess whether the other information in the offering document is consistent with the financial information with which the auditor is associated.

Effective Date

19-1. This ISA (UK and Ireland) is effective for audits of financial statements for periods commencing on or after 15 December 2004.

INTERNATIONAL STANDARD ON AUDITING (UK AND IRELAND) 570

GOING CONCERN

CONTENTS

International Standard on Auditing (UK and Ireland) (ISA (UK and Ireland)) 570 "Going Concern" should be read in the context of the Auditing Practices Board's Statement "The Auditing Practices Board - Scope and Authority of Pronouncements (Revised)" which sets out the application and authority of ISAs (UK and Ireland).

Introduction

1. The purpose of this International Standard on Auditing (UK and Ireland) (ISA (UK and Ireland)) is to establish standards and provide guidance on the auditor's responsibility in the audit of financial statements with respect to the going concern assumption used in the preparation of the financial statements, including considering management's[1a] assessment of the entity's ability to continue as a going concern.

1-1. This ISA (UK and Ireland) contains standards and guidance for the auditor in relation to the going concern basis that is generally presumed in financial statements which are required to be properly prepared in accordance with the Act[1b], and to give a true and fair view. In the absence of specific legal or other provisions to the contrary, the principles and procedures embodied in the ISA (UK and Ireland) apply also to the audit of the financial statements of other entities. This ISA (UK and Ireland) does not establish standards nor provide guidance about going concern in any other context, such as that of an engagement to report on an entity's future viability.

1-2. This ISA (UK and Ireland) uses the terms 'those charged with governance' and 'management'. The term 'governance' describes the role of persons entrusted with the supervision, control and direction of an entity. Ordinarily, those charged with governance are accountable for ensuring that the entity achieves its objectives, and for the quality of its financial reporting and reporting to interested parties. Those charged with governance include management only when they perform such functions.

1-3. In the UK and Ireland, those charged with governance include the directors (executive and non-executive) of a company or other body, the members of an audit committee where one exists, the partners, proprietors, committee of management or trustees of other forms of entity, or equivalent persons responsible for directing the entity's affairs and preparing its financial statements.

1-4. 'Management' comprises those persons who perform senior managerial functions.

1-5. In the UK and Ireland, depending on the nature and circumstances of the entity, management may include some or all of those charged with governance (e.g. executive directors). Management will not normally include non-executive directors.

2. **When planning and performing audit procedures and in evaluating the results thereof, the auditor should consider the appropriateness of management's[1a] use of the going concern assumption in the preparation of the financial statements.**

2-1. **The auditor should consider any relevant disclosures in the financial statements.**

[1a] In the UK and Ireland, those charged with governance are responsible for the preparation of the financial statements and the assessment of the entity's ability to continue as a going concern.

[1b] For Great Britain, 'the Act' refers to the Companies Act 1985. For Northern Ireland, the equivalent legislation is provided by the Companies (Northern Ireland) Order 1986 and for the Republic of Ireland by the Companies Acts 1963 to 2003.

Management's Responsibility[1a]

3. The going concern assumption is a fundamental principle in the preparation of financial statements. Under the going concern assumption, an entity is ordinarily viewed as continuing in business for the foreseeable future with neither the intention nor the necessity of liquidation, ceasing trading or seeking protection from creditors pursuant to laws or regulations. Accordingly, assets and liabilities are recorded on the basis that the entity will be able to realize its assets and discharge its liabilities in the normal course of business.

4. Some financial reporting frameworks contain an explicit requirement[1] for management[1a] to make a specific assessment of the entity's ability to continue as a going concern, and standards regarding matters to be considered and disclosures to be made in connection with going concern. For example, International Accounting Standard 1 (revised 2003), "Presentation of Financial Statements," requires management to make an assessment of an enterprise's ability to continue as a going concern.[2]

4-1. Appendix 1 to this ISA (UK and Ireland) summarizes, in relation to going concern, the legal and professional accounting requirements in the UK and Ireland with which those charged with governance comply in preparing financial statements.

4-2. An important consequence of the legal and professional accounting requirements in the UK and Ireland is that, when preparing financial statements, those charged with governance should satisfy themselves as to whether the going concern basis is appropriate. Even if it is appropriate, it may still be necessary for the financial statements to contain additional disclosures, for instance relating to the adoption of that basis, in order to give a true and fair view.

---

[1] The detailed requirements regarding management's responsibility to assess the entity's ability to continue as a going concern and related financial statement disclosures may be set out in accounting standards, legislation or regulation.

[2] IAS 1, "Presentation of Financial Statements," paragraphs 23 and 24 state: "When preparing financial statements, management shall make an assessment of an entity's ability to continue as a going concern. Financial statements shall be prepared on a going concern basis unless management either intends to liquidate the entity or to cease trading, or has no realistic alternative but to do so. When management is aware, in making its assessment, of material uncertainties related to events or conditions that may cast significant doubt upon the entity's ability to continue as a going concern, those uncertainties shall be disclosed. When financial statements are not prepared on a going concern basis, that fact shall be disclosed, together with the basis on which the financial statements are prepared and the reasons why the entity is not a going concern.

In assessing whether the going concern assumption is appropriate, management takes into account all available information about the future, which is at least, but is not limited to, twelve months from the balance sheet date. The degree of consideration depends on the facts in each case. When an entity has a history of profitable operations and ready access to financial resources, a conclusion that the going concern basis of accounting is appropriate may be reached without detailed analysis. In other cases, management may need to consider a wide range of factors relating to current and expected profitability, debt repayment schedules and potential sources of replacement financing before it can satisfy itself that the going concern basis is appropriate."

5. In other financial reporting frameworks, there may be no explicit requirement for management to make a specific assessment of the entity's ability to continue as a going concern. Nevertheless, since the going concern assumption is a fundamental principle in the preparation of the financial statements, management[1a] has a responsibility to assess the entity's ability to continue as a going concern even if the financial reporting framework does not include an explicit responsibility to do so.

6. When there is a history of profitable operations and a ready access to financial resources, management[1a] may make its assessment without detailed analysis.

7. Management's[1a] assessment of the going concern assumption involves making a judgment, at a particular point in time, about the future outcome of events or conditions which are inherently uncertain. The following factors are relevant:

    •   In general terms, the degree of uncertainty associated with the outcome of an event or condition increases significantly the further into the future a judgment is being made about the outcome of an event or condition. For that reason, most financial reporting frameworks that require an explicit management assessment specify the period for which management is required to take into account all available information.

    •   Any judgment about the future is based on information available at the time at which the judgment is made. Subsequent events can contradict a judgment which was reasonable at the time it was made.

    •   The size and complexity of the entity, the nature and condition of its business and the degree to which it is affected by external factors all affect the judgment regarding the outcome of events or conditions.

8. Examples of events or conditions, which may give rise to business risks, that individually or collectively may cast significant doubt about the going concern assumption are set out below. This listing is not all-inclusive nor does the existence of one or more of the items always signify that a material uncertainty[3] exists.

    Financial

    •   Net liability or net current liability position.

    •   Necessary borrowing facilities have not been agreed.

    •   Fixed-term borrowings approaching maturity without realistic prospects of renewal or repayment; or excessive reliance on short-term borrowings to finance long-term assets.

---

[3] The phrase "material uncertainty" is used in IAS 1 in discussing the uncertainties related to events or conditions which may cast significant doubt on the enterprise's ability to continue as a going concern that should be disclosed in the financial statements. In other financial reporting frameworks, and elsewhere in the ISA's (UK and Ireland), the phrase "significant uncertainties" is used in similar circumstances.

- Major debt repayment falling due where refinancing is necessary to the entity's continued existence.

- Major restructuring of debt.

- Indications of withdrawal of financial support by debtors and other creditors.

- Negative operating cash flows indicated by historical or prospective financial statements.

- Adverse key financial ratios.

- Substantial operating losses or significant deterioration in the value of assets used to generate cash flows.

- Major losses or cash flow problems which have arisen since the balance sheet date.

- Arrears or discontinuance of dividends.

- Inability to pay creditors on due dates.

- Inability to comply with the terms of loan agreements.

- Reduction in normal terms of trade credit by suppliers.

- Change from credit to cash-on-delivery transactions with suppliers.

- Inability to obtain financing for essential new product development or other essential investments.

- Substantial sales of fixed assets not intended to be replaced.

Operating

- Loss of key management without replacement.

- Loss of key staff without replacement.

- Loss of a major market, franchise, license, or principal supplier.

- Labor difficulties or shortages of important supplies.

- Fundamental changes in the market or technology to which the entity is unable to adapt adequately.

- Excessive dependence on a few product lines where the market is depressed.

- Technical developments which render a key product obsolete.

Other

- Non-compliance with capital or other statutory requirements.

- Pending legal or regulatory proceedings against the entity that may, if successful, result in claims that are unlikely to be satisfied.

- Changes in legislation or government policy expected to adversely affect the entity.

- Issues which involve a range of possible outcomes so wide that an unfavorable result could affect the appropriateness of the going concern basis.

The significance of such events or conditions often can be mitigated by other factors. For example, the effect of an entity being unable to make its normal debt repayments may be counterbalanced by management's plans to maintain adequate cash flows by alternative means, such as by disposal of assets, rescheduling of loan repayments, or obtaining additional capital. Similarly, the loss of a principal supplier may be mitigated by the availability of a suitable alternative source of supply.

Auditor's Responsibility

9. The auditor's responsibility is to consider the appropriateness of management's[1a] use of the going concern assumption in the preparation of the financial statements, and consider whether there are material uncertainties about the entity's ability to continue as a going concern that need to be disclosed in the financial statements. The auditor considers the appropriateness of management's use of the going concern assumption even if the financial reporting framework used in the preparation of the financial statements does not include an explicit requirement for management to make a specific assessment of the entity's ability to continue as a going concern.

9-1. The auditor also considers whether there are adequate disclosures regarding the going concern basis in the financial statements in order that they give a true and fair view.

9-2. The auditor's procedures necessarily involve a consideration of the entity's ability to continue in operational existence for the foreseeable future. In turn, that necessitates consideration both of the current and the possible future circumstances of the business and the environment in which it operates.

10. The auditor cannot predict future events or conditions that may cause an entity to cease to continue as a going concern. Accordingly, the absence of any reference to going concern uncertainty in an auditor's report cannot be viewed as a guarantee as to the entity's ability to continue as a going concern.

Planning the Audit and Performing Risk Assessment Procedures

11. **In obtaining an understanding of the entity, the auditor should consider whether there are events or conditions and related business risks which may cast significant doubt on the entity's ability to continue as a going concern.**

12. **The auditor should remain alert for audit evidence of events or conditions and related business risks which may cast significant doubt on the entity's ability to continue as a going concern in performing audit procedures throughout the audit. If such events or conditions are identified, the auditor should, in addition to performing the procedures in paragraph 26, consider whether they affect the auditor's assessment of the risks of material misstatement.**

13. The auditor considers events and conditions relating to the going concern assumption when performing risk assessment procedures, because this allows for more timely discussions with management, review of management's plans and resolution of any identified going concern issues.

14. In some cases, management[1a] may have already made a preliminary assessment when the auditor is performing risk assessment procedures. If so, the auditor reviews that assessment to determine whether management has identified events or conditions, such as those discussed in paragraph 8, and management's plans to address them.

15. If management[1a] has not yet made a preliminary assessment, the auditor discusses with management the basis for their intended use of the going concern assumption, and inquires of management whether events or conditions, such as those discussed in paragraph 8, exist. The auditor may request management to begin making its assessment, particularly when the auditor has already identified events or conditions relating to the going concern assumption.

16. The auditor considers the effect of identified events or conditions when assessing the risks of material misstatement and, therefore, their existence may affect the nature, timing and extent of the auditor's further procedures in response to the assessed risks.

Evaluating Management's[1a] Assessment

17. **The auditor should evaluate management's[1a] assessment of the entity's ability to continue as a going concern.**

17-1. **The auditor should assess the adequacy of the means by which the those charged with governance have satisfied themselves that:**

   (a) **It is appropriate for them to adopt the going concern basis in preparing the financial statements; and**

(b) The financial statements include such disclosures, if any, relating to going concern as are necessary for them to give a true and fair view.

For this purpose:

(i) The auditor should make enquiries of those charged with governance and examine appropriate available financial information; and

(ii) Having regard to the future period to which those charged with governance have paid particular attention in assessing going concern (see paragraphs 18 and 18-1 below), the auditor should plan and perform procedures specifically designed to identify any material matters which could indicate concern about the entity's ability to continue as a going concern.

18. The auditor should consider the same period as that used by management[1a] in making its assessment under the applicable financial reporting framework. If management's assessment of the entity's ability to continue as a going concern covers less than twelve months from the balance sheet date, the auditor should ask management to extend its assessment period to twelve months from the balance sheet date.

18-1. In the UK and Ireland, if the period used by the those charged with governance in making their assessment is less than one year from the date of approval of the financial statements, and they have not disclosed that fact in the financial statements, the auditor does so within the audit report (see paragraphs 31-4 and 31-5).

18-2. In assessing going concern, those charged with governance take account of all relevant information of which they are aware at the time. The nature of the exercise entails that those charged with governance look forward, and there will be some future period to which they will pay particular attention in assessing going concern. It is not possible to specify a minimum length for this period: it is recognized in any case that any such period would be artificial and arbitrary since in reality there is no 'cut off point' after which there should be a sudden change in the approach adopted by those charged with governance. The length of the period is likely to depend upon such factors as:

• The entity's reporting and budgeting systems; and

• The nature of the entity, including its size or complexity.

Where the period considered by those charged with governance has been limited, for example, to a period of less than one year from the date of approval of the financial statements, those charged with governance will have determined whether, in their opinion, the financial statements require any additional disclosure to explain adequately the assumptions that underlie the adoption of the going concern basis.

18-3. The basis for the auditor's procedures is the information upon which those charged with governance have based their assessment and the reasoning of those charged with governance. The auditor assesses whether this constitutes sufficient appropriate audit evidence for the purpose of the audit and whether the auditor concurs with the judgment of those charged with governance about the need for additional disclosures.

18-4. The following factors in particular may affect the information available to the auditor, and whether the auditor considers this information constitutes sufficient audit evidence for the purpose of the audit.

(a) *The nature of the entity (its size and the complexity of its circumstances, for instance)*. This ISA (UK and Ireland) applies to the audits of the financial statements of all sizes of entity. The larger or more complex the entity the more sophisticated is likely to be the information available and needed to support the assessment of whether it is appropriate to adopt the going concern basis.

(b) *Whether the information relates to future events, and if so how far into the future those events lie*. The information relating to the period falling after one year from the balance sheet date is often prepared in far less detail and subject to a greater degree of estimation than the information relating to periods ending on or before one year from the balance sheet date.

19. Management's[1a] assessment of the entity's ability to continue as a going concern is a key part of the auditor's consideration of the going concern assumption. As noted in paragraph 7, most financial reporting frameworks requiring an explicit management assessment specify the period for which management is required to take into account all available information.[4]

19-1. A determination of the sufficiency of the evidence supplied to the auditor by those charged with governance will depend on the particular circumstances. However, to be sufficient the evidence may not require formal cash flow forecasts and budgets to have been prepared for the period ending one year from the date of approval of the financial statements. Although such forecasts and budgets are likely to provide the most persuasive evidence, alternative sources of evidence may also be acceptable. Often, the auditor through discussion with those charged with governance of their plans and expectations for that period may be able to obtain satisfaction that those charged with governance have in fact paid particular attention to a period of one year from the date of approval of the financial statements. Appendix 2 illustrates circumstances where formal budgets and forecasts have, with justification, not been provided for the entire twelve month period yet the auditor is able to conclude that those charged with governance have paid particular attention to the period ending one year from the date of approval of the financial statements.

---

[4] For example, IAS 1 defines this as a period that should be at least, but is not limited to, twelve months from the balance sheet date.

FRS 18 does not specify this period but does require that where the foreseeable future considered by the directors has been limited to a period of less than one year from the date of approval of the financial statements, that fact should be disclosed in the financial statements.

20.   In evaluating management's[1a] assessment, the auditor considers the process management followed to make its assessment, the assumptions on which the assessment is based and management's plans for future action. The auditor considers whether the assessment has taken into account all relevant information of which the auditor is aware as a result of the audit procedures.

20-1.   The auditor may need to consider some or all of the following matters:

- Whether the period to which those charged with governance have paid particular attention in assessing going concern is reasonable in the entity's circumstances and in the light of the need for those charged with governance to consider the ability of the entity to continue in operational existence for the foreseeable future.

- The systems, or other means (formal or informal), for timely identification of warnings of future risks and uncertainties the entity might face.

- Budget and/or forecast information (cash flow information in particular) produced by the entity, and the quality of the systems (or other means, formal or informal) in place for producing this information and keeping it up to date.

- Whether the key assumptions underlying the budgets and/or forecasts appear appropriate in the circumstances.

- The sensitivity of budgets and/or forecasts to variable factors both within the control of those charged with governance and outside their control.

- Any obligations, undertakings or guarantees arranged with other entities (in particular, lenders, suppliers and group companies) for the giving or receiving of support.

- The existence, adequacy and terms of borrowing facilities, and supplier credit.

- The plans of those charged with governance for resolving any matters giving rise to the concern (if any) about the appropriateness of the going concern basis. In particular, the auditor may need to consider whether the plans are realistic, whether there is a reasonable expectation that the plans are likely to resolve any problems foreseen and whether those charged with governance are likely to put the plans into practice effectively.

20-2.   The extent of the procedures is influenced primarily by the excess of the financial resources available to the entity over the financial resources that it requires. The entity's procedures (and the auditor's procedures) need not always be elaborate in order to provide sufficient appropriate audit evidence. For example, the auditor may not always need to examine budgets and forecasts for this purpose. This is particularly likely to be the case in respect of entities with uncomplicated circumstances. Many smaller companies fall into this category. Thus for example:

- Regarding the systems or other means for timely identification of warnings of future risks and uncertainties, those charged with governance might consider that it is appropriate simply to keep abreast of developments within their individual business and their business sector. In the circumstances, the auditor might concur with those charged with governance; or

- Those charged with governance might not, as a matter of course, prepare periodic cash flow and other budgets, forecasts or other management accounts information apart from the accounting records required by law and outline plans for the future. In the view of those charged with governance, this might be acceptable where the business is stable. In the circumstances the auditor might concur with those charged with governance. Hence the auditor's procedures regarding budgets, forecasts and related issues might comprise discussion of the outline plans of those charged with governance in the light of other information available to the auditor.

21. As noted in paragraph 6, when there is a history of profitable operations and a ready access to financial resources, management[1a] may make its assessment without detailed analysis. In such circumstances, the auditor's conclusion about the appropriateness of this assessment normally is also made without the need for performing detailed procedures. When events or conditions have been identified which may cast significant doubt about the entity's ability to continue as a going concern, however, the auditor performs additional audit procedures, as described in paragraph 26.

The Auditor's Examination of Borrowing Facilities

21-1. In examining borrowing facilities the auditor could decide, for example, that it is necessary:

(a) To obtain confirmations of the existence and terms of bank facilities; and

(b) To make an own assessment of the intentions of the bankers relating thereto.

The latter assessment could involve the auditor examining written evidence or making notes of meetings which the auditor would hold with those charged with governance and, occasionally, with those charged with governance and the entity's bankers. In making an assessment of the bankers' intentions the auditor ascertains, normally through enquiries of those charged with governance, whether the bankers are aware of the matters that are causing the auditor to decide that such an assessment is necessary. It is also important that the relationships between the auditor, those charged with governance and the bankers are clarified and understood.

21-2. The auditor might be more likely to decide that it is necessary to obtain confirmations of the existence and terms of bank facilities, and to make an independent assessment of the intentions of the bankers relating thereto, in cases where, for example:

- There is a low margin of financial resources available to the entity.

- The entity is dependent on borrowing facilities shortly due for renewal.

- Correspondence between the bankers and the entity reveals that the last renewal of facilities was agreed with difficulty, or that, since the last review of facilities, the bankers have imposed additional conditions as a prerequisite for continued lending.

- A significant deterioration in cash flow is projected.

- The value of assets granted as security for the borrowings is declining.

- The entity has breached the terms of borrowing covenants, or there are indications of potential breaches.

21-3. The auditor considers whether any inability to obtain sufficient appropriate audit evidence regarding the existence and terms of borrowing facilities and the intentions of the lender relating thereto, and/or the factors giving rise to this inability, need to be:

- Disclosed in the financial statements in order that they give a true and fair view; and/or

- Referred to (by way of an explanatory paragraph or a qualified opinion) in the auditor's report.

Period Beyond Management's[1a] Assessment

22. **The auditor should inquire of management as to its knowledge of events or conditions and related business risks beyond the period of assessment used by management[1a] that may cast significant doubt on the entity's ability to continue as a going concern.**

23. The auditor is alert to the possibility that there may be known events, scheduled or otherwise, or conditions that will occur beyond the period of assessment used by management[1a] that may bring into question the appropriateness of management's use of the going concern assumption in preparing the financial statements. The auditor may become aware of such known events or conditions during the planning and performance of the audit, including subsequent events procedures.

24. Since the degree of uncertainty associated with the outcome of an event or condition increases as the event or condition is further into the future, in considering such events or conditions, the indications of going concern issues will need to be significant before the auditor considers taking further action. The auditor may need to ask management[1a] to determine the potential significance of the event or condition on their going concern assessment.

25. The auditor does not have a responsibility to design audit procedures other than inquiry of management to test for indications of events or conditions which cast significant doubt on the entity's ability to continue as a going concern beyond the

period assessed by management[1a] which, as discussed in paragraph 18, would be at least twelve months from the balance sheet date.

Further Audit Procedures When Events or Conditions are Identified

26.   When events or conditions have been identified which may cast significant doubt on the entity's ability to continue as a going concern, the auditor should:

(a)   Review management's[1a] plans for future actions based on its going concern assessment;

(b)   Gather sufficient appropriate audit evidence to confirm or dispel whether or not a material uncertainty exists through carrying out audit procedures considered necessary, including considering the effect of any plans of management and other mitigating factors; and

(c)   Seek written representations from management[5] regarding its plans for future action.

26-1. The auditor should consider the need to obtain written confirmations of representations from those charged with governance regarding:

(a)   The assessment of those charged with governance that the company is a going concern;

(b)   Any relevant disclosures in the financial statements.

26-2. Such written confirmations are necessary in respect of matters material to the financial statements when those representations are critical to obtaining sufficient appropriate audit evidence. In view of their importance, it is appropriate for such confirmations to be provided by those charged with governance, rather than other levels of the entity's management.

26-3. If they are unable to obtain such written confirmations of representations as they consider necessary from those charged with governance, the auditor considers whether:

•   There is a limitation on the scope of the auditor's work which requires a qualified opinion or disclaimer of opinion; or

•   The failure of those charged with governance to provide the written confirmations could indicate that there is concern.

---

[5] In the UK and Ireland the auditor obtains written representations from those charged with governance.

27. Events or conditions which may cast significant doubt on the entity's ability to continue as a going concern may be identified in performing risk assessment procedures or in the course of performing further audit procedures. The process of considering events or conditions continues as the audit progresses. When the auditor believes such events or conditions may cast significant doubt on the entity's ability to continue as a going concern, certain audit procedures may take on added significance. The auditor inquires of management as to its plans for future action, including its plans to liquidate assets, borrow money or restructure debt, reduce or delay expenditures, or increase capital. The auditor also considers whether any additional facts or information are available since the date on which management[1a] made its assessment. The auditor obtains sufficient appropriate audit evidence that management's plans are feasible and that the outcome of these plans will improve the situation.

28. Audit procedures that are relevant in this regard may include:

- Analyzing and discussing cash flow, profit and other relevant forecasts with management.

- Analyzing and discussing the entity's latest available interim financial statements.

- Reviewing the terms of debentures and loan agreements and determining whether any have been breached.

- Reading minutes of the meetings of shareholders, those charged with governance and relevant committees for reference to financing difficulties.

- Inquiring of the entity's lawyer regarding the existence of litigation and claims and the reasonableness of management's assessments of their outcome and the estimate of their financial implications.

- Confirming the existence, legality and enforceability of arrangements to provide or maintain financial support with related and third parties and assessing the financial ability of such parties to provide additional funds.

- Considering the entity's plans to deal with unfilled customer orders.

- Reviewing events after period end to identify those that either mitigate or otherwise affect the entity's ability to continue as a going concern.

29. When analysis of cash flow is a significant factor in considering the future outcome of events or conditions the auditor considers:

(a) The reliability of the entity's information system for generating such information; and

(b) Whether there is adequate support for the assumptions underlying the forecast.

In addition the auditor compares:

(c)   The prospective financial information for recent prior periods with historical results; and

(d)   The prospective financial information for the current period with results achieved to date.

Audit Conclusions and Reporting

30.   **Based on the audit evidence obtained, the auditor should determine if, in the auditor's judgment, a material uncertainty exists related to events or conditions that alone or in aggregate, may cast significant doubt on the entity's ability to continue as a going concern.**

30-1.   **The auditor should document the extent of the auditor's concern (if any) about the entity's ability to continue as a going concern.**

30-2.   The auditor might be more likely to conclude that there is a significant level of concern about the entity's ability to continue as a going concern if, for example, indications such as those in paragraph 8 are present. However, where such indications are present, the auditor may have obtained sufficient appropriate evidence causing the auditor to conclude that there is not a significant level of concern about the entity's ability to continue as a going concern.

30-3.   The auditor could consider that there is a significant level of concern about the entity's ability to continue as a going concern, or the auditor could disagree with the preparation of the financial statements on the going concern basis. In such cases (whether or not this is because of potential insolvency) the auditor might decide to write to those charged with governance drawing their attention to the need to consider taking suitable advice. In particular, those charged with governance of an entity may need to obtain advice from specialist accountants or lawyers on the appropriateness and implications of continuing to trade while they know, or ought to know, that the entity is insolvent.

31.   A material uncertainty exists when the magnitude of its potential impact is such that, in the auditor's judgment, clear disclosure of the nature and implications of the uncertainty is necessary for the presentation of the financial statements not to be misleading.

31-1.   **The auditor should consider whether the financial statements are required to include disclosures relating to going concern in order to give a true and fair view.**

31-2.   In particular, if the future period to which those charged with governance have paid particular attention is, as described in paragraph 18-2, not very long, those charged with governance will have determined whether, in their opinion, the financial statements require any additional disclosures to explain adequately the assumptions that underlie the adoption of the going concern basis. The auditor assesses whether to concur with the judgments of those charged with governance regarding the need for additional disclosures and their adequacy. Disclosure, however, does not eliminate the need to make appropriate judgments about the suitability of the future period as an adequate basis for assessing the position.

31-3. To avoid repetition, the text in the financial statements might refer readers to specific disclosures located elsewhere in the annual report (for instance in the Operating and Financial Review). The auditor takes account of such specified disclosures in considering the adequacy of disclosures in the financial statements.

31-4. **If the period to which those charged with governance have paid particular attention in assessing going concern is less than one year from the date of approval of the financial statements, and those charged with governance have not disclosed that fact, the auditor should do so within the section of the auditor's report setting out the basis of the audit opinion, unless the fact is clear from any other references in the auditor's report[6].**

31-5. Where, in forming their opinion, the auditor's assessment of going concern is based on a period to which those charged with governance have paid particular attention which is less than one year from the date of approval of the financial statements, it is appropriate for the auditor to disclose that fact within the basis of the audit opinion, unless it is disclosed in the financial statements or accompanying information (for example, the Operating and Financial Review). In deciding whether to disclose the fact, the auditor assesses whether the evidence supplied by those charged with governance is sufficient to demonstrate that those charged with governance have, in assessing going concern, paid particular attention to a period of one year from the date of approval of the financial statements.

31-6. The auditor qualifies the audit opinion if the auditor considers that those charged with governance have not taken adequate steps to satisfy themselves that it is appropriate for them to adopt the going concern basis. This might arise, for example, when the auditor does not consider that the future period to which those charged with governance have paid particular attention in assessing going concern is reasonable in the entity's circumstances. This is a limitation on the scope of the auditor's work, as the auditor is unable to obtain all the information and explanations which they consider necessary for the purpose of their audit.

Going Concern Assumption Appropriate but a Material Uncertainty Exists

32. If the use of the going concern assumption is appropriate but a material uncertainty exists, the auditor considers whether the financial statements:

---

[6] If the non-disclosure of the fact in the financial statements is a departure from the requirements of the applicable financial reporting framework, the auditor would give a qualified opinion ("except for").

(a) Adequately describe the principal events or conditions that give rise to the significant doubt on the entity's ability to continue in operation and management's plans to deal with these events or conditions; and

(b) State clearly that there is a material uncertainty related to events or conditions which may cast significant doubt on the entity's ability to continue as a going concern and, therefore, that it may be unable to realize its assets and discharge its liabilities in the normal course of business.

33. **If adequate disclosure is made in the financial statements, the auditor should express an unqualified opinion but modify the auditor's report by adding an emphasis of matter paragraph that highlights the existence of a material uncertainty relating to the event or condition that may cast significant doubt on the entity's ability to continue as a going concern and draws attention to the note in the financial statements that discloses the matters set out in paragraph 32.** In evaluating the adequacy of the financial statement disclosure, the auditor considers whether the information explicitly draws the reader's attention to the possibility that the entity may be unable to continue realizing its assets and discharging its liabilities in the normal course of business. The following is an example of such a paragraph when the auditor is satisfied as to the adequacy of the note disclosure:

"Without qualifying our opinion, we draw attention to Note X in the financial statements which indicates that the Company incurred a net loss of ZZZ during the year ended December 31, 20X1 and, as of that date, the Company's current liabilities exceeded its total assets by ZZZ. These conditions, along with other matters as set forth in Note X, indicate the existence of a material uncertainty which may cast significant doubt about the Company's ability to continue as a going concern."

In extreme cases, such as situations involving multiple material uncertainties that are significant to the financial statements, the auditor may consider it appropriate to express a disclaimer of opinion instead of adding an emphasis of matter paragraph.

33-1. The emphasis of matter paragraph describes clearly the nature of the matters giving rise to the auditor's concern and refers to the relevant disclosures in the financial statements. The auditor uses judgment to decide the extent to which it is necessary for the description in the auditor's report to repeat information taken from the notes to the financial statements. The extent of the auditor's concern is one factor affecting the nature and extent of the description in the auditor's report. The prime consideration is clarity of communication. The description is normally identified within the auditor's report through the use of the sub-heading 'Going concern'.

33-2. The auditor might have concluded that there is a significant level of concern about the entity's ability to continue as a going concern. In these cases the auditor does not normally regard the disclosures as adequate unless (in addition to any disclosures otherwise required, for example by accounting standards) the following matters are included in the financial statements:

(a) A statement that the financial statements have been prepared on the going concern basis;

(b) A statement of the pertinent facts;

(c) The nature of the concern;

(d) A statement of the assumptions adopted by those charged with governance, which should be clearly distinguishable from the pertinent facts;

(e) (Where appropriate and practicable) a statement regarding the plans of those charged with governance for resolving the matters giving rise to the concern; and

(f) Details of any relevant actions by those charged with governance.

The guidance above regarding disclosures in the financial statements does not constitute an accounting standard.

34. **If adequate disclosure is not made in the financial statements, the auditor should express a qualified or adverse opinion, as appropriate (ISA (UK and Ireland) 700, "The Auditor's Report on Financial Statements," paragraphs 45–46). The report should include specific reference to the fact that there is a material uncertainty that may cast significant doubt about the entity's ability to continue as a going concern.** The following is an example of the relevant paragraphs when a qualified opinion is to be expressed:

"The Company's financing arrangements expire and amounts outstanding are payable on March 19, 20X1. The Company has been unable to re-negotiate or obtain replacement financing. This situation indicates the existence of a material uncertainty which may cast significant doubt on the Company's ability to continue as a going concern and therefore it may be unable to realize its assets and discharge its liabilities in the normal course of business. The financial statements (and notes thereto) do not disclose this fact.

In our opinion, except for the omission of the information included in the preceding paragraph, the financial statements give a true and fair view of (present fairly, in all material respects,) the financial position of the Company at December 31, 20X0 and the results of its operations and its cash flows for the year then ended in accordance with ..."

Illustrative examples of auditor's reports tailored for use with audits conducted in accordance with ISAs (UK and Ireland) are given in the most recent version of the APB Bulletin, "Auditor's Reports on Financial Statements".

The following is an example of the relevant paragraphs when an adverse opinion is to be expressed:

"The Company's financing arrangements expired and the amount outstanding was payable on December 31, 20X0. The Company has been unable to re-negotiate or obtain replacement financing and is considering filing for bankruptcy. These events indicate a material uncertainty which may cast significant doubt on the Company's ability to continue as a going concern and therefore it may be unable to realize its assets and discharge its liabilities in the normal course of business. The financial statements (and notes thereto) do not disclose this fact.

In our opinion, because of the omission of the information mentioned in the preceding paragraph, the financial statements do not give a true and fair view of (or do not present fairly) the financial position of the Company as at December 31, 20X0, and of its results of operations and its cash flows for the year then ended in accordance with....(and do not comply with...)..."

Illustrative examples of auditor's reports tailored for use with audits conducted in accordance with ISAs (UK and Ireland) are given in Appendix 2 and the most recent version of the APB Bulletin, "Auditor's Reports on Financial Statements".

Going Concern Assumption Inappropriate

35.   **If, in the auditor's judgment, the entity will not be able to continue as a going concern, the auditor should express an adverse opinion if the financial statements have been prepared on a going concern basis.** If, on the basis of the additional audit procedures carried out and the information obtained, including the effect of management's plans, the auditor's judgment is that the entity will not be able to continue as a going concern, the auditor concludes, regardless of whether or not disclosure has been made, that the going concern assumption used in the preparation of the financial statements is inappropriate and expresses an adverse opinion.

36.   When the entity's management[1a] has concluded that the going concern assumption used in the preparation of the financial statements is not appropriate, the financial statements need to be prepared on an alternative authoritative basis. If on the basis of the additional audit procedures carried out and the information obtained the auditor determines the alternative basis is appropriate, the auditor can issue an unqualified opinion if there is adequate disclosure but may require an emphasis of matter in the auditor's report to draw the user's attention to that basis.

36-1. **In rare circumstances, in order to give a true and fair view, those charged with governance may have prepared the financial statements on a basis other than that of going concern. If the auditor considers this other basis to be appropriate in the specific circumstances, and if the financial statements contain the necessary disclosures, the auditor should not qualify the auditor's report in this respect.**

36-2. Some enterprises are formed for a specific purpose, such as a joint venture to undertake a construction project, and are wound up or dissolved when the purpose is achieved. Under these circumstances the financial statements may be prepared on a basis that reflects the fact that assets may need to be realized other than in the ordinary course of operations. In these circumstances the auditor may wish, without qualifying the audit opinion, to refer in the auditor's report to the basis on which the financial statements are prepared; the auditor may do this in the introductory paragraph of the report.

Management Unwilling to Make or Extend its Assessment

37.   **If management[1a] is unwilling to make or extend its assessment when requested to do so by the auditor, the auditor should consider the need to modify the auditor's report as a result of the limitation on the scope of the auditor's work.** In certain circumstances, such as those described in paragraphs 15, 18 and 24, the auditor may believe that it is necessary to ask management to make or extend its assessment. If management is unwilling to do so, it is not the auditor's responsibility to rectify the lack of analysis by management, and a modified report may be appropriate because it may not be possible for the auditor to obtain sufficient appropriate evidence regarding the use of the going concern assumption in the preparation of the financial statements.

38.   In some circumstances, the lack of analysis by management may not preclude the auditor from being satisfied about the entity's ability to continue as a going concern. For example, the auditor's other procedures may be sufficient to assess the appropriateness of management's[1a] use of the going concern assumption in the preparation of the financial statements because the entity has a history of profitable operations and a ready access to financial resources. In other circumstances, however, the auditor may not be able to confirm or dispel, in the absence of management's assessment, whether or not events or conditions exist which indicate there may be a significant doubt on the entity's ability to continue as a going concern, or the existence of plans management has put in place to address them or other mitigating factors. In these circumstances, the auditor modifies the auditor's report as discussed in ISA (UK and Ireland) 700, "The Auditor's Report on Financial Statements," paragraphs 36–44.

Regulated Entities

38-1. When the auditor of a regulated financial entity considers that it might be necessary to either qualify the audit opinion or add an explanatory paragraph to the audit report, the auditor may have a duty to inform the appropriate regulator at an early stage in the audit. In such cases the regulator might, if it has not already done so, specify corrective action to be taken by the entity. At the time at which the auditor formulates the audit report, the auditor takes account of matters such as:

*   Any views expressed by the regulator.

*   Any legal advice obtained by those charged with governance.

*   The actual and planned corrective action.

Significant Delay in the Signature or Approval of Financial Statements

39.   When there is significant delay in the signature or approval of the financial statements by management[1a] after the balance sheet date, the auditor considers the reasons for the delay. When the delay could be related to events or conditions relating to the going concern assessment, the auditor considers the need to perform additional audit procedures, as described in paragraph 26, as well as the effect on the auditor's conclusion regarding the existence of a material uncertainty, as described in paragraph 30.

Application to Groups

39-1. The principles and procedures set out in this ISA (UK and Ireland) apply also to the audit of consolidated financial statements.

39-2. It may be appropriate, on the grounds of materiality, for the group financial statements to be prepared on the going concern basis even though it is inappropriate for the individual financial statements of one or more members of the group to be prepared on the going concern basis.

Effective Date

40.   This ISA (UK and Ireland) is effective for audits of financial statements for periods commencing on or after 15 December 2004.

Public Sector Perspective

Additional guidance for auditors of public sector bodies in the UK and Ireland is given in:

- Practice Note 10 "Audit of Financial Statements of Public Sector Bodies in the United Kingdom (Revised)"

- Practice Note 10(I) "Audit of Central Government Financial Statements in the Republic of Ireland (Revised)"

1.   *The appropriateness of the use of the going concern assumption in the preparation of the financial statements is generally not in question when auditing either a central government or those public sector entities having funding arrangements backed by a central government. However, where such arrangements do not exist, or where central government funding of the entity may be withdrawn and the existence of the entity may be at risk, this ISA (UK and Ireland) will provide useful guidance. As governments corporatize and privatize government entities, going concern issues will become increasingly relevant to the public sector.*

Appendix 1

Preparation of the Financial Statements: Note on Legal and Professional Requirements

Company Law and Accounting Standards

1. The UK Companies Act 1985 specifies certain accounting principles which should normally be adopted in preparing the financial statements of a company. One of these principles is that:

   'the company shall be presumed to be carrying on business as a going concern' (paragraph 10 of Schedule 4 to the Act).[7]

   However such a presumption is not conclusive and may be disregarded if the facts of the particular situation so require. The term 'going concern' is not defined in the Act but, as discussed below, is explained in International Accounting Standard (IAS) 1 'Presentation of Financial Statements' and Financial Reporting Standard (FRS) 18 'Accounting Policies'.

2. Paragraph 15 of Schedule 4 to the UK Companies Act 1985 states that departures from the Act's accounting principles *may* be made if it appears to the directors that there are 'special reasons' for doing so.[8] The financial statements must disclose any such departure, the reasons for it and its effect. 'Special reasons' would include circumstances where the directors conclude, on the basis of the facts as they appear to them, that it is appropriate to depart from the going concern presumption.

3. Furthermore, in addition to that particular provision of the UK Companies Act 1985, section 226 of the Act contains an overriding requirement for directors to prepare financial statements which give a true and fair view of the state of affairs of the company as at the end of the financial year and of its profit or loss for the financial year[9].

4. If compliance with the provisions of the Act would not be *sufficient* to give a true and fair view, the Act requires the directors to give the necessary additional information in the financial statements. If, in 'special circumstances', compliance with the provisions of the Act is *inconsistent* with the requirement to give a true and fair view, the Act requires the directors to depart from the particular provision to the extent necessary to give a true and fair view. The financial statements must disclose the particulars of any such departure, the reasons for it and its effect.

5. Accordingly, directors cannot assume that preparing the financial statements on the going concern basis and in accordance with the other provisions of the Act will necessarily result in the financial statements giving a true and fair view. Whilst, in general, compliance with accounting standards is also necessary to meet the

---

[7] In the Republic of Ireland the equivalent is Section 5(a), Companies (Amendment) Act, 1986.
[8] In the Republic of Ireland the equivalent is Section 6, Companies (Amendment) Act 1986.
[9] In the Republic of Ireland the equivalent is Section 3(b), Companies (Amendment) Act 1986.

requirement to prepare financial statements giving a true and fair view, such compliance is not of itself sufficient to ensure that a true and fair view is given in all cases.

Accounting Standards and the Definition of 'Going Concern'

6. FRS 18 states that "The information provided by financial statements is usually most relevant if prepared on the hypothesis that the entity is able to continue in existence for the foreseeable future. This hypothesis is commonly referred to as the going concern assumption."

7. FRS 18 requires that:

    "An entity should prepare its financial statements on a going concern basis, unless

    (a) the entity is being liquidated or has ceased trading, or

    (b) the directors have no realistic alternative but to liquidate the entity or to cease trading,

    in which circumstances the entity may, if appropriate, prepare its financial statements on a basis other than that of going concern."

8. FRS 18 also requires that "When preparing financial statements, directors should assess whether there are significant doubts about an entity's ability to continue as a going concern." and, in relation to that assessment, the following information should be disclosed in the financial statements:

    "(a) any material uncertainties of which the directors are aware in making their assessment, related to events or conditions that may cast significant doubt upon the entity's ability to continue as a going concern.

    (b) where the foreseeable future considered by the directors has been limited to a period of less than one year from the date of approval of the financial statements, that fact.

    (c) when the financial statements are not prepared on a going concern basis, that fact, together with the basis on which the financial statements are prepared and the reason why the entity is not regarded as a going concern."

9. The requirements of IAS 1 are consistent with those of FRS 18 with the exception that, if the foreseeable future considered by the directors has been limited to a period of less than one year from the date of approval of the financial statements, IAS 1 does not require disclosure of that fact. IAS 1 states that "In assessing whether the going concern assumption is appropriate, management takes into account all available information about the future, which is at least, but not limited to, twelve months from the balance sheet date.

Appendix 2

Illustrative Examples of the Auditor's Assessment of Whether Evidence Provided by Those Charged With Governance, Concerning the Attention They Have Paid to the Period One Year From the Date of Approval of the Financial Statements, is Sufficient

The appendix is illustrative only and does not form part of the Auditing Standards. The purpose of the appendix is to illustrate the application of the Auditing Standards to assist in clarifying their meaning in a number of commercial situations. The examples focus on particular aspects of the situations illustrated and are not intended to be a comprehensive discussion of all the relevant factors that might influence either the directors' or auditor's assessment of the appropriateness of the going concern basis. As the auditor would need to exercise judgment in the circumstances described it is possible that different auditors may arrive at different conclusions. This does not, however, detract from the examples which demonstrate thought process and the implications for an audit report once certain conclusions have been reached by the auditor. These examples neither modify nor override the Auditing Standards.

Example 1 - A small company producing specialized computer application software

Extract from the auditor's risk assessment

This owner managed company employs a few highly trained and highly paid computer system designers to design application software for use by transportation enterprises, such as airlines and bus companies, in preparing their timetables and fare structures. Few companies are engaged in this field and the supply of suitably trained staff is limited. The system designers, who met at University, have been with the company since its formation. They all have an equity interest in the company.

Although the company has only been in existence for five years it has established a reputation for excellence in its field. Its reputation derives from the skill and expertise of its individual employees rather than from anything attaching to the company itself.

A significant amount of time is spent by the designers in pure research activities developing new products. In addition the time needed to develop individual systems relating to an established product can be considerable. In addition to design of new systems the company maintains those systems it has installed on a contractual basis and undertakes training courses in the use of the systems for the employees of its customers.

The company is thinly capitalized and relies primarily on advances from its customers supplemented by short term bank borrowings for its day to day cash requirements.

The company employs a part time book-keeper to prepare the financial statements, cash flow forecasts and maintain the books of account.

The company has usually been in a position to choose which contracts it accepts and has not had difficulty in recovering its costs. The company is not economically dependent on any one transportation enterprise.

The company updates each month a rolling cash flow projection with a six month time horizon. The company does not prepare projections for a longer period as it perceives its management need is to be able to manage effectively its short term cash flow. The company has negotiated a line of credit with its bankers which it would be able to utilize to overcome short term cash shortages.

Assessment by the auditor of whether there is sufficient evidence that the directors have paid particular attention to a period of twelve months

When the auditor assesses whether the directors have, in assessing going concern, paid particular attention to a period of one year from the expected date of approval of the financial statements the auditor:

(a) Reviews the cash flow forecasts for the six month period from the expected date of approval of the financial statements; and

(b) Then enquires of the directors the steps they have taken to assess the appropriateness of the going concern basis for the subsequent six month period.

The directors inform the auditor that they do not consider there is any need for cash flow forecasts to be prepared beyond six months because:

• The cash flow forecasts show a net cash inflow for the period;

• They have reviewed in detail the assumptions implicit in the forecast with the bookkeeper and concur with them;

• The company has a significant back-log of orders which will occupy half of the designers for at least the next year;

• The company is actively tendering for both systems design and maintenance contracts in the United Kingdom and Europe and is considering expanding into the Americas;

• The company has recently renewed its arrangements with its bankers for a further year;

• The design employees seem to be settled and stimulated and there is no reason to believe that they will leave the company in the foreseeable future; and

• In the unlikely event that the company did not win many of the tenders it could modify its existing expansion plans which have been necessitated by an increase in maintenance contracts. Rather than employ new staff to undertake this work existing staff could be reassigned to it.

The auditor concludes that the directors have paid particular attention to the period ending one year after their approval of the financial statements.

Example 2 - An enterprise in the fashion industry

Extract from the auditor's risk assessment

This company employing 1,000 people designs and manufactures ladies fashion wear. Its business is seasonal and it presents two major collections per year: one in the spring and one in the autumn.

The company has attracted established designers and they are regarded as one of the leading manufacturers.

Almost all of the company's sales orders are received from the major retailers when they show their collections. Although some of the garments are manufactured prior to the showing of the collection the majority of them will be manufactured in the four months immediately following the showing.

The company's finance director is a qualified accountant with a staff of 6. Because of the seasonal nature of the business the company prepares its detailed budgets and cash flow forecasts until the end of the next season. The company's year end is 30 June and the directors expect to approve the financial statements during October. Detailed cash flow forecasts are only available to the end of February in the following year a period of only four months from the approval of the financial statements.

The company which has been marginally profitable over the last few years has a small line of credit with its bank but is financed primarily through the factoring of its debtors.

Assessment by the auditor of whether there is sufficient evidence that the directors have paid particular attention to a period of twelve months

When the auditor assesses whether the directors have, in assessing going concern, paid particular attention to a period of one year from the expected date of approval of the financial statements the auditor would:

(a)   Review the cash flow forecasts for the four month period from the expected date of approval of the financial statements; and

(b)   Then enquire of the directors the steps they have taken to assess the appropriateness of the going concern basis for the subsequent eight month period.

The directors inform the auditor that they do not consider there is any need for additional cash flow forecasts to be prepared beyond the end of February in the following year because:

•   The cash flow forecasts show a net cash inflow for the period and the present cash position is strong because of a recent sale of debtors from the present collection;

•   The directors have reviewed in detail the assumptions implicit in the forecast and concur with them;

- The designers are working on the next collection and they believe, based on discussions with some of the retailers, that they have some good general ideas which will appeal to their customers if translated into imaginative detailed designs;

- Discussions with the major retailers indicate that they expect demand to be high next season;

- The company's relationship with its factor is good and they do not expect any difficulties in selling their debtors in the future;

- The company anticipates no major capital expenditures in the next twelve months. Most of the machinery is less than five years old and in any event is financed by lease arrangements rather than by purchase; and

- The company has recently renewed its arrangements with its bankers for a further year.

The auditor concludes that the directors have paid particular attention to the period ending one year after their approval of the financial statements.

The auditor's options when the auditor concludes that the directors have not paid particular attention to the period ending one year after the approval of the financial statements

The two examples above illustrate that the auditor may conclude that the directors have paid particular attention, to the period ending one year after the approval of the financial statements, even though they have not prepared cash flow forecasts for that period.

The auditor may conclude in slightly different situations that the directors have not paid particular attention to the period ending one year after the approval of the financial statements. If this is the case the auditor needs to consider the impact on the auditor's report which may be either:

(a) The auditor may conclude that there is a significant level of concern about the entity's ability to continue as a going concern (but the auditor does not disagree with the use of the going concern basis). In which case the directors include a note to the financial statements and the auditor includes an emphasis of matter paragraph when setting out the basis of their opinion (in accordance with paragraph 33 of the ISA (UK and Ireland)); or, less probably;

(b) The auditor may conclude that the directors have not paid particular attention to the period ending one year from the date of approval of the financial statements but there is no significant level of concern. Then if the directors:

    (i) Refer to the period paid particular attention to, in the annual report, the auditor need not refer to the period in the basis of opinion (in accordance with paragraph 31-5 of the ISA (UK and Ireland)); however

(ii) If the directors do not refer to the period paid particular attention to, the auditor would do so in the auditor's report in accordance with paragraph 31-4 of the ISA (UK and Ireland)[10]; or

(c) The auditor may conclude that the directors have not taken adequate steps to satisfy themselves that it is appropriate to adopt the going concern basis. Accordingly, there is a limitation of scope which gives rise to a qualified auditor's report (in accordance with paragraph 31-6 of the ISA (UK and Ireland)).

---

[10] If the non-disclosure in the financial statements of the period paid particular attention to is a departure from the requirements of the applicable financial reporting framework, the auditor would give a qualified opinion ("except for").

INTERNATIONAL STANDARD ON AUDITING (UK AND IRELAND) 580

MANAGEMENT REPRESENTATIONS

CONTENTS

International Standard on Auditing (UK and Ireland) (ISA (UK and Ireland)) 580 "Management Representations" should be read in the context of the Auditing Practices Board's Statement "The Auditing Practices Board - Scope and Authority of Pronouncements (Revised)" which sets out the application and authority of ISAs (UK and Ireland).

Introduction

1.   The purpose of this International Standard on Auditing (UK and Ireland) (ISA (UK and Ireland)) is to establish standards and provide guidance on the use of management representations as audit evidence, the procedures to be applied in evaluating and documenting management representations and the action to be taken if management refuses to provide appropriate representations.

1-1.   This ISA (UK and Ireland) uses the terms 'those charged with governance' and 'management'. The term 'governance' describes the role of persons entrusted with the supervision, control and direction of an entity. Ordinarily, those charged with governance are accountable for ensuring that the entity achieves its objectives, and for the quality of its financial reporting and reporting to interested parties. Those charged with governance include management only when they perform such functions.

1-2.   In the UK and Ireland, those charged with governance include the directors (executive and non-executive) of a company or other body, the members of an audit committee where one exists, the partners, proprietors, committee of management or trustees of other forms of entity, or equivalent persons responsible for directing the entity's affairs and preparing its financial statements.

1-3.   'Management' comprises officers those persons who perform senior managerial functions.

1-4.   In the UK and Ireland, depending on the nature and circumstances of the entity, management may include some or all of those charged with governance (e.g. executive directors). Management will not normally include non-executive directors.

2.   **The auditor should obtain appropriate representations from management.**

2-1.   **Written confirmation of appropriate representations from management, as required by paragraph 4 below, should be obtained before the audit report is issued.**

Acknowledgment by Management of its Responsibility for the Financial Statements

3.   **The auditor should obtain audit evidence that management[1a] acknowledges its responsibility for the fair presentation of the financial statements in accordance with the applicable financial reporting framework, and has approved the financial statements.** The auditor can obtain audit evidence of management's acknowledgment of such responsibility and approval from relevant minutes of meetings of those

---

[1a]   In the UK and Ireland, those charged with governance are responsible for the preparation of the financial statements.

charged with governance or by obtaining a written representation from management or a signed copy of the financial statements.

3-1. **In the UK and Ireland, the auditor should obtain evidence that those charged with governance acknowledge their collective responsibility for the preparation of the financial statements and have approved the financial statements.**

3-2. In the UK and Ireland, the directors of a company have a legal collective responsibility to prepare company and, where appropriate, group financial statements that give a true and fair view.

3-3. When the auditor has responsibility for reporting on the financial statements of a group of companies, acknowledgement by the directors of their responsibility for the financial statements applies to both the group financial statements and the financial statements of the parent undertaking.

Representations by Management as Audit Evidence

4. **The auditor should obtain written representations from management on matters material to the financial statements when other sufficient appropriate audit evidence cannot reasonably be expected to exist.** The possibility of misunderstandings between the auditor and management is reduced when oral representations are confirmed by management in writing. Matters which might be included in a letter from management or in a confirmatory letter to management are contained in the example of a management representation letter in the Appendix to this ISA (UK and Ireland).[1b]

4-1. It is advisable for the auditor to discuss the relevant matters with those responsible for giving written representations before they sign them to ensure that they understand what it is that they are being asked to confirm.

5. Written representations requested from management may be limited to matters that are considered either individually or collectively material to the financial statements. Regarding certain items it may be necessary to inform management of the auditor's understanding of materiality.

5.a. **The auditor should obtain written representations from management that:**

(a) **It acknowledges its responsibility for the design and implementation of internal control to prevent and detect error; and**

(b) **It believes the effects of those uncorrected financial statements misstatements aggregated by the auditor during the audit are immaterial, both individually and in the aggregate, to the financial statements taken as a**

[1b] The example letter does not include all management representations that ISAs (UK and Ireland) require the auditor to obtain. Appendix 2 gives a summary of the management representations the auditor is required by other ISAs (UK and Ireland) to obtain as at 15 December 2004.

whole. A summary of such items should be included in or attached to the written representations.

6. During the course of an audit, management makes many representations to the auditor, either unsolicited or in response to specific inquiries. When such representations relate to matters which are material to the financial statements, the auditor will need to:

   (a) Seek corroborative audit evidence from sources inside or outside the entity;

   (b) Evaluate whether the representations made by management appear reasonable and consistent with other audit evidence obtained, including other representations; and

   (c) Consider whether the individuals making the representations can be expected to be well informed on the particular matters.

7. Representations by management cannot be a substitute for other audit evidence that the auditor could reasonably expect to be available. For example, a representation by management as to the cost of an asset is not a substitute for the audit evidence of such cost that an auditor would ordinarily expect to obtain. If the auditor is unable to obtain sufficient appropriate audit evidence regarding a matter which has, or may have, a material effect on the financial statements and such audit evidence is expected to be available, this will constitute a limitation in the scope of the audit, even if a representation from management has been received on the matter.

8. In certain instances, audit evidence other than that obtained by performing inquiry may not be reasonably expected to be available; therefore the auditor obtains a written representation by management. For example, the auditor may not be able to obtain other audit evidence to corroborate management's intention to hold a specific investment for long-term appreciation.

8-1. In some exceptional cases, the matter may be of such significance the auditor refers to the representations in the auditor's report as being relevant to an understanding of the basis of the audit opinion.

8-2. When the auditor has responsibility for reporting on group financial statements, where appropriate the auditor obtains written confirmation of representations relating to specific matters regarding both the group financial statements and the financial statements of the parent undertaking. The means by which the auditor obtains these representations depends on the group's methods of delegation of management control and authority. The auditor may be able to obtain the required representations regarding the group financial statements from the management of the parent undertaking because of the level of their involvement in the management of the group. Alternatively, the auditor may obtain certain representations regarding matters material to the group financial statements directly from the management of the subsidiary undertakings, or by seeing relevant representations by management to the auditors of those subsidiary undertakings, in addition to those obtained from the management of the parent undertaking.

9. **If a representation by management is contradicted by other audit evidence, the auditor should investigate the circumstances and, when necessary, reconsider the reliability of other representations made by management.**

9-1. The investigation of apparently contradictory audit evidence regarding a representation received usually begins with further enquiries of management, to ascertain whether the representation has been misunderstood or whether the other audit evidence has been misinterpreted, followed by corroboration of management's responses. If management is unable to provide an explanation or if the explanation is not considered adequate, further audit procedures may be required to resolve the matter.

Documentation of Representations by Management

10. The auditor would ordinarily include in audit working papers evidence of management's representations in the form of a summary of oral discussions with management or written representations from management.

11. A written representation is ordinarily more reliable audit evidence than an oral representation and can take the form of:

    (a) A representation letter from management;

    (b) A letter from the auditor outlining the auditor's understanding of management's representations, duly acknowledged and confirmed by management; or

    (c) Relevant minutes of meetings of the board of directors or similar body or a signed copy of the financial statements.

11-1. A signed copy of the financial statements for a company may be sufficient evidence of the directors' acknowledgement of their collective responsibility for the preparation of the financial statements where it incorporates a statement to that effect. A signed copy of the financial statements, however, is not, by itself, sufficient appropriate evidence to confirm other representations given to the auditor as it does not, ordinarily, clearly identify and explain the specific separate representations.

Basic Elements of a Management Representation Letter

12. When requesting a management representation letter, the auditor would request that it be addressed to the auditor, contain specified information and be appropriately dated and signed.

13. A management representation letter would ordinarily be dated the same date as the auditor's report. However, in certain circumstances, a separate representation letter regarding specific transactions or other events may also be obtained during the course of the audit or at a date after the date of the auditor's report, for example, on the date of a public offering.

13-1. Written representations required as audit evidence are obtained before the audit report is issued.

14. A management representation letter would ordinarily be signed by the members of management who have primary responsibility for the entity and its financial aspects (ordinarily the senior executive officer and the senior financial officer) based on the best of their knowledge and belief. In certain circumstances, the auditor may wish to obtain representation letters from other members of management. For example, the auditor may wish to obtain a written representation about the completeness of all minutes of the meetings of shareholders, the board of directors and important committees from the individual responsible for keeping such minutes.

14-1. In the UK and Ireland, it is usually appropriate for the auditor to request that the management representation letter be discussed and agreed by those charged with governance and signed on their behalf by the chairman and secretary, before they approve the financial statements, to ensure that all those charged with governance are aware of the representations on which the auditor intends to rely in expressing the auditor's opinion on those financial statements. For the audit of statutory financial statements, the auditor may also wish to consider whether to take the opportunity to remind the directors that it is an offence to mislead the auditor (UK: Section 389A of the Companies Act 1985; Ireland: Section 197(i), Companies Act, 1990).

Action if Management Refuses to Provide Representations

15. **If management refuses to provide a representation that the auditor considers necessary, this constitutes a scope limitation and the auditor should express a qualified opinion or a disclaimer of opinion.** In such circumstances, the auditor would evaluate any reliance placed on other representations made by management during the course of the audit and consider if the other implications of the refusal may have any additional effect on the auditor's report.

Effective Date

15-1. This ISA (UK and Ireland) is effective for audits of financial statements for periods commencing on or after 15 December 2004.

Appendix

This example letter does not include all representations that ISAs (UK and Ireland) require the auditor to obtain. A summary of such representations as at 15 December 2004 is included in Appendix 2. Additionally, in the UK and Ireland representations from those charged with governance would include acknowledgment of any responsibilities they may have in law in relation to the preparation of financial statements and providing information to the auditor. An example of such a representation for directors of a UK company incorporated under the Companies Act 1985 is:

> "We acknowledge as directors our responsibilities under the Companies Act 1985 for preparing financial statements which give a true and fair view and for making accurate representations to you. All the accounting records have been made available to you for the purpose of your audit and all the transactions undertaken by the company have been properly reflected and recorded in the accounting records. All other records and related information, including minutes of all management and shareholders meetings, have been made available to you."

In the Republic of Ireland reference would be made to the Companies Acts 1963 – 2003.

Example of a Management Representation Letter

The following letter is not intended to be a standard letter. Representations by management will vary from one entity to another and from one period to the next.

Although seeking representations from management on a variety of matters may serve to focus management's attention on those matters, and thus cause management to specifically address those matters in more detail than would otherwise be the case, the auditor needs to be cognizant of the limitations of management representations as audit evidence as set out in this ISA (UK and Ireland).

(Entity Letterhead)

(To Auditor)   (Date)

This representation letter is provided in connection with your audit of the financial statements of ABC Company for the year ended December 31, 19X1 for the purpose of expressing an opinion as to whether the financial statements give a true and fair view of (present fairly, in all material respects,) the financial position of ABC Company as of December 31, 19X1 and of the results of its operations and its cash flows for the year then ended in accordance with (indicate applicable financial reporting framework).

We acknowledge our responsibility for the fair presentation of the financial statements in accordance with (indicate applicable financial reporting framework).[1]

We confirm, to the best of our knowledge and belief, the following representations:

---

[1] If required add "On behalf of the board of directors (or similar body)."

Include here representations relevant to the entity. Such representations may include:

- There have been no irregularities involving management or employees who have a significant role in internal control or that could have a material effect on the financial statements.

- We have made available to you all books of account and supporting documentation and all minutes of meetings of shareholders and the board of directors (namely those held on March 15, 19X1 and September 30, 19X1, respectively).

- We confirm the completeness of the information provided regarding the identification of related parties.

- The financial statements are free of material misstatements, including omissions.

- The Company has complied with all aspects of contractual agreements that could have a material effect on the financial statements in the event of noncompliance. There has been no noncompliance with requirements of regulatory authorities that could have a material effect on the financial statements in the event of noncompliance.

- The following have been properly recorded and when appropriate, adequately disclosed in the financial statements:

  (a) The identity of, and balances and transactions with, related parties.

  (b) Losses arising from sale and purchase commitments.

  (c) Agreements and options to buy back assets previously sold.

  (d) Assets pledged as collateral.

- We have no plans or intentions that may materially alter the carrying value or classification of assets and liabilities reflected in the financial statements.

- We have no plans to abandon lines of product or other plans or intentions that will result in any excess or obsolete inventory, and no inventory is stated at an amount in excess of net realizable value.

- The Company has satisfactory title to all assets and there are no liens or encumbrances on the company's assets, except for those that are disclosed in Note X to the financial statements.

- We have recorded or disclosed, as appropriate, all liabilities, both actual and contingent, and have disclosed in Note X to the financial statements all guarantees that we have given to third parties.

- Other than . . . described in Note X to the financial statements, there have been no events subsequent to period end which require adjustment of or disclosure in the financial statements or Notes thereto.

- The . . . claim by XYZ Company has been settled for the total sum of XXX which has been properly accrued in the financial statements. No other claims in connection with litigation have been or are expected to be received.

- There are no formal or informal compensating balance arrangements with any of our cash and investment accounts. Except as disclosed in Note X to the financial statements, we have no other line of credit arrangements.

- We have properly recorded or disclosed in the financial statements the capital stock repurchase options and agreements, and capital stock reserved for options, warrants, conversions and other requirements.

_____

(Senior Executive Officer)

_____

(Senior Financial Officer)

Appendix 2

Specific Management Representations the Auditor is Required by Other ISAs (UK and Ireland) to Obtain

This appendix sets out the specific management representations required by ISAs (UK and Ireland) in issue at 15 December 2004. It is not a comprehensive list of the only representations that the auditor needs to obtain. As stated in paragraph 4 of this ISA (UK and Ireland), the auditor should obtain written representations from management on matters material to the financial statements when other sufficient appropriate audit evidence cannot reasonably be expected to exist. Also, as stated in paragraph 14-1, in the UK and Ireland, it is usually appropriate for the auditor to request that the management representation letter be discussed and agreed by those charged with governance and signed on their behalf by the chairman and secretary, before they approve the financial statements, to ensure that all those charged with governance are aware of the representations on which the auditor intends to rely in expressing the auditor's opinion on those financial statements.

240 - The Auditor's Responsibility to Consider Fraud in an Audit of Financial Statements

90.   The auditor should obtain written representations from management[2] that:

   (a)   It acknowledges its responsibility for the design and implementation of internal control to prevent and detect fraud;

   (b)   It has disclosed to the auditor the results of its assessment of the risk that the financial statements may be materially misstated as a result of fraud;

   (c)   It has disclosed to the auditor its knowledge of fraud or suspected fraud affecting the entity involving:

      (i)   Management[3];

      (ii)   Employees who have significant roles in internal control; or

      (iii)   Others where the fraud could have a material effect on the financial statements; and

(d)   It has disclosed to the auditor its knowledge of any allegations of fraud, or suspected fraud, affecting the entity's financial statements communicated by employees, former employees, analysts, regulators or others.

---

[2]   In the UK and Ireland the auditor obtains written representations from those charged with governance.
[3]   In the UK and Ireland, and those charged with governance.

250 Section A - Consideration of Laws and Regulations in an Audit of Financial Statements

23. The auditor should obtain written representations that management[4] has disclosed to the auditor all known actual or possible noncompliance with laws and regulations whose effects should be considered when preparing financial statements.

23-1. Where applicable, the written representations should include the actual or contingent consequences which may arise from the non-compliance.

260 - Communication of Audit Matters with Those Charged With governance

11-19. The auditor should seek to obtain a written representation from those charged with governance that explains their reasons for not correcting misstatements brought to their attention by the auditor.

545 - Auditing Fair Value Measurements and Disclosures

63. The auditor should obtain written representations from management regarding the reasonableness of significant assumptions, including whether they appropriately reflect management's intent and ability to carry out specific courses of action on behalf of the entity where relevant to the fair value measurements or disclosures.

550 - Related Parties

15/115. The auditor should obtain a written representation from management[5] concerning:

(a) The completeness of information provided regarding the identification of related parties; and

(b) The adequacy of related party disclosures in the financial statements.

570 - Going Concern

26. When events or conditions have been identified which may cast significant doubt on the entity's ability to continue as a going concern, the auditor should:

....

(c) Seek written representations from management[6] regarding its plans for future action.

---

[4] In the UK and Ireland the auditor obtains this written representation from those charged with governance.
[5] In the UK and Ireland the auditor obtains written representations from those charged with governance.
[6] In the UK and Ireland the auditor obtains written representations from those charged with governance.

26-1. The auditor should consider the need to obtain written confirmations of representations from those charged with governance regarding:

(a) The assessment of those charged with governance that the company is a going concern;

(b) Any relevant disclosures in the financial statements.

INTERNATIONAL STANDARD ON AUDITING (UK AND IRELAND) 600

USING THE WORK OF ANOTHER AUDITOR

CONTENTS

International Standard on Auditing (UK and Ireland) (ISA (UK and Ireland)) 600 "Using the Work of Another Auditor" should be read in the context of the Auditing Practices Board's Statement "The Auditing Practices Board - Scope and Authority of Pronouncements (Revised)" which sets out the application and authority of ISAs (UK and Ireland).

Introduction

1. The purpose of this International Standard on Auditing (UK and Ireland) (ISA (UK and Ireland)) is to establish standards and provide guidance when an auditor, reporting on the financial statements of an entity, uses the work of another auditor on the financial information of one or more components included in the financial statements of the entity. This ISA (UK and Ireland) does not deal with those instances where two or more auditors are appointed as joint auditors nor does it deal with the auditor's relationship with a predecessor auditor. Further, when the principal auditor concludes that the financial statements of a component are immaterial, the standards in this ISA (UK and Ireland) do not apply. When, however, several components, immaterial in themselves, are together material, the procedures outlined in this ISA (UK and Ireland) would need to be considered.

1-1. The statutory requirements relating to companies incorporated in the UK and Ireland for other auditors to co-operate with principal auditors are explained in more detail in paragraphs 15-1 to 15-5 below and in the attached Appendix. In certain parts of the public sector where the responsibilities of principal and other auditors are governed by statutory provisions, these override the provisions of this ISA (UK and Ireland). This ISA (UK and Ireland) does not deal with those instances where two or more auditors are appointed as joint auditors nor does it deal with the auditor's relationship with predecessor auditors.

2. **When the principal auditor uses the work of another auditor, the principal auditor should determine how the work of the other auditor will affect the audit.**

3. "Principal auditor" means the auditor with responsibility for reporting on the financial statements of an entity when those financial statements include financial information of one or more components audited by another auditor.

4. "Other auditor" means an auditor, other than the principal auditor, with responsibility for reporting on the financial information of a component which is included in the financial statements audited by the principal auditor. Other auditors include affiliated firms, whether using the same name or not, and correspondents, as well as unrelated auditors.

5. "Component" means a division, branch, subsidiary, joint venture, associated company or other entity whose financial information is included in financial statements audited by the principal auditor.

5-1. This ISA (UK and Ireland) uses the terms 'those charged with governance' and 'management'. The term 'governance' describes the role of persons entrusted with the supervision, control and direction of an entity. Ordinarily, those charged with governance are accountable for ensuring that the entity achieves its objectives, and for the quality of its financial reporting and reporting to interested parties. Those charged with governance include management only when they perform such functions.

5-2. In the UK and Ireland, those charged with governance include the directors (executive and non-executive) of a company or other body, the members of an audit committee where one exists, the partners, proprietors, committee of management or trustees of other forms of entity, or equivalent persons responsible for directing the entity's affairs and preparing its financial statements.

5-3. 'Management' comprises those persons who perform senior managerial functions.

5-4. In the UK and Ireland, depending on the nature and circumstances of the entity, management may include some or all of those charged with governance (e.g. executive directors). Management will not normally include non-executive directors.

Acceptance as Principal Auditor

6. **The auditor should consider whether the auditor's own participation is sufficient to be able to act as the principal auditor.** For this purpose the principal auditor would consider:

   (a) The materiality of the portion of the financial statements which the principal auditor audits;

   (b) The principal auditor's degree of knowledge regarding the business of the components;

   (c) The risk of material misstatements in the financial statements of the components audited by the other auditor; ~~and~~

   (d) The performance of additional procedures as set out in this ISA (UK and Ireland) regarding the components audited by the other auditor resulting in the principal auditor having significant participation in such audit; and

   (e) The nature of the principal auditor's relationship with the firm acting as other auditor.

The Principal Auditor's Procedures

7. **When planning to use the work of another auditor, the principal auditor should consider the professional competence of the other auditor in the context of the specific assignment.** Some of the sources of information for this consideration could be common membership of a professional organization, common membership of, or affiliation, with another firm or reference to the professional organization to which the other auditor belongs. These sources can be supplemented when appropriate by inquiries with other auditors, bankers, *etc.* and by discussions with the other auditor.

7-1. **In the UK and Ireland, when planning to use the work of another auditor, the principal auditor's consideration of the professional competence of the other** auditor should include consideration of the professional qualifications, experience and resources of the other auditor in the context of the specific assignment.

7-2. The principal auditor considers the standing of any firm with which the other auditor is affiliated and also considers making reference to the other auditor's professional organization. The principal auditor's assessment may be influenced by the review of the previous work of the other auditor.

8. **The principal auditor should perform procedures to obtain sufficient appropriate audit evidence, that the work of the other auditor is adequate for the principal auditor's purposes, in the context of the specific assignment.**

9. The principal auditor would advise the other auditor of:

(a) The independence requirements regarding both the entity and the component and obtain written representation as to compliance with them;

(b) The use that is to be made of the other auditor's work and report and make sufficient arrangements for the coordination of their efforts at the initial planning stage of the audit. The principal auditor would inform the other auditor of matters such as areas requiring special consideration, procedures for the identification of intercompany transactions that may require disclosure and the timetable for completion of the audit; and

(c) The accounting, auditing and reporting requirements and obtain written representation as to compliance with them.

10. The principal auditor might also, for example, discuss with the other auditor the audit procedures applied, review a written summary of the other auditor's procedures (which may be in the form of a questionnaire or checklist) or review working papers of the other auditor. The principal auditor may wish to perform these procedures during a visit to the other auditor. The nature, timing and extent of procedures will depend on the circumstances of the engagement and the principal auditor's knowledge of the professional competence of the other auditor. This knowledge may have been enhanced from the review of previous audit work of the other auditor.

11. The principal auditor may conclude that it is not necessary to apply procedures such as those described in paragraph 10 because sufficient appropriate audit evidence previously obtained that acceptable quality control policies and procedures are complied with in the conduct of the other auditor's practice. For example, when they are affiliated firms the principal auditor and the other auditor may have a continuing, formal relationship providing for procedures that give that audit evidence such as periodic inter-firm review, tests of operating policies and procedures and review of working papers of selected audits.

12. **The principal auditor should consider the significant findings of the other auditor.**

13.	The principal auditor may consider it appropriate to discuss with the other auditor and the management of the component, the audit findings or other matters affecting the financial information of the component and may also decide that supplementary tests of the records or the financial information of the component are necessary. Such tests may, depending on the circumstances, be performed by the principal auditor or the other auditor.

13-1.	In the UK and Ireland, the principal auditor may also consider it appropriate to discuss with those charged with governance of the component the audit findings or other matters affecting the financial information of the component. The principal auditor may consider it appropriate to request copies of reports to management or those charged with governance issued by the other auditor.

14.	The principal auditor would document in the audit working papers the components whose financial information was audited by other auditors, their significance to the financial statements of the entity as a whole, the names of the other auditors and any conclusions reached that individual components are immaterial. The principal auditor would also document the procedures performed and the conclusions reached. For example, working papers of the other auditor that have been reviewed would be identified and the results of discussions with the other auditor would be recorded. However, the principal auditor need not document the reasons for limiting the procedures in the circumstances described in paragraph 11, provided those reasons are summarized elsewhere in documentation maintained by the principal auditor's firm.

Cooperation Between Auditors

15.	**The other auditor, knowing the context in which the principal auditor will use the other auditor's work, should cooperate with the principal auditor.** For example, the other auditor would bring to the principal auditor's attention any aspect of the other auditor's work that cannot be carried out as requested. Similarly, subject to legal and professional considerations, the other auditor will need to be advised of any matters that come to the attention of the principal auditor which may have an important bearing on the other auditor's work.

15-1.	In the UK and Ireland, the other auditor carries out the audit work in the knowledge that the financial information on which the other auditor reports is to be included within the financial statements which are reported on by the principal auditor. In many circumstances when the component is a subsidiary undertaking, there is a statutory obligation on the other auditor, and the component which the other auditor audits, to give the principal auditor such information and explanations as the principal auditor may reasonably require for the purpose of the principal auditor's audit. Where there is no statutory obligation on the other auditor and the principal auditor advises that the principal auditor intends to use the other auditor's work, the other auditor may require permission from the component to communicate with the principal auditor on matters pertaining to the component's audit. If the component refuses such permission, the other auditor brings this to the attention of the principal auditor so that the principal auditor can discuss and agree an appropriate course of action with those charged with governance of the entity which they audit.

15-2. If the other auditor identifies a matter which the other auditor considers likely to be relevant to the principal auditor's work, the other auditor may communicate directly with the principal auditor, providing consent is obtained by the component or there exists a statutory obligation, or it may require reference to the matter to be made within the other auditor's audit report.

15-3. In the UK and Ireland the other auditor has sole responsibility for the other auditor's audit opinion on the financial statements of the component which the other auditor audits. Accordingly, the other auditor plans and executes the audit in a manner which enables the other auditor to report on the component without placing reliance on the principal auditor necessarily informing the other auditor of matters which have come to the principal auditor's attention and which may have an important bearing on the financial statements of the component. This may involve the other auditor seeking representations directly from the management or those charged with governance of the entity audited by the principal auditor.

15-4. In the UK and Ireland there is no obligation, statutory or otherwise, on the principal auditor to provide information to the other auditor. However, in undertaking the audit work the principal auditor may identify matters which the principal auditor considers to be relevant to the other auditor's work. In these circumstances, the principal auditor discusses and agrees an appropriate course of action with those charged with governance of the entity which they audit.

15-5. The course of action agreed with those charged with governance may involve the principal auditor communicating directly with the other auditor, or those charged with governance informing the component or the other auditor. However, there may be circumstances where sensitive commercial considerations dictate that information cannot be passed on to the component or the other auditor. In this event, the principal auditor is not required to take further action as to do so would be in breach of the principle of client confidentiality.

Reporting Considerations

16. **When the principal auditor concludes that the work of the other auditor cannot be used and the principal auditor has not been able to perform sufficient additional procedures regarding the financial information of the component audited by the other auditor, the principal auditor should express a qualified opinion or disclaimer of opinion because there is a limitation in the scope of the audit.**

17. If the other auditor issues, or intends to issue, a modified auditor's report, the principal auditor would consider whether the subject of the modification is of such a nature and significance, in relation to the financial statements of the entity on which the principal auditor is reporting, that a modification of the principal auditor's report is required.

17-1. When the principal auditor is satisfied that the work of the other auditors is adequate for the purposes of the audit, no reference to the other auditors is made in the principal auditor's report.

Division of Responsibility

18. While compliance with the guidance in the preceding paragraphs is considered desirable, the local regulations of some countries permit a principal auditor to base the audit opinion on the financial statements taken as a whole solely upon the report of another auditor regarding the audit of one or more components. **When the principal auditor does so, the principal auditor's report should state this fact clearly and should indicate the magnitude of the portion of the financial statements audited by the other auditor.** When the principal auditor makes such a reference in the auditor's report, audit procedures are ordinarily limited to those described in paragraphs 7 and 9.

18-1. In the UK and Ireland the principal auditor has sole responsibility for the principal auditor's audit opinion and a reference to the other auditor in the principal auditor's report may be misunderstood and interpreted as a qualification of the principal auditor's opinion or a division of responsibility, which is not acceptable.

Effective Date

18-2. This ISA (UK and Ireland) is effective for audits of financial statements for periods commencing on or after 15 December 2004.

Public Sector Perspective

Additional guidance for auditors of public sector bodies in the UK and Ireland is given in:

- Practice Note 10 "Audit of Financial Statements of Public Sector Bodies in the United Kingdom (Revised)"

- Practice Note 10(I) "Audit of Central Government Financial Statements in the Republic of Ireland (Revised)"

1. *The basic principles in this ISA (UK and Ireland) apply to the audit of financial statements in the public sector, however, supplementary guidance on additional considerations when using the work of other auditors in the public sector is needed. For example, the principal auditor in the public sector has to ensure that, where legislation has prescribed compliance with a particular set of auditing standards, the other auditor has complied with those standards. In respect to public sector entities, the Public Sector Committee has supplemented the guidance included in this ISA (UK and Ireland) in its Study 4 "Using the Work of Other Auditors—A Public Sector Perspective."*

Appendix

Statutory Framework at 15 December 2004

1. If a parent company and its subsidiary undertaking are companies incorporated in Great Britain, section 389A(3) of the Companies Act 1985 imposes a duty on the subsidiary undertaking and its auditors to 'give to the auditors of any parent company of the undertaking such information and explanations as they may reasonably require for the purposes of their duties as auditors of that company'. Similar obligations regarding companies incorporated in Northern Ireland and the Republic of Ireland are set out in Article 397A(3) of the Companies (Northern Ireland) Order 1986 and section 196(1) of the Companies Act 1990 respectively.

2. Where a parent company is incorporated in Great Britain but its subsidiary undertaking is not, section 389A(4) of the Companies Act 1985 imposes a duty on the parent company, if required by its auditors to do so, to 'take all such steps as are reasonably open to it to obtain from the subsidiary undertaking such information and explanations as they may reasonably require for the purposes of their duties as auditors of that company'. Similar obligations on parent companies incorporated in Northern Ireland and the Republic of Ireland are set out in Article 397A(4) of the Companies (Northern Ireland) Order 1986 and section 196(2) of the Companies Act 1990 respectively.

INTERNATIONAL STANDARD ON AUDITING (UK AND IRELAND) 610

CONSIDERING THE WORK OF INTERNAL AUDIT

CONTENTS

International Standard on Auditing (UK and Ireland) (ISA (UK and Ireland)) 610 "Considering the Work of Internal Audit" should be read in the context of the Auditing Practices Board's Statement "The Auditing Practices Board - Scope and Authority of Pronouncements (Revised)" which sets out the application and authority of ISAs (UK and Ireland).

Introduction

1. The purpose of this International Standard on Auditing (UK and Ireland) (ISA (UK and Ireland)) is to establish standards and provide guidance to external auditors in considering the work of internal auditing. This ISA (UK and Ireland) does not deal with instances when personnel from internal auditing assist the external auditor in carrying out external audit procedures. The audit procedures noted in this ISA (UK and Ireland) need only be applied to internal auditing activities which are relevant to the audit of the financial statements.

1-1. This ISA (UK and Ireland) uses the terms 'those charged with governance' and 'management'. The term 'governance' describes the role of persons entrusted with the supervision, control and direction of an entity. Ordinarily, those charged with governance are accountable for ensuring that the entity achieves its objectives, and for the quality of its financial reporting, and reporting to interested parties. Those charged with governance include management only when they perform such functions.

1-2. In the UK and Ireland, those charged with governance include the directors (executive and non-executive) of a company or other body, the members of an audit committee where one exists, the partners, proprietors, committee of management or trustees of other forms of entity, or equivalent persons responsible for directing the entity's affairs and preparing its financial statements.

1-3. 'Management' comprises those persons who perform senior managerial functions.

1-4. In the UK and Ireland, depending on the nature and circumstances of the entity, management may include some or all of those charged with governance (e.g. executive directors). Management will not normally include non-executive directors.

2. **The external auditor should consider the activities of internal auditing and their effect, if any, on external audit procedures.**

3. "Internal auditing" means an appraisal activity established within an entity as a service to the entity. Its functions include, amongst other things, monitoring internal control.

4. While the external auditor has sole responsibility for the audit opinion expressed and for determining the nature, timing and extent of external audit procedures, certain parts of internal auditing work may be useful to the external auditor.

Scope and Objectives of Internal Auditing

5. The scope and objectives of internal auditing vary widely and depend on the size and structure of the entity and the requirements of its management. Ordinarily, internal auditing activities include one or more of the following:

    *   Monitoring of internal control. The establishment of adequate internal control is a responsibility of management which demands proper attention on a continuous

basis. Internal auditing is ordinarily assigned specific responsibility by management for reviewing controls, monitoring their operation and recommending improvements thereto.

- Examination of financial and operating information. This may include review of the means used to identify, measure, classify and report such information and specific inquiry into individual items including detailed testing of transactions, balances and procedures.

- Review of the economy, efficiency and effectiveness of operations including non-financial controls of an entity.

- Review of compliance with laws, regulations and other external requirements and with management policies and directives and other internal requirements.

- Special investigations into particular areas, for example, suspected fraud.

Relationship Between Internal Auditing and the External Auditor   *see BS5 #81 APB*   *reason for threat*

6. The role of internal auditing is determined by management[1], and its objectives differ from those of the external auditor who is appointed to report independently on the financial statements. The internal audit function's objectives vary according to management's requirements[2]. The external auditor's primary concern is whether the financial statements are free of material misstatements.

7. Nevertheless some of the means of achieving their respective objectives are often similar and thus certain aspects of internal auditing may be useful in determining the nature, timing and extent of external audit procedures.

8. Internal auditing is part of the entity. Irrespective of the degree of autonomy and *threat* objectivity of internal auditing, it cannot achieve the same degree of independence as required of the external auditor when expressing an opinion on the financial statements. The external auditor has sole responsibility for the audit opinion expressed, and that responsibility is not reduced by any use made of internal auditing. All judgments relating to the audit of the financial statements are those of the external auditor.

---

[1] In the UK and Ireland those charged with governance, rather than management, are usually responsible for determining the role of internal auditing.

[2] For Listed Companies in the UK and Ireland, "The Combined Code on Corporate Governance" (FRC 2003) contains guidance to assist company boards in making suitable arrangements for their audit committees.

see
E85
pp81 APB

Understanding and Preliminary Assessment of Internal Auditing

9.   The external auditor should obtain a sufficient understanding of internal audit activities to identify and assess the risks of material misstatement of the financial statements and to design and perform further audit procedures.

10.   Effective internal auditing will often allow a modification in the nature and timing, and a reduction in the extent of audit procedures performed by the external auditor but cannot eliminate them entirely. In some cases, however, having considered the activities of internal auditing, the external auditor may decide that internal auditing will have no effect on external audit procedures.

10-1.   The effectiveness of internal auditing may be an important factor in the external auditor's evaluation of the control environment and assessment of audit risk.

11.   The external auditor should perform an assessment of the internal audit function when internal auditing is relevant to the external auditor's risk assessment.

12.   The external auditor's preliminary assessment of the internal audit function will influence the external auditor's judgment about the use which may be made of internal auditing in making risk assessments and thereby modifying the nature, timing and extent of further external audit procedures.

13.   When obtaining an understanding and performing an assessment of the internal audit function, the important criteria are:

(a)   Organizational Status: specific status of internal auditing in the entity and the effect this has on its ability to be objective. In the ideal situation, internal auditing will report to the highest level of management and be free of any other operating responsibility. Any constraints or restrictions placed on internal auditing by management would need to be carefully considered. In particular, the internal auditors will need to be free to communicate fully with the external auditor.

(b)   Scope of Function: the nature and extent of internal auditing assignments performed. The external auditor would also need to consider whether management acts on internal audit recommendations and how this is evidenced.

(c)   Technical Competence: whether internal auditing is performed by persons having adequate technical training and proficiency as internal auditors. The external auditor may, for example, review the policies for hiring and training the internal auditing staff and their experience and professional qualifications.

(d)   Due Professional Care: whether internal auditing is properly planned, supervised, reviewed and documented. The existence of adequate audit manuals, work programs and working papers would be considered.

Timing of Liaison and Coordination

14. When planning to use the work of internal auditing, the external auditor will need to consider internal auditing's tentative plan for the period and discuss it at as early a stage as possible. Where the work of internal auditing is to be a factor in determining the nature, timing and extent of the external auditor's procedures, it is desirable to agree in advance the timing of such work, the extent of audit coverage, materiality levels and proposed methods of sample selection, documentation of the work performed and review and reporting procedures.

15. Liaison with internal auditing is more effective when meetings are held at appropriate intervals during the period. The external auditor would need to be advised of and have access to relevant internal auditing reports and be kept informed of any significant matter that comes to the internal auditor's attention which may affect the work of the external auditor. Similarly, the external auditor would ordinarily inform the internal auditor of any significant matters which may affect internal auditing.

Evaluating the Work of Internal Auditing

16. **When the external auditor intends to use specific work of internal auditing, the external auditor should evaluate and perform audit procedures on that work to confirm its adequacy for the external auditor's purposes.**

17. The evaluation of specific work of internal auditing involves consideration of the adequacy of the scope of work and related programs and whether the assessment of the internal auditing remains appropriate. This evaluation may include consideration of whether:

    (a) The work is performed by persons having adequate technical training and proficiency as internal auditors and the work of assistants is properly supervised, reviewed and documented;

    (b) Sufficient appropriate audit evidence is obtained to be able to draw reasonable conclusions;

    (c) Conclusions reached are appropriate in the circumstances and any reports prepared are consistent with the results of the work performed; and

    (d) Any exceptions or unusual matters disclosed by internal auditing are properly resolved.

18. The nature, timing and extent of the audit procedures performed on the specific work of internal auditing will depend on the external auditor's judgment as to the risk of material misstatement of the area concerned, the assessment of internal auditing and the evaluation of the specific work by internal auditing. Such audit procedures may include examination of items already examined by internal auditing, examination of other similar items and observation of internal auditing procedures.

18-1. In the event that the external auditor concludes that the work of internal auditing is not adequate for the external auditor's purposes, the external auditor extends the audit procedures beyond those originally planned to ensure that sufficient appropriate audit evidence is obtained to support the conclusions reached.

19. The external auditor would record conclusions regarding the specific internal auditing work that has been evaluated and the audit procedures performed on the internal auditor's work.

19-1. The auditor considers whether amendments to the external audit program are required as a result of matters identified by internal auditing.

Effective Date

19-2. This ISA (UK and Ireland) is effective for audits of financial statements for periods commencing on or after 15 December 2004.

Public Sector Perspective

Additional guidance for auditors of public sector bodies in the UK and Ireland is given in:

- Practice Note 10 "Audit of Financial Statements of Public Sector Bodies in the United Kingdom (Revised)"

- Practice Note 10(I) "Audit of Central Government Financial Statements in the Republic of Ireland (Revised)"

1. *The basic principles in this ISA (UK and Ireland) apply to the audit of financial statements in the public sector. Supplementary guidance on additional considerations, when considering the work of internal auditing in the public sector is provided in the Public Sector Committee's Study 4 "Using the Work of Other Auditors—A Public Sector Perspective."*

INTERNATIONAL STANDARD ON AUDITING (UK AND IRELAND) 620

USING THE WORK OF AN EXPERT

CONTENTS

International Standard on Auditing (UK and Ireland) (ISA (UK and Ireland)) 620 "Using the Work of an Expert" should be read in the context of the Auditing Practices Board's Statement "The Auditing Practices Board - Scope and Authority of Pronouncements (Revised)" which sets out the application and authority of ISAs (UK and Ireland).

Introduction

1. The purpose of this International Standard on Auditing (UK and Ireland) (ISA (UK and Ireland)) is to establish standards and provide guidance on using the work of an expert as audit evidence.

1-1. This ISA (UK and Ireland) uses the terms 'those charged with governance' and 'management'. The term 'governance' describes the role of persons entrusted with the supervision, control and direction of an entity. Ordinarily, those charged with governance are accountable for ensuring that the entity achieves its objectives, and for the quality of its financial reporting, and reporting to interested parties. Those charged with governance include management only when they perform such functions.

1-2. In the UK and Ireland, those charged with governance include the directors (executive and non-executive) of a company or other body, the members of an audit committee where one exists, the partners, proprietors, committee of management or trustees of other forms of entity, or equivalent persons responsible for directing the entity's affairs and preparing its financial statements.

1-3. 'Management' comprises those persons who perform senior managerial functions.

1-4. In the UK and Ireland, depending on the nature and circumstances of the entity, management may include some or all of those charged with governance (e.g. executive directors). Management will not normally include non-executive directors.

2. **When using the work performed by an expert, the auditor should obtain sufficient appropriate audit evidence that such work is adequate for the purposes of the audit.**

3. "Expert" means a person or firm possessing special skill, knowledge and experience in a particular field other than accounting and auditing.

4. The auditor's education and experience enable the auditor to be knowledgeable about business matters in general, but the auditor is not expected to have the expertise of a person trained for or qualified to engage in the practice of another profession or occupation, such as an actuary or engineer.

5. An expert may be:

    (a) Contracted by the entity;

    (b) Contracted by the auditor;

    (c) Employed by the entity; or

    (d) Employed by the auditor.

When the auditor uses the work of an expert employed by the audit firm, the auditor will be able to rely on the firm's systems for recruitment and training that determine that expert's capabilities and competence, as explained in ISA (UK and Ireland) 220, "Quality Control for Audits of Historical Financial Information" instead of needing to evaluate them for each audit engagement.

5-1. If the auditor determines that it is appropriate to seek to use the work of an expert, the auditor considers whether an appropriate expert is already employed by the auditor or the entity. If neither the auditor or the entity employ an appropriate expert, the auditor considers asking those charged with governance to engage an appropriate expert subject to the auditor being satisfied as to the expert's competence and objectivity (see paragraphs 8 to 10-1 below). If those charged with governance are unable or unwilling to engage an expert, the auditor may consider engaging an expert or whether sufficient appropriate audit evidence can be obtained from other sources. If unable to obtain sufficient appropriate audit evidence, the auditor considers the possible need to modify the auditor's report.

5-2. Although the auditor may use the work of an expert, the auditor has sole responsibility for the audit opinion.

Determining the Need to Use the Work of an Expert

6. In obtaining an understanding of the entity and performing further procedures in response to assessed risks, the auditor may need to obtain, in conjunction with the entity or independently, audit evidence in the form of reports, opinions, valuations and statements of an expert. Examples are:

- Valuations of certain types of assets, for example, land and buildings, plant and machinery, works of art, and precious stones.

- Determination of quantities or physical condition of assets, for example, minerals stored in stockpiles, underground mineral and petroleum reserves, and the remaining useful life of plant and machinery.

- Determination of amounts using specialized techniques or methods, for example, an actuarial valuation.

- The measurement of work completed and to be completed on contracts in progress.

- Legal opinions concerning interpretations of agreements, statutes and regulations.

7. When determining the need to use the work of an expert, the auditor would consider:

    (a) The engagement team's knowledge and previous experience of the matter being considered;

    (b) The risk of material misstatement based on the nature, complexity, and materiality of the matter being considered; and

(c) The quantity and quality of other audit evidence expected to be obtained.

Competence and Objectivity of the Expert

8. **When planning to use the work of an expert, the auditor should evaluate the professional competence of the expert.** This will involve considering the expert's:

   (a) Professional certification or licensing by, or membership in, an appropriate professional body; and

   (b) Experience and reputation in the field in which the auditor is seeking audit evidence.

8-1. **In the UK and Ireland, when planning to use the work of an expert the auditor should assess the professional qualifications, experience and resources of the expert.**

9. **The auditor should evaluate the objectivity of the expert.**

10. The risk that an expert's objectivity will be impaired increases when the expert is:

    (a) Employed by the entity; or

    (b) Related in some other manner to the entity, for example, by being financially dependent upon or having an investment in the entity.

    If the auditor is concerned regarding the competence or objectivity of the expert, the auditor needs to discuss any reservations with management and consider whether sufficient appropriate audit evidence can be obtained concerning the work of an expert. The auditor may need to undertake additional audit procedures or seek audit evidence from another expert (after taking into account the factors in paragraph 7).

10-1. If the auditor is unable to obtain sufficient appropriate audit evidence concerning the work of an expert, the auditor considers the possible need to modify the auditor's report.

Scope of the Expert's Work

11. **The auditor should obtain sufficient appropriate audit evidence that the scope of the expert's work is adequate for the purposes of the audit.** Audit evidence may be obtained through a review of the terms of reference which are often set out in written instructions from the entity to the expert. Such instructions to the expert may cover matters such as:

    • The objectives and scope of the expert's work.

- A general outline as to the specific matters the auditor expects the expert's report to cover.

- The intended use by the auditor of the expert's work, including the possible communication to third parties of the expert's identity and extent of involvement.

- The extent of the expert's access to appropriate records and files.

- Clarification of the expert's relationship with the entity, if any.

- Confidentiality of the entity's information.

- Information regarding the assumptions and methods intended to be used by the expert and their consistency with those used in prior periods.

In the event that these matters are not clearly set out in written instructions to the expert, the auditor may need to communicate with the expert directly to obtain audit evidence in this regard. In obtaining an understanding of the entity, the auditor also considers whether to include the expert during the engagement team's discussion of the susceptibility of the entity's financial statements to material misstatement.

Evaluating the Work of the Expert

12. **The auditor should evaluate the appropriateness of the expert's work as audit evidence regarding the assertion being considered.** This will involve evaluation of whether the substance of the expert's findings is properly reflected in the financial statements or supports the assertions, and consideration of:

- Source data used.

- Assumptions and methods used and their consistency with prior periods.

- When the expert carried out the work.

- Results of the expert's work in the light of the auditor's overall knowledge of the business and of the results of other audit procedures.

13. When considering whether the expert has used source data which is appropriate in the circumstances, the auditor would consider the following procedures:

   (a) Making inquiries regarding any procedures undertaken by the expert to establish whether the source data is relevant and reliable; and

   (b) Reviewing or testing the data used by the expert.

14. The appropriateness and reasonableness of assumptions and methods used and their application are the responsibility of the expert. The auditor does not have the same expertise and, therefore, cannot always challenge the expert's assumptions and

methods. However, the auditor will need to obtain an understanding of the assumptions and methods used and to consider whether they are appropriate and reasonable, based on the auditor's knowledge of the business and the results of other audit procedures.

15. **If the results of the expert's work do not provide sufficient appropriate audit evidence or if the results are not consistent with other audit evidence, the auditor should resolve the matter.** This may involve discussions with the entity and the expert, applying additional audit procedures, including possibly engaging another expert, or modifying the auditor's report.

Reference to an Expert in the Auditor's Report

16. **When issuing an unmodified auditor's report, the auditor should not refer to the work of an expert.** Such a reference might be misunderstood to be a qualification of the auditor's opinion or a division of responsibility, neither of which is intended.

17. If, as a result of the work of an expert, the auditor decides to issue a modified auditor's report, in some circumstances it may be appropriate, in explaining the nature of the modification, to refer to or describe the work of the expert (including the identity of the expert and the extent of the expert's involvement). In these circumstances, the auditor would obtain the permission of the expert before making such a reference. If permission is refused and the auditor believes a reference is necessary, the auditor may need to seek legal advice.

Effective Date

17-1. This ISA (UK and Ireland) is effective for audits of financial statements for periods commencing on or after 15 December 2004.

INTERNATIONAL STANDARD ON AUDITING (UK AND IRELAND) 700

THE AUDITOR'S REPORT ON FINANCIAL STATEMENTS

CONTENTS

International Standard on Auditing (UK and Ireland) (ISA (UK and Ireland)) 700 "The Auditor's Report on Financial Statements" should be read in the context of the Auditing Practices Board's Statement "The Auditing Practices Board - Scope and Authority of Pronouncements (Revised)" which sets out the application and authority of ISAs (UK and Ireland).

Introduction

1. The purpose of this International Standard on Auditing (UK and Ireland) (ISA (UK and Ireland)) is to establish standards and provide guidance on the form and content of the auditor's report issued as a result of an audit performed by an independent auditor of the financial statements of an entity. Much of the guidance provided can be adapted to auditor reports on financial information other than financial statements.

1-1. This ISA (UK and Ireland) uses the terms 'those charged with governance' and 'management'. The term 'governance' describes the role of persons entrusted with the supervision, control and direction of an entity. Ordinarily, those charged with governance are accountable for ensuring that the entity achieves its objectives, and for the quality of its financial reporting and reporting to interested parties. Those charged with governance include management only when they perform such functions.

1-2. In the UK and Ireland, those charged with governance include the directors (executive and non-executive) of a company or other body, the members of an audit committee where one exists, the partners, proprietors, committee of management or trustees of other forms of entity, or equivalent persons responsible for directing the entity's affairs and preparing its financial statements.

1-3. 'Management' comprises those persons who perform senior managerial functions.

1-4. In the UK and Ireland, depending on the nature and circumstances of the entity, management may include some or all of those charged with governance (e.g. executive directors). Management will not normally include non-executive directors.

2. **The auditor should review and assess the conclusions drawn from the audit evidence obtained as the basis for the expression of an opinion on the financial statements.**

3. This review and assessment involves considering whether the financial statements have been prepared in accordance with an acceptable financial reporting framework[1] being either International Accounting Standards (IASs) or relevant national standards or practices. It may also be necessary to consider whether the financial statements comply with statutory requirements.

4. **The auditor's report should contain a clear written expression of opinion on the financial statements taken as a whole.**

---

[1] The Framework of International Standards on Auditing also identifies another authoritative and comprehensive financial reporting framework. Reporting in accordance with this third type of framework is covered in ISA 800, "The Auditor's Report on Special Purpose Audit Engagements."

Basic Elements of the Auditor's Report

5.   The auditor's report includes the following basic elements, ordinarily in the following layout:

   (a)   Title;

   (b)   Addressee;

   (c)   *Opening or introductory paragraph*

      (i)   Identification of the financial statements audited;

      (ii)   A statement of the responsibility of the entity's management[2] and the responsibility of the auditor;

   (d)   *Scope paragraph (describing the nature of an audit)*

      (i)   A reference to the ISAs or relevant national standards or practices;

      (ii)   A description of the work the auditor performed;

   (e)   *Opinion paragraph* containing

      (i)   A reference to the financial reporting framework used to prepare the financial statements (including identifying the country of origin[3] of the financial reporting framework when the framework used is not International Accounting Standards); and

      (ii)   An expression of opinion on the financial statements;

   (f)   Date of the report;

   (g)   Auditor's address; and

   (h)   Auditor's signature.

   A measure of uniformity in the form and content of the auditor's report is desirable because it helps to promote the reader's understanding and to identify unusual circumstances when they occur.

---

[2]   In the UK and Ireland, those charged with governance are responsible for the preparation of the financial statements.

[3]   In some circumstances it also may be necessary to refer to a particular jurisdiction within the country of origin to identify clearly the financial reporting framework used.

Title

6.   **The auditor's report should have an appropriate title.** It may be appropriate to use the term "Independent Auditor" in the title to distinguish the auditor's report from reports that might be issued by others, such as by officers of the entity, the board of directors, or from the reports of other auditors who may not have to abide by the same ethical requirements as the independent auditor.

Addressee

7.   **The auditor's report should be appropriately addressed as required by the circumstances of the engagement and local regulations.** The report is ordinarily addressed either to the shareholders or the board of directors of the entity whose financial statements are being audited.

7-1   In the UK and Ireland, the Companies Act requires that the auditor's report on the financial statements of a company is addressed to its members because the audit is undertaken on their behalf. The auditor's report on financial statements of other types of reporting entity is addressed to the appropriate person or persons, as defined by statute or by the terms of the individual engagement.

Opening or Introductory Paragraph

8.   **The auditor's report should identify the financial statements of the entity that have been audited, including the date of and period covered by the financial statements.**

9.   **The report should include a statement that the financial statements are the responsibility of the entity's management[4] and a statement that the responsibility of the auditor is to express an opinion on the financial statements based on the audit.**

9-1.   **In the UK and Ireland:**

  (a)   **The auditor should distinguish between the auditor's responsibilities and the responsibilities of those charged with governance by including in the auditor's report a reference to a description of the relevant responsibilities of those charged with governance when that description is set out elsewhere in the financial statements or accompanying information; or**

---

[4]   The level of management responsible for the financial statements will vary according to the legal situation in each country.

In the UK and Ireland, those charged with governance are responsible for the preparation of the financial statements. Thus it is the directors of a company who are required by law to prepare annual accounts which consist of a balance sheet and profit and loss account together with accompanying notes and which give a true and fair view of the state of affairs of the company (or group) at the end of the financial year and of the profit or loss of the company (or group) for that year.

(b) **Where the financial statements or accompanying information do not include an adequate description of the relevant responsibilities of those charged with governance, the auditor's report should include a description of those responsibilities.**

9-2. An appreciation of the interrelationship between the responsibilities of those who prepare financial statements and those who audit them is also necessary to achieve an understanding of the nature and context of the opinion expressed by the auditor. Readers need to be aware that it is those charged with governance of the reporting entity and not the auditor who determines the accounting policies followed. In the UK and Ireland, the auditor's report therefore also sets out the respective responsibilities of those charged with governance and the auditor.

10. Financial statements are the representations of management[2]. The preparation of such statements requires management[2] to make significant accounting estimates and judgments, as well as to determine the appropriate accounting principles and methods used in preparation of the financial statements. This determination will be made in the context of the financial reporting framework that management[2] chooses, or is required, to use. In contrast, the auditor's responsibility is to audit these financial statements in order to express an opinion thereon.

11. *An illustration of these matters in an opening (introductory) paragraph is:*

> *"We have audited the accompanying[5] balance sheet of the ABC Company as of December 31, 20X1, and the related statements of income and cash flows for the year then ended. These financial statements are the responsibility of the Company's management. Our responsibility is to express an opinion on these financial statements based on our audit."*

Illustrative examples of auditor's reports tailored for use with audits conducted in accordance with ISAs (UK and Ireland) are given in the most recent version of the APB Bulletin, "Auditor's Reports on Financial Statements".

Scope Paragraph

12. **The auditor's report should describe the scope of the audit by stating that the audit was conducted in accordance with ISAs (UK and Ireland) or in accordance with relevant national standards or practices as appropriate.** "Scope" refers to the auditor's ability to perform audit procedures deemed necessary in the circumstances. The reader needs this as an assurance that the audit has been carried out in accordance with established standards or practices. Unless otherwise stated, the auditing standards or practices followed are presumed to be those of the country indicated by the auditor's address.

---

[5] The reference can be by page numbers.

13. **The report should include a statement that the audit was planned and performed to obtain reasonable assurance about whether the financial statements are free of material misstatement.**

13-1. In the UK and Ireland, the auditor's statement that the audit was planned and performed to obtain reasonable assurance about whether the financial statements are free of material misstatement, includes reference to material misstatement caused by fraud or other irregularity or error.

14. **The auditor's report should describe the audit as including:**

    (a) **Examining, on a test basis, evidence to support the financial statement amounts and disclosures;**

    (b) **Assessing the accounting principles used in the preparation of the financial statements;**

    (c) **Assessing the significant estimates made by management[2] in the preparation of the financial statements; and**

    (d) **Evaluating the overall financial statement presentation.**

14-1. **In the UK and Ireland, the accounting principles used in the preparation of financial statements are established by legislation. The auditor should consider whether the accounting policies are appropriate to the reporting entity's circumstances, consistently applied and adequately disclosed.**

15. **The report should include a statement by the auditor that the audit provides a reasonable basis for the opinion.**

16. *An illustration of these matters in a scope paragraph is:*

> *"We conducted our audit in accordance with International Standards on Auditing (or refer to relevant national standards or practices). Those Standards require that we plan and perform the audit to obtain reasonable assurance about whether the financial statements are free of material misstatement. An audit includes examining, on a test basis, evidence supporting the amounts and disclosures in the financial statements. An audit also includes assessing the accounting principles used and significant estimates made by management, as well as evaluating the overall financial statement presentation. We believe that our audit provides a reasonable basis for our opinion."*

Illustrative examples of auditor's reports tailored for use with audits conducted in accordance with ISAs (UK and Ireland) are given in the most recent version of the APB Bulletin, "Auditor's Reports on Financial Statements".

16-1. In the UK and Ireland:

(a) In some circumstances, the auditor may be required to report whether the financial statements have been properly prepared in accordance with regulations or other requirements, but is not required to report on whether they give a true and fair view. Where the special circumstances of the reporting entity require or permit the adoption of policies or accounting bases which do not normally permit a true and fair view to be given, the auditor refers to those circumstances in the paragraphs dealing with the respective responsibilities of those charged with governance and the auditor (unless the matter is included in a separate statement given by those charged with governance) and may draw attention to them in the basis of opinion section of the report.

(b) The auditor may wish to include additional comment in this part of the auditor's report to highlight matters which they regard as relevant to a proper understanding of the basis of their opinion.

Opinion Paragraph

17. **The opinion paragraph of the auditor's report should clearly indicate the financial reporting framework used to prepare the financial statements (including identifying the country of origin of the financial reporting framework when the framework used is not International Accounting Standards) and state the auditor's opinion as to whether the financial statements give a true and fair view (or are presented fairly, in all material respects,) in accordance with that financial reporting framework and, where appropriate, whether the financial statements comply with statutory requirements.**

18. The terms used to express the auditor's opinion are "give a true and fair view"[6] or "present fairly, in all material respects," and are equivalent. Both terms indicate, amongst other things, that the auditor considers only those matters that are material to the financial statements.

19. The financial reporting framework is determined by IASs, rules issued by recognized standard setting bodies, and the development of general practice within a country, with an appropriate consideration of fairness and with due regard to local legislation. To advise the reader of the context in which the auditor's opinion is expressed, the auditor's opinion indicates the framework upon which the financial statements are based. The auditor refers to the financial reporting framework in such terms as:

   "...in accordance with International Accounting Standards (or [title of financial reporting framework with reference to the country of origin])..."

---

[6] In the UK and Ireland, the auditor ordinarily is required by law or regulations to evaluate whether the financial statements give a true and fair view.

Illustrative examples of auditor's reports tailored for use with audits conducted in accordance with ISAs (UK and Ireland) are given in the most recent version of the APB Bulletin, "Auditor's Reports on Financial Statements".

This designation will help the user to better understand which financial reporting framework was used in preparing the financial statements. When reporting on financial statements that are prepared specifically for use in another country, the auditor considers whether appropriate disclosure has been made in the financial statements about the financial reporting framework that has been used.

19-1. For accounting periods commencing on or after 1 January 2005, the consolidated financial statements of UK companies that are admitted to trading on a regulated market and Irish listed companies must be prepared under EU adopted IFRS. Other companies may choose to use EU adopted IFRS; those who do not will be able to continue to prepare their financial statements in accordance with UK and Irish standards.

20. In addition to an opinion on the true and fair view (or fair presentation, in all material respects,), the auditor's report may need to include an opinion as to whether the financial statements comply with other requirements specified by relevant statutes or law.

21. An illustration of these matters in an opinion paragraph is:

"In our opinion, the financial statements give a true and fair view of (or 'present fairly, in all material respects,') the financial position of the Company as of December 31, 20X1, and of the results of its operations and its cash flows for the year then ended in accordance with International Accounting Standards (or [title of financial reporting framework with reference to the country of origin[7]]) (and comply with ...[8])."

Illustrative examples of auditor's reports tailored for use with audits conducted in accordance with ISAs (UK and Ireland) are given in the most recent version of the APB Bulletin, "Auditor's Reports on Financial Statements".

22. [9]

Other requirements specified by relevant statutes and law in the UK and Ireland

22-1. Further opinions or information to be included in the auditor's report may be determined by specific statutory requirements applicable to the reporting entity, or, in some circumstances, by the terms of the auditor's engagement. Such matters may be required to be dealt with by a positive statement in the auditor's report or only by exception. For example, in the Republic of Ireland the auditor is required to state whether, in the auditor's opinion, proper books of account have been kept, whereas

---

[7] See footnote 3.
[8] Refer to relevant statutes or law.
[9] Deleted by the IAASB.

company legislation in the United Kingdom requires the auditor to report only when a company has not maintained proper accounting records.

22-2. Where further opinions are required by statute or other regulation, matters which result in qualification of such an opinion may also result in a qualification of the auditor's opinion on the financial statements: for example, if proper accounting records have not been maintained and as a result it proves impracticable for the auditor to obtain sufficient evidence concerning material matters in the financial statements, the auditor's report indicates that the scope of the examination was limited and includes a qualified opinion or disclaimer of opinion on the financial statements arising from that limitation, as required by paragraphs 37 and 38.

Date of Report

23. **The auditor should date the report as of the completion date of the audit.** This informs the reader that the auditor has considered the effect on the financial statements and on the report of events and transactions of which the auditor became aware and that occurred up to that date.

23-1. **In the UK and Ireland, the date of an auditor's report on a reporting entity's financial statements is the date on which the auditor signed the report expressing an opinion on those statements.**

24. **Since the auditor's responsibility is to report on the financial statements as prepared and presented by management[2], the auditor should not date the report earlier than the date on which the financial statements are signed or approved by management[10].**

24-1. **In the UK and Ireland, the auditor should not date the report earlier than the date on which all other information contained in a report of which the audited financial statements form a part have been approved by those charged with governance and the auditor has considered all necessary available evidence.**

24-2. The auditor is not in a position to form the opinion until the financial statements (and any other information contained in a report of which the audited financial statements form a part) have been approved by those charged with governance and the auditor has completed the assessment of all the evidence the auditor considers necessary for the opinion or opinions to be given in the auditor's report. This assessment includes events occurring up to the date the opinion is expressed. The auditor therefore plans the conduct of audits to take account of the need to ensure, before expressing an opinion on financial statements, that those charged with governance have approved the financial statements and any accompanying financial information and that the auditor has completed a sufficient review of post balance sheet events.

---

[10] In the UK and Ireland, the financial statements are signed or approved by those charged with governance.

24-3. The date of the auditor's report is, therefore, the date on which, following:

    (a) receipt of the financial statements and accompanying documents in the form approved by those charged with governance for release;

    (b) review of all documents which the auditor is required to consider in addition to the financial statements (for example the directors' report, chairman's statement or other review of an entity's affairs which will accompany the financial statements); and

    (c) completion of all procedures necessary to form an opinion on the financial statements (and any other opinions required by law or regulation) including a review of post balance sheet events

the auditor signs (in manuscript) the auditor's report expressing an opinion on the financial statements for distribution with those statements.

24-4. The form of the financial statements and other financial information approved by those charged with governance, and considered by the auditor when signing a report expressing the auditor's opinion, may be in the form of final drafts from which printed documents will be prepared. Subsequent production of printed copies of the financial statements and auditor's report does not constitute the creation of a new document. Copies of the report produced for circulation to shareholders or others may therefore reproduce a printed version of the auditor's signature showing the date of actual signature.

24-5. If the date on which the auditor signs the report is later than that on which those charged with governance approved the financial statements, the auditor takes such steps as are appropriate:

    (a) to obtain assurance that those charged with governance would have approved the financial statements on that later date (for example, by obtaining confirmation from specified individual members of the board to whom authority has been delegated for this purpose); and

    (b) to ensure that their procedures for reviewing subsequent events cover the period up to that date.

24-6. The copy of the auditor's report that is delivered to the registrar of companies is required to state the name of the auditor and be signed by the auditor. Where the auditor signs the auditor's report in a form from which a final printed version is produced, the auditor may sign copies for identification purposes in order to provide the registrar with appropriately signed copies. No further active procedures need be followed at that later date.

Auditor's Address

25.   **The report should name a specific location, which is ordinarily the city where the auditor maintains the office that has responsibility for the audit.**

Auditor's Signature

26.   **The report should be signed in the name of the audit firm, the personal name of the auditor or both, as appropriate.** The auditor's report is ordinarily signed in the name of the firm because the firm assumes responsibility for the audit.

26-1. In the UK and Ireland, where required by relevant law and regulations, the report also states the auditor's status as a registered auditor.

The Auditor's Report

27.   **An *unqualified opinion* should be expressed when the auditor concludes that the financial statements give a true and fair view (or are presented fairly, in all material respects,) in accordance with the identified financial reporting framework.** An unqualified opinion also indicates implicitly that any changes in accounting principles or in the method of their application, and the effects thereof, have been properly determined and disclosed in the financial statements.

27-1. In the UK and Ireland, an unqualified opinion entails concluding whether inter alia:

- The financial statements have been prepared using appropriate accounting principles, which have been consistently applied;

- Any departures from relevant legislation, regulations or the identified financial reporting framework are justified and adequately explained in the financial statements; and

- There is adequate disclosure of all information relevant to the proper understanding of the financial statements.

28.   *The following is an illustration of the entire auditor's report incorporating the basic elements set forth and illustrated above. This report illustrates the expression of an unqualified opinion.*

"AUDITOR'S REPORT

(APPROPRIATE ADDRESSEE)

We have audited the accompanying[11] balance sheet of the ABC Company as of December 31, 20X1, and the related statements of income, and cash flows for the year then ended. These financial statements are the responsibility of the Company's management. Our responsibility is to express an opinion on these financial statements based on our audit.

We conducted our audit in accordance with International Standards on Auditing (or refer to relevant national standards or practices). Those Standards require that we plan and perform the audit to obtain reasonable assurance about whether the financial statements are free of material misstatement. An audit includes examining, on a test basis, evidence supporting the amounts and disclosures in the financial statements. An audit also includes assessing the accounting principles used and significant estimates made by management, as well as evaluating the overall financial statement presentation. We believe that our audit provides a reasonable basis for our opinion.

In our opinion, the financial statements give a true and fair view of (or 'present fairly, in all material respects,') the financial position of the Company as of December 31, 20X1, and of the results of its operations and its cash flows for the year then ended in accordance with International Accounting Standards (or [title of financial reporting framework with reference to the country of origin[12]]) (and comply with ...[13]).

AUDITOR

Date

Address"

Illustrative examples of auditor's reports tailored for use with audits conducted in accordance with ISAs (UK and Ireland) are given in the most recent version of the APB Bulletin, "Auditor's Reports on Financial Statements".

Modified Reports

29.   An auditor's report is considered to be modified in the following situations:

Matters That Do Not Affect the Auditor's Opinion

(a)   Emphasis of matter

---

[11]   See footnote 5.
[12]   See footnote 3.
[13]   See footnote 8.

Matters That Do Affect the Auditor's Opinion

(b)   Qualified opinion,

(c)   Disclaimer of opinion, or

(d)   Adverse opinion.

Uniformity in the form and content of each type of modified report will further the user's understanding of such reports. Accordingly, this ISA (UK and Ireland) includes suggested wording to express an unqualified opinion as well as examples of modifying phrases for use when issuing modified reports.

Illustrative examples of auditor's reports tailored for use with audits conducted in accordance with ISAs (UK and Ireland) are given in the most recent version of the APB Bulletin, "Auditor's Reports on Financial Statements".

Matters That Do Not Affect the Auditor's Opinion

30.   In certain circumstances, an auditor's report may be modified by adding an emphasis of matter paragraph to highlight a matter affecting the financial statements which is included in a note to the financial statements that more extensively discusses the matter. The addition of such an emphasis of matter paragraph does not affect the auditor's opinion. The paragraph would preferably be included after the opinion paragraph and would ordinarily refer to the fact that the auditor's opinion is not qualified in this respect.

31.   **The auditor should modify the auditor's report by adding a paragraph to highlight a material matter regarding a going concern problem.**

32.   **The auditor should consider modifying the auditor's report by adding a paragraph if there is a significant uncertainty (other than a going concern problem), the resolution of which is dependent upon future events and which may affect the financial statements.** An uncertainty is a matter whose outcome depends on future actions or events not under the direct control of the entity but that may affect the financial statements.

32-1.   The emphasis of matter paragraph describes the matter giving rise to the significant uncertainty and its possible effects on the financial statements, including (where practicable) quantification. Where it is not possible to quantify the potential effects of the resolution of the uncertainty, the auditor includes a statement to that effect. Reference may be made to notes in the financial statements but such a reference is not a substitute for sufficient description of the significant uncertainty so that a reader can appreciate the principal points at issue and their implications.

32-2.   Communication with the reader is enhanced by the use of an appropriate sub-heading differentiating the emphasis of matter paragraph from other matters included in the section describing the basis of the auditor's opinion.

32-3. In determining whether an uncertainty is significant, the auditor considers:

(a) the risk that the estimate included in financial statements may be subject to change;

(b) the range of possible outcomes; and

(c) the consequences of those outcomes on the view shown in the financial statements.

32-4. Uncertainties are regarded as significant when they involve a significant level of concern about the validity of the going concern basis or other matters whose potential effect on the financial statements is unusually great. A common example of a significant uncertainty is the outcome of major litigation.

32-5. An unqualified opinion indicates that the auditor considers that appropriate estimates and disclosures relating to significant uncertainties are made in the financial statements. It remains unqualified notwithstanding the inclusion of an emphasis of matter paragraph describing a significant uncertainty.

32-6. When the auditor concludes that the estimate of the outcome of a significant uncertainty is materially misstated or that the disclosure relating to it is inadequate, the auditor issues a qualified opinion.

33. *An illustration of an emphasis of matter paragraph for a significant uncertainty in an auditor's report follows:*

"In our opinion ... (remaining words are the same as illustrated in the opinion paragraph—paragraph 28 above).

Without qualifying our opinion we draw attention to Note X to the financial statements. The Company is the defendant in a lawsuit alleging infringement of certain patent rights and claiming royalties and punitive damages. The Company has filed a counter action, and preliminary hearings and discovery proceedings on both actions are in progress. The ultimate outcome of the matter cannot presently be determined, and no provision for any liability that may result has been made in the financial statements."

Illustrative examples of auditor's reports tailored for use with audits conducted in accordance with ISAs (UK and Ireland) are given in the most recent version of the APB Bulletin, "Auditor's Reports on Financial Statements".

(An illustration of an emphasis of matter paragraph relating to going concern is set out in ISA (UK and Ireland) 570, "Going Concern.")

34. The addition of a paragraph emphasizing a going concern problem or significant uncertainty is ordinarily adequate to meet the auditor's reporting responsibilities regarding such matters. However, in extreme cases, such as situations involving

multiple uncertainties that are significant to the financial statements, the auditor may consider it appropriate to express a disclaimer of opinion instead of adding an emphasis of matter paragraph.

35. In addition to the use of an emphasis of matter paragraph for matters that affect the financial statements, the auditor may also modify the auditor's report by using an emphasis of matter paragraph, preferably after the opinion paragraph, to report on matters other than those affecting the financial statements. For example, if an amendment to other information in a document containing audited financial statements is necessary and the entity refuses to make the amendment, the auditor would consider including in the auditor's report an emphasis of matter paragraph describing the material inconsistency. An emphasis of matter paragraph may also be used when there are additional statutory reporting responsibilities.

Matters That Do Affect the Auditor's Opinion

36. An auditor may not be able to express an unqualified opinion when either of the following circumstances exist and, in the auditor's judgment, the effect of the matter is or may be material to the financial statements:

(a) There is a limitation on the scope of the auditor's work; or

(b) There is a disagreement with management[2] regarding the acceptability of the accounting policies selected, the method of their application or the adequacy of financial statement disclosures.

The circumstances described in (a) could lead to a qualified opinion or a disclaimer of opinion. The circumstances described in (b) could lead to a qualified opinion or an adverse opinion. These circumstances are discussed more fully in paragraphs 41–46.

36-1. In the UK and Ireland, when the auditor concludes that the financial statements of a company do not comply with accounting standards, the auditor assesses:

(a) Whether there are sound reasons for the departure;

(b) Whether adequate disclosure has been made concerning the departure from accounting standards;

(c) Whether the departure is such that the financial statements do not give a true and fair view of the state of affairs and profit or loss.

In normal cases, a departure from accounting standards will result in the issue of a qualified or adverse opinion on the view given by the financial statements.

36-2. In the UK and Ireland, where no explanation is given for a departure from accounting standards, its absence may of itself impair the ability of the financial statements to give a true and fair view of the company's state of affairs and profit or loss. When the auditor concludes that this is so, a qualified or adverse opinion on the view given by the financial statements is appropriate, in addition to a reference (where appropriate) to the departure from accounting standards and the reasons for the departure.

37. A *qualified opinion* should be expressed when the auditor concludes that an unqualified opinion cannot be expressed but that the effect of any disagreement with management[2], or limitation on scope is not so material and pervasive as to require an adverse opinion or a disclaimer of opinion. A qualified opinion should be expressed as being 'except for' the effects of the matter to which the qualification relates.

38. A *disclaimer of opinion* should be expressed when the possible effect of a limitation on scope is so material and pervasive that the auditor has not been able to obtain sufficient appropriate audit evidence and accordingly is unable to express an opinion on the financial statements.

39. An *adverse opinion* should be expressed when the effect of a disagreement is so material and pervasive to the financial statements that the auditor concludes that a qualification of the report is not adequate to disclose the misleading or incomplete nature of the financial statements.

40. Whenever the auditor expresses an opinion that is other than unqualified, a clear description of all the substantive reasons should be included in the report and, unless impracticable, a quantification of the possible effect(s) on the financial statements. Ordinarily, this information would be set out in a separate paragraph preceding the opinion or disclaimer of opinion and may include a reference to a more extensive discussion, if any, in a note to the financial statements.

40-1. Whilst reference may be made to relevant notes in the financial statements, such reference is not a substitute for sufficient description of the circumstances in the auditor's report so that a reader can appreciate the principal points at issue and their implications for an understanding of the financial statements.

Circumstances That May Result in Other Than an Unqualified Opinion

Limitation on Scope

41. A limitation on the scope of the auditor's work may sometimes be imposed by the entity (for example, when the terms of the engagement specify that the auditor will not carry out an audit procedure that the auditor believes is necessary). However, when the limitation in the terms of a proposed engagement is such that the auditor believes the need to express a disclaimer of opinion exists, the auditor would ordinarily not accept such a limited engagement as an audit engagement, unless required by statute. Also, a statutory auditor would not accept such an audit engagement when the limitation infringes on the auditor's statutory duties.

Limitation of scope imposed by the entity before accepting an audit engagement in the UK and Ireland

41-1. If the auditor is aware, before accepting an audit engagement, that those charged with governance of the entity, or those who appoint its auditor, will impose a limitation on the scope of the audit work which the auditor considers likely to result in the need to issue a disclaimer of opinion on the financial statements, the auditor should not accept that engagement, unless required to do so by statute[14].

41-2. Agreeing to such a restriction on the scope of the audit work would seriously threaten the auditor's independence and make it impossible for the auditor to meet with integrity and rigour the requirements of ISAs (UK and Ireland). The acceptance of such a limited engagement as an audit engagement would be incompatible with the auditor's obligations to:

- Conduct any audit of financial statements in accordance with applicable legislation;

- Conduct any audit of financial statements in accordance with Auditing Standards contained in the ISAs (UK and Ireland); and

- Comply with the APB ethical standards.

Furthermore, the auditor, by accepting the engagement on such restricted terms, might be regarded as complicit in an arrangement to enable the entity to observe the form of any legal or regulatory audit requirements but to evade complying with the substance of those obligations.

Limitation on scope imposed by the entity after accepting an audit engagement in the UK and Ireland

41-3. If the auditor becomes aware, after accepting an audit engagement, that those charged with governance of the entity, or those who appointed them as its auditor, have imposed a limitation on the scope of the audit work which they consider likely to result in the need to issue a disclaimer of opinion on the financial statements, the auditor should request the removal of the limitation. If the limitation is not removed, the auditor should consider resigning from the audit engagement.

---

[14] There are certain circumstances in which (regardless of any limitation imposed on the scope of the audit work) the auditor is required by statute to accept an audit engagement, for example the majority of appointments of the national audit agencies to audit the accounts of certain public sector bodies. However, in general, there is no such requirement in the private sector; there may be a statutory requirement for the entity to appoint auditors, but this does not create an obligation for any auditors to accept appointment.

41-4. If the limitation is not removed, the auditor considers the factors discussed in paragraph 41-2 above and may often decide that resignation from the audit engagement is appropriate. If, after careful consideration of all the circumstances (for example, where third party interests are involved), the auditor concludes that it is appropriate to continue with the engagement, the auditor includes in the audit report a full description of the events which led to the disclaimer. On completion of the audit for that year, however, the auditor will follow the requirements of paragraph 41-1 when deciding whether to undertake the audit for the following period[15].

41-5. In cases where the auditor resigns immediately, or continues with the audit for that year but does not seek reappointment, the auditor needs to comply with:

(a) Any statutory or regulatory requirements for a statement of the circumstances of ceasing to hold office;[16] and

(b) The requirements of APB ethical standards concerning the response to enquiries from any proposed successor auditor seeking information which could affect the decision whether or not they may properly accept appointment.

The fact that such a limitation has been imposed on the scope of the auditor's work may be a matter to which the auditor refers in both cases.

41-6. Where a significant limitation of scope has arisen during the course of the audit work the auditor should consider whether an obligation arises under statute, as discussed in ISA (UK and Ireland) 250, Part B, to make a report to the appropriate regulators.

Limitation on scope imposed by circumstances

42. A scope limitation may be imposed by circumstances (for example, when the timing of the auditor's appointment is such that the auditor is unable to observe the counting of physical inventories). It may also arise when, in the opinion of the auditor, the entity's accounting records are inadequate or when the auditor is unable to carry out an audit procedure believed to be desirable. In these circumstances, the auditor would attempt to carry out reasonable alternative procedures to obtain sufficient appropriate audit evidence to support an unqualified opinion.

43. **When there is a limitation on the scope of the auditor's work that requires expression of a qualified opinion or a disclaimer of opinion, the auditor's report should describe the limitation and indicate the possible adjustments to the**

---

[15] Auditors in the Republic of Ireland are required by the Companies Act 1963 (section 160, para 2(c)) to give the company notice in writing of their unwillingness to be re-appointed, where this is the case.

[16] For example, in the case of a limited company incorporated in the United Kingdom, on ceasing to hold office for any reason, the auditor is required under section 394(1) Companies Act 1985 (or Article 58(1) Companies (No 2) (Northern Ireland) Order 1990) to make'... a statement of any circumstances connected with his ceasing to hold office which he considers should be brought to the attention of the members or creditors of the company or, if he considers that there are no such circumstances, a statement that there are none.' Similar requirements exist in the Republic of Ireland (section 185 Companies Act, 1990).

financial statements that might have been determined to be necessary had the limitation not existed.

43-1. In the UK and Ireland, in considering whether a limitation of scope results in a lack of evidence necessary to form an opinion, the auditor assesses:

(a) The quantity and type of evidence which may reasonably be expected to be available to support the particular figure or disclosure in the financial statements; and

(b) The possible effect on the financial statements of the matter for which insufficient evidence is available. When the possible effect is, in the opinion of the auditor, material to the financial statements, there will be insufficient evidence to support an unqualified opinion.

44. *Illustrations of these matters are set out below.*

Limitation on Scope—Qualified Opinion

"We have audited ... (remaining words are the same as illustrated in the introductory paragraph—paragraph 28 above).

Except as discussed in the following paragraph, we conducted our audit in accordance with ... (remaining words are the same as illustrated in the scope paragraph—paragraph 28 above).

We did not observe the counting of the physical inventories as of December 31, 20X1, since that date was prior to the time we were initially engaged as auditors for the Company. Owing to the nature of the Company's records, we were unable to satisfy ourselves as to inventory quantities by other audit procedures.

In our opinion, except for the effects of such adjustments, if any, as might have been determined to be necessary had we been able to satisfy ourselves as to physical inventory quantities, the financial statements give a true and ... (remaining words are the same as illustrated in the opinion paragraph—paragraph 28 above).

Illustrative examples of auditor's reports tailored for use with audits conducted in accordance with ISAs (UK and Ireland) are given in the most recent version of the APB Bulletin, "Auditor's Reports on Financial Statements".

Limitation on Scope—Disclaimer of Opinion

"We were engaged to audit the accompanying balance sheet of the ABC Company as of December 31, 20X1, and the related statements of income and cash flows for the year then ended. These financial statements are the responsibility of the Company's management. (Omit the sentence stating the responsibility of the auditor).

(The paragraph discussing the scope of the audit would either be omitted or amended according to the circumstances.)

(Add a paragraph discussing the scope limitation as follows:)

We were not able to observe all physical inventories and confirm accounts receivable due to limitations placed on the scope of our work by the Company.

Because of the significance of the matters discussed in the preceding paragraph, we do not express an opinion on the financial statements.

Illustrative examples of auditor's reports tailored for use with audits conducted in accordance with ISAs (UK and Ireland) are given in the most recent version of the APB Bulletin, "Auditor's Reports on Financial Statements".

Disagreement with Management[2]

45. The auditor may disagree with management[2] about matters such as the acceptability of accounting policies selected, the method of their application, or the adequacy of disclosures in the financial statements. **If such disagreements are material to the financial statements, the auditor should express a qualified or an adverse opinion.**

46. *Illustrations of these matters are set out below.*

Disagreement on Accounting Policies-Inappropriate Accounting Method—Qualified Opinion

"We have audited ... (remaining words are the same as illustrated in the introductory paragraph—paragraph 28 above).

We conducted our audit in accordance with ... (remaining words are the same as illustrated in the scope paragraph—paragraph 28 above).

As discussed in Note X to the financial statements, no depreciation has been provided in the financial statements which practice, in our opinion, is not in accordance with International Accounting Standards. The provision for the year ended December 31, 20X1, should be xxx based on the straight-line method of depreciation using annual rates of 5% for the building and 20% for the equipment. Accordingly, the fixed assets should be reduced by accumulated depreciation of xxx and the loss for the year and accumulated deficit should be increased by xxx and xxx, respectively.

In our opinion, except for the effect on the financial statements of the matter referred to in the preceding paragraph, the financial statements give a true and ... (remaining words are the same as illustrated in the opinion paragraph—paragraph 28 above)."

Illustrative examples of auditor's reports tailored for use with audits conducted in accordance with ISAs (UK and Ireland) are given in the most recent version of the APB Bulletin, "Auditor's Reports on Financial Statements".

Disagreement on Accounting Policies—Inadequate Disclosure—Qualified Opinion

"We have audited ... *(remaining words are the same as illustrated in the introductory paragraph—paragraph 28 above).*

We conducted our audit in accordance with ... *(remaining words are the same as illustrated in the scope paragraph—paragraph 28 above).*

On January 15, 20X2, the Company issued debentures in the amount of xxx for the purpose of financing plant expansion. The debenture agreement restricts the payment of future cash dividends to earnings after December 31, 19X1. In our opinion, disclosure of this information is required by ...[17] .

In our opinion, except for the omission of the information included in the preceding paragraph, the financial statements give a true and ... *(remaining words are the same as illustrated in the opinion paragraph—paragraph 28 above)."*

Illustrative examples of auditor's reports tailored for use with audits conducted in accordance with ISAs (UK and Ireland) are given in the most recent version of the APB Bulletin, "Auditor's Reports on Financial Statements".

Disagreement on Accounting Policies—Inadequate Disclosure—Adverse Opinion

"We have audited ... *(remaining words are the same as illustrated in the introductory paragraph—paragraph 28 above).*

We conducted our audit in accordance with ... *(remaining words are the same as illustrated in the scope paragraph—paragraph 28 above).*

(Paragraph(s) discussing the disagreement).

In our opinion, because of the effects of the matters discussed in the preceding paragraph(s), the financial statements do not give a true and fair view of (or do not 'present fairly') the financial position of the Company as of December 20, 19X1, and of the results of its operations and its cash flows for the year then ended in accordance with International Accounting Standards (or [title of financial reporting framework with reference to the country of origin[18]]) (and do not comply with ...[19])."

Illustrative examples of auditor's reports tailored for use with audits conducted in accordance with ISAs (UK and Ireland) are given in the most recent version of the APB Bulletin, "Auditor's Reports on Financial Statements".

---

[17] See footnote 8.
[18] See footnote 3.
[19] See footnote 8.

Effective Date

47. This ISA (UK and Ireland) is effective for audits of financial statements for periods commencing on or after 15 December 2004.

Public Sector Perspective

Additional guidance for auditors of public sector bodies in the UK and Ireland is given in:

- Practice Note 10 "Audit of Financial Statements of Public Sector Bodies in the United Kingdom (Revised)"

- Practice Note 10(I) "Audit of Central Government Financial Statements in the Republic of Ireland (Revised)"

1. *While the basic principles contained in this ISA (UK and Ireland) apply to the audit of financial statements in the public sector, the legislation giving rise to the audit mandate may specify the nature, content and form of the auditor's report.*

2. *This ISA (UK and Ireland) does not address the form and content of the auditor's report in circumstances where financial statements are prepared in conformity with a disclosed basis of accounting, whether mandated by legislation or ministerial (or other) directive, and that basis results in financial statements which are misleading.*

3. *Paragraph 17 of this standard requires the auditor to indicate clearly the financial reporting framework used to prepare the financial statements. Where a public sector entity has adopted International Public Sector Accounting Standards as the financial reporting framework, the auditor should clearly state that fact in the audit opinion. For example:*

   "In our opinion, the financial statements present fairly, in all material respects, the financial position of the [public sector entity] as of December 31, 20X1 and of its financial performance and its cash flows for the year then ended in accordance with International Public Sector Accounting Standards."

Appendix

Forming an opinion on financial statements[1]

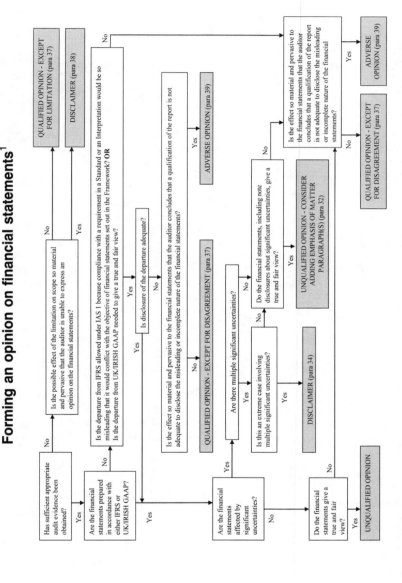

[1] This flowchart does not cover modified reports involving going concern problems. Refer to the most recent version of the APB Bulletin, "Auditor's Reports on Financial Statements".

INTERNATIONAL STANDARD ON AUDITING (UK AND IRELAND) 710

COMPARATIVES

CONTENTS

International Standard on Auditing (UK and Ireland) (ISA (UK and Ireland)) 710 "Comparatives" should be read in the context of the Auditing Practices Board's Statement "The Auditing Practices Board - Scope and Authority of Pronouncements (Revised)" which sets out the application and authority of ISAs (UK and Ireland).

Introduction

1. The purpose of this International Standard on Auditing (UK and Ireland) (ISA (UK and Ireland)) is to establish standards and provide guidance on the auditor's responsibilities regarding comparatives. It does not deal with situations when summarized financial statements are presented with the audited financial statements (for guidance see ISA (UK and Ireland) 720 "Other Information in Documents Containing Audited Financial Statements," and ISA 800 "The Auditor's Report on Special Purpose Audit Engagements").

1-1. This ISA (UK and Ireland) uses the terms 'those charged with governance' and 'management'. The term 'governance' describes the role of persons entrusted with the supervision, control and direction of an entity. Ordinarily, those charged with governance are accountable for ensuring that the entity achieves its objectives, and for the quality of its financial reporting and reporting to interested parties. Those charged with governance include management only when they perform such functions.

1-2. In the UK and Ireland, those charged with governance include the directors (executive and non-executive) of a company or other body, the members of an audit committee where one exists, the partners, proprietors, committee of management or trustees of other forms of entity, or equivalent persons responsible for directing the entity's affairs and preparing its financial statements.

1-3. 'Management' comprises those persons who perform senior managerial functions.

1-4. In the UK and Ireland, depending on the nature and circumstances of the entity, management may include some or all of those charged with governance (e.g. executive directors). Management will not normally include non-executive directors.

1-5. ISA (UK and Ireland) 510 "Opening Balances" establishes standards and guidance regarding opening balances, including when the financial statements are audited for the first time or when the financial statements for the prior period were audited by another auditor.

2. **The auditor should determine whether the comparatives comply in all material respects with the financial reporting framework applicable to the financial statements being audited.**

2-1. **The auditor should obtain sufficient appropriate audit evidence that amounts derived from the preceding period's financial statements are free from material misstatements and are appropriately incorporated in the financial statements for the current period.**

3. The existence of differences in financial reporting frameworks between countries results in comparative financial information being presented differently in each framework. Comparatives in financial statements, for example, may present amounts (such as financial position, results of operations, cash flows) and appropriate

disclosures of an entity for more than one period, depending on the framework. The frameworks and methods of presentation are referred to in this ISA (UK and Ireland) as follows:

(a) *Corresponding figures* where amounts and other disclosures for the preceding period are included as part of the current period financial statements, and are intended to be read in relation to the amounts and other disclosures relating to the current period (referred to as "current period figures" for the purpose of this ISA (UK and Ireland)). These corresponding figures are not presented as complete financial statements capable of standing alone, but are an integral part of the current period financial statements intended to be read only in relationship to the current period figures; and

(b) *Comparative financial statements* where amounts and other disclosures for the preceding period are included for comparison with the financial statements of the current period, but do not form part of the current period financial statements.

(Refer to Appendix 1 to this ISA (UK and Ireland) for discussion of these different reporting frameworks.)

4. Comparatives are presented in compliance with the applicable financial reporting framework. The essential audit reporting differences are that:

(a) For corresponding figures, the auditor's report only refers to the financial statements of the current period; whereas

(b) For comparative financial statements, the auditor's report refers to each period that financial statements are presented.

5. This ISA (UK and Ireland) provides guidance on the auditor's responsibilities for comparatives and for reporting on them under the two frameworks in separate sections.

5-1. In the UK and Ireland the corresponding figures method of presentation is usually required.

Corresponding Figures

The Auditor's Responsibilities

6. **The auditor should obtain sufficient appropriate audit evidence that the corresponding figures meet the requirements of the applicable financial reporting framework.** The extent of audit procedures performed on the corresponding figures is significantly less than for the audit of the current period figures and is ordinarily limited to ensuring that the corresponding figures have been correctly reported and are appropriately classified. This involves the auditor evaluating whether:

(a)   Accounting policies used for the corresponding figures are consistent with those of the current period or whether appropriate adjustments and/or disclosures have been made; and

(b)   Corresponding figures agree with the amounts and other disclosures presented in the prior period or whether appropriate adjustments and/or disclosures have been made.

6-1. **In the UK and Ireland, the auditor should obtain sufficient appropriate audit evidence that:**

(a)   **The accounting policies used for the corresponding amounts are consistent with those of the current period and appropriate adjustments and disclosures have been made where this is not the case;**

(b)   **The corresponding amounts agree with the amounts and other disclosures presented in the preceding period and are free from errors in the context of the financial statements of the current period; and**

(c)   **Where corresponding amounts have been adjusted as required by relevant legislation and accounting standards, appropriate disclosures have been made.**

7.   When the financial statements of the prior period have been audited by another auditor, the incoming auditor evaluates whether the corresponding figures meet the conditions specified in paragraph 6 above and also follows the guidance in ISA (UK and Ireland) 510 "Initial Engagements—Opening Balances."

8.   When the financial statements of the prior period were not audited, the incoming auditor nonetheless assesses whether the corresponding figures meet the conditions specified in paragraph 6 above and also follows the guidance in ISA (UK and Ireland) 510 "Initial Engagements—Opening Balances."

9.   If the auditor becomes aware of a possible material misstatement in the corresponding figures when performing the current period audit, the auditor performs such additional audit procedures as are appropriate in the circumstances.

Reporting

10.   **When the comparatives are presented as corresponding figures, the auditor should issue an audit report in which the comparatives are not specifically identified because the auditor's opinion is on the current period financial statements as a whole, including the corresponding figures.**

11.   The auditor's report would make specific reference to the corresponding figures only in the circumstances described in paragraphs 12, 13, 15(b), and 16 through 19.

12. **When the auditor's report on the prior period, as previously issued, included a qualified opinion, disclaimer of opinion, or adverse opinion and the matter which gave rise to the modification is:**

   (a) **Unresolved, and results in a modification of the auditor's report regarding the current period figures, the auditor's report should also be modified regarding the corresponding figures; or**

   (b) **Unresolved, but does not result in a modification of the auditor's report regarding the current period figures, the auditor's report should be modified regarding the corresponding figures.**

12-1. With respect to situations described in 12(b), if corresponding amounts are required by law or regulation, the reference is in the form of a qualification on the grounds of non-compliance with that requirement. If corresponding amounts are presented solely as good practice, the reference is made in the auditor's report in the form of an explanatory paragraph.

13. When the auditor's report on the prior period, as previously issued, included a qualified opinion, disclaimer of opinion, or adverse opinion and the matter which gave rise to the modification is resolved and properly dealt with in the financial statements, the current report does not ordinarily refer to the previous modification. However, if the matter is material to the current period, the auditor may include an emphasis of matter paragraph dealing with the situation.

13-1. In some circumstances the auditor may consider it appropriate to qualify the audit opinion on the current period's financial statements. For example, if a provision which the auditor considered should have been made in the previous period is made in the current period.

14. In performing the audit of the current period financial statements, the auditor, in certain unusual circumstances, may become aware of a material misstatement that affects the prior period financial statements on which an unmodified report has been previously issued.

15. **In such circumstances, the auditor should consider the guidance in ISA (UK and Ireland) 560 "Subsequent Events" and:**

   (a) **If the prior period financial statements have been revised and reissued with a new auditor's report, the auditor should obtain sufficient appropriate audit evidence that the corresponding figures agree with the revised financial statements; or**

   (b) **If the prior period financial statements have not been revised and reissued, and the corresponding figures have not been properly restated and/or appropriate disclosures have not been made, the auditor should issue a modified report on the current period financial statements modified with respect to the corresponding figures included therein.**

16. If, in the circumstances described in paragraph 14, the prior period financial statements have not been revised and an auditor's report has not been reissued, but the corresponding figures have been properly restated and/or appropriate disclosures have been made in the current period financial statements, the auditor may include an emphasis of matter paragraph describing the circumstances and referencing to the appropriate disclosures. In this regard, the auditor also considers the guidance in ISA (UK and Ireland) 560 "Subsequent Events."

Incoming Auditor—Additional Requirements

Prior Period Financial Statements Audited by Another Auditor

17. In some jurisdictions, the incoming auditor is permitted to refer to the predecessor auditor's report on the corresponding figures in the incoming auditor's report for the current period. **When the auditor decides to refer to another auditor, the incoming auditor's report should indicate:**

   (a) **That the financial statements of the prior period were audited by another auditor;**

   (b) **The type of report issued by the predecessor auditor and, if the report was modified, the reasons therefor; and**

   (c) **The date of that report.**

17-1. In the UK and Ireland the incoming auditor does not refer to the predecessor auditor's report on the corresponding figures in the incoming auditor's report for the current period. The incoming auditor assumes audit responsibility for the corresponding figures only in the context of the financial statements as a whole. The incoming auditor reads the preceding period's financial statements and, using the knowledge gained during the current audit, considers whether they have been properly reflected as corresponding figures in the current period's financial statements.

17-2. Although the incoming auditor is not required to re-audit the financial statements of the preceding period, if the incoming auditor becomes aware of a possible material misstatement of corresponding figures, the procedures in paragraphs 14 - 16 apply.

Prior Period Financial Statements Not Audited

18. **When the prior period financial statements are not audited, the incoming auditor should state in the auditor's report that the corresponding figures are unaudited.** Such a statement does not, however, relieve the auditor of the requirement to perform appropriate audit procedures regarding opening balances of the current period. Clear disclosure in the financial statements that the corresponding figures are unaudited is encouraged.

18-1. If the auditor is not able to obtain sufficient appropriate audit evidence regarding the corresponding figures, or if there is not adequate disclosure, the auditor considers the implications for the auditor's report.

19. **In situations where the incoming auditor identifies that the corresponding figures are materially misstated, the auditor should request management[1a] to revise the corresponding figures or if management refuses to do so, appropriately modify the report.**

Comparative Financial Statements

The Auditor's Responsibilities

20. **The auditor should obtain sufficient appropriate audit evidence that the comparative financial statements meet the requirements of the applicable financial reporting framework.** This involves the auditor evaluating whether:

   (a) Accounting policies of the prior period are consistent with those of the current period or whether appropriate adjustments and/or disclosures have been made; and

   (b) Prior period figures presented agree with the amounts and other disclosures presented in the prior period or whether appropriate adjustments and disclosures have been made.

21. When the financial statements of the prior period have been audited by another auditor, the incoming auditor evaluates whether the comparative financial statements meet the conditions in paragraph 20 above and also follows the guidance in ISA (UK and Ireland) 510 "Initial Engagements—Opening Balances."

22. When the financial statements of the prior period were not audited, the incoming auditor nonetheless evaluates whether the comparative financial statements meet the conditions specified in paragraph 20 above and also follows the guidance in ISA (UK and Ireland) 510 "Initial Engagements—Opening Balances."

23. If the auditor becomes aware of a possible material misstatement in the prior year figures when performing the current period audit, the auditor performs such additional audit procedures as are appropriate in the circumstances.

Reporting

24. When the comparatives are presented as comparative financial statements, the auditor should issue a report in which the comparatives are specifically identified because the auditor's opinion is expressed individually on the financial statements of

---

[1a] In The UK and Ireland, those charged with governance are responsible for the preparation of the financial statements.

each period presented. Since the auditor's report on comparative financial statements applies to the individual financial statements presented, the auditor may express a qualified or adverse opinion, disclaim an opinion, or include an emphasis of matter paragraph with respect to one or more financial statements for one or more periods, while issuing a different report on the other financial statements.

25.　When reporting on the prior period financial statements in connection with the current year's audit, if the opinion on such prior period financial statements is different from the opinion previously expressed, the auditor should disclose the substantive reasons for the different opinion in an emphasis of matter paragraph. This may arise when the auditor becomes aware of circumstances or events that materially affect the financial statements of a prior period during the course of the audit of the current period.

Incoming Auditor—Additional Requirements

Prior Period Financial Statements Audited by Another Auditor

26.　**When the financial statements of the prior period were audited by another auditor,**

　　(a)　**The predecessor auditor may reissue the audit report on the prior period with the incoming auditor only reporting on the current period; or**

　　(b)　**The incoming auditor's report should state that the prior period was audited by another auditor and the incoming auditor's report should indicate:**

　　　　(i)　**That the financial statements of the prior period were audited by another auditor;**

　　　　(ii)　**The type of report issued by the predecessor auditor and if the report was modified, the reasons therefor; and**

　　　　(iii)　**The date of that report.**

27.　In performing the audit on the current period financial statements, the incoming auditor, in certain unusual circumstances, may become aware of a material misstatement that affects the prior period financial statements on which the predecessor auditor had previously reported without modification.

28.　**In these circumstances, the incoming auditor should discuss the matter with management and, after having obtained management's authorization, contact the predecessor auditor and propose that the prior period financial statements be restated. If the predecessor agrees to reissue the audit report on the restated financial statements of the prior period, the auditor should follow the guidance in paragraph 26.**

29.   If, in the circumstances discussed in paragraph 27, the predecessor does not agree with the proposed restatement or refuses to reissue the audit report on the prior period financial statements, the introductory paragraph of the auditor's report may indicate that the predecessor auditor reported on the financial statements of the prior period before restatement. In addition, if the incoming auditor is engaged to audit and applies sufficient audit procedures to be satisfied as to the appropriateness of the restatement adjustment, the auditor may also include the following paragraph in the report:

> We also audited the adjustments described in Note X that were applied to restate the 19X1 financial statements. In our opinion, such adjustments are appropriate and have been properly applied.

Prior Period Financial Statements Not Audited

30.   **When the prior period financial statements are not audited, the incoming auditor should state in the auditor's report that the comparative financial statements are unaudited.**   Such a statement does not, however, relieve the auditor of the requirement to carry out appropriate audit procedures regarding opening balances of the current period. Clear disclosure in the financial statements that the comparative financial statements are unaudited is encouraged.

31.   **In situations where the incoming auditor identifies that the prior year unaudited figures are materially misstated, the auditor should request management to revise the prior year's figures or if management refuses to do so, appropriately modify the report.**

Effective Date

32.   This ISA (UK and Ireland) is effective for audits of financial statements for periods commencing on or after 15 December 2004.

Discussion of Financial Reporting Frameworks for Comparatives

1. Comparatives covering one or more preceding periods provide the users of financial statements with information necessary to identify trends and changes affecting an entity over a period of time.

2. Under financial reporting frameworks (both implicit and explicit) prevailing in a number of countries, comparability and consistency are desirable qualities for financial information. Defined in broadest terms, comparability is the quality of having certain characteristics in common and comparison is normally a quantitative assessment of the common characteristics. Consistency is a quality of the relationship between two accounting numbers. Consistency (for example, consistency in the use of accounting principles from one period to another, the consistency of the length of the reporting period, *etc.*) is a prerequisite for true comparability.

3. There are two broad financial reporting frameworks for comparatives: the corresponding figures and the comparative financial statements.

4. Under the corresponding figures framework, the corresponding figures for the prior period(s) are an integral part of the current period financial statements and have to be read in conjunction with the amounts and other disclosures relating to the current period. The level of detail presented in the corresponding amounts and disclosures is dictated primarily by its relevance to the current period figures.

5. Under the comparative financial statements framework, the comparative financial statements for the prior period(s) are considered separate financial statements. Accordingly, the level of information included in those comparative financial statements (including all statement amounts, disclosures, footnotes and other explanatory statements to the extent that they continue to be of significance) approximates that of the financial statements of the current period.

Appendix 2

Example Auditor's Reports

Illustrative examples of auditor's reports tailored for use with audits conducted in accordance with ISAs (UK and Ireland) are given in the most recent version of the APB Bulletin, "Auditor's Reports on Financial Statements".

Example A   *Corresponding Figures: Example Report for the circumstances described in paragraph 12a*

AUDITOR'S REPORT

(APPROPRIATE ADDRESSEE)

We have audited the accompanying[1] balance sheet of the ABC Company as of December 31, 19X1, and the related statements of income and cash flows for the year then ended. These financial statements are the responsibility of the Company's management. Our responsibility is to express an opinion on these financial statements based on our audit.

We conducted our audit in accordance with International Standards on Auditing (or refer to applicable national standards or practices). Those Standards require that we plan and perform the audit to obtain reasonable assurance about whether the financial statements are free of material misstatement. An audit includes examining, on a test basis, evidence supporting the amounts and disclosures in the financial statements. An audit also includes assessing the accounting principles used and significant estimates made by management, as well as evaluating the overall financial statement presentation. We believe that our audit provides a reasonable basis for our opinion.

As discussed in Note X to the financial statements, no depreciation has been provided in the financial statements which practice, in our opinion, is not in accordance with International Accounting Standards (or refer to applicable national standards). This is the result of a decision taken by management at the start of the preceding financial year and caused us to qualify our audit opinion on the financial statements relating to that year. Based on the straight-line method of depreciation and annual rates of 5% for the building and 20% for the equipment, the loss for the year should be increased by XXX in 19X1 and XXX in 19X0, the fixed assets should be reduced by accumulated depreciation of XXX in 19X1 and XXX in 19X0, and the accumulated loss should be increased by XXX in 19X1 and XXX in 19X0.

In our opinion, except for the effect on the financial statements of the matter referred to in the preceding paragraph, the financial statements give a true and fair view of (or 'present fairly, in all material respects,') the financial position of the Company as of December 31,

---

[1]   The reference can be by page numbers.

19X1, and of the results of its operations and its cash flows for the year then ended in accordance with ...[2] (and comply with ...[3]).

AUDITOR

Date
Address

---

[2] Indicate International Accounting Standards or applicable national standards.
[3] Reference to applicable statutes or laws.

Example B *Corresponding Figures: Example Report for the circumstances described in paragraph 12b*

AUDITOR'S REPORT

(APPROPRIATE ADDRESSEE)

We have audited the accompanying[4] balance sheet of the ABC Company as of December 31, 19X1, and the related statements of income and cash flows for the year then ended. These financial statements are the responsibility of the Company's management. Our responsibility is to express an opinion on these financial statements based on our audit.

We conducted our audit in accordance with International Standards on Auditing (or refer to applicable national standards or practices). Those Standards require that we plan and perform the audit to obtain reasonable assurance about whether the financial statements are free of material misstatement. An audit includes examining, on a test basis, evidence supporting the amounts and disclosures in the financial statements. An audit also includes assessing the accounting principles used and significant estimates made by management, as well as evaluating the overall financial statement presentation. We believe that our audit provides a reasonable basis for our opinion.

Because we were appointed auditors of the Company during 19X0, we were not able to observe the counting of the physical inventories at the beginning of that (period) or satisfy ourselves concerning those inventory quantities by alternative means. Since opening inventories enter into the determination of the results of operations, we were unable to determine whether adjustments to the results of operations and opening retained earnings might be necessary for 19X0. Our audit report on the financial statements for the (period) ended (balance sheet date) 19X0 was modified accordingly.

In our opinion, except for the effect on the corresponding figures for 19X0 of the adjustments, if any, to the results of operations for the (period) ended 19X0, which we might have determined to be necessary had we been able to observe beginning inventory quantities as at ..., the financial statements give a true and fair view of (or 'present fairly, in all material respects,') the financial position of the Company as of December 31, 19X1, and of the results of its operations and its cash flows for the year then ended in accordance with ...[5] (and comply with ....[6]).

AUDITOR

Date
Address

---

[4] The reference can be by page numbers.
[5] Indicate International Accounting Standards or applicable national standards.
[6] Reference to applicable statutes or laws.

Example C *Comparative Financial Statements: Example Report for the circumstances described in paragraph 24*

AUDITOR'S REPORT

(APPROPRIATE ADDRESSEE)

We have audited the accompanying[7] balance sheets of the ABC Company as of December 31, 19X1 and 19X0, and the related statements of income and cash flows for the years then ended. These financial statements are the responsibility of the Company's management. Our responsibility is to express an opinion on these financial statements based on our audits.

We conducted our audits in accordance with International Standards on Auditing (or refer to applicable national standards or practices). Those Standards require that we plan and perform the audit to obtain reasonable assurance about whether the financial statements are free of material misstatement. An audit includes examining, on a test basis, evidence supporting the amounts and disclosures in the financial statements. An audit also includes assessing the accounting principles used and significant estimates made by management, as well as evaluating the overall financial statement presentation. We believe that our audits provide a reasonable basis for our opinion.

As discussed in Note X to the financial statements, no depreciation has been provided in the financial statements which practice, in our opinion, is not in accordance with International Accounting Standards (or refer to applicable national standards). Based on the straight-line method of depreciation and annual rates of 5% for the building and 20% for the equipment, the loss for the year should be increased by XXX in 19X1 and XXX in 19X0, the fixed assets should be reduced by accumulated depreciation of XXX in 19X1 and XXX in 19X0, and the accumulated loss should be increased by XXX in 19X1 and XXX in 19X0.

In our opinion, except for the effect on the financial statements of the matter referred to in the preceding paragraph, the financial statements give a true and fair view of (or 'present fairly, in all material respects,') the financial position of the Company as of December 31, 19X1 and 19X0, and of the results of its operations and its cash flows for the years then ended in accordance with ...[8] (and comply with ....[9]).

AUDITOR

Date
Address

---

[7] The reference can be by page numbers.
[8] Indicate International Accounting Standards or applicable national standards.
[9] Reference to applicable statutes or laws.

Example D   *Corresponding Figures: Example Report for the circumstances described in paragraph 17*

AUDITOR'S REPORT

(APPROPRIATE ADDRESSEE)

We have audited the accompanying[10] balance sheet of the ABC Company as of December 31, 19X1, and the related statements of income and cash flows for the year then ended. These financial statements are the responsibility of the Company's management. Our responsibility is to express an opinion on these financial statements based on our audit. The financial statements of the Company as of December 31, 19X0, were audited by another auditor whose report dated March 31, 19X1, expressed an unqualified opinion on those statements.

We conducted our audit in accordance with International Standards on Auditing (or refer to applicable national standards or practices). Those Standards require that we plan and perform the audit to obtain reasonable assurance about whether the financial statements are free of material misstatement. An audit includes examining, on a test basis, evidence supporting the amounts and disclosures in the financial statements. An audit also includes assessing the accounting principles used and significant estimates made by management, as well as evaluating the overall financial statement presentation. We believe that our audit provides a reasonable basis for our opinion.

In our opinion, the financial statements give a true and fair view of (or 'present fairly, in all material respects,') the financial position of the Company as of December 31, 19X1, and of the results of its operations and its cash flows for the year then ended in accordance with ...[11] (and comply with ...[12]).

AUDITOR

Date
Address

---

[10] The reference can be by page numbers.
[11] Indicate International Accounting Standards or applicable national standards.
[12] Reference to applicable statutes or laws.

Example E *Comparative Financial Statements: Example Report for the circumstances described in paragraph 26b*

AUDITOR'S REPORT

(APPROPRIATE ADDRESSEE)

We have audited the accompanying[13] balance sheet of the ABC Company as of December 31, 19X1, and the related statements of income and cash flows for the year then ended. These financial statements are the responsibility of the Company's management. Our responsibility is to express an opinion on these financial statements based on our audit. The financial statements of the Company as of December 31, 19X0, were audited by another auditor whose report dated March 31, 19X1, expressed a qualified opinion due to their disagreement as to the adequacy of the provision for doubtful receivables.

We conducted our audit in accordance with International Standards on Auditing (or refer to applicable national standards or practices). Those Standards require that we plan and perform the audit to obtain reasonable assurance about whether the financial statements are free of material misstatement. An audit includes examining, on a test basis, evidence supporting the amounts and disclosures in the financial statements. An audit also includes assessing the accounting principles used and significant estimates made by management, as well as evaluating the overall financial statement presentation. We believe that our audit provides a reasonable basis for our opinion.

The receivables referred to above are still outstanding at December 31, 19X1 and no provision for potential loss has been made in the financial statements. Accordingly, the provision for doubtful receivables at December 31, 19X1 and 19X0 should be increased by XXX, the net profit for 19X0 decreased by XXX and the retained earnings at December 31, 19X1 and 19X0 reduced by XXX.

In our opinion, except for the effect on the financial statements of the matter referred to in the preceding paragraph, the 19X1 financial statements referred to above give a true and fair view of (or 'present fairly, in all material respects,') the financial position of the Company as of December 31, 19X1, and of the results of its operations and its cash flows for the year then ended in accordance with ...[14] (and comply with ...[15]).

AUDITOR

Date
Address

---

[13] The reference can be by page numbers.
[14] Indicate International Accounting Standards or applicable national standards.
[15] Reference to applicable statutes or laws.

INTERNATIONAL STANDARD ON AUDITING (UK AND IRELAND) 720 (REVISED)

SECTION A - OTHER INFORMATION IN DOCUMENTS CONTAINING AUDITED FINANCIAL STATEMENTS

SECTION B - THE AUDITOR'S STATUTORY REPORTING RESPONSIBILITY IN RELATION TO DIRECTORS' REPORTS

CONTENTS

International Standard on Auditing (UK and Ireland) (ISA (UK and Ireland)) 720 "Other Information in Documents Containing Audited Financial Statements" should be read in the context of the Auditing Practices Board's Statement "The Auditing Practices Board - Scope and Authority of Pronouncements (Revised)" which sets out the application and authority of ISAs (UK and Ireland).

This ISA (UK and Ireland) adopts the text of ISA 720 issued by the International Auditing and Assurance Standards Board. Supplementary material added by the APB is differentiated by the use of grey shading.

SECTION A – OTHER INFORMATION IN DOCUMENTS CONTAINING AUDITED FINANCIAL STATEMENTS

Introduction

1. The purpose of this Section of this International Standard on Auditing (UK and Ireland) (ISA (UK and Ireland)) is to establish standards and provide guidance on the auditor's consideration of other information, on which the auditor has no obligation to report, in documents containing audited financial statements. This ISA (UK and Ireland) applies when an annual report is involved; however, it may also apply to other documents, such as those used in securities offerings[1].

1-1. The standards and guidance in this Section apply to all other information included in documents containing audited financial statements, including the directors' report. Further standards and guidance on the auditor's statutory reporting obligations in relation to directors' reports are set out in Section B.

1-2. This Section of this ISA (UK and Ireland) is primarily directed towards the auditor's consideration of other information contained in an entity's published annual report. It is not intended to address issues which may arise if financial information is extracted from that document.

1-3. This ISA (UK and Ireland) uses the terms 'those charged with governance' and 'management'. The term 'governance' describes the role of persons entrusted with the supervision, control and direction of an entity. Ordinarily, those charged with governance are accountable for ensuring that the entity achieves its objectives, and for the quality of its financial reporting and reporting to interested parties. Those charged with governance include management only when they perform such functions.

1-4. In the UK and Ireland, those charged with governance include the directors (executive and non-executive) of a company or other body, the members of an audit committee where one exists, the partners, proprietors, committee of management or trustees of other forms of entity, or equivalent persons responsible for directing the entity's affairs and preparing its financial statements.

1-5. 'Management' comprises those persons who perform senior managerial functions.

1-6. In the UK and Ireland, depending on the nature and circumstances of the entity, management may include some or all of those charged with governance (e.g. executive directors). Management will not normally include non-executive directors.

---

[1] The guidance in this ISA (UK and Ireland) is limited to Annual Reports and statutory audits. Guidance on other information issued with investment circulars is covered in Statement of Investment Reporting Standard (SIR) 1000.

2. **The auditor should read the other information to identify material inconsistencies with the audited financial statements.**

2-1. **If, as a result of reading the other information, the auditor becomes aware of any apparent misstatements therein, or identifies any material inconsistencies with the audited financial statements, the auditor should seek to resolve them.**

3. A "material inconsistency" exists when other information contradicts information contained in the audited financial statements. A material inconsistency may raise doubt about the audit conclusions drawn from audit evidence previously obtained and, possibly, about the basis for the auditor's opinion on the financial statements.

4. An entity ordinarily issues on an annual basis a document which includes its audited financial statements together with the auditor's report thereon. This document is frequently referred to as the "annual report." In issuing such a document, an entity may also include, either by law or custom, other financial and non-financial information. For the purpose of this ISA (UK and Ireland), such other financial and non-financial information is called "other information."

4-1. When the auditor reads the other information, the auditor does so in the light of the knowledge the auditor has acquired during the audit. The auditor is not expected to verify any of the other information. The audit engagement partner (and, where appropriate, other senior members of the engagement team who can reasonably be expected to be aware of the more important matters arising during the audit and to have a general understanding of the entity's affairs), reads the other information with a view to identifying significant misstatements therein or matters which are inconsistent with the financial statements.

4-2. Guidance to auditors in the UK and Ireland on the consideration of other information where the annual financial statements accompanied by the auditor's report are published on an entity's website, or in Great Britain where companies can meet their statutory reporting obligations to shareholders by distributing annual financial statements and certain other reports electronically, is given in the Appendix to this Section[2].

5. Examples of other information include a report by management or those charged with governance on operations, financial summaries or highlights, employment data, planned capital expenditures, financial ratios, names of officers and directors and selected quarterly data.

---

[2] In Great Britain The Companies Act (Electronic Communications) Order 2000 enables companies to meet, subject to certain conditions, their statutory reporting obligations to shareholders by distributing annual financial statements and certain other reports electronically, or to post their financial statements on their web site and advise shareholders of this.

5-1. Further examples relevant in the UK and Ireland are a directors' report required by statute (see Section B), statements relating to corporate governance, as required by the Listing Rules, a chairman's statement, a voluntary Operating and Financial Review and non-statutory financial information included within the annual report[3].

5-2. If the auditor believes that the other information is misleading, and the auditor is unable to resolve the matter with management and those charged with governance, the auditor considers the implications for the auditor's report and what further actions may be appropriate. The auditor has regard to the guidance in paragraphs 18-5 and 18-6 below.

6. In certain circumstances, the auditor has a statutory or contractual obligation to report specifically on other information. In other circumstances, the auditor has no such obligation. However, the auditor needs to give consideration to such other information when issuing a report on the financial statements, as the credibility of the audited financial statements may be undermined by inconsistencies which may exist between the audited financial statements and other information.

6-1. The credibility of the audited financial statements may also be undermined by misstatements within the other information.

7. Some jurisdictions require the auditor to apply specific procedures to certain of the other information, for example, required supplementary data and interim financial information. If such other information is omitted or contains deficiencies, the auditor may be required to refer to the matter in the auditor's report.

7-1. In the UK and Ireland an example of this type of work for a listed company would include the auditor's review of whether the Corporate Governance Statement reflects the company's compliance with the provisions of the Combined Code specified by the Listing Rules for review by the auditor.

8. When there is an obligation to report specifically on other information, the auditor's responsibilities are determined by the nature of the engagement and by local legislation and professional standards. When such responsibilities involve the review of other information, the auditor will need to follow the guidance on review engagements in the appropriate ISAs (UK and Ireland).

---

[3] The APB recognises that in some circumstances the presentation of non-statutory financial information and associated narrative explanations with the statutory results may help shareholders understand better the financial performance of a company. However, the APB is concerned that in other circumstances such non-statutory information in annual reports has the potential to be misleading and shareholders may sometimes be misinformed by the manner in which non-statutory information is presented. The APB believes that the potential for non-statutory information to be misleading is considerable when undue and inappropriate prominence is given to the non-statutory information, when there is no description of the non-statutory information and, where appropriate, the adjusted numbers are not reconciled to the statutory financial information.

Access to Other Information

9.   In order that an auditor can consider other information included in the annual report, timely access to such information will be required. The auditor therefore needs to make appropriate arrangements with the entity to obtain such information prior to the date of the auditor's report[4]. In certain circumstances, all the other information may not be available prior to such date. In these circumstances, the auditor would follow the guidance in paragraphs 20-23[5].

Consideration of Other Information

10.   The objective and scope of an audit of financial statements are formulated on the premise that the auditor's responsibility is restricted to information identified in the auditor's report. Accordingly, the auditor has no specific responsibility to determine that other information is properly stated.

Material Inconsistencies

11.   **If, on reading the other information, the auditor identifies a material inconsistency, the auditor should determine whether the audited financial statements or the other information needs to be amended.**

11-1.   **If the auditor identifies a material inconsistency the auditor should seek to resolve the matter through discussion with those charged with governance.**

11-2.   If the auditor concludes that the other information contains inconsistencies with the financial statements, and the auditor is unable to resolve them through discussion with those charged with governance, the auditor considers requesting those charged with governance to consult with a qualified third party, such as the entity's legal counsel and considers the advice received.

12.   **If an amendment is necessary in the audited financial statements and the entity refuses to make the amendment, the auditor should express a qualified or adverse opinion.**

13.   **If an amendment is necessary in the other information and the entity refuses to make the amendment, the auditor should consider including in the auditor's report an emphasis of matter paragraph describing the material inconsistency or taking other actions.** The actions taken, such as not issuing the auditor's report or withdrawing from the engagement, will depend upon the particular circumstances and the nature and significance of the inconsistency. The auditor would also consider obtaining legal advice as to further action.

---

[4]   ISA (UK and Ireland) 700 requires that "The auditor should not date the report earlier than the date on which all other information contained in a report of which the audited financial statements form a part have been approved by those charged with governance and the auditor has considered all necessary available evidence.'

[5]   Paragraphs 19 to 23 are not applicable in an audit conducted in compliance with ISAs(UK and Ireland).

13-1. In circumstances where the auditor has no issues with the financial statements themselves, and the emphasis of matter is being used to report on matters other than those affecting the financial statements, an emphasis of matter paragraph in relation to a material inconsistency does not give rise to a qualified audit opinion.

Material Misstatements of Fact

14. While reading the other information for the purpose of identifying material inconsistencies, the auditor may become aware of an apparent material misstatement of fact.

15. For the purpose of this ISA(UK and Ireland), a "material misstatement of fact" in other information exists when such information, not related to matters appearing in the audited financial statements, is incorrectly stated or presented.

15-1. A material misstatement of fact in other information would potentially include an inconsistency between information obtained by the auditor during the audit (such as information obtained as part of the planning process or analytical procedures, or as management representations) and information which is included in the other information.

16. **If the auditor becomes aware that the other information appears to include a material misstatement of fact, the auditor should discuss the matter with the entity's management**[6] When discussing the matter with the entity's management, the auditor may not be able to evaluate the validity of the other information and management's responses to the auditor's inquiries, and would need to consider whether valid differences of judgment or opinion exist.

16-1. **The auditor should consider whether the other information requires to be amended.**

17. **When the auditor still considers that there is an apparent misstatement of fact, the auditor should request management[7] to consult with a qualified third party, such as the entity's legal counsel and should consider the advice received.**

18. **If the auditor concludes that there is a material misstatement of fact in the other information which management refuses to correct, the auditor should consider taking further appropriate action.** The actions taken could include such steps as notifying those charged with governance in writing of the auditor's concern regarding the other information and obtaining legal advice.

---

[6] In the UK and Ireland the auditor discusses such matters with, and obtains responses from, those charged with governance.

[7] In the UK and Ireland the auditor requests those charged with governance to consult with a qualified third party.

18-1.   In the UK and Ireland the auditor requests those charged with governance to correct any material misstatements of fact in the other information.

18-2.   **If an amendment is necessary in the other information and the entity refuses to make the amendment, the auditor should consider including in the auditor's report an emphasis of matter paragraph describing the material misstatement.**

18-3.   In circumstances where the auditor has no issues with the financial statements, and the emphasis of matter is being used to report on matters other than those affecting the financial statements, an emphasis of matter paragraph in relation to a material misstatement of fact in the other information does not give rise to a qualified audit opinion.

18-4.   The auditor has regard to the nature of the inconsistency or misstatement that in the auditor's opinion exists. A distinction may be drawn between a matter of fact and one of judgment. It is generally more difficult for the auditor to take issue with a matter of judgment (such as the view of those charged with governance of the likely out-turn for the following year) than a factual error. Although an auditor does not substitute the auditor's judgment for that of those charged with governance in such matters, there may be circumstances in which the auditor is aware that the expressed view of those charged with governance is significantly at variance with the entity's internal assessment or is so unreasonable as not to be credible to someone with the auditor's knowledge.

Further Actions Available to the Auditor

18-5.   The auditor of a limited company in the United Kingdom or the Republic of Ireland may use the auditor's right to be heard at any general meeting of the members on any part of the business of the meeting which concerns the auditor as auditor[8].

18-6.   The auditor may also consider resigning from the audit engagement. In the case of auditors of limited companies in the United Kingdom or the Republic of Ireland, the requirements for the auditor to make a statement on ceasing to hold office as auditor apply[9]. When making a statement in these circumstances, the considerations set out in paragraph 18-4 above would normally be applicable.

Availability of Other Information After the Date of the Auditor's Report

Paragraphs 19 to 23 are not applicable in an audit conducted in accordance with ISAs (UK and Ireland). ISA (UK and Ireland) 700, "The Auditor's Report on Financial Statements" requires that "The auditor should not date the report earlier than the date on which all other information contained in a report of which the audited financial statements forma part have been approved by those charged with governance and the auditor has considered all necessary available evidence.".

---

[8]   The relevant reference for Great Britain is section 390 of the Companies Act 1985, for Northern Ireland is Article 398 of the Companies (Northern Ireland) Order 1986 and for the Republic of Ireland is section 193(5) of the Companies Act 1990.

[9]   The relevant reference for Great Britain is section 394 of the Companies Act 1985, for Northern Ireland is Article 401A of the Companies (Northern Ireland) Order 1986 and for the Republic of Ireland is section 185 of the Companies Act 1990.

19. When all the other information is not available to the auditor prior to the date of the auditor's report, the auditor would read the other information at the earliest possible opportunity thereafter to identify material inconsistencies.

20. If, on reading the other information, the auditor identifies a material inconsistency or becomes aware of an apparent material misstatement of fact, the auditor would determine whether the audited financial statements or the other information need revision.

21. When revision of the audited financial statements is appropriate, the guidance in ISA (UK and Ireland) 560, "Subsequent Events" would be followed.

22. When revision of the other information is necessary and the entity agrees to make the revision, the auditor would carry out the audit procedures necessary under the circumstances. The audit procedures may include reviewing the steps taken by management to ensure that individuals in receipt of the previously issued financial statements, the auditor's report thereon and the other information are informed of the revision.

23. **When revision of the other information is necessary but management refuses to make the revision, the auditor should consider taking further appropriate action.** The actions taken could include such steps as notifying those charged with governance in writing of the auditor's concern regarding the other information and obtaining legal advice.

Effective Date

23-1. This Section of this ISA (UK and Ireland) is effective for audits of financial statements for periods commencing on or after 1 April 2005 and ending on or after 31 March 2006.

Public Sector Perspective

Additional guidance for auditors of public sector bodies in the UK and Ireland is given in:

- Practice Note 10 "Audit of Financial Statements of Public Sector Bodies in the United Kingdom (Revised)"

- Practice Note 10(I) "Audit of Central Government Financial Statements in the Republic of Ireland (Revised)"

1. This ISA (UK and Ireland) is applicable in the context of the audit of financial statements. In the public sector, the auditor may often have a statutory or contractual obligation to report specifically on other information. As paragraph 8 of Section A of this ISA (UK and Ireland) indicates, the procedures stated in this ISA (UK and Ireland) would not be adequate to satisfy legislative or other audit requirements related to, for example, the expression of an opinion on the reliability of performance indicators and

other information contained in the annual report. It would be inappropriate to apply this ISA (UK and Ireland) in circumstances where the auditor does have an obligation to express an opinion on such information. In the absence of specific auditing requirements in relation to "other information," the broad principles contained in this ISA (UK and Ireland) are applicable.

**THE AUDITING
PRACTICES BOARD**

Appendix

Electronic Publication of the Auditor's Report

Introduction

1. In Great Britain The Companies Act 1985 (Electronic Communications) Order 2000 (the Electronic Communications Order) enables companies to meet, subject to certain conditions, their statutory reporting obligations to shareholders by distributing annual financial statements and certain other reports[10] electronically, or to post their financial statements on their web site and advise shareholders of this.

2. Various types of financial information can be found on web sites including information that has been audited (for example the annual financial statements), information which the auditor may have reviewed (for example interim financial information) and information with which the auditor has had no direct involvement, such as financial highlights from a company's Annual Report or may never have seen, such as presentations for analysts. In addition, web sites typically contain a considerable amount of non-financial information.

3. The purpose of this Appendix is to provide guidance to auditors on the consideration of other information not only if companies decide to take advantage of the Electronic Communications Order, but also in the more common current situation where the annual financial statements accompanied by the auditor's report are published on an entity's web site[11].

The Auditor's Consideration of Other Information Issued with the Annual Report

Checking Information Presented Electronically

4. When companies include the annual financial statements and the auditor's report on their web site or, in Great Britain, decide to distribute annual financial statements to their shareholders electronically, the auditor:

    (a) Reviews the process by which the financial statements to be published electronically are derived from the financial information contained in the manually signed accounts;

    (b) Checks that the proposed electronic version is identical in content with the manually signed accounts; and

    (c) Checks that the conversion of the manually signed accounts into an electronic format has not distorted the overall presentation of the financial information, for example, by highlighting certain information so as to give it greater prominence.

---

[10] Other reports include Summary Financial Statements.
[11] This guidance is generally applicable both to auditors in Great Britain (where the Electronic Communications Order applies) and in Northern Ireland and the Republic of Ireland (where it does not).

5.   It is recommended that the auditor retains a printout or disk of the final electronic version for future reference if necessary.

Auditor's Report Wording

6.   The auditor considers whether the wording of the auditor's report is suitable for electronic distribution. Issues include:

*   Identifying the financial statements that have been audited and the information that has been reviewed, or read, by the auditor.

*   Identifying the nationality of the accounting and auditing standards applied.

*   Limiting the auditor's association with any other information distributed with the Annual Report.

Identification of the Financial Statements That Have Been Audited

7.   In Annual Reports produced in a hard copy format, the auditor's report usually identifies the financial statements which have been audited by reference to page numbers. The use of page numbers is often not a suitable method of identifying particular financial information presented on a web site[12] The auditor's report therefore needs to specify in another way the location and description of the information that has been audited.

8.   The APB recommends that the auditor's report describes, by name, the primary statements that comprise the financial statements. The same technique can also be used to specify the information that has been reviewed or, because it is included in the Annual Report, read by the auditor.

9.   The auditor ensures that the auditor's statutory report on the full financial statements is not associated with extracts from, or summaries of, those audited financial statements.

Identification of the Nationality of the Accounting and Auditing Standards Applied

10. Auditor's reports on web sites will be accessible internationally, and it is therefore important that the auditor's report indicates clearly the nationality of the accounting standards used in the preparation of the financial statements and the nationality of the auditing standards applied. For the same reason, the auditor ensures that the auditor's report discloses sufficient of the auditor's address to enable readers to understand in which country the auditor is located.

---

[12] The audited financial statements can be presented on the web site using a variety of webfile formats. As at the date of this Bulletin, examples of these are the Portable Document Format (PDF) or Hypertext Mark-up Language (HTML). Page numbers generally continue to be an effective referencing mechanism for PDF files but this is not always the case when data is represented in HTML.

Limitation of the Auditor's Association With any Other Information Distributed With the Annual Report

11. In addition to the Annual Report many companies publish on their web sites a considerable volume of financial and non-financial information. This information could take the form of additional analyses or alternative presentations of audited financial information. Users of the web site are likely to find it difficult to distinguish financial information which the auditor has audited, or read, from other data. This issue is exacerbated when there are hyperlinks which allow users to move easily from one area of the web site to another.

12. The auditor gives careful consideration to the use of hyperlinks between the audited financial statements and information contained on the web site that has not been subject to audit or 'reading' by the auditor ('other information'). To avoid possible misunderstandings concerning the scope of the audit, the auditor requests those charged with governance to ensure that hyperlinks contain warnings that the linkage is from audited to unaudited information.

13. Sometimes audited information is not included in the financial statements themselves (e.g. certain information relating to directors' remuneration may be set out as part of a company's corporate governance disclosures). The APB is of the view that companies should be encouraged to make disclosures that are required to be audited, as part of the financial statements or included in the Annual Report in such a way that it is clear which elements of it have been audited. In other circumstances the auditor assesses whether the scope of the audit will be capable of being clearly described. If this cannot be achieved to the satisfaction of the auditor it may be necessary to describe the particulars that have been audited within the auditor's report.

14. The auditor is concerned to establish that the auditor's report on the financial statements is not inappropriately associated with other information. The auditor takes steps to satisfy themselves that information that they have audited or, because it is included in the Annual Report, read, is distinguished from other information in a manner appropriate to the electronic format used by the entity. Techniques that can be used to differentiate material within a web site include

- Icons or watermarks.

- Colour borders.

- Labels/banners such as 'annual report' or 'audited financial statements'.

The appropriate mode of differentiation between audited and unaudited information will be dependent on the electronic format selected, and the nature and extent of other information presented on the web site. The method of differentiation would normally also be clearly stated in an introduction page within the web site.

15. During the course of the audit, the auditor discusses with the those charged with governance or, where appropriate, the audit committee how the financial statements and auditor's report will be presented on the entity's web site with a view to minimizing

the possibility that the auditor's report is inappropriately associated with other information. If the auditor is not satisfied with the proposed electronic presentation of the audited financial statements and auditor's report, the auditor requests that the presentation be amended. If the presentation is not amended the auditor will, in accordance with the terms of the engagement, not give consent for the electronic release of the audit opinion.

16. If the auditor's report is used without the auditor's consent, and the auditor has concerns about the electronic presentation of the audited financial statements or the auditor's report and appropriate action is not taken by those charged with governance, the auditor seeks legal advice as necessary. The auditor also considers whether it would be appropriate to resign.

SECTION B - THE AUDITOR'S STATUTORY REPORTING RESPONSIBILITY IN RELATION TO DIRECTORS' REPORTS

Introduction

1. The purpose of this Section of this International Standard on Auditing (UK and Ireland) (ISA (UK and Ireland)) is to establish standards and provide guidance on the auditor's statutory reporting responsibility in relation to directors' reports.

2. In the United Kingdom and the Republic of Ireland, legislation[13] requires the auditor of a company to state in the auditor's report whether, in the auditor's opinion, the information given in the directors' report is consistent with the financial statements.

3. "Information given in the directors' report" includes information that is included by way of cross reference to other information presented separately from the directors' report. For example, a UK company may decide to present a voluntary Operating and Financial Review (OFR) which includes some or all of the matters required for the Business Review section of the directors' report. Rather than duplicate the information, the company may cross refer from the Business Review section in the directors' report to the relevant information provided in the OFR.

4. The auditor is not required to verify, or report on, the completeness of the information in the directors' report. If, however, the auditor becomes aware that information that is required by law or regulations to be in the directors' report has been omitted the auditor communicates the matter to those charged with governance. This communication includes situations where the required information is presented separately from the directors' report without appropriate cross references.

The Auditor's Procedures

5. **The auditor should read the information in the directors' report and assess whether it is consistent with the financial statements.**

6. Much of the information in the directors' report is likely to be extracted or directly derived from the financial statements and will therefore be directly comparable with them. Some financial information may, however, be more detailed or prepared on a different basis from that in the financial statements. Where the financial information is more detailed, the auditor agrees the information to the auditor's working papers or the entity's accounting records. Where the financial information has been prepared on a different basis, the auditor considers whether there is adequate disclosure of the

---

[13] Relevant legislation includes:
  * In Great Britain, with effect for financial years that commence on after 1 April 2005, section 235 of the Companies Act 1985 as amended by "The Companies Act 1985 (Operating and Financial Review and Directors' Report etc.) Regulations 2005" (SI 2005/1011).
  * In Northern Ireland, with effect for financial years that commence on after 1 April 2005, Article 243 of the Companies (Northern Ireland) Order 1986 as amended by "The Companies (1986 Order) (Operating and Financial Review and Directors' Report etc.) Regulations (Northern Ireland) 2005" (Statutory Rule 2005 No.61).
  * In the Republic of Ireland, Section 15 of the Companies (Amendment) Act 1986.

differences in the bases of preparation to enable an understanding of the differences in the information, and checks the reconciliation of the information to the financial statements.

7. **If the auditor identifies any inconsistencies between the information in the directors' report and the financial statements the auditor should seek to resolve them.**

8. Inconsistencies include:

    - Differences between amounts or narrative appearing in the financial statements and the directors' report.

    - Differences between the bases of preparation of related items appearing in the financial statements and the directors' report, where the figures themselves are not directly comparable and the different bases are not disclosed.

    - Contradictions between figures contained in the financial statements and narrative explanations of those figures in the directors' report.

    The auditor ordinarily seeks to resolve inconsistencies through discussion with management and those charged with governance.

9. **If the auditor is of the opinion that the information in the directors' report is materially inconsistent[14] with the financial statements, and has been unable to resolve the inconsistency, the auditor should state that opinion and describe the inconsistency in the auditor's report.**

10. **If an amendment is necessary to the financial statements and management and those charged with governance refuse to make the amendment, the auditor should express a qualified or adverse opinion on the financial statements.**

11. The Appendix to this Section includes illustrative wording for the auditor's report. Example A, where the auditor has concluded that information in the directors' report is consistent with the information in the financial statements. Example B, where the auditor has concluded that information in the directors' report is not consistent with the information in the financial statements.

Documentation

12. **The auditor should document:**

    (a) **The results of those procedures performed to assess whether the information in the directors' report is consistent with the financial statements, including details of any material inconsistencies identified and how they were resolved; and**

---

[14] Materiality is addressed in ISA (UK and Ireland) 320 "Audit Materiality". An inconsistency is "material" if it could influence the economic decisions of users.

   (b)   **The conclusion reached as to whether the information in the directors' report
         is consistent with the financial statements.**

Effective Date

13.   This Section of this ISA (UK and Ireland) is effective for audits of financial statements
      for periods commencing on or after 1 April 2005 and ending on or after 31 March 2006.

Appendix

Illustrative Wording for the Auditor's Report

Example A. Extracts from an auditor's report with an unmodified opinion on the directors' report

Respective responsibilities of directors and auditors

[*Details of other responsibilities as are applicable – for examples see the illustrative reports in the APB Bulletin "Auditor's Reports on Financial Statements in Great Britain and Northern Ireland"*[15]]

We report to you whether in our opinion the information given in the directors' report is consistent with the financial statements. [The information given in the directors' report includes that specific information presented in the Operating and Financial Review that is cross referred from the Business Review section of the directors' report.[16]]

Basis of audit opinion

.....

Opinion

In our opinion:

- [*Opinion on the financial statements and other opinions, if any, that are required.*]

- The information given in the directors' report is consistent with the financial statements.

---

[15] Illustrative reports for the Republic of Ireland are given in the APB Bulletin "Auditor's Reports on Financial Statements in the Republic of Ireland".

[16] Include and tailor as necessary to clarify the information covered by the auditor's opinion.

Example B - Extracts from an auditor's report with a modified opinion on the directors' report (financial statements prepared under UK GAAP)

Respective responsibilities of directors and auditors

[Details of other responsibilities as are applicable – for examples see the illustrative reports in the APB Bulletin "Auditor's Reports on Financial Statements in Great Britain and Northern Ireland"[3]]

We report to you whether in our opinion the information given in the directors' report is consistent with the financial statements. [The information given in the directors' report includes that specific information presented in the Operating and Financial Review that is cross referred from the Business Review section of the directors' report.[4]]

Basis of audit opinion

.....

Opinion

In our opinion:

- [*Opinion on the financial statements and other opinions, if any, that are required.*]

Material inconsistency between the financial statements and the directors' report

In our opinion, the information given in the seventh paragraph of the Business Review in the directors' report is not consistent with the financial statements. That paragraph states without amplification that "the company's trading for the period resulted in a 10% increase in profit over the previous period's profit". The profit and loss account, however, shows that the company's profit for the period includes a profit of £Z which did not arise from trading but arose from the disposal of assets of a discontinued operation. Without this profit on the disposal of assets the company would have reported a profit for the year of £Y, representing a reduction in profit of 25% over the previous period's profit on a like for like basis. Except for this matter, in our opinion the information given in the directors' report is consistent with the financial statements.

Section 5: STANDARDS FOR INVESTMENT REPORTING

2006 ACTIVITIES

Ethical Standards

As discussed on page 15, in October 2006 the ESRA was issued in final form. The ESRA represents the 'applicable ethical standards issued by the Auditing Practices Board' referred to in paragraph 18 of SIR 1000, *'Investment Reporting Standards Applicable to All Engagements in Connection with an Investment Circular'*. The ESRA is included in Section 3 of this Compendium.

Application of the SIRs to the Republic of Ireland

The SIRs have been drafted with reference to legislation and regulations implementing the Prospectus Directive in the United Kingdom. Bulletin 2006/4, *'Regulatory and Legislative Background to the Application of Standards for Investment Reporting in the Republic of Ireland'*, which was published in April 2006, provides an explanation of the background to the legislative and regulatory environment in Ireland and provides a mapping of legislative and technical references within the SIRs, as published, to the Irish equivalent.

STANDARDS FOR INVESTMENT REPORTING

1000 – INVESTMENT REPORTING STANDARDS APPLICABLE TO ALL ENGAGEMENTS IN CONNECTION WITH AN INVESTMENT CIRCULAR

CONTENTS

SIR 1000 contains basic principles and essential procedures ("Investment Reporting Standards"), indicated by paragraphs in bold type, with which a reporting accountant is required to comply in the conduct of all engagements in connection with an investment circular prepared for issue in connection with a securities transaction governed wholly or in part by the laws and regulations of the United Kingdom.

SIR 1000 also includes explanatory and other material, including appendices, in the context of which the basic principles and essential procedures are to be understood and applied. It is necessary to consider the whole text of the SIR to understand and apply the basic principles and essential procedures.

The definitions in the glossary of terms set out in Appendix 4 are to be applied in the interpretation of this and all other SIRs. Terms defined in the glossary are underlined the first time that they occur in the text.

This SIR replaces SIR 100 "Investment circulars and reporting accountants" issued in December 1997.

To assist readers, SIRs contain references to, and extracts from, certain legislation and chapters of the Rules of the UK Listing Authority. Readers are cautioned that these references may change subsequent to publication.

Introduction

1. The application of Standards for Investment Reporting (SIRs) is best understood by reference to the following four defined terms used throughout the SIRs:

    (a) **investment circular** is a generic term defined as *"Any document issued by an entity pursuant to statutory or regulatory requirements relating to securities on which it is intended that a third party should make an investment decision, including a prospectus, listing particulars, a circular to shareholders or similar document"*;

    (b) **reporting accountant** is defined as *"An accountant engaged to prepare a report for inclusion in, or in connection with, an investment circular. The reporting accountant may or may not be the auditor of the entity issuing the investment circular. The term "reporting accountant" is used to describe either the engagement partner or the engagement partner's firm[1]. The reporting accountant could be a limited company or an engagement principal employed by the company;*

    (c) **public reporting engagement** is defined as *"An engagement in which a reporting accountant expresses a conclusion that is published in an investment circular, and which is designed to enhance the degree of confidence of the intended users of*

---

[1] Where the term applies to the engagement partner, it describes the responsibilities or obligations of the engagement partner. Such obligations or responsibilities may be fulfilled by either the engagement partner or a member of the engagement partner's team.

the report about the 'outcome²' of the directors' evaluation or measurement of 'subject matter' against 'suitable criteria'"; and

(d) **private reporting engagement** is defined as *"An engagement, in connection with an investment circular, in which a reporting accountant does not express a conclusion that is published in an investment circular".* Private reporting engagements are likely to involve the reporting accountant reporting privately to one or more of an issuer, sponsor or regulator.

2. In order to provide flexibility to develop SIRs for a wide range of possible public reporting engagements, the description of public reporting engagement includes three generic terms. Their meanings are as follows:

(a) the **"subject matter"** of the engagement is that which is being evaluated or measured against suitable criteria. Examples of subject matter are the entity's financial position and the directors' expectation of the issuer's profit for the period covered by a profit forecast;

(b) criteria are the benchmarks used to evaluate or measure the subject matter. **"Suitable criteria"** are usually derived from laws and regulations and are required by directors to enable them to make reasonably consistent evaluations or measurements of the subject matter. With respect to public reporting engagements the suitable criteria for specific types of engagement are described in the individual SIR dealing with such engagements. Where the reporting accountant's engagement requires it to consider only certain criteria, such criteria are described as "reporting accountant's criteria". Reporting accountant's criteria are set out in the SIRs. Where a SIR has not been issued with respect to a particular type of reporting engagement, the reporting accountant uses those criteria that are specified by legislation or regulation. The evaluation or measurement of a subject matter solely on the basis of the reporting accountant's own expectations, judgments and individual experience would not constitute suitable criteria; and

(c) the **"outcome"** of the evaluation or measurement of a subject matter is the information that results from the directors applying the suitable criteria to the subject matter. Examples of outcomes are historical financial information and a directors' profit forecast and related disclosures that are included in an investment circular.

3. Not all engagements performed by a reporting accountant are public reporting engagements. Examples of engagements that are not public reporting engagements include:

• Engagements involving the preparation of a comfort letter.

• Engagements involving the preparation of a long form report.

---

² The "outcome" is sometimes described as "subject matter information."

Such engagements are private reporting engagements.

4.   This SIR establishes basic principles and essential procedures for the work of reporting accountants that are common to all reporting engagements (both public and private) relating to investment circulars. Other SIRs set out basic principles and essential procedures to address the particular issues and requirements arising on specific public reporting engagements. These comprise:

(a)   SIR 2000 "Investment reporting standards applicable to public reporting engagements on historical financial information";

(b)   SIR 3000 "Investment reporting standards applicable to public reporting engagements on profit forecasts"; and

(c)   SIR 4000 "Investment reporting standards applicable to public reporting engagements on pro forma financial information.

5.   Appendix 1 summarises public reporting engagements that reporting accountants may be required to undertake under the Prospectus Rules.

Engagement acceptance and continuance

6.   **The reporting accountant should accept (or continue where applicable) a reporting engagement only if, on the basis of a preliminary knowledge of the engagement circumstances, nothing comes to the attention of the reporting accountant to indicate that the requirements of relevant ethical standards and guidance, issued by the Auditing Practices Board and the professional bodies of which the reporting accountant is a member, will not be satisfied. (SIR 1000.1)**

7.   **The reporting accountant should accept (or continue where applicable) a reporting engagement only if:**

(a)   **the scope of the engagement is expected to be sufficient to support the required report;**

(b)   **the reporting accountant expects to be able to carry out the procedures required by the SIRs; and**

(c)   **those persons who are to perform the engagement collectively possess the necessary professional competencies. (SIR 1000.2)**

8.   In determining whether the scope of the engagement is expected to be sufficient to support the required report, the reporting accountant considers whether there appear to be any significant limitations on the scope of the reporting accountant's work.

9.   A reporting accountant may be requested to perform reporting engagements on a wide range of matters. Some engagements may require specialised skills and

knowledge. In these circumstances the reporting accountant considers using internal or external specialists having the appropriate skills.

Agreeing the terms of the engagement

10. **The reporting accountant should agree the terms of the engagement with those from whom they accept instructions. All the terms of the engagement should be recorded in writing. (SIR 1000.3)**

11. Generally, a letter is prepared by the reporting accountant, covering all aspects of the engagement, and accepted in writing by the directors of the issuer and, where relevant, the sponsor. With respect to a public reporting engagement the letter will record the reporting accountant's understanding of what constitutes the subject matter of the engagement, the suitable criteria, and the information that constitutes the outcome of the evaluation or measurement of the subject matter against the suitable criteria.

12. As an alternative to a letter drafted by the reporting accountant, an instruction letter may be issued by the directors and, where relevant, the sponsor. In these circumstances, its terms are formally acknowledged by the reporting accountant in writing, clarifying particular aspects of the instructions and covering any matters that may not have been addressed.

13. This letter, or exchange of letters (together referred to as "the engagement letter"), provides evidence of the contractual relationship between the reporting accountant, the entity and, where relevant, the sponsor. It sets out clearly the scope and limitations of the work to be performed by the reporting accountant. It also confirms the reporting accountant's acceptance of the engagement and includes a summary of the reporting accountant's responsibilities and those of the directors and, where relevant, the sponsor as they relate to the reporting accountant's role.

14. The engagement letter establishes a direct responsibility to the other parties from the reporting accountant. It is also the mechanism by which the scope of the reporting accountant's contribution is defined and agreed. If in the course of the engagement the terms of the engagement are changed, such changes are similarly agreed, and recorded in writing.

15. The engagement letter will usually set out the form of any reports (public or private) required (including, in each case, the nature of any opinion to be expressed by the reporting accountant). Accordingly, it is important to clarify those from whom the reporting accountant has agreed to accept instructions including, where relevant, sponsors, and determine their requirements and the scope of such reports, at an early stage.

16. **The engagement letter should specify those reports that are intended for publication in the investment circular and any other reports that are required. The engagement letter should specify, in respect of each report, to whom it is to be addressed. (SIR 1000.4)**

17. The engagement letter sets out the express terms governing the reporting accountant's contractual responsibilities in connection with the transaction to those instructing them. Reporting accountants do not accept responsibility beyond the matters or entities in respect of which they are specifically instructed. Nor are they expected to comment or report on matters which more properly fall within the skill and experience of other experts or advisers. They understand, however, the need to apply their own professional skill and experience in interpreting and carrying out their instructions. The reporting accountant may find information outside the defined scope of the engagement that it believes should be disclosed, because, in its view such information is material to the purpose of the investment circular or to the proposed transaction. The reporting accountant discusses such matters with the directors of the issuer and the sponsor, where relevant, and agrees a course of action.

Ethical requirements

18. **In the conduct of an engagement involving an investment circular, the reporting accountant should comply with the applicable ethical standards issued by the Auditing Practices Board. The reporting accountant should also adhere to the relevant ethical guidance of the professional bodies of which the reporting accountant is a member. (SIR 1000.5)**

19. While it is not the responsibility of the reporting accountant to judge the appropriateness, or otherwise, of a proposed transaction, in respect of which they have been engaged, there may be rare circumstances where a reporting accountant considers the proposed transaction, or their proposed association with the transaction, to be so inappropriate that the reporting accountant cannot properly commence work or continue to act.

Legal and regulatory requirements

20. **The reporting accountant should be familiar with the applicable laws and regulations governing the report which is to be given. (SIR 1000.6)**

21. The principal legal and regulatory requirements applicable to reporting accountants in the United Kingdom are summarised in Appendix 2. Readers are cautioned that these references may change subsequent to publication of this SIR.

Quality control

22. **The reporting accountant should comply with the applicable standards and guidance set out in International Standard on Quality Control (UK and Ireland) 1 and ISA (UK and Ireland) 220. (SIR 1000.7)**

23. International Standard on Quality Control (UK and Ireland) 1 "Quality control for firms that perform audits and reviews of historical financial information, and other assurance

and related services engagements" provides standards and guidance on the system of quality control that a firm establishes.

24. The quality control procedures that an engagement partner applies are those set out in ISA (UK and Ireland) 220 "Quality control for audits of historical financial information". In applying ISA (UK and Ireland) 220, the terms "audit" and "audit engagement" are read as "reporting accountant's engagement" and the term "auditor's report" is read as "reporting accountant's report".

25. **When undertaking any engagement involving an investment circular a <u>partner</u> with appropriate experience should be involved in the conduct of the work. (SIR 1000.8)**

26. Reporting accountants are frequently from a firm that is also the auditor of the entity. The audit partner, although having knowledge of the entity, may not have the necessary experience to take responsibility for all aspects of an engagement involving an investment circular. The extent of involvement of a partner with the requisite experience of dealing with investment circulars is determined, for example, by the expertise required to make the reports that the reporting accountant has agreed to provide and the experience of the audit partner.

27. In some cases it may be appropriate for the partner with the requisite experience of dealing with investment circulars to act as a second partner. In other cases it may be appropriate for such a partner to be the lead engagement partner.

Planning and performing the engagement

28. **The reporting accountant should develop and document a plan for the work so as to perform the engagement in an effective manner. (SIR 1000.9)**

29. Planning is an essential component of all reporting accountant's engagements. Examples of the main matters to be considered include:

- The terms of the engagement.

- Ethical considerations.

- Whether the timetable is realistic.

- The reporting accountant's understanding of the entity and its environment.

- Identifying potential problems that could impact the performance of the engagement.

- The need for the involvement of specialists.

30. Planning is not a discrete phase, but rather an iterative process throughout the engagement. As a result of unexpected events, changes in conditions or the evidence

obtained from the results of evidence-gathering procedures, the reporting accountant may need to revise the overall strategy and engagement plan, and thereby the resulting planned nature, timing and extent of further procedures.

31. A preliminary review of the available information may provide an indication of potential issues that might need to be addressed in carrying out the engagement. If the preliminary review indicates that there are factors which may give rise to a qualification or other modification of any report, then such factors are reported immediately to the directors and, where relevant, the sponsor.

32. Changes in circumstances, or unexpected results of work carried out, may require the plan to be amended as work progresses. Any such amendments are documented. Where the changes affect the work set out in the engagement letter, the engagement letter is also amended as necessary following agreement with the directors, and where relevant, the sponsor.

33. **The reporting accountant should consider materiality in planning its work in accordance with its instructions and in determining the effect of its findings on the report to be issued. (SIR 1000.10)**

34. Matters are material if their omission or misstatement could, individually or collectively, influence the economic decisions of users of the outcome. Materiality depends on the size and nature of the omission or misstatement judged in light of the surrounding circumstances. The size or nature of the matter, or a combination of both, could be the determining factor.

35. In certain circumstances, such as private reporting engagements to report the results of agreed-upon procedures, materiality may have been determined for the reporting accountant within the scope of the engagement.

36. **The reporting accountant should obtain sufficient appropriate evidence on which to base the report provided. (SIR 1000.11)**

37. The reporting accountant, either directly or indirectly, will seek to obtain evidence derived from one or more of the following procedures: inspection, observation, enquiry, confirmation, computation and analytical procedures. The choice of which of these, or which combination, is appropriate will depend on the circumstances of each engagement and on the form of opinion (if any) to be given. Guidance on considerations applicable in particular circumstances is given in other SIRs which address the particular issues and requirements arising on specific engagements.

38. The evidence gathered in support of an individual report takes account of the information gathered and conclusions drawn in support of other reporting engagements in connection with the transaction.

39. **If the reporting accountant becomes aware of any withholding, concealment or misrepresentation of information, it should take steps, as soon as practicable, to consider its obligation to report such findings and, if necessary, take legal advice to determine the appropriate response. (SIR 1000.12)**

40. In preparing any report the reporting accountant relies on information supplied to it by the directors, employees or agents of the entity that is the subject of the reporting accountant's enquiries. The engagement letter may limit the extent of the reporting accountant's responsibility where information which is material to the report has been withheld from, concealed from or misrepresented to the reporting accountant. Notwithstanding any such limitation, the reporting accountant does not accept such information without further inquiry where, applying its professional skill and experience to the engagement, the information provided, prima facie, gives rise to doubts about its validity.

41. The reporting accountant normally informs the directors of the issuer and the sponsor, where relevant, as soon as practicable, of any withholding, concealment or misrepresentation of information. The reporting accountant's duty of confidentiality would ordinarily preclude reporting to a third party. However, in certain circumstances, that duty of confidentiality is overridden by law, for example, in the case of suspected money laundering it may be appropriate to report the matter direct to the appropriate authority. The reporting accountant may need to seek legal advice in such circumstances, giving due consideration to any public interest considerations.

42. **The reporting accountant should obtain appropriate written confirmation of representations from the directors of the entity. (SIR 1000.13)**

43. Written confirmation of representations made by the directors on matters material to the reporting accountant's report is ordinarily obtained. These representations also encompass statements or opinions attributed to directors, management, employees or agents of an entity, which are relied upon by the reporting accountant.

44. This may be achieved by the directors confirming that they have read a final draft of the report and that to the best of their knowledge and belief:

    (a) they have made available to the reporting accountant all significant information, relevant to the report, of which they have knowledge;

    (b) the report is factually accurate, no material facts have been omitted and the report is not otherwise misleading; and

    (c) the report accurately reflects any opinion or statements attributed therein to the directors, management, employees or agents of the entity.

45. Representations by the directors of the entity cannot replace the evidence that the reporting accountant could reasonably expect to be available to support any opinion given, if any. An inability to obtain sufficient appropriate evidence regarding a matter could represent a limitation of scope even if a representation has been received on the matter.

Documentation

46. **The reporting accountant should document matters that are significant in providing evidence that supports the report provided and in providing evidence that the engagement was performed in accordance with SIRs. (SIR 1000.14)**

47. **The reporting accountant should record in the working papers (or, if applicable, the report) the reporting accountant's reasoning on all significant matters that require the exercise of judgment, and related conclusions. (SIR 1000.15)**

48. The information to be recorded in working papers is a matter of professional judgment since it is neither necessary nor practical to document every matter considered by the reporting accountant. When applying professional judgment in assessing the extent of documentation to be prepared and retained, the reporting accountant may consider what is necessary to provide an understanding of the work performed and the basis of the principal decisions taken to another person, such as a reporting accountant, who has no previous experience with the engagement. That other person may, however, only be able to obtain an understanding of detailed aspects of the engagement by discussing them with the reporting accountant who prepared the documentation.

49. The form and content of working papers are affected by matters such as:

    * The nature and scope of the engagement.

    * The form of the report and the opinion, if any, to be given.

    * The nature and complexity of the entity's business.

    * The nature and condition of the entity's accounting and internal control systems.

    * The needs in the particular circumstances for direction, supervision and review of the work of members of the reporting accountant's team.

    * The specific methodology and technology that the reporting accountant uses.

Professional scepticism

50. **The reporting accountant should plan and perform an engagement with an attitude of professional scepticism. (SIR 1000.16)**

51. An attitude of professional scepticism is essential to ensure that the reporting accountant makes a critical assessment, with a questioning mind, of the validity of evidence obtained and is alert to evidence that contradicts or brings into question the reliability of documents or representations.

52. Whilst the reporting accountant may proceed on the basis that information and explanations provided by the directors and management of the issuer are reliable, it assesses them critically and considers them in the context of its knowledge and

findings derived from other areas of its work. The reporting accountant is alert for, and, where appropriate reports, on a timely basis, to the directors and sponsors, where relevant, any inconsistencies it considers to be significant. The extent to which the reporting accountant is required to perform further procedures on the information and explanations received will depend upon the reporting accountant's specific instructions, and the level of assurance, if any, it is to provide and the requirements of relevant SIRs.

Reporting

53. **In all reports the reporting accountant should:**

    (a) **address reports only to those parties who are party to the engagement letter (and on the basis agreed in the engagement letter) or to a relevant regulatory body;**

    (b) **identify the matters to which the report relates;**

    (c) **address all matters that are required by the engagement letter;**

    (d) **explain the basis of the reporting accountant's work;**

    (e) **give, where applicable, a clear expression of opinion;**

    (f) **include the reporting accountant's manuscript or printed signature;**

    (g) **include the reporting accountant's address; and**

    (h) **date the report. (SIR 1000.17)**

54. **In all public reporting engagements the reporting accountant should explain the basis of the reporting accountant's opinion by including in its report:**

    (a) **a statement as to the reporting accountant's compliance, or otherwise, with applicable Standards for Investment Reporting; and**

    (b) **a summary description of the work performed by the reporting accountant. (SIR 1000.18)**

55. Certain of the reports prepared in connection with investment circulars are public reporting engagements and, therefore, intended for publication in the investment circular. Examples of such reports are accountant's reports, reports on profit forecasts and reports on pro forma financial information. Additional basic principles and essential procedures on the expression of opinions or conclusions relating to these example public reporting engagements are provided as follows:

    (a) accountant's reports on historical financial information, in SIR 2000;

    (b)   reports on profit forecasts, in SIR 3000; and

    (c)   reports on pro forma financial information, in SIR 4000.

56.   In private reporting engagements the reporting accountant would ordinarily include in its report:

    (a)   a statement of compliance with this SIR; and

    (b)   either a summary description of the work performed or a cross reference to the description of work to be performed in the engagement letter.

In some private reporting engagements those engaging the reporting accountant agree with the reporting accountant the procedures to be performed[3]. In such cases it may be unnecessary for the report of the reporting accountant to repeat the description of the procedures that is set out in the engagement letter.

57.   **Before signing the report, the reporting accountant should consider whether it is appropriate to make the required report, having regard to the scope of the work performed and the evidence obtained. (SIR 1000.19)**

58.   The date of a report is the date on which the reporting accountant signs the report as being suitable for release. However, the reporting accountant should not sign the report (whether modified or not) unless sufficient appropriate evidence has been obtained and all relevant procedures have been finalised. Such procedures include the review procedures of both the engagement partner and the engagement quality control reviewer.

59.   As noted in paragraph 15 above, the engagement letter usually sets out the form of the report to be issued, including, where applicable, the form of opinion to be expressed. The reporting accountant ensures that the form of report or opinion is consistent with the terms of the engagement letter.

60.   The level of assurance, if any, provided by the reporting accountant may vary from engagement to engagement. This reflects the wide range of characteristics of the matters to which the engagements undertaken by reporting accountants relate. To avoid any misunderstanding by the user of the report as to the scope of the opinion or the level of assurance provided, it is important that the matters to which the engagements undertaken by reporting accountants relate are clearly identified and that the reporting accountant's opinion or other assurance is expressed in terms that are appropriate to the particular engagement. Standards and guidance on the form and scope of reports appropriate in particular circumstances is given in other SIRs which address particular issues and requirements relevant to individual reports.

61.   In certain circumstances the Prospectus Rules require, "a declaration by those responsible for certain parts of the registration document that, having taken all

---

[3]   These are often referred to as "agreed-upon procedures engagements"

reasonable care to ensure that such is the case, the information contained in the part of the registration document for which they are responsible is, to the best of their knowledge, in accordance with the facts and contains no omission likely to affect its import". The reporting accountant is responsible for its reports included in investment circulars and ordinarily includes this declaration (when satisfied it is able to do so) at the end of each public report included in an investment circular to which the Prospectus Rules apply.

Modified opinions

62. **The reporting accountant should not express an unmodified opinion when the following circumstances exist and, in the reporting accountant's judgment, the effect of the matter is or may be material:**

    (a) **there is a limitation on the scope of the reporting accountant's work, that is, circumstances prevent, or there are restrictions imposed that prevent, the reporting accountant from obtaining evidence required to reduce engagement risk to the appropriate level; or**

    (b) **the outcome is materially misstated. (SIR 1000.20)**

63. Where not precluded by regulation, the reporting accountant expresses a qualified opinion when the effect of a matter described in paragraph 62 is not so material or pervasive as to require an adverse opinion or a disclaimer of opinion. When giving a qualified opinion, the opinion is expressed "except for" the matter to which the qualification relates.

64. Some regulations require a positive and unmodified opinion. Consequently, in the event that the reporting accountant is unable to report in the manner prescribed it considers, with the parties to whom it is to report, whether the outcome can be amended to alleviate its concerns, or whether the outcome should be omitted from the investment circular.

Pre-existing financial information

65. With respect to historical financial information, where the issuer already has available:

    (a) audited annual financial statements; or

    (b) audited or reviewed financial information, which meet the requirements of the applicable rules in respect of the preparation and presentation of historical financial information to be included in the investment circular,

    it may choose to include these financial statements, or financial information, in the investment circular together with the pre-existing reports of the auditor. In these circumstances the audit firm is not required by the Prospectus Rules to consent to the inclusion of its reports in the investment circular.

Consent

66. **Where the reporting accountant is required to give consent to the inclusion of its public report, or references to its name, in an investment circular the reporting accountant should, before doing so, consider its public report in the form and context in which it appears, or is referred to, in the investment circular as a whole by:**

    (a) **comparing its public report together with the information being reported on to the other information in the rest of the investment circular and assessing whether the reporting accountant has any cause to believe that such other information is inconsistent with the information being reported on; and**

    (b) **assessing whether the reporting accountant has any cause to believe that any information in the investment circular is misleading.**

    When the reporting accountant believes information in the investment circular is either inconsistent with its public report, together with the information being reported on, or misleading, the reporting accountant should withhold its consent until the reporting accountant is satisfied that its concerns are unwarranted or until the investment circular has been appropriately amended. (SIR 1000.21)

67. **The reporting accountant should give consent to the inclusion of any report in an investment circular only when all relevant reports that it has agreed to make, in that investment circular, have been finalised. (SIR 1000.22)**

68. In order to comply with the relevant legislation or regulations, the issuer of an investment circular may ask a reporting accountant to provide a consent letter, consenting to the inclusion of public reports in investment circulars in a number of different circumstances. An example consent letter is set out in Appendix 3. The various circumstances include:

    (a) under the Prospectus Rules. These relate to a prospectus issued by an issuer (other than under the Listing Rules). No consent is required to the inclusion of previously issued reports. Where a reporting accountant prepares an accountant's report on a financial information table for the purposes of the prospectus, the reporting accountant's consent must be obtained. A statement referring to the reporting accountant's consent to the inclusion of such report in the prospectus is required, by item 23.1 of Annex I of the Prospectus Rules, to be included in the Prospectus;

    (b) under the Listing Rules. Where these relate to listing particulars prepared in connection with an application for admission of securities to listing, the same consent requirements, that is item 23.1 of Annex I of the Prospectus Rules, apply;

    (c) under the Listing Rules. Where these relate to a Class 1 circular, paragraph 13.4.1 (6) of the Listing Rules sets out similar consent requirements;

(d) under the City Code. In connection with a takeover, Rule 28.4 requires a similar consent requirement in respect of a public report on a profit forecast. Rule 28.5 requires a similar consent in connection with a subsequent document issued in connection with the offer; and

(e) under the AIM Rules. The consent requirements of item 23.1 of Annex I of the Prospectus Rules apply.

69. Whilst the reporting accountant's reporting responsibilities do not extend beyond its report, the process of giving consent involves an awareness of the overall process whereby the investment circular is prepared, and may entail discussions with those responsible for the document as a whole in relation to its contents.

70. In deciding whether to give its consent, a reporting accountant reads the final version of the investment circular with a view to assessing the overall impression given by the document, having regard to the purposes for which it has been prepared, as well as considering whether there are any inconsistencies between its report and the information in the rest of the document. As part of this process the reporting accountant considers whether it has any cause to believe that any information in the investment circular may be misleading such that the reporting accountant would not wish to be associated with it.

71. For this purpose the engagement partner uses the knowledge of the partners and professional staff working on the engagement. If particular issues are identified the engagement partner may make enquiries of partners and professional staff previously engaged on the audit of financial statements that are the basis of financial information in the investment circular, and any other partners and professional staff who may have been previously consulted regarding such issues, including the engagement quality review partner who is independent of the engagement. The engagement partner is not expected to make enquiries more widely within the reporting accountant's firm.

72. Because of the degree of knowledge required and the increased responsibility that may be assumed, it is inappropriate for a reporting accountant to provide consent unless the reporting accountant has been commissioned to undertake work specifically in connection with the relevant document in relation to the matter for which consent is sought. Hence, if an investment circular includes a reference to a report or opinion, previously provided by the reporting accountant, which is already in the public domain, the reporting accountant is not expected to provide consent to the inclusion of that information and does not generally do so. As discussed in paragraph 65, an example would be the inclusion or incorporation by reference in a prospectus of a previously published audit report or interim review report.

73. An exception to this general rule would be where the reporting accountant has previously consented to the inclusion in an investment circular of that earlier report or opinion and it is being repeated or referred to in connection with the same transaction in respect of which it was originally issued. For example, as noted in paragraph 68 above, Rule 28.5 of the City Code requires a profit forecast made and reported on in one document to be confirmed in any subsequent document in connection with the same offer, and for the reporting accountant to indicate that it has no objection to its

report continuing to apply. In such a case, before issuing its consent the reporting accountant makes enquiries as to whether there have been any material events subsequent to the date of its original report which might require modification of or disclosure in that report.

74. Letters of consent are dated the same date as the relevant document. The City Code requires the letter of consent to be available for public inspection. The letter of consent may be made available for public inspection in other cases.

Events occurring between the date of the reporting accountant's report and the completion date of the transaction

75. **If, in the period between the date of the reporting accountant's report and the completion date of the transaction, the reporting accountant becomes aware of events and other matters which, had they occurred and been known at the date of the report, might have caused it to issue a different report or withhold consent, the reporting accountant should discuss the implications of them with those responsible for the investment circular and take additional action as appropriate. (SIR 1000.23)**

76. If, as a result of discussion with those responsible for the investment circular concerning an event that occurred prior to the completion date of the transaction, the reporting accountant is either uncertain about or disagrees with the course of action proposed, it may consider it necessary to take legal advice with respect to its responsibilities in the particular circumstances.

77. After the date of its report, the reporting accountant has no obligation to perform procedures or make enquiries regarding the investment circular.

Effective date

78. A reporting accountant is required to comply with the Investment Reporting Standards contained in this SIR for reports signed after 31 August 2005. Earlier adoption is encouraged.

Appendix 1

SUMMARY OF POSSIBLE REPORTING ACCOUNTANT'S PUBLIC REPORTING ENGAGEMENTS UNDER THE PROSPECTUS RULES

In the following table possible reporting accountant's responsibilities, as set out in the Prospectus Rules, are shaded.

Applicable annex:	Shares	Debt, units < €50k	Debt, units =/> €50k	Derivatives, units < €50K	Derivatives, units =/> €50K	Asset backed securities, units < €50k	Asset backed securities, units =/> €50k	Depository receipts, units < €50k	Depository receipts, units =/> €50k	Banks issuing anything other than equity securities
Registration document	I, II	IV	IX	IV	IX	VII	VII	X	X	XI
Securities note	III	V	XIII	XII	XII	VIII	VIII	X	X	As relevant instrument type
Historical financial information	I, 20.1	IV, 13.1	IX, 11.1	IV, 13.1	IX, 11.1	VII, 8.2	VII, 8.2 bis	X, 20.1	X, 20.1 bis	XI, 11.1
Number of years	3 years with latest 2 years on new GAAP	2 years with latest year on new GAAP	2 years with latest year on new GAAP	2 years with latest year on new GAAP	2 years with latest year on new GAAP	2 years with latest year on new GAAP	2 years with latest year on new GAAP	3 years with latest 2 years on new GAAP	3 years with latest 2 years on new GAAP	2 years with latest year on new GAAP

	Shares	Debt, units < €50k	Debt, units =/> €50k	Derivatives, units < €50k	Derivatives, units =/> €50K	Asset backed securities, units < €50k	Asset backed securities, units =/> €50k	Depository receipts, units < €50k	Depository receipts, units =/> €50k	Banks issuing anything other than equity securities
GAAP	National GAAP or IFRS[1] as applicable to EU issuer. IFRS or GAAP equivalent to IFRS for non-EU issuers	National GAAP or IFRS[1] as applicable to EU issuer. IFRS or GAAP equivalent to IFRS for non-EU issuers	National GAAP or IFRS[1] as applicable to EU issuer. Non-EU issuers may use local GAAP with a narrative description of differences	National GAAP or IFRS[1] as applicable to EU issuer. IFRS or GAAP equivalent to IFRS for non-EU issuers	National GAAP or IFRS[1] as applicable to EU issuer. Non-EU issuers may use local GAAP with a narrative description of differences	National GAAP or IFRS[1] as applicable to EU issuer. IFRS or GAAP equivalent to IFRS for non-EU issuers	National GAAP or IFRS[1] as applicable to EU issuer. Non-EU issuers may use local GAAP with a narrative description of differences	National GAAP or IFRS[1] as applicable to EU issuer. IFRS or GAAP equivalent to IFRS for non-EU issuers	National GAAP or IFRS[1] as applicable to EU issuer. Non-EU issuers may use local GAAP with a narrative description of differences	National GAAP or IFRS[1] as applicable to EU issuer. IFRS or GAAP equivalent to IFRS for non-EU issuers
Issuers operating less than one year	Special purpose financial information must be included	Special purpose financial information must be included	No additional requirements	Special purpose financial information must be included	No additional requirements	Special purpose financial information must be included	No additional requirements	Special purpose financial information must be included	No additional requirements	Special purpose financial information must be included
Report on financial information	Auditor's report or accountant's report as applicable	Auditor's report or accountant's report as applicable	Auditor's report or accountant's report as applicable	Auditor's report or accountant's report as applicable	Auditor's report or accountant's report as applicable	Auditor's report or accountant's report as applicable	Auditor's report or accountant's report as applicable	Auditor's report or accountant's report as applicable	Auditor's report or accountant's report as applicable	Auditor's report or accountant's report as applicable

1 In this table the expression IFRS is intended to refer to "those IFRSs as adopted for use in the European Union".

	Shares	Debt, units < €50k	Debt, units =/> €50k	Derivatives, units < €50K	Derivatives, units =/> €50K	Asset backed securities, units < €50k	Asset backed securities, units =/> €50k	Depository receipts, units < €50k	Depository receipts, units =/> €50k	Banks issuing anything other than equity securities
Age of latest financial information	I, 20.5	IV, 13.4	IX, 11.4	IV, 13.4	IX, 11.4	-	-	X, 20.4	X, 20.4	XI, 11.4
Age of audited information	No more than 15 months if unaudited interims or 18 months if audited interims	No more than 18 months	No more than 18 months	No more than 18 months	No more than 18 months	No requirements	No requirements	No more than 15 months if unaudited interims or 18 months if audited interims	No more than 15 months if unaudited interims or 18 months if audited interims	No more than 18 months
Pro forma financial information	I, 20.2 & II	-	-	-	-	-	-	-	-	-
Information	Required to show effect of significant gross changes	No requirements	No requirements	No requirements	No requirements	No requirements	No requirements	No requirements	No requirements	No requirements
Report on proper compilation	Required, where pro forma included	No requirements	No requirements	No requirements	No requirements	No requirements	No requirements	No requirements	No requirements	No requirements

	Shares	Debt, units < €50k	Debt, units =/> €50k	Derivatives, units < €50k	Derivatives, units =/> €50K	Asset backed securities, units < €50k	Asset backed securities, units =/> €50k	Depository receipts, units < €50k	Depository receipts, units =/> €50k	Banks issuing anything other than equity securities
Profit forecasts and estimates	I, 13	IV, 9	IX, 8	IV, 9	IX, 8	-	-	X, 13	X, 13	XI, 8
Disclosure of assumptions	Required	Required	Required	Required	Required	No requirements	No requirements	Required	Required	Required
Report on proper compilation	Required	Required	No requirements	Required	No requirements	No requirements	No requirements	Required	Required	Required
Outstanding forecasts	Update statement required	No requirements	No requirements	No requirements	No requirements	No requirements	No requirements	Update statement required	Update statement required	No requirements

Appendix 2

PRINCIPAL LEGAL AND REGULATORY REQUIREMENTS

The description of legal and regulatory requirements provided in this appendix is intended to be a guide and not intended to be a definitive interpretation of such requirements.

The FSA Handbook

1   In July 2005 the then existing listing rules were modified to take account of the implementation of the Prospectus Directive in the United Kingdom. At the same time the opportunity was taken to revise the rules applying to the continuing obligations of listed companies.

2   The FSA Handbook now includes three parts relevant to securities and their issuers, namely: the "Prospectus Rules", the "Listing Rules" and the "Disclosure Rules".

3   The Prospectus Rules effect the practical implementation of the Prospectus Directive. They apply to all prospectuses required to be issued by UK companies either offering securities to the public or seeking admission of securities to a regulated market. The annexes to the PD Regulation provide detailed rules on prospectuses and, in particular, the content requirements of prospectuses. In respect of prospectus content requirements, the Prospectus Rules reproduce the Annexes to the PD Regulation. Accordingly, references to the contents requirements in Annexes to the Prospectus Rules are also references to the Annexes to the PD Regulation.

4   The Prospectus Rules also make it clear that the FSA expect "CESR's recommendations for the consistent implementation of the European Commission's Regulation on Prospectuses no. 809/2004"[1] to be followed by issuers when preparing a prospectus.

5   The Listing Rules provide the rules and guidance applicable to issuers of securities both seeking admission to, and once admitted to, the Official List. They include the conditions for admission to listing, the requirements concerning Sponsors under the Listing Rules, Class 1 and related party transactions and the requirements for listing particulars when a prospectus is not required to be prepared.

6   The Disclosure Rules contain rules and guidance in relation to the publication and control of "inside information" and the disclosure of transactions by persons discharging managerial responsibilities and their connected persons.

7   The annexes to the Prospectus Rules provide that historical financial information for the last three completed financial years, where it exists, is to be included in a prospectus. This information can either be extracted or incorporated by reference from the issuer's annual financial statements or presented in the prospectus specifically for

---

[1]   "CESR" is the Committee of European Securities Regulators. Its recommendations were issued in February 2005 and are sometimes referred to as the "Level 3 Guidance of the Lamfalussy Process". This guidance can be accessed on the CESR website www.cesr-eu.org.

that purpose. The Prospectus Rules provide that where the accounting framework to be applied in an issuer's next annual financial statements is different from that previously applied, at least some of the historical financial information must be represented on the basis of those new policies. The historical financial information must either be accompanied by the auditor's report on the statutory financial statements or by a new opinion by reporting accountants where the information has been presented for the purpose of the prospectus.

8   Where an issuer with listed equity securities proposes to undertake a Class 1 acquisition, Listing Rule 13.5 requires that certain historical financial information is presented in relation to the target and, where relevant, the target's subsidiary undertakings. The last three years historical financial information must be presented in a financial information table on a basis consistent with accounting policies of the issuer. Unless the target is itself admitted to trading on an EU regulated market or on an overseas regulated market or listed on an overseas investment exchange, the financial information table must be reported on by a reporting accountant. However, if there is no report by reporting accountants on the financial information table itself, it is necessary for the issuer to consider whether any material adjustment is required to achieve consistency between the target's historical financial information and the accounting policies of the issuer, in which event a reconciliation of key financial statement components must be presented and the reconciliation reported on by reporting accountants.

9   If an issuer chooses to include a profit forecast or <u>profit estimate</u> in a prospectus the registration document may be required to contain the following information:

(a)   a statement setting out the principal assumptions upon which the issuer has based its forecast or estimate. See item 13.1 of Annex I to the Prospectus Rules for more detailed requirements regarding assumptions; and

(b)   a report prepared by independent accountants or auditors stating that in the opinion of the independent accountants or auditors the forecast or estimate has been properly compiled on the basis stated and that the basis of accounting used for the profit forecast or estimate is consistent with the accounting policies of the issuer.

The profit forecast or estimate must be prepared on a basis comparable with the historical financial information.

10   If a profit forecast in a prospectus has been published which is still outstanding, the issuer must provide a statement setting out whether or not that forecast is still correct as at the time of the registration document, and an explanation of why such forecast is no longer valid if that is the case.

11   Where an issuer includes pro forma financial information in a prospectus, (relating to shares, transferable securities equivalent to shares and certain other securities convertible into shares), Annex I item 20.2 and Annex II of the Prospectus Rules require any such information to be reported on by the reporting accountants. The

Listing Rules also require a reporting accountant's report on any pro forma financial information that an issuer chooses to include in a Class 1 circular.

12   Where a statement or report attributed to an expert (including reporting accountants) is included in a prospectus at the issuer's request, the Prospectus Rules require a statement of consent from the expert. This is discussed in more detail in paragraphs 66 to 74 in the body of this SIR. The consent of the auditor is not required where reports (audit or review) previously issued by the auditor are included in a prospectus.

13   Other rules apply in particular circumstances. By replication of the Prospectus Rules requirements an expert is required, by the Listing Rules, to consent to the inclusion of any report in any listing particulars. However, the consent of the auditor is not required where reports (audit or review) previously issued by the auditor are included in the listing particulars.

14   The Listing Rules also require pro forma financial information in a Class 1 circular to be reported on by an issuer's reporting accountants and to contain provisions requiring an expert's consent to any report included in a Class 1 circular.

Admission to the Main Market of the London Stock Exchange

15   A two-stage admission process applies to companies who want to have their securities admitted to the Main Market for listed securities of the London Stock Exchange. The securities need to be admitted to the Official List by the UK Listing Authority (UKLA), a division of the Financial Services Authority, and also admitted to trading by the London Stock Exchange. To be admitted to trading the Admission and Disclosure Standards need to be met. Once both processes are complete the securities are officially listed on the Exchange.

AIM requirements

16   Under the AIM Rules of the London Stock Exchange, companies seeking admission to AIM must publish an AIM admission document. This is the case whether or not they are required by the Prospectus Rules to prepare a prospectus (because they are also making an offer of securities to the public which is not exempt from the requirement to produce a prospectus).

17   The AIM Rules provide that the content of an admission document should be based on the share disclosure requirements in the Prospectus Rules, modified to allow issuers to elect not to include certain financial information where no prospectus is required, notably profit forecasts and pro forma financial information. However, if such information is included the Prospectus Rules requirements must be followed.

The Professional Securities Market

18   From 1 July 2005, issuers listing debt, convertibles or depository receipts in London will have a choice of being admitted to a regulated market or the Professional Securities Market, which is a market operated and regulated by the London Stock Exchange. Issuers listing on the Professional Securities Market will not be required to

report historical financial information under IFRSs or an EU approved equivalent standard either in listing documents or as a continuing obligation requirement.

The City Code

19 Where a document sent to shareholders in connection with an offer falling within the scope of the City Code contains a profit forecast or estimate, with certain exceptions, Rule 28.3 of the City Code requires that forecast or estimate to be reported on by reporting accountants and by the financial advisers. The City Code's requirements for such reports are similar to those under the Prospectus Rules. In certain circumstances, the City Code also provides for a reporting accountant to report on merger benefit statements (Rule 19.1) and interim financial information (Rule 28.6 (c)).

Companies legislation

20 In the United Kingdom, financial information presented in an investment circular may constitute "non statutory accounts" within the meaning of section 240 of the Companies Act 1985. The document in which the financial information is presented will usually, therefore, contain a statement complying with section 240(3) of the Companies Act 1985. However, this statement is only appropriate where the financial information comprises non-statutory accounts of the company issuing the document. No statement is needed in respect of financial information on a target company in an acquisition circular, for example, unless the directors of the target company explicitly accept responsibility for that part of the document. The statement is also the responsibility of the directors of the company publishing the document, not the reporting accountants.

Financial Services and Markets Act 2000

21 Upon implementation of the Prospectus Directive into UK law with effect from 1 July 2005, the existing regime regarding the issue of prospectuses in the UK whether in connection with an official listing of securities or a public offer was repealed.

22 Under Part VI, the FSA's function is a statutory one. Part VI covers not only the whole process by which securities are admitted to official listing but also the obligations to which companies are subject once they have obtained listing. The Listing Rules represent listing rules for the purposes of Part VI.

23 Prospectus Rule 5.5 (in relation to prospectuses), and regulation 6 of The Financial Services and Markets Act 2000 (Official Listing of Securities) Regulations 2001 (in relation to listing particulars, i.e. not prospectuses within the meaning of the Prospectus Directive) provide that each person:

(a) who accepts, and is stated in the particulars as accepting, responsibility for the particulars or for any part of the particulars; or

(b) who has authorised the contents of, or any part of, the particulars;

is deemed to accept responsibility for the particulars (or that part of them).

24 This raises potential issues for reporting accountants, for example:

- If they are involved in advising on an investment circular but are not named in it.

- If they issue a report or letter which is included in the investment circular.

25 In the first example the Prospectus Rules and The Financial Services and Markets Act 2000 (Official Listing of Securities) Regulations 2001 relieve professional advisers from responsibility for the circular where they are solely giving advice as to the contents of the listing particulars in a professional capacity.

26 In the second example the Prospectus Rules and The Financial Services and Markets Act 2000 (Official Listing of Securities) Regulations 2001 limit the responsibility of experts, including reporting accountants, to the part for which they accept responsibility and only if the part for which they accept responsibility is included in (or substantially in) the form and context to which they have agreed.

Appendix 3

EXAMPLE OF A CONSENT LETTER

The Directors
ABC plc

Dear Sirs

We hereby give our consent to the inclusion in the [describe Investment Circular] dated [ ]
issued by ABC plc of [our accountant's report]/[our report relating to the profit estimate for
the year ended 20 ,]/[our report relating to the profit forecast for the year ending 20 ,]/[our
report relating to the pro forma financial information for the year ended 20] dated [ ] [[and]
the references to our name[2]] in the form and context in which [it]/[they] are included, as
shown in the enclosed proof of the [describe Investment Circular] which we have signed for
identification.

[We also hereby authorise the contents of the [report[s]] referred to above which [is/are]
included in the Prospectus for the purposes of Prospectus Rule [5.5.3R (2)(f)] [5.5.4R (2)(f)]
OR [We also hereby authorise the contents of the [report[s]] referred to above which [is/
are] included in the Listing Particulars for the purposes of Regulation 6(1)(e) of The
Financial Services and Markets Act 2000 (Official Listing of Securities) Regulations 2001.]
OR [We also hereby authorise the contents of the report[s] referred to above which [is/are]
included in the Admission Document for the purposes of the Schedule Two to the AIM
Rules][3]

Yours faithfully

Reporting accountant

---

[2] This is required only when a statement is attributed to a reporting accountant as an expert outside the
     context of a report from the reporting accountant included in the investment circular.
[3] This paragraph is not required in respect of a Class 1 Circular.

Appendix 4

GLOSSARY OF TERMS

Accountant's report - A report by a reporting accountant included in an investment circular, in which the reporting accountant normally expresses a "true and fair, for the purposes of the investment circular" opinion on historical financial information relating to the issuer and its subsidiaries in accordance with SIR 2000 "Investment Reporting Standards applicable to public reporting engagements on historical financial information ".

Admission and Disclosure Standards - The Admission and Disclosure Standards published by the London Stock Exchange, for companies admitted or seeking to be admitted to trading by the Exchange.

Agreed-upon procedures [engagements] - An engagement where the reporting accountant is engaged to carry out procedures of an audit or assurance nature, that the reporting accountant, the entity and any appropriate third parties have agreed, and to report on factual findings. The recipients of the report must form their own conclusions from the report by the reporting accountant. The report is restricted to those parties that have agreed to the procedures to be performed, since others, unaware of the reasons for the procedures, may misinterpret the results.

AIM - The Alternative Investment Market operated by the London Stock Exchange plc. The market is for smaller growing companies. Securities admitted to AIM are unlisted.

AIM Admission Document - The document prepared in connection with an application for admission of an issuer's securities to trading on AIM. If upon admission a prospectus is required in accordance with the Prospectus Rules, such prospectus may serve as the AIM Admission Document.

AIM Rules - The Rules of the Alternative Investment Market.

CESR - The Committee of European Securities Regulators.

Circular - A circular issued by any company to its shareholders and/or holders of its debt securities in connection with a transaction, which does not constitute a prospectus, listing particulars or AIM admission document.

City Code - The City Code on Takeovers and Mergers, published by the Panel on Takeovers and Mergers.

Class 1 circular - A circular relating to a Class 1 transaction.

Class 1 transaction - A transaction where one or more of a number of specified percentage ratios exceed a predetermined level as specified in Chapter 10 of the Listing Rules.

Comfort letter - A private letter from the reporting accountant, usually prepared at the request of the issuer and/or the sponsor, where relevant. It is intended to provide the addressees with comfort (in the form of an opinion or a report on the results of specific procedures carried out by the reporting accountants) regarding matters relevant to the addressees' responsibilities.

Completion date of the transaction - The date by which any offer contained in the circular must have been accepted or application made for shares or other securities to be issued, or the date on which shareholders vote to approve the transaction.

Consent letter - A letter whereby the reporting accountant consents to the inclusion in an investment circular of references to its name or the inclusion of any of its reports or letters which are to be published therein.

Due diligence - The process whereby the directors of the issuer and other parties, whether as principal or in an advisory capacity, satisfy themselves that the transaction is entered into after due and careful enquiry and that all relevant regulatory and/or legal requirements have been properly complied with. There is no generally accepted definition of required procedures for this purpose and where others (such as reporting accountants) are engaged to carry out work that will form part of the process, it is for the instructing parties to make clear what is required of those others in the particular circumstances.

Engagement partner - The partner or other person in the firm who is responsible for the engagement and its performance, and for reports that are issued on behalf of the firm, and who, where required, has the appropriate authority from a professional, legal or regulatory body.

Financial information - The term is used to signify the specific information presented in the form of a table upon which a reporting accountant reports. Typically, this information encompasses a number of accounting periods.

Financial statements - A balance sheet, profit and loss account (or other form of income statement), statement of cash flow, and statement of total recognised gains and losses (or statement of changes in equity), notes and other statements and explanatory material. In order to avoid confusion the term financial information is used throughout the SIRs to refer to the information upon which the reporting accountant reports. When the term financial statements is used within the SIRs this refers to financial statements from which the financial information has been derived by the issuer.

FSA - Financial Services Authority.

FSMA - Financial Services and Markets Act 2000.

IFRSs - International Financial Reporting Standards issued by the International Accounting Standards Board. This term incorporates all International Financial Reporting Standards, International Accounting Standards (IASs) and Interpretations originated by the International Financial Reporting Interpretations Committee (IFRIC) or the former Standards Interpretation Committee of the IASC.

Investment circular - A generic term describing any document issued by an entity pursuant to statutory or regulatory requirements relating to securities on which it is intended that a third party should make an investment decision, including a prospectus, listing particulars, circular to shareholders or similar document.

ISAs (UK and Ireland) - International Standards on Auditing (UK and Ireland) issued by the Auditing Practices Board.

Issuer - For the purposes of the Prospectus Rules "A legal person who issues or proposes to issue securities". For the purposes of the Listing Rules "Any company or other legal person or undertaking (including a public sector issuer), any class of whose securities has been admitted to listing, or is the subject of an application for admission to listing".

Listing particulars - A document not being a Prospectus prepared in connection with an admission of securities to the Official List.

Listing Rules - The part of the FSA's Handbook entitled "Listing Rules" governing the conduct of companies whose securities are admitted to the Official List.

London Stock Exchange - The London Stock Exchange plc.

Long form report - A private report with a restricted circulation, normally prepared by the reporting accountants on the instructions of, and addressed to, the sponsor, where relevant, and the directors of the issuer as part of their due diligence, dealing with agreed matters including commentary on financial and other information in an orderly and relevant form for a specific purpose.

Main Market - The London Stock Exchange's market for larger and established companies. Securities admitted to the Main Market are listed.

Nominated adviser - A corporate broker, investment banker or other professional adviser approved by the London Stock Exchange to act as a nominated adviser to an AIM company under the AIM Rules.

Ofex - An independent, self regulated, UK market for smaller companies.

Official List - The Official List maintained by the FSA.

Outcome - The outcome of the evaluation or measurement of a subject matter is the information that results from the directors applying the suitable criteria to the subject matter. Examples of outcomes are historical financial information and a directors' profit forecast and related disclosures that are included in an investment circular.

Partner - Any individual with authority to bind a firm of reporting accountants with respect to the performance of any engagement in connection with an investment circular.

PD Regulation - The implementing EU Regulation 809/2004 that provides the detailed rules concerning Prospectuses and their contents. Much of the text of this regulation is included within the Prospectus Rules.

Private reporting engagement - An engagement in which a reporting accountant does not express a conclusion that is published in an investment circular.

Professional Securities Market - A market for debt, convertibles and depository receipts, which is operated and regulated by the London Stock Exchange. This is not a regulated market as defined by the Prospectus and Transparency Directives.

Profit estimate - Historical financial information for a financial period which has expired but for which the results have not yet been published.

Profit forecast - The PD Regulation defines a profit forecast as "a form of words which expressly states or by implication indicates a figure or a minimum or maximum figure for the likely level of profits or losses for the current financial period and/or financial periods subsequent to that period, or contains data from which calculation of such a figure for future profits or losses may be made, even if no particular figure is mentioned and the word "profit" is not used. Where a profit forecast relates to an extended period and/or is subject to significant uncertainty it is sometimes referred to as a projection.

Pro forma financial information - Financial information such as net assets, profit or cash flow statements that demonstrate the impact of a transaction on previously published financial information together with the explanatory notes thereto.

Projection - See "Profit forecast".

Prospectus - The document issued in accordance with the Prospectus Rules in connection with either a public offer or an admission of securities to trading on a regulated market.

Prospectus Regulations - The UK statutory instrument which makes amendments to Part VI of FSMA and to certain secondary legislation.

Prospectus Rules - The FSA's Handbook part "Prospectus Rules" which together with the PD Regulation and the changes to FSMA Part VI made by the Prospectus Regulations, implement the Prospectus Directive into UK law. In respect of Prospectus content requirements, the Prospectus Rules reproduce the Annexes to the PD Regulation. Accordingly, references to the contents requirements in Annexes to the Prospectus Rules are also references to the Annexes to the PD Regulation.

Public offer - An offer to the public in any form to subscribe for securities in an issuer.

Public reporting engagement - An engagement in which a reporting accountant expresses a conclusion that is published in an investment circular and which is designed to enhance the degree of confidence of the intended users of the report about the "outcome" of the directors' evaluation or measurement of "subject matter" (usually financial information) against "suitable criteria".

Report - This term encompasses letters that the reporting accountant may be required to send by regulation or arising from the terms of the engagement.

Reporting accountant - An accountant engaged to prepare a report for inclusion in, or in connection with, an investment circular. The reporting accountant may or may not be the auditor of the entity issuing the investment circular. The term "reporting accountant" is used to describe either the engagement partner or the engagement partner's firm. The reporting accountant could be a limited company or an engagement principal employed by the company.

Reporting accountant's criteria - A subset of suitable criteria which the reporting accountant's engagement requires the reporting accountant to consider. Reporting accountant's criteria are set out in appendices to the SIRs.

Securities - Are as defined by Article 4 of the EU's Markets in Financial Instruments Directive with the exception of money-market instruments having a maturity of less than twelve months.

Sponsor - For the purposes of SIRs, "sponsor" is a generic term which includes any one or more of the following to whom the reporting accountant has agreed, in its engagement letter, to address a relevant report:

(a)   a person approved, under section 88 of FSMA, by the FSA as a sponsor. The FSA's sponsor regime applies to applications for admission to listing and major transactions. The sponsor regime is designed to ensure that effective due diligence is undertaken on issuers and transactions to ensure that issuers are eligible for listing, that major transactions are properly evaluated and that all relevant information has been included in the investment circular. Listing Rule 8.2.1 sets out the circumstances when an issuer must appoint a sponsor;

(b)   a nominated adviser approved by the London Stock Exchange in connection with an application for admission to AIM and subsequent transactions by a company with securities traded on AIM; and

(c)   in connection with any transaction, any party, other than the issuer, who may have specific responsibility for the preparation and/or contents of an investment circular.

Subject matter - The subject matter of an engagement is that which is being evaluated or measured against "suitable criteria". Examples of subject matter are the entity's financial position and the directors' expectation of the issuer's profit for the period covered by a profit forecast.

Suitable criteria - Criteria are the benchmarks used to evaluate or measure the subject matter. Suitable criteria are usually derived from laws and regulations and are required by directors to enable them to make reasonably consistent evaluations or measurements of the subject matter. With respect to public reporting engagements the suitable criteria for specific types of engagement are described in the individual SIR dealing with such engagements.

STANDARDS FOR INVESTMENT REPORTING

2000 – INVESTMENT REPORTING STANDARDS APPLICABLE TO PUBLIC REPORTING ENGAGEMENTS ON HISTORICAL FINANCIAL INFORMATION

CONTENTS

Appendices
1 *Bold letter paragraphs included in ISAs (UK and Ireland) that are unlikely to apply to the reporting accountant's exercise in relation to historical financial information in investment circulars*
2 *Examples of engagement letter clauses*
3 *Example of an accountant's report on historical financial information*

ANNEXURE

Accounting conventions commonly used in the preparation of historical financial information in investment circulars[1]

---

[1] The Annexure has been compiled by the APB from a number of sources. It does not include either basic principles, essential procedures or guidance promulgated by the APB.

SIR 2000 contains basic principles and essential procedures ("Investment Reporting Standards") indicated by paragraphs in bold type, with which a reporting accountant is required to comply in the conduct of an engagement involving the examination of historical financial information which is intended to give a true and fair view, for the purposes of the relevant investment circular, included within an investment circular prepared for issue in connection with a securities transaction governed wholly or in part by the laws and regulations of the United Kingdom.

SIR 2000 also includes explanatory and other material, including appendices, in the context of which the basic principles and essential procedures are to be understood and applied. It is necessary to consider the whole text of the SIR to understand and apply the basic principles and essential procedures.

For the purposes of the SIRs, an investment circular is defined as: "any document issued by an entity pursuant to statutory or regulatory requirements relating to listed or unlisted securities on which it is intended that a third party should make an investment decision, including a prospectus, listing particulars, circular to shareholders or similar document".

SIR 1000 "Investment reporting standards applicable to all engagements in connection with an investment circular" contains basic principles and essential procedures that are applicable to all engagements involving an investment circular. The definitions in the glossary of terms set out in Appendix 4 of SIR 1000 are to be applied in the interpretation of this and all other SIRs. Terms defined in the glossary are underlined the first time that they occur in the text.

This SIR replaces SIR 200 "Accountants' reports on historical financial information in investment circulars" issued in December 1997.

To assist readers, SIRs contain references to, and extracts from, certain legislation and chapters of the Rules of the UK Listing Authority. Readers are cautioned that these references may change subsequent to publication.

Introduction

1. The purpose of this Standard for Investment Reporting (SIR) is to establish standards and provide guidance on the reporting accountant's responsibilities and procedures when preparing an "accountant's report" on historical financial information. The work required to prepare an "accountant's report" is referred to in this SIR as the "reporting accountant's exercise". The objective of the reporting accountant's exercise is to enable the reporting accountant to express an opinion as to whether, for the purposes of the relevant investment circular, the financial information gives a true and fair view of the state of affairs and profits, cash flows and statements of changes in equity of the issuer, or where applicable the target.

2. **When the reporting accountant is engaged to prepare an accountant's report, the reporting accountant should obtain sufficient appropriate evidence to express an opinion as to whether the financial information presents a true and fair view, for the purposes of the investment circular. (SIR 2000.1)**

3. An engagement to prepare an accountant's report is a public reporting engagement as described in SIR 1000. The description of a public reporting engagement includes three generic terms having the following meanings in the context of an engagement to report on historical financial information:

   (a) with respect to historical financial information the "**subject matter**" is the entity's financial position for the periods being reported on;

   (b) the "**suitable criteria**" are the requirements of the applicable financial reporting framework, the PD Regulation, and Listing Rules together with any "accepted conventions", as set out in the Annexure, that are applicable; and

   (c) with respect to historical financial information the "**outcome**" is the directors' historical financial information that is included in the investment circular and which has resulted from the directors applying the suitable criteria to the subject matter. The reporting accountant expresses an opinion (in the "**accountant's report**") as to whether the historical financial information gives, for the purposes of the investment circular, a true and fair view.

4. The Prospectus Rules set out certain requirements, derived from the PD Regulation, relating to the presentation of historical financial information in a prospectus. Annex I of the PD Regulation (and there are equivalent requirements in a number of the other annexes) requires that historical financial information is either audited or "reported on as to whether or not, for the purposes of the registration document, it gives a true and fair view, in accordance with auditing standards applicable in a Member State or an equivalent standard." SIR 2000 is regarded as an equivalent standard for the purposes of the PD Regulation[2].

5. With respect to Class 1 acquisitions, Chapter 13 of the Listing Rules sets out requirements for a financial information table relating to a target company and the accountant's opinion on that table. The accountant's opinion is required to state whether, for the purposes of the Class 1 circular, the financial information table gives a true and fair view of the financial matters set out in it, and whether the financial information table has been prepared in a form that is consistent with the accounting policies adopted in the listed company's latest annual accounts.

6. In this SIR, accountant's opinions on such financial information tables are described as "accountant's reports".

7. An accountant's report is likely to be used where the issuer's audited annual financial statements do not meet the standards of preparation and presentation prescribed in the applicable rules and need, therefore, to be adjusted in order that historical financial information which complies with the applicable rules can be presented. For example, where the entity is seeking a listing, the financial information for the last two years is required to be prepared and presented in a form consistent with that which will be

---

[2] In respect of prospectus content requirements, the Prospectus Rules reproduce the Annexes to the PD Regulation. Accordingly, references to the contents requirements in the Annexes to the Prospectus Rules are also references to the Annexes to the PD Regulation.

adopted in the issuer's next published annual financial statements, having regard to accounting standards and policies and legislation applicable to such annual financial statements. In the context of Class 1 circulars, the objective may be to present the financial information of the target for all periods in a form which is consistent and comparable with the accounting policies adopted by the listed company in its latest annual accounts.

8. In addition, an accountant's report is used where the issuer has a complex financial history and there are no underlying financial statements that have been audited. Conventions for accounting where there are complex financial histories are described in the Annexure.

9. The nature of the accountant's report is such that the objective of the reporting accountant's exercise does not differ in essence from that of an auditor. The underlying requirement of this SIR is that the reporting accountant will, in conducting the work necessary to provide the accountant's report, perform or rely on work that meets those requirements of ISAs (UK and Ireland) that are applicable to the reporting accountant's exercise. The reporting accountant applies ISAs (UK and Ireland) on the basis set out in this SIR in the context of the following:

    (a) the reporting accountant is often reporting on financial information that has been included in, or formed part of, financial statements which have themselves already been subject to audit by an independent auditor. In consequence, there may be available to the reporting accountant a body of independent evidence relating to the historical financial information which would not be available to an auditor examining the financial information for the first time;

    (b) the financial information being examined may relate to accounting periods in circumstances where financial statements for one, and possibly two, subsequent periods have been prepared and audited. These circumstances mean that in assessing risks that may affect the historical financial information in relation to earlier periods the reporting accountant has the benefit of information relating to uncertainties affecting the financial information which would not have been available to an auditor auditing the information for the first time; and

    (c) the reporting accountant does not have the statutory reporting responsibilities of an auditor.

10. This SIR provides standards that address those aspects of the reporting accountant's exercise that require the reporting accountant to perform procedures directly, for example risk assessment procedures. It also provides guidance on the application of ISAs (UK and Ireland) to the reporting accountant's exercise.

11. This SIR recognises that the reporting accountant may wish to use evidence previously obtained by the auditor who audited the historical financial statements for the relevant period covered by the reporting accountant's exercise. Guidance is provided on the steps that the reporting accountant undertakes, including initial planning considerations, in order to assess the suitability of the audit evidence for this purpose.

12. Subject to the considerations set out in this SIR, references in the ISAs (UK and Ireland) to the auditor performing audit procedures or obtaining audit evidence may be read as references to the reporting accountant being satisfied that the procedures have been performed, or the evidence obtained, either by the reporting accountant or an auditor.

13. Certain requirements of ISAs (UK and Ireland) will not apply to the reporting accountant's exercise, for example, when the requirement of an ISA (UK and Ireland) is predicated on a continuing relationship between an auditor and the entity being audited, or because of the specific nature of the reporting accountant's responsibilities, under applicable regulations, as discussed in this SIR. A summary of the bold letter paragraphs included in ISAs (UK and Ireland) that are unlikely to apply to the reporting accountant's exercise is included in Appendix 1 of this SIR.

14. This SIR also provides guidance to the reporting accountant in the context of assessing whether the financial information shows a true and fair view, for the purposes of the investment circular. In situations where the issuer has a historical record of audited financial statements, the true and fair view for the purposes of the investment circular may be a financial reporting framework such as International Financial Reporting Standards. In situations where the issuer has a complex financial history the conventions to support the true and fair view for the purposes of the investment circular are set out in the Annexure.

15. The structure of this SIR reflects the order of the ISAs (UK and Ireland) and the contents are intended to be read in conjunction with the ISAs (UK and Ireland).

Pre-existing financial information

16. With respect to historical financial information, where the issuer already has available:

    (a) audited annual financial statements; or

    (b) audited or reviewed interim financial information,

    which meet the requirements of the applicable rules in respect of the preparation and presentation of historical financial information to be included in the investment circular, it may choose to include these financial statements, or financial information, in the investment circular together with the pre-existing reports of the auditor. In these circumstances an accountant's report is not prepared and this SIR does not apply to such circumstances. Furthermore, in these circumstances the audit firm is not required by the Prospectus Rules to consent to the inclusion of its reports in the investment circular.

17. Notwithstanding that the audit firm is not required to give consent, a reporting accountant that is also the auditor of the company may become aware that the financial statements are defective. For example a material error may have been detected in the original financial statements. If the reporting accountant does become aware that the financial statements are defective and that the directors have not

revised them as required by the Companies Act 1985, it discusses the matter with those charged with governance. If the directors do not decide to revise the financial statements the reporting accountant considers the need to take legal advice.

True and fair view, for the purposes of the investment circular

18. **The reporting accountant should:**

    (a) **obtain an understanding of the purpose of the investment circular;**

    (b) **ascertain which financial reporting framework is required to be used by the applicable regulations and which, if any, accepted conventions as to the preparation and presentation of historical financial information for inclusion in investment circulars are to be applied; and**

    (c) **review the appropriateness of the accounting policies,**

    in order to determine whether the proposed historical financial information prepared by the issuer is capable of giving a true and fair view, for the purposes of the investment circular. (SIR 2000.2)

19. Where historical financial information is presented in a prospectus the Prospectus Rules generally determine the applicable financial reporting framework. The Prospectus Rules require the most recent year's financial information to be presented in a form consistent with that which will be adopted in the issuer's next published annual financial statements, having regard to the accounting standards, policies and legislation applicable to such annual financial statements.

20. The reporting accountant satisfies itself that the directors have performed a thorough review of the accounting policies used in preparing the historical financial information in determining the accounting policies appropriate for the business following the transaction that is the subject of the prospectus. The reporting accountant also considers whether the policies are consistent with the applicable financial reporting framework, and accounting policies used in the relevant industry. Where the reporting accountant does not agree with the directors' final proposed accounting policies they refer to the guidance on reporting set out in paragraphs 72 to 76 of this SIR.

21. Where information is presented in a Class 1 circular, the suitable criteria are those set out in the Listing Rules. These rules require financial information to be presented in a form consistent with the accounting policies adopted in the issuer's latest annual consolidated accounts.

22. The directors have regard to, and make appropriate disclosure of, accepted conventions which have been developed for the preparation and presentation of historical financial information in investment circulars (including those relating to additional disclosures). These conventions have been developed to assist the directors, to the extent consistent with established accounting principles, to fulfil the criteria set out in the relevant regulations, present the information in an easily

analysable form, and give a true and fair view for the purposes of the applicable investment circular.

23. The Annexure provides a summary of these conventions including, among others, conventions that address:

- Making adjustments to previously published financial statements and dealing with entities which have not previously prepared consolidated accounts.

- Carve outs.

- Acquisitions.

- Newly formed issuers.

In certain circumstances applying the conventions may result in combined or aggregated, rather than consolidated, financial information being presented in order to meet the requirement to present financial information that gives a true and fair view, for the purposes of the investment circular.

General professional considerations

24. SIR 1000.3 and SIR 1000.4 set out basic principles and essential procedures applicable to agreeing the terms of the engagement. Paragraphs 11 to 15 and paragraph 17 of SIR 1000 provide guidance with respect to these basic principles and essential procedures. SIR 1000.5 sets out the basic principles and essential procedures with respect to the ethical requirements that apply to a reporting accountant.

25. Where the evidence used by the reporting accountant includes that contained within the working papers of an auditor, the working papers of the reporting accountant identify the papers reviewed and the nature of the work performed. Whilst it is not necessary for the working papers to replicate all of the detailed findings contained in the auditor's working papers reporting accountants do document the basis on which the auditor addressed the particular risks identified in the reporting accountant's risk assessment procedures.

26. In considering the requirements of ISA (UK and Ireland) 240 "The auditor's responsibility to consider fraud in an audit of financial statements" and ISA (UK and Ireland) 250 "Section A - Consideration of Laws and Regulations in an audit of financial statements. Section B - The auditor's right and duty to report to regulators in the financial sector" for the auditor to report any matters arising to certain authorities, the reporting accountant will need to assess the effect of these requirements when reporting in terms of the true and fair view, for the purposes of the investment circular. Where matters arise which may potentially require disclosure by the reporting accountant and the reporting accountant is unsure how to proceed, the reporting accountant takes legal advice.

27. In applying ISAs (UK and Ireland) 240, 250 and 260 "Communication of audit matters with those charged with governance", the reporting accountant considers who, in relation to the investment circular, should be regarded as a person charged with governance. Where the issuer has already formed an audit committee, the reporting accountant communicates with the audit committee in accordance with the guidance set out in this SIR. In the absence of an audit committee those responsible for governance will usually be the directors of the issuer.

Planning

28. **The reporting accountant should perform and document risk assessment procedures to support the reporting accountant's exercise. (SIR 2000.3)**

29. In addition to those matters that a reporting accountant considers when applying SIR 1000, a reporting accountant may consider:

- Any previous modifications to the audit report on underlying financial statements and the potential impact on the approach to the reporting accountant's exercise.

- The nature of adjustments to previously published historical financial information which may be proposed by the preparer of the historical financial information (for example as a result of changing the applicable accounting framework) and the sources of evidence to support an examination of the adjustments.

- The interaction with other roles undertaken by the reporting accountant in connection with the transaction, for example preparing a long form report.

- Staffing, including relevant experience and skills linked to investment circular reporting, and sources of consultation.

- Liaison with the auditor and arrangements for terms of access to the auditor's working papers, or equivalent evidence if maintained in machine readable form.

- The nature and timing of procedures to support any decision to rely on evidence obtained by the auditor.

- Whether the financial reporting framework applicable to the audited financial statements is the same as that applicable to the financial information contained in the investment circular.

- Whether there are any special circumstances concerning the appointment, resignation or reporting responsibilities of the auditor.

- Whether there is evidence of any limitation having been placed on the work of the auditor.

- Whether corrections or adjustments to subsequent financial statements indicate possible inadequacies in the audits of earlier periods.

30. **Where the reporting accountant is considering using audit evidence obtained by an auditor as part of the evidence for the reporting accountant's exercise, the reporting accountant should consider the professional qualification, independence and professional competence of the auditor and the quality control systems applied by the audit firm to that engagement. (SIR 2000.4)**

31. Matters that the reporting accountant considers include:

    • The integrity and experience of the auditor.

    • Whether the auditor was required to apply ISAs (UK and Ireland) or equivalent standards.

    • Whether there is any evidence that the auditor has not complied with applicable independence requirements.

Understanding of the entity, its environment and risk assessment

32. **The reporting accountant should obtain an understanding of the entity and its environment, including its internal control, sufficient to identify and assess the risks of material misstatement of the historical financial information covered by the accountant's report whether due to fraud or error, and sufficient to design and perform further procedures. (SIR 2000.5)**

33. Such an understanding is ordinarily obtained by:

    (a) meeting the directors and management of the entity;

    (b) visiting the entity's premises;

    (c) discussing the financial information and recent results with management;

    (d) applying analytical procedures to the financial information; and

    (e) obtaining from management an understanding of the principal transaction flows, internal controls and reporting arrangements of the business.

34. If this process indicates that there are factors which may give rise to a modification of the accountant's report then such factors are reported immediately to those responsible for the investment circular, usually the directors and any other responsible parties.

35. In considering areas of risk in relation to the periods for which historical financial information is presented, the reporting accountant has regard to the probability that misstatements in earlier periods, if they exist, are likely to have been detected in subsequent periods. Account is also taken of the fact that other uncertainties,

particularly those affecting subjective matters in the historical financial information, may have been resolved with the passage of time.

36. **When performing the risk assessment, the reporting accountant should take into account all other relevant work performed in connection with the investment circular. (SIR 2000.6)**

37. The reporting accountant may be undertaking other relevant work related to the transaction giving rise to the accountant's report. For example, the reporting accountant may have been commissioned to prepare a long form report, or a comfort letter on a statement of sufficiency of working capital.

38. If other relevant work has been performed by another firm the reporting accountant requests the issuer to provide access to such work. If the reporting accountant is not allowed access to such work they consider the implications for their report.

Materiality

39. The reporting accountant determines materiality for the purposes of the reporting accountant's work independently from the auditor, if any, who audited the underlying financial statements, and accordingly the reporting accountant's assessment of materiality may differ from that of the auditor. In determining materiality for the purposes of reporting on historical financial information, regard is had to the context in which the opinion is to be given (which includes the fact that the information may relate to a trend of results over a three year period).

The reporting accountant's procedures

40. **The reporting accountant should perform procedures to obtain sufficient appropriate evidence as to whether the work of an auditor, which the reporting accountant plans to use, is adequate for the reporting accountant's purposes. Where the reporting accountant concludes that the auditor's work is not adequate, does not have access to the auditor's working papers, or an audit has not previously been performed, the reporting accountant should perform procedures that compensate for this. The procedures of the auditor and the reporting accountant, taken together, should meet the requirements of ISAs (UK and Ireland) unless:**

   (a) **a requirement is not applicable to the reporting accountant's engagement; or**

   (b) **it is not practicable for the reporting accountant to undertake such procedures.**

   If the reporting accountant decides not to meet a requirement of ISAs (UK and Ireland) that is not listed in Appendix 1, it should document the reason for not meeting the requirement and why its omission does not have an impact on its opinion. (SIR 2000.7)

41. In determining the procedures to be performed in response to the assessed risk of material misstatement at the assertion level, the reporting accountant considers the extent to which the procedures that the reporting accountant wishes to perform have previously been performed by an auditor. Where such procedures have been performed by an auditor, the reporting accountant may, subject to the considerations discussed in this SIR, use the evidence obtained by the auditor from those procedures as part of the reporting accountant's own evidence.

42. The nature of ISAs (UK and Ireland) requires reporting accountants to exercise professional judgment in applying them. In exceptional circumstances reporting accountants may judge it necessary to depart from a basic principle or essential procedure of a standard to achieve more effectively the objective of the engagement. When such a situation arises the reporting accountant documents the reason for the departure unless the basic principle or essential procedure is one of those set out in Appendix 1. Appendix 1 identifies bold letter paragraphs that are unlikely to apply to the reporting accountant's exercise and sets out some of the generic reasons why a bold letter paragraph may not be applicable.

43. Where applicable auditing standards have changed during the period covered by the historical financial information, or it is not practicable for the reporting accountant to undertake procedures that meet the requirements of ISAs (UK and Ireland), the reporting accountant considers the implications for the reporting accountant's exercise, having regard to its risk assessment. The reporting accountant may be able to conclude that it is unnecessary to apply certain bold letter paragraphs in the ISAs (UK and Ireland) throughout the three year period covered by the accountant's report because:

    (a) it is sufficient to apply them with respect to the latest period only, because sufficient appropriate evidence relating to earlier periods can be obtained from the latest period; or

    (b) the auditing standards that were applicable at the time met the same objectives as the requirements of ISAs (UK and Ireland)[3].

    In such cases the reporting accountant documents the reason or justification for not meeting the requirement and why omitting it does not have an impact on its opinion.

44. **When the reporting accountant intends to use audit evidence obtained by the auditor, it should evaluate whether the audit procedures performed by the auditor adequately respond to the reporting accountant's assessment of the risks (including significant risks requiring special audit consideration) of material misstatement of the financial information to be included in the investment circular. (SIR 2000.8)**

---

[3] Prior to the adoption of ISAs (UK and Ireland) applicable auditing standards in the United Kingdom were "Statements of Auditing Standards" (SASs) issued by the Auditing Practices Board. For the purposes of SIR 2000 the SASs are deemed to meet the same objectives as the requirements of ISAs (UK and Ireland).

45. **The reporting accountant's procedures should include:**

    (a) **examining material adjustments from previously published historical financial statements made during the course of preparing the historical financial information and considering the responsible party's basis for satisfying itself that the adjustments are necessary and whether they have been correctly determined;**

    (b) **evaluating whether all necessary adjustments to previously published historical financial statements have been made; and**

    (c) **where the information is based on previously published financial statements, comparing the historical financial information to those financial statements and assessing whether the information has been accurately extracted therefrom. (SIR 2000.9)**

46. In certain areas, use of the work of the auditor may be the only practicable means of obtaining the evidence necessary to support the reporting accountant's opinion[4]. The timing of the reporting accountant's own work will inevitably be dictated by the timing of the preparation of the historical financial information and the related investment circular and this may be some time after the end of the periods to which the report relates.

Evidence

47. The reporting accountant reconsiders the matters considered at the planning stage as described in paragraphs 29 and 31.

48. Where the financial information to be reported on has previously been subject to audit, the auditor's working papers will be a useful source for the evidence which the reporting accountant may need to support its opinion on the financial information.

49. If planning to use the work of the auditor, the reporting accountant considers whether:

    (a) the work of the auditor was conducted to an appropriate materiality level; and

    (b) the auditor appears to have complied with the auditing standards applicable to the auditor's work.

50. The reporting accountant accepts evidence in audit working papers as being prima facie truthful and genuine, but in considering that evidence adopts an attitude of professional scepticism, whether the audit working paper was produced by an auditor from the reporting accountant's own firm or by another auditor. However, with respect to audit working papers obtained from the reporting accountant's own firm, the

---

[4] Procedures which require the reporting accountant to be physically present at a client site at a relevant date (for example attendance at physical inventory counting) will clearly be impossible to perform.

reporting accountant is more familiar with the detailed quality control procedures that will have been applied in the conduct of the audit. The application of professional scepticism will include considering the evidence contained in the audit working papers in the light of the understanding of the entity and its environment, including its internal control and such other evidence as the reporting accountant obtains directly.

51. The extent to which independent testing of the evidence obtained by the auditor (for example, reperformance of tests performed by the auditor) will be necessary is a matter for the reporting accountant's judgment on the basis of the information available at the time, including the reporting accountant's evaluation of the auditor's work.

52. **The reporting accountant should evaluate the quality of the audit evidence obtained by the auditor that the reporting accountant intends to rely on. Where the reporting accountant concludes that such audit evidence is either not sufficient or is inappropriate for the purposes of the reporting accountant's exercise the reporting accountant should obtain evidence directly. Where the evidence is not available, the reporting accountant should consider the implications for its report. (SIR 2000.10)**

53. Where the reporting accountant intends to rely on internal controls, the reporting accountant performs tests of control when unable to rely on the auditor's tests of such internal controls. This is likely to arise when:

    (a) the auditor has not performed tests of those internal controls; or

    (b) the auditor has performed tests of internal controls but the internal controls have subsequently changed.

54. Where relevant information is not available from the audit working papers, the reporting accountant will need to obtain the relevant evidence directly. The audit working papers are unlikely for example, to contain information concerning post balance sheet events up to the date of signing the accountant's report or to contain evidence relating to any adjustments made to the financial statements in preparing the historical financial information.

Obtaining access to information in audit working papers

55. When the company's auditor, or former auditor, is not appointed as the reporting accountant, the auditor will be aware that the reporting accountant may need access to information contained in the audit working papers. The auditor or former auditor is normally prepared, in accordance with relevant professional guidance, to make the audit working papers available to reporting accountants for the purpose of work under this SIR.

56. Access may be granted only on the basis that the auditor accepts no responsibility or liability to the reporting accountant in connection with the use of the audit working

papers by the reporting accountant. This has no effect on the reporting accountant's judgment regarding the extent to which reliance is placed on the working papers.

57. In cases where the reporting accountant is not able to obtain access to information in audit working papers, the reporting accountant will have no option other than to obtain the relevant evidence directly.

58. Irrespective of whether the reporting accountant has access to the auditor's working papers, the reporting accountant seeks to obtain, either from the directors or from the auditor, copies of all relevant communications sent by the auditor to those charged with governance of the entity, including those required to be sent by auditing standards applicable at the time, and copies of any responses to such communications made by management. A relevant communication would, for example, be one that discussed internal control and other weaknesses.

Related parties

59. Paragraphs 7(a) and 107(a) of ISA (UK and Ireland) 550 "Related Parties" require prior years' working papers to be reviewed for names of known related parties. These paragraphs do not apply in respect of the earliest period where more than one period is to be reported on.

Events occurring up to the date of the accountant's report

60. Unless a post balance sheet event indicates that there has been an error in the preparation of the historical financial information in an earlier period, the reporting accountant will, having regard to the convention for treating post balance sheet events for the purposes of historical financial information in an investment circular (as referred to in the Annexure), only consider the impact of post balance sheet events occurring up to the date of the accountant's report on the final period presented.

Events occurring between the date of the accountant's report and the completion date of the transaction

61. **If, in the period between the date of the accountant's report and the <u>completion date of the transaction</u>, the reporting accountant becomes aware of events and other matters which, had they occurred and been known at the date of the report, might have caused it to issue a different report or to withhold consent, the reporting accountant should discuss the implications of them with those responsible for the investment circular and take additional action as appropriate. (SIR 2000.11)**

62. After the date of the accountant's report, the reporting accountant has no obligation to perform procedures or make enquiries regarding the investment circular.

63. Under Chapter 3 of the Prospectus Rules, a supplementary prospectus must be prepared if, after the date the prospectus has been formally approved by the FSA and before the final closing of the offer of securities to the public or the commencement of trading in the relevant securities, there is a significant change affecting any matter contained in the document or a significant new matter has arisen (or a material mistake or inaccuracy is noted).

64. If, as a result of discussions with those responsible for the investment circular concerning a subsequent event that occurred prior to the completion date of the transaction, the reporting accountant is either uncertain about or disagrees with the course of action proposed, the reporting accountant may consider it necessary to take legal advice with respect to an appropriate course of action.

Going concern

65. References to an emphasis of matter relating to a material uncertainty regarding going concern that is relevant at the time the accountant's report is signed, and which will not be resolved by a satisfactory outcome to the transaction to which the investment circular relates, will be included in the basis of opinion section of the reporting accountants' report.

66. Where the matter or uncertainty will be resolved if the outcome of transactions to which the investment circular containing the report relates is satisfactory (for example the successful raising of money through a share issue or shareholder approval of a transaction), the reporting accountant will consider whether adequate disclosure of that matter or uncertainty is made in the basis of preparation note to the historical financial information. If adequate disclosure is made in the historical financial information it is unlikely to be necessary for the reporting accountant to include an emphasis of matter in the basis of opinion section of its report.

Representations

67. SIR 1000.13 sets out the basic principles and essential procedures with respect to obtaining written confirmation of representations from the directors of the entity.

68. A number of specific representations are required by ISAs (UK and Ireland). Where representations have been obtained by the auditor, subject to the considerations set out in this SIR, it may not be necessary for the reporting accountant to seek further representations covering the same matters, other than in relation to the period since the audit opinion relating to the final period included in the historical financial information was given.

69. Representations additional to those pursuant to ISAs (UK and Ireland) that a reporting accountant may consider for incorporation in the letter of representation or board minute include:

- Confirmation from the directors or management of the entity that they are responsible for the preparation of the historical financial information.

- Confirmation that any adjustments made to historical financial statements for the purposes of preparing the historical financial information are necessary, have been correctly determined and that there are no other adjustments that are necessary.

70. In relation to a Class 1 acquisition, the acquirer may not be in a position to make representations in relation to the historical financial information of the target entity on matters such as fraud, non-compliance with laws and regulation and related parties. In such circumstances representations may be sought from the management of the target entity.

Joint reporting accountants

71. When joint reporting accountants are appointed, the division of work as between them is a matter for agreement. The arrangements between the joint reporting accountants may form part of the engagement letter. Irrespective of any such arrangement, the joint reporting accountants are jointly and severally responsible for the report to be given. Each of the joint reporting accountants participates in the planning of the engagement and they agree upon the scope of work and any changes subsequently found to be necessary thereto. Each of the joint reporting accountants has regard to the considerations set out in this SIR in respect of using the work of an auditor in determining the extent to which it is appropriate to rely on the evidence obtained by the other reporting accountants or the extent to which they consider it necessary to carry out their own work. Each of the joint reporting accountants reviews the work of the other to the extent considered necessary and records the results of that review. A common set of working papers is normally maintained.

Reporting

72. SIRs 1000.17, 1000.18, 1000.19 and 1000.20 set out the basic principles and essential procedures with respect to reporting.

73. The reporting accountant's opinion is usually expressed in terms of whether, for the purpose of the relevant investment circular, the financial information gives a true and fair view of the state of affairs and profits, cash flows and statement of changes in equity.

74. When there is a limitation on the scope of the reporting accountant's work, the reporting accountant considers whether the limitation results in a lack of evidence necessary to form an opinion. When the possible effect is, in the opinion of the reporting accountant, material to the financial information, there will be insufficient evidence to support an unqualified opinion. The nature of the work of reporting accountants is such that in the absence of reliable contemporary evidence relating to significant accounts and balances it may not be possible to form an opinion on the financial information. This might be the case where there has been no audit of the

underlying financial information in the past or where the auditor has given a qualified opinion because of a limitation in the scope of work.

75. As a consequence of the purpose for which financial information is presented and the importance which may be attached to it by readers of the document, a reporting accountant does not normally agree to be associated with financial information where a disclaimer of opinion needs to be given on the information for the entire period.

76. The reporting accountant needs to be satisfied that the financial information adequately describes the applicable financial reporting framework in the description of the basis of preparation, and makes reference to this in the report.

Other information - references to previous audit opinions

77. The reporting accountant's opinion is arrived at independently of any audit opinion previously given on the financial statements which form the basis for the financial information to be reported on. It is not part of the reporting accountant's role to explain (where this is the case) why the reporting accountant's opinion differs from the opinion of the auditor. In some cases, however, there may be an obligation on an issuer to disclose details of qualifications or disclaimers contained in audit reports prepared by the statutory auditor. In such cases, the reporting accountant considers the disclosures made by the issuer relating to such qualifications or disclaimers and whether any matters disclosed might give rise to questions as to how the reporting accountant has dealt with matters giving rise to the qualifications or disclaimers. If the reporting accountant is not satisfied with the disclosures, the reporting accountant discusses the matter with those responsible for the investment circular and ensures that the appropriate information is included by the issuer or is included in the accountant's report. Where the audit has been undertaken by another firm, the reporting accountant does not normally refer to the name of the auditor in the accountant's report.

Comparatives

78. The reporting accountant is required to provide a report on each period included in the historical financial information to which the reporting requirement relates. In consequence the financial information does not constitute "comparatives" as contemplated by ISA (UK and Ireland) 710 "Comparatives". Accordingly ISA (UK and Ireland) 710 is not applicable to the work of the reporting accountant.

Consent in the context of investment circulars containing a report by a reporting accountant

79. Paragraphs 66 to 74 of SIR 1000 deal with consent in relation to the inclusion of an accountant's report in an investment circular.

Effective date

80. A reporting accountant is required to comply with the Investment Reporting Standards contained in this SIR for reports signed after 31 August 2005. Earlier adoption is encouraged.

Appendix 1

BOLD LETTER PARAGRAPHS INCLUDED IN ISAs (UK AND IRELAND) THAT ARE UNLIKELY TO APPLY TO THE REPORTING ACCOUNTANT'S EXERCISE IN RELATION TO HISTORICAL FINANCIAL INFORMATION IN INVESTMENT CIRCULARS.

This summary is illustrative and is included as a convenient source of reference only. It should not be used as a substitute for a reading of the full text of SIR 2000. The summary identifies bold letter paragraphs that are unlikely to apply to the reporting accountant's exercise. The Appendix either cross-refers to paragraphs within SIR 2000 which discuss aspects of ISAs (UK and Ireland) or includes separate discussion below.

ISAs (UK and Ireland) are regularly revised and from time to time new ISAs (UK and Ireland) are issued. Also, there may be extant bold letter paragraphs that, for one reason or another, are not applicable to a particular engagement. Particular bold letter paragraphs in ISAs (UK and Ireland) are unlikely to apply to the reporting accountant's exercise for the following reasons, among others:

- Equivalent and overriding requirements are set out in SIRs, for example ethical requirements.

- The concept of a recurring engagement, or an ongoing relationship with a client, although relevant to audits is usually not relevant to engagements to report on an investment circular.

- The requirement for the reporting accountant to report on three years may remove the need to consider prior years' working papers for the first year reported on.

- With respect to an Initial Public Offering (IPO) there may be no practical distinction between management and those charged with corporate governance.

ISA (UK and Ireland)	SIR 2000 Reference or comment
200 Objective and General Principles Governing an Audit of Financial Statements	
"The auditor should comply with the Code of Ethics for Professional Accountants issued by the International Federation of Accountants." (4)	Paragraph 24 (Paragraph 18 of SIR 1000).
"In the UK and Ireland the relevant ethical pronouncements with which the auditor should comply are the APB's Ethical Standards and the ethical pronouncements relating to the work of auditors issued by the auditor's relevant professional body." (4-1)	Paragraph 24 (Paragraph 18 of SIR 1000).

ISA (UK and Ireland)	SIR 2000 Reference or comment
210 Terms of Audit Engagements	
"On recurring audits, the auditor should consider whether circumstances require the terms of the engagement to be revised and whether there is a need to remind the client of the existing terms of the engagement." (10)	The concept of recurring audits does not apply to investment circulars.
"An auditor who, before the completion of the engagement, is requested to change the engagement to one which provides a lower level of assurance, should consider the appropriateness of doing so." (12)	Changing the engagement to one which provides a lower level of assurance is not permitted by the PD Regulation.
"The auditor should not agree to a change of engagement where there is no reasonable justification for doing so." (18)	The regulation does not provide the opportunity to vary the nature of the engagement.
300 Planning an Audit of Financial Statements	
"The auditor should perform the following activities prior to starting an initial audit: (b) Communicate with the previous auditor, where there has been a change of auditors, in compliance with relevant ethical requirements. (28)	Not applicable as there is not an ongoing relationship.
330 The Auditor's Procedures in Response to Assessed Risks	
"If the auditor plans to use audit evidence about the operating effectiveness of controls obtained in prior audits, the auditor should obtain audit evidence about whether changes in those specific controls have occurred subsequent to the prior audit. The auditor should obtain audit evidence about whether such changes have occurred by performing inquiry in combination with observation or inspection to confirm the understanding of those specific controls". (39)	Paragraphs 52 and 53.
"If the auditor plans to rely on controls that have changed since they were last tested, the auditor should test the operating effectiveness of such controls in the current audit". (40)	Paragraphs 52 and 53.
"If the auditor plans to rely on controls that have not changed since they were last tested, the auditor should test the operating effectiveness of such controls at least once in every third audit." (41)	Paragraphs 52 and 53.
"When there are a number of controls for which the auditor determines that it is appropriate to use audit evidence obtained in prior audits, the auditor should test the operating effectiveness of some controls each audit." (43)	Paragraphs 52 and 53.
510 Initial engagements – Opening Balances and Continuing Engagements – Opening Balances	
"The auditor should also obtain sufficient appropriate audit evidence for the matters set out in paragraph 2 for continuing audit engagements (see paragraphs 10-1 and 10-2". (2-1)	Not applicable as the reporting accountant's exercise is not a continuing engagement.

ISA (UK and Ireland)	SIR 2000 Reference or comment
550 Related Parties	
IAS 24	
"The auditor should review information provided by those charged with governance and management identifying the names of all known related parties and should perform the following audit procedures in respect of the completeness of this information: (a) Review prior year working papers for names of known related parties;" (7)	Paragraph 59 explains that this does not apply in respect of the earliest period where more than one period is to be reported on.
FRS 8	
"(a) Review prior year working papers for names of known related parties;" (107)	Paragraph 59 explains that this does not apply in respect of the earliest period where more than one period is to be reported on.
560 Subsequent Events	
"When, after the date of the auditor's report but before the financial statements are issued, the auditor becomes aware of a fact which may materially affect the financial statements, the auditor should consider whether the financial statements need amendment, should discuss the matter with management and should take the action appropriate in the circumstances." (9)	Paragraphs 61 to 64.
"When management does not amend the financial statements in circumstances where the auditor believes they need to be amended and the auditor's report has not been released to the entity, the auditor should express a qualified opinion or an adverse opinion." (11)	Paragraphs 61 to 64.
"When, after the financial statements have been issued, the auditor becomes aware of a fact which existed at the date of the auditor's report and which, if known at that date, may have caused the auditor to modify the auditor's report, the auditor should consider whether the financial statements need revision, should discuss the matter with management, and should take the action appropriate in the circumstances." (14)	Paragraphs 61 to 64.
"The new auditor's report should include an emphasis of a matter paragraph referring to a note to the financial statements that more extensively discusses the reason for the revision of the previously issued financial statements and to the earlier report issued by the auditor." (16)	Paragraphs 61 to 64.
710 Comparatives	
All paragraphs.	Paragraph 78.

Appendix 2

EXAMPLES OF ENGAGEMENT LETTER CLAUSES

These examples of engagement letter clauses are intended for consideration in the context of an accountant's report. They should be tailored to the specific circumstances and supplemented by such other clauses as are relevant and appropriate.

For a prospectus

Financial information upon which the report is to be given

We understand that the directors of ABC plc will include in the Prospectus historical financial information for the [three] years ended [   ] in relation to ABC plc, the last [two years] of which will be presented and prepared in a form consistent with that which will be adopted in ABC plc's next published annual financial statements, having regard to accounting standards and policies and legislation applicable to such annual financial statements in accordance with the requirements of Annex I item 20.1 of the Prospectus Rules.

Responsibilities

The directors of ABC plc are responsible for the historical financial information.

It is our responsibility to form an opinion as to whether the financial information gives a true and fair view for the purposes of the Prospectus and to report our opinion to the directors of ABC plc.

Scope of work

We shall expect to obtain such relevant and reliable evidence as we consider sufficient to enable us to draw reasonable conclusions therefrom. The nature and extent of our procedures will vary according to our assessment of the appropriate sources of evidence. Our work will be directed to those matters which in our view materially affect the overall financial information upon which our opinion is to be given, and will not be directed to the discovery of errors or misstatements which we consider to be immaterial.

It is expected that a substantial part of the evidence which we may require will be contained in the audit files of LMN Accountants. ABC plc has agreed that it will use its best endeavours to ensure that the relevant audit files are made available to us.

Our work may also depend upon receiving without undue delay full co-operation from all relevant officials of ABC plc and their disclosure to us of all the accounting records of ABC plc and all other records and related information (including certain representations) as we may need for the purposes of our examination.

For a Class 1 circular

Financial information upon which the report is to be given

We understand that the directors of ABC plc will include in the Class 1 Circular a historical financial information table for the [three] years ended [ ] in relation to XYZ Limited which will be presented and prepared in a form consistent with the accounting policies adopted in ABC plc's latest annual consolidated accounts in accordance with the requirements of chapter 13 of the Listing Rules.

Responsibilities

The directors of ABC plc are responsible for the historical financial information table.

It is our responsibility to form an opinion as to whether the financial information gives a true and fair view for the purposes of the Class 1 circular and whether the financial information table has been prepared in a form that is consistent with the accounting policies adopted in ABC plc's latest annual accounts and to report our opinion to the directors of ABC plc.

Scope of work

We shall expect to obtain such relevant and reliable evidence as we consider sufficient to enable us to draw reasonable conclusions therefrom. The nature and extent of our procedures will vary according to our assessment of the appropriate sources of evidence. Our work will be directed to those matters which in our view materially affect the overall financial information upon which our opinion is to be given, and will not be directed to the discovery of errors or misstatements which we consider to be immaterial.

It is expected that a substantial part of the evidence which we may require will be contained in the audit files of LMN Accountants. ABC plc has agreed that it will use its best endeavours to ensure that the relevant audit files are made available to us.

Our work may also depend upon receiving without undue delay full co-operation from all relevant officials of ABC plc and XYZ Limited and their disclosure to us of all the accounting records of XYZ Limited and all other records and related information (including certain representations) as we may need for the purposes of our examination.

Appendix 3

EXAMPLE OF AN ACCOUNTANT'S REPORT ON HISTORICAL FINANCIAL INFORMATION

Date

Reporting accountant's address

Addressees, as agreed between the parties in the engagement letter

Dear Sirs

[ABC plc]/[XYZ Limited]

We report on the financial information set out [in paragraphs .... to ....]. This financial information has been prepared for inclusion in the [describe document[1]] dated..........of ABC plc on the basis of the accounting policies set out in paragraph [ ]. This report is required by [Relevant Regulation] and is given for the purpose of complying with that [Relevant Regulation] and for no other purpose.

Responsibilities

[As described in paragraph [ ]] [T/t]he Directors of ABC plc are responsible for preparing the financial information [on the basis of preparation set out in [*note x to the financial information*]] [and in accordance with [*the applicable financial reporting framework*]].

It is our responsibility to form an opinion [on the financial information] [as to whether the financial information gives a true and fair view, for the purposes of the [describe document], and to report our opinion to you.

Basis of opinion

We conducted our work in accordance with Standards for Investment Reporting issued by the Auditing Practices Board in the United Kingdom. Our work included an assessment of evidence relevant to the amounts and disclosures in the financial information. It also included an assessment of significant estimates and judgments made by those responsible for the preparation of the financial information and whether the accounting policies are appropriate to the entity's circumstances, consistently applied and adequately disclosed.

We planned and performed our work so as to obtain all the information and explanations which we considered necessary in order to provide us with sufficient evidence to give reasonable assurance that the financial information is free from material misstatement whether caused by fraud or other irregularity or error.

---

[1] For example, "prospectus", "listing particulars", "Class 1 circular" and "AIM admission document."

Opinion

In our opinion, the financial information gives, for the purposes of the [describe document] dated ....., a true and fair view of the state of affairs of [ABC plc]/[XYZ Limited] as at the dates stated and of its profits, cash flows and [recognised gains and losses] [changes in equity] for the periods then ended in accordance with the basis of preparation set out in note x [and in accordance with [*the applicable financial reporting framework*] as described in note y] [and has been prepared in a form that is consistent with the accounting policies adopted in [ABC plc's] latest annual accounts[2]].

Declaration[3]

For the purposes of [Prospectus Rule [5.5.3R(2)(f)] [5.5.4R (2)(f)]] [Paragraph a of Schedule Two of the AIM Rules] we are responsible for [this report as part] [the following part(s)] of the [prospectus] [registration document] [AIM admission document] and declare that we have taken all reasonable care to ensure that the information contained [in this report][those parts] is, to the best of our knowledge, in accordance with the facts and contains no omission likely to affect its import. This declaration is included in the [prospectus] [registration document] [AIM admission document] in compliance with [item 1.2 of annex I of the PD Regulation] [item 1.2 of annex III of the PD Regulation] [Schedule Two of the AIM Rules].

Yours faithfully

Reporting accountant

---

[2] The wording in these square brackets is appropriate for inclusion where the report relates to historical financial information included in a Class 1 circular.
[3] This declaration is a requirement of the Prospectus Rules and is appropriate for inclusion when the report is included in a Prospectus, see Appendix 2 of SIR 1000. It is also appropriate for inclusion in an AIM admission document under Schedule Two of the AIM Rules.

ACCOUNTING CONVENTIONS COMMONLY USED IN THE PREPARATION OF HISTORICAL FINANCIAL INFORMATION IN INVESTMENT CIRCULARS

This Annexure has been compiled by the APB from a number of sources to describe conventions commonly used for the preparation of historical financial information intended to show a true and fair view for the purposes of an investment circular. It does not include either basic principles, essential procedures, or guidance promulgated by the APB.

Introduction

1   Preparers[1] have regard to accepted conventions which have been developed for the preparation and presentation of historical financial information in investment circulars. They seek to assist preparers, to the extent consistent with established accounting principles, to meet the obligation that the historical financial information should give a true and fair view for the purposes of the relevant investment circular. These conventions also take into account the requirement contained in the Prospectus Directive that the information should be presented in an easily analysable and comprehensible form. The conventions are described in the material presented below.

Disclosure of the financial reporting framework adopted

2   Preparers summarise the applicable financial reporting framework within the notes to the financial information. Where one of the conventions described in this Annexure is applied and its application has a material effect on the financial information or is necessary for an understanding of the basis of preparation of the financial information, it is appropriate to describe the treatment adopted in the basis of preparation note in the historical financial information.

Adjustments to the financial information

3   Preparers make adjustments, only in respect of material items, in order to:

(a)   present the financial information for all relevant years on the basis of consistent, acceptable and appropriately applied accounting policies, in accordance with the applicable requirements;

(b)   correct errors; and

(c)   record adjusting post balance sheet events where appropriate (see paragraph 13 below).

---

[1]   The directors and management of an entity are responsible for the preparation and presentation of the financial statements of an entity. In this Annexure they are collectively referred to as "the preparers".

4   The historical financial information presented will be based on the records of the entity whose historical financial information is presented in the investment circular (referred to as "the entity" throughout this Annexure), for the periods reported on. These records reflect the representations and intentions of the entity's management at the time the underlying financial information was drawn up. Matters such as the selection of accounting policies, accounting estimates and valuation judgments form part of the responsibilities of management in compiling a record of their stewardship.

5   In presenting historical financial information in an investment circular, except insofar as necessary to achieve the objectives set out above, preparers do not seek to replace accounting policies, accounting estimates or valuation judgments with alternatives subsequently selected by themselves. They consider whether the specific application of the basis of accounting originally adopted by management falls within an acceptable range of alternatives (if not, the conclusion will usually be that an error has occurred, which may need to be adjusted). Furthermore, it is not normally appropriate for adjustments to be made to eliminate items of earned income or expenses incurred, nor, in any circumstances, to recognise notional items of income or expense. The historical financial information presented in the investment circular is thus a version of the historical record as presented by the entity's management and adjustments are introduced only to achieve those specific objectives set out in paragraph 3 of this Annexure.

Trend of results

6   The historical financial information included in an investment circular presents a trend of results for the relevant period. In this respect the financial information may be distinguished from the financial information contained in statutory accounts.

7   Notional, or other, adjustments that impact net profits or net assets are not introduced in order to make the "track record" more consistent with the entity's expected operations or structure following the transaction. Such adjustments would anticipate future events and are not consistent with the principle that the historical financial information should record the events which actually occurred during the period of the historical financial information.

Adjustments for change in basis of accounting

8   Adjustments are made to ensure that, wherever practicable, the financial information is stated on the basis of consistent accounting policies. Under the PD Regulation (subject to certain transitional provisions in Article 35 of the PD Regulation), the financial information for the most recent year (where audited historical financial information is required for the latest 2 financial years) or most recent 2 years (where audited historical financial information is required for the latest 3 financial years) is required to be prepared and presented in a form consistent with that which will be adopted in the issuer's next published annual financial statements (having regard to accounting standards and policies and legislation applicable to such annual financial statements). The requirements do not prevent entities from presenting the financial

information for all periods in a form which is consistent with that which will be adopted in the next published financial statements if they so choose. In other contexts such as in a Class 1 transaction, the objective may be for the financial information for all periods to be presented in a form consistent with the accounting policies adopted by the acquirer in its latest annual consolidated accounts.

9   When considering the adjustments that may be necessary where a new International Financial Reporting Standard or other relevant accounting standard has been introduced during, or (where applicable under the regulations) subsequent to, the period to which the regulations apply, a relevant factor will be whether the requirements for implementing the new accounting standard provide that it should be applied retroactively once adopted. Where adoption of a new accounting standard leads to the inclusion of a prior year adjustment in the accounts, adjustments are made, to the extent practicable, to reflect the effect of the policy in any relevant earlier period. Where the adoption of a new accounting standard does not lead to the inclusion of a prior year adjustment, for example where the accounting standard is stated to apply to transactions first accounted for after a certain date; no such adjustment is made to the financial information. Where an entity chooses to adopt a new accounting standard early and this is permitted or encouraged, although not required, by that standard, the financial information reflects the same treatment as adopted by the entity.

10   Although adjustments may be made for changes in accounting policies, adjustments are not normally made for changes in the methods of applying an accounting policy (whether a one-off change or a series of gradual refinements) or otherwise to correct the entity's accounting estimates, provided that there were no errors. The effect of correcting an estimate in a later period is normally reflected in the result of that period. Consideration may be given to whether an understanding of the trend of results would be assisted by separate or additional disclosure in relation to changes in the methods of applying accounting policies or the impact of a correction of an accounting estimate.

11   Occasionally, an accounting policy may have been applied on the basis of considerations other than relevant economic ones (for example where financial statements measure the carrying amount of depreciable fixed assets in accordance with depreciation policies which are influenced by taxation considerations - as is the case in certain jurisdictions). Those presenting historical financial information in an investment circular may determine that an adjustment is necessary in order for the financial information to present a true and fair view, for the purposes of the relevant investment circular.

Audit qualifications relating to non-compliance with accounting standards

12   Where the auditor's report(s) on the underlying financial statements was qualified on grounds, for example, of failure to comply with an applicable accounting standard or disagreement over an accounting treatment, it may be possible to make adjustments so as to remove the need for a similar qualification in a report on the adjusted historical financial information.

Post balance sheet events

13 In determining whether adjustment is to be made for post balance sheet events, subject to the guidance set out above, it is normal practice to consider events only up to the date on which the audit report on the relevant underlying financial statements was originally signed by the auditors except in relation to the final period presented. In respect of this final period, it will be necessary for post balance sheet events to be reflected up to the date on which the historical financial information to be presented in the investment circular is approved by the responsible party. Where the financial information is based upon financial records which were not audited, the relevant date for post balance sheet event considerations in the earlier periods is normally taken to be the date at which the underlying balance sheet was finalised.

Presentation of the financial information

14 Subject to the requirements of any applicable regulation, the financial information is presented on a consistent and comparable basis from period to period and includes such presentational changes to the financial information as are necessary in order to achieve this.

15 Presentational changes might be made to:

(a) present the financial information in a comparable way; and

(b) give due prominence to matters of particular importance in the context of the document in which the financial information is included.

16 The financial information contained in the entity's records may not have been presented on a comparable basis from period to period because the convention for presenting financial information adopted in earlier periods may have been different from that adopted in later periods.

17 Whenever practicable, financial information is presented in such a way that information which a user of the investment circular might wish to compare, is in fact comparable. Presentational changes of this nature may be categorised as follows:

(a) reclassifications (for example, cost of sales reclassified as distribution costs);

(b) re-analyses (for example, restatements of analyses between continuing and discontinued activities);

(c) grossing up of items netted off in earlier periods (for example, matched assets and liabilities previously left off balance sheet);

(d) derivation or computation of information undisclosed in earlier periods (for example, profit and loss account subtotals or cash flow statements); and

**THE AUDITING
PRACTICES BOARD**

(e) harmonisation of note disclosures (for example the editing of notes for earlier periods to integrate them with notes for later periods).

18 For example, a business classed as a continuing operation in one year may have been designated a discontinued activity in financial statements drawn up for a later period. It will be desirable for the relevant information within continuing operations in the earlier periods to be reclassified as discontinued. Where separate disclosure of information relating to entities acquired during the period has been presented in the financial statements, it is customary to reclassify such information for the purposes of the historical financial information as continuing activities, other than in respect of acquisitions made in the final period of the track record.

19 Changes are not, however, made to the presentation adopted in the financial statements on which the financial information is based, unless such changes are consistent with the requirement to give a true and fair view for the purposes of the investment circular.

20 Where it is considered that the significance of certain items to an understanding of the financial information may be obscured by the presentation adopted in the financial statements, it is usually appropriate for that presentation to be changed, relevant disclosures to be made or relevant explanations to be introduced to highlight their significance. This approach may be adopted for example to highlight certain categories of expense, such as proprietors' remuneration, in the trading record of a company seeking flotation. It may also be adopted to highlight the results of different classes of business, particularly in cases where there are proposals that a class of business is to be discontinued.

21 However, in all cases, changes in presentation would be inappropriate if they are in conflict with applicable accounting standards.

22 As noted above, in certain cases regulatory requirements stipulate that information for the most recent two of the three years is to be presented on a basis comparable with that which would be adopted in an issuer's next annual financial statements. In such cases, in order that the reader is able to relate the first year's information to the final two years, preparers may present financial information for the second year on the basis originally reported (and thus comparable with the first year) as well as on the adjusted basis required by the regulation.

Issues connected with underlying financial statements

23 Where the entity has prepared accounts consolidating all its subsidiaries during the period, the financial information will, subject to any adjustments made, be the information set out in the consolidated accounts.

24 There may be cases where historical financial information is to be prepared for an entity in circumstances where consolidated financial statements do not exist. This may arise for example where the business is a sub-group, the parent company of which was exempt from the requirement to prepare consolidated accounts, or where the

business comprises companies under common ownership but which were not constituted as a legal sub-group.

Unconsolidated accounts

25   Where there has been a legal sub-group it will usually be appropriate, for ease of analysis and comprehension, for the accounts of the subsidiaries to be consolidated into the accounts of the parent company. For this purpose, specially prepared consolidated accounts may be compiled by the relevant entity, applying the normal conventions for consolidation.

Entities under common management and control

26   Where the entities have been under common management and control but do not form a legal group, the historical financial information will normally be presented on a combined or aggregated basis. Under this method, the results and net assets of the relevant entities are aggregated (with eliminations for intercompany transactions and balances), as are the related share capital balances and reserves. If the information is not presented on a combined or aggregated basis then separate historical financial information for entities accounting for substantially the whole of the historical revenue earning record is likely to be required.

Carve outs

27   Where a business has formed part of a larger group ("overall group") during the three year period, but has not been accounted for separately, it may be desirable to present a separate track record (a "carve out") for that business ("carve out business"), derived from the records of the overall group. This approach may be preferable to the alternative approach of presenting the track record of the overall group, with appropriate disclosures of operations discontinuing or not acquired. Circumstances where a carve out approach might be followed include flotations of businesses in a demerger and Class 1 acquisitions of divisions of a selling group.

28   When considering whether it is appropriate to present carve out financial information, the following factors will be relevant:

(a)   the extent to which the carve out business has been separately managed and financially controlled within the overall group; and

(b)   the extent to which it is practicable to identify the historical financial information attributable to the carve out business.

29   Where the omission of the results and assets of those operations not the subject of the transaction concerned would be misleading in the context of the circumstances in which the historical financial information is to be presented, it will generally be appropriate to adopt the approach of presenting financial information on the overall group. Disclosures are made to assist the user to understand the contribution made by the operations not the subject of the transaction concerned. However, each case will need to be assessed on its own facts and circumstances.

30 In preparing the track record for the carve out business, the guidance in paragraph 5 of this Annexure will be relevant. The objective will be, so far as possible, to present a historical record reflecting the events which actually occurred in the reporting period. Whilst it may be possible to identify certain transactions and balances which clearly relate to the carve out business, there will often be cases where the accounting records do not differentiate between items which relate to the carve out business and items which relate to the remainder of the overall group's business. Examples include management overheads, funding arrangements and shared assets. The guidance below discusses some of the elements typically encountered in preparing a carve out track record.

31 Clear and comprehensive disclosure in the notes to the historical financial information will normally be needed in the basis of preparation in order for the nature of the historical financial information to be clearly understood. The description would be expected to give a general indication of the process adopted for the preparation of the historical financial information, and describe any factors which are particularly important to an understanding of the manner in which the information has been prepared.

32 The accounting policies to be adopted in the carve out accounts will need to reflect the requirements relating to the presentation of historical financial information and may differ from those previously adopted. The question of functional currency is also considered having regard to the economic environment of the carve out business, which may lead to the adoption of a different functional currency from that of the overall group.

Allocations

33 Where transactions or balances are not accounted for within the overall group in a manner which clearly attributes them to the carve out business, it will generally be desirable for a method for allocating the relevant amounts to the carve out business to be identified with a view to providing the fairest approximation to the amounts actually attributable to the carve out business. The method adopted is applied on a rational and consistent basis. It will not, however, be appropriate to make allocations where there is no rational or consistent basis for doing so.

Bases for allocating transactions and balances

34 The appropriate basis for allocating group income and expenditure to a carve out business will vary according to the circumstances. It may, for example, be appropriate to allocate centrally accounted-for human resources costs on the basis of headcount (but account might be taken also of relative levels of staff turnover or other factors which indicate greater or less than average use in deciding whether the approach was in fact appropriate). The costs of a head office accounts department might be allocated by reference to the relevant sizes of the carve out business and remaining group. Again if other factors suggest that size is not a good indicator – if for example a disproportionate number of the accounting team are engaged in work for one part of the business and not the other – refinements to the approach might be considered appropriate.

35 It is important to recognise that the purpose of the allocation is to attribute an appropriate element of the overall group record to the carve out business. As a consequence, the position shown will frequently not be that which might have existed if the carve out business had been a stand-alone business. The position will be affected by the arrangements which apply to the group as a whole, which are a matter of historical fact and which it is not the purpose of the carve out financial information to alter. Frequently, disclosure will be made accompanying the financial information highlighting that the information presented may not be representative of the position which may prevail after the transaction.

36 Where an element of overall group third party debt is to be assumed by the carve out business, it may be appropriate to allocate an appropriate element of such debt to the carve out business during the historical track record period. The basis for such an allocation may be by reference to the terms of the separation agreement. In other cases, the debt may be treated as part of the carve out business' balance with the overall group. Finance lease borrowings would be expected to be allocated in line with the allocation of the related asset. The allocation of interest income/costs would follow the way in which the related debt and debt instruments have been apportioned.

Relationship with the remaining group

37 In addition to transactions with 'third parties', the results of the business will also include transactions with the part of the overall group which is not part of the carve out business (the "remaining group"). Hence, for example, sales which were previously regarded as 'intra group' will need to be re-examined to determine whether they relate to entities within the carve out business or outside it.

38 The remaining group will normally also be regarded as a related party for the purposes of disclosing related party transactions, and it will normally be necessary to identify the extent of the relationships between the carve out business and the remaining group. Balances with the remaining group may have comprised elements of trading balances and short term or long term funding balances, which may or may not have been interest bearing. Balances of a trading nature will normally be presented as an element of debtors or creditors. Balances which are considered to be funding in nature (having regard inter alia to the use made of the balances, the period for which they remain outstanding and the level of other capital) will normally be classified according to their general nature. Where the balance is interest bearing and has other characteristics of debt, it will be presented in the manner of debt financing. Where the balance does not have the characteristics of debt, it will be re-classified from creditors into capital and be presented in the manner of equity, typically aggregated with the share capital and reserves of companies comprising the carve out business, as 'parent company net investment' in the carve out business.

39 Balances with the remaining group may also contain elements of third party debtors or creditors which have been accounted for on behalf of the carve out business by the remaining group. Examples might be VAT costs, payroll taxes, certain customers or suppliers common to the carve out business and the remaining group, and external funding balances. Such elements of the balance with the remaining group would be expected to be reallocated to the appropriate third party captions.

THE AUDITING
PRACTICES BOARD

40   Consolidation journals within the overall group accounting records will need to be analysed and, if appropriate, allocated to the carve out business.

Pension costs

41   Where employees of the carve out business participate in a pension scheme relating to the overall group, the track record of the carve out business would reflect the apportioned costs applicable to the carve out business. The accounting implications of any pension surplus/deficit attributable to the carve out business would also normally be expected to be reflected in the track record.

Acquisitions

42   Acquisitions will be treated in accordance with the guidance in paragraphs 50 to 52 of this Annexure. It should be noted that acquisitions previously regarded as too small for separate disclosure in the overall group accounts may become sufficiently material to require separate disclosure in the context of the carve out business.

Disposals, non recurring and exceptional items

43   Non recurring and exceptional items are generally allocated to the carve out business and accounted for in accordance with the applicable accounting standard. The treatment of disposals follows that described in paragraph 53 of this Annexure.

Taxation

44   Tax charges are generally allocated to the carve out business to reflect the proportion of the overall group charge attributable to the carve out business. The approach will typically involve the aggregation of the tax charges actually incurred by the companies within the carve out business (and will therefore reflect the benefits, reliefs and charges arising as a result of membership of the overall group), after taking account of the tax effects of any adjustments. Where the information relating to the tax charges actually incurred is not available, the tax charge may be recomputed on the basis of the results of the carve out business. The tax rate applied is selected having regard to the tax position of the overall group and might thus include the impact of benefits, reliefs and charges arising as a result of membership of the overall group, to the extent that they would have been available to or imposed upon the carve out business.

Cash flow statements

45   A cash flow statement is prepared for the carve out business based on the carve out information. Where the overall group operates a central cash account, cash flows relating to centrally settled costs are allocated to the carve out business to the extent that the related balances are allocated to the carve out business.

Investments in subsidiaries, joint ventures and associates

46   The status of an entity in the overall group's accounts (that is, whether it is recorded as a subsidiary, joint venture or associate) may be the result of investments in the relevant

entity by more than one group company. If not all the investing companies are to be part of the carve out business, this may mean that the status of the entity in the track record of the carve out business is different from that within the overall group. Additional or new disclosures may therefore be required.

Treatment of other items

47   Dividends are expected to be reflected in the track record of the carve out business where companies within the carve out business have paid dividends to members of the remaining group.

48   In relation to the disclosure of directors' remuneration, it is normal to present information for those individuals who are to be directors of the carve out business or who were employed by the overall group in a capacity equivalent to that of a director of the carve out business. The information disclosed will reflect the salaries and benefits paid in respect of services to the carve out business by any member of the overall group to those individuals (irrespective of whether the individuals were directors or not) during the period covered by the track record. No information is presented for proposed directors of the carve out business who were not employed by the overall group, or for individuals who served as directors of companies within the carve out group but who are not to be directors of the carve out group's holding company following the transaction.

49   A segmental analysis is prepared for the carve out business to reflect the segments which the carve out business has decided to adopt.

Acquisitions

50   Entities acquired during the period covered by the historical financial information will typically be accounted for, in the records of the acquiring entity, in accordance with the accounting treatment applicable, having regard to the set of accounting standards adopted. Hence, for example, if the accounting standards require acquisition accounting, the acquired subsidiary will be accounted for from the date of acquisition by the acquiring entity.

51   Chapter 13 of the Listing Rules states that, in the case of a Class 1 acquisition when, during the three year period to be covered by the historical financial information (or in the lesser period up to the date of the acquisition if the target's business has been in operation for less than 3 years), the target has acquired or has agreed to acquire an undertaking which would have been classified, at the date of the acquisition, as a Class 1 acquisition, financial information on that undertaking must be given, which covers as a minimum the period from the beginning of the three year period to the date of acquisition.

52   Generally (and typically where the acquisition has been or will be accounted for under the acquisition method), the requirement outlined in paragraph 50 of this Annexure leads to a separate table of historical financial information covering the results of the acquired subsidiary undertaking during the period prior to acquisition. The Listing Rules contain no express contents requirements for acquisitions which would have

been classified as smaller than Class 1 (ie a Class 2 or Class 3 transaction), although Listing Rule 13.3 contains contents requirements applicable to all circulars. Additional financial information may be required where the financial information presented in the entity's own track record does not account for substantially all of the track record of the business during the three year period.

Disposals

53 Disposals of subsidiaries or a discontinuation of a material section of the business are reflected by separate analysis between the continuing business and the disposed or discontinued business, either under the relevant headings in the profit and loss table or in the notes to the historical financial information. It is not normally appropriate to make adjustments to eliminate the results of subsidiaries that have been disposed of or discontinued operations from the trading record. However, it may not be necessary to introduce the results of a subsidiary that has been disposed of or a discontinued operation into specially prepared consolidated accounts or combined accounts prepared having regard to the considerations set out in paragraphs 25 to 49 of this Annexure, unless the inclusion of such information is relevant to an understanding of the business to which the historical financial information relates.

Financial information on newly formed issuers

54 In many cases, investment circulars are prepared in relation to newly formed companies (for example start up businesses, investment trusts, newly formed holding companies etc). Generally such companies will not have prepared accounts for a financial year at the time the investment circular is to be issued and consequently financial statements will need to be prepared for the purposes of the investment circular.

Unincorporated entities and entities producing limited accounting information

55 Acquisitions may involve entities which do not prepare financial information which meets the standards required for statutory accounts in the UK (and additionally may not have been subject to the disciplines of an external audit). The accounting conventions adopted may be devised for internal management accounting purposes rather than to meet more generally applicable accounting standards. In such cases, it may not be possible to present financial information meeting the requirements of the relevant regulations. The decision as to what information to present will depend upon the degree to which the information can be regarded as sufficiently relevant and reliable having regard to the purpose for which it is presented. Frequently the purpose will be to assist shareholders in a decision; it is for those responsible for the investment circular to weigh up the balance between depriving shareholders of information which may be relevant to a decision and being satisfied that the information presented is of sufficient quality to be properly used as the basis for a decision. Where there is significant doubt about the quality of the financial information available, those responsible for the investment circular would be advised not to present it in the investment circular. This may lead to very limited financial information appearing in the relevant investment circular. In the case of an investment circular regulated by the UK

Listing Authority, the position should be discussed in advance with the UK Listing Authority.

Changes in the legal form of entities

56   There may be circumstances where businesses have been carried on during the period covered by the report by different legal entities with the consequence that the relevant financial information may be found in the accounts of different legal entities. A typical example is a management buy-out, where prior to the buy-out, the business might have been accounted for in the financial statements of a subsidiary undertaking of the vendor, but, following the buy-out, the financial information may be that of the entity formed to effect the acquisition.

57   In cases where the legal entity accounting for the business has changed (for example where a business has been transferred from one entity to another – typically a newly formed company) but where there is no essential change in the underlying business, it is normal for the financial information to be presented as part of a single table, with the results of the predecessor entity shown next to those of the successor entity (generally on a combined basis in the period during which the transaction took place).

58   A consequence of the change in legal entity may be a change in the capital structure. Frequently, where there is a management buy-out, debt becomes a significant part of the capitalisation of the business. In order to highlight for the reader the potential lack of comparability between periods, a statement is often included within the introduction or beneath the profit and loss account (and in the relevant notes) referring to the change in capital structure and alerting the reader to the fact that the information relating to financing costs may not be comparable throughout the period. In certain cases, where the effect is material to an appreciation of the figures, it may also be necessary to draw attention to a discontinuity in values attributed to balance sheet items. In circumstances where, as in the case of a management buy-out, fair value adjustments have been made during the period covered by the historical financial information, it is inappropriate to attempt to show the impact of such adjustments on the results prior to the acquisition. However, the impact of the fair value adjustments is, where practicable, highlighted in respect of the post-acquisition results.

Earnings per share

59   In cases where there has been a capital reorganisation since the date at which the last balance sheet was drawn up, it will usually be appropriate for the earnings per share figures disclosed to be adjusted to reflect the reorganisation (to the extent that it involves issues of shares for no consideration, issues containing a bonus element, share splits etc). In such cases, the number of shares used in the earnings per share calculation is adjusted so that the shares originally in issue are replaced by the number of new shares, representing the shares originally in issue, following the reorganisation. Where shares have been issued during the period, this is taken into account in calculating the equivalent weighted average number of post-reorganisation shares. Where the reconstruction involves conversions, for example of preference shares or loan stock, the earnings figures used in the calculation of earnings per share may also

THE AUDITING PRACTICES BOARD

need to be adjusted to eliminate the effect of any related preference dividends or interest.

60   Difficulties may also arise over the relevance of the earnings per share figure in certain cases, for example where prior to flotation a new holding company has been created. In such cases an earnings per share figure based on the share capital of the subsidiary may be of limited significance to investors. Accordingly, it is usually appropriate to include a supplementary earnings per share figure, in addition to the historical earnings per share figure, based on the relevant number of shares in the new parent company (before the issue of shares to raise new funds). This approach is also generally adopted in the case of a carve out business which did not have share capital during the reporting period. Where the effect is material and where practicable, the number of shares used for the purposes of the calculation is adjusted to reflect variations in the levels of capital funding the operations arising, for example, from issues of equity for cash during the period under review. In some circumstances, such as where there has been a management buy out during the period reported on, the differences in the capital structure may be such that a comparison of the earnings per share figures is not meaningful. Where this is the case, the statement to be included beneath the profit and loss table mentioned above generally refers also to the lack of comparability of the earnings per share information.

Reporting currency

61   Where historical financial information is to be presented on a target entity, and that target has reported historically in a currency other than that of the acquiring entity, it is normal to present the financial information in the target's original reporting currency.

Extraction without material adjustment

62   In a Class 1 circular, the listed company must (in addition to citing the source of the information) state whether the financial information that has been extracted from audited accounts was extracted without material adjustment. It is not possible to prescribe conditions for determining whether an adjustment will be a material adjustment in any given case, although presentational changes which do not have the effect of altering net assets, are normally permitted to be made. The UK Listing Authority will need to agree the approach in individual cases.

STANDARDS FOR INVESTMENT REPORTING

3000 – INVESTMENT REPORTING STANDARDS APPLICABLE TO PUBLIC REPORTING ENGAGEMENTS ON PROFIT FORECASTS

CONTENTS

Appendices
1   *The regulatory background*
2   *Reporting accountant's criteria*
3   *Other regulatory provisions relevant to the preparers of profit forecasts*
4   *Examples of engagement letter clauses*
5   *Examples of management representation letter clauses*
6   *Example of a report on a profit forecast*
7   *Example of a report on a profit estimate that is not subject to assumptions*

SIR 3000 contains basic principles and essential procedures ("Investment Reporting Standards"), indicated by paragraphs in bold type, with which a reporting accountant is required to comply in the conduct of an engagement to report on a profit forecast which is included within an investment circular prepared for issue in connection with a securities transaction governed wholly or in part by the law and regulations of the United Kingdom.

SIR 3000 also includes explanatory and other material, including appendices, in the context of which the basic principles and essential procedures are to be understood and applied. It is necessary to consider the whole text of the SIR to understand and apply the basic principles and essential procedures.

For the purposes of SIRs, an investment circular is defined as: "any document issued by an entity pursuant to statutory or regulatory requirements relating to listed or unlisted securities on which it is intended that a third party should make an investment decision, including a prospectus, listing particulars, circular to shareholders or similar document".

SIR 1000 "Investment reporting standards applicable to all engagements involving an investment circular" contains basic principles and essential procedures that are applicable to all engagements involving an investment circular. The definitions in the Glossary of terms set out in Appendix 4 of SIR 1000 are to be applied in the interpretation of this and all other SIRs. Terms defined in the glossary are underlined the first time that they occur in the text.

To assist readers, SIRs contain references to, and extracts from, certain legislation and chapters of the Rules of the UK Listing Authority. Readers are cautioned that these references may change subsequent to publication.

Introduction

1. Standard for Investment Reporting (SIR) 1000 "Investment Reporting Standards applicable to all engagements in connection with an investment circular" establishes the Investment Reporting Standards applicable to all engagements involving investment circulars. The purpose of this SIR is to establish specific additional Investment Reporting Standards and provide guidance for a reporting accountant engaged to report publicly on profit forecasts to be included in an investment circular under the PD Regulation, other regulations with similar requirements[1], the City Code, or if required by the London Stock Exchange in respect of an AIM Admission Document.

2. An engagement to report publicly on the proper compilation of a profit forecast is a public reporting engagement as described in SIR 1000. The description of a public reporting engagement includes three generic terms having the following meanings in the context of an engagement to report on the proper compilation of a profit forecast:

---

[1] In the UK the Prospectus Directive is implemented into law through amendments to Part VI of FSMA and to certain secondary legislation. The Annexes to the PD Regulation have been incorporated into the Prospectus Rules issued by the FSA.

(a) with respect to a profit forecast the "**subject matter**" is the directors' expectation of the issuer's profit for the period of the forecast;

(b) "**suitable criteria**" to be used by directors in the preparation of the profit forecast are provided by the requirements of the PD Regulation and the guidance[2] issued by CESR (CESR Recommendations). In forming its opinion as to whether the profit forecast has been properly compiled the reporting accountant considers whether certain of those criteria ("**reporting accountant's criteria**") have been properly applied. Reporting accountant's criteria are set out in Appendix 2 of this SIR; and

(c) with respect to a profit forecast the "**outcome**"[3] is the directors' profit forecast and related disclosures, that is included in the investment circular, and on which the reporting accountant expresses an opinion (in the "**reporting accountant's report**") as to whether that forecast is properly compiled on the basis stated and the basis of accounting used is consistent with the accounting policies of the issuer.

3. The PD Regulation defines a profit forecast as "a form of words which expressly states or by implication indicates a figure or a minimum or maximum figure for the likely level of profits or losses for the current financial period and/or financial periods subsequent to that period, or contains data from which a calculation of such a figure for future profits or losses may be made, even if no particular figure is mentioned and the word "profit" is not used"[4]. Where a profit forecast relates to an extended period and/or is subject to significant uncertainty it is sometimes referred to as a projection.

4. A profit forecast may include historical financial information relating to a past period. For example, a forecast made on 15 October 20xx for the profit for the year ended 31 December 20xx may include the profit for the six months ended 30 June 20xx included in the issuer's half yearly report and amounts extracted from management accounts for July and August. A profit estimate is historical financial information for a financial period which has expired but for which the results have not yet been published.

5. In this SIR requirements relating to "profit forecasts" also apply to statements typically referred to as "profit estimates" or "projections". The Investment Circular Reporting Standards in this SIR are applied to the whole period of the profit forecast including historical financial information included therein.

The nature of profit forecasts

6. A profit forecast is, by definition, uncertain because events and circumstances may not occur as expected or may not be predicted at all, or because the directors may take actions different to those previously intended. A profit forecast will usually include

---

[2] CESR issued "CESR's Recommendations for the Consistent Implementation of the European Commission's Regulation on Prospectuses No. 809/2004" in February 2005.
[3] The "outcome" is sometimes described as "subject matter information".
[4] The definition of a profit forecast in the City Code is similar to that used by the PD Regulation.

disclosures which provide information to assist the intended users understand the uncertainties involved.

7. A profit forecast is usually based on assumptions, relating to the expected outcome of future events and possible actions by the entity. As assumptions on which any forward-looking element of a profit forecast is based are a critical element of the profit forecast, the various regulations require, among other things, the disclosure of the principal assumptions which could have a material effect on the achievement of the profit forecast including those within the influence and control of the directors.

8. The extent to which a profit forecast will differ materially from the actual out-turn will depend on a profit forecast's particular circumstances. The length of the period into the future to which the profit forecast relates is only one, and not necessarily the most significant, factor. For example, an established business may be able to predict with greater certainty its results for the following year, particularly if it operates in a very stable environment, than a start-up business or an established business entering a new field.

9. Profit forecasts are inherently uncertain and the probability that a profit forecast will correctly predict the actual out-turn is dependent upon the many factors which determine that uncertainty. The fact that a profit forecast does not correctly predict the actual out-turn does not mean that the profit forecast was not properly compiled.

10. The Institute of Chartered Accountants in England and Wales issued guidance entitled "Prospective Financial Information – Guidance for UK directors" in September 2003 ("ICAEW Guidance") to assist directors in meeting the needs of the intended users of such information and of regulators and to promote the production of high quality prospective financial information, including profit forecasts.

11. As explained in Appendix 1 of this SIR the CESR Recommendations state that profit forecasts should be:

(a) reliable;

(b) understandable;

(c) comparable; and

(d) relevant.

Directors are required to form a judgment as to whether the profit forecast is relevant to the purpose of the investment circular[5] and, therefore, whether or not it is appropriate for the profit forecast to be included in the investment circular. The directors' judgment

---

[5] The ICAEW Guidance considers that a profit forecast will only be "relevant" if it:
(a) has the ability to influence economic decisions of investors;
(b) is provided in time to influence the economic decisions of investors; and
(c) has predictive value or, by helping to confirm or correct past evaluations or assessments, it has confirmatory value.

in this regard will be influenced by the applicable regulatory requirements. The role of the reporting accountant is to report on whether a profit forecast, that the directors have decided to include in an investment circular, has been properly compiled. The role of the reporting accountant does not include questioning the directors' decision to include a profit forecast in an investment circular.

12. In order to provide an opinion on the proper compilation of a profit forecast the reporting accountant carries out the procedures required by this SIR and SIR 1000, and any others it considers necessary, to satisfy itself that the profit forecast is:

    (a)   reliable[6];

    (b)   understandable[7]; and

    (c)   comparable[8].

Consequently, these three principles are considered to be suitable criteria for the evaluation of profit forecasts by the reporting accountant (see Appendix 2 of this SIR).

Reliability

13. The ICAEW Guidance explains that to be **reliable** a profit forecast will possess the following attributes:

    (a)   it can be depended upon by the intended users as a faithful representation of what it either purports to represent or could reasonably be expected to represent;

    (b)   it is neutral because it is free from deliberate or systematic bias intended to influence a decision or judgment to achieve a predetermined result;

    (c)   it is free from material error;

    (d)   it is complete within the bounds of what is material; and

    (e)   it is prudent in that a degree of caution is applied in making judgments under conditions of uncertainty.

The ICAEW Guidance explains that a profit forecast will be a faithful representation where it reflects an entity's strategies, plans and risk analysis in a way that is appropriate for the purpose for which the profit forecast is being prepared. The fact that a profit forecast does not correctly predict the actual out-turn once reported, does not necessarily mean that it was not reliable when made.

14. A profit forecast, including the assumptions used, is more likely to possess the above attributes when the issuer has undertaken an analysis of the underlying business and

---

[6] The business analysis principle in the ICAEW Guidance.
[7] The reasonable disclosure principle in the ICAEW Guidance.
[8] The subsequent validation principle in the ICAEW Guidance.

its strategies, plans and risks (the directors' business analysis) and when the forecast is prepared as a faithful representation of that business analysis, taking prudent account of the risk analysis. The reliability of a profit forecast is, therefore, a function of:

(a) the quality of the analysis undertaken; and

(b) the degree to which that analysis is reflected in the profit forecast.

Understandability

15. To be **understandable** a profit forecast contains the information necessary for intended users to appreciate the degree of uncertainty attaching to the information and how that uncertainty might impact it. This requires the disclosure of assumptions and other matters relevant to the basis of preparation of the profit forecast which are of importance in assisting the intended users' understanding of the profit forecast. The omission of important information may prevent a profit forecast from being understandable and equally, if the disclosure is too complex or too extensive the understandability of the profit forecast may be also impaired. What constitutes reasonable disclosure will therefore depend upon the particular circumstances of each profit forecast but will need to take into consideration:

(a) sources of uncertainty and the related assumptions made relating to uncertainties;

(b) the factors that will affect whether assumptions will be borne out in practice; and

(c) alternative outcomes, being the consequences of assumptions not being borne out.

Comparability

16. The usefulness of a profit forecast is derived partly from its **comparability**, namely the expectation that it will be possible to compare it to the actual results and that it can be compared to equivalent information for other reporting periods. For this to be the case profit forecasts need to be prepared and presented on a basis comparable with the actual financial information for that period and will involve the application of the accounting policies used by the entity in preparing the historical financial information included in the investment circular.

Compilation process

17. The compilation of a profit forecast is the gathering, classification and summarisation of relevant financial information. The process followed by the preparer would be expected to include:

(a) an appropriate analysis of the business (what is appropriate will depend on a number of factors including the complexity and predictability of the business and the length of the period being forecast and accordingly the content, degree of detail and presentation of such analyses may vary significantly);

(b)   identification of material uncertainties;

(c)   selection of appropriate assumptions;

(d)   where relevant, identification of and reference to, appropriate third party information (eg. market research reports);

(e)   arithmetic computation of the profit forecast;

(f)   appropriate sensitivity analysis;

(g)   appropriate disclosures to enable the intended users to understand the profit forecast; and

(h)   appropriate consideration of the profit forecast and approval of it by the directors of the entity.

Engagement acceptance and continuance

18.   SIR 1000.1 and SIR 1000.2 set out the basic principles and essential procedures, with respect to engagement acceptance and continuance, which are applicable to all engagements involving an investment circular.

19.   When accepting or continuing an engagement to report publicly on a profit forecast, the reporting accountant ascertains whether the directors intend to comply with all relevant regulatory requirements, in particular those that are the basis of the reporting accountant's criteria set out in Appendix 2 of this SIR.

Agreeing the terms of the engagement

20.   SIR 1000.3 and SIR 1000.4 set out the basic principles and essential procedures with respect to agreeing the terms of the engagement. Examples of engagement letter clauses are set out in Appendix 4 of this SIR.

Ethical requirements

21.   SIR 1000.5 sets out the basic principles and essential procedures with respect to the ethical requirements that apply to a reporting accountant[9].

---

[9]   In January 2006 the APB issued an Exposure Draft of an Ethical Standard for Reporting Accountants (ESRA).

Legal and regulatory requirements

22. The PD Regulation requires any profit forecast or estimate included in a <u>prospectus</u> to be reported on by independent accountants or auditors (referred to in this SIR as "a reporting accountant") and specifies the form of opinion to be given[10]. The City Code contains provisions in relation to profit forecasts included in offer documents and requires reports from the auditors or reporting accountants in certain circumstances.

23. SIR 1000.6 sets out the basic principles with respect to the legal and regulatory requirements applicable to a reporting accountant.

24. Appendices 1, 2 and 3 to this SIR set out those provisions of the PD Regulation, the CESR Recommendations relating to the implementation of the PD Regulation, and the City Code, that provide the suitable criteria for directors. Those provisions that are the basis of criteria for a reporting accountant expressing an opinion on whether the profit forecast has been properly compiled are set out in Appendix 2 of this SIR.

Quality control

25. SIR 1000.7 and SIR 1000.8 set out the basic principles and essential procedures with respect to the quality control of engagements to report on profit forecasts.

Planning and performing the engagement

26. SIR 1000.9 and SIR 1000.10 set out the basic principles and essential procedures with respect to the planning of all reporting engagements. Additional essential procedures and guidance are set out below.

27. **The reporting accountant should obtain an understanding of the key factors affecting the subject matter sufficient to identify and assess the risk of the profit forecast not being properly compiled and sufficient to design and perform evidence gathering procedures including:**

    (a) **the background to and nature of the circumstances in which the profit forecast, which is included in the investment circular, was made;**

    (b) **the entity's business; and**

    (c) **the procedures adopted, or planned to be adopted, by the directors for the preparation of the profit forecast. (SIR 3000.1)**

28. The reporting accountant gains an understanding of the background to and nature of the circumstances in which the profit forecast is being prepared, by discussion with the

---

[10] The PD Regulation requirements are reproduced verbatim in the Prospectus Rules issued by the FSA.

directors or management of the issuer and by reading relevant supporting documentation. In particular, the reporting accountant ascertains whether the profit forecast is being made for the first time or whether it is a forecast that has previously been made by the issuer that may be required to be updated by the directors.

29. The reporting accountant uses professional judgment to determine the extent of the understanding required of the entity's business. In a start-up situation or where an established business is entering a new field the reporting accountant's understanding of the prospective business is necessarily limited to general knowledge of the field being entered and an understanding of the business analysis undertaken by the entity.

30. Reporting on the proper compilation of a profit forecast generally requires an understanding of the entity's management accounting, budgeting and forecasting systems and procedures beyond that normally considered necessary for an audit of historical financial statements.

31. Discussion with the preparers of a profit forecast will identify the process by which the profit forecast has been, or will be prepared, the extent to which the ICAEW guidance has been followed, the sources of information used, areas of significant uncertainty where assumptions have been made and the basis for those assumptions and how those assumptions have been documented. Specific matters for consideration include:

- The organisational structure of the entity and the extent to which subsidiaries or local operating units have been involved in the preparation of the profit forecast.

- Whether the profit forecast is prepared on a basis comparable with the most recent historical financial information in the investment circular.

- The extent to which the period of the forecast includes historical financial information.

- Whether the profit forecast will be capable of comparison to subsequently published historical financial information.

32. Where profit forecasts are regularly prepared by the entity either for internal management purposes or for publication, the reporting accountant considers the closeness to actual out-turns achieved in previous forecasts and the analysis of any variances. As well as helping to provide an understanding of the entity's business this may be helpful in identifying those aspects of the business which are subject to significant uncertainty.

33. **The reporting accountant should consider materiality and public reporting engagement risk in planning its work in accordance with its instructions and in determining the effect of its findings on the report to be issued. (SIR 3000.2)**

Materiality

34. The ICAEW Guidance states that in order for a profit forecast to be *reliable* it will, amongst other things, be free of material error. An error in the context of the proper compilation of a profit forecast includes:

   • Assumptions that are not consistent with the analysis of the business.

   • Mathematical or clerical mistakes in the compilation of the profit forecast.

   • Misapplication of accounting policies.

   • Misapplication of a stated assumption.

   • Known misstatements in historical financial information embodied in the forecast without adjustment.

35. Additionally, there may be deficiencies in the presentation of a profit forecast which may impair the understandability or comparability of the forecast in a way that is material. An error could, therefore, also include:

   (a) failure to disclose an assumption or other explanation which is necessary for an understanding of the forecast; or

   (b) presenting the forecast in a way that it is not capable of being compared with subsequent published results.

36. Matters are material if their omission or misstatement could, individually or collectively, influence the economic decisions of the intended users of the profit forecast. Materiality depends on the size and nature of the omission or misstatement judged in light of the surrounding circumstances. The size or nature of the matter, or a combination of both, could be the determining factor.

37. Evaluating whether an omission or misstatement could influence economic decisions of the intended users of the profit forecast, and so be material, requires consideration of the characteristics of those intended users. The intended users are assumed to:

   (a) have a reasonable knowledge of business and economic activities and accounting and a willingness to study the profit forecast with reasonable diligence; and

   (b) make reasonable economic decisions on the basis of the profit forecast.

   The determination of materiality, therefore, takes into account how intended users with such characteristics could reasonably be expected to be influenced in making economic decisions.

38. The fact that the out-turn differs from the forecast does not necessarily mean that the forecast was not properly compiled as, for example, actual economic conditions may have differed from those reasonably assumed in the preparation of the profit forecast.

Public reporting engagement risk

39. "Public reporting engagement risk" is the risk that the reporting accountant expresses the positive and unmodified opinion required by the PD Regulation or the City Code when the profit forecast has not been properly compiled on the basis stated or the basis of accounting used for the profit forecast is not consistent with the accounting policies of the issuer.

40. SIR 1000.11 and SIR 1000.12 set out the basic principles and essential procedures, with respect to obtaining evidence, that are applicable to all engagements involving an investment circular. Additional basic principles, essential procedures and guidance relating to engagements to report on profit forecasts are set out below.

41. **To form an opinion that the profit forecast has been properly compiled, the reporting accountant should obtain sufficient appropriate evidence that the forecast is free from material error in its compilation by:**

    (a) **obtaining evidence that the directors have applied the criteria set out in Appendix 2 of this SIR;**

    (b) **checking that the profit forecast has been accurately computed based upon the disclosed assumptions and the preparer's accounting policies;**

    (c) **considering whether the assumptions used are consistent with the directors' business analysis and the reporting accountant's own knowledge of the business; and**

    (d) **where applicable, evaluating the basis on which any historical financial information included in the profit forecast has been prepared. (SIR 3000.3)**

42. The reporting accountant considers the business analysis carried out by the preparer of the profit forecast and whether there is prima facie evidence that it has been used by the directors in compiling the profit forecast. The extent and nature of the analysis that is necessary to support a forecast, and therefore the extent of the reporting accountant's consideration of such analysis, will be dependent upon the specific circumstances in which the forecast is being prepared. The reporting accountant discusses the preparer's plans, strategies and risk analysis with the preparer of the profit forecast, considers documentary support for them and assesses whether they are consistent with the analysis of the business. Where the outcome is dependent upon the intent of the directors and management the reporting accountant will ordinarily obtain representations from the directors concerning such matters.

43. The preparer can be expected to document the assumptions that have been made relating to matters significant to the profit forecast. The reporting accountant will, therefore, obtain from preparers of the profit forecast details of those assumptions

identified as being relevant to the compilation of the profit forecast. It will usually be the case that not all of the assumptions made in support of the profit forecast will be published. This is because only those that are material to an understanding of the profit forecast are required to be disclosed.

44. There may be a range of appropriate assumptions which can be used as the basis for a profit forecast and the resulting forecast may differ significantly depending on which assumptions are adopted. The reporting accountant is not required to express an opinion on the appropriateness of the assumptions used or the achievability of the results reflected in a profit forecast. The reporting accountant does however:

   (a) consider if any of the assumptions adopted by the directors which, in the opinion of the reporting accountant are necessary for a proper understanding of the profit forecast, have not been adequately disclosed; and

   (b) consider whether any material assumption made by the directors appears to be unrealistic.

45. When checking whether the profit forecast has been accurately computed the reporting accountant considers whether cash flow statements and balance sheets have been prepared to act as checks against omissions and inconsistencies. If cash flow statements and balance sheets have not been prepared, in circumstances where the reporting accountant considers this to be necessary, the reporting accountant discusses with the directors whether their preparation is necessary in order to properly compile the profit forecast.

Historical financial information

46. **When evaluating the basis on which any historical financial information included in the profit forecast has been prepared the reporting accountant should:**

   (a) **consider whether any element of that historical financial information has been audited or reviewed by the auditors and, if so, the results of that audit or review;**

   (b) **evaluate the suitability of unaudited historical financial information included in the profit forecast;**

   (c) **evaluate how the historical financial information has been embodied into the profit forecast; and**

   (d) **if adjustments have been made to previously published historical financial information evaluate whether the adjustments appear appropriate in the circumstances. (SIR 3000.4)**

47. If historical financial information has been audited or reviewed the reporting accountant evaluates the scope of the audit or review procedures performed. In performing such an evaluation the reporting accountant ordinarily seeks access to the working papers of the auditor or reviewer and considers whether the results of those

procedures indicate that the historical financial information may be unreliable or reveal uncertainties that ought to require the directors to make and disclose assumptions in the forecast.

48. In order to evaluate the suitability of unaudited historical financial information included in the profit forecast the reporting accountant[11]:

   (a) understands the internal control environment of the entity relevant to the historical financial information;

   (b) discusses with the management of the issuer the accounting policies applied and any differences from the method of preparing the entity's published financial statements;

   (c) enquires of management, including internal audit, whether there have been any changes in the financial reporting systems or internal controls, or any breakdowns in systems and controls, which might affect the reliability of the financial information;

   (d) enquires about changes in the entity's procedures for recording, classifying and summarising transactions, accumulating information for disclosure, and preparing the financial information;

   (e) considers the accuracy of unaudited historical financial information by comparing it to audited financial statements for the same period;

   (f) compares the historical financial information to previous budgets or forecasts prepared by the entity in respect of the period covered by the historical financial information and gains an understanding of the reasons for any significant differences; and

   (g) checks the historical financial information used in the profit forecast agrees to, or reconciles with, the underlying accounting records of the entity.

49. Where the reporting accountant determines that it is not able to obtain sufficient appropriate evidence from the above procedures to indicate that the financial information for the expired part of the forecast period forms a suitable basis for inclusion in the profit forecast the reporting accountant discusses the matter with the directors of the issuer and, if appropriate, the issuer's advisers.

50. In considering historical financial information included in a profit forecast, it is important that the reporting accountant understands the manner in which such information has been included in the profit forecast. Where different systems or processes have been used to produce prospective financial information and the historical information, there is a risk that there may be inconsistencies in the cut-off

---

[11] Some of these procedures may already have been performed as part of a review.

between these two sources of information which could lead to a material error in the compilation of the profit forecast.

Consistent accounting policies

51. **The reporting accountant should compare the accounting policies used in connection with the profit forecast with those used by the entity in preparing the most recent historical financial information in the investment circular, and evaluate whether they are consistent with each other and continue to be appropriate so far as concerns the profit forecast. (SIR 3000.5)**

52. Where the profit forecast relates to the expansion of an existing business the reporting accountant's primary consideration is the consistency of the accounting policies used. However, the reporting accountant also considers the ongoing appropriateness of the accounting policies in the light of the business plans underlying the profit forecast.

53. Where the profit forecast relates to a start-up situation the reporting accountant considers the appropriateness of the accounting policies chosen.

Presentation of the profit forecast

54. **The reporting accountant should consider whether it has become aware of anything to cause it to believe that:**

    (a) **the profit forecast is presented in a way that is not understandable;**

    (b) **a material assumption is unrealistic;**

    (c) **an assumption or other information which appears to it to be material to a proper understanding of the profit forecast has not been disclosed; or**

    (d) **the profit forecast is not capable of subsequently being compared with historical financial information.**

    If the reporting accountant is aware of such matters it should discuss them with the parties responsible for the profit forecast and with those persons to whom its report is to be addressed and consider whether it is able to issue its opinion. (SIR 3000.6)

55. The ICAEW Guidance provides guidance to directors with regard to the matters that should be disclosed in connection with a profit forecast. This covers both the manner in which the profit forecast is presented and the use of disclosure to deal with uncertainty. It is important that useful information is not obscured through the inclusion of immaterial items or the use of headings or financial measures which are not meaningful to, or may be misunderstood by, the intended users.

56. When evaluating the presentation of a profit forecast the reporting accountant considers whether the components of the profit forecast are clearly described and whether the descriptions are adequate to allow an intended user to understand the

profit forecast. For example, if a profit forecast is presented as a single figure for profit before tax, and this was to be achieved by the inclusion of a significant non-recurring profit from the sale of a fixed asset, consideration is given as to whether additional disclosure is necessary to make the profit forecast understandable.

57. When evaluating whether the disclosures made in respect of a profit forecast are sufficient to make it understandable, the reporting accountant considers whether the degree of uncertainty inherent in the information is clearly disclosed. Disclosure of an assumption may not make the profit forecast understandable if the significance of that assumption is not apparent from the disclosure made.

58. Where a profit forecast is subject to significant uncertainty it is common practice for the preparers to perform a sensitivity analysis in respect of those assumptions which are either believed to be subject to the greatest uncertainty and/or where the profit forecast is most sensitive to variations in such assumptions. The reporting accountant considers such sensitivity analysis, as it may assist in the identification of material assumptions or other aspects of the profit forecast where the uncertainty requires additional disclosure to enable it to be understood.

59. The manner in which the profit forecast is presented in the investment circular will also be considered in respect of whether the profit forecast is capable of being compared with subsequent historical financial information. The choice of captions and disclosure or emphasis of particular numbers or attributes may determine how the profit forecast will be interpreted and consideration is given as to whether this is consistent with the purpose for which the profit forecast has been prepared.

Representation letter

60. SIR 1000.13 sets out the basic principles and essential procedures, with respect to representation letters, that are applicable to all engagements involving an investment circular. Examples of representation letter clauses are set out in Appendix 5 of this SIR.

61. Some of the assumptions used in the compilation of a profit forecast will be dependent on the intent of the directors and management. Consequently the representations of directors and management as to their intent are a particularly important source of evidence for the reporting accountant.

Documentation

62. SIR 1000.14 and SIR 1000.15 set out the basic principles and essential procedures with respect to the reporting accountant's working papers.

Professional scepticism

63. SIR 1000.16 sets out the basic principle with respect to the attitude of professional scepticism adopted by the reporting accountant in planning and performing an engagement.

Reporting

64. SIR 1000.17, SIR 1000.18 and SIR 1000.19 set out the basic principles and essential procedures, with respect to reporting, that are applicable to all engagements involving an investment circular. Additional basic principles and essential procedures relating to engagements to report on profit forecasts are set out below.

Responsibilities

65. **In all reports on profit forecasts in investment circulars the reporting accountant should explain the extent of its responsibility in respect of the profit forecast by including in its report:**

    (a) **a statement that the reporting accountant's responsibility is to form an opinion (as required by the relevant regulatory requirement) on the compilation of the profit forecast and to report its opinion to the addressees of the report; and**

    (b) **a statement that the profit forecast and the assumptions on which it is based are the responsibility of the directors. (SIR 3000.7)**

Basis of preparation of the profit forecast

66. **The reporting accountant should include a basis of preparation section of its report that cross refers to disclosures that explain the basis of preparation of the profit forecast including:**

    (a) **assumptions made;**

    (b) **the accounting policies applied; and**

    (c) **where appropriate, the source of historical financial information embodied in the profit forecast. (SIR 3000.8)**

67. Where the entity is reporting on the expansion of an established business it is usual for it to report that the basis of accounting is consistent with the existing accounting policies. Where the accounting policies used in the profit forecast differ from those previously published a more detailed explanation of the accounting policies used in the preparation of the profit forecast will be appropriate.

Basis of opinion

68. SIR 1000.18 sets out the basic principles and essential procedures, with respect to the basis of the reporting accountant's opinion, that are applicable to all engagements involving an investment circular. Additional basic principles and essential procedures relating to engagements to report on profit forecasts are set out below.

69. **The reporting accountant should explain the basis of its opinion by including in its report a statement that where the profit forecast and any assumptions on which it**

is based relate to the future and may, therefore, be affected by unforeseen events, the reporting accountant does not express any opinion as to whether the actual results achieved will correspond to those shown in the profit forecast. (SIR 3000.9)

70. By its nature financial information relating to the future is inherently uncertain. For a profit forecast to be understandable sufficient information must be disclosed to allow an intended user to understand this uncertainty. As the reporting accountant is not required to form or express an opinion on the achievability of the result shown in the profit forecast, it is inappropriate for the reporting accountant to include in the basis of preparation section of its report cautionary language relating to uncertainty beyond that referred to above.

Expression of opinion

71. **The report should contain a clear expression of opinion that complies with applicable regulatory requirements. (SIR 3000.10)**

72. In forming its opinion the reporting accountant takes account of those events or information which the reporting accountant becomes aware of occurring up to the date on which the reporting accountant signs the report, that affect the opinion expressed in the report.

73. The investment circular in which the reporting accountant's report is included may be made available in other countries, such as the United States of America, which have their own standards for accountants when reporting on profit forecasts. In such circumstances, the reporting accountant considers whether to include a reference to the fact that a report issued in accordance with the SIRs should not be relied upon as if it had been issued in accordance with the standards applicable in that other country. An example of such a reference is included in the example reports set out in Appendices 6 and 7 of this SIR.

Modified opinions

74. SIR 1000.20 sets out the basic principles and essential procedures, with respect to modified opinions, that are applicable to all engagements involving an investment circular. Additional basic principles and essential procedures relating to engagements to report on profit forecasts are set out below.

75. **The reporting accountant should not express an unmodified opinion when the directors have not applied the criteria set out in Appendix 2 of this SIR and in the reporting accountant's judgment the effect of not doing so is, or may be, material. (SIR 3000.11)**

76. The PD and other regulations, such as the City Code, usually require a positive and unmodified opinion. Consequently, in the event that the reporting accountant concludes that it is unable to report in the manner prescribed it invites those responsible for the profit forecast to consider whether the profit forecast can be

amended to alleviate its concerns or whether the profit forecast should be omitted from the investment circular.

77. Examples of reports on a profit forecast and a profit estimate expressing such positive and unmodified opinions are set out in Appendices 6 and 7 of this SIR.

Consent

78. SIR 1000.21 and SIR 1000.22 set out the basic principles and essential procedures with respect to the giving of consent by the reporting accountant.

79. The reporting accountant considers whether disclosures in the investment circular, such as those in the "Risk Factors" section, are consistent with the assumptions and other disclosures made in connection with the profit forecast before consent is given by the reporting accountant to its report on the profit forecast being included in the investment circular.

Events occurring between the date of the reporting accountant's report and the completion date of the transaction

80. SIR 1000.23 sets out the basic principles and essential procedures with respect to events occurring between the date of the reporting accountant's report and the completion date of the transaction.

81. Under Sections 81 and 87G of the FSMA, Prospectus Rule 3.4, and Listing Rule 4.4.1, a supplementary investment circular must be prepared if, after the date the investment circular has been formally approved by a regulator and before dealings in the relevant securities commence, the issuer becomes aware that there has been a significant change affecting any matter contained in the document or a significant new matter has arisen, the inclusion of information in respect of which would have been required if it had arisen at the time of its preparation. A similar obligation arises under Article 16 of the Prospectus Directive in respect of the period following registration of the investment circular during which an agreement in respect of the securities can be entered into in pursuance of the offer contained in the investment circular.

82. If, as a result of discussion with those responsible for the investment circular concerning an event that occurred prior to the completion date of the transaction, the reporting accountant is either uncertain about or disagrees with the course of action proposed the reporting accountant may consider it necessary to take legal advice with respect to its responsibilities in the particular circumstances.

83. After the date of its report, the reporting accountant has no obligation to perform procedures or make enquiries regarding the investment circular.

Effective date

84. A reporting accountant is required to comply with the Investment Reporting Standards contained in this SIR for reports signed after 31 March 2006. Earlier adoption is encouraged.

Appendix 1

THE REGULATORY BACKGROUND

Prospectus Directive Requirements

The **Prospectus Directive** and **PD Regulation** determine the requirements for the content of a prospectus. In determining whether the PD Regulation has been complied with, the FSA will take into account whether a person has complied with the CESR Recommendations.

The PD Regulation requires that where an issuer chooses to include a profit forecast (including a profit estimate) in a prospectus it must:

(a) be prepared on a basis comparable with the historical financial information in the prospectus;

(b) include a statement setting out the principal assumptions upon which the issuer has based its forecast or estimate. There must be a clear distinction between assumptions about factors which the members of the administrative, management or supervisory bodies can influence and assumptions about factors which are exclusively outside the influence of the members of the administrative, management or supervisory bodies; the assumptions must be readily understandable by investors, be specific and precise and not relate to the general accuracy of the estimates underlying the forecast; and

(c) other than for issuers of high denomination debt and derivative securities, include a report prepared by independent accountants or auditors stating that in their opinion the forecast or estimate has been properly compiled on the basis stated and that the basis of accounting used for the profit forecast or estimate is consistent with the accounting policies of the issuer.

The CESR Recommendations provide further guidance concerning the principles that should be applied in preparing a profit forecast in a prospectus. In addition to due care and diligence being taken to ensure that profit forecasts or estimates are not misleading to investors, the following principles should be taken into consideration when profit forecasts are being compiled. Profit forecasts and estimates should be:

(a) *reliable* - they should be supported by a thorough analysis of the issuer's business and should represent factual and not hypothetical strategies, plans and risk analysis; (a criterion for a reporting accountant see Appendix 2 of this SIR)

(b) *understandable* - they should contain disclosure that is not too complex or extensive for investors to understand; (a criterion for a reporting accountant see Appendix 2 of this SIR)

(c) *comparable* - they should be capable of justification by comparison with outcomes in the form of historical financial information (a criterion for a reporting accountant see Appendix 2 of this SIR); and

(d) **relevant** - they must have an ability to influence economic decisions of investors and provided on a timely basis so as to influence such decisions and assist in confirming or correcting past evaluations or assessments. (Not a criterion for a reporting accountant see paragraph 11 of this SIR).

The City Code

The City Code requires that:

(a) all communications to shareholders in an offer, including forecasts, must maintain the highest standard of accuracy and fair presentation;

(b) assumptions should be drafted in a way that allows shareholders to understand their implications; and

(c) the forecast is compiled with due care and consideration by the directors and the disclosure of assumptions should provide useful information to assist shareholders to help them to form a view as to the reasonableness and reliability of the forecast.

Notes 1(c) and (d) to Rule 28.2 of the City Code state:

"The forecast and the assumptions on which it is based are the sole responsibility of the directors. However, a duty is placed on the financial advisers to discuss the assumptions with their client and to satisfy themselves that the forecast has been made with due care and consideration. Auditors or consultant accountants must satisfy themselves that the forecast, so far as the accounting policies and calculations are concerned, has been properly compiled on the basis of the assumptions made.

Although the accountants have no responsibility for the assumptions, they will as a result of their review be in a position to advise the company on what assumptions should be listed in the circular and the way in which they should be described. The financial advisers and accountants obviously have substantial influence on the information about assumptions to be given in the circular; neither should allow an assumption to be published which appears to be unrealistic, or one to be omitted which appears to be important, without commenting appropriately in its report".

Whilst the City Code does not explicitly identify the principles contained in the CESR Recommendations those principles are consistent with the requirement of the Code.

**THE AUDITING
PRACTICES BOARD**

Appendix 2

REPORTING ACCOUNTANT'S CRITERIA

	PD Regulation	Annex I[1] of PD Regulation	CESR Recommendations
A statement setting out the principal assumptions upon which the issuer has based its forecast or estimate.		13.1	
There must be a clear distinction between assumptions about factors which the members of the administrative, management or supervisory bodies can influence and assumptions about factors which are exclusively outside the influence of the members of the administrative, management or supervisory bodies; the assumptions must be readily understandable by investors, be specific and precise and not relate to the general accuracy of the estimates underlying the forecast.		13.1	
The profit forecast or estimate must be prepared on a basis comparable with the historical financial information.		13.3	
The following principles should be taken into consideration when profit forecasts or estimates are being compiled. Profit forecasts or estimates should be • **Understandable,** ie Profit forecasts or estimates should contain disclosure that is not too complex or extensive for investors to understand; • **Reliable,** ie Profit forecasts should be supported by a thorough analysis of the issuer's business and should represent factual and not hypothetical strategies, plans and risk analysis; • **Comparable,** ie Profit forecasts or estimates should be capable of justification by comparison with outcomes in the form of historical financial information;			para 41

[1] The column illustrates Annex I as an example. Other annexes to the PD Regulation contain identical requirements with respect to profit forecasts. See Appendix 1 of SIR 1000.

Appendix 3

OTHER REGULATORY PROVISIONS RELEVANT TO THE PREPARERS OF PROFIT FORECASTS

	PD Regulation	Annex I of PD Regulation	CESR Recommendations
(8) Voluntary disclosure of profit forecasts in a share registration document should be presented in a consistent and comparable manner and accompanied by a statement prepared by independent accountants or auditors. This information should not be confused with the disclosure of known trends or other factual data with material impact on the issuer's prospects. Moreover, they should provide an explanation of any changes in disclosure policy relating to profit forecasts when supplementing a prospectus or drafting a new prospectus.	Recital 8		
Profit forecast means a form of words which expressly states or by implication indicates a figure or a minimum or maximum figure for the likely level of profits or losses for the current financial period and/or financial periods subsequent to that period, or contains data from which a calculation of such a figure for future profits or losses may be made, even if no particular figure is mentioned and the word "profit" is not used.	Article 2		
Profit estimate means a profit forecast for a financial period which has expired and for which results have not yet been published.	Article 2		
If an issuer chooses to include a profit forecast or profit estimate the registration document must contain the information set out in items 13.1 and 13.2.		13	
A report prepared by independent accountants or auditors stating that in the opinion of the independent accountants or auditors the forecast or estimate has been properly compiled on the basis stated and that the basis of accounting used for the profit forecast or estimate is consistent with the accounting policies of the issuer.		13.2	

	PD Regulation	Annex I of PD Regulation	CESR Recommendations
If a profit forecast in a prospectus has been published which is still outstanding, then provide a statement setting out whether or not that forecast is still correct as at the time of the registration document, and an explanation of why such forecast is no longer valid if that is the case.		13.4	
The inclusion of a profit forecast or estimate in a prospectus is the responsibility of the issuer and persons responsible for the prospectus and due care and diligence must be taken to ensure that profit forecasts or estimates are not misleading to investors.			para 40
The following principles should be taken into consideration when profit forecasts or estimates are being compiled. Profit forecasts or estimates should be • **Relevant**, ie profit forecasts and estimates must have an ability to influence economic decisions of investors and provided on a timely basis so as to influence such decisions and assist in confirming or correcting past evaluations or assessments.			para 41
Where an issuer provides a profit forecast or estimate in a registration document, if the related schedules so requires, it must be reported on by independent accountants or auditors in the registration document (as described in item 13.2 of Annex I of the Regulation). Where the issuer does not produce a single prospectus, upon the issuance of the securities note and summary at a later time, the issuer should either: • Confirm the profit forecasts or estimates; or • State that the profit forecasts or estimates are no longer valid or correct; or • Make appropriate alteration of profit forecasts or estimates. In this case they must be reported upon as described in item 13.2 of Annex I of the Regulation.			para 42
If an issuer has made a statement other than in a previous prospectus that would constitute a profit forecast or estimate if made in a prospectus, for instance, in a regulatory announcement, and that statement is still outstanding at the time of publication of the prospectus, the issuer should consider whether the forecasts or estimates are still material and valid and choose whether or not to include them in the prospectus. CESR considers that there is a presumption that an outstanding forecast made other than in a previous prospectus will be material in the case of share issues (especially in the context of an IPO). This is not necessarily the presumption in case of non-equity securities.			paras 43 & 44

	PD Regulation	Annex I of PD Regulation	CESR Recommendations
When there is an outstanding profit forecast or estimate in relation to a material undertaking which the issuer has acquired, the issuer should consider whether it is appropriate to make a statement as to whether or not the profit forecast or estimate is still valid or correct. The issuer should also evaluate the effects of the acquisition and the profit forecast made by that undertaking on its own financial position and report on it as it would have done if the profit forecast or estimate had been made by the issuer.			paras 45 & 46
The forecast or estimate should normally be of profit before tax (disclosing separately any non-recurrent items and tax charges if they are expected to be abnormally high or low). If the forecast or estimate is not of profit before tax, the reasons for presenting another figure from the profit and loss account must be disclosed and clearly explained. Furthermore the tax effect should be clearly explained. When the results are published relating to a period covered by a forecast or estimate, the published financial statements must disclose the relevant figure so as to enable the forecast and actual results to be directly compared.			paras 47 & 48
CESR recognises that often in practice, there is a fine line between what constitutes a profit forecast and what constitutes trend information as detailed in item 12 of Annex I of the Regulation. A general discussion about the future or prospects of the issuer under trend information will not normally constitute a profit forecast or estimate as defined in Articles 2.10 and 2.11 of the Regulation. Whether or not a statement constitutes profit forecasts or estimates is a question of fact and will depend upon the circumstances of the particular issuer.			para 49
This is a non-exhaustive list of factors that an issuer is expected to take into consideration when preparing forecasts: • Past results, market analysis, strategic evolutions, market share and position of the issuer • Financial position and possible changes therein • Description of the impact of an acquisition or disposal, change in strategy or any major change in environmental matters and technology • Changes in legal and tax environment • Commitments towards third parties.			para 50

THE AUDITING PRACTICES BOARD

Appendix 4

EXAMPLES OF ENGAGEMENT LETTER CLAUSES

The examples of engagement letter clauses are intended for consideration in the context of a public reporting engagement on a profit forecast. They should be tailored to the specific circumstances and supplemented by such other clauses as are relevant and appropriate.

Financial information upon which the report is to be given

The [investment circular] will contain a profit [forecast] [estimate] for the company for the period [ending] [ended] [date] (the "PFI") prepared and presented in accordance with [item 13 of Annex I of the PD Regulation] [the requirements of the City Code] [other applicable regulation]. We will prepare a report on the profit [forecast] [estimate] addressed to [...] expressing our opinion on the profit [forecast] [estimate], in the form described below, to be included in the [investment circular].

We will ask the Directors to make certain representations to us regarding the PFI. If the PFI is intended only to be a hypothetical illustration, or the Directors are unable to make such representations to us, we will not wish to be associated with the PFI and accordingly, will be unable to report publicly on it.

Responsibilities

The preparation and presentation of the profit forecast will be the responsibility solely of the Directors. [This responsibility includes the identification and disclosure of the assumptions underlying the profit forecast. (omit if no assumptions)] The Directors are also responsible for ensuring that the PFI is prepared and presented in accordance with [item 13 of Annex I of the PD Regulation] [the requirements of the City Code] [other applicable regulation].

We will require the Directors to formally adopt the PFI before we report on it. We understand that the Directors will have regard to the guidance issued by The Institute of Chartered Accountants in England & Wales entitled "Prospective Financial Information – Guidance for UK directors" in preparing the PFI.

It is our responsibility to form an opinion as to whether the profit [forecast] [estimate] has been properly compiled on the basis stated and whether such basis is consistent with the accounting policies normally adopted by ABC plc.

If the results of our work are satisfactory, and having regard to the requirements of [item 13.2 of Annex I of the PD Regulation] [the City Code] [other applicable regulation], we shall prepare a report on the profit [forecast] [estimate] for inclusion in the [investment circular]. An illustration of the form of our report is attached.

Scope of work

Our work will be undertaken in accordance with Standard for Investment Reporting (SIR) 3000 "Investment Reporting Standards Applicable to Public Reporting Engagements on Profit Forecasts" issued by the Auditing Practices Board and will be subject to the limitations described therein.

We draw your attention in particular to paragraph 75 of SIR 3000 which would preclude us from expressing any opinion if the Directors have not complied with the regulatory requirements set out in Appendix 2 of that SIR.

As the purpose of our engagement is restricted as described above and since the PFI and the assumptions on which it is based relate to the future and may be affected by unforeseen events, we will not provide any opinion as to how closely the actual result achieved will correspond to the profit [forecast] [estimate]. Accordingly we neither confirm nor otherwise accept responsibility for the ultimate accuracy and achievability of the PFI.

Assumptions

We will discuss the assumptions with the persons responsible for preparing the PFI together with the evidence they have to support the assumptions, but we will not seek to independently verify or audit those assumptions. We are not responsible for identifying the assumptions.

In the event that anything comes to our attention to indicate that any of the assumptions adopted by the Directors which, in our opinion, are necessary for a proper understanding of the PFI have not been disclosed or if any material assumption made by the Directors appears to us to be unrealistic we will inform the directors so that steps can be taken to resolve the matter. However, we are required to comment in our report if an assumption is published which appears to us to be unrealistic or an assumption is omitted which appears to us to be important to an understanding of the PFI.

Appendix 5

EXAMPLES OF MANAGEMENT REPRESENTATION LETTER CLAUSES

Similar clauses to those below could be amended to be used in connection with a report on a profit estimate.

Introduction

We refer to the forecast of *[insert description of items forecast],* profit for the financial year and earnings per share of ABC plc ("the Company") and its subsidiaries together ("the ABC Group") for the year ending *[date]* ("the profit forecast") set out on page [•] of the [Prospectus]/[Circular]/[Offer Document] to be issued on *[date]*. We acknowledge that we are solely responsible for the profit forecast and the assumptions on which it is based as set out on page [•] and confirm on behalf of the Directors [and Proposed Directors] of the Company to the best of our knowledge and belief, having made appropriate enquiries of officials of the Company, the following representations made to you in the course of your work:

Specific representations

- The profit forecast is based on our assessment of the financial position and results of operations and cash flow for the period and is presented on a basis consistent with the accounting policies [normally] [to be] adopted by the ABC Group and has been prepared in accordance with relevant legislative requirements.[1]

- We believe the forecast results are likely to be achieved although achievement of the forecast may be favourably or unfavourably affected by unforeseeable and uncontrollable events.

- We have made available to you all significant information relevant to the profit forecast of which we have knowledge.

- All significant assumptions have been disclosed and the assumptions underlying the profit forecast are reasonable and appropriate.

- The results shown in the [audited/unaudited] financial results for the six months ended *[date]* and the unaudited management accounts for the [•] months ended *[date]* which are included in the profit forecast have been prepared in accordance with the accounting policies [normally] [to be] adopted by the ABC Group and are free from material misstatement.

---

[1] The reporting accountant may also wish to obtain a representation that the profit forecast has been prepared in accordance with 'Prospective Financial Information - Guidance for UK directors' published by the Institute of Chartered Accountants in England and Wales.

- There are no contingencies, (other than those which have been taken into account in making the forecast), that are material in the context of the profit forecast which should be disclosed or taken into account in the profit forecast.

- The profit forecast is presented in a manner which is balanced and fair and not misleading and contains all information necessary for a proper understanding of the profit forecast.

- The profit forecast together with the assumptions and the representations in this letter have been approved by the board of directors.

Representations in respect of specific assumptions such as;

- The assumed like for like increase in sales of 5% in the last quarter of 200X incorporates expected price increases of 2% based on preliminary discussions with three of our major customers.

- The assumed increase in gross margin of 2 percentage points from 1 July 200X is based on manufacturing cost savings as a result of the realisation of efficiencies resulting from the factory reorganisation which we expect to be completed by the end of May 200X.

- The assumed increase in sales prices by 2% more than the general level of inflation in 200Y is based upon the expectation that our major competitor will announce a price increase of at least that amount in November 200X. Our expectation takes account of similar timing of increases in previous years and information derived from conversations with mutual customers.

- The opening of two new sales outlets in the current financial year assumes that negotiations to agree a lease on one out of the three potential units in Guildford will be completed and that refitting and pre-opening will be completed within 10 weeks which is 25% longer than the historical average due to additional building works being required in one of the potential sites.

- The profit forecast assumes that a forward sale of $x million will be designated as a hedge against expected US$ income.

Appendix 6

EXAMPLE OF A REPORT ON A PROFIT FORECAST

Date

Reporting accountant's address

Addressees, as agreed between the parties in the engagement letter

Dear Sirs

[ABC plc]

We report on the profit forecast comprising [*insert description of items comprising the prospective financial information, e.g.* [forecast of turnover, operating profit, profit before tax and earnings per share]//[projected profit and loss account]] of ABC plc ("the Company") and its subsidiaries (together "the ABC Group") for the [*specify period*] ending [*date*] (the "Profit Forecast"). The Profit Forecast, and the material assumptions upon which it is based, are set out on pages [●] to [●] of the [*describe document*] ("the [Document]") issued by the Company dated [*date*]. This report is required by [Relevant Regulation] [guidance issued by the London Stock Exchange with respect to the AIM market] and is given for the purpose of complying with that [Relevant Regulation] [guidance issued by the London Stock Exchange] and for no other purpose.

[*Substitute the following text for the last sentence of the immediately preceding paragraph, where a profit forecast is made by an offeree in the context of a takeover.* This report is required by Rule 28.3(b) of the City Code and is given for the purpose of complying with that rule and for no other purpose. Accordingly, we assume no responsibility in respect of this report to the Offeror or any person connected to, or acting in concert with, the Offeror or to any other person who is seeking or may in future seek to acquire control of the Company (an "Alternative Offeror") or to any other person connected to, or acting in concert with, an Alternative Offeror.]

Responsibilities

It is the responsibility of the Directors of ABC plc to prepare the Profit Forecast in accordance with the requirements of the [PD Regulation]/[Listing Rules]/[City Code] [guidance issued by the London Stock Exchange].

It is our responsibility to form an opinion as required by the [PD Regulation]/[Listing Rules]/ [City Code] [guidance issued by the London Stock Exchange] as to the proper compilation of the Profit Forecast and to report that opinion to you.

Basis of preparation of the Profit Forecast

The Profit Forecast has been prepared on the basis stated on page [ ] of the [Document][1] and is based on the [audited/unaudited] interim financial results for the [six] months ended [date], the unaudited management accounts for the [x] months ended [date] and a forecast to [date]. The Profit Forecast is required to be presented on a basis consistent with the accounting policies of the ABC Group.

Basis of opinion

We conducted our work in accordance with the Standards for Investment Reporting issued by the Auditing Practices Board in the United Kingdom. Our work included [evaluating the basis on which the historical financial information included in the Profit Forecast has been prepared and] considering whether the Profit Forecast has been accurately computed based upon the disclosed assumptions and the accounting policies of the ABC Group. Whilst the assumptions upon which the Profit Forecast are based are solely the responsibility of the Directors, we considered whether anything came to our attention to indicate that any of the assumptions adopted by the Directors which, in our opinion, are necessary for a proper understanding of the Profit Forecast have not been disclosed and whether any material assumption made by the Directors appears to us to be unrealistic.

We planned and performed our work so as to obtain the information and explanations we considered necessary in order to provide us with reasonable assurance that the Profit Forecast has been properly compiled on the basis stated.

Since the Profit Forecast and the assumptions on which it is based relate to the future and may therefore be affected by unforeseen events, we can express no opinion as to whether the actual results reported will correspond to those shown in the Profit Forecast and differences may be material.

[*This paragraph may be omitted if the document is not to be distributed outside the UK* - Our work has not been carried out in accordance with auditing or other standards and practices generally accepted in the United States of America [or other jurisdictions] and accordingly should not be relied upon as if it had been carried out in accordance with those standards and practices.]

---

[1]   The disclosures presented with the profit forecast should explain the basis on which the forecast has been prepared. This will include identification of the accounting policies used and the financial information used in compiling the forecast. Typically this may include reference to audited/unaudited financial statements of the entity for an interim period, unaudited management accounts and management's forecast for the period for which no management accounts are available.

Opinion

In our opinion, the Profit Forecast has been properly compiled on the basis [stated] [of the assumptions made by the Directors/][2] and the basis of accounting used is consistent with the accounting policies of the ABC Group[3].

Declaration[4]

For the purposes of [Prospectus Rule [5.5.3R(2)(f)] [5.5.4R(2)(f)] [guidance issued by the London Stock Exchange] we are responsible for [this report as part] [the following part(s) of the [prospectus] [registration document] [AIM admission document] and declare that we have taken all reasonable care to ensure that the information contained [in this report] [those parts] is, to the best of our knowledge, in accordance with the facts and contains no omission likely to affect its import. This declaration is included in the [prospectus] [registration document] [AIM admission document] in compliance with [item 1.2 of annex I of the PD Regulation] [item 1.2 of annex III of the PD Regulation] [guidance issued by the London Stock Exchange].

Yours faithfully

Reporting Accountant

---

[2] The City Code requires 'on the basis of the assumptions made by the Directors' but the PD Regulation requires 'on the basis stated'.
[3] Where the accounting policies used in the profit forecast either differ from those used by the company in its latest published financial statements or where the company has never published financial statements reference should be made to the accounting policies which have been used.
[4] This declaration is a requirement of the PD Regulation and is appropriate for inclusion when the report is included in a Prospectus, see Appendix 2 of SIR 1000.

Appendix 7

EXAMPLE OF A REPORT ON A PROFIT ESTIMATE THAT IS NOT SUBJECT TO ASSUMPTIONS

Date

Reporting accountant's address

Addressees, as agreed between the parties in the engagement letter

Dear Sirs

[ABC plc]

We report on the profit estimate comprising [*insert description of items comprising the prospective financial information, e.g. [*estimate of turnover, operating profit, profit before tax and earnings per share]/[estimated profit and loss account]*] of ABC plc ("the Company") and its subsidiaries (together "the ABC Group") for the [*specify period*] ended [*date*] (the "Profit Estimate"). The Profit Estimate and the basis on which it is prepared is set out on pages [•] to [•] of the [*describe document*] ("the [Document]") issued by the Company dated [*date*]. This report is required by [Relevant Regulation] [guidance issued by the London Stock Exchange with respect to the AIM market] and is given for the purpose of complying with that [Relevant Regulation] [guidance issued by the London Stock Exchange] and for no other purpose.

[*Substitute the following text for the last sentence of the immediately preceding paragraph, where a profit estimate is made by an offeree in the context of a takeover.* This report is required by Rule 28.3(b) of the City Code and is given for the purpose of complying with that rule and for no other purpose. Accordingly, we assume no responsibility in respect of this report to the Offeror or any person connected to, or acting in concert with, the Offeror or to any other person who is seeking or may in future seek to acquire control of the Company (an "Alternative Offeror") or to any other person connected to, or acting in concert with, an Alternative Offeror.]

Responsibilities

It is the responsibility of the directors of ABC plc to prepare the Profit Estimate in accordance with the requirements of the [PD Regulation]/[Listing Rules]/[City Code]. In preparing the Profit Estimate the directors of ABC plc are responsible for correcting errors that they have identified which may have arisen in unaudited financial results and unaudited management accounts used as the basis of preparation for the Profit Estimate.

It is our responsibility to form an opinion as required by the [PD Regulation]/[Listing Rules]/ [City Code] as to the proper compilation of the Profit Estimate and to report that opinion to you.

Basis of preparation of the Profit Estimate

The Profit Estimate has been prepared on the basis stated on page [ ] of the [Document][1] and is based on the [audited/unaudited] interim financial results for the [six] months ended [date], the unaudited management accounts for the [x] months ended [date] and an estimate for the [month] to [date]. The Profit Estimate is required to be presented on a basis consistent with the accounting policies of the ABC Group.

Basis of opinion

We conducted our work in accordance with the Standards for Investment Reporting issued by the Auditing Practices Board in the United Kingdom. Our work included evaluating the basis on which the historical financial information for the [x] months to [date] included in the Profit Estimate has been prepared and considering whether the Profit Estimate has been accurately computed using that information and whether the basis of accounting used is consistent with the accounting policies of the ABC Group.

We planned and performed our work so as to obtain the information and explanations we considered necessary in order to provide us with reasonable assurance that the Profit Estimate has been properly compiled on the basis stated.

However, the Profit Estimate has not been audited. The actual results reported, therefore, may be affected by revisions required to accounting estimates due to changes in circumstances, the impact of unforeseen events and the correction of errors in the [interim financial results] [management accounts]. Consequently we can express no opinion as to whether the actual results achieved will correspond to those shown in the Profit Estimate and the difference may be material.

[*This paragraph may be omitted if the document is not to be distributed outside the UK* Our work has not been carried out in accordance with auditing or other standards and practices generally accepted in the United States of America [or other jurisdictions] and accordingly should not be relied upon as if it had been carried out in accordance with those standards and practices.]

Opinion

In our opinion, the Profit Estimate has been properly compiled on the basis stated and the basis of accounting used is consistent with the accounting policies of the ABC Group[2].

---

[1] The disclosures presented with the profit estimate should explain the basis on which the estimate has been prepared. This will include identification of the accounting policies used and the financial information used in compiling the estimate. Typically this may include reference to audited/unaudited financial statements of the entity for an interim period, unaudited management accounts and management's estimate (which may itself be based on other forms of management information for the period for which no management accounts are available.

[2] Where the accounting policies used in the profit estimate either differ from those used by the company in its latest published financial statements or where the company has never published financial statements reference should be made to the accounting policies which have been used.

Declaration[3]

For the purposes of [Prospectus Rule [5.5.3R(2)(f)] [5.5.4R(2)(f)] [guidance issued by the London Stock Exchange] we are responsible for [this report as part] [the following part(s) of the [prospectus] [registration document] [AIM admission document] and declare that we have taken all reasonable care to ensure that the information contained [in this report] [those parts] is, to the best of our knowledge, in accordance with the facts and contains no omission likely to affect its import. This declaration is included in the [prospectus] [registration document] [AIM admission document] in compliance with [item 1.2 of annex I of the PD Regulation] [item 1.2 of annex III of the PD Regulation] [guidance issued by the London Stock Exchange].

Yours faithfully

Reporting Accountant

---

[3] This declaration is a requirement of the PD Regulation and is appropriate for inclusion when the report is included in a Prospectus, see Appendix 2 of SIR 1000.

STANDARDS FOR INVESTMENT REPORTING

4000 - INVESTMENT REPORTING STANDARDS APPLICABLE TO PUBLIC REPORTING ENGAGEMENTS ON PRO FORMA FINANCIAL INFORMATION

CONTENTS

ANNEXURE
Sections of TECH 18/98 "Pro forma financial information – Guidance for preparers
under the Listing Rules" (published by the Institute of Chartered Accountants in
England & Wales) that remain relevant

SIR 4000 contains basic principles and essential procedures ("Investment Reporting Standards"), indicated by paragraphs in bold type, with which a reporting accountant is required to comply in the conduct of an engagement to report on pro forma financial information, which is included within an investment circular prepared for issue in connection with a securities transaction governed wholly or in part by the laws and regulations of the United Kingdom.

SIR 4000 also includes explanatory and other material, including appendices, in the context of which the basic principles and essential procedures are to be understood and applied. It is necessary to consider the whole text of the SIR to understand and apply the basic principles and essential procedures.

For the purposes of the SIRs, an investment circular is defined as: "any document issued by an entity pursuant to statutory or regulatory requirements relating to listed or unlisted securities on which it is intended that a third party should make an investment decision, including a prospectus, listing particulars, circular to shareholders or similar document".

SIR 1000 "Investment reporting standards applicable to all engagements involving an investment circular" contains basic principles and essential procedures that are applicable to all engagements involving an investment circular. The definitions in the glossary of terms set out in Appendix 4 of SIR 1000 are to be applied in the interpretation of this and all other SIRs. Terms defined in the glossary are underlined the first time that they occur in the text.

To assist readers, SIRs contain references to, and extracts from, certain legislation and chapters of the Rules of the UK Listing Authority. Readers are cautioned that these references may change subsequent to publication.

Introduction

1. Standard for Investment Reporting (SIR) 1000 "Investment Reporting Standards applicable to all engagements in connection with an investment circular" establishes the Investment Reporting Standards applicable to all engagements involving investment circulars. The purpose of this SIR is to establish specific additional Investment Reporting Standards and provide guidance for a reporting accountant engaged to report publicly on pro forma financial information to be included in an investment circular under the PD Regulation, the Listing Rules[1], or if required by the London Stock Exchange in respect of an AIM Admission Document.

2. An engagement to report publicly on the proper compilation of pro forma financial information is a public reporting engagement as described in SIR 1000. The description of a public reporting engagement includes three generic terms having the following meanings in the context of an engagement to report on the proper compilation of pro forma financial information:

---

[1] In the UK the Prospectus Directive is implemented into law through amendments to Part VI of FSMA and to certain secondary legislation. The Annexes to the PD Regulation have been incorporated into the Prospectus Rules issued by the FSA.

(a) with respect to pro forma financial information the "**subject matter**" is the impact that the transaction, that is the subject of the investment circular, would have had on the earnings of the issuer (assuming that the transaction had been undertaken at the commencement of the financial period used for the illustration) or on the assets and liabilities of the issuer (assuming that the transaction had been undertaken at the end of the financial period used for the illustration);

(b) "**suitable criteria**" to be used by directors in the preparation of the pro forma financial information are provided by the requirements of the PD Regulation and the guidance issued by CESR[2] (CESR Recommendations). In forming its opinion as to whether the pro forma financial information has been properly compiled the reporting accountant considers whether certain of those criteria ("**reporting accountant's criteria**") have been properly applied. Reporting accountant's criteria are set out in Appendix 1 of this SIR; and

(c) with respect to pro forma financial information the "**outcome**"[3] is the pro forma financial information and related disclosures that are included in the investment circular and on which the reporting accountant expresses an opinion (in the "**reporting accountant's report**") as to whether that information is properly compiled on the basis stated and whether such basis is consistent with the accounting policies of the issuer.

The nature of pro forma financial information

3. For the purpose of this SIR "pro forma financial information" is defined to include financial information such as net assets, profit or cash flow statements that demonstrate the impact of a transaction on previously published financial information together with the explanatory notes thereto. Under item 1 of Annex II of the PD Regulation the pro forma financial information must be accompanied by introductory text describing the transaction, the businesses or entities involved, the period to which it refers and its purpose and limitations.

4. The Institute of Chartered Accountants in England and Wales (ICAEW) issued guidance entitled "Pro forma financial information - Guidance for preparers under the Listing Rules"[4] in September 1998 (the "ICAEW Guidance") to assist directors when preparing pro forma financial information for inclusion in documents subject to approval by the FSA prior to their issue. While aspects of this guidance remain of assistance to directors there are differences between the requirements of the PD Regulation, the CESR Recommendations and the requirements on which the ICAEW guidance was based. The Annexure has been prepared to assist in determining which parts of the ICAEW guidance continue to be relevant.

---

[2] CESR issued "CESR's Recommendations for the Consistent Implementation of the European Commission's Regulation on Prospectuses No. 809/2004" in February 2005.
[3] The "outcome" is sometimes described as "subject matter information".
[4] TECH 18/98

Compilation process

5. The compilation of pro forma information is the gathering, classification and summarisation of relevant financial information. The process followed by the preparer would be expected to include the following:

    (a) the accurate extraction of information from sources permitted under the PD Regulation;

    (b) the making of adjustments to the source information that are arithmetically correct, appropriate and complete for the purpose for which the pro forma financial information is presented;

    (c) arithmetic computation of the pro forma information;

    (d) consideration of accounting policies;

    (e) appropriate disclosure to enable the intended users to understand the pro forma financial information; and

    (f) appropriate consideration of the pro forma financial information and approval by the directors of the entity.

Engagement acceptance and continuance

6. SIR 1000.1 and SIR 1000.2 set out the basic principles and essential procedures, with respect to engagement acceptance and continuance, that are applicable to all engagements involving an investment circular.

7. When accepting or continuing an engagement to report publicly on pro forma information, the reporting accountant ascertains whether the directors intend to comply with all relevant regulatory requirements, in particular those that constitute the reporting accountant's criteria set out in Appendix 1 of this SIR.

Agreeing the terms of the engagement

8. SIR 1000.3 and SIR 1000.4 set out the basic principles and essential procedures with respect to agreeing the terms of the engagement. Examples of engagement letter clauses are set out in Appendix 3 of this SIR.

Ethical requirements

9. SIR 1000.5 sets out the basic principles and essential procedures with respect to the ethical requirements that apply to a reporting accountant[5].

Legal and regulatory requirements

10. The PD Regulation requires any pro forma financial information included in a prospectus to be reported on by independent accountants or auditors (referred to in this SIR as the "reporting accountant") and specifies the form of opinion to be given. The Listing Rules require any pro forma financial information included in a Class 1 circular to be reported on in the same way. References in the SIR to the PD Regulation apply equally to the Listing Rules where those Rules apply.

11. SIR 1000.6 sets out the basic principles with respect to the legal and regulatory requirements applicable to a reporting accountant.

12. Appendices 1 and 2 to this SIR set out those provisions of the PD Regulation and the CESR Recommendations, relating to the implementation of the Regulation, that provide the suitable criteria for directors. Those provisions that constitute criteria for a reporting accountant expressing an opinion on whether the pro forma information has been properly compiled are set out in Appendix 1 of this SIR.

Quality control

13. SIR 1000.7 and SIR 1000.8 set out the basic principles and essential procedures with respect to the quality control of engagements to report on pro forma financial information.

Planning and performing the engagement

14. SIR 1000.9 and SIR 1000.10 set out the basic principles and essential procedures with respect to the planning of all reporting engagements. Additional basic principles, essential procedures and guidance are set out below.

15. **The reporting accountant should obtain an understanding of the key factors affecting the subject matter sufficient to identify and assess the risk of the pro forma financial information not being properly compiled and sufficient to design and perform evidence gathering procedures including:**

    (a) **the nature of the transaction being undertaken by the issuer;**

---

[5] In January 2006 the APB issued an Exposure Draft of an Ethical Standard for Reporting Accountants (ESRA).

(b) **the entity's business; and**

(c) **the procedures adopted, or planned to be adopted, by the directors for the preparation of the pro forma financial information. (SIR 4000.1)**

16. The reporting accountant gains an understanding of the transaction, in respect of which the pro forma financial information is being prepared, by discussion with the directors or management of the issuer and by reading relevant supporting documentation.

17. The reporting accountant uses professional judgment to determine the extent of the understanding required of the entity's business.

18. Other matters for consideration by the reporting accountant include the availability of evidence to provide factual support for the proposed adjustments and the accounting policies that will form the basis of the adjustments to the pro forma financial information.

19. **The reporting accountant should consider materiality and public reporting engagement risk in planning its work in accordance with its instructions and in determining the effect of its findings on the report to be issued. (SIR 4000.2)**

Materiality

20. Matters are material if their omission or misstatement could, individually or collectively, influence the economic decisions of the intended users of the pro forma financial information. Materiality depends on the size and nature of the omission or misstatement judged in light of the surrounding circumstances. The size or nature of the matter, or a combination of both, could be the determining factor.

21. A misstatement in the context of the compilation of pro forma financial information includes, for example:

- Use of an inappropriate source for the unadjusted financial information.

- Incorrect extraction of the unadjusted financial information from an appropriate source.

- In relation to adjustments, the misapplication of accounting policies or failure to use the accounting policies adopted in the last, or to be adopted in the next, financial statements.

- Failure to make an adjustment required by the PD regulation.

- Making an adjustment that does not comply with the PD regulation.

- A mathematical or clerical mistake.

- Inadequate, or incorrect, disclosures.

22. Evaluating whether an omission or misstatement could influence economic decisions of the intended users of the pro forma financial information, and so be material, requires consideration of the characteristics of those intended users. The intended users are assumed to:

    (a) have a reasonable knowledge of business and economic activities and accounting and a willingness to study the pro forma financial information with reasonable diligence; and

    (b) make reasonable economic decisions on the basis of the pro forma financial information.

    The determination of materiality, therefore, takes into account how intended users with such characteristics could reasonably be expected to be influenced in making economic decisions.

Public reporting engagement risk

23. "Public reporting engagement risk" is the risk that the reporting accountant expresses an inappropriate opinion when the pro forma financial information has not been properly compiled on the basis stated or that basis is not consistent with the accounting policies of the issuer[6].

24. SIR 1000.11 and SIR 1000.12 set out the basic principles and essential procedures, with respect to obtaining evidence, that are applicable to all engagements involving an investment circular. Additional basic principles, essential procedures and guidance relating to engagements to report on pro forma financial information are set out below.

25. **The reporting accountant should obtain sufficient appropriate evidence that the pro forma financial information is free from material error in its compilation by:**

    (a) **checking that the unadjusted financial information of the issuer has been accurately extracted from a source that is both appropriate and in accordance with the relevant regulation;**

    (b) **obtaining evidence that the directors have applied the criteria set out in Appendix 1 of this SIR and, therefore, that the adjustments are appropriate and complete for the purpose for which the pro forma financial information is presented; and**

    (c) **checking that the calculations within the pro forma financial information are arithmetically correct. (SIR 4000.3)**

26. Item 5 of Annex II of the PD Regulation permits pro forma financial information to be published only in respect of:

---

[6] The PD Regulation requires a positive and unmodified opinion – for this reason there is no risk that the reporting accountant will inappropriately modify its opinion.

(a)   the current financial period;

(b)   the most recently completed financial period; and

(c)   the most recent interim period for which relevant unadjusted information has been or will be published or is being published in the same investment circular.

Unadjusted financial information of the issuer

27.   The reporting accountant considers whether the period in respect of which the pro forma financial information is proposed to be published is permitted under the PD Regulation. The reporting accountant also considers whether the source of the unadjusted financial information for the issuer is appropriate and whether the source of the unadjusted financial information is clearly stated.

28.   The reporting accountant is not required to perform specific procedures on the unadjusted financial information of the issuer other than as described in paragraph 27. However, if the reporting accountant has reason to believe that the unadjusted financial information is, or may be, unreliable, or if a report thereon has identified any uncertainties or disagreements, the reporting accountant considers the effect on the pro forma financial information.

29.   The reporting accountant checks the extraction of the unadjusted financial information from the source concerned.

Adjustments

30.   Item 6 of Annex II to the PD Regulation requires pro forma adjustments to be:

(a)   clearly shown and explained;

(b)   directly attributable to the transaction; and

(c)   factually supportable.

31.   In addition, in respect of a pro forma profit and loss or cash flow statement, they must be clearly identified as to those adjustments which are expected to have a continuing impact on the issuer and those which are not.

32.   More detailed guidance for directors concerning the implementation of these requirements is provided by the CESR Recommendations and those parts of the ICAEW Guidance that remain relevant (see Annexure).

33.   The reporting accountant considers the way in which the directors have fulfilled their responsibilities. With its understanding of the transaction and the entity's business as background the reporting accountant discusses with the directors the steps the directors have taken to identify relevant adjustments and whether such adjustments are permitted to be made.

34. If, as a result of these enquiries, the reporting accountant becomes aware of a significant adjustment which, in its opinion, ought to be made for the purposes of the pro forma financial information it discusses the position with the directors of the issuer and, if necessary, the issuer's advisers. If the reporting accountant is not able to agree with the directors and the issuer's advisers as to how the matter is to be resolved it considers the consequences for its report.

35. The reporting accountant considers the adjustments to assess whether they are "directly attributable" to the transaction whose impact is being illustrated by the pro forma financial information, that is, they are an integral part of the transaction concerned. If a potential adjustment is not directly attributable to the transaction or transactions described in the investment circular, it cannot be made (although it may be appropriate to disclose by way of note to the pro forma financial information the nature of a prohibited potential adjustment and the effect it would have had if it had been permissible to include it).

36. In assessing whether adjustments are directly attributable to the transaction the reporting accountant considers whether the adjustments relate to future events and/or decisions. This is because adjustments that are related to the transaction being illustrated but which are dependent on actions to be taken once the transaction has been completed, cannot be said to be "directly attributable".

37. The reporting accountant considers whether the adjustments have been clearly shown and explained and, in respect of a pro forma profit and loss or cash flow statement, whether they have been clearly identified as to those which are expected to have a continuing impact on the issuer (that is, relate to events or circumstances that are expected to recur) and to those which are not.

38. The reporting accountant obtains appropriate evidence that the directors of the issuer have factual support for each adjustment. Sources of such evidence would include published financial statements, other financial information or valuations disclosed elsewhere in the investment circular, purchase and sale agreements and other agreements relating to the transaction.

Omitted adjustments

39. In view of the specific restrictions on the nature of the adjustments permitted to be made under item 6 of Annex II of the PD Regulation, the directors may not be permitted to make all the adjustments that they would otherwise wish to. For example, an adjustment which is directly attributable but which is not factually supportable could not be included in pro forma financial information.

40. If any adjustments are excluded because of the requirement in item 6 of Annex II of the PD Regulation for adjustments to be factually supportable, the reporting accountant considers the effect on the pro forma financial information and in particular whether the exclusion renders the pro forma financial information misleading. In such circumstances, the reporting accountant may consider that disclosure in the notes to the pro forma financial information of the fact that such an adjustment has not been

made is sufficient in the context of the overall purpose of the pro forma financial information.

41. However, if the reporting accountant concludes that an omitted adjustment is so fundamental as to render the pro forma statement misleading in the context of the investment circular, it discusses the matter with the directors and, if necessary, the issuer's advisers and in the event that acceptable changes to the disclosures are not made, considers whether it is able to issue its report.

Checking the calculations

42. The reporting accountant ascertains whether the adjustments made in the pro forma financial information are included under the appropriate financial statement caption as well as the arithmetical accuracy of the calculations within the pro forma financial information itself.

Consistent accounting policies

43. **The reporting accountant should evaluate whether the adjustments made to the unadjusted financial information are consistent with the accounting policies adopted in the last, or to be adopted in the next, financial statements of the entity presenting the pro forma financial information. (SIR 4000.4)**

44. It is the responsibility of the directors of the issuer to ensure that in accordance with item 4 of Annex II of the PD Regulation the pro forma financial information is prepared in a manner consistent with either the accounting policies adopted in the last, or to be adopted in the next, financial statements of the issuer.

45. Where the reporting accountant is not the auditor of the issuer or has not otherwise reported on the financial information relating to the subject of the transaction, it evaluates the steps taken to ensure that the pro forma financial information has been prepared in a manner consistent with the accounting policies of the issuer. Guidance for directors with respect to the consistency of accounting policies is provided by the ICAEW Guidance.

Presentation of pro forma financial information

46. **The reporting accountant should consider whether it has become aware of anything to cause it to believe that the pro forma financial information is presented in a way that is not understandable or is misleading in the context in which it is provided. If the reporting accountant is aware of such matters it should discuss them with the parties responsible for the pro forma financial information and with those persons to whom its report is to be addressed, and consider whether it is able to issue its report. (SIR 4000.5)**

47. The reporting accountant reads the pro forma financial information to assess whether:

    (a)   as required by item 1 of Annex II of the PD Regulation, the pro forma financial information includes a description of the transaction, the businesses or entities involved and the period to which it refers and clearly states the purpose for which it has been prepared, that it has been prepared for illustrative purposes only and that, because of its nature, it addresses a hypothetical situation and, therefore, does not represent the company's actual financial position or results;

(b) in accordance with the normal form of presentation under item 3 of Annex II of the PD Regulation, the pro forma financial information is presented in columnar format composed of (a) the historical unadjusted information, (b) the pro forma adjustments and (c) the resulting pro forma financial information in the final column; and

(c) disclosures, in the notes to the pro forma financial information, concerning omitted adjustments are satisfactory (see paragraphs 40 and 41 above).

Representation letter

48. SIR 1000.13 sets out the basic principles and essential procedures, with respect to representation letters, that are applicable to all engagements involving an investment circular. Examples of management representation letter clauses are set out in Appendix 4 of this SIR.

Documentation

49. SIR 1000.14 and SIR 1000.15 set out the basic principles and essential procedures with respect to the reporting accountant's working papers.

Professional scepticism

50. SIR 1000.16 sets out the basic principle with respect to the attitude of professional scepticism adopted by the reporting accountant in planning and performing an engagement.

Reporting

51. SIRs 1000.17, SIR 1000.18 and SIR 1000.19 set out the basic principles and essential procedures, with respect to reporting, that are applicable to all engagements involving an investment circular. Additional basic principles and essential procedures relating to engagements to report on pro forma financial information are set out below.

Responsibilities

52. **In all reports on pro forma financial information in investment circulars the reporting accountant should explain the extent of its responsibility in respect of the pro forma financial information by including in its report:**

    (a) **a statement that the reporting accountant's responsibility is to form an opinion (as required by the applicable regulatory requirements) on the proper compilation of the pro forma financial information and to report its opinion to the addressees of the report; and**

(b)   a statement that the pro forma financial information is the responsibility of the directors. (SIR 4000.6)

53.   The reporting accountant's responsibility in relation to the opinion required by the PD Regulation is limited to the provision of the report and the opinion expressed.

Basis of preparation of the pro forma financial information

54.   **The reporting accountant should include a basis of preparation section of its report that cross refers to disclosures that explain the basis of preparation of the pro forma financial information. (SIR 4000.7)**

55.   The basis of preparation section of the report will make clear whether the accounting policies applied in the preparation of the pro forma information are those adopted by the entity in preparing the last published financial statements or those that it plans to adopt in the next published financial statements.

Expression of opinion

56.   **The report on the pro forma financial information should contain a clear expression of opinion that complies with applicable regulatory requirements. (SIR 4000.8)**

57.   In forming its opinion the reporting accountant takes account of those events which the reporting accountant becomes aware of occurring up to the date on which the reporting accountant signs the report, that affect the opinion expressed in the report.

58.   In providing the opinion required by the PD Regulation the reporting accountant is not providing any assurance in relation to any source financial information on which the pro forma financial information is based beyond that opinion. In particular, the reporting accountant is not refreshing or updating any opinion that it may have given in any other capacity on that source financial information.

59.   The investment circular in which the reporting accountant's report is included may be made available in other countries, such as the United States of America, which have their own standards for accountants when reporting on pro forma financial information. In such circumstances, the reporting accountant considers whether to include a reference to the fact that a report issued in accordance with the SIRs should not be relied upon as if it had been issued in accordance with the standards applicable in that other country. An example of such a reference is included in the example report set out in Appendix 5 of this SIR.

Modified opinions

60.   SIR 1000.20 sets out the basic principles and essential procedures, with respect to modified opinions, that are applicable to all engagements involving an investment circular. Additional basic principles and essential procedures relating to engagements to report on pro forma financial information are set out below.

61. In the event that the reporting accountant concludes that it is unable to report in the manner prescribed it considers, with the parties to whom it is to report, whether the pro forma financial information can be amended to alleviate its concerns or whether the pro forma information should be omitted from the investment circular and the requirement for information to be given on the effect of the transaction satisfied in some other way.

62. **As the PD Regulation requires a positive and unmodified opinion, the reporting accountant should not express an opinion when the directors have not applied the criteria set out in Appendix 1 of this SIR and, in the reporting accountant's judgment the effect of not doing so is, or may be, material. (SIR 4000.9)**

63. An example of a report on pro forma financial information expressing a positive and unmodified opinion, pursuant to the PD Regulation, is set out in Appendix 5 of this SIR.

Consent

64. SIR 1000.21 and SIR 1000.22 set out the basic principles and essential procedures with respect to the giving of consent by the reporting accountant.

Events occurring between the date of the reporting accountant's report and the completion date of the transaction

65. SIR 1000.23 sets out the basic principles and essential procedures with respect to events occurring between the date of the reporting accountant's report and the completion date of the transaction.

66. Under Section 81 and 87G of the FSMA, Prospectus Rule 3.4 and Listing Rule 4.4.1, a supplementary investment circular must be prepared if, after the date the investment circular has been formally approved by a regulator and before dealings in the relevant securities commence, the issuer becomes aware that there has been a significant change affecting any matter contained in the document or a significant new matter has arisen, the inclusion of information in respect of which would have been required if it had arisen at the time of its preparation. A similar obligation arises, under Article 16 of the Prospectus Directive, in respect of the period following registration of the investment circular during which an agreement in respect of the securities can be entered into in pursuance of the offer contained in the investment circular.

67. If, as a result of discussions with those responsible for the investment circular concerning an event that occurred prior to the completion date of the transaction, the reporting accountant is either uncertain about or disagrees with the course of action proposed it may consider it necessary to take legal advice with respect to its responsibilities in the particular circumstances.

68. After the date of its report, the reporting accountant has no obligation to perform procedures or make enquiries regarding the investment circular.

Effective date

69. A reporting accountant is required to comply with the Investment Reporting Standards contained in this SIR for reports signed after 31 March 2006. Earlier adoption is encouraged.

Appendix 1

REPORTING ACCOUNTANT'S CRITERIA

	Annex I of PD Regulation	Annex II of PD Regulation	CESR Recommendations
In the case of a significant gross change, a description of how the transaction might have affected the assets and liabilities and earnings of the issuer, had the transaction been undertaken at the commencement of the period being reported on or at the date reported. This requirement will normally be satisfied by the inclusion of pro forma financial information.	20.2		
The pro forma information must normally be presented in columnar format composed of: a) the historical unadjusted information; b) the pro forma adjustments; and c) the resulting pro forma financial information in the final column		3	
The sources of the pro forma financial information have to be stated.		3	
The pro forma information must be prepared in a manner consistent with the accounting policies adopted by the issuer in its last or next financial statements and shall identify the following: a) the basis upon which it is prepared; b) the source of each item of information and adjustment.		4	
Pro forma adjustments related to the pro forma financial information must be: a) clearly shown and explained.		6	
Pro forma adjustments related to the pro forma financial information must be: b) directly attributable to the transaction.		6	

	Annex I of PD Regulation	Annex II of PD Regulation	CESR Recommendations
"Directly attributable to transactions". Pro forma information should only reflect matters that are an integral part of the transactions which are described in the prospectus. In particular, pro forma financial information should not include adjustments which are dependent on actions to be taken once the current transactions have been completed, even where such actions are central to the issuer's purpose in entering into the transactions.			Para 88
Pro forma adjustments related to the pro forma financial information must be: c) factually supportable.		6	
"Factually supportable". The nature of the facts supporting an adjustment will vary according to the circumstances. Nevertheless, facts are expected to be capable of some reasonable degree of objective determination. Support might typically be provided by published accounts, management accounts, other financial information and valuations contained in the document, purchase and sale agreements and other agreements to the transaction covered by the prospectus. For instance in relation to management accounts, the interim figures for an undertaking being acquired may be derived from the consolidation schedules underlying that undertaking's interim statements.			Para 87
In respect of a pro forma profit and loss or cash flow statement, the adjustments must be clearly identified as to those expected to have a continuing impact on the issuer and those which are not.		6	
The accounting treatment applied to adjustments should be presented and prepared in a form consistent with the policy the issuer would adopt in its last or next published financial statements.			Para 89[1]

[1] Paragraph 89 of the CESR guidance also makes recommendations that do not constitute criteria but provide useful guidance with respect to this criterion.

Appendix 2

OTHER REGULATORY PROVISIONS RELEVANT TO THE PREPARERS OF PRO FORMA FINANCIAL INFORMATION

	PD Regulation	Annex I of PD Regulation	Annex II of PD Regulation	CESR Recommendations
(9) Pro forma financial information is needed in case of significant gross change, i.e. a variation of more than 25% relative to one or more indicators of the size of the issuer's business, in the situation of an issuer due to a particular transaction, with the exception of those situations where merger accounting is required.	Recital 9			
For these purposes, "Significant gross change" is described in recital 9 of the PD Regulation. Thus, in order to assess whether the variation to an issuer's business as a result of a transaction is more than 25%, the size of the transaction should be assessed relative to the size of the issuer by using appropriate indicators of size prior to the relevant transaction. A transaction will constitute a significant gross change where at least one of the indicators of size is more than 25%. A non-exhaustive list of indicators of size is provided below: - Total assets - Revenue - Profit or loss Other indicators of size can be applied by the issuer especially where the stated indicators of size produce an anomalous result or are inappropriate to the specific industry of the issuer; in these cases the issuers should address these anomalies by agreement of the competent authority. The appropriate indicators of size should refer to figures from the issuer's last or next published annual financial statements.				Paras 90 to 94

	PD Regulation	Annex I of PD Regulation	Annex II of PD Regulation	CESR Recommendations
Pro forma financial information should be preceded by an introductory explanatory paragraph that states in clear terms the purpose of including this information in the prospectus	Article 5			
This pro forma financial information is to be presented as set out in Annex II and must include the information indicated therein.		20.2		
Pro forma financial information must be accompanied by a report prepared by independent accountants or auditors.				
The pro forma information must include a description of the transaction, the businesses or entities involved and the period to which it refers.			1	
The pro forma information must clearly state the purpose to which it has been prepared			1	
The pro forma information must clearly state that it has been prepared for illustrative purposes only			1	
The pro forma information must clearly state that, because of its nature, it addresses a hypothetical situation and, therefore, does not represent the company's actual financial position or results.			1	
In order to present pro forma financial information, a balance sheet and profit and loss account, and accompanying explanatory notes, depending on the circumstances may be included			2	

	PD Regulation	Annex I of PD Regulation	Annex II of PD Regulation	CESR Recommendations
Where applicable the financial statements of the acquired businesses or entities must be included in the prospectus.			3	
Pro forma information may only be published in respect of: a) the current financial period; b) the most recently completed financial period; and/or c) the most recent interim period for which relevant unadjusted information has been or will be published or is being published in the same document			5	

Appendix 3

EXAMPLES OF ENGAGEMENT LETTER CLAUSES

The examples of engagement letter clauses are intended for consideration in the context of a public reporting engagement on pro forma financial information. They should be tailored to the specific circumstances and supplemented by such other clauses as are relevant and appropriate.

Financial information upon which the report is to be given

The [investment circular] will include a pro forma [balance sheet/profit and loss account] together with a description of the basis of presentation (including the accounting policies used) and supporting notes to illustrate how the transaction might have affected the financial information of the company had the transaction been undertaken at the beginning of the period[s] concerned or as at the date[s] stated (the "pro forma financial information").

Responsibilities

The pro forma financial information, which will be the responsibility solely of the directors, will be prepared for illustrative purposes only. This is required to be prepared in accordance with items 1 to 6 of Annex II of the PD Regulation.

It is our responsibility to form an opinion as to whether the pro forma financial information has been properly compiled on the basis stated and that such basis is consistent with the accounting policies of ABC plc.

If the results of our work are satisfactory, and having regard to the requirements of item 7 of Annex II of the PD Regulation, we shall prepare a report on the pro forma financial information for inclusion in the [*describe document*]. An illustration of the form of our report is attached.

Scope of work

Our work will be undertaken in accordance with Standard for Investment Reporting (SIR) 4000 "Investment Reporting Standards Applicable to Public Reporting Engagements on Pro Forma Financial Information" issued by the Auditing Practices Board and will be subject to the limitations described therein.

We draw your attention in particular to paragraph 62 of SIR 4000 which would preclude us from expressing any opinion if the directors have not complied with the regulatory requirements set out in Appendix 1 of that SIR.

Appendix 4

EXAMPLES OF MANAGEMENT REPRESENTATION LETTER CLAUSES

The following are examples of management representation letter clauses relating to a report on pro forma financial information, issued pursuant to the PD Regulation or Listing Rules, which may be obtained from the issuer. Alternatively they may form the basis for a board minute.

Introduction

We refer to the pro forma financial information set out in Part [...] of the [investment circular] dated...to be issued in connection with [...] dated. We acknowledge that we are solely responsible for the pro forma financial information and confirm on behalf of the Directors of the Company to the best of our knowledge and belief, having made appropriate enquiries of officials of the Company [and the directors and officials of the target company], the following representations made to you in the course of your work.

Specific representations

- We acknowledge as duly appointed officials of the Company our responsibility for the pro forma financial information (which has been prepared in accordance with [CESR's Recommendations for the Consistent Implementation of the European Commission's Regulation on Prospectuses No. 809/2004"] [and, to the extent applicable, with Technical Release TECH 18/98 published by the Institute of Chartered Accountants in England and Wales].

- We have considered the pro forma financial information and we confirm that, in our opinion, as required by item 20.2 of Annex I of the PD Regulation, the pro forma financial information provides investors with information about the impact of the transaction by illustrating how that transaction might have affected the [assets and liabilities] [and] [earnings] of the issuer, had the transaction been undertaken at the commencement of the period being reported on or at the date reported. Furthermore, we confirm that, in our opinion, the pro forma financial information is not misleading.

- We have considered the adjustments included in the pro forma financial information. We confirm that, in our opinion, the pro forma financial information includes all appropriate adjustments permitted by item 6 of Annex II of the PD Regulation, of which we are aware, necessary to give effect to the transaction as if the transaction had been undertaken [at the date reported on} [at the commencement of the period being reported on].

- [We have considered those adjustments which have been omitted by virtue of not being permitted to be included by item 6 of Annex II of the PD Regulation and the disclosures made in respect thereof. In our opinion the omission of these adjustments does not render the pro forma financial information misleading.]

- [*Where the accounting policies in the issuer's next financial statements are used.* The accounting policies used in compiling the pro forma financial information are those to be adopted in the Company's next financial statements, and all changes necessary to reflect those policies have been made.]

- [*Any specific representations relating to information included in the pro forma financial information.*]

Appendix 5

EXAMPLE REPORT ON PRO FORMA FINANCIAL INFORMATION IN ACCORDANCE WITH THE PD REGULATION OR THE LISTING RULES

Date

Reporting accountant's address

Addressees, as agreed between the parties in the engagement letter

Dear Sirs,

[ABC plc]

We report on the pro forma [financial information] (the "Pro forma financial information") set out in Part [...] of the [investment circular] dated......., which has been prepared on the basis described [in note x], for illustrative purposes only, to provide information about how the [transaction] might have affected the financial information presented on the basis of the accounting policies [adopted/to be adopted[1]] by ABC plc in preparing the financial statements for the period [ended/ending] [*date*]. This report is required by [Relevant Regulation] [guidance issued by the London Stock Exchange with respect to the AIM market] and is given for the purpose of complying with that [Relevant Regulation] [guidance issued by the London Stock Exchange] and for no other purpose.

Responsibilities

It is the responsibility of the directors of ABC plc to prepare the Pro forma financial information in accordance with [item 20.2 of Annex I of the PD Regulation] [guidance issued by the London Stock Exchange].

It is our responsibility to form an opinion, as required by [item 7 of Annex II of the PD Regulation] [guidance issued by the London Stock Exchange], as to the proper compilation of the Pro forma financial information and to report that opinion to you.

In providing this opinion we are not updating or refreshing any reports or opinions previously made by us on any financial information used in the compilation of the Pro forma financial information, nor do we accept responsibility for such reports or opinions beyond that owed to those to whom those reports or opinions were addressed by us at the dates of their issue.

Basis of Opinion

We conducted our work in accordance with the Standards for Investment Reporting issued by the Auditing Practices Board in the United Kingdom. The work that we performed for the

---

[1] See paragraph 44 of SIR 4000

purpose of making this report, which involved no independent examination of any of the underlying financial information, consisted primarily of comparing the unadjusted financial information with the source documents, considering the evidence supporting the adjustments and discussing the Pro forma financial information with the directors of ABC plc.

We planned and performed our work so as to obtain the information and explanations we considered necessary in order to provide us with reasonable assurance that the Pro forma financial information has been properly compiled on the basis stated and that such basis is consistent with the accounting policies of ABC plc.

[*This paragraph may be omitted if the document is not to be distributed outside the UK* - Our work has not been carried out in accordance with auditing or other standards and practices generally accepted in the United States of America [or other jurisdictions] and accordingly should not be relied upon as if it had been carried out in accordance with those standards and practices.]

Opinion

In our opinion:

(a)   the Pro forma financial information has been properly compiled on the basis stated; and

(b)   such basis is consistent with the accounting policies of ABC plc.

Declaration[2]

For the purposes of [Prospectus Rule [5.5.3R(2)(f)] [5.5.4R(2)(f)]] [guidance issued by the London Stock Exchange] we are responsible for [this report as part] [the following part(s)] of the [prospectus] [registration document] [AIM Admission Document] and declare that we have taken all reasonable care to ensure that the information contained [in this report] [those parts] is, to the best of our knowledge, in accordance with the facts and contains no omission likely to affect its import. This declaration is included in the [prospectus] [registration document] [AIM Admission Document] in compliance with [item 1.2 of Annex I of the PD Regulation] [item 1.2 of Annex III of the Prospectus Regulation] [guidance issued by the London Stock Exchange].

Yours faithfully

Reporting accountant

---

[2]   This declaration is a requirement of the Prospectus Rules and is appropriate for inclusion when the report is included in a Prospectus, see Appendix 2 of SIR 1000. It is also appropriate for inclusion in an AIM admission document under Schedule Two of the AIM Rules.

SECTIONS OF TECH 18/98 "PRO FORMA FINANCIAL INFORMATION – GUIDANCE FOR PREPARERS UNDER THE LISTING RULES"[1] (PUBLISHED BY THE INSTITUTE OF CHARTERED ACCOUNTANTS IN ENGLAND & WALES) THAT REMAIN RELEVANT

This Annexure has been compiled by the APB to indicate those paragraphs of TECH 18/98 that continue to be relevant. (There are differences between the requirements of the PD Regulation and the CESR Recommendations compared to the requirements on which TECH 18/98 was based.) The Annexure does not include either basic principles, essential procedures, or guidance promulgated by the APB.

Paragraphs in TECH 18/98	Application under the PD Regulation
1 to 5	*Not applicable*
6	Principles still applicable, save that under Item 20.2 of Annex I of the PD Regulation inclusion of pro forma information is now normally included where there has been a "significant gross change" (as defined in Recital (9))
7 and 8	Principles still applicable
9	*Not applicable – replaced by the following:* *Item 20.2 of Annex 1 of the PD Regulation. In the case of a significant gross change, a description of how the transaction might have affected the assets and liabilities and earnings of the issuer, had the transaction been undertaken at the commencement of the period being reported on or at the date reported.* *This requirement will normally be satisfied by the inclusion of pro forma financial information.* *This pro forma financial information is to be presented as set out in Annex II and must include the information indicated therein.* *Pro forma financial information must be accompanied by a report prepared by independent accountants or auditors.*
10 and 11	Principles still applicable
12 to 19	Principles still applicable save that there is no express requirement under the PD Regulation for all appropriate adjustments to be included, nor for the pro forma financial information not to be misleading
20	*Not applicable – replaced by the following (the words **emphasised** are additional to the original Listing Rule and certain other words have been deleted):* *Item 1 of Annex II of the PD Regulation. The pro forma information **must include a description of the transaction, the businesses or entities involved and the period to which it refers**, and must clearly state the following:* *a) the purpose **to** which it has been prepared;* *b) the fact that it has been prepared for illustrative purposes only;* *c) the fact that because of its nature, **the pro forma financial information addresses a hypothetical situation and, therefore, does not represent the company's actual financial position or results.***

---

[1] This Annexure applies to TECH 18/98 which was published by the ICAEW in 1998 and is available for download from its website. The ICAEW has indicated that it intends to update and reissue TECH 18/98. When it is reissued this Annexure will no longer be applicable and should not be used.

	Item 2 of Annex II of the PD Regulation *In order to present pro forma financial information, a balance sheet and profit and loss account, and accompanying explanatory notes, depending on the circumstances may be included.*
21 to 24	Principles still applicable
25	*Not applicable – replaced by the following:* *Item 3 of Annex II of the PD Regulation. Pro forma financial information must **normally** be presented in columnar format, **composed of**:* *a) the **historical** unadjusted information;* *b) the pro forma adjustments; and* *c) the **resulting** pro forma financial information **in the final column**.* ***The sources of the pro forma financial information have to be stated and, if applicable, the financial statements of the acquired businesses or entities must be included in the prospectus*** *Item 4 of Annex II of the PD Regulation. The pro forma information must be prepared in a manner consistent with the accounting policies adopted by the issuer in its **last or next** financial statements and shall identify the following:* *a) the basis upon which it is prepared;* *b) the source of each item of information and adjustment.*
26	Principles still applicable
27	Principles still applicable, save that the accounting policies to be used in the next financial statements may also be applied
28 to 29	Principles still applicable
30	*Not applicable*
31 and 32	Principles still applicable
33	*Not applicable*
34	Applicable, save that the words "*and, in the case of a pro forma balance sheet or net asset statement, as at the date on which such periods end or ended*" are omitted
35 to 43	Principles still applicable
44 and 45	*Not applicable*
46 to 71	Principles still applicable
72 to 74	*Not applicable*

Section 6: GUIDANCE

DEVELOPMENTS IN 2006

During 2006 the APB issued:

- three revised Practice Notes;

- two updated Practice Notes containing interim guidance;

- five consultation drafts of Practice Notes (for three of which 'near final' versions have been issued); and

- six Bulletins.

Revised Practice Notes

Practice Note 10 – Public Sector Audits in the United Kingdom

In January the APB issued Practice Note 10 (Revised), *'Audit of Financial Statements of Public Sector Bodies in the United Kingdom'*. The revision provides updated guidance for auditors following the replacement of the APB's SASs with International Standards on Auditing (ISAs) (UK and Ireland). It also takes account of legal and regulatory developments affecting public sector bodies in the United Kingdom since the previous Practice Note 10 (Revised) was issued in April 2001.

The standards governing the conduct and reporting of the audit of financial statements in the public sector are a matter for the national audit agencies and certain regulators to determine. However, the heads of the national audit agencies in the UK have chosen to adopt the APB's engagement standards and quality control standards as the basis of their approach to the audit of financial statements.

Practice Note 10(I) – Public Sector Audits in the Republic of Ireland

In July the APB issued Practice Note 10(I) (Revised), *'Audit of Central Government Financial Statements in the Republic of Ireland'*. The revision provides updated guidance for auditors following the introduction of ISAs (UK and Ireland) and takes account of legal and regulatory developments in the Republic of Ireland since the previous Practice Note 10(I) (Revised) was issued in January 2002.

Practice Note 14 – Registered Social Landlords

In March the APB published Practice Note 14 (Revised), *'The Audit of Registered Social Landlords in the United Kingdom'*. The revision provides updated guidance for auditors following the introduction of ISAs (UK and Ireland) and takes account of legal and regulatory developments affecting RSLs since the previous Practice Note 14 (Revised) was issued in November 2003.

Updated Practice Notes Containing Interim Guidance

Practice Note 12 – Money Laundering

In April the APB issued an update to Practice Note 12 (Revised), *'Money Laundering - Interim Guidance for Auditors in the United Kingdom'*, which was originally issued in August 2004. This updated version, which reflects a number of changes to legislation arising from the Serious and Organised Crime and Police Act 2005, was submitted to HM Treasury for approval under the Proceeds of Crime Act 2002. The guidance in the Practice Note was further updated in January 2007 to reflect the implementation of section 102 of the Serious and Organised Crime and Police Act 2005. When approval is received from HM Treasury the APB will publish Practice Note 12 (Revised) in final form.

Practice Note 16 – Bank Confirmations

In October the APB issued an update to Practice Note 16 (revised), *'Bank Reports for Audit Purposes (Revised) – Interim guidance'*. In October 2005 the APB had issued as a consultation draft a proposed revision of Practice Note 16 (Revised) which reflected discussions between the audit profession and the British Bankers' Association (BBA). A number of respondents to the October 2005 consultation draft recommended more extensive changes to the process by which auditors request bank confirmations and banks respond. Further discussions are taking place between the audit profession and the BBA in this regard but changes to Practice Note 16 (Revised) beyond those contemplated in the consultation draft are not expected for a number of months. In the circumstances the APB considered that it would be helpful to issue the October 2005 consultation draft as interim guidance.

Consultation Drafts of Practice Notes

Practice Note 15 – Occupational Pension Schemes

In August the APB published a consultation draft of a revision of Practice Note 15, *'The Audit of Occupational Pension Schemes in the United Kingdom'*. The consultation period ended in November 2006.

The proposed revised Practice Note provides updated guidance for auditors following the introduction of ISAs (UK and Ireland) and incorporates the supplementary guidance that was set out in Bulletin 2005/5, *'Audit Risk and Fraud - Supplementary Guidance for Auditors of Occupational Pension Schemes'*. References to the role and powers of Opra have been replaced by equivalent material in relation to The Pensions Regulator. The guidance on reporting on contributions has been revised to reflect the introduction of materiality as a consideration by The Occupational Pension Schemes (Administration and Audited Accounts) (Amendment) Regulations 2005.

Practice Note 19 – Banks and Building Societies

In May the APB published a consultation draft of a revision of Practice Note 19, *'The Audit of Banks and Building Societies in the United Kingdom'*. The consultation period ended in August 2006.

The proposed revised Practice Note provides updated guidance for auditors following the introduction of ISAs (UK and Ireland), reflects recent changes in legislation and regulation and incorporates the guidance in Bulletin 2006/6, *'Audit Risk and Fraud – Supplementary Guidance for Auditors of Banks and Building Societies'*. In the revised Practice Note, the guidance for banks and building societies has been combined into a single document in recognition that there is now insufficient guidance that is unique to building societies to merit maintaining a separate Practice Note.

Following consideration of comments received during the consultation period, a 'near-final' version of Practice Note 19 (Revised) was issued in electronic form on the APB's website in December 2006.

Practice Note 20 – Insurers

In July the APB published a second consultation draft of a revision of Practice Note 20, *'The Audit of Insurers in the United Kingdom'*. The consultation period ended in September 2006.

The first consultation draft was issued in December 2005. The consensus view of commentators was that substantial redrafting of the proposed revision was needed. The main concerns that the APB sought to address in the second consultation draft were:

- Requests for additional guidance on certain audit areas such as accounting estimates;

- Suggestions that the guidance included in the Practice Note should focus on matters specific to the audit of insurers and should not repeat 'generic' auditing guidance already contained in the ISAs (UK and Ireland);

- Suggestions that the Practice Note was too long and could usefully be shortened by eliminating 'educational' material about the insurance sector;

- Comments that a number of lists within the Practice Note (e.g. of audit risks) mixed life assurance and general insurance and, as a consequence, would not be applicable to every audit; and

- Concerns that the revision included too much material specific to the Lloyd's market, particularly now that syndicates have moved to an annual accounting basis.

Following consideration of comments received during the consultation period, a 'near-final' version of Practice Note 20 (Revised) was issued in electronic form on the APB's website in December 2006.

Practice Note 21 – Investment Businesses

In March the APB published a consultation draft of a revision of Practice Note 21, *'The Audit of Investment Businesses in the United Kingdom'*. The consultation period ended in June 2006.

The proposed revised Practice Note provides updated guidance for auditors following the introduction of ISAs (UK and Ireland) and incorporates the supplementary guidance in Bulletins 2001/7, *'Supplementary Guidance for Auditors of Investment Businesses following "N2"'*, and 2005/2, *'Audit Risk and Fraud – Supplementary Guidance for Auditors of Investment Businesses'*. It also takes account of other regulatory developments since the current Practice Note was issued in 2000.

During 2006 a number of legislative and regulatory changes have been made which impact the need for a statutory audit for some smaller investment businesses and the nature of audit work undertaken for regulatory purposes for some smaller investment businesses. Requirements in relation to statutory audits are contained in The Companies Act 1985 Regulations 2006 (SI 2006 No. 2782). The APB will extend its revision of Practice Note 21 to reflect these developments but, as a result, the Practice Note will not be finalised until later in 2007.

Practice Note 24 – Friendly Societies

In February the APB published a consultation draft of a revision of Practice Note 24, *'The Audit of Friendly Societies in the United Kingdom'*. The consultation period ended in May 2006.

The proposed revised Practice Note provides updated guidance for auditors following the introduction of ISAs (UK and Ireland) and incorporates the supplementary guidance in Bulletin 2004/6 that was issued at the end of 2004. Bulletin 2004/6 responded to the publication by the FSA of new rules that extended the scope of the auditor's work on the regulatory returns of directive friendly societies carrying on long-term insurance business. The proposed revised Practice Note also takes account of the FSA requirements that became effective on 31 December 2005 for auditors to engage Reviewing Actuaries in respect of the FSC 1 regulatory returns of Non-Directive Incorporated Societies.

Following consideration of comments received during the consultation period, a 'near-final' version of Practice Note 24 (Revised) was issued in electronic form on the APB's website in December 2006.

Consultation Paper on Practice Note 13 and Smaller Entity Audit Documentation

In January 2007 the APB issued a consultation paper which seeks views on whether Practice Note 13, *'The audit of small businesses'*, should be updated. The consultation paper also provides draft guidance that is intended to help auditors to understand what audit documentation is required by ISAs (UK and Ireland). It sets out how these requirements are influenced by the special considerations of a smaller entity audit and provides illustrative examples of audit documentation that are relevant to the requirements of the audit risk and fraud standards. The consultation paper asks whether it would be appropriate for the APB to issue such illustrative guidance.

Bulletins

Bulletin 2006/1 – Example Auditor's Reports in the Republic of Ireland

In January the APB published Bulletin 2006/1, *'Auditor's Reports on Financial Statements in the Republic of Ireland'*.

The example auditor's reports:

- Reflect changes to the reporting and accounting provisions of the Companies Act 1963 to 2005;

- Illustrate how to describe the financial reporting framework when an entity prepares its financial statements in accordance with International Financial Reporting Standards (IFRSs) as adopted by the EU;

- Take account of the introduction of ISAs (UK and Ireland);

- Illustrate the inclusion in auditor's reports of 'emphasis of matter paragraphs' rather than 'fundamental uncertainty' paragraphs; and

- Reflect changes to corporate governance reporting requirements following the publication of the 2003 Combined Code.

The Bulletin provides examples of the form and content of auditor's reports under ISA (UK and Ireland) 700, *'The Auditor's Report on Financial Statements'*, and company law in the Republic of Ireland.

Bulletin 2006/2 – Illustrative Auditor's Reports for the United Kingdom Public Sector

In January the APB published Bulletin 2006/2, *'Illustrative Auditor's Reports on Public Sector Financial Statements in the United Kingdom'*. The Bulletin provides examples of the form and content of auditor's reports under ISA (UK and Ireland) 700, *'The Auditor's Report on Financial Statements'*, and other regulatory requirements relevant to public sector bodies in the United Kingdom. It supports the guidance given in Practice Note 10 (Revised), *'Audit of Financial Statements of Public Sector Bodies in the United Kingdom'*, which was also published in January (see above).

Bulletin 2006/3 – Auditor's Reports on Abbreviated Accounts

In April the APB published Bulletin 2006/3, *'The Special Auditor's Report on Abbreviated Accounts in the United Kingdom'*.

Many small and medium sized companies avail themselves of their entitlement to submit abbreviated accounts to the Registrar of Companies. The auditors of such companies are required to make a 'special report' that the company is entitled to deliver abbreviated accounts and that the abbreviated accounts have been properly prepared.

This Bulletin supersedes Bulletin 1997/1 and updates the APB guidance:

- For changes in legislation, in particular, the Companies Act 1985 (International Accounting Standards and Other Accounting Amendments) Regulations 2004;

- For changes in terminology pursuant to the replacement of SAS 600 by ISA (UK and Ireland) 700 *'The Auditor's Report on Financial Statements'*; and

- To extend the guidance to cover Northern Ireland.

Bulletin 2006/4 – Standards for Investment Reporting in Ireland

As described on page 753 of Section 5, in April the APB published Bulletin 2006/4, *'Regulatory and Legislative Background to the Application of Standards for Investment Reporting in the Republic of Ireland'*, which provides some of the background to the legislative and regulatory environment in Ireland and provides a mapping of legislative and technical references within the SIRs, as published, to the Irish equivalent.

Bulletin 2006/5 – Combined Code

In September the APB published Bulletin 2006/5, *'The Combined Code on Corporate Governance: Requirements of Auditors under the Listing Rules of the Financial Services Authority and the Irish Stock Exchange'*.

The Bulletin provides updated guidance for auditors when reviewing a company's statement made in relation to the 'Combined Code on Corporate Governance' issued by the Financial Reporting Council and takes account of:

- The issuance of 'Internal Control: Revised Guidance for Directors on the Combined Code' (Turnbull Guidance) in October 2005; and

- The issuance of revised Listing Rules in 2005.

The Turnbull Review Group made only a small number of changes to the Turnbull Guidance as originally issued. One of these changes is that the board's statement on internal control should confirm that necessary actions have been, or are being, taken to remedy any significant failings or weaknesses in internal control. The effect of this development for the auditor's review required by the Listing Rules is discussed in the Bulletin.

Bulletin 2006/6 – Example Auditor's Reports in the United Kingdom

In September the APB published Bulletin 2006/6, *'Auditor's Reports on Financial Statements in the United Kingdom'*, which replaces Bulletin 2005/4.

The Bulletin provides illustrative examples of both unmodified and modified auditor's reports of financial statements of companies incorporated in the United Kingdom for periods commencing on or after 1 April 2005.

The example auditor's reports take account of:

- Changes made to the Companies Act 1985 and the Companies (Northern Ireland) Order 1986 to require the auditor to give a positive opinion as to the consistency of the directors' report with the financial statements; and

- The revised standard formulation for expressing compliance with IFRSs as adopted by the European Union.

In response to feedback received, the revised Bulletin also provides examples of unmodified reports of publicly traded companies that are not required to prepare group accounts.

BULLETIN 2002/2

THE UNITED KINGDOM DIRECTORS' REMUNERATION REPORT REGULATIONS 2002

CONTENTS

Introduction

1. With effect from 1 August 2002 the United Kingdom Government brought into force 'The Directors' Remuneration Report Regulations 2002'[1] (the Regulations) which will be effective for financial years ending on or after 31 December 2002[2]. These Regulations require 'quoted companies' to prepare a Directors' Remuneration Report, for each financial year, that contains specified information, some of which is required to be audited.

The Directors' Remuneration Report

2. The directors of a 'quoted company' are required to produce for each financial year a Directors' Remuneration Report which is required to be approved by the board of directors and signed on behalf of the directors by a director or the secretary of the company. The required content of the Directors' Remuneration Report is set out in Schedule 7A to the Companies Act 1985 (the Act).

3. A 'quoted company' is defined as a company incorporated under the Act:

    *   whose equity share capital has been included in the official list; or which

    *   is officially listed in an EEA[3] State; or which

    *   is admitted to dealing on either the New York Stock Exchange or the exchange known as Nasdaq.

    The definition does not include companies that have been admitted to trading on the Alternative Investment Market (AIM).

Requirements of Schedule 6 to the Companies Act 1985

4. Schedule 6 to the Act requires a company to produce certain information concerning directors' remuneration by way of notes to the company's financial statements. The Regulations exempt a quoted company from disclosing the information specified in paragraphs 2 to 14 in Part I of Schedule 6. A quoted company is, however, required to disclose the information specified in paragraph 1 in Part I of Schedule 6 in the notes to the company's financial statements.

---

[1] These Regulations are set out in Statutory Instrument 2002 No. 1986 which can be downloaded from http://www.legislation.hmso.gov.uk/si/si2002/20021986.htm

[2] SI 2002/1986 applies to companies incorporated in Great Britain. Northern Ireland is responsible for its own companies legislation and it is expected that in due course the Companies (Northern Ireland) Order 1986 will be amended to introduce the same requirements as those set out in the Regulations

[3] EEA is the European Economic Area

5. Part I of Schedule 6 will continue to apply in its entirety to companies which are not quoted and Parts II and III of that Schedule will apply to both quoted and unquoted companies.

6. The table set out below shows which of the requirements of Schedules 6 and 7A apply to quoted and unquoted companies respectively and the requirements with respect to audit.

Requirement	Quoted companies	Unquoted companies	Required to be audited
Schedule 6 to the Companies Act 1985 Disclosure of Information: Emoluments and other Benefits of Directors and others (These disclosures are required to be made in the notes to the financial statements)			
Part I, paragraph 1	✓	✓	✓
Part I, paragraphs 2-14		✓	✓
Part II	✓	✓	✓
Part III	✓	✓	✓
Schedule 7A to the Companies Act 1985 Directors' Remuneration Report (These disclosures are required to be made in the Directors' Remuneration Report)			
Part 2 (relating to information about remuneration committees, performance related remuneration and liabilities in respect of directors' contracts)	✓		
Part 3 (relating to detailed information about directors' remuneration)	✓		✓

Requirements of auditors

7. In addition to reporting on the financial statements, the company's auditors are required, through an amendment to Section 235 of the Act, to report to the company's members as to whether the 'auditable part' of the Directors' Remuneration Report has been properly prepared in accordance with the Companies Act 1985. The 'auditable part' of the Directors' Remuneration Report is the part which contains the information required by Part 3 of Schedule 7A.

8. The auditors are also required to carry out such investigations as will enable them to form an opinion as to whether the auditable part of the Directors' Remuneration Report is in agreement with the accounting records and returns.

9. To the extent that the requirements of Schedule 6 or Part 3 of Schedule 7A are not complied with, the auditors are required to include in their report, so far as they are reasonably able to do so, a statement giving the required particulars.

Reporting on the Directors' Remuneration Report

10. The auditors have to report on the Directors' Remuneration Report within their report on the financial statements. To communicate the opinion required of the auditors in the most effective way the APB recommends that the opinion paragraph of the auditors' report for quoted companies be drafted along the following lines:

In our opinion:

- the financial statements give a true and fair view of the state of the [group's and the] company's affairs as at ... and of [the group's] [its] profit [loss] for the year then ended; and

- the financial statements and the part of the Directors' Remuneration Report to be audited have been properly prepared in accordance with the Companies Act 1985.

---

11. An illustration of an auditors' report for a quoted company incorporated in Great Britain is set out in Appendix 1. In Appendix 1 the changes that need to be made to the example auditors' report illustrated in Appendix 1 to Bulletin 2001/2 are shown as marked up text.

12. As the auditors are not required to audit all of the information contained in the Directors' Remuneration Report they will need, in their report, to describe accurately which elements of the Directors' Remuneration Report they have audited.

13. Companies, therefore, need to make the disclosures that are required to be audited in such a way that it is clear which elements have been audited. One way of doing this would be for the audited disclosures to be set out in a discrete section under a suitable heading such as 'audited information'.

14. It would be unsatisfactory for auditors, in their report, to describe what they have audited in an uninformative manner such as 'the disclosures required by Part 3 of Schedule 7A to the Companies Act' as this would require readers of the auditors' report to have a detailed knowledge of the requirements.

15. The auditors assess whether the scope of their audit will be capable of being clearly described. If this cannot be achieved to their satisfaction by cross-reference, they set out the particulars that have been audited within the auditors' report.

16. The auditors make arrangements with the directors, well in advance of the year end, to ensure that the audited disclosures will be clearly distinguished from those that have not been audited. Illustrative terms of engagement are set out in Appendix 2 to this Bulletin.

Difference between the disclosures required by Schedule 6 and Schedule 7A

17. As described above, the Regulations will continue to apply paragraph 1 of Schedule 6 to the Act to quoted companies. The consequence of this will be that the financial statements of quoted companies will disclose aggregate directors' emoluments that may differ from the aggregate directors' remuneration disclosed in the Directors' Remuneration Report. This arises because the Act's definition of 'emoluments' differs from its definition of 'remuneration'.

18. Both of these disclosures will be reported on by the auditors. Where both disclosures have been prepared in accordance with the relevant requirements of the Act any difference between the disclosures is not an 'inconsistency'[4] between the financial statements and the information in the Directors' Remuneration Report. Where the difference between the disclosures of directors' emoluments and remuneration are material the auditors encourage the directors to provide an explanation of the difference.

Disclosure requirements in the Listing Rules

19. Following the introduction of the Regulations the APB understands that the United Kingdom Listing Authority (the UKLA) is aware that a certain level of duplication exists between the requirements of the Regulations and the requirements of Listing Rule 12.43A (c) relating to directors' remuneration. The UKLA is currently considering the most appropriate way of addressing this issue.

20. In the meantime additional care will need to be taken when auditing the disclosure of directors' remuneration. This is because not all of the requirements of Listing Rule 12.43A (c) are duplicated in the Regulations.

The auditors' responsibilities with respect to the unaudited part of the Directors' Remuneration Report

21. Although the Regulations do not require the Directors' Remuneration Report to be included in the Annual Report it is likely that many quoted companies will continue their practice of including directors' remuneration disclosures in the Annual Report. As the information given in Part 2 of the Directors' Remuneration Report is neither

---

4   SAS 160 'Other information in documents containing audited financial statements (Revised) at SAS 160.1 requires: **Auditors should read the other information. If as a result they ...identify any material inconsistency with the audited financial statements, they should seek to resolve them'.**

required to be audited nor reviewed by the auditors it constitutes 'other information'. Statement of Auditing Standards 160 'Other information in documents containing audited financial statements' requires auditors to read such 'other information' and if they become aware of any apparent misstatements or identify material inconsistencies with the financial statements to seek to resolve them.

Issuing the Directors' Remuneration Report as a separate document

22. If a quoted company issues its Directors' Remuneration Report as a separate document the scope of the auditors' report included in the Annual Report will, nevertheless, be required to encompass the auditable part of the Directors' Remuneration Report. For this reason, the requirements of SAS 160 apply to the content of a separate Directors' Remuneration Report, notwithstanding the fact that the Report is not included in a document containing audited financial statements.

23. When the Directors' Remuneration Report is issued as a separate document, although not required by the Act, the auditors:

   • when their report is unqualified, encourage the directors to indicate within the Directors' Remuneration Report where the auditors' report, prepared in accordance with Section 235 of the Act, may be found; or

   • when their report expresses either a qualified or adverse opinion or disclaims an opinion, which is relevant to the Directors' Remuneration Report, require the directors to reproduce the relevant parts of the auditors' report as part of the Directors' Remuneration Report. In the event that the directors do not agree to do so, the auditors consider whether to resign.

The auditors' statement on the Summary Financial Statement

24. Following the introduction of the Regulations the Government has amended the Companies (Summary Financial Statement) Regulations 1995[5] to expand the disclosure required in a Summary Financial Statement in relation to directors' remuneration.

25. Certain of the companies which are permitted under section 251 of the Act to produce a Summary Financial Statement will fall within the category of companies required to produce a Directors' Remuneration Report (ie quoted companies). Such companies that prepare summarised financial statements will be required to include either the whole, or a summary, of certain information concerning directors' remuneration contained in the notes to the financial statements and in the Directors' Remuneration Report.

---

[5] These amendments are set out in Statutory Instrument 2002 No. 1780 which can be downloaded from http/www.legislation.hmso.gov.uk/si/si2002/20021780.htm

26. The relevant information is the aggregate amount of directors' emoluments (from the notes to the company's financial statements)[6], a statement of the company's policy on directors' remuneration for the next following financial year and the performance graph (the last two items are required by the Regulations but are not required to be audited).

27. These requirements apply to companies and groups, whether or not they are banking or insurance companies and groups.

28. A revised illustrative example of the 'Auditors' Statement on the Summary Financial Statement' reflecting the requirements of the amended Companies (Summary Financial Statement) Regulations is set out as Appendix 3 to this Bulletin. In Appendix 3 the changes that need to be made to the example Statement on the summary financial statement illustrated in Appendix 5 to Bulletin 2001/2 are shown as marked up text.

Superseded guidance

29. With the publication of this Bulletin the following guidance issued by the APB is withdrawn:

- Bulletin 1999/5 - Appendix 3

- Bulletin 2001/2 - Appendices 1 and 5

---

[6] This is a summary of all the information required by paragraph 1(1) of Part I to Schedule 6 to the Act

Appendix 1

Withdrawn by Bulletin 2005/4. For examples see Bulletin 2006/6.

Appendix 2

ILLUSTRATIVE TERMS OF ENGAGEMENT FOR A QUOTED COMPANY

Audit of directors' remuneration disclosures

The disclosures that quoted companies are required to make with respect to directors' remuneration are specified in:

- paragraph 1 in Part I of Schedule 6 to the Companies Act 1985; and

- Schedule 7A to the Companies Act 1985.

The disclosures specified by paragraph 1 of Part 1 of Schedule 6 are required to be given in notes to the annual accounts whereas the disclosures specified by Schedule 7A are required to be given in the Directors' Remuneration Report[7].

With respect to the disclosures specified by Schedule 7A we are only required to report on that part of the Directors' Remuneration Report which contains the information required by Part 3 of that Schedule. You have agreed that the disclosures in the Directors' Remuneration Report that are required to be audited will be clearly and unambiguously identified as such. If the disclosures are not capable of being clearly described to our satisfaction we will need to set out all the particulars that we have audited within the auditors' report.

The Companies Act requires that we include in our report any required particulars omitted by the directors if we are reasonably able to do so.

---

[7] Unquoted companies are required to make the disclosures specified by the whole of Part 1 of Schedule 6 of the Companies Act 1985 in the notes to the annual accounts. Schedule 7A does not apply to unquoted companies.

Appendix 3

Withdrawn by Bulletin 2005/4. For example see Bulletin 2007/1.

BULLETIN 2004/1

THE AUDITORS' ASSOCIATION WITH PRELIMINARY ANNOUNCEMENTS

CONTENTS

Introduction

1. Bulletin 1998/7, "The Auditors' Association with Preliminary Announcements" was issued in July 1998. It provided guidance to auditors to assist them in discharging their responsibilities with regard to 'Preliminary Statements' of annual results by listed companies under Listing Rule 12.40.

2. This Bulletin provides updated guidance for auditors on their responsibilities with regard to preliminary announcements of annual results. The updated Bulletin:

    (a) reflects changes to the Listing Rules; and

    (b) emphasises the need for auditors to consider the way in which non-statutory information is presented in preliminary announcements before agreeing to their release.

    With immediate effect this Bulletin supersedes Bulletin 1998/7 which is withdrawn.

3. In this Bulletin the term "Preliminary Announcement" encompasses:

    (a) disclosures required by the Listing Rules[1]; and

    (b) such additional information (highlights, Chairman's Statement, narrative disclosures, management commentary, press release etc) that is released to a Regulatory Information Service[2] as part of a preliminary announcement.

    Any presentation to analysts or trading statement is not included within the definition of preliminary announcement.

4. Preliminary announcements play a key part in the annual financial reporting cycle, being the first public communication of companies' full year results and year-end financial position. Preliminary announcements are relied on to provide timely, sufficient and accurate information to ensure an orderly and efficient market. Preliminary announcements form one of the focal points for investor interest, primarily because they confirm or update market expectations. Because of this the auditors of listed companies have a legitimate and important role to play in the process leading to the orderly release of preliminary announcements.

5. Both the content and the preparation of the preliminary announcement are the responsibility of the company's directors. The directors of a listed company are

---

[1] The Listing Rules require a preliminary statement of annual results which must include any significant additional information necessary for the purpose of assessing the results being announced (Rule 12.40 (a)). The minimum financial information required is set out in Listing Rule 12.52.

[2] Regulatory Information Service is the term for any organisation through which the Listing Rules require listed companies to disseminate price sensitive information. In the Republic of Ireland all price sensitive information must be sent to the Company Announcements Office of the Irish Stock Exchange.

required by the Listing Rules to have agreed the preliminary statement with the auditors before it is notified to a Regulatory Information Service.

6. The Listing Rules do not indicate what form the agreement with the auditors should take or the extent of work expected of the auditors before they give their agreement. This Bulletin provides guidance on the procedures that would normally be carried out by the auditors and on communicating the outcome of such procedures to the directors.

7. Many companies provide more information in their preliminary announcement than that required by the Listing Rules with respect to the preliminary statement. In the opinion of the APB it is neither practical nor desirable for auditors to agree to anything less than the entire content of the preliminary announcement notwithstanding that the Listing Rules may not require such agreement.

8. There is an expectation that the information in a preliminary announcement will be consistent with that in the audited financial statements. The risk of later changes to the figures in the preliminary announcement is not completely extinguished unless the preliminary announcement is issued at the same time that the full financial statements are approved by the directors and the auditors have signed their opinion on them. This is the practice of many companies.

9. It has also been the accepted practice of some companies and their auditors to issue the preliminary announcement, with the auditors' agreement, when the audit is at an advanced stage but before the audit report on the financial statements has been signed.

10. Although the APB would not wish to prevent auditors from agreeing to the release of preliminary announcements before the audit report has been signed there is, in such circumstances, an unavoidable risk that the company may wish to revise its preliminary announcement in the light of audit findings or other developments arising between the preliminary announcement being notified to a Regulatory Information Service and the completion of the audit.

11. This Bulletin provides guidance to auditors on interpreting the expression 'advanced stage'.

12. There is no requirement for a preliminary announcement to include an auditors' report. In the view of the APB this is appropriate, as it is unlikely that a communication, that contains both a clear expression of opinion and sets out the information necessary for a proper understanding of that opinion, can be developed without producing a report of excessive length and complexity; which would be out of place in the context of the preliminary announcement as a whole. However, to avoid possible misunderstanding and to make explicit their agreement to the preliminary announcement the auditors issue a letter to the company signifying their agreement (see Appendix 1).

Listing Rule requirements

13. Under Listing Rule 12.40 a company must notify a Regulatory Information Service without delay after Board approval of its preliminary statement of annual results and in any event, within 120 days of the end of the period to which the statement relates (in exceptional circumstances the Listing Authority[3] may grant an extension of this time limit). The preliminary statement must:

   (a) have been agreed with the company's auditors;

   (b) show the figures in the form of a table, consistent with the presentation to be adopted in the annual accounts for that financial year, including at least the items required for a half-yearly report (see Listing Rules 12.52 and 12.59);

   (c) if the auditors' report is likely to be qualified, give details of the nature of the qualification; and

   (d) include any significant additional information necessary for the purpose of assessing the results being announced.

14. Listing Rule 12.40(a)(ii), through a cross reference to Listing Rule 12.52, requires that at least the following figures presented in the form of a table, consistent with the presentation to be adopted in the annual accounts for that financial year, must be included in a preliminary statement:

   (a) a profit and loss account comprising the following:

   (i) net turnover;

   (ii) operating profit or loss;

   (iii) interest payable less interest receivable (net);

   (iv) profit or loss before taxation and extraordinary items;

   (v) taxation on profits on ordinary activities (United Kingdom [Irish] taxation and, if material, overseas and share of associated undertakings' taxation to be shown separately);

   (vi) profit or loss on ordinary activities after tax;

   (vii) minority interests;

---

[3] In the UK the term "Listing Authority" refers to the United Kingdom Listing Authority of the Financial Services Authority ("FSA") acting in its capacity as the competent authority for the purposes of Part VI of the Financial Services and Markets Act 2000. In the Republic of Ireland, the Irish Stock Exchange is the competent authority for the purposes of the EU Directives referred to in the European Communities (Stock Exchange) Regulations 1984 (S.I. No.282).

(viii) profit or loss attributable to shareholders, before extraordinary items;

(ix) extraordinary items (net of taxation);

(x) profit or loss attributable to shareholders;

(xi) rates of dividend(s) paid and proposed and amount absorbed thereby; and

(xii) earnings per share expressed as pence per share;

(b) a balance sheet;

(c) a cash flow statement; and

(d) comparative figures in respect of (a) to (c) above for the corresponding period in the preceding financial year.

15. In accordance with Listing Rule 12.40(a)(ii), through a cross reference to Listing Rule 12.59, the Listing Authority may authorise the omission from the preliminary statement of annual results of any information in addition to the items of information referred to in Listing Rule 12.58, either on the grounds referred to in Listing Rule 12.58 or if it considers such omission otherwise necessary or appropriate.

Companies Act requirements

16. In the United Kingdom, preliminary announcements[4] constitute non-statutory accounts under section 240 of the Companies Act 1985[5] and, therefore, must include a statement indicating:

(a) that they are not the statutory accounts;

---

[4] In the Republic of Ireland, a preliminary announcement made by a single entity constitutes abbreviated accounts under section 19 of the Companies (Amendment) Act, 1986. A preliminary announcement made by a group constitutes abbreviated group accounts under regulation 40 of the European Communities (Companies: Group Accounts) Regulations, 1992. This states that where a parent undertaking publishes abbreviated group accounts relating to any financial year, it shall also publish a statement indicating:
(a) that the abbreviated group accounts are not the group accounts, copies of which are required by law to be annexed to the annual return,
(b) whether the copies of the group accounts so required to be annexed have in fact been so annexed,
(c) whether the auditors have made a report under section 193 of the Companies Act, 1990 in respect of the group accounts which relate to any financial year with which the abbreviated group accounts purport to deal, and
(d) whether the report of the auditors contained any qualifications.
The statement required for a single entity is similar.
[5] The equivalent legislation in Northern Ireland is Article 243(3) of the Companies (Northern Ireland) Order, 1986.

(b) whether statutory accounts for any relevant financial year have been delivered to the registrar of companies;

(c) whether the auditors have reported on the statutory accounts for any such year; and

(d) if so, whether it was qualified or contained a statement under section 237(2) or (3).

The ASB's Statement on Preliminary Announcements

17. The ASB's Statement issued in July 1998 contains recommendations as to the contents of preliminary announcements issued by listed companies. The ASB's Statement is intended to have persuasive rather than mandatory force and is not an accounting standard.

18. The ASB's recommended contents for a preliminary announcement are similar to their recommendations regarding interim statements. The ASB also encourages the publication of a commentary on and, to the extent necessary to support the commentary, a separate presentation of the final interim period (ie the second half or, if quarterly reporting is adopted, the fourth quarter of the year) figures.

19. The ASB's Statement states that it would be helpful if the preliminary announcement clearly stated that the auditors' report on the full financial statements has yet to be signed, if that is the case.

Terms of engagement

20. It is in the interests of both the auditors and the company that the auditors' role in respect of the preliminary announcement is set out in writing; typically by including relevant paragraphs in the audit engagement letter. To avoid misunderstandings the engagement letter describes the auditors' understanding of the process of 'agreeing' the preliminary announcement.

21. In circumstances where the auditors are to agree to a preliminary announcement based on financial statements on which their audit is not complete the engagement letter includes cautionary language to the effect that there is an unavoidable risk that the company may wish to revise its preliminary announcement in the light of audit findings or other developments occurring before the completion of the audit. (See Appendix 3).

22. Matters that may be dealt with in the engagement letter include:

(a) the responsibility of the directors to prepare the preliminary announcement;

(b) the fact that the auditors will conduct their work in accordance with this Bulletin;

(c) a statement as to whether the auditors believe it is management's intention that the preliminary announcement will be based on audited financial statements or on draft financial statements upon which the auditors have not issued a report;

(d) a statement that the auditors will issue a letter confirming their agreement to the preliminary announcement; and

(e) a statement explaining the inherent limitations of the auditors' work.

23. Examples of suitable paragraphs for inclusion in a letter of engagement are given in Appendix 2 for circumstances where the preliminary announcement is to be based on audited financial statements and in Appendix 3 for circumstances where the preliminary announcement is to be based on draft financial statements.

Procedures

Planning

24. Where the preliminary announcement is to be based on draft financial statements the company's timetable should allow the auditors to have completed the audit other than for those matters set out in paragraph 28 below.

Preliminary announcements based on audited financial statements

25. Arising from the requirements of the Listing Rules, there is an expectation on the part of users that the information in a preliminary announcement will be consistent with that in the audited financial statements. The only way of achieving absolute certainty of this is for the audit of the financial statements to have been completed and the contents of the preliminary announcement to have been extracted from audited financial statements that had been approved and signed by the directors and upon which the auditors have signed their report.

Preliminary announcements based on draft financial statements

26. Companies may wish to issue their preliminary announcement before the audit is complete. There are additional risks for directors in these circumstances if further information comes to light as a result of the auditors' procedures that the directors decide should be reflected in the financial statements and gives rise to the need for a revised announcement by the company. Before agreeing to the release of the preliminary announcement, therefore, the directors will need to ensure they are satisfied that the information it contains will be consistent with the information that will be contained in the audited financial statements.

27. The auditors will need to be satisfied that any matters outstanding with respect to their audit will be unlikely to result in changes to the information contained in the preliminary announcement. This means that the audit of the financial statements must be at an advanced stage and that, subject only to unforeseen events, the auditors expect to be in a position to issue their report on the financial statements incorporating the amounts upon which the preliminary announcement is based, and know what that report will say.

28. This means completing the audit, including a review by an independent partner as described in paragraphs 58 to 66 of SAS 240 Revised, 'Quality control for audit work', subject only to the following:

   (a) clearing outstanding audit matters which the auditors are satisfied are unlikely to have a material impact on the financial statements or disclosures in the preliminary announcement;

   (b) completing audit procedures on the detail of note disclosures to the financial statements that will not have a material impact on the primary financial statements and completing their reading of the other information in the annual report in accordance with SAS 160 'Other information in documents containing audited financial statements';

   (c) updating the subsequent events review to cover the period between the issue of the preliminary announcement and the date of the auditors' report on the financial statements; and

   (d) obtaining written representations, where relevant, from management and establishing that the financial statements have been reviewed and approved by the directors.

All preliminary announcements

29. The following procedures will normally be carried out by the auditors in relation to the preliminary announcement itself regardless of whether it is based on draft financial statements or extracted from audited financial statements:

   (a) checking that the figures in the preliminary announcement covering the full year have been accurately extracted from the audited or draft financial statements; and reflect the presentation to be adopted in the audited financial statements. For example, any summarisation should not change the order in which items are presented where this is specified by law or accounting standards;

   (b) considering whether the information (including the management commentary) is consistent with other expected contents of the annual report of which the auditors are aware; and

   (c) considering whether the financial information in the preliminary announcement is misstated. A misstatement exists when the information is stated incorrectly or presented in a misleading manner. A misstatement may arise, for example, as a result of an omission of a significant change of accounting policy disclosed or due to be disclosed in the audited financial statements.

30. Auditors consider whether the preliminary announcement includes a statement by directors as required by section 240 of the Companies Act 1985[6] and whether the preliminary announcement includes the minimum information required by Listing Rule 12.52, subject to any omissions authorised by the Listing Authority under Listing Rule

---

[6] See footnotes 4 and 5 for the equivalent legislation in Northern Ireland and the Republic of Ireland.

12.59, and any significant additional information necessary for the purpose of assessing the results under Listing Rule 12.40(a)(iv).

Non-statutory figures and management commentary

31. The FSA and APB recognise that in some circumstances the presentation of non-statutory financial information[7] and associated narrative explanations with the statutory results may help shareholders understand better the financial performance of a company. However, the FSA and APB are concerned that in other instances such non-statutory information has the potential to be misleading[8] and shareholders may sometimes be misinformed by the manner in which non-statutory information is included in preliminary announcements with which auditors are associated. In those circumstances the APB believes that the potential for non-statutory information to be misleading is considerable when inappropriate prominence is given to the non-statutory information, when there is no description of the non-statutory information and, where appropriate, the adjusted numbers are not reconciled to the statutory financial information[9].

32. In this context where the preliminary announcement includes non-statutory information, before agreeing to its release, auditors consider whether:

   (a) appropriate prominence is given to statutory financial information and related narrative explanations compared to the prominence given to non-statutory financial information and its related narrative explanations;

   (b) non-statutory financial information is reconciled, where appropriate, to the statutory financial information and sufficient prominence is given to that reconciliation;

   (c) non-statutory financial information is clearly and accurately described; and

   (d) the non-statutory information is not otherwise misleading in the form and context in which it appears.

---

[7] Non-statutory financial information includes the adjustment of statutory financial information to:
   - exclude certain items to give alternative earnings numbers eg earnings before interest, tax, depreciation and amortisation (EBITDA),
   - exclude certain business segments or activities, or
   - reflect significant non-adjusting post balance sheet events eg disposals or acquisitions.

[8] Listing Rule 9.3A requires that "A company must take all reasonable care to ensure that any statement or forecast or any other information it notifies to a Regulatory Information Service or makes available through the UK Listing Authority is not misleading, false or deceptive and does not omit anything likely to affect the import of such statement, forecast or other information."

[9] The UK Listing Authority's January 2003 newsletter 'List!' included the warning that "*Issuers need to consider whether publishing non-GAAP earnings without giving sufficient prominence to the GAAP numbers may give a misleading presentation of financial performance*". More recently in Consultation Paper 203, "Review of the Listing Regime" (paragraph 10.13) the UKLA expressed the view that "*We believe that where issuers do include non-statutory figures in announcements such figures must be presented in a balanced fashion. By 'balanced' we mean that issuers will be expected not to give undue prominence to the non-statutory figures and not to be selective when choosing which numbers are presented, so that the presentation of information should not be designed to give an overly favourable impression to the reader. A 'balanced' presentation should also mean that issuers provide investors with all necessary information to understand the context and the relevance of such figures, including reconciliations with the statutory number provided*".

If the auditors do not believe that the preliminary announcement satisfies these conditions, they seek to resolve the issues arising with the directors. If they are unable to resolve the issues the auditors consider whether to withhold their consent to the release of the announcement.

33. An important feature of preliminary announcements is a management commentary on the company's performance during the year and its position at the year-end. Such management commentary may include comments on the final interim period in the preliminary announcement and separate presentation of the final interim period figures to the extent this is necessary to support the management commentary. The extent of information on the final interim period will vary from company to company and in some cases this may only consist of a reference to the key figures in the management commentary.

34. Auditors read the management commentary, any other narrative disclosures and any final interim period figures and consider whether they are in conflict with the information that they have obtained in the course of their audit. If they become aware of any apparent inconsistencies with information obtained during their audit or with the draft financial statements, they seek to resolve them with the directors. If they are unable to resolve the matters the auditors will not agree to the publication of the preliminary announcement.

35. If they are available, auditors will also read the text, or draft thereof, of any Chairman's Statement, operating and financial review ("OFR") or similar document to be included in the annual report from which the management commentary in the preliminary announcement will usually be derived.

Directors' approval of the preliminary announcement

36. The ASB's Statement recommends that the preliminary announcement should state the date on which it was approved by the board of directors. Auditors do not agree to the preliminary announcement until its entire content has been formally approved by the board or by a duly authorised committee[10] of the board.

Qualification of the audit opinion

37. The Listing Rules require that, if the auditors' report (on the financial statements) is likely to be qualified, the preliminary statement should give details of the nature of the qualification. The APB considers that similar disclosure should be made when the preliminary statement is based on audited financial statements on which the auditors have qualified their opinion. In doing this, care should be taken to ensure compliance with section 240[11] of the Companies Act which states that an auditors' report on the statutory accounts (under section 235) may not be published with non-statutory accounts.

---

[10] The revised Combined Code published by the Financial Reporting Council in July 2003 states that for reporting years beginning on or after 1 November 2003 one of the main roles and responsibilities of the audit committee is "to monitor the integrity of the financial statements of the company, and any formal announcements relating to the company's financial performance, reviewing significant financial reporting judgements contained in them"(Combined Code provision C.3.2).

[11] See footnotes 4 and 5 for the equivalent legislation in Northern Ireland and the Republic of Ireland.

38. The Listing Rules do not refer to a situation where an auditors' report contains an explanatory paragraph dealing with a fundamental uncertainty. Where the auditors' report does, or will, contain an explanatory paragraph dealing with a fundamental uncertainty, the auditors do not agree to the preliminary announcement unless the directors have explained the fundamental uncertainty in the preliminary announcement. This is because the auditors must regard the fundamental uncertainty as a matter that is highly relevant to the reported financial position. There is, however, no need for the preliminary announcement to refer to the auditors in this context - it is for management to explain the relevant issues.

39. If the precise details of the matters giving rise to a qualified opinion or explanatory paragraph are critical to a full appreciation of the auditors' report, the APB strongly recommends that auditors should normally not agree to a preliminary announcement containing information about a qualification before the matter has been resolved. Where reference is made in a preliminary announcement to a qualified opinion or a fundamental uncertainty, the directors should give adequate prominence to that information in the announcement and the auditors should be satisfied in this regard. If the auditors have concerns about the appropriateness of the wording of a statement referring to a qualified opinion they are encouraged to seek legal advice.

Communication of agreement

40. The APB encourages the auditors to make explicit their agreement to the issue of the preliminary announcement by sending a letter to the directors. An example of such a letter is given in Appendix 1.

41. Similarly, if the auditors are not in agreement with the content of the preliminary announcement, they communicate this to the directors by sending them a letter setting out the reasons for their disagreement, advising the directors that the preliminary announcement should not be released to a Regulatory Information Service.

42. The auditors may become aware that a company has released its preliminary announcement without first obtaining their agreement. There may be a number of reasons for this ranging from innocent oversight on the part of the directors to the directors knowingly releasing a preliminary announcement with which the auditors disagree. The action that the auditors take depends on the particular circumstances. In circumstances where a preliminary announcement is inadvertently released without the auditors' knowledge, but with which the auditor do in fact agree, the auditors may wish to remind the directors of their obligation under the Listing Rules to obtain the auditors' agreement.

43. However, at the other end of the spectrum where the auditors become aware that the directors have released an announcement with which they disagree they take legal advice with a view to notifying the Listing Authority of the fact that they had not agreed to the announcement.

Appendix 1

EXAMPLE LETTER TO DIRECTORS INDICATING AUDITORS' AGREEMENT WITH PRELIMINARY ANNOUNCEMENT

Dear Sirs

In accordance with the terms of our engagement letter dated [ ], we have reviewed the attached proposed preliminary announcement of XYZ plc for the year ended [ ]. Our work was conducted having regard to Bulletin 2004/1 issued by the Auditing Practices Board. As directors you are responsible for preparing and issuing the preliminary announcement.

Our responsibility is solely to give our agreement to the preliminary announcement having carried out the procedures specified in the Bulletin as providing a basis for such agreement. In this regard we agree to the preliminary announcement being notified to [a Regulatory Information Service] [and/or the Company Announcements Office of the Irish Stock Exchange, as appropriate].

[As you are aware we are not in a position to sign our report on the annual financial statements as they have not yet been approved by the directors and we have not yet ... [insert significant procedures that are yet to be completed, for example completing the subsequent events review and obtaining final representations from directors ...]. Consequently there can be no absolute certainty that we will be in a position to issue an unmodified audit opinion on financial statements consistent with the results and financial position reported in the preliminary announcement. However, at the present time, we are not aware of any matters that may give rise to a modification to our report. In the event that such matters do come to our attention we will inform you immediately.]

Yours faithfully

Appendix 2

EXAMPLE TERMS OF ENGAGEMENT; AUDIT COMPLETED

Extract from Letter of Engagement

The Listing Rules state that 'a preliminary statement of the annual results .... must have been agreed with the company's auditors'. As directors of the company, you are responsible for preparing and issuing the preliminary statement of annual results and ensuring that we agree with its release.

We undertake to review the preliminary announcement having regard to Bulletin 2004/1 'The auditors' association with preliminary announcements' issued by the Auditing Practices Board. Accordingly, our review will be limited to checking the accuracy of extraction of the financial information in the preliminary announcement from the audited financial statements of the company for that year, considering whether any non-statutory financial information and associated narrative explanations may be misleading and reading the management commentary, including any comments on or separate presentation of the final interim period figures, and considering whether it is in conflict with the information that we obtained in the course of our audit.

You will provide us with such information and explanations as we consider necessary for the purposes of our work. We shall request sight of the preliminary announcement in sufficient time to enable us to complete our work. The Board/committee of the Board will formally approve the preliminary announcement before we agree to it.

EXAMPLE TERMS OF ENGAGEMENT, AUDIT NOT COMPLETED

Extract from Letter of Engagement

The Listing Rules state that ' a preliminary statement of the annual results ...... must have been agreed with the company's auditors'. As directors of the company, you are responsible for preparing and issuing the preliminary statement of annual results and ensuring that we agree with its release.

We undertake to review the preliminary announcement having regard to Bulletin 2004/1 'The auditors' association with preliminary announcements' issued by the Auditing Practices Board. Accordingly, our review will be limited to checking the accuracy of extraction of the financial information in the preliminary announcement from the latest available draft financial statements of the company for that year, considering whether any non-statutory financial information and associated narrative explanations may be misleading and reading the management commentary, including any comments on or separate presentation of the final interim period figures, and considering whether it is in conflict with the information that we have obtained in the course of our audit.

You will provide us with such information and explanations as we consider necessary for the purposes of our work. We shall request sight of the preliminary announcement in sufficient time to enable us to complete our work. The Board/committee of the Board will formally approve the preliminary announcement before we agree to it. You will also make available to us the proposed text of the company's annual report.

We will not agree to the release of the preliminary announcement until the audit is complete subject only to the following:

(a) clearing outstanding audit matters which we are satisfied are unlikely to have a material impact on the financial statements or disclosures in the preliminary announcement;

(b) completing audit procedures on the detail of note disclosures to the financial statements and completing our reading of the other information in the annual report;

(c) updating the subsequent events review to cover the period between the date of the preliminary announcement and the date of the auditors' report on the financial statements; and

(d) obtaining written representations, where relevant, from management and establishing that the financial statements have been reviewed and approved by the directors.

The scope of our work will be necessarily limited in that, we will only be able to check the consistency of the preliminary announcement with draft financial statements on which our audit is incomplete. Accordingly, we shall not, at that stage, know whether further adjustments may be required to those draft financial statements. Consequently, there is an unavoidable risk that the company may wish to revise its preliminary announcement in the light of audit findings or other developments occurring between the preliminary announcement being notified to [a Regulatory Information Service] [and/or the Company Announcements Office of the Irish Stock Exchange, as appropriate] and the completion of the audit.

In the event that we disagree with the release of the preliminary announcement we will send you a letter setting out the reasons why.

THE AUDITING PRACTICES BOARD

BULLETIN 2005/1

AUDIT RISK AND FRAUD
– SUPPLEMENTARY GUIDANCE FOR
AUDITORS OF CHARITIES

CONTENTS

Introduction

1.   In December 2004 a series of International Standards on Auditing (ISAs) (UK and Ireland) were issued by the Auditing Practices Board (APB) to replace Statements of Auditing Standards (SASs). The ISAs (UK and Ireland) are effective for audits of accounting periods commencing on or after 15 December 2004.

2.   Three of these ISAs (UK and Ireland), which concern the areas of audit risk and fraud, include a number of requirements that are additional to those set out in the SASs they replace. This Bulletin provides supplementary guidance for auditors of charities on these additional requirements, by replacing the sections of Practice Note (PN) 11 'The Audit of Charities in the United Kingdom (Revised)' which cover:

*   SAS 210: 'Knowledge of the business';

*   SAS 300: 'Accounting and internal control systems and audit risk assessments'; and

*   SAS 110: 'Fraud and error'.

3.   Whilst this Bulletin addresses those aspects of auditing standards that have changed most significantly due to the introduction of the ISAs (UK and Ireland), the APB appreciates that other aspects of PN 11 will also need to be updated, and plans to revise the whole Practice Note in due course.

ISAs (UK and Ireland) apply to the conduct of all audits in respect of accounting periods commencing on or after 15 December 2004. This includes audits of the financial statements of charities. The purpose of the following paragraphs is to identify the special considerations arising from the application of certain 'bold letter' requirements (which are indicated by grey-shaded boxes below) to the audit of charities, and to suggest ways in which these can be addressed. This Bulletin does not contain commentary on all of the bold letter requirements included in ISAs (UK and Ireland) 315, 330 and 240 and reading it should not be seen as an alternative to reading the relevant ISAs (UK and Ireland) in their entirety.

Audit Risk

Requirements of ISA (UK and Ireland) 315: Obtaining an Understanding of the Entity and its Environment and Assessing the Risks of Material Misstatement

Background note

The purpose of this ISA (UK and Ireland) is to establish standards and to provide guidance on obtaining an understanding of the entity and its environment, including its internal control, and on assessing the risks of material misstatement in a financial statement audit.

4. The principles of obtaining and using knowledge of the charity to be audited are the same as those applying to the audit of any entity. The auditor's responsibilities in this respect are not related to the level of fee charged for the audit : for example, the same knowledge and understanding of the client charity are required in respect of audits carried out on an honorary basis as for audits carried out for a commercial fee.

Understanding the Entity and Its Environment, Including Its Internal control

The auditor should obtain an understanding of relevant industry, regulatory, and other external factors including the applicable financial reporting framework (ISA (UK and Ireland) 315 para 22).

The regulatory framework

5. Provision for the oversight of charities in the United Kingdom is different in England and Wales, Scotland and Northern Ireland and the auditor needs to ascertain and understand the applicable law and regulations of the jurisdiction within which the charity operates. This involves keeping up to date with laws and regulations relating to charities generally, and to the client charity in particular.

6. A key element in understanding the entity is a knowledge and understanding of the charity's governing document. There are many different types of governing instrument or constitution which will determine the objects of the charity and the powers of its trustees, and the audit approach needs to be adapted accordingly. Particular issues include any limitations in objectives placed on the charity by its governing document, or terms and restrictions placed on material gifts or donations received.

7. The accounting requirements under which charities report depend on how they are constituted and the relevant national jurisdiction within the United Kingdom. The principal categories are as follows:

    *   non-company charities in England and Wales – the Charities Act 1993;

    *   non-company charities in Scotland – the Law Reform (Miscellaneous Provisions) (Scotland) Act 1990;

    *   charitable companies – the Companies Act 1985; and/or

    *   exempt charities – dependent on how they are constituted and on any specific statutes or regulations that apply to them.

8. The financial statements of a charity which are prepared to give a true and fair view are required to be prepared in accordance with applicable law and regulations, Financial Reporting Standards[1], and Statements of Standard Accounting Practice, irrespective

---

[1] Charities are required to follow the Charities SORP, which specifies adherence to UK Financial Reporting Standards. In addition, charitable companies are prohibited by SI 2004/2947 from adopting International Financial Reporting Standards.

of whether they are subject to audit, independent examination or reporting under section 249A of the Companies Act. The Statement of Recommended Practice 'Accounting and Reporting by Charities' (the Charities SORP) (including updates to the SORP)[2] issued by the Charity Commission in October 2000 and developed in accordance with the Accounting Standards Board's (ASB's) stated practice, supplements these general accounting principles and is intended to apply to all charities in the United Kingdom and the Republic of Ireland (unless a separate SORP exists for a particular class of charities) regardless of their size, constitution or complexity and indicates the current view of best practice in accounting for charities. In addition, FRS 18 – Accounting Policies – requires a statement that financial statements have been prepared in accordance with the relevant SORP, and details of any departures from the recommended practice and disclosures. Consequently, it is normally necessary to follow the guidance set out in the Charities SORP in order to give a true and fair view.

9. Trustees of small unincorporated charities in England and Wales which are within the income thresholds defined by legislation may elect to prepare financial statements on a receipts and payments basis. In Scotland, the trustees can elect to do this if there is no requirement in the trust deed for audited accounts. Financial statements prepared on this basis are not required to give a true and fair view. Separate guides on the preparation of financial statements on this basis are available from the Charity Commission and the Office of the Scottish Charity Regulator.

Non-departmental public bodies

10. A number of non-departmental public bodies are charities. The auditors of such bodies are responsible for expressing an opinion on both the view given by the body's financial statements[3] and on whether the expenditure of the body is in accordance with the purposes intended by Parliament. In addition, the Treasury requires sponsor departments of such bodies to include, in the terms of engagement for the auditors of a non-departmental public body appointed by the Secretary of State of the sponsor department, a responsibility to report to the department any significant matters arising out of their audit work, including losses incurred owing to failures of internal control, misconduct, fraud or other irregularity.

Practice Note 10 (Revised) 'Audit of financial statements of public sector entities in the United Kingdom' provides guidance for auditors of public bodies on the form of reports required and factors to be taken into account in the conduct of their work.

The auditor should obtain an understanding of the nature of the entity (ISA (UK and Ireland) 315 para 25).

---

[2] A revised version of the SORP is due to be issued shortly after the date of this Bulletin.
[3] These financial statements should comply with Treasury guidance (Executive Non-Departmental Public Bodies: Annual Reports and Accounts Guidance) to the extent that the guidance does not conflict with the charities SORP.

Special features of charities

11. Knowledge of the charity's activities and organisation is essential for ascertaining the risk of material misstatement arising from fraud, error, or non-compliance with applicable law and regulations. The auditor considers special features of charities (ie the nature and sources of income, restricted funds, trading and charitable status, taxation and operating structures and branches), in order to plan and carry out audit work effectively and efficiently, and to provide a yardstick against which to evaluate the evidence gained from audit procedures.

12. Sources of income often include grants, for example from public authorities or other charities. Such grants are often made for specific purposes and are subject to conditions, breach of which can have serious implications for the charity. Developments in the public sector mean that auditors of a public authority donor may have, or seek, the right of access to the charity's records to follow through and verify the use made of the grant. In addition grants from public bodies are increasingly subject to clawback provisions requiring repayment if a charity breaches specified conditions.

13. Where charities receive funding to undertake operational activities, the auditor ascertains whether such income is received under contract (which is generally unrestricted income) or by way of grant for provision of a specific service, (which normally gives rise to restricted income). As well as distinguishing whether the income is restricted or not, the nature of the terms and conditions may affect taxation considerations (eg the VAT treatment).

14. The trustees of smaller charities may not have formal documentation of their activities which can be used to chart the charities' progress through the year, although auditors may be able to encourage trustees to keep such records. The most useful source of information in these circumstances is likely to be discussion with the trustees.

Branches

15. The auditor needs a clear understanding of the legal structure of a charity. A charity may operate through branches to raise funds or carry out particular aspects of its charitable activities. The auditor needs to understand whether the structure adopted by a charity falls within the definition of a branch in the Charities SORP. The principles set out in the Charities SORP apply whether operations are carried out in the UK or overseas.

16. Branches which fall within the Charities SORP definition will be accounted for as part of the whole charity. Therefore the omission of branches where material will affect the audit opinion. The auditor also needs to be aware that some charities will use the term "branches" outside of its Charities SORP meaning to describe a network of charities which are administratively autonomous and as such are separate accounting entities. The constitutional provisions in such cases may require careful consideration.

17. Joint venture situations whereby two or more charities jointly control an entity or undertake joint arrangements in partnership to carry out an activity are sometimes

applicable. The auditor needs to understand the structure adopted in such arrangements and how they are differentiated from participating interests in associates. The Charities SORP provides guidance on this issue and the accounting methods to be adopted.

18. The auditor will also need to consider the terms on which branches raise funds. Local appeals may be for specific purposes, and where this is the case such funds will be restricted in the accounts of the main charity.

Overseas operations

19. The considerations noted above apply equally where activities are carried out overseas. The auditor takes into account the fact that significant aspects of a charity's business may be conducted in conditions or locations which impede access. In these circumstances auditors will need to ensure that they are able to assess the full extent of the activities, and have the necessary understanding of the regulatory environment in which significant activities are carried out – for example in relation to taxation and employment law. The auditor also needs to be aware of the Charity Commission's guidance on charities working internationally.

Connected entities

20. The structure and management of any connected entities should be considered, in particular the degree to which connected entities are managed and controlled by the trustees and management of the charity. Where the charity is not a company and/or where the connected entity is not a subsidiary, the auditor of the connected entity normally owes duties of confidentiality to that entity. In these cases the charity's auditor will ordinarily wish to put arrangements in place through the trustees of the charity and directors of the connected entity to allow the connected entity, and its auditor, to give the auditor of the charity such information and explanations as may reasonably be required for the purposes of the auditor's duties. The charity's auditor also considers discussing his particular responsibilities under the 1993 Act and the Regulations with the auditor of the connected entity, so that these are fully understood.

The auditor should obtain an understanding of the entity's selection and application of accounting policies and consider whether they are appropriate for its business and consistent with the applicable financial reporting framework and accounting policies used in the relevant industry (ISA (UK and Ireland) 315 para 28).

Incoming resources

21. The Charities SORP states that incoming resources should be recognised when prudent and practical. Recognition is dependent on legal entitlement, reasonable certainty of receipt and the monetary value being measurable with reasonable certainty. The use of autonomous branches, agents or loosely affiliated volunteer groups for fund-raising needs to be considered when determining the appropriate method of income recognition. The auditor of a charity needs to understand clearly the basis and terms on which such fund-raising services are provided to it.

Estimates

22. The Charities SORP provides detailed guidance on appropriate accounting policies and measurement bases. In applying these policies and bases the use of estimates and estimation techniques will often be necessary to determine the monetary value of assets and liabilities and to determine the allocation of costs within the statement of financial activities. The auditor seeks to ensure that techniques selected by trustees enable the financial statements to give a true and fair view. The auditor ensures that the financial statements disclose a description of those estimation techniques adopted, including underlying principles, that are significant in order to comply with FRS 18 'Accounting Policies' and the Charities SORP.

The auditor should obtain an understanding of the entity's objectives and strategies, and the related business risks that may result in material misstatement of the financial statements (ISA (UK and Ireland) 315 para 30).

23. The auditor considers the possibility of non-compliance by the charity with its governing document which may cause the financial statements not to give a true and fair view. Each charity is bound to comply with the terms of its governing document which may, for example, take the form of a trust deed, a will, a constitution or the Memorandum and Articles of Association of a company. The governing document sets out the objects of the charity and determines the powers of its trustees, and may also set out more detailed rules for conducting its work. Failure to comply with the governing document's terms may constitute a breach of trust and, in particular, in England and Wales may form grounds for intervention by the Charity Commission.

24. In order fully to understand the charity's business risks and strategies, the auditor also considers the ways in which the charity organises its affairs including, for example, the use of volunteer staff and branch offices, and the carrying out of overseas and/or trading activities.

The auditor should obtain an understanding of the measurement and review of the entity's financial performance (ISA (UK and Ireland) 315 para 35).

25. The auditor obtains an understanding of the performance indicators used by the differing levels of management, e.g. trustees, audit committee (if in existence), chief executive, finance director, department heads. The auditor also considers what steps have been taken by trustees and senior management in respect of cost allocations and setting a reserves policy.

The auditor should obtain an understanding of internal control relevant to the audit (ISA (UK and Ireland) 315 para 41).

26. The maintenance of an effective system of internal control is at least as important, if not more so, for charities as it is for other entities, since it is a fundamental duty of charity trustees to protect the property of their charity and to secure its application for the objects of the charity. Failure to do so can render the trustees personally liable for any loss occasioned to the charity. Guidance leaflets entitled 'Internal financial controls for

charities' and 'The hallmarks of an effective charity' have been published by the Charity Commission, and these provide a useful point of reference for auditors.

The regulatory framework

27. Certain charities, for example registered friendly societies[4], are subject to specific reporting requirements in respect of internal controls. Where there is such a requirement, auditors plan their work bearing in mind the need to report if a satisfactory system of control over transactions has not been maintained.

The operations of charities

28. There is a very wide variation between different charities in terms of size, activity and organisation, so that there can be no 'standard' approach to internal control systems and audit risk assessments. Charities undertake a variety of activities, through varying structures that may include both UK and overseas branches that will present widely different risks. Internal control systems will be developed in relation to the specific risks associated with income sources, the activities undertaken, and location and staffing arrangements.

Control environment

29. The role, attitude and actions of the trustees are fundamental in shaping the control environment of a charity. Factors to consider include:

- the amount of time committed by trustees to the charity's affairs;

- the skills and qualifications of individual trustees;

- the frequency and regularity of trustee meetings and the level of attendance at these meetings;

- the form and content of trustee meetings;

- the independence of trustees from each other;

- the division of duties between trustees;

- the supervision by the trustees of relatively informal working arrangements which are common when employing volunteers;

- the degree of involvement in, or supervision of, the charity's transactions on the part of individual trustees;

---

[4] The requirements, applicable to friendly societies, of the Industrial and Provident Societies Act regarding internal control are dealt with in Practice Note 14 (Revised) The audit of registered social landlords in the United Kingdom.

- The level of delegation by trustees to senior management and the formality of this delegation; and

- The committee structure of the organisation.

30. Other features of the control environment will depend on the size, activities, organisation and corporate governance structures of the charity but might include:

- a recognised plan of the charity's structure showing clearly the areas of responsibility and lines of authority and reporting. Where the charity does not have staff, and is administered entirely by the trustees, there can still be an agreed division of duties, provided there is adequate monitoring by the body of trustees as a whole;

- segregation of duties where charities have more than one member of staff (whether paid or not). In larger charities, such segregation could include involvement of staff from outside the finance department in certain transactions, for example in providing a first signatory for cheques;

- supervision by trustees of activities of staff where segregation of duties is not practical;

- competence, training and qualification of paid staff and any volunteers appropriate to the tasks they have to perform;

- involvement of the trustees in the recruitment, appointment and supervision of senior executives;

- access of trustees to independent professional advice where necessary;

- budgetary controls in the form of estimates of income and expenditure for each financial year and comparison of actual results with the estimates on a regular basis; and

- communication of results of such reviews to the trustees on a regular basis so as to facilitate their review of performance and enable them to initiate action where necessary.

The auditor should obtain an understanding of the entity's process for identifying business risks relevant to financial reporting objectives and deciding about actions to address those risks, and the results thereof (ISA (UK and Ireland) 315 para 76).

31. The Charities SORP requires charities with income in excess of £250,000 to include a statement in the annual trustees report confirming that the major risks to which the charity is exposed, as identified by the trustees, have been reviewed and systems have been established to mitigate those risks. As a result of this, charities will often maintain a risk register. Where this is the case, the auditor reviews this register. In smaller charities this may not be the case and so the auditor refers to paragraph 79 of ISA (UK and Ireland) 315.

The auditor should obtain an understanding of the information system, including the related business processes, relevant to financial reporting, including the following areas:

- The classes of transactions in the entity's operations that are significant to the financial statements.

- The procedures, within both IT and manual systems, by which those transactions are initiated, recorded, processed and reported in the financial statements.

- The related accounting records, whether electronic or manual, supporting information, and specific accounts in the financial statements, in respect of initiating, recording, processing and reporting transactions.

- How the information system captures events and conditions, other than classes of transactions, that are significant to the financial statements.

- The financial reporting process used to prepare the entity's financial statements, including significant accounting estimates and disclosures (ISA (UK and Ireland) 315 para 81).

32. For charities it is important that the systems in place are able to capture accurately any restrictions placed on income (whether imposed by the donor or as a result of the charity's fundraising initiatives). The systems should also ensure the documentation supporting the restrictions on the income is retained and easily accessible. The auditor assesses these systems as part of the process of obtaining an understanding of the information systems.

The auditor should obtain a sufficient understanding of control activities to assess the risks of material misstatement at the assertion level and to design further audit procedures responsive to assessed risks (ISA (UK and Ireland) 315 para 90).

33. Aspects of the control activities which are special to charities are described below. Control activities which are not specific to charities, such as segregation of duties or physical security of tangible assets are not included in the examples but are also relevant to the auditors' assessment of the components of audit risk.

Control activities

34. The following tables set out some of the control activities which are special to charities. A particular difficulty for charity trustees in establishing control activities can stem from the use of volunteers (often on a part-time basis) who are not formally accountable to them, unlike employees. Nevertheless, it is important for charities raising a significant proportion of income through volunteers, for example street collectors, to ensure that those volunteers are adequately supervised and controlled. The tables are not intended to be comprehensive: there may be other control activities which will be relevant to a particular charity's activities and control activities which are of general application (such as segregation of duties or physical security of tangible assets) which are not included in the examples given below. The nature and extent of the activities will clearly depend on the size of the charity.

Table 1: cash donations

Source	Examples of controls
Collecting boxes and tins	• numerical control over boxes and tins • satisfactory sealing of boxes and tins so that any opening prior to recording cash is apparent • regular collection and recording of proceeds from collecting boxes • dual control over counting and recording of proceeds
Other cash receipts	• clear directions to staff on how to handle cash donations • advice to donors on where to make donations securely
Postal receipts	• unopened mail kept securely • dual control over the opening of mail • immediate recording of donations on opening of mail or receipt • agreement of bank paying-in slips to record of receipts by an independent person
Receipts over the internet	• sending a confirmation of receipt to the donor • controls over the writing up of daybooks

Table 2: other donations

Source	Examples of controls
Gift aid	• establish procedures to ensure donations are initially recorded correctly with tax compliance issues being met • regular checks and follow-up procedures to ensure due amounts are received • regular checks to ensure all tax repayments have been obtained • structured archive system in place to ensure documentation is retained for 7 years
Legacies	• comprehensive correspondence files maintained in respect of each legacy, and numerically controlled searches of agency reports of legacies receivable • regular reports and follow-up procedures undertaken in respect of outstanding legacies • security of chattels received as legacies and procedures to establish their value and proper realisation
Donations in kind/ intangible income	• in case of charity shops, separation of recording, storage and sale of stock • all types of activity: immediate recording of donated assets • procedures for recording donated services

Table 3: other income

Source	Examples of controls
Fund-raising activities	• records maintained for each fund-raising event • other controls maintained over receipts appropriate to the type of activity and receipt (as set out in tables 1 and 2) • controls maintained over expenses as for administrative expenses
Central and local government grants and loans	• regular checks that all sources of income or funds are fully utilised and appropriate claims made • ensuring income or funds are correctly applied in accordance with the terms of the grant or loan • comprehensive records of applications made and follow-up procedures for those not discharged

Table 4: fixed assets

Source	Examples of controls
Existence of assets	• a register of fixed assets maintained, including donated assets
Valuation	• donated assets recorded at approximate market value, where appropriate depreciation calculated and recorded in accordance with proper assessment of future benefits deriving from assets' use

Table 5: use of funds

Resource	Examples of controls
Restricted funds	• separate records maintained of relevant revenue, expenditure and assets • terms controlling application of funds • oversight of application of fund monies by independent personnel or trustees
Grants to beneficiaries	• records maintained, as appropriate, of requests for material grants received and their treatment • appropriate checks made on applications and applicants for grants, and that amounts paid are intra vires • records maintained of all grant decisions, checking that proper authority exists, that adequate documentation is presented to decision-making meetings, and that any conflicts of interest are recorded

> • controls to ensure grants made are properly spent by the recipient for the specified purpose, for example requirements for returns with supporting documentation or auditors' reports concerning expenditure, or monitoring visits.

Branch operations

35. Many charities carry out their operations through branches based either in the United Kingdom or overseas. Set out below are the control activities that the charity may implement:

- regular reports or returns to the charity's head office by any branch, office or individual representative of the charity, checks to ensure that all these are received, and a mechanism for monitoring branch activities, for example by comparison of expenditure to budget;

- prompt investigation of any report of the misuse of the charity's name;

- internal controls of equivalent standard to those of the main charity in any branch where the trustees of the charity have direct control;

- existence of an accounts manual and the standardisation of procedures at all branches;

- proper acknowledgements of remittances to and from abroad;

- clarity of instructions and guidelines as to receipt and transfer of income to identify the point at which it belongs to the main charity;

- controls over recruitment and appointment of staff to run branch operations;

- defined authorisation limits and responsibilities for local staff in ordering and paying for goods and services;

- if the amounts involved are material, periodic checks by internal audit or head office personnel;

- retention of documents for local inspection (for example at overseas locations if local law requires this) or for periodic transmission to the head office; and

- in the case of overseas branches, controls over treasury operations, for example to ensure that unspent cash balances are held in hard currencies and in secure holdings where the overseas economy is inflationary and conditions are unstable.

Assessing the Risks of Material Misstatement

> The auditor should identify and assess the risks of material misstatement at the financial statement level, and at the assertion level for classes of transactions, account balances, and disclosures (ISA (UK and Ireland) 315 para 100).

36. Factors which may affect the assessment of the risk of material misstatement in charities include:

    • the extent to which an atmosphere of trust exists;

    • the complexity and extent of regulation;

    • the significance of donations and cash receipts;

    • the extent of donations over the internet or by credit card;

    • the valuation of donations in kind;

    • difficulties of the charity in establishing ownership and timing of voluntary income where funds are raised by non-controlled bodies;

    • lack of predictable income or precisely identifiable relationship between expenditure and income which makes it difficult for the charity to ensure that income to which it is entitled is actually received;

    • uncertainty of future income which can make consideration of future operations and viability of the charity difficult;

    • the objects and powers given by charities' governing documents are often narrow. Failure to act in accordance with those objects and powers is likely to have consequences for the financial statements, and therefore the auditors' report;

    • restricted funds held by many charities which require special considerations as to use and accounting;

    • the extent and nature of trading activities must be compatible with the entity's charitable status;

    • the complexity of tax rules (whether Income, CGT, VAT or business rates) relating to charities;

    • difficulties in identification and quantification of liabilities arising from constructive obligations[5];

---

5   See also paragraph 123 of the Charities SORP.

THE AUDITING PRACTICES BOARD

- the sensitivity of certain key statistics, such as the proportion of resources used in administration and fund-raising;

- the need to maintain adequate resources for future expenditure while avoiding the build up of reserves which could appear excessive to potential donors or be incompatible with the entity's charitable status.

37. A common feature of most charities is the receipt of voluntary income, which may be received by way of cash donations or donations in kind. Unlike the income of commercial entities, voluntary income will not always be supported by invoices or equivalent documentation. Obtaining assurance as to the completeness and accuracy of recorded donations can therefore be difficult.

38. The level of income from donations cannot be predicted with any great accuracy, as people's pattern of giving may change due, for example, to economic hardship or competing demands on limited resources. It is also difficult to establish a relationship between donations and other figures in the financial statements, as expenditure levels may not have any direct relationship with such income. Where voluntary cash donations are received, the trustees need to make arrangements to institute appropriate controls, to the extent practicable, to ensure that all income is properly accounted for, and the charity's auditors are likely to rely on evidence concerning those controls in order to form a view on the completeness of the income shown in its financial statements.

As part of the risk assessment, the auditor should determine which of the risks identified are, in the auditor's judgment, risks that require special audit consideration (such risks are defined as "significant risks") (ISA (UK and Ireland) 315 para 108).

For significant risks, to the extent the auditor has not already done so, the auditor should evaluate the design of the entity's related controls, including relevant control activities, and determine whether they have been implemented (ISA (UK and Ireland) 315 para 113).

39. The completeness of incoming resources, overseas operations and restricted funds are likely to be significant risks affecting charity audits, and audit procedures in respect of these are commented on further below. Examples of substantive procedures to address these risks are described in paragraphs 42 to 52.

Requirements of ISA (UK and Ireland) 330: The Auditor's Procedures in Response to Assessed Risks

Background note

The purpose of this ISA (UK and Ireland) is to establish standards and provide guidance on determining overall responses and designing and performing further audit procedures to respond to the assessed risks of material misstatement at the financial statement and assertion levels in a financial statement audit.

When the auditor has determined that it is not possible or practicable to reduce the risks of material misstatement at the assertion level to an acceptably low level with audit evidence obtained only from substantive procedures, the auditor should perform tests of relevant controls to obtain audit evidence about their operating effectiveness (ISA (UK and Ireland) 330 para 25).

40. When considering whether donations and gifts receivable by a charity are properly recorded, auditors seek evidence to determine whether the accounting records reflect cash and other forms of donation from the point at which the charity is entitled to them. Where the auditors are satisfied, through evaluation and testing, that there are appropriate and effective controls, they can use the results of their internal control testing as a source of audit evidence about the completeness of recorded transactions.

When, in accordance with paragraph 108 of ISA (UK and Ireland) 315, the auditor has determined that an assessed risk of material misstatement at the assertion level is a significant risk and the auditor plans to rely on the operating effectiveness of controls intended to mitigate that significant risk, the auditor should obtain the audit evidence about the operating effectiveness of those controls from tests of controls performed in the current period. (ISA (UK and Ireland) 330 para 44).

41. For significant risks the auditor does not rely on audit evidence obtained in a prior audit. Accordingly, if the auditor plans to rely on the operating effectiveness of controls to mitigate identified significant risks, the auditor obtains the evidence in the current period.

When the auditor has determined that an assessed risk of material misstatement at the assertion level is a significant risk, the auditor should perform substantive procedures that are specifically responsive to that risk (ISA (UK and Ireland) 330 para 51).

Sources and completeness of incoming resources

42. The incoming resources of charities often involve a number of different sources, ranging from grants from government departments to occasional cash donations by members of the public in response to street collections. Whilst it is the trustees' responsibility to safeguard the assets and incoming resources of the charity, the voluntary nature of some elements of its incoming resources raises considerations concerning the methods available to the trustees for the purposes of ensuring that all incoming resources to which the charity is entitled are correctly accounted for. These considerations differ from those in commercial concerns: the amount of voluntary donations cannot in many cases be determined in advance, nor can a charity be regarded as necessarily entitled to funds, even when the amounts can be predicted, before they are donated to it. Trustees of a charity cannot be held responsible for the security of money or other assets which are intended for its use until that money or assets are, or should be, within the control of the charity. Trustees should, however, establish procedures to ensure appropriate recording and safeguarding as soon as such assets come within their control.

43. Possible substantive procedures regarding completeness of incoming resources include the following:

- *recognition of incoming resources from professional fund-raisers:* income recognition can be a complex issue where a charity obtains resources by means of fund-raising organisations[6]. The agreement (between the charity and the fund raiser) and other documents relating to the transaction can be checked by the auditor to see whether all donations received in the charity's name have been transmitted to it or otherwise accounted for;

- *recognition of incoming resources from branches, associates or subsidiaries:* if charities use branches, associates or subsidiaries to raise funds, the auditor can check the arrangements made by the main charity to determine at what point incoming resources are recognised;

- *recognition of legacy income:* legacy income should only be recognised when it becomes reasonably certain that the legacy will be received and the value of the incoming resources can be measured with sufficient reliability (SORP, p89). Sources of audit evidence as to whether legacy income has been correctly recorded include correspondence from solicitors and legacy fundraising agencies;

- *informal fund-raising groups:* where informal fund-raising groups raise money or other resources for charitable purposes on a voluntary basis, without knowledge of any particular charity, criteria for recognising income are not met until the funds raised are notified to the recipient charity. In general neither trustees nor auditors have an obligation to estimate the extent of income from such sources before this point. Even if a legal entitlement on the part of the charity to the resulting income may arise under trust law, it would normally be inappropriate for the charity to account for income from such sources since its ultimate cash realisation, so far as the charity itself is concerned, cannot be determined with sufficient certainty;

- *grants receivable:* in the case of grant funded charities, an examination of the grant applications and correspondence is a useful way of verifying completeness of incoming resources. Wherever possible the auditor seeks to obtain direct confirmation of the amounts receivable from the grant provider; and

- *Non-cash donations:* satisfactory operation of internal controls may enable the auditor to obtain sufficient appropriate audit evidence as to the recognition and measurement of donations made by way of goods, other assets or services. The trustees of a charity should develop procedures for recording donations in kind and ensure that the policy for valuing the assets or services received is consistent with the Charities SORP. The basis of any valuation of non-cash donations should be clearly stated in the notes to the financial statements and consistently applied. The auditor considers whether the policy is reasonable in the circumstances and has been properly applied.

---

[6] The Charities Act 1992, Section 59 requires there to be an agreement between the charity and the fund raiser in a prescribed form.

44. Analytical procedures may also be used as a source of audit evidence about the completeness of incoming resources. Whilst the degree of inherent uncertainty affecting donated incoming resources may restrict the reliance which can be placed on such techniques in respect of donations, they nevertheless provide a source of additional corroborative evidence to supplement that drawn from the auditor's consideration of relevant controls over completeness of incoming resources from donations. The auditor therefore undertakes analytical procedures to assess whether such incoming resources are consistent with his knowledge of the charity and its activities over the period, and considers undertaking other forms of analytical review.

45. In the case of larger charities with more complex operations, there are specialist publications and sources of information which can be referred to for general information about charities as well as comparative figures and statistics. These sources include 'trade' journals, umbrella organisations, and the Charity Commission. Available statistics include responses to mailshots (i.e. donations received), and industry norms such as sales per square foot for trading operations in different areas.

Overseas operations

46. Overseas operations can take a number of forms including branches, joint ventures with other charities, projects managed by local agents or partners through to the grant funding of autonomous local organisations.

47. Where the overseas operations form part of the charity, audit evidence will be required to support material expenditure of money in the field. An understanding of the structure of the charity will also be needed in determining at what point expenditure is incurred. Where the overseas operations are part of the charity, the transfer of funds by itself does not give rise to expenditure as such funds remain under the control of the charity.

48. Procedures may include:

   • consideration of internal control procedures put in place by the charity, and how adherence to procedures is monitored;

   • obtaining evidence from field officers' reports as to work undertaken;

   • comparison of accounting returns of expenditure with field reports and plans for consistency and reasonableness;

   • analytical review of accounting returns received from overseas branches or local agents;

   • consideration of any inspection or internal control visit reports undertaken by any internal audit function; and

   • consideration of audit work undertaken by local auditors.

49. Where material assets are held or material funds are applied by overseas branches or subsidiaries the auditor seeks observational evidence by way of site visits. Such visits

may provide valuable evidence of the existence of tangible fixed assets and of project work being undertaken by the charity.

50. Where a charity makes a significant grant to an overseas organisation that is autonomous from the charity, the auditor seeks evidence to support:

- receipt of funding by that organisation; and

- that the charity has exercised reasonable diligence in ensuring application of the funds for charitable purposes (see ICTA 1988 s506(3)).

Appropriate procedures by the charity may involve the vetting of applications, reviewing project reports received, setting thresholds for site visits to projects involving significant grant funding, reviewing accounts and the local certification of expenditure.

Restricted funds

51. Restricted funds (including endowments) which are subject to specific trusts as to their application may give rise to a significant risk of misstatement. The auditor considers:

- the terms or conditions attaching to restricted funds;

- any funds that are in deficit;

- any income funds which are held in illiquid assets thereby preventing application of the fund; and

- the expenditure of the capital of an endowed fund without express authority.

52. Audit procedures may include:

- consideration of internal control procedures put in place by the charity to identify restricted funds whether imposed by the donor or as a result of the charity's fund raising initiatives;

- consideration of the methods used in cost allocation;

- comparison of expenditure (whether out of income or capital) with the terms of the restricted fund, and appeal documentation, bid submissions and related reports to donors;

- consideration of the recoverability of negative balances; and

- consideration of the ability of the fund to meet its obligations in view of its underlying assets.

The auditor should perform audit procedures to evaluate whether the overall presentation of the financial statements, including the related disclosures, are in accordance with the applicable financial reporting framework (ISA (UK and Ireland) 330 para 65).

53. Examples of points that the auditor considers as part of the overall assessment of whether the financial statements prepared on the accruals basis give a true and fair view include:

- consistency of accounting policies adopted with the Charities SORP;

- recognition of income on a gross basis;

- adequacy of analysis of incoming resources;

- allocation of costs between SOFA expenditure headings;

- capitalisation of expenditure on fixed assets;

- accounting treatment of historic or inalienable assets;

- accounting for constructive obligations.

The legal and regulatory framework of charities is such that a checklist approach to compliance with the SORP and statutes is likely to be necessary.

Fraud

Requirements of ISA (UK and Ireland) 240: The Auditor's Responsibility to Consider Fraud in an Audit of Financial Statements

Background note

The purpose of this ISA(UK and Ireland) is to establish basic principles and essential procedures and to provide guidance on the auditor's responsibility to consider fraud in an audit of financial statements and expand on how the standards and guidance in ISA (UK and Ireland) 315 and ISA (UK and Ireland) 330 are to be applied in relation to the risks of material misstatement due to fraud.

Special features of charities

54. The trustees of a charity are responsible for the prevention and detection of fraud in relation to the charity, even if they have delegated some of their executive functions to senior staff. They are expected to safeguard charity assets and reserves through the implementation of appropriate systems of control. The auditor of a charity is responsible for forming an opinion as to whether financial statements show a true and fair view and to this end the auditor plans, performs and evaluates audit work in order to have a reasonable expectation of detecting material misstatements in the financial statements arising from error or fraud.

55. Many charities receive funds which have restrictions placed upon them. These funds are held on trust and must be applied to the purpose for which they were given. The misappropriation of funds constitutes a breach of trust, whether it was intentional or

accidental. In planning, performing and evaluating the audit work the auditor considers the risk of material misstatement arising from such breaches of trust.

56. The auditor considers the possibility that the charity's records of incoming resources to which it is legally entitled may be incomplete as a result of fraud. A common type of fraud against charities is the diversion of donations to bank or building society accounts which they do not control. Sources of audit evidence as to whether incoming resources from appeals and other 'non-routine' sources have been fully recorded can involve the assessment and testing of internal controls, and comparison of donations actually received by the charity to past results for similar appeals, to budgets and to statistics for response rates for charities in general.

When obtaining an understanding of the entity and its environment, including its system of internal control, the auditor should consider whether the information obtained indicates that one or more fraud risk factors are present (ISA (UK and Ireland) 240 para 48).

57. Certain features of charities may increase the risk of fraud. These include:

- widespread branches or operations, such as those established in response to emergency appeals in countries where there is no effective system of law and order;

- the use of volunteer and/or inexperienced staff;

- transactions (income and expenditure) often undertaken in cash;

- unpredictable patterns of giving (in cash, by cheque, and through donations in kind) by members of the public, both in terms of timing and point of donation;

- the limited involvement of trustees in key decision making or monitoring.

A more comprehensive list of features which may increase the risk of fraud is contained in appendix 1 to ISA (UK and Ireland) 240.

58. Reviewing the minutes of meetings of the board of trustees, finance committee and audit committee helps the auditor evaluate whether one or more fraud risk factors are present.

When performing analytical procedures to obtain an understanding of the entity and its environment, including its internal control, the auditor should consider unusual or unexpected relationships that may indicate risks of material misstatement due to fraud (ISA (UK and Ireland) 240 para 53).

59. A particular difficulty in applying analytical procedures to the audit of charities is that certain items in the financial statements can be very difficult to predict. The usefulness of individual procedures depends on the scale and nature of activities undertaken, but examples of measures that can be adopted include:

- comparison of actual income and expenditure to prior years' figures and trends;

- comparison of actual to budgeted results;

- comparison of actual expenditure to the auditor's own estimate of the expenditure that would be reasonable for the particular transaction under review;

- comparison of results of an individual branch to those of similar branches of the main charity;

- checking charity shops' sales revenue between different periods (eg monthly) and to other shops operating in similar locations;

- analysis of efficiency ratios such as staff or administration costs as a percentage of benefits delivered or grants made, or the ratio of operating costs to income (in this respect, care needs to be taken to compare the results of charities of similar sizes, since larger charities tend to benefit from economies of scale); and

- comparison of actual cash donations received as a result of fund-raising activities to the amount which could be expected on the basis of charity statistics, if any are available. It is likely to be helpful to analyse voluntary income into its different sources and then design analytical techniques appropriate to each source. For example, funds can be raised through television or radio appeals, street collections, trading activities, special events, telephone canvassing and postal appeals. The income raised through special events may be predicted and controlled through budgeting, whereas industry statistics and the charity's own past experience may provide a useful indication of the amount likely to be raised from a postal appeal.

If the auditor has identified a fraud or has obtained information that indicates that a fraud may exist, the auditor should communicate these matters as soon as practicable to the appropriate level of management (ISA (UK and Ireland) 240 para 93).

60. The appropriate level of management for most charities will be the Board of trustees. However, for large charities where the fraud or suspected fraud is not being perpetrated by senior management then the appropriate level of management will be the senior management team.

The auditor should document communications about fraud made to management, those charged with governance, regulators and others (ISA (UK and Ireland) 240 para 109).

(1) reporting to management

61. The auditor is required to communicate findings to 'the appropriate level of management', unless the suspected or actual instance of fraud casts doubt on the integrity of the directors or equivalents (in a charity, the trustees). In this case, 'the auditor should make a report direct to a proper authority in the public interest, without delay and without informing the directors in advance'.

62. In the case of charities where the trustees are not involved in the day-to-day management of the charity, having delegated this function to staff, and it is the latter who are suspected of involvement in fraud, the auditor may consider that it is appropriate to communicate with the trustees in the first instance. In this case the auditor is required to communicate findings as soon as practicable.

(2) reporting to the addressees of the auditor's report on the financial statements

63. Even where the addressees of the auditor's report are the trustees, and the auditor suspects them of involvement in a fraud or is aware that the matter has already been communicated fully to them, the report on the financial statements is required to include details of any fundamental uncertainty, or disagreement over disclosure of a suspected or actual instance of fraud or error having a material effect on the financial statements. In the case of a charitable company, the auditor's report is addressed to the members of the company, who may not all be trustees.

(3) reporting to third parties

64. The regulatory framework within which a charity operates does not alter the nature of the auditor's responsibility to consider fraud and error in an audit of financial statements. However, the framework does affect the circumstances in which the auditor reports to third parties, the form of the report and the persons or bodies to whom the report is made. The section in PN 11 providing guidance on SAS 620 deals with reports to the regulators of charities.

65. The auditor normally reports actual or suspected frauds to certain third parties, in particular to a 'proper authority' in the public interest. The auditor only reports to an authority 'with a proper interest to receive the information'.

66. In the case of charities, the proper authority is ordinarily the Charity Commission for charities established in England and Wales (other than exempt charities), the Office of the Scottish Charity Regulator for charities based in Scotland, the Charities Branch of the Department for Social Development for charities in Northern Ireland, and, in any part of the United Kingdom, the Police.

67. Charities undertake a wide range of activities (some of which are themselves regulated). Where a charity is subject to a regulatory regime in addition to that resulting from its charitable status, its auditor assesses whether to report a suspected fraud to the relevant other regulator. For example, in England and Wales 'exempt' charities are subject to other regulatory authorities, which may be regarded as proper authorities: for example certain universities, or grant maintained schools in England and Wales, which are regulated by the Department for Education and Skills (or its agencies) as the funding authority; other charities throughout the United Kingdom may be registered friendly societies, whose auditors have a statutory duty to report to the Financial Services Authority.

68. Auditors of unincorporated charities in England & Wales have a statutory duty to report to the Charity Commission in certain circumstances, as set out in the section of PN 11 dealing with the application to charities of SAS 620. It is unlikely that auditors of such

charities will encounter suspected frauds of sufficient gravity to consider reporting in the public interest which do not also give rise to a statutory duty to report.

BULLETIN 2005/3

GUIDANCE FOR AUDITORS ON FIRST-TIME APPLICATION OF IFRSs IN THE UNITED KINGDOM AND THE REPUBLIC OF IRELAND

CONTENTS

Appendices

1: Equivalent Legislative References for Northern Ireland and Comparative Legislative References for the Republic of Ireland

2: Example review report

Introduction

Objective

1. This Bulletin provides auditors with guidance on issues that may arise when companies (and other entities that are subject to audit) undertake the transition from United Kingdom, or Republic of Ireland, Generally Accepted Accounting Practice (UK/ ROI GAAP) to International Financial Reporting Standards (IFRSs)[1].

2. Regulation EC 1606/2002[2] (IAS Regulation) requires European Union companies with securities that are admitted to trading on a regulated market of any Member State to prepare their consolidated financial statements in conformity with IFRSs as adopted for use in the European Union.

3. At the same time as IFRSs take effect in 2005, changes to legal accounting requirements also enter into force in UK and ROI law, arising mainly from the Fair Value Directive and the Modernisation Directive. Consequently, there is substantial complexity in the interaction of legal issues, accounting standards, and auditing requirements.

4. As this Bulletin reflects the requirements of the Companies Act 1985 (CA 1985) it is of direct application to audits of entities that are incorporated in Great Britain. The UK DTI has published 'Guidance for British Companies on Changes to the Accounting and Reporting Provisions of the Companies Act 1985' ("DTI Guidance")[3], which describes the main changes to the CA 1985, as well as highlighting certain practical issues. Appendix 1 of this Bulletin sets out a table of the equivalent legislative references for Northern Ireland and of comparative legislative references for the Republic of Ireland.

5. IFRS 1 'First-time adoption of International Financial Reporting Standards' has been issued to enable preparers to ensure that an entity's first IFRS financial statements, and its interim reports for part of the period covered by those financial statements, contain high quality information that:

    (a) is transparent for users and comparable over all periods presented;

    (b) provides a suitable starting point for accounting under IFRSs; and

    (c) can be generated at a cost that does not exceed the benefits to users.

---

[1] IFRSs is a defined term which incorporates all International Financial Reporting Standards, International Accounting Standards (IASs) and Interpretations originated by the International Financial Reporting Interpretations Committee (IFRIC) or the former Standards Interpretation Committee of the IASC. Details of all IFRSs can be found at the IASB website at www.iasb.org; IASB publications include helpful executive summaries of the standards. Unless otherwise stated, references in this Bulletin to IFRSs encompass both the IFRSs as issued by the IASB and IFRSs as adopted for use in the European Union (which may not be the same).

[2] EC 1606/2002 can be found on the Europa website at http://europa.eu.int/eur-lex/pri/en/oj/dat/2002/ l_243/l_24320020911en00010004.pdf. Subsequent EC Regulations adopt specific IFRSs.

[3] This can be found on the DTI website at http://www.dti.gov.uk/cld/guidance.doc

Appended to IFRS 1 is 'Guidance on Implementing IFRS 1', which explains how the requirements of IFRS 1 interact with the requirements of those IFRSs that are most likely to involve questions that are specific to first time adopters. The guidance also includes an illustrative example of how a first time adopter might disclose how the transition to IFRSs affected its reported financial position, financial performance and cash flows as required by IFRS 1.

6. APB published two earlier drafts of this Bulletin in August 2004 and April 2005 to provide auditors with interim guidance. Since then, a number of uncertainties have been resolved and there have been various developments in auditing and financial reporting that are reflected in this Bulletin. In particular:

- The European Commission has adopted the majority of the extant IFRSs and Interpretations, apart from certain parts of IAS 39 on financial instruments and various very recent pronouncements from the IASB.[4]

- Further implementing legislation in the UK and the ROI has been passed,[5] as well as other guidance issued, for example on IFRS and distributable profits.

- Consensus has emerged in Europe about the specific wording to be used in auditor's reports when describing the financial reporting framework.

7. In spite of the progress made in resolving many of the legal and regulatory issues, there are some remaining uncertainties that are relevant to auditors. The APB will therefore continue to keep the situation under review.

Limitations of the Bulletin

8. The Bulletin does not give guidance on every aspect of the introduction of IFRSs in the UK and ROI. Specifically, it does not deal with the following:

(a) *Reporting on the opening IFRS balance sheet and/or the 2004 comparatives:* These represent non-statutory assurance engagements that are beyond the scope of this Bulletin.[6]

(b) *Identification of key differences between UK/ROI GAAP and IFRSs:* While the Bulletin refers to some differences between UK/ROI GAAP and IFRSs as examples, it does not provide a comprehensive list of differences.

(c) *Identification of those company law requirements that still apply to accounts prepared under IFRSs:* In the case of the CA 1985, this is provided in the DTI Guidance.

---

[4] Information about adopted IFRSs can be found on the Europa website at http://europa.eu.int/comm/internal_market/accounting/ias_en.htm#comments.

[5] See the DTI website at http://www.dti.gov.uk/cld/ for further details.

[6] The International Auditing and Assurance Standards Board (IAASB) has issued a non-authoritative paper on the subject 'First Time Adoption of International Financial Reporting Standards – Guidance for Auditors on Reporting Issues', in the form of a series of questions and answers.

(d) *The Companies Act 1985 (Operating and Financial Review and Directors' Report) Regulations 2005.*

Responsibilities of the directors

General responsibilities of the directors

9. Under company law, the directors are responsible for preparing financial statements. Implicitly, this requires them to take reasonable steps to ensure that the entity will cope with the introduction of IFRSs, where applicable. The directors, through the entity's management, need to consider the specific impacts of IFRSs on the financial statements and whether proper accounting records will be maintained. The auditor considers whether management has put in place procedures with subsidiaries and branches such that the relevant accounting information will be received by the parent company on a timely basis to enable the group accounts to be properly prepared under IFRSs.

Analysing the impact on the business

10. When preparing an "impact analysis" the entity will need to consider the effect of the introduction of IFRSs on:

(a) computer and other data systems, internal controls and systems for preparing financial statements, for example systems capable of capturing all requisite information on financial instrument fair values, hedging arrangements and embedded derivatives;

(b) the financial statements themselves, including interim results in the year of change. For example, how the financial statements should communicate the effect of the introduction of IFRSs to the users of the entity's financial statements;

(c) business-critical issues that arise from the financial statements, for example the calculation of debt covenants and borrowing powers limitations in the entity's constitutional documents, or the impact on distributable profits where IFRSs are adopted in individual entity financial statements; and

(d) other regulatory concerns, for example changes to the measurement of regulatory capital as a result of changes in the financial statements.

Management plans that address the issues identified

11. Given the likely pervasiveness of the changes introduced by IFRSs, it is unlikely that any company, group or other entity moving to IFRSs will have financial statements and/or a business so straightforward that no formal plan is necessary. Matters likely to be included in a plan, depending on the size and complexity of the organisation, are:

• Creating an appropriate overall project steering structure.

• Defining the individual projects (for critical accounting policies or line items).

- Planning to resource these projects, including estimates for costs, time, external resources, (eg for input from specialists), staffing levels for the changeover period, hardware capacity and new software.

- Developing a testing and implementation strategy.

- Identifying constraints such as staff availability and the realistic ability to secure further resources.

- Developing a high-level milestone plan to co-ordinate the overall programme of projects.

- Reviewing and updating the plan to reflect actual progress.

- Identifying alternative actions for systems issues which will not be addressed in time (contingency or damage limitation plans).

12. The auditor considers how the impact analysis and management plans affect its risk assessment for the audit during the period of transition from UK/ROI GAAP to IFRSs.

SUMMARY OF SIGNIFICANT ISSUES COVERED IN THE BULLETIN

13. In relation to the audit of IFRS information for the first time, certain issues are likely to be of particular importance. The Bulletin discusses the issues by relevant ISAs (UK and Ireland). The main features of the guidance are as follows:

   (a) There are major implications for audit risk (Paragraph 67)

   (b) Auditors are likely to need to perform additional procedures on comparatives and opening balances for both full year financial statements (Paragraph 75) and interim reports (Paragraph 149)

   (c) The need for audit staff to have appropriate knowledge and understanding of IFRSs (Paragraph 16) and the increased likelihood for the need for consultation with those responsible for technical financial reporting issues (Paragraph 22)

   (d) There are implications for the auditor's consideration of laws and regulations, including:

      (i) The need to consider whether companies have complied with the legal requirement to prepare group accounts in accordance with IFRSs as adopted for use in the EU (Paragraph 28)

      (ii) The requirement for auditors of parent companies to consider whether directors have secured that the individual accounts of subsidiary undertakings prepare their statutory accounts following the same financial reporting framework, unless in their opinion there is a good reason for not doing so (Paragraph 39)

   (e) Going concern issues may arise in relation to the impact of IFRSs on debt covenants (Paragraphs 105 – 109)

   (f) The introduction of IFRSs will give rise to complexities regarding taxation (Paragraphs 51 – 52) and the distribution of profits (Paragraphs 49 – 50)

   (g) Uncertainties for interim reports caused by the possible need for companies to anticipate the adoption of some IFRSs for use in the EU (Paragraphs 152 – 154)

   (h) Careful consideration will need to be given to the tailoring of auditor's reports especially with respect to:

      (i) The need to refer to the applicable financial reporting framework (Paragraphs 119 – 122).

      (ii) Parent companies adopting IFRSs but also taking advantage of the Section 230 exemption (Paragraphs 42 – 43 and 123 – 124)

      (iii)   The use of different financial reporting frameworks for group and parent company financial statements gives rise to separate auditor's reports for these if they are presented in separate sections of the Annual Report (Paragraph 44).

(i)   The disclosures required in the year of transition to IFRSs, including:

      (i)   Reconciliations of IFRS information to previous GAAP (Paragraph 16)

      (ii)   More extensive disclosure of estimation uncertainty (Paragraphs 93 – 94)

(j)   Potential difficulties relating to the audit of fair value information (Paragraphs 95 – 97)

APPLICATION OF ISAS (UK AND IRELAND): SPECIFIC ISSUES

14. This section highlights some of the specific issues raised by the introduction of IFRSs in the application of ISAs (UK and Ireland).

International Standard on Quality Control (UK and Ireland)

ISQC 1 'Quality Control for Firms that Perform Audits and Reviews of Historical Financial Information, and other Assurance and Related Services Engagements'

15. ISQC 1 requires a firm of auditors to establish policies and procedures designed to provide reasonable assurance that it has sufficient personnel with the capabilities, competence, and commitment to ethical principles necessary to perform its engagements in accordance with professional standards and regulatory and legal requirements, and to enable the firm or engagement partners to issue reports that are appropriate in the circumstances. ISQC 1 requires firms to assign appropriate staff with the necessary capabilities, competence and time to perform engagements in accordance with professional standards and regulatory and legal requirements, and to enable the firm or engagement partners to issue reports that are appropriate in the circumstances.

16. Audit staff require knowledge and understanding of IFRSs. In the year of transition it will be particularly important for audit staff to have sufficient knowledge of both UK/ROI GAAP and IFRSs in order to audit the reconciliations between the two required by IFRS 1. Without such knowledge and understanding they may fail to

    (a) detect improper or incorrect reconciling items such as changes in previous estimates or correction of errors;

    (b) consider an omission from the reconciling items or items which have been incorrectly included within other reconciliation amounts; or

    (c) identify incorrect IFRS figures (where UK/ROI GAAP figures have been left unchanged) which may result in no reconciling item being shown at all.

International Standards on Auditing (UK and Ireland)

ISA (UK & Ireland) 200 'Objective and General Principles Governing an Audit of Financial Statements'

Ethical Standards for Auditors

17. If the auditor is asked to assist the directors with their preparations for the introduction of IFRSs, careful consideration will need to be given to the implications of this for the auditor's independence and objectivity.

18. APB Ethical Standard 5 (ES 5) states that for listed companies, or significant affiliates of such an entity, the threats to the auditor's objectivity and independence that would be created are too high to allow the audit firm to undertake an engagement to provide any accounting services save in certain exceptional circumstances[7]. ES 5 also prohibits audit firms from accepting an engagement to provide a valuation to an audit client where the valuation would both involve a significant degree of subjective judgment, and is material to the financial statements.

19. These prohibitions do not extend to separate engagements to provide assurance to those charged with governance on the application of IFRSs, or to provide advice on accounting policies, or train management in IFRS-related matters. In order to help ensure that engagements of this nature are not confused with the statutory audit, it is advisable for auditors to clarify responsibilities for each engagement in separate engagement letters.

ISA (UK & Ireland) 210 'Terms of Audit Engagements'

Clarifying with directors their responsibilities

20. To avoid confusion as to the respective responsibilities of directors and auditors, concerning the introduction of IFRSs, the auditors communicate formally with the directors to avoid any misunderstandings. The directors are responsible for ensuring that the entity is prepared for the introduction of IFRSs and the auditors will wish to state explicitly in writing that the issue will be considered by them only in so far as it affects their audit responsibilities under statute and ISAs (UK and Ireland). This could be done by updating the audit engagement letter.

21. Particular matters that auditors may wish to clarify in the engagement letter are that the directors are responsible for:

    (a) analysing the impact of the introduction of IFRSs on the business;

    (b) developing plans to mitigate the effects identified by this analysis;

    (c) assessing any impact of the introduction of IFRSs on the appropriateness of adopting the going concern basis in preparing the financial statements; and

    (d) the preparation of financial statements as required under IFRSs, including comparative figures, and the disclosures needed to give a fair presentation and hence give a true and fair view.[8]

---

[7] 'Accounting services' are defined as the provision of services that involve the maintenance of accounting records or the preparation of financial statements that are then subject to audit.

[8] The Financial Reporting Council (FRC) has issued a paper "The Implications of New Accounting and Auditing Standards for the "True and Fair View" and Auditors' Responsibilities" which can be found on the FRC website at www.frc.org.uk.

ISA (UK & Ireland) 220 'Quality Control for Audits of Historical Financial Information'

22. ISA (UK and Ireland) 220 addresses consultation, both within the audit team and with others within and outside the audit firm. The auditor considers the need for consultation on those matters deemed critical for an entity in its IFRS financial statements in the year of transition. Consultations are more likely at this time with those responsible for technical financial reporting issues within the audit firm and externally in cases where internal technical expertise is not available.

23. It will also be important at this time to ensure differences of opinion, particularly those on financial reporting issues relating to the application of IFRSs, are dealt with properly. Similarly, the engagement quality control review is likely to focus on the significant judgments made by the engagement team relating to the application of IFRSs.

ISA (UK & Ireland) 240 'The Auditor's Responsibility to Consider Fraud in an Audit of Financial Statements'

24. The introduction of IFRSs may lead to significant changes in financial reporting for many entities. Substantial changes to accounting systems may give greater opportunity for aggressive earnings management and, in extreme cases, fraud. Auditors consider the increased risk of fraud in planning and designing the audit procedures to be performed in the year an entity converts to IFRSs.

25. ISA (UK and Ireland) 240 requires the members of the engagement team to discuss the susceptibility of the entity's financial statements to material misstatements due to fraud. In the year of transition to IFRSs, this discussion will encompass the increased risk of fraud and its non-detection arising from the transition in the context of the specific circumstances of the entity.

ISA (UK & Ireland) 250, Section A 'Consideration of Laws and Regulations in an Audit of Financial Statements'

26. ISA (UK & Ireland) 250, Section A states that the auditor should obtain sufficient appropriate audit evidence about compliance with those laws and regulations generally recognized by the auditor to have an effect on the determination of material amounts and disclosures in financial statements. The auditor should have a sufficient understanding of these laws and regulations in order to consider them when auditing the assertions related to the determination of the amounts to be recorded and the disclosures to be made.

27. Some of the relevant sources of law and regulation identified in the footnotes to paragraphs 20 and 20-1 of ISA (UK & Ireland) 250, Section A, are disapplied (or at least partially so) by the requirements of the IAS Regulation, for example the statutory formats in Schedule 4A CA 1985 for group accounts.[9]

---

[9] The DTI Guidance lists at paragraph 4.21, those provisions in Part VII (Accounts and Audit) of the Companies Act 1985 that still apply.

28. The auditor considers whether an entity falls within the mandatory requirement to prepare its consolidated financial statements in accordance with IFRSs adopted for use in the European Union. This is important because, should any entity fail to follow IFRSs when *required* to do so, auditors would be required to qualify their audit report on the grounds of non-compliance with company law.

The IAS Regulation

29. The IAS Regulation requires certain companies[10] to prepare their consolidated financial statements in accordance with IFRSs adopted for use in the European Union, for accounting periods beginning on or after 1 January 2005. This requirement applies to companies:

   (a) that are subject to the law of a Member State; and

   (b) whose securities are admitted (as at the balance sheet date) to trading on a regulated market (publicly traded companies); and

   (c) that are required by Member State law to prepare group accounts.

30. The IAS Regulation also contains Member State options[11], one of which is to permit or require adopted IFRSs to be used by:

   (a) publicly traded companies, in their individual company accounts; and

   (b) non publicly traded companies, in both, or either of, their group and individual company accounts.

   The UK and ROI have introduced a permissive regime in relation to this Member State option. This means that, from 2005 and until such time as ASB's standards become the same as IASB's, there will be two regimes of Generally Accepted Accounting Practice in the UK and ROI: IFRSs as adopted for use in the EU and UK/ROI GAAP[12].

---

[10] In the EC IAS Regulation 'company' has the same meaning as in Article 48 of the Treaty of Rome (DTI Guidance, paragraph 4.8).

[11] One Member State option allows deferral to 2007 of the mandatory requirement to follow IFRS for companies that already follow an internationally accepted GAAP or those that only have listed debt securities. The DTI has stated that the UK will not take up this Member State option. However, the 2005 ROI Regulations provide for deferral of the obligation to prepare IFRS accounts to 2007 in respect of debt listed securities in the ROI.

[12] ASB has begun to effect UK convergence to IFRSs by issuing its first 'convergence standards', namely FRSs 20-26, to bring certain aspects of UK accounting standards more into line with IFRSs in 2005. It has also issued (in March 2005) an Exposure Draft on the future role of the Board, including its approach to convergence with IFRS. See www.frc.org.uk/asb.

Subject to the law of a Member State

31. For companies to be subject to the law of a Member State, they have to be incorporated in a Member State. From 1 May 2004, Member States include the Accession States (i.e. those that joined the EU in May 2004)[13].

32. The corollary to this is that companies incorporated in a jurisdiction outside the EU, e.g. the USA, and hence not subject to any EU Member State's law, will not be subject to the mandatory requirement to follow IFRSs even if they have securities admitted to trading on a regulated market in an EU Member State.

Securities traded on a regulated market

33. There are several regulated markets in the UK and ROI. It should be noted that not all markets on which listed securities are traded are necessarily "regulated markets" as defined by the Prospectus Directive. An example is the Professional Securities Market, which is operated and regulated by the London Stock Exchange. Issuers listed on such non regulated markets are not required to adopt IFRSs.

Required to prepare group accounts

34. As stated in the DTI Guidance, the test as to whether a company is required to prepare group accounts, for the purpose of the EC Regulation, is by reference to the European Seventh Directive, as adopted into the CA 1985. The relevant Sections are 227 for companies and 255A for banks and insurance companies.

35. The CA 1985 has recently been amended (as outlined in Section 5 of the DTI Guidance), to implement parts of the Modernisation Directive and take up some options in the existing Seventh Directive. In particular, there will no longer be a requirement for a company to have a "participating interest" in its investee for a parent/subsidiary relationship to exist.[14]

Voluntary adoption of IFRSs

36. The new legislation allows publicly traded companies to prepare their individual accounts in accordance with adopted IFRSs. The individual accounts of other group companies may also be prepared in accordance with adopted IFRSs, subject to the consistency requirements discussed in paragraphs 38 to 41. Non-publicly traded companies are also able to apply IFRSs as adopted for use in the EU, in:

   (a) their group accounts; or

---

[13] The complete list of Member States at any time can be found at http://www.europa.eu.int?abc/index_en.htm

[14] This amendment is permitted by Article 2.1 of the Modernisation Directive, although the amendment to the 1985 Act does not extend to removing the parallel requirement to have a participating interest in an associate undertaking. The Accounting Standards Board has in turn issued amendments to FRS 2 to bring it into line with the revised parts of the 1985 Act. The requirements in FRS 5 to consolidate quasi-subsidiaries are not relevant to the legal requirement to consolidate.

(b)   their individual company accounts; or

(c)   both their group and individual company accounts.

37.   There are no specific formalities required in order to make a voluntary move to IFRSs; however, the CA 1985 has a number of restrictions that are discussed in the following paragraphs.

All companies within a group to report using the same accounting framework

38.   Those entities that adopt IFRSs for their group financial statements will prepare those group financial statements under IFRSs regardless of which financial reporting framework is used in the preparation and presentation of the individual statutory accounts of the parent and its subsidiaries. Consequently, the directors of the parent company will need to ensure that management has put systems in place to ensure that all necessary information is available from subsidiaries, on a timely basis, in order to permit proper preparation of IFRS group accounts.

39.   The CA 1985 states (in Section 227C(1)) that the directors of a *parent* company must secure that the individual accounts of the parent and each of its subsidiary undertakings are all prepared using the same financial reporting framework "except to the extent that in their opinion there are good reasons for not doing so"[15]. This provision is intended to provide a degree of flexibility where there are genuine grounds for using different accounting frameworks within a group. Paragraph 4.16 of the DTI Guidance gives some examples of what might constitute 'good reasons'. These examples relate to very specific circumstances and the Guidance notes that the key point is that "the directors of the parent company must be able to justify any inconsistency, to shareholders, regulators or other interested parties."

40.   Auditors enquire as to whether the directors have considered the question and documented their reasons and the auditors consider the acceptability of such reasons, including any advice the directors have taken. If the auditors doubt whether the directors are correct in their opinion that there is a 'good reason', the auditors discuss their concerns with those charged with governance. If, having considered the reason given, the auditors continue to have doubts as to whether there is a justification, they may consider seeking legal advice and consider the implications for their audit report.

41.   The requirement to have a "good reason" where all companies in a group do not use the same accounting framework is a parent company responsibility; it is not an issue for the directors or auditors of any individual subsidiary as long as the subsidiary has properly followed a legally acceptable GAAP which has been clearly disclosed.

---

[15]   There are various exemptions to this as laid out in Paragraph 4.14 of the DTI Guidance. The 2004 Regulations also provide a partial exemption (in new Section 227C(5) of the 1985 Act), such that if a parent company prepares both its consolidated and its individual accounts under IFRS, it is not required to ensure that all its subsidiary undertakings also use IFRSs, although it must still ensure that all its GB subsidiary undertakings use the same GAAP as each other, again unless there are good reasons for not doing so.

Parent company individual financial statements

42. Under Section 230 of the CA 1985, a parent company need not present its individual profit and loss account, nor certain related notes, where it has presented group financial statements[16]. The DTI Guidance states that taking the Section 230 exemption (which it describes as a publication exemption) should not affect the ability of a parent company to be treated as a "first time adopter" and hence to take advantage of exemptions for first time use under the provisions of IFRS 1.

43. IAS 1 and IFRS 1 both require an "explicit and unreserved statement of compliance with IFRSs" in order to be a first-time adopter. In view of the fact that Paragraph 8 of IAS 1 'Presentation of Financial Statements' requires a profit and loss account to be presented in a set of IFRS financial statements, and in order for the statement of compliance with IFRSs not to be misleading, it will be important for an IFRS parent company (particularly one taking advantage of the IFRS 1 exemptions) to indicate that the compliance statement is based on its full IFRS financial statements, of which those presented are an extract (excluding the profit and loss account and related notes). This impacts the auditor's description of the financial reporting framework in the auditor's report as discussed in the ISA (UK and Ireland) 700 section of this Bulletin.

44. If the group financial statements are prepared under IFRSs but the parent company does not adopt IFRSs in its individual financial statements, the parent and group will present information on different bases. Section 240(2) of the CA 1985 requires group and individual accounts to be published but does not specify whether these accounts should be presented in separate sections of the annual report or combined into a single set of primary statements and notes. Where different financial reporting frameworks are applied, the DTI Guidance notes that using separate sections of the annual report is likely to lead to clearer presentation. The approach taken to the presentation of the parent company financial information will affect the auditor's report (as discussed under ISA (UK and Ireland) 700).

The decision to move is irreversible

45. The CA 1985 makes a company's decision to switch to IFRSs irreversible, except under certain limited circumstances. The exceptions are laid out in new Sections 226(5) and 227(6) to the CA 1985 and relate to where, for example, companies and groups cease to be publicly traded and when a company becomes a subsidiary of an undertaking that does not prepare its accounts in accordance with IFRSs.

---

[16] The Section 230 exemption relates only to the profit and loss account and, by virtue of Section 261(2), the notes to the profit and loss account. The parent individual IFRS financial statements will, however, still need to include the other primary statements and note disclosures required by IFRS, including a cash flow statement and a statement of changes in shareholders' equity.

Applicable law: remaining elements of the Companies Act 1985 and related regulation

46. Entities that switch to IFRSs still have to follow aspects of UK company accounting and reporting law, as indicated by the European Commission[17] and by the DTI Guidance (at Paragraphs 4.18-4.21). The auditors need to be aware of which elements of the accounting and reporting provisions of the CA 1985 are still applicable and which are not.[18]

Duty to maintain proper accounting records

47. Auditors are required by Section 237(1) (a) of CA 1985 to investigate whether proper accounting records have been kept by the company and proper returns adequate for their audit have been received from branches not visited by them. That requirement is in relation to the accounting records of individual companies, not the group. Where individual companies within a group have adopted IFRSs, the auditors will need to consider whether the legal responsibility to maintain proper accounting records has been satisfied by appropriate changes in accounting systems and records.

48. If a group's consolidated accounts are prepared under IFRSs, but the individual accounts of all (or most of) the companies within the group remain on UK/ROI or other local GAAP(s), the primary accounting records from which the IFRS consolidated accounts are created may still be based on local GAAP. There is no legal requirement for management to change or adapt accounting systems at the individual company level to capture the new or different accounting information required for IFRS consolidated accounts. The responsibility for ensuring that the necessary information and records are available lies with the parent company's management. In these circumstances, where the requisite adjustments to apply IFRSs to subsidiary financial information is made by way of consolidation adjustments, the group auditor considers whether it is possible to obtain sufficient appropriate audit evidence. If not there may be a limitation on the scope of the auditor's work. (See comments on limitations of scope in the ISA (UK and Ireland) 700 section of the Bulletin).

Distributable profits

49. ISA (UK & Ireland) 250 Section A refers to the laws relating to distributions under Section 263 CA 1985. Group accounts are not relevant to determining the ability of a parent company to make a distribution. However, companies choosing to switch to

---

[17] The guidance from the European Commission on which elements of the accounting directives will continue to apply to IFRS companies can be found at http://europa.eu.int/comm/internal_market/accounting/docs/ias/200311-comments/ias-200311-comments_en.pdf.

[18] The DTI Guidance provides useful guidance to small companies in relation to publication exemptions and abbreviated accounts in Paragraphs 4.25-4.31.

IFRSs in their individual accounts may produce 'relevant accounts' that result in a different amount of distributable profits from the amount that would have been determined under UK/ROI accounting standards[19].

50. The amount of profits a company has available for distribution may change as a result of the transition to IFRSs. When a distribution is being considered, the last set of audited financial statements, which are the relevant accounts for the purpose of Section 270 of the CA 1985, may be under UK/ROI GAAP. Nevertheless, the directors may know that, in the following accounting period (which will already have begun), the changes introduced by IFRSs may have a significant detrimental impact on distributable reserves, thus potentially affecting the directors' assessment of their common law duty not to make a distribution out of capital, as well as their general fiduciary duties.

Taxes Acts

51. Compliance with the Taxes Acts is addressed in ISA (UK & Ireland) 250 Section A. The Chancellor of the Exchequer announced in 2003 that the law would be amended to allow IFRS accounts to be used as the basis of corporation tax assessments for companies (as with distributable profits, only individual financial statements of companies are relevant; group accounts are not used to assess UK corporation tax liabilities). The 2004 Finance Act reflects this move for accounting periods beginning on or after 1 January 2005 and the overall stated aim of Her Majesty's Revenue and Customs (HMRC) is to achieve broadly equivalent tax treatment whether UK/ROI GAAP or IFRS accounts comprise the starting point for corporation tax computations, even where there are material differences in accounting treatment.

52. In the Chancellor's 2004 Pre-Budget Report, the government considered the transitional adjustments arising from certain changes in accounting for financial instruments and decided to defer any tax effects from the transition, in this respect, until the impact could be determined and managed. For most companies, this deferral will operate until accounting periods beginning on or after 1 January 2006 (i.e. for their 2005 accounting periods). In July 2005 it was announced that for tax purposes most transitional adjustments relating to financial instruments will be spread over 10 years from 2006. The position will be reviewed again in 2006 when more information is available and further transitional measures may be introduced. Transactions occurring following transition will be taxed in accordance with IFRSs. Measures were introduced in the Finance Act 2005 to enable securitisation vehicles to continue applying existing UK/ROI accounting standards for tax purposes for accounting periods ending before 1 January 2007 and to address specific technical issues.[20]

---

[19] Auditors will be aware of the guidance on this subject issued in 2003 by the Institutes of Chartered Accountants in England and Wales and of Scotland, which has been supplemented by guidance on the impact on distributable profits of new pension accounting standards and of new standards (UITF Abstracts) on share-based payment and the presentation of shares in ESOP trusts. Draft guidance has been published on IFRSs and distributable profits, which will also be relevant to the application of converged UK standards. See www.icaew.co.uk or www.icas.org.uk.

[20] HMRC has published guidance on tax and IFRS, with links to legislation and commentary, which can be accessed at http://www.hmrc.gov.uk/practitioners/int_accounting.htm#note15

Listing Rules

53. Companies subject to the mandatory application of IFRSs under the IAS Regulation will also be subject to the requirements of the regulated market on which their securities are traded. Where the authorities over such markets make pronouncements in relation to the introduction of IFRSs, regard to these may be relevant in order for the company to maintain its listing.[21]

54. In September 2003 the FSA wrote to the Company Secretaries of all Listed Issuers and amongst other things noted "That a consequence of not being in a position to adopt IFRSs will be that issuers are unable to meet the reporting requirements and deadlines of the Listing Rules. Failure by issuers to submit preliminary or interim results within the required timescale is likely to result in the suspension of the issuer's securities". However, the FSA has subsequently allowed, by concession, that companies' first set of interim accounts under IFRSs may be presented up to 120 days after the relevant period end, rather than the usual 90 days.[22] Companies must inform the market that they are taking advantage of this concession before the end of the half-year period to which the interim accounts relate in order to be claimed. In April 2005 the FSA wrote to the Chief Executives of all Listed Issuers regarding IFRS readiness, reminding them, among other things, that a failure to submit interim results within the required timescale is likely to result in the suspension of the issuer's securities.

ISA (UK & Ireland) 250, Section B 'The Auditor's Right and Duty to Report to Regulators in the Financial Sector'

55. Entities that are required to maintain a certain level of regulatory capital may be affected by the introduction of IFRSs. Auditors consider whether the introduction of IFRSs impacts on their assessment of going concern and on their responsibility to report matters of material significance to a regulator.[23]

ISA (UK & Ireland) 260 'Communication of Audit Matters With Those Charged With Governance'

56. Auditors may identify issues related to the introduction of IFRSs which they consider they should report to those charged with governance. These may be matters which need to be formally communicated because they represent material weaknesses in internal control. However, in addition, they may report other matters which have come to light as a result of the enquiries made about the introduction of IFRSs. For example, where, after making enquiries, the auditors conclude that management has not sufficiently considered all the potential impacts of the introduction of IFRSs, or that management do not have a "good reason" for individual companies in the group not

---

[21] Auditors will be aware that the regime for regulated markets changed in the UK from 1 July 2005 as a result, inter alia, of the implementation of the requirements of the EU Prospectus Directive.

[22] The text of the FSA's letter to Chief Executives of listed companies can be found at http://www.fsa.gov.uk/pubs/ceo/ceo_letter_25oct04.pdf.

[23] The FSA announced in April 2005 the changes in its regulatory accounting rules in the light of new accounting standards. The changes are published in (Policy Statement) PS 05/5 entitled "Implications of a changing accounting framework" and reflect the introduction of IFRSs. The document can be downloaded from http://www.fsa.gov.uk/pubs/policy/ps05_05.pdf.

preparing their individual accounts using the same accounting framework (paragraph 39).

57. The auditors also consider all relevant aspects of the financial reporting framework, covering not only IFRSs but also those statutory and regulatory requirements which still apply. Auditors consider whether the accounting policies adopted by an entity in its first IFRS financial statements comply with the requirements of IAS 8, which includes a hierarchy of sources of guidance where no IFRS or Interpretation is available. Where IFRSs are silent on a subject it would be permissible for entities to continue to follow existing practice as long as it did not run counter to similar standards or the IASB's 'Framework for the Preparation and Presentation of Financial Statements'.

58. Auditors consider the qualitative aspects of financial reporting in the context of IFRSs and in particular the selection of accounting policies. When auditors identify that an entity has adopted an accounting policy that was not available to it under UK/ROI GAAP, where it could have continued to apply its existing policy, they draw such circumstances to the attention of those charged with governance.

59. The disclosure requirements in respect of the transition to IFRSs, as required by paragraphs 38-43 of IFRS 1, are substantial. As well as auditing the disclosures given by the entity for compliance with the standard, auditors consider whether the entity's approach to disclosure leads to information that is as clear as possible, given the complexity of the exercise. The overall requirement for fair presentation will be of particular importance in the transition period.

ISA (UK & Ireland) 300 'Planning an Audit of Financial Statements'

60. The introduction of IFRSs is likely to be a major factor in the planning of the audit for the year of implementation. Auditors consider how their audit plan is likely to be affected by the change and how to ensure that all members of the audit team are fully briefed and have sufficient knowledge of IFRSs.

Initial risk assessment at the planning stage

61. Audit risk is likely to be increased in the year of transition to IFRSs. As part of their risk assessment process, auditors ascertain by enquiry of management:

- The major changes likely to the entity's financial statements due to the introduction of IFRSs.

- The impact of the introduction of IFRSs on key systems which generate specific accounting information.

- The extent to which fair value accounting has been adopted for certain items, including financial instruments.

62. Auditors also direct their enquiries more specifically in order to understand management's views on:

- Any increased risk of error in accounting information or other information supporting items in the financial statements.

- The potential impact, if any, on the going concern basis.

- The possible impact on specific financial statement amounts or disclosures.

63. The auditor's conclusions from these initial inquiries may be that no particular procedures need to be performed, that is, where the entity's management considers that the effect on the financial statements is minimal and the auditor's judgment is that, based on its knowledge of the business and its systems, the conclusion is reasonable. In the far more likely situation where management identifies the introduction of IFRSs as being of potential financial statement significance, the auditors obtain an understanding of management's impact analysis and detailed plans to deal with the introduction of IFRSs.

64. In considering the entity's 'impact analysis', the auditors might, for example, enquire about factors such as:

- Whether the impact analysis was carried out systematically and the quality of records documenting that process.

- Whether all significant business units were involved in the process.

- The skills, knowledge and experience of the staff involved in the impact analysis.

65. In considering management's statements about plans and implementation progress, auditors might, for example, consider whether:

- Financial reporting and systems replacement/modification projects are being led by staff with experience of such projects (whether internal or provided by external advisors).

- Resources have been committed to the projects identified, whether relating to systems changes or financial reporting issues.

- Information or test results are available, whether generated internally or obtained from external IT suppliers, on relevant accounting systems.

- Timescales have been allocated to the projects identified.

- Progress against plans is being monitored rigorously and regularly.

- Slippage against the plan has resulted in positive action or reprioritisation

Lack of any of the above may indicate a higher risk that plans or progress reports are unreliable.

Comparatives and opening balances

66. At the planning stage auditors consider the work required on opening balances and comparatives. (See the discussion on ISA (UK and Ireland) 510 and ISA (UK and Ireland) 710 below.)

ISA (UK & Ireland) 315 'Obtaining an Understanding of the Entity and Its Environment and Assessing the Risks of Material Misstatement' and ISA (UK & Ireland) 330 'The Auditor's Procedures in Response to Assessed Risks'

67. The increase in overall audit risk in the year of transition of an entity to IFRSs is likely to be substantial (and some increase is also possible in the periods leading up to the change). Some of the main factors leading to the increase in audit risk are as follows:

- In 2005/6 companies will have limited practical experience of working with IFRSs. The application in the UK and ROI of existing accounting standards is based on experience that has built up over many years; this accumulated knowledge base does not exist for IFRSs.

- One of the major difficulties faced by both preparers and auditors is the identification of all differences between the old and new accounting frameworks. Although UK and ROI accounting standards are, in some ways, similar to IFRSs, there are some major differences, for example in relation to accounting for business combinations, and a large number of smaller differences that are less immediately obvious (so that some may assume some old and new standards are the same when in fact they are not). Moreover, the interaction between different IFRSs, for example IFRS 1 and the other IFRSs, is complex.

- Major changes may be necessary to financial reporting systems and the controls over them, in order to produce the necessary information for IFRS financial statements. As well as increasing the risk of error, this also increases the opportunity for fraud.

- There may be opportunities for aggressive earnings management by companies. For example, management may wish to set an advantageous starting figure for earnings under IFRSs in the year of transition, conscious of the implications for future years. This could involve setting the figure as *low* as possible in a year of such a major change, while attention is focussed on the changeover itself, so giving leeway for flattering increases in earnings in future years.

- Recent changes to IFRSs, some of which are being introduced into UK/ROI GAAP as well, bring new challenges for auditors and preparers. In particular, the valuation of certain items, such as employee share options and non-traded financial instruments, are subject to many variables and can be subjective.

- Entities applying IFRSs for the first time are required by IFRS 1 (paragraph 41) to distinguish between GAAP changes and the correction of prior period errors when describing the changes to their financial statements. There is a risk that past errors may not be disclosed as such.

- There are a number of possible consequences of implementing IFRSs, including changes to a company's tax base and charge, restrictions on or reductions to distributable profits and breaches of accounts-based debt or similar covenants. All these could have substantial implications for the financial statements and even, perhaps, for the ability of the company to remain a going concern.

68. As noted above under ISA (UK and Ireland) 240 and below under ISA (UK and Ireland) 540, directors and managers will need to be aware of the greater risk of error and opportunities for fraud that could arise where an entity has to make major adaptations to its systems or where the systems are functioning incorrectly. The extent of change and the urgency may cause a relaxation of formal testing and program change control procedures.

69. Auditors use the entity's impact analysis and detailed plans for the implementation of IFRSs to aid identification of risks of misstatement in the IFRS financial statements.

70. Auditors consider extending their risk assessment procedures as a result of the introduction of IFRSs and in particular consider:

    (a) making enquiries of any consultants used by the company, (whether internal teams or external consultants), about the success or otherwise of the IFRS conversion process, the problems identified and how they were remedied and the areas of main concern for the business; and

    (b) investigating changes in systems and controls that have been implemented as part of the IFRS conversion project.

ISA (UK & Ireland) 320 'Audit Materiality'[24]

71. The definition of 'material' in IAS 1 'Presentation of Financial Statements' (which is in line with the IASB's 'Framework for the Preparation and Presentation of Financial Statements') is:

    "Omissions or misstatements of items are material if they could, individually or collectively, influence the economic decisions of users taken on the basis of the financial statements. Materiality depends on the size and nature of the omission or misstatement judged in the surrounding circumstances. The size or nature of the item, or a combination of both, could be the determining factor."

72. UK and ROI accounting standards do not define 'materiality' or 'material'. However, the discussion of materiality in the ASB's Statement of Principles (paragraphs 3.28 – 3.32) includes the following:

    "An item of information is material to the financial statements if its misstatement or omission might reasonably be expected to influence the economic decisions of

---

[24] In January 2005 the APB published an exposure draft of a revised version of ISA (UK and Ireland) 320. See www.frc.org.uk/apb for details.

users of those financial statements, including their assessment of management's stewardship.

Whether information is material will depend on the size and nature of the item in question judged in the particular circumstances of the case..."

73. As these definitions of 'material' are not inconsistent with each other auditors adopt the same approach to determining materiality for an audit of IFRS financial statements as for an audit of UK/ROI GAAP financial statements[25]. However, the application of IFRSs may impact the benchmark upon which materiality has been calculated (eg profit before tax may be reduced) giving rise to a potential need to adjust the recording of uncorrected misstatements of prior periods (see section on ISA (UK and Ireland) 520)

74. One aspect to be considered in light of possible pressure on management to achieve a particular result is highlighted by Paragraph 8 of IAS 8 (December 2003), in the context of the application of accounting policies:

"IFRSs set out accounting policies that the IASB has concluded result in financial statements containing relevant and reliable information about the transactions, other events and conditions to which they apply. Those policies need not be applied when the effect of applying them is immaterial. However, it is inappropriate to make, or leave uncorrected, immaterial departures from IFRSs to achieve a particular presentation of an entity's financial position, financial performance or cash flows."

ISA (UK & Ireland) 510 'Initial Engagements – Opening Balances and Continuing Engagements – Opening Balances' and ISA (UK & Ireland) 710 'Comparatives'

Opening balances and comparatives under IFRSs and the impact on the audit

75. The issues of comparatives and opening balances for any particular year's audit are closely linked. It is unlikely to be possible to audit the first financial statements under IFRSs without performing procedures on the opening IFRS balance sheet[26] and then rolling these forward to the 2005 comparative figures and ultimately the 2005 figures themselves. For a 31 December preparer, the opening IFRS balance sheet will be as at 1 January 2004 (ie. the 31 December 2003 balance sheet as previously published under UK/ROI GAAP, but converted to IFRSs).

76. In this context, however, it is important to note that Section 235 of CA 1985 does not bring the comparative figures of the previous year, presented alongside the current period financial statements, within the scope of the auditor's report, nor does the auditor's report make direct reference to the comparative figures. Nevertheless, IAS 1 requires comparative figures to be presented (as they are by UK and Irish company

---

[25] An exception to this is related parties: see paragraph 99 for details.
[26] It is important to distinguish between ISA (UK and Ireland) 510 opening balances, which refers to the current period opening balance sheet, and the opening IFRS balance sheet as required by IFRS 1, which refers to the opening balance sheet, as described here.

law under UK/ROI GAAP) and auditors have specific responsibilities with regard to opening balances to the extent they affect and determine current period figures in the financial statements.

77. Overall, it is unlikely that the usual level of audit work for continuing engagements, as outlined in ISAs UK & Ireland) 510 and 710, will be sufficient to ensure that opening balances in the year of transition to IFRSs are not materially misstated. The additional work required to be carried out will depend on the nature and complexity of the changes on a case-by-case basis. ISA (UK and Ireland) 510 and ISA (UK and Ireland) 710, which deal with the audit of opening balances and comparatives for incoming auditors, provide useful guidance on additional procedures.

78. In light of the expected pressure on time and resources in the 2005 reporting season, auditors are encouraged to carry out relevant procedures on the IFRS opening balance sheet and 2005 comparatives, to the extent these are necessary for completion of the audit on the 2005 financial statements, as early as possible. Companies may wish their auditors to give some level of private or public assurance on 2004 figures. This work will constitute an engagement separate from the statutory audit; however, auditors can use any such work, updated and amended as necessary, for the purposes of the procedures required by ISAs (UK & Ireland) 510 and 710.

The application of IFRS 1

79. Auditors refer to the requirements of IFRS 1 in order to assess whether the directors of the audited entity have dealt with the opening position correctly. Companies that are classed as 'first-time adopters' of IFRSs are those making an explicit and unreserved statement of compliance with IFRSs when presenting their first annual financial statements under IFRSs. Broadly, IFRS 1 requires first-time adopters to prepare an opening balance sheet under IFRSs at the date of transition, which is the beginning of the earliest period for which an entity presents full comparative information under IFRSs in its first IFRS financial statements.[27]

80. The opening IFRS balance sheet should be prepared in accordance with IFRSs that are in force as at the reporting date[28] (IFRSs which are not yet mandatory can also be adopted if early adoption is permitted by the IFRS in question). IFRS 1 therefore requires IFRSs to be applied as if they always had been. The exceptions to this rule are that:

(a) the transitional arrangements in each IFRS should not be followed;

(b) IFRS 1 gives specific exemptions to the general rule on retrospective adjustment for all standards; and

(c) IFRS 1 also prohibits retrospective application of certain IFRSs.

---

[27] Hence, for a 2005 first-time adopter that is a 31 December preparer, the date of transition will be 1 January 2003.

[28] So for 2005 first-time adopters that are 31 December preparers, the reporting date is 31 December 2005.

81. Broadly speaking, entities have a choice in applying some, all, or none of the exemptions to retrospective restatement given in IFRS 1 but must disclose which exemptions have been taken. Auditors consider the completeness and accuracy of the disclosure of the exemptions in the financial statements and consider whether the consequential implications for the opening balance sheet and restated comparatives have been taken into account (for example, if past business combinations have not been restated as permitted by IFRS 1, there may be consequential requirements to amend the opening balance sheet figures for assets and liabilities recognised in the business combination, including goodwill). This will be necessary in order for the auditors to assess whether the closing balance sheet at the reporting date has been properly prepared, not merely to assess whether comparative information has been properly presented.[29]

82. Auditors consider whether only differences between UK requirements and IFRSs are included as reconciling items in the opening balance sheet and comparatives. In particular, corrections of errors and revisions of estimates in past results should not be included as reconciling items from UK/ROI GAAP to IFRSs, but should be accounted for as required by IAS 8.

Different first-time adoption dates

83. In the light of implementation difficulties regarding, for example, distributable profits, it is highly likely that many UK listed groups may choose not to move their parent and subsidiary individual financial statements to IFRSs at the same time as their consolidated financial statements. Similarly, where there is a "good reason"[30] some subsidiaries may remain under UK GAAP while the rest of the group's subsidiaries move over to IFRSs. IFRS 1 gives guidance (at paragraphs 24-25) on situations where parents and subsidiaries become first-time adopters at different times.

ISA (UK & Ireland) 520 'Analytical Procedures'

Analytical procedures as risk assessment and substantive procedures

84. Whilst analytical procedures are still likely to be important to the auditor, the lack of historical information in relation to a particular entity arising through the wholesale change in its accounting basis means that additional care will be required in the auditor's use of analytical techniques. As well as a lack of historical data for a particular company or group, industry figures and information may not be available other than on a UK/ROI GAAP basis. A related issue is that some IFRSs require prospective application, so there will be no restated comparative figures for analytical review purposes. Analytical procedures might therefore be of reduced effectiveness throughout the audit.

85. Auditors consider whether they need to perform additional, alternative, substantive procedures in order to compensate for the inability to carry out certain analytical

---

[29] IFRS 1 was published with application guidance which will be useful to both preparers and auditors in applying IFRS 1 in practice.

[30] See paragraph 41.

procedures that have been used as substantive procedures in the past. The usefulness of analytical procedures in the overall review of the financial statements may also be weakened and lead the auditors to conclude that additional alternative procedures are necessary.

Analytical procedures in the overall review at the end of the audit

Uncorrected misstatements

86. One of the principal considerations when carrying out the overall review of the financial statements is "The potential impact on the financial statements of the aggregate of uncorrected misstatements (including those arising from bias in making accounting estimates) identified during the course of the audit and the preceding period's audit, if any". Where the adoption of IFRSs gives rise to a lower level of materiality than that used under UK/ROI GAAP the auditors consider whether their evaluation of misstatements identified in the prior year audit needs to be revised.

87. The reference to the uncorrected misstatements of previous periods is of particular relevance in the context of paragraph 41 of IAS 8:

> "Financial statements do not comply with IFRSs if they contain either material errors or immaterial errors made intentionally to achieve a particular presentation of an entity's financial position, financial performance or cash flows. Potential current period errors discovered in that period are corrected before the financial statements are authorised for issue. However, material errors are sometimes not discovered until a subsequent period, and these prior period errors are corrected in the comparative information presented in the financial statements for that subsequent period."

88. The decision to leave errors uncorrected in the prior period will have been based on an assessment of materiality in the context of UK/ROI GAAP. That assessment will now be made in the context of IFRS figures. Auditors, therefore, examine the schedule of unadjusted differences from the prior period audit and consider whether retrospective restatement is necessary because of a combination of the requirements of IAS 8 in this respect and the reassessment of materiality in the context of the IFRS figures. As well as quantitative aspects, auditors also consider qualitative factors in forming their judgment.

89. One point of difference between IFRSs and UK/ROI GAAP is in relation to how errors are corrected. IAS 8 (revised December 2003) requires all errors to be corrected by prior period adjustment. Accounting standards only relate to material items, so by definition IAS 8 is referring to all material errors. The UK standard, FRS 3 'Reporting Financial Performance', requires only 'fundamental errors' to be corrected in this way, all others being corrected through the profit and loss account in the period in which they are discovered.[31] Auditors consider whether any errors discovered during the

---

[31] The previous version of IAS 1 made a distinction between fundamental errors and other material prior period errors. The distinction has been eliminated because the definition of fundamental error was difficult to interpret consistently.

course of the audit of the first IFRS accounts, which relate to prior periods, should be corrected by prior period adjustment. As required by IFRS 1, any restatement of errors made under previous GAAP should be clearly differentiated (in the entity's explanation of the transition to IFRSs) from items relating to the restatement of prior year comparatives to comply with IFRSs.

ISA (UK & Ireland) 540 'Audit of Accounting Estimates'[32]

Errors vs. changes in estimate

90. Accounting estimates are dealt with in IAS 1 and IAS 8 'Accounting Policies, Changes in Accounting Estimates and Errors'. The IAS 8 definitions of 'changes in accounting estimates' and 'prior period errors' are fundamental to the decisions that management have to make when differentiating between circumstances giving rise to either a retrospective restatement of an error, or prospective application of a change in an accounting estimate.

91. Care should be taken that management does not use hindsight when assessing the calculation of estimates for comparative information as IFRS 1 specifically prohibits the restatement of estimates at the date of transition to IFRSs or in comparative figures, unless objective evidence is available to show that the estimates were in error. The principle set out in IFRS 1 is that an entity's estimates under IFRSs at the date of transition to IFRSs shall be consistent with estimates made for the same date under previous GAAP (after adjustments to reflect any differences in accounting policies), unless there is objective evidence that those estimates were in error.

92. Where IFRSs require estimates to be made that were not required under UK/ROI GAAP, the lack of track record and management experience in making such estimates will lead to greater risk of misstatement. Auditors consider whether additional audit procedures are required with regard to such estimates.

Disclosure of estimation uncertainty

93. IAS 1, at paragraph 116, requires disclosure in the financial statements of information about the key assumptions concerning the future and other key sources of estimation uncertainty at the balance sheet date that have a significant risk of causing a material adjustment to the carrying amounts of assets and liabilities within the next financial year.[33] These disclosures relate to the estimates that require management's most difficult, subjective or complex judgments. The disclosures required by IAS 1 are different to, and may be more extensive than, those required by paragraph 55(b) of FRS 18. The Basis for Conclusions to IAS 1 indicates the IASB's expectation that disclosure in accordance with this requirement would be made in respect of relatively few assets or liabilities (or classes of them).

---

[32] In January 2005 the APB published an exposure draft of a revised version of ISA (UK and Ireland) 540. See www.frc.org.uk/apb for details.

[33] This disclosure requirement does not apply to assets and liabilities measured at fair value based on recently observed market prices.

94. IAS 1, at paragraph 113, also requires an entity to disclose in its financial statements the judgments, apart from those involving estimations, management has made in applying the entity's accounting policies that have the most significant effect on the amounts recognised in the financial statements, for example whether the substance of the relationship between the entity and a special purpose entity indicates that the special purpose entity is controlled by the entity. Auditors consider extending their evaluations of these types of disclosure, bearing in mind they go beyond the requirements of FRS 18.

ISA (UK and Ireland) 545 'Auditing Fair Value Measurements and Disclosures'

95. IFRSs require certain assets and liabilities to be recognised at fair value rather than historical cost. Incorporating more fair values in financial statements (also reflected in recent changes to ASB standards), may give rise to difficulties for auditors, particularly on transition to IFRSs, for example:

- Paragraphs 16-19 of IFRS 1 permit companies to elect to use fair value at transition as deemed cost for some assets, such amounts will not previously have been audited.

- IFRS 2 'Share-based Payment' does not prescribe particular techniques for valuing employee (and other) share options, but sets out general requirements for valuation, which require management and possibly external expert judgment in selecting a model and adapting it to the particular circumstances. This is in the context of several complicating factors, such as the fact that established models are not necessarily suited to non-traded options, a lack of established techniques and standards against which the auditors can judge an expert's work and the difficulty in obtaining and assessing some of the inputs to any valuation model, such as share price volatility.

- IFRS 3 'Business Combinations' and IAS 38 'Intangible Assets' require many more intangibles to be fair-valued separately from goodwill than is currently the case under FRS 10. Auditing valuations of unique intangibles is likely to be particularly difficult due to subjective assumptions and the potential to use different techniques which might give different answers.

- Fair value information is required for leases of land and buildings under IAS 17 'Leases' (Paragraphs 14-19). On first-time adoption, entities may need to look back many years to obtain the information, in turn raising potential audit issues.

96. Even though the EC has "carved out" some aspects of fair values from IAS 39 'Financial Instruments: Recognition and Measurement', fair value measurements are still required for many financial instruments.[34] Application guidance has been issued

---

[34] In June 2005 the IASB published an amendment to the fair value option in IAS 39. In July 2005, the European Commission's Accounting Regulatory Committee supported the Commission's proposal to endorse the "IAS 39 Fair Value Option", which should lead to a removal of one part of the carve-out, but (as at November 2005) the difference with respect to hedge accounting remains.

by the IASB on IAS 39; guidance has also been issued by the ASB on whether and to what extent the full version of IAS 39 can be applied in Europe.[35] Given the complexity of the issue, auditors consider whether an entity has made full and clear disclosure of the extent to which it has applied IAS 39.[36]

97. Guidance on the audit of fair values in financial statements has been introduced for the first time in the UK and Ireland by ISA (UK and Ireland) 545. The standard anticipates the types of difficulties noted above and attention is drawn, in particular, to the following paragraphs of the standard.

- Paragraph 10 requires the auditors to assess the management process for determining fair values and the controls over it, recognising management's primary responsibility for producing the relevant fair value information.

- Paragraphs 17 and 56 require consideration by auditors of the entity's use and disclosure of fair value information according to the relevant financial reporting framework. The issue of disclosure is particularly important as several of the standards discussed above have substantial disclosure requirements.

- Paragraph 24 deals with situations where alternative valuation methodologies are permitted by accounting standards, requiring auditors to consider the suitability of those used.

- The importance of the work of an expert in the context of fair values is highlighted in Paragraphs 29-32.

- Paragraph 39 addresses the auditor's evaluation of the significant assumptions used by management.

ISA (UK & Ireland) 550 'Related Parties'

98. Auditing standards on related parties are closely linked to the underlying accounting framework. From 2005 two accounting frameworks will be in use in the UK and Ireland – IFRS (including IAS 24 "Related party disclosures") and UK/ROI GAAP (including FRS 8 "Related party disclosures"). To accommodate the differences between the two frameworks, ISA (UK and Ireland) 550 has separate parts for use where the financial statements being audited are intended to comply with IAS 24 and FRS 8 respectively.

99. Although the requirements of IAS 24 and FRS 8 are broadly similar, there are a number of differences that may have an impact on the auditor's evaluation of the adequacy of the disclosure of related party transactions. These differences include:

---

[35] This guidance is available on the ASB website at http://www.asb.org.uk/images/uploaded/documents/ASB%20Guidance%20on%20Applic%20of%20IAS%2039%20-%20attach%20to%20262.pdf.

[36] The FSA wrote to listed companies in October 2004 warning them on clarity of disclosure on this issue. The letter is at http://www.fsa.gov.uk/pubs/ceo/ceo_letter_25oct04.pdf.

- The use of different, but similar, definitions of terms such as related party transaction.

- IAS 24 requires disclosure of an outstanding balance between an entity and its related parties even if there have been no transactions between those parties within the reporting period. FRS 8 does not require such disclosure.

- IAS 24 requires the disclosure of related party transactions and outstanding balances in separate financial statements of a parent, investor or venturer. FRS 8 provides an exemption for such disclosure.

- IAS 24 does not reflect that aspect of the FRS 8 definition of materiality which, uniquely, requires assessment of materiality from the point of view of the related party as well as the point of view of the reporting entity.

- Both standards require disclosures of controlling parties. IAS 24 does not contemplate the situation where an entity does not know the identity of its ultimate controlling party and, therefore, does not have the requirement, which is included in FRS 8, to disclose that fact.

ISA (UK & Ireland) 560 'Subsequent Events'

100. IAS 10 'Events After the Balance Sheet Date' and the recent UK/ROI standard FRS 21 of the same title are substantially the same as SSAP 17 'Post-Balance Sheet Events'. The main difference, which has been facilitated by a change in company law, relates to the treatment of dividends declared after the end of an accounting period but before the accounts are approved. Under UK/ROI GAAP, until now, these have been treated as a liability in the accounts of the period just passed, but in future they will only be disclosed as they do not meet the recognition criteria of a liability at the period end.

101. FRS 21 (along with enabling changes to UK legislation) will change UK accounting practice to bring it into line with IAS 10. This will affect single entity accounts and so may affect a parent company in a group which relies on the receipt of dividends from subsidiaries to distribute on to its own shareholders. The change in treatment of dividends paid may affect the period in which the receipt of the dividend can be recorded in the parent's 'relevant accounts'. This may be relevant to the assessment of compliance with laws and regulations under ISA (UK and Ireland) 250 Section A as discussed above.

ISA (UK & Ireland) 570 'Going Concern'

Foreseeable future

102. IAS 1 requires that management make an assessment of the entity's ability to continue as a going concern. IAS 1 addresses going concern on a similar but not identical basis to FRS 18 'Accounting Policies', the relevant UK/ROI standard. Guidance regarding 'the future period to which the directors have paid particular attention in assessing going concern' differs slightly between IAS 1 and FRS 18, as do the detailed disclosure requirements.

103. It is technically possible for management to meet the requirements of IAS 1 by looking forward 12 months from the balance sheet date rather than 12 months from the date of approval of the financial statements. However, this is only possible in circumstances where there is no other information available about the future. If, in such circumstances, the directors do not disclose the length of the future period to which they have paid particular attention, ISA (UK and Ireland) 570 requires the auditors to disclose the length of the period considered in an emphasis of matter paragraph within their report.

104. For UK listed companies, Listing Rule 9.8.6R(3) requires the annual report and accounts to include a statement by the directors that the business is a going concern with supporting assumptions or qualifications as necessary. The rule refers to guidance on the interpretation of this point issued by ICAEW[37]. This guidance is closely aligned to the requirements of ISA (UK and Ireland) 570. It is unlikely that any reason will arise for management to change their approach to the assessment of going concern due to the switch from FRS 18 to IAS 1.

Borrowing powers and debt covenants

105. Listed companies may have limits, in their Articles of Association or other constitutional documents, on the extent to which they can borrow funds without obtaining specific shareholder consent. These provisions are usually expressed by reference to the consolidated financial statements, generally an adjusted net assets position. The legal drafting usually uses, as the starting point before adjustments, balances on share capital and reserves as a proxy for net assets.

106. Similar, but more extensive, financial covenants are often found in debt instruments and borrowing agreements, including those for straightforward bank loans and overdrafts. As well as limiting borrowing, these will often include limits on ratios between interest and earnings and even absolute minimum levels for tangible net assets.

107. Both of these types of arrangement may be affected by the introduction of IFRSs through:

(a) increases in the type and extent of liabilities recognised, for example in relation to financial instruments measured at fair value; and

(b) changes in the value of net assets, again through the recognition of new assets or liabilities or the use of new measurement bases.

108. Where applicable, the auditors consider whether the directors have made provision to obtain approval for an increase in the company's borrowing powers from the shareholders in general meeting in sufficient time for the introduction of IFRSs. In the case of financial covenants in debt agreements, auditors consider whether clauses exist that allow the use of 'frozen GAAP' (i.e. GAAP that was being used when the

---

[37] Guidance on Going Concern and Financial Reporting for directors of listed companies in the United Kingdom, ICAEW November 1994. http://www.icaew.co.uk/index.cfm?AUB=TB21_67522.MNXI_67522

agreement was signed is continued for the life of the agreement for covenant purposes, ignoring new accounting requirements); where there is no clause allowing the use of 'frozen GAAP', the auditors consider, in their review of going concern, whether any necessary renegotiation of covenants has taken place in good time and any risk of default by the borrower or termination by the lender as a result of the change in the financial statements caused by the introduction of IFRSs.

109. Where any breach of an undertaking to a lender has taken place before the year end, the auditors consider whether the liability to which it relates has been treated correctly as current or non-current in the balance sheet, depending on the requirements of Paragraphs 65-67 of IAS 1.

ISA (UK & Ireland) 580 'Management Representations'

110. In the periods leading up to the period of transition, auditors may in many cases require, as part of their audit evidence, management assurances on matters such as the potential impact of the introduction of IFRSs on the business. The auditors consider obtaining written representation on these points.

111. In the year of transition, auditors may wish to use the management representation letter to clarify the responsibilities of the directors in relation to the transition to IFRSs. Specific representations are likely to be required by auditors that the directors have obtained all necessary information from subsidiaries that have not adopted IFRSs, to enable adjustments to be made to their financial statements for the purposes of consolidation into the group accounts.

112. Auditors consider the need to obtain representations on management's intentions for future actions, where these will have a direct impact on the accounting treatment of certain items. For example, the treatment of non-current assets held for sale arises from management intention to sell the assets.

ISA (UK & Ireland) 600 'Using the Work of Another Auditor'

113. Co-operation between the principal auditors and the other auditors will be vital in the year of transition to IFRSs. This is particularly the case where the subsidiaries (and parent) are following UK/ROI or another national GAAP in their financial statements, but the group financial statements are prepared under IFRSs. While this is no different, in theory, from those existing situations where a UK/ROI parent owns foreign subsidiaries that report locally under other accounting frameworks, in 2005 there may be substantially more group companies than in the past preparing their statutory accounts under one accounting framework, but reporting for consolidation purposes to the parent under another.

114. Principal auditors consider the extent to which they will need to instruct the other auditors about the need to perform additional procedures and provide information relevant to the transition. The principal auditors also consider whether they will need to perform further procedures in relation to the other auditors' work, which may require additional visits to the other auditors. The principal auditors may wish to ascertain whether other auditors have made enquiries about the introduction of IFRSs in relation

to the entities they are auditing, particularly in those subsidiaries which comprise major parts of the group's business. This will be relevant whether or not the subsidiary entities in question are required to follow IFRSs; their results will still be required to be included in the group accounts of a parent following IFRSs.

ISA (UK & Ireland) 620 'Using the Work of an Expert'

115. There is likely to be a wider range of circumstances in which auditors consider the need to use the work of an expert because of the increased use of valuations in IFRSs as noted under ISA (UK and Ireland) 545 above.

116. Auditors consider the need to use the work of an expert as early as possible in the planning process in the year of transition, to ensure that expert advice can be obtained in a timely fashion. However specialised the work of an expert, auditors assess it and consider the impact of this assessment on the audit report in the context of ISA (UK and Ireland) 620.

ISA (UK & Ireland) 700 'The Auditor's Report on Financial Statements'

'True and fair'/'present fairly'

117. IAS 1 requires management to prepare financial statements that 'present fairly' the financial position, performance and cash flows of the company. However, the CA 1985 continues to require the auditors to report whether the financial statements give a true and fair view. (A company following UK/ROI GAAP will still be required to prepare financial statements that present a true and fair view.) New Section 262(2A) of the CA 1985 makes clear that the terms "present fairly" and "true and fair view" should be read as having the same meaning. There is, therefore, no discrepancy between the standard management brings to bear in its preparation of IFRS financial statements and the auditor's opinion on them.[38]

118. Section 235 of CA 1985 includes a new requirement (Section 235(1A)) for the auditor's report to identify the financial reporting framework applied in the preparation of the financial statements. It is important to appreciate the context in which this reference is made, the DTI Guidance notes that "The requirement that an audit opinion states whether the annual or consolidated accounts give a true and fair view in accordance with the relevant financial reporting framework clarifies the context in which the audit opinion was given, it does not represent a restriction of the scope of that opinion".

Reference to the financial reporting framework

119. The requirement for IFRSs to be adopted for use in the EU gives rise to a potential for differences to exist between IFRSs as issued by the IASB and IFRSs as adopted for use in the European Union. While there has been considerable attention given to IAS 39 'Financial Instruments: Recognition and Measurement' (where the EC has adopted

---

[38] A view supported by the Financial Reporting Council (FRC) in its paper "The Implications of New Accounting and Auditing Standards for the "True and Fair View" and Auditors' Responsibilities".

a so-called 'carved-out' version), the difference between the effective date of a standard established by IASB and when that standard is adopted into EU law, for the purposes of the IAS Regulation, may also give rise to further differences in the future.

120. Differences between IFRSs as issued by the IASB and IFRSs adopted for use in the European Union raise an issue concerning the description of the financial reporting framework a company is following in both the financial statements and the auditor's report thereon. The APB's view is for auditors to express an opinion in the terms 'true and fair view, in accordance with IFRSs as adopted for use in the European Union'.[39]

121. Many companies will be in a position of complying with both IFRSs as issued by the IASB and IFRSs as adopted for use in the European Union[40]. Consequently, the entity may also wish the auditors to express an opinion in terms of 'true and fair view, in accordance with IFRSs'. In these circumstances, it is preferable to state separately a second opinion with regard to full IFRSs to avoid confusing readers of the auditor's report and to leave intact the opinion required by law on compliance with IFRSs as adopted by the EU. The example auditors' reports set out in Bulletin 2005/4 'Auditor's Reports on Financial Statements' illustrate this point (see for example Appendix 1, Example 7).

122. For a minority of companies compliance with IFRSs as issued by the IASB may not ensure compliance with IFRSs as adopted for use in the European Union. Such situations will require auditors to consider carefully how to refer to the financial reporting framework in their audit reports. Auditors may need to take legal advice depending on the precise circumstances. However, the overriding requirement, in all circumstances, is for the *company* to provide full and clear disclosure of the accounting policies that have been adopted, so that users of financial statements can make an informed assessment about what the company has done and how its results are affected by the decisions it has made. Consequently, auditors consider carefully the disclosure made and, where it is in their view deficient:

(a) discuss the relevant disclosures with those charged with governance; and

(b) consider the implications for their report.

---

[39] This is also the consensus view that has emerged across Europe following a consultation paper issued by FEE (the Fédération des Experts Comptables Européens). More details can be found at www.fee.be.

[40] In relation to IAS 39 the ASB has produced guidance on what it believes to be the correct approach to the situation in the UK and Ireland. It is assumed, for the purposes of this Bulletin, that most companies:
(a) will follow the more restrictive hedge accounting rules in the IASB's IAS 39, as recommended by the ASB; and
(b) will not use the 'full fair value' option in the IASB's IAS 39 (although the European Commission may be about to endorse a revised version of the full fair value option which will remove this particular difference).
Consequently, the majority of companies are expected to be in compliance with both full IFRSs and the EU carved-out version.

THE AUDITING PRACTICES BOARD

Group accounts and the parent's own individual financial statements

123. As described in the ISA (UK and Ireland) 250 section of this Bulletin, the introduction of IFRSs may give rise to issues regarding the presentation of the parent company financial statements where different accounting frameworks are applied and/or the Section 230 exemption is applied. To address this, companies may decide to present the financial statements in separate sections of the annual report.

124. Where companies adopt the separate sections approach, separate audit reports will be prepared for the group and parent company financial statements and, as recommended by the DTI Guidance, where advantage has been taken of the Section 230 exemption, the reference to the framework used in the auditor's report needs to make clear that it is "IFRSs as adopted for use in the European Union *and as applied in accordance with the provisions of the 1985 Act*".[41] An illustrative example of an auditor's report on parent company accounts prepared under IFRSs and using the Section 230 exemption is set out in Appendix 1, Example 11 of Bulletin 2006/6.

Statements of compliance with and departures from IFRSs

125. An unqualified opinion may be expressed only when the auditors are able to conclude that the financial statements give a true and fair view in accordance with the identified financial reporting framework. In all other circumstances the auditors are required to disclaim an opinion or to issue a qualified or adverse opinion. Accordingly, the auditors do not express an unqualified opinion that financial statements have been prepared in accordance with IFRSs if the financial statements contain any departure from IFRSs and the departure has a material effect on the financial statements.

126. When the auditors report on whether the financial statements have been prepared in accordance with IFRSs and those financial statements contain a material departure from IFRSs, such a departure results in a disagreement with management regarding the acceptability of the accounting policies selected, the method of their application, or the adequacy of disclosures in the financial statements[42]. In the light of paragraph 41 of IAS 8, auditors consider whether failure to correct misstatements produces financial statements that are so seriously misleading that an adverse opinion is required, rather than a qualified opinion.

Limitations of scope

127. As noted in the section on ISA (UK and Ireland) 250 individual companies within the group may continue to prepare their financial statements under UK/ROI GAAP and adjustments required to bring the group financial statements into line with IFRSs may be made only as consolidation adjustments. In such circumstances, the auditors pay

---

[41] See Paragraph 43 regarding the need to explain the company's approach.

[42] Paragraph 17 of IAS 1 (revised December 2003) allows an entity to depart from the requirements of a standard in the rare circumstances that management concludes that compliance with the requirement would be so misleading that it would conflict with the objective of fair presentation. A departure from the requirements of a particular IFRS made under the provisions of paragraph 17 of IAS 1does not constitute a departure from IFRSs for this purpose.

particular attention to whether this approach is adequate in order to permit the auditors to form an opinion on the consolidated financial statements.

128. Given the pervasive nature of the change to the basis of accounting, it may be the case that the auditors will be subject to a limitation of scope if the entity simply adjusts the information provided in consolidation schedules by accounting systems based on UK/ ROI GAAP. Auditors, therefore, assess whether the company has put in place new or adapted accounting systems to record the information required for consolidated financial statements to be prepared under IFRSs to the necessary level of detail and accuracy for the auditors to obtain sufficient audit evidence. Where this is not the case, the auditors consider the implications for their audit report.

ISA (UK & Ireland) 720 "Other Information in Documents Containing Audited Financial Statements"

129. Companies that are subject to the mandatory application of adopted IFRSs are unlikely to wish to wait for the first period of application (accounting periods beginning on or after 1 January 2005) to communicate with users of their financial statements about the likely impact of the change. The Committee of European Securities Regulators (CESR) has issued a Recommendation to regulators to give guidance for listed companies on this point.[43] The FSA has drawn the attention of publicly traded companies to the Recommendation in an article in its publication LIST!, and in its letter to Chief Executives dated 15 April 2005.

130. Commentary following the publication of the CESR recommendation has indicated that there are likely to be variations in practice in the periods leading up to 2005:

(a) some companies may provide disclosures about the transition to IFRSs at the same time and alongside their 2004 published interim and annual financial statements; whereas

(b) other companies may provide such information separately and at different times.

131. Where such information is issued in conjunction with the financial statements, the auditors have regard to the requirements of ISA (UK and Ireland) 720. Where companies disclose such information in the notes to the financial statements, the auditors consider the implications for their report.[44]

132. Paragraph 36 of IFRS 1 requires one year of comparatives to be given under IFRSs, paragraph 37 considers the situation where older comparative financial information is also presented under the previous GAAP of the entity. Such presentation is permitted,

---

[43] The recommendation can be downloaded from the CESR website at www.cesr-eu.org.Broadly, the CESR guidance suggests various "milestones" of disclosure leading up to 2005. The milestones coincide with the publication of the 2003 annual financial statements, the 2004 annual financial statements, the 2005 interim financial statements and the 2005 annual financial statements. At each milestone, publicly traded companies are encouraged to provide investors with certain specified information.

[44] IAPS 1014, published by the IAASB, provides guidance on this matter.

but the standard requires it to be clearly labelled as not being prepared under IFRSs as well as a description to be given of the main adjustments that would be required for the information to be compliant with IFRSs (such adjustments do not need to be quantified).

REVIEW OF INTERIM FINANCIAL INFORMATION UNDER IFRSs

133. This section sets out guidance for auditors undertaking an engagement to review interim financial information in accordance with Bulletin 1999/4 "Review of Interim Financial Information" on interim financial information published before a company's full annual financial statements are published under IFRSs for the first time.

Listing Rules[45]

134. The Listing Rules require that the accounting policies and presentation applied to interim figures must be consistent with those in the latest published annual accounts, save where they are to be changed in the subsequent annual financial statements, in which case the new accounting policies and presentation should be followed, and the changes and reasons therefore should be disclosed in the interim report. Accordingly, for listed companies that are adopting IFRSs in their annual financial statements, interim financial information for the accounting period must also be prepared using the new accounting policies and presentation that follows from the adoption of those standards.

135. The Listing Rules also require that the interim financial information must contain enough information to enable a comparison to be made with the corresponding period of the preceding financial year.

Accounting Standards[45]

136. Under UK/ROI GAAP, the guidance in the ASB's Statement "Interim Reports" is persuasive rather than mandatory. Under IFRSs, however, there are specific requirements governing the content and presentation of interim reports, which may result in significant changes for some companies.

137. The FSA has indicated[46] that, in line with the recommendation of the Committee of European Securities Regulators (CESR), issuers should prepare 2005 interims on the basis of the IFRS measurement and recognition principles that are expected to apply at the year end and comparatives should be restated. The FSA reiterated this view in June 2005[47], stating that this should include IFRSs not yet adopted for use in the EU but which are expected to be adopted in time to be applied to the full 2005 financial statements.

138. IAS 34 "Interim Financial Reporting" has been adopted for use in the EU. However, as the IAS Regulation applies only to annual financial statements, and given the FSA's statement described above, the standard is not considered mandatory in respect of interim financial statements.

---

[45] Reference should be made to the Listing Rules, IFRS 1 and IAS 34 for full details of the specific requirements in relation to interim financial reports.

[46] December 2004 edition of List!

[47] June 2005 edition of List!

139. IAS 34 requires that if an entity's interim financial report is in compliance with it, that fact shall be stated. IAS 34 also states (in paragraph 19) that an interim financial report shall not be described as complying with International Financial Reporting Standards unless it complies with all IFRSs. Thus, the choice of following only endorsed standards or anticipating unendorsed standards in the interim financial statements will mean that care will be required as to what a company claims to be compliant with. The overriding consideration should be for full and clear disclosure of both the standards followed and any uncertainties about the likely adoption of any new or revised IFRSs that are followed before their adoption by the EU.

140. For companies that adopt IAS 34 "Interim Financial Reporting" for their interim report, that standard prescribes the minimum content of an interim financial report and the principles for recognition and measurement in complete or condensed financial statements for an interim period.

141. IFRS 1 requires that, if an entity presents an interim financial report under IAS 34, the interim financial report include reconciliations of the figures reported under previous GAAP to the IFRS figures, giving sufficient detail to enable users to understand the material adjustments to the balance sheet, income statement and cash flow statement. Even where an entity is not reporting under IAS 34, this information is likely to be necessary in order to give a clear picture to the market about the impact of IFRSs.

Guidance for auditors

142. The review procedures outlined in Bulletin 1999/4 assume that the auditor has audited the latest annual financial statements and has reviewed the corresponding financial information for the preceding year. The adoption of IFRSs gives rise to some particular issues in relation to the auditor's review of the interim financial information in the year of adoption. These include the extent to which the auditor needs to perform procedures on:

(a) adjustments made to the opening balance sheet and comparative information to reflect the adoption of IFRSs; and

(b) new systems, or changes to existing systems, that generate financial information needed to reflect IFRSs.

143. Members of the engagement team need to have obtained an understanding of IFRSs commensurate with their responsibilities and sufficient as a whole to perform the engagement competently. When assessing the risks of material misstatements the auditors consider the possible effect of management's lack of experience of accounting under IFRSs (see paragraph 67).

144. Paragraph 20 of Bulletin 1999/4 addresses the situation when the auditor did not audit the previous financial statements. It notes that Auditing Standards require the auditors to obtain sufficient appropriate evidence that opening balances do not contain errors or misstatements which materially affect the current period's financial statements and obtain an understanding of, and where appropriate test, accounting and internal control systems.

145. Similarly, paragraph 38 of Bulletin 1999/4 addresses changes in accounting policy. It states that:

> "Auditors review the adjustments and disclosures made. If the auditors do not consider that accounting policy changes have been properly reflected in the financial information, they consider the implications for their review report."

146. The illustrative procedures set out in Appendix 2 of Bulletin 1999/4 include:

> "(q) considering whether the classification and presentation of disclosures is appropriate and in accordance with Stock Exchange requirements, including consideration of the proper presentation of comparative figures, changes thereto and disclosure thereof."

147. When performing a review of interim financial information for which IFRSs have been adopted for the first time, the auditor considers whether the relevant requirements of paragraphs 38 to 46 of IFRS 1 have been complied with, reviewing the adjustments and disclosures made in accordance therewith. These requirements include disclosure of details of changes to the comparative figures.

148. Guidance for the auditor in relation to opening balances and comparatives and the impact on the audit of the annual financial statements is given in the section of this draft bulletin dealing with ISA (UK and Ireland) 510 and ISA (UK and Ireland) 710. This guidance indicates that overall, it is unlikely that the usual level of audit work for continuing engagements, as outlined in ISAs (UK and Ireland) 510 and 710, will be sufficient to ensure that opening balances in the year of transition to IFRSs are not materially misstated and additional procedures, such as those for incoming auditors (for which guidance is given in ISAs (UK and Ireland) 510 and 710) will be required.

149. Paragraph 75 includes the statement that "It is unlikely to be possible to audit the first financial statements under IFRSs without performing procedures on the opening IFRS balance sheet and then rolling these forward to the 2005 comparative figures and ultimately the 2005 figures themselves." The auditor is unlikely to be able to issue a review conclusion on interim financial information until these procedures have been performed and the auditor has considered the results.

New systems, or changes to existing systems, that give rise to financial information needed to reflect IFRSs

150. In addition to the guidance in paragraph 20 of Bulletin 1999/4, the illustrative procedures set out in Appendix 2 of Bulletin 1999/4 include:

> "(i) enquiring about changes in the company's procedures for recording, classifying and summarising transactions, accumulating information for disclosure, and preparing the financial information;"

The adoption of IFRSs will require some companies to change, or introduce new, accounting systems (e.g. to record the information necessary for compliance with IAS 39 "Financial Instruments: Recognition and Measurement" or IFRS 2 "Share-based

Payment"). As noted above, where this is the case, the considerations for the auditor are similar to those where the auditor did not audit the previous financial statements. In particular, the auditor needs to obtain an understanding of, and where appropriate test, accounting and internal control systems to determine whether those systems provide the necessary information to enable the preparation of financial statements in accordance with the new accounting policies.

Reference to financial reporting framework in the auditor's review report

151. In the section on "Directors' responsibilities" in the review report the auditor adds a paragraph emphasising the fact that IFRSs as adopted in the EU have been followed for the first time. The precise wording adopted by the auditor will depend on the nature and level of disclosure made by the directors in the interim financial report. Example wording of an interim review report is set out in Appendix 2.

152. As noted in Paragraph 139 above differences may exist between the effective date of a standard established by IASB and when that standard is adopted by the European Union, for the purposes of the IAS Regulation. In such circumstances companies may face a situation, when preparing interim information, where an IFRS that has been issued by the IASB has yet to be formally adopted for use in the EU. The company may wish to anticipate the standard's adoption in its interim report, in the expectation that the EC will have adopted the standard in time for its application in the company's annual financial statements.

153. As it is possible that any standard may not be formally adopted within the relevant timescale, this approach carries certain risks, and the auditors discuss the decision with those charged with governance to ensure they are aware of those risks. The position of the particular pronouncement in the adoption process (including existence or otherwise of adoption advice by EFRAG (the European Financial Reporting Advisory Group)) will be relevant in assessing these risks. Again, disclosure by the company on this point should be very clear, to ensure that readers of the interim review understand which standards the company is complying with.

154. Where a company anticipates the adoption of a new or revised IFRS by the EC which has a significant impact on the company's results, the auditors consider the disclosures made by the company and may conclude that it is appropriate to highlight the uncertainty in their report. Illustrative wording of this nature is given in the example interim review report in Appendix 2.

Reporting timetable

155. As noted in paragraph 54 the FSA has given companies a concession relating to the timing of the publication of their first set of half yearly accounts under IFRSs.

Appendix 1

Equivalent Legislative References for Northern Ireland and Comparative Legislative References for the Republic of Ireland.

Legislative references in Northern Ireland

The legal requirements in Northern Ireland are very similar to those in Great Britain. The following table shows the corresponding references to those contained in the Bulletin in relation to Great Britain.

Legislative references in the Republic of Ireland

The principal legislation relating to the form and content of group accounts is contained in the Companies (Amendment) Act 1986 and the European Communities (Companies: Group Accounts) Regulations 1992 (SI 201of 1992), which implement the EU Seventh Directive and amend certain provisions of the Companies Acts 1963 to (then) 1990 relating to group accounts.

Implementation of the IAS Regulation in the Republic of Ireland follows a broadly equivalent approach to that in the United Kingdom, with the exception that application of the requirement to prepare accounts following IFRS has been deferred until 2007 in the case of listed debt securities. The following table shows the comparative legislative references to those contained in this Bulletin in relation to Great Britain.

Bulletin Paragraph Reference	GB Legislation Reference (all references to Companies Act 1985)	Equivalent NI Legislative Reference	Comparative ROI Legislative Reference
4	The Companies Act 1985 (International Accounting Standards and Other Accounting Amendments) Regulations 2004 (Statutory Instrument 2004/2947) - *Implement the IAS Regulation, the Accounts Modernisation and Fair Value Directives.*	The Companies (1986 Order) (International Accounting Standards and Other Accounting Amendments) Regulations (Northern Ireland) 2004 (Statutory Rule 2004/496)	European Communities (International Financial Reporting Standards and Miscellaneous Amendments) Regulations 2005, SI 116 of 2005. European Communities (Fair Value Accounting) Regulation 2004, SI 765 of 2004
8(c)	The Companies Act 1985	The Companies (Northern Ireland) Order 1986	The Companies Acts 1963 to 2003.
27	Schedule 4A CA 1985	Schedule 4A of the Companies (Northern Ireland) Order 1986	Schedule Part 1, Companies (Amendment) Act 1986

Bulletin Paragraph Reference	GB Legislation Reference (all references to Companies Act 1985)	Equivalent NI Legislative Reference	Comparative ROI Legislative Reference
34	S 227 – requirement to produce consolidated accounts companies	Article 235	S 150 Companies Act 1963
34	S 255A –requirement to produce consolidated accounts banks and insurance companies	Article 263A	S 150 Companies Act 1963
39	S 227C(1) requirement that the directors of a parent company should ensure that all the individual companies (including the parent) within a group follow the same accounting framework "except to the extent that in their opinion there are good reasons for not doing so" .	Article 235C (1)	S 150 Companies Act 1963
39 (footnote 15)	S 227C (5) –provision of partial exemption re. S 227C(1)	Article 235C (5)	S 150(C) (1) Companies Act 1963, as amended by European Communities (International Financial Reporting Standards and Miscellaneous Amendments) Regulations 2005
42	S 230 – publication exemption for Profit and Loss account.	Article 238	S 3(2) Companies (Amendment) Act 1986
42 (footnote 16)	S 261 (2) – publication exemption – notes to Profit and Loss	Article 269 (2)	Schedule Part IV 23 Companies (Amendment) Act 1986
44	S 240 (2) – requirement for consolidated and individual accounts to be published together	Article 248 (2)	S 150 Companies Act 1963
45	S 226(5) decision to switch to IFRS irreversible except where companies and groups cease to be publicly traded.	Article 234 (5)	S 148 (5) (b) and (c) Companies Act 1963, as amended by European Communities (International Financial Reporting Standards and Miscellaneous Amendments) Regulations 2005

Bulletin Paragraph Reference	GB Legislation Reference (all references to Companies Act 1985)	Equivalent NI Legislative Reference	Comparative ROI Legislative Reference
45	S 227(6) – decision to switch to IFRS irreversible except where company becomes a subsidiary of an undertaking that does not prepare its accounts in accordance with IFRS.	Article 234 (5) and Article 235 (6)	S 148 (5) (a) Companies Act 1963, as amended by European Communities (International Financial Reporting Standards and Miscellaneous Amendments) Regulations 2005
47	S 237 (1) – auditors required to investigate whether proper accounting records kept	Article 245(1)	S 194 Companies Act 1990
49	S 263 – laws relating to distributions	Article 271	Part IV Companies Act 1983
76	S 235 – comparatives not within scope of auditor's report	Article 243	S 193 Companies Act 1990
117	S 262 (2A) – terms – "present fairly" and "true and fair view" read as having the same meaning.	Article 270 (2A)	Schedule 1, 1(B) – European Communities (International Financial Reporting Standards and Miscellaneous Amendments) Regulations 2005
118	S 235 (1A) – auditor's report to identify financial reporting framework applied in the preparation of the financial statements	Article 243 (1A)	S 8 (4) Companies Act 1990, as amended by European Communities (International Financial Reporting Standards and Miscellaneous Amendments) Regulations 2005

Appendix 2

Example Review Report

INDEPENDENT REVIEW REPORT TO XYZ PLC

Introduction

We have been instructed by the company to review the financial information for the [three months] [six months] [nine months] ended ... which comprises [specify primary financial statements and the related notes that have been reviewed].[48] We have read the other information contained in the interim report and considered whether it contains any apparent misstatements or material inconsistencies with the financial information.

Directors' responsibilities

The interim report, including the financial information contained therein, is the responsibility of, and has been approved by the directors. The directors are responsible for preparing the interim report in accordance with the Listing Rules of the Financial Services Authority.

As disclosed in note X, the next annual financial statements of the [group/company] will be prepared in accordance with IFRSs as adopted for use in the European Union.*** [This interim report has been prepared in accordance with International Accounting Standard 34, "Interim Financial Reporting" and the requirements of IFRS 1, "First Time Adoption of International Financial Reporting Standards" relevant to interim reports.][49]

The accounting policies are consistent with those that the directors intend to use in the next annual financial statements. [There is, however, a possibility that the directors may determine that some changes to these policies are necessary when preparing the full annual financial statements for the first time in accordance with IFRSs as adopted for use in the European Union. This is because, as disclosed in note Y, the directors have anticipated that [new] [revised] IFRS X, which has yet to be formally adopted for use in the EU will be so adopted in time to be applicable to the next annual financial statements.][50]

Review work performed

We conducted our review in accordance with guidance contained in Bulletin 1999/4 issued by the Auditing Practices Board for use in the United Kingdom. A review consists principally of making enquiries of [group] management and applying analytical procedures to the financial information and underlying financial data and based thereon, assessing whether the disclosed accounting policies have been consistently applied unless otherwise disclosed. A review excludes audit procedures such as tests of controls and verification

---

[48] Review reports of entities that do not publish their interim reports on a web site or publish them using 'PDF' format may continue to refer to the pages of the interim report.

[49] This wording should be tailored accordingly to reflect the approach adopted by the directors (see Paragraphs 138 – 141).

[50] This wording should be tailored accordingly to reflect the approach adopted by the directors and the disclosures given in the interim report (see Paragraphs 139 and 153).

of assets, liabilities and transactions. It is substantially less in scope than an audit and, therefore, provides a lower level of assurance. Accordingly, we do not express an audit opinion on the financial information.

Review conclusion

On the basis of our review we are not aware of any material modifications that should be made to the financial information as presented for the [three] [six] [nine] months ended ....

ABC & Company   *Designation*
Date   *Address*

*** Subsequent to this Bulletin being printed the Accounting Regulatory Committee (ARC) of the European Commission indicated that it was supportive of the following standard formulation for use in the notes to the accounts and in the auditor's report " ... in accordance with International Financial Reporting Standards as adopted by the EU" or (abbreviated version) "in accordance with IFRSs as adopted by the EU". The ARC wording differs slightly from that used in the Appendix and auditors may wish to use the ARC's wording in their reports. *(See APB Press Notice No. 25 of 21 December 2005)*

BULLETIN 2006/3

THE SPECIAL AUDITOR'S REPORT ON ABBREVIATED ACCOUNTS IN THE UNITED KINGDOM

CONTENTS

Introduction

1.   This Bulletin supersedes Bulletin 1997/1 "The Special Auditors' Report on Abbreviated Accounts in Great Britain": It updates the guidance previously given in that Bulletin:

(a)   For changes in legislation, in particular, "The Companies Act 1985 (International Accounting Standards and Other Accounting Amendments) Regulations 2004"[1];

(b)   For changes in terminology pursuant to the replacement of SAS 600 by ISA (UK and Ireland) 700 "The Auditor's Report on Financial Statements"; and

(c)   To extend it to cover Northern Ireland[2].

Entitlement to deliver abbreviated accounts to the Registrar of Companies

2.   For accounting periods commencing on or after 1 January 2005, all UK companies have a choice as to whether to prepare their individual accounts using International Financial Reporting Standards (IFRSs) as adopted by the EU (IAS individual accounts) or UK Generally Accepted Accounting Practice (GAAP) (Companies Act individual accounts). Non-publicly traded companies will also have a choice between preparing UK GAAP group accounts and group accounts using IFRSs as adopted by the EU.

3.   Companies which qualify as "small" or "medium-sized" in relation to a financial year and that are preparing Companies Act individual accounts are entitled to take advantage of certain special provisions which allow "abbreviated accounts" to be delivered to the Registrar of Companies (Registrar), rather than copies of the "full" financial statements required by section 226 of the Companies Act 1985 (CA 1985). These provisions are not available to companies preparing IAS individual accounts, as the format of accounts on which they are based does not apply to companies using IFRSs as adopted by the EU. The special provisions regarding abbreviated accounts are set out in sections 246 (for small companies) and 246A (for medium-sized companies) of CA 1985. The relevant size and eligibility criteria are set out in section 247 of CA 1985. Section 247A of CA 1985 specifies cases in which the special provisions do not apply.

4.   If the directors of a small or medium-sized company intend to deliver abbreviated accounts to the Registrar, the "full" financial statements required by sections 226 and 227 of CA 1985 and the directors' report required by section 234 of CA 1985 must still be prepared and sent to members of the company.

5.   Abbreviated accounts may only be prepared for an individual company. There is no provision in the Act for "abbreviated group accounts". Small and medium-sized groups are entitled, under section 248 of CA 1985, to exemption from the requirement

---

[1]   Statutory Instrument 2004 No. 2947
[2]   See Appendix 4

to prepare group accounts. If an eligible group does not take advantage of this exemption, it must deliver to the Registrar a copy of the "full" group accounts that it prepares for its members.

6. Except when a company's directors have taken advantage of the exemption from audit by virtue of section 249AA (dormant companies), sections 246(8) and 246A(4) of CA 1985 require the abbreviated accounts to include a statement, in a prominent position above the director's signature, that the accounts are prepared in accordance with the special provisions of Part VII of CA 1985 relating to small or medium-sized companies.

Special report of the auditor

7. If abbreviated accounts prepared in accordance with the relevant provisions are delivered to the Registrar, section 247B(2) of CA 1985 requires that they be accompanied by a copy of a special report of the auditor. This requirement does not apply if the directors have taken advantage of the exemption from audit conferred on certain categories of small company by section 249A(1) or (2) or section 249AA (dormant companies) of CA 1985.

8. The elements of the special report of the auditor are set out in the following paragraphs and illustrated in Appendices 1 to 3 of this Bulletin.

Title and addressee

9. The Act does not state to whom the special report of the auditor should be addressed. In the absence of any requirement the auditor addresses the report to the company. It is appropriate to use the term "Independent Auditor" in the title.

Introductory paragraph

10. The auditor identifies the abbreviated accounts examined.

Respective responsibilities

11. The auditor includes a description of its responsibilities and also states that the directors are responsible for preparing the abbreviated accounts in accordance with the relevant section of the Companies Act 1985.

Basis of opinion

12. The auditor indicates that its work was limited to determining whether the company is entitled to deliver abbreviated accounts to the Registrar and whether the abbreviated accounts to be delivered are properly prepared in accordance with the relevant provisions.

Opinion

13. Legal advice has indicated that, although abbreviated accounts must be properly prepared in accordance with the relevant provisions, they are not required to give a true and fair view (in practice, they will not do so).

14. Section 247B(2) of CA 1985 requires the auditor to state that in its opinion:

    (a) the company is entitled to deliver abbreviated accounts prepared in accordance with the relevant provision to the Registrar; and

    (b) the abbreviated accounts to be delivered are properly prepared in accordance with the relevant provision.

15. The fact that the auditor's report under section 235 of CA 1985 on the "full" financial statements was qualified, or contained an emphasis of matter paragraph dealing with a significant uncertainty, does not prevent the abbreviated accounts from being prepared in accordance with the relevant provisions. The matter in question may, however, affect the company's eligibility as "small" or "medium-sized". The auditor therefore considers whether the maximum effect of the matter giving rise to the qualification or emphasis of matter would cause two or more of the criteria for determining eligibility (that is, the turnover, employee or balance sheet totals) to exceed the relevant limits. An auditor may be unable to properly assess the criteria for small or medium sized eligibility where an adverse opinion or disclaimer of opinion has been given under section 235 of CA 1985.

16. CA 1985 does not envisage a qualified opinion being expressed on the abbreviated accounts. An auditor unable to make the positive statements required reports this fact to the directors. In such circumstances, the directors cannot deliver the abbreviated accounts to the Registrar.

Other information required

17. Under section 247B(3) of CA 1985, if the auditor's report under section 235 of CA 1985 on the "full" financial statements:

    (a) was qualified, the special report is required to set out the qualified report in full (together with any further material necessary to understand the qualification);

    (b) contained a statement under section 237(2) (accounts, records or returns inadequate or accounts not agreeing with records or returns), or section 237(3) (failure to obtain necessary information and explanations) of CA 1985, the special report is required to set out the statement in full.

18. These are, however, minimum requirements and do not preclude the inclusion in the special auditor's report of other information which the auditor considers important to a proper understanding of that report. In particular, when the auditor's report under section 235 of CA 1985 is unqualified but contains an emphasis of matter paragraph, the APB considers that it is necessary for the auditor to include such a paragraph

(together with any further material necessary to understand it) in the special auditor's report.

19. As noted above, when a qualified report or an emphasis of matter paragraph includes a reference to a note to the "full" financial statements, without stating explicitly all the relevant information contained in that note, the auditors add the necessary information to their report on the abbreviated accounts, immediately following the reproduction of the text of their report on the "full" financial statements.

20. Similarly, where the auditor's report under section 235 of CA 1985 contains an "other matter" paragraph, the auditor considers whether this matter affects users' understanding of the abbreviated accounts, and therefore whether the paragraph needs to be included in the special report on the abbreviated accounts. For example, if the auditor's report drew attention to an inconsistency between the directors' report and the "full" financial statements:

- for a small-sized company, where the abbreviated accounts may exclude the directors' report, the "other matter" paragraph is unlikely to be included in the special report of the auditor as it does not affect the reader's understanding of the information in the abbreviated accounts;

- for a medium-sized company the directors' report is filed with the abbreviated accounts and consequently the "other matter" paragraph is likely to be included in the special report of the auditor.

Date

21. The auditor dates the special report on the date on which it is signed. The auditor does not sign the special report until the directors have approved and signed the abbreviated accounts. It is desirable that the auditor completes and signs its special report on the date that it completes and signs its report on the "full" financial statements to avoid the impression that the special report in any way "updates" the auditor's report on the "full" financial statements. Where the auditor dates its special report after the date of its report on the "full" financial statements the basis of the opinion of the special report states that it has not considered the effects of any events between the two dates.

Change of auditor

22. Where there is to be a change of auditor, it is preferable for the auditor who reported on the "full" financial statements to report on the abbreviated accounts for that financial year. Where this is not possible, the new auditor performing the latter function can accept the "full" financial statements audited by its predecessor as a basis for its work, unless it has grounds to doubt the company's eligibility to deliver abbreviated accounts (for example, because a qualified opinion affects the criteria for determining eligibility). If there is a need to refer in the special report to the predecessor auditor's report on the "full" financial statements, the new auditor indicates in its report by whom the audit of the "full" financial statements was carried out.

Appendix 1

Example of a special report on the abbreviated accounts of a small company

INDEPENDENT AUDITOR'S REPORT TO XYZ LIMITED UNDER SECTION 247B OF THE COMPANIES ACT 1985

We have examined the abbreviated accounts set out on pages ... to ... , together with the financial statements of XYZ Limited for the year ended ... prepared under section 226 of the Companies Act 1985.

Respective responsibilities of directors and auditors

The directors are responsible for preparing the abbreviated accounts in accordance with section 246 of the Companies Act 1985. It is our responsibility to form an independent opinion as to whether the company is entitled to deliver abbreviated accounts prepared in accordance with sections 246(5) and (6)[3] of the Act to the Registrar of Companies and whether the abbreviated accounts have been properly prepared in accordance with those provisions and to report our opinion to you.

Basis of opinion

We conducted our work in accordance with Bulletin 2006/3 "The special auditor's report on abbreviated accounts in the United Kingdom" issued by the Auditing Practices Board. In accordance with that Bulletin we have carried out the procedures we consider necessary to confirm, by reference to the financial statements, that the company is entitled to deliver abbreviated accounts and that the abbreviated accounts to be delivered are properly prepared[4].

Opinion

In our opinion the company is entitled to deliver abbreviated accounts prepared in accordance with sections 246(5) and (6) of the Companies Act 1985, and the abbreviated accounts have been properly prepared in accordance with those provisions.

[Other information[5]]

Registered auditors   *Address*
Date

---

[3] This example assumes that company has taken advantage of both sections 246(5) and (6) of CA 1985; in other cases the references in this paragraph and the opinion paragraph would be amended accordingly

[4] Add appropriate wording where special report is dated after the signing of the auditor's report on the full financial statements (see paragraph 21).

[5] This section is only included in the circumstances described in paragraphs 17 to 20 (see Appendix 3).

Appendix 2

Example of a special report on the abbreviated accounts of a medium-sized company

INDEPENDENT AUDITOR'S REPORT TO XYZ LIMITED UNDER SECTION 247B OF THE COMPANIES ACT 1985

We have examined the abbreviated accounts set out on pages ... to ... , together with the financial statements of XYZ Limited for the year ended ... prepared under section 226 of the Companies Act 1985.

Respective responsibilities of directors and auditors

The directors are responsible for preparing the abbreviated accounts in accordance with section 246A of the Companies Act 1985. It is our responsibility to form an independent opinion as to whether the company is entitled to deliver abbreviated accounts prepared in accordance with section 246A(3) of the Act to the Registrar of Companies and whether the abbreviated accounts have been properly prepared in accordance with that provision and to report our opinion to you.

Basis of opinion

We conducted our work in accordance with Bulletin 2006/3 "The special auditor's report on abbreviated accounts in the United Kingdom" issued by the Auditing Practices Board. In accordance with that Bulletin we have carried out the procedures we consider necessary to confirm, by reference to the financial statements, that the company is entitled to deliver abbreviated accounts and that the abbreviated accounts to be delivered are properly prepared[6].

Opinion

In our opinion the company is entitled to deliver abbreviated accounts prepared in accordance with section 246A(3) of the Companies Act 1985, and the abbreviated accounts have been properly prepared in accordance with that provision.

[Other information[7]]

Registered auditors   *Address*
Date

---

[6] Add appropriate wording where special report is dated after the signing of the auditor's report on the full financial statements (see paragraph 21)

[7] This section is only included in the circumstances described in paragraphs 17 to 20 (see Appendix 3).

Appendix 3

Example of a special report on the abbreviated accounts of a small company including other information - emphasis of matter paragraph regarding a significant uncertainty (going concern)

INDEPENDENT AUDITOR'S REPORT TO XYZ LIMITED UNDER SECTION 247B OF THE COMPANIES ACT 1985

We have examined the abbreviated accounts set out on pages ... to ... , together with the financial statements of XYZ Limited for the year ended ... prepared under section 226 of the Companies Act 1985.

Respective responsibilities of directors and auditors

The directors are responsible for preparing the abbreviated accounts in accordance with section 246 of the Companies Act 1985. It is our responsibility to form an independent opinion as to whether the company is entitled to deliver abbreviated accounts prepared in accordance with sections 246(5) and (6) of the Act to the Registrar of Companies and whether the abbreviated accounts have been properly prepared in accordance with those provisions and to report our opinion to you.

Basis of opinion

We conducted our work in accordance with Bulletin 2006/3 "The special auditor's report on abbreviated accounts in the United Kingdom" issued by the Auditing Practices Board. In accordance with that Bulletin we have carried out the procedures we consider necessary to confirm, by reference to the financial statements, that the company is entitled to deliver abbreviated accounts and that the abbreviated accounts to be delivered are properly prepared[8].

Opinion

In our opinion the company is entitled to deliver abbreviated accounts prepared in accordance with sections 246(5) and (6) of the Companies Act 1985, and the abbreviated accounts have been properly prepared in accordance with those provisions.

---

[8] Add appropriate wording where special report is dated after the signing of the auditor's report on the full financial statements (see paragraph 21).

Other information

On ...[9] we reported as the auditor to the members of the company on the financial statements prepared under section 226 of the Companies Act 1985 and our report included the following paragraph[10]

"Emphasis of matter - Going concern

In forming our opinion, which is not qualified, we have considered the adequacy of the disclosure made in note x to the financial statements concerning the company's ability to continue as a going concern. The company incurred a net loss of £X during the year ended 31 December 20X1 and, at that date, the company's current liabilities exceeded its total assets by £Y. These conditions, along with the other matters explained in note x to the financial statements, indicate the existence of a material uncertainty which may cast significant doubt about the company's ability to continue as a going concern. The financial statements do not include the adjustments that would result if the company was unable to continue as a going concern."[11]

Registered auditors   *Address*
Date

---

[9] The date of the auditor's report on the financial statements.
[10] In this example, the "other information" section of the report on the abbreviated accounts reproduces an emphasis of matter paragraph from the auditor's report on the financial statements (see paragraph 18). In other cases where this section is included (see paragraphs 17 and 20), the first sentence is worded appropriately, for example: "On ... we reported as the auditor to the shareholders of the company on the financial statements prepared under section 226 of the Companies Act 1985 and our report [was as follows]/[included the following statement] (*as appropriate*): ..."
[11] Further material necessary to understand the explanatory paragraph may be added (see paragraph 19).

Appendix 4

Northern Ireland

The guidance given in this Bulletin in respect of companies incorporated in Great Britain is wholly applicable in relation to companies incorporated in Northern Ireland, subject to substitution of the legislative references given below.

	Companies Act 1985	Companies (Northern Ireland) Order 1986
Annual financial statements	s226	Art. 234
Auditor's report	s235	Art. 243
Duties of auditors	s237(2)	Art. 245(2)
	s237(3)	Art. 245(3)
Special provisions for small companies	s246	Art. 254
Special provisions for medium-sized companies	s246A	Art. 254A
Qualification of company as small or medium-sized	s247	Art. 255
Cases in which special provisions do not apply	s247A	Art. 255A
Special auditor's report	s247B	Art. 255B
Exemption for small and medium-sized groups	s248	Art 256
Exemptions from audit	s249A	Art. 257A
Dormant companies	s249AA	Art. 257AA

BULLETIN 2006/5

THE COMBINED CODE ON CORPORATE GOVERNANCE: REQUIREMENTS OF AUDITORS UNDER THE LISTING RULES OF THE FINANCIAL SERVICES AUTHORITY AND THE IRISH STOCK EXCHANGE

CONTENTS

Introduction

1. This Bulletin provides guidance for auditors when reviewing a company's statement made in relation to "The Combined Code on Corporate Governance" ("Combined Code") in accordance with Listing Rule ("LR") 9.8.10R of the Financial Services Authority ("FSA") or LR 6.8.9 of the Irish Stock Exchange ("ISE"). It replaces the guidance in:

    - APB Bulletin 2004/3, "The Combined Code on Corporate Governance: Requirements of Auditors under the Listing Rules of the Financial Services Authority" published in November 2004; and

    - APB Bulletin 2004/4 "The Combined Code on Corporate Governance: Requirements of Auditors under the Listing Rules of the Irish Stock Exchange" published in December 2004.

2. This Bulletin reflects the following:

    (a) The issuance of "Internal Control: Revised Guidance for Directors on the Combined Code" ("Turnbull Guidance") by the Financial Reporting Council in October 2005. The Turnbull Review Group made only a small number of changes to the Turnbull Guidance as first issued in 1999. One of these changes is that the board's statement on internal control should confirm that necessary actions have been, or are being, taken to remedy any significant failings or weaknesses identified from its review of the effectiveness of the system of internal control. This development is set out in paragraph 36 of the revised Turnbull Guidance and is discussed in paragraphs 40 to 44 in this Bulletin.

    (b) The issuance of revised Listing Rules in July 2005. Although there has been no change to the substance of the requirements of the Listing Rules in this regard the text of the rules differs from the previous rules.

3. This Bulletin provides guidance for auditors of both:

    (a) companies listed on the Official List maintained by the FSA that are incorporated in the United Kingdom; and

    (b) companies listed on the Official List maintained by the ISE that are incorporated in Ireland.

    The text of the applicable revised Listing Rules issued by the FSA is set out in Appendix 1. Appendix 2 sets out the references to the equivalent Listing Rules of the ISE. In the remainder of this Bulletin reference is made to the "Listing Rules" and footnotes provide the specific references to the Listing Rules issued by the FSA and the ISE.

**THE AUDITING
PRACTICES BOARD**

4.   This Bulletin does not address the report to shareholders on executive directors' remuneration that is required by the Listing Rules[1].

Requirements of the Listing Rules relating to corporate governance matters

Requirement for companies to "comply or explain"

5.   The FSA Listing Rules require listed companies[2] that are incorporated in the United Kingdom to include in their annual report and accounts a two-part disclosure statement in relation to the Combined Code. The Listing Rules of the ISE have a similar requirement with respect to listed companies that are incorporated in the Republic of Ireland. The first part of the disclosure statement is to explain how the company has applied the principles set out in Section 1 of the Combined Code, in a manner that would enable shareholders to evaluate how the principles have been applied[3].

6.   The second part of the disclosure statement requires the company to either[4]:

(a)   Comply - include "*a statement as to whether the listed company has complied throughout the accounting period with all relevant provisions set out in Section 1 of the Combined Code"; or*

(b)   Explain – include "*a statement as to whether the listed company has not complied throughout the accounting period with all relevant provisions set out in Section 1 of the Combined Code and if so, setting out:*

(i)   *those provisions, if any, it has not complied with;*

(ii)   *in the case of provisions whose requirements are of a continuing nature, the period within which, if any, it did not comply with some or all of those provisions; and*

(iii)   *the company's reasons for non-compliance".*

7.   It is expected that listed companies will comply with the provisions of the Combined Code most of the time. However, it is recognised that departures from the provisions of the Code may be justified in particular circumstances. The auditor has no responsibility to review or otherwise assess and comment upon a company's decision to depart from the provisions of the Code. It is for shareholders and others to evaluate any such departure and the company's explanation for it.

---

[1]   FSA LR 9.8.6R(7) and LR 9.8.8R; ISE LR 6.8.6(8) and LR 6.8.8.
[2]   A listed company is defined by the FSA and the Irish Stock Exchange as "a company that has any class of its securities listed".
[3]   FSA LR 9.8.6R(5); ISE LR 6.8.6(6)
[4]   FSA LR 9.8.6R(6); ISE LR 6.8.6(7)

8.   The Listing Rules[5] requires an overseas company with a primary listing to disclose in its annual report and accounts certain matters relating to its corporate governance. There are no requirements relating to auditors in respect of these Listing Rules.

Review of the company's disclosure statement by the auditor

9.   The Listing Rules[6] require that *"A listed company must ensure that the auditors review the parts of the statement that relate to the following provisions of the Combined Code C1.1, C2.1, and C3.1 to C3.7."* They require the auditor to review nine of the ten objectively verifiable Combined Code provisions relating to accountability and audit.

10. The tenth accountability and audit Combined Code provision (C.1.2 on going concern) is addressed by different Listing Rules[7]. These Listing Rules require the directors to make a statement that the business is a going concern, together with supporting assumptions or qualifications as necessary. This statement is required to be included in the annual report and accounts and to be reviewed by the auditor before publication.

The auditor's review of the statement of compliance

11. The scope of the auditor's review required by the Listing Rules[8], in comparison to the totality of the Combined Code, is narrow. The auditor is not required to review the directors' narrative statement of how they have applied the Code principles and is required only to review the directors' compliance statement in relation to nine of the forty-eight Code provisions applicable to companies. Nevertheless, because the directors' narrative statement comprises other information included in a document containing audited financial statements there is a broader requirement under Auditing Standards[9] for the auditor to read such "other information" and if the auditor becomes aware of any apparent misstatements therein, or identifies any material inconsistencies with the audited financial statements, to seek to resolve them.

12. The Listing Rules are silent as to whether the auditor should report on the auditor's review of the directors' compliance statement and whether any such report should be published or referred to in the annual report. The APB is of the view that if the auditor's report itself contains a description of the auditor's responsibilities (including the auditor's responsibilities under the Listing Rules), as discussed in paragraphs 24 to 29, there is no necessity for a separate auditor's report dealing with the auditor's review of corporate governance matters.

13. Because of the limited nature of the auditor's review and in order to avoid the possibility of misunderstandings arising the APB recommends that:

---

[5]   FSA LR 9.8.7R; ISE LR 6.8.7
[6]   FSA LR 9.8.10R(2); ISE LR 6.8.9(2)
[7]   FSA LR 9.8.6R(3) and LR 9.8.10R(1); ISE LR 6.8.6(3) and LR 6.8.9(1)
[8]   FSA LR 9.8.10R; ISE LR 6.8.9
[9]   ISA (UK and Ireland) 720 (Revised) Section A, "Other information in documents containing audited financial statements".

(a) the auditor's engagement letter explains the scope of the auditor's review. Example paragraphs are set out in Appendix 3; and

(b) prior to the release of the annual report and accounts the auditor communicates, and discusses, with those charged with governance the factual findings of the auditor's review.

Combined Code provisions that the auditor is required to review

14. The provisions of the Combined Code that the auditor is required to review are set out below, together with a reference to the specific procedures recommended by the APB:

Provision	Detailed recommendation	Specific procedures
C.1.1	The directors should explain in the annual report their responsibility for preparing the accounts and there should be a statement by the auditors about their reporting responsibilities.	23-29
C.2.1	The board should, at least annually, conduct a review of the effectiveness of the group's system of internal controls and should report to shareholders that they have done so. The review should cover all material controls, including financial, operational and compliance controls and risk management systems.	30-55
C.3.1	The board should establish an audit committee of at least three, or in the case of smaller companies[10] two, members, who should all be independent non-executive directors. The board should satisfy itself that at least one member of the audit committee has recent and relevant financial experience.	56-59
C.3.2	The main role and responsibilities of the audit committee should be set out in written terms of reference and should include: • to monitor the integrity of the financial statements of the company, and any formal announcements relating to the company's financial performance, reviewing significant financial reporting judgements contained in them; • to review the company's internal financial controls and, unless expressly addressed by a separate board risk committee composed of independent directors,	60

---

[10] In the UK, a smaller company is one that is below the FTSE 350 throughout the year immediately prior to the reporting year. The Irish Stock Exchange considers a smaller company to be one that is included in the ISEQ Small Cap Index throughout the year immediately prior to the reporting year.

	or by the board itself, to review the company's internal control and risk management systems; • to monitor and review the effectiveness of the company's internal audit function; • to make recommendations to the board, for it to put to the shareholders for their approval in general meeting, in relation to the appointment, re-appointment and removal of the external auditor and to approve the remuneration and terms of engagement of the external auditor; • to review and monitor the external auditor's independence and objectivity and the effectiveness of the audit process, taking into consideration relevant UK professional and regulatory requirements; • to develop and implement policy on the engagement of the external auditor to supply non-audit services, taking into account relevant ethical guidance regarding the provision of non-audit services by the external audit firm; and to report to the board, identifying any matters in respect of which it considers that action or improvement is needed and making recommendations as to the steps to be taken.		
C.3.3	The terms of reference of the audit committee, including its role and the authority delegated to it by the board, should be made available. A separate section of the annual report should describe the work of the committee in discharging those responsibilities.	61	
C.3.4	The audit committee should review arrangements by which staff of the company may, in confidence, raise concerns about possible improprieties in matters of financial reporting or other matters. The audit committee's objective should be to ensure that arrangements are in place for the proportionate and independent investigation of such matters and for appropriate follow-up action.	62	
C.3.5	The audit committee should monitor and review the effectiveness of the internal audit activities. Where there is no internal audit function, the audit committee should consider annually whether there is a need for an internal audit function and make a recommendation to the board, and the reasons for the absence of such a function should be explained in the relevant section of the annual report.	63	
C.3.6	The audit committee should have primary responsibility for making a recommendation on the appointment,	64	

	reappointment and removal of the external auditors. If the board does not accept the audit committee's recommendation, it should include in the annual report, and in any papers recommending appointment or re- appointment, a statement from the audit committee explaining the recommendation and should set out reasons why the board has taken a different position.	
C.3.7	The annual report should explain to shareholders how, if the auditor provides non-audit services, auditor objectivity and independence is safeguarded.	65-67

General procedures

15. Paragraphs 16 to 22 set out general procedures relating to the auditor's review of the statement of compliance. These general procedures are applicable to all of the nine provisions of the Combined Code that the auditor is required to review.

16. In relation to all elements of the corporate governance disclosures relating to the provisions of the Combined Code that are within the scope of the auditor's review, the auditor obtains appropriate evidence to support the compliance statement made by the company. The type of procedures usually performed include:

    (a) reviewing the minutes of the meetings of the board of directors, and of relevant board committees;

    (b) reviewing supporting documents prepared for the board of directors or board committees that are relevant to those matters specified for review by the auditor;

    (c) making enquiries of certain directors (such as the chairman of the board of directors and the chairmen of relevant board committees) and the company secretary to satisfy themselves on matters relevant to those provisions of the Combined Code specified for review by the auditor; and

    (d) attending meetings of the audit committee (or the full board if there is no audit committee) at which the annual report and accounts, including the statement of compliance, are considered and approved for submission to the board of directors.

17. The auditor may request the directors to provide written confirmation of oral representations made during the course of the review.

Non-compliance with provisions of the Combined Code

18. Where the auditor becomes aware of any provision of the Combined Code that is within the scope of the auditor's review and with which the company has not complied, the auditor establishes that the departure is described in the directors' statement of compliance. However, the auditor is not required to, and does not, perform additional

procedures to investigate the appropriateness of reasons given for non-compliance with the provision.

19. Where there is a departure from a provision specified for the auditor's review but there is proper disclosure of this fact and of the reasons for the departure, as envisaged by the Listing Rules[11], the auditor does not refer to this in its report on the financial statements.

20. However, where the auditor considers that there is not proper disclosure of a departure from a provision of the Combined Code specified for the auditor's review the auditor reports this in the auditor's report on the financial statements. Paragraph 55 describes the way in which such a matter (which does not give rise to a qualified opinion on the financial statements) is reported and provides an example of such an opinion.

Auditor's association with company's corporate governance disclosures

21. The auditor would not wish to be associated with either the statement of compliance or the company's narrative statement of how it has applied the Code principles if the auditor has reason to believe that they may be misleading. The auditor, therefore, reads both of these statements and considers whether any information in either of them is apparently misstated or materially inconsistent with other information of which the auditor has become aware in the course of either the review of the company's compliance statement (insofar as it relates to the nine provisions of the Combined Code that the auditor is required to review under the Listing Rules) or the audit of the financial statements.

22. The auditor is not expected actively to search for misstatements or inconsistencies. However, if the auditor becomes aware of such a matter the auditor discusses it with the directors in order to establish the significance of the lack of proper disclosure. If such lack of proper disclosure is considered significant by the auditor and the directors cannot be persuaded to amend the disclosure to the auditor's satisfaction, the auditor considers the implications for the auditor's reporting responsibilities and the auditor may need to take legal advice.

Specific procedures

Responsibilities of the directors and the auditor

> **C.1.1** The directors should explain in the annual report their responsibility for preparing the accounts and there should be a statement by the auditors about their reporting responsibilities.

---

[11] FSA LR 9.8.10R; ISE LR 6.8.9

Directors' responsibilities

23. While the content of the statement of the directors' responsibilities is determined by the directors, the auditor establishes that the directors' responsibility for preparing the accounts is explained in the annual report.

Auditor's responsibilities

24. The auditor has different responsibilities with respect to the various component parts of the annual report. For example, the auditor is required to "audit" the financial statements, "review" the company's compliance with certain aspects of the Combined Code and "read" all information in the annual report that is not subject to any other requirement. The auditor reads such "other information" because the credibility of the financial statements and the related auditor's report may be undermined by material inconsistencies between the financial statements and the "other information", or by apparent misstatements within the other information.

25. In some instances the auditor has to report positively the results of the work whereas in other instances the auditor only has to report by exception. The APB is of the view that users of annual reports will find it difficult to understand the scope of the auditor's involvement in the absence of a clear statement of the auditor's responsibilities towards the whole annual report.

26. The key elements of a statement of the auditor's responsibilities relate to the requirements of:

   (a) statute and Auditing Standards with respect to the audit of the financial statements;

   (b) statute with respect to the auditor's opinion as to whether the information given in the directors report for the financial year for which the financial statements are prepared is consistent with those financial statements;

   (c) statute and the Listing Rules where the auditor is only required to report by exception;

   (d) the Listing Rules for the auditor to review the statement concerning the company's compliance with certain provisions of the Combined Code; and

   (e) Auditing Standards to read the "other information" in the annual report.

27. A description of the auditor's responsibilities may either be included as a separate section of the auditor's report on the financial statements or set out as a separate statement within the annual report. The APB encourages auditors to include a description of the auditor's responsibilities within the auditor's report on the financial statements. Illustrative examples of auditor's reports containing descriptions of the

auditor's responsibilities are given in the most recent version of the APB Bulletin "Auditor's Reports on Financial Statements"[12].

28. The content of the statement of the auditor's responsibilities ought to be determined by the auditor regardless of whether it is published as a separate statement, or incorporated into the auditor's report on the financial statements.

29. Appendix 3 to this Bulletin includes illustrative paragraphs that may be included in the auditor's engagement letter to describe the auditor's responsibilities with respect to the company's compliance with the Listing Rules[13]. In practice the auditor tailors the engagement letter to the specific circumstances of the engagement.

Internal control

> **C.2.1 The board should, at least annually, conduct a review of the effectiveness of the group's system of internal controls and should report to shareholders that they have done so. The review should cover all material controls, including financial, operational and compliance controls and risk management systems.**

The auditor's responsibilities with respect to the directors' narrative statement

30. The annual report will contain a narrative statement of how the company has applied Code principle C.2. The Turnbull Guidance recommends that, "In its narrative statement of how the company has applied Code Principle C.2, the board should, as a minimum, disclose that there is an ongoing process for identifying, evaluating and managing the significant risks faced by the company, that it has been in place for the year under review and up to the date of approval of the annual report and accounts, that is regularly reviewed by the board...".[14] The Turnbull Guidance also states that "The annual report and accounts should include such meaningful, high-level information as the board considers necessary to assist shareholders' understanding of the main features of the company's risk management processes and system of internal control, and should not give a misleading impression"[15]. The content of such narrative statements is likely, therefore, to vary widely from company to company.

31. Although the Listing Rules do not require the auditor to review the narrative statement, there are requirements under Auditing Standards for the auditor to read the other information (of which the company's narrative statement forms a part) issued with the audited financial statements and to seek to resolve any apparent misstatements or material inconsistencies with the audited financial statements.

---

[12] At the date of publication of this Bulletin the most recent version was Bulletin 2005/4
[13] FSA LR 9.8.10R; ISE LR 6.8.9
[14] Paragraph 34 of the Turnbull Guidance.
[15] Paragraph 33 of the Turnbull Guidance

Auditor's review of compliance

32. The Turnbull Guidance[16], recommends that the company discloses a summary of the process the board (and where applicable, its committees) has adopted in reviewing the effectiveness of the system of internal control. The Turnbull Guidance[17] describes the directors' process for reviewing effectiveness and in particular states[18]: *"The board should define the process to be adopted for its review of the effectiveness of internal control. This should encompass both the scope and frequency of the reports it receives and reviews during the year, and also the process for its annual assessment, such that it will be provided with sound, appropriately documented, support for its statement on internal control in the company's annual report and accounts".*

33. The objective of the auditor's review of compliance is to assess whether the company's summary of the process the board (and where applicable its committees) has adopted in reviewing the effectiveness of the system of internal control, is both supported by the documentation prepared by or for the directors and appropriately reflects that process.

34. To achieve this objective the auditor, in addition to the procedures outlined in paragraph 16;

    (a) obtains an understanding, through enquiry of the directors, of the process defined by the board for its review of the effectiveness of all material internal controls and compares that understanding to the statement made by the board in the annual report and accounts;

    (b) reviews the documentation prepared by or for the directors to support their statement made in connection with Code provision C.2.1 and assesses whether or not it provides sound support for that statement; and

    (c) relates the statement made by the directors to the auditor's knowledge of the company obtained during the audit of the financial statements. As explained in paragraph 36, the scope of the directors' review will be considerably broader in its scope than the knowledge the auditor can be expected to have based on their audit.

35. The auditor considers whether the directors' statement covers the year under review and the period to the date of approval of the annual report and accounts, as recommended by the Turnbull Guidance[19].

36. In carrying out the review, the auditor will have regard to the knowledge of the company the auditor has obtained from the audit work. To enable the auditor to

---

[16] Paragraphs 26-32 and 36 of the Turnbull Guidance.
[17] Paragraphs 26-32 of the Turnbull Guidance.
[18] Paragraph 27 of the Turnbull Guidance.
[19] Paragraph 26 of the Turnbull Guidance.

perform the audit and express an opinion on the financial statements, the auditor is required by Auditing Standards[20] to obtain an understanding of the entity and its environment, including its internal control, sufficient to identify and assess the risks of material misstatement of the financial statements. Consequently, the auditor's assessment required by Auditing Standards will be considerably narrower in scope than the review performed by the directors for the purpose of reporting on compliance with Code provision C.2.1.

37. The auditor, therefore, is not expected to assess whether all risks and controls have been addressed by the directors or that risks are satisfactorily addressed by internal controls. In order to communicate this fact to users of the annual report, the following sentence is included in the auditor's report on the financial statements.

> "We are not required to consider whether the board's statements on internal control cover all risks and controls, or form an opinion on the effectiveness of the company's corporate governance procedures or its risk and control procedures."

38. However, ISA (UK and Ireland) 260 "Communication of audit matters with those charged with governance" requires, among other things, that the auditor communicates, on a timely basis, to those charged with governance material weaknesses in internal control identified during the audit. A material weakness in internal control is a deficiency in design or operation which could adversely affect the entity's ability to record, process, summarize and report financial and other relevant data so as to result in a material misstatement in the financial statements. A material weakness in control identified by the auditor will be considered by the directors, in the context of the reports they receive and review during the year as part of their overall process for undertaking an annual assessment of the effectiveness of the company's internal control procedures, and it may be considered by them to be a significant failing or weakness as described in the Turnbull Guidance.

39. In view of the obligations placed on directors by the Turnbull Guidance the APB recommends that any material weaknesses in internal control identified by the auditor be reported to those charged with governance as soon as is practicable. The auditor does not wait until the financial statement audit has been completed before reporting such weaknesses. In this way, the directors will be aware of the weaknesses that the auditor has identified and be able to take account of them in making their statements on internal control[21].

---

[20] ISA (UK and Ireland) 315, "Obtaining an understanding of the entity and its environment and assessing the risks of material misstatement".

[21] The auditor has a responsibility under ISA (UK and Ireland) 260 to consider whether there is adequate two-way communication between the auditor and those charged with governance, such that an effective audit can take place. As part of this responsibility, amongst other things, the auditor will need to consider the appropriateness and timeliness of actions taken by those charged with governance in response to the recommendations made by the auditor including those regarding material weaknesses in internal control.

Actions taken by the directors to remedy significant failings or weaknesses

40. A revision made to the Turnbull Guidance in October 2005 was to expand the existing recommendation regarding the board's statement on internal control in the annual report in relation to Code provision C2.1. The recommendation was expanded to say that the board should in its statement on internal control, *"confirm that necessary actions have been or are being taken to remedy any significant failings or weaknesses identified from that review"*[22] (The reference to "that review" relates to the board's annual review of the effectiveness of the system of internal control).

41. The auditor's review responsibility with respect to this recommendation includes:

   (a) reviewing the documentation prepared by or for the directors supporting their statement made in connection with Code provision C2.1 that discusses those failings or weaknesses, if any, in internal control that they have assessed as "significant" and assessing whether or not it provides sound support for that statement;

   (b) discussing with the directors the actions they have already taken, or consider necessary to take, with respect to the identified significant failings or weaknesses; and

   (c) relating the statement made by the directors to the auditor's knowledge of the company obtained during the audit of the financial statements.

42. With respect to 41(c) above, the auditor assesses whether the directors, in making their statement, have taken into consideration the material weaknesses in internal control reported to those charged with governance by the auditor in accordance with ISA (UK and Ireland) 260 (See paragraph 38 above).

43. However, the auditor is not required to assess either the directors' decision as to what constitutes a significant failing or weakness, or whether the actions, taken or to be taken by the directors, will in fact remedy the significant failings or weaknesses identified by the directors. The APB recommends that a statement to this effect be included in the engagement letter (see Appendix 3).

44. If the auditor:

   (a) considers that the documentation and discussions do not support the directors' confirmation that necessary actions have been, or are being, taken or

   (b) based on its audit findings is aware of material weaknesses in internal control that have not been considered by the directors

---

[22] Paragraph 36 of the Turnbull Guidance

it discusses the position with the directors. If the auditor is not satisfied with the directors' explanations it considers the consequences for its opinion (see paragraph 54).

Internal control aspects of problems disclosed in the annual report

45. The Turnbull Guidance[23] also recommends that the board discloses *"the process it has applied to deal with material internal control aspects of any significant problems disclosed in the annual report and accounts"*.

46. This may be a difficult recommendation for directors to satisfy, and for the auditor to review, because what is meant by "significant problems" is not defined and the word "problem" encompasses more than financial matters. A directors' description, for example, of difficulties obtaining raw materials at a remote overseas location may be seen as a significant problem by directors of some companies but not the directors of others. Even when the directors have identified a problem it may not always be clear whether the problem has material internal control aspects. A significant loss-making contract, for example, will necessitate an assessment of whether the problem is attributable to changes in circumstances that could not reasonably have been foreseen as opposed to weaknesses in internal control.

47. The auditor's review responsibility with respect to this recommendation includes:

    (a) discussing with the directors the steps the directors have taken to determine what "significant problems" are disclosed in the annual report and accounts; and

    (b) assessing whether disclosures made by the board of the processes it has applied to deal with material internal control aspects of any significant problems disclosed in the annual report and accounts appropriately reflect those processes.

48. The auditor is not required to assess whether the processes described by the directors will, in fact, remedy the problem described in the annual report and accounts.

49. If the auditor is aware of a significant problem that is disclosed in the annual report and accounts for which the board has not disclosed the material internal control aspects it discusses the position with the directors of the company.

50. If the auditor is not able to agree with the directors as to how the matter should be resolved it considers the consequences for its opinion (see paragraph 54).

Failure to conduct a review

51. The Listing Rules[24] require the company to disclose if the board has failed to conduct a review of the effectiveness of internal control. The Turnbull Guidance[25] recommends

---

[23] Paragraph 36 of the Turnbull Guidance.
[24] FSA LR 9.8.6R(6)(b); ISE LR 6.8.6(7)(b)
[25] Paragraph 37 of the Turnbull Guidance

that where it has not made the required disclosures the board should state that fact and provide an explanation. The auditor considers whether this recommendation is met and whether the explanation is consistent with the auditor's understanding.

Groups of companies

52. The Turnbull Guidance establishes that, for groups of companies, the review of effectiveness should be from the perspective of the group as a whole[26]. Accordingly, the auditor's consideration of the board's description of its process for reviewing the effectiveness of internal control encompasses the group as a whole.

53. Where material joint ventures and associated companies have not been dealt with as part of the group for the purposes of applying the Turnbull Guidance, this fact should be disclosed by the board[27]. The auditor assesses, based on the auditor's knowledge of the group obtained during the audit of the financial statements, whether any material joint ventures or associated companies have not been dealt with and, therefore, if such a disclosure is necessary.

Reporting by exception

54. If the auditor concludes:

(a) that the board's summary of the process it has applied in reviewing the effectiveness of internal control is either not supported by or does not appropriately reflect the auditor's understanding of the process undertaken (paragraphs 32 to 39);

(b) that the documentation and discussions do not support the directors' confirmation that necessary actions have been, or are being taken; (paragraphs 40 to 44);

(c) that the processes disclosed to deal with material internal control aspects of significant problems disclosed in the annual report and accounts do not appropriately reflect the auditor's understanding of the process undertaken (paragraphs 45 to 50);

(d) that no disclosure has been made by the board that it has failed to conduct a review of the effectiveness of internal control (paragraph 51);

(e) where the board discloses that it has not reviewed the effectiveness of internal control, that its explanation is not consistent with the auditor's understanding (paragraph 51); or

---

[26] Paragraph 13 of the Turnbull Guidance
[27] Paragraph 38 of the Turnbull Guidance

(f) that no disclosure has been made by the board that a material joint venture or associated company has not been dealt with as part of the group (paragraphs 52 to 53),

they report this in their report on the financial statements.

55. However, as this does not give rise to a qualified audit opinion on the financial statements the APB recommends that the auditor's comments be included under the heading "Other matter" which would be included in the auditor's report below the auditor's opinion and any emphasis of matter related to the auditor's report on the financial statements as illustrated below:

Opinion
[Standard opinion wording for an auditor's report on group (not including parent company) financial statements of a publicly traded company incorporated in Great Britain[28]]

Emphasis of matter
Where applicable any emphasis of matter paragraph relating to the auditor's report on the financial statements.

Other matter
We have reviewed the board's description of its process for reviewing the effectiveness of internal control set out on page x of the annual report. In our opinion the board's comments concerning ... do not appropriately reflect our understanding of the process undertaken by the board because.....

An audit committee of independent non-executive directors

C.3.1 The board should establish an audit committee of at least three, or in the case of smaller companies[29] two, members, who should all be independent non-executive directors. The board should satisfy itself that at least one member of the audit committee has recent and relevant financial experience.

Auditor's review of compliance

56. When reviewing the company's compliance with this provision of the Combined Code the APB recommends that the auditor performs the following procedures:

(a) Checking that the audit committee comprises at least three, or in the case of smaller companies two, members.

---

[28] See Example 7 in Bulletin 2005/4

[29] In the UK a smaller company is one that is below the FTSE 350 throughout the year immediately prior to the reporting year. The Irish Stock Exchange considers a smaller company to be one that is included in the ISEQ Small Cap Index throughout the year immediately prior to the reporting year.

(b) Obtaining an understanding of the process adopted by the board for determining whether:

    (i) the members of the audit committee are all independent non-executive directors (see paragraphs 57 to 58); and

    (ii) at least one member of the audit committee has recent and relevant financial experience (see paragraph 59).

(c) Reviewing evidence such as minutes and other documentation supporting the board's view that the non-executive directors on the audit committee are independent and, where appropriate, have recent and relevant financial experience.

57. Provision A.3.1 of the Combined Code, requires the board to identify in the annual report each non-executive director it considers to be independent. This provision includes guidance on how independence might be interpreted by listing a number of relationships or circumstances that may indicate that a director is not independent[30]. The Code makes clear, however, that notwithstanding such relationships or circumstances the company is entitled to explain why a director is considered independent.

58. It is not the auditor's responsibility to satisfy itself whether directors are properly described as being "independent" non-executives. Nor does the auditor lay down more precise criteria with respect to the meaning of the term "independent" than those set out in the Combined Code. When reviewing the company's compliance with this provision of the Combined Code the APB recommends that the review procedures be limited to establishing that the audit committee is comprised of non-executive directors who are identified in the annual report as being, in the opinion of the board, independent. However, if the auditor doubts whether the directors are properly described as being "independent" non-executives the auditor communicates those concerns to the audit committee and the board of directors.

59. Similarly, it is not the auditor's responsibility to satisfy itself whether the company is correct in concluding that a particular audit committee member has "recent and relevant financial experience". Nor should the auditor lay down more precise criteria with respect to the meaning of the term "recent and relevant financial experience". When reviewing the company's compliance with this provision of the Combined Code the APB recommends that the review procedures be limited to considering the process adopted by the board for determining that at least one member of the audit committee has "recent and relevant financial experience". However, if the auditor doubts whether

---

[30] A footnote to A.3.1 explains 'A.2.2 states that the chairman should on appointment meet the independence criteria set out in this provision, but thereafter the test of independence is not appropriate in relation to the chairman'.

the company is correct in concluding that a particular audit committee member has "recent and relevant financial experience" the auditor communicates those concerns to the audit committee and the board of directors.[31]

Role and responsibilities of the audit committee[32]

C.3.2   The main role and responsibilities of the audit committee should be set out in written terms of reference and should include:

- to monitor the integrity of the financial statements of the company, and any formal announcements relating to the company's financial performance, reviewing significant financial reporting judgements contained in them;
- to review the company's internal financial controls and, unless expressly addressed by a separate board risk committee composed of independent directors, or by the board itself, to review the company's internal control and risk management systems;
- to monitor and review the effectiveness of the company's internal audit function;
- to make recommendations to the board, for it to put to the shareholders for their approval in general meeting, in relation to the appointment, re-appointment and removal of the external auditor and to approve the remuneration and terms of engagement of the external auditor;
- to review and monitor the external auditor's independence and objectivity and the effectiveness of the audit process, taking into consideration relevant UK professional and regulatory requirements;
- to develop and implement policy on the engagement of the external auditor to supply non-audit services, taking into account relevant ethical guidance regarding the provision of non-audit services by the external audit firm; and to report to the board, identifying any matters in respect of which it considers that action or improvement is needed and making recommendations as to the steps to be taken.

Auditor's review of compliance

60.   When reviewing the company's compliance with this provision of the Combined Code the APB recommends that the auditor obtains a copy of the terms of reference of the audit committee and reviews whether the roles and responsibilities of the audit committee described in the terms of reference reflect the recommendations of Code provision C.3.2. It is not the auditor's responsibility to consider whether the audit committee has fulfilled its roles and responsibilities.

---

[31] The Combined Code recommends that the board should satisfy itself that at least one member of the audit committee has recent and relevant financial experience. Where this is not the case there is a need for an explanation such as the board has concluded that the audit committee "collectively" has recent and relevant financial experience.

[32] In Ireland Section 42(2) of the Companies (Auditing and Accounting) Act 2003 requires the board of directors to establish an audit committee and sets out its responsibilities.

Terms of reference of the audit committee

C.3.3 **The terms of reference of the audit committee, including its role and the authority delegated to it by the board, should be made available[23]. A separate section of the annual report should describe the work of the committee in discharging those responsibilities.**

Auditor's review of compliance

61. When reviewing the company's compliance with this provision of the Combined Code the APB recommends that the auditor performs the following procedures:

    (a) Reviewing whether the terms of reference of the audit committee are included on the company's website or that the terms of reference have been reasonably made available or communicated by another method.

    (b) Reviewing whether a description of the work performed by the audit committee in discharging its responsibilities, is included in a separate section of the annual report, and is not materially inconsistent with the information that the auditor has obtained in the course of the audit work on the financial statements.

Arrangements by which company's staff may raise concerns

C.3.4 **The audit committee should review arrangements by which staff of the company may, in confidence, raise concerns about possible improprieties in matters of financial reporting or other matters. The audit committee's objective should be to ensure that arrangements are in place for the proportionate and independent investigation of such matters and for appropriate follow-up action.**

Auditor's review of compliance

62. When reviewing the company's compliance with this provision of the Combined Code the APB recommends that the auditor performs the following procedures:

    (a) Reviewing supporting documentation to determine whether there is evidence that the audit committee has reviewed the arrangements and, if necessary, discussing with members of the audit committee what review procedures they performed.

    (b) Reviewing documentation supporting the company's arrangements for the proportionate and independent investigation of concerns raised in confidence by staff relating to possible improprieties in matters of financial reporting or other matters and for appropriate follow-up action. It is not the responsibility of the auditor to consider whether such arrangements will facilitate "proportionate and independent" investigation or "appropriate" follow-up action but the auditor reviews the process by which the audit committee satisfies itself that the recommendation of the Combined Code has been satisfied.

Monitoring and review of the effectiveness of the internal audit activities

> **C.3.5** **The audit committee should monitor and review the effectiveness of the internal audit activities. Where there is no internal audit function, the audit committee should consider annually whether there is a need for an internal audit function and make a recommendation to the board, and the reasons for the absence of such a function should be explained in the relevant section of the annual report.**

Auditor's review of compliance

63. When reviewing the company's compliance with this provision of the Combined Code the APB recommends that the auditor performs the following procedures:

   (a) Where there is an internal audit function discussing with the audit committee chairman and reviewing the supporting documentation to establish that the audit committee has monitored and reviewed the effectiveness of the internal audit activities. It is not the auditor's responsibility to consider whether the internal audit activities are effective.

   (b) Where there is no internal audit function, reviewing whether:

   (i) the audit committee has considered whether there is a need for an internal audit function;

   (ii) there is documentation that evidences the audit committee's recommendation to the board;

   (iii) the reasons for the absence of such a function are explained in the relevant section of the annual report. It is not the auditor's responsibility to consider whether the reasons given are appropriate.

Appointment, reappointment and removal of the external auditor

> **C.3.6** **The audit committee should have primary responsibility for making a recommendation on the appointment, reappointment and removal of the external auditors. If the board does not accept the audit committee's recommendation, it should include in the annual report, and in any papers recommending appointment or re-appointment, a statement from the audit committee explaining the recommendation and should set out reasons why the board has taken a different position.**

Auditor's review of compliance

64. When reviewing the company's compliance with this provision of the Combined Code the APB recommends that the auditor performs the following procedures:

(a) Reviewing documentation, for example inclusion in the terms of reference of the audit committee, which explains that the audit committee has primary responsibility for making a recommendation on the appointment, reappointment and removal of the external auditors.

(b) Reviewing documentation that evidences the audit committee's recommendation to the board.

(c) Where the board has not accepted the audit committee's recommendation, reviewing whether there is included in the annual report and in any papers recommending appointment or re-appointment of the auditors:

    (i) a statement from the audit committee explaining its recommendation; and

    (ii) a statement from the board setting out reasons why the board has taken a different position from that recommended by the audit committee.

Non-audit activities

> **C.3.7 The annual report should explain to shareholders how, if the auditor provides non-audit services, auditor objectivity and independence is safeguarded.**

Auditor's review of compliance

65. When reviewing the company's compliance with this provision of the Combined Code the APB recommends that the auditor establishes whether the annual report includes a statement explaining to shareholders how, if the auditor provides non-audit services, auditor objectivity and independence is safeguarded.

66. The auditor considers the explanation of how auditor objectivity and independence is safeguarded in the context of the information of which they are aware. While it is not the auditor's responsibility to establish that the audit committee has fulfilled its responsibilities as set out in the terms of reference recommended by the Combined Code (to review and monitor the independence and objectivity of the external auditor and to develop and implement policy on the engagement of the external auditor to supply non- audit services taking into account relevant ethical guidance regarding the provision of non-audit services by the external auditor[24]) the auditor will be aware of whether the audit committee has undertaken these responsibilities and:

(a) notifies the audit committee and the board of directors if they believe these responsibilities have not been undertaken; and

(b) considers the requirements of Auditing Standards in relation to other information issued with audited financial statements if they believe the explanation is misleading.

67. APB Ethical Standards ("ESs") 1 to 5 set out the integrity, objectivity and independence requirements for auditors in the audit of financial statements. ES1[33] requires the audit engagement partner to ensure that those charged with governance of the audit client are appropriately informed on a timely basis of all significant facts and matters that bear upon the auditors "objectivity and independence". In relation to non-audit services, ES5[34] requires the audit engagement partner to ensure that those charged with governance are informed of any inconsistencies between APB Ethical Standards and the company's policy for the supply of non-audit services by the audit firm and any apparent breach of that policy.

Directors' statement on going concern

> **C.1.2 The directors should report that the business is a going concern, with supporting assumptions or qualifications as necessary.**

Auditor's review of compliance

68. The Listing Rules[35] require the directors of certain listed companies[36] to include in the annual report and accounts a statement that:

> *"the business is a going concern, together with supporting assumptions or qualification as necessary, that has been prepared in accordance with "Going Concern and Financial Reporting: Guidance for directors of listed companies registered in the United Kingdom, published in November 1994[37]".*

69. The Listing Rules[38] require a listed company to ensure that the auditor reviews the directors' going concern statement. In order for the auditor to meet the review requirements of this rule the auditor:

   (a) assesses the consistency of the directors' going concern statement with the knowledge obtained in the course of the audit of the financial statements. This knowledge will primarily have been obtained in meeting Auditing Standards[39] relating to going concern; and

   (b) assesses whether the directors' statement meets the disclosure requirements of the guidance for directors referred to in the Listing Rules[40]. Illustrative suggested disclosures for directors are set out in paragraphs 47 to 54 of that guidance.

---

[33] Paragraph 49
[34] Paragraph 35
[35] FSA LR 9.8.6R(3); ISE LR 6.8.6R(3)
[36] In the case of the FSA the Listing Rule applies to companies incorporated in the United Kingdom and in the case of the ISE the Listing Rule applies to companies incorporated in the Republic of Ireland.
[37] Going Concern and Financial Reporting: Guidance for directors of listed companies registered in the UK, ICAEW, November 1994. This guidance can be downloaded from the ICAEW web-site.
[38] FSA LR 9.8.10R(1); ISE LR 6.8.9(1)
[39] ISA (UK and Ireland) 570, 'The going concern basis in financial statements".
[40] FSA 9.8.6R(3); ISE LR 6.8.6(3)

70. The auditor does not assess or report on whether the directors have complied with any other detailed requirements of the guidance for directors. In particular, as the auditor does not express an opinion on the ability of the company to continue in operational existence they do not undertake additional procedures that would support such an opinion.

71. Paragraph 49 of the guidance for directors (dealing with going concern) provides the following illustrative example of the basic disclosure that directors make when the going concern presumption is appropriate:

> "After making enquiries, the directors have a reasonable expectation that the company has adequate resources to continue in operational existence for the foreseeable future. For this reason, they continue to adopt the going concern basis in preparing the accounts".

72. It is particularly important that the directors' statement on going concern is not inconsistent with any disclosures regarding going concern in either the financial statements or the auditor's report thereon. Where going concern matters are discussed in the financial statements one method of achieving consistency is for the directors' statement to include a cross reference to the relevant note to the financial statements.

Reporting requirements derived from other Auditing Standards

73. Auditing Standards set out the auditor's responsibilities in relation to other information in documents containing audited financial statements. These responsibilities extend to the Combined Code disclosures where there is either a material misstatement of fact or a material inconsistency with the audited financial statements. Application of these Standards requires that:

   (a) Where the auditor identifies a material inconsistency between the audited financial statements and the Combined Code disclosures the auditor determines whether the audited financial statements or the Combined Code disclosures need to be amended and seeks to resolve the matter through discussion with those charged with governance:

      (i) If an amendment is necessary in the audited financial statements and the entity refuses to make the amendment, the auditor expresses a qualified or adverse opinion on the financial statements.

      (ii) If an amendment is necessary in the Combined Code disclosures and the entity refuses to make the amendment, the auditor considers including in the auditor's report an emphasis of matter paragraph describing the material inconsistency[41] or taking other actions.

---

[41] As explained in paragraph 55, the APB recommends that the auditor's comments be included under the heading 'other matter' which would be included in the auditor's report below the auditor's opinion.

(b) Where the auditor identifies a material misstatement of fact in the Combined Code disclosures the auditor discusses the matter with those charged with governance. Where, after discussion, the auditor still considers that there is an apparent misstatement of fact, the auditor requests those charged with governance to consult with a qualified third party, such as the entity's legal counsel, and considers the advice received.

If the auditor concludes that an amendment is necessary in the Combined Code disclosures, which the entity refuses to correct, the auditor considers taking further appropriate action and considers including in the auditor's report an emphasis of matter paragraph describing the material misstatement.

Appendix 1

Extracts from the FSA Listing Rules[42]

Additional information

LR 9.8.6R   In the case of a *listed company* incorporated in the *United Kingdom*, the following additional items must be included in its annual report and accounts:

(3)   a statement made by the *directors* that the business is a going concern, together with supporting assumptions or qualifications as necessary, that has been prepared in accordance with "Going Concern and Financial Reporting: Guidance for Directors of listed companies registered in the United Kingdom", published in November 1994;

(5)   a statement of how the *listed company* has applied the principles set out in Section 1 of the *Combined Code*, in a manner that would enable shareholders to evaluate how the principles have been applied;

(6)   a statement as to whether the *listed company* has;

(a)   complied throughout the accounting period with all relevant provisions set out in Section 1 of the *Combined Code*; or

(b)   not complied throughout the accounting period with all relevant provisions set out in Section 1 of the *Combined Code* and if so, setting out:

i.   those provisions, if any, it has not complied with;

ii.   in the case of provisions whose requirements are of a continuing nature, the period within which, if any, it did not comply with some or all of those provisions; and

iii.   the *company's* reasons for non-compliance; ...

LR 9.8.7R   An *overseas company* with a *primary listing* must disclose in its annual report and accounts:

(1)   whether or not it complies with the corporate governance regime of its country of incorporation;

(2)   the significant ways in which its actual corporate governance practices differ from those set out in the *Combined Code*; and

---

[42] See Appendix 2 for references to equivalent Irish Stock Exchange Listing Rules

(3) the unexpired term of the service contract of any *director* proposed for election or re-election at the forthcoming annual general meeting and, if any *director* for election or re-election does not have a service contract, a statement to that effect.

Auditors report

LR 9.8.10R

A *listed company* must ensure that the auditors review each of the following before the annual report is published:

(1) LR 9.8.6R (3) (statement by the directors that the business is a going concern); and

(2) the parts of the statement required by LR9.8.6R (6) (corporate governance) that relate to the following provisions of the *Combined Code:*

a. C1.1;

b. C.2.1; and

c. C3.1 to C3.7

Appendix 2

Equivalent Irish Stock Exchange Listing Rules

FSA Listing Rule	Equivalent Listing Rule of the Irish Stock Exchange
LR 9.8.6R	LR 6.8.6
LR 9.8.6R (3)	LR 6.8.6 (3)
LR 9.8.6R (5)	LR 6.8.6 (6)
LR 9.8.6R (6)	LR 6.8.6 (7)
LR 9.8.6R (7)	LR 6.8.6 (8)
LR 9.8.7R	LR 6.8.7
LR 9.8.8R	LR 6.8.8
LR 9.8.10R	LR 6.8.9
LR 9.8.10R(1)	LR 6.8.9(1)
LR 9.8.10R(2)	LR 6.8.9(2)

Appendix 3

Example Terms of Engagement Paragraphs

The following is an illustrative example of paragraphs that may be included in the auditor's engagement letter dealing with the auditor's responsibilities with respect to the company's compliance with FSA LR 9.8.10R or ISE LR 6.8.9. In practice the auditor tailors the engagement letter to the specific circumstances of the engagement.

The auditor may wish to include a statement in its engagement letter limiting the auditor's liability in respect of the engagement to review the directors' corporate governance disclosures. The auditor is recommended to take legal advice concerning the wording of such a statement and how it is communicated.

Review of the company's disclosures relating to corporate governance and going concern.

Responsibilities of directors

As directors of the company you are responsible for ensuring that the company complies with the Listing Rules of the [Financial Services Authority including rules LR 9.8.6R (3), (5) and (6) "Additional information" and LR 9.8.10R "Auditors report"] [Irish Stock Exchange including rules LR 6.8.6 (3), (6) and(7) "Additional information" and LR 6.8.9 "Auditors Report"].

Responsibilities of the auditor

Listing Rule [9.8.10R] [6.8.9] states that "A listed company must ensure that the auditors review each of the following before the annual report is published:

(1) [LR9.8.6R (3)] [LR 6.8.6 (3)] (statement by the directors that the business is a going concern); and

(2) the parts of the statement required by [LR 9.8.6R (6)] [LR 6.8.6(7) (corporate governance) that relate to the following provisions of the Combined Code:

    (a) C1.1;

    (b) C2.1; and

    (c) C3.1 to C3.7.

As we have agreed, we will carry out the review required of us by the Listing Rules having regard to the guidance published in APB Bulletin 2006/5. We are not required to form an opinion on the company's corporate governance procedures.

Having finalised our review we expect to communicate and discuss with you the factual findings of our review.

Scope of review

You will provide us with such information and explanations as we consider necessary. We may request you to provide written confirmation of oral representations which you make to us during the course of our review. We shall request sight of all documents or statements which are due to be issued with either the statement of compliance or the going concern statement and all documentation prepared by or for the board in support of the company's statements.

As we have agreed we will attend the meeting of the audit committee [full board] at which the annual report and accounts, including the going concern statement and the statement of compliance, are considered and approved for submission to the board of directors.

Internal control

With respect to Code Provision C.2.1, our work will be restricted to:

(a)   assessing, based on enquiry of the directors, the supporting documentation prepared by or for the directors and our knowledge obtained during the audit of the financial statements, whether the company's summary of the process the board (and where applicable its committees) has adopted in reviewing the effectiveness of internal control appropriately reflects that process; and

(b)   assessing whether the company's disclosures of the processes it has applied to deal with material internal control aspects of any significant problems disclosed in the annual report and accounts appropriately reflects those processes.

As our work is not designed to:

(a)   consider whether the board's statements on internal control cover all risks and controls; or

(b)   form an opinion on the effectiveness of the company's risk and control procedures; or

(c)   assess either the directors' decision as to what constitutes a significant failing or weakness, or whether the actions, taken or to be taken, will in fact remedy the significant failings or weaknesses identified by the directors,

our work on internal control will not be sufficient to enable us to express any assurance as to whether or not your internal controls are effective. In addition our financial statement audit should not be relied upon to draw to your attention matters that may be relevant to your consideration as to whether or not your system of internal control is effective.

Going concern

With respect to the company's going concern statement our work will be restricted to a consideration of whether the statement provides the disclosures required by [LR 9.8.6R (3)] [LR 6.8.6 (3)] and is not inconsistent with the information of which we are aware from our audit work on the financial statements. We will not carry out the additional work necessary to give an opinion that the company has adequate resources to continue in operational existence.

Statement of auditor's responsibilities

Code provision C.1.1 recommends, among other things, that there should be a statement in the annual report about the auditor's reporting responsibilities. As we have agreed we will incorporate a description of our reporting responsibilities in our audit report on the financial statements.

BULLETIN 2006/6

AUDITOR'S REPORTS ON FINANCIAL STATEMENTS IN THE UNITED KINGDOM

CONTENTS

Note: Readers are advised to use the navigation aids (shaded above) to assist in locating particular example auditor's reports.

Introduction

1. The purpose of this Bulletin is to provide illustrative examples of:

   (a) unmodified auditor's reports for audits of financial statements of companies incorporated in Great Britain or Northern Ireland for periods commencing on or after 1 April 2005 (see Appendix 1);

   (b) modified auditor's reports (excluding going concern issues) (see Appendices 2 and 4); and

   (c) modified auditor's reports arising from going concern issues (see Appendix 3).

2. For the purposes of this Bulletin companies are classified as either:

   (a) "publicly traded companies" – defined as "those whose securities are admitted to trading on a regulated market in any Member State in the European Union"; or

   (b) "non-publicly traded companies" – defined as "those who do not have any securities that are admitted to trading on a regulated market in any Member State in the European Union" (EU).

3. This is the second edition of the Bulletin referred to in various paragraphs of ISA (UK and Ireland) 700 "The auditor's report on financial statements". It supersedes Bulletin 2005/4.

4. The example auditor's reports included in the Bulletin take account of:

   (a) changes made to the Companies Act 1985 (CA 1985) and the Companies (Northern Ireland) Order 1986 to require the auditor to give a positive opinion as to the consistency of the directors' report with the financial statements[1] (see paragraphs 6 and 7);

   (b) the revised standard formulation for expressing compliance with the financial reporting framework applicable to companies subject to Regulation 1606/2002/EC ("IAS Regulation"). This formulation was proposed by the European Commission to the meeting of The Accounting Regulatory Committee (ARC) held on 30 November 2005. As the revised formulation was determined after the publication of Bulletin 2005/4 the wording differs slightly from that used in the example auditor's reports in that Bulletin (see paragraphs 8 and 9); and

   (c) changes made to certain of the example auditor's reports in order to conform with the presentation of the other reports.

5. The Bulletin does not address:

---

[1] This subject is dealt with in International Standard on Auditing (ISA) (UK and Ireland) 720 (Revised) Section B – "The auditor's statutory reporting responsibility in relation to directors' reports.

(a) the changes to the auditor's report and the directors' responsibility statement that may be necessary when the Companies Bill is enacted;

(b) the changes to the structure of the auditor's report contemplated by ISA 700 (Revised). The APB has concluded that the revision of ISA (UK and Ireland) 700 should be deferred until progress has been made in resolving the following issues:

- o the finalisation of the Companies Bill which will impact the responsibilities of auditors and directors.

- o whether the revised ISA 700 will be approved for adoption in the EU.

- o finalisation of the exposure drafts of ISAs 705 and 706 that address modifications to the auditor's report.

Change to the Companies Act 1985

6. In 2005 Statutory Instrument 2005 No. 1011 "The Companies Act 1985 (Operating and Financial Review and Directors' Report etc)) Regulations 2005" amended the CA 1985 so that the auditor must give a positive opinion as to the consistency of the directors' report with the financial statements. This regulation applies to financial years beginning on or after 1 April 2005.

7. A similar change has been made with respect to companies incorporated in Northern Ireland by Statutory Rule 2005 No. 61 "The Companies (1986 Order) (Operating and Financial Review and Directors' Report etc) Regulations (Northern Ireland) 2005. This regulation similarly applies to financial years beginning on or after 1 April 2005.

International Financial Reporting Standards

Reference to the accounting framework in the auditor's report

8. As the APB supports the ARC formulation discussed in paragraph 4(b) it takes the view that the accounting framework used by companies adopting IFRSs as adopted by the EU should be referred to in the auditor's opinion in the following terms:

> *"true and fair view, in accordance with IFRSs as adopted by the European Union".*

The example auditor's reports included in the Appendices have been prepared on this basis. As explained in paragraph 4(b) this wording differs slightly from that used in Bulletin 2005/4.

9. Many companies will be in a position of complying with both IFRSs as issued by the IASB and "IFRSs as adopted by the European Union", and may request the auditor to express an opinion in terms of "true and fair view, in accordance with IFRSs". In these

circumstances the APB believes that it is preferable for the auditor to state a second separate opinion with regards to IFRSs as issued by the IASB in order to avoid confusing readers of the auditor's report, and to leave intact the opinion required by law on compliance with IFRSs as adopted by the European Union. To accomplish this the second opinion is clearly separated from the opinion required by CA 1985 by use of an appropriate heading. Where applicable, the example auditor's reports set out in Appendix 1 illustrate this point.

Different financial reporting frameworks used for group and parent company financial statements

10. A significant development arising from the use of IFRSs as adopted by the EU, as the financial reporting framework for group financial statements, is that group and parent company financial statements may be prepared in accordance with different financial reporting frameworks.

11. The example unmodified reports in Appendix 1 illustrate, among other things, the following scenarios for auditor's reports on the group and parent company financial statements of publicly traded companies:

> IFRSs as adopted by the EU used for group financial statements (required for publicly traded companies) and either:
> i) IFRSs as adopted by the EU used for parent company financial statements; or
> ii) UK GAAP used for parent company financial statements.

In such instances, companies may choose to present the financial statements of the group and the parent company in separate sections of the annual report and in such circumstances separate auditor's reports might be provided[2]. Appendix 1 includes example auditor's reports for situations where the group and parent company financial statements are presented separately or together (see also paragraph 14 below).

12. Where separate auditor's reports are provided on the group and parent company financial statements the illustrative examples assume that:

(a) the auditor's responsibilities with respect to the Corporate Governance Statement are described in the auditor's report on the group financial statements; and

(b) the Directors Remuneration Report is reported on in the auditor's report on the parent company financial statements[3]

However, other approaches may be adopted.

---

[2] The Companies Act 1985 does not require the directors to sign the group balance sheet and thereby evidence their approval of it. Where separate financial statements are presented the auditor obtains evidence of the directors' approval of the group financial statements before signing the auditor's report on those financial statements.

[3] In the Directors' Remuneration Report the information subject to audit relates to each person who has served as a director of the company.

Exemption for presentation of parent company profit and loss account

13. Bulletin 2005/3 discusses the exemption in Section 230 CA 1985,[4] which allows a parent company not to publish its profit and loss account and certain related information. Where advantage has been taken of the Section 230 exemption and the parent company financial statements have been prepared in accordance with "IFRSs as adopted by the European Union" the financial reporting framework is described in the auditor's report as:

> "true and fair view, in accordance with IFRSs as adopted by the European Union *and as applied in accordance with the provisions of the Companies Act 1985".*

14. Where the group and parent company financial statements are both prepared in accordance with "IFRSs as adopted by the European Union" it is likely that issuers may wish to present those financial statements separately so that the Section 230 exemption can be utilised without giving rise to, what might be considered to be, a modified auditor's report on the group financial statements. This is illustrated in example reports 11 and 12 in Appendix 1.

15. The example unmodified reports in Appendix 1 illustrate the impact of the Section 230 exemption and the company's decision whether or not to present the group and parent company financial statements and auditor's reports separately in the annual report.

Statement of directors' responsibilities

16. Appendix 5 is an illustrative example of a statement of directors' responsibilities for a non-publicly traded company preparing its parent company financial statements under UK GAAP. The APB has not prepared an illustrative example of a statement of directors' responsibilities for a publicly traded company as the directors' responsibilities, which are in part dependent on the particular regulatory environment, will vary dependent on the rules of the market on which its securities are admitted to trading.

Additional example auditor's reports

17. Three additional example auditor's reports have been included in this edition of the Bulletin. These examples are:

(a) An unmodified auditor's report for a publicly traded company that does not prepare group accounts and prepares financial statements in accordance with IFRSs as adopted by the European Union (ie a publicly traded company having no subsidiaries). (Example 14 in Appendix 1)

---

[4] Article 238 of the Companies (Northern Ireland) Order 1986.

(b) An unmodified auditor's report for a publicly traded company that does not prepare group accounts and prepares financial statements in accordance with UK GAAP (ie a publicly traded company having no subsidiaries). (Example 15 in Appendix 1)

(c) An extract from an auditor's report with a modified opinion on the directors' report. (Appendix 4)

18. The numbering of examples provided in Appendices to the previous edition of this Bulletin has been retained.

Appendix 1

Unmodified auditor's reports on financial statements

This Appendix contains updated examples of unmodified auditor's reports for:

- *Non-publicly traded companies incorporated in Great Britain (example reports 1 - 4); and*

- *Publicly traded companies incorporated in Great Britain (example reports 5 - 15)*

The example auditor's reports take into account the following factors illustrated in the navigation aids on pages 1042 and 1043:

- *Whether the company prepares group financial statements;*

- *Whether the financial statements are prepared using "IFRSs as adopted by the European Union";*

- *Whether the group financial statements comply with both "IFRSs as adopted by the European Union" and IFRSs as issued by the International Accounting Standards Board;*

- *Whether the parent company financial statements are prepared using "IFRSs as adopted by the European Union";*

- *Whether the Section 230 exemption from presenting the parent company profit and loss account or income statement has been taken;*

- *Whether group and parent company financial statements are presented separately (i.e. two separate auditor's reports).*

Application to Northern Ireland

The example auditor's reports can be used with respect to companies incorporated in Northern Ireland subject to changing references to the "Companies Act 1985" to references to the "Companies (Northern Ireland) Order 1986".

In Northern Ireland, the requirement for a Directors' Remuneration Report was introduced in 2005 by Statutory Rule 2005 No. 56 "The Directors' Remuneration Report Regulations (Northern Ireland) 2005". This statutory rule came into operation on 30th March 2005 and is, therefore, effective for financial years commencing on or after 1 April 2005.

Directors' Remuneration Report

The provisions of CA 1985, and the Companies (Northern Ireland) Order 1986, relating to the Directors Remuneration Report apply to "quoted companies". The definition of a quoted company differs from that of a publicly traded company. For the purposes of the examples it is assumed that non-publicly traded companies are not quoted companies and that publicly traded companies are quoted companies.

Navigation aid (1) to the examples of unmodified auditor's reports on financial statements where the company does not prepare group accounts

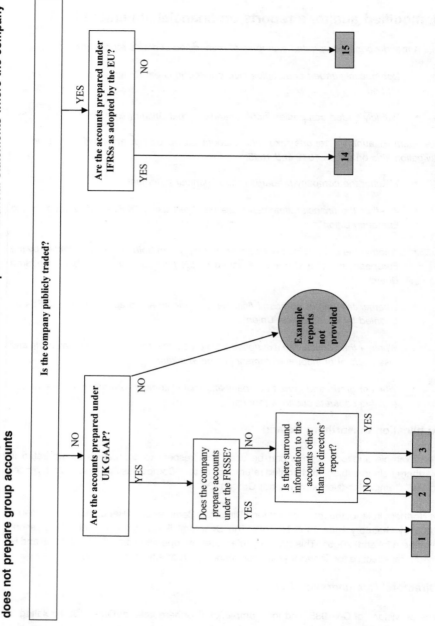

Navigation aid (2) to the examples of unmodified auditor's reports on financial statements where the company prepares group accounts

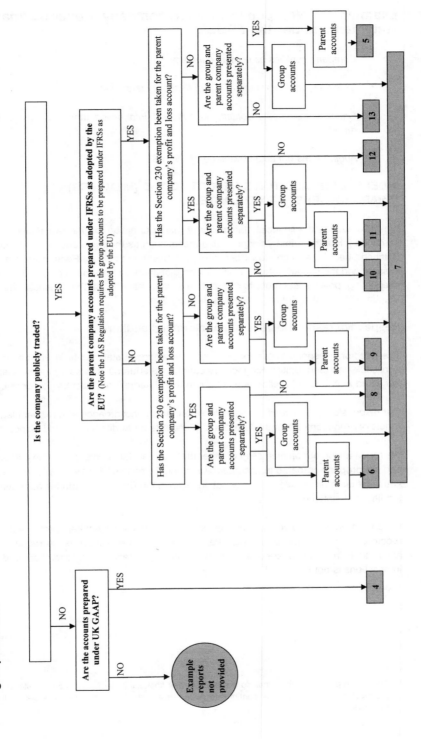

Example 1 – Non-publicly traded company preparing financial statements under the FRSSE:

- *Company qualifies as a small company.*

- *Company does not prepare group financial statements.*

- *Financial statements contain no surround information other than the directors' report.*

- *Auditor does not take advantage of ES PASE.*

INDEPENDENT AUDITOR'S REPORT TO THE [MEMBERS] [SHAREHOLDERS] OF XYZ LIMITED

We have audited the financial statements of (name of entity) for the year ended ... which comprise [state the primary financial statements such as the Profit and Loss Account, the Balance Sheet, [the Cash Flow Statement,] the Statement of Total Recognised Gains and Losses] and the related notes[5]. These financial statements have been prepared under the accounting policies set out therein and the requirements of the Financial Reporting Standard for Smaller Entities [(Effective January 2005)].

Respective responsibilities of directors and auditors

The directors' responsibilities for preparing the financial statements in accordance with applicable law and United Kingdom Accounting Standards (United Kingdom Generally Accepted Accounting Practice) are set out in the Statement of Directors' Responsibilities.

Our responsibility is to audit the financial statements in accordance with relevant legal and regulatory requirements and International Standards on Auditing (UK and Ireland).

We report to you our opinion as to whether the financial statements give a true and fair view and are properly prepared in accordance with the Companies Act 1985. We also report to you whether in our opinion the information given in the Directors' Report is consistent with the financial statements.

In addition we report to you if, in our opinion, the company has not kept proper accounting records, if we have not received all the information and explanations we require for our audit, or if information specified by law regarding directors' remuneration and other transactions is not disclosed.

---

[5] Auditor's reports of entities that do not publish their financial statements on a web site or publish them using 'PDF' format may continue to refer to the financial statements by reference to page numbers.

We read the Directors' Report and consider the implications for our report if we become aware of any apparent misstatements within it[6].

Basis of audit opinion

We conducted our audit in accordance with International Standards on Auditing (UK and Ireland) issued by the Auditing Practices Board. An audit includes examination, on a test basis, of evidence relevant to the amounts and disclosures in the financial statements. It also includes an assessment of the significant estimates and judgments made by the directors in the preparation of the financial statements, and of whether the accounting policies are appropriate to the company's circumstances, consistently applied and adequately disclosed.

We planned and performed our audit so as to obtain all the information and explanations which we considered necessary in order to provide us with sufficient evidence to give reasonable assurance that the financial statements are free from material misstatement, whether caused by fraud or other irregularity or error. In forming our opinion we also evaluated the overall adequacy of the presentation of information in the financial statements.

Opinion

In our opinion:

- the financial statements give a true and fair view, in accordance with United Kingdom Generally Accepted Accounting Practice applicable to Smaller Entities, of the state of the company's affairs as at .... and of its profit [loss] for the year then ended;

- the financial statements have been properly prepared in accordance with the Companies Act 1985; and

- the information given in the Directors' Report is consistent with the financial statements.

Registered auditors   *Address*
Date

---

[6] CA 1985 requires the auditor to report on the consistency of the Directors' Report with the financial statements. Consequently the paragraph that addresses the "read" requirement in auditing standards need refer only to apparent misstatements and not include a reference to consistency.

Example 2 – Non-publicly traded company – Auditor's report on individual company financial statements:

- *Company does not prepare group financial statements.*

- *Company does not meet the Companies Act definition of a quoted company.*

- *UK GAAP used for individual company financial statements.*

- *Financial statements contain no surround information other than the directors' report.*

INDEPENDENT AUDITOR'S REPORT TO THE [MEMBERS] [SHAREHOLDERS] OF XYZ LIMITED

We have audited the financial statements of (name of entity) for the year ended ... which comprise [state the primary financial statements such as the Profit and Loss Account, the Balance Sheet, the Cash Flow Statement, the Statement of Total Recognised Gains and Losses] and the related notes[7]. These financial statements have been prepared under the accounting policies set out therein.

Respective responsibilities of directors and auditors

The directors' responsibilities for preparing the financial statements in accordance with applicable law and United Kingdom Accounting Standards (United Kingdom Generally Accepted Accounting Practice) are set out in the Statement of Directors' Responsibilities.

Our responsibility is to audit the financial statements in accordance with relevant legal and regulatory requirements and International Standards on Auditing (UK and Ireland).

We report to you our opinion as to whether the financial statements give a true and fair view and are properly prepared in accordance with the Companies Act 1985. We also report to you whether in our opinion the information given in the Directors' Report is consistent with the financial statements.

In addition we report to you if, in our opinion, the company has not kept proper accounting records, if we have not received all the information and explanations we require for our audit, or if information specified by law regarding directors' remuneration and other transactions is not disclosed.

We read the Directors' Report and consider the implications for our report if we become aware of any apparent misstatements within it[8].

---

[7] Auditor's reports of entities that do not publish their financial statements on a web site or publish them using 'PDF' format may continue to refer to the financial statements by reference to page numbers.

[8] CA 1985 requires the auditor to report on the consistency of the Directors' Report with the financial statements. Consequently the paragraph that addresses the "read" requirement in auditing standards need refer only to apparent misstatements and not include a reference to consistency.

Basis of audit opinion

We conducted our audit in accordance with International Standards on Auditing (UK and Ireland) issued by the Auditing Practices Board. An audit includes examination, on a test basis, of evidence relevant to the amounts and disclosures in the financial statements. It also includes an assessment of the significant estimates and judgments made by the directors in the preparation of the financial statements, and of whether the accounting policies are appropriate to the company's circumstances, consistently applied and adequately disclosed.

We planned and performed our audit so as to obtain all the information and explanations which we considered necessary in order to provide us with sufficient evidence to give reasonable assurance that the financial statements are free from material misstatement, whether caused by fraud or other irregularity or error. In forming our opinion we also evaluated the overall adequacy of the presentation of information in the financial statements.

Opinion

In our opinion:

- the financial statements give a true and fair view, in accordance with United Kingdom Generally Accepted Accounting Practice, of the state of the company's affairs as at .... and of its profit [loss] for the year then ended;

- the financial statements have been properly prepared in accordance with the Companies Act 1985; and

- the information given in the Directors' Report is consistent with the financial statements.

Registered auditors   *Address*
Date

Example 3 – Non-publicly traded company – Auditor's report on individual company financial statements:

- *Company does not prepare group financial statements.*

- *Company does not meet the Companies Act definition of a quoted company.*

- *UK GAAP used for individual company financial statements.*

- *Financial statements contain surround information other than the directors' report.*

INDEPENDENT AUDITOR'S REPORT TO THE [MEMBERS] [SHAREHOLDERS] OF XYZ LIMITED

We have audited the financial statements of (name of entity) for the year ended ... which comprise [state the primary financial statements such as the Profit and Loss Account, the Balance Sheet, the Cash Flow Statement, the Statement of Total Recognised Gains and Losses] and the related notes[9]. These financial statements have been prepared under the accounting policies set out therein.

Respective responsibilities of directors and auditors

The directors' responsibilities for preparing the Annual Report and the financial statements in accordance with applicable law and United Kingdom Accounting Standards (United Kingdom Generally Accepted Accounting Practice) are set out in the Statement of Directors' Responsibilities.

Our responsibility is to audit the financial statements in accordance with relevant legal and regulatory requirements and International Standards on Auditing (UK and Ireland).

We report to you our opinion as to whether the financial statements give a true and fair view and are properly prepared in accordance with the Companies Act 1985. We also report to you whether in our opinion the information given in the Directors' Report is consistent with the financial statements. [The information given in the Directors' Report includes that specific information presented in the Operating and Financial Review that is cross referred from the Business Review section of the Directors' Report.][10]

In addition we report to you if, in our opinion, the company has not kept proper accounting records, if we have not received all the information and explanations we require for our audit, or if information specified by law regarding directors' remuneration and other transactions is not disclosed.

We read other information contained in the Annual Report, and consider whether it is consistent with the audited financial statements. This other information comprises only [the

---

[9] Auditor's reports of entities that do not publish their financial statements on a web site or publish them using 'PDF' format may continue to refer to the financial statements by reference to page numbers.

[10] Include and tailor as necessary to clarify the information covered by the auditor's opinion.

Directors' Report, the Chairman's Statement and the Operating and Financial Review][11]. We consider the implications for our report if we become aware of any apparent misstatements or material inconsistencies with the financial statements. Our responsibilities do not extend to any other information.

Basis of audit opinion

We conducted our audit in accordance with International Standards on Auditing (UK and Ireland) issued by the Auditing Practices Board. An audit includes examination, on a test basis, of evidence relevant to the amounts and disclosures in the financial statements. It also includes an assessment of the significant estimates and judgments made by the directors in the preparation of the financial statements, and of whether the accounting policies are appropriate to the company's circumstances, consistently applied and adequately disclosed.

We planned and performed our audit so as to obtain all the information and explanations which we considered necessary in order to provide us with sufficient evidence to give reasonable assurance that the financial statements are free from material misstatement, whether caused by fraud or other irregularity or error. In forming our opinion we also evaluated the overall adequacy of the presentation of information in the financial statements.

Opinion

In our opinion:

- the financial statements give a true and fair view, in accordance with United Kingdom Generally Accepted Accounting Practice, of the state of the company's affairs as at .... and of its profit [loss] for the year then ended;

- the financial statements have been properly prepared in accordance with the Companies Act 1985; and

- the information given in the Directors' Report is consistent with the financial statements.

Registered auditors   *Address*
Date

---

[11] The other information that is 'read' is the content of the printed Annual Report other than the financial statements. The description of the information that has been read is tailored to reflect the terms used in the Annual Report.

Example 4 – Non-publicly traded company – Auditor's report on group and parent company financial statements:

- Group and parent company financial statements not presented separately.

- Company prepares group financial statements.

- Company does not meet the Companies Act definition of a quoted company.

- UK GAAP used for group and parent company financial statements.

- Section 230 exemption taken for parent company's own profit and loss account.

INDEPENDENT AUDITOR'S REPORT TO THE [MEMBERS] [SHAREHOLDERS] OF XYZ LIMITED

We have audited the group and parent company financial statements (the "financial statements") of (name of entity) for the year ended ... which comprise [state the primary financial statements such as the Group Profit and Loss Account, the Group and Company Balance Sheets, the Group Cash Flow Statement, the Group Statement of Total Recognised Gains and Losses] and the related notes[12]. These financial statements have been prepared under the accounting policies set out therein.

Respective responsibilities of directors and auditors

The directors' responsibilities for preparing the Annual Report and the financial statements in accordance with applicable law and United Kingdom Accounting Standards (United Kingdom Generally Accepted Accounting Practice) are set out in the Statement of Directors' Responsibilities.

Our responsibility is to audit the financial statements in accordance with relevant legal and regulatory requirements and International Standards on Auditing (UK and Ireland).

We report to you our opinion as to whether the financial statements give a true and fair view and are properly prepared in accordance with the Companies Act 1985. We also report to you whether in our opinion the information given in the Directors' Report is consistent with the financial statements. [The information given in the Directors' Report includes that specific information presented in the Operating and Financial Review that is cross referred from the Business Review section of the Directors' Report.][13]

In addition we report to you if, in our opinion, the company has not kept proper accounting records, if we have not received all the information and explanations we require for our audit, or if information specified by law regarding directors' remuneration and other transactions is not disclosed.

---

[12] Auditor's reports of entities that do not publish their financial statements on a web site or publish them using 'PDF' format may continue to refer to the financial statements by reference to page numbers.

[13] Include and tailor as necessary to clarify the information covered by the auditor's opinion.

We read other information contained in the Annual Report, and consider whether it is consistent with the audited financial statements. This other information comprises only [the Directors' Report, the Chairman's Statement and the Operating and Financial Review][14]. We consider the implications for our report if we become aware of any apparent misstatements or material inconsistencies with the financial statements. Our responsibilities do not extend to any other information.

Basis of audit opinion

We conducted our audit in accordance with International Standards on Auditing (UK and Ireland) issued by the Auditing Practices Board. An audit includes examination, on a test basis, of evidence relevant to the amounts and disclosures in the financial statements. It also includes an assessment of the significant estimates and judgments made by the directors in the preparation of the financial statements, and of whether the accounting policies are appropriate to the group's and company's circumstances, consistently applied and adequately disclosed.

We planned and performed our audit so as to obtain all the information and explanations which we considered necessary in order to provide us with sufficient evidence to give reasonable assurance that the financial statements are free from material misstatement, whether caused by fraud or other irregularity or error. In forming our opinion we also evaluated the overall adequacy of the presentation of information in the financial statements.

Opinion

In our opinion:

- the financial statements give a true and fair view, in accordance with United Kingdom Generally Accepted Accounting Practice, of the state of the group's and the parent company's affairs as at .... and of the group's profit[loss] for the year then ended;

- the financial statements have been properly prepared in accordance with the Companies Act 1985; and

- the information given in the Directors' Report is consistent with the financial statements.

Registered auditors   *Address*
Date

---

[14] The other information that is 'read' is the content of the printed Annual Report other than the financial statements. The description of the information that has been read is tailored to reflect the terms used in the Annual Report.

Example 5 – Publicly traded company – Auditor's report on parent company financial statements:

- *Group and parent company financial statements presented separately.*

- *IFRSs as adopted by the European Union used for group and parent company financial statements.*

- *Company does meet the Companies Act definition of a quoted company.*

- *Section 230 exemption not taken for parent company's own income statement.*

- *Corporate governance statement reported on in the report on the group financial statements.*

- *Directors' Remuneration Report reported on in the report on the parent company financial statements.*

INDEPENDENT AUDITOR'S REPORT TO THE [MEMBERS] [SHAREHOLDERS] OF XYZ PLC

We have audited the parent company financial statements of (name of entity) for the year ended ... which comprise [state the primary financial statements such as the Income Statement, the Balance Sheet, the Cash Flow Statement, the Statement of Changes in Equity/Statement of Recognised Income and Expense] and the related notes[15]. These parent company financial statements have been prepared under the accounting policies set out therein. We have also audited the information in the Directors' Remuneration Report that is described as having been audited.[16]

We have reported separately on the group financial statements of (name of entity) for the year ended .... [That report is modified by the inclusion of an emphasis of matter] [The opinion in that report is (qualified)/(an adverse opinion)/(a disclaimer of opinion)].

Respective responsibilities of directors and auditors

The directors' responsibilities for preparing the Annual Report, the Directors' Remuneration Report and the parent company financial statements in accordance with applicable law and International Financial Reporting Standards (IFRSs) as adopted by the European Union are set out in the Statement of Directors' Responsibilities.

---

[15] Auditor's reports of entities that do not publish their financial statements on a web site or publish them using 'PDF' format may continue to refer to the financial statements by reference to page numbers.

[16] Part 3 of Schedule 7A to the Companies Act 1985 sets out the information in the Directors' Remuneration Report that is subject to audit. Companies should describe clearly which disclosures within the Directors' Report have been audited.

Our responsibility is to audit the parent company financial statements and the part of the Directors' Remuneration Report to be audited in accordance with relevant legal and regulatory requirements and International Standards on Auditing (UK and Ireland).

We report to you our opinion as to whether the parent company financial statements give a true and fair view and whether the parent company financial statements and the part of the Directors' Remuneration Report to be audited have been properly prepared in accordance with the Companies Act 1985. We also report to you whether in our opinion the information given in the Directors' Report is consistent with the parent company financial statements. [The information given in the Directors' Report includes that specific information presented in the Operating and Financial Review that is cross referred from the Business Review section of the Directors' Report.][17]

In addition we report to you if, in our opinion, the company has not kept proper accounting records, if we have not received all the information and explanations we require for our audit, or if information specified by law regarding directors' remuneration and other transactions is not disclosed.

We read other information contained in the Annual Report and consider whether it is consistent with the audited parent company financial statements. The other information comprises only [the Directors' Report, the unaudited part of the Directors' Remuneration Report, the Chairman's Statement and the Operating and Financial Review][18]. We consider the implications for our report if we become aware of any apparent misstatements or material inconsistencies with the parent company financial statements. Our responsibilities do not extend to any other information.

Basis of audit opinion

We conducted our audit in accordance with International Standards on Auditing (UK and Ireland) issued by the Auditing Practices Board. An audit includes examination, on a test basis, of evidence relevant to the amounts and disclosures in the parent company financial statements and the part of the Directors' Remuneration Report to be audited. It also includes an assessment of the significant estimates and judgments made by the directors in the preparation of the parent company financial statements, and of whether the accounting policies are appropriate to the company's circumstances, consistently applied and adequately disclosed.

We planned and performed our audit so as to obtain all the information and explanations which we considered necessary in order to provide us with sufficient evidence to give reasonable assurance that the parent company financial statements and the part of the Directors' Remuneration Report to be audited are free from material misstatement, whether caused by fraud or other irregularity or error. In forming our opinion we also evaluated the

---

[17] Include and tailor as necessary to clarify the information covered by the auditor's opinion.

[18] The other information that is 'read' is the content of the printed Annual Report other than the financial statements. The description of the information that has been read is tailored to reflect the terms used in the Annual Report.

overall adequacy of the presentation of information in the parent company financial statements and the part of the Directors' Remuneration Report to be audited.

Opinion

In our opinion:

- the parent company financial statements give a true and fair view, in accordance with IFRSs as adopted by the European Union, of the state of the company's affairs as at .... and of its profit[loss] for the year then ended;

- the parent company financial statements and the part of the Directors' Remuneration Report to be audited have been properly prepared in accordance with the Companies Act 1985; and

- the information given in the Directors' Report is consistent with the parent company financial statements.

Registered auditors   *Address*
Date

Example 6 – Publicly traded company – Auditor's report on parent company financial statements:

- *Group and parent company financial statements presented separately.*

- *IFRSs as adopted by the European Union used for group financial statements.*

- *UK GAAP used for parent company financial statements.*

- *Company does meet the Companies Act definition of a quoted company.*

- *Section 230 exemption taken for parent company's own profit and loss account.*

- *Corporate governance statement reported on in the report on the group financial statements.*

- *Directors' Remuneration Report reported on in the report on the parent company financial statements.*

INDEPENDENT AUDITOR'S REPORT TO THE [MEMBERS] [SHAREHOLDERS] OF XYZ PLC

We have audited the parent company financial statements of (name of entity) for the year ended ... which comprise [state the primary financial statements such as the Balance Sheet] and the related notes[19]. These parent company financial statements have been prepared under the accounting policies set out therein. We have also audited the information in the Directors' Remuneration Report that is described as having been audited[20].

We have reported separately on the group financial statements of (name of entity) for the year ended .... [That report is modified by the inclusion of an emphasis of matter] [The opinion in that report is (qualified)/(an adverse opinion)/(a disclaimer of opinion)].

Respective responsibilities of directors and auditors

The directors' responsibilities for preparing the Annual Report, the Directors' Remuneration Report and the parent company financial statements in accordance with applicable law and United Kingdom Accounting Standards (United Kingdom Generally Accepted Accounting Practice) are set out in the Statement of Directors' Responsibilities.

Our responsibility is to audit the parent company financial statements and the part of the Directors' Remuneration Report to be audited in accordance with relevant legal and regulatory requirements and International Standards on Auditing (UK and Ireland).

---

[19] Auditor's reports of entities that do not publish their financial statements on a web site or publish them using 'PDF' format may continue to refer to the financial statements by reference to page numbers.

[20] Part 3 of Schedule 7A to the Companies Act 1985 sets out the information in the Directors' Remuneration Report that is subject to audit. Companies should describe clearly which disclosures within the Directors' Report have been audited.

We report to you our opinion as to whether the parent company financial statements give a true and fair view and whether the parent company financial statements and the part of the Directors' Remuneration Report to be audited have been properly prepared in accordance with the Companies Act 1985. We also report to you whether in our opinion the Directors' Report is consistent with the parent company financial statements. [The information given in the Directors' Report includes that specific information presented in the Operating and Financial Review that is cross referred from the Business Review section of the Directors' Report.][21]

In addition we report to you if, in our opinion, the company has not kept proper accounting records, if we have not received all the information and explanations we require for our audit, or if information specified by law regarding directors' remuneration and other transactions is not disclosed.

We read other information contained in the Annual Report and consider whether it is consistent with the audited parent company financial statements. The other information comprises only [the Directors' Report, the unaudited part of the Directors' Remuneration Report, the Chairman's Statement and the Operating and Financial Review][22]. We consider the implications for our report if we become aware of any apparent misstatements or material inconsistencies with the parent company financial statements. Our responsibilities do not extend to any other information.

Basis of audit opinion

We conducted our audit in accordance with International Standards on Auditing (UK and Ireland) issued by the Auditing Practices Board. An audit includes examination, on a test basis, of evidence relevant to the amounts and disclosures in the parent company financial statements and the part of the Directors' Remuneration Report to be audited. It also includes an assessment of the significant estimates and judgments made by the directors in the preparation of the parent company financial statements, and of whether the accounting policies are appropriate to the company's circumstances, consistently applied and adequately disclosed.

We planned and performed our audit so as to obtain all the information and explanations which we considered necessary in order to provide us with sufficient evidence to give reasonable assurance that the parent company financial statements and the part of the Directors' Remuneration Report to be audited are free from material misstatement, whether caused by fraud or other irregularity or error. In forming our opinion we also evaluated the overall adequacy of the presentation of information in the parent company financial statements and the part of the Directors' Remuneration Report to be audited.

Opinion

In our opinion:

---

[21] Include and tailor as necessary to clarify the information covered by the auditor's opinion.

[22] The other information that is 'read' is the content of the printed Annual Report other than the financial statements. The description of the information that has been read is tailored to reflect the terms used in the Annual Report.

- the parent company financial statements give a true and fair view, in accordance with United Kingdom Generally Accepted Accounting Practice, of the state of the company's affairs as at ....;

- the parent company financial statements and the part of the Directors' Remuneration Report to be audited have been properly prepared in accordance with the Companies Act 1985; and

- the information given in the Directors' Report is consistent with the parent company financial statements.

Registered auditors   *Address*
Date

Example 7 – Publicly traded company – Auditor's report on group (not including parent company) financial statements:

- Group and parent company financial statements presented separately.

- IFRSs as adopted by the European Union used for group financial statements.

- Company does meet the Companies Act definition of a quoted company.

- Corporate governance statement reported on in the report on the group financial statements.

- Directors' Remuneration Report reported on in the report on the parent company financial statements.

INDEPENDENT AUDITOR'S REPORT TO THE [MEMBERS] [SHAREHOLDERS] OF XYZ PLC

We have audited the group financial statements of (name of entity) for the year ended ... which comprise [state the primary financial statements such as the Group Income Statement, the Group Balance Sheet, the Group Cash Flow Statement, the Group Statement of Changes in Equity/Statement of Recognised Income and Expense] and the related notes[23]. These group financial statements have been prepared under the accounting policies set out therein.

We have reported separately on the parent company financial statements of (name of entity) for the year ended and on the information in the Directors' Remuneration Report that is described as having been audited. [That report is modified by the inclusion of an emphasis of matter] [The opinion in that report is (qualified)/(an adverse opinion)/(a disclaimer of opinion)].

Respective responsibilities of directors and auditors

The directors' responsibilities for preparing the Annual Report and the group financial statements in accordance with applicable law and International Financial Reporting Standards (IFRSs) as adopted by the European Union are set out in the Statement of Directors' Responsibilities.

Our responsibility is to audit the group financial statements in accordance with relevant legal and regulatory requirements and International Standards on Auditing (UK and Ireland).

We report to you our opinion as to whether the group financial statements give a true and fair view and whether the group financial statements have been properly prepared in accordance with the Companies Act 1985 and Article 4 of the IAS Regulation. We also

---

[23] Auditor's reports of entities that do not publish their financial statements on a web site or publish them using 'PDF' format may continue to refer to the financial statements by reference to page numbers.

report to you whether in our opinion the information given in the Directors' Report is consistent with the group financial statements. [The information given in the Directors' Report includes that specific information presented in the Operating and Financial Review that is cross referred from the Business Review section of the Directors' Report.][24]

In addition we report to you if, in our opinion, we have not received all the information and explanations we require for our audit, or if information specified by law regarding director's remuneration and other transactions is not disclosed.

We review whether the Corporate Governance Statement reflects the company's compliance with the nine provisions of the [2003[25]] Combined Code specified for our review by the Listing Rules of the Financial Services Authority, and we report if it does not. We are not required to consider whether the board's statements on internal control cover all risks and controls, or form an opinion on the effectiveness of the group's corporate governance procedures or its risk and control procedures.

We read other information contained in the Annual Report and consider whether it is consistent with the audited group financial statements. The other information comprises only [the Directors' Report, the Chairman's Statement, the Operating and Financial Review and the Corporate Governance Statement][26]. We consider the implications for our report if we become aware of any apparent misstatements or material inconsistencies with the group financial statements. Our responsibilities do not extend to any other information.

Basis of audit opinion

We conducted our audit in accordance with International Standards on Auditing (UK and Ireland) issued by the Auditing Practices Board. An audit includes examination, on a test basis, of evidence relevant to the amounts and disclosures in the group financial statements. It also includes an assessment of the significant estimates and judgments made by the directors in the preparation of the group financial statements, and of whether the accounting policies are appropriate to the group's circumstances, consistently applied and adequately disclosed.

We planned and performed our audit so as to obtain all the information and explanations which we considered necessary in order to provide us with sufficient evidence to give reasonable assurance that the group financial statements are free from material misstatement, whether caused by fraud or other irregularity or error. In forming our opinion we also evaluated the overall adequacy of the presentation of information in the group financial statements.

---

[24] Include and tailor as necessary to clarify the information covered by the auditor's opinion.

[25] In June 2006 the Financial Reporting Council issued a revised version of the Combined Code. An announcement is expected from the Financial Services Authority regarding the period from which the reference to 2003 should be changed to 2006.

[26] The other information that is 'read' is the content of the printed Annual Report other than the financial statements. The description of the information that has been read is tailored to reflect the terms used in the Annual Report.

Opinion

In our opinion:

- the group financial statements give a true and fair view, in accordance with IFRSs as adopted by the European Union, of the state of the group's affairs as at .... and of its profit[loss] for the year then ended;

- the group financial statements have been properly prepared in accordance with the Companies Act 1985 and Article 4 of the IAS Regulation; and

- the information given in the Directors' Report is consistent with the group financial statements.

[Separate opinion in relation to IFRSs

As explained in Note x to the group financial statements, the group in addition to complying with its legal obligation to comply with IFRSs as adopted by the European Union, has also complied with the IFRSs as issued by the International Accounting Standards Board.

In our opinion the group financial statements give a true and fair view, in accordance with IFRSs, of the state of the group's affairs as at ...and of its profit [loss] for the year then ended.]

Registered auditors   *Address*
Date

Example 8 – Publicly traded company – Auditor's report on group and parent company financial statements:

- *Group and parent company financial statements not presented separately.*

- *IFRSs as adopted by the European Union used for group financial statements.*

- *UK GAAP used for parent company financial statements.*

- *Company does meet the Companies Act definition of a quoted company.*

- *Section 230 exemption taken for parent company's own profit and loss account.*

INDEPENDENT AUDITOR'S REPORT TO THE [MEMBERS] [SHAREHOLDERS] OF XYZ PLC

We have audited the group and parent company financial statements (the "financial statements") of (name of entity) for the year ended ... which comprise [state the primary financial statements such as the Group Income Statement, the Group and Parent Company Balance Sheets, the Group Cash Flow Statement, the Group Statement of Changes in Equity/Statement of Recognised Income and Expense] and the related notes[27]. These financial statements have been prepared under the accounting policies set out therein. We have also audited the information in the Directors' Remuneration Report that is described as having been audited[28].

Respective responsibilities of directors and auditors

The directors' responsibilities for preparing the Annual Report and the group financial statements in accordance with applicable law and International Financial Reporting Standards (IFRSs) as adopted by the European Union, and for preparing the parent company financial statements and the Directors' Remuneration Report in accordance with applicable law and United Kingdom Accounting Standards (United Kingdom Generally Accepted Accounting Practice) are set out in the Statement of Directors' Responsibilities.

Our responsibility is to audit the financial statements and the part of the Directors' Remuneration Report to be audited in accordance with relevant legal and regulatory requirements and International Standards on Auditing (UK and Ireland).

We report to you our opinion as to whether the financial statements give a true and fair view and whether the financial statements and the part of the Directors' Remuneration Report to be audited have been properly prepared in accordance with the Companies Act 1985 and

---

[27] Auditor's reports of entities that do not publish their financial statements on a web site or publish them using 'PDF' format may continue to refer to the financial statements by reference to page numbers.

[28] Part 3 of Schedule 7A to the Companies Act 1985 sets out the information in the Directors' Remuneration Report that is subject to audit. Companies should describe clearly which disclosures within the Directors' Report have been audited.

whether, in addition, the group financial statements have been properly prepared in accordance with Article 4 of the IAS Regulation. We also report to you whether in our opinion the information given in the Directors' Report is consistent with the financial statements. [The information given in the Directors' Report includes that specific information presented in the Operating and Financial Review that is cross referred from the Business Review section of the Directors' Report.][29]

In addition we report to you if, in our opinion, the company has not kept proper accounting records, if we have not received all the information and explanations we require for our audit, or if information specified by law regarding directors' remuneration and other transactions is not disclosed.

We review whether the Corporate Governance Statement reflects the company's compliance with the nine provisions of the [2003[30]] Combined Code specified for our review by the Listing Rules of the Financial Services Authority, and we report if it does not. We are not required to consider whether the board's statements on internal control cover all risks and controls, or form an opinion on the effectiveness of the group's corporate governance procedures or its risk and control procedures.

We read other information contained in the Annual Report and consider whether it is consistent with the audited financial statements. The other information comprises only [the Directors' Report, the unaudited part of the Directors' Remuneration Report, the Chairman's Statement, the Operating and Financial Review and the Corporate Governance Statement][31]. We consider the implications for our report if we become aware of any apparent misstatements or material inconsistencies with the financial statements. Our responsibilities do not extend to any other information.

Basis of audit opinion

We conducted our audit in accordance with International Standards on Auditing (UK and Ireland) issued by the Auditing Practices Board. An audit includes examination, on a test basis, of evidence relevant to the amounts and disclosures in the financial statements and the part of the Directors' Remuneration Report to be audited. It also includes an assessment of the significant estimates and judgments made by the directors in the preparation of the financial statements, and of whether the accounting policies are appropriate to the group's and company's circumstances, consistently applied and adequately disclosed.

We planned and performed our audit so as to obtain all the information and explanations which we considered necessary in order to provide us with sufficient evidence to give reasonable assurance that the financial statements and the part of the Directors'

---

[29] Include and tailor as necessary to clarify the information covered by the auditor's opinion.

[30] In June 2006 the Financial Reporting Council issued a revised version of the Combined Code. An announcement is expected from the Financial Services Authority regarding the period from which the reference to 2003 should be changed to 2006.

[31] The other information that is 'read' is the content of the printed Annual Report other than the financial statements. The description of the information that has been read is tailored to reflect the terms used in the Annual Report.

Remuneration Report to be audited are free from material misstatement, whether caused by fraud or other irregularity or error. In forming our opinion we also evaluated the overall adequacy of the presentation of information in the financial statements and the part of the Directors' Remuneration Report to be audited.

Opinion

In our opinion:

- the group financial statements give a true and fair view, in accordance with IFRSs as adopted by the European Union, of the state of the group's affairs as at .... and of its profit[loss] for the year then ended;

- the group financial statements have been properly prepared in accordance with the Companies Act 1985 and Article 4 of the IAS Regulation;

- the parent company financial statements give a true and fair view, in accordance with United Kingdom Generally Accepted Accounting Practice, of the state of the parent company's affairs as at ....;

- the parent company financial statements and the part of the Directors' Remuneration Report to be audited have been properly prepared in accordance with the Companies Act 1985; and

- the information given in the Directors' Report is consistent with the financial statements.

[Separate opinion in relation to IFRSs

As explained in Note x to the group financial statements, the group in addition to complying with its legal obligation to comply with IFRSs as adopted by the European Union, has also complied with the IFRSs as issued by the International Accounting Standards Board.

In our opinion the group financial statements give a true and fair view, in accordance with IFRSs, of the state of the group's affairs as at ...and of its profit [loss] for the year then ended.]

Registered auditors   *Address*
Date

Example 9 – Publicly traded company – Auditor's report on parent company financial statements:

- *Group and parent company financial statements presented separately.*

- *IFRSs as adopted by the European Union used for group financial statements.*

- *UK GAAP used for parent company financial statements.*

- *Company does meet the Companies Act definition of a quoted company.*

- *Section 230 exemption not taken for parent company's own profit and loss account.*

- *Corporate governance statement reported on in the report on the group financial statements.*

- *Directors' Remuneration Report reported on in the report on the parent company financial statements.*

INDEPENDENT AUDITOR'S REPORT TO THE [MEMBERS] [SHAREHOLDERS] OF XYZ PLC

We have audited the parent company financial statements of (name of entity) for the year ended ... which comprise [state the primary financial statements such as the Profit and Loss Account, the Balance Sheet, the Statement of Total Recognised Gains and Losses] and the related notes[32]. These parent company financial statements have been prepared under the accounting policies set out therein. We have also audited the information in the Directors' Remuneration Report that is described as having been audited[33].

We have reported separately on the group financial statements of (name of entity) for the year ended .... [That report is modified by the inclusion of an emphasis of matter] [The opinion in that report is (qualified)/(an adverse opinion)/(a disclaimer of opinion).]

Respective responsibilities of directors and auditors

The directors' responsibilities for preparing the Annual Report, the Directors' Remuneration Report and the parent company financial statements in accordance with applicable law and United Kingdom Accounting Standards (United Kingdom Generally Accepted Accounting Practice) are set out in the Statement of Directors' Responsibilities.

---

[32] Auditor's reports of entities that do not publish their financial statements on a web site or publish them using 'PDF' format may continue to refer to the financial statements by reference to page numbers.

[33] Part 3 of Schedule 7A to the Companies Act 1985 sets out the information in the Directors' Remuneration Report that is subject to audit. Companies should describe clearly which disclosures within the Directors' Report have been audited.

Our responsibility is to audit the parent company financial statements and the part of the Directors' Remuneration Report to be audited in accordance with relevant legal and regulatory requirements and International Standards on Auditing (UK and Ireland).

We report to you our opinion as to whether the parent company financial statements give a true and fair view and whether the parent company financial statements and the part of the Directors' Remuneration Report to be audited have been properly prepared in accordance with the Companies Act 1985. We also report to you whether in our opinion the information given in the Directors' Report is consistent with the parent company financial statements. [The information given in the Directors' Report includes that specific information presented in the Operating and Financial Review that is cross referred from the Business Review section of the Directors' Report.][34]

In addition we report to you if, in our opinion, the company has not kept proper accounting records, if we have not received all the information and explanations we require for our audit, or if information specified by law regarding directors' remuneration and other transactions is not disclosed.

We read other information contained in the Annual Report and consider whether it is consistent with the audited parent company financial statements. The other information comprises only [the Directors' Report, the unaudited part of the Directors' Remuneration Report, the Chairman's Statement and the Operating and Financial Review][35]. We consider the implications for our report if we become aware of any apparent misstatements or material inconsistencies with the parent company financial statements. Our responsibilities do not extend to any other information.

Basis of audit opinion

We conducted our audit in accordance with International Standards on Auditing (UK and Ireland) issued by the Auditing Practices Board. An audit includes examination, on a test basis, of evidence relevant to the amounts and disclosures in the parent company financial statements and the part of the Directors' Remuneration Report to be audited. It also includes an assessment of the significant estimates and judgments made by the directors in the preparation of the parent company financial statements, and of whether the accounting policies are appropriate to the company's circumstances, consistently applied and adequately disclosed.

We planned and performed our audit so as to obtain all the information and explanations which we considered necessary in order to provide us with sufficient evidence to give reasonable assurance that the parent company financial statements and the part of the Directors' Remuneration Report to be audited are free from material misstatement, whether caused by fraud or other irregularity or error. In forming our opinion we also evaluated the overall adequacy of the presentation of information in the parent company financial statements and the part of the Directors' Remuneration Report to be audited.

---

[34] Include and tailor as necessary to clarify the information covered by the auditor's opinion.

[35] The other information that is 'read' is the content of the printed Annual Report other than the financial statements. The description of the information that has been read is tailored to reflect the terms used in the Annual Report.

Opinion

In our opinion:

- the parent company financial statements give a true and fair view, in accordance with United Kingdom Generally Accepted Accounting Practice, of the state of the company's affairs as at .... and of its profit[loss] for the year then ended;

- the parent company financial statements and the part of the Directors' Remuneration Report to be audited have been properly prepared in accordance with the Companies Act 1985; and

- the information given in the Directors' Report is consistent with the parent company financial statements.

Registered auditors   *Address*
Date

Example 10 – Publicly traded company – Auditor's report on group and parent company financial statements:

- *Group and parent company financial statements not presented separately.*

- *IFRSs as adopted by the European Union used for group financial statements.*

- *UK GAAP used for parent company financial statements.*

- *Company does meet the Companies Act definition of a quoted company.*

- *Section 230 exemption not taken for parent company's own profit and loss account.*

INDEPENDENT AUDITOR'S REPORT TO THE [MEMBERS] [SHAREHOLDERS] OF XYZ PLC

We have audited the group and parent company financial statements (the "financial statements") of (name of entity) for the year ended ... which comprise [state the primary financial statements such as the Group Income Statement, the Parent Company Profit and Loss Account, the Group and Parent Company Balance Sheets, the Group Cash Flow Statement, the Group Statement of Changes in Equity/Statement of Recognised Income and Expense, the Parent Company Statement of Total Recognised Gains and Losses] and the related notes[36]. These financial statements have been prepared under the accounting policies set out therein. We have also audited the information in the Directors' Remuneration Report that is described as having been audited[37].

Respective responsibilities of directors and auditors

The directors' responsibilities for preparing the Annual Report and the group financial statements in accordance with applicable law and International Financial Reporting Standards (IFRSs) as adopted by the European Union, and for preparing the parent company financial statements and the Directors' Remuneration Report in accordance with applicable law and United Kingdom Accounting Standards (United Kingdom Generally Accepted Accounting Practice) are set out in the Statement of Directors' Responsibilities.

Our responsibility is to audit the financial statements and the part of the Directors' Remuneration Report to be audited in accordance with relevant legal and regulatory requirements and International Standards on Auditing (UK and Ireland).

We report to you our opinion as to whether the financial statements give a true and fair view and whether the financial statements and the part of the Directors' Remuneration Report to be audited have been properly prepared in accordance with the Companies Act 1985 and

---

[36] Auditor's reports of entities that do not publish their financial statements on a web site or publish them using 'PDF' format may continue to refer to the financial statements by reference to page numbers.

[37] Part 3 of Schedule 7A to the Companies Act 1985 sets out the information in the Directors' Remuneration Report that is subject to audit. Companies should describe clearly which disclosures within the Directors' Report have been audited.

whether, in addition, the group financial statements have been properly prepared in accordance with Article 4 of the IAS Regulation. We also report to you whether in our opinion the information given in the Directors' Report is consistent with the financial statements. [The information given in the Directors' Report includes that specific information presented in the Operating and Financial Review that is cross referred from the Business Review section of the Directors' Report.][38]

In addition we report to you if, in our opinion, the company has not kept proper accounting records, if we have not received all the information and explanations we require for our audit, or if information specified by law regarding directors' remuneration and other transactions is not disclosed.

We review whether the Corporate Governance Statement reflects the company's compliance with the nine provisions of the [2003[39]] Combined Code specified for our review by the Listing Rules of the Financial Services Authority, and we report if it does not. We are not required to consider whether the board's statements on internal control cover all risks and controls, or form an opinion on the effectiveness of the group's corporate governance procedures or its risk and control procedures.

We read other information contained in the Annual Report and consider whether it is consistent with the audited financial statements. The other information comprises only [the Directors' Report, the unaudited part of the Directors' Remuneration Report, the Chairman's Statement, the Operating and Financial Review and the Corporate Governance Statement][40]. We consider the implications for our report if we become aware of any apparent misstatements or material inconsistencies with the financial statements. Our responsibilities do not extend to any other information.

Basis of audit opinion

We conducted our audit in accordance with International Standards on Auditing (UK and Ireland) issued by the Auditing Practices Board. An audit includes examination, on a test basis, of evidence relevant to the amounts and disclosures in the financial statements and the part of the Directors' Remuneration Report to be audited. It also includes an assessment of the significant estimates and judgments made by the directors in the preparation of the financial statements, and of whether the accounting policies are appropriate to the group's and company's circumstances, consistently applied and adequately disclosed.

We planned and performed our audit so as to obtain all the information and explanations which we considered necessary in order to provide us with sufficient evidence to give reasonable assurance that the financial statements and the part of the Directors'

---

[38] Include and tailor as necessary to clarify the information covered by the auditor's opinion.

[39] In June 2006 the Financial Reporting Council issued a revised version of the Combined Code. An announcement is expected from the Financial Services Authority regarding the period from which the reference to 2003 should be changed to 2006.

[40] The other information that is 'read' is the content of the printed Annual Report other than the financial statements. The description of the information that has been read is tailored to reflect the terms used in the Annual Report.

Remuneration Report to be audited are free from material misstatement, whether caused by fraud or other irregularity or error. In forming our opinion we also evaluated the overall adequacy of the presentation of information in the financial statements and the part of the Directors' Remuneration Report to be audited.

Opinion

In our opinion:

- the group financial statements give a true and fair view, in accordance with IFRSs as adopted by the European Union, of the state of the group's affairs as at .... and of its profit[loss] for the year then ended;

- the group financial statements have been properly prepared in accordance with the Companies Act 1985 and Article 4 of the IAS Regulation;

- the parent company financial statements give a true and fair view, in accordance with United Kingdom Generally Accepted Accounting Practice, of the state of the parent company's affairs as at .... and of its profit [loss] for the year then ended;

- the parent company financial statements and the part of the Directors' Remuneration Report to be audited have been properly prepared in accordance with the Companies Act 1985; and

- the information given in the Directors' Report is consistent with the financial statements.

[Separate opinion in relation to IFRSs

As explained in Note x to the group financial statements, the group in addition to complying with its legal obligation to comply with IFRSs as adopted by the European Union, has also complied with the IFRSs as issued by the International Accounting Standards Board.

In our opinion the group financial statements give a true and fair view, in accordance with IFRSs, of the state of the group's affairs as at ...and of its profit [loss] for the year then ended.]

Registered auditors   *Address*
Date

Example 11 – Publicly traded company – Auditor's report on parent company financial statements:

- Group and parent company financial statements presented separately.

- IFRSs as adopted by the European Union used for both group and parent company financial statements.

- Company does meet the Companies Act definition of a quoted company.

- Section 230 exemption taken for parent company's own income statement.

- Corporate governance statement reported on in the report on the group financial statements.

- Directors' Remuneration Report reported on in the report on the parent company financial statements.

INDEPENDENT AUDITOR'S REPORT TO THE [MEMBERS] [SHAREHOLDERS] OF XYZ PLC

We have audited the parent company financial statements of (name of entity) for the year ended ... which comprise [state the primary financial statements such as the Balance Sheet, the Cash Flow Statement, the Statement of Changes in Equity/Statement of Recognised Income and Expense] and the related notes[41]. These parent company financial statements have been prepared under the accounting policies set out therein. We have also audited the information in the Directors' Remuneration Report that is described as having been audited[42].

We have reported separately on the group financial statements of (name of entity) for the year ended .... [That report is modified by the inclusion of an emphasis of matter] [The opinion in that report is (qualified)/(an adverse opinion)/(a disclaimer of opinion).]

Respective responsibilities of directors and auditors

The directors' responsibilities for preparing the Annual Report, the Directors' Remuneration Report and the parent company financial statements in accordance with applicable law and International Financial Reporting Standards (IFRSs) as adopted by the European Union are set out in the Statement of Directors' Responsibilities.

---

[41] Auditor's reports of entities that do not publish their financial statements on a web site or publish them using 'PDF' format may continue to refer to the financial statements by reference to page numbers.

[42] Part 3 of Schedule 7A to the Companies Act 1985 sets out the information in the Directors' Remuneration Report that is subject to audit. Companies should describe clearly which disclosures within the Directors' Report have been audited.

Our responsibility is to audit the parent company financial statements and the part of the Directors' Remuneration Report to be audited in accordance with relevant legal and regulatory requirements and International Standards on Auditing (UK and Ireland).

We report to you our opinion as to whether the parent company financial statements give a true and fair view and whether the parent company financial statements and the part of the Directors' Remuneration Report to be audited have been properly prepared in accordance with the Companies Act 1985. We also report to you whether in our opinion the information given in the Directors' Report is consistent with the parent company financial statements. [The information given in the Directors' Report includes that specific information presented in the Operating and Financial Review that is cross referred from the Business Review section of the Directors' Report.][43]

In addition we report to you if, in our opinion, the company has not kept proper accounting records, if we have not received all the information and explanations we require for our audit, or if information specified by law regarding directors' remuneration and other transactions is not disclosed.

We read other information contained in the Annual Report and consider whether it is consistent with the audited parent company financial statements. The other information comprises only [the Directors' Report, the unaudited part of the Directors' Remuneration Report, the Chairman's Statement and the Operating and Financial Review][44]. We consider the implications for our report if we become aware of any apparent misstatements or material inconsistencies with the parent company financial statements. Our responsibilities do not extend to any other information.

Basis of audit opinion

We conducted our audit in accordance with International Standards on Auditing (UK and Ireland) issued by the Auditing Practices Board. An audit includes examination, on a test basis, of evidence relevant to the amounts and disclosures in the parent company financial statements and the part of the Directors' Remuneration Report to be audited. It also includes an assessment of the significant estimates and judgments made by the directors in the preparation of the parent company financial statements, and of whether the accounting policies are appropriate to the company's circumstances, consistently applied and adequately disclosed.

We planned and performed our audit so as to obtain all the information and explanations which we considered necessary in order to provide us with sufficient evidence to give reasonable assurance that the parent company financial statements and the part of the Directors' Remuneration Report to be audited are free from material misstatement, whether caused by fraud or other irregularity or error. In forming our opinion we also evaluated the overall adequacy of the presentation of information in the parent company financial statements and the part of the Directors' Remuneration Report to be audited.

---

[43] Include and tailor as necessary to clarify the information covered by the auditor's opinion.

[44] The other information that is 'read' is the content of the printed Annual Report other than the financial statements. The description of the information that has been read is tailored to reflect the terms used in the Annual Report.

Opinion

In our opinion:

- the parent company financial statements give a true and fair view, in accordance with IFRSs as adopted by the European Union as applied in accordance with the provisions of the Companies Act 1985, of the state of the company's affairs as at ....;

- the parent company financial statements and the part of the Directors' Remuneration Report to be audited have been properly prepared in accordance with the Companies Act 1985; and

- the information given in the Directors' Report is consistent with the parent company financial statements.

Registered auditors   *Address*
Date

Example 12 – Publicly traded company – Auditor's report on group and parent company financial statements:

- *Group and parent company financial statements not presented separately.*

- *IFRSs as adopted by the European Union used for both group and parent company financial statements.*

- *Company does meet the Companies Act definition of a quoted company.*

- *Section 230 exemption taken for parent company's own income statement.*

INDEPENDENT AUDITOR'S REPORT TO THE [MEMBERS] [SHAREHOLDERS] OF XYZ PLC

We have audited the group and parent company financial statements (the "financial statements") of (name of entity) for the year ended ... which comprise [state the primary financial statements such as the Group Income Statement, the Group and Parent Company Balance Sheets, the Group and Parent Company Cash Flow Statements, the Group and Parent Company Statements of Changes in Equity/Statements of Recognised Income and Expense] and the related notes[45]. These financial statements have been prepared under the accounting policies set out therein. We have also audited the information in the Directors' Remuneration Report that is described as having been audited[46].

Respective responsibilities of directors and auditors

The directors' responsibilities for preparing the Annual Report, the Directors' Remuneration Report and the financial statements in accordance with applicable law and International Financial Reporting Standards (IFRSs) as adopted by the European Union are set out in the Statement of Directors' Responsibilities.

Our responsibility is to audit the financial statements and the part of the Directors' Remuneration Report to be audited in accordance with relevant legal and regulatory requirements and International Standards on Auditing (UK and Ireland).

We report to you our opinion as to whether the financial statements give a true and fair view and whether the financial statements and the part of the Directors' Remuneration Report to be audited have been properly prepared in accordance with the Companies Act 1985 and, as regards the group financial statements, Article 4 of the IAS Regulation. We also report to you whether in our opinion the information given in the Directors' Report is consistent with the financial statements. [The information given in the Directors' Report includes that

---

[45] Auditor's reports of entities that do not publish their financial statements on a web site or publish them using 'PDF' format may continue to refer to the financial statements by reference to page numbers.

[46] Part 3 of Schedule 7A to the Companies Act 1985 sets out the information in the Directors' Remuneration Report that is subject to audit. Companies should describe clearly which disclosures withinh the Directors' Report have been audited.

specific information presented in the Operating and Financial Review that is cross referred from the Business Review section of the Directors' Report.][47]

In addition we report to you if, in our opinion, the company has not kept proper accounting records, if we have not received all the information and explanations we require for our audit, or if information specified by law regarding directors' remuneration and other transactions is not disclosed.

We review whether the Corporate Governance Statement reflects the company's compliance with the nine provisions of the [2003[48]] Combined Code specified for our review by the Listing Rules of the Financial Services Authority, and we report if it does not. We are not required to consider whether the board's statements on internal control cover all risks and controls, or form an opinion on the effectiveness of the group's corporate governance procedures or its risk and control procedures.

We read other information contained in the Annual Report and consider whether it is consistent with the audited financial statements. The other information comprises only [the Directors' Report, the unaudited part of the Directors' Remuneration Report, the Chairman's Statement, the Operating and Financial Review and the Corporate Governance Statement][49]. We consider the implications for our report if we become aware of any apparent misstatements or material inconsistencies with the financial statements. Our responsibilities do not extend to any other information.

Basis of audit opinion

We conducted our audit in accordance with International Standards on Auditing (UK and Ireland) issued by the Auditing Practices Board. An audit includes examination, on a test basis, of evidence relevant to the amounts and disclosures in the financial statements and the part of the Directors' Remuneration Report to be audited. It also includes an assessment of the significant estimates and judgments made by the directors in the preparation of the financial statements, and of whether the accounting policies are appropriate to the group's and company's circumstances, consistently applied and adequately disclosed.

We planned and performed our audit so as to obtain all the information and explanations which we considered necessary in order to provide us with sufficient evidence to give reasonable assurance that the financial statements and the part of the Directors' Remuneration Report to be audited are free from material misstatement, whether caused by fraud or other irregularity or error. In forming our opinion we also evaluated the overall adequacy of the presentation of information in the financial statements and the part of the Directors' Remuneration Report to be audited.

---

[47] Include and tailor as necessary to clarify the information covered by the auditor's opinion.

[48] In June 2006 the Financial Reporting Council issued a revised version of the Combined Code. An announcement is expected from the Financial Services Authority regarding the period from which the reference to 2003 should be changed to 2006.

[49] The other information that is 'read' is the content of the printed Annual Report other than the financial statements. The description of the information that has been read is tailored to reflect the terms used in the Annual Report.

Opinion

In our opinion:

- the group financial statements give a true and fair view, in accordance with IFRSs as adopted by the European Union, of the state of the group's affairs as at .... and of its profit[loss] for the year then ended;

- the parent company financial statements give a true and fair view, in accordance with IFRSs as adopted by the European Union as applied in accordance with the provisions of the Companies Act 1985, of the state of the parent company's affairs as at ....;

- the financial statements and the part of the Directors' Remuneration Report to be audited have been properly prepared in accordance with the Companies Act 1985 and, as regards the group financial statements, Article 4 of the IAS Regulation; and

- the information given in the Directors' Report is consistent with the financial statements.

[Separate opinion in relation to IFRSs

As explained in Note x to the group financial statements, the group in addition to complying with its legal obligation to comply with IFRSs as adopted by the European Union, has also complied with the IFRSs as issued by the International Accounting Standards Board.

In our opinion the group financial statements give a true and fair view, in accordance with IFRSs, of the state of the group's affairs as at ...and of its profit [loss] for the year then ended.]

Registered auditors   *Address*
Date

Example 13 – Publicly traded company – Auditor's report on group and parent company financial statements:

- *Group and parent company financial statements not presented separately.*

- *IFRSs as adopted by the European Union used for both group and parent company financial statements.*

- *Company does meet the Companies Act definition of a quoted company.*

- *Section 230 exemption not taken for parent company's own income statement.*

INDEPENDENT AUDITOR'S REPORT TO THE [MEMBERS] [SHAREHOLDERS] OF XYZ PLC

We have audited the group and parent company financial statements (the "financial statements") of (name of entity) for the year ended ... which comprise [state the primary financial statements such as the Group and Parent Company Income Statements, the Group and Parent Company Balance Sheets, the Group and Parent Company Cash Flow Statements, the Group and Parent Company Statements of Changes in Equity/Statement of Recognised Income and Expense] and the related notes[50]. These financial statements have been prepared under the accounting policies set out therein. We have also audited the information in the Directors' Remuneration Report that is described as having been audited[51].

Respective responsibilities of directors and auditors

The directors' responsibilities for preparing the Annual Report, the Directors' Remuneration Report and the financial statements in accordance with applicable law and International Financial Reporting Standards (IFRSs) as adopted by the European Union are set out in the Statement of Directors' Responsibilities.

Our responsibility is to audit the financial statements and the part of the Directors' Remuneration Report to be audited in accordance with relevant legal and regulatory requirements and International Standards on Auditing (UK and Ireland).

We report to you our opinion as to whether the financial statements give a true and fair view and whether the financial statements and the part of the Directors' Remuneration Report to be audited have been properly prepared in accordance with the Companies Act 1985 and, as regards the group financial statements, Article 4 of the IAS Regulation. We also report to you whether in our opinion the information given in the Directors' Report is consistent with the financial statements. [The information given in the Directors' Report includes that

---

[50] Auditor's reports of entities that do not publish their financial statements on a web site or publish them using 'PDF' format may continue to refer to the financial statements by reference to page numbers.

[51] Part 3 of Schedule 7A to the Companies Act 1985 sets out the information in the Directors' Remuneration Report that is subject to audit. Companies should describe clearly which disclosures within the Directors' Report have been audited.

specific information presented in the Operating and Financial Review that is cross referred from the Business Review section of the Directors' Report.][52]

In addition we report to you if, in our opinion, the company has not kept proper accounting records, if we have not received all the information and explanations we require for our audit, or if information specified by law regarding directors' remuneration and other transactions is not disclosed.

We review whether the Corporate Governance Statement reflects the company's compliance with the nine provisions of the [2003[53]] Combined Code specified for our review by the Listing Rules of the Financial Services Authority, and we report if it does not. We are not required to consider whether the board's statements on internal control cover all risks and controls, or form an opinion on the effectiveness of the group's corporate governance procedures or its risk and control procedures.

We read other information contained in the Annual Report and consider whether it is consistent with the audited financial statements. The other information comprises only [the Directors' Report, the unaudited part of the Directors' Remuneration Report, the Chairman's Statement, the Operating and Financial Review and the Corporate Governance Statement][54]. We consider the implications for our report if we become aware of any apparent misstatements or material inconsistencies with the financial statements. Our responsibilities do not extend to any other information.

Basis of audit opinion

We conducted our audit in accordance with International Standards on Auditing (UK and Ireland) issued by the Auditing Practices Board. An audit includes examination, on a test basis, of evidence relevant to the amounts and disclosures in the financial statements and the part of the Directors' Remuneration Report to be audited. It also includes an assessment of the significant estimates and judgments made by the directors in the preparation of the financial statements, and of whether the accounting policies are appropriate to the group's and company's circumstances, consistently applied and adequately disclosed.

We planned and performed our audit so as to obtain all the information and explanations which we considered necessary in order to provide us with sufficient evidence to give reasonable assurance that the financial statements and the part of the Directors' Remuneration Report to be audited are free from material misstatement, whether caused by fraud or other irregularity or error. In forming our opinion we also evaluated the overall adequacy of the presentation of information in the financial statements and the part of the Directors' Remuneration Report to be audited.

---

[52] Include and tailor as necessary to clarify the information covered by the auditor's opinion.

[53] In June 2006 the Financial Reporting Council issued a revised version of the Combined Code. An announcement is expected from the Financial Services Authority regarding the period from which the reference to 2003 should be changed to 2006.

[54] The other information that is 'read' is the content of the printed Annual Report other than the financial statements. The description of the information that has been read is tailored to reflect the terms used in the Annual Report.

Opinion

In our opinion:

- the financial statements give a true and fair view, in accordance with IFRSs as adopted by the European Union, of the state of the group's and the parent company's affairs as at .... and of the group's and the parent company's profit[loss] for the year then ended;

- the financial statements and the part of the Directors' Remuneration Report to be audited have been properly prepared in accordance with the Companies Act 1985 and, as regards the group financial statements, Article 4 of the IAS Regulation; and

- the information given in the Directors' Report is consistent with the financial statements.

[Separate opinion in relation to IFRSs

As explained in Note x to the group financial statements, the group in addition to complying with its legal obligations to comply with IFRSs as adopted by the European Union, has also complied with the IFRSs as issued by the International Accounting Standards Board.

In our opinion the group financial statements give a true and fair view, in accordance with IFRSs, of the state of the group's affairs as at ...and of its profit [loss] for the year then ended.]

Registered auditors   *Address*
Date

Example 14 – Publicly traded company that does not prepare group accounts:

- IFRSs as adopted by the European Union used for financial statements.

- Company does meet the Companies Act definition of a quoted company.

INDEPENDENT AUDITOR'S REPORT TO THE [MEMBERS] [SHAREHOLDERS] OF XYZ PLC

We have audited the financial statements of (name of entity) for the year ended ... which comprise [state the primary financial statements such as the Income Statement, the Balance Sheet, the Cash Flow Statement, the Statement of Changes in Equity/Statement of Recognised Income and Expense] and the related notes[55]. These financial statements have been prepared under the accounting policies set out therein. We have also audited the information in the Directors' Remuneration Report that is described as having been audited.[56]

Respective responsibilities of directors and auditors

The directors' responsibilities for preparing the Annual Report, the Directors' Remuneration Report and the financial statements in accordance with applicable law and International Financial Reporting Standards (IFRSs) as adopted by the European Union are set out in the Statement of Directors' Responsibilities.

Our responsibility is to audit the financial statements and the part of the Directors' Remuneration Report to be audited in accordance with relevant legal and regulatory requirements and International Standards on Auditing (UK and Ireland).

We report to you our opinion as to whether the financial statements give a true and fair view and whether the financial statements and the part of the Directors' Remuneration Report to be audited have been properly prepared in accordance with the Companies Act 1985. We also report to you whether in our opinion the information given in the Directors' Report is consistent with the financial statements. [The information given in the Directors' Report includes that specific information presented in the Operating and Financial Review that is cross referred from the Business Review section of the Directors' Report.][57]

In addition we report to you if, in our opinion, the company has not kept proper accounting records, if we have not received all the information and explanations we require for our

---

[55] Auditor's reports of entities that do not publish their financial statements on a web site or publish them using 'PDF' format may continue to refer to the financial statements by reference to page numbers.

[56] Part 3 of Schedule 7A to the Companies Act 1985 sets out the information in the Directors' Remuneration Report that is subject to audit. Companies should describe clearly which disclosures within the Directors' Report have been audited.

[57] Include and tailor as necessary to clarify the information covered by the auditor's opinion.

audit, or if information specified by law regarding directors' remuneration and other transactions is not disclosed.

We review whether the Corporate Governance Statement reflects the company's compliance with the nine provisions of the [2003[58]] Combined Code specified for our review by the Listing Rules of the Financial Services Authority, and we report if it does not. We are not required to consider whether the board's statements on internal control cover all risks and controls, or form an opinion on the effectiveness of the company's corporate governance procedures or its risk and control procedures.

We read other information contained in the Annual Report and consider whether it is consistent with the audited financial statements. The other information comprises only [the Directors' Report, the unaudited part of the Directors' Remuneration Report, the Chairman's Statement and the Operating and Financial Review][59]. We consider the implications for our report if we become aware of any apparent misstatements or material inconsistencies with the financial statements. Our responsibilities do not extend to any other information.

Basis of audit opinion

We conducted our audit in accordance with International Standards on Auditing (UK and Ireland) issued by the Auditing Practices Board. An audit includes examination, on a test basis, of evidence relevant to the amounts and disclosures in the financial statements and the part of the Directors' Remuneration Report to be audited. It also includes an assessment of the significant estimates and judgments made by the directors in the preparation of the financial statements, and of whether the accounting policies are appropriate to the company's circumstances, consistently applied and adequately disclosed.

We planned and performed our audit so as to obtain all the information and explanations which we considered necessary in order to provide us with sufficient evidence to give reasonable assurance that the financial statements and the part of the Directors' Remuneration Report to be audited are free from material misstatement, whether caused by fraud or other irregularity or error. In forming our opinion we also evaluated the overall adequacy of the presentation of information in the financial statements and the part of the Directors' Remuneration Report to be audited.

---

[58] In June 2006 the Financial Reporting Council issued a revised version of the Combined Code. An announcement is expected from the Financial Services Authority regarding the period from which the reference to 2003 should be changed to 2006.

[59] The other information that is 'read' is the content of the printed Annual Report other than the financial statements. The description of the information that has been read is tailored to reflect the terms used in the Annual Report.

Opinion

In our opinion:

- the financial statements give a true and fair view, in accordance with IFRSs as adopted by the European Union, of the state of the company's affairs as at .... and of its profit[loss] for the year then ended;

- the financial statements and the part of the Directors' Remuneration Report to be audited have been properly prepared in accordance with the Companies Act 1985; and

- the information given in the Directors' Report is consistent with the financial statements.

[Separate opinion in relation to IFRSs

As explained in Note x to the financial statements, the company in addition to complying with IFRSs as adopted by the European Union, has also complied with the IFRSs as issued by the International Accounting Standards Board.

In our opinion the financial statements give a true and fair view, in accordance with IFRSs, of the state of the company's affairs as at ... and of its profit [loss] for the year then ended.]

Registered auditors   *Address*
Date

Example 15 – Publicly traded company that does not prepare group accounts:

- *UK GAAP used for financial statements.*

- *Company does meet the Companies Act definition of a quoted company.*

INDEPENDENT AUDITOR'S REPORT TO THE [MEMBERS] [SHAREHOLDERS] OF XYZ PLC

We have audited the financial statements of (name of entity) for the year ended ... which comprise [state the primary financial statements such as the Profit and Loss Account, the Balance Sheet, the Cash Flow Statement, the Statement of Total Recognised Gains and Losses] and the related notes[60]. These financial statements have been prepared under the accounting policies set out therein. We have also audited the information in the Directors' Remuneration Report that is described as having been audited[61].

Respective responsibilities of directors and auditors

The directors' responsibilities for preparing the Annual Report, the Directors' Remuneration Report and the financial statements in accordance with applicable law and United Kingdom Accounting Standards (United Kingdom Generally Accepted Accounting Practice) are set out in the Statement of Directors' Responsibilities.

Our responsibility is to audit the financial statements and the part of the Directors' Remuneration Report to be audited in accordance with relevant legal and regulatory requirements and International Standards on Auditing (UK and Ireland).

We report to you our opinion as to whether the financial statements give a true and fair view and whether the financial statements and the part of the Directors' Remuneration Report to be audited have been properly prepared in accordance with the Companies Act 1985. We also report to you whether in our opinion the information given in the Directors' Report is consistent with the financial statements. [The information given in the Directors' Report includes that specific information presented in the Operating and Financial Review that is cross referred from the Business Review section of the Directors' Report.][62]

In addition we report to you if, in our opinion, the company has not kept proper accounting records, if we have not received all the information and explanations we require for our audit, or if information specified by law regarding directors' remuneration and other transactions is not disclosed.

---

[60] Auditor's reports of entities that do not publish their financial statements on a web site or publish them using 'PDF' format may continue to refer to the financial statements by reference to page numbers.

[61] Part 3 of Schedule 7A to the Companies Act 1985 sets out the information in the Directors' Remuneration Report that is subject to audit. Companies should describe clearly which disclosures within the Directors' Report have been audited.

[62] Include and tailor as necessary to clarify the information covered by the auditor's opinion.

We review whether the Corporate Governance Statement reflects the company's compliance with the nine provisions of the [2003[63]] Combined Code specified for our review by the Listing Rules of the Financial Services Authority, and we report if it does not. We are not required to consider whether the board's statements on internal control cover all risks and controls, or form an opinion on the effectiveness of the company's corporate governance procedures or its risk and control procedures.

We read other information contained in the Annual Report and consider whether it is consistent with the audited financial statements. The other information comprises only [the Directors' Report, the unaudited part of the Directors' Remuneration Report, the Chairman's Statement and the Operating and Financial Review][64]. We consider the implications for our report if we become aware of any apparent misstatements or material inconsistencies with the financial statements. Our responsibilities do not extend to any other information.

Basis of audit opinion

We conducted our audit in accordance with International Standards on Auditing (UK and Ireland) issued by the Auditing Practices Board. An audit includes examination, on a test basis, of evidence relevant to the amounts and disclosures in the financial statements and the part of the Directors' Remuneration Report to be audited. It also includes an assessment of the significant estimates and judgments made by the directors in the preparation of the financial statements, and of whether the accounting policies are appropriate to the company's circumstances, consistently applied and adequately disclosed.

We planned and performed our audit so as to obtain all the information and explanations which we considered necessary in order to provide us with sufficient evidence to give reasonable assurance that the financial statements and the part of the Directors' Remuneration Report to be audited are free from material misstatement, whether caused by fraud or other irregularity or error. In forming our opinion we also evaluated the overall adequacy of the presentation of information in the financial statements and the part of the Directors' Remuneration Report to be audited.

---

[63] In June 2006 the Financial Reporting Council issued a revised version of the Combined Code. An announcement is expected from the Financial Services Authority regarding the period from which the reference to 2003 should be changed to 2006.

[64] The other information that is 'read' is the content of the printed Annual Report other than the financial statements. The description of the information that has been read is tailored to reflect the terms used in the Annual Report.

Opinion

In our opinion:

- the financial statements give a true and fair view, in accordance with United Kingdom Generally Accepted Accounting Practice, of the state of the company's affairs as at .... and of its profit[loss] for the year then ended;

- the financial statements and the part of the Directors' Remuneration Report to be audited have been properly prepared in accordance with the Companies Act 1985; and

- the information given in the Directors' Report is consistent with the financial statements.

Registered auditors   *Address*
Date

Appendix 2

Modified auditor's reports on financial statements (excluding going concern issues)

Note: Example auditor's reports addressing going concern issues are included in Appendix 3. Illustrative wording for an auditor's report with a modified opinion on the consistency of the directors' report with the financial statements is provided by Appendix 4.

This Appendix gives illustrative examples of modified auditor's reports on financial statements and includes:

- Examples of auditor's reports where the matter does not affect the auditor's opinion for example, emphasis of matter paragraphs; and

- Examples of auditor's reports where the matter does affect the auditor's opinion for example:

  ○ Qualified opinions;

  ○ Disclaimers of opinion; or

  ○ Adverse opinions.

The example auditor's reports are designed to illustrate the modified auditor's reports that might be issued for the different reporting situations illustrated in the navigation aid on page 1086 and do not depend on the accounting framework adopted. In most cases the examples have been based on Example 2 in Appendix 1 (ie a non-publicly traded company incorporated in Great Britain that does not prepare group financial statements and prepares its parent company financial statements under United Kingdom Generally Accepted Acounting Practice). There are some exceptions where the example illustrates an issue relating to compliance with IFRSs as adopted by the European Union.

Tailoring of the examples will be required if they are to be used in other circumstances. Preceding each example is a description of the background to the particular modification. The full text of the example unmodified auditor's reports are included in Appendix 1 but for the purpose of illustrating the modification only those sections of the auditor's report affected by the modification are included. Deletions to the examples in Appendix 1, arising from the modification, are shown as struck out text .

Navigation aid to the examples of modified auditor's reports (excluding going concern issues)

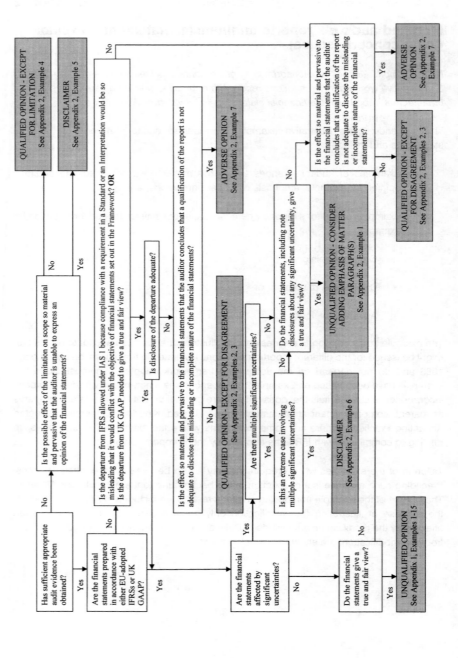

Appendix 2 – Extracts from modified auditor's reports

Matters that do not affect the auditor's opinion

1   Emphasis of matter – Possible outcome of a lawsuit, unable to quantify effect on financial statements.

Matters that do affect the auditor's opinion

Qualified opinion – Disagreement

2   Disagreement – Inappropriate accounting treatment of debtors.

3   Disagreement – Prior period qualification unresolved and results in a modification of the auditor's report regarding the current period.

Qualified opinion – Limitation on scope

4   Limitation on scope – Auditor not appointed at the time of the stocktake.

Disclaimer of opinion

5   Disclaimer – Unable to observe all physical stock and confirm trade debtors.

6   Disclaimer – Multiple material/significant uncertainties.

Adverse opinion

7   Adverse opinion – No provision made for losses expected to arise on certain long-term contracts.

Example 1 – Unqualified opinion – Emphasis of matter. Possible outcome of a lawsuit, unable to quantify effect on financial statements.

- *UK non-publicly traded company prepares UK GAAP financial statements.*

- *A lawsuit alleges that the company has infringed certain patent rights and claims royalties and punitive damages. The company has filed a counter action, and preliminary hearings and discovery proceedings on both actions are in progress.*

- *The ultimate outcome of the matter cannot presently be determined, and no provision for any liability that may result has been made in the financial statements.*

- *The company makes relevant disclosures in the financial statements.*

- *The auditor issues an unqualified auditor's report with an emphasis of matter paragraph describing the situation giving rise to the emphasis of matter and its possible effects on the financial statements, including that the effect on the financial statements of the resolution of the uncertainty cannot be quantified.*

Basis of audit opinion

We conducted our audit in accordance with International Standards on Auditing (UK and Ireland) issued by the Auditing Practices Board. An audit includes examination, on a test basis, of evidence relevant to the amounts and disclosures in the financial statements. It also includes an assessment of the significant estimates and judgments made by the directors in the preparation of the financial statements, and of whether the accounting policies are appropriate to the company's circumstances, consistently applied and adequately disclosed.

We planned and performed our audit so as to obtain all the information and explanations which we considered necessary in order to provide us with sufficient evidence to give reasonable assurance that the financial statements are free from material misstatement, whether caused by fraud or other irregularity or error. In forming our opinion we also evaluated the overall adequacy of the presentation of information in the financial statements.

Opinion

In our opinion:

- the financial statements give a true and fair view, in accordance with United Kingdom Generally Accepted Accounting Practice, of the state of the company's affairs as at ... and of its profit [loss]for the year then ended;

- the financial statements have been properly prepared in accordance with the Companies Act 1985; and

- the information given in the Directors' Report is consistent with the financial statements.

Emphasis of matter – possible outcome of a lawsuit

In forming our opinion on the financial statements, which is not qualified, we have considered the adequacy of the disclosures made in note x to the financial statements concerning the possible outcome of a lawsuit, alleging infringement of certain patent rights and claiming royalties and punitive damages, where the company is the defendant. The company has filed a counter action, and preliminary hearings and discovery proceedings on both actions are in progress. The ultimate outcome of the matter cannot presently be determined, and no provision for any liability that may result has been made in the financial statements.

Registered auditors   *Address*
Date

Example 2 – Qualified opinion – Disagreement. Inappropriate accounting treatment of debtors.

- *UK non-publicly traded company prepares UK GAAP financial statements.*

- *The debtors shown on the balance sheet include an amount of £Y due from a company which has ceased trading. XYZ plc has no security for this debt.*

- *The auditor's opinion is that the company is unlikely to receive any payment and full provision of £Y should have been made.*

- *The auditor does not believe that the effect of the disagreement is so material and pervasive that the financial statements as a whole are misleading and issues a qualified opinion – except for disagreement about the accounting treatment of debtors.*

Qualified opinion arising from disagreement about accounting treatment

Included in the debtors shown on the balance sheet is an amount of £Y due from a company which has ceased trading. XYZ plc has no security for this debt. In our opinion the company is unlikely to receive any payment and full provision of £Y should have been made. Accordingly, debtors should be reduced by £Y, deferred taxes should be reduced by £X and profit for the year and retained earnings should be reduced by £Z.

Except for the financial effect of not making the provision referred to in the preceding paragraph, in our opinion the financial statements:

- give a true and fair view, in accordance with United Kingdom Generally Accepted Accounting Practice, of the state of the company's affairs as at ... and of its profit [loss]for the year then ended; and

- have been properly prepared in accordance with the Companies Act 1985.

In our opinion the information given in the Directors' Report is consistent with the financial statements.

Registered auditors   *Address*
Date

Example 3 – Qualified opinion – Disagreement. Prior period qualification unresolved and results in a modification of the auditor's report regarding the current period figures.

- *UK non-publicly traded company prepares UK GAAP financial statements.*

- *Included in the debtors shown on the balance sheet of 31 December 20X4 and 31 December 20X5 is an amount of £Y which is the subject of litigation and against which no provision has been made. The auditor considers that a full provision of £Y should have been made in the year ended 31 December 20X4.*

Qualified opinion arising from disagreement over accounting treatment

Included in the debtors shown on the balance sheets of 31 December 20X4 and 31 December 20X5 is an amount of £Y which is the subject of litigation and against which no provision has been made. In our opinion, full provision of £Y should have been made in the year ended 31 December 20X4. Accordingly, debtors at 31 December 20X4 and 20X5 should be reduced by £Y, deferred taxes at 31 December 20X4 and 20X5 should be reduced by £X, and profit for the year ended 31 December 20X4 and retained earnings at 31 December 20X4 and 20X5 should be reduced by £Z.

In our opinion the financial statements give a true and fair view, in accordance with United Kingdom Generally Accepted Accounting Practice, of the company's profit [loss] for the year ended 31 December 20X5.

Except for the financial effect of not making the provision referred to in the preceding paragraph, in our opinion the financial statements:

- give a true and fair view, in accordance with United Kingdom Generally Accepted Accounting Practice, of the state of the company's affairs as at 31 December 20X5 and of its profit [loss] for the year then ended; and

- have been properly prepared in accordance with the Companies Act 1985.

In our opinion the information given in the Directors' Report is consistent with the financial statements.

Registered auditor
Date

Address

Example 4 – Qualified opinion – Limitation on scope. Auditor not appointed at the time of the stocktake.

- *UK non-publicly traded company prepares UK GAAP financial statements.*

- *The evidence available to the auditor was limited because they did not observe the counting of the physical stock as of 31 December 20X1, since that date was prior to the time the auditor was initially engaged as auditor for the company. Owing to the nature of the company's records, the auditor was unable to satisfy themselves as to stock quantities by other audit procedures.*

- *The limitation in audit scope causes the auditor to issue a qualified opinion – except for any adjustments that might have been found to be necessary had they been able to obtain sufficient evidence concerning stock.*

- *The limitation of scope was determined by the auditor not to be so material and pervasive as to require a disclaimer of opinion.*

Basis of audit opinion

We conducted our audit in accordance with International Standards on Auditing (UK and Ireland) issued by the Auditing Practices Board, except that the scope of our work was limited as explained below.

An audit includes examination, on a test basis, of evidence relevant to the amounts and disclosures in the financial statements. It also includes an assessment of the significant estimates and judgments made by the directors in the preparation of the financial statements, and of whether the accounting policies are appropriate to the company's circumstances, consistently applied and adequately disclosed.

We planned ~~and performed~~ our audit so as to obtain all the information and explanations which we considered necessary in order to provide us with sufficient evidence to give reasonable assurance that the financial statements are free from material misstatement, whether caused by fraud or other irregularity or error. However, with respect to stock having a carrying amount of £X the evidence available to us was limited because we did not observe the counting of the physical stock as of 31 December 20X1, since that date was prior to our appointment as auditor of the company. Owing to the nature of the company's records, we were unable to obtain sufficient appropriate audit evidence regarding the stock quantities by using other audit procedures.

In forming our opinion we also evaluated the overall adequacy of the presentation of information in the financial statements.

Qualified opinion arising from limitation in audit scope

Except for the financial effects of such adjustments, if any, as might have been determined to be necessary had we been able to satisfy ourselves as to physical stock quantities, in our opinion the financial statements:

- give a true and fair view, in accordance with United Kingdom Generally Accepted Accounting Practice, of the state of the company's affairs as at 31 December 20X1 and of its profit [loss]for the year then ended; and

- have been properly prepared in accordance with the Companies Act 1985.

In respect solely of the limitation on our work relating to stocks:

- we have not obtained all the information and explanations that we considered necessary for the purpose of our audit; and

- we were unable to determine whether proper accounting records had been maintained.

In our opinion the information given in the Directors' Report is consistent with the financial statements.

Registered auditors   *Address*
Date

Example 5 – Disclaimer of opinion. Unable to observe all physical stock and confirm trade debtors.

- UK non-publicly traded company prepares UK GAAP financial statements.

- The evidence available to the auditor was limited because the auditor was not able to observe all physical stock and confirm trade debtors due to limitations placed on the scope of the auditor's work by the directors of the Company.

- As a result, the auditor has been unable to form a view on the financial statements and issues a modified opinion disclaiming the view given by the financial statements.

Basis of audit opinion

We conducted our audit in accordance with International Standards on Auditing (UK and Ireland) issued by the Auditing Practices Board, except that the scope of our work was limited as explained below.

An audit includes examination, on a test basis, of evidence relevant to the amounts and disclosures in the financial statements. It also includes an assessment of the significant estimates and judgments made by the directors in the preparation of the financial statements, and of whether the accounting policies are appropriate to the company's circumstances, consistently applied and adequately disclosed

We planned and performed our audit so as to obtain all the information and explanations which we considered necessary in order to provide us with sufficient evidence to give reasonable assurance that the financial statements are free from material misstatement, whether caused by fraud or other irregularity or error. However, the evidence available to us was limited because we were unable to observe the counting of physical stock having a carrying amount of £X and send confirmation letters to trade debtors having a carrying amount of £Y due to limitations placed on the scope of our work by the directors of the company. As a result of this we have been unable to obtain sufficient appropriate audit evidence concerning both stock and trade debtors. Because of the significance of these items, we have been unable to form a view on the financial statements.

In forming our opinion we also evaluated the overall adequacy of the presentation of information in the financial statements.

Opinion: disclaimer on view given by the financial statements

Because of the possible effect of the limitation in evidence available to us, we are unable to form an opinion as to whether the financial statements:

- give a true and fair view, in accordance with United Kingdom Generally Accepted Accounting Practice, of the state of the company's affairs as at ... and of its profit [loss]for the year then ended; and

- have been properly prepared in accordance with the Companies Act 1985.

In respect solely of the limitation of our work referred to above:

- we have not obtained all the information and explanations that we considered necessary for the purpose of our audit; and

- we were unable to determine whether proper accounting records have been maintained.

Notwithstanding our disclaimer on the view given by the financial statements, in our opinion the information given in the Directors' Report is consistent with the financial statements.

Registered auditors   *Address*
Date

Example 6 – Disclaimer of opinion. Multiple material/ significant uncertainties.

As discussed in ISA (UK and Ireland) 700 paragraph 34 the addition of a paragraph emphasising a going concern problem or significant uncertainty is ordinarily adequate to meet the auditor's reporting responsibilities regarding such matters. However, in extreme cases, such as situations involving multiple uncertainties that are significant to the financial statements, the auditor may consider it appropriate to express a disclaimer of opinion instead of adding an emphasis of matter paragraph.

This example does not include a description of the multiple material/significant uncertainties that might lead to a disclaimer of opinion because circumstances will vary and auditors will have to use their judgment when deciding whether it is an extreme case involving multiple uncertainties that are significant to the financial statements. Often, if such matters were considered individually, because the company makes relevant disclosures in the financial statements, the auditor would normally issue an unqualified auditor's report with an emphasis of matter paragraph setting out the basis of the auditor's opinion, describing the situation giving rise to the emphasis of matter and its possible effects on the financial statements, including (where practicable) quantification but the audit opinion would be unqualified.

Opinion: disclaimer on view given by the financial statements

In forming our opinion on the financial statements, we have considered the adequacy of the disclosures made in the financial statements concerning the following matters:

- [Significant uncertainty 1]

- [Significant uncertainty 2]

- [Significant uncertainty 3]

Because of the potential significance, to the financial statements, of the combined effect of the three matters referred to in the paragraph above, we are unable to form an opinion as to whether the financial statements:

- give a true and fair view, in accordance with United Kingdom Generally Accepted Accounting Practice, of the state of the company's affairs as at ... and of its profit [loss]for the year then ended; and

- have been properly prepared in accordance with the Companies Act 1985.

Notwithstanding our disclaimer on the view given by the financial statements, in our opinion the information given in the Directors' Report is consistent with the financial statements.

Registered auditors   *Address*
Date

Example 7 – Adverse opinion. No provision made for losses expected to arise on certain long-term contracts.

- UK non-publicly traded company prepares UK GAAP financial statements.

- No provision has been made for losses expected to arise on certain long-term contracts currently in progress, as the directors consider that such losses should be off-set against amounts recoverable on other long-term contracts.

- In the auditor's opinion, provision should be made for foreseeable losses on individual contracts as required by [specify accounting standards].

- The auditor issues an adverse opinion due to the failure to provide for the losses and quantifies the impact on the profit for the year the contract work in progress and deferred taxes payable at the year end.

Adverse opinion on the financial statements

As more fully explained in note x to the financial statements no provision has been made for losses expected to arise on certain long-term contracts currently in progress, as the directors consider that such losses should be off-set against amounts recoverable on other long-term contracts. In our opinion, provision should be made for foreseeable losses on individual contracts as required by [specify accounting standards]......... If losses had been so recognised the effect would have been to reduce the carrying amount of contract work in progress by £X, deferred taxes payable by £Y, and the profit for the year and retained earnings at 31 December 20X1 by £Z.

In view of the effect of the failure to provide for the losses referred to above, in our opinion the financial statements do not give a true and fair view, in accordance with United Kingdom Generally Accepted Accounting Practice, of the state of the company's affairs as at 31 December 20X1 and of its profit [loss]for the year then ended.

In all other respects, in our opinion the financial statements have been properly prepared in accordance with the Companies Act 1985.

Notwithstanding our adverse opinion on the financial statements, in our opinion the information given in the Directors' Report is consistent with the financial statements.

Registered auditors   *Address*
Date

Appendix 3

Modified auditor's reports arising from going concern issues – Extracts from modified reports

Note: Example auditor's reports addressing issues other than going concern are included in Appendix 2.

The auditor's reports included in Appendix 3 are illustrative examples only and it has not been possible to describe all of the facts that the auditors would have to consider when forming their opinion. Auditors use their professional judgment when deciding what form of modified auditor's report to give, taking into account the particular circumstances of the reporting entity.

The Appendix gives illustrative examples of modified auditor's reports on financial statements arising from the going concern issues illustrated in the navigation aid on page 1099.

Preceding each example auditor's report is a description of the background to the particular modification. The full text of the example unmodified auditor's reports is included in Appendix 1 but for the purpose of illustrating the modification, only those sections of the auditor's report affected by the modification are included. Deletions to the examples in Appendix 1, arising from the modification, are shown as struck out text.

Navigation aid to the example modified auditor's reports arising from going concern issues

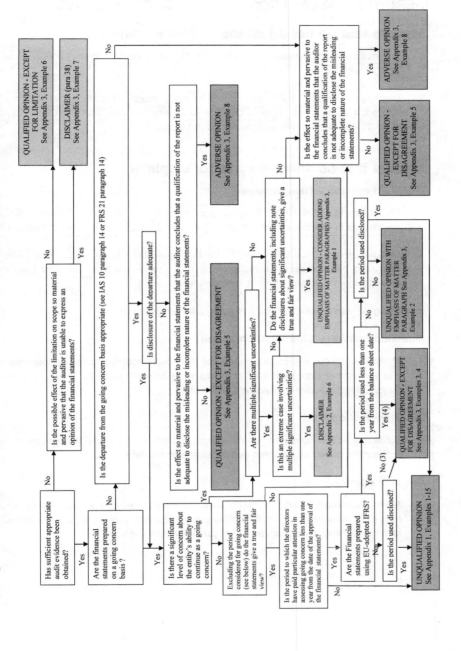

Appendix 3 – EXTRACTS FROM MODIFIED AUDITOR'S REPORTS ARISING FROM GOING CONCERN ISSUES

Matters that do not affect the auditor's opinion

1   Emphasis of matter – Material uncertainty about the company's ability to continue as a going concern.

2   Emphasis of matter – IFRSs as adopted by the European Union financial statements where the going concern period considered by directors complies with IAS 1 but not ISA (UK and Ireland) 570 and this fact is not disclosed.

Matters that do affect the auditor's opinion

Qualified opinion – Disagreement

3   Disagreement – UK GAAP financial statements where the going concern period considered by directors does not comply with FRS 18 and this fact is not disclosed.

4   Disagreement – IFRSs as adopted by the European Union financial statements where the going concern period considered by directors is less than one year from the balance sheet date and so does not comply with IAS 1.

5   Disagreement – Non-disclosure of going concern problems.

Qualified opinion – Limitation on scope

6   Limitation on scope – Evidence available to auditor regarding going concern status was limited because cash flow forecasts were only prepared for a period of nine months from approval of financial statements

Disclaimer of opinion

7   Disclaimer – The company has not prepared profit or cash flow projections for an appropriate period subsequent to the balance sheet date.

Adverse opinion

8   Adverse opinion – Significant level of concern about the company's ability to continue as a going concern that is not disclosed in the financial statements and the financial statements have been prepared on a going concern basis.

Example 1 – Unqualified opinion – Emphasis of matter. Material uncertainty about the company's ability to continue as a going concern.

- UK non-publicly traded company prepares UK GAAP financial statements.

- The Company incurred a net loss of £X during the year ended 31 December 20X1 and, as of that date, the Company's current liabilities exceeded its total assets by £Y.

- These conditions, along with other matters set forth in the notes to the financial statements, indicate the existence of a material uncertainty, which may cast significant doubt about the Company's ability to continue as a going concern.

- The Company makes relevant disclosures in the financial statements including that referred to in paragraphs 32 and 33 of ISA (UK and Ireland) 570 "Going Concern".

- The auditor issues an unqualified auditor's report with an emphasis of matter paragraph describing the situation giving rise to the emphasis of matter and its possible effects on the financial statements, including (where practicable) quantification.

Basis of audit opinion

We conducted our audit in accordance with International Standards on Auditing (UK and Ireland) issued by the Auditing Practices Board. An audit includes examination, on a test basis, of evidence relevant to the amounts and disclosures in the financial statements. It also includes an assessment of the significant estimates and judgments made by the directors in the preparation of the financial statements, and of whether the accounting policies are appropriate to the company's circumstances, consistently applied and adequately disclosed

We planned and performed our audit so as to obtain all the information and explanations which we considered necessary in order to provide us with sufficient evidence to give reasonable assurance that the financial statements are free from material misstatement, whether caused by fraud or other irregularity or error. In forming our opinion we also evaluated the overall adequacy of the presentation of information in the financial statements.

Opinion

In our opinion:

- the financial statements give a true and fair view, in accordance with United Kingdom Generally Accepted Accounting Practice, of the state of the company's affairs as at 31 December 20X1 and of its profit [loss]for the year then ended;

- the financial statements have been properly prepared in accordance with the Companies Act 1985; and

- the information given in the Directors' Report is consistent with the financial statements.

Emphasis of matter – Going concern

In forming our opinion on the financial statements, which is not qualified, we have considered the adequacy of the disclosure made in note x to the financial statements concerning the company's ability to continue as a going concern. The company incurred a net loss of £X during the year ended 31 December 20X1 and, at that date, the company's current liabilities exceeded its total assets by £Y. These conditions, along with the other matters explained in note x to the financial statements, indicate the existence of a material uncertainty which may cast significant doubt about the company's ability to continue as a going concern. The financial statements do not include the adjustments that would result if the company was unable to continue as a going concern.

Registered auditors   *Address*
Date

Example 2 – Unqualified opinion – Emphasis of matter. Financial statements where the going concern period considered by directors complies with IAS 1 but not ISA (UK and Ireland) 570 and this fact is not disclosed.

- UK publicly traded company uses IFRSs as adopted by the European Union for financial statements.

- The balance sheet date being audited is 31 December 20X1.

- The date of approval of the financial statements was 31 May 20X2.

- In assessing whether the going concern assumption is appropriate the directors have taken into account the period up to 31 March 20X3 which is:

  - 15 months from the balance sheet date ie more than the 12 months from the balance sheet date required by IAS 1; but only

  - 10 months from the date of approval of the financial statements ie less than the 12 months from the date of approval of the financial statements required by ISA (UK and Ireland) 570.

- The directors have refused to either extend their assessment period to twelve months from the date of approval of the financial statements or to disclose the fact that the period they have used for their assessment is less than twelve months from the date of approval of the financial statements.

- The auditor issues an unqualified auditor's report with an emphasis of matter paragraph disclosing the fact that the going concern period considered by the directors is less than one year from the date of approval of the financial statements and that this fact has not been disclosed.

Basis of audit opinion

We conducted our audit in accordance with International Standards on Auditing (UK and Ireland) issued by the Auditing Practices Board. An audit includes examination, on a test basis, of evidence relevant to the amounts and disclosures in the financial statements and the part of the Directors' Remuneration Report to be audited. It also includes an assessment of the significant estimates and judgments made by the directors in the preparation of the financial statements, and of whether the accounting policies are appropriate to the company's circumstances, consistently applied and adequately disclosed.

We planned and performed our audit so as to obtain all the information and explanations which we considered necessary in order to provide us with sufficient evidence to give reasonable assurance that the financial statements and the part of the Directors' Remuneration Report to be audited are free from material misstatement, whether caused by fraud or other irregularity or error. In forming our opinion we also evaluated the overall adequacy of the presentation of information in the financial statements and the part of the Directors' Remuneration Report to be audited.

Opinion

In our opinion:

- the financial statements give a true and fair view, in accordance with IFRSs as adopted by the European Union, of the state of the company's affairs as at 31 December 20X1 and of its profit [loss]for the year then ended;

- the financial statements and the part of the Directors' Remuneration Report to be audited have been properly prepared in accordance with the Companies Act 1985 and Article 4 of the IAS Regulation; and

- the information given in the Directors' Report is consistent with the financial statements.

Emphasis of matter – Going concern

In forming our opinion on the financial statements, which is not qualified, we have considered the adequacy of the disclosures made in note x to the financial statements concerning the period used by the directors in assessing whether the going concern assumption is appropriate. In making their assessment the directors have considered the period up to 31 March 20X3 which is less than twelve months from the date of approval of the financial statements and the directors have not disclosed this fact. International Standards on Auditing (UK and Ireland) require the auditor to draw this fact to the attention of readers of the financial statements.

Registered auditors   *Address*
31 May 20X2

Example 3 – Qualified opinion – Disagreement. Financial statements where the going concern period considered by directors does not comply with FRS 18 and this fact is not disclosed.

- UK non-publicly traded company prepares UK GAAP financial statements.

- In assessing whether it is appropriate to prepare the financial statements on a going concern basis, the directors have paid particular attention to a period ending on 30 September 20X3 which is less than one year from the date of approval of the financial statements on 31 October 20X2.

- The directors have not disclosed this fact in the financial statements breaching the requirements of paragraph 61(b) of Financial Reporting Standard 18 "Accounting policies". FRS 18 requires the disclosure of the fact that " the foreseeable future considered by the directors has been limited to a period of less than one year from the date of approval of the financial statements".

- Although the auditor has concluded that there is no significant level of concern about going concern, the failure to disclose the fact that the foreseeable future considered by the directors has been limited to a period of less than one year from the date of approval of the financial statements is a breach of FRS 18 and the auditor issues a qualified "except for" opinion describing the disagreement over the departure from FRS 18.

Qualified opinion arising from departure from FRS 18 'Accounting policies'

In assessing whether it is appropriate to prepare the financial statements on a going concern basis the directors have paid particular attention to a period ending on 30 September 20X3 which is less than twelve months from the date of approval of the financial statements. This fact has not been disclosed in the financial statements, contrary to the requirements of Financial Reporting Standard 18 'Accounting policies'.

Except for the absence of the disclosure referred to above in our opinion the financial statements:

- give a true and fair view, in accordance with United Kingdom Generally Accepted Accounting Practice, of the state of the company's affairs as at 31 December 20X1 and of its profit [loss]for the year then ended; and

- have been properly prepared in accordance with the Companies Act 1985.

In our opinion the information given in the Directors' Report is consistent with the financial statements.

Registered auditors
31 October 20X2

Address

Example 4 – Qualified opinion – Disagreement. Financial statements where the going concern period considered by directors does not comply with IAS 1.

- UK publicly traded company uses IFRSs as adopted by the European Union for financial statements.

- The balance sheet date being audited is 31 December 20X1.

- The date of approval of the financial statements was 31 May 20X2.

- In assessing whether the going concern assumption is appropriate the directors have taken into account the period up to 30 November 20X2 which is:

  ○ only 11 months from the balance sheet date ie less than the 12 months from the balance sheet date required by IAS 1; and

  ○ only 6 months from the date of approval of the financial statements ie less than the 12 months from the date of approval of the financial statements required by ISA (UK and Ireland) 570.

- The directors have refused to either extend their assessment period to a period of more than twelve months from the balance sheet date (to comply with IAS 1) or twelve months from the date of approval of the financial statements (to comply with ISA (UK and Ireland) 570) or to disclose the fact that the period they have used for their assessment is less than twelve months from the date of approval of the financial statements (to comply with ISA (UK and Ireland) 570).

- The auditor:

  ○ includes an emphasis of matter paragraph explaining that in making their going concern assessment the directors have considered a period which is less than twelve months from the date of approval of the financial statements and the directors have not disclosed this fact; and

  ○ issues a qualified "except for" opinion describing the disagreement over the disclosing the fact that the going concern period considered by the directors is less than the twelve months from the balance sheet date required by IAS 1.

Qualified opinion arising from departure from IAS 1 'Presentation of financial statements'

In assessing whether it is appropriate to prepare the financial statements on a going concern basis the directors have paid particular attention to a period ending on 30 November 20X2 which is less than twelve months from the balance sheet date. This is contrary to the requirements of International Accounting Standard 1 'Presentation of financial statements'.

Except for the non-compliance with IAS 1 referred to above in our opinion:

- the financial statements give a true and fair view, in accordance with IFRSs as adopted by the European Union, of the state of the company's affairs as at 31 December 20X1 and of its profit [loss]for the year then ended; and

- the financial statements and the part of the Directors' Remuneration Report to be audited have been properly prepared in accordance with the Companies Act 1985.

In our opinion the information given in the Directors' Report is consistent with the financial statements.

Emphasis of matter – Going concern

In forming our opinion on the financial statements, we have considered the adequacy of the disclosures made in note x to the financial statements concerning the period used by the directors in assessing whether the going concern assumption is appropriate. In making their assessment the directors have considered the period up to 30 November 20X2 which is less than twelve months from the date of approval of the financial statements and the directors have not disclosed this fact. International Standards on Auditing (UK and Ireland) require the auditor to draw this fact to the attention of readers of the financial statements. Our opinion is not further qualified in respect of this matter.

Registered auditors   *Address*
31 May 20X2

Example 5 – Qualified opinion – Disagreement. Non-disclosure of going concern problems.

- UK non-publicly traded company prepares UK GAAP financial statements.

- Neither the financial statements nor the directors' report disclose that the Company's financing arrangements expire and amounts outstanding are payable on 19 July 20X2 and that the Company has been unable to re-negotiate or obtain replacement financing.

- This situation indicates the existence of a material uncertainty which may cast significant doubt on the Company's ability to continue as a going concern and therefore it may be unable to realise its assets and discharge its liabilities in the normal course of business.

- The auditor concludes that there is a significant level of concern about going concern and disagrees with the failure to disclose this information in the financial statements. The auditor issues a qualified except for opinion describing the disagreement.

Qualified opinion arising from omission of information concerning going concern

The company's financing arrangements expire and amounts outstanding are payable on 19 July 20X2. The company has been unable to re-negotiate or obtain replacement financing. This situation indicates the existence of a material uncertainty which may cast significant doubt on the company's ability to continue as a going concern and therefore it may be unable to realise its assets and discharge its liabilities in the normal course of business. The financial statements (and notes thereto) do not disclose this fact.

Except for the omission of the information included in the preceding paragraph, in our opinion the financial statements:

- give a true and fair view, in accordance with United Kingdom Generally Accepted Accounting Practice, of the state of the company's affairs as at 31 December 20X1 and of its profit [loss]for the year then ended; and

- have been properly prepared in accordance with the Companies Act 1985.

In our opinion the information given in the Directors' Report is consistent with the financial statements.

Registered auditors   *Address*
Date

Example 6 – Qualified opinion – Limitation of scope. Evidence available to auditor regarding going concern status was limited because cash flow forecasts were only prepared for a period of nine months from approval of financial statements.

- UK non-publicly traded company prepares UK GAAP financial statements.

- The evidence available to the auditor was limited because the company had prepared cash flow forecasts and other information needed for the assessment of the appropriateness of the going concern basis of preparation of the financial statements only for a period of nine months from the date of approval of the financial statements.

- Although this fact is disclosed in the financial statements had the information been available the auditor might have formed a different opinion.The auditor considers that those charged with governance have not taken adequate steps to satisfy themselves that it is appropriate for them to adopt the going concern basis.

- The auditor does not consider that the future period to which those charged with governance have paid particular attention in assessing going concern is reasonable in the entity's circumstances. The auditor considers that the particular circumstances of the company and the nature of the company's business require that such information be prepared, and reviewed by the directors and auditor for a period of at least twelve months from the date of approval of the financial statements.

- The auditor issues an 'except for' qualified opinion referring to the adjustments that might have been found to be necessary had they obtained sufficient evidence concerning the appropriateness of the going concern basis of preparation of the financial statements.

Basis of audit opinion

We conducted our audit in accordance with International Standards on Auditing (UK and Ireland) issued by the Auditing Practices Board, except that the scope of our work was limited as explained below.

An audit includes examination, on a test basis, of evidence relevant to the amounts and disclosures in the financial statements. It also includes an assessment of the significant estimates and judgments made by the directors in the preparation of the financial statements, and of whether the accounting policies are appropriate to the company's circumstances, consistently applied and adequately disclosed

We planned ~~and performed~~ our audit so as to obtain all the information and explanations which we considered necessary in order to provide us with sufficient evidence to give reasonable assurance that the financial statements are free from material misstatement, whether caused by fraud or other irregularity or error. However, the evidence available to us was limited because the company has prepared cash flow forecasts and other information needed for the assessment of the appropriateness of the going concern basis of preparation of the financial statements for a period of only nine months from the date of approval of these financial statements. We consider that the directors have not taken adequate steps to satisfy themselves that it is appropriate for them to adopt the going concern basis because the circumstances of the company and the nature of the business require that such information be prepared, and reviewed by the directors and ourselves, for a period of at least twelve months from the date of approval of the financial statements. Had this information been available to us we might have formed a different opinion.

In forming our opinion we also evaluated the overall adequacy of the presentation of information in the financial statements.

Qualified opinion arising from limitation in audit scope

Except for any adjustments that might have been found to be necessary had we been able to obtain sufficient evidence concerning the appropriateness of the going concern basis of preparation of the financial statements, in our opinion the financial statements:

- give a true and fair view, in accordance with United Kingdom Generally Accepted Accounting Practice, of the state of the company's affairs as at 31 December 20X1 and of its profit [loss]for the year then ended; and

- have been properly prepared in accordance with the Companies Act 1985.

In respect solely of the limitation on our work relating to the assessment of the appropriateness of the going concern basis of preparation of the financial statements we have not obtained all the information and explanations that we considered necessary for the purpose of our audit.

In our opinion the information given in the Directors' Report is consistent with the financial statements.

Registered auditors   *Address*
Date

Example 7 – Disclaimer of opinion. Going concern – company has not prepared profit or cash flow projections for an appropriate period subsequent to the balance sheet date.

- UK non-publicly traded company prepares UK GAAP financial statements.

- The evidence available to the auditor to confirm the appropriateness of preparing the financial statements on the going concern basis was limited because the company has not prepared profit or cash flow projections for an appropriate period subsequent to the balance sheet date.

- The auditor considers that the circumstances of the company and the nature of the company's business requires that such information be prepared, and reviewed by the directors and the auditor, for a period of at least twelve months from the date of approval of the financial statements.

- The auditor concludes that the possible effect of this limitation on scope is so material and pervasive that the auditor has been unable to obtain sufficient appropriate audit evidence and accordingly is unable to form an opinion on whether or not it is appropriate to prepare the financial statements on a going concern basis. As a result, the auditor issues an opinion disclaiming the view given by the financial statements.

Basis of audit opinion

We conducted our audit in accordance with International Standards on Auditing (UK and Ireland) issued by the Auditing Practices Board, except that the scope of our work was limited as explained below.

An audit includes examination, on a test basis, of evidence relevant to the amounts and disclosures in the financial statements. It also includes an assessment of the significant estimates and judgments made by the directors in the preparation of the financial statements, and of whether the accounting policies are appropriate to the company's circumstances, consistently applied and adequately disclosed

We planned and performed our audit so as to obtain all the information and explanations which we considered necessary in order to provide us with sufficient evidence to give reasonable assurance that the financial statements are free from material misstatement, whether caused by fraud or other irregularity or error. However, the evidence available to us to confirm the appropriateness of preparing the financial statements on the going concern basis was limited because the company has not prepared any profit or cash flow projections for an appropriate period subsequent to the balance sheet date. As a result, and in the absence of any alternative evidence available to us, we have been unable to form a view as to the applicability of the going concern basis, the circumstances of which, together with the effect on the financial statements should this basis be inappropriate, are set out in note x to the financial statements.

In forming our opinion we also evaluated the overall adequacy of the presentation of information in the financial statements.

Opinion: disclaimer on view given by the financial statements

Because of the possible effect of the limitation in evidence available to us, we are unable to form an opinion as to whether the financial statements:

- give a true and fair view, in accordance with United Kingdom Generally Accepted Accounting Practice, of the state of the company's affairs as at 31 December 20.. and of its profit [loss]for the year then ended; and

- have been properly prepared in accordance with the Companies Act 1985.

In respect solely of the limitation of our work referred to above we have not obtained all the information and explanations that we considered necessary for the purpose of our audit.

Notwithstanding our disclaimer on the view given by the financial statements, in our opinion the information given in the Directors' Report is consistent with the financial statements.

Registered auditors   *Address*
Date

Example 8 – Adverse opinion. Significant level of concern about the company's ability to continue as a going concern that is not disclosed in the financial statements.

- UK non-publicly traded company prepares UK GAAP financial statements.

- Although there is a significant level of concern about the company's ability to continue as a going concern the financial statements and notes do not disclose this fact and the directors have prepared the financial statements on the going concern basis.

- The auditor considers that the financial statements should disclose that there is a material uncertainty, which may cast significant doubt on the company's ability to continue as a going concern.

- The effect of this disagreement is so material and pervasive to the amounts included within the financial statements that the auditor concludes that a qualification of the report is not adequate to disclose the misleading or incomplete nature of the financial statements.

- The auditor issues an adverse audit opinion stating that, because the material uncertainty regarding going concern is not disclosed, the financial statements do not give a true and fair view.

Adverse opinion on financial statements

As explained in note x to the financial statements the company's financing arrangements expired and the amount outstanding was payable on 31 December 20X1. The company has been unable to re-negotiate or obtain replacement financing and is considering entering insolvency proceedings. These events indicate a material uncertainty which may cast significant doubt on the company's ability to continue as a going concern and therefore it may be unable to realise its assets and discharge its liabilities in the normal course of business. The financial statements (and notes thereto) do not disclose this fact and have been prepared on the going concern basis.

In our opinion, because of the omission of the information referred to above, the financial statements do not give a true and fair view, in accordance with United Kingdom Generally Accepted Accounting Practice, of the state of the company's affairs as at 31 December 20X1 and of its profit [loss]for the year then ended.

In all other respects, in our opinion the financial statements have been properly prepared in accordance with the Companies Act 1985.

Notwithstanding our adverse opinion on the financial statements, in our opinion the information given in the Directors' Report is consistent with the financial statements.

Registered auditors   *Address*
Date

Appendix 4

Extract from an auditor's report with a modified opinion on the directors' report (financial statements prepared under UK GAAP)[65]

Respective responsibilities of directors and auditors

[Details of directors' and the auditor's other responsibilities as are applicable – for examples see Appendix 1]

We also report to you whether in our opinion the information given in the Directors' Report is consistent with the financial statements. [The information given in the Directors' Report includes that specific information presented in the Operating and Financial Review that is cross referred from the Business Review section of the Directors' Report.][66]

Basis of audit opinion

...

Opinion

In our opinion:

- *[Opinion on the financial statements and other opinions, if any, that are required.]*

Emphasis of matter – ...[include if applicable]

Material inconsistency between the financial statements and the directors' report

In our opinion, the information given in the seventh paragraph of the Business Review in the Directors' Report is not consistent with the financial statements. That paragraph states without amplification that "the company's trading for the period resulted in a 10% increase in profit over the previous period's profit". The profit and loss account, however, shows that the company's profit for the period includes a profit of £Z which did not arise from trading but arose from the disposal of assets of a discontinued operation. Without this profit on the disposal of assets the company would have reported a profit for the year of £Y, representing a reduction in profit of 25% over the previous period's profit on a like for like basis. Except for this matter, in our opinion the information given in the Directors' Report is consistent with the financial statements.

Registered auditors   *Address*
Date

---

[65] This example is also included as Example B in the Appendix to ISA (UK and Ireland) 720 (Revised) "Section B – The auditor's statutory reporting responsibility in relation to Directors' Reports"
[66] Include and tailor as necessary to clarify the information covered by the auditor's opinion.

Appendix 5

Illustrative statement of directors' responsibilities

Example wording of a description of the directors' responsibilities for inclusion in the annual report of a non-publicly traded company incorporated in the United Kingdom preparing its financial statements under UK GAAP

Statement of directors' responsibilities

The directors are responsible for preparing the Annual Report and the financial statements in accordance with applicable law and regulations.

Company law requires the directors to prepare financial statements for each financial year. Under that law the directors have elected to prepare the financial statements in accordance with United Kingdom Generally Accepted Accounting Practice (United Kingdom Accounting Standards and applicable law). The financial statements are required by law to give a true and fair view of the state of affairs of the company and of the profit or loss of the company for that period. In preparing these financial statements, the directors are required to:

- select suitable accounting policies and then apply them consistently;

- make judgments and estimates that are reasonable and prudent[67];

- state whether applicable UK Accounting Standards have been followed, subject to any material departures disclosed and explained in the financial statements;[68]

- prepare the financial statements on the going concern basis unless it is inappropriate to presume that the company will continue in business.[69]

The directors are responsible for keeping proper accounting records that disclose with reasonable accuracy at any time the financial position of the company and enable them to ensure that the financial statements comply with the [Companies Act 1985] [Companies (Northern Ireland) Order 1986]. They are also responsible for safeguarding the assets of the company and hence for taking reasonable steps for the prevention and detection of fraud and other irregularities.

The directors are responsible for the maintenance and integrity of the corporate and financial information included on the company's website. Legislation in the United Kingdom governing the preparation and dissemination of financial statements may differ from legislation in other jurisdictions.[70]

---

[67] Paragraph 12 of Part II of Schedule 4 to CA 1985 requires that the amount of any item "shall be determined on a prudent basis".

[68] This bullet does not apply to small and medium sized companies as defined by CA 1985.

[69] Included where no separate statement on going concern is made by the directors.

[70] Where the financial statements are published on the internet.

The APB has not prepared an illustrative example of a statement of directors' responsibilities for a publicly traded company as the directors' responsibilities, which are in part dependent on the particular regulatory environment, will vary dependent on the rules of the market on which its securities are admitted to trading.

BULLETIN 2007/1

EXAMPLE REPORTS BY AUDITORS UNDER COMPANY LEGISLATION IN GREAT BRITAIN

CONTENTS

Introduction

1. The purpose of this Bulletin is to provide updated illustrative examples of reports by auditors under the Companies Act 1985 (CA 1985) originally published in Appendix 1 of Practice Note 8 'Reports by auditors under company legislation in the United Kingdom'. Illustrative examples of auditor's reports on financial statements are provided in Bulletin 2006/6 'Auditor's Reports on Financial Statements in the United Kingdom'.

2. In order to understand the legislative background giving rise to the need for these reports this Bulletin should be read in conjunction with Practice Note 8 which was issued in October 1994, and Bulletin 1999/6 'The auditor's statement on the summary financial statement'. Both of these documents can be downloaded from the Auditing Practices Board's web site www.frc.org.uk/apb.

3. The wording of the example reports by auditors is based on current legislative requirements and, in some cases, on ISA (UK and Ireland) 700 'The Auditor's Report on Financial Statements' issued by the APB in December 2004. Changes to these example reports may be needed when the Companies Act 2006 (CA 2006) comes into force.

4. During the period between the issuance of this Bulletin and CA 2006 coming into force, the APB will consider whether to update the whole of Practice Note 8 to reflect the requirements of CA 2006.

5. Examples of two of the fifteen reports by auditors included in Appendix 1 to Practice Note 8 are not included in this Bulletin. With respect to Example 6 the report is no longer required by CA 1985 and with respect to Example 4 updated examples are included in APB Bulletin 2006/3 'The Special Auditor's Report on Abbreviated Accounts in the United Kingdom'. However, to assist users of the Bulletin the numbering of the examples used in Practice Note 8 has been retained.

6. With respect to Example 5 'Auditor's statement on a summary financial statement' the example in Practice Note 8 was superseded by the examples in Appendix 1 to Bulletin 1999/6 and Appendix 3 to Bulletin 2002/2. Example 5 in this Bulletin supersedes all of these examples.

7. Unless otherwise indicated in a footnote, these example reports are effective immediately upon publication.

Example 1 – Auditor's report on revised financial statements: revision by replacement[1]

This example is based on the following assumptions:

- *Non-publicly traded company that does not prepare group accounts.*

- *UK GAAP used for individual company accounts.*

- *Financial statements contain no surround information other than the directors' report.*

REPORT OF THE INDEPENDENT AUDITOR TO THE [MEMBERS] [SHAREHOLDERS] OF XYZ LIMITED

We have audited the revised financial statements of XYZ Limited for the year ended ... which comprise [state the primary financial statements such as the Profit and Loss Account, the Balance Sheet, the Cash Flow Statement, the Statement of Total Recognised Gains and Losses] and the related notes[2]. These revised financial statements have been prepared under the accounting policies set out therein and replace the original financial statements approved by the directors on....

The revised financial statements have been prepared under the Companies (Revision of Defective Accounts and Report) Regulations 1990 and accordingly do not take account of events which have taken place after the date on which the original financial statements were approved.

Respective responsibilities of directors and auditors

As described in the Statement of Directors' Responsibilities the company's directors are responsible for the preparation of revised financial statements in accordance with applicable law and United Kingdom Accounting Standards (United Kingdom Generally Accepted Accounting Practice).[3]

---

[1] This example report is effective for accounting periods commencing on or after 1 April 2005.

[2] Auditor's reports of entities that do not publish their financial statements on a web site or publish them using 'PDF' format may continue to refer to the financial statements by reference to page numbers.

[3] If the directors' responsibilities with respect to revised financial statements are not set out in a separate statement, the auditors will include a description in their report, for example:
'Under section 245 (or section 245B) of the Companies Act 1985 the directors have the authority to revise financial statements or a directors' report if they do not comply with the Act[, or, where applicable, Article 4 of the IAS Regulation]. The revised financial statements must be amended in accordance with the Companies (Revision of Defective Accounts and Report) Regulations 1990. These require that the revised financial statements show a true and fair view as if they were prepared and approved by the directors as at the date of the original financial statements and accordingly do not take account of events which have taken place after the date on which the original financial statements were approved.' (This example does not make reference to Article 4 of the IAS Regulation as such a reference is only included when the entity is required to prepare consolidated financial statements in accordance with IFRSs as adopted by the EU and the restatement is in respect of such consolidated financial statements.)

Our responsibility is to audit the revised financial statements in accordance with relevant legal and regulatory requirements and International Standards on Auditing (UK and Ireland).

We report to you our opinion as to whether the revised financial statements give a true and fair view and are properly prepared in accordance with the Companies Act 1985 as they have effect under the Companies (Revision of Defective Accounts and Report) Regulations 1990. We also report to you whether in our opinion the information given in the [revised][4] Directors' Report is consistent with the revised financial statements.

In addition we report to you if, in our opinion, the company has not kept proper accounting records, if we have not received all the information and explanations we require for our audit, or if information specified by law regarding directors' remuneration and other transactions is not disclosed.

We read the [revised][4] Directors' Report and consider the implications for our report if we become aware of any apparent misstatements within it.

We are also required to report whether in our opinion the original financial statements failed to comply with the requirements of the Companies Act 1985 in the respects identified by the directors.

Basis of audit opinion

We conducted our audit in accordance with International Standards on Auditing (UK and Ireland) issued by the Auditing Practices Board. An audit includes examination, on a test basis, of evidence relevant to the amounts and disclosures in the revised financial statements. It also includes an assessment of the significant estimates and judgments made by the directors in the preparation of the revised financial statements, and of whether the accounting policies are appropriate to the company's circumstances, consistently applied and adequately disclosed.

The audit of revised financial statements includes the performance of additional procedures to assess whether the revisions made by the directors are appropriate and have been properly made.

We planned and performed our audit so as to obtain all the information and explanations which we considered necessary in order to provide us with sufficient evidence to give reasonable assurance that the revised financial statements are free from material misstatement, whether caused by fraud or other irregularity or error. In forming our opinion we also evaluated the overall adequacy of the presentation of information in the revised financial statements.

---

[4] The word 'revised' will be needed if the Directors' Report has also been revised.

Opinion

In our opinion:

- the revised financial statements give a true and fair view, in accordance with United Kingdom Generally Accepted Accounting Practice, seen as at the date the original financial statements were approved, of the state of the company's affairs as at .... and of its profit [loss] for the year then ended;

- the revised financial statements have been properly prepared in accordance with the provisions of the Companies Act 1985 as they have effect under the Companies (Revision of Defective Accounts and Report) Regulations 1990;

- the original financial statements for the year ended... failed to comply with the requirements of the Companies Act 1985 in the respects identified by the directors in the statement contained in note [x] to these revised financial statements; and

- the information given in the [revised][4] Directors' Report is consistent with the revised financial statements.

Registered auditors   *Address*
Date

Example 2 – Auditor's report on revised financial statements: revision by supplementary note[5]

This example is based on the following assumptions:

- *Non-publicly traded company that does not prepare group accounts.*

- *UK GAAP used for individual company accounts.*

- *Financial statements contain no surround information other than the directors' report.*

REPORT OF THE INDEPENDENT AUDITOR TO THE [MEMBERS] [SHAREHOLDERS] OF XYZ LIMITED

We have audited the revised financial statements of XYZ Limited for the year ended.... which comprise [state the primary financial statements such as the Profit and Loss Account, the Balance Sheet, the Cash Flow Statement, the Statement of Total Recognised Gains and Losses] and the related notes.[6] The revised financial statements replace the original financial statements approved by the directors on... and consist of the attached supplementary note together with the original financial statements which were circulated to [members] [shareholders] on....

The revised financial statements have been prepared under the Companies (Revision of Defective Accounts and Report) Regulations 1990 and accordingly do not take account of events which have taken place after the date on which the original financial statements were approved.

Respective responsibilities of directors and auditors

As described in the Statement of Directors' Responsibilities the company's directors are responsible for the preparation of revised financial statements in accordance with applicable law and United Kingdom Accounting Standards (United Kingdom Generally Accepted Accounting Practice).[7]

---

[5] This example report is effective for accounting periods commencing on or after 1 April 2005.

[6] Auditor's reports of entities that do not publish their financial statements on a web site or publish them using 'PDF' format may continue to refer to the financial statements by reference to page numbers.

[7] If the directors' responsibilities with respect to revised financial statements are not set out in a separate statement, the auditors will include a description in their report, for example:
'Under section 245 (or section 245B) of the Companies Act 1985 the directors have the authority to revise financial statements or a directors' report if they do not comply with the Act [, or, where applicable, Article 4 of the IAS Regulation]. The revised financial statements must be amended in accordance with the Companies (Revisions of Defective Accounts and Report) Regulations 1990. These require that the revised financial statements show a true and fair view as if they were prepared and approved by the directors as at the date of the original financial statements and accordingly do not take account of events which have taken place after the date on which the original financial statements were approved.' (This example does not make reference to Article 4 of the IAS Regulation as such a reference is only included when the entity is required to prepare consolidated financial statements in accordance with IFRSs as adopted by the EU and the restatement is in respect of such consolidated financial statements.)

Our responsibility is to audit the revised financial statements in accordance with relevant legal and regulatory requirements and International Standards on Auditing (UK and Ireland).

We report to you our opinion as to whether the revised financial statements give a true and fair view and are properly prepared in accordance with the Companies Act 1985 as they have effect under the Companies (Revision of Defective Accounts and Report) Regulations 1990. We also report to you whether in our opinion the information given in the [revised][8] Directors' Report is consistent with the financial statements.

In addition we report to you if, in our opinion, the company has not kept proper accounting records, if we have not received all the information and explanations we require for our audit, or if information specified by law regarding directors' remuneration and transactions is not disclosed.

We read the [revised][8] Directors' Report and consider the implications for our report if we become aware of any apparent misstatements within it.

We are also required to report whether in our opinion the original financial statements failed to comply with the requirements of the Companies Act 1985 in the respects identified by the directors.

Basis of audit opinion

We conducted our audit in accordance with International Standards on Auditing (UK and Ireland) issued by the Auditing Practices Board. An audit includes examination, on a test basis, of evidence relevant to the amounts and disclosures in the revised financial statements. It also includes an assessment of the significant estimates and judgments made by the directors in the preparation of the revised financial statements, and of whether the accounting policies are appropriate to the company's circumstances, consistently applied and adequately disclosed.

The audit of revised financial statements includes the performance of additional procedures to assess whether the revisions made by the directors are appropriate and have been properly made.

We planned and performed our audit so as to obtain all the information and explanations which we considered necessary in order to provide us with sufficient evidence to give reasonable assurance that the revised financial statements are free from material misstatement, whether caused by fraud or other irregularity or error. In forming our opinion we also evaluated the overall adequacy of the presentation of information in the revised financial statements.

---

[8]   The word 'revised' will be needed if the Directors' Report has also been revised.

Opinion

In our opinion:

- the revised financial statements give a true and fair view, in accordance with United Kingdom Generally Accepted Accounting Practice, seen as at the date the original financial statements were approved, of the state of the company's affairs as at .... and of its profit [loss] for the year then ended;

- the revised financial statements have been properly prepared in accordance with the provisions of the Companies Act 1985 as they have effect under the Companies (Revision of Defective Accounts and Report) Regulations 1990;

- the original financial statements for the year ended .... failed to comply with the requirements of the Companies Act 1985 in the respects identified by the directors in the statement contained in the supplementary note; and

- the information given in the [revised][8] Directors' Report is consistent with the revised financial statements.

Registered auditors   *Address*
Date

Example 3 – Auditor's report on revised directors' report

REPORT OF THE INDEPENDENT AUDITOR TO THE [MEMBERS] [SHAREHOLDERS] OF XYZ LIMITED

We have considered the information given in the revised directors' report for the year ended.... The revised directors' report replaces the original directors' report approved by the directors on... [and consists of the attached supplementary note together with the original report which was circulated to [members] [shareholders] on...][9]. The revised directors' report has been prepared under the Companies (Revision of Defective Accounts and Report) Regulations 1990 and accordingly does not take account of events which have taken place after the date on which the original directors' report was approved.

Respective responsibilities of directors and auditors

The directors are responsible for the preparation of the revised directors' report.

Our responsibility is to report to you whether the revised directors' report is consistent with the annual financial statements.

Basis of opinion

Our consideration has been directed towards matters of consistency alone and not to whether the revised directors' report complies with the requirements of the Companies Act 1985.

Opinion

In our opinion the information given in the revised directors' report is consistent with the annual financial statements for the year ended... which were circulated to [members] [shareholders] on....

Registered auditors   *Address*
Date

---

[9] Omit the words in brackets when the revision is by way of a full replacement.

Example 4 – Report on abbreviated accounts

Updated guidance on reporting on abbreviated accounts, including example reports, is provided by Bulletin 2006/3 'The Special Auditor's Report on Abbreviated Accounts in the United Kingdom'.

Example 5 – Auditor's statement on a summary financial statement[10]

The following example supersedes the examples provided in Bulletin 1999/6 'The auditors' statement on the summary financial statement' and Bulletin 2002/2 'The United Kingdom Directors' Remuneration Report Regulations 2002', and is for entities that prepare UK GAAP consolidated financial statements.

INDEPENDENT AUDITOR'S STATEMENT TO THE [MEMBERS] [SHAREHOLDERS] OF XYZ PLC

We have examined the summary financial statement [which comprises the Summary Consolidated Profit and Loss Account, Summary Consolidated Balance Sheet, Summary Consolidated Statement of Total Recognised Gains and Losses, [Summary Consolidated Cash Flow Statement][11] [and the Summary Directors' Remuneration Report][12] [set out on pages....][13].

Respective responsibilities of directors and auditors

The directors are responsible for preparing the [*summarised annual report*] in accordance with United Kingdom law.

Our responsibility is to report to you our opinion on the consistency of the summary financial statement within the [*summarised annual report*] with the full annual financial statements [, the Directors' Report][14] [and the Directors' Remuneration Report][12], and its compliance with the relevant requirements of section 251 of the Companies Act 1985 and the regulations made thereunder.

We also read the other information contained in the [*summarised annual report*] and consider the implications for our report if we become aware of any apparent misstatements or material inconsistencies with the summary financial statement.

Basis of opinion

We conducted our work in accordance with Bulletin 1999/6 'The auditor's statement on the summary financial statement' issued by the Auditing Practices Board. Our report on the

---

[10] This example report is effective for accounting periods commencing on or after 1 January 2005.

[11] The wording in the example is for entities preparing UK GAAP consolidated financial statements. For entities preparing consolidated financial statements under IFRSs as adopted by the EU the equivalent wording would be 'Summary Consolidated Income Statement, Summary Consolidated Balance Sheet, Summary Consolidated Statement of [Changes in Equity]/[Recognised Income and Expense], Summary Consolidated Cash Flow Statement'.

[12] A Summary Directors' Remuneration Report is needed only when a summary financial statement is prepared by a quoted company.

[13] Reports of entities that do not publish their summary financial statement on a web site or publish it using 'PDF' format may continue to refer to the summary financial statement by reference to page numbers.

[14] There is no requirement for an entity to include a Summary Directors' Report. If the directors include information in the summary financial statement that is derived from the Directors' Report the auditor is required to report that such information is consistent with the Directors' Report.

company's full annual financial statements describes the basis of our audit opinion[s] on those financial statements [and the Directors' Remuneration Report][12].

Opinion

In our opinion the summary financial statement is consistent with the full annual financial statements [, the Directors' Report][14] [and the Directors' Remuneration Report][12] of XYZ plc for the year ended ... and complies with the applicable requirements of section 251 of the Companies Act 1985, and the regulations made thereunder. [We have not considered the effects of any events between the date on which we signed our report on the full annual financial statements (insert date) and the date of this statement.][15]

Registered auditors   *Address*
Date

---

[15] Include this sentence where the date of this statement is after the date of the auditor's report on the full annual financial statements.

Example 6 – Report on entitlement to exemption from preparing group financial statements

Subsections (3) and (4) of section 248 of CA 1985 (auditors' report on entitlement to claim exemption from preparation of group accounts) were repealed by Statutory Instrument 1996 No. 189 'The Companies Act 1985 (Miscellaneous Accounting Amendments) Regulations 1996'.

Example 7 – Statement on a company's ability to make a distribution[16]

This example is based on the assumption that the financial statements have been prepared in accordance with UK GAAP.

STATEMENT OF THE INDEPENDENT AUDITOR TO THE [MEMBERS] [SHAREHOLDERS] OF XYZ LIMITED PURSUANT TO SECTION 271(4) OF THE COMPANIES ACT 1985

We have audited the financial statements of XYZ Limited for the year ended... in accordance with International Standards on Auditing (UK and Ireland) issued by the Auditing Practices Board and have expressed a qualified opinion thereon in our report dated....

Respective responsibilities of directors and auditors

As set out in the Statement of Directors' Responsibilities in the financial statements for the year ended [date], the directors are responsible for the preparation of the financial statements in accordance with applicable law and United Kingdom Accounting Standards. They are also responsible for considering whether the company, subsequent to the balance sheet date, has sufficient distributable profits to make a distribution at the time the distribution is made.

Our responsibility is to report whether, in our opinion, the subject matter of our qualification of our auditor's report on the financial statements for the year ended ... is material for determining, by reference to those financial statements, whether the distribution proposed by the company is permitted under section 263[17] [section 264/265] of the Companies Act 1985. We are not responsible for giving an opinion on whether the company has sufficient distributable reserves to make the distribution proposed at the time it is made.

Basis of opinion

We have carried out such procedures as we considered necessary to evaluate the effect of the qualified opinion for the determination of profits available for distribution.

Opinion

In our opinion the subject matter of the qualification is not material for determining, by reference to those financial statements, whether [the distribution of £...]/[the interim/final dividend for the year ended... of £...]/[any distribution] proposed by the company is permitted under section 263[17] [section 264/265] of the Companies Act 1985.

Registered auditors   *Address*
Date

---

[16] This example report is effective for accounting periods commencing on or after 15 December 2004.
[17] The reference in all cases to section 263 in this example is extended to cover also section 264 in the case of a public company and also sections 264 and 265 if the public company is also an 'investment company'.

Notes:

1 As an alternative the auditor's statement might be expressed in terms of the company's ability to make potential distributions up to a specific level. This may be particularly appropriate where the amount of the dividend has not yet been determined. In such circumstances the opinion paragraph would be worded as follows:

'In our opinion the subject matter of the qualification is not material for determining, by reference to those financial statements, whether a distribution of not more than £... by the company is permitted under section 263[17] [section 264/265] of the Companies Act 1985'.

2 Where the auditor concludes that the subject matter of the qualification is material to either a specific distribution which is proposed or to any distribution, then an adverse opinion is given. In such circumstances the opinion paragraph would be worded as follows:

'Adverse opinion
In our opinion the subject matter of the qualification is material for determining, by reference to those financial statements, whether [the distribution of £...]/[the interim/final dividend for the year ended ... of £...]/[any distribution] proposed by the company is permitted under section 263[17] [section 264/265] of the Companies Act 1985.'

3 In this example it is assumed that a separate report is given regarding the company's ability to make a distribution. However, as an alternative, this matter is sometimes addressed in the auditor's report on the financial statements by adding a separate statement after the audit opinion paragraph. That statement might be worded as follows:

'Statement of the independent auditors to the members of XYZ Limited pursuant to section 271(4) of the Companies Act 1985

*Basis of opinion
We have carried out such procedures as we considered necessary to evaluate the effect of the qualified opinion for the determination of profits available for distribution.*

*Opinion
In our opinion the subject matter of the above qualification is not material for determining, by reference to those financial statements, whether [the distribution of £...]/[the interim/final dividend for the year ended .... of £....]/[any distribution] proposed by the company is permitted under section 263[17] [section 264/ 265] of the Companies Act 1985.'*

Example 8 – Statement when a private company wishes to re-register as a public company[18]

This example is used when the company's financial statements were prepared within seven months before its application to re-register as a public company.

If the company's financial statements were not prepared within seven months then this statement must be made in respect of a specially prepared balance sheet which must be audited by the auditor. This statement is made in addition to a separate report made by the auditor on such a specially prepared balance sheet (see Example 9).

STATEMENT OF THE INDEPENDENT AUDITOR TO XYZ LIMITED FOR THE PURPOSE OF SECTION 43(3)(b) OF THE COMPANIES ACT 1985

We have examined the balance sheet and related notes of XYZ Limited as at... [which formed part of the financial statements for the year then ended]/[which were prepared for the purpose of the proposed re-registration of XYZ Limited as a public company] and audited by [us]/[ABC LLP].

Respective responsibilities of directors and auditors

As described on page... the company's directors are responsible for the preparation of the balance sheet and related notes. It is our responsibility to form an independent opinion, based on our examination, and to report our opinion to you.

Basis of opinion

The scope of our work, for the purpose of this statement, was limited to an examination of the relationship between the company's net assets and its called-up share capital and undistributable reserves as stated in the audited balance sheet.

Opinion

Where opinion on [financial statements]/[specially prepared balance sheet] is unqualified

[In our opinion the audited balance sheet at... shows that the amount of the company's net assets (within the meaning given to that expression by section 264(2) of the Companies Act 1985) was not less than the aggregate of its called-up share capital and undistributable reserves.]

---

[18] This example report is effective for accounting periods commencing on or after 15 December 2004.

Where opinion on financial statements is qualified but the qualification is not 'material' for the purposes of this statement

[We audited the financial statements of XYZ Limited for the year ended ...in accordance with International Standards on Auditing (UK and Ireland) issued by the Auditing Practices Board and expressed a qualified opinion thereon.

[Description of qualified opinion.]

In our opinion the matter giving rise to our qualification is not material for determining by reference to the balance sheet at ... whether, at that date, the amount of the company's net assets (within the meaning given to that expression by section 264(2) of the Companies Act 1985) was not less than the aggregate of its called-up share capital and undistributable reserves.]

Registered auditors   *Address*
Date

Example 9 – Report on balance sheet prepared other than in respect of an accounting reference period for the purpose of a private company re-registering as a public company[19]

This example is used when the latest financial statements are not eligible for use as they were prepared more than seven months before the company's application to re-register as a public company, or because at the time they were prepared the balance sheet did not meet the test in s43(3)(b) of CA 1985. In these circumstances it is necessary for the company to prepare a balance sheet which is required to be audited. In such circumstances the statement in Example 8 is also made in respect of the prepared balance sheet.

This example is based on the assumption that the balance sheet has been prepared in accordance with UK GAAP.

REPORT OF THE INDEPENDENT AUDITOR TO XYZ LIMITED FOR THE PURPOSE OF SECTION 43(3)(c) OF THE COMPANIES ACT 1985

We have audited the balance sheet and related notes of (name of entity) as at...set out on pages... to.... which have been prepared under the accounting policies set out therein.

Respective responsibilities of directors and auditors

As described on page... the company's directors are responsible for the preparation of the balance sheet in accordance with applicable law and United Kingdom Accounting Standards.

Our responsibility is to audit the balance sheet in accordance with relevant legal and regulatory requirements and International Standards on Auditing (UK and Ireland).

Basis of audit opinion

We conducted our audit in accordance with International Standards on Auditing (UK and Ireland) issued by the Auditing Practices Board. An audit includes examination, on a test basis, of evidence relevant to the amounts and disclosures. It also includes an assessment of the significant estimates and judgments made by the directors in the preparation of the balance sheet and related notes, and of whether the accounting policies are appropriate to the company's circumstances, consistently applied and adequately disclosed.

We planned and performed our audit so as to obtain all the information and explanations which we considered necessary in order to provide us with sufficient evidence to give reasonable assurance that the balance sheet is free from material misstatement, whether caused by fraud or other irregularity or error. In forming our opinion we also evaluated the overall adequacy of the presentation of information in the balance sheet.

---

[19] This example report is effective for accounting periods commencing on or after 15 December 2004.

Opinion

Unqualified[20]

In our opinion the balance sheet as at ... has been properly prepared in accordance with the provisions of the Companies Act 1985, which would have applied had the balance sheet been prepared for a financial year of the company.

Qualified

[Description of qualified opinion]

Except for the financial effect of the matter referred to in the preceding paragraph, in our opinion the balance sheet has been properly prepared in accordance with the provisions of the Companies Act 1985, which would have applied had the balance sheet been prepared for a financial year of the company.

In our opinion, the matter giving rise to our qualification is not material for determining by reference to the balance sheet at .... whether, at that date, the amount of the company's net assets was less than the aggregate of its called-up share capital and undistributable reserves.

Registered auditors   *Address*
Date

---

[20] The meaning of unqualified report is set out in section 46 of CA 1985.

Example 10 – Report when a private company wishes to redeem or purchase its own shares out of capital

REPORT OF THE INDEPENDENT AUDITOR TO THE DIRECTORS OF XYZ LIMITED PURSUANT TO SECTION 173(5) OF THE COMPANIES ACT 1985

We report on the attached statutory declaration of the directors dated..., prepared pursuant to the Companies Act 1985, in connection with the company's proposed [purchase]/ [redemption] of... (number) [ordinary]/[preferred] shares by a payment out of capital.

Basis of opinion

We have inquired into the company's state of affairs in order to review the bases for the statutory declaration.

Opinion

In our opinion the amount of £... specified in the statutory declaration as the permissible capital payment for the shares to be [purchased]/[redeemed] is properly determined in accordance with sections 171 and 172 of the Companies Act 1985.

We are not aware of anything to indicate that the opinion expressed by the directors in their statutory declaration as to any of the matters mentioned in section 173(3) of the Companies Act 1985 is unreasonable in all the circumstances.

Registered auditors   *Address*
Date

Example 11 – Report when a private company wishes to provide financial assistance for the purchase of its own shares or those of its holding company[21]

REPORT OF THE INDEPENDENT AUDITOR TO THE DIRECTORS OF XYZ LIMITED PURSUANT TO SECTION 156(4) OF THE COMPANIES ACT 1985

We report on the attached [statutory declaration]/[statement] of the directors dated ..., prepared pursuant to the Companies Act 1985, in connection with the proposal that the company should give financial assistance for the purchase of ... (number) of the company's [ordinary]/[preferred] shares.

Basis of opinion

We have enquired into the state of the company's affairs in order to review the bases for the [statutory declaration]/[statement].

Opinion

We are not aware of anything to indicate that the opinion expressed by the directors in their [statutory declaration]/[statement] as to any of the matters mentioned in section 156(2) of the Companies Act 1985 is unreasonable in all the circumstances.

Registered auditors   *Address*
Date

---

[21] When CA 2006 comes into force this report will no longer be required.

Example 12 – Report when a public company wishes to allot shares otherwise than for cash

REPORT OF THE INDEPENDENT [PERSON] [AUDITOR][22] TO XYZ PLC FOR THE PURPOSES OF SECTION 103(1) OF THE COMPANIES ACT 1985

We report on the value of the consideration for the allotment to... [name of allottee] of... [number] shares, having a nominal value of [...] each, to be issued at a premium of... pence per share. The shares and share premium are to be treated as fully paid up.

The consideration for the allotment to [name of allottee] is the freehold building situated at... [address] and... [number] shares, having a nominal value of [...] each, in LMN PLC.

Basis of valuation

The freehold building was valued on the basis of its open market value by [name of specialist], a Fellow of the Royal Institution of Chartered Surveyors, on... and in our opinion it is reasonable to accept such a valuation.

The shares in LMN PLC were valued by us on... on the basis of the price shown in the Stock Exchange Daily Official List at....

Opinion

In our opinion, the methods of valuation of the freehold building and the shares in LMN PLC were reasonable in all the circumstances. There appears to have been no material change in the value of either part of the consideration since the date(s) at which the valuations were made.

On the basis of the valuations, in our opinion, the value of the total consideration is not less than £... (being the total amount to be treated as paid up on the shares allotted together with the share premium).

Registered auditors   *Address*
Date

---

[22] Section 108 of CA 1985 requires the valuation and report required by section 103 to be made by an independent person, that is to say a person qualified at the time of the report to be appointed, or continue to be, an auditor of the Company. In circumstances where the auditor is designated by legislation as being eligible to carry out a valuation, paragraph 56 of ES 5 'Non-Audit services provided to audit clients' disapplies the general prohibition in paragraph 54 of ES5 on audit firms undertaking an engagement to provide any valuation to an audit client where the valuation involves a significant degree of subjective judgment and has a material effect on the financial statements. In such circumstances the audit engagement partner considers the threats to the auditor's objectivity and independence and applies relevant safeguards.

Example 13 – Report when non-cash assets are transferred to a public company by certain of its members

REPORT OF THE INDEPENDENT [PERSON] [AUDITOR][23] TO XYZ PLC FOR THE PURPOSES OF SECTION 104(4) OF THE COMPANIES ACT 1985

We report on the transfer of non-cash assets to XYZ PLC ('the Company') by subscribers to the Company's memorandum of association.

The consideration to be received by the Company is a freehold building situated at... [address] ('the consideration to be received').

The consideration to be given by the Company is... [number] shares, having a nominal value of £1 each, in LMN PLC ('the consideration to be given').

Basis of valuation

The freehold building was valued on the basis of its open market value by [name of specialist], a Fellow of the Royal Institution of Chartered Surveyors, on... and in our opinion it is reasonable to accept such a valuation.

The shares in LMN PLC were valued by us on... on the basis of the price shown in the Stock Exchange Daily Official List at....

Opinion

In our opinion, the methods of valuation of the freehold building and the shares in LMN PLC were reasonable in all the circumstances. There appears to have been no material change in the value of the consideration to be received or the consideration to be given since the date(s) at which the valuations were made.

On the basis of the valuations, in our opinion, the value of the consideration to be received by the Company is not less than the value of the consideration to be given by the Company.

Registered auditors   *Address*
Date

---

[23] Section 109 (via section 108) of CA 1985 requires the valuation and report required by Section 104(4) to be made by an independent person, that is to say a person qualified at the time of the report to be appointed, or continue to be, an auditor of the Company. In circumstances where the auditor is designated by legislation as being eligible to carry out a valuation, paragraph 56 of ES 5 'Non-Audit services provided to audit clients' disapplies the general prohibition in paragraph 54 of ES5 on audit firms undertaking an engagement to provide any valuation to an audit client where the valuation involves a significant degree of subjective judgment and has a material effect on the financial statements. In such circumstances the audit engagement partner considers the threats to the auditor's objectivity and independence and applies relevant safeguards.

Example 14 – Report on initial accounts when a public company wishes to make a distribution[24]

This example is based on the assumption that the initial accounts have been prepared in accordance with UK GAAP.

REPORT OF THE INDEPENDENT AUDITOR TO THE DIRECTORS OF XYZ PLC UNDER SECTION 273(4) OF THE COMPANIES ACT 1985

We have audited the initial accounts of XYZ PLC for the period from .... to ... which comprise [state the primary financial statements such as the Profit and Loss Account, the Balance Sheet, the Cash Flow Statement, the Statement of Total Recognised Gains and Losses] and the related notes. The initial accounts have been prepared under the accounting policies set out therein.

Respective responsibilities of directors and auditors

As described on page ... the directors are responsible for the preparation of the initial accounts in accordance with applicable law and United Kingdom Accounting Standards.

Our responsibility is to audit the initial accounts in accordance with relevant legal and regulatory requirements and International Standards on Auditing (UK and Ireland). We report to you our opinion as to whether the initial accounts have been properly prepared within the meaning of section 273 of the Companies Act 1985.

Basis of audit opinion

We conducted our audit in accordance with International Standards on Auditing (UK and Ireland) issued by the Auditing Practices Board. An audit includes examination, on a test basis, of evidence relevant to the amounts and disclosures in the initial accounts. It also includes an assessment of the significant estimates and judgments made by the directors in the preparation of the initial accounts, and of whether the accounting policies are appropriate to the company's circumstances, consistently applied and adequately disclosed.

We planned and performed our audit so as to obtain all the information and explanations which we considered necessary in order to provide us with sufficient evidence to give reasonable assurance that the initial accounts are free from material misstatement, whether caused by fraud or other irregularity or error. In forming our opinion we also evaluated the overall adequacy of the presentation of information in the initial accounts.

---

[24] This example report is effective for accounting periods commencing on or after 15 December 2004.

Opinion

In our opinion the initial accounts for the period from... to... have been properly prepared within the meaning of section 273 of the Companies Act 1985.

Registered auditors   *Address*
Date

Example 15 – Report on ceasing to hold office

No circumstances connected with ceasing to hold office as auditor

STATEMENT TO THE DIRECTORS OF XYZ LIMITED ON CEASING TO HOLD OFFICE AS AUDITOR

In accordance with section 394 of the Companies Act 1985, we confirm that there are no circumstances connected with our ceasing to hold office that we consider should be brought to the attention of the company's [members] [shareholders] or creditors.

Registered auditors   *Address*
Date

Circumstances connected with ceasing to hold office that the auditor considers should be brought to the attention of the members or creditors of the company

STATEMENT OF CIRCUMSTANCES RELATING TO:

- **[THE INTENTION OF PQR NOT TO SEEK RE-APPOINTMENT AS AUDITORS OF XYZ LIMITED AT THE CONCLUSION OF OUR TERM OF OFFICE];or**

- **[THE RESIGNATION OF PQR AS AUDITORS OF XYZ LIMITED]; or**

- **[THE REMOVAL OF PQR AS AUDITORS OF XYZ LIMITED]**

In accordance with section 394 of the Companies Act 1985, we consider that the following circumstances connected with our ceasing to hold office should be brought to the attention of the [members] [shareholders] and creditors:

[Set out circumstances]

Unless the company applies to the court, this statement of circumstances, which we consider should be brought to the attention of [members] [shareholders] and creditors of the company, must be sent within 14 days to every person entitled under section 238 of the Companies Act 1985 to be sent copies of the company's accounts. This is a requirement of section 394(3) of that Act.

Registered auditors   *Address*
Date

PRACTICE NOTE 12 (REVISED)

MONEY LAUNDERING – INTERIM GUIDANCE FOR AUDITORS IN THE UNITED KINGDOM

CONTENTS

INTRODUCTION

1.   Practice Note 12 (Revised), "Money Laundering", was last issued as interim guidance in April 2006 and has been updated to take account of section 102 of the Serious and Organised Crime and Police Act ("SOCPA") which was brought into force in 2006.

2.   **Practice Note 12 (Revised) reflects the legislation effective at 31st December 2006. Auditors need to be alert to subsequent changes in legislative requirements including:**

   •   **prescription as to the forms to be used for reporting suspicions of money laundering, and**

   •   **additional requirements arising from the Third EU Money Laundering Directive.**

3.   Practice Note 12 (Revised) focuses on the impact of the anti-money laundering legislation on auditors' responsibilities when auditing and reporting on financial statements. It does not provide general guidance on the legislation. The Consultative Committee of Accountancy Bodies has issued "Anti-Money Laundering (Proceeds of Crime and Terrorism) – Second Interim Guidance for Accountants" ("CCAB Guidance") which provides general guidance on the legislation[1].

4.   The Serious Organised Crime Agency ("SOCA")[2] has adopted reporting guidance and disclosure forms previously issued by the National Criminal Intelligence Service ("NCIS") (http://www.soca.gov.uk/financialIntel/index.html). These may change over time.

5.   The anti-money laundering legislation is complex and uncertainty inevitably exists as to how the courts will interpret it in practice. Notwithstanding this, it is expected that the courts will take into account guidance issued by authoritative bodies. To obtain a full understanding of the legal requirements in the United Kingdom, auditors also refer to the relevant provisions of the legislation and, if necessary, obtain legal advice.

Key changes

6.   The key changes introduced by the Proceeds of Crime Act 2002 ("POCA"), (as subsequently amended by SOCPA) and the Money Laundering Regulations 2003 (the "ML Regulations") are as follows:

---

[1]   Cross references in the Practice Note to "CCAB Guidance" are to the second interim guidance published by the CCAB on the 16 February 2004 and subsequently updated on 9 March 2004. If, subsequent to the publication of this Practice Note, the CCAB updates the second interim guidance the cross references should be taken as referring to the latest CCAB Guidance. (http://www.icaew.co.uk/viewer/index.cfm?AUB=TB2I_31571).

[2]   From 1 April 2006 the body previously named the National Criminal Intelligence Service ("NCIS") became part of the new Serious Organised Crime Agency.

- Part 7 of POCA consolidated, updated and reformed criminal law in the United Kingdom with regard to money laundering. The definition of money laundering[3] was extended to comprise three principal money laundering offences[4] (behaviour that directly constitutes money laundering). These include possessing, or in any way dealing with, or concealing, the proceeds of any crime and includes crime committed by an entity or an individual. Under the previous anti-money laundering legislation money laundering reporting duties of auditors extended only to the suspected proceeds of drug trafficking or terrorist funds unless as a result of their work the auditors would themselves have committed a money laundering offence.

- Whilst POCA and the ML Regulations do not extend the scope of the audit, auditors, who are now within the regulated sector[5], are required to report where:

  - they know or suspect, or have reasonable grounds[6] to know or suspect, that another person is engaged in money laundering;

  - they can identify the other person or the whereabouts of any of the laundered property or that they believe, or it is reasonable to expect them to believe that

---

3   Section 340(11) of POCA states that "Money laundering is an act which:
    (a) constitutes an offence under section 327, 328 or 329,
    (b) constitutes an attempt, conspiracy or incitement to commit an offence specified in paragraph (a),
    (c) constitutes aiding, abetting, counselling or procuring the commission of an offence specified in paragraph (a), or
    (d) would constitute an offence specified in paragraph (a), (b) or (c) if done in the United Kingdom."
4   The principal money laundering offences defined under POCA are:
    • s327 "Concealing" criminal property (including concealing or disguising its nature, source, location, disposition, movement, ownership or rights attaching; converting, transferring or removing from any part of the UK).
    • s328 "Arranging" (entering into or becoming concerned in an arrangement which the business or an individual knows or suspects facilitates the acquisition, retention, use or control of criminal property by or on behalf of another person).
    • s329 "Acquiring, using or possessing criminal property".
5   For the purposes of this Practice Note this includes both the businesses in the regulated sector defined in the Proceeds of Crime Act 2002 Schedule 9 Part 1 (as amended by Statutory Instrument 2003/3074 "The Proceeds of Crime Act 2002 (Business in the Regulated Sector and Supervisory Authorities) Order 2003" in November 2003) and also relevant businesses as defined in paragraph 2(2) of the Money Laundering Regulations 2003. Businesses in the regulated sector and relevant businesses are collectively referred to hereinafter as the 'regulated sector' in this Practice Note. The regulated sector includes (but is not restricted to) businesses engaged in the following activities in the United Kingdom:
    • banking, investment business and other FSMA 2000 regulated activities
    • accountancy or audit services
    • money service operators
    • estate agency work
    • operating a casino
    • insolvency practitioners
    • tax services
    • legal services involving participation in financial or real property transactions
    • formation, operation or management of a company or a trust
    • dealing in goods of any description which involves accepting a total cash payment of 15,000 euro or more.
6   More detailed guidance on what is meant by "reasonable grounds" is given in section 6 of the CCAB Guidance.

the information will or may assist in identifying that other person or the whereabouts of the laundered property; and

-   the information has come to the auditors in the normal course of their 'regulated' business.

•   Failure by an auditor to report knowledge or suspicion of, or reasonable grounds to know or suspect, money laundering in relation to the proceeds of any crime is a criminal offence[7]. Auditors are required to report offences committed in the United Kingdom and any involvement or dealings in the United Kingdom with the proceeds of conduct occurring overseas which would constitute an offence punishable by imprisonment for a maximum term in excess of 12 months in any part of the United Kingdom if it occurred there. [8] Where the auditor knows or has reasonable grounds to believe that the money laundering is taking place wholly abroad, the auditor is not required to report if the money laundering was lawful in the country where it occurred.[9] Auditors (partners and staff) will face criminal penalties[10] if they breach the requirements.

•   The requirement to report is not just related to matters that might be considered material to the financial statements; auditors have to report knowledge or suspicion, or reasonable grounds for knowledge or suspicion, of crimes that

---

[7]   Subject to the provisions of POCA section 330(6) relating to legal professional privilege.

[8]   SOCPA section 102 amended POCA so that it is not a money laundering offence for a person to deal with the proceeds of conduct which that person knows, or believes on reasonable grounds, occurred in a particular country or territory outside the United Kingdom, and which was not, at the time it occurred, unlawful under the criminal law then applying in that country or territory, and does not constitute an offence that would be punishable by imprisonment for a maximum term in excess of 12 months in any part of the United Kingdom if it occurred there. Partners and staff in audit firms do not therefore need to make reports about the proceeds of such conduct (i.e. lawful and non-serious overseas conduct). In addition, a report is not required in respect of the proceeds of overseas conduct which would amount to one of the following offences in the United Kingdom (notwithstanding that the penalty for such offences is in excess of 12 months' imprisonment):
(a) an offence under the Gaming Act 1968;
(b) an offence under the Lotteries and Amusements Act 1976; or
(c) an offence under section 23 or 25 of the Financial Services and Markets Act 2000.

[9]   See POCA sections 330(7A), 331(6A) and 332(7), inserted by SOCPA section 102.

[10] Criminal penalties are covered under sections 334 and 336(6) of POCA. The maximum penalty for the three principal money laundering offences on conviction on indictment is fourteen years imprisonment. The maximum penalty on conviction on indictment is five years imprisonment for the following offences:
•   a person in the regulated sector other than a nominated officer failing to disclose (section 330),
•   the nominated officer failure to disclose offences (section 331 for the regulated sector, section 332 for those outside this sector),
•   the giving of consent by a nominated officer inappropriately to prohibited acts (section 336(5)), and
•   the 'tipping off' offence (section 333).
Furthermore in all cases, an unlimited fine can be imposed.
On summary conviction, the maximum penalty for all the above offences is six months' imprisonment and/or a fine not exceeding the statutory maximum. A person guilty of an offence under section 339(1A) of making a disclosure under section 330, 331, 332 or 338 otherwise than in the form prescribed by the Secretary of State or otherwise than in the manner so prescribed is liable on summary conviction to a fine not exceeding level 5 on the standard scale.

potentially have no material financial statement impact. POCA does not contain de minimis concessions that affect the reporting requirements of auditors.

- Firms must take appropriate measures so that partners and staff are made aware of the provisions of POCA, the ML Regulations and TA 2000 and are given training in how to recognise and deal with actual or suspected money laundering activities.

- Auditors are required to adopt more rigorous client identification procedures and appropriate anti-money laundering procedures.

7. In the United Kingdom, POCA came into force on 24 February 2003, although the failure to report offences under POCA sections 330 to 332 did not generally apply to auditors until the ML Regulations came into force on 1 March 2004. The principal money laundering offences, consent provisions and 'tipping off' offences have therefore applied to auditors from 24 February 2003[11]. However, auditors, who were not within the regulated sector before 1 March 2004, only need to report knowledge or suspicions of money laundering if part or all of the information that gave rise to that knowledge or suspicion came to the attention of the auditor on or after that date (or if a report is necessary for another reason, such as because the auditor would otherwise commit one of the main money laundering offences). The amendments to POCA introduced by SOCPA came into force on 1 July 2005, other than the amendments in SOCPA section 102[8], which came into force on 15 May 2006.

The Proceeds of Crime Act 2002

8. For a number of years auditors in the United Kingdom have been required to report to an appropriate authority where they suspect the laundering of money which either derives from drug trafficking or is related to terrorist offences. There were also certain reporting duties relating to the laundering of the proceeds of other crime under the Criminal Justice Act. Partners and staff in audit firms must continue to report non-compliance with certain laws related to terrorism[12] (see Appendix Two of the CCAB Guidance) but POCA extends both the definition of what money laundering comprises and the auditor's reporting responsibilities. The anti-money laundering legislation now imposes a duty to report money laundering in respect of all criminal property. Property is criminal property if:

(a) It constitutes a person's benefit from criminal conduct or it represents such a benefit (in whole or in part and whether directly or indirectly); and

(b) The alleged offender knows or suspects that it constitutes or represents such a benefit.

---

[11] Information on the transitional provisions is given in Statutory Instrument 2003/120 "The Proceeds of Crime Act 2002 (Commencement No. 4, Transitional Provisions and Savings) Order 2003". Similar transitional provisions exist in respect of information which came to the auditor's attention prior to 1 March 2004 (see section 25 of the CCAB Guidance).

[12] The Terrorism Act 2000 (as amended by the Anti-terrorism, Crime and Security Act 2001) and associated regulations.

9. POCA establishes three principal money laundering offences[4] which extend the definition of money laundering to encompass offences relating to the possession, acquisition, use, concealment or conversion of criminal property and involvement in arrangements relating to criminal property. These principal offences apply to all persons and businesses whether or not they are within the regulated sector.

10. In addition, under section 330 of POCA those persons working in the regulated sector are required to report knowledge or suspicion, or reasonable grounds for knowledge or suspicion, that another person is engaged in money laundering to a nominated officer where that knowledge or suspicion, or reasonable grounds for knowledge or suspicion, came to those persons in the course of their business or employment in the regulated sector. In audit firms the nominated officer is usually known as a Money Laundering Reporting Officer ("MLRO") and is referred to as such in this Practice Note.[13] If as a result of that report the MLRO has knowledge or suspicion of, or reasonable grounds to know or suspect money laundering, the MLRO then has a responsibility to report to SOCA. Features of the anti-money laundering legislation include:

    *   Money laundering comprises three principal money laundering offences[4] which are defined in sections 327, 328 and 329 of POCA with further regulated sector offences defined in sections 330 and 331 of POCA. The principal money laundering offences include concealing, disguising, converting, transferring, removing, arranging, using, acquiring or possessing property which constitutes or represents a benefit from criminal conduct. POCA does not contain de minimis concessions that affect the reporting requirements of auditors with the result that reports need to be made irrespective of the quantum of the benefits derived from, or the seriousness of the offence.

    *   Where they have knowledge, suspicion or reasonable grounds to know or suspect that another person is engaged in money laundering, partners and staff in audit firms are required to make a disclosure to their firm's MLRO or, in the case of sole practitioners, to SOCA, regardless of whether that person is a client or a third party[7].

    *   Partners and staff in audit firms need to be alert to the dangers of disseminating information that is likely to tip off a money launderer or prejudice an investigation ('tipping off')[14] as this may constitute a criminal offence under the anti-money laundering legislation.

11. Auditors who consider that the actions they plan to take, or may be asked to take, will result in themselves committing a principal money laundering offence are required to

---

[13] Section 7(2) of the ML Regulations exempts sole practitioners from the requirements relating to internal reporting procedures but the external reporting obligations under POCA remain. There is no obligation on a sole practitioner to appoint an MLRO where the sole practitioner does not employ any staff, or act in association with any other person. Where no MLRO is appointed and a sole practitioner has knowledge or suspicion of, or reasonable grounds to know or suspect, money laundering the sole practitioner has a responsibility to report to SOCA.

[14] See guidance on 'tipping off' in paragraphs 35 to 37.

obtain prior consent to those actions from their MLRO and the MLRO is required to seek appropriate prior consent from SOCA (see paragraphs 46 and 47).

The Money Laundering Regulations 2003

12. The Money Laundering Regulations 2003 replace the Money Laundering Regulations 1993 and 2001. The ML Regulations extend the 'regulated sector' to which POCA refers to include the provision by way of business of audit services by a person who is eligible for appointment as a company auditor under Section 25 of the Companies Act 1989 or Article 28 of the Companies (Northern Ireland) Order 1990[15]. For the purposes of this Practice Note "person" is interpreted as referring to a UK audit firm that is designated as a "Registered Auditor"[16] and the ML Regulations apply to all partners and staff within that UK audit firm who are involved in providing audit services in the UK.

13. Where a Registered Auditor is not providing audit services the ML Regulations will nevertheless often apply as they also cover "the provision by way of business of accountancy services by a body corporate or unincorporate or, in the case of a sole practitioner, by an individual"[17].

14. The ML Regulations impose requirements on businesses in the regulated sector relating to systems and training to prevent money laundering, identification procedures for clients, record keeping procedures and internal reporting procedures.

FIRM-WIDE PRACTICES

Money Laundering Reporting Officer

15. The ML Regulations require relevant businesses to appoint a nominated officer (usually known as the MLRO). There is no obligation for a sole practitioner who does not employ any staff, or act in association with any other person, to appoint an MLRO. Auditors are required to report where they know or suspect, or have reasonable grounds to know or suspect, that another person is engaged in money laundering. Partners and staff in audit firms discharge their responsibilities by reporting to their MLRO or, in the case of sole practitioners, to SOCA and, where appropriate, by obtaining consent from the MLRO or SOCA to continue with any prohibited activities. The MLRO is responsible for deciding, on the basis of the information provided by the partners and staff, whether further enquiry is required, whether the matter should be reported to SOCA and for making the report to SOCA. Partners and staff seek advice from the MLRO who acts as the main source of guidance and if necessary is the liaison point for communication with lawyers, SOCA and the relevant law enforcement

---

[15] Regulation 2(2)k of the Money Laundering Regulations 2003.
[16] A Registered Auditor is defined as "A firm entered on the register as eligible for appointment as company auditor under section 25 of the 1989 Act, article 28 of the NI Order 1990, or section 185 of the RI 1990 Act."
[17] Regulation 2(j) of the Money Laundering Regulations 2003.

agency. More detailed guidance on the role of the MLRO is given in section 15 of the CCAB Guidance.

Training

16. Firms are required to take appropriate measures so that partners and staff are made aware of the relevant provisions of POCA, the ML Regulations and the TA 2000 and are given training in how to recognise and deal with activities which may be related to money laundering. Guidance on training is given in section 16 of the CCAB Guidance. The level of training provided to individuals needs to be appropriate to both the level of exposure of the individual to money laundering risk and their role and seniority within the firm. Senior members of the firm whatever their role need to understand the requirements of POCA and the ML Regulations.

17. Apart from the training referred to in paragraph 16 above, additional training or expertise in criminal law is not required under POCA. However, ISA (UK and Ireland) 250 'Consideration of laws and regulations in an audit of financial statements' requires an auditor to obtain a general understanding of the legal and regulatory framework applicable to the entity and the industry to help identify possible or actual instances of non-compliance with those laws and regulations which provide a legal framework within which the entity conducts its business and which are central to the entity's ability to conduct its business and hence to its financial statements.

Client identification procedures

18. Appropriate identification procedures, as required by the ML Regulations are now mandatory when accepting appointment as auditor. Guidance on identification procedures is given in section 18 of the CCAB Guidance.

19. Auditing standards on quality control for audits state that acceptance of client relationships and specific audit engagements includes considering the integrity of the principal owners, key management and those charged with governance of the entity. This involves the auditor making appropriate enquiries and may involve discussions with third parties, the obtaining of written references and searches of relevant databases. These procedures may provide some of the relevant client identification information but will need to be extended to comply with the ML Regulations.

20. Annual reappointment as auditor does not, in itself, require the client identification procedures to be re-performed. However, if there has been a change in the client's circumstances, such as changes in beneficial ownership, control or directors, and this information was relied upon originally as part of the client identification procedures then, depending on the auditor's assessment of risk, the procedures may need to be re-performed and documented, to provide evidence of the decision.

Engagement letters

21. It may be helpful for the auditor to explain to the client the reason for requiring evidence of identity and this can be achieved by including an additional paragraph in the audit engagement letter. Where client identification procedures start before the

engagement letter is drafted it might be helpful for the auditor to address this in pre-engagement letter communications with the potential client. The following is an illustrative paragraph that could be included for this purpose:

"Client identification
As with other professional services firms, we are required to identify our clients for the purposes of the UK anti-money laundering legislation. We are likely to request from you, and retain, some information and documentation for these purposes and/or to make searches of appropriate databases. If we are not able to obtain satisfactory evidence of your identity within a reasonable time, there may be circumstances in which we are not able to proceed with the audit appointment."

22. It may also be helpful to inform clients of the auditor's responsibilities under POCA to report knowledge or suspicion, or reasonable grounds to know or suspect, that a money laundering offence has been committed and the restrictions created by the 'tipping off' rules on the auditor's ability to discuss such matters with their clients, although it is not necessary to do so. The following is an illustrative paragraph that could be included in the audit engagement letter for this purpose:

"Money laundering disclosures
The provision of audit services is a business in the regulated sector under the Proceeds of Crime Act 2002 and, as such, partners and staff in audit firms have to comply with this legislation which includes provisions that may require us to make a money laundering disclosure in relation to information we obtain as part of our normal audit work. It is not our practice to inform you when such a disclosure is made or the reasons for it because of the restrictions imposed by the 'tipping off' provisions of the legislation."

23. Whether or not to include these illustrative paragraphs in the audit engagement letter is a policy decision to be taken by individual firms to be applied on all audit engagements, irrespective of particular client situations. However, unless the policy is applied in a consistent manner there is a possibility that inclusion of these paragraphs might be interpreted by law enforcement as 'tipping off'.

IMPACT OF LEGISLATION ON AUDIT PROCEDURES

Identification of knowledge or suspicions

24. ISA (UK and Ireland) 250 establishes standards and provides guidance on the auditor's responsibility to consider law and regulations in an audit of financial statements. The anti-money laundering legislation does not require the auditor to extend the scope of the audit, save as referred to in paragraph 32 below, but the normal audit work could give rise to knowledge or suspicion, or reasonable grounds for knowledge or suspicion, that will need to be reported. Such knowledge or suspicion may arise in relation to:

•   law and regulations relating directly to the preparation of the financial statements;

- law and regulations which provide a legal framework within which the entity conducts its business; and

- other law and regulations.

25. Auditing standards on law and regulations require the auditor to obtain sufficient appropriate audit evidence about compliance with those laws and regulations that have an effect on the determination of material amounts and disclosures in the financial statements. This may cause the auditor to be suspicious that, for example, breaches of the Companies Act or tax offences have taken place, which may be criminal offences resulting in the acquisition of criminal property.

26. Auditing standards on law and regulations also require the auditor to perform procedures to help identify possible or actual instances of non-compliance with those laws and regulations which provide a legal framework within which the entity conducts its business and which are central to the entity's ability to conduct its business[18] and hence to its financial statements. These procedures consist of:

- obtaining a general understanding of the legal and regulatory framework applicable to the entity and the industry and of the procedures followed to ensure compliance with that framework;

- inspecting correspondence with the relevant licensing or regulatory authorities;

- enquiring of those charged with governance as to whether they are on notice of any such possible instances of non-compliance with law or regulations; and

- obtaining written representation that those charged with governance have disclosed to the auditor all known actual or possible non-compliance with laws and regulations whose effects should be considered when preparing financial statements, together with, where applicable, the actual or contingent consequences which may arise from the non-compliance.

This work may give the auditor grounds to suspect that criminal offences have been committed.

27. Laws relating to money laundering will be central to an entity's business, if that business is within the regulated sector as defined by POCA and the ML Regulations[5]. When auditing the financial statements of businesses within the regulated sector the auditor reviews the steps taken by the entity to comply with the ML Regulations, assesses their effectiveness and obtains management representations concerning compliance with the ML Regulations. If the client's systems are thought to be ineffective the auditor considers whether there is a responsibility to report 'a matter of material significance' to the regulator and the possible impact of fines, following non-compliance with the ML Regulations or POCA. Where the entity's business is outside

---

[18] For example, non-compliance with certain laws and regulations may cause the entity to cease operations, or call into question the entity's status as a going concern.

the regulated sector, although the auditor's reporting responsibilities under the money laundering legislation are unchanged, the entity's management is not required to implement the ML Regulations. Whilst the principal money laundering offences apply to these entities, the laws relating to money laundering are unlikely to be considered by the auditor to be central to an entity's business for the purposes of ISA (UK and Ireland) 250.

28. In relation to other laws and regulations, auditing standards on laws and regulations require the auditor to be alert to the fact that audit procedures applied for the purpose of forming an opinion on the financial statements may bring instances of possible non-compliance with laws and regulations to the auditor's attention and to be alert for those instances that might incur obligations for partners and staff in audit firms to report money laundering offences. There are also a number of offences under the TA 2000, which trigger an obligation to make a report. For example, someone is engaged in money laundering under section 18 of the TA 2000 if they enter into or become concerned in an arrangement which facilitates the retention or control of terrorist property[19]. More detailed guidance on offences under the TA 2000 is given in Appendix Two of the CCAB Guidance.

29. The auditor also gives consideration to whether any contingent liabilities might arise in this area. For example, there may be regulatory or criminal fines for non-compliance with POCA or the ML Regulations. In certain circumstances, even where POCA has been complied with, civil claims may arise or recovery actions by the Assets Recovery Agency may give rise to contingent liabilities. The auditor will remain alert to the fact that discussions with the client on such matters may give rise to a risk of 'tipping off' (see paragraphs 35 to 37).

30. In some situations the audit client may have obtained legal advice to the effect that certain actions or circumstances do not give rise to criminal conduct and therefore cannot give rise to criminal property. As explained in auditing standards on law and regulations, whether an act constitutes non-compliance with law or regulations may involve consideration of matters which do not lie within the competence and experience of individuals trained in the audit of financial information. Provided that the auditor considers that the advice has been obtained from a suitably qualified and independent lawyer and that the lawyer was made aware of all relevant circumstances known to the auditor, the auditor may rely on such advice, provided the auditor has complied with auditing standards on using the work of an expert.

31. The anti-money laundering legislation requires United Kingdom auditors to report conduct which takes place overseas if that conduct would constitute an offence in any part of the United Kingdom (subject to the SOCPA section 102 amendment[8]). The anti-money laundering legislation does not change the scope of the audit and does not therefore impose any requirement for the UK parent company auditor to change or add to the normal instructions to auditors of overseas subsidiaries. However, when considering non-UK parts of the group audit the UK parent company auditor will need

---

[19] Terrorist property includes "money or other property which is likely to be used for the purposes of terrorism" irrespective of whether those funds come from a legitimate source or not.

to consider whether information obtained as part of the group audit procedures (for example reports made by non-UK subsidiary auditors, discussions with non-UK subsidiary auditors or discussions with UK and non-UK directors) gives rise to knowledge or suspicion, or reasonable grounds for knowledge or suspicion, such that there is a requirement for the UK parent company auditor to report to SOCA.

Further enquiry

32. Once the auditor suspects a possible breach of law or regulations, the auditor will need to make further enquiries to assess the implications of this for the audit of the financial statements. Auditing standards on laws and regulations require that when the auditor becomes aware of information concerning a possible instance of non-compliance, the auditor should obtain an understanding of the nature of the act and the circumstances in which it has occurred, and sufficient other information to evaluate the possible effect on the financial statements. Providing that the auditor is satisfied that the auditor knows or suspects, or has reasonable grounds to know or suspect, that another person is engaged in money laundering, a disclosure must be made to the firm's MLRO or, for sole practitioners, to SOCA. The anti-money laundering legislation does not require the auditor to undertake any additional enquiries to determine further details of the predicate criminal offence. If the auditor is genuinely uncertain as to whether or not there are grounds to make a disclosure, the auditor may wish to seek advice from the MLRO.

33. The auditor may have knowledge or suspicion that money laundering offences have occurred where an audit client is the victim of the crime; for example a company involved in the retail business is likely to have been the victim of shoplifting offences. Where the auditor can identify the money launderer or the whereabouts of any of the laundered property, or believe, or it is reasonable to expect the auditor to believe, that the information or other matter will or may assist in identifying the money launderer or the whereabouts of any of the laundered property, the auditor is required to report knowledge or suspicion of money laundering arising from such crimes because they constitute money laundering under the anti-money laundering legislation. Such situations are likely to be reported using limited intelligence value reports (see paragraph 39).

34. Where the auditor has made a report to the MLRO and the MLRO has decided that further enquiry is necessary, subject to compliance with legislation relating to 'tipping off', the auditor will need to be made aware of the outcome of the enquiry to determine whether there are any implications for the audit report or the decision to accept reappointment as auditor.

'Tipping off'

35. In the United Kingdom, 'tipping off' is an offence under section 333 of the Proceeds of Crime Act 2002. It arises when an individual discloses matters where:

   (a) There is knowledge or suspicion that a disclosure (internal or external) has already been made; and

(b) That disclosure is likely to prejudice any investigation which might be conducted following the disclosure in (a).

Whilst 'tipping off' requires a person to have knowledge or suspicion that a disclosure has been made, a further offence of prejudicing an investigation is included in section 342 of POCA. Under this provision, it is an offence to make any disclosure which is likely to prejudice an investigation of which a person has knowledge or suspicion, or to falsify, conceal, destroy or otherwise dispose of, or cause or permit the falsification, concealment, destruction or disposal of, documents relevant to such an investigation.

36. In performing any further enquiries in the context of the audit of the financial statements the auditor needs to be aware that the auditor is under an obligation under the money laundering legislation not to disclose information to any person if doing so is likely to tip off or prejudice an investigation (referred to in this Practice Note as 'tipping off'). The risk of committing an offence of 'tipping off' is greatest if management and/or the directors are themselves involved in the suspected criminal activity. To minimise any risk of 'tipping off' it is important that any further enquiries represent only steps that the auditor would have performed as part of the normal audit work (although even these steps may in some circumstances amount to 'tipping off') and that the MLRO is consulted before any further enquiry is performed. There is potentially a risk of 'tipping off' if the auditor does not act on suspicions when management and/or the directors might have expected the auditor to take some action. In these circumstances, the auditor seeks advice from the MLRO. Guidance on 'tipping off' is provided in Section 9 of the CCAB Guidance.

37. The auditor will also need to consider whether continuing to act for the company could itself constitute money laundering, for example if it amounted to aiding or abetting the commission of one of the principal money laundering offences in sections 327, 328 or 329 of POCA, or if it amounted to one of the principal money laundering offences itself, in particular the offence of becoming involved in an arrangement under section 328 of POCA. In those circumstances the auditor may want to consider whether to resign, but should firstly contact their MLRO, both to report the suspicions and to seek guidance in respect of 'tipping off'. If the auditor wishes to continue to conduct the audit the auditor may need to seek appropriate consent from SOCA for such an action to be taken (see paragraphs 46 and 47).

Reporting to the MLRO

38. In the United Kingdom, the auditor is required to report to their MLRO or, in the case of sole practitioners, to SOCA where they know or suspect, or have reasonable grounds to know or suspect, that another person is engaged in money laundering. Money Laundering reports need to be made irrespective of the quantum of the benefits derived from, or the seriousness of, the offence. There are no de minimis concessions applicable to the auditor contained in POCA, the ML Regulations or the TA 2000. There is no provision for the auditor not to make a report even where the auditor considers

that the matter has already been reported (although in such cases the 'limited intelligence value' report form may be appropriate)[20]. However, following amendments to POCA introduced by SOCPA, the auditor is no longer required to report where the auditor cannot identify the money launderer and the whereabouts of any of the laundered property, and the auditor does not believe, and it is unreasonable to expect the auditor to believe, that the information or other matter will or may assist in identifying the money launderer or the whereabouts of any of the laundered property.

39. The format of the internal report made to the MLRO is not specified by the ML Regulations. MLROs determine the form in which partners and staff in audit firms report knowledge or suspicion of, or reasonable grounds to know or suspect, money laundering offences internally to their MLRO. Reporting as soon as is practicable to the MLRO is the individual responsibility of the partner or audit staff member and although suspicions would normally be discussed within the engagement team before deciding whether or not to make an internal report to the MLRO this should not delay the report to the MLRO and, even where the rest of the engagement team disagrees, an individual should not be dissuaded from reporting to the MLRO if the individual still considers that it is necessary. Wherever possible the form of the internal report to the MLRO follows the guidance provided by SOCA in relation to standard disclosure reports and reports of limited intelligence value. In the case of a sole practitioner, who is not required to appoint an MLRO, the sole practitioner reports directly to SOCA wherever possible using the SOCA disclosure forms (http://www.soca.gov.uk/financialIntel/disclosure.html#forms). The SOCA reporting guidance permits aggregated reporting of suspicious activity that meets the SOCA criteria for "limited intelligence value" reporting. These criteria are defined in SOCA guidance notes for completing the limited intelligence value report form available on the SOCA website.

40. Guidance on the reporting of knowledge and suspicions by the MLRO to SOCA is given in section 20 of the CCAB Guidance.

41. During the course of the audit work the auditor might obtain knowledge or form a suspicion about a prohibited act that would be a criminal offence under POCA sections 327, 328 or 329 but it has yet to occur. Because attempting or conspiring to commit a money laundering offence is in itself a money laundering offence, it is possible that in some circumstances a report might need to be made.

42. When reporting to the MLRO partners and staff in audit firms follow their firm's internal reporting procedures. The timing of reporting by the MLRO to SOCA, or in the case of a sole practitioner their report to SOCA, is governed by section 331(4) of POCA which requires the disclosure to be made "as soon as is practicable" after the information or other matter comes to the attention of the MLRO.

43. Both standard and limited intelligence value reports are to be made as soon as is practicable. In practice this does not always mean "immediately" and provided that during the engagement no time sensitive information is discovered (that may, for

---

[20] SOCA is currently reviewing its system for reporting, including the use of 'standard' and 'limited intelligence value' reports.

example, allow the recovery of proceeds of crime if communicated immediately) then SOCA will accept aggregate limited intelligence value reports no later than one month following the completion of an audit. For the purposes of this Practice Note "completion of the audit" is interpreted as being no later than the date the auditor's report is signed, although if there is likely to be a significant gap between the date the audit work is completed and the date the auditor's report is signed the auditor considers submitting the limited intelligence value report earlier.

44. Partners and staff in audit firms follow their firm's internal documentation procedures when considering whether to include documentation relating to money laundering reporting in the audit working papers.

Legal privilege

45. Legal privilege can provide a defence for a professional legal adviser to a charge of failing to report knowledge or suspicion of money laundering and is generally available to the legal profession when giving legal advice to a client or acting in relation to litigation.[21] If the auditor is given access to client information over which legal professional privilege may be asserted (for example, correspondence between clients and solicitors in relation to legal advice or litigation) and that information gives grounds to suspect money laundering, the auditor considers whether the auditor is nevertheless obliged to report to the MLRO. There is some ambiguity about how the issue of legal privilege is interpreted and a prudent approach is to assume that legal privilege does not extend to the auditor and where the auditor is in possession of client information which is clearly privileged (for example, a solicitor's advice to an audit client), the auditor seeks legal advice to determine whether that privilege can be extended to the auditor. Guidance on legal privilege is given in section 12 of the CCAB Guidance.

Reporting to obtain appropriate consent

46. In addition to the auditor's duty to report knowledge or suspicion of, or reasonable grounds to know or suspect, money laundering under POCA sections 330 and 331, the auditor may need to obtain appropriate consent to perform an act which could otherwise constitute a principal money laundering offence by the auditor under POCA sections 327 to 329 (a "prohibited act"). For example, if the auditor suspected that the audit report was necessary in order for financial statements to be issued in connection

---

[21] Statutory Instrument 2006/308 "The Proceeds of Crime Act 2002 and Money Laundering Regulations 2003 (Amendment) Order 2006" extends this defence to accountants, auditors or tax advisers who satisfy certain conditions where the information on which their suspicion of money laundering is based comes to their attention in privileged circumstances (as defined in POCA section 330(10)). The Government has stated that this defence is intended to apply in the very limited circumstances of the accountants, auditors or tax advisers carrying out the same functions as lawyers in relation to legal advice. Examples may be where a client provides information in connection with the provision by the auditor of advice on legal issues such as tax or company law. The giving of such advice would not normally arise as a result of an audit engagement, but may arise where the auditor has an additional contract with the client, to provide advisory services. In such circumstances, the auditor may discuss their money laundering suspicions with the MLRO without requiring the MLRO to make a disclosure to SOCA.

with a transaction involving the proceeds of crime, or if the auditor was to sign off an auditor's report on financial statements for a company that was a front for illegal activity, the auditor might be involved in an arrangement which facilitated the acquisition, retention, use or control of criminal property under section 328 of POCA. In these circumstances, in addition to the normal procedures, the auditor would generally need to obtain appropriate consent from SOCA via the MLRO as soon as is practicable. Consent may be given expressly or may be deemed to have been given following the expiry of certain time limits specified in section 336 of POCA. Where applicable the auditor understands the applicable time limits. Further guidance on seeking appropriate consent is given in section 20 of the CCAB Guidance.

47. Appropriate consent from SOCA will protect the auditor from committing a principal money laundering offence but will not relieve the auditor from any civil liability or other professional, legal or ethical obligations. As an alternative to seeking appropriate consent, the auditor may wish to consider resignation from the audit but, in such circumstances, is still required to disclose suspicions to the MLRO and will wish to consider the possibility of 'tipping off'. Further guidance on resignation is given in paragraphs 54 to 56 below and on communication with relevant law enforcement agencies in relation to 'tipping off' is given in paragraph 52.

Reporting to regulators

48. Reporting to SOCA does not relieve the auditor from other statutory duties. Examples of statutory reporting responsibilities include:

   • *audits of entities in the financial sector*: the auditor has a statutory duty to report matters of 'material significance' to the FSA which come to the auditor's attention in the course of the audit work;

   • *audits of entities in the public sector*: auditors of some public sector entities may be required to report on the entity's compliance with requirements to ensure the regularity and propriety of financial transactions. Activity connected with money laundering may be a breach of those requirements; and

   • *audits of other types of entity*: auditors of some other entities are also required to report matters of 'material significance' to regulators (for example, charities and occupational pension schemes).

49. Knowledge or suspicion, or reasonable grounds for knowledge or suspicion, of involvement of the entity's directors in money laundering, or of a failure of a regulated business to comply with the ML Regulations would normally be regarded as being of material significance to a regulator and so give rise to a statutory duty to report to the regulator in addition to the requirement to report to SOCA. In determining whether such a duty arises, the auditor follows the requirements of auditing standards on reporting to regulators in the financial sector and considers the specific guidance dealing with each area set out in related Practice Notes, subject to compliance with legislation relating to 'tipping off'.

50. Auditing standards on law and regulations require that when the auditor becomes aware of suspected or actual non-compliance with law and regulations which gives rise to a statutory duty to report, the auditor should, subject to compliance with legislation relating to 'tipping off', make a report to the appropriate authority without undue delay. There is a potential conflict between the auditor's statutory duty to report to the regulator and the offence of 'tipping off'. Further guidance is set out in section 22 of the CCAB Guidance.

The auditor's report on financial statements

51. Where it is suspected that money laundering has occurred the auditor will need to apply the concept of materiality when considering whether the auditor's report on the financial statements needs to be qualified or modified, taking into account whether:

- the crime itself has a material effect on the financial statements;

- the consequences of the crime have a material effect on the financial statements; or

- the outcome of any subsequent investigation by the police or other investigatory body may have a material effect on the financial statements.

52. If it is known that money laundering has occurred and that directors or senior staff of the company were knowingly involved, the auditor will need to consider whether the auditor's report is likely to include a qualified opinion on the financial statements. Any disclosure in the auditor's report is subject to compliance with legislation relating to 'tipping off'. It might be necessary for the auditor through the MLRO to discuss with the relevant law enforcement agency (notified to them by SOCA) whether disclosure in the report on the financial statements, either through qualifying the opinion or referring to fundamental uncertainty, could constitute 'tipping off'. If so, the auditor through the MLRO will need to agree an acceptable form of words with the relevant law enforcement agency. Whilst an attempt may be made to seek the views of the relevant law enforcement agency it must be borne in mind that the agency may not be willing or able to agree a form of words to use in communicating with the client. In such circumstances, the auditor is advised to consider whether it would be appropriate to seek legal advice. Although appropriate consent cannot be given to 'tipping off', it is unlikely that the auditor who uses a form of words agreed with the relevant law enforcement agency will commit a 'tipping off' offence provided that the auditor does not know or suspect that the disclosure will prejudice an investigation. Such knowledge or suspicion is an essential element of the 'tipping off' offences under POCA sections 333 and 342.

53. Timing may be the crucial factor. Any delay in issuing the audit report pending the outcome of an investigation is likely to be impracticable and could in itself lead to issues of 'tipping off'. The auditor also considers the potential dangers of 'tipping off' by not issuing a qualified auditor's report in situations where management and/or the directors might expect the auditor to qualify the report. The auditor seeks advice from the MLRO who acts as the main source of guidance and if necessary is the liaison point for communication with lawyers, SOCA and the relevant law enforcement

agency. If an audit report has to be issued, and agreement with the relevant law enforcement agency cannot be reached, firms may need to seek legal advice before issuing a qualified audit report. As a last resort it may be necessary to make an application to the court in respect of the content of the qualified audit report. See section 22 of CCAB Guidance for guidance on the interaction of different reporting duties.

Resignation and communication with successor auditors

54. The auditor may wish to resign from the position as auditor if the auditor believes that the client or an employee is engaged in money laundering or any other illegal act, particularly where a normal relationship of trust can no longer be maintained. Where the auditor intends to cease to hold office there may be a conflict between the requirements under section 394 of the Companies Act 1985 for the auditor to deposit a statement at a company's registered office of any circumstances that the auditor believes need to be brought to the attention of members or creditors and the risk of 'tipping off'. This may arise if the circumstances connected with the resignation of the auditor include knowledge or suspicion of money laundering. See section 24 of CCAB Guidance for guidance on cessation of work and resignation.

55. Where such disclosure of circumstances may amount to 'tipping off', the auditor seeks to agree the wording of the section 394 disclosure with the relevant law enforcement agency and, failing that, seeks legal advice. The auditor also considers the potential dangers of 'tipping off' by not making a disclosure of circumstances connected with money laundering in situations where management and/or the directors might expect the section 394 disclosures to refer to the facts and circumstances that give rise to the auditor's suspicions of money laundering. The auditor seeks advice from the MLRO who acts as the main source of guidance and if necessary is the liaison point for communication with lawyers, SOCA and the relevant law enforcement agency. The auditor may as a last resort need to apply to the court for direction as to what is included in the section 394 statement.

56. The offence of 'tipping off' may also cause a conflict with the need to communicate with the prospective successor auditor in accordance with ethical requirements relating to changes in professional appointment. Whilst the existing auditor might feel obliged to mention any knowledge or suspicion regarding suspected money laundering, to do so may run the risk of 'tipping off'. Expressing such concerns orally rather than in writing does not alleviate the issue. CCAB ethical guidance[22] suggests that any money laundering disclosures that have been made would not be made known to the successor auditor. However, (subject to 'tipping off' considerations), it may be necessary to communicate the underlying circumstances which gave rise to the disclosure. The approach adopted when an auditor is contacted by a successor auditor follows that described in paragraphs 54 and 55 in relation to the section 394 statement.

---

[22] For example, section 210, paragraph 12 of the ICAEW Code of Ethics, states 'Disclosure of money laundering or terrorist suspicion reporting by the existing accountant to the potential successor should be avoided because this information may be discussed with the client or former client.'

Appendix 1

Examples of situations that may give rise to money laundering offences that auditors may encounter during the course of the audit

These are examples of some of the situations that auditors may encounter during the course of the audit and some of the factors that auditors may wish to bear in mind when considering reporting suspicions of money laundering. They are intended to demonstrate the breadth of the money laundering legislation. This is not an exhaustive list of offences, nor a guide as to how such offences must be dealt with. The best way to deal with suspected money laundering will vary according to the particular facts of each case and should be dealt with in accordance with the firm's procedures.

The examples are based on the legislation and SOCA guidance current at the time the Practice Note was finalised. Auditors will wish to consider whether SOCA guidance has been updated as well as the extent to which they are prepared to follow any SOCA guidance, particularly if SOCA states in its guidance that in a particular type of case no report at all is required.

1. Offences where the client is the victim (for example, shoplifting)

The auditor acts for a large retail client. The auditor discovers there has been significant stock shrinkage in a number of stores. The client attributes at least some of this to shoplifting. In addition, the auditor is aware that some of the stores hold files detailing instances when the police have been called to deal with shoplifters caught by the security guards.

POCA does not require the auditor to undertake further enquiry outside the auditor's normal audit work to determine whether an offence has occurred or to find out further details of the offence. Accordingly, the auditor does not need to review the files containing the details of the police being called, unless the auditor would otherwise have done so for the purposes of the audit.

Where the auditor does not believe that the information will or may assist in identifying the shoplifter or the whereabouts of any of the goods stolen by the shoplifter, for example where the identity of the shoplifters cannot be deduced from the information in the auditor's possession (as opposed to information that the client may have) and the proceeds have disappeared without trace, the auditor decides not to make a report to the MLRO.

In the less likely circumstances that the auditor believes that the information possessed will or may assist in identifying the shoplifter or the whereabouts of any of the goods stolen by the shoplifter, the auditor will make a report to the MLRO briefly describing the situation.

2. Offences that indicate dishonest behaviour (for example, overpayments not returned)

Some customers of the audit client have overpaid their invoices and some have paid twice. The auditor discovers that the audit client has a policy of retaining all overpayments by customers and crediting them to the profit and loss account if they are not claimed within a year.

The auditor considers whether the retention of the overpayments might amount to theft by the audit client from its customer. If so, the client will be in possession of the proceeds of its crime, a money laundering offence.

SOCA guidance states that in the case of minor irregularities where there is nothing to suggest dishonest behaviour, the person making the report may be satisfied that no criminal property is involved and therefore a report is not required. Otherwise, where dishonest behaviour is suspected and a report is necessary, a limited intelligence value report may be appropriate.

The auditor considers whether there are any indications that the company has acted honestly, for example whether the client attempted to return the overpayments to its customers, or that the overpayments were mistakenly overlooked. If there are no such indications, the auditor concludes that the client may have acted dishonestly. Following the firm's procedures, which take into account the SOCA guidance about minor irregularities where dishonest behaviour is suspected, and about multiple suspicions of limited intelligence value which arise during the course of one audit, the auditor decides to make a report to the MLRO at the end of the audit, briefly describing the situation and any other matters of limited intelligence value.

3. Companies Act offences that are criminal offences (for example, loans to Directors)

The audit client is a public company with a number of subsidiaries. On one of the subsidiary audits, the auditor discovers that the subsidiary has guaranteed a £20,000 loan made by a bank to one of its directors.

The auditor knows that loans to directors and persons connected to them, and the giving of guarantees or security for loans to directors, are prohibited by section 330 of the Companies Act 1985. The auditor also knows that in the case of relevant companies only (which include public companies and subsidiaries of public companies), such loans can give rise to criminal offences under section 342(2) of the Companies Act 1985, and the director may also commit an offence. The auditor considers whether any of the exemptions apply (e.g. short-term loans up to a certain value, certain inter-company loans, certain small loans, loans approved at general meetings to enable a director to perform the director's duties), and whether the company could claim that it did not know the relevant circumstances at the time of the loan.

The auditor concludes that there are reasonable grounds to suspect that an offence has been committed and that the director is in possession of the proceeds of the company's crime. The auditor decides to make a full report to his MLRO without waiting until the end of the audit.

THE AUDITING PRACTICES BOARD

4. Companies Act offences that are civil offences (for example, **illegal dividend payments**)

During the course of the audit, the auditor discovers that the audit client has paid a dividend based on draft accounts. Audit adjustments subsequently reduce distributable reserves to the extent that the dividend is now illegal under the Companies Act 1985.

The auditor recognises that the payment of an illegal dividend is not per se a criminal offence because the Companies Act 1985 imposes only civil sanctions on companies making illegal distributions and decides not to report the matter to the MLRO.

5. Offences that involve saved costs (for example, **environmental offences**)

The client has a factory which manufactures some of the goods sold in its retail business. In the course of reviewing board minutes, the auditor discovers that the client has been disposing of waste from the factory without a proper licence. There are concerns that pollutants from the waste have been leaking into a nearby river. The client is currently in discussion with the relevant licensing authorities to try to get proper authorisation.

The auditor has reasonable grounds to suspect that the client may have committed offences of disposing of waste without the relevant licence and of polluting the nearby river. The client has saved the costs of applying for a licence. It is also apparent that its methods of disposing of the waste are cheaper than processing it properly. These saved costs represent the benefit of the client's crime. The client is in possession of the benefit of a crime and the auditor therefore suspects that it has committed a money laundering offence.

The firm's procedures follow SOCA guidance in stating that in the case of regulatory matters, where the relevant government agency is already aware of an offence which also happens to be an instance of suspected money laundering, a limited intelligence value report can be made. A limited intelligence value report can also be made where the only benefit from criminal conduct is in the form of cost savings.

The authorities are aware of the licensing issue and the pollution of the nearby river. As the only benefit to the company is in the form of cost savings, the auditor decides to include this matter in the limited intelligence value report to the MLRO at the end of the audit.

6. Offences committed overseas that are criminal offences under UK law (for example, **bribery**)

The client plans to expand its retail operations into a country where it has not operated before. Construction of its first outlets is underway and it is in consultation with the overseas Government about obtaining the necessary permits to sell its goods (although these negotiations are proving difficult). The client has engaged a consultancy firm to oversee the implementation of its plans and liaise 'on the ground', although it is not clear to the auditor exactly what the firm's role is. The auditor notices that the payments made to the firm are very large, particularly in comparison to the services provided. The auditor reviews the expenses claimed by the consultant and notes that some of these are for significant sums to meet government officials' expenses.

The auditor considers whether the payments may be for the consultant to use in paying bribes, for example to obtain the necessary permits. The country is one where corruption and facilitation payments are known to be widespread. The auditor makes some enquiries about the consultancy firm but cannot establish that it is a reputable business.

Taking into account compliance with legislation relating to 'tipping off' the auditor questions the client's Finance Director about the matter and the FD admits that the consultant has told him that some 'facilitation payments' will be necessary to move the project along and the FD agreed that some payments should be made to get the local officials to do the jobs that they should be doing anyway; for example, to get the traffic police to let the construction vehicles through nearby road blocks. The FD thought that such payments were acceptable in the country in question.

The auditor suspects that bribes have been paid and the auditor is aware that bribery, including the bribery of government officials, is a criminal offence under UK law. Accordingly, the auditor decides to make a full report to the MLRO. Even after SOCPA Section 102 comes into force this disclosure is still likely to be required. Bribery of foreign public officials, by UK nationals and corporations, is a criminal offence even where it occurs wholly outside the UK, under Part 12 of the Anti-terrorism Crime and Security Act 2001. An exemption from making a money laundering disclosure is unlikely, where the overseas bribery has been undertaken by a third party on behalf of a UK national or corporation.

7. Offences committed overseas that are not criminal offences under UK law (for example, breach of exchange controls and importing religious material)

During the course of the audit, the auditor forms a suspicion that one of the overseas subsidiaries has been in breach of a number of local laws. In particular:

- Dividends have been paid to the parent company in breach of local exchange control requirements.

- The subsidiary has imported religious materials intended for the preaching of a particular faith, which is contrary to the laws of that jurisdiction.

Money laundering offences include conduct occurring overseas which would constitute an offence if it had occurred in the UK. Because the UK has no exchange control legislation and the preaching of any faith is allowed it is possible that neither of the offences committed by the overseas subsidiary constitute offences under UK law. The auditor considers whether any other offence might have been committed if this conduct took place in the UK, but the auditor decides not to make a report to the MLRO in these circumstances.

Appendix 2

Guidance as to whom the anti-money laundering legislation applies

To whom does the reporting requirement apply?

The requirement to make a report under section 330 and 331 of POCA applies to information which comes to a person in the course of a business, or an MLRO, in the regulated sector. That information may relate to money laundering by persons or businesses inside or outside the regulated sector.

The offence of failing to report that another person is engaged in money laundering applies to all money laundering, including conduct taking place overseas that would be an offence if it took place in the United Kingdom. For that reason there may be an obligation to report information arising from the audit of non-UK companies or their subsidiaries.

When is an auditor in the UK regulated sector?

The regulated sector includes the provision, in the UK, by way of business, of audit services by a person who is eligible for appointment as a company auditor under s.25 of the Companies Act 1989 or Article 28 of the Companies (Northern Ireland) Order 1990.[23]

A person is eligible for appointment as a company auditor if the person is a member of a recognised supervisory body, (which is a body established in the UK which maintains and enforces rules as to the eligibility of persons to seek appointment as a company auditor and the conduct of company audit work, and which is recognised by the Secretary of State by Order) and is eligible for appointment under the rules of that body.

For the purposes of this Practice Note "person" is interpreted as referring to a UK audit firm that is designated as a "Registered Auditor" and the ML Regulations apply to all partners and staff within that UK audit firm who are involved in providing audit services in the UK.

Where they become involved in the provision of audit services in the UK by a UK audit firm which is subject to POCA and the ML Regulations, such persons may also include:

- Experts from other disciplines within the UK audit firm.

- Experts from outside the UK audit firm.

- Employees of non-UK audit firms for example, an auditor from an overseas office of an international firm.

Where they are not involved in the provision of audit services in the UK by a UK audit firm such persons may fall within other parts of the regulated sector, for example the provision of accountancy services by way of business is within the regulated sector regardless of

---

[23] POCA Schedule 9, Part 1, paragraph 1(1)(k).

whether the person providing the services is or is not a member of a UK professional auditing/accountancy body.

It is unlikely that it will be practicable or desirable for a UK audit firm which is within the regulated sector to distinguish for reporting purposes between partners and staff who are providing services in the regulated sector and those who are not. Accordingly, UK audit firms may choose to impose procedures across the firm requiring all partners and staff to report to the firm's MLRO (see section 13 of the CCAB Guidance)[24].

The following table illustrates how the reporting requirements might apply to a number of different audit/client scenarios.[25] This table is intended as a guide and it is recognised that there may be factual scenarios which do not fall within the categories above. In case of any doubt, auditors should refer to the provisions of POCA and the ML Regulations, which take precedence over any guidance in this Appendix.

---

[24] Persons outside the regulated sector are not obliged to report to their MLRO under POCA section 330 and section 331 (the 'failure to report' offence), but can make voluntary reports under POCA section 337 of information they obtain in the course of their trade, profession, business or employment which causes them to know or suspect, or gives reasonable grounds for knowing or suspecting, that another person is engaged in money laundering. Such reports are protected from breach of client confidentiality in the same way as reports made under POCA section 330 and section 331.

[25] The audit/client reporting scenarios do not take into account section 102 of SOCPA (see footnote 8).

	Offence discovered as part of audit of:	
Persons	**UK companies (including UK subsidiaries of UK or non-UK companies)**	**Non-UK companies (including non-UK subsidiaries of UK or non-UK companies)**
• working in UK for UK audit firm	Yes	Yes
• working in UK for non-UK audit firm[26]	Possibly. Where the auditor or audit firm is not eligible for appointment as a UK company auditor, in practice, it is likely that the auditor or firm would be providing accountancy services and therefore fall within the UK regulated sector.	
• seconded to UK audit firm	Yes	Yes
• working temporarily outside UK or on foreign secondments, or working permanently outside UK but employed by a UK audit firm	The position of an auditor working temporarily outside the UK or on foreign secondments, or working permanently outside the UK but employed by a UK audit firm, is more difficult. For example the duty to report may be influenced by the terms of the secondment. The following is a non-exhaustive list of issues to consider and firms may wish to take legal advice in relation to the need for their employees to comply with the UK's money laundering reporting regime as well as any local legal requirements. Issues to consider include: • If the auditor's work outside the UK is part of a UK audit then in some circumstances that information may have come to the auditor's attention in the course of engaging in regulated activities in the UK and therefore be reportable. • In the case of an auditor working permanently outside the UK for a UK firm, it may be appropriate to consider whether the auditor is working at a separate firm or at a branch office of a UK firm. • An auditor should be particularly cautious about any decision not to make a report on their return to the UK if the information relates to work that the auditor is undertaking in the UK. • Regardless of the strict legal position, firms may wish to consider putting in place a business-wide anti-money laundering strategy to protect their global reputation and UK regulated business (see Section 13 of the CCAB Guidance). • An auditor working permanently or temporarily outside the UK considers the anti-money laundering legislation in their host country.	
• working permanently outside UK for non-UK audit firm	No	No

---

[26] It is recognised that it would not be possible for a non-UK audit firm or auditor to be appointed as the auditor of a UK company. However, these categories have been included for completeness.

PRACTICE NOTE 16

BANK REPORTS FOR AUDIT PURPOSES (REVISED) – INTERIM GUIDANCE

CONTENTS

Preface

Practice Note (PN)16 – Bank Reports for Audit Purposes, was originally issued in 1998.

In October 2005 the APB issued as a consultation draft a proposed revision of PN 16 which reflected discussions between the audit profession and the British Bankers' Association (BBA). The relatively minor changes to the original Practice Note were to:

- encourage auditors to submit requests for information earlier;

- incorporate supplementary material from the ICAEW publication Audit 3/02 issued in September 2002;

- recommend the provision of a main account name and number by the auditor, to facilitate banks in identifying the appropriate customer more readily; and

- clarify that auditors do not need a new authority to disclose information every time that they ask for confirmation of bank details.

No changes were made to the detailed information set out in the requests for standard and supplementary information (Appendices 1 and 2).

A number of respondents to the October 2005 consultation draft recommended more extensive changes to the process by which auditors request bank confirmations and banks respond. Further discussions are taking place between the audit profession and the BBA in this regard but further changes to PN 16 are not expected for a number of months. In the circumstances the APB believes that it would be helpful to clarify the status of PN 16 and to issue the October 2005 consultation draft as interim guidance.

Introduction

1. ISA (UK and Ireland) 500 'Audit evidence' requires the auditor to obtain sufficient appropriate audit evidence to be able to draw reasonable conclusions on which to base the audit opinion. In addition, paragraph 5 of ISA (UK and Ireland) 505 refers explicitly to confirmations of bank balances and other information obtained from bankers. This Practice Note provides guidance to auditors seeking evidence from an entity's bankers about balances, transactions or arrangements.

2. A commonly adopted procedure in the audit of an entity's financial statements is for the auditor to obtain direct confirmation from the entity's banker(s) of balances and other amounts which appear in the balance sheet and other information which may be disclosed in the notes to the financial statements, for example information on guarantees and foreign exchange transactions. Bank confirmations are a valuable source of audit evidence because they provide independent evidence regarding the reliability of an entity's records

3. The auditor considers the risks in relation to relevant financial statement assertions when deciding whether to obtain a bank confirmation. Ordinarily auditors will wish to obtain confirmation of balances, facilities and security arrangements.

4. When an entity has a complex relationship with its bank, including using the bank as a custodian of its assets, providing trade finance or undertaking derivative or commodity transactions, the auditor will often decide to obtain supplementary information. Auditors will base their decision on their knowledge of the entity's business and on discussions with directors and management and will request information when they know, or suspect, that there are banking relationships relevant to the audit.

5. Banks are aware of the information required from requests for standard and supplementary information. The requirements are published in appendices 1 and 2 of this Practice Note (and additionally can be found at the British Bankers' Association (BBA) website). The purpose of providing two types of request form is to help auditors obtain comprehensive information when their clients have complex business operations with banks while minimising the banks' costs in relation to responding to auditors' requests regarding clients that have less complex relationships. The arrangements are also designed to facilitate timely and accurate responses by banks.

6. As indicated in appendices 1 and 2, the auditor's request will specify whether the auditor is requesting the 'standard information' (for clients with simple banking relationships) or the nature of the supplementary information required (for clients with more complex banking relationships). If the auditor requires information additional to that which has been predefined as 'standard' or 'supplementary' this needs to be clearly specified in an attachment to the bank confirmation request letter under the heading 'additional information'.

7. Auditors need to be aware that, where supplementary and/or additional information is requested, banks may charge their customers an additional fee for providing the information and responses to auditors are likely to take longer to process.

Authority to disclose

8. Banks require the explicit written authority of their customers to disclose the information requested. The BBA has requested that, where possible, this takes the form of an ongoing standing authority rather than as a separate authority each time information is requested. Auditors need to satisfy themselves that an authority is in place and up to date. A new authority will be needed in the case of a new audit client: other circumstances where banks may need an updated authority include client changes such as new group entities or auditor changes such as re-organisation as a limited liability partnership (LLP) or merger with another practice. An illustrative letter providing authority to a bank to disclose information to the entity's auditor is included as Appendix 3.

Disclaimers

9. The bank confirmation request letter indicates that neither the request from the auditor, nor the bank's response, will create any contractual or other duty between the bank and the auditor. In addition, the banks may add a disclaimer at the end of their reply to the effect that their response is given solely for the purposes of the audit without creating any responsibility to the auditor on the part of the bank, its employees or agents and that it does not relieve the auditor from other enquiries or from performance of any other duty.

10. The APB is of the view that the inclusion of the introductory statement and of a disclaimer of the nature described above does not significantly impair the value of the information given as audit evidence. The information given by a bank ought not to be regarded as inaccurate or likely to be inaccurate simply because the giving of it is not actionable. Accordingly, the auditor can reasonably rely upon information given by a banker, provided it is not clearly wrong, suspicious or inconsistent in itself, ambiguous or in conflict with other evidence gathered in the course of the audit.

Bank confirmation process

11. The key steps to be taken by the auditor in initiating the process agreed with the BBA are as follows:

(a) A request for a bank confirmation is to be issued on the auditor's own note paper and sent to the bank branch with which the client has the prime business arrangement. The branch will either respond on behalf of the bank or forward the request to a specialist department.

(b) The bank confirmation request is to specify:

(i) The names of all entities covered by the request, together with the main account number and sort code of the principal entity or the holding company. Entity names are often similar in nature and the identification of the relevant client is not always straightforward. The provision of the principal entity or holding company account number and sort code will assist in the identification of the customer. Banks still have a responsibility to identify all relevant accounts using the main account details, rather than rely solely on the information in the request;

(ii) whether the auditor is requesting 'standard information' and, where appropriate, the nature of supplementary information required;

(iii) details of 'additional information' if so required;

(iv) the date for which the auditor is requesting confirmation (the audit confirmation date);

(v) a statement that the bank's response will not create a contractual relationship between the bank and the auditor;

(vi) a statement requesting the bank to advise the auditor if the authority is insufficient to allow the bank to provide full disclosure of the information requested; and

(vii) a contact name and telephone number.

(c) The bank confirmation request should reach the branch at least one month in advance of the audit confirmation date. Where such notice cannot be provided, special arrangements may need to be made with the bank. It is advisable to allow more time at busy periods such as those covering December and March year ends. In straightforward circumstances the banks will endeavour to provide the information within one month from the confirmation date but where it is necessary for them to obtain information from different branches or where there is a request for non-standard information, a response may take up to two months. For example, in responding to requests for bank reports, banks may need to consult a number of business divisions internally, including those responsible for:

- account balances, including loans, whether in sterling or a foreign currency;

- money market deposits;

- securities;

- contingent liabilities (including acceptances, endorsements, guarantees, irrevocable letters of credit and assets pledged as collateral security);

- commitments (including documentary credits and short-term trade related facilities, forward asset purchases and forward deposits placed, undrawn note issuance and revolving underwriting facilities and undrawn formal standby facilities, credit lines and other commitments to lend);

- derivatives (including futures and forwards, forward rate agreements, swaps, options, caps, collars and floors);

- leasing;

- factoring and invoice discounting.

12. In order to expedite the provision of responses to requests for bank reports, auditors and banks may find it helpful to use the pro forma acknowledgement provided at Appendix 5. The purpose of the acknowledgement is to provide auditors with assurance that the request for the bank report has been received, and with a point of contact within the bank to whom enquiries can be addressed. The named contact may be an account relationship manager, an assistant to the account relationship manager or a contact within a national or regional service centre, depending on the bank's internal arrangements.

13. It is also helpful if envelopes are headed 'Bank report for audit purposes' and are addressed to the account relationship manager at the branch maintaining the main banking relationship with the customer. Heading the envelope in this way will ensure that processing starts without delay in the event that the relationship manager is away from the office.

Bank acknowledgements

14. Where auditors include the acknowledgement with a request for a bank report, banks return the acknowledgement to the auditor as soon as possible.

Responses to requests

15. The bank report is an essential element of the audit process for many entities and the information it contains is required on a timely basis. For listed companies and other entities subject to tight reporting deadlines the information may be needed sooner than the periods described in 11 (c) above and auditors may wish to discuss with listed clients' bankers the possibility of accelerating responses to such confirmation requests. Failure to respond to bank confirmations within a reasonable time can have a significant effect on customers and may result in a qualified audit report. It also means that the bank has not provided the customer with a service integral to the lending relationship and may create difficulties for the bank when it comes to reviewing facilities provided.

Minor omissions or discrepancies

16. Minor omissions or discrepancies in the information provided by the bank may be dealt with informally by telephone or e-mail, although auditors may request written confirmation of changes to the information provided.

Debit and credit balances

17. A customer may maintain several accounts with a bank, some in debit and others in credit, perhaps at different branches of the bank. The standard and supplementary requests for information request details of all bank accounts.

Guarantees and other third party securities

18. The provision of information about guarantees and other third party securities has, on occasion, resulted in significant delays in the completion of bank reports because banks have been unable to release the information sought without specific customer consent. When banks do not have sufficient authority to provide full disclosure of the information requested, they advise the auditor of that fact and indicate, where that is the case, that such guarantees or third party securities exist. The auditor can then obtain details of the arrangement from the entity, for example by asking to see the relevant facility letter or loan agreement. In some cases, these procedures will suffice. In other cases, auditors will require further independent evidence, and in such cases they can ask banks for the specific information to be provided once consent from the guarantor or third party has been received.

Accrued interest and charges

19. Banks frequently receive requests for information about accrued interest and charges on a daily basis. The provision of this information falls outside this Practice Note and the request may be declined if the bank cannot generate the data from its computerised records or if the audit confirmation date has passed.

Appendix 1

Standard request for information

The following is an extract from the BBA advice to banks regarding receipt of a standard request for information for audit purposes.

The following information must always be disclosed upon receipt of a request for information for audit purposes. Responses must be given in the order as below and if no information is available then this must be stated as 'None' in the response.

1   **Account and Balance Details**

-    Give full titles of all Bank accounts including loans, (whether in sterling or another currency) together with their account numbers and balances. For accounts closed during the 12 months up to the audit confirmation date give the account details and date of closure.

Note. Also give details where your Customer's name is joined with that of other parties and where the account is in a trade name.

-    State if any account or balances are subject to any restriction(s) whatsoever. Indicate the nature and extent of the restriction e.g. garnishee order.

2   **Facilities**

Give the following details of all loans, overdrafts, and associated guarantees and indemnities:

-    term

-    repayment frequency and/or review date

-    details of period of availability of agreed finance i.e. finance remaining undrawn

-    detail the facility limit.

3   **Securities**

With reference to the facilities detailed in (2) above give the following details:

-    Any security formally charged (date, ownership and type of charge). State whether the security supports facilities granted by the Bank to the customer or to another party.

Note. Give details if a security is limited in amount or to a specific borrowing or if to your knowledge there is a prior, equal or subordinate charge.

-    Where there are any arrangements for set-off of balances or compensating balances e.g. back to back loans, give particulars (i.e. date, type of document and accounts covered) of any acknowledgement of set-off, whether given by specific letter of set-off or incorporated in some other document.

4   **Additional Banking Relationships**

State if you are aware of the customer(s) having any additional relationships with branches or subsidiaries of the Bank not covered by the response. Supply a list of branches etc.

Appendix 2

Request for supplementary information

The following is an extract from the BBA advice to banks regarding receipt of a supplementary request for information for audit purposes.

Request for Trade Finance information

On occasion Auditors may request Trade Finance information. Responses must be given in the order as below and if no information is available then this must be stated as 'None' in the response.

1	**Trade Finance** Give the currencies and amounts of the following:
	(a) Letters of Credit
	(b) Acceptances
	(c) Bills discounted with recourse to the customer or any subsidiary or related party of the customer.
	(d) Bonds, Guarantees, Indemnities or other undertakings given to the Bank by the customer in favour of third parties (including separately any such items in favour of any subsidiary or related party of the customer). Give details of the parties in favour of whom guarantees or undertakings have been given, whether such guarantees or undertakings are written or oral and their nature.
	(e) Bonds, Guarantees, Indemnities or other undertakings given by you, on your customer's behalf, stating whether there is recourse to your customer and/or to its parent or any other company within the group.
	(f) Other contingent liabilities not already detailed.
	Note. For each item state the nature and extent of any facility limits and details of period of availability of agreed facility.
2	**Securities**
	With reference to the facilities detailed in the above section give the following:
	• Details of any security formally charged (date, ownership and type of charge). State whether the security supports facilities granted by the Bank to the customer or to another party.
	Note. Give details if a security is limited in amount or to a specific borrowing or if to your knowledge there is prior, equal or subordinate charge.
	• Where there are any arrangements for set-off of balances or compensating balances e.g. back to back loans, give particulars (i.e. date, type of document and accounts covered) of any acknowledgement of set-off, whether given by specific letter of set-off or incorporated in some other document.

Request for Derivatives and Commodity Trading information

On occasion Auditors may request Derivatives and Commodity Trading information. Responses must be given in the order as below and if no information is available then this must be stated as 'None' in the response:

1	**Derivatives and Commodity Trading** Give the currencies, amounts and maturity dates on a contract by contract basis of all outstanding derivative contracts including the following: (a) foreign exchange contracts (b) forward rate agreements (c) financial futures (d) interest rate swaps (e) option contracts (f) bullion contracts (g) commodity contracts (h) swap arrangements (near and far dates) (i) others (indicate their nature). *Note. Indicate the nature and extent of any facility limits, detail period of availability of agreed facilities.*
2	**Securities** With reference to facilities detailed in the above section give the following: • Details of any security formally charged (date, ownership and type of charge). State whether the security supports facilities granted by the Bank to the customer or to another party. Note. Give details if a security is limited in amount or to a specific borrowing or if to your knowledge there is prior, equal or subordinate charge. • Where there are any arrangements for set-off balances of compensating balances e.g. back to back loans, give particulars (i.e. date, type of document and accounts covered) of any acknowledgement of set-off, whether given by specific letter of set-off or incorporated in some other document.

Request for Custodian Arrangements information

On occasion Auditors may request Custodian Arrangements information. Responses must be given in the order as below and if no information is available then this must be stated as 'None' in the response:

1	**Custodian Arrangements** Give details of the nature and quantity of any assets held but not charged.

Appendix 3

Bank confirmation request letter – Illustration

[xxxx Bank PLC
25 xxx Street
Warrington
Cheshire WA1 1XQ]

Dear Sirs

In accordance with the agreed practice for provision of information to auditors, please forward information on our mutual client(s) as detailed below on behalf of the bank, its branches and subsidiaries. This request and your response will not create any contractual or other duty with us.

Companies or other business entities (attach a separate listing if necessary)

[Parent Company Ltd
Subsidiary 1 Ltd
Subsidiary 2 Ltd]

Main account number

Sort code

Audit confirmation date *[e.g. 31 March 2006]*

Information Required	*Tick*
Standard	
Trade finance	
Derivative and commodity trading	
Custodian arrangements	
Other information (see attached)	

The Authority to Disclose Information signed by your customer is attached / already held by you (delete as appropriate). Please advise us if this Authority is insufficient for you to provide full disclosure of the information requested.

The contact name is *[John Caller]*
Telephone *[01 234 5678]*

Yours faithfully

[XXX Accountants]

Appendix 4

Authority to disclose information – Illustration

xxxxx Bank PLC
25 xxx Street
Warrington
Cheshire WA1 1XQ]

[Parent Company Ltd,
Subsidiary 1 Ltd,
Subsidiary 2 Ltd]

I/ We authorise [xxxx Bank PLC] including all branches and subsidiaries to provide to our auditor [*XXX Accountants*] any information that they may request from you regarding all and any of our accounts and dealings with you.

_____

signature(s)

Appendix 5

Bank acknowledgement of auditor request

PART A – This Part To Be Completed By The Auditor

This acknowledgement should be returned to:

[Name and address of auditor][1]

Please contact [name] if you have any queries on this letter:

Tel. No. ....

E-mail* ....   * If available.

PART B – This Part To Be Completed By The Bank

Thank you for your request for a bank report for audit purposes in respect of

....

(customer's name, main account number and sort code)

The request was received on:

.... (day/month/year)

Your request is being processed and the letter will be completed once we have gathered the information sought. In the event of your needing to contact us, please address any enquiries to:

Name of individual or section responsible ....

Bank   ....

Address   ....

            ....

            ....

Tel. No.   ....

E-mail*   ....   * If available.

---

[1]   The name and address should be positioned so as to fit the window in a standard envelope

Section 7: GLOSSARY OF TERMS[1]

Access controls—Procedures designed to restrict access to on-line terminal devices, programs and data. Access controls consist of "user authentication" and "user authorization." "User authentication" typically attempts to identify a user through unique logon identifications, passwords, access cards or biometric data. "User authorization" consists of access rules to determine the computer resources each user may access. Specifically, such procedures are designed to prevent or detect:

(a) Unauthorized access to on-line terminal devices, programs and data;

(b) Entry of unauthorized transactions;

(c) Unauthorized changes to data files;

(d) The use of computer programs by unauthorized personnel; and

(e) The use of computer programs that have not been authorized.

Accounting estimate—An approximation of the amount of an item in the absence of a precise means of measurement.

Accounting records—Generally include the records of initial entries and supporting records, such as checks and records of electronic fund transfers; invoices; contracts; the general and subsidiary ledgers; journal entries and other adjustments to the financial statements that are not reflected in formal journal entries; and records such as work sheets and spreadsheets supporting cost allocations, computations, reconciliations and disclosures.

Accounting services—The provision of services that involve the maintenance of accounting records or the preparation of financial statements that are then subject to audit.

Adverse opinion—(see Modified auditor's report)

---

[1] Where accounting terms have not been defined in the IAASB pronouncements, reference should be made to the Glossary of Terms published by the International Accounting Standards Board.

Affiliate—Any undertaking which is connected to another by means of common ownership, control or management.

Agreed-upon procedures engagement—An engagement in which an auditor is engaged to carry out those procedures of an audit nature to which the auditor and the entity and any appropriate third parties have agreed and to report on factual findings. The recipients of the report form their own conclusions from the report by the auditor. The report is restricted to those parties that have agreed to the procedures to be performed since others, unaware of the reasons for the procedures may misinterpret the results.

Analytical procedures—Evaluations of financial information made by a study of plausible relationships among both financial and non-financial data. Analytical procedures also encompass the investigation of identified fluctuations and relationships that are inconsistent with other relevant information or deviate significantly from predicted amounts.

Annual report—A document issued by an entity, ordinarily on an annual basis, which includes its financial statements together with the auditor's report thereon.

Anomalous error—(see Audit sampling)

Application controls in information technology— Manual or automated procedures that typically operate at a business process level. Application controls can be preventative or detective in nature and are designed to ensure the integrity of the accounting records. Accordingly, application controls relate to procedures used to initiate, record, process and report transactions or other financial data.

Appropriateness—The measure of the quality of evidence, that is, its relevance and reliability in providing support for, or detecting misstatements in, the classes of transactions, account balances, and disclosures and related assertions.

Assertions—Representations by management, explicit or otherwise, that are embodied in the financial statements.

Assess—Analyze identified risks to conclude on their significance. "Assess," by convention, is used only in relation to risk. (also see Evaluate)

Assistants—Personnel involved in an individual audit other than the auditor.

Association—(see Auditor association with financial information)

Assurance—(see Reasonable assurance)

Assurance engagement—An engagement in which a practitioner expresses a conclusion designed to enhance the degree of confidence of the intended users other than the responsible party about the outcome of the evaluation or measurement of a subject matter against criteria. The outcome of the evaluation or measurement of a subject matter is the information that results from applying the criteria (also see Subject matter information). Under the "International Framework for Assurance Engagements" there are two types of

see DOI/08/03

assurance engagement a practitioner is permitted to perform: a reasonable assurance engagement and a limited assurance engagement.

Limited assurance engagement—The objective of a limited assurance engagement is a reduction in assurance engagement risk to a level that is acceptable in the circumstances of the engagement, but where that risk is greater than for a reasonable assurance engagement, as the basis for a negative form of expression of the practitioner's conclusion.

Reasonable assurance engagement—The objective of a reasonable assurance engagement is a reduction in assurance engagement risk to an acceptably low level in the circumstances of the engagement as the basis for a positive form of expression of the practitioner's conclusion.

Assurance engagement risk—The risk that the practitioner expresses an inappropriate conclusion when the subject matter information is materially misstated.

Attendance—Being present during all or part of a process being performed by others; for example, attending physical inventory taking will enable the auditor to inspect inventory, to observe compliance of management's procedures to count quantities and record such counts and to test-count quantities.

Audit documentation—The record of audit procedures performed, relevant audit evidence obtained, and conclusions the auditor reached (terms such as "working papers" or "workpapers" are also sometimes used).

Audit evidence—All of the information used by the auditor in arriving at the conclusions on which the audit opinion is based. Audit evidence includes the information contained in the accounting records underlying the financial statements and other information.

Audit firm—(see Firm)

Audit matters of governance interest—Those matters that arise from the audit of financial statements and, in the opinion of the auditor, are both important and relevant to those charged with governance in overseeing the financial reporting and disclosure process. Audit matters of governance interest include only those matters that have come to the attention of the auditor as a result of the performance of the audit.

Audit of financial statements—The objective of an audit of financial statements is to enable the auditor to express an opinion whether the financial statements are prepared, in all material respects, in accordance with an applicable financial reporting framework. An audit of financial statements is an assurance engagement (see Assurance engagement).

Audit opinion—(see Opinion)

Audit plan—Converts the audit strategy into a more detailed plan and includes the nature, timing and extent of audit procedures to be performed by engagement team members in order to obtain sufficient appropriate audit evidence to reduce audit risk to an acceptably low level.

Audit program—(see Audit plan)

Audit risk—Audit risk is the risk that the auditor expresses an inappropriate audit opinion when the financial statements are materially misstated. Audit risk is a function of the risk of material misstatement (or simply, the "risk of material misstatement") (i.e., the risk that the financial statements are materially misstated prior to audit) and the risk that the auditor will not detect such misstatement ("detection risk"). The risk of material misstatement has two components: inherent risk and control risk (as described at the assertion level below). Detection risk is the risk that the auditor's procedures will not detect a misstatement that exists in an assertion that could be material, individually or when aggregated with other misstatements.

> *Control risk*—Control risk is the risk that a misstatement that could occur in an assertion and that could be material, individually or when aggregated with other misstatements, will not be prevented or detected and corrected on a timely basis by the entity's internal control.

> *Inherent risk*—Inherent risk is the susceptibility of an assertion to a misstatement, that could be material, individually or when aggregated with other misstatements assuming that there were no related internal controls.

Audit sampling—The application of audit procedures to less than 100% of items within an account balance or class of transactions such that all sampling units have a chance of selection. This will enable the auditor to obtain and evaluate audit evidence about some characteristic of the items selected in order to form or assist in forming a conclusion concerning the population from which the sample is drawn. Audit sampling can use either a statistical or a non-statistical approach.

> *Anomalous error*—An error that arises from an isolated event that has not recurred other than on specifically identifiable occasions and is therefore not representative of errors in the population.

> *Confidence levels*—The mathematical complements of sampling risk.

> *Expected error*—The error that the auditor expects to be present in the population.

> *Non-sampling risk*—Arises from factors that cause the auditor to reach an erroneous conclusion for any reason not related to the size of the sample. For example, most audit evidence is persuasive rather than conclusive, the auditor might use inappropriate procedures, or the auditor might misinterpret evidence and fail to recognize an error.

> *Non-statistical sampling*—Any sampling approach that does not have the characteristics of statistical sampling.

> *Population*—The entire set of data from which a sample is selected and about which the auditor wishes to draw conclusions. A population may be divided into strata, or sub-populations, with each stratum being examined separately. The term population is used to include the term stratum.

Sampling risk—Arises from the possibility that the auditor's conclusion, based on a sample, may be different from the conclusion reached if the entire population were subjected to the same audit procedure.

Sampling unit—The individual items constituting a population, for example checks listed on deposit slips, credit entries on bank statements, sales invoices or debtors' balances, or a monetary unit.

Statistical sampling—Any approach to sampling that has the following characteristics:

(a) Random selection of a sample; and

(b) Use of probability theory to evaluate sample results, including measurement of sampling risk.

Stratification—The process of dividing a population into subpopulations, each of which is a group of sampling units which have similar characteristics (often monetary value).

Tolerable error—The maximum error in a population that the auditor is willing to accept.

Total error—Either the rate of deviation or total misstatement.

Audit team—All audit professionals who, regardless of their legal relationship with the auditor or audit firm, are assigned to a particular audit engagement in order to perform the audit task (e.g. audit partner(s), audit manager(s) and audit staff).

Auditor—The engagement partner. The term "auditor" is used to describe either the engagement partner or the audit firm. Where it applies to the engagement partner, it describes the obligations or responsibilities of the engagement partner. Such obligations or responsibilities may be fulfilled by either the engagement partner or a member of the audit team. Where it is expressly intended that the obligation or responsibility be fulfilled by the engagement partner, the term "engagement partner" rather than "auditor" is used. (The term "auditor" may be used when describing related services and assurance engagements other than audits. Such reference is not intended to imply that a person performing a related service or assurance engagement other than an audit need necessarily be the auditor of the entity's financial statements.)

Existing auditor—The auditor of the financial statements of the current period.

External auditor—Where appropriate the term "external auditor" is used to distinguish the external auditor from an internal auditor.

Incoming auditor—The auditor of the financial statements of the current period, where either the financial statements of the prior period have been audited by another auditor (in this case the incoming auditor also known as a successor auditor), or the audit is an initial audit engagement.

Internal auditor—A person performing an internal audit.

Other auditor—An auditor, other than the principal auditor, with responsibility for reporting on the financial information of a component, which is included in the financial statements audited by the principal auditor. Other auditors include affiliated firms, whether using the same name or not, and correspondents, as well as unrelated auditors.

Predecessor auditor—The auditor who was previously the auditor of an entity and who has been replaced by an incoming auditor.

Principal auditor—The auditor with responsibility for reporting on the financial statements of an entity when those financial statements include financial information of one or more components audited by another auditor.

Proposed auditor—An auditor who is asked to replace an existing auditor.

Successor auditor—An auditor replacing an existing auditor (also known as an incoming auditor).

Auditor association with financial information—An auditor is associated with financial information when the auditor attaches a report to that information or consents to the use of the auditor's name in a professional connection.

Chain of command—All persons who have a direct supervisory, management or other oversight responsibility over either any audit partner of the audit team or over the conduct of audit work in the audit firm. This includes all partners, principals and shareholders who may prepare, review or directly influence the performance appraisal of any audit partner of the audit team as a result of their involvement with the audit engagement.

Close family—Any non-dependent parent, child or sibling.

See immediate family pg 1194

Comparatives—Comparatives in financial statements may present amounts (such as financial position, results of operations, cash flows) and appropriate disclosures of an entity for more than one period, depending on the framework. The frameworks and methods of presentation are as follows:

(a) Corresponding figures where amounts and other disclosures for the preceding period are included as part of the current period financial statements, and are intended to be read in relation to the amounts and other disclosures relating to the current period (referred to as "current period figures"). These corresponding figures are not presented as complete financial statements capable of standing alone, but are an integral part of the current period financial statements intended to be read only in relationship to the current period figures.

(b) Comparative financial statements where amounts and other disclosures for the preceding period are included for comparison with the financial statements of the current period, but do not form part of the current period financial statements.

Comparative financial statements—(see Comparatives)

Compilation engagement—An engagement in which accounting expertise, as opposed to auditing expertise, is used to collect, classify and summarize financial information.

Component—A division, branch, subsidiary, joint venture, associated company or other entity whose financial information is included in financial statements audited by the principal auditor.

Comprehensive basis of accounting—A comprehensive basis of accounting comprises a set of criteria used in preparing financial statements which applies to all material items and which has substantial support.

Computer-assisted audit techniques—Applications of auditing procedures using the computer as an audit tool (also known as CAATs).

Computer information systems (CIS) environment—Exists when a computer of any type or size is involved in the processing by the entity of financial information of significance to the audit, whether that computer is operated by the entity or by a third party.

Confidence levels—(see Audit sampling)

Confirmation—A specific type of inquiry that is the process of obtaining a representation of information or of an existing condition directly from a third party.

Contingent fee basis—Any arrangement made at the outset of an engagement under which a pre-determined amount or a specified commission on or percentage of any consideration or saving is payable to the audit firm upon the happening of a specified event or the achievement of an outcome (or alternative outcomes). Differential hourly fee rates, or arrangements under which the fee payable will be negotiated after the completion of the engagement, do not constitute contingent fee arrangements.

Continuing auditor—(see Auditor)

Control activities—Those policies and procedures that help ensure that management directives are carried out. Control activities are a component of internal control.

Control environment—Includes the governance and management functions and the attitudes, awareness and actions of those charged with governance and management concerning the entity's internal control and its importance in the entity. The control environment is a component of internal control.

Control risk—(see Audit risk)

Corporate governance—(see Governance)

Corresponding figures—(see Comparatives)

Criteria—The benchmarks used to evaluate or measure the subject matter including, where relevant, benchmarks for presentation and disclosure. Criteria can be formal or less formal. There can be different criteria for the same subject matter. Suitable criteria are required for reasonably consistent evaluation or measurement of a subject matter within the context of professional judgment.

Suitable criteria—Exhibit the following characteristics:

- ○ Relevance: relevant criteria contribute to conclusions that assist decision-making by the intended users.

- ○ Completeness: criteria are sufficiently complete when relevant factors that could affect the conclusions in the context of the engagement circumstances are not omitted. Complete criteria include, where relevant, benchmarks for presentation and disclosure.

- ○ Reliability: reliable criteria allow reasonably consistent evaluation or measurement of the subject matter including, where relevant, presentation and disclosure, when used in similar circumstances by similarly qualified practitioners.

- ○ Neutrality: neutral criteria contribute to conclusions that are free from bias.

- ○ Understandability: understandable criteria contribute to conclusions that are clear, comprehensive, and not subject to significantly different interpretations.

Current period figures—Amounts and other disclosures relating to the current period.

Database—A collection of data that is shared and used by a number of different users for different purposes.

Detection risk—(see Audit risk)

Disclaimer of opinion—(see Modified auditor's report)

Electronic Data Interchange (EDI)—The electronic transmission of documents between organizations in a machine-readable form.

Emphasis of matter paragraph(s)—(see Modified auditor's report)

Employee fraud—Fraud involving only employees of the entity subject to the audit.

Encryption (cryptography)—The process of transforming programs and information into a form that cannot be understood without access to specific decoding algorithms (cryptographic keys). For example, the confidential personal data in a payroll system may be encrypted against unauthorized disclosure or modification. Encryption can provide an effective control for protecting confidential or sensitive programs and information from unauthorized access or modification. However, effective security depends upon proper controls over access to the cryptographic keys.

Engagement letter—An engagement letter documents and confirms the auditor's acceptance of the appointment, the objective and scope of the audit, the extent of the auditor's responsibilities to the client and the form of any reports.

Engagement partner—The partner or other person in the firm who is responsible for the engagement and its performance, and for report that is issued on behalf of the firm, and who, where required, has the appropriate authority from a professional, legal or regulatory body.

Engagement quality control review—A process designed to provide an objective evaluation, before the report is issued, of the significant judgments the engagement team made and the conclusions they reached in formulating the report.

Engagement quality control reviewer—A partner, other person in the firm, suitably qualified external person, or a team made up of such individuals, with sufficient and appropriate experience and authority to objectively evaluate, before the report is issued, the significant judgments the engagement team made and the conclusions they reached in formulating the report.

Engagement team—All personnel performing an engagement, including any experts contracted by the firm in connection with that engagement.

For the purposes of APB Ethical Standards, engagement team comprises all persons who are directly involved in the acceptance and performance of a particular audit. This includes the audit team, professional personnel from other disciplines involved in the audit engagement and those who provide quality control or direct oversight of the audit engagement, but it does not include experts contracted by the firm.

Entity's risk assessment process—A component of internal control that is the entity's process for identifying business risks relevant to financial reporting objectives and deciding about actions to address those risks, and the results thereof.

Environmental matters—

(a) Initiatives to prevent, abate, or remedy damage to the environment, or to deal with conservation of renewable and non-renewable resources (such initiatives may be required by environmental laws and regulations or by contract, or they may be undertaken voluntarily);

(b) Consequences of violating environmental laws and regulations;

(c) Consequences of environmental damage done to others or to natural resources; and

(d) Consequences of vicarious liability imposed by law (for example, liability for damages caused by previous owners).

Environmental performance report—A report, separate from the financial statements, in which an entity provides third parties with qualitative information on the entity's commitments towards the environmental aspects of the business, its policies and targets in that field, its achievement in managing the relationship between its business processes and environmental risk, and quantitative information on its environmental performance.

Environmental risk—In certain circumstances, factors relevant to the assessment of inherent risk for the development of the overall audit plan may include the risk of material misstatement of the financial statements due to environmental matters.

Error—An unintentional misstatement in financial statements, including the omission of an amount or a disclosure.

Ethics partner—The partner or other person in the audit firm having responsibility for the adequacy of the firm's policies and procedures relating to integrity, objectivity and independence, their compliance with APB Ethical Standards and the effectiveness of their communication to partners and staff within the firm and providing related guidance to individual partners.

Evaluate—Identify and analyze the relevant issues, including performing further procedures as necessary, to come to a specific conclusion on a matter. "Evaluation," by convention, is used only in relation to a range of matters, including evidence, the results of procedures and the effectiveness of management's response to a risk. (also see Assess)

Existing auditor—(see Auditor)

Expected error— (see Audit sampling)

Experienced auditor—An individual (whether internal or external to the firm) who has a reasonable understanding of (i) audit processes, (ii) ISAs (UK and Ireland) and applicable legal and regulatory requirements, (iii) the business environment in which the entity operates, and (iv) auditing and financial reporting issues relevant to the entity's industry.

Expert—A person or firm possessing special skill, knowledge and experience in a particular field other than accounting and auditing.

External audit—An audit performed by an external auditor.

External auditor—(see Auditor)

External confirmation—The process of obtaining and evaluating audit evidence through a direct communication from a third party in response to a request for information about a particular item affecting assertions made by management in the financial statements.

Fair value—The amount for which an asset could be exchanged, or a liability settled, between knowledgeable, willing parties in an arm's length transaction.

Financial interest—An equity or other security, debenture, loan or other debt instrument of an entity, including rights and obligations to acquire such an interest and derivatives directly related to such an interest.

Firewall—A combination of hardware and software that protects a WAN, LAN or PC from unauthorized access through the Internet and from the introduction of unauthorized or harmful software, data or other material in electronic form.

Firm—A sole practitioner, partnership or corporation, or other entity of professional accountants.

For the purpose of APB Ethical Standards, audit firm includes network firms in the UK and Ireland which are controlled by the audit firm or its partners.

Forecast—Prospective financial information prepared on the basis of assumptions as to future events which management expects to take place and the actions management expects to take as of the date the information is prepared (best-estimate assumptions).

Fraud—An intentional act by one or more individuals among management, those charged with governance, employees, or third parties, involving the use of deception to obtain an unjust or illegal advantage. Two types of intentional misstatement are relevant to the auditor: misstatements resulting from fraudulent financial reporting and misstatements resulting from misappropriation of assets (also see Fraudulent financial reporting and Misappropriation of assets).

Fraudulent financial reporting—Involves intentional misstatements, including omissions of amounts or disclosures in financial statements, to deceive financial statement users.

General IT-controls— Polices and procedures that relate to many applications and support the effective functioning of application controls by helping to ensure the continued proper operation of information systems. General IT-controls commonly include controls over data center and network operations; system software acquisition, change and maintenance; access security; and application system acquisition, development, and maintenance.

Going concern assumption—Under this assumption, an entity is ordinarily viewed as continuing in business for the foreseeable future with neither the intention nor the necessity of liquidation, ceasing trading or seeking protection from creditors pursuant to laws or regulations. Accordingly, assets and liabilities are recorded on the basis that the entity will be able to realize its assets and discharge its liabilities in the normal course of business.

Governance—Describes the role of persons entrusted with the supervision, control and direction of an entity. Those charged with governance ordinarily are accountable for ensuring that the entity achieves its objectives, financial reporting, and reporting to interested parties. Those charged with governance include management only when it performs such functions.

In the UK and Ireland, those charged with governance include the directors (executive and non-executive) of a company or other body, the members of an audit committee where one exists, the partners, proprietors, committee of management or trustees of other forms of entity, or equivalent persons responsible for directing the entity's affairs and preparing its financial statements.

Government business enterprises—Businesses that operate within the public sector ordinarily to meet a political or social interest objective. They are ordinarily required to operate commercially, that is, to make profits or to recoup through user charges a substantial proportion of their operating costs.

Immediate family—A spouse (or equivalent) or dependent.

See close family Pg 1188

Incoming auditor—(see Auditor)

Independence[2]—Comprises:

(a) Independence of mind—the state of mind that permits the provision of an opinion without being affected by influences that compromise professional judgment, allowing an individual to act with integrity, and exercise objectivity and professional judgment; and

(b) Independence in appearance—the avoidance of facts and circumstances that are so significant a reasonable and informed third party, having knowledge of all relevant information, including any safeguards applied, would reasonably conclude a firm's, or a member of the assurance team's, integrity, objectivity or professional skepticism had been compromised.

Independent partner—A partner or other person performing the function of a partner who is not a member of the audit team. The experience required of the independent partner is determined by the nature of the audit engagement and the seniority and experience of the audit engagement partner.

Information system relevant to financial reporting—A component of internal control that includes the financial reporting system, and consists of the procedures and records established to initiate, record, process and report entity transactions (as well as events and conditions) and to maintain accountability for the related assets, liabilities and equity.

Inherent risk—(see Audit risk)

Initial audit engagement—An audit engagement in which either the financial statements are audited for the first time; or the financial statements for the prior period were audited by another auditor.

Inquiry—Inquiry consists of seeking information of knowledgeable persons, both financial and non-financial, throughout the entity or outside the entity.

Inspection (as an audit procedure)—Examining records or documents, whether internal or external, or tangible assets.

---

[2] As defined in the IFAC *Code of Ethics for Professional Accountants*. APB Ethical Standard 1 defines independence as freedom from situations and relationships which make it probable that a reasonable and informed third party would conclude that objectivity either is impaired or could be impaired. Independence is related to and underpins objectivity. However, whereas objectivity is a personal behavioural characteristic concerning the auditors' state of mind, independence relates to the circumstances surrounding the audit, including the financial, employment, business and personal relationships between the auditors and their client.

Inspection (in relation to completed engagements)—Procedures designed to provide evidence of compliance by engagement teams with the firm's quality control policies and procedures;

Intended users—The person, persons or class of persons for whom the practitioner prepares the assurance report. The responsible party can be one of the intended users, but not the only one.

Interim financial information or statements—Financial information (which may be less than a complete set of financial statements as defined above) issued at interim dates (usually half-yearly or quarterly) in respect of a financial period.

Internal auditing—An appraisal activity established within an entity as a service to the entity. Its functions include, amongst other things, examining, evaluating and monitoring the adequacy and effectiveness of internal control.

Internal auditor—(see Auditor)

Internal control—The process designed and effected by those charged with governance, management and other personnel to provide reasonable assurance about the achievement of the entity's objectives with regard to reliability of financial reporting, effectiveness and efficiency of operations and compliance with applicable laws and regulations. Internal control consists of the following components:

(a) The control environment;

(b) The entity's risk assessment process;

(c) The information system, including the related business processes, relevant to financial reporting, and communication;

(d) Control activities; and

(e) Monitoring of controls.

Investigate—Inquire into matters arising from other procedures to resolve them.

IT environment—The policies and procedures that the entity implements and the IT infrastructure (hardware, operating systems, etc.) and application software that it uses to support business operations and achieve business strategies.

Key audit partner—An audit partner, or other person performing the function of an audit partner, of the engagement team (other than the audit engagement partner) who is involved at the group level and is responsible for key decisions or judgments on significant matters, such as on significant subsidiaries or divisions of the audit client, or on significant risk factors that relate to the audit of that client.

Key management position—Any position at the audit client which involves the responsibility for fundamental management decisions at the audit client (e.g. as a CEO or CFO), including an ability to influence the accounting policies and the preparation of the financial statements of the audit client. A key management position also arises where there are contractual and factual arrangements which in substance allow an individual to participate in exercising such a management function in a different way (e.g. via a consulting contract).

Limited assurance engagement—(see Assurance engagement)

Limitation on scope—A limitation on the scope of the auditor's work may sometimes be imposed by the entity (for example, when the terms of the engagement specify that the auditor will not carry out an audit procedure that the auditor believes is necessary). A scope limitation may be imposed by circumstances (for example, when the timing of the auditor's appointment is such that the auditor is unable to observe the counting of physical inventories). It may also arise when, in the opinion of the auditor, the entity's accounting records are inadequate or when the auditor is unable to carry out an audit procedure believed desirable.

Listed entity[3]—An entity whose shares, stock or debt are quoted or listed on a recognized stock exchange, or are marketed under the regulations of a recognized stock exchange or other equivalent body.

Local Area Network (LAN)—A communications network that serves users within a confined geographical area. LANs were developed to facilitate the exchange and sharing of resources within an organization, including data, software, storage, printers and telecommunications equipment. They allow for decentralized computing. The basic components of a LAN are transmission media and software, user terminals and shared peripherals.

Management—Comprises officers and others who also perform senior managerial functions. Management includes those charged with governance only in those instances when they perform such functions.

In the UK and Ireland, depending on the nature and circumstances of the entity, management may include some or all of those charged with governance (e.g. executive directors). Management will not normally include non-executive directors.

Management fraud—Fraud involving one or more members of management or those charged with governance.

Management representations—Representations made by management to the auditor during the course of an audit, either unsolicited or in response to specific inquiries.

Material inconsistency—Exists when other information contradicts information contained in the audited financial statements. A material inconsistency may raise doubt about the audit conclusions drawn from audit evidence previously obtained and, possibly, about the basis for the auditor's opinion on the financial statements.

---

[3]   As defined in the IFAC *Code of Ethics for Professional Accountants*.

Material misstatement of fact—Exists in other information when such information, not related to matters appearing in the audited financial statements, is incorrectly stated or presented.

Material weakness—A weakness in internal control that could have a material effect on the financial statements.

Materiality—Information is material if its omission or misstatement could influence the economic decisions of users taken on the basis of the financial statements. Materiality depends on the size of the item or error judged in the particular circumstances of its omission or misstatement. Thus, materiality provides a threshold or cutoff point rather than being a primary qualitative characteristic which information must have if it is to be useful.

Misappropriation of assets—Involves the theft of an entity's assets and is often perpetrated by employees in relatively small and immaterial amounts. However, it can also involve management who are usually more capable of disguising or concealing misappropriations in ways that are difficult to detect.

Misstatement—A misstatement of the financial statements that can arise from fraud or error (also see Fraud and Error).

Modified auditor's report—An auditor's report is considered to be modified if either an emphasis of matter paragraph(s) is added to the report or if the opinion is other than unqualified:

Matters that Do Not Affect the Auditor's Opinion

Emphasis of matter paragraph(s)—An auditor's report may be modified by adding an emphasis of matter paragraph(s) to highlight a matter affecting the financial statements which is included in a note to the financial statements that more extensively discusses the matter. The addition of such an emphasis of matter paragraph(s) does not affect the auditor's opinion. The auditor may also modify the auditor's report by using an emphasis of matter paragraph(s) to report matters other than those affecting the financial statements.

Matters that Do Affect the Auditor's Opinion

Adverse opinion—An adverse opinion is expressed when the effect of a disagreement is so material and pervasive to the financial statements that the auditor concludes that a qualification of the report is not adequate to disclose the misleading or incomplete nature of the financial statements.

Disclaimer of opinion—A disclaimer of opinion is expressed when the possible effect of a limitation on scope is so material and pervasive that the auditor has not been able to obtain sufficient appropriate audit evidence and accordingly is unable to express an opinion on the financial statements.

Qualified opinion—A qualified opinion is expressed when the auditor concludes that an unqualified opinion cannot be expressed but that the effect of any disagreement with management, or limitation on scope is not so material and pervasive as to require an adverse opinion or a disclaimer of opinion.

Monitoring (in relation to quality control)—A process comprising an ongoing consideration and evaluation of the firm's system of quality control, including a periodic inspection of a selection of completed engagements, designed to enable the firm to obtain reasonable assurance that its system of quality control is operating effectively.

Monitoring of controls—A process to assess the effectiveness of internal control performance over time. It includes assessing the design and operation of controls on a timely basis and taking necessary corrective actions modified for changes in conditions. Monitoring of controls is a component of internal control.

National practices (auditing)—A set of guidelines not having the authority of standards defined by an authoritative body at a national level and commonly applied by auditors in the conduct of an audit, review, other assurance or related services.

National standards (auditing)—A set of standards defined by law or regulations or an authoritative body at a national level, the application of which is mandatory in conducting an audit, review, other assurance or related services.

Network firm[4]—An entity under common control, ownership or management with the firm or any entity that a reasonable and informed third party having knowledge of all relevant information would reasonably conclude as being part of the firm nationally or internationally.

For the purpose of APB Ethical Standards, a network firm is any entity:

(i)   controlled by the audit firm or

(ii)   under common control, ownership or management or

(iii)   otherwise affiliated or associated with the audit firm through the use of a common name or through the sharing of significant common professional resources.

Non-compliance—Refers to acts of omission or commission by the entity being audited, either intentional or unintentional, that are contrary to the prevailing laws or regulations.

Non-sampling risk—(see Audit sampling)

Non-statistical sampling—(see Audit sampling)

Observation—Consists of looking at a process or procedure being performed by others, for example, the observation by the auditor of the counting of inventories by the entity's personnel or the performance of control activities.

---

[4] As defined in the IFAC *Code of Ethics for Professional Accountants*.

Opening balances—Those account balances which exist at the beginning of the period. Opening balances are based upon the closing balances of the prior period and reflect the effects of transactions of prior periods and accounting policies applied in the prior period.

Opinion—The auditor's report contains a clear written expression of opinion on the financial statements as a whole. An unqualified opinion is expressed when the auditor concludes that the financial statements give a true and fair view (or are presented fairly, in all material respects,) in accordance with the applicable financial reporting framework (also see Modified auditor's report).

Other auditor—(see Auditor)

Other information—Financial or non-financial information (other than the financial statements or the auditor's report thereon) included – either by law or custom – in the annual report.

Overall audit strategy—Sets the scope, timing and direction of the audit, and guides the development of the more detailed audit plan.

Partner—Any individual with authority to bind the firm with respect to the performance of a professional services engagement.

PCs or personal computers (also referred to as microcomputers)—Economical yet powerful self-contained general purpose computers consisting typically of a monitor (visual display unit), a case containing the computer electronics and a keyboard (and mouse). These features may be combined in portable computers (laptops). Programs and data may be stored internally on a hard disk or on removable storage media such as CDs or floppy disks. PCs may be connected to on-line networks, printers and other devices such as scanners and modems.

Person in a position to influence the conduct and outcome of the audit—This is:

(a) Any person who is directly involved in the audit (the engagement team), including:

    (i) the audit partners, audit managers and audit staff (the audit team);

    (ii) professional personnel from other disciplines involved in the audit (for example, lawyers, actuaries, taxation specialists, IT specialists, treasury management specialists);

    (iii) those who provide quality control or direct oversight of the audit;

(b) Any person, who forms part of the chain of command for the audit within the audit firm;

(c) Any person within the audit firm who, due to any other circumstances, may be in a position to exert such influence.

Personnel—Partners and staff.

Planning—Involves establishing the overall audit strategy for the engagement and developing an audit plan, in order to reduce audit risk to an acceptably low level.

Population—(see Audit sampling)

Post balance sheet events—(see Subsequent events)

Practitioner—A professional accountant in public practice.

Predecessor auditor—(see Auditor)

Principal auditor—(see Auditor)

Professional accountant—Those persons who are members of a professional accountancy body, whether in public practice (including a sole practitioner, partnership or corporate body), industry, commerce, the public sector or education.

Professional accountant in public practice[5]— A professional accountant, irrespective of functional classification (e.g. audit, tax or consulting) in a firm that provides professional services. This term is also used to refer to a firm of professional accountants in public practice.

Professional skepticism—An attitude that includes a questioning mind and a critical assessment of evidence.

Professional standards—IAASB engagement standards, as defined in the IAASB's 'Preface to the International Standards on Quality Control, Auditing, Assurance and Related Services', and relevant ethical requirements, which ordinarily comprise Parts A and B of the IFAC *Code of Ethics for Professional Accountants* and relevant national ethical requirements.[6]

Programming controls—Procedures designed to prevent or detect improper changes to computer programs that are accessed through on-line terminal devices. Access may be restricted by controls such as the use of separate operational and program development libraries and the use of specialized program library software. It is important for on-line changes to programs to be adequately documented, controlled and monitored.

Projection—Prospective financial information prepared on the basis of:

---

[5] As defined in the IFAC *Code of Ethics for Professional Accountants*.
[6] In the UK and Ireland the relevant ethical pronouncements with which the auditor complies are the APB's Ethical Standards and the ethical pronouncements relating to the work of auditors issued by the auditor's relevant professional body - see the Statement 'The Auditing Practices Board – Scope and Authority of Pronouncements'.

(a) Hypothetical assumptions about future events and management actions which are not necessarily expected to take place, such as when some entities are in a start-up phase or are considering a major change in the nature of operations; or

(b) A mixture of best-estimate and hypothetical assumptions.

Proposed auditor—(see Auditor)

Prospective financial information—Financial information based on assumptions about events that may occur in the future and possible actions by an entity. Prospective financial information can be in the form of a forecast, a projection or a combination of both. (see Forecast and Projection)

Public sector—National governments, regional (for example, state, provincial, territorial) governments, local (for example, city, town) governments and related governmental entities (for example, agencies, boards, commissions and enterprises).

Qualified opinion—(see Modified auditor's report)

Quality controls—The policies and procedures adopted by a firm designed to provide it with reasonable assurance that the firm and its personnel comply with professional standards and regulatory and legal requirements, and that reports issued by the firm or engagement partners are appropriate in the circumstances.

Reasonable assurance (in the context of an audit engagement)—A high, but not absolute, level of assurance, expressed positively in the auditor's report as reasonable assurance, that the information subject to audit is free of material misstatement.

Reasonable assurance (in the context of quality control)—A high, but not absolute, level of assurance.

Reasonable assurance engagement—(see Assurance engagement)

Recalculation—Consists of checking the mathematical accuracy of documents or records.

Related party—Related party and related party transaction are defined in International Accounting Standard (IAS) 24, 'Related Party Disclosures' as:

Related party— A party is related to an entity if:

(a) Directly, or indirectly through one or more intermediaries, the party:

(i) Controls, is controlled by, or is under common control with, the entity (this includes parents, subsidiaries and fellow subsidiaries);

(ii) Has an interest in the entity that gives it significant influence over the entity; or

(iii) Has joint control over the entity;

(b) The party is an associate (as defined in IAS 28, 'Investments in Associates') of the entity;

(c) The party is a joint venture in which the entity is a venturer (see IAS 31, 'Interest in Joint Ventures');

(d) The party is a member of the key management personnel of the entity or its parent;

(e) The party is a close member of the family of any individual referred to in (a) or (d);

(f) The party is an entity that is controlled, jointly controlled or significantly influenced by, or for which significant voting power in such entity resides with, directly or indirectly, any individual referred to in (d) or (e); or,

(g) The party is a post-employment benefit plan for the benefit of employees of the entity, or of any entity that is a related party of the entity.

Related party transaction— A transfer of resources, services or obligations between related parties, regardless of whether a price is charged.

The above definitions of "related party" and "related party transaction" apply when the financial statements being audited are intended to comply with IAS 24. If the financial statements being audited are intended to comply with Financial Reporting Standard 8, 'Related Party Disclosures', the definitions included therein are used (see the Appendix to ISA (UK and Ireland) 550, 'Related Parties').

Related services—Comprise agreed-upon procedures and compilations.

Reperformance—The auditor's independent execution of procedures or controls that were originally performed as part of the entity's internal controls, either manually or through the use of CAATs.

Responsible party—The person (or persons) who:

(a) In a direct reporting engagement, is responsible for the subject matter; or

(b) In an assertion-based engagement, is responsible for the subject matter information (the assertion), and may be responsible for the subject matter.

The responsible party may or may not be the party who engages the practitioner (the engaging party).

Review (in relation to quality control)—Appraising the quality of the work performed and conclusions reached by others.

Review engagement—The objective of a review engagement is to enable an auditor to state whether, on the basis of procedures which do not provide all the evidence that would be required in an audit, anything has come to the auditor's attention that causes the auditor to believe that the financial statements are not prepared, in all material respects, in accordance with an applicable financial reporting framework.

Review procedures—The procedures deemed necessary to meet the objective of a review engagement, primarily inquiries of entity personnel and analytical procedures applied to financial data.

Risk assessment procedures—The audit procedures performed to obtain an understanding of the entity and its environment, including its internal control, to assess the risks of material misstatement at the financial statement and assertion levels.

Risk of material misstatement—(see Audit Risk)

Sampling risk—(see Audit sampling)

Sampling unit—(see Audit sampling)

Scope of an audit—The audit procedures deemed necessary in the circumstances to achieve the objective of the audit.

Scope of a review—The review procedures deemed necessary in the circumstances to achieve the objective of the review.

Scope limitation—(see Limitation on scope)

Segment information—Information in the financial statements regarding distinguishable components or industry and geographical aspects of an entity.

Significance—The relative importance of a matter, taken in context. The significance of a matter is judged by the practitioner in the context in which it is being considered. This might include, for example, the reasonable prospect of its changing or influencing the decisions of intended users of the practitioner's report; or, as another example, where the context is a judgment about whether to report a matter to those charged with governance, whether the matter would be regarded as important by them in relation to their duties. Significance can be considered in the context of quantitative and qualitative factors, such as relative magnitude, the nature and effect on the subject matter and the expressed interests of intended users or recipients.

Significant risk—A risk that requires special audit consideration.

Small entity—Any entity in which:

(a) There is concentration of ownership and management in a small number of individuals (often a single individual); and

(b) One or more of the following are also found:

　　(i) Few sources of income;

(ii)　Unsophisticated record-keeping; and

(iii)　Limited internal controls together with the potential for management override of controls.

Small entities will ordinarily display characteristic (a), and one or more of the characteristics included under (b).

In the UK and Ireland, company law provides a lighter reporting regime for companies that are defined, by legislation, as small. A company qualifies as "small" if it meets particular thresholds in respect of turnover, balance sheet total/gross assets and number of employees and certain other criteria. The thresholds and other criteria are subject to change and reference to the relevant legislation should be made to determine what they are in respect of a particular accounting period.

For the purpose of the APB Ethical Standards, a small entity is defined in 'APB Ethical Standard – Provisions Available for Small Entities'.

Special purpose auditor's report—A report issued in connection with the independent audit of financial information other than an auditor's report on financial statements, including:

(a)　Financial statements prepared in accordance with a comprehensive basis of accounting other than International Accounting Standards or national standards;

(b)　Specified accounts, elements of accounts, or items in a financial statement;

(c)　Compliance with contractual agreements; and

(d)　Summarized financial statements.

Staff—Professionals, other than partners, including any experts the firm employs.

Statistical sampling—(see Audit sampling)

Stratification—(see Audit sampling)

Subject matter information—The outcome of the evaluation or measurement of a subject matter. It is the subject matter information about which the practitioner gathers sufficient appropriate evidence to provide a reasonable basis for expressing a conclusion in an assurance report.

Subsequent events—International Accounting Standard (IAS) 10, 'Events After the Balance Sheet Date' identifies two types of events both favorable and unfavorable occurring after period end:

(a)　Those that provide further evidence of conditions that existed at period end; and

(b)　Those that are indicative of conditions that arose subsequent to period end.

Substantive procedures—Audit procedures performed to detect material misstatements at the assertion level; they include:

(a) Tests of details of classes of transactions, account balances and disclosures; and

(b) Substantive analytical procedures.

Successor auditor—(see Auditor)

Sufficiency—Sufficiency is the measure of the quantity of audit evidence. The quantity of the audit evidence needed is affected by the risk of misstatement and also by the quality of such audit evidence.

Suitable criteria—(see Criteria)

Suitably qualified external person (for the purpose of ISQC 1)—An individual outside the firm with the capabilities and competence to act as an engagement partner, for example a partner of another firm, or an employee (with appropriate experience) of either a professional accountancy body whose members may perform audits and reviews of historical financial information, other assurance or related services engagements, or of an organization that provides relevant quality control services.

Summarized financial statements—Financial statements summarizing an entity's annual audited financial statements for the purpose of informing user groups interested in the highlights only of the entity's financial performance and position.

Supreme Audit Institution—The public body of a State which, however designated, constituted or organized, exercises by virtue of law, the highest public auditing function of that State.

Test—The application of procedures to some or all items in a population.

Tests of control—Tests performed to obtain audit evidence about the operating effectiveness of controls in preventing, or detecting and correcting, material misstatements at the assertion level.

Those charged with governance—(see Governance)

Tolerable error—(see Audit sampling)

Total error—(see Audit sampling)

Transaction logs—Reports that are designed to create an audit trail for each on-line transaction. Such reports often document the source of a transaction (terminal, time and user) as well as the transaction's details.

Uncertainty— A matter whose outcome depends on future actions or events not under the direct control of the entity but that may affect the financial statements.

Understanding of the entity and its environment—The auditor's understanding of the entity and its environment consists of the following aspects:

(a) Industry, regulatory, and other external factors, including the applicable financial reporting framework.

(b) Nature of the entity, including the entity's selection and application of accounting policies.

(c) Objectives and strategies and the related business risks that may result in a material misstatement of the financial statements.

(d) Measurement and review of the entity's financial performance.

(e) Internal control.

Unqualified opinion—(see Opinion)

Walk-through test—Involves tracing a few transactions through the financial reporting system.

Wide Area Network (WAN)—A communications network that transmits information across an expanded area such as between plant sites, cities and nations. WANs allow for on-line access to applications from remote terminals. Several LANs can be interconnected in a WAN.

Working papers—The material prepared by and for, or obtained and retained by, the auditor in connection with the performance of the audit. Working papers may be in the form of data stored on paper, film, electronic media or other media.

Appendix: APB STANDARDS AND GUIDANCE AT 1 JANUARY 2007

---

[1] In November 2005 APB issued a revised version of ISA 230 that is effective for audits of accounting periods commencing on or after 15 June 2006.

Ethical Standards

Practice Notes

Bulletins

2001/4	Supplementary guidance for auditors of building societies in the United Kingdom following 'N2'.	*December 2001*
2001/5	Supplementary guidance for auditors of banks in the United Kingdom following 'N2'.	*December 2001*
2001/7	Supplementary guidance for auditors of investment businesses in the United Kingdom following 'N2'.	*December 2001*
2002/1	The duty of auditors in the Republic of Ireland to report to the Director of Corporate Enforcement	*July 2002*
2002/2	The United Kingdom directors' remuneration report regulations 2002	*October 2002*
2002/3	Guidance for reporting accountants of stakeholder pension schemes in the United Kingdom	*November 2002*
2003/1	Corporate Governance: Requirements of public sector auditors (central government)	*November 2003*
2003/2	Corporate Governance: Requirements of public sector auditors (NHS bodies)	*November 2003*
2004/1	The auditors' association with preliminary announcements	*January 2004*
2004/2	Corporate Governance: Requirements of public sector auditors (local government bodies)	*June 2004*
2004/5	Supplementary guidance for auditors of insurers in the UK (Revised)	*December 2004*
2004/6	Supplementary guidance for auditors of friendly societies in the UK	*December 2004*
2005/1	Audit risk and fraud: Supplementary guidance for the auditors of charities.	*February 2005*
2005/2	Audit risk and fraud: Supplementary guidance for the auditors of investment businesses.	*April 2005*
2005/3	Guidance for auditors on first-time application of IFRSs in the United Kingdom and the Republic of Ireland	*November 2005*
2005/5	Audit risk and fraud: Supplementary guidance for the auditors of pension schemes.	*May 2005*
2005/6	Audit risk and fraud: Supplementary guidance for the auditors of banks and building societies.	*May 2005*
2005/7	Integrity, objectivity and independence – Guidance for reporting accountants undertaking engagements in connection with an investment circular.[2]	*July 2005*

---

[2] Will be withdrawn with effect from 1 April 2007 as this guidance is replaced by APB Ethical Standards for Reporting Accountants issued in October 2006 and effective from 1 April 2007.

2006/1	Auditor's reports on financial statements in the Republic of Ireland	*January 2006*
2006/2	Illustrative auditor's reports on public sector financial statements in the United Kingdom	*January 2006*
2006/3	The special auditor's report on abbreviated accounts in the United Kingdom	*April 2006*
2006/4	Regulatory and legislative background to the application of Standards for Investment Reporting in the Republic of Ireland	*April 2006*
2006/5	The Combined Code on Corporate Governance: Requirements of auditors under the Listing Rules of the Financial Services Authority and the Irish Stock Exchange	*September 2006*
2006/6	Auditor's reports on financial statements in the United Kingdom	*September 2006*
2007/1	Example reports by auditors under company legislation in Great Britain	*January 2007*

Statement of Standards for Reporting Accountants

Audit exemption reports	*October 1994*

Statements of Investment Reporting Standards

1000	Investment reporting standards applicable to all engagements in connection with an investment circular	*June 2005*
2000	Investment reporting standards applicable to public reporting engagements on historical financial information	*June 2005*
3000	Investment reporting standards applicable to public reporting engagements on profit forecasts	*January 2006*
4000	Investment reporting standards applicable to public reporting engagements on pro forma financial information	*January 2006*